Handbook of Reading Research, Volume V

In a time of pressures, challenges, and threats to public education, teacher preparation, and funding for educational research, the fifth volume of the *Handbook of Reading Research* takes a hard look at why we undertake reading research, how school structures, contexts, and policies shape students' learning, and, most importantly, how we can realize greater impact from the research conducted. A comprehensive volume, with a "gaps and game changers" frame, this handbook not only synthesizes current reading research literature, but also informs promising directions for research, pushing readers to address problems and challenges in research design or method.

Bringing the field authoritatively and comprehensively up-to-date since the publication of the *Handbook of Reading Research, Volume IV*, this volume presents multiple perspectives that will facilitate new research development, tackling topics including:

- Diverse student populations and sociocultural perspectives on reading development
- Digital innovation, literacies, and platforms
- Conceptions of teachers, reading, readers, and texts, and the role of affect, cognition, and social-emotional learning in the reading process
- New methods for researching reading instruction, with attention to equity, inclusion, and education policies
- Language development and reading comprehension
- Instructional practices to promote reading development and comprehension for diverse groups of readers

Each volume of this handbook has come to define the field for the period of time it covers, and this volume is no exception, providing a definitive compilation of current reading research. This is a must-have resource for all students, teachers, reading specialists, and researchers focused on and interested in reading and literacy research, and improving both instruction and programs to cultivate strong readers and teachers.

Elizabeth Birr Moje is Dean of the School of Education, George Herbert Mead Collegiate Professor of Education, an Arthur F. Thurnau Professor, and a Faculty Associate in the Institute for Social Research and Latina/o Studies at the University of Michigan, USA.

Peter P. Afflerbach is Professor of Reading in the Department of Teaching and Learning, Policy and Leadership at the University of Maryland, USA.

Patricia Enciso is Professor of Literacy, Literature, and Equity Studies in the Department of Teaching and Learning at the College of Education and Human Ecology, and Faculty Associate in Latinx Studies at The Ohio State University, USA.

Nonie K. Lesaux is Juliana W. and William Foss Thompson Professor of Education and Society at the Harvard Graduate School of Education, USA.

Handbook of Reading Research, Volume V

Edited by Elizabeth Birr Moje, Peter P. Afflerbach, Patricia Enciso, and Nonie K. Lesaux

MICHELLE KWOK, EDITORIAL ASSISTANT

Routledge
Taylor & Francis Group
NEW YORK AND LONDON

First published 2020
by Routledge
52 Vanderbilt Avenue, New York, NY 10017

and by Routledge
2 Park Square, Milton Park, Abingdon, Oxon, OX14 4RN

Routledge is an imprint of the Taylor & Francis Group, an informa business

© 2020 Taylor & Francis

The right of Elizabeth Birr Moje, Peter P. Afflerbach, Patricia Enciso, and Nonie K. Lesaux to be identified as the authors of the editorial material, and of the authors for their individual chapters, has been asserted in accordance with sections 77 and 78 of the Copyright, Designs and Patents Act 1988.

All rights reserved. No part of this book may be reprinted or reproduced or utilised in any form or by any electronic, mechanical, or other means, now known or hereafter invented, including photocopying and recording, or in any information storage or retrieval system, without permission in writing from the publishers.

Trademark notice: Product or corporate names may be trademarks or registered trademarks, and are used only for identification and explanation without intent to infringe.

Library of Congress Cataloging-in-Publication Data
A catalog record for this title has been requested

ISBN: 978-1-138-93736-9 (hbk)
ISBN: 978-1-138-93737-6 (pbk)
ISBN: 978-1-315-67630-2 (ebk)

Typeset in Bembo
by Swales & Willis, Exeter, Devon, UK

Contents

Preface   *ix*

PART I
Game Changers in Reading Research: Setting the Stage   1

1 Game Changers in Reading Research   3
   Elizabeth Birr Moje, Peter P. Afflerbach, Patricia Enciso, and Nonie K. Lesaux

PART II
How Increasingly Diversified Populations Change the Game for Readers, Teachers, Leaders, and Reading Researchers   15

2 Demographic Realities and Methodological Flexibility in Literacy Teaching and Research   17
   C. Patrick Proctor and Chris K. Chang-Bacon

3 Social and Cultural Diversity as Lens for Understanding Student Learning and the Development of Reading Comprehension   37
   Carol D. Lee

4 A Sociocultural Perspective on Readers, Reading, Reading Instruction and Assessment, Reading Policy, and Reading Research   57
   Peter Smagorinsky, Mary Guay, Tisha Lewis Ellison, and Arlette Ingram Willis

PART III
How Do Expanding Forms of Texts and Everyday Communication Change the Game for Readers, Teachers, Leaders, and Reading Researchers?   77

5 Reading Multiple and Non-Traditional Texts: New Opportunities and New Challenges   79
   Ivar Bråten, Jason L. G. Braasch, and Ladislao Salmerón

Contents

6	Who Reads What, in Which Formats, and Why? *Margaret Mackey*	99
7	Digital Reading: A Research Assessment *Naomi S. Baron*	116
8	Multimodal Critical Inquiry: Nurturing Decolonial Imaginaries *Gerald Campano, T. Philip Nichols, and Grace D. Player*	137

PART IV
How Do Expanding Conceptualizations of Readers Change the Game for Teachers, Leaders, and Reading Researchers? — **153**

9	The Language for School Literacy: Widening the Lens on Language and Reading Relations *Paola Uccelli, Emily Phillips Galloway, and Wenjuan Qin*	155
10	Readers' Individual Differences in Affect and Cognition *Emily Fox*	180
11	Continuities between Early Language Development and Reading Comprehension *Kiren S. Khan and Laura M. Justice*	197
12	What Do We Know Today about the Complexity Of Vocabulary Gaps and What Do We Not Know? *Jeannette Mancilla-Martinez and Janna B. McClain*	216
13	The Role of Knowledge in Understanding and Learning from Text *Gina N. Cervetti and Tanya S. Wright*	237
14	Defining Deep Reading Comprehension for Diverse Readers *Laura K. Allen and Danielle S. McNamara*	261

PART V
How Do Expanding Conceptions of Teacher, Reader, and Text Interaction Change the Game for Reading Researchers, Teachers, Leaders, and Policy Makers? — **277**

15	The Joint Development of Literacy and Self-Regulation in Early Childhood: Implications for Research and Practice *Emily C. Hanno, Stephanie M. Jones, and Dana C. McCoy*	279

16	Literacy Instruction and Individual Differences in Students' Cognitive Development *Jin Kyoung Hwang and Carol McDonald Connor*	307
17	Social and Cultural Differences in Reading Development: Instructional Processes, Learning Gains, and Challenges *Allison Skerrett*	328
18	Learning Academic Language, Comprehending Text *Dianna Townsend, Ana Taboada Barber, and Hannah Carter*	345
19	High Quality Language Environments Promote Reading Development in Young Children and Older Learners *Perla B. Gámez*	365
20	Expanding Teaching and Learning with Disciplinary Texts: The Case of Reading and Science *Cynthia Greenleaf and Kathleen Hinchman*	384
21	Literacy Instruction and Digital Innovation: Trends and Affordances for Digital Equity in Classrooms *Silvia Noguerón-Liu and Jayne C. Lammers*	406
22	Restorying Critical Literacies *Ebony Elizabeth Thomas, Jane Bean-Folkes, and James Joshua Coleman*	424
23	More Connected and More Divided than Ever: Toward a Cosmopolitan Ethics of Digital Literacies *David B. Sabey and Kevin M. Leander*	436

PART VI
How Do Research Methods Change the Game for Reading Researchers and Policy Makers — 453

24	The Use of Video Data in Reading Research *Brian Rowan, Bridget Maher, and Mark White*	455
25	Examining the Process of Reading in Media Text Environments: A Methodological Perspective *Byeong-Young Cho*	464
26	How Can Neuroscience Bridge Gaps in Reading Research? *Kimberly G. Noble and Katrina R. Simon*	487

Contents

27 Qualitative Case Study Methodology Driven by Sociocultural Perspectives   492
    Carmen M. Martínez-Roldán

PART VII
Minding the Gaps: Translating Reading Research as the Game is Changing   **499**

28 Concluding Thoughts from the Editors   501

Contributor Biographies   *506*
Index   *512*

Preface

We begin Volume V of the *Handbook of Reading Research* by raising questions that ground this research in the demands of the past, present, and future. As in previous volumes, some of these questions are fundamental and perennial: How do we define "reading"? What is the current state of reading research, and what are the possibilities moving forward? What are the challenges of studying reading development and learning in the United States and around the world? What research methods might help us more fully attend to the challenges of reading development and learning? In this volume, we explore these questions as well as others that reflect the unique and rapidly evolving demands of the current era, one filled with both gaps and possibilities. Although the word "gaps" may call up the oft-used language of achievement or opportunity, our use of the word is meant to convey the disconnect we see between research production and research applications. In this time of increasing access to rapidly changing texts, tools, and technologies; new forms of social engagement and connection; evolving workplace and societal demands with respect to the literacy skills of the individual; and growing linguistic and ethno-racial diversity, researchers are presented with new opportunities and new responsibilities to conduct research that builds understanding across groups and breaks down unproductive disciplinary, methodological, and discursive differences. We therefore situate our review of the latest advances in reading research in the phenomena that are changing the playing field of reading, learning to read, and teaching others to read.

Minding the Gaps

As the editors of this volume, we have chosen to explore several areas of opportunity and disconnect in reading research. Ultimately, understanding – and narrowing or closing – these gaps will help us match the science of reading, learning to read, and teaching reading to the diversity of today's classrooms, the complexities of a new digital age, and the changing demands of 21st-century workforce and community participation. In this volume, we note four gaps that persist in reading research, each of which is tightly related to and implicated by or in the other three. These gaps are:

- *Translational research gap:* This focuses on the gap between the research conducted in laboratories or other controlled settings and research conducted in practice. The focus here is on both the gap between basic and applied research, and the gap that occurs as researchers translate – or fail to translate – both basic and applied research into discourse and knowledge that

Preface

is meaningful and useful in contexts of teaching and learning. This translational gap has enormous implications for the implementation gap because it is often the case that many critical dimensions of research findings are lost in translation from controlled settings to actual conditions of teaching and learning.

- *Implementation gap*: This gap exists between what we know about how reading develops and what we know about how to teach people to read – and what actually occurs in classrooms across this increasingly diverse nation, especially under conditions of poor resources, low-quality curricula, little sustained teacher education and professional development, and high accountability demands on teachers. In other words, how do practitioners actually *do* the things that we know from research could make a difference in people's reading and learning lives? Why do the findings of research so rarely find their way into practice in any sustained or scaled way? Why does the gap between what we *know* and what we *do* rarely seem to close?

- *Relevance gap*: This gap refers to the disconnect between high-quality research and what practitioners really want or need to know to do their instructional work. It may be that the answer to the questions posed regarding the implementation gap lies in the relevance gap, which could be a matter of researchers not addressing the most pressing questions that education practitioners have. How, as researchers, do we close this gap without giving up the integrity of questions we care about and believe are important? When should researchers follow the questions of practitioners and when should researchers' questions drive the field? What do we need to know about how to prepare readers to productively and critically engage with and within various communicative practices, particularly as those practices continue to quickly evolve?

- *Bridging gap*: Finally, the chapters address the gap in or lack of communication between and among complementary research fields, each of which could contribute to closing other gaps. How do we begin to look across various methods, epistemologies, and questions with the goal of advancing our knowledge? How do we ensure that we draw from multiple perspectives and methods without compromising the quality and integrity with respect to theories, methods, and perspectives?

To explore these gaps, we begin the volume by framing the "game changers" that demand a new approach to reading research. We then offer 23 expert reviews of both basic and applied research findings in areas with a strong existing research base. Building from our framework focused on gaps, these reviews offer significant substantive or methodological advances and are organized by their focus on addressing gaps related to readers' identities and experiences; reading instructional practices, texts, and contexts; and reading research methodologies. These chapters offer not only syntheses but also implications for future research. Importantly, the authors themselves also bring diverse perspectives, methods, backgrounds, and experiences in the field, broadly-defined.

Following the 23 research reviews, we offer four snapshots of new research methods. Rather than provide a complete instruction manual for how to engage in a certain method, authors were asked to present a compelling portrait of what the particular method could offer to reading research. These design and methods essays are meant to inspire game-changing research to help reading scholars contribute to closing gaps.

We conclude the volume with our thoughts about the obstacles that stand in our way as we seek to close gaps, and we ponder what gap-closing work could do in the face of the game-changing conditions of the past decade and the next. In a departure from past volumes of the handbook, the conclusion starts by considering a major obstacle in gap closing: the way media present the problems of reading and education. We raise questions about how future research might close gaps in today's challenging contexts, especially in the face of media influences on the value of evidence and knowledge production. This new generation of research has implications for the development of literacy programs, teaching practice, teacher education, systems of instruction in and out of school, conditions of schooling, and education policies.

It should be noted that the volume is organized around the field's dominant theory that comprehension and meaning making occur at the intersection of a reader, a text, and an activity, all situated in particular and multiple contexts, with parts focusing on those four dimensions (readers, texts, instructional activity, and contexts) of the interactive model of reading. However, because reading is about the intersection of those dimensions, in many cases a chapter dedicated to understanding readers might also implicate how texts works, or a chapter focused on instruction will, of necessity, attend to who readers are. Indeed, the blurring of the dimensions – although challenging for editors trying to organize the handbook parts – is a testament to the fact that the science of reading is never simple. Reading itself is a complex process, learning to read is more complex, and teaching people to read may be the most complex process of all.

Part I: Game Changers in Reading Research: Setting the Stage

In this introductory chapter, we – the editors – set the stage for the handbook by describing what we consider to be key *game changers* of the current era that shape the conduct of research, its transformative potential, and our abilities as researchers to close the gaps we have described. Some of these game changers were present, or were beginning to develop, when the last volume of the handbook was published, but, by and large, the changes we have outlined in Chapter 1 are new or are having a new impact. Some game changers will be unpacked even further in several chapters, and so we nod to them, but do not fully delineate them. Others that are less central to reading research, but that nevertheless have an impact on the work we do, receive more attention in this initial chapter.

Part II: How Increasingly Diversified Populations Change the Game for Readers, Teachers, Leaders, and Reading Researchers

Part II introduces the volume through a *demographic lens*, as Proctor and Chang-Bacon examine the characteristics of the student population and the teaching force before looking to current research and educational approaches that recognize the racial, ethnic, and linguistic breadth that characterizes children and youth in schools today. Pointing to the gap between increasingly culturally diverse student populations and the continuing static demography of the teaching population, Proctor and Chang-Bacon argue that literacy research and education must embrace a broad range of methods that will shape learning, education policies, and lifelong opportunities for future generations.

Lee's chapter moves us from a demographic lens to an incisive analysis of the complex culturally shaped "problem space" that attends classroom interactions, text selections, curricular reforms, and assessments of reading comprehension. Like Proctor and Chang-Bacon, Lee recognizes the negative consequences for youth whose reading competence is assessed under assumptions of knowledge, experiences, and timelines that may not be universal. Lee argues for research methods informed by cross-disciplinary scholarship that recognize youth capacity – and motivation – to recruit and generate knowledge from multiple, diverse pathways as they produce and interpret texts in school and across the lifespan. Lee's interrogation of the limitations of existing assessments of comprehension, standards, and conceptions of text complexity suggests implications for the design of culturally-informed and supportive learning environments.

Finally, Smagorinsky, Guay, Lewis Ellison, and Willis examine reading and reading research through a sociocultural lens. Focusing primarily on African American students' historical achievement gap in reading as determined by school testing, the authors explore the ways in which reading is subject to social and cultural mediation in practice, policy, and research, all of which contribute to our understanding of the state of reading development in the U.S. and its schools. The authors question a common assumption that views reading as an isolated act between reader and text – a view that minimizes readers' unique backgrounds and experiences while defining "normalcy" in relation to the dominant culture. Ultimately, their review argues for the inclusion of more diverse perspectives across all facets of reading development assessment, practice, policy, and research.

Part III: How Do Expanding Forms of Texts and Everyday Communication Change the Game for Readers, Teachers, Leaders, and Reading Researchers?

Over the past decade, digital platforms have contributed to a surge in the availability of various types of texts for readers of all ages, with specific purposes and practices that extend well beyond the "one reader-one text" models that have long defined reading research. In a comprehensive review of models for multi-text reading across print and digital texts, Bråten, Braasch, and Salmerón outline the range of reader intentions and "epistemic thinking" with multiple texts, within and outside of classroom settings. While emphasizing the value of well-developed and useful starting points in existing research, they point to the astounding gap between current theoretical frameworks for understanding teacher-directed text analyses and readers' self-directed, online critical reading across texts and platforms.

This gap in our understanding of readers' digital experiences becomes especially apparent in Mackey's review of online events during the summer of 2016, a pivotal time in the shifting landscape of reading and reading research due to the proliferation of non-traditional texts and mobile devices, the 25th anniversary of the World Wide Web, and the consequential role that social media played during the U.S. presidential election and the U.K. Brexit vote. Mackey confirms the trend toward an increasing range of digital texts and the related difficulty of accessing reliable data about readers' usage, digital format, and content. Ultimately, her analysis contributes to our understanding of how readers select and interact with text in the digital age and highlights the importance of monitoring how critical, social, and deep reading play out across a range of text types and reading conditions.

Similarly, Baron's review of international research on digital reading points to gaps in our understanding of the potential differences between how people read on digital screens versus print – in other words, exploring the question of whether the container matters. Baron synthesizes existing research on learners' interactions with digital text and, like Mackey, she highlights the complexity and importance of obtaining reliable or focused demographic, cognitive, perceptual, and usage data. Baron concludes by suggesting future research questions focused on building a deeper, more meaningful understanding of digital reading with implications for pedagogical practice.

Finally, in the last chapter of this part, Campano, Nichols, and Player continue with questions about digital access and reader agency through the lens of multimodalities and colonization in literacy research. They argue that rather than explore diverse modes in ways that can reproduce hierarchies of competence and exclusion through a "confrontation between different literate traditions" (Rasmussen, 2012, p. 3), researchers should, instead, recognize the power of considering multimodalities through a postcolonial lens, whether in digital or face-to-face composing and reading. Through multimodal literacies, across print and digital platforms, a "multiplicity of identities (even within the self), languages, literacies, and meaning-making practices" (p. 106) are mobilized and reclaimed. This analysis has implications for practice and future research.

Part IV: How Do Expanding Conceptualizations of Readers Change the Game for Teachers, Leaders, and Reading Researchers?

In recent years, reading research has faced many opportunities – and responsibilities – to better match and reflect the growing diversity (cultural, linguistic, and economic) among learners in the U.S., and to consider how these dimensions of diversity necessarily influence the conceptualization of reading and inform effective models of instruction. At the same time, there has been a well-warranted press to ensure that we are taking a sufficiently comprehensive view of the reader, focusing on the role of cognitive and non-cognitive factors in text comprehension, or by examining the pathway between language acquisition and reading comprehension, across different developmental stages, for example. In turn, this set of chapters is a reminder that a more expansive view of the reader should inform a next generation of theories, research, and instructional approaches, to ensure a 21st century knowledge base.

In their introductory chapter to this part, Uccelli, Phillips Galloway, and Qi examine the findings from studies conducted on adolescents' academic language – studies using both qualitative and quantitative methods. Uccelli and colleagues outline four research developments that have helped to transform the field's understanding of academic language, all of which point to a need for a more inclusive definition of this notion of school-relevant language. To this end, Uccelli and colleagues offer a new term, Language for School Literacy, defined as "the repertoire of discourse practices and academic language skills that learners gradually internalize as they flexibly enact the socio-cultural norms of reading, writing, and learning at school" (p. 156). At a time when the school-age population continues to diversify on many dimensions, and the press for developing students' academic language continues to increase, this more inclusive and integrated conceptualization of academic language offers an important contribution, and brings with it implications for future research and classroom practice.

Expanding the discussion of learner diversity, Fox explores the relationship between readers' affect-related and cognitively-based individual differences. Highlighting the role that readers' feelings and beliefs play in their interaction with and comprehension of texts, Fox argues that understanding this affective diversity is key to understanding why and how people read, as well as their reading-related outcomes. Fox concludes with suggestions aimed at closing the gaps between affect and cognition within the theoretical frameworks used to explore reading, and in the context of instructional practice.

Next, Khan and Justice address the divides in research, theory, and practice related to children's early language acquisition and later reading outcomes. This chapter seeks to bridge the gap between these bodies of work by highlighting connections between early language acquisition and future reading outcomes and by proposing a developmental model of reading comprehension designed to connect early and middle childhood. Khan and Justice also highlight classroom practices that have the most potential to foster the language-related skills that are key to later reading success, suggesting an interconnected view of language and reading development that has the potential to support instructional continuity across grade levels and, ultimately, "provide a more coherent learning pathway for children" (p. 206).

Building on this discussion of early language and reading development, Mancilla-Martinez and McClain attend to the gaps as they relate to our understanding of children's vocabulary learning. In this chapter, they synthesize the research related to the complex factors that influence how children from diverse backgrounds acquire vocabulary, paying special attention to the gaps between what we know and do not know when it comes to children's language environments, language acquisition processes, and their opportunities to hear and use increasingly sophisticated and diverse vocabulary at school and at home. Mancilla-Martinez and McClain close by discussing promising practice-based approaches that support children's vocabulary development and by suggesting areas for future research.

Like vocabulary, prior knowledge plays an important role in helping children understand and comprehend texts. In their chapter, Cervetti and Wright explore and synthesize the research related to different types of topic, domain, general, and cultural knowledge, drawing connections between these forms of knowledge and children's language and reading development. Though a great deal of research has been conducted on the topic of knowledge and its relation to children's reading skills, much of this research has resulted in a largely singular instructional focus and approach – one aimed at activating children's prior knowledge to support their interaction with and comprehension of various texts. Cervetti and Wright argue that opportunities remain to further explore how supporting children to explicitly build and integrate knowledge shapes their language and reading skills. Ultimately, bridging the gap between our understanding of knowledge activation, knowledge building, and knowledge integration has implications for designing and enhancing discipline-specific and conceptually-rich instructional practice.

Allen and McNamara close this part with an examination of the role of higher-order thinking and metacognition among diverse groups of learners. In their literature review, they explore distinctions between surface and deep comprehension with a focus on adolescent and adult readers, younger developing readers, second language learners, and adult literacy learners. They identify gaps between theoretical understandings of the role of higher-order thinking and metacognitive strategies, which research has shown to support children's reading comprehension, and applications of these theories in practice. Too often, they argue, educational practice prioritizes a linear conception of literacy skill development that introduces higher-order and metacognitive strategies only after readers have mastered basic decoding skills. Allen and McNamara conclude by offering suggestions for bridging these translation and implementation gaps.

Part V: How Do Expanding Conceptions of Teacher, Reader, and Text Interaction Change the Game for Reading Researchers, Teachers, Leaders, and Policy Makers?

Building on previous parts, Part V explores expanding conceptions of reading, readers, and texts in the contexts of learning and teaching people to read. Because the chapters in this part are situated within the contexts of teaching and learning, the authors have necessarily paid particular attention to the implementation gap – the gap between what is known about reading instruction and instructional responses in practice.

This part begins with chapters that focus on expanded conceptions of individual readers. Hanno, Jones, and McCoy move past assumptions that the relationship between self-regulation and reading is unidirectional, moving from self-regulation to reading, and review current literature to offer a conceptual model of the bidirectional relationship between self-regulation and reading through early literacy development, which has significant implications for practice. The authors review six intervention studies that encapsulate the bi-directional relationship between literacy development and self-regulation, and close by offering implications for instructional practice and research.

In the next chapter, Hwang and Connor continue to review studies on individual readers, expanding conceptions of the differences and influences that contribute to an individual's cognitive development in relation to reading. Also moving beyond a one-way directional view of reading proficiency, Hwang and Connor offer the Lattice Model as a way to portray reading development as a complex web of cognitive, linguistic, and comprehension processes that are influenced by an individuals' learning experiences in the home, school, and community. The

Lattice Model supports the notion of a reciprocal effect of reading comprehension on cognitive development.

Next, Skerrett examines the social and cultural differences in reading development and instruction. Following a review of the foundations of sociocultural perspectives on literacy, Skerrett discusses studies on aspects of reading instruction that have largely been informed by sociocultural perspectives, including those that explore reading identity, choice texts, shared texts, instruction across contexts, and integrating sociocultural and cognitive factors in reading instruction. In so doing, Skerrett attends to the individual reader as situated across multiple contexts, and thus provides an expanded conception of the influences of reading instruction.

Moving from readers to texts, Townsend, Barber, and Carter attend to what has long been a contested term: academic language. Informed by work in the area of Systemic Functional Linguistics (SFL), the authors define *academic language* and *academic literacy* as two, often overlapping, categories of instructional targets. They review intervention studies intended to improve academic language at the elementary and secondary levels and contrast this body of research with intervention studies aimed at improving academic literacy skills. In so doing, they clarify the distinction between these two overlapping, but distinct, domains, and discuss implications for future studies on the relationship between academic literacy, vocabulary, and reading comprehension. The authors raise questions about how to attend to ideological and raciolinguistical issues of what counts as academic language and literacy while drawing on a "neutral" framework, such as SFL, and call for instruction that makes space for critical conversations that explore the functions of academic language.

Gamez continues with a chapter that considers what it might look like for classrooms to make space for critical conversations, not just with an eye toward the functions of language, but also toward the ways in which classroom discussions influence reading comprehension, overall. Gamez expands notions of what makes for high-quality language experiences in school and at home, moving from a focus solely on the quantity of teacher or caregiver words to one that considers the syntactical complexity and vocabulary diversity of dialogue. She concludes by suggesting practical applications to increase high quality conversations in classrooms, including intentional read-aloud opportunities for younger readers and, for adolescent readers, text-based classroom discussion amongst peers.

Moving from primarily spoken language to language in written texts, Greenleaf and Hinchman delve into the research-based practices that support students to engage with disciplinary texts. Focusing on the domain of science, the authors take a "social practices" view of disciplinary literacy, exploring the role of texts in disciplinary inquiry and knowledge building, and the characteristics of such texts. Their review of the research reveals implementation gaps, particularly around how students learn to read specialized texts from a developmental perspective in contrast to a social practices view. When it comes to teaching with disciplinary texts, gaps exist between what is known about how to support teachers to use disciplinary texts in their classrooms and what is known about teachers' understanding of the epistemologies and practices of their discipline. The authors call for more research on literacy instruction that simultaneously develops requisite skills, strategies, and dispositions for discipline-specific reading and reasoning; builds knowledge about subjects of study; and meaningfully engages with the lives and languages students bring to the classroom.

Also expanding our conception of texts in instruction, Nogueron-Liu and Lammers's chapter reviews studies about the features and affordances of digital tools, and their implications for classroom-based practices. Literacy practices within classrooms can be understood as activities mediated by a wide range of meaning-making tools – including multiple languages, media, texts on various platforms (e.g., print books, CD-ROMs, websites), and devices to access content. The authors argue that by framing new technologies as mediational tools, researchers can better understand the history embedded in digital platforms and software, and the ways in which they are constructed, adopted, and changed. The authors review studies that reveal how new forms and practices for reading texts can be shaped by the features of available digital tools, which are in turn driven by different equity-based goals. Teachers then select digital tools based on their needs to meet curriculum standards, as well as their efforts to teach and introduce new literacy dispositions.

Next, Thomas, Bean-Folkes, and Coleman review the history of critical literacy from its beginnings in the early 20th century, "for the place where a story *begins* influences the meaning that can be derived from that story" (p. 432). In restoring the traditions of critical literacy, the authors provide implications for youth who use participatory media sites to become civically involved, to construct and understand themselves in the context of the narratives that make up their world, and to choose to read texts that reflect themselves. The authors review studies of teaching practices that question and disrupt the status quo and discuss the hurdles that educators and researchers may face in bridging the definition, relevance, implementation, and translation gaps.

Finally, Sabey and Leander consider the relationships amongst ethics, digital literacies, and education within the global dynamics of this era. They begin by framing digital literacies as social practices that produce localizing and globalizing movements and contribute to the homogenization and heterogenization of the political, social, and cultural forces within any cultural realm of interpretation or "figured world" (p. 437). Within these tensions, the authors consider how literacy scholarship can engage more directly with the development of ethical digital social practices, to which they turn to the theory of cosmopolitanism. They review literature on the applications of cosmopolitanism to present a framework on how "unsettling encounters," "critical reflections," and "hospitable dialogues" all play roles in cosmopolitan interactions, with a goal towards more ethical digital literacy education (p. 439 ff).

Part VI: How Do Research Methods Change the Game for Reading Researchers and Policy Makers

As noted at the beginning of this preface, the handbook does not only review research; it also aims to frame future research agendas. To this end, this set of chapters focuses on research methods that offer significant advances to bridging gaps amongst reading research methodologies; reading instructional practices, texts, and contexts; and readers' identities and experiences. Each chapter in this part is not intended to be an exhaustive review of the particular method, nor is it intended to teach readers how to enact the method, but rather to make readers aware of the assumptions that undergird the approach, the goals of using the approach, and the possibilities for using the approach to address, if not close, the gaps that frame this volume.

First, Rowan, Maher, and White examine the use of video data in reading research. The authors describe trends and opportunities related to video data collection, storage, labeling, and analysis in the context of qualitative and quantitative studies. Rowan and colleagues highlight the promise of video data as a potentially powerful tool for addressing or closing gaps in reading research, particularly in terms of bridging new and traditional research methods, narrowing the gap between basic and applied research, and addressing issues of classroom implementation. They close by describing their own research, which incorporates video data and suggests implications for future scholarship.

Next, Cho explores methods for studying reading across various forms of media, including through the use of concurrent verbal protocols, cued verbal reports, task-based discourses, ethnographic interviews, eye movement measures, and log files. In an increasingly complex digital age, Cho argues that researchers can and should use diverse research methods and measures to better understand readers' cognitive engagement with a variety of media and text types. Ultimately, his review provides a reminder that "theory and methodology are symbiotic" and that a consistently evolving conception of research methods will be key to bridging understanding and implementation gaps given the multifaceted, complex, and complicated nature of reading in different media text environments.

Seeking to bridge gaps within and between disciplines, Noble and Simon explore methods for studying the neurobiological basis of reading. The authors acknowledge the high costs associated with neuroscientific methods such as brain imaging, but they argue that there is, in fact, substantial value inherent in exploring reading by getting under the hood through this relatively new approach. Noble and Simon outline three central and promising areas of neuroscientific reading research ripe for further review, including the use of neuroscience to elucidate differences in the brain that may not be detectable through behavioral approaches alone, the use of neuroscience to predict reading impairments that may not otherwise be observable in very young children, and the use of neuroscience to generate evidence that is particularly compelling for decisionmakers and stakeholders across the fields of research, policy, and practice.

Finally, Martínez-Roldán illustrates the use of multiple methods for exploring how community and linguistic diversity mediate reading. These methods include some that are familiar – a traditional qualitative case study method, for example – as well as some that may be considered novel, such as a combination of a sociocultural approach influenced by Vygotsky's concept of mediation and by Cultural-Historical Activity Theory (CHAT). Martínez-Roldán describes how such an approach, which is characterized by a focus on both the use of cultural tools in learning and a conception of learning as an "activity system," can be used both to address translation and implementation gaps related to bilingual children's language and reading development and, ultimately to "generate social change and combat inequalitites" (p. 492). The chapter closes with a discussion of the author's use of this generative research approach to bridge gaps between researchers, teachers, and teacher candidates who seek to understand and respond to emergent bilingual learners' unique strengths and needs.

Part I
Game Changers in Reading Research
Setting the Stage

1

Game Changers in Reading Research

Elizabeth Birr Moje, Peter P. Afflerbach, Patricia Enciso, and Nonie K. Lesaux

---

To frame Volume V of the *Handbook of Reading Research*, we situate the examination of reading research in today's contexts of reading, learning to read, teaching reading, and using what we read in the world. In thinking about how reading is studied and practiced, however, we focus on uncovering some of the social, economic, and political conditions of research, teaching, and learning contexts—conditions that shape how reading occurs; develops; and is learned, taught, and studied. These contextual conditions also contribute to widening, mediating, and/or shrinking the gaps highlighted across the volume. Specifically, we interrogate the factors that change the game, in ways that may be positive or negative, for students, teachers, leaders, and researchers.

Whether researchers are concerned with examining the relationships between knowledge and comprehension processes, documenting the social and cultural practices that shape meaning making, or analyzing the impact of digital technologies on reading, they invoke interrelated systems with different levels and loci of influence, from macro (state and societal systems), to meso (school and education policies and systems), to micro (classrooms, informal learning spaces, homes, and families). The graphic in Figure 1.1 represents just some of the conditions that are changing the game for teachers, school leaders, families, policy makers, and reading researchers. Beyond state and national systems, researchers also recognize the influence of global inequalities, economies, and migrations requiring new approaches to educational practice and research that value diverse ways of knowing, being, and doing.

Many demands press on and push out of these systems, posing challenges both to teaching reading and to the conduct of reading research within the real conditions of schooling. These game-changing demands necessitate that we work *as a field* to close the gaps. Intersecting conditions across interlocking systems make intervening in any one condition—or outcome of a condition—in any given space incredibly difficult for teachers, leaders, policy makers, and researchers, especially if these players are not attempting to reach across the gaps. This volume highlights gaps in reading education and research that have widened and, we argue, must be addressed by our field. In particular, educators and researchers are increasingly aware of the responsibility to understand readers more fully—as social, emotional, cognitive, and cultural beings whose quality of life depends, in part, on supportive and informed learning environments. Taking up this responsibility, we identify the game-changing conditions that have shaped contemporary contexts for reading research and have influenced the organization of this volume and the research reviews that follow.

Classroom systems
- increased access to multiple texts
- new literacy practices
- more, and more robust, curricular demands
- increased testing
- greater inclusion across the reading skill spectrum
- growth in linguistic, cultural, racial/ethnic diversity

School and education policies and systems
- diminishing school resources
- decreasing school oversight
- lower teacher pay and benefits
- advances in assessment
- improved access to data
- increased accountability demands
- reduced teacher preparation requirements
- increased demand for teaching particular reading skills

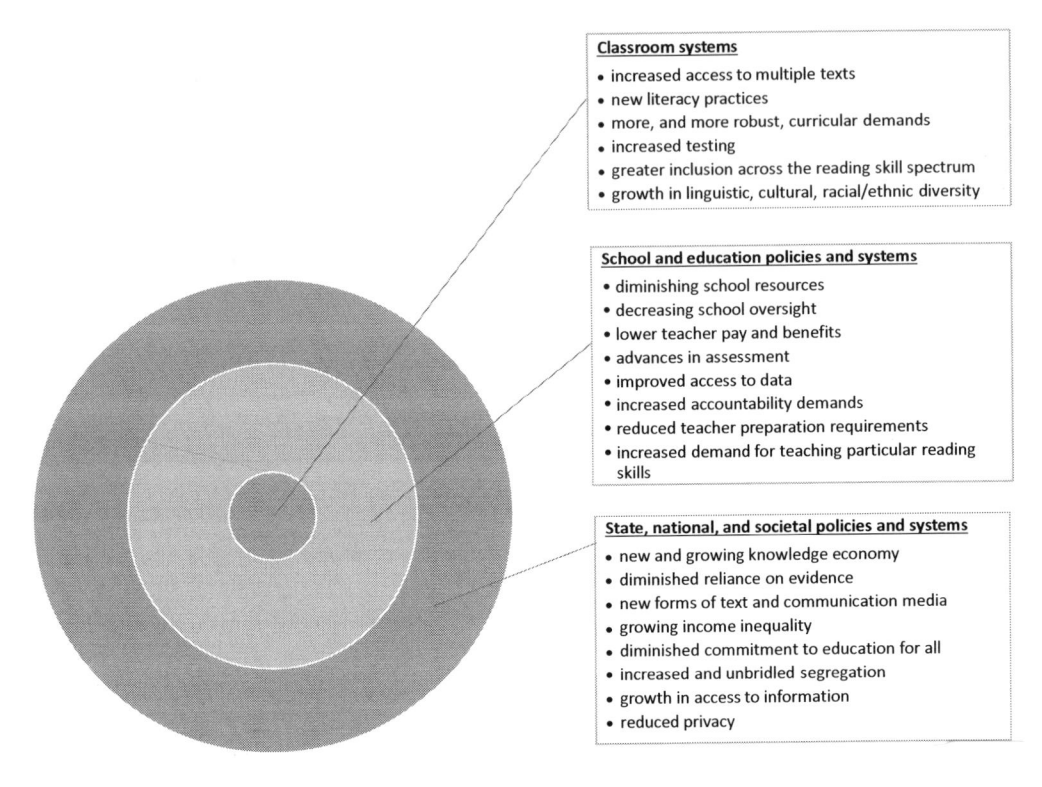

State, national, and societal policies and systems
- new and growing knowledge economy
- diminished reliance on evidence
- new forms of text and communication media
- growing income inequality
- diminished commitment to education for all
- increased and unbridled segregation
- growth in access to information
- reduced privacy

Figure 1.1 Conditions of education contexts that shape reading research and practice

Describing the Game Changers

Some of the conditions or game changers we outline below are familiar to those who have followed 21st-century literacies work in which education is shaped by an increasingly global, information-oriented "fast times" economy (c.f. Gee, 2000). Increasing availability of information—both filtered and unfiltered, edited and unedited, accurate and questionable—for example, is a game changer in terms of our thinking about what and how students need to learn, and especially about how they learn to read. Availability of information has also intensified in the sense that information is delivered constantly and in multiple forms (image, word, sound). Sometimes one bit of information delivered in a particular medium conflicts with other bits, delivered in different media, requiring readers to make sense of these various forms simultaneously, and at a speed not required in reading print on paper. The speed of access to that information has also changed how we think about literacy, and reading, in particular. Children and youth, some argue, do not only need to learn to read for meaning but also need to learn how to seek, sort, and evaluate the information they read because so much information is produced so quickly, and often with little verification or editing.

At the national level, other demands were ushered in with the education reforms of the Clinton, Bush, and Obama administrations. The disaggregating of test data promoted by every presidential administration since the Clinton administration revealed the ways that many children were, actually, being left behind. Disaggregation of data also illuminated the fact that who got left behind depended a great deal on race, socioeconomic status, and language skill (see Proctor and Chang-Bacon, Chapter 2, this volume, for specific analysis of these demographic challenges to learning literacy and to academic and economic success writ large). Moreover, many U.S. policy makers argued that no child was learning at the levels necessary to ensure U.S. success in a global market; similar trends in global policy contexts—especially in Western developed countries—can also be seen as more and more countries sought increased learning outcomes for their children and youth (World Bank, 2019).

Coupled with decreasing economic prominence and increasing trade imbalances, the United States responded similarly in the late 1990s and early 2000s as it did in the Sputnik era of the 1950s, casting the education system as one in crisis, and demanding new standards and new accountability. The fear of being left behind globally inspired discourses of competition ("race to the top") as an antidote to the pending "crisis." Competition discourses worldwide revolve around what are variously referred to as "market-based education reforms" that purport to make the work of educating children more competitive, thus allowing the market (i.e., parents, and in some cases, youth) to decide on education practices by choosing the best options for their children or themselves (Plank & Sykes, 2003). The notion of choice is meant to give people options on a variety of dimensions, from quality of offerings and pedagogy; to the perspectives or values espoused in a given school setting; to the size, location, safety, schedule, and other dimensions of school operation. The fact that opportunities to choose are mediated by social, economic, and political realities of people's lives (Hanushek, Kain, Rivkin, & Branch, 2007) is often overlooked in the discourses of choice and competition, creating game-changing conditions in a range of school contexts (Bifulco & Ladd, 2006; Saporito, 2014). These market-based reforms are often associated with public charters, voucher movements, and alternative routes to teacher certification.

In addition to thinking about these demands, we approached this handbook focused on the ways in which a new global economy produces material effects on education practice, policy, and research. A dominant theme throughout the handbook, therefore, is the question of how reading researchers need to account for these effects in their work. What some might think of as distal influences on reading, learning to read, teaching reading, and conducting reading research, we actually posit as game changers—ones that demand reading researchers do a better job of closing gaps. In what follows, we describe several of these game changers, noting that some chapters in this volume take these game changers on in very specific ways. For those game changers not addressed in the handbook as independent chapters, we draw attention to the conditions they produce and the questions these changes should raise for reading researchers.

A Changing Ethnic, Racial, and Socioeconomic Landscape

Increasing migration across national and local boundaries has dramatically shaped the composition of not only U.S. classrooms, but also classrooms around the world. As Proctor and Chang-Bacon (this volume, Chapter 2) describe, the U.S. student population is increasingly diverse, even in locations outside major cities. What has not changed radically, however, is the teaching workforce, which remains largely homogeneous. The contrast between the racial, cultural, and linguistic backgrounds of predominantly monolingual, white, female teachers and their plurilingual, racialized, religiously and culturally diverse student populations is a game changer, especially when considering that reading instruction and research can be skewed toward assumptions of universal childhoods (Bloch, Kennedy, Lightfoot, & Weyenberg 2006; Dumas & Nelson, 2016) and equitably resourced learning environments (Cook-Harvey, Darling-Hammond, Lam, Mercer, & Roc, 2016).

In their chapter, Proctor and Chang-Bacon explicitly address the demands and implications of forging research and educational change within the context of widening demographic and economic differences in school and community contexts. Recognizing demographic changes as well as long histories of racialization, Lee (this volume, Chapter 3) and other authors outline precisely how researchers and educators might realize new relations of trust and engagement with youth who desire and deserve more robust learning environments. The gap among theory, research, and teaching, however, remains and demands cross-system investment in a vision of equity and change.

Workforce and Changes in the U.S. and Global Economy

A global economy has changed the way people in any country think about educating children, youth, and adults for the world of work and for active community participation. Although often cast as the effects of a more technological, information-based economy, the reality is that the diminished U.S. manufacturing and labor portfolio has simply reduced options for our students. It is worth noting that service jobs actually still exist in large numbers in our society, but that wages for those jobs have not kept pace with inflation (Bailey & Belfield, 2019; Krugman, 1997, 2017), suggesting that the demand for "knowledge workers" might be overstated.

Despite these economic analyses that call attention to wage rather than knowledge disparities, it remains the case that attention to literacy—and reading in particular—is a crucial need in a society whose "game" has changed in these ways. Given that the U.S. economy is no longer based on manufacturing, learning to read is a necessary ingredient of full participation in a society that depends on and demands literacy. "Learning to read" signifies more than the ability to call out words or to answer multiple choice questions on a test. It involves reading widely and deeply for meaning, and using what one reads to do real work in the real world, and sifting through the welter of information that comes to individuals in an information economy. It also refers to developing the skills and competencies that allow a reader to question and challenge received knowledge in a given text, or taken-for-granted assumptions about how the world works, that shape disciplines and other domains of practice. In sum, 8th or 10th grade basic literacy skills are insufficient for life; it is more difficult than ever before to be successful in a society in which the great majority of high-paying jobs require at least a college education and, typically, advanced degrees, which has implications for reading research and educational practice.

New Forms of Text and New Communication Practices

In this knowledge economy, for better and for worse, youth and adults communicate identity, knowledge, and aspiration across digital platforms offering boundless exposure to and interaction with texts, images, and sounds. Although communication is the primary driver for digital connectivity, youth and teachers are also reading and interpreting a continuously changing flow of new textual forms. This scenario produces both generative change in the conceptualization of text and challenging gaps in identifying when, what, and how reading is happening.

Bråten, Braasch, and Salmerón (this volume, Chapter 5), Mackey, (this volume, Chapter 6), and Baron (this volume, Chapter 7), all frame and address the question of "what is a text" in terms of the container. Does it matter if the text is read online or in hard copy? As a fundamental focus for basic reading research this question of text form is a game changer: Where, when and how does reading happen if the text is not sourced and vetted? What happens when readers are searching for information and constructing meaning across platforms with multiple online and offline texts? What is happening to readers, by readers, and with readers as they read and create texts for new purposes?

Some of the greatest implementation gaps between research and schools appear to lie in teachers' and school leaders' assumptions about what new text forms do and do not do, and in how to use different media to enhance learning, rather than to distract from it. Many researchers are creating, evaluating, and/or implementing digital platforms to support comprehension (c.f. Allen & McNamara, this volume, Chapter 14), community reading with youth (Noguerón-Liu and Lammers, this volume, Chapter 21) and disciplinary literacy in science education (Greenleaf and Hinchman, this volume, Chapter 20). Importantly, many researchers address the problem of "the text" across different domains of reading and literacy education. As their research suggests, reading researchers will continue to need rigorous, open-minded, and systematic cross-domain research on texts and the power of texts in all their forms in a new decade.

Testing

Within education systems, and throughout society, testing exerts both obvious and nuanced influence on reading theory, practice, and research. Tests have an impact on how students, teachers, parents, administrators, legislators, and the general public conceptualize growth in literacy, the appropriateness of curriculum and instruction, suitable assessment, and learning outcomes. It is difficult to overstate the influence of testing on how reading curriculum, instruction, and student learning occur in the everyday. In some respects, 21st-century schooling has been marked by an ever-escalating race to teach and learn at an ever faster, development-defying pace, so that youth will eventually be competitive in a fast-paced global economy. Testing mediates the discourse between reading research and reading practice, and therefore is responsible for connections and gaps in how the two communicate. For decades, testing has been—and likely will continue to be—a game changer.

Reading assessment, as part of the overall testing context, has been addressed in multiple chapters as a game changer for researchers who have developed innovative approaches to contextualizing and illuminating students' knowledge, language skills, and motivations to read (see Fox, Chapter 10; Khan and Justice, Chapter 11; Mancilla-Martinez and McClain, Chapter 12; Cervetti and Wright, Chapter 13). Although there is promise in the reading assessment space, the larger testing movement has, in many cases and contexts, simultaneously reframed children's reading development timelines and teachers' focus on the relationship between learning to read and measurable outcomes. This kind of thinking is part of the market-based reform ethic, which produces strategies that promote competition, such as pay for performance or value-added models applied to assessment. These models examine what the teacher has done to make a difference in child learning, but do not account for all the challenging conditions that the child might experience in life or in school classrooms.

This story is not new. As early as 1987, Alexander, James, and Glaser described the phenomenon of habitual testing constraining the broad conceptualization and appreciation of academic subjects and student development when conducting a review of results of the National Assessment of Educational Progress (NAEP):

> unfortunately, we are apt to measure what we can, and eventually come to value what is measured over what is left unmeasured. The shift is subtle and occurs gradually.
>
> (p. 23)

As a result, particular aspects of students' reading development—those most frequently measured by consequential tests—become the markers of progress as well as the foci of reading research design and rationale. Testing figures in how society regards schools, teachers, and students and how it conceptualizes achievement, accountability, and quality. As test scores receive most attention, an expected result is that positive influences on students' reading test scores will receive attention, and many other influences will be ignored. Testing and test scores are interwoven into the microsystems of daily classroom life, and into economic and political macrosystems of our society. Thus, testing has changed the game for teachers, leaders, and reading researchers by exerting a profound influence on both reading research and reading instruction practice at all grades (but especially at the primary grades).

Increasing Demands for Student Learning

Prompted by less-than-desirable results produced in the No Child Left Behind—and corresponding testing regime—of the 1990s, together with the warnings about the turn to a knowledge economy during the same era, the Council of Chief State School Officers (CCSSO) and the National Governors Association (NGA) worked to produce more robust learning opportunities for students, on the assumption that the poor test performance was a result of inadequate curriculum and/or instruction. The approach was to try to unify U.S. education through the establishment of common learning standards, resulting in the Common Core State Standards for English Language Arts and Literacy in History/Social Studies, Science, and Technical Subjects (as well as Common Core State Standards for Mathematics, rendered in a separate document). As described by the framers in the final document,

> the Standards are meant to be, (1) research and evidence based, (2) aligned with college and work expectations, (3) rigorous, and (4) internationally benchmarked. A particular standard was included in the document only when the best available evidence indicated that its mastery was essential for college and career readiness in a 21st-century, globally competitive society.
>
> (CCSSO & NGACBP, 2010, p. 3)

The document is also intended to be "a living work, as new and better evidence emerges, the Standards will be revised accordingly" (2010, p. 3), although to our knowledge, no revision of the Standards has been offered in the past nine years since their launch, despite significant advancements in literacy research and notable critiques of gaps in the standards (many of which are presented in this volume).

More noteworthy, the standards were just that: end goals, standards for learning, rather than curricula or professional practice guides. Teachers and school leaders were expected to achieve these standards without corresponding attention to professional development, the creation or curating of viable text resources, or the development of curricular materials. To be sure, numerous groups—including reading researchers and commercial publishers—have crafted materials, professional development opportunities, and text resources purported to be aligned with the CCSS, but no official documents or strategies were developed to accompany the standards. As the launch date makes clear, the standards have been in place for nine years, but the results of national testing regimes such as the National Assessment of Education Progress (NAEP, 2019) show a [non-significant] *decrease* in scores since 2009 (with a modest increase in scores at both 4th and 8th grade from 1992, well before the new standards were launched). Only one state, Mississippi, made statistically significant gains in reading, although their gains bring them only equal to the average score of 4th-grade students in the United States, which remains well below proficient according to NAEP metrics.

In this volume, with a lens towards forward progress and momentum, researchers look to pedagogies that support and extend students' knowledge and language development (Cervetti and Wright, Chapter 13) and toward assessments and related activities that address unique configurations of students' knowledge and language capacity relative to narrative forms and complexities (Allen and McNamara, Chapter 14). They also view students' and teachers' knowledge in a dynamic, flexible relationship with their linguistic repertoires and the academic discipline they are studying (Townsend, Chapter 18 and Uccelli, Chapter 9). Reading researchers are addressing the demand for increased student learning, for a highly diverse population, including and especially multilingual learners. Going forward, the challenge will be translating and implementing research findings across larger landscapes of classrooms and communities. Although standards will be with us for some time, the core of reading education will have to continue to focus on the interrelated practices of language in use, knowledge production, and conceptual understanding across varied narrative forms and within specific disciplinary domains.

Children Experiencing Stress(ors); Teachers Experiencing Burn-Out

One game changer that is not examined in its own chapter in this volume is the increasing level of student anxiety and trauma witnessed in the latter half of the decade between publication of HRR4 (2010) and this volume (2020). School districts around the United States are experiencing unprecedented levels of trauma, stress, and anxiety, especially in neighborhoods where youth are regularly policed, where drugs and guns are endangering lives, and where economic growth is a dire issue (Fine et al., 2003; Morsy & Rothstein, 2019). The trauma of experiencing hunger and housing insecurity, daily exposure to violence, and toxic living conditions is felt by students and teachers in many communities across all regions of the U.S. and world (Dutro, 2019; World Health Organization, 2017). Both youth living in under-resourced and well-resourced communities also experience stressors associated with bullying, high-stakes testing, toxic political discourses, and sexual harassment, often promulgated through social media (Nutt, 2018; Shalaby, 2017).

The increase in documented stress and anxiety is precipitous and unprecedented, as evidenced by the highest U.S. suicide rate in 28 years, at 13%, an increase of 24% between 1999 and 2014 (Curtin, Warner, & Hedegaard, 2016). In addition, teachers in challenging school environments name the trauma their students experience as the greatest job challenge they face, producing what is being labeled as "secondary trauma" (Walker, 2019). Even a cursory search in the popular press paints a frightening picture of this game changing condition of schooling, especially when one attends to the fact that schools and schooling-related processes themselves can cause trauma (Gaffney, 2019). As Lee (this volume, Chapter 3) points out, it is difficult to learn to read—or learn anything—when experiencing threat. Indeed, threats to any student's well-being, especially among indigenous youth, youth of color, and youth who identify as LGBTQ, means that the conditions of schooling that increasingly define human value in terms of test results and compliance are barely tolerable for youth or teachers.

In their review of research on protective factors in early childhood literacy and development, Hanno, Jones, and McCoy (this volume, Chapter 15) highlight the significance of "burnout cascade" and the ways both children and adults experience heightened stress and fractured relationships when teachers feel inadequate and unable to cope with children's needs. They argue, as do other researchers, that knowledge about and attention to one's own and others' cultural histories (Thomas, Bean-Folkes, and Coleman, this volume, Chapter 22), capacity to listen (Sabey and Leander, this volume, Chapter 23), and perception of students as competent and multifaceted (Lee, Chapter 3; Campano, Nichols, and Player, this volume, Chapter 8) can create more humanizing and expansive opportunities for learning. How, then, can these concerns become visible, prioritized features of research in reading education? If schooling and classroom conditions, interactions, and instruction are actually increasing stress, then what needs to change?

Declines in the Teacher Workforce and in Teacher Preparation

In relation to the stress experienced by teachers, a game changer not featured as its own topic in this volume is the decline in the number of well-prepared teachers in the U.S. That is, we have a teaching workforce and teacher preparation landscape that is shifting alongside many other conditions that relate to educating today's students to high levels of literacy. Specifically, the United States has witnessed increasing shortages in the overall teacher labor market since the 2008 recession when teacher salaries stagnated and many traditional teacher benefits (e.g., pension plans) were reduced or cut altogether. Furthermore, as noted in a 2019 Economic Policy Institute report, "The current national estimates of the teacher shortage likely understate the magnitude of the problem because the estimates consider the *new* qualified teachers needed to meet *new* demand" (Garcia & Weiss, 2019, p. 4). Exacerbating the numerical shortage is the lack of qualified teachers (Garcia & Weiss, 2019; Sutcher, Darling-Hammond, & Carver-Thomas, 2016). Specifically, according to the Center for American Progress (Partelow, 2019), enrollment in teacher preparation programs has declined by one-third since 2010, suggesting that there is a shortage of *prepared* teachers (Sutcher et al., 2016). The decline in teachers prepared in accredited programs is coupled with a small increase in individuals prepared in alternative certification programs; however, these programs are not required to report on outcomes (or any other data) under the Higher Education act, thus making it impossible to track completion numbers, quality of preparation, or years of service with any certainty (Partelow, 2019).

The declines tracked in teacher preparation programs vary significantly, with Oklahoma experiencing the highest decline at 80% and Massachusetts the lowest, at 15%. Michigan, which has seen a 67% decline in enrollment also had a largest decline in completers of U.S.-based teacher preparation programs, at 54%, although Oklahoma was not far behind. Coupling declining enrollments with drops in completion results in classrooms populated by teachers who are not accredited by teacher education programs. In Michigan, the shortage is so dire—especially in mathematics, sciences, world languages, and special education—that the substitute teacher pool has been depleted. Requirements for long-term (extended) substitute teachers—people who can teach an entire year in the same school—have been reduced to 60 credit hours in any subjects (i.e., not necessarily in a program of study). Some public charter schools in Detroit, Michigan, for example, employ extended substitute teachers as 100% of their teaching force (Wilkinson & French, 2019), which means that all day, every day, and all year long, children are being taught to be "college and career ready" by people who have not themselves graduated from college.

Research sheds light on the reasons for the declines; although providing details of the specific findings is beyond the scope of this chapter, the Economic Policy Institute report implicated working conditions—including many outlined above—together with lack of preparation (especially related to being asked to teach outside of one's expertise) and salaries as the most reported and/or observed explanations for teachers choosing not to enter, and choosing to leave, the profession (Garcia & Weiss, 2019).

Finally, whether a product of a diminishing workforce or a result of market-based reforms, changes in teacher certification and professional education standards are evident nationwide. According to data from the U.S. Department of Education's National Teacher and Principal Survey in 2015–2016, 8.8% of teachers do not have a standard state certificate or a professional certificate; 17.1% took a route to certification not associated with a higher education institution (USDOE, 2017).

These statistics, taken together with the fact that in the 2015–2016 academic year, 22.4% of teachers had been teaching for five or fewer years, and 9.4% had been teaching less than two years (USDOE, 2017), shed light on major issues in developing reading skills and competencies to a high degree among all students. Ultimately, it is clear that the nation's children, especially those in the most economically challenged areas of the country, where teacher shortages are at higher levels (Garcia & Weiss, 2019), are not being taught by the most prepared teachers, especially when it comes to both primary grades reading instruction and disciplinary literacy instruction (see Greenleaf and Hinchman, Chapter 21, on the importance and challenge of sophisticated disciplinary literacy teaching).

Given the gap between what we know about how the act of reading occurs and what we know about how to teach the process of reading to large and diverse groups of children simultaneously, these statistics highlight a major game changer in reading instruction and reading research. Teaching reading is a complex practice that requires sophisticated knowledge of language and linguistics, of reading processes and practices, of child development, and of the specialized learning needs of children from all backgrounds. Layer those knowledge demands at the level of the teacher with the need to understand the cultural and linguistic practices among an increasingly diverse population of children, while also meeting new standards that will be routinely tested under ever-changing testing regimes, and it should be clear that the game has changed significantly for teachers, school leaders, and reading researchers. It is especially ironic—or tragic—that this game-changing shortage of well-prepared teachers, irrespective of their training pathway, comes at a time when classrooms are more diverse, texts are more fluid and people's reach through text and text media is more global, the economy has changed and with it what learners need, accountability demands are on the rise, and learners are experiencing higher rates of stress and trauma.

What Is Reading Research in These Game-Changing Times?

As we described, the world is changing; societies are changing. Correspondingly, the work of educating the population is changing. These changes result from the complex dynamics of local and distant politics, economics, and preferences for particular reading research and practice. Policymakers and parents demand higher standards for student learning, with outcomes measured on increasingly high-stakes tests. Meanwhile underpaid, and in many cases underprepared, teachers are navigating the challenges posed by student needs and profiles even as they are learning to use new and multiple text media and technological tools that change dramatically from day to day and that provide access to increasingly unfiltered and unedited information. Game changing, indeed.

These changes therefore have implications for reading research. Changing contexts and demands within the complex systems of reading education, reading teacher education, and research on literacy learning and teaching require that we take a hard, informed look at what reading research is, why we do it, and how we know what we know (i.e., What counts as evidence? What doesn't count?). Finally, reading researchers need to ascertain how knowledge and knowledge production matter for children and youth, their teachers, school leaders, and those who influence reading policies in schools and school systems. The focus here is on the new demands and whether our "old" purposes, assumptions, methods, and designs are up to the task of producing research that addresses the contexts and conditions of change. This motivation requires that we ask questions, such as:

- Who are the students we teach, and in what ways are they different or similar as students in relation to prior generations?
- Who comprises the teaching workforce in the U.S. and around the world?
- What are the implications of these differences in student and teaching populations for their teaching and learning—the everyday collaboration in the classroom? What do those implications mean for literacy teacher education and for literacy research?

- What do we know about individual student readers' development? How is development understood in contexts of migration, war and civil/or unrest, and economic inequality?
- What do we know about reading as a cultural and social practice, again in the contexts of migration, war and/or civil unrest, and economic inequality?
- What does the lack of high-quality teacher preparation mean for the implications of the two prior questions? How do teachers who may know little about individual development and about cultural and social practices engage with and support today's diverse groups of learners?
- What do we know about the changing nature of texts, how they influence reader behaviors individually and socially, and how they are used in varying contexts?
- What do we know about instruction that considers students' individual reading development, social and cultural practices, and the demands of new texts and new ways of communicating? How can we translate these ideas into practice in ways that help teachers and school leaders with the game changers they face?
- Finally, how do we know these things? What are the most sophisticated designs and methods for researching reading? What are the most appropriate avenues of inquiry? How can we work across fields, disciplines, and epistemologies, to bridge gaps in the knowledge of reading researchers and to design even more sophisticated research designs than we have had in the past?

Each of the "what do we know" questions begs a corresponding, "what do we do with what we know" question. This handbook is published in the midst of challenging times for society, both domestic and global, and there are no easy solutions for closing the gaps made salient by these game changers. The chapters that follow take up these questions and offer the beginnings of multiple research paths forward. We invite readers to take up these questions throughout the handbook and to consider how the next decade of researchers can respond.

References

Bailey, T. R., & Belfield, C. R. (2019). The false dichotomy between academic learning and occupational skills. *Daedalus, 148*(4), 164–178. Retrieved from https://doi-org.proxy.lib.umich.edu/10.1162/daed_a_01765

Bifulco, R., & Ladd, H. F. (2006). School choice, racial segregation, and test-score gaps: Evidence from North Carolina's charter school program. *Journal of Policy Analysis and Management, 26*, 31–56.

Bloch, M., Kennedy, D., Lightfoot, T., & Weyenberg, D. (2006). *The child in the world/the world in the child: Education and the configuration of a universal, modern, and globalized childhood*. Palgrave Macmillan US.

Cook-Harvey, C., Darling-Hammond, L., Lam, L., Mercer, C., & Roc, M. (2016). *Executive Summary Equity and ESSA: Leveraging Educational Opportunity Through the Every Student Succeeds Act*. Retrieved December 2019 from www.hunt-institute.org/wp-content/uploads/2016/11/ESSA-Summary_11.10.16.pdf.

Curtin, S. C., Warner, M., & Hedegaard, H. (2016, April). *NCHS Data Brief No. 241: Increase in suicide in the United States, 1999–2014*. Retrieved December, 2019 from cdc.gov..

Dumas, M. J., & Nelson, J. D. (2016). (Re)imagining black boyhood: Toward a critical framework for educational research. *Harvard Educational Review, 86*(1), Spring 2016, 27–47.

Dutro, E. (2019). *The vulnerable heart of literacy: Centering trauma as powerful pedagogy*. New York, NY: Teachers College Press.

Fine, M., Freudenberg, N., Payne, Y., Perkins, T., Smith, K., & Wanzer, K. (2003). Anything can happen with police around": Urban youth evaluate strategies of surveillance in public places. *Journal of Social Issues, 59*, 141–158. doi:10.1111/1540-4560.t01-1-00009

Gaffney, C. (2019). When schools cause trauma. *Teaching Tolerance, 62*. Retrieved December 1, 2019 from. tolerance.org.

Garcia, E., & Weiss, E. (2019). The teacher shortage is real, large and growing, and worse than we thought. *The perfect storm in the teacher labor market*. Washington, DC: Economic Policy Institute. Retrieved December, 2019 from epi.org.

Gee, J. P. (2000). Teenagers in new times: A new literacy studies perspective. *Journal of Adolescent & Adult Literacy, 43*, 412–420.

Hanushek, E. A., Kain, J. F., Rivkin, S. G., & Branch, G. F. (2007). Charter school quality and parental decision making with school choice. *Journal of Public Economics, 91*, 823–848.

Krugman, P. R. (1997). *The age of diminished expectations: U.S. economic policy in the 1990s*. Cambridge, MA: MIT Press.

Krugman, P. R. (2017). Opinion | Why don't all jobs matter? (2017, April 17). *The New York Times*. Retrieved from www.nytimes.com/2017/04/17/opinion/why-dont-all-jobs-matter.html

Morsy, L., & Rothstein, R. (2019). *Toxic stress and children's outcomes African American children growing up poor are at greater risk of disrupted physiological functioning and depressed academic achievement*. Washington, DC: Education Policy Institute. Retrieved from www.epi.org/files/pdf/164823.pdf

NAEP. (2019). *The nation's report card: Reading*. Washington, DC: National Center for Education Statistics.

National Governors Associations Center for Best Practices, Council of Chief State School Officers. (2010). *Common core state standards*. Washington, DC: National Governors Association Center for Best Practices, Council of Chief State School Officers.

No Child Left Behind Act. (2001). Pub. L. No. 107–110, 115 Stat. 1425.

Nutt, A. E. (2018, May 10). "Why kids and teens may face far more anxiety these days. *The Washington Post*. Retrieved from www.washingtonpost.com/news/to-your-health/wp/2018/05/10/why-kids-and-teens-may-face-far-more-anxiety-these-days/

Partelow, L. (2019, December). *What to make of declining enrollment in teacher preparation programs*. Washington, DC: Center for American Progress. Retrieved December 7, 2019 americanprogress.org.

Plank, D. N., & Sykes, G. (2003). *Choosing choice: School choice in international perspective*. New York, NY: Teachers College Press.

Saporito, S. (2014). Private choices, public consequences: Magnet school choice and segregation by race and poverty. *Social Problems, 50*, 181–203.

Shalaby, C. (2017). *Troublemakers: Lessons in freedom from young children at school*. New York, NY: The New Press.

Sutcher, L., Darling-Hammond, L., & Carver-Thomas, D. (2016). *A coming crisis in teaching? Teacher supply, demand, and shortages in the U.S.* Learning Policy Institute, September 2016. Retrieved November, 2019 from https://learningpolicyinstitute.org/product/coming-crisis-teaching.

U.S. Department of Education. (2017). *Teacher shortage areas nationwide listing. 1990–1991 through 2017–2018.* June 2017. Washington, DC: Author.

Walker, T. (2019, October). "I didn't know it had a name": Secondary traumatic stress and educators. *neaToday*. Washington, DC: National Education Association.

Wilkinson, M., & French, R. (2019, August 9). Michigan school leaders decry explosion of untrained teachers in classrooms. Lansing, MI: Bridge Magazine.

World Bank. (2019). The education crisis: Being in school is not the same as learning. Retrieved December 18, 2019, from www.worldbank.org/en/news/immersive-story/2019/01/22/pass-or-fail-how-can-the-world-do-its-homework

World Health Statistics. (2017). Monitoring Health for the SDGs, Sustainable Development Goals.

Part II
How Increasingly Diversified Populations Change the Game for Readers, Teachers, Leaders, and Reading Researchers

2
Demographic Realities and Methodological Flexibility in Literacy Teaching and Research

C. Patrick Proctor and Chris K. Chang-Bacon

The ability to comprehend text and interrogate its credibility has become increasingly critical in an era of information saturation. As a result, literacy, now more than ever, is the foundation upon which content knowledge and informed civic participation are built, which places a special emphasis on quality literacy instruction for children and youth. The unique racial, ethnic, and linguistic pluralities in the United States interact with this reality, demanding that we as educators and researchers become more linguistically and methodologically flexible as we tackle thorny issues of generalizable literacy research and the means by which that research is translated into practice across tremendous variability in the instructional contexts in which children and youth are learning.

Our goal in this chapter is to present a vision of literacy education and literacy research for the current era. We argue that, when it comes to literacy, both education and research are inescapably impacted by racial, ethnic, and linguistic diversity. This requires that we, as educators and as researchers, be methodologically flexible in the means by which we structure literacy teacher education and literacy research. In other words, the dramatically heterogeneous set of demographic circumstances and variable policy landscapes that define national and international contexts have a profound impact on how we prepare teachers for literacy instruction, and for how we tackle the empirical questions and findings that guide literacy research. We see these as related issues, and thus envision educators and researchers engaged in mutual and ongoing exploration of questions about how languages and literacies vary across instructional and demographic contexts, with implications for a broader and more comprehensive understanding of literacy and its development vis-à-vis instructional practice.

In the first section of this chapter, we describe a demographic lens of race, ethnicity, and language through which literacy education and research are refracted. This section includes attention to student and teacher demographics, the mismatch between them, and the policies that have historically affected the means by which teachers are trained and researchers are constrained. In the second section, we turn specifically to literacy teacher education, defined broadly as teacher preparation (pre-service) and professional development (in-service). We locate literacy within these domains of teacher education, describing their characteristics, how literacy is framed within them, and specifically how the demographic lens creates a need for methodological flexibility in relation to how teachers are prepared to deliver literacy instruction. In the third and final section, we turn to literacy research and explore how demographic realities are, or are not, reflected in this arena. We argue that attention to demographic range (among both participants and literacy researchers themselves) is critical for informing our understandings of research findings and their relation to practice. We finally argue that methodological flexibility is critical to informing good literacy practice.

We note that, in our focus on demography, we do not directly engage issues of sexuality, disability, neurodiversity, and other critical dimensions of identity and culture that can impact literacy teaching and learning. We focus specifically on race, ethnicity, and language because we view these as core to many national contexts in which children and youth develop literacy, in part through schooling. Additionally in this chapter, we focus specifically on the U.S. context where race, ethnicity, and language are core to the country's founding, and thus relevant to both its failings and its potentialities with respect to literacy and schooling.

Ultimately, then, our challenge to the reader is simple: to apply this demographic lens to contemporary understandings of literacy, and to reflect on whether and how methodological flexibility allows us to better focus on these critical demographics in literacy work. It is our hope to set this challenge specifically for this *Handbook of Reading Research*, and more generally for literacy educators and researchers working in today's exhilarating and fraught contexts.

The Demographic Lens: Students, Teachers, and Policy

Any profession must respond to the demographic realities of its time. In education, this response involves alignment between student populations, teacher practice, and educational policy. Literacy itself is likewise affected by a complex interplay across these categories. Literacy standards inform student outcomes (and vice versa), while teachers are expected to respond to policy changes and meet standardized performance benchmarks in the face of varied levels of student need and language background. Paradoxically, education has been critiqued as "conservative" (Lortie, 1975), slow to respond to change as a profession. Below we use the demographic lens to highlight a paradox characterized by heterogeneity in the U.S. student population, alongside a "conservatism" in teacher demographics, contextualized in a shifting landscape of literacy standards and educational policy.

Student Populations

Demographically, 2014 was the first year in U.S. history in which White, English-speaking students comprised less than half of the public school enrolled population (NCES, 2017a). This shift is primarily driven by an increase in the enrollment of Latinx students, which rose from 9.0 million to 12.5 million between 2003–2013 (19% to 25% of total enrollment) and is projected to increase to 14.7 million in 2025 (29%; NCES, 2017b). Approximately one in five students is growing up speaking a language other than English at home (Ryan, 2013). These bilingual children and youth constitute the fastest growing population in U.S. schools (Shin, 2013), where English dominates as the language of instruction. While the majority of English learners were born in the U.S. (Batalova, Fix, & Murray, 2005), immigration contributes to an evolving linguistic landscape, with a record 42.2 million immigrants living in the U.S. as of 2014 (13.2% of the nation's population). This figure is projected to increase to 20% by 2060 (Colby & Ortman, 2015). In such a context, the availability of technology and the increasingly fluid nature of global migration has led to increasing numbers of transnational youth who maintain significant ties to two or more countries (Oliveira, 2017; Skerrett, 2015).

While not a perfect correlation, there is no denying the associations between race, language status, and poverty in the U.S. Kochhar and Fry (2014) note that, between 2007 and 2013, median disparities in wealth ratios increased from 10 to 12.9 and 8.2 to 10.3 between Black and

Latinx household net worth and White household net worth, respectively. In real dollars, this means that the 2013 median household net worth for White families was $81,400 but just $11,000 and $13,700 for Black and Latinx families, respectively. Recent reports also indicate that low-income students are now a majority in U.S. public schools (Southern Education Foundation, 2015), with students of color being more likely than their White peers to attend high-poverty schools (National Equity Atlas, 2016). Economic instability and the adverse childhood experiences associated with poverty are stable predictors of literacy outcomes for children and youth in the U.S. Indeed, Phillips (2016) notes that poverty can affect early neurobiological development with implications for working memory, attentional control, error processing, impulse control, and self-regulation, all of which are known predictors of reading outcomes, and also impact the likelihood of students being drawn into school disciplinary systems from an early age.

In addition, the push in recent decades for inclusion and mainstreaming of students with special needs intersects with the broadening demographic realities of U.S. classrooms. Mixed evidence indicates that students of color and English learners are both overrepresented in some disability categories (e.g., intellectual disabilities, general learning disabilities; Artiles, Klingner, Sullivan, & Fierros, 2010; Sullivan, 2011), but also underrepresented, for example, in being diagnosed with autism spectrum disorders (Jo et al., 2015; Mandell et al., 2009; Zuckerman et al., 2013, 2014). Both sets of findings point to systems for identifying students with special needs that have not kept pace with demographic and linguistic variability in U.S. schools.

Teacher Demographics

Unlike the rapidly evolving student population in U.S. schools, inertia grips the teacher demographic and sets up a demographic paradox. While students of color now comprise more than half the public school population, teachers of color are just 18% of the teacher workforce (U.S. Department of Education, 2016). And even though every state in the U.S. has a low ratio of teachers-of-color to students-of-color, this difference is most pronounced in the most diverse states, notably California and Nevada, states in the Southwest and Mid Atlantic (Boser, 2014), and in large urban centers.

The implications of this demographic paradox for literacy achievement have been thrown into sharp relief in recent years. Research has long demonstrated that U.S. schools privilege literacy practices that reflect White middle class language norms, while literacy practices that decenter those norms are often unrecognized or actively delegitimized (Delpit & Dowdy, 2008; Heath, 1982; Michaels, 1981). Delegitimization of non-White norms and expectations has been linked to the potential for imbalance in student disciplinary practices, especially suspensions and expulsions, which have been shown to affect Black and Latinx students at alarmingly disproportionate rates (see Gregory, Skiba, & Noguera, 2010 for a review). This trend is stable across the Pre-K-12 spectrum. Gilliam, Maupin, Reyes, Accavitti, and Shic (2016) found evidence of implicit bias against Black children in varied disciplinary contexts, while Okonofua and Eberhardt (2015), working with K-12 teachers, showed that student race exerted both a direct and an indirect effect on how teachers felt about when and how to discipline White versus Black students. In terms of consequences, students of color have been shown to be disproportionately removed from class relative to their White peers for comparable disciplinary infractions (Fenning & Rose, 2007; Wald & Losen, 2003).

Arcia (2006) showed how such actions have clear implications for literacy outcomes. In a three-year longitudinal study (2001–2004) Arcia compared students who had been suspended at least once during that period (n = 49,327) to matched students who had received no suspensions during that time (n = 42,809). Analyses of state reading achievement data showed that non-suspended students' reading performance was significantly higher than for suspended students, and that number of days suspended (i.e., 1–10; 11–20; or ≥ 21) was inversely associated with reading outcomes. Yet when children of color are rated by teachers of color, they are considered to be less disruptive (Dee, 2005; Downey & Pribesh, 2004; Wright, 2015) and to have better work habits (Farkas, Grobe, Sheehan, & Shuan, 1990) relative to ratings provided by White teachers.

Linguistic differences further complicate the demographic paradox. The majority of U.S. teachers are monolingual English-speakers (Howard, 2016), and the majority of schooling takes place exclusively in English. Thus, multilingual students are expected to accommodate the monolingualism of the teachers and texts they encounter in schools. This raises barriers to parent and family involvement (Cherng, 2016; Toldson & Lemmons, 2013), literacy instruction that engages students' full range of language abilities (Durán, 2017; Escamilla, 2009; García & Kleifgen, 2010), and assessment of students within and across languages (Proctor, Silverman, & Harring, 2017; Soltero-González, Escamilla, & Hopewell, 2012). Linguistic research also demonstrates the legitimacy and inevitability of dialect variation (Adger, Wolfram, & Christian, 2007; Lippi-Green, 2012; Rickford, 1999) alongside findings that suggest such variation remains stigmatized in educational settings (Bacon, 2017; Smith, 2016), particularly when used by students of color (Baker-Bell, 2013; Flores & Rosa, 2015). Teachers unfamiliar with their students' linguistic aptitudes may misinterpret dialectal differences as decoding errors (Wheeler, Cartwright, & Swords, 2012), as a lack of grammatical awareness (Dyson & Smitherman, 2009), or may dismiss students' language use altogether as "broken" English (DeBose, 2007).

Shifting Policy Landscapes

The demographic paradox between teacher and student populations intersects with shifting educational policies and literacy standards. Without doubt, the need for a highly literate population has resulted in unprecedented attention to education reform and teacher quality issues among policymakers (Cochran-Smith & Villegas, 2016). Since the Clinton-era *Goals 2000: Educate America Act* of 1994, we have seen a persistent focus on standards-and-outcomes based education reform, predicated on particular beliefs about what students need to know for a literacy-heavy economy, and, just as importantly, on being able to measure that knowledge. Following the Clinton Administration, George W. Bush launched the *No Child Left Behind Act*, which built on Goals 2000 in part by establishing penalties for schools that underperformed on standards-aligned literacy assessments. Under Barack Obama's *Race to the Top* initiative and the *Every Student Succeeds Act*, assessment paradigms remained in place, along with the requirement that high-stakes tests be attached to academically challenging literacy standards aligned with college entrance requirements and the state's career and technical education standards (ASCD, 2016).

More recently, the Common Core State Standards (CCSS) and the Next Generation Science Standards (NGSS) provide, for states that have adopted them, a set of linguistically complex standards that are founded on the types of language and literacy skills deemed relevant for 21st century knowledge economies. Holding aside concerns about banking models of education (Freire, 1970), the CCSS have been the subject of focus among literacy educators and researchers specifically for their linguistic dimensions. Similar literacy expectations emerge in the NGSS, specifically around discipline-specific ways in which scientists speak, write, and reason (Lehrer & Schauble, 2006; McNeill, Lowenhaupt, & Katsch-Singer, in press), and in the service of constructing and critiquing scientific knowledge (Pruitt, 2014).

Some have suggested that these standards lack sufficient supports and direction for a systematic implementation by districts, schools, and teachers (e.g., Calderón, Slavin, & Sánchez, 2011). On the other hand, López (2016) notes that it is "the focus on the explicit use of language as the medium of content acquisition that is lauded by scholars who have dedicated their careers to promoting equitable education ..." (p. 8). This includes the *Understanding Language* group (http://ell.stanford.edu/) who have argued that the insertion of language into content learning is critical, and provides meaningful opportunities to leverage the standards in service of threaded literacy instruction (e.g., Bunch, Kibler, & Pimentel, 2012). Rymes, Flores, and Pomerantz (2016) further suggested that these new standards "articulate the need for students to apply language knowledge purposefully, yet flexibly, to accomplish specific tasks in particular contexts" (p. 258). Here, then, we see the direct injection of language and linguistic possibilities into language arts and science standards, which can be viewed through the demographic lens as a start point for teachers and students to make instructional sense of them.

Summary

In this section, we established a demographic lens by highlighting key characteristics, incongruities, and challenges across students, teachers, and educational policy. From a teaching perspective, the reality of the demographic paradox is fraught, with implications for cultural, racial, and linguistic mismatches that can affect learning outcomes for students, particularly in the midst of linguistically intricate language, literacy, and content standards. In this time in history, students come from broad experiential and linguistic starting points, but are held to common sets of linguistic standards that are typically only in English, and implemented by teachers whose backgrounds are often more aligned with the standards than with the students. The need for broader representation and increased linguistic awareness among teachers is a clear implication of the demographic paradox. Second is the need to assess the monolingualism of our standards and the research that informs these standards to consider how broad linguistic variability interacts with large-scale implementation of linguistically complex expectations. We explore these factors below as they relate to teacher education and literacy research.

Teacher Education

Good literacy instruction requires good teachers who are knowledgeable about how language and literacy develop, and the most effective ways to teach to that development. Across demographic and policy contexts, Sleeter (2014) reminds us that "[t]eachers do not just teach reading, or fifth graders, or social justice, or English learners, or standards; they do all of these things simultaneously" (p. 151). As it stands, we have two primary approaches for promoting quality literacy instruction in schools: teacher preparation and professional development (PD), both of which are forms of teacher education. While it is beyond the scope of this chapter to provide a comprehensive review of teacher preparation and PD, we highlight these two domains as critical vehicles for aligning teachers' literacy instruction viewed through the demographic lens. In this section, we frame literacy practices in the context of teacher education and then focus on how demographic shifts intersect with both teacher preparation and professional development. Based on these factors, we conclude by offering five critical competencies for literacy teacher education to better reflect the demographic realities of today's schools and classrooms.

Literacy in Teacher Education

There is no question that literacy research has made substantial strides since the National Reading Panel (NRP, 2000) identified reading comprehension, phonics, phonemic awareness, fluency, and vocabulary (the "big 5") as key targets of literacy instruction. For example, the quantitative role of language in both reading and writing has undergone substantive investigation with broadly representative grade levels and demographic groups. Selected findings suggest that a limited focus on vocabulary is insufficient for understanding and impacting literacy outcomes, and more instructional attention to malleable linguistic factors is merited in literacy instruction, for example, morphology (Bowers, Kirby, & Deacon, 2010; Carlisle, 2010; Goodwin & Ahn, 2013; Kieffer & Lesaux, 2012; Kieffer, Petscher, Proctor, & Silverman, 2016), syntax (Foorman, Koon, Petscher, Mitchell, & Truckenmiller, 2015; Geva & Farnia, 2012; Proctor, Silverman, Harring, & Montecillo, 2012), and teacher language use (Gámez & Lesaux, 2015; Silverman, Proctor, Harring, Doyle, Mitchell, & Meyer, 2014). Likewise, qualitative research has continued to highlight the affordances of understanding literacy as situated and contextualized practice (Barton, 2007). Ethnographic and case-study research demonstrate the importance of considering context (Azano, 2015; Baird, Kibler, & Palacios, 2015; Rogers & Street, 2012; Scales et al., 2017) and identity (Hall, 2016; Hall, Johnson, Juzwik, Wortham, & Mosley, 2010; Muhammad, 2012; Wagner, 2016). Furthermore, research on multimodal composition has cautioned against "textual bias" in literacy instruction (Horner, 2013), which may fail to cover the range of literacy practices students engage with on a daily basis across digital, visual, and sound-based mediums (Bartels, 2017; Dalton, 2012; Stornaiuolo, Higgs, & Hull, 2013; Wargo, 2017). In the aggregate, these advances in literacy research have provided increasingly nuanced suggestions for advancing school-based literacy outcomes while expanding definitions of literacy overall, with implications for the knowledge base of teachers.

To this day, however, coverage of the "big 5" can serve as a limited bar by which teacher education is evaluated. For example, the National Council for Teacher Quality (NCTQ) released its highly-contested 2014 *Teacher Prep Review* in which standards for early reading, English learners, and struggling readers were almost entirely based on the NRP report (Greenberg, Walsh, & McKee, 2015). By contrast, the International Literacy Association (2010) *Standards for Reading Professionals* articulates a more contemporary focus on dimensions of reading research, including major theories of reading and writing, motivation and engagement, first language, second language, and bilingual reading development, and disciplinary literacy. Such discrepancies are indicative of broad variability in teacher education.

Beyond professional organizations, a range of suggestions have been made for how to frame, and teach, literacy development in teacher education. Fillmore and Snow (2002) argued for an emphasis on equipping teachers with foundational knowledge of educational linguistics. Lucas and Villegas (2013) advocated a focus on second language acquisition principles in their framework for linguistically responsive teaching. Valdés, Capitelli, and Alvarez (2011) contended that grounding teacher preparation in sociolinguistic knowledge positions all students as possessing legitimate literacy competencies. Alim (2005, 2010) and Fairclough (1999) pushed for teachers to explore the relationships between power, ideology, and language use in society. Finally, Bunch (2013) and Galguera (2011) argued for *pedagogical language knowledge*, or "knowledge directly related to disciplinary teaching and learning situated in the particular (and multiple) contexts in which teaching and learning take place" (Bunch, 2013, p. 307).

As these varied approaches suggest, teacher preparation and PD will differ with respect to how literacy is addressed. At the teacher preparation level, students require a broad understanding of literacy development, instructional approaches, and learning environments. Professional development models can assume some foundational knowledge, but must respond to expressed needs in a given setting (e.g., Raphael, Au, & Goldman, 2009).

Demographics and Literacy in Teacher Education

While teacher preparation programs have been targeted for failing to attend to the racial (Ball & Tyson, 2011; Castro, 2010; Milner, 2010; Silverman, 2010), linguistic (Endo, 2015; Lucas &

Villegas, 2013; Schleppegrell, 2007a, 2007b), and socioeconomic (DeCastro-Ambrosetti & Cho, 2005; White, Mistry, & Chow, 2013) variability of contemporary classrooms, programs that develop teacher candidates' understandings around the complexities of language, race, and identity have shown some promise (Godley, Reaser, & Moore; 2015; Jupp & Lensmire, 2016). Furthermore, community-based field placements have been shown to help some teacher candidates complexify their understanding of literacy practices and development, and to strengthen teacher-family relationships within communities (Bain & Moje, 2012; Brayko, 2013). While important advances, these approaches have also been criticized for their singular focus on helping the traditional White teacher candidate engage with multilingual and multiracial students (Willis, 2003) while sidelining teacher candidates of color (Brown, 2014).

Professional development approaches have also been criticized for overlooking demographic realities (Bolgatz, 2005; Coles-Ritchie & Smith, 2016). Teachers have described professional development for "diversity" as ineffective, unnecessary, or an imposition (Gay, 2005; Wiseman & Fox, 2010). Many see such conversations as separate from, or even at the expense of, academic instruction (Pollock, Bocala, Deckman, & Dickstein-Staub, 2016). Teachers report coming away from such sessions maintaining the belief that they must simply renounce individual prejudices, rather than interrogate systems of structural inequality and how such systems might play out instructionally (Cross, 2010; Vaught & Castagno, 2008).

In the meantime, teachers continue to report feeling unprepared to implement culturally and linguistically responsive literacy pedagogies (Gándara & Santibañez, 2016; Samson & Collins, 2012). For example, nationally, less than 30% of teachers of English learners (ELs) report having opportunities for PD targeting race, ethnicity, and language (Ballantyne, Sanderman, & Levy, 2008). While this figure climbs to 38% in urban areas, two thirds of this PD consists of fewer than eight hours over the course of the school year (Rotermund, DeRoche, & Ottem, 2017). Another survey of special education teachers found that teachers of ELs received a median of only three hours of EL-based professional training over a five-year period (Zehler et al., 2003). This general trend holds in states with large EL populations. In California, for example, Gándara, Maxwell-Jolly, and Driscoll (2005) found that approximately half of teachers whose classrooms consisted of at least 50% of EL students received professional development or only one session on EL instruction over five years.

When teachers in preservice or PD contexts do receive language-specific professional development, it most often tracks back to a methods focus (e.g., Bartolomé, 1994) in which instructional approaches for scaffolding and differentiation of instruction are privileged.[1] Far less common are efforts to restructure school- or district-level systems to better support linguistically diverse populations. Expedient acquisition of academic English for the purpose of performance on standardized literacy assessments thus becomes the primary emphasis, often at the expense of interrogating the social, cognitive, and linguistic complexities students navigate and how those interact with instruction.

Summary

Teacher preparation faces a dual front in training teachers for literacy instruction. The first is that preparation programs must work with current students to confront and resolve the tensions that arise as a function of the demographic paradox. The second is that teacher preparation programs need to diversify the pool of students who are coming into teaching. Haddix (2017) further contends that while teacher diversification is necessary, it too is insufficient, and teacher education must be restructured to support the preparation of a more racially and linguistically diverse teacher core.

Professional development research also finds that teachers often feel unprepared for working with multilingual and multiracial populations and indicate dissatisfaction with the content of PD that addresses literacy, demography, and policy. One potential reason for dissatisfaction is that there appear to be more frameworks and macro theories than there are actionable approaches that address the implementation of transformative literacy practices. In light of this, we recommend a set of five core literacy competencies that should be threaded into coursework and professional development for literacy teacher education.

1. *Foundational and contemporary literacy research.* There have been volumes written establishing a scientific foundation for reading development among children and adolescents. Notable among these are *Preventing Reading Difficulties in Young Children* (Snow, Burns, & Griffin, 1998) and the National Reading Panel Report (NRP, 2000). As we noted above, however, literacy researchers continue to make strides in understanding what are malleable dimensions of literacy instruction, coupled with how instruction might be tailored to address variation in language, race, culture, and other critical contextual factors. These constantly evolving research foundations should be tracked and updated so that pre- and in-service teachers are provided with state-of-the-art literacy knowledge for effective instruction.

2. *First, second, and simultaneous language development.* Demographic trends in the U.S. show that multilingualism is typical and thus knowledge of language acquisition and its implications for instruction is critical (Takanishi & Le Menestrel, 2017). By language, we do not mean English language, but rather monolingual, bi- and multi-lingual, and dialectal languages that characterize the linguistic realities of the U.S. student population. Working with teachers in pre- and in-service settings requires an interrogation of what are the languages spoken in the schools and classrooms where teachers are working and how those languages are understood and leveraged in the service of meeting standards and acquiring literacy and content knowledge.

3. *Language development and disability.* Intersecting with the second recommendation, late diagnoses and underrepresentation in special educational services (Samson & Lesaux, 2009) alongside overrepresentation and misinterpretation of data (Klingner & Eppollito, 2014) reflect the range of challenges that arise with demographic shifts and their intersections with literacy, language, and cognition. To date, the convergences between these issues are limited, and oftentimes confusing. Increased attention to issues of language and disability are critical for developing awareness of these complexities and are key to working with multilingual and multiracial populations.

4. *Functional roles of language.* It is becoming increasingly clear that understanding how language functions across disciplinary contexts and modalities is important for literacy instruction. As Brisk and Kaveh (2019) argue, "[c]ontent area teachers must develop an identity as language teachers in charge of building students' linguistic resources to be able to function expressing and comprehending knowledge in the discipline" (p. 9).

5. *Socio- and Racio-linguistics.* A focus on the social and linguistic contexts of teaching and learning environments undergirds how we understand language and literacy in teaching contexts. Emerging scholarship articulates a *raciolinguistic* perspective, arguing that language and race are systemically interconnected in ways that highlight how language functions to privilege some and marginalize others in schools and society (Alim, Rickford, & Ball, 2016; Flores & Rosa, 2015). Working with pre- and in-service teachers to interrogate these systems should undergird efforts that target each of the previous recommendations.

These core competencies should be considered in light of recent research on the characteristics of effective professional development (e.g., Birman, Desimone, Porter, & Garet, 2000; Darling-Hammond & Richardson, 2009; Desimone, Porter, Garet, Yoon, & Birman, 2002; Salinas, Dwyer, Paratore, & O'Brien, 2012). This research broadly suggests that effective PD is: 1) *sustained* in its duration to allow for deeper subject-area focus, more opportunities for active learning, and more coherence with teachers' experiences; 2) *collective* in its approach to participation among teachers from the same department, grade, or subject area who work together in service of a shared professional culture; 3) *active* in promoting learning via professional learning activities including classroom observations, common planning, and reviewing student work; and 4) *coherent*, with clear links to school and system policies, standards and assessments, and other PD. With these characteristics in mind, we see promise in embedding the five core literacy competencies into impactful PD and teacher education more broadly. Expanding the scope of literacy teacher education should be accompanied by a similar broadening of methods used in literacy research to inform teacher education and practice.

Literacy Research

As with the teaching profession, literacy research must respond to demographic and policy changes. First, sampling procedures must be designed to maximize the likelihood that findings are generalizable to the populations that characterize U.S. schools. Second, literacy research must be operationalized to eventually inform classroom practice (Snow, 2015). No single study or method can accomplish these tasks entirely. Below, we argue for broadening the scope of literacy research, both in terms of populations and methodological approaches.

Demographic Trends in Literacy Research

If demographic realities interact with how we think about literacy teacher education, then they also ought to be reflected in literacy research itself. We begin by acknowledging that the same inertia that grips the demographics of the teaching profession also manifests among literacy researchers and the broader gatekeepers to literacy research and publication. Indeed, Rogers (2017) noted that scholars of color rarely serve as editors of literacy journals. In a telling review, she found that, since their inceptions (in 1952 and 1969, respectively), the two journals associated with the Literacy Research Association, *Literacy Research: Theory, Method, and Practice* and *Journal of Literacy Research*, had a combined total of 165 White editors and only 14 editors of color. This, alongside the cumulative effect of repeated citations of certain scholars versus others, in multiple journals over time, begets a literacy research paradigm that amounts to "research policing" (Brooks, 2017) and excludes the variety of perspectives and approaches that are necessary to advance literacy research in needed ways.

In terms of sampled populations, the degree to which demographic realities inform literacy research is more challenging to evaluate given the sheer quantity of literacy research that is produced annually. Indeed, in our research for this chapter, we were unable to locate any published analyses that characterized the range of sample diversity represented in literacy research with respect to race, ethnicity, or language background. In an attempt to get an initial sense of where literacy research might be and where it is going with respect to this question, we conducted our own constrained retrospective and prospective analyses.

Retrospectively, we reviewed two major publication outlets noted for high quality literacy research: *Reading Research Quarterly* and *Scientific Studies of Reading*. We reviewed empirical studies published from both journals from 1996–1997, 2006–2007, and 2016–2017. We assessed the diversity of the research samples in these journals by noting the reported demographics with respect to race and language. Prospectively, we reviewed recently funded literacy-focused grants by the National Center for Educational Research through the Institute of Education Sciences. In so doing, we sought to get a general sense of the demographic characteristics of funded literacy research and the priorities of federal funding to date. Findings from these studies are likely to be published in literacy research journals and might be considered one barometer of sample variability to come in the future.

Table 2.1 shows that the retrospective analysis yielded 14 studies from each decade, resulting in 42 overall. Generally, racial and ethnic diversity were better represented than language diversity. Across all three time points, approximately half of the studies (48%) were conducted among predominantly (85%–100%) White populations, or did not report racial demographics. This percentage varied, from 50% in 1996–1997, to 36% in 2006–2007, and 58% in 2016–2017. Notably, the 2016–2017 studies tended to dedicate more space to discussions of overall demographic characteristics than the 1996–1997 studies. Linguistically, fully 74% of the studies were conducted among predominantly monolingual populations, or did not report linguistic characteristics of the samples. These percentages were consistent across decades, with the only notable difference being that the 2016–2017 studies were more likely to explicitly report that research was conducted among English-speaking populations.

Prospectively, the outlook for language representation in literacy research remains similarly limited. Just three of the 57 projects funded in 2016 by NCER fell under the category "English Learners," and four additional projects were explicitly designed to focus on Spanish-speaking children or dual language programs. Together, these comprised just 12% of funded projects.

Table 2.1 Overview of empirical studies reviewed for reporting of ethnolinguistic diversity, by race (primarily White) and language (primarily monolingual)

	Primarily White (PW)	*Did not report race (DNRR)*	*Combined PW + DNRR*	*Primarily Monolingual (PM)*	*Did not report language (DNRL)*	*Combined PM + DNRL*
2016 RRQ (7 studies)	2	2	4	3	2	5
2016 SSR (7 studies)	2	2	4	3	2	5
2016 Total (14 studies)	4 (29%)	4 (29%)	8 (58%)	6 (43%)	4 (29%)	10 (72%)
2006 RRQ (7 studies)	1	0	1	0*	5	5
2006 SSR (7 studies)	2	2	4	1	4	5
2006 Total (14 studies)	3 (21%)	2 (14%)	5 (36%)	1 (7%)	9 (64%)	10 (71%)
1996 RRQ (7 studies)	0	2	2	0*	5	5
1997 SSR (7 studies)	1	4	5	0*	6	6
1996/7 Total (14 studies)	1 (7%)	6 (43%)	7 (50%)	0* (0%)	11 (79%)	11 (79%)
OVERALL TOTAL (42 studies)	8 (19%)	12 (29%)	20 (48%)	7 (16%)	24 (57%)	31 (74%)

NCER also holds periodic "Technical Working Groups" (TWGs) in which researchers and other stakeholders convene to discuss the state of research, or gaps in research, on particular topics. While none of the seven TWGs between 2012–2015 convened specifically around the topic of linguistic diversity, the need for further research on English learning was discussed in five of the seven TWGs (NCER, 2016).

These brief analyses of sample composition and research foci suggest that racial and ethnic diversity are well-represented relative to linguistic diversity, which continues to lag. The review suggests that students designated as ELLs are at times excluded from broader analyses or the focus of research on special populations of language learners who are separate from the broader student population. While these approaches are methodologically valid, and have yielded important literacy insights, they also mask the demographic realities of today's multilingual and multiracial classrooms.

In this context, one takeaway from these findings is to consider the relative value and meaning of two broadly-used categories: English learner (EL) and Individualized Education Plan (IEP). Practically, carrying such labels results in the provision of individualized linguistic, cognitive, or behavioral supports in schools. Analytically, these labels can sometimes create unnecessary or unhelpful confounds. For example, EL designations are primarily determined via English language assessments. If, for example, the researcher is trying to learn about how language functions to predict reading comprehension, an EL analytic category may serve to explain away variation in the outcome that could be better understood with greater nuance using more precise measurement approaches.

Methodological Trends

Literacy researchers are frequently concerned with uncovering findings that have direct applicability to instructional practice. Given the inherent messiness of teaching and schools, these questions of diversity in literacy research should apply not only to demographics, but also to methodologies. Different approaches to conducting research are crucial if we want to know what processes are involved in a given outcome (e.g., vocabulary knowledge predicts reading comprehension), and how to teach to the development of those processes (e.g., approaches to vocabulary instruction that best promote its growth, which in turn boosts reading comprehension). In short, we want to know what works, why, and how. However, the translation of literacy research to practice has historically privileged a narrow range of research methodologies (primarily correlational designs) that identify those literacy skills that should be taught, alongside a similarly narrow view of the type of research that specifies how those skills are translated for practitioners (primarily randomized-control and quasi-experimental designs).

Pressley (2000) articulated this concern in his critique of the National Reading Panel (2000) approach to identifying phonics, phonemic awareness, fluency, vocabulary, and comprehension as the "big 5" literacy skills on which practitioners ought to focus. He argued that it was "puzzling that scientists as good as the ones on the Panel could have convinced themselves to take these conceptually and methodologically narrow approaches" (p. 169). Thus, in the early 21st century, there was concern among literacy researchers about privileging correlational and experimental designs to identify the literacy skills that children should be taught.[2]

Almost two decades later, it feels as if not much has changed. In the present policy era, the What Works Clearinghouse (WWC; http://ies.ed.gov/ncee/Wwc/) has emerged as an arbiter for translating instructional research to practitioners. The WWC has as its primary goal "to provide educators with the information they need to make evidence-based decisions," through the use of "high quality" research. In this context, experimental designs, notably the randomized-control trial (RCT), reflect the gold standard. Riehl (2006) notes that the progression from correlational research to the RCT invokes a medical model to which the educational community is expected to aspire, and a model to which the literacy research community has been especially subjected.

The need for methodologically sound studies to guide the translation from literacy research to practice is clear. However, there is serious concern as to whether, by themselves, experimental designs are the most effective means of guiding that translation. Ginsburg and Smith (2016) provide a comprehensive overview of why RCTs in the social sciences are particularly challenging and vulnerable to a host of validity threats, both internal and external. Threats to external validity are clear in that most RCTs in the education field are conducted at a single time point and are typically not replicated elsewhere (see also Pressley, 2000). Thus, we cannot know if results of a given curricular intervention would generalize to different settings with a new set of teachers and learners. As the authors put it, "no one argues that the results of a single RCT will necessarily generalize to different populations at different times and places" (p. 5). In addressing internal validity issues, Ginsburg and Smith (2016) highlight fully 12 potential threats to RCT implementation by examining 27 WWC-approved studies in mathematics from grades 1–12. While too long to enumerate here, the analysis makes clear that the unmapped social factors that impinge on the conduct of RCTs in educational research can serve to undermine the credibility of many reported findings.

The Institute of Education Sciences Practice Guides (http://ies.ed.gov/ncee/wwc/Publication#/ContentTypeId:3) represent a relatively recent attempt to aggregate experimental and quasi-experimental studies on a given topic (e.g., reading comprehension instruction, English learners, writing, struggling readers). To date, Practice Guide findings are somewhat broadly disseminated to teachers and teacher educators through the Regional Educational Laboratories (http://ies.ed.gov/ncee/edlabs/) system, which arranges for broad-exposure PD for teachers in targeted districts, and through other national clearinghouse outlets. The question that arises from such dissemination is one of relevance. Gaps open before the practitioner who may struggle with texts, strategies, words, or approaches used in approved experimental studies that were tested in less-than-generalizable schooling conditions (Gitlin & Margonis, 1995).

As a result, there is a clear need to integrate diverse methodological approaches in literacy research so that we are not just asking *what works*, but also asking *why* and *how*. Indeed, Riehl (2006) notes that medical research, while often deferential to the authority of the RCT, is also characterized by a strong case-study focus that provides context to experimental findings. In educational research broadly, and literacy research specifically, we lack a coherent set of guidelines for determining whether methodologies other than experimental and quasi-experimental designs meet rigorous empirical standards. However, such models do exist in medical research. Collingridge and Gantt (2008) outline standards for rigor in three qualitative research domains: ethnography, existential phenomenology, and grounded theory, along with associated theoretical frameworks for data collection. In education, the federal Department of Education showed the will and ability to articulate rigor beyond the RCT when Kratochwill et al. (2010) detailed procedures for effective single-subject designs in educational research. However, beyond these attempts, methodological range is not particularly well-represented when research findings are communicated with literacy practitioners. We contend that it is attention to exactly this kind of methodological detail and range that is needed to broaden our understanding of the why and how of effective literacy instruction in today's districts, schools, and classrooms (McHugh, Park, Zong, & Yang, 2018).

A Practical Example

To illustrate what might be possible with a more diverse methodological framework guiding the research-to-practice paradigm, we offer the following description of two literacy studies with very different methodologies, that can serve to supplement one another. One study (August, Branum-Martin, Cardenas-Hagan, & Francis, 2009) is a WWC-approved study that reported on the evaluation of a language-based science curriculum in a single large district in the Rio Grande Valley of Texas. A total of 40 classrooms of students, with ten teachers in five middle schools (890 total students, 98% Latinx, 562 ELs) participated. Each teacher had four classes, and those classes were randomly assigned to treatment or control. The treatment condition received a science instructional approach that targeted vocabulary development, oral explanations, and small group work to promote talk and language development via content instruction. The researchers used multi-level ANCOVAs to assess treatment effects on vocabulary and science content knowledge outcomes at post-intervention. A Likert-based fidelity measure was used to rate instructional quality for science instruction for the treatment and control groups. Results showed treatment effects on district-aligned, researcher-developed measures of science and vocabulary. These findings were used in a recent IES Practice Guide (Baker et al., 2014) to recommend: a) direct instruction of academic vocabulary; b) using media to promote language comprehension; and c) using small group work to discuss and write about content. However, there is no explanatory mechanism provided in the study that contextualizes the nature of the instruction or the small group interactions that took place.

The second study (Farnsworth, 2012) used a participant-observational multi-case methodology to qualitatively assess how kindergarten-aged English learners "participate in knowledge construction in peer groups while developing language" (p. 253). Farnsworth (2012) situated her study in the anti-bilingual context of an Arizona kindergarten classroom in a school where bilingual environmental print had recently been ordered removed as the result of a recent state program audit. Data sources included classroom observations, video recording, student and teacher interviews, and classroom artifacts. Discourse analysis of small group (n = 4) discussions of focal students comprising a small mathematics group were used to make sense of how students worked to construct arguments. The study examined the types of language children used in their small group discussions, particularly the means by which sophisticated argumentation skills were developed via conversations that might otherwise have been considered off-topic or non-academic. Findings articulated how students in small groups: a) learn to position themselves in these discussions; b) develop voices of authority; and c) use varied linguistic forms to develop arguments and argumentation skills. A broader methodological perspective to inform instructional recommendations might contextualize the findings of the August et al. (2009) RCT with Farnsworth's (2012) multi-case study to unpack the Practice Guide recommendation to use small group work to discuss academic content. While the August et al. study used small groups in its instructional model and found effects on a content-based assessment, Farnsworth's study gave us a glimpse into the nature of small group discussions in a specific educational context. Other studies that use qualitative or mixed approaches to further unpack the broad recommendations associated with August et al.'s study would invariably provide greater ecological validity to the recommendations, and would also illuminate other important instructional details that RCTs fail to unearth, and that are germane to differing contexts in which instruction takes place.

Conclusion

We began this chapter noting that in an era of information ubiquity, from both digital and print sources, literacy skills are more critical than ever. Language and literacy are the primary drivers of human communication, and viewed through a demographic lens, the sheer range of linguistic, ethnic, and race-specific factors that are likely to affect how literacy is taught and how it develops is awe-inspiring. We have argued that teachers, teacher educators, and literacy researchers must use this demographic lens to be mindful about what we are learning about literacy and its development, and how we provide literacy instruction for children and youth in this moment in history. We have further argued that what counts as quality research has been constrained in recent years due to the impact of policy expectations that limit translatable research to causal and correlational designs. Broader conversations across literacy studies that employ a spectrum of methods to answer diverse research questions will invariably spur more nuanced empirical insights and deeper instructional recommendations for today's distributed and multifaceted literacy contexts. Ultimately, then, literacy education and research must evolve to meet the representational demands of our times. We hope this chapter sets that stage for this *Handbook of Reading Research* and for us as literacy educators and scholars who continue to learn, teach, and grow.

Acknowledgment

The authors would like to thank María Carlo, Marilyn Cochran-Smith, and Jeanne Paratore for their helpful insights and comments on early drafts of this chapter.

Notes

1 See, for example, the impressive efforts by the Massachusetts Department of Elementary and Secondary Education in their Rethinking Equity and Teaching for English Language Learners (RETELL) initiative to train *all* in-service teachers, in a relatively short period of time, for endorsement to work with EL students in mainstream settings. http://www.doe.mass.edu/retell/
2 See Gee (1999), Snow (2000), and Gee (2000) for a thorough, and occasionally acerbic, debate on this topic.

References

Adger, C., Wolfram, W., & Christian, D. (2007). *Dialects in schools and communities* (2nd ed.). Mahwah, NJ: Lawrence Erlbaum Associates.
Alim, H. S. (2005). Critical language awareness in the United States: Revisiting issues and revising pedagogies in a resegregated society. *Educational Researcher, 34*(7), 24–31.
Alim, H. S. (2010). Critical language awareness. Sociolinguistics and language education. In N. H. Hornberger & S. McKay (Eds.), *Sociolinguistics and language education* (pp. 205–231). Bristol, UK: Multilingual Matters.
Alim, H. S., Rickford, J. R., & Ball, A. F. (Eds.). (2016). *Raciolinguistics: How language shapes our ideas about race.* New York, NY: Oxford University Press.
Arcia, E. (2006). Achievement and enrollment status of suspended students: Outcomes in a large, multicultural school district. *Education and Urban Society, 38*, 359–369.
Artiles, A. J., Klingner, J. K., Sullivan, A., & Fierros, E. (2010). Shifting landscapes of professional practices: English learner special education placement in English-only states. In P. Gándara & M. Hopkins (Eds.), *Forbidden language: English learners and restrictive language policies* (pp. 102–117). New York, NY: Teachers College Press.
ASCD. (2016). *Elementary and secondary education act: Comparison of the no child left behind act to the every student succeeds act.* Alexandria, VA: Author.
August, D., Branum-Martin, L., Cardenas-Hagan, E., & Francis, D. J. (2009). The impact of an instructional intervention on the science and language learning of middle grade English language learners. *Journal of Research on Educational Effectiveness, 2*(4), 345–376. doi:10.1080/19345740903217623
Azano, A. P. (2015). Addressing the rural context in literacies research. *Journal of Adolescent & Adult Literacy, 59*(3), 267–269.
Bacon, C. K. (2017). Dichotomies, dialects, and deficits: Confronting the "Standard English" myth in literacy and teacher education. *Literacy Research: Theory, Method, and Practice, 66*(1), 341–357.

Bain, R. B., & Moje, E. B. (2012). Mapping the teacher education terrain for novices. *Phi Delta Kappan*, *93*(5), 62–65.

Baird, A. S., Kibler, A., & Palacios, N. (2015). "Yo te estoy ayudando; estoy aprendiendo también/I am helping you; I am learning too:" A bilingual family's community of practice during home literacy events. *Journal of Early Childhood Literacy*, *15*(2), 147–176.

Baker, S., Lesaux, N., Jayanthi, M., Dimino, J., Proctor, C. P., Morris, J., … Newman-Gonchar, R. (2014). *Teaching academic content and literacy to English learners in elementary and middle school (NCEE 2014-4012)*. Washington, DC: National Center for Education Evaluation and Regional Assistance (NCEE), Institute of Education Sciences, U.S. Department of Education. Retrieved from the NCEE website http://ies.ed.gov/ncee/wwc/publications_reviews.aspx.

Baker-Bell, A. (2013). "I never really knew the history behind African American language:" Critical language pedagogy in an Advanced Placement English Language Arts Class. *Equity & Excellence in Education*, *46*, 355–370.

Ball, A. F., & Tyson, C. A. (2011). *Studying diversity in teacher education*. Lanham, MD: Rowman & Littlefield.

Ballantyne, K. G., Sanderman, A. R., & Levy, J. (2008). *Educating English language learners: Building teacher capacity*. Washington, DC: National Clearinghouse for English Language Acquisition. Retrieved from http://www.ncela.gwu.edu/practice/mainstream_teachers.htm.

Bartels, J. T. (2017). Snapchat and the sophistication of multimodal composition. *English Journal*, *106*(5), 90–92.

Bartolomé, L. (1994). Beyond the methods fetish: Toward a humanizing pedagogy. *Harvard Educational Review*, *64*(2), 173–195.

Barton, D. (2007). *Literacy: An introduction to the ecology of written language*. Malden, MA: Blackwell.

Batalova, J., Fix, M., & Murray, J. (2005). *English language learner adolescents: Demographics and literacy achievements*. Report to the Center for Applied Linguistics. Washington, DC: Migration Policy Institute.

Birman, B. F., Desimone, L., Porter, A. C., & Garet, M. S. (2000). Designing professional development that works. *Educational Leadership*, *17*, 613–649.

Bolgatz, J. (2005). *Talking race in the classroom*. New York, NY: Teachers College Press.

Boser, U. (2014). *Teacher diversity revisited: A new state-by-state analysis*. Washington, DC: Center for American Progress.

Bowers, P. N., Kirby, J. R., & Deacon, S. H. (2010). The effects of morphological instruction on literacy skills: A systematic review of the literature. *Review of Educational Research*, *80*(2), 144–179.

Brayko, K. (2013). Community-based placements as contexts for disciplinary learning: A study of literacy teacher education outside of school. *Journal of Teacher Education*, *64*(1), 47–59.

Brisk, M., & Kaveh, Y. (2019). *Teacher education for bi/multilingual students*. The Oxford Encyclopedia of Global Perspectives on Teacher Education.

Brooks, M. (2017). Other: Multiraciality, community, and cross-racial research. *Journal of Literacy Research*, *49*, 544–558.

Brown, K. D. (2014). Teaching in color: A critical race theory in education analysis of the literature on preservice teachers of color and teacher education in the US. *Race Ethnicity and Education*, *17*(3), 326–345.

Bunch, G. C. (2013). Pedagogical language knowledge: Preparing mainstream teachers for English learners in the new standards era. *Review of Research in Education*, *37*(1), 298–341.

Bunch, G. C., Kibler, A., & Pimentel, S. (2012). *Realizing opportunities for English learners in the common core English language arts and disciplinary literacy standards*. Stanford, CA: Understanding Language Initiative.

Calderón, M., Slavin, R., & Sánchez, M. (2011). Effective instruction for English learners. *The Future of Children*, *21*(1), 103–127.

Carlisle, J. F. (2010). Effects of instruction in morphological awareness on literacy achievement: An integrative review. *Reading Research Quarterly*, *45*(4), 464–487.

Castro, A. J. (2010). Themes in the research on preservice teachers' views of cultural diversity implications for researching millennial preservice teachers. *Educational Researcher*, *39*(3), 198–210.

Cherng, H. Y. S. (2016). Is all classroom conduct equal? Teacher contact with parents of racial/ethnic minority and immigrant adolescents. *Teachers College Record*, *118*(11), n11.

Cochran-Smith M., & Villegas A. M. (2016) Preparing teachers for diversity and high-poverty schools: A research-based perspective. In J. Lampert, & B. Burnett (Eds.), *Teacher education for high poverty schools. education, equity, economy*, Vol. 2. Cham: Springer.

Cochran-Smith, M., Villegas, A. M., Abrams, L., Chavez Moreno, L., Mills, T., & Stern, R. (2016). Research on teacher preparation: Charting the landscape of a sprawling field. In D. H. Gitomer & C. A. Bell (Eds.), *Handbook of research on teaching* (5th ed., pp. 439–547). Washington, DC: American Educational Research Association.

Colby, S. L., & Ortman, J. M. (2015). *Projections of the size and composition of the US population: 2014 to 2060.* Washington, DC: US Census Bureau.

Coles-Ritchie, M., & Smith, R. R. (2017). Taking the risk to engage in race talk: Professional development in elementary schools. *International Journal of Inclusive Education, 21*(2), 172–186.

Collingridge, D. S., & Gantt, E. E. (2008). The quality of qualitative research. *American Journal of Medical Quality, 23,* 389–395.

Cross, B. E. (2010). New racism, reformed teacher education, and the same ole' oppression. *Educational Studies, 38*(3), 263–274.

Dalton, B. (2012). Multimodal composition and the common core state standards. *The Reading Teacher, 66*(4), 333–339.

Darling-Hammond, L., & Richardson, N. (2009). Teacher learning: What matters? *Educational Leadership, February,* 46–53.

DeBose, C. E. (2007). The Ebonics phenomenon, language planning, and the hegemony of standard English. In H. S. Alim & J. Baugh (Eds.), *Talkin Black talk: Language, education and social change* (pp. 30–43). New York, NY: Teachers College Press.

DeCastro-Ambrosetti, D., & Cho, G. (2005). Do parents value education? Teachers' perceptions of minority parents. *Multicultural Education, 13*(2), 44–46.

Dee, T. S. (2005). A teacher like me. *Does Race, Ethnicity, or Gender Matter? The American Economic Review, 95,* 158–165.

Delpit, L., & Dowdy, J. K. (Eds.). (2008). *The skin that we speak: Thoughts on language and culture in the classroom.* New York, NY: The New Press.

Desimone, L. M., Porter, A. C., Garet, M. S., Yoon, K. S., & Birman, B. F. (2002). Effects of professional development on teachers' instruction: Results from a three-year longitudinal study. *Educational Evaluation and Policy Analysis, 24,* 81–112.

Downey, D. B., & Pribesh, S. (2004). When race matters: Teachers' evaluations of students' classroom behavior. *Sociology of Education, 77,* 267–282.

Durán, L. (2017). Audience and young bilingual writers: Building on strengths. *Journal of Literacy Research, 49*(1), 92–114.

Dyson, A. H., & Smitherman, G. (2009). The right (write) start: African American Language and the discourse of sounding right. *Teachers College Record, 111*(4), 973–998.

Endo, R. (2015). From unconscious deficit views to affirmation of linguistic varieties in the classroom: White preservice teachers on building critical self-awareness about linguicism's causes and consequences. *Multicultural Perspectives, 17*(4), 207–214.

Escamilla, K. (2009). English language learners: Developing literacy in second language learners—Report of the National Literacy Panel on language-minority children and youth. *Journal of Literacy Research, 41,* 432–452. doi:10.1080/10862960903340165

Fairclough, N. (1999). Global capitalism and critical awareness of language. *Language Awareness, 8*(2), 71–83.

Farkas, G., Grobe, R. P., Sheehan, D., & Shuan, Y. (1990). Cultural resources and school success: Gender, ethnicity, and poverty groups within an urban school district. *American Sociological Review, 55,* 127–142.

Farnsworth, M. (2012). Who's coming to my party? Peer talk as a bridge to oral language proficiency. *Anthropology and Education Quarterly, 43,* 253–270.

Fenning, P., & Rose, J. (2007). Overrepresentation of African American students in exclusionary discipline the role of school policy. *Urban Education, 42*(6), 536–559.

Fillmore, L. W., & Snow, C. E. (2002). What teachers need to know about language. In C. T. Adger, C. E. Snow, & D. Christian (Eds.), *What teachers need to know about language* (pp. 7–54). Washington, DC: Center for Applied Linguistics and Delta Systems.

Flores, N., & Rosa, J. (2015). Undoing appropriateness: Raciolinguistic ideologies and language diversity in education. *Harvard Educational Review, 85*(2), 149–171.

Foorman, B. R., Koon, S., Petscher, Y., Mitchell, A., & Truckenmiller, A. (2015). Examining general and specific factors in the dimensionality of oral language and reading in 4th–10th grades. *Journal of Educational Psychology, 107*(3), 884.

Freire, P. (1970). *Pedagogy of the oppressed* (M. B. Ramos, Trans.). New York, NY: Continuum.

Galguera, T. (2011). Participant structures as professional learning tasks and the development of pedagogical language knowledge among preservice teachers. *Teacher Education Quarterly, 38,* 85–106.

Gámez, P. B., & Lesaux, N. K. (2015). Early-adolescents' reading comprehension and the stability of the middle school classroom-language environment. *Developmental Psychology, 51,* 447–458.

Gándara, P., Maxwell-Jolly, J., & Driscoll, A. (2005). *Listening to teachers of English language learners: A survey of California teachers' challenges, experiences, and professional development needs.* Santa Cruz, CA: The Center for the Future of Teaching and Learning. Retrieved from http://files.eric.ed.gov/fulltext/ED491701.pdf

Gándara, P., & Santibañez, L. (2016). The teachers our English Language learners need. *Educational Leadership, 73*(5), 32–37.

García, O., & Kleifgen, J. A. (2010). *Educating emergent bilinguals: Policies, programs, and practices for English language learners.* New York, NY: Teachers College Press.

Gay, G. (2005). Politics of multicultural teacher education. *Journal of Teacher Education, 56,* 221–228.

Gee, J. (1999). *An introduction to discourse analysis: Theory and method.* London; New York, NY: Routledge.

Gee, J. (2000). Identity as an analytic lens for research in education. *Review of Research in Education, 25,* 99–125.

Geva, E., & Farnia, F. (2012). Developmental changes in the nature of language proficiency and reading fluency paint a more complex view of reading comprehension in ELL and EL1. *Reading and Writing, 25*(8), 1819–1845.

Gilliam, W. S., Maupin, A. N., Reyes, C. R., Accavitti, M., & Shic, F. (2016). *Do early educators' implicit biases regarding sex and race relate to behavior expectations and recommendations of preschool expulsions and suspensions?* New Haven, CT: Yale University, Child Study Center. Retrieved from https://medicine.yale.edu/childstudy/zigler/publications/Preschool%20Implicit%20Bias%20Policy%20Brief_final_9_26_276766_5379_v1.pdf

Ginsburg, A., & Smith, M. S. (2016). *Do randomized control trials meet the "Gold Standard"? A study of the usefulness of RCTs in the What Works Clearinghouse.* Washington, DC: American Enterprise Institute.

Gitlin, A., & Margonis, F. (1995). The political aspect of reform: Teacher resistance as good sense. *American Journal of Education, 103*(4), 377–405.

Godley, A. J., Reaser, J., & Moore, K. G. (2015). Pre-service English language arts teachers' development of critical language awareness for teaching. *Linguistics and Education, 32,* 41–54.

Goodwin, A. P., & Ahn, S. (2013). A meta-analysis of morphological interventions in English: Effects on literacy outcomes for school-age children. *Scientific Studies of Reading, 17*(4), 257–285.

Greenberg, J., Walsh, K., & McKee, A. (2015). *2014 teacher prep review: A review of the nation's teacher preparation programs. Revised.* Washington, DC: National Council on Teacher Quality.

Gregory, A., Skiba, R. J., & Noguera, P. A. (2010). The achievement gap and the discipline gap: Two sides of the same coin? *Educational Researcher, 39*(1), 59–68.

Haddix, M. M. (2017). Diversifying teaching and teacher education: Beyond rhetoric and toward real change. *Journal of Literacy Research, 49*(1), 141–149.

Hall, L. A. (2016). The role of identity in reading comprehension development. *Reading & Writing Quarterly, 32*(1), 56–80.

Hall, L. A., Johnson, A. S., Juzwik, M. M., Wortham, S. E., & Mosley, M. (2010). Teacher identity in the context of literacy teaching: Three explorations of classroom positioning and interaction in secondary schools. *Teaching and Teacher Education, 26*(2), 234–243.

Heath, S. B. (1982). What no bedtime story means: Narrative skills at home and school. *Language in Society, 11*(1), 49–76.

Horner, B. (2013). Ideologies of literacy, "academic literacies," and composition studies. *Literacy in Composition Studies, 1*(1), 1–9.

Howard, G. R. (2016). *We can't teach what we don't know: White teachers, multiracial schools.* New York, NY: Teachers College Press.

International Literacy Association. (2010). *Standards for reading professionals.* Newark, DE: International Literacy Association. Retrieved from https://www.literacyworldwide.org/get-resources/standards/standards-for-reading-professionals.

Jo, H., Schieve, L. A., Rice, C. E., Yeargin-Allsopp, M., Tian, L. H., Blumberg, S. J., … Boyle, C. A. (2015). Age at autism spectrum disorder (ASD) diagnosis by race, ethnicity, and primary household language among children with special health care needs, United States, 2009–2010. *Maternal and Child Health Journal, 19*(8), 1687–1697.

Jupp, J. C., & Lensmire, T. J. (2016). Second-wave white teacher identity studies: Toward complexity and reflexivity in the racial conscientization of white teachers. *International Journal of Qualitative Studies in Education, 29*(8), 985–988.

Kids Count Data Center. (2017). *Linguistic isolation still a challenge for some kids in immigrant families.* Retrieved May 3, 2017 from http://datacenter.kidscount.org/updates/show/150-linguistic-isolation-still-a-challenge?utm_source=eblast&utm_medium=email&utm_campaign=KIDS-COUNT

Kieffer, M. J., & Lesaux, N. K. (2012). Knowledge of words, knowledge about words: Dimensions of vocabulary in first and second language learners in sixth grade. *Reading and Writing: An Interdisciplinary Journal, 25,* 347–373.

Kieffer, M. J., Petscher, Y., Proctor, C. P., & Silverman, R. D. (2016). Is the whole greater than the sum of its parts? Modeling the contributions of language comprehension skills to reading comprehension in the upper elementary grades. *Scientific Studies of Reading, 20*(6), 436–454.

Klingner, J., & Eppollito, A. (2014). *English language learners: Differentiating between language acquisition and learning disabilities.* Arlington, VA: Council For Exceptional Children.

Kochhar, R., & Fry, R. (2014). *Wealth inequality has widened along racial, ethnic lines since end of Great Recession.* Pew Research Center. Retrieved from www.pewresearch.org/fact-tank/2014/12/12/racial-wealth-gaps-great-recession/

Kratochwill, T. R., Hitchcock, J., Horner, R. H., Levin, J. R., Odom, S. L., Rindskopf, D. M., & Shadish, W. R. (2010). *Single-case designs technical documentation.* Retrieved from What Works Clearinghouse website http://ies.ed.gov/ncee/wwc/pdf/wwc_scd.pdf.

Lehrer, R., & Schauble, L. (2006). Scientific thinking and science literacy: Supporting development in learning in contexts. In W. Damon, R. M. Lerner, K. A. Renninger, & I. E. Sigel (Eds.), *Handbook of child psychology* (Vol. 4, 6th ed., pp. 153–196). Hoboken, NJ: Wiley.

Lippi-Green, R. (2012). *English with an accent: Language, ideology and discrimination in the United States* (2nd ed.). New York, NY: Routledge.

López, F. (2016). Language education policies in the Common Core era. In C. P. Proctor, A. Boardman, & E. H. Hiebert (Eds.), *Teaching emergent bilingual students: Flexible approaches in an era of new standards* (pp. 3–19). New York, NY: The Guilford Press.

Lortie, D. C. (1975). *Schoolteacher: A sociological study.* Chicago, IL: University of Chicago Press.

Lucas, T., & Villegas, A. M. (2013). Preparing linguistically responsive teachers: Laying the foundation in preservice teacher education. *Theory into Practice, 52*(2), 98–109.

Mandell, D. S., Wiggins, L. D., Carpenter, L. A., Daniels, J., DiGuiseppi, C., Durkin, M. S., … Kirby, R. S. (2009). Racial/ethnic disparities in the identification of children with autism spectrum disorders. *American Journal of Public Health, 99*(3), 493–498.

McHugh, M., Park, M., Zong, J., & Yang, K. (2018). *Effectively serving children in a superdiverse classroom: Implications for the early education system.* Webinar, February 24, 2018. Washington, DC: Migration Policy Institute.

McNeill, K. L., Lowenhaupt, R. J., & Katsch-Singer, R. (in press). Instructional leadership in the era of NGSS: Principals' understandings of science practices. *Science Education, 102*(3).

Michaels, S. (1981). "Sharing time": Children's narrative styles and differential access to literacy. *Language in Society, 10*(3), 423–442.

Milner, H. R. (2010). What does teacher education have to do with teaching? Implications for diversity studies. *Journal of Teacher Education, 61*(1–2), 118–131.

Muhammad, G. E. (2012). Creating spaces for Black adolescent girls to "write it out!". *Journal of Adolescent & Adult Literacy, 56*(3), 203–211.

National Center for Education Statistics. (2017a). *The condition of education, 2017.* Retrieved from http://nces.ed.gov/programs/coe/.

National Center for Education Statistics. (2017b). *Racial/ethnic enrollment in public schools.* Retrieved from https://nces.ed.gov/programs/coe/indicator_cge.asp.

National Center for Educational Research. (2016). *Technical working group meeting summaries.* Retrieved from http://ies.ed.gov/ncer/whatsnew/techworkinggroup/.

National Equity Atlas. (2016). *Percent of students in high-poverty schools: United States, All public schools, 2010-2014.* Retrieved from http://nationalequityatlas.org/node/35536

National Reading Panel. (2000). *Teaching children to read: An evidence-based assessment of the scientific research literature on reading and its implications for reading instruction: Reports of the subgroups.* Washington, DC: National Institute of Child Health and Development.

Okonofua, J. A., & Eberhardt, J. L. (2015). Two strikes: Race and the disciplining of young students. *Psychological Science, 26*, 617–624.

Oliveira, G. (2017). Between Mexico and New York City: Mexican maternal migration's influences on separated siblings' social and educational lives. *Anthropology & Education Quarterly, 48*(2), 159–175.

Phillips, D. A. (2016). Stability, security, and social dynamics in early childhood environments. In N. K. Lesaux & S. M. Jones (Eds.), *The leading edge of early childhood education: Linking science to policy for a new generation* (pp. 7–29). Cambridge, MA: Harvard Education Press.

Pollock, M., Bocala, C., Deckman, S. L., & Dickstein-Staub, S. (2016). Caricature and hyperbole in preservice teacher professional development for diversity. *Urban Education, 51*(6), 629–658.

Pressley, M. (2000). Effective beginning reading instruction. *Journal of Literacy Research, 34*, 165–188.

Proctor, C. P., Boardman, A., & Hiebert, E. H. (Eds.) (2016). *Teaching emergent bilingual students: Flexible approaches in an era of new standards.* New York, NY: Guilford Publications.

Proctor, C. P., Silverman, R. D., Harring, J. R., & Montecillo, C. (2012). The role of vocabulary depth in predicting reading comprehension among English monolingual and Spanish–English bilingual children in elementary school. *Reading and Writing, 25*(7), 1635–1664.

Proctor, C. P., Silverman, R. D., & Harring, J. R. (2017) Linguistic interdependence between Spanish language and English language and reading: A longitudinal exploration from second through fifth grade. *Bilingual Research Journal, 40*(4), 372–391. doi: 10.1080/15235882.2017.1383949

Pruitt, S. L. (2014). The next generation science standards: The features and challenges. *Journal of Science Teacher Education, 25*(2), 145–156.

Raphael, T. E., Au, K. H., & Goldman, S. R. (2009). Whole school instructional improvement through the standards-based change process: A developmental model. In J. V. Hoffman & Y. M. Goodman (Eds.), *Literacies for changing times: An historical perspective on the future of reading research, public policy, and classroom practices* (pp. 198–230). New York, NY: Routledge.

Rickford, J. R. (1999). *African American vernacular English: Features, evolution, educational implications.* Hoboken, NJ: Wiley-Blackwell.

Riehl, C. (2006). Feeling better: A comparison of medical research and education research. *Educational Researcher, 35*(5), 24–29.

Rogers, A., & Street, B. V. (2012). *Adult literacy and development: Stories from the field.* London: Niace.

Rogers, R. (2017, December). Literacy research, racial consciousness, and equitable flows of knowledge. *Presidential address delivered at the annual meeting of the Literacy Research Association,* Tampa Bay, FL.

Rotermund, S., DeRoche, J., & Ottem, R. (2017). *Teacher professional development by selected teacher and school characteristics: 2011–12.* Washington, DC: National Center for Education Statistics. Retrieved from https://files.eric.ed.gov/fulltext/ED573871.pdf

Ryan, C. (2013). *Language use in the United States: American community survey reports.* Washington, DC: U.S. Census Bureau. Retrieved from www.census.gov/prod/2013pubs/acs-22.pdf

Rymes, B., Flores, N., & Pomerantz, A. (2016). The common core state standards and English learners: Finding the silver lining. *Language, 92*(4), e257–e273.

Salinas, A., Dwyer, J., Paratore, J. R., & O'Brien, L. (2012). *Integrating technology in early childhood education: What we know and what we should do.* Washington, DC: PublicBroadcasting Service.

Samson, J. F., & Collins, B. A. (2012). *Preparing all teachers to meet the needs of English Language Learners: Applying research to policy and practice for teacher effectiveness.* Washington, DC: Center for American Progress.

Samson, J. F., & Lesaux, N. K. (2009). Language-minority learners in special education: Rates and predictors of identification for services. *Journal of Learning Disabilities, 42*(2), 148–162.

Scales, R. Q., Wolsey, T. D., Young, J., Smetana, L., Grisham, D. L., Lenski, S., ... Chambers, S. A. (2017). Mediating factors in literacy instruction: How novice elementary teachers navigate new teaching contexts. *Reading Psychology, 38*(6), 604–651.

Schleppegrell, M. J. (2007a). The linguistic challenges of mathematics teaching and learning: A research review. *Reading & Writing Quarterly, 23*(2), 139–159.

Schleppegrell, M. J. (2007b). At last: The meaning in grammar. *Research in the Teaching of English, 42*(1), 121–128.

Shin, S. J. (2013). *Bilingualism in schools and society: Language, identity, and policy.* New York, NY: Routledge.

Silverman, R. D., Proctor, C. P., Harring, J. R., Meyer, A., Doyle, B., & Mitchell, M. (2014). Teachers' instruction and students' vocabulary and comprehension: An exploratory study with English monolingual and Spanish-English bilingual students in grades 3-5. *Reading Research Quarterly, 49,* 31–60.

Silverman, S. K. (2010). What is diversity? An inquiry into preservice teacher beliefs. *American Educational Research Journal, 47*(2), 292–329.

Skerrett, A. (2015). *Teaching transnational youth—Literacy and education in a changing world.* New York, NY: Teachers College Press.

Sleeter, C. (2014). Toward teacher education research that informs policy. *Educational Researcher, 44*(3), 146–153.

Smith, P. (2016). A distinctly American opportunity: Exploring non-standardized English (es) in literacy policy and practice. *Policy Insights from the Behavioral and Brain Sciences, 3,* 194–202.

Snow, C. E. (2000). On the limits of reframing: Rereading the National Academy of Sciences report on reading. *Journal of Literacy Research, 32,* 113–120.

Snow, C. E. (2015). Rigor and Realism: Doing educational science in the real world. *Educational Researcher, 44,* 460–466.

Snow, C. E., Burns, M. S., & Griffin, P. (Eds). (1998). *Preventing reading difficulties in young children.* Washington, DC: National Academies Press.

Soltero-González, L., Escamilla, K., & Hopewell, S. (2012). Changing teachers' perceptions about the writing abilities of emerging bilingual students: Towards a holistic bilingual perspective on writing assessment. *International Journal of Bilingual Education and Bilingualism, 15*(1), 71–94.

Southern Education Foundation. (2015). *A new majority: Low income students now a majority in the nation's public schools*. Retrieved from www.southerneducation.org/getattachment/4ac62e27-5260-47a5-9d02-14896ec3a531/A-New-Majority-2015-Update-Low-Income-Students-Now.aspx

Stornaiuolo, A., Higgs, J., & Hull, G. A. (2013). Social media as authorship: Methods for studying literacies and communities online. In P. Albers, T. Holbrook, & A. S. Flint (Eds.), *New literacy research methods* (pp. 224–237). New York, NY: Routledge.

Sullivan, A. L. (2011). Disproportionality in special education identification and placement of English language learners. *Exceptional Children, 77*(3), 317–334.

Takanishi, R., & Le Menestrel, S. (2017). *Promoting the educational success of children and youth learning English: Promising futures*. Washington, DC: National Academies Press.

Toldson, I. A., & Lemmons, B. P. (2013). Social demographics, the school environment, and parenting practices associated with parents' participation in schools and academic success among Black, Hispanic, and White students. *Journal of Human Behavior in the Social Environment, 23*(2), 237–255.

U.S. Department of Education. (2016). *The state of racial diversity in the education workforce*. Retrieved from www2.ed.gov/rschstat/eval/highered/racial-diversity/state-racial-diversity-workforce.pdf

U.S. Department of Education, Office of Postsecondary Education. (2014). *Preparing and credentialing the nation's teachers: The secretary's ninth report on teacher quality*. Retrieved from www2.ed.gov/about/reports/annual/teachprep/index.html

Valdés, G., Capitelli, S., & Alvarez, L. (2011). Realistic expectations: English language learners and the acquisition of "academic" English. In G. Valdés, S. Capitelli, & L. Alvarez (Eds.), *Latino children learning English: Steps in the journey* (pp. 15–41). New York, NY: Teachers College Press.

Vaught, S. E., & Castagno, A. E. (2008). "I don't think I'm a racist": Critical race theory, teacher attitudes, and structural racism. *Race Ethnicity and Education, 11*(2), 95–113.

Wagner, C. J. (2016). Teaching young dual language learners to be writers: Rethinking writing instruction through the lens of identity. *Journal of Education, 196*(1), 31–40.

Wald, J., & Losen, D. (2003). Defining and redirecting a school-to-prison pipeline. *New Directions for Youth Development, 2003*(99), 9–15.

Wargo, J. M. (2017). Rhythmic rituals and emergent listening: Intra-activity, sonic sounds and digital composing with young children. *Journal of Early Childhood Literacy, 17*(3), 392–408.

Wheeler, R., Cartwright, K. B., & Swords, R. (2012). Factoring AAVE into reading assessment and instruction. *The Reading Teacher, 65*(6), 416–425.

White, E. S., Mistry, R. S., & Chow, K. A. (2013). How do teachers talk about economic inequality? The complexity of teaching at a socioeconomically integrated elementary school. *Analyses of Social Issues and Public Policy, 13*(1), 370–394.

Willis, A. I. (2003). Parallax: Addressing race in preservice literacy education. In S. Greene & D. Abt-Perkins (Eds.), *Making race visible: Literacy research for cultural understanding* (pp. 51–70). New York, NY: Teachers College Press.

Wiseman, A., & Fox, R. K. (2010). Supporting teachers' development of cultural competence through teacher research. *Action in Teacher Education, 32*, 26–37.

Wright, A. C. (2015). *Teachers' perceptions of students' disruptive behavior: The effect of racial congruence and consequences for school suspension*. Unpublished manuscript, University of California, Santa Barbara, CA.

Zehler, A. M., Fleischman, H. L., Hopstock, P. J., Stephenson, T. G., Pendzick, M. L., & Sapru, S. (2003). *Descriptive study of services to LEP students and LEP students with disabilities*. Minneapolis, MN: National Center of Educational Outcomes, University of Minnesota.

Zuckerman, K. E., Mattox, K., Donelan, K., Batbayar, O., Baghaee, A., & Bethell, C. (2013). Pediatrician identification of Latino children at risk for autism spectrum disorder. *Pediatrics, 132*(3), 445–453.

Zuckerman, K. E., Sinche, B., Mejia, A., Cobian, M., Becker, T., & Nicolaidis, C. (2014). Latino parents' perspectives on barriers to autism diagnosis. *Academic Pediatrics, 14*(3), 301–308.

3
Social and Cultural Diversity as Lens for Understanding Student Learning and the Development of Reading Comprehension

Carol D. Lee

In order to address the question of social and cultural differences as factors in understanding competencies in reading comprehension, it is useful to start with a discussion of what is entailed in reading comprehension. The attention to issues of social and cultural differences, in regard to reading comprehension, typically grows out of concerns about the persistent achievement gaps in reading as measured by standardized assessments (National Center for Education Statistics, 2013), typically those used for the accountability of students, schools, districts, and states. Among the challenges of these, as our primary indicators of gaps in reading comprehension achievement, are the constraints of what such assessments typically measure (Lee, 2014; Lee & Goldman, 2015). They are timed. They typically do not account for the role of prior knowledge along multiple dimensions. The responses are typically multiple choice with particular forced logic to response options. They have limited genres and often do not measure comprehension across academic disciplines, and when they do include texts from different disciplines, the number of texts per discipline is limited. Some evidence that these are issues of concern to the field include efforts by the Educational Testing Service to develop new comprehension measures – the GISA – that attempts to capture some indicators of relevant prior knowledge, to situate the task of comprehension as more social and attached to meaningful goals rather than as decontextualized tasks, and to develop separate assessments in three disciplines – science, history, and literature (Kim et al., 2016). In addition, PARCC and Smarter Balance, the new assessments explicitly aligned to the Common Core State Standards in English Language Arts introduce new directions (Herman & Linn, 2013): asking students to provide evidence from texts to support answers; organizing conceptually related text sets by disciplinary areas (e.g. narrative texts; social science texts; science texts) and asking students to synthesize across texts; and asking students to construct written arguments based on text sets. These assessments, although timed and largely multiple choice, are more authentic and require more critical, discipline focused comprehension. However, cross state data from the 2014–15 and 2015–16 administration of the PARCC ELA assessment document highlight the persistent disparities in outcomes associated with race, ethnicity and class (http://parcconline.org/images/Consortium_and_State_Tables_FINAL_3_7_16.pdf). As with other initiatives, increasing the complexity of the reading assessments does not shift the persistent disparities.

Current research articulates reading comprehension as entailing the reader, the task, the text, and the context (Valencia, Wixson, & Pearson, 2014). This conception suggests that displays of competence must be understood as outgrowths of relationships across these four factors. There is fairly straightforward evidence that the relationships across these factors are dynamic and contextual (Kintsch, 1998; McNamara, Kintsch, Songer, & Kintsch, 1996; Spiro, 1980; van den Broek, Lorch, Linderholm, & Gustafson, 2001). For example, we know expert readers (like ourselves) who are befuddled when reading legal or medical documents, but are quite expert readers in our disciplines. Wineburg and Grossman (1998) conducted professional development with high school literature and history teachers, asking each group to read texts in the other groups' discipline, this resulted in each group not being deeply comfortable with reading another discipline. Teachers from the two disciplines saw their tasks quite differently, with one group focusing largely on literal summaries while the other focused on discipline specific interpretive problems. There are many studies documenting the reading habits of adolescents outside of school in areas they find interesting, when those same adolescents struggle with reading in school (Fisher, 2003; Moje, 2000; Moje & Tysvaer, 2010). These cases exemplify ways in which competence in reading comprehension can vary based on what the reader brings (interests, goals, specific skills), what is the task, what sort of complexities does the text pose, and about the context of reading that may influence goals, effort, and ability.

In addition to the dynamic relations among these four factors, there are also important issues with regard to the skills entailed in comprehension. Baseline skills include decoding (Juel, 1991; Snow, Burns, & Griffin, 1998), an array of knowledge with regard to vocabulary (e.g. roots, affixes, structural transformations – translating from noun form to verb form, etc. – synonyms, antonyms, using context clues to differentiate among different meanings of the same word) (August, Carlo, Dressler, & Snow, 2005; Hiebert & Kamil, 2005; Nagy, Diakidoy, & Anderson, 1993; Stahl & Nagy, 2005), deconstructing syntax (Brewer, 1977; Richek, 1976), and detecting basic text structures (e.g. expository – chronology, cause/effect, problem/solution; narrative) (Graesser, McNamara, & Louwerse, 2003; Meyer, Brandt, & Bluth, 1980; van Dijk, 1972). It is well established that these foundational skills are an important prerequisite for basic comprehension. At the same time, there is a substantive body of research documenting the way that when some of these foundational skills are lacking, there are other competencies that can accommodate and facilitate comprehension (Bransford & Johnson, 1972; Stahl & Miller, 1989). This proposition was central to the argument with regard to whole language instruction (e.g. children can use the comprehension of pictures in a children's book to facilitate comprehension even when they cannot pronounce or recognize all the words on the page) (Stahl & Miller, 1989).

Thus reading comprehension entails dynamic meaning-making processes. A reader cannot predict in advance the problems any given text will present and must have a flexible toolkit of meaning-making resources and must have a schema-tool kit for noticing what features (language and structure) of texts may potentially signal particular kinds of comprehension and interpretive problems. As students move through the grades, such comprehension and interpretive problems become increasingly specific to disciplines and increasingly complex (e.g. texts that are longer, more dense, uses of academic language, and structurally more complex) (Biancarosa & Snow, 2004; Lee & Spratley, 2009). The requisite skill set may shift from section to section within a given text. Thus the toolkit must be both broad and flexible. The requisite toolkit must also be adaptive to the task the reader is engaging with, whether it is a given text or a set of texts, with some texts only requiring recall while others require comparisons, extrapolating and organizing information to construct arguments, or critiquing (e.g. authorial intent and bias; using criteria based on the epistemological tools the reader brings to inform interpretations). And the requisite toolkit should be responsive to the contexts under which comprehension is taking place (individually, in social interactions with others, for achieving personal goals or for high stakes accountability).

Thus to consider how social and cultural differences come into play in acts of comprehension and how we as teachers and researchers can understand the variation and influences on social and cultural differences makes the problem space of reading comprehension even more complex. In order to tackle such complexity, we need grounding in core propositions undergirding human learning and development initially in order to warrant our interpretations of such social and cultural variation. Such warrants have been powerful influences on how, in both research and practice, we have interpreted social and cultural differences and assumptions the field has made about what such differences contribute to the persistent disparities in assessments of reading comprehension associated with what we think of as race, ethnicity, and the experience of poverty (Lee, 2016a). Historically, researchers have argued that deficiencies in language capacities (Bereiter & Engelmann, 1966; Hart & Risley, 1995), in mental functioning (Gould, 1981; Hernstein & Murray, 1994; Jensen, 1969), and in the social organization of families and communities (E. Jensen, 2009; Traub, 1999), have been the primary levers accounting for disparities in assessment outcomes in reading. More current theorizing around what are called non-cognitive factors (Becker & Luthar, 2002; Heckman, 2012; Heckman & Rubinstein, 2001), including executive functioning, have emerged as new deficit warrants.

The Affordances of a Human Development Perspective

I want to make the case that social and cultural diversity are normative for the human species. I start with this argument because it forms the basis for conceptualizing such diversity as an opportunity to examine generativity in any domain, including understanding how and under what circumstances humans comprehend and interrogate texts within and across contexts. Without such grounding it is much easier to conceptualize such diversity as a problem rather an opportunity.

Humans survive as a species because our abilities to engage in symbolic reasoning provide us with tools for navigating what are, inevitably, shifts in the material and biological world we occupy (Quartz & Sejnowski, 2002). Such symbolic reasoning entails interpretive perceptions (of the self, of others, of settings, of tasks) (Dweck, 1999; Eccles, O'Neil, & Wigfield, 2005) and knowledge that evolves from our construction of schema (e.g. cognitive structures that identify the salient features of a phenomenon that allow us to recognize a phenomenon and variations of that phenomenon, with the flexibility of building new knowledge from existing knowledge as well as constructing new schema) (Markus, 1977; Rumelhart, 1980). Our perceptions and knowledge are deeply intertwined with what some think of as a uniquely human symbolic technology: language (Pinker, 1994; Streeter, 1976). And our perceptions and knowledge develop through our relationships and interactions with other human beings (Bell, 2010; Bowlby, 1969). We know that infants in utero learn to recognize the sounds of their mothers' voices and significant others in their environment; that new borns pay more attention to human faces than to objects; that infants mirror the actions of their caregivers, following someones eye gaze (Meltzoff, 1988; Meltzoff & Moore, 1977). Among the earliest tasks in human development that continues across the life course, is to learn to read the internal states of others (Flavell & Miller, 1998; Kunda, 1999). Infants and young children are driven to explore, to learn to be independent in controlling their bodies, and to navigate through developmental trajectories across the life course, fulfilling their ego-related demands and perceptions of need. It is these dispositions that drive human behavior and such dispositions are filtered largely through the attribution of emotional salience – do we feel safe, efficacious, and do a set of experiences meet our criteria for relevance (Maslow, 1943).

There is a wonderful film called *Babies* that documents the first year of life of four infants from Mongolia, Namibia, Tokyo, and San Francisco. There are no adults talking in this film. We only see and hear from the babies. This film clearly shows that each of these infants works to accomplish the fundamental life tasks I have articulated, but in very different ways, with very different kinds of social supports, and toward very different social goals. They are physiologically pre-disposed to explore in order to accomplish these fundamental tasks (to stand, to grasp, to walk, to use language, to get what they want, to establish relationships with others, to explore their material and social worlds) through their participation in the practices of their diverse cultural niches (Rogoff, 2003; Super & Harkness, 1986).

It is the dynamic interplay between physiological processes rooted in our biology and our participation in cultural practices that creates the ecology of human development (Cole, 2007; Fischer & Bidell, 1998; Wilson, 1998). It is important to understand these relationships in light of current scientific findings, particularly in the field of epigenetics (Plotsky & Meaney, 1993; Russo, Martienssen, & Riggs, 1996). Work in epigenetics shows how inherited genetic markers that predispose a person toward a personality trait or a possible disease can be moderated or turned off by cultural experiences in the world. In addition, emerging work around the impact of toxic stress on physiological processes that can contribute to health outcomes (Adam et al., 2015; Geronimus, 2013) as well as research on contexts, experiences, and belief systems that can moderate the impacts of toxic stress (American Psychological Association Task Force on Resilience and Strength in Black Children and Adolescents, 2008; Bowman, 1989; Miller & MacIntosh, 1999; Spencer, 1987; Spencer et al., 2006), offer another layer of findings about the integral interplay of the biologic and the cultural. These findings, I argue, are essential to counter the historic dominant hegemonic discourses around human biology as deterministic and human biology as sources of deficits.

I raise these core orienting propositions around the interplay of biology and culture because the drivers around these relationships emerge from our evolution as a species, and thus we ignore them at our peril (Lee, 2010). From these grounding propositions, I want to take up their implications for the design of learning environments that take diversity as a resource and then as specific implications for understanding and facilitating reading comprehension, within and across settings.

Features of Robust Learning Environments

I extrapolate from these core propositions that robust learning environments are ones that address the salience of perceptions, cognition, and emotions. These psycho-social constructs of necessity are diverse and not unitary. Such environments are designed to support students in wrestling with the following questions:

Perceptions

- Am I able to do this?
- Will effort matter?
- Is this task meaningful to me and worth my effort?
- What supports are available to help me wrestle with this task?

Cognitions

- What knowledge and strategies are available to me to wrestle with this task?
- What do I think is the task and as a consequence how do I think about resources available to me to wrestle with this task?

Emotions

- Do I feel safe in attempting to wrestle with this task?
- Do I feel that some set of my needs are being met as I wrestle with this task?
- How do I weigh the risks versus the opportunities entailed in doing this work?
- Are my positive emotions strong enough to deal with the negative feelings I have about this?

These relationships among perceptions, cognition, and emotions as underlying mechanisms that fuel human behavior, tell us that relationships matter, relationships between the learner and other people, the learner and the task, and the learner and the setting matter (Ainsworth, Blehar, Waters, & Wall, 1978; Fox & Hane, 2008; Goodenow, 1993). My point here is that thinking only of the cognitive demands of a targeted task, in this case reading comprehension, is insufficient to motivate learners to be engaged and to persist in meaningful goal directed behavior, especially in the face of challenges.

A third meaningful contribution to this argument is the role of ecological systems theory (Bronfenbrenner & Morris, 2006), the idea that people learn within and across settings, and that the influences on people's development comes not only from the direct settings in which they participate, the settings that those influencing the person participate, and the broader macro level ideologies and institutional configurations in which development evolves (Weisner, 2002). This also means that people bring with them knowledge, beliefs, and relationships as they move across settings. This is a reason why it is important to consider the prior knowledge, belief systems, language resources, and dispositions that learners construct from their participation in the multiple cultural communities in which they participate. And the processes and challenges of development differ on account of where in the life course, in this case, the learner is (Damon & Lerner, 2008; Spencer, 2006; Swanson, Edwards, & Spencer, 2010; Zelazo, 2013). The task for the purpose of this chapter is reading and comprehending texts, within particular settings such as schools and across diverse settings outside of school.

These foundational questions can also be understood in light of the literature in human development around resources for navigating risks and resilience (Masten, 2015; Spencer et al., 2006). Conceptualizing these questions under the umbrella of understanding sources of risk and resilience are essential for how we contextualize how we think about social and cultural diversity. How we conceptualize this problem space is important because of both the historical metanarratives around who faces risks and what are sources of resilience (Lee, 2009). In thinking about social and cultural diversity, we must consider the historic and institutionalized sources of risk which particular communities face (Churchill, 2004; Massey & Denton, 1993; Mills, 1997; Tate, 2008). These include the ways that racism, the structuring of poverty, and hegemonic ideologies around ethnicity, immigrant status, gender, sexual and gender orientation, and special needs, institutionalize opportunities and challenges. Spencer's PVEST (Spencer, 2006) framework posits that populations, particularly children and adolescents, disenfranchised by these hegemonic beliefs and institutionalized stigmatizing practices must wrestle both with the normative challenges of life course development (some of which I have described) along with the navigation and identity challenges that emerge from the institutionalization of racism, poverty, and other destabilizing ideologies. PVEST essentially argues that it is not simply the objective nature of risks that one faces that determines outcomes, but rather the relationships between the resources that are strategically focused on the nature of the risks faced that influence outcomes for individuals and populations. This means that in order to address the questions I identify in designing robust learning environments, designers (researchers, teachers, policy makers) must anticipate both normative developmental challenges and tasks as well as those that arise out of hegemonic institutionalized ideologies. Historically, one approach has been to argue that resources for resilience need to be based on normative assumptions about a set of practices and belief systems associated with the politically and ideologically dominant group (Graham, 1992); while other approaches argue that sources of resilience need to be rooted in drawing on cultural practices and belief systems carried across generations in a given cultural community that have sustained resilience in the face of challenge, as well as learning to interrogate the political, structural, and economic tools used to oppress particular communities (Gay, 1995; Gutiérrez, Morales, & Martinez, 2009; Ladson-Billings, 1995; Lomawaima, 2004; McCarty & Lee, 2014; Moll & Gonzales, 2004). The former approach presumes a singular normative pathway for development. Latter approaches presume a diverse set of pathways for development (Paris & Winn, 2013).

In order for robust learning environments to support students wrestling with core foundational psycho-social states, such environments must seek to accomplish the following (Lee, 2007):

- Position the learner as competent.
- Anticipate sources of vulnerability.
- Examine and scaffold resources the learner brings.
- Make public the social good and utility.
- Make problem solving explicit and public.
- Provide supports as learners are engaged in complex problem solving.
- Provide expansive opportunities.
- Remain adaptive and dynamic.

Implications for the Design of Robust Environments to Support Reading Comprehension

I have tried to lay two foundational warrants: (1) reading comprehension as entailing dynamic systems of meaning making; and (2) human learning and development as rooted in diverse pathways, informed mutually by biological processes and participation in cultural practices that entail dynamic relationships among perceptions, cognition, emotions, and relationships. I will now address the implications for designing robust environments that support children and adolescents in learning to read texts across academic disciplines in K-12 school settings.

I have argued that students are more likely to engage and persist when the processes for meaning making with texts are made explicit and public, and when they have opportunities to explore this kind of problem solving with supports that make them feel competent, and toward goals they construe as relevant. I will address here making meaning making processes explicit and relevant.

Comprehension Made Explicit

Historically, standards for comprehension have presumed substantive differences in goals by grade level. On the contrary, comprehension processes are few, and remain relatively stable across grade levels (e.g. monitoring comprehension, making and testing predictions, making connections across stretches of text, attending to language and structure, summarizing). At one level, the CCSS's (National Governors Association, 2010) overarching standards reflect this parsimony, although the standards continue to articulate relatively arbitrary differences in standards across grade levels. Such core processes entail what Kintsch (1998) calls text based models (e.g. extrapolating meaning directly from the text) and situation models (e.g. extrapolating from the text to the world outside the text) that themselves are interactive. However, there are also micro level processes (beyond basic decoding) that can guide how we make meaning from texts. In many respects, the big, stable processes I have identified represent outcomes of comprehension more than micro level processes through which these outcomes are achieved. Examples of such micro-level processes include:

- Vocabulary – using context clues, syntax, and knowledge of roots and affixes to infer meaning.
- Sentence comprehension – using the ability to deconstruct the elements of sentences of different structures to infer meaning.
- Text structure – detecting explicit and implicit indicators of logical relationships among ideas in a text.
- Cohesion – detecting antecedents and linguistic markers of relationships.

All of these processes are embedded in a student's knowledge about how a particular language works. However, there is not sufficient attention to making such micro-level processes explicit in our schools, nor are they typically reflected in commercial literacy curricula. For example, sentence diagramming is not routinely taught, and the teaching of roots and affixes is not systematic. Minimally these micro-level processes are relevant from middle school through high school.

Another important dimension of comprehension, important for making problem solving explicit, involves the demands of reading in the content areas, which is especially important in middle school and high school. In a recent IES funded study (Goldman et al., 2016), researchers in Project READI identified categories of knowledge required to navigate critical reading and argumentation in the disciplines. READI examined the breadth of knowledge that novices need to learn to bring to bear in the disciplines of literature, history, and science. These demands in the reading of history texts has been well documented (Perfetti, Britt, & Georgi, 1995; Seixas, 1993; Wineburg, 1991, 2002; Wineburg & Wilson, 1988). Research on the comprehension of texts in science is emerging (Greenleaf, Brown, Goldman, & Ko, 2013; Lemke, 1998; Pearson, Moje, & Greenleaf, 2010). Micro-level comprehension processes in literature still remain relatively situated in literary theory, with some efforts to extrapolate to middle and high school literature classrooms (Appleman, 2000; Grossman, 2001; Lee, 2011; Lee, Goldman, Levine, & Magliano, 2016; Levine & Horton, 2013; Smith, 1989, 1991). Extrapolating from extant studies in the disciplines, Project READI defined the following categories of knowledge at work in disciplinary reasoning with texts: epistemology, key concepts, strategies, types of texts, and language use. Making explicit epistemological orientations toward the task, understanding key concepts as schema for interrogating big ideas, deploying discipline specific strategies for tackling texts, understanding the anticipated logic of different text genres within disciplines, and understanding and using the academic language registers of the discipline represent fundamental requisites for inducting novice readers into inquiries in the discipline.

Taking these three fundamental tasks of reading comprehension (engaging macro level comprehension processes, strategically deploying micro level comprehension processes, and drawing across the multiple kinds of disciplinary knowledge required for content area reading) as necessary tools for novice readers to develop, with increasingly complex texts and tasks across the grade levels and subject matters, I will now address how social and cultural diversity in knowledge, language, beliefs, and dispositions can present themselves as resources to support reading comprehension in the depth and breadth I have described.

Culturally and Socially Diverse Repertoires as Resources for a Multi-Dimensional Framing of Reading Comprehension

First, it should be noted that reasoning through the symbolic functions of language are endemic to the human species (Pinker, 1994, 2007). We all reason through and with language. Written texts have evolved from inscriptions in caves to engravings on stone to writings on papyrus. In many ways the printing press democratized making meaning with and from written texts, and digital medium has expanded this democratization exponentially. In addition, there are cognitive and social similarities between the reading of written texts (which now include words, pictures, and graphic displays) and the reading of multi-media (our sensemaking of fictional movies and documentaries, of lyrics about human relationships and human and political conundrums, of art, etc.) (Tan, 2013; The New London Group, 1996). Cognitive research has shown that humans without instruction construct narrative schema (e.g. human behavior as goal directed, entailing causal links among actions, with consequences) that are deployed in making sense of experience in the world and that facilitate the long-term memory of events (Bruner, 1990; Trabasso & van den Broek, 1985; Turner, 1996). Researchers in early story comprehension (Stein & Glenn, 1979) have documented how young children, even before they can read, encapsulate stories in narrative schema. Thus research on the meaning making repertoires that, for our purposes, youth from non-dominant communities develop outside of school, provide one lens for conceptualizing and noticing culturally diverse resources to support reading comprehension.

In my own work in Cultural Modeling, I have documented how epistemologies around language play and skill in interpreting figuration among speakers of African-American English can be made explicit in order to scaffold epistemologies and skills in noticing and interpreting various forms of figuration in literature (Lee, 1991, 1995, 2007, 2008). Such skills in everyday speech are typically tacit, and thus examining what I call cultural data sets of signifying (a genre of ritual insult) (Smitherman, 1977) among this linguistic community can make public and explicit strategies that then have the potential to be generalizable beyond the oral context. In a similar vein, adolescents across ethnic groups highly value rap lyrics (Alim, Ibrahim, & Pennycook, 2008) and other popular music genres which require the identification and interpretation of such tropes as irony, satire, symbolism, and unreliable narration, all relevant interpretive problems in literature, but also in history. Research in Cultural Modeling has documented the positive transfer of such skills to literature texts (Lee, 1995, 2007).

There is another body of growing research on translingualism, documenting the metalinguistic skills that youth who are English Language Learners, with sufficient language competencies in English and their first language (often Spanish in these studies) develop and critically deploy in translating in both everyday and official capacities for their parents and families (Orellana, 2009; Orellana & Eksner, 2006; Orellana & Reynolds, 2008; Orellana, Dorner, & Pulido, 2003; Valdes, 2002). These metalinguistic repertoires include detecting and interpreting linguistic markers of points of view, of differential positioning, of the salience of particular registers in both languages, and the appropriateness of particular registers for particular contexts. Orellana has developed instructional interventions in elementary classrooms which scaffold such repertoires for reading comprehension and composition.

Another important body of research that has not been taken up in classrooms, but represents important findings, is work around the role of culture in comprehension. Some of this early work was carried out at the Center for the Study of Reading in the 1970's by Richard Anderson and colleagues (Reynolds, Taylor, Steffensen, Shirey, & Anderson, 1982; Steffensen, Joag-Dev, & Anderson, 1979). Building on well-established documentation on the role of prior knowledge in comprehension and how such prior knowledge is retained in long term memory through schemata (Anderson, 2004; Anderson & Pearson, 1988; Bartlett, 1932; Rumelhart, 1980), these studies demonstrated how the interpretation of the same story can be different based on the cultural knowledge the reader brings to bear. In one story about a wedding, readers from the U.S. and India read the same story and recall very different details about the event, based on cultural differences in what a wedding entails. On a more generic level, Bransford (1972) documented how the depth of understanding of a text about baseball differed based on the level of expert knowledge of the reader. Thus it is quite possible that access to texts among culturally diverse learners may be significantly related to the relevant schema they bring to the text. This has important implications for text selection in schools and within disciplines. For example, while Steinbeck's *The Grapes of Wrath* has a 5th grade readability level, it is not likely that upper middle class 5th graders will have the same conceptual access to the themes and character development as students whose families are undocumented immigrant/migrant workers. And if in the literature classroom, we want to teach generative knowledge about text structures, interpretive problems, and problems of point of view, for example, we do not need to limit ourselves to selecting only texts from the European and Euro-American canon.

Epistemology is another important source of knowledge influencing how readers make sense of texts. There is important research in the area of indigenous knowledge systems (Megan Bang et al., 2014; Brayboy, 2005; Jones, Brayboy & Maughan, 2009; Semali & Kincheloe, 2002), documenting how indigenous communities in the Americas and other parts of the world develop across generations epistemological dispositions to conceptualize interdependent and equal relations between humans and the natural world. For example, many indigenous communities see plants and animals as relatives, and memorialize such relations in stories and proverbs (Bang, Medin, & Altran, 2007; Ross, Medin, & Cox, 2007). Bang and colleagues (Dehghani et al., 2013) have examined storybooks for young children about the natural world written by indigenous and non-indigenous authors. They have found indigenous authors are more likely to foreground relationships between humans and the natural world as embedded and to portray these relationships as psychologically meaningful. These findings are consistent with research Bang and others (Bang & Medin, 2010; Bang, Medin, Washinawatok, & Chapman, 2010; Bang, Warren, Rosebery, & Medin, 2012) have conducted cross-culturally, examining conceptions of relations between humans and the natural world, and in curriculum development in science interventions they have developed to scaffold such indigenous epistemologies regarding the natural world to promote scientific inquiry in schools. Although they have not yet directly examined how children from indigenous backgrounds who have been socialized in such epistemologies engage with science texts written for young children by indigenous authors, the extant research would suggest these children bring relevant schema to the comprehension and interpretation of such texts.

The point of these exemplars is that they provide illustrations of knowledge structures, epistemologies, and language repertoires that youth, in this case, from non-dominant communities develop outside of formal schooling, that provide resources for making text comprehension, including the comprehension and interpretation of discipline specific texts, public and explicit, through scaffolding.

I have argued that research on human learning posits that the ability to feel efficacious promotes engagement and motivation, dispositions we inherit from our evolution as a species, including the physiological processes through which we impute salience to experience, including emotional attributions, including the ways in which a learning environment makes explicit and provides supports for problem solving. I have illustrated in this section meaningful relationships between meaning making processes in everyday contexts, particularly around narratives – including the ways we narrativize both the political and scientific world (stories of agents engaged in goal directed behaviors, including events that are causally linked), and often narrativize through figurative tropes, engaging processes required to tackle complex written texts.

Social Contexts and Diverse Interactional Styles as Resources for Robust Literacy Learning Environments

Other important dimensions of robust learning environments have to do with how they make us feel connected, how they impact the relationships we build and the relevance we impute to tasks we are expected to accomplish. Accomplishing these goals often include the social organization of settings. Here research in informal settings outside of K-12 schooling offers examples of culturally diverse forms of social organization that have demonstrated the capacity to engage youth from non-dominant groups in robust literacy learning, including the interrogation of complex texts.

In Cultural Modeling classrooms, working with youth who are speakers of African-American English (AAE), the invocation of African-American rhetorical strategies of language production and interactions have repeatedly engaged students in complex literary reasoning (Lee, 2005b). Such strategies include highly valenced prosody, multi-party overlapping talk, high use of gesture, as well as AAE dialect. In our analyses of video recordings over many years, these strategies are invoked by students when they are most engaged in the critical reasoning of challenging problems in the literature being studied. In Cultural Modeling classrooms, the design included not only scaffolding linguistic repertoires, epistemological dispositions toward figuration, and tacit knowledge of meaning making strategies relevant to literary texts, but equally important is the selection and sequencing of texts that would invite identity wrestling around issues of race and ethnicity and opportunities to interrogate how, through these texts, characters wrestled with the persistent challenges of racism and poverty. In the most recent iteration, a four year longitudinal intervention in Project READI funded by IES, we found that an affirmative sense of racial identity was correlated positively with literacy outcomes that included grades, close transfer comprehension assessments developed by the project, and far transfer assessments on EPAS, the ACT sequence for 9th, 10th and 11th graders (Lee, 2016b). We found similar findings associated with a measure of literary epistemology valuing multiple meanings and multiple readings, and the specific strategies and practices in the Cultural Modeling framework, including valuing the social relevance of literature to one's life (Yukhymenko-Lescroart et al., 2016).

The Migrant Student Leadership Institute at UCLA (Gutiérrez, 2014; Gutiérrez, 2008) spearheaded and conceptualized by Kris Gutiérrez, is an example of what she calls social design experiments (Gutiérrez & Jurow, 2016). The program worked with high school students whose families were migrant workers, with the goal of engaging them in literacy practices that would both help prepare them for college while simultaneously engaging them in interrogating the political and economic forces with which they and their families had to navigate. This included examinations of inter-generational practices and belief systems that have historically sustained their communities. Manuel Espinoza (2009) who worked on the project, called it "educational sanctuary." The curriculum integrated science and the social sciences, for example, to examine environmental racism affecting their lives. Students read such texts as the "Tuskegee Study of Untreated Syphillis in the Negro Male," the U.S. sponsored Guatemalan STD Study from the 1940's, as well as C. Wright Mills' *The Sociological Imagination* and Paulo Freire's *Pedagogy of the Oppressed*, among others, and wrote critical arguments around their analyses and engaged in a hybrid cultural practice of critical autobiography called "testimonios." From the 2001–2003 cohort, in comparison to a control group admitted to the program but who did not attend, a statistically significant percentage of students enrolled in this program went on to be accepted into the prestigious University of California system (Nunez, 2009). The design principles from this intervention included scaffolding linguistic repertoires, structuring literacy supports that meet relevant goals of students, building a network of adult and peer relationships that address youths' need for safety and a sense of self-efficacy. For example, there is a video of the adult teacher/mentors having students, together, lift another student off the ground and carry him up the stairs in an area on campus. The avowed goal of this metaphoric activity was to embody the propositions that the students had to work together, collaboratively, to achieve challenging goals and to demonstrate that they belonged on the UCLA campus. This program is an example of designing literacy rich robust learning environments, in this case for youth from non-dominant communities, that addresses both the breadth of socio-emotional needs of youth at an important life course transition as well as making the complex demands of critical reading of difficult texts explicit, public, accessible, and relevant. The rich discussions, the testimonios, and the written arguments provided insights to both students and their mentor/teachers of the internal reasoning of individual students in processing texts, but also expansive opportunities for students to share their thinking about texts with one another.

There are additional compelling exemplars of robust literacy learning environments designed in out-of-school contexts that illustrate how cultural diversity serves as a resource for helping students learn to engage with complex texts. These are literate rich settings where making public how to tackle complex problems of text comprehension is scaffolded through recruiting cultural repertoires (knowledge, beliefs, epistemologies, social networks), building supportive relationships with peers and mentors, and co-constructing socially meaningful goals toward which the recruitment of literacy practices serves important purposes are normative. There is an emerging body of research on the literate practices in these settings and especially around the role of these settings in engaging literacy as a tool for identity wrestling. Winn's (Fisher, 2003, 2005) research has documented mentor–mentee relationships in spoken word community based settings that engage adolescents in critically examining poetry from the Black Arts Movement of the 1970's, for thinking about how these young people draw on such texts in creating their own politically insightful poetic forms, as well as support for incarcerated adolescent girls to engage in critical engagement with and the production of texts (Winn, 2010).

A growing focus in supporting what we might think of as critical literacies (e.g. the investigation of texts that examine the underpinnings and institutional configurations that create and sustain persistent historical inequalities) has emerged as an important paradigm shift in literacy research in and across settings, which is not limited to schooling. This shift is buttressed by the idea that for non-dominant populations in particular, learning to examine, navigate, and resist institutionalized forms of oppression are critical tasks across the life course, in addition to the normative tasks of development, a proposition reflected in Spencer's (Spencer et al., 2006) PVEST model for understanding how sources of risk and resilience unfold. This emerging body of work conceptualizes literacy – reading texts and producing texts, including multi-modal texts – as generative tools for life course development, and not simply technical tools for workforce preparation. This work is unfolding in both out-of-school and school settings. Across these programs of research, students are typically invited to examine texts of some complexity for the purpose of gaining knowledge that can be used to engage in social action, often political action. This work stretches the bounds of the kinds of texts that should be examined (e.g. street fiction, hip hop texts, as well as, for example, texts rooted in critical race theory, feminist thought, etc., which is often not the focus of more standard conceptions of appropriate text sets for adolescents). This work also stretches the boundaries of languages, language registers, and language varieties that serve as the medium of communication, revisiting the dialect and bilingual debates of the past (August & Shanahan, 2006; Farr, 1991; Gándara, Moran, & Garcia, 2004; Lee, 2005a; Scott, Straker, & Katz, 2009). This body of research reveals that text-based processing and modes of representing comprehension are connected to both what we know about generic comprehension as well as discipline specific comprehension; and often pushes the boundaries of what our field sees as discipline specific modes of reasoning about texts. This emerging research includes Majors (Majors, 2003, 2015) work connecting text based reasoning and argumentation in African-American beauty salons with school based literacies; Lyiscott's (Lyiscott, 2017; Van Orman & Lyiscott, 2013) Cyphers for Justice, where adolescents, including incarcerated youth, and preservice teachers critique and produce social justice texts as springboards for political action; Morrell (2004, Morrell & Duncan-Andrade, 2002) and Duncan-Andrade's (Duncan-Andrade, 2004; Duncan-Andrade & Morrell, 2005) work with hip hop literacies in high school literature classrooms; Kinloch's (2007, 2010) research documenting how urban adolescents critically examine issues of gentrification and the privileging of particular language varieties; Paris's (2010, 2011) research in what he calls borderland communities (Anzaldúa, 1987), where youth are reading and producing texts that examine their intersectional identities around race, ethnicity, class, and citizenship statuses; San Pedro's (2014, 2015) research with indigenous youth learning to navigate the conflicting epistemologies behind Native American literature and settler colonial historical narratives; and Alim's (2009, Alim et al., 2008) cross cultural studies of hip-hop linguistic practices as pedagogical resources.

Collectively, this work builds on earlier research on the significance of cultural practices to literacy learning (Ball, 1992; Ball & Farr, 2003; Delpit, 1995; Gay, 1995; Gutiérrez, Baquedano-Lopez, & Tejeda, 1999; Ladson-Billings, 1995; Ladson-Billings & Tate, 1995; Lee, 2007; Mahiri, 1998; McCarty, 2002; Valdes, 1996), but extends that work in numerous ways. It expands the range of texts to be interrogated, adds new dimensions for the rationale behind text selection, expands the goals of literacy beyond a technocratic emphasis. Like earlier work, it emphasizes the role of emotional salience and relationships, of the importance of relevance, and engages in design principles to develop and sustain a sense of self-efficacy among learners, all goals I have argued are endemic to human development and functioning, and therefore essential targets for learning. Both the older and the more current work open opportunities to examine the diverse pathways through which meaning making from and with texts unfolds within and across communities of practice.

Conundrums of the Paradigm Shift

There are both theoretical and practice based conundrums that these investigations into diverse literacy practices present. Theoretically, we need syntheses of findings from across these programs of research to understand the diversity, but also the underlying processes that undergird such diversity. I noted earlier that the film *Babies* documented the underlying tasks of development in the first year of life that are common to the enterprise of growing from birth to one year of age, as well as the diverse pathways and the diverse social goals that fuel such development. In a similar vein, I have tried to outline both generic macro and micro level comprehension processes entailed in reading comprehension, but in understanding such processes as entailing characteristics of the person, the text and the task. With these examples of programs of research designing for and documenting diverse pathways for interrogating texts within and across different cultural communities, including the intersectionality across communities, we need to better understand how these pathways link to what we think of as foundational processes. We may find in such syntheses that the dynamic relationships entailed in comprehension are such that some of our foundational propositions need to be re-visited.

At the level of practice, particularly in the contexts of formal schooling, teachers, designers of curriculum, and assessment developers need to be more deeply grounded in the micro-analyses of sources of complexity in the range of texts and genres that these critical pedagogical models I have described invite students to examine. If the knowledge gleaned by students – no matter the context of learning – is to be generative, it needs to be metacognitive, explicit, and understood as probabilistic and not deterministic. There is also the challenge of helping students learn to navigate diverse linguistic communities and their requirements for participation: moving from another national language or English language dialect to academic registers required by the academy, particularly post-secondary; learning to communicate to multiple valued audiences – one's community, the larger public. There are daunting institutional challenges to the development of such pedagogical content knowledge (Shulman, 1986) to be endemic to teaching and learning (Snow, Griffin, & Burns, 2006): the policy and ideological constraints around the thinking of critical literacy as the work of schooling; the constraints of existing standards (including the CCSS) and assessments; and the epistemological shifts required. At the same time, these islands of critical literacy, in schools and non-school settings, offer hope for many kinds of transformations: in how youth, particularly youth from non-dominant communities, view the generative functions of text-based literacies; in how such youth come to use the tools of literacy to work toward social and political transformations around issues of equity; and of how youth learn to become themselves producers of new knowledge.

Closing

I have tried to situate discussions of how social and cultural differences in communities can be understood to support literacy learning and development in a broader context of understanding literacy learning as just one task of human development in literate societies. I agree wholeheartedly with calls for attention to the social world and cultural differences around promoting multiculturalism in our schools and society. At the same time, I want to frame our interrogations of such diversity in human terms, in terms of the scientific investigation of what fuels human learning. It just so happens that the learning task in this volume is on reading comprehension, but we could put forth the same warrants for features of learning environments that are robust if the task were mathematical reasoning or scientific reasoning. It turns out that in reading comprehension we have a universal task of the species, namely the use of and interrogation of language as a resource for meaning making. Because of this, so much of what we do in comprehending texts has parallels in other language based genres (oral storytelling, proverbs, narratives in television and movies, in music lyrics, and in metaphors we live by (Lakoff and Johnson, 1980). We all interrogate language all the time. Understanding the wide range of variation in how we use language is in fact the stuff of reading comprehension.

References

Adam, E. K., Heissel, J. A., Zeiders, K. H., Richeson, J. A., Ross, E. C., Ehrlich, K. B., … Malanchuk, O. (2015). Developmental histories of perceived racial discrimination and diurnal cortisol profiles in adulthood: A 20-year prospective study. *Psychoneuroendocrinology*, 62, 279–291.
Ainsworth, M., Blehar, M., Waters, E., & Wall, S. (1978). *Patterns of attachment*. Hillsdale, NJ: Erlbaum.
Alim, H. S. (2009). Hip hop nation language. *Linguistic Anthropology: A Reader*, 272–289.
Alim, H. S., Ibrahim, A., & Pennycook, A. (2008). *Global linguistic flows: Hip hop cultures, youth identities, and the politics of language*. New York, NY: Routledge.
American Psychological Association Task Force on Resilience and Strength in Black Children and Adolescents. (2008). *Resilience in African American children and adolescence: A vision for optimal development*. Washington, DC.
Anderson, R. (2004). Role of the reader's schema in comprehension, learning, and memory. In R. B. Ruddell & N. J. Unrau (Eds.), *Theoretical models and processes of reading* (5th ed.) (pp. 594–606). Newark, DE: International Reading Association.
Anderson, R. C., & Pearson, P. D. (1988). A schema-theoretic view of basic processes in reading comprehension. In P. Carrell, J. Devine, & D. Eskey (Eds.), *Interactive approaches to second language reading* (pp. 37–55). Cambridge, UK: Cambridge University Press.
Anzaldúa, G. (1987). *Borderlands: La frontera* (Vol. 3). San Francisco, CA: Aunt Lute.
Appleman, D. (2000). *Critical encounters in high school English: Teaching literary theory to adolescents*. New York, NY: Teachers College Press.
August, D., Carlo, M., Dressler, C., & Snow, C. (2005). The critical role of vocabulary development for English language learners. *Learning Disabilities Research and Practice*, 20, 50–57.
August, D., & Shanahan, T. (2006). *Developing literacy in second-language learners: Report of the national literacy panel on language-minority children and youth*. Mahwah, NJ: Lawrence Erlbaum.
Ball, A. (1992). Cultural preferences and the expository writing of African-American adolescents. *Written Communication*, 9(4), 501–532.

Ball, A., & Farr, M. (2003). Language varieties, culture and teaching the English language arts. In J. Flood, D. Lapp, J. Squire, & J. Jensen (Eds.), *Handbook of research on teaching the English language arts* (2nd ed., pp. 435–445). Mahwah, NJ: Lawrence Erlbaum.

Bang, M., Curley, L., Kessel, A., Marin, A., Suzukovich, E. S., III, & Strack, G. (2014). Muskrat theories, tobacco in the streets, and living chicago as indigenous land. *Environmental Education Research, 20*(1), 37–55.

Bang, M., & Medin, D. (2010). Cultural processes in science education: Supporting the navigation of multiple epistemologies. *Science Education, 94*(6), 1008–1026.

Bang, M., Medin, D., Washinawatok, K., & Chapman, S. (2010). Innovations in culturally based science education through partnerships and community. In M. Khine & I. Saleh (Eds.), *New science of learning* (pp. 569–592). New York, NY: Springer.

Bang, M., Medin, D. L., & Altran, S. (2007). Cultural mosaics and mental models of nature. *Proceedings of the National Academy of Sciences, 104,* 13868–13874.

Bang, M., Warren, B., Rosebery, A. S., & Medin, D. (2012). Desettling expectations in science education. *Human Development, 55*(5–6), 302–318.

Bartlett, F. C. (1932). *Remembering: A study in experimental and social psychology.* Cambridge, UK: Cambridge University Press.

Becker, B. E., & Luthar, S. S. (2002). Social-emotional factors affecting achievement outcomes among disadvantaged students: Closing the achievement gap. *Educational Psychologist, 37,* 197–214.

Bell, D. C. (2010). *The dynamics of connection: How evolution and biology create caregiving and attachment.* Lanham, MD: Lexington.

Bereiter, C., & Engelmann, S. (1966). *Teaching disadvantaged children in pre-school.* Englewood Cliffs, NJ: Prentice Hall.

Biancarosa, G., & Snow, C. (2004). *Reading next - a vision for action and research in middle and high school literacy: A report to carnegie corporation in New York.* Washington, DC: Alliance for Excellent Education.

Bowlby, J. (1969). *Attachment. Attachment and loss* (Vol. 1). London: Hogarth.

Bowman, P. (1989). Research perspectives on black men: Role strain and adaptation across the adult life cycle. In R. Jones (Ed.), *Black adult development and aging* (pp. 117–150). Berkeley, CA: Cobbs & Henry.

Bransford, J., & Johnson, M. (1972). Contextual prerequisites for understanding: Some investigations of comprehension and recall. *Journal of Verbal Learning and Verbal Behavior, 11,* 717–726.

Brayboy, B. M. J. (2005). Toward a tribal critical race theory in education. *The Urban Review, 37*(5), 425–446.

Brewer, W. (1977). Memory for the pragmatic implications of sentences. *Memory and Cognition, 5,* 673–678.

Bronfenbrenner, U., & Morris, P. A. (2006). The bioecological model of human development. In R. M. Lerner & W. Damon (Eds.), *Handbook of child psychology: Theoretical models of human development* (pp. 793–828). John Wiley & Sons Inc.

Bruner, J. (1990). *Acts of meaning.* Cambridge, MA: Harvard University Press.

Churchill, W. (2004). *Kill the Indian, save the man: The genocidal impact of American Indian residential schools.* San Fracisco, CA: City Lights Publisher.

Cole, M. (2007). Phylogeny and cultural history in ontogeny. *Journal of Physiology, 101,* 236–246.

Damon, W., & Lerner, R. M. (2008). The scientific study of child and adolescent development: Important issues in the field today. In W. Damon & R. M. Lerner (Eds.), *Child and adolescent development an advanced course* (pp. 3–18). Hoboken, NJ: Wiley and Sons.

Dehghani, M., Bang, M., Medin, D., Marin, A., Leddon, E., & Waxman, S. (2013). Epistemologies in the text of children's books: Native-and non-native-authored books. *International Journal of Science Education, 35*(13), 2133–2151.

Delpit, L. (1995). *Other people's children: Cultural conflict in the classroom.* New York, NY: The New Press.

Duncan-Andrade, J. M. (2004). Your best friend or your worst enemy: Youth popular culture, pedagogy, and curriculum in urban classrooms. *The Review of Education, Pedagogy, and Cultural Studies, 26*(4), 313–337.

Duncan-Andrade, J. M., & Morrell, E. (2005). Turn up that radio, teacher: Popular cultural pedagogy in new century urban schools. *Journal of School Leadership, 15*(3), 284.

Dweck, C. S. (1999). *Self-theories: Their role in motivation, personality and development.* Philadelphia, PA: The Psychology Press.

Eccles, J., O'Neil, S., & Wigfield, A. (2005). Ability self-perceptions and subjective task values in adolescents and children. In K. Moore & L. Lippman (Eds.), *What do children need to flourish: Conceptualizing and measuring indicators of positive development* (pp. 237–270). New York, NY: Springer.

Espinoza, M. (2009). A case study of the production of educational sanctuary in one migrant classroom. *Pedagogies: An International Journal, 4*(1), 44–62.

Farr, M. (1991). Dialects, culture and teaching the English language arts. In J. Flood, J. Jenson, D. Lapp, & J. Squire (Eds.), *Handbook of research on teaching the English language arts* (pp. 365–371). New York, NY: Macmillan.

Fischer, K. W., & Bidell, T. R. (1998). Dynamic development of psychological structures in action and thought. In W. Damon & R. M. Lerner (Eds.), *Handbook of child psychology: Theoretical models of human development* (Vol. 1, 5th ed., pp. 467–562). New York, NY: Wiley & Sons.

Fisher, M. (2003). Open mics and open minds: Spoken word poetry in African diaspora participatory literacy communities. *Harvard Educational Review, 73*(3), 362–389.

Fisher, M. T. (2005). From the coffee house to the school house: The promise and potential of spoken word poetry in school contexts. *English Education, 37*(2), 115–131.

Flavell, J. H., & Miller, P. H. (1998). Social cognition. In D. Kuhn & R. Siegler (Eds.), *Handbook of child psychology* (Vol. 2, 5th ed., pp. 851–898). New York, NY: Wiley.

Fox, N. A., & Hane, A. A. (2008). Studying the biology of human attachment. In J. Cassidy & P. R. Shaver (Eds.), *Handbook of attachment: Theory, research and clinical applications* (pp. 811–829). New York, NY: Guilford Press.

Gándara, P., Moran, R., & Garcia, E. (2004). Chapter 2: Legacy of brown: Lau and language policy in the United States. *Review of Research in Education, 28*(1), 27–46.

Gay, G. (1995). Curriculum theory and multicultural education. In J. Banks & C. A. M. Banks (Eds.), *Handbook of research on multicultural education* (pp. 25–43). New York, NY: Macmillan Publishing Company.

Geronimus, A. (2013). Jedi public health: Co-creating an identity-safe culture to promote health equity. In A. Geronimus, S. A. James, M. Destin, L. F. Graham, M. L. Hatzenbuehler, M. C. Murphy, J. A. Pearson, A. Omari & J. P. Thomson (Eds.), *Mapping "race": Critical approaches to health disparities research* (pp. 105–116). Population Health, 2.

Goldman, S. R., Britt, M. A., Brown, W., Cribb, G., George, M., Greenleaf, C., … Project READI (2016). Disciplinary literacies and learning to read for understanding: A conceptual framework for disciplinary literacy. *Educational Psychologist, 51*, 1–28.

Goodenow, C. (1993). Classroom belonging among early adolescent students: Relationships to motivation and achievement. *Journal of Early Adolescence, 13*, 21–43.

Gould, S. J. (1981). *The mismeasure of man.* New York, NY: W.W. Norton.

Graesser, A. C., McNamara, D. S., & Louwerse, M. M. (2003). What do readers need to learn in order to process coherence relations in narrative and expository text? In A. P. Sweet & C. Snow (Eds.), *Rethinking reading comprehension* (pp. 82–98). New York, NY: Guilford Publications.

Graham, S. (1992). Most of the subjects were white and middle class": Trends in published research on African Americans in selected APA journals, 1970–1989. *American Psychologist, 47*(5), 629–639.

Greenleaf, C., Brown, W., Goldman, S. R., & Ko, M. (2013). *Readi for science: Promoting scientific literacy practices through text-based investigations for middle and high school science teachers and students. Presented at workshop on literacy for science.* Washington, DC: National Research Council.

Grossman, P. (2001). *Research on the teaching of literature: Finding a place* (4th ed.). New York, NY: Macmillan Press.

Gutiérrez, K. (2014). The science of justice: Migrant youth and sociocritial literacies in science. In C. f. t. S. o. R. a. E. i. Education (Ed.), *The elusive quest for civil rights in education* (pp. 12–13). Philadelphia, PA: University of Pennsylvania.

Gutiérrez, K., Baquedano-Lopez, P., & Tejeda, C. (1999). Rethinking diversity: Hybridity and hybrid language practices in the third space. *Mind, Culture, and Activity, 6*(4), 286–303.

Gutiérrez, K., Morales, P. L., & Martinez, D. (2009). Re-mediating literacy: Culture, difference, and learning for students from non-dominant communities. *Review of Research in Educational Research, 33*, 212–245.

Gutiérrez, K. D. (2008). Developing a sociocritical literacy in the third space. *Reading Research Quarterly, 43*(2), 148–164.

Gutiérrez, K. D., & Jurow, A. S. (2016). Social design experiments: Toward equity by design. *Journal of the Learning Sciences, 25*(4), 565–598.

Hart, B., & Risley, R. T. (1995). *Meaningful differences in the everyday experience of young American children.* Baltimore, MD: Brookes.

Heckman, J. J. (2012). An effective strategy for promoting social mobility. *Boston Review,* 10155–10162.

Heckman, J. J., & Rubinstein, Y. (2001). The importance of noncognitive skills: Lessons from the ged testing program. *American Economic Review, 91*, 145–149.

Herman, J., & Linn, R. (2013). On the road to assessing deeper learning: The status of smarter balanced and parcc assessment consortia. Cresst report 823. *National Center for Research on Evaluation, Standards, and Student Testing (CRESST).*

Hernstein, R., & Murray, C. (1994). *The bell curve: Intelligence and class structure in American life*. New York, NY: Free Press.

Hiebert, E. H., & Kamil, M. (2005). *Teaching and learning vocabulary: Bringing research to practice*. Hillsdale, NJ: Lawrence Erlbaum.

Jensen, A. (1969). How much can we boost iq and scholastic achievement. *Harvard Educational Review, 39*, 1–123.

Jensen, E. (2009). *Teaching with poverty in mind: What being poor does to kids' brains and what schools can do about it*. Alexandria, VA: Association for Supervision and Curriculum Development.

Jones Brayboy, B. M., & Maughan, E. (2009). Indigenous knowledges and the story of the bean. *Harvard Educational Review, 79*(1), 1–21.

Juel, C. (1991). Beginning reading. In R. Barr, M. L. Kamil, P. B. Mosenthal, & P. D. Pearson (Eds.), *Handbook of reading research* (Vol. 2, pp. 759–788). New York, NY: Longman.

Kim, J., Hemphill, L., Troyer, M., Jones, S., LaRusso, M., Kim, H.-Y., … Snow, C. (2016). The experimental effects of the strategic adolescent reading intervention (stari) on a scenarios-based reading comprehension assessment. *Society for Research on Educational Effectiveness*.

Kinloch, V. (2007). The white-ification of the hood": Power, politics, and youth performing narratives of community. *Language Arts, 85*(1), 61.

Kinloch, V. (2010). *Harlem on our minds: Place, race, and the literacies of urban youth*. New York, NY: Teachers College Press.

Kintsch, W. (1998). *Comprehension: A paradigm for cognition*. New York, NY: Cambridge University Press.

Kunda, Z. (1999). *Social cognition: Making sense of people*. Cambridge, MA: MIT Press.

Ladson-Billings, G. (1995). Toward a theory of culturally relevant pedagogy. *American Educational Research Journal, 32*(3), 465–491.

Ladson-Billings, G., & Tate, W. (1995). Toward a critical race theory of education. *Teachers College Record, 97*(1), 47–68.

Lakoff, G., & Johnson, M. (1980). *Metaphors we live by*. Chicago, IL: University of Chicago Press.

Lee, C. D. (1991). Big picture talkers/words walking without masters: The instructional implications of ethnic voices for an expanded literacy. *Journal of Negro Education, 60*(3), 291–305.

Lee, C. D. (1995). A culturally based cognitive apprenticeship: Teaching African American high school students' skills in literary interpretation. *Reading Research Quarterly, 30*(4), 608–631.

Lee, C. D. (2005a). Culture and language: Bi-dielectical issues in literacy. In P. L. Anders & J. Flood (Eds.), *Culture and language: Bi-dielectical issues in literacy* (pp. 241–274). Newark, DE: International Reading Association.

Lee, C. D. (2005b). Double voiced discourse: African American vernacular English as resource in cultural modeling classrooms. In A. F. Ball & S. W. Freedman (Eds.), *New literacies for new times: Bakhtinian perspectives on language, literacy, and learning for the 21st century* (pp. 129–147). New York, NY: Cambridge University Press.

Lee, C. D. (2007). *Culture, literacy and learning: Taking bloom in the midst of the whirlwind*. New York, NY: Teachers College Press.

Lee, C. D. (2008). Cultural modeling as opportunity to learn: Making problem solving explicit in culturally robust classrooms and implications for assessment. In P. Moss, D. Pullin, J. P. Gee, E. Haertel, & L. J. Young (Eds.), *Assessment, equity, and opportunity to learn* (pp. 136–169). New York, NY: Cambridge University Press.

Lee, C. D. (2009). Historical evolution of risk and equity. *Interdisciplinary Issues and Critiques Review of Research in Education, 33*, 63–100.

Lee, C. D. (2010). Soaring above the clouds, delving the ocean's depths understanding the ecologies of human learning and the challenge for education science. *Educational Researcher, 39*(9), 643–655.

Lee, C. D. (2011). Education and the study of literature. *Scientific Study of Literature, 1*(1), 49–58.

Lee, C. D. (2014). Reading gaps and complications of scientific studies of learning. In S. Harper (Ed.), *The elusive quest for civil rights in education: Evidence-based perspectives from leading scholars on the 50th anniversary of the civil rights act* (pp. 14–17). Philadelphia, PA: Center for the Study of Race and Equity in Education, The University of Pennsylvania.

Lee, C. D. (2016a). Influences of the experience of race as a lens for understanding variation in displays of competence in reading comprehension. In P. Afflerbach (Ed.), *Handbook of individual differences in reading: Reader, text, and context* (pp. 286–304). New York, NY: Routledge.

Lee, C. D. (2016b). Slipping into the breaks and looking around: Exploring the roles of racial identity and psycho-social development on academic outcomes through literature. *Paper presented at the annual meeting of the American Educational Research Association*, Washington, DC.

Lee, C. D., & Goldman, S. R. (2015). Assessing literary reasoning: Text and task complexities. *Theory into Practice, 54*(3), 213–227.

Lee, C. D., Goldman, S. R., Levine, S., & Magliano, J. P. (2016). Epistemic cognition in literary reasoning. In J. Green, W. Sandoval, & I. Bråten (Eds.), *Handbook of epistemic cognition* (pp. 165–183). New York, NY: Taylor & Francis.

Lee, C. D., & Spratley, A. (2009). *Reading in the disciplines and the challenges of adolescent literacy*. New York, NY: Carnegie Foundation of New York.

Lemke, J. (1998). Multiplying meaning: Visual and verbal semiotics in scientific text. In J. R. Martin & R. Veel (Eds.), *Reading science: Critical and functional perspectives on discourse of science* (pp. 87–113). New York, NY: Routledge.

Levine, S., & Horton, W. S. (2013). Using affective appraisal to help readers construct literary interpretations. *Scientific Study of Literature, 3*(1), 105–136.

Lomawaima, K. T. (2004). Educating native Americans. In J. Banks & C. Banks (Eds.), *Handbook of research on multicultural education* (2nd ed., pp. 441–461). San Francisco, CA: Jossey-Bass.

Lyiscott, J. (2017). Racial identity and liberation literacies in the classroom. *English Journal, 106*(4), 47.

Mahiri, J. (1998). *Shooting for excellence: African American and youth culture in new century schools*. New York, NY: Teachers College Press and National Council of Teachers of English.

Majors, Y. (2015). *Shop talk*. New York, NY: Teachers College Record.

Majors, Y. J. (2003). Shoptalk: Teaching and learning in an African American hair salon. *Mind, Culture, and Activity, 10*(4), 289–310.

Markus, H. (1977). Self schemas and processing information abut the self. *Journal of Personality and Social Psychology, 35*, 63–78.

Maslow, A. H. (1943). A theory of human motivation. *Psychological Review, 50*(4), 370.

Massey, D., & Denton, N. (1993). *American apartheid: Segregation and the making of the underclass*. Cambridge, MA: Harvard University Press.

Masten, A. S. (2015). *Ordinary magic: Resilience in development*. New York City, NY: Guilford Publications.

McCarty, T., & Lee, T. (2014). Critical culturally sustaining/revitalizing pedagogy and indigenous education sovereignty. *Harvard Educational Review, 84*(1), 101–124.

McCarty, T. L. (2002). *A place to be navajo: Rough rock and the struggle for self-determination in indigenous schooling*. Mahwah, NJ: Lawrence Erlbaum.

McNamara, D. S., Kintsch, E., Songer, N. B., & Kintsch, W. (1996). Are good texts always better? Text coherence, background knowledge, and levels of understanding in learning from text. *Cognition and Instruction, 14*, 1–43.

Meltzoff, A. N. (1988). Imitation, objects, tools, and the rudiments of language in human ontogeny. *Human Evolution, 3*, 509–516.

Meltzoff, A. N., & Moore, M. K. (1977). Imitation of facial and manual gestures by human neonates. *Science, 198*, 75–78.

Meyer, B. J. F., Brandt, D. M., & Bluth, G. J. (1980). Use of top-level structure in text: Key for reading comprehension of ninth-grade students. *Reading Research Quarterly, 16*, 72–103.

Miller, D. B., & MacIntosh, R. (1999). Promoting resilience in urban African American adolescents: Racial socialization and identity as protective factors. *Social Work Research, 23*, 159–269.

Mills, C. W. (1997). *The racial contract*. Ithaca, NY: Cornell University Press.

Moje, E. B. (2000). To be part of the story: The literacy practices of gangsta adolescents. *Teachers College Record, 102*, 652–690.

Moje, E. B., & Tysvaer, N. (2010). *Adolescent literacy development in out-of-school time: A practitioner's guide*. New York, NY: Carnegie.

Moll, L., & Gonzales, N. (2004). Engaging life: A funds of knowledge approach to multicultural education. In J. Banks & C. A. M. Banks (Eds.), *Handbook of research on multicultural education* (2nd ed.) (pp. 699–715). New York, NY: Jossey-Bass.

Morrell, E. (2004). *Becoming critical researchers: Literacy and empowerment for urban youth* (Vol. 227). New York, NY: Peter Lang.

Morrell, E., & Duncan-Andrade, J. (2002). Promoting academic literacy with urban youth through engaging hip-hop culture. *English Journal, 91*(6), 88–93.

Nagy, W. E., Diakidoy, J., & Anderson, R. (1993). The acquisition of morphology: Learning the contribution of suffixes to the meanings of derivatives. *Journal of Reading Behavior, 25*, 155–170.

National Center for Education Statistics. (2013). *The nation's report card: Trends in academic progress (nces 2013 456)*. Washington, DC.

National Governors Association. (2010). *Common core state standards initiative*: CCSSO Council of Chief State School Officers.
The New London Group. (1996). A pedagogy of multiliteracies: Designing social futures. *Harvard Educational Review, 66*(1), 60–92.
Nunez, A. (2009). Creating pathways to college for migrant students: Assessing a migrant outreach program. *Journal of Education for Students Placed at Risk, 14*(3), 226–237.
Orellana, M. (2009). *Translating immigrant childhoods: Children's work as culture and language brokers*. New Brunswick, NJ: Rutgers University Press.
Orellana, M., & Eksner, H. (2006). Power in cultural modeling: Building on the bilingual language practices of immigrant youth in germany and the United States. *National Reading Conference Yearbook, 55*, 224–234.
Orellana, M., & Reynolds, J. (2008). Cultural modeling: Leveraging bilingual skills for school paraphrasing tasks. *Reading Research Quarterly, 43*(1), 48–65.
Orellana, M. F., Dorner, L., & Pulido, L. (2003). Accessing assets: Immigrant youth's work as family translators or" para-phrasers. *Social Problems, 50*(4), 505–524.
Paris, D. (2010). Texting identities: Lessons for classrooms from multiethnic youth space. *English Education, 42*(3), 278–292.
Paris, D. (2011). A friend who understand fully': Notes on humanizing research in a multiethnic youth community. *International Journal of Qualitative Studies in Education, 24*(2), 137–149.
Paris, D., & Winn, M. T. (2013). *Humanizing research: Decolonizing qualitative inquiry with youth and communities*. Los Angeles: Sage.
Pearson, P. D., Moje, E., & Greenleaf, C. (2010). Literacy and science: Each in the service of the other. *Science, 328*(5977), 459–463.
Perfetti, C. A., Britt, M. A., & Georgi, M. C. (1995). *Text-based learning and reasoning: Studies in history*. Hillsdale, NJ: Lawrence Erlbaum.
Pinker, S. (1994). *The language instinct: The new science of language and mind* (Vol. 7529). London: Penguin UK.
Pinker, S. (2007). *The stuff of thought: Language as a window into human nature*. New York, NY: Penguin.
Plotsky, P. M., & Meaney, M. J. (1993). Early, postnatal experience alters hypothalamic corticotropin-releasing factor (crf) mrna, median eminence crf content and stress-induced release in adult rats. *Brain Research. Molecular Brain Research, 18*(3), 195–200.
Quartz, S. R., & Sejnowski, T. J. (2002). *Liars, lovers, and heroes: What the new brain science reveals about how we become who we are*. New York, NY: William Morrow.
Reynolds, R., Taylor, M., Steffensen, M., Shirey, L., & Anderson, R. (1982). Cultural schemata and reading comprehension. *Reading Research Quarterly, 17*(3), 353–365.
Richek, M. (1976). Effect of sentence complexity on the reading comprehension of syntactic structures. *Journal of Educational Psychology, 68*, 800–806.
Rogoff, B. (2003). *The cultural nature of human development*. New York, NY: Oxford University Press.
Ross, N. O., Medin, D. L., & Cox, D. (2007). Epistemological models and culture conflict: Menominee and European American hunters in wisconsin. *Ethos, 35*(4), 478–515.
Rumelhart, D. (1980). Schemata: The building blocks of cognition. In R. Spiro, B. Bruce, & W. Brewer (Eds.), *Theoretical issues in reading comprehension: Perspectives from cognitive psychology, linguistics, artificial intelligence and education* (pp. 33–58). Hillsdale, NJ: Erlbaum.
Russo, E. A., Martienssen, R. A., & Riggs, A. D. (Eds.). (1996). *Epigenetic mechanisms of gene regulation*. Plainview, NY: Cold Spring Harbor Laboratory Press.
San Pedro, T. J. (2014). Internal and environmental safety zones: Navigating expansions and contractions of identity between indigenous and colonial paradigms, pedagogies, and classrooms. *Journal of American Indian Education, 53*, 42–62.
San Pedro, T. J. (2015). Silence as shields: Agency and resistances among native American students in the urban southwest. *Research in the Teaching of English, 50*(2), 132.
Scott, J., Straker, D. Y., & Katz, L. (2009). *Affirming students' right to their own language*. Urbana, IL: National Council of Teachers of English.
Seixas, P. (1993). The community of inquiry as a basis for knowledge and learning: The case of history. *American Educational Research Journal, 30*(2), 305–326.
Semali, L. M., & Kincheloe, J. L. (2002). *What is indigenous knowledge? Voices from the academy*. New York, NY: Routledge.
Shulman, L. (1986). Those who understand: Knowledge growth in teaching. *Educational Researcher, 15*(2), 4–14.
Smith, M. (1989). Teaching the interpretation of irony in poetry. *Research in the Teaching of English, 23*, 254–272.

Smith, M. (1991). *Understanding unreliable narrators: Reading between the lines in the literature classroom*. Urbana, IL: National Council of Teachers of English.

Smitherman, G. (1977). *Talkin and testifyin: The language of black America*. Boston, MA: Houghton Mifflin.

Snow, C., Burns, M. S., & Griffin, P. (1998). *Preventing reading difficulties in young children*. Washington, DC: National Academy Press.

Snow, C., Griffin, D., & Burns, M. S. (2006). *Knowledge to support the teaching of reading: Preparing teachers for a changing world*. San Francisco, CA: Jossey-Bass.

Spencer, M. B. (1987). Black children's ethnic identity formation: Risk and resilience in castelike minorities. In J. Phinney & M. Rotheram (Eds.), *Children's ethnic socialization: Pluralism and development* (pp. 103–116). Newbury Park, CA: Sage.

Spencer, M. B. (2006). Phenomenology and ecological systems theory: Development of diverse groups. In W. Damon & R. M. Lerner (Eds.), *Handbook of child psychology* (Vol. 1, 6th ed., pp. 829–893). New York, NY: Wiley.

Spencer, M. B., Harpalani, V., Cassidy, E., Jacobs, C., Donde, S., & Goss, T. N. (2006). Understanding vulnerability and resilience from a normative development perspective: Implications for racially and ethnically diverse youth. In D. Chicchetti & E. Cohen (Eds.), *Handbook of developmental psychopathology* (Vol. 1), (pp. 627–672). Hoboken, NJ: Wiley.

Spiro, R. (1980). Constructive processes in prose comprehension and recall. In R. Spiro, B. Bruce, & W. Brewer (Eds.), *Theoretical issues in reading comprehension* (pp. 245–278). Hillsdale, NJ: Erlbaum.

Stahl, S., & Miller, P. (1989). Whole language and language experience approaches for beginning reading: A quantitative research synthesis. *Review of Educational Research, 59*, 87–116.

Stahl, S., & Nagy, W. E. (2005). *Teaching word meanings*. Hillsdale, NJ: Lawrence Erlbaum.

Steffensen, M., Joag-Dev, C., & Anderson, R. (1979). A cross-cultural perspective on reading comprehension. *Reading Research Quarterly, 15*(1), 10–29.

Stein, N. L., & Glenn, C. G. (1979). An analysis of story comprehension in elementary school children. In R. O. Freedle (Ed.), *New directions in discourse processing* (Vol. 2), (pp. 53–119). Norwood, NJ: Ablex.

Streeter, L. A. (1976). Language perception of 2-month-old infants shows effects of both innate mechanisms and experience. *Nature, 259*, 39–41.

Super, C., & Harkness, S. (1986). The developmental niche: A conceptualization at the interface of child and culture. *International Journal of Behavioral Development, 9*, 545–569.

Swanson, D. P., Edwards, M. C., & Spencer, M. B. (Eds.). (2010). *Adolescence: Development during a global era*. New York, NY: Elsevier.

Tan, E. S. (2013). *Emotion and the structure of narrative film: Film as an emotion machine*. New York, NY: Routledge.

Tate, W. (2008). "Geography of opportunity": Poverty, place, and educational outcomes. *Educational Researcher, 37*(7), 397–411.

Trabasso, T., & van den Broek, P. (1985). Causal thinking and the representation of narrative events. *Journal of Memory and Language, 24*, 612–630.

Traub, J. (1999). What no school can do. *The New York Times Magazine, January, 162*, 52–56.

Turner, M. (1996). *The literary mind*. New York, NY: Oxford University Press.

Valdes, G. (1996). *Con respeto: Bridging the distances between culturally diverse families and schools*. New York, NY: Teachers College Press.

Valdes, G. (2002). *Expanding the definitions of giftedness: The case of young interpreters from immigrant countries*. Mahwah, NJ: Lawrence Erlbaum.

Valencia, S. W., Wixson, K., & Pearson, P. D. (2014). Putting text complexity in context: Refocusing on comprehension of complex text. *Elementary School Journal, 115*, 270–289.

van den Broek, P., Lorch, R. F., Linderholm, T., & Gustafson, M. (2001). The effects of readers' goals on inference generation and memory for texts. *Memory & Cognition, 29*, 1081–1087.

van Dijk, T. A. (1972). *Some aspects of text grammars: A study in theoretical linguistics and poetics*. The Hague: Mouton.

Van Orman, K., & Lyiscott, J. (2013). Politely disregarded: Street fiction, mass incarceration, and critical praxis. *English Journal, 102*(4), 59.

Weisner, T. S. (2002). Ecocultural understanding of children's developmental pathways. *Human Development, 174*, 275–281.

Wilson, E. O. (1998). *Consilience: The unity of knowledge*. New York, NY: Knopf.

Wineburg, S. (1991). Historical problem solving: A study of the cognitive processes used in the evauation of documentary and pictorial evidence. *Journal of Educational Psychology, 83*(1), 73–87.

Wineburg, S. (2002). *Historical thinking and other unusual acts: Charting the future of teaching the past*. Philadelphia, PA: Temple University Press.

Wineburg, S., & Grossman, P. (1998). Creating a community of learners among high school teachers. *Phi Delta Kappan, 73*, 684–689.

Wineburg, S., & Wilson, S. M. (1988). Peering at history through different lenses: The role of disciplinary perspectives in teaching hisory. *Teachers College Record, 89*(4), 525–539.

Winn, M. T. (2010). 'Our side of the story': Moving incarcerated youth voices from margins to center. *Race Ethnicity and Education, 13*(3), 313–325.

Yukhymenko-Lescroart, M. A., Briner, S. W., Magliano, J. P., Lawless, K., Burkett, C., McCarthy, K. S., ... Goldman, S. R. (2016). Development and initial validation of the literature epistemic cognition scale (lecs). *Learning and Individual Differences, 51*, 242–248.

Zelazo, P. D. (2013). Developmental psychology: A new. *The Oxford Handbook of Developmental Psychology, Vol. 1: Body and Mind, 1*, 3.

4

A Sociocultural Perspective on Readers, Reading, Reading Instruction and Assessment, Reading Policy, and Reading Research

Peter Smagorinsky, Mary Guay, Tisha Lewis Ellison, and Arlette Ingram Willis

---

This chapter positions readers in relation to their environments, and reading and reading research as social acts. A person's orientation to print texts – our concern here, rather than in relation to texts produced through other semiotic systems – is rooted in enculturation that begins in homes and communities, and is subject to interpretation in schools when students' reading practices depart from norms set by members of the dominant culture. A sociocultural perspective questions an assumption common in policy and assessment that views reading as an isolated act between reader and text that minimizes readers' instantiation of meaning into texts (that is, their *encoding* of meaning; Smagorinsky, 2001). This assumption tends to consider social factors to be irrelevant (as critiqued by Berliner, 2014) and limits reading to its technical, testable, and decoding features (Smagorinsky, 2009a). As this chapter goes to press, the SAT has announced the development of an "adversity score" to adjust for environmental factors in an effort to address inequity, albeit in ways that immediately invited critique (e.g., Williams, 2019). Reading research in turn is conducted by people socialized to worldviews, research paradigms, and other ideological perspectives that are a consequence of mediated human development (Cole, 1996; Vygotsky, 1987; Wertsch, 1985). This socialization has consequences for the sorts of research questions posed, research goals articulated, research methods employed, interpretive assumptions and procedures, and other factors. Reading is thus subject to social mediation in its conception, practice, and investigation, all of which contribute to how knowledge is constructed about the state of reading development in the U.S. and its schools.

This chapter will illustrate sociocultural phenomena primarily through the lens of African American students' historical achievement gap in reading, as determined in school (Tatum, 2005). This gap has been attributed to genetic inferiority by highly-placed scholars (Herrnstein & Murray, 1994) who reflect views that remain in circulation in the public consciousness (Byrd & Hughey, 2015), in spite of evidence from cultural psychology (Cole, 1996) that foregrounds socialization rather than genetics to account for human diversity. The construction of African

American literacy thus provides a suitable case through which to consider the role of sociocultural contexts in the reading development of people from nondominant cultures.

We begin by detailing how reading is a social, cultural, and historical phenomenon that goes well beyond simple decoding of the text before a reader. This analysis suggests that not only is reading a sociocultural phenomenon, reading research itself is socially constructed. Investigative conclusions often follow from ideological assumptions that are manifested in the conduct of research into reading instruction, development, and performance, both in and out of school. We then situate reading instruction and assessment within the U.S. national policy context, which in turn influences what should be valued in school. We conclude with the recommendation that an understanding of the phenomenon of reading is best informed by multiple perspectives that do not assume the normativity of dominant cultures or the definitive authority of standardized reading tests in measuring reading facility. Rather, attention to cultural pluralism suggests that taking account of varied angles on readers and reading will, and should, complicate the policy imperative to impose standardization on people of diverse socialization.

Reading as a Social, Cultural, and Historical Phenomenon

Cole, John-Steiner, Scribner, and Souberman titled their collection of essential Vygotsky (1978) essays *Mind in Society*, under the assumption that thinking is social in origin: People learn not only words but also ways of thinking through their engagement with the people who surround them, so as to address the problems presented by their environments (Tulviste, 1991). Literacy practices are thus historical in that they represent new iterations of long-standing traditions; cultural in that they are suited to the specific needs developed over time within a community of practice; and social in that they are put into practice as part of engagement with others, both in immediate interpersonal exchanges and more enduringly as artifacts produced for subsequent attention (Witte, 1992).

The acts of producing or reading a text of any sort are historical, cultural, and social. A text is a collection of signs amenable to interpretation. In print literacy, which is the primary consideration in most of what is considered reading research, the meaning of these signs follows from how the squiggles on a page are constructed, coded, decoded, and encoded. Consider the following six versions of the same idea:

Thinking is social in origin.
Мышление имеет социальное происхождение.
思考是社会的起源。
การคิดเป็นเรื่องของสังคมในที่มา.
التفكير اجتماعي في الأصل.
थनिकनिग इस सोचजिल् इन ओरगिनि.

These squiggles represent textual codes in six different symbol systems originating in different cultures: English, Russian, Chinese, Thai, Arabic, and Sanskrit. No one is born knowing how to read any of them. Rather, enculturation to reading follows from the extant practices of the people who surround the reader, with some nations and cultures accommodating multiple languages and textual conventions simultaneously, such that there is no single home or first language (e.g., for the South African context, with 11 official languages, see Makalela, 2016). The inscription of meaning is only available to readers and writers familiar with the codes that structure texts and their component parts, including not only the meaning of specific signs, but also the order in which they are read, how the syntax is structured, how such factors as modes of argumentation are realized in textual structure and emphasis, and other factors. Knowing these linguistic features is a consequence of socialization to historical cultural traditions for engaging with text.

The culture of school serves some students better than others, because some have far fewer adaptations to make in order to fit. In general, White middle-class students in the U.S. tend to fit well with the social and academic expectations of schools much better than students from other social, cultural, and economic groups (Ogbu, 2003; Smagorinsky, 2017). Students from other groups who have learned to think and act differently are often viewed as deficient because they adhere to different norms. This deficit perspective is taken by Stotsky (1999), who rejects multicultural approaches as diluted and academically unchallenging. She argues that the absence of sufficient Greek and Latin word roots in multicultural texts confirms that "our" language is lost when others are included.

For students from outside the dominant culture who are subjected to deficit judgments, school can become a place where they feel rejected and where their cultural identities are denied. These students tend to feel out of place with the process and expectations of public education (Heath, 1983; Lee, 2007). Yet, they are often the ones required to make the greatest adaptations. Schools, meanwhile, remain relatively stable, accommodating their historical values and not those that structure the lives of marginalized students (Portes & Smagorinsky, 2010). As a result, school often perpetuates the inequities that, ideally, it is designed to help to alleviate.

Our discussion of "reading" thus begins with an account of how literacy, along with literacy education, including reading, does not follow from a single approach to socialization to learning. As Haddix and Sealy-Ruiz (2012) and others have argued, this cultural orientation to texts needs to take into account how people learn to engage textually in their daily lives. Their research on African American cultural speech genres and social languages suggests that school instruction could do more to build on students' experiential frameworks to advance their knowledge of school subjects. If not, their emotional resistance to how school is conducted may alienate them to the point of dropping out and finding their potential fulfilled elsewhere (Wong, Eccles, & Sameroff, 2003).

The idea of building academic knowledge upon students' worlds of experience is not new, nor is it confined to students from minoritized heritages. It was central to Vygotsky's (1987) notion that robust concepts are only available through the interplay between academic (what he called in translation "scientific" concepts) and everyday (in his parlance, "spontaneous") concepts, developed in the 1920s and 1930s. It is a commonly invoked form of pedagogy, regardless of students' racial socialization, to connect school learning to popular culture (Alvermann, 2011) and other home-grown interests. The racial dimension suggests the need to admit a broader range of home-and-community knowledge and practice that represents the whole school population's enculturation. Doing so would require schools to consider broader educational restructuring that produces diversity in relation to students' home socialization, rather than avenues to assimilation to established educational practices (Gutiérrez, Rymes, & Larson, 1995).

In the policy world, the emotional engagement that students develop with school as an institution, and with particular people and places within school, is irrelevant. Yet students' emotional engagement with school is associated with their investment in its academic mission (Furlong et al., 2003). The U.S., among many Western societies, has grounded its educational thinking in European Enlightenment rationalism (McCagg, 1989). This perspective has produced the idea of "cold cognition" (Roth, 2007): thinking unencumbered by emotion, an idea that has been engrained in U.S. educational practice since the founding of public schools. Literary reading, for example, has long been governed by the values of New Criticism, which takes a "scientific" view of reading that emphasizes *explication de texte*, i.e., the detached analysis and decoding of the technical aspects of literature (Applebee, 1993). New Criticism fell into a period of doubt and disrepute among many literature teachers through the influence of "transactional" theories of reading, often traced to Rosenblatt (1996) and thus to Dewey (1902), that emphasize readers' constructive roles in relation to texts, rather than solely focusing attention on authors' inferred intended meaning. New Criticism has been revived in the recent Common Core State Standards (CCSS), in which a reader's personal life, emotional engagement with characters, cultural orientation to society, and other factors that cannot be found in the text itself, should not be summoned to inform the quest for meaning (see Shanahan, 2013, for advocacy of this perspective; Tampio, 2018, for a critique).

We thus proceed with the assumption that human cognition and intellectual development, including learning how to read, are grounded in historical, cultural, and social mediation. Schools tend to rely on the structures they have inherited to occupy the present and anticipate the future. Schools in the U.S. have long been complicit in *deculturalization*, i.e., the use of schools to replace family languages and cultures with those of the dominant group (Spring, 2016). From a cultural perspective, reading instruction has embedded Christian didactics in McGuffy primers (Luke, 1997), character education reading lists (see Smagorinsky & Taxel, 2005), and other curricular structures, texts, and practices. Curriculum and instruction have often elided or forbidden texts and ideologies from other perspectives, including Arizona's rejection of the Ethnic Studies Program, whose critical perspective was deemed anti-American (Acosta, 2013), the suppression of hip-hop culture in school (Baszile, 2009), and the muffling of other perspectives that do not fit the values embedded in schools designed and run according to the values of the dominant White population, particularly the upper and middle classes (see Bates, 2011, for the challenges facing poor White students in school). The act of reading is thus not cultural only where the eyeballs meet the page. It is embedded in a variety of broader social institutions and practices that shape education, reading, ideology, and everything else that meets at the intersection provided by the community school.

Socialization to Reading Begins at Home

Attention to children's socialization to reading at home and in community life got its greatest boost from Heath (1983), in one of the most influential studies of literacy in the field's history. Her *Ways with Words*, as of this writing, has been referenced roughly 15,500 times in published scholarship. Three-and-a-half decades after its publication, this ten-year ethnographic study of three rural communities in the Appalachian Piedmont has averaged about 420 references a year, according to a search run via Harzing's *Publish or Perish* software. Its insights have held up well beyond its time and place of data collection, suggesting remarkable durability and significance in helping to explain literacy as a function of far more than the decoding of texts, often considered the basic definition of reading both historically (e.g., Gough, 1972) and in current policy (Coleman & Pimentel, 2012).

Sociocultural literacy theories argue that readers infuse print texts (and other textual forms) with cultural meaning as they *encode* them in relation to their worldly experiences (Smagorinsky, 2001). Heath (1982, 1983) found that members of culturally distinctive communities approached reading in ways that were markedly different, and that were grounded in broader cultural values. Reading, as she found, involves more than cognitive textual processing. Rather, reading manifests how cultures view the purpose and act of reading print in relation to the conduct of their lives and the value systems that motivate their approach to living, and thus their ways with words.

Children from what Heath (1982) dubbed "Maintown," which represented "mainstream middle-class school-oriented culture" (p. 49), made the easiest transition to school. The reading practices at home were similar to those required in school, including question-and-answer routines about the text and its contents and form. The other two focal communities experienced home and school reading quite differently. White fundamentalist Christian families were oriented to the *Holy Bible* as the principal source of knowledge, one not to be questioned. These families viewed the written word as containing immutable, doctrinaire truth. When their children attended school, they struggled with textual ambiguity because their orientation and approach to reading and writing came from a single sacred text that located all authority and agency in the printed word and its authors. Culture shaped their understanding of how texts function, which worked within their primary social centers of home and faith community, but not when school required them to question a text's contents.

The African American community Heath (1982, 1983) studied was not oriented to reading as a valuable way to spend time. Their community life was organized around social interaction and performative activity rather than around quiet, isolated reading. Solitary reading was interpreted as anti-social and therefore was discouraged; children were told to get outside and play instead. Reading in this community worked against the more important value of social engagement. By extrapolation, the tendency of schools and many teachers to value quiet, individual work over noisy, contentious interaction and collaboration works in favor of students raised according to that priority (Rothstein-Fisch & Trumbull, 2008).

Heath (1982, 1983) studied one relatively small area in a remote part of the U.S., and so readers should be cautious about generalizing to all African American families and communities, or to all Christian families from the fundamentalist community she studied. Yet, many others have confirmed her conclusion that school structures are often not hospitable to the ways of knowing fostered in many African American households. For example, Noguera (2003), among others, has found that this disjuncture between home socialization and school expectations has produced pathologizing assumptions about Black youth that evaluate them in ways that are alien to how they have learned to conduct themselves within the confines of their own communities. The performance of African American students on school tasks and standardized tests has served as a means by which they are assessed as exhibiting, as a demographic group, low literacy rates (Howard, 2001). This is not to say that children and youth from other cultures and racial groups are exempt from these challenges and consequences, only that African American students as a group have experienced them consistently and systemically, as evidenced by their assignment to low-track and remedial classrooms in disproportionate numbers (Yonezawa, Wells, & Serna, 2002).

In the wake of Heath's (1982, 1983) intensive study, a number of African American scholars have argued that one way of understanding the difficulty that minoritized students have in transitioning to school is to conduct ethnographies in which a site is studied in depth for at least a year (Athanases & Heath, 1995). These studies, according to their advocates, enable a researcher to "[identify and give] voice to alternative world views" (Delpit, 1988, p. 282). Researchers in this conception study, understand, interpret, and present the world from a population's emic perspective, rather than allowing them to be characterized by outsiders relying on assumptions, tools, standards, and expectations based on their own cultures of origin, and using strictly numerical reductions of the literacy potential and performance of people at the site.

Sociocultural theories that accompany the ethnographic tradition have not, to date, been embraced by federal reading stakeholders as a viable framework to examine reading improvement, instruction, and intervention, nor has its reliance on non-numeric reductions of data, often in narrative form. The use of experimental and quasi-experimental studies is positioned as more valid and "scientific" than other methods of educational research, as a "gold standard," reflecting the history of hyperrationality that underpins much of educational research and policy (Manuel, Goodwyn, & Zancanella, 2016). Denzin's (2009) critique of the National Research Council's reluctance to include multiple forms of evidence in federal funding of research can be extended to a history of such positioning in federal reforms of reading research. One consequence of this exclusive value on a single research paradigm is that research like Heath's (1982, 1983) is excluded from consideration, leaving her findings, and those from studies in her tradition, outside the purview of educational policy, regardless of their influence on research and practice and stature in many areas of inquiry.

Sociocultural research that involves case studies, ethnographic accounts, narrative inquiry, and other non-numeric data is designed to provide detail and nuance, rather than to produce broad generalizations about performance or one-shot measures of achievement. It is concerned with understanding the effects of activity, culture, language, and systems of knowing of everyday life and experience that shape cognitive frameworks, worldviews, literacy practices, and other ways of thinking. Experimental research's minimization of variables to focus on outcomes leads to generalizations and recommendations for "best" and "high-leverage practices" that have been questioned from a sociocultural perspective more oriented to situated literacy learning (Philip et al., 2018; Smagorinsky, 2009b, 2018). Yet the search for silver bullets has great policy appeal over approaches that rely on messy, time-consuming, labor-intensive, small-sample ethnographic and other qualitative methods that do not produce black-and-white conclusions for one and all to follow. As a result, the privileged research base that was conducted within the experimental tradition dictates policies driven by the assumption that students are all more or less the same, and that only teachers' instruction and students' application matter. What Berliner (2014) calls *exogenous*, or outside variables, thus play little role in policy, which is enamored of such factors as *grit* (Duckworth, 2016) as the means by which poverty and discrimination can be overcome to produce better reading test scores, regardless of students' socialization in homes and community life (Dixson & Rousseau, 2005).

Kirkland's (2014) comparison of research paradigms enacted in and out of school illustrates how different research traditions function according to assumptions and practices that yield very different findings. School assessments, according to Kirkland, are definitive and discriminatory when they isolate students in one-off standardized tests of little interest to them, raising questions about the assessments' reliability and validity. African American students tend to do relatively poorly on these measures, and test scores have official status in determining literacy rates and in turn create the image of illiterate Black youth, an impression that in turn constructs whole views of the African American population in the White public imaginary (Leonardo, 2009; Steele, 2011).

Kirkland (2014) finds, however, that assessing students outside school through more fine-grained, long-term collections and analyses of verbal data produces a very different view of this population. When in community settings and engaged in literacy practices of their choice, when participating socially instead of working in isolation, and when studied in light of their own interests and goals through nuanced means that include their own perspectives – the world views that Delpit (1988) hopes to elicit from minoritized people – these same youth come across much differently. They create a compelling range of texts in a variety of cultural settings (Hill, 2009) that are creative, vital, and provide agency. They build on home-and-community-cultivated identities and language practices to produce texts that depict and interpret their experiences and surroundings. They have a medium through which to tell their own stories, which are otherwise ignored in their school experiences (Rhym, 2018). They are anything but the dull and linguistically-challenged people pathologized in school, where test scores have insurmountable power in determining their learning and literate identities and create the public and policy perspectives on their human potential. These policies are often enacted with the help of researchers who assert context-free claims about their assessment procedures and products (e.g., Pianta & Hamre, 2009; Rowan & Correnti, 2009), those that carry the assumption of color-blindness (Richeson & Nussbaum, 2004) without considering factors such as poverty and enculturation that question their validity (e.g., Berliner, 2014; Learned & Moje, 2015; Smagorinsky, 2009b; Willis, 2009).

These oppositional interpretations of one population from studies conducted in different sites using different methods illustrate the problem of the *social construction of data* (Smagorinsky, 1995). Both qualitative and quantitative research methods may be open-ended (see Tukey, 1977, for exploratory data analysis in quantitative methods). Yet the acknowledgement of researchers' constructive role in generating and analyzing data is more likely associated with qualitative methods that avoid claims to providing a single authoritative portrait of a people or practices, which is how numeric test data tend to be characterized. A sociocultural perspective on literacy research and practice assumes that social science data are human constructions that embody a researcher's worldview and socialization, applied to the conduct of other human beings (McGregor & Murnane, 2010). These filters can shape which questions are asked, which cultural framework they emerge from, how they are investigated, how the data are reduced and analyzed, and from whose perspective the interpretation of those analyses is constructed.

Rather than studying reading solely as a school-based practice, many researchers have positioned the home as a child's first and most critical site of socialization to literacy practices. To fight back against the sort of pathologization of African American people and families that concern Noguera (2003) and others taking an emic perspective on this population, researchers have spent time with African American families to document their literacy practices. These studies have taken place in both impoverished and more affluent, professional homes. Cushman (1999), for instance, studied itinerant families navigating the public housing system as a consequence of economic instability. Her positionality demonstrates the difficulty that many university researchers have when trying to understand the lives of people living on the margins of society. Her participants lived amidst rats and conditions that were often unsanitary and always unpredictable. Being trusted and accepted as a university ethnographer – as investigators who "don't study villages … they study *in* villages" to use Geertz's (1973, p. 22; emphasis in original) phrase – in such a setting requires the development of a strong relationship, often built on commonality, that takes time to develop.

Cushman's own life circumstances provided her with an entrée to public housing residents living on the margins of society, something that is unavailable to most researchers, who are overwhelmingly White (National Center for Education Statistics, 2018) and rarely from impoverished backgrounds, given that even getting an undergraduate degree is associated with family affluence (Zinshteyn, 2016). The residents had a Black Cherokee heritage, and Cushman's racial background included White Cherokee blood (see Cushman, 2013). She had also been homeless herself during her doctoral studies, providing rare intersubjectivity – broadly speaking, reaching a shared understanding of the situation – with her participants and a means of forming a relationship based on shared experience. This perspective and set of experiences gave her an empathic view of the residents and the means by which they learned about and worked within the bureaucratic tangle of the public housing system, requiring a knowledge of reading the word and the world, as Freire (1985) phrased it, that structured their living conditions. Achieving intersubjectivity with research participants from backgrounds different from one's own is a long-acknowledged challenge for researchers (Rosenthal, 1966), and may help account for the Whiteness of many research populations studied by White investigators who have difficulty getting access to people who may distrust their motives, given the history of pathologization in judging one culture by the values of a dominant culture (Padilla, 2008).

This example might reinforce the idea that all African American or minoritized families are living in abject poverty, which is true for some but not all members of this demographic, even as those who occupy the middle class may experience similar types and degrees of discrimination (Sellers, Bonham, Neighbors, & Amell, 2009). Other scholars have studied families with greater literacy affordances, challenging deficit assumptions and documenting what is possible in families living on the economic margins. Again, though, access to studying these populations outside school is critical; not all university researchers would be welcomed into African American homes to study their literacy practices, given the distrust that might meet their requests for access (Coker & Huang, 2010). African American families have often been subject to misrepresentations and cultural-deficit viewpoints in research that overlooks their rich and complex literacy practices (Milner, 2013). These stereotypes suggest that African American families are non-existent, limited, and underachieving, in large part because literacy measures are based on their school assessment, independent of how they engage in literacy practices in home and community settings, even as family literacy scholars have critiqued these deficit views (Arzubiaga, Artiles, King, & Harris-Murri, 2008; Auerbach, 1989; Compton-Lilly, Rogers, & Lewis, 2012; Gadsden, 2004).

Sub-Saharan Black African-descent people in the U.S. still bear the legacy of centuries of indentured servitude, slavery, segregation, violence, exclusion, and discriminatory means that continue through to the present day in the form of such practices of bank-loan redlining, political gerrymandering, voter suppression, microaggressions, and other means of oppression (Lipsitz, 1998). In the 1800s, the fear of a liberated Black population empowered by literacy produced prohibitions against their learning to read and write, traumatizing enslaved families (Leary, 2005), whose reading and writing were forbidden to perpetuate a cycle of illiterate families (Mubenga, 2006). White allies were often subject to punishment if they contributed to their slaves' literacy (Williams, 2005). Formal education in former slave states following emancipation placed Black children in schools that were badly under-resourced, and racially segregated "separate-but-equal" schools were denied adequate funding and resources until the Brown v. Board of Education 1954 decision forced integration.

Yet legal integration ended neither segregation nor discrimination (Orfield, With Schley, Glass, & Reardon, 1993). Centuries later, reports from the National Assessment of Educational Progress (NAEP) and National Center for Education Statistics (NCES) (National Assessment of Educational Progress and National Center for Education Statistics, 2017) describe a chronic academic gap between African American children's test scores in reading and math and those of White peers (Bohrnstedt, Kitmitto, Ogut, Sherman, & Chan, 2015). The variable of race is in turn complicated by factors such as the relation between race and poverty (Myers, Kim, & Mandala, 2004) and other extra-scholastic, intersectional factors that are often effaced in educational policy (Berliner, 2014).

This lag has been attributed to a variety of deficiencies in both homes and schools, including a lack of resources, unstable home lives, race itself, and ineffective teachers (Howard, 2013), compounded by persistent systemic racism governing schools (Darling-Hammond, 1998; Lewis, 2009; Scott, Brown, Jean-Baptiste, & Barbarin, 2012). African Americans' literacy rates, as measured by assessments conducted according to instruments developed to accompany the White-infused curriculum and instruction of schools (Berchini, 2016), have been reported as unacceptably low and in need of school remediation.

Parents' interactions support and play a critical role in children's literacy skills at home (Compton-Lilly, 2007; Edwards, 2004; Heath, 2010; Lewis, 2013). Despite how African American parents have been labeled as "hard to reach" by schools (Davies, 1988), research in African American homes, often by African American researchers whose access is predicated on participants' trust of their motives, finds the parents often participating in some form of literacy-focused practices with their children. Anderson, Hiebert, Scott, and Wilkinson (1985) view parental engagement as fundamental to language socialization; in schools, however, some forms of socialization get preferential treatment and others are viewed as being in deficit to them. Parents' role and involvement play a pivotal role in the support of their children's school success (Howard, 2015), in that parents can offer human (education), social (relationships), financial (access) (Yan, 1999), and cultural capital (skill) support (Bourdieu, 1986).

As positioning theory (Harré & Van Langenhove, 1999) would assume, however, the social practices produced by different forms of support become hierarchically constructed in the context of school. The more similar a home's practices are to those expected in school, the more familiar and comfortable the school experience is to the student, and the greater the chances the student will be evaluated as a success, as found by Heath (1983). Discrepant socialization can produce reliance on different speech genres and literacy practices from those typically made available in school (Majors, 2015). Simply providing support for literacy at home, then, may not prepare children and youth for achievement as students in school. Nor, in turn, does school necessarily prepare students for literacy learning and practice outside school (Considine, Horton, & Moorman, 2009).

Research centered on families, then, complicates assumptions about the socialization of readers in home and community. African American parents, contrary to stereotype, are often actively involved with their children's school work (e.g., speaking with children about their school experiences, providing access to books at home). When these practices support students' gravitation to school norms, this engagement produces positive outcomes in reading and math assessments (Halle, Kurtz-Costes, & Mahoney, 1997). African American family socialization can enhance school-based learning, complicating the idea that racialized cultures are separate and incompatible. Longitudinal research conducted from pre-school to high school (Hoover-Dempsey et al., 2005; Vondra, Dowell Hommerding, & Shaw, 1999) finds that inner-city African American parents provided involvement, support, and motivation to promote academic achievement and teacher-student relationships.

The question posed by many minoritized scholars, however, is how their people's identities, communicative practices, ways of knowing, speech genres, and other aspects of culture can be responded to, supported, and sustained, not how they can be abandoned to assimilate to White school norms and the testing apparatus that enforces them (e.g., Four Arrows, 2013; Gutiérrez, 2008; Paris & Alim, 2017). Parents' involvement in reading African American children's literature with young children contributed to gains in children learning print, comprehension, and vocabulary skills (McNair, 2013). For McNair, such "culturally sensitive reading material enhances information processing in African American children" because "reading material depicts verbal and visual content that is consistent with the sociocultural experiences of African American children," and parents' involvement in their children's literate lives promoted their literacy development and provided teachers a foundation on which to build in school (p. 473; cf. Bell & Clark, 1998).

Yet the correspondence between these home literacy practices and those assessed in school is often weak. The Common Core State Standards (CCSS) have been critiqued for their implementation, inequalities, unoriginality, and cultural insensitivity, in particular for African American students (Lewis Ellison, 2017). Many African American parents are not aware of the standards and accompanying exams and do not understand the benefits, processes, or results, leaving them disadvantaged in discussing their children's education with people in schools (Abdullah, 2013; Bell, 2012; Lewis Ellison, 2017; Milner, 2006; Osburn, Stegman, Suitt, & Ritter, 2004). These concerns are important when considering children's literacy development, academic achievement, and cultural competence. When some parents know how to navigate parent-school relationships better than others, their children are advantaged in school assessments (Hill & Taylor, 2004).

Standardized tests typically are developed in alignment with White, middle-class literacy practices (Whiting & Ford, 2009). Bodovski (2010), for instance, studied the complex web of intersections between race and social class that produce differential parenting strategies that have consequences for educational outcomes among children, again relying on assimilative criteria rather than culturally-sustaining measures that are attentive to how people of color define their own identities, communicative practices, social processes, speech genres, and other aspects of social life (Paris & Alim, 2017). This *concerted cultivation* (Lareau, 2003) produces distinctive differences in child-rearing according to class, race, and gender distinctions, echoing Heath's (1983) findings that cultural practices in home settings shape cognitive and social processes that may be out of synch with how learning is assessed in schools during literacy lessons and on standardized tests (Troy, 2016). However, racial and ethnic group identity and socialization play a critical role in student achievement (King, Akua, & Russell, 2014). The home-based cultural competencies that children bring to the classroom, families' sociocultural contexts of literacy development (cognitive, linguistic, behavioral, and interpersonal), and the consequences of these textual conceptions and literacy practices in school contexts must be acknowledged to reach fair conclusions about these students and their families (Scott et al., 2012).

The Policy Context as Sociocultural Structure

Federal policies serve as critical contexts in that they often shape instruction, giving credence to the aphorism that "what you test is what you get" or, as Resnick and Resnick (1989) put it, "You get what you assess" (p. 66). No Child Left Behind (NCLB) and Race To The Top (RTTT), two federal mandates, imposed testing on U.S. schools to force what policymakers considered to be accountability measures (McGuinn, 2016). Although they are claimed by some to be race-neutral (Santos, Cabrera, & Fosnacht, 2010), others find tests to involve a racial bias (Morgan et al., 2010), suggesting that politics and race are incontrovertibly associated with how students are perceived in relation to their education, and how racialized perspectives shape assumptions and beliefs about the role of bias in assessment.

U.S. federal education reform policy has targeted educational inequalities among racial groups. Histories of federal reform policies that address reading (Allington, 2006; Pressley, Duke, & Boling, 2004; Shanahan, 2011), however, have tended to diminish the role of race, with a few exceptions (Gutiérrez, 2001; Prendergast, 2002; Shannon, 1992; Willis, 1997; Willis & Harris, 1997). The social construct of race requires greater attention if reading is to be understood in relation to the social contexts that shape the reading experience.

In the mid-20th century, politics, research, and education reform intersected to address consequences of poverty in education. The passage of the Civil Rights Act 1964 and President Johnson's "War on Poverty" set the stage for Johnson's 1965 State of the Union address, in which he committed aid to public schools serving low-income families. The Elementary and Secondary Education Act was passed in 1965 and worked in concert with the Civil Rights Act to address racial and social inequality, along with poverty (Frankenburg, 2018), providing Title I funding to address educational inequality for poor children and children of color.

During this period, some reading researchers became interested in the intersection of reading and readers' socioeconomic status (Bond & Dykstra, 1964). These studies focused on how communities were organized (urban, suburban, small town, and rural); what occupations they supported (industrial, agrarian, etc.); community conditions (stable, transitional, volatile, etc.); and the demographic markers that characterized community members (sex, age, race/ethnicity, preschool experience). The dominant work, however, assumed the neutrality of social contexts and the availability of what Newman, Griffin, and Cole (1989) call a *problem isomorph*: a test item that is interpreted in the same way by all test-takers. This assumption provides the tests with the veneer of unassailable assessment authority rather than, as argued by Newman et al., identifying the degree to which test-takers are consonant with the means of measurement. This belief enabled researchers to eliminate poor people of color from research samples, in turn allowing for research findings to be normed in accordance with other sorts of students to provide the standards by which they are measured as readers, inevitably in deficit.

Nature, Nurture, and Reading

We have thus far focused on the social construction of race in reading research. Although African American students are not any more neurologically prone to reading difficulties than any other population, those from low-income homes may be especially at-risk for reading difficulties, although they may not be uniquely so relative to other racial groups (Washington, 2001). Shifrer, Muller, and Callahan (2010) argue that rather than being biologically handicapped as readers, African American children are more prone to be diagnosed as dyslexic than are children from other demographic groups (cf. Hoyles & Hoyles, 2010), suggesting that neurology cannot explain all facets of identification. These perspectives highlight a critical tension in reading research and instruction grounded in the nature vs. nurture debate first identified by Galton (1869). Do difficulties with reading or other academic or intelligence measure reside within individual people, giving them a biological explanation with only such variables as orthographic system responsible for differences and not readers' cultures (Paulesu et al., 2001)? Or are academic struggles with reading or other learning disabilities (Dudley-Marling, 2019) social constructions whose assessments might change if the environment itself were restructured, if the diagnostic tools were changed, and if the people forming judgments were to take a different perspective (see Newman et al., 1989)? Or are both nature and nurture (and, most critically here, the social construction of diagnosis) all in play when identifying and assisting struggling readers and in their engagements with print text?

The "nature" part of the debate is now well-established. The condition known as dyslexia, in spite of disagreements about what it is and how to identify it (Worthy, Lammert, Long, Salmerón, & Godfrey, 2018), recurs in families and thus likely exhibits a genetic component, although the specific genes that result in dyslexia have not been identified (Elliott & Grigorenko, 2014; Vellutino, Fletcher, Snowling, & Scanlon, 2004). The hazards of identification are evident in the estimates of its presence in the whole population, which range between 3%–20% of the population (Elliott & Grigorenko, 2014). This ambiguity muddies the waters of understanding precisely what is involved when children struggle to read in school, and suggest that other factors may be at work in a diagnosis. These issues are especially confounding when race enters the diagnostic picture. In a common sort of conclusion from research, for instance, Morgan, Farkas, Tufis, and Sperling (2008) found that "children with reading problems in first grade were significantly more likely to display poor task engagement, poor self-control, externalizing behavior problems, and internalizing behavior problems in third grade. … Academic underachievement and problem behaviors frequently co-occur" in school (p. 417). What constitutes a "behavior problem," however, is often a cultural judgment. Wallace, Goodkind, Wallace, and Bachman (2008), among many others, report differential suspension rates for Black and White students, suggesting that Black students' behavior is prone to be interpreted as problematic by a teaching force that is roughly 85% White (U.S. Department of Education, 2016). The history of Black and White cultural differences often suggests that different sorts of socialization may lead to a misinterpretation of each other's intentions (Kochman, 1981). It is worth questioning, then, what it means to be diagnosed as a struggling reader in the context of school, where it is common for White adults to make cultural judgments (e.g., what counts as problematic behavior in relation to reading struggles) about children of color, including their performance as readers and their scores on school-administered test data that confirm their biases.

Christian and Bloome (2004) locate this interpretive problem in Bourdieu's (1994) construct of symbolic capital, i.e.,

> the privileged social status and social position that a person may have within a particular situation. … In classrooms and in schools, learning to read is often who you are: how well a child learns to read in comparison to other students provides a social position in a social hierarchy of "becoming readers." That social position is part of the child's social identity.
>
> *(p. 367)*

From this perspective, the biological makeup that is central to much discourse surrounding reading disorders is not paramount. Rather, it is among the human features, both biological and social, that produce the person who is then open to interpretation. If reading does have a neurological dimension (assumed by Ehri, 2002), and if social construction affects virtually all interpretive human activity (assumed by Cole, 1996), then it's likely that both are in play when trying to understand why some people are diagnostically considered more able readers than others. Nature provides the material, nurture produces the social consequences. These social consequences might include the problem that people of color, no matter what their natural endowment might provide, are often interpreted by White teachers, researchers, and policymakers according to criteria established in middle-class White populations, against which they often appear in deficit rather following a different order (Gillborn, 2005).

Discussion

This chapter has featured the construct of race, particularly that of African Americans, as an illustration of the sociocultural dimensions of readers, reading, reading assessment and policy, reading curriculum and instruction, and reading research. Race is not an absolute variable; it works at the intersection with other demographic phenomena including gender, social class, able-bodiedness, and other factors (Cole, 2009). Discussions of race are complicated by the abundance of mixed-race families in a pluralistic world (see Parker, Horowitz, Morin, & Lopez, 2015), even as mixed-race people must often declare a racial heritage to appease people from both within and without their cultural groups (Hobbs, 2014). Yet race has emerged as a critical factor in reading and other educational fields (Tatum, 2005) and is a key variable to address if socialization to school affects educational outcomes. African American scholars have recently begun to assert the need for emic perspectives on the experiences of African American people, rather than having them judged according to norms established with the dominant culture by researchers from the dominant culture (Emdin, 2016; Love, 2019). These challenges call for non-assimilative approaches to educational reform that emphasize the diversity of the human experience and accentuate the qualities and potentials of children and youth (and adults) whose cultural ways of knowing serve them well at home and in community life, if not necessarily in established school instruction and assessment derived from White middle-class norms (Gutiérrez, 2008).

The "Reading Wars" have been contested between proponents of phonics and whole language instruction for beginning readers (Pearson, 2004). They also have a racial dimension, with African American and White researchers often at odds with whether differential reading scores emerge from dysfunctional individuals, families, and communities, or monolithic schools that rhetorically celebrate diversity while retaining their fundamental structures, values, and practices. Although such binaries can mask nuance, the divide between how African American students are perceived appears to emerge in large part from the eyes of the beholder, themselves shaped by socialization to assumptions and norms to which people like themselves adhere. A sociocultural perspective enables an understanding of how people and their abilities and potentials are constructed from different cultural perspectives.

This review suggests that more perspectives should be included in judgments about various demographic groups' literacy development, and that the insights available from each should be included in reading policy and practice. Otherwise, minoritized groups will continue to be judged in deficit to norms established with populations whose historical cultural means and ends lead them to practices that may be poorly aligned with the deep structure of schools (Smagorinsky, 2020) – the institutionalized curriculum and assessment, dress codes, codes of conduct, approved speech genres and social languages, conventions for interaction, composition of administration and faculty, the physical arrangement of schools, the hidden curriculum, and other structural factors that organize the educational process according to a specific value system – established without their consultation and without attention to the diversity that is so critical to their mission statements and purported values.

References

Abdullah, K. (2013, December 20). Q&A: Common Core an education "re-set" for African American students. *New America Media*. Retrieved April 7, 2017 from http://newamericamedia.org/2013/12/qa-common-core-an-education-re-set-for-african-american-students.php

Acosta, C. (2013). Pedagogies of resiliency and hope in response to the criminalization of Latin@ students. *Journal of Language and Literacy Education, 9*(2), 63–71.

Allington, R. L. (2006). Reading lessons and federal policymaking: An overview and introduction of the special issue. *Elementary School Journal, 107*(1), 2–15.

Alvermann, D. E. (2011). Popular culture and literacy practices. In M. L. Kamil, P. D. Pearson, E. B. Moje, & P. P. Afflerbach (Eds.), *Handbook of reading research: Vol. IV* (pp. 541–560). New York, NY: Routledge.

Anderson, R. C., Hiebert, E. H., Scott, J. A., & Wilkinson, I. A. G. (1985). *Becoming a nation of readers: The report of the Commission on Reading*. Washington, DC: National Academy of Education, National Institute of Education, & Center for the Study of Reading.

Applebee, A. N. (1993). *Literature in the secondary school: Studies of curriculum and instruction in the United States*. NCTE Research Report No. 250. Urbana, IL: National Council of Teachers of English.

Arzubiaga, A. E., Artiles, A. J., King, K. A., & Harris-Murri, N. (2008). Beyond research on cultural minorities: Challenges and implications of research as situated cultural practice. *Exceptional Children, 74*(3), 309–327. Retrieved April 6, 2017 from http://aartiles.faculty.asu.edu/publications_files/2008_Arzubiaga-etal.pdf

Athanases, S. Z., & Heath, S. B. (1995). Ethnography in the study of the teaching and learning of English. *Research in the Teaching of English, 29*(3), 262–287.

Auerbach, E. (1989). Toward a social-contextual approach to family literacy. *Harvard Educational Review, 59*(2), 165–181.

Baszile, D. T. (2009). Deal with it we must: Education, social justice, and the curriculum of hip hop culture. *Equity & Excellence in Education, 42*, 6–19.

Bates, V. C. (2011). Sustainable school music for poor, white, rural students. *Action, Criticism, and Theory for Music Education, 10*(2), 100–127.

Bell, C. M. (2012). Closing the achievement gap: Identifying social, societal, familial and psychological factors affecting Black students' academic performance. *The Public Purpose, 10*, 1–20. Retrieved April 7, 2017 from https://american.edu/spa/publicpurpose/upload/Bell_12.pdf

Bell, Y., & Clark, T. (1998). Culturally relevant reading material as related to comprehension and recall in African American Children. *Journal of Black Psychology, 24*(4), 455–475.

Berchini, C. (2016). Curriculum matters: The Common Core, authors of color, and inclusion for inclusion's sake. *Journal of Adolescent & Adult Literacy, 60*(1), 55–62.

Berliner, D. C. (2014). Exogenous variables and value-added assessments: A fatal flaw. *Teachers College Record, 116*(1), 1–31.

Bodovski, K. (2010). Parental practices and educational achievement: Social class, race, and Habitus. *British Journal of Sociology of Education, 31*(2), 139–156.

Bohrnstedt, G., Kitmitto, S., Ogut, B., Sherman, D., & Chan, D. (2015). *School composition and the Black–White achievement gap* (NCES 2015-018). Washington, DC: U.S. Department of Education, National Center for Education Statistics. Retrieved September 24, 2015 from http://nces.ed.gov/pubsearch

Bond, G., & Dykstra, R. (1964). *Conference on coordination of accepted proposals for the Cooperative Research Program in First Grade Reading Instruction. Final Report*. (Report Number CRP-F-062). Minneapolis, MN: University of Minnesota. (ERIC Document Reproduction Service No. ED 003 422).

Bourdieu, P. (1986). The forms of capital. In J. Richardson (Ed.), *Handbook of theory and research for the sociology of education* (pp. 241–258). New York, NY: Greenwood.

Bourdieu, P. (1994). *Raisons pratiques: Sur la théorie de l'action*. Paris, FR: Seuil. [*Practical reason: On the theory of action*, Cambridge, UK: Polity Press, 1998].

Byrd, W. C., & Hughey, M. W. (2015, September 28). Born that way? 'Scientific' racism is creeping back into our thinking. Here's what to watch out for. *The Washington Post*. Retrieved May 4, 2019 from www.washingtonpost.com/news/monkey-cage/wp/2015/09/28/born-that-way-scientific-racism-is-creeping-back-into-our-thinking-heres-what-to-watch-out-for/?utm_term=.7ea2e9a0f647

Christian, B., & Bloome, D. (2004). Learning to read is who you are. *Reading & Writing Quarterly, 20*, 365–384.

Coker, A. D., & Huang, -H.-H. (2010). Examining issues affecting African American participation in research studies. *Journal of Black Studies, 40*(4), 619–636.

Cole, E. R. (2009). Intersectionality and research in psychology. *American Psychologist, 64*(3), 170–180.

Cole, M. (1996). *Cultural psychology: A once and future discipline*. Cambridge, MA: Harvard University Press.

Coleman, D., & Pimentel, S. (2012). *Revised publishers' criteria for the Common Core State Standards in English Language Arts and Literacy, Grades 3–12*. Washington, DC: National Governors' Association & Common Core State Standards Initiative. Retrieved April 26, 2019 from www.corestandards.org/assets/Publishers_Criteria_for_3-12.pdf

Compton-Lilly, C. (2007). *Re-reading families: The literate lives of urban children, the intermediate years*. New York, NY: Teachers College Press.

Compton-Lilly, C., Rogers, R., & Lewis, T. Y. (2012). Analyzing epistemological considerations related to diversity: An integrative critical literature review of family literacy scholarship. *Reading Research Quarterly, 47*(1), 33–60.

Considine, D., Horton, J., & Moorman, G. (2009). Teaching and reading the millennial generation through media literacy. *Journal of Adolescent & Adult Literacy, 52*(6), 471–481.

Cushman, E. (1999). Critical literacy and institutional language. *Research in the Teaching of English, 33*, 245–274.

Cushman, E. (2013). *The Cherokee syllabary: Writing the people's perseverance*. Norman, OK: University of Oklahoma Press.

Darling-Hammond, L. (1998). Unequal opportunity: Race and education. *Brookings Review, 16*(2), 28–32.

Davies, D. (1988). Benefits and barriers to parent involvement. *Community Education Research Digest, 2*, 11–19.

Delpit, L. D. (1988). The silenced dialogue: Power and pedagogy in educating other people's children. *Harvard Educational Review, 58*(3), 280–298.

Denzin, N. K. (2009). The elephant in the living room: Or, extending the conversation about the politics of evidence. *Qualitative Research, 9*(2), 139–160.

Dewey, J. (1902). *The child and the curriculum*. Chicago, IL: University of Chicago Press.

Dixson, A. D., & Rousseau, C. K. (2005). And we are still not saved: Critical race theory in education ten years later. *Race Ethnicity and Education, 8*(1), 7–27.

Duckworth, A. (2016). *Grit: The power of passion and perseverance*. New York, NY: Scribner.

Dudley-Marling, C. (2019). Learning disabilities: Theory matters. In P. Smagorinsky, J. Tobin, & K. Lee (Eds.), *Dismantling the disabling environments of education: Creating new cultures and contexts for accommodating difference* (pp. 25–46). New York, NY: Peter Lang.

Edwards, P. A. (2004). *Children literacy development: Making it happen through school, family, and community involvement*. Boston, MA: Allyn & Bacon.

Ehri, L. C. (2002). Phases of acquisition in learning to read words and implication of teaching. In R. Stainthorp & P. Tomlinson (Eds), *Learning and teaching reading, 7*(28) (pp. 7–28). London, UK: British Journal of Education Psychology Monograph Series II.

Elliott, J. G., & Grigorenko, E. L. (2014). *The dyslexia debate*. New York, NY: Cambridge University Press.

Emdin, C. (2016). *For White folks who teach in the hood...and the rest of y'all too*. Boston, MA: Beacon Press.

Four Arrows. (2013). *Teaching truly: A curriculum to indigenize mainstream education*. New York, NY: Peter Lang.

Frankenburg, E. (2018). *Using socioeconomic-based strategies to further racial integration in k-12 schools*. San Antonio, TX: Intercultural Development Research Association. Retrieved May 3, 2019 from https://files.eric.ed.gov/fulltext/ED582810.pdf

Freire, P. (1985). Reading the world and reading the word: An interview with Paulo Freire. *Language Arts, 62*(1), 15–21.

Furlong, M. J., Whipple, A. D., St. Jean, G., Simental, J., Soliz, A., & Punthuna, S. (2003). Multiple contexts of school engagement: Moving toward a unifying framework for educational research and practice. *The California School Psychologist, 8*, 99–113.

Gadsden, V. L. (2004). Family literacy and culture. In B. H. Wasik (Ed.), *Handbook of family literacy* (pp. 401–426). Mahwah, NJ: Erlbaum.

Galton, F. (1869). *Hereditary genius*. London, UK: Macmillan.

Geertz, C. (1973). *The interpretation of cultures: Selected essays by Clifford Geertz*. New York, NY: Basic Books.

Gillborn, D. (2005). Education policy as an act of white supremacy: Whiteness, critical race theory and education reform. *Journal of Education Policy, 20*(4), 485–505.

Gough, P. B. (1972). One second of reading. *Visible Language, 6*(4), 291–320.

Gutiérrez, K. D. (2001). What's new in the English language arts: Challenging policies and practices, ¿y Qué? *Language Arts, 78*, 564–569.

Gutiérrez, K. D. (2008). Developing a sociocritical literacy in the third space. *Reading Research Quarterly, 43*(2), 148–164.

Gutiérrez, K. D., Rymes, B., & Larson, J. (1995). Script, counterscript, and underlife in the classroom: James Brown versus Brown v. Board of Education. *Harvard Educational Review. 65*(3), 445–472.

Haddix, M., & Sealy-Ruiz, Y. (2012). Cultivating digital and popular literacies as empowering and emancipatory acts among urban youth. *Journal of Adolescent and Adult Literacy, 56*(3), 189–192.

Halle, T. G., Kurtz-Costes, B., & Mahoney, J. L. (1997). Family influences on school achievement in low-income, African American children. *Journal of Educational Psychology, 89*(3), 527–537.

Harré, R., & Van Langenhove, L. (1999). *Positioning theory: Moral contexts of intentional action.* Oxford, UK: Blackwell.

Heath, S. B. (1982). What no bedtime story means: Narrative skills at home and school. *Language in Society, 11,* 49–76. Retrieved May 3, 2019 from www.shirleybriceheath.net/pdfs/LANGLRN_WhtNoBedtimeStryMns.pdf

Heath, S. B. (1983). *Ways with words: Language, life, and work in communities and classrooms.* New York, NY: Cambridge University Press.

Heath, S. B. (2010). Family literacy or community learning? Some critical questions on perspective. In K. Dunsmore & D. Fisher (Eds.), *Bringing literacy home* (pp. 15–41). Newark, DE: International Reading Association.

Herrnstein, R. J., & Murray, C. (1994). *The bell curve: Intelligence and class structure in American life.* New York, NY: Simon and Schuster.

Hill, M. L. (2009). *Beats, rhymes, and classroom life: Hip-hop pedagogy and the politics of identity.* New York, NY: Teachers College Press.

Hill, N. E., & Taylor, L. C. (2004). Parental school involvement and children's academic achievement: Pragmatics and issues. *Current Directions in Psychological Science, 13*(4), 161–164.

Hobbs, A. (2014). *A chosen exile: A history of racial passing in American life.* Cambridge, MA: Harvard University Press.

Hoover-Dempsey, K. V., Walker, J. M. T., Sandler, H. M., Whetsel, D., Green, C. L., Wilkins, A. S., & Closson, K. (2005). Why do parents become involved? Research findings and implications. *The Elementary School Journal, 106*(2), 105–130.

Howard, E. D. (2015). *African American parents' perceptions of public school: African American parents' involvement in their children's education* (Unpublished doctoral dissertation). East Tennessee State University, Johnson City, TN.

Howard, T. C. (2001). Telling their side of the story: African-American students' perceptions of culturally relevant teaching. *The Urban Review, 33*(2), 131–149.

Howard, T. C. (2013). *Why race & culture matter in schools: Closing the achievement gap in America's classrooms.* New York, NY: Teachers College Press.

Hoyles, A., & Hoyles, M. (2010). Race and dyslexia. *Race Ethnicity and Education, 13*(2), 209–231.

Johnson, L. B. (1965). *Public papers of the presidents of the United States: Lyndon B. Johnson (Containing the public messages, speeches, and statements of the President, 1963–1964), Book I.* Washington, DC: United States Printing Office.

King, J. E., Akua, C., & Russell, L. (2014). Liberating urban education for human freedom. In H. R. Milner & K. Lomotey (Eds.), *Handbook of urban education* (pp. 24–49). New York, NY: Routledge.

Kirkland, D. E. (2014, November). The lies "big data" tell: Rethinking the literate performances of black males through a modified meta-analysis of qualitative "little" data. Paper presented at the annual convention of the National Council of Teachers of English, National Harbor, MD.

Kochman, T. (1981). *Black and white styles in conflict.* Chicago, IL: University of Chicago Press.

Lareau, A. (2003). *Unequal childhoods.* Berkeley, CA: University of California Press.

Learned, J. & Moje, E. B. (2015). School contexts and the production of individual differences. In P. P. Afflerbach (Ed.), *Handbook of individual differences in reading: Reader, text, and context,* (pp. 177–195). New York, NY: Taylor & Francis.

Leary, J. D. (2005). *Crimes against humanity. Post traumatic slave syndrome: America's legacy of enduring injury and healing.* Milwaukie, OR: Uptone Press.

Lee, C. D. (2007). *The role of culture in academic literacies: Conducting our blooming in the midst of the whirlwind.* New York, NY: Teachers College Press.

Lee, J., Grigg, W., & Donahue, P., (2007). *The nation's report card: Reading 2007.* (NCES 2007 496). Washington, DC: National Center for Education Statistics.

Leonardo, Z. (2009). *Race, whiteness, and education.* New York, NY: Routledge.

Lewis Ellison, T. (2017). The matter in parents' stories: African American urban mothers' counter stories about the Common Core State Standards and quality teaching. *Urban Education, 52,* 1–31.

Lewis, T. Y. (2009). New report says Black-White reading and math achievements improve but racial gap remains. *The St. Louis American.* Retrieved from www.stlamerican.com/news/local_news/new-report-says-black-white-reading-and-math-achievements-improve/article_b10f0228-2f61-5b6d-ac1e-7adf6141b787.html

Lewis, T. Y. (2013). "We txt 2 sty cnnectd:" An African American mother and son communicate: Digital literacies, meaning-making, and activity theory systems. *Journal of Education*, *193*(2), 1–13.

Lipsitz, G. (1998). *The possessive investment in whiteness: How White people profit from identity politics*. Philadelphia, PA: Temple University Press.

Love, B. (2019). *We want to do more than survive: Abolitionist teaching and the pursuit of educational freedom*. Boston, MA: Beacon Press.

Luke, A. (1997). Textbooks and primers. In D. Wagner, B. Street, R. Venezky, & E. Nisbet (Eds.), *Literacy: An international handbook*. New York, NY: Garland Press. Retrieved May 3, 2019 from https://pages.gseis.ucla.edu/faculty/kellner/ed270/Luke/WAGNER.html

Majors, Y. J. (2015). *Shoptalk: Lessons in teaching from an African American hair salon*. New York, NY: Teachers College Press.

Makalela, L. (2016). Ubuntu translanguaging: An alternative framework for complex multilingual encounters. *Southern African Linguistics and Applied Language Studies*, *34*(3), 187–196. doi:10.2989/16073614.2016.1250350

Manuel, J., Goodwyn, A., & Zancanella, D. (2016). English through the looking glass, retrospect and prospect: Global perspectives and common ground. *English Teaching: Practice & Critique*, *15*(1), 2–6. Retrieved May 3, 2019 from doi:10.1108/ETPC-03-2016-0045

McCagg, W. O. (1989). The origins of defectology. In W. O. McCagg & L. Siegelbaum (Eds.), *The disabled in the Soviet Union: Past and present, theory and practice* (pp. 39–62). Pittsburgh, PA: University of Pittsburgh Press.

McGregor, S. L. T., & Murnane, J. A. (2010). Paradigm, methodology and method: Intellectual integrity in consumer scholarship. *International Journal of Consumer Studies*, *34*, 419–427.

McGuinn, P. (2016). From no child left behind to the every student succeeds act: Federalism and the education legacy of the Obama administration. *Publius: The Journal of Federalism*, *46*(3), 392–415.

McNair, J. (2013). "I never knew there were so many books about us": Parents and children reading and responding to African American children's literature together. *Children's Literature in Education*, *44*(3), 191–207.

Milner, H. R. (2006). The promise of Black teachers' success with Black students. *Educational Foundations*, *20*, 89–104.

Milner, H. R. (2013). Analyzing poverty, learning, and teaching through a critical race theory lens. *Review of Research in Education*, *37*, 1–53.

Morgan, A. T. A., Marsiske, M., Dzierzewski, J., Jones, R. N., Whitfield, K. E., Johnson, K. E., & Cresci, M. K. (2010). Race-related cognitive test bias in the ACTIVE study: A MIMIC model approach. *Experimental Aging Research*, *36*(4), 426–452.

Morgan, P. L., Farkas, G., Tufis, P. A., & Sperling, R. A. (2008). Are reading and behavior problems risk factors for each other? *Journal of Learning Disabilities*, *41*(5), 417–436. doi:10.1177/0022219408321123.

Mubenga, P. (2006). *Closing the achievement gap between African American children and their Caucasian counterparts using collaborative learning setting*. Washington, DC: Institute of Education Sciences, U.S. Department of Education, (ERIC Document Reproduction No. ED490762).

Myers, S. L., Kim, H., & Mandala, C. (2004). The effect of school poverty on racial gaps in test scores: The case of the Minnesota basic standards tests. *The Journal of Negro Education*, *73*(1), 81–98.

National Assessment of Educational Progress and National Center for Education Statistics. (2017). *NAEP Reading Report Card*. Washington, DC: National Center for Education Statistics.

National Center for Education Statistics. (2018). *The condition of education 2018* (NCES 2018-144), *characteristics of postsecondary faculty*. Washington, DC: U.S. Department of Education. Retrieved April 27, 2019 from https://nces.ed.gov/programs/coe/indicator_csc.asp

Newman, D., Griffin, P., & Cole, M. (1989). *The construction zone: Working for cognitive change in school*. New York, NY: Cambridge University Press.

Noguera, P. (2003). The trouble with black boys: The role and influence of environmental and cultural factors on the academic performance of African American males. *Urban Education*, *38*(4), 431–459.

Ogbu, J. U. (2003). *Black American students in an affluent suburb: A study of academic disengagement*. New York, NY: Routledge.

Orfield, G., With Schley, S., Glass, D., & Reardon, S. (1993). *The growth of segregation in American schools: Changing patterns of separation and poverty since 1968*. Alexandria, VA: National School Boards Association Council of Urban Boards of Education. Retrieved April 7, 2017 from http://files.eric.ed.gov/fulltext/ED366689.pdf

Osburn, M. Z., Stegman, C. E., Suitt, L. D., & Ritter, G. (2004). Parents' perceptions of standardized testing: Its relationship and effect on student achievement. *Journal of Educational Research & Policy Studies, 4*(1), 75–95.

Padilla, A. M. (2008). Social cognition, ethnic identity, and ethnic specific strategies for coping with threat due to prejudice and discrimination. In C. Willis-Esqueda (Ed.), *Motivational aspects of prejudice and racism* (pp. 7–42). New York, NY: Springer.

Paris, D., & Alim, H. S. (Eds.) (2017). *Culturally sustaining pedagogies: Teaching and learning for justice in a changing world*. New York, NY: Teachers College Press.

Parker, K., Horowitz, J. M., Morin, R., & Lopez, M. H. (2015, June 11). *Multiracial in America: Proud, diverse and growing in numbers*. Washington, DC: Pew Research Center. Retrieved May 21, 2019 from www.pewsocialtrends.org/2015/06/11/multiracial-in-america/

Paulesu, E., De´monet, J.-F., Fazio, F., McCrory, E., Chanoine, V., Brunswick, N., … Frith, U. (2001). Dyslexia: Cultural diversity and biological unity. *Science, 291*, 2165–2167.

Pearson, P. D. (2004). The reading wars. *Educational Policy, 18*(1), 216–252.

Philip, T. M., Souto-Manning, M., Anderson, L., Horn, I., Andrews, D. J. C., Stillman, J., & Varghese, M. (2018). Making justice peripheral by constructing practice as "core": How the increasing prominence of core practices challenges teacher education. *Journal of Teacher Education*. doi:10.1177/0022487118798324

Pianta, R. C., & Hamre, B. K. (2009). Conceptualization, measurement, and improvement of classroom processes: Standardized observation can leverage capacity. *Educational Researcher, 38*, 109–119.

Portes, P., & Smagorinsky, P. (2010). Static structures, changing demographics: Educating for shifting populations in stable schools. *English Education, 42*, 236–248.

Prendergast, C. (2002). The economy of literacy: How the Supreme Court stalled the civil rights movement. *Harvard Educational Review, 72*, 206–229.

Pressley, M., Duke, N. K., & Boling, E. (2004). The educational science and scientifically-based instruction we need: Lessons from reading research and policymaking. *Harvard Educational Review, 74*(1), 30–61.

Resnick, L. B., & Resnick, D. P. (1989). *Tests as standards of achievement in schools*. Pittsburgh, PA: Learning, Research, and Development Center. Retrieved December 5, 2018 from https://files.eric.ed.gov/fulltext/ED335421.pdf

Rhym, D. (2018). *Where do rappers come from?: Hip-hop as a remixing of the African-American oral tradition and how it engaged three African-American students* (Unpublished doctoral dissertation). The University of Georgia.

Richeson, J. A., & Nussbaum, R. J. (2004). The impact of multiculturalism versus color-blindness on racial bias. *Journal of Experimental Social Psychology, 40*, 417–423.

Rosenblatt, L. M. (1996). *Literature as exploration* (5th ed.). New York, NY: Modern Language Association.

Rosenthal, R. (1966). *Experimenter effects in behavioral research*. New York, NY: Appleton-Century-Crofts.

Roth, W.-M. (2007). Emotion at work: A contribution to third-generation cultural-historical activity theory. *Mind, Culture, and Activity, 14*(1-2), 40–63.

Rothstein-Fisch, C., & Trumbull, E. (2008). *Managing diverse classrooms: How to build on students' cultural strengths*. Alexandria, VA: Association for Supervision and Curriculum Development.

Rowan, B., & Correnti, R. (2009). Studying reading instruction with teacher logs: Lessons from the Study of Instructional Improvement. *Educational Researcher, 38*, 120–131.

Santos, J. L., Cabrera, N. L., & Fosnacht, K. J. (2010). Is "race-neutral" really race-neutral? Disparate impact towards underrepresented minorities in post-209 UC System admissions. *The Journal of Higher Education, 81*(6), 675–701.

Scott, K. S., Brown, J., Jean-Baptiste, E., & Barbarin, O. (2012). A socio-cultural conception of literacy practices in African American families. In B. Wasik (Ed.), *Handbook of family literacy* (2nd ed.) (pp. 239–254). New York, NY: Taylor & Francis.

Sellers, S. L., Bonham, V., Neighbors, H. W., & Amell, J. W. (2009). Effects of racial discrimination and health behaviors on mental and physical health of middle-class African American men. *Health Education & Behavior, 36*(1), 31–44.

Shanahan, T. (2011). Education policy and the language arts. In D. Lapp & D. Fisher (Eds.), *Handbook of research on teaching the English language arts* (pp. 152–158). Newark, DE: International Reading Association.

Shanahan, T. (2013). Letting the text take center stage: How the Common Core State Standards will transform English Language Arts instruction. *American Educator, 37*(3), 43.

Shannon, P. (Ed.). (1992). *Becoming political: Readings and writings in the politics of literacy education*. Portsmouth, NH: Heinemann.

Shifrer, D., Muller, C., & Callahan, R. (2010). Disproportionality and learning disabilities: Parsing apart race, socioeconomic status, and language. *Journal of Learning Disabilities, 44*(3), 246–257.

Smagorinsky, P. (1995). The social construction of data: Methodological problems of investigating learning in the zone of proximal development. *Review of Educational Research, 65*, 191–212.

Smagorinsky, P. (2001). If meaning is constructed, what is it made from?: Toward a cultural theory of reading. *Review of Educational Research, 71*, 133–169.

Smagorinsky, P. (2009a). The cultural practice of reading and the standardized assessment of reading instruction: When incommensurate worlds collide. *Educational Researcher, 38*(7), 522–527.

Smagorinsky, P. (2009b). Is it time to abandon the idea of "best practices" in the teaching of English? *English Journal, 98*(6), 15–22.

Smagorinsky, P. (2017). Misfits in school literacy: Whom are U. S. schools designed to serve? In D. Appleman & K. Hinchman (Eds.), *Adolescent literacy: A handbook of practice-based research* (pp. 199–214). New York, NY: Guilford.

Smagorinsky, P. (2018). Literacy in teacher education: "It's the context, stupid". *Journal of Literacy Research, 50*(3), 281–303.

Smagorinsky, P. (2020). *Learning to teach English and Language Arts: A Vygotskian perspective on beginning teachers' pedagogical concept development*. London, UK: Bloomsbury.

Smagorinsky, P., & Taxel, J. (2005). *The discourse of character education: Culture wars in the classroom*. Mahwah, NJ: Erlbaum.

Spring, J. (2016). *Deculturalization and the struggle for equality: A brief history of the education of dominated cultures in the United States*. New York, NY: Routledge.

Steele, C. M. (2011). *Whistling Vivaldi: How stereotypes affect us and what we can do*. New York, NY: W. W. Norton.

Stotsky, S. (1999). *Losing our language: How multicultural classroom instruction is undermining our children's ability to read, write, and reason*. New York, NY: Free Press.

Tampio, N. (2018). A democratic critique of the Common Core English Language Arts (ELA) Standards. *Democracy & Education, 26*(1), 1–7.

Tatum, A. (2005). *Teaching reading to Black adolescent males: Closing the achievement gap*. Portland, ME: Stenhouse.

Troy, G. (2016, June 25). The racist origins of the SAT. *The Daily Beast*. Retrieved March 6, 2019 from www.thedailybeast.com/the-racist-origins-of-the-sat?ref=scroll

Tukey, J. W. (1977). *Exploratory data analysis*. Reading, MA: Addison-Wesley.

Tulviste, P. (1991). *The cultural-historical development of verbal thinking*. Commack, NY: Nova Science.

U.S. Department of Education. (2016, July). *The state of racial diversity in the educator workforce*. Washington, DC: Author. Retrieved March 7, 2019 from www2.ed.gov/rschstat/eval/highered/racial-diversity/state-racial-diversity-workforce.pdf

Vellutino, F. R., Fletcher, J. M., Snowling, M. J., & Scanlon, D. M. (2004). Specific reading disability (dyslexia): What have we learned in the past four decades? *Journal of Child Psychology and Psychiatry, 45*(1), 2–40.

Vondra, J. I., Dowell Hommerding, K., & Shaw, D. D. (1999). *Stability and change in infant attachment in a low-income sample*. Monographs of the Society for Research in Child Development, 64(3, Serial No. 258). Retrieved April 7, 2017 from www.jstor.org/stable/3181561.

Vygotsky, L. S. (1978). *Mind in society: The development of higher psychological processes* (M. Cole, V. John-Steiner, S. Scribner, & E. Souberman, Eds.). Cambridge, MA: Harvard University Press.

Vygotsky, L. S. (1987). Thinking and speech. In L. S. Vygotsky (Ed.), *Collected works* (Vol. 1, pp. 39–285) (R. Rieber & A. Carton, Eds; N. Minick, Trans.). New York, NY: Plenum.

Wallace, J. M., Jr., Goodkind, S., Wallace, C. M., & Bachman, J. G. (2008). Racial, ethnic, and gender differences in school discipline among U.S. high school students: 1991–2005. *Negro Educational Review, 59*, 47–62.

Washington, J. (2001). Early literacy skills in African-American children: Research considerations. *Learning Disabilities Research and Practice 16*(4), 213–221.

Wertsch, J. V. (1985). *Vygotsky and the social formation of mind*. Cambridge, MA: Harvard University Press.

Whiting, G. W., & Ford, D. Y. (2009). Cultural bias in testing. In E. M. Anderman & L. H. Anderman (Eds.), *Psychology of classroom learning: An encyclopedia* (pp. 296–300). Detroit, MI: Macmillan.

Williams, H. A. (2005). *Self-taught: African American education in slavery and freedom*. Chapel Hill, NC: University of North Carolina Press.

Williams, T. C. (2019, May 17). The SAT's bogus 'adversity score'. *New York Times*. Retrieved May 21, 2019 from www.nytimes.com/2019/05/17/opinion/sat-adversity-score.html

Willis, A. I. (1997). Historical considerations. *Language Arts, 74*(5), 387–397.

Willis, A. I. (2009). EduPolitical research: Reading between the lines. *Educational Researcher, 38*, 528–536. doi:10.3102/0013189X09347584

Willis, A. I., & Harris, V. J. (1997). Expanding the boundaries: A reaction to the First Grade Reading Studies. *Reading Research Quarterly, 32*(4), 439–445.

Witte, S. (1992). Context, text, intertext: Toward a constructivist semiotic of writing. *Written Communication, 9*, 237–308.

Wong, C. A., Eccles, J. S., & Sameroff, A. (2003). The influence of ethnic discrimination and ethnic identification on African American adolescents' school and socioemotional adjustment. *Journal of Personality, 71*(6), 1197–1232.

Worthy, J., Lammert, C., Long, S. L., Salmerón, C., & Godfrey, V. (2018). "What if we were committed to giving *every* individual the services and opportunities they need?": Teacher educators' understandings, perspectives, and practices surrounding dyslexia. *Research in the Teaching of English, 53*(2), 125–148.

Yan, W. (1999). Successful African-American students: The role of parental involvement. *Journal of Negro Education, 68*, 5–22.

Yonezawa, S., Wells, A. A., & Serna, I. (2002). Choosing tracks: "Freedom of choice" in detracking schools. *American Educational Research Journal, 39*(1), 37–67.

Zinshteyn, M. (2016, April 25). The growing college-degree wealth gap. *The Atlantic*. Retrieved April 27, 2019 from www.theatlantic.com/education/archive/2016/04/the-growing-wealth-gap-in-who-earns-college-degrees/479688/

Part III
How Do Expanding Forms of Texts and Everyday Communication Change the Game for Readers, Teachers, Leaders, and Reading Researchers?

5

Reading Multiple and Non-Traditional Texts

New Opportunities and New Challenges

Ivar Bråten, Jason L. G. Braasch, and Ladislao Salmerón

Introduction

The purpose of this chapter is to review theory and research on the reading of multiple and non-traditional texts, discuss implications for educational research and practice, and suggest directions for future theoretical and empirical work. Reading multiple texts involves trying to construct meaning from multiple textual resources that present consistent, componential (i.e., information across different texts is part of a larger whole not specified in any single text), or conflicting information on the same situation, issue, or phenomenon (Bråten, Anmarkrud, Brandmo, & Strømsø, 2014; Goldman, 2004). Such textual resources may be digital as well as printed. Compared to printed texts, digital texts afford new opportunities in terms of accessibility, coverage, and topicality, yet pose new challenges due to relaxed parameters for publishing and the consequential need to differentiate useful and reliable texts from those that are not (Britt & Gabrys, 2000; Leu & Maykel, 2016; Lucassen, Muilwijk, Noordzij, & Schraagen, 2013). Still, well into the 21st century, digital texts cannot be considered non-traditional in and of themselves. Accordingly, we will reserve the term non-traditional texts for digital texts embedded in social activity. More specifically, the reading of non-traditional texts is taken to involve forms of social interaction in digital contexts that have traditionally required face-to-face encounters, such as the reading of instant messages, web forums, blogs, and online comments (Bråten, Stadtler, & Salmerón, 2018). Also, when reading such non-traditional texts, individuals typically engage with multiple texts dealing with the same situation, issue, or phenomenon, for example, when reading several answers to a question posted on a web forum or reading a number of online comments to a particular newspaper article.

Our treatment of the reading of multiple and non-traditional texts thus spans reading contexts ranging from the reading of multiple traditional texts in print, as when a high school class reads documents distributed by their teacher to complete a history assignment, to the reading of multiple non-traditional texts online, as when a couple reads conflicting evaluations of the same hotel on a travel forum website to decide on accommodation for their upcoming weekend trip. In a middle position, as it were, is the reading of multiple traditional texts online, as when undergraduate students read a set of published articles retrieved via the university library's website on their laptops to prepare a class presentation on a particular course-related issue. Of course, all these reading contexts are ubiquitous in the 21st century information society (Bråten & Braasch, 2017; Goldman et al., 2011). It is therefore somewhat paradoxical that much, if not most, of what researchers know about reading is based on individuals reading a single text (cf., McNamara & Magliano, 2009). Given this state of affairs, it can be argued that increased attention to reading contexts involving multiple and non-traditional texts is required to improve the ecological validity of the work that we, as a field, produce. Accordingly, our discussion of emergent conceptualizations and empirical findings regarding the reading of multiple and non-traditional texts in this chapter highlights the need to better align the world of reading research with the world of real life reading, both in and out of school.

The remainder of this chapter is divided into three main sections. In the first, we provide a theoretical background by discussing relevant frameworks for understanding how the reading of multiple and non-traditional texts is similar to and differs from the reading of single and traditional texts. In the second, we review empirical work on the role of individual and contextual factors in multiple text comprehension, the similarities and differences between reading printed and digital texts, and the reading of non-traditional texts in digital contexts. Finally, in the third main section, we summarize the outcome of our conceptual and empirical analysis, discuss implications for the conceptualization of the reading process and instructional practice, and note future work that is needed in this area of research.

Theoretical Background

The past 20 years has seen an increased interest in theory development for the purposes of better understanding the affordances and challenges of reading to understand multiple and non-traditional texts. In this section, we present and discuss several prominent frameworks that have resulted from these efforts. They include the Documents Model Framework (DMF), the Multiple-Document Task-based Relevance Assessment and Content Extraction (MD-TRACE) model, the Disciplinary Literacy conceptual framework, the Semantics, Surface, and Source (3S) model of credibility evaluation, and the New Literacies framework.

The Documents Model Framework

The DMF is arguably the most influential framework for describing how readers mentally represent multiple, and at times conflicting, messages in terms of the information sources conveying them (Britt, Perfetti, Sandak, & Rouet, 1999; Britt & Rouet, 2012; Britt, Rouet, & Braasch, 2013; Perfetti, Rouet, & Britt, 1999; Rouet, 2006). The framework specifies that readers of multiple texts will ideally create two additional mental structures above and beyond those described in models of single text comprehension (e.g., Kintsch, 1998; van den Broek, 2010). First, to optimize their understandings of the situation or phenomenon described by texts, readers should construct an *integrated mental model*, which is a mental representation of the global situation described in multiple texts as relationships among the semantic content (Britt & Rouet, 2012). An integrated mental model could entail ideas unique to single texts, ideas shared across multiple texts, and ideas offered by multiple texts that contradict one another. The DMF additionally proposes that readers should construct an *intertext model*, which is a mental representation that uses source features (e.g., authors, publication venues, perspectives, and so forth) as organizational components (Britt & Rouet, 2012). Intertext links are mentally represented as relationships between information sources – referred to as document nodes – and their respective content assertions (e.g., "Author A claims ...", "Author B claims ..."). Intertext links also function as connections between the document nodes themselves (e.g., "Author A disagrees with Author B"). In this way, the DMF describes how readers *ideally* comprehend multiple diverse texts, in terms of their respective information sources.

The Multiple-Document Task-based Relevance Assessment and Content Extraction Model

The MD-TRACE model specifies a general sequence of processes readers might cycle through when interacting with complex texts (including multiple or non-traditional texts) to complete an overarching reading task (Rouet & Britt, 2011). In Step 1, readers interpret task goals based on provided instructions (e.g., write an essay on whether we should use products containing GMOs). Readers might also plan a set of procedures they could engage in to satisfy their task goals. The result is a "task model," a mental representation of the task that presumably guides inquiry into the topic (Rouet & Britt, 2011). In Step 2, readers assess information needs given the current states of their task products (their essays) (Rouet & Britt, 2011). Step 3 reflects a set of sub-processes including a) selecting a document, b) reading and comprehending the document, and c) integrating current ideas with those from prior-read documents. In Step 4, task products are created or updated. Finally, in Step 5, readers assess the sufficiency of their task products. As such, at any point in time, readers can cycle back through earlier steps if they perceive their products have not sufficiently addressed their task goals. For example, based on the current states of their task products, readers might decide there are additional informational needs. As a result, they may return to search engines to click on the titles of additional texts to evaluate whether they might provide additional supports for their GMO essays. Thus, decisions to return to earlier steps appear to be contingent on readers' perceptions about the adequacy of their final products.

The MD-TRACE model also outlines *internal* resources that readers should bring to bear to optimally navigate the described sequence (Rouet & Britt, 2011). These include general world and specific domain knowledge, knowledge of which source characteristics are important to consider within the discipline, and appropriate search, processing, evaluation, and integration strategies. It additionally outlines *external* resources relevant to the processing sequence including task specifications, texts, search devices or organizers, and any products generated along the way (e.g., notes taken during reading) (Rouet & Britt, 2011).

The Disciplinary Literacy Conceptual Framework

Goldman et al.'s (2016) framework describes the discipline-specific nature of what students need to know about knowledge construction, representation, and communication. How multiple and non-traditional texts are read and knowledge represented in the discipline of science, for example, requires guidance from a different set of beliefs about the nature of knowledge (i.e., epistemic beliefs; Hofer & Bendixen, 2012) than do processes specific to other disciplines (e.g., history). Goldman et al. (2016) offered core constructs to improve the articulation of knowledge in three disciplines (science, history, literature) that readers would ideally use to build multiple levels of textual representation previously specified in models of single and multiple text comprehension. Thus, their framework can be viewed as an extension of the DMF and MD-TRACE models that importantly highlights the ways that reading and literacy practices are similar and differ across various disciplines.

For example, readers' beliefs about knowledge in science might guide them towards reliable practices for finding and selecting relevant texts on the topic of GMOs. These beliefs might also direct their evaluations of textual information, including a primary text's arguments and any information that accompanies them (e.g., supporting and counter-arguments posted in a comments section). More specifically, readers' epistemic beliefs concerning science could lead them towards practices for evaluating whether available claims are valid or invalid, whether forms of evidence are reasonable or unreasonable, whether authors' credentials make them knowledgeable, credible sources on the topic, and so forth. Ultimately these types of evaluation practices help determine whether readers will or will not integrate currently processed information with ideas from prior-read texts.

In contrast, the same students' practices might look very different if tasked to write an essay on a history topic (e.g., What preconditions gave rise to the Arab Spring?) because such a task could be guided by a different set of beliefs about knowledge specific to that discipline. Readers' epistemic beliefs concerning history could lead them towards an altogether different set of reliable practices for evaluating whether available claims are valid or invalid, whether forms of evidence are reasonable or unreasonable, whether claims and evidence have been corroborated across multiple sources, in what ways status as primary versus secondary documents helps readers differentiate whether they should or should not trust the information, and so forth (VanSledright & Maggioni, 2016). Thus, Goldman et al.'s (2016) framework emphasizes that there are distinctive characteristics of learners' epistemic thinking that guide all aspects of reading and representing information within a discipline, from initiating a task model to final assessments of whether the task product sufficiently addresses the overarching task goal.

The Semantics, Surface, and Source Model of Credibility Evaluation

The 3-S model of Lucassen and colleagues (2011, 2013) describes three strategies information seekers can use when making credibility assessments about information they find online. As such, this model focuses prominently on reading on the Internet and on reading of non-traditional texts. Regarding a first strategy, individuals may consider the semantic features of information, for example the accuracy of the information. Individuals verify available information against their relevant domain knowledge and use the extent to which information is verified as an index of credibility. Thus, with respect to establishing credibility via this strategy, domain expertise is the primary lens by which readers can decide upon the factual accuracy of any information they come across (Lucassen et al., 2013; Lucassen & Schraagen, 2011).

A second strategy involves a consideration of the "surface features" of online information, including a website's design or aesthetics, the length of an article, and the number of embedded references, images, and links, to name but a few (e.g., "this information seems credible because it is long, looks serious, and has a lot of links"). By comparison, those with lower domain expertise tend to rely more heavily on surface features due to their inherent inability to disentangle what is factually accurate (Lucassen et al., 2013).

According to a third strategy, information seekers can consider any relevant prior experience they may have had with particular sources (e.g., "this information seems credible because it was published by the BBC, which I consider to be a trustworthy source"). In using this strategy, individuals use source features found on websites such as the logo in the corner or a link with "about us" information as indices of credibility. Thus, whereas semantic and surface features involve the content of a website and its layout, respectively, source features inform on the information provider, or who has produced the information (Lucassen et al., 2013). Taken together, information users rely on these three strategies in concert to help decide whether they will trust the texts they encounter.

The New Literacies Framework

On a surface level, the new literacies framework identifies a similar set of five component practices as the MD-TRACE model. However, whereas the MD-TRACE stems from a more traditional reading comprehension literature, the new literacies framework explicitly focuses on online reading comprehension and – in doing so – also highlights facets of problem-solving and question-answering specific to non-traditional types of texts found in online environments (Kinzer & Leu, 2017; Leu, Kinzer, Coiro, Castek, & Henry, 2013). In the first step, readers identify important problems to solve or questions they would like to answer (rather than interpreting pre-specified task instructions, as in MD-TRACE). For example, a reader might set out to learn more about GMOs as a result of reading a scathing opinion article a friend posted via social media. In a second step, the individual reads for the purpose of locating information that might help in answering the question of interest. To find information on the topic, for example, the reader will need to a) generate key words that return useful websites, b) read a set of links returned from the search engine to infer which websites might be useful, and c) to skim and scan information presented within the websites (Leu et al., 2013). In a third step, the reader decides upon which information is reliable by critically evaluating the available information (based on accuracy, reliability, potential biases, and so forth) (Leu et al., 2013). In a fourth step, the individual synthesizes information deemed useful for answering the question into a coherent understanding of what was read. In a final step, the reader communicates the constructed response to an intended audience. To return to the example, the reader might leave a reply to the posting of the opinion article to share what was learned about GMOs based on the recent inquiry. Thus, in describing these five general practices, Leu and colleagues (2013) have also taken great strides in beginning to identify the new skills, strategies, dispositions, and social practices with which readers must be proficient to successfully conduct online inquiry.

As a caveat, many Internet reading experiences do not directly reflect the sequence of steps outlined by the new literacies framework. For example, readers do not always have concrete research questions in mind but may, rather, arrive at research questions in a more "bottom up" fashion. Thus, readers may sometimes rapidly toggle amongst several component processes – entering and revising search terms, skimming and scanning links and accessed texts – before a preliminary research question of interest materializes. Furthermore, in evaluating and synthesizing information during reading, readers may realize that there is not enough (reliable) information. This may guide them towards adapting the question to suit the available information, or in choosing an altogether new query of interest. Thus, the new literacies framework richly describes a logical sequence of steps readers might go through to solve a problem. However, authentic reading experiences may follow different paths, different iterations amongst the steps, different entry points into the processes, and so forth. As additional empirical data are collected regarding readers' engagement with these component processes, patterns may emerge that warrant a need to revise the framework to account for more varied approaches towards reading in an information age.

Summary

To summarize, the reviewed models extend our understandings of multiple and non-traditional text reading. Taken together, they describe a set of processes, strategies, and skills that – when optimally functioning – could result in effective, efficient comprehension. The models do, however, differ in terms of the grain sizes with which they operate. For example, although both the DMF and MD-TRACE were developed from a rich history of research on single and traditional text comprehension, the former is more fine-grained in its description of multiple text reading processes compared to the latter. The DMF specifically describes how readers mentally represent multiple texts in terms of the information sources conveying them. The MD-TRACE is much broader in scope by offering a general sequence of processes that readers cycle through to complete an overarching reading task (of which constructing and modifying a documents model is but one facet). The Disciplinary Literacy conceptual framework can be viewed as an extension of these models that essentially highlights a) the ways reading and literacy practices are similar and differ across various disciplines, and b) the epistemic thinking within each discipline that guides multiple text processing and representation.

By comparison, the 3-S and new literacies frameworks explicitly focus on *online* reading comprehension and – in doing so – highlight the kinds of processes, strategies, and skills that are described as uniquely important when reading non-traditional texts in online environments (for further discussion of such processes, strategies, and skills, see sections on the reading of digital and non-traditional texts below). These models also differ in terms of grain size. Whereas the 3-S is fine-grained in its specific description of three strategies that individuals can use when making credibility assessments about online information, the new literacies model is much broader in scope, offering a sequence of steps one could take when reading online to solve a problem or answer a question (of which evaluating websites for credibility is but one facet). Thus, the 3-S model might be considered a more constrained articulation of a sub-process falling within the broader conceptualization of online reading represented by the new literacies model.

Finally, we note that all reviewed models outline *internal* (i.e., individual) and *external* (i.e., contextual) resources relevant for successful multiple or non-traditional text comprehension. Important *internal* resources include prior knowledge, thinking about knowledge and knowing, and appropriate strategic processing. The models also agree that there are key *external* resources that can facilitate optimal reading and comprehension of multiple and non-traditional texts. Such resources include task specifications, textual materials, search devices or organizers, and products generated along the way (e.g., self-generated text). In the next section, we review empirical evidence regarding a number of these individual and contextual factors with a focus on multiple text comprehension.

Empirical Work

The Role of Individual and Contextual Factors in Multiple Text Comprehension

Construction of meaning from multiple texts represents a great challenge for readers regardless of age. Theorists assume that how readers meet this challenge depends on individual as well as contextual factors. This assumption has considerable empirical backing. Moreover, emerging evidence suggests that interactions among individual and contextual factors may affect multiple text comprehension.

Individual Factors in Multiple Text Comprehension

Since Wineburg's (1991) landmark study in the area of multiple text reading, a number of studies have provided evidence that what readers already know about the topic discussed across texts impacts their multiple text comprehension. Thus, while research in the 1990s (Rouet, Britt, Mason, & Perfetti, 1996; Stahl, Hynd, Britton, McNish, & Bosquet, 1996; Wineburg, 1991) indicated that students with limited prior knowledge may have difficulties integrating information across multiple historical texts, more recent research (Bråten, Anmarkrud et al., 2014; Bråten & Strømsø, 2010a, 2010b; Bråten, Strømsø, & Britt, 2009; Gil, Bråten, Vidal-Abarca, & Strømsø, 2010a; Strømsø & Bråten, 2009; Strømsø, Bråten, & Britt, 2010) has shown that students' prior knowledge is a predictor of their comprehension when reading multiple texts on a scientific issue. Presumably, prior knowledge contributes to comprehension because it facilitates bridging inferences that create interconnection and coherence in complex, divergent text materials. Compared to the reading of single texts, multiple text reading may represent an added complexity in this regard because it requires the building of links and coherence not only within but also across texts (Britt & Rouet, 2012; Goldman, 2004).

In addition to individual differences with respect to prior knowledge about the topic or domain, individual differences with respect to readers' beliefs about that topic or domain knowledge, that is their epistemic beliefs, seem to matter in terms of multiple text comprehension (for reviews, see Bråten, Britt, Strømsø, & Rouet, 2011; Bråten, Strømsø, & Ferguson, 2016). There is thus a growing research base indicating that beliefs concerning the certainty, simplicity, and source of knowledge, as well as regarding the justification of knowledge claims, are related to a readers ability to construct integrated understandings from the reading of multiple texts (Barzilai & Ka'adan, 2017; Barzilai & Zohar, 2012; Bråten, Ferguson, Strømsø, & Anmarkrud, 2013, 2014; Bråten & Strømsø, 2010b; Bråten, Strømsø, & Samuelstuen, 2008; Kammerer, Bråten, Gerjets, & Strømsø, 2013; Mason, Ariasi, & Boldrin, 2011; Mason, Boldrin, & Ariasi, 2010; Pieschl, Stahl, & Bromme, 2008; Strømsø & Bråten, 2009; Strømsø, Bråten, & Samuelstuen, 2008). In general, this body of research has shown that viewing knowledge as tentative rather than certain, complex rather than simple, originating in expert authors rather than the reader, and justified by rules of inquiry and cross-checking of knowledge sources rather than own opinion and experience predict students' abilities to synthesize information from expository texts expressing diverse and even contradictory viewpoints on a particular topic. Basically, adaptive epistemic beliefs in the context of multiple text reading seem well aligned with the open, ill-structured problem that trying to construct meaning from multiple, often conflicting, texts represents.

Arguably, prior knowledge and adaptive epistemic beliefs may have limited value to readers if they cannot motivate themselves to apply those resources in the service of multiple text comprehension. Accordingly, there is evidence to suggest that individual differences in motivation play a role in the context of multiple text reading (Bråten, Ferguson, Anmarkrud, & Strømsø, 2013: Strømsø & Bråten, 2009; Strømsø et al., 2010). For example, Strømsø and Bråten (2009) found that topic interest, specifically students' self-reported individual interest and engagement in issues and activities concerning the topic of climate change, uniquely explained variance in multiple text comprehension when entered into a regression equation together with measures of prior knowledge and epistemic beliefs concerning the same topic. Moreover, Bråten, Ferguson, Anmarkrud, and Strømsø (2013) demonstrated that readers' beliefs in their capabilities to understand what they read in science, that is their science reading self-efficacy, was a unique positive predictor of multiple text comprehension when several other relevant individual difference variables were controlled. Because readers must persist in reading several texts on the same topic and engage in building coherence across those texts, it may generally require more energy and engagement to learn from and comprehend multiple texts than to work with one coherent text on the same topic (Bråten, Ferguson, Anmarkrud, & Strømsø, 2013). The role of reading motivation therefore may be more pronounced in multiple text contexts than in single text contexts.

Compared to the individual difference variables discussed above, strategic processing may be conceived as a more proximal contributor to multiple text comprehension, that is, as a contributor through which those other individual difference variables work (Bråten, Anmarkrud et al., 2014). Again, this area of research owes much to Wineburg (1991), who found that historians heavily relied on a strategic approach including "corroboration" and "sourcing" when trying to comprehend multiple texts on a historical event. While corroboration involved comparing across texts and examining potential discrepancies among them, sourcing involved noting and using information about the source of a text (e.g., its author or text genre). Whereas the historians used these strategies to piece together a coherent interpretation of the event described across texts, high school students participating in Wineburg's study seldom used corroboration and sourcing when reading the same texts.

Building on Wineburg's (1991) seminal work, many researchers have provided evidence for a link between deeper-level intertextual processing during reading and multiple text comprehension, using methodologies ranging from verbal protocols (Anmarkrud, Bråten, & Strømsø, 2014; Goldman, Braasch, Wiley, Graesser, & Brodowinska, 2012; Strømsø, Bråten, & Samuelstuen, 2003; Wolfe & Goldman, 2005) to note taking (Britt & Sommer, 2004; Hagen, Braasch, & Bråten, 2014; Kobayashi, 2009a, 2009b), reading patterns (i.e., linear vs. nonlinear reading; Bråten, Ferguson, Anmarkrud, & Strømsø, 2013; Salmerón, Gil, Bråten, & Strømsø, 2010), and task-specific self-reported multiple text comprehension strategies (Bråten, Anmarkrud et al., 2014; Bråten & Strømsø, 2011). The sourcing strategy initially described by Wineburg has been given particular attention by researchers in the last decade. Thus, quite a few correlational studies have demonstrated that the extent to which students consider trustworthiness based on source features may predict their learning and comprehension when reading about controversial issues in multiple texts (Anmarkrud et al., 2014; Barzilai & Eseth-Alkalai, 2015; Barzilai, Tzadok, & Eshet-Alkalai, 2015; Bråten et al., 2009; Goldman et al., 2012; List, Alexander, & Stephens, 2017; Strømsø et al., 2010; Wiley et al., 2009). In addition, recent intervention work has strengthened the idea that students' consideration of source feature information during reading promotes comprehension of multiple texts (Barzilai & Ka'adan, 2017; Braasch, Bråten, Strømsø, Anmarkrud, & Ferguson, 2013; Mason, Junyent, & Tornatora, 2014; Wiley et al., 2009).

Several studies indicate that readers' strategic processing mediates the effects of prior knowledge, epistemic beliefs, and motivation on multiple text comprehension (Barzilai & Eseth-Alkalai, 2015; Barzilai et al., 2015; Bråten, Anmarkrud et al., 2014; Kobayashi, 2009b). For example, Bråten, Anmarkrud et al. (2014), in a path analytic study, found that readers' knowledge about the topic of the texts, beliefs about the justification of knowledge claims, and reading motivation indirectly affected their multiple text comprehension through their use of deeper-level intertextual strategies. Of note is that such strategies involve intentional attempts to control and modify meaning construction during multiple text reading (cf., Afflerbach, Pearson, & Paris, 2008). Presumably, when there is a high amount of content overlap between texts, automatic, bottom-up resonance (i.e., associative) processes (O'Brien & Myers, 1999) may drive intertextual integration during reading (Beker, Jolles, Lorch, & van den Brock, 2016); otherwise, top-down strategic processing may be necessary (Kurby, Britt, & Magliano, 2005).

Contextual Factors in Multiple Text Comprehension

Readers' processing and comprehension of multiple texts have been shown to be influenced by the reading task (for review, see Bråten, Gil, & Strømsø, 2011). Most empirical work on this issue concerns the effects of "general purpose instructions" (McCrudden & Schraw, 2007) to construct arguments based on textual content versus other general purpose instructions, most notably to summarize information across texts (Bråten & Strømsø, 2010a; Gil et al., 2010a; Gil, Bråten, Vidal-Abarca, & Strømsø, 2010b; Hagen et al., 2014; Le Bigot & Rouet, 2007; Naumann, Wechsung, & Krems, 2009; Stadtler, Scharrer, Skodzik, & Bromme, 2014; Wiley et al., 2009; Wiley & Voss, 1999). In general, this body of research indicates that argument tasks can lead to more elaborative processing and a deeper understanding than summary tasks. As discussed below, such positive effects of argument tasks may be moderated by individual difference variables, however.

In addition to the reading task, several aspects of the nature of the textual materials seem to influence multiple text processing and comprehension. These include the type of texts that readers encounter, such as primary versus secondary source texts (Rouet et al., 1996), informational versus policy-related texts (i.e., explanatory texts with and without recommendations for personal and public policy changes; Blaum, Griffin, Wiley, & Britt, 2017), and popular and social media texts versus textbooks or scholarly essays (Bråten, Braasch, Strømsø, & Ferguson, 2015;

List et al., 2017). In particular, research has focused on the role of conflicting information across sources in promoting strategic multiple text processing and comprehension, with a number of studies (Braasch, Rouet, Vibert, & Britt, 2012; Ferguson, Bråten, Strømsø, & Anmarkrud, 2013; Kammerer & Gerjets, 2014; Kammerer, Kalbfell, & Gerjets, 2016; Rouet, Le Bigot, de Pereyra, & Britt, 2016; Salmerón, Macedo-Rouet, & Rouet, 2016; Saux et al., 2017; Strømsø, Bråten, Britt, & Ferguson, 2013) indicating that the presence of conflicts may increase not only adaptive text processing, especially sourcing, but also the integration of information across texts (for review, see Braasch & Bråten, 2017).

Interacting Factors in Multiple Text Comprehension

Importantly, individual and contextual factors seem to affect multiple text processing and comprehension interactively as well as independently. For example, research has indicated that argument tasks, such as instructions to read for the purpose of constructing arguments, may not be equally beneficial for all readers of multiple texts. Rather, their effects may be moderated by readers' prior knowledge about the topic of the texts (Gil et al., 2010a, 2010b) as well as their epistemic beliefs concerning the certainty of knowledge (Bråten, Gil et al., 2011; Bråten & Strømsø, 2010a; Gil et al., 2010b). In brief, readers lacking prior knowledge or believing that knowledge about the topic is certain rather than tentative and evolving, may have a hard time trying to construct arguments from multiple texts and actually be better off when given the simpler task of summarizing information presented in a set of texts. In the same vein, research by Kobayashi (2009a) and Hagen et al. (2014) suggests that elaborative intertextual processing plays a more pronounced role when readers are tasked to identify or construct arguments than when they are given other reading tasks, such as producing a summary.

In addition to such interactions between reading task instructions and individual factors, a few multiple text studies have indicated interactions between the nature of the reading materials and individual factors (Barzilai & Eseth-Alkalai, 2015; Trevors, Feyzi-Behnagh, Azevedo, & Bouchet, 2016), between different individual factors (Ferguson & Bråten, 2013), and between different contextual factors (Stadtler et al., 2014). As an example of interactions between the nature of the reading materials and individual differences, Barzilai and Eseth-Alkalai (2015) found that presenting conflicting information across texts promoted sourcing only among readers believing in uncertain knowledge and the need to justify knowledge claims through critical thinking and evidence. In turn, readers' sourcing activities predicted their integration of information from multiple texts in written arguments.

Moreover, there is also some evidence to suggest that different individual difference variables may interactively affect multiple text comprehension. For example, Ferguson and Bråten (2013) used cluster analysis to investigate interactions between students' prior knowledge about the topic of the texts and their epistemic beliefs when reading multiple conflicting texts on a socio-scientific topic. These authors found that students who had high prior knowledge and, at the same time, believed that knowledge claims should be justified by checking multiple external sources for consistency rather than relying on their own personal opinions were particularly well positioned to construct integrated understandings from the texts.

Finally, different contextual factors may interact to affect multiple text comprehension. Stadtler et al. (2014) compared the effects of argument and summary reading tasks, using reading materials that either signaled the existence of conflicting claims across texts through rhetorical means (e.g., by starting a text with the following phrase: "Contrary to what some health professionals argue, …") or not. In that study, beneficial effects of an argument task on readers' sourcing were observed only among participants presented with reading materials in which intertextual conflicts were explicitly signaled.

Reading Printed versus Digital Texts

Four decades ago, research on the similarities and differences between reading printed and digital texts was initiated with a focus on ergonomic aspects, such as the colors of the text and background and the size of the screen (for a review, see Dillon, 1992). This research raised strong concerns about potential drawbacks of digital reading as compared to print reading, for example, about digital texts being slower to read. For several reasons, it is difficult to extrapolate from the early findings to the current situation. First, the rise of the Internet and the proliferation of mobile devices in the late 1990s have profoundly affected the availability and interconnectedness of digital texts. Second, current readers are not unfamiliar with digital texts, as was the case when the early comparison studies were conducted (Dillon, 1992). Finally, the improved quality of digital screens has brought the visual experience of reading digital and printed texts much closer (Benedetto, Drai-Zerbib, Pedrotti, Tissier, & Baccino, 2013).

From a psychological perspective, comparisons of how readers process printed and digital texts have addressed three main issues in the last decades. These concern preference, comprehension, and self-regulation of reading. Regarding preference, the extent to which readers prefer digital rather than printed texts has been found to depend on their age. Thus, when interviewed in small scale studies, middle and high school students born around 2000 (so-called "millenials") have expressed a clear preference for reading using digital media, such as e-books or tablets, as opposed to reading printed books (Jones & Brown, 2011; Moje, Overby, Tysvaer, & Morris, 2008; Tveit & Mangen, 2014). When asked to explain their experiences with different media, students from the 3rd to 10th grade seem to associate digital reading with more positive and less negative affect (e.g., more fun, less tiring), and perceive that it improves their cognitive processing (e.g., increased attention, better memory; Tveit & Mangen, 2014). This perception of improved cognitive processing is not necessarily associated with better performance, however (see below). Presumably due to their preference for digital media, digital reading may also increase reading engagement for young students, particularly for struggling readers (Fletcher & Nicholas, 2016; Maynard, 2010). A note of caution is needed when interpreting such findings, however, because there may be a novelty effect underlying young students' preference for digital devices (cf., Clark, 1983). Interestingly, a large scale study with young British students that focused on their actual reading experiences found that those who read only digital texts reportedly enjoyed reading much less than those who read only printed or both types of texts (Picton, 2014).

That reader preference may depend on age is evidenced by the fact that older, undergraduate readers (born in the mid-1990s) have been shown to display an opposite pattern compared to younger readers, with adult readers strongly preferring printed rather than digital texts (Rowlands, Nicholas, Jamali, & Huntington, 2007). Moreover, this preference for printed texts among adult readers seems to be consistent across countries, ranging from the U.S. to Germany and Japan (Baron, 2015; Kurata, Ishita, Miyata, & Minami, 2017), across levels of experience with digital reading, ranging from "digital immigrants" to "digital natives" (Kretzschmar et al., 2013; Kurata et al., 2017), and across reading purposes, ranging from study-related reading to reading for pleasure (Baron, 2015; Kurata et al., 2017). In fact, even people who spend more time reading on screen than on paper have been shown to clearly prefer reading printed texts (Kurata et al., 2017). At this point, we can only speculate about the reasons that adults prefer reading printed texts. However, small scale studies have suggested that adult readers perceive that print reading facilitates concentration, memory, and comprehension, compared to digital reading (Baron, 2015). With respect to the reading of narratives, in particular, it has been argued that print reading facilitates readers' immersion in fictional worlds (i.e., phenomenological immersion) to a greater extent than does digital reading (Mangen, 2008). It is thus possible that more experience with reading both printed and digital texts may have led adult readers to prefer the former.

Regarding the issue of whether print reading actually improves comprehension compared to digital reading, results are mixed, however. Thus, while some research comparing print and digital reading has not found any difference in terms of comprehension performance (Holzinger et al., 2011; Kretzschmar et al., 2013: Margolin, Driscoll, Toland, & Kegler, 2013; Singer & Alexander, 2017), other studies have indicated that digital reading may have negative effects on comprehension (Ackerman & Goldsmith, 2011; Mangen, Walgermo, & Brønnick, 2013). Attempts to clarify this issue have investigated variables that might moderate the relationship between students' reading and their comprehension performance. In particular, it has been suggested that reading digital compared to printed texts may affect the way readers perceive their current understanding of the texts as well as their subsequent regulation of study time (Ackerman & Goldsmith, 2011; Ackerman & Lauterman, 2012; Lauterman & Ackerman, 2014), with digital reading possibly generating a false feeling of knowing, which, in turn, could have detrimental effects on comprehension. Accordingly, in a series of studies comparing undergraduates' reading of identical printed or digital texts, Ackerman and colleagues (Ackerman & Goldsmith, 2011, Exp. 1; Lauterman & Ackerman, 2014) found that when reading digital texts, students tended to overestimate their understanding. As a likely result of this overestimation, students also spent less time reading and achieved poorer comprehension when reading digital texts (Ackerman & Goldsmith, 2011, Exp. 2). Such difficulties monitoring and regulating their digital reading have been found to be particularly pronounced among students preferring to read on paper (Lauterman & Ackerman, 2014), which suggests that motivational aspects linked to media preferences can influence students' self-regulation during reading. Of note is, however, that Singer and Alexander (2017) failed to replicate the findings reported by Ackerman and colleagues in a follow-up study.

Finally, the reading of hypertext has received particular attention from researchers interested in digital reading. Hypertext denotes a digital document that includes links to related documents, creating a network of information. Hypertext therefore requires that readers choose which links to navigate and which to ignore during reading, which allows them to adjust the reading experience to their needs and potentially improve comprehension, to a greater extent than when reading non-navigable documents (Fesel, Segers, Clariana, & Verhoeven, 2015). For successful comprehension to occur, however, readers need to navigate between conceptually related units of information and simultaneously pay attention to those units in order to integrate them (van den Broek & Kendeou, 2015). In contrast, if readers navigate documents in an incoherent sequence (Salmerón, Cañas, Kintsch, & Fajardo, 2005) or overuse a quick scanning of the documents (Salmerón, Naumann, García, & Fajardo, 2017), comprehension difficulties may occur. To prevent such difficulties, hypertexts typically include overviews, that is, navigable graphical representations that display the structure of the hypertext. Such overviews can scaffold comprehension by facilitating readers' organization of their mental hypertext representations (Amadieu & Salmerón, 2014), especially if readers pay close attention to overviews at the beginning of reading sessions (Salmerón, Baccino, Cañas, Madrid, & Fajardo, 2009; Salmerón & García, 2011).

Reading Non-traditional Texts in Digital Contexts

Much reading on the Internet takes the form of social activity that mimics face-to-face interaction. In Web 2.0, authors tend to adopt a style closer to oral than written language (Warschauer & Grimes, 2007). Readers, for their part, are expected to participate in "dialogues" by sharing (at least some of) what they read or comment on the writings of others. These features of non-traditional texts may have consequences for digital reading that we address in the following sub-sections.

Language in Non-traditional Texts

Web blogs and forums are major digital spaces for social interactions in Web 2.0. In such spaces, people typically share information and provide comments. In the context of schooling, blogs and forums might be seen as empowering students in the sense of giving them independent access to academic content. Popular examples are scientific blogs, which often present complex scientific content from the school curriculum in simplified ways. Even when such blogs contain high-quality content, they may come with certain costs, however. This is because blogs tend to use less academic language, with most sentences starting with pronouns, verbs referring to actions rather than relations, and long sentences sequencing rather than embedding information (Snow, 2010). In this way, extensive blog use may limit students' exposure to helpful models of academic language, which is essential to comprehending academic texts and the phenomena under study (Snow, 2010).

The same concern applies to web forums, where any user can post questions and receive answers and recommendations from other users. Such forums are used for a variety of purposes, asking for advice on class assignments as well as personal problems (Shah & Kitzie, 2012). However, an additional concern about web forums is that comments vary greatly in terms of authors' competence and the quality of the information they provide. On the positive side, recent research has indicated that students, from early elementary school onward, are rather unwilling to accept information provided by non-expert authors in web forums, at least when expert sources also participate in the discussions (Salmerón et al., 2016; Winter & Krämer, 2012). More problematic, however, is the argumentative style of many forum comments. Academic texts typically present reasons and evidence to support claims and dismiss purely personal views as unreliable. In contrast, authors in web forums often provide personal anecdotal experiences in support of their claims (Betsch, Ulshöfer, Renkewitz, & Betsch, 2011; Warschauer & Grimes, 2007). This argumentative style seems particularly appealing to younger students. For example, Salmerón et al. (2016) found that 5th- and 6th-graders were more likely to recommend expert messages referring to personal experiences than expert messages referring to other information resources (e.g., a hospital web page) in support of author claims. The same study showed that even 8th- and 9th-graders recommended messages referring to personal experiences to the same extent as messages referring to other information sources. In sum, despite the new opportunities they represent, encouraging the use of blogs and forums in order to increase students' engagement with curricular content may require that teachers provide additional instruction targeting academic vocabulary and the rhetoric of academic language and argumentation (Snow, 2010).

Social Interaction in Reading Non-traditional Texts

Somewhat ironically, engaging in different forms of social interaction during reading may sometimes result in communication problems. We discuss such effects in relation to two typical online social contexts: micro-blogging (e.g., Twitter) and news comments. On micro-blogging sites, users share brief comments, which can be grouped by topic by means of hashtags. Readers decide whether or not they will repost a comment to share it with their connections. One might argue that such decision-making regarding reposting is likely to engage readers in deeper processing of messages, which, in turn, will boost comprehension. Alternatively, this decision-making process might come with a cognitive cost that is detrimental to comprehension. Recently, Jiang, Hou, and Wang (2016) tried to clarify this issue by having two groups of undergraduate students read a series of messages dealing with controversial topics on a micro-blogging site. In one group, participants could repost any messages they wanted, whereas in the other group, participants just read the messages with no social actions allowed. Results showed that participants in the "reposting group" reported a higher cognitive load during reading and obtained lower scores on a comprehension test, particularly with respect to the messages they actually reposted. Sparrow, Liu, and Wegner (2011) found that users who expected to have future access to information (e.g., because they thought the information was stored in a computer) had poorer recall for that information than for information that could not be stored. One possibility is that the social act of sharing induces a perception of "storage" because readers expect connected users to respond to the shared information, with this resulting in a more shallow encoding of the information.

Another social context relevant to the reading of non-traditional texts involves online news. In this scenario, readers can comment on particular pieces of news and potentially use such comments to expand the information provided in the news in order to form an educated opinion on the issues in question. In a large scale study, including a sample representative of the U.S. population, Anderson, Brossard, Scheufele, Xenos, and Ladwig (2014) presented participants with an online newspaper article on the pros and cons of nanotechnology, which was followed by either civil (polite) or uncivil (insulting) comments. In Western media, uncivil online comments are quite frequent (Coe, Kenski, & Rains, 2014). Anderson et al. (2014) found that uncivil comments led to more polarized attitudes among participants. Thus, in a non-traditional reading scenario involving intense social discussion, readers may disregard balanced views presented in original articles and instead move closer towards extreme views voiced by uncivil agents in online comments.

Conclusions, Implications, and Future Directions

The theoretical and empirical work discussed in this chapter highlights the relevance and importance of focusing on multiple and non-traditional texts within reading research. Thus, our discussion of several viable theoretical frameworks as well as related empirical evidence, indicates that multiple and non-traditional texts, while offering many new opportunities in terms of engagement, integrated understanding, and social interaction, also pose a range of new challenges compared to the reading of single traditional texts. Current conceptualizations address the increased complexity involved in dealing with such texts, most notably with respect to searching for information, attending to sources, evaluating the relevance and credibility of information, and integrating information across texts. Accordingly, empirical work confirms that effective and efficient processing and comprehension of multiple and non-traditional texts demand much of readers regardless of age, with this burgeoning research base indicating that a range of individual and contextual factors, as well as their interaction, affect how well readers are able to reap the potential benefits of the new literacy landscape.

Despite the remarkable progress that has been made in this area of reading research in this century, however, there is much to be explicated and investigated regarding the reading of multiple and non-traditional texts. In terms of theory, there is a clear need to expand well-established conceptualizations of the reading process and reading comprehension, rooted in the single-text paradigm (McNamara & Magliano, 2009), to encompass the reading of multiple and non-traditional texts. Thus, although several frameworks relevant to the reading of multiple and non-traditional texts already exist (Britt et al., 2013; Goldman et al., 2016; Leu et al., 2013; Lucassen et al., 2013; Rouet & Britt, 2011), those frameworks may only deal with some aspects of these forms of reading or lack the explanatory power and specificity necessary to derive specific, testable hypotheses from them. Attempts to forge a more coherent theory from the promising, albeit somewhat rudimentary, frameworks that currently exist, is thus an important agenda for future reading research. Of note is that such a theory also needs to build on and incorporate basic insights gained from research on single-text reading. Moreover, further theoretical clarification and refinement need to proceed in parallel with empirical work aiming to confirm (or disconfirm) specific relationships and effects initially postulated. Presumably, intervention work will be an important element of these efforts.

In addition to its implications for (re-)conceptualizing reading within reading research, a shift of emphasis towards multiple and non-traditional texts also has instructional implications. While school-based intervention work targeting multiple-text processing and comprehension has produced promising results (for review, see Bråten & Braasch, 2017; Bråten et al., 2018), there is a need for much more experimental work that meets "best evidence" criteria (Slavin, 1986) and, thus, allows for causal inferences. And while many students use a lot of time engaging with non-traditional texts in digital contexts outside school (Naumann, 2015), challenges involved in the processing and interpretation of such texts are not systematically addressed within reading instruction in school, if attended to at all. This gap between reading instruction in school and students' reading out of school may have serious consequences because students are not really trained to become competent readers in the online social contexts where they do much, if not most, of their reading, with research-based knowledge of whether or how students transfer what they learn in schooled reading contexts to unschooled contexts essentially lacking. Recent research has suggested, however, that time spent on online reading involving social interactions may be negatively related to students' print reading skills (Duncan, McGeown, Griffiths, Stothard, & Dobai, 2015; Naumann, 2015).

Take, for example, the crucial 21st century literacy skills of sourcing and critical evaluation of knowledge claims by considering the reasons and evidence presented in support of those claims (Alexander & the Disciplined Reading and Learning Laboratory, 2012; Bråten & Braasch, 2017). To the extent that such competencies are taught in school, for example, within disciplinary literacy practices in history and science (Britt, Richter, & Rouet, 2014; Goldman et al., 2016), it is an open question whether this will have any consequences for how students engage and cope with multiple and non-traditional texts out of school. The risk is, therefore, that students, unaffected by the school's efforts to teach them such critical reading skills, will disregard essential features of source credibility (i.e., expertise and trustworthiness) and rely on claims justified by personal opinions and experiences rather than reasons and evidence when reading in online social contexts out of school. Moreover, such "uncritical habits of mind" may continue into adult life, potentially influencing not only individual attitude formation, knowledge generation, and action tendencies, but also democratic discourse at the level of society. The most pertinent issue, then, is how the school's reading instruction can be brought to life in the sense of addressing and targeting students' real life reading of multiple and non-traditional texts in ways that matter for their development as critical readers and learners both in and out of school. Importantly, this seems to require that students' reading of non-traditional texts in digital contexts, hitherto representing an essentially out-of-school activity, is no longer proceeding parallel to and largely unaffected by instructional efforts to promote reading skills but, rather, given due attention within the school's reading instruction. It goes without saying that designing and evaluating the effects of instructional efforts to address this issue are a formidable challenge to future reading researchers.

In addition to the broad implications for theory and instruction discussed above, and the calls for further theoretical and empirical work accompanying those implications, several more specific issues are in need of future research. These include (but are not limited to) interactions among individual and contextual factors in the processing and comprehension of not only multiple but also non-traditional texts, effects of print versus digital reading on self-regulation and comprehension, and effects of the social process of sharing textual information on depth of processing and comprehension performance. The exponential increase in the availability and accessibility of multiple and non-traditional texts on almost any topic has changed the landscape of reading in the last decades. Hopefully, this chapter will contribute to bringing the reading of multiple and non-traditional texts to the forefront of reading research as well.

References

Ackerman, R., & Goldsmith, M. (2011). Metacognitive regulation of text learning: On screen versus on paper. *Journal of Experimental Psychology: Applied, 17*, 18–32.

Ackerman, R., & Lauterman, T. (2012). Taking reading comprehension exams on screen or on paper? A metacognitive analysis of learning texts under time pressure. *Computers in Human Behavior, 28*, 1816–1828.

Afflerbach, P., Pearson, P. D., & Paris, S. G. (2008). Clarifying differences between reading skills and reading strategies. *The Reading Teacher, 61*, 364–373.

Alexander, P. A., & the Disciplined Reading and Learning Research Laboratory. (2012). Reading into the future: Competence for the 21st century. *Educational Psychologist, 47*, 259–280.

Amadieu, F., & Salmerón, L. (2014). Concept maps for comprehension and navigation of hypertexts. In R. Hanewald & D. Ifenthaler (Eds.), *Digital knowledge maps in education* (pp. 41–59). New York, NY: Springer.

Anderson, A. A., Brossard, D., Scheufele, D. A., Xenos, M. A., & Ladwig, P. (2014). The "Nasty effect:" Online incivility and risk perceptions of emerging technologies. *Journal of Computer-Mediated Communication, 19*, 373–387.

Anmarkrud, Ø., Bråten, I., & Strømsø, H. I. (2014). Multiple-documents literacy: Strategic processing, source awareness, and argumentation when reading multiple conflicting documents. *Learning and Individual Differences, 30*, 64–76.

Baron, N. S. (2015). *Words onscreen: The fate of reading in a digital world*. New York, NY: Oxford University Press.

Barzilai, S., & Eseth-Alkalai, Y. (2015). The role of epistemic perspectives in comprehension of multiple author viewpoints. *Learning and Instruction, 36*, 86–103.

Barzilai, S., & Ka'adan, I. (2017). Learning to integrate divergent information sources: The interplay of epistemic cognition and epistemic metacognition. *Metacognition and Learning, 12*, 192–232.

Barzilai, S., Tzadok, E., & Eshet-Alkalai, Y. (2015). Sourcing while reading divergent expert accounts: Pathways from views of knowing to written argumentation. *Instructional Science, 43*, 737–766.

Barzilai, S., & Zohar, A. (2012). Epistemic thinking in action: Evaluating and integrating online sources. *Cognition and Instruction, 30*, 39–85.

Beker, K., Jolles, D., Lorch, R. F., & van den Broek, P. (2016). Learning from texts: Activation of information from previous texts during reading. *Reading and Writing, 29*, 1161–1178.

Benedetto, S., Drai-Zerbib, V., Pedrotti, M., Tissier, G., & Baccino, T. (2013). E-readers and visual fatigue. *PLoS ONE, 8*(12), e83676.

Betsch, C., Ulshöfer, C., Renkewitz, F., & Betsch, T. (2011). The influence of narrative vs. statistical information on perceiving vaccination risks. *Medical Decision Making, 31*, 742–753.

Blaum, D., Griffin, T. D., Wiley, J., & Britt, M. A. (2017). Thinking about global warming: Effect of policy-related documents and prompts on learning about causes of climate change. *Discourse Processes, 54*, 303–316.

Braasch, J. L. G., & Bråten, I. (2017). The Discrepancy-Induced Source Comprehension (D-ISC) model: Basic assumptions and preliminary evidence. *Educational Psychologist, 52*, 167–181.

Braasch, J. L. G., Bråten, I., Strømsø, H. I., Anmarkrud, Ø., & Ferguson, L. E. (2013). Promoting secondary school students' evaluation of source features of multiple documents. *Contemporary Educational Psychology, 38*, 180–195.

Braasch, J. L. G., Rouet, J. F., Vibert, N., & Britt, M. A. (2012). Readers' use of source information in text comprehension. *Memory & Cognition, 40*, 450–465.

Bråten, I., Anmarkrud, Ø., Brandmo, C., & Strømsø, H. I. (2014). Developing and testing a model of direct and indirect relationships between individual differences, processing, and multiple-text comprehension. *Learning and Instruction, 30*, 9–24.

Bråten, I., & Braasch, J. L. G. (2017). Key issues in research on students' critical reading and learning in the 21st century information society. In C. Ng & B. Bartlett (Eds.), *Improving reading and reading engagement in the 21st century: International research and innovations* (pp. 77–98). Singapore: Springer.

Bråten, I., Braasch, J. L. G., Strømsø, H. I., & Ferguson, L. E. (2015). Establishing trustworthiness when students read multiple documents containing conflicting scientific evidence. *Reading Psychology, 36*, 315–349.

Bråten, I., Britt, M. A., Strømsø, H. I., & Rouet, J. F. (2011). The role of epistemic beliefs in the comprehension of multiple expository texts: Toward an integrated model. *Educational Psychologist, 46*, 48–70.

Bråten, I., Ferguson, L. E., Anmarkrud, Ø., & Strømsø, H. I. (2013). Prediction of learning and comprehension when adolescents read multiple texts: The roles of word-level processing, strategic approach, and reading motivation. *Reading and Writing, 26*, 321–348.

Bråten, I., Ferguson, L. E., Strømsø, H. I., & Anmarkrud, Ø. (2013). Justification beliefs and multiple-documents comprehension. *European Journal of Psychology of Education, 28*, 879–902.

Bråten, I., Ferguson, L. E., Strømsø, H. I., & Anmarkrud, Ø. (2014). Students working with multiple conflicting documents on a scientific issue: Relations between epistemic cognition while reading and sourcing and argumentation in essays. *British Journal of Educational Psychology, 84*, 58–85.

Bråten, I., Gil, L., & Strømsø, H. I. (2011). The role of different task instructions and reader characteristics when learning from multiple expository texts. In M. T. McCrudden, J. P. Magliano, & G. Schraw (Eds.), *Text relevance and learning from text* (pp. 95–122). Greenwich, CT: Information Age.

Bråten, I., Stadtler, M., & Salmerón, L. (2018). The role of sourcing in discourse comprehension. In M. F. Schober, D. N Rapp, & M. A. Britt (Eds.), *Handbook of discourse processes* (2nd. ed., pp. 141–166). New York, NY: Routledge.

Bråten, I., & Strømsø, H. I. (2010a). Effects of task instruction and personal epistemology on the understanding of multiple texts about climate change. *Discourse Processes, 47*, 1–31.

Bråten, I., & Strømsø, H. I. (2010b). When law students read multiple documents about global warming: Examining the role of topic-specific beliefs about the nature of knowledge and knowing. *Instructional Science, 38*, 635–657.

Bråten, I., & Strømsø, H. I. (2011). Measuring strategic processing when students read multiple texts. *Metacognition and Learning, 6*, 111–130.

Bråten, I., Strømsø, H. I., & Britt, M. A. (2009). Trust matters: Examining the role of source evaluation in students' construction of meaning within and across multiple texts. *Reading Research Quarterly, 44*, 6–28.

Bråten, I., Strømsø, H. I., & Ferguson, L. E. (2016). The role of epistemic beliefs in the comprehension of single and multiple texts. In P. Afflerbach (Ed.), *Handbook of individual differences in reading: Reader, text, and context* (pp. 67–79). New York, NY: Routledge.

Bråten, I., Strømsø, H. I., & Samuelstuen, M. S. (2008). Are sophisticated students always better? The role of topic-specific personal epistemology in the understanding of multiple expository texts. *Contemporary Educational Psychology, 33*, 814–840.

Britt, M. A., & Gabrys, G. L. (2000). Teaching advanced literacy skills for the World Wide Web. In C. R. Wolfe (Ed.), *Learning and teaching on the World Wide Web* (pp. 73–90). San Diego, CA: Academic Press.

Britt, M. A., Perfetti, C. A., Sandak, R., & Rouet, J. F. (1999). Content integration and source separation in learning from multiple texts. In S. R. Goldman, A. C. Graesser, & P. van den Broek (Eds.), *Narrative, comprehension, causality, and coherence: Essays in honor of Tom Trabasso* (pp. 209–233). Mahwah, NJ: Erlbaum.

Britt, M. A., Richter, T., & Rouet, J. F. (2014). Scientific literacy: The role of goal-directed reading and evaluation in understanding scientific information. *Educational Psychologist, 49*, 104–122.

Britt, M. A., & Rouet, J. F. (2012). Learning with multiple documents: Component skills and their acquisition. In J. R. Kirby & M. J. Lawson (Eds.), *Enhancing the quality of learning: Dispositions, instruction, and learning processes* (pp. 276–314). New York, NY: Cambridge University Press.

Britt, M. A., Rouet, J. F., & Braasch, J. L. G. (2013). Documents as entities: Extending the situation model theory of comprehension. In M. A. Britt, S. R. Goldman, & J. F. Rouet (Eds.), *Reading: From words to multiple texts* (pp. 160–179). New York, NY: Routledge.

Britt, M. A., & Sommer, J. (2004). Facilitating textual integration with macro-structure focusing tasks. *Reading Psychology, 25*, 313–339.

Clark, R. E. (1983). Reconsidering research on learning from media. *Review of Educational Research, 53*, 445–459.

Coe, K., Kenski, K., & Rains, S. A. (2014). Online and uncivil? Patterns and determinants of incivility in newspaper website comments. *Journal of Communication, 64*, 658–679.

Dillon, A. (1992). Reading from paper versus screens: A critical review of the empirical literature. *Ergonomics, 35*, 1297–1326.

Duncan, L. G., McGeown, S. P., Griffiths, Y. M., Stothard, S. E., & Dobai, A. (2015). Adolescent reading skill and engagement with digital and traditional literacies as predictors of reading comprehension. *British Journal of Psychology, 107*, 209–238.

Ferguson, L. E., & Bråten, I. (2013). Student profiles of knowledge and epistemic beliefs: Changes and relations to multiple-text comprehension. *Learning and Instruction, 25*, 49–61.

Ferguson, L. E., Bråten, I., Strømsø, H. I., & Anmarkrud, Ø. (2013). Epistemic beliefs and comprehension in the context of reading multiple documents: Examining the role of conflict. *International Journal of Educational Research, 62*, 100–114.

Fesel, S. S., Segers, E., Clariana, R. B., & Verhoeven, L. (2015). Quality of children's knowledge representations in digital text comprehension: Evidence from pathfinder networks. *Computers in Human Behavior, 48*, 135–146.

Fletcher, J., & Nicholas, K. (2016). Reading for 11–13-year-old students in the digital age: New Zealand case studies. *Education, 3–13*, 1–12.

Gil, L., Bråten, I., Vidal-Abarca, E., & Strømsø, H. I. (2010a). Summary versus argument tasks when working with multiple documents: Which is better for whom? *Contemporary Educational Psychology, 35*, 157–173.

Gil, L., Bråten, I., Vidal-Abarca, E., & Strømsø, H. I. (2010b). Understanding and integrating multiple science texts: Summary tasks are sometimes better than argument tasks. *Reading Psychology, 31*, 30–68.

Goldman, S. R. (2004). Cognitive aspects of constructing meaning through and across multiple texts. In N. Shuart-Faris & D. Bloome (Eds.), *Uses of intertextuality in classroom and educational research* (pp. 317–351). Greenwich, CT: Information Age.

Goldman, S. R., Braasch, J. L. G., Wiley, J., Graesser, A. C., & Brodowinska, K. M. (2012). Comprehending and learning from Internet sources: Processing patterns of better and poorer learners. *Reading Research Quarterly, 47*, 356–381.

Goldman, S. R., Britt, M. A., Brown, W., Cribb, G., George, M., Greenleaf, C., Lee, C., Shanahan, C., & Project READI. (2016). Disciplinary literacies and learning to read for understanding: A conceptual framework for disciplinary literacy. *Educational Psychologist, 51*, 219–246.

Goldman, S. R., Ozuru, Y., Braasch, J. L. G., Manning, F. H., Lawless, K. A., Gomez, K. W., & Slanovits, M. J. (2011). Literacies for learning: A multiple source comprehension illustration. In N. L. Stein & S. W. Raudenbush (Eds.), *Developmental cognitive science goes to school* (pp. 30–44). New York, NY: Routledge.

Hagen, Å. M., Braasch, J. L. G., & Bråten, I. (2014). Relationships between spontaneous note-taking, self-reported strategies, and comprehension when reading multiple texts in different task conditions. *Journal of Research in Reading, 37*, 141–157.

Hofer, B. K., & Bendixen, L. D. (2012). Personal epistemology: Theory, research, and future directions. In K. R. Harris, S. Graham, & T. Urdan (Eds.), *APA educational psychology handbook: Vol. 1. Theories, constructs, and critical issues* (pp. 227–256). Washington, DC: American Psychological Association.

Holzinger, A., Baernthaler, M., Pammer, W., Katz, H., Bjelic-Radisic, V., & Ziefle, M. (2011). Investigating paper vs. screen in real-life hospital workflows: Performance contradicts perceived superiority of paper in the user experience. *International Journal of Human-Computer Studies, 69*, 563–570.

Jiang, T., Hou, Y., & Wang, Q. (2016). Does micro-blogging make us "shallow"? Sharing information online interferes with information comprehension. *Computers in Human Behavior, 59*, 210–214.

Jones, T., & Brown, C. (2011). Reading engagement: A comparison between E-books and traditional print books in an elementary classroom. *International Journal of Instruction, 4*, 1308–1470.

Kammerer, Y., Bråten, I., Gerjets, P., & Strømsø, H. I. (2013). The role of Internet-specific epistemic beliefs in laypersons' source evaluations and decisions during Web search on a medical issue. *Computers in Human Behavior, 29*, 1193–1203.

Kammerer, Y., & Gerjets, P. (2014). Quellenbewertungen und Quellenverweise beim Lesen und Zusammenfassen wissenschaftsbezogener Informationen aus multiplen Webseiten [Source evaluations and source references when reading and summarizing science-related information from multiple web pages]. *Unterrichtswissenschaft, 42*, 7–23.

Kammerer, Y., Kalbfell, E., & Gerjets, P. (2016). Is this information source commercially biased? How contradictions between web pages stimulate the consideration of source information. *Discourse Processes, 53*, 430–456.

Kintsch, W. (1998). *Comprehension: A paradigm for cognition*. New York, NY: Cambridge University Press.

Kinzer, C. K., & Leu, D. J. (2017). New Literacies and new literacies within changing digital environments. In M. A. Peters (Ed.), *Encyclopedia of educational philosophy and theory*. Singapore: Springer.

Kobayashi, K. (2009a). Comprehension of relations among controversial texts: Effects of external strategy use. *Instructional Science, 37*, 311–324.

Kobayashi, K. (2009b). The influence of topic knowledge, external strategy use, and college experience on students' comprehension of controversial texts. *Learning and Individual Differences, 19*, 130–134.

Kretzschmar, F., Pleimling, D., Hosemann, J., Füssel, S., Bornkessel-Schlesewsky, I., & Schlesewsky, M. (2013). Subjective impressions do not mirror online reading effort: Concurrent EEG-eyetracking evidence from the reading of books and digital media. *PloS ONE, 8*(2), e56178.

Kurata, K., Ishita, E., Miyata, Y., & Minami, Y. (2017). Print or digital? Reading behavior and preferences in Japan. *Journal of the Association for Information Science and Technology, 68*, 884–894.

Kurby, C. A., Britt, M. A., & Magliano, J. P. (2005). The role of top-down and bottom-up processes in between-text integration. *Reading Psychology, 26,* 335–362.

Lauterman, T., & Ackerman, R. (2014). Overcoming screen inferiority in learning and calibration. *Computers in Human Behavior, 35,* 455–463.

Le Bigot, L., & Rouet, J. F. (2007). The impact of presentation format, task assignment, and prior knowledge on students' comprehension of multiple online documents. *Journal of Literacy Research, 39,* 445–470.

Leu, D. J., Kinzer, C. K., Coiro, J., Castek, J., & Henry, L. A. (2013). New literacies: A dual-level theory of the changing nature of literacy, instruction, and assessment. In D. E. Alvermann, N. J. Unrau, & R. B. Ruddell (Eds.), *Theoretical models and processes of reading* (6th ed., pp. 1150–1181). Newark, DE: International Reading Association.

Leu, D. J., & Maykel, C. (2016). Thinking in new ways and in new times about reading. *Literacy Research and Instruction, 55,* 122–127.

List, A., Alexander, P. A., & Stephens, L. A. (2017). Trust but verify: Examining the association between students' sourcing behaviors and ratings of text trustworthiness. *Discourse Processes, 54,* 83–104.

Lucassen, T., Muilwijk, R., Noordzij, M. L., & Schraagen, J. M. (2013). Topic familiarity and information skills in online credibility evaluation. *Journal of the American Society for Information Science and Technology, 64,* 254–264.

Lucassen, T., & Schraagen, J. M. (2011). Factual accuracy and trust in information: The role of expertise. *Journal of the American Society for Information Science and Technology, 62,* 1232–1242.

Mangen, A. (2008). Hypertext fiction reading: Haptics and immersion. *Journal of Research in Reading, 31,* 404–419.

Mangen, A., Walgermo, B. R., & Brønnick, K. (2013). Reading linear texts on paper versus computer screen: Effects on reading comprehension. *International Journal of Educational Research, 58,* 61–68.

Margolin, S. J., Driscoll, C., Toland, M. J., & Kegler, J. L. (2013). E-readers, computer screens, or paper: Does reading comprehension change across media platforms? *Applied Cognitive Psychology, 27,* 512–519.

Mason, L., Ariasi, N., & Boldrin, A. (2011). Epistemic beliefs in action: Spontaneous reflections about knowledge and knowing during online information searching and their influence on learning. *Learning and Instruction, 21,* 137–151.

Mason, L., Boldrin, A., & Ariasi, N. (2010). Searching the Web to learn about a controversial topic: Are students epistemically active? *Instructional Science, 38,* 607–633.

Mason, L., Junyent, A. A., & Tornatora, M. C. (2014). Epistemic evaluation and comprehension of web-source information on controversial science-related topics: Effects of a short-term instructional intervention. *Computers & Education, 76,* 143–157.

Maynard, S. (2010). The impact of e-books on young children's reading habits. *Publishing Research Quarterly, 26,* 236–248.

McCrudden, M. T., & Schraw, G. (2007). Relevance and goal-focusing in text processing. *Educational Psychology Review, 19,* 113–139.

McNamara, D. S., & Magliano, J. (2009). Toward a comprehensive model of comprehension. *Psychology of Learning and Motivation, 51,* 297–384.

Moje, E. B., Overby, M., Tysvaer, N., & Morris, K. (2008). The complex world of adolescent literacy: Myths, motivations, and mysteries. *Harvard Educational Review, 78,* 107–154.

Naumann, A. B., Wechsung, I., & Krems, J. F. (2009). How to support learning from multiple hypertext sources. *Behavior Research Methods, 41,* 639–646.

Naumann, J. (2015). A model of online reading engagement: Linking engagement, navigation, and performance in digital reading. *Computers in Human Behavior, 53,* 263–277.

O'Brien, E. J., & Myers, J. L. (1999). Text comprehension: A view from the bottom up. In S. R. Goldman, A. C. Graesser, & P. van den Broek (Eds.), *Narrative, comprehension, causality, and coherence: Essays in honor of Tom Trabasso* (pp. 35–54). Mahwah, NJ: Erlbaum.

Perfetti, C. A., Rouet, J. F., & Britt, M. A. (1999). Towards a theory of documents representation. In H. van Oostendorp & S. R. Goldman (Eds.), *The construction of mental representations during reading* (pp. 99–122). Mahwah, NJ: Erlbaum.

Picton, I. (2014). *The impact of ebooks on the reading motivation and reading skills of children and young people: A rapid literature review.* London: National Literacy Trust.

Pieschl, S., Stahl, E., & Bromme, R. (2008). Epistemological beliefs and self-regulated learning with hypertext. *Metacognition and Learning, 3,* 17–37.

Rouet, J. F. (2006). *The skills of document use.* Mahwah, NJ: Erlbaum.

Rouet, J. F., & Britt, M. A. (2011). Relevance processes in multiple document comprehension. In M. T. McCrudden, J. P. Magliano, & G. Schraw (Eds.), *Text relevance and learning from text* (pp. 19–52). Greenwich, CT: Information Age.

Rouet, J. F., Britt, M. A., Mason, R. A., & Perfetti, C. A. (1996). Using multiple sources of evidence to reason about history. *Journal of Educational Psychology, 88*, 478–493.

Rouet, J. F., Le Bigot, L., de Pereyra, G., & Britt, M. A. (2016). Whose story is this? Discrepancy triggers readers' attention to source information in short narratives. *Reading and Writing, 29*, 1549–1570.

Rowlands, I., Nicholas, D., Jamali, H. R., & Huntington, P. (2007). What do faculty and students really think about e-books? *Aslib Proceedings, 59*, 489–511.

Salmerón, L., Baccino, T., Cañas, J. J., Madrid, R. I., & Fajardo, I. (2009). Do graphical overviews facilitate or hinder comprehension in hypertext? *Computers & Education, 53*, 1308–1319.

Salmerón, L., Cañas, J. J., Kintsch, W., & Fajardo, I. (2005). Reading strategies and hypertext comprehension. *Discourse Processes, 40*, 171–191.

Salmerón, L., & García, V. (2011). Reading skills and children's navigation strategies in hypertext. *Computers in Human Behavior, 27*, 1143–1151.

Salmerón, L., Gil, L., Bråten, I., & Strømsø, H. I. (2010). Comprehension effects of signalling relationships between documents in search engines. *Computers in Human Behavior, 26*, 419–426.

Salmerón, L., Macedo-Rouet, M., & Rouet, J. F. (2016). Multiple viewpoints increase students' attention to source features in social question and answer forum messages. *Journal of the Association for Information Science and Technology, 67*, 2404–2419.

Salmerón, L., Naumann, J., García, V., & Fajardo, I. (2017). Scanning and deep processing of information in hypertext: An eye-tracking and cued retrospective think-aloud study. *Journal of Computer Assisted Learning, 33*, 222–233.

Saux, G., Britt, M. A., Le Bigot, L., Vibert, N., Burin, D., & Rouet, J. F. (2017). Conflicting but close: Readers' integration of information sources as a function of their disagreement. *Memory and Cognition, 45*, 151–167.

Shah, C., & Kitzie, V. (2012). Social Q&A and virtual reference: Comparing apples and oranges with the help of experts and users. *Journal of the American Society for Information Science and Technology, 63*, 2020–2036.

Singer, L. M., & Alexander, P. A. (2017). Reading across mediums: Effects of reading digital and print texts on comprehension and calibration. *Journal of Experimental Education, 85*, 155–172.

Slavin, R. E. (1986). Best-evidence synthesis: An alternative to meta-analytic and traditional reviews. *Educational Researcher, 15*, 5–11.

Snow, C. E. (2010). Academic language and the challenge of reading for learning about science. *Science, 328*, 450–452.

Sparrow, B., Liu, J., & Wegner, D. M. (2011). Google effects on memory: Cognitive consequences of having information at our fingertips. *Science, 333*, 776–778.

Stadtler, M., Scharrer, L., Skodzik, T., & Bromme, R. (2014). Comprehending multiple documents on scientific controversies: Effects of reading goals and signaling rhetorical relationships. *Discourse Processes, 51*, 93–116.

Stahl, S. A., Hynd, C. R., Britton, B. K., McNish, M. M., & Bosquet, D. (1996). What happens when students read multiple source documents in history? *Reading Research Quarterly, 31*, 430–456.

Strømsø, H. I., & Bråten, I. (2009). Beliefs about knowledge and knowing and multiple-text comprehension among upper secondary students. *Educational Psychology, 29*, 425–445.

Strømsø, H. I., Bråten, I., & Britt, M. A. (2010). Reading multiple texts about climate change: The relationship between memory for sources and text comprehension. *Learning and Instruction, 18*, 513–527.

Strømsø, H. I., Bråten, I., Britt, M. A., & Ferguson, L. E. (2013). Spontaneous sourcing among students reading multiple documents. *Cognition and Instruction, 31*, 176–203.

Strømsø, H. I., Bråten, I., & Samuelstuen, M. S. (2003). Students' strategic use of multiple sources during expository text reading. *Cognition and Instruction, 21*, 113–147.

Strømsø, H. I., Bråten, I., & Samuelstuen, M. S. (2008). Dimensions of topic-specific epistemological beliefs as predictors of multiple text understanding. *Learning and Instruction, 18*, 513–527.

Trevors, G., Feyzi-Behnagh, R., Azevedo, R., & Bouchet, F. (2016). Self-regulated learning processes vary as a function of epistemic beliefs and contexts: Mixed method evidence from eye tracking and concurrent and retrospective reports. *Learning and Instruction, 42*, 31–46.

Tveit, Å. K., & Mangen, A. (2014). A joker in the class: Teenage readers' attitudes and preferences to reading on different devices. *Library & Information Science Research, 36*, 179–184.

van den Broek, P. (2010). Using texts in science education: Cognitive processes and knowledge representation. *Science, 328*, 453–456.

van den Broek, P., & Kendeou, P. (2015). Building coherence in web-based and other non-traditional reading environments: Cognitive opportunities and challenges. In R. J. Spiro, M. DeSchryver, M. S. Hagerman, P. M. Morsink, & P. Thompson (Eds.), *Reading at a crossroads? Disjunctures and continuities in current conceptions and practices* (pp. 104–114). New York, NY: Routledge.

VanSledright, B., & Maggioni, L. (2016). Epistemic cognition in history. In J. A. Greene, W. A. Sandoval, & I. Bråten (Eds.), *Handbook of epistemic cognition* (pp. 128–146). New York, NY: Routledge.

Warschauer, M., & Grimes, D. (2007). Audience, authorship, and artifact: The emergent semiotics of Web 2.0. *Annual Review of Applied Linguistics, 27*, 1–23.

Wiley, J., Goldman, S. R., Graesser, A. C., Sanchez, C. A., Ash, I. K., & Hemmerick, J. (2009). Source evaluation, comprehension, and learning in internet science inquiry tasks. *American Educational Research Association Journal, 46*, 1060–1106.

Wiley, J., & Voss, J. F. (1999). Constructing arguments from multiple sources: Tasks that promote understanding and not just memory for text. *Journal of Educational Psychology, 91*, 301–311.

Wineburg, S. (1991). Historical problem solving: A study of the cognitive processes used in the evaluation of documentary and pictorial evidence. *Journal of Educational Psychology, 83*, 73–87.

Winter, S., & Krämer, N. C. (2012). Selecting science information in Web 2.0: How source cues, message sidedness, and need for cognition influence users' exposure to blog posts. *Journal of Computer-Mediated Communication, 18*, 80–96.

Wolfe, M. B. W., & Goldman, S. R. (2005). Relations between adolescents' text processing and reasoning. *Cognition and Instruction, 23*, 467–502.

6

Who Reads What, in Which Formats, and Why?

Margaret Mackey

Who is reading what seems like a straightforward question. Answers, however, are surprisingly difficult to pin down, being short-term in nature, frequently provisional in their warrant, and very often contradictory.

The bound paper book is not dead yet, as we will see; the contemporary picture is complex. The codex culture was relatively easy to enumerate. Bestseller lists have their limitations (they silently elide the true bestsellers, the Bibles, cookbooks, and dictionaries, for example), but they offer something like a specific tally, with numbers attached. Circulation figures for newspapers and magazines are reassuringly concrete. But that era has vanished.

This chapter begins with the watershed summer of 2016 and uses the developments of that season to set up categories for discussing a complex and fast-moving scenario. In Part I, "What is going on?", a brief outline of that summer's developments under five headings is expanded into a broader exploration of each of these topics. Part II, "Why it matters," discusses the importance of choice and its implications for achievement. Part III, "How we assess it," looks at the difficulties of assembling and assessing evidence in the volatile conditions of contemporary literacy choices. Finally, Part IV, "How we read what we read in the 21st century," investigates the implications of our new cultural arrangements for forms of social, deep, and critical reading.

Part I: What Is Going On? Five Snapshots of a Complicated World

A brief overview of a single season, summer 2016, provides a small case study of the complexities of what people read, on what platforms, and for what purposes. It was a lively season that raised many questions about possible directions for a reading culture. I first present the highlights of that summer and then discuss subsequent trends and movements in more detail.

- The summer of 2016 was dominated by two texts, neither of them a conventional novel: the augmented reality (AR) app game, *Pokémon GO*, and the script of a stage play, *Harry Potter and the Cursed Child* (Rowling, Tiffany, & Thorne, 2016). Each of these titles, of course, is part of a much larger textual universe; and they represent a striking component of contemporary life: reading is frequently entwined with a host of related texts, and written texts form just one element of a franchise of related titles crossing media boundaries.

- The summer of 2016 represented a turning point (at least for the moment) in how we assess the impact of e-books and e-reading. A steady rise in the percentage of readers using electronic platforms was turned back in 2016; though e-reading remains important, it is no longer advancing so steadily.
- The billionth iPhone was sold in the summer of 2016. Smartphones and tablet computers represent a breakthrough in portability, being as mobile and easy to carry as a book, a fact with many disruptive consequences that are still being assessed.
- The summer of 2016 marked the 25th anniversary of the World Wide Web, which caused its own kind of reading revolution – particularly, but not exclusively, with regard to information seeking behaviours.
- The exploitation of algorithms on social media was already a concern in 2016. This last topic, of course, has only increased in significance since we now have reason to question the impact of the "harvesting" of social media data on at least two major events of 2016: the Brexit vote in the United Kingdom, and the Presidential election in the United States.

All these glimpses of a cultural scene in flux offer only snapshots of a fast-moving scenario. Looking back today, however, it seems clear that each of these five pointers represents a significant shift in reading behaviours. What can we learn from an expanded view of each topic?

- Franchises play an important role in recruiting reader interest and participation.

Two blockbusters, in different formats, dominated media news of summer 2016. *Pokémon GO* was an Augmented Reality app game, and *Harry Potter and the Cursed Child* was a print book of a playscript, featuring a new Harry Potter story by J. K. Rowling. The Harry Potter playscript sold two million copies in North America within two days of its launch (www.hollywoodreporter.com/news/harry-potter-cursed-child-script-916817). The distribution of *Pokémon GO* reached 100 million downloads worldwide in a matter of weeks (http://expandedramblings.com/index.php/pokemon-go-statistics/). Ypulse, a youth marketing research group, found that American 13–33-year-olds, in August 2016, cited *Pokémon Go* as their favourite app, beating out (in order) Snapchat, Facebook, Instagram, Spotify, YouTube, Twitter, Pinterest, Tumblr, and Facebook Messenger, to rule the Top Ten (www.ypulse.com/post/view/millennials-teens-15-favorite-apps-right-now).

A year after its release, in June 2017, *Pokémon Go* was still attracting 60 million monthly users (compared to 100 million at its peak, the previous August). Total revenues stood at $1.2 billion, with 752 million downloads (Minotti, 2017, n.p.) Similarly, the Harry Potter franchise remained dominant. *Harry Potter and the Cursed Child* was the runaway number one title of 2016, selling 4.1 million copies; for comparison, *The Girl on the Train*, the number two title for that year according to *Fortune*, sold 836,000 copies (http://fortune.com/2017/06/26/harry-potter-20th-anniversary/). In 2018, the Pottermore website reported sales of half a billion copies of Harry Potter (the seven books of the series and the three companion volumes), cumulating from the publication of the first book in 1997. Audiobook versions add to the numbers: the Pottermore news team said on February 1, 2018, that "more than 4 billion Harry Potter minutes" have been consumed in audiobook form since 2016. The books have been translated into more than 80 languages. Overall, and on average, "this means one in fifteen people in the world owns a Harry Potter book" (https://www.pottermore.com/news/500-million-harry-potter-books-have-now-been-sold-worldwide, 2018).

It is difficult to think of two larger text universes than *Pokémon* and *Harry Potter*. They represent many different kinds of reading experiences – the taxonomic precision of the Pokémon collector's guidebook or the rules for the games is a sharp contrast to the multi-volume expansiveness of Rowling's narrative fiction, which was reshaped further for movies and videogames. Entering these worlds through words is only one part of the experience, and readers who engage with them do not feel that this reading is a stand-alone encounter. Reading as only one fraction of a broader story experience is now a commonplace occurrence of our culture.

- Any account of book reading habits and access now must include information about format as well as content – and venue also matters.

In the early part of the decade, e-reading increased from 17% of American adults reporting they had read an e-book in 2011 all the way up to 28% in 2016, according to findings from the Pew Research Center (Perrin, 2016). But 2016 seems to represent the peak for e-reading, at least for the moment. A January 2018 survey found a dip to 26%. Meanwhile, the slippage of those reporting reading a paper book (from 71% in 2011 to as low as 63% in 2015) began to level out in 2016, and by 2018 had climbed back to 67%. But these two categories do not exhaust the possibilities; an increasing number of American adults listen to audiobooks. The percentage rises from 11% in 2011 to 18% in 2018 – nearly one in five (Perrin, 2018). Altogether 74% of Americans have read a book in any format over the past twelve months prior to January 2018 (Perrin, 2018).

Access to reading material is not a politically neutral issue. The publishing industry in English-speaking countries is still very white, both in terms of personnel and also in terms of product. "We Need Diverse Books" is a campaign that aims to broaden the range and appeal of what is made available to young people (https://diversebooks.org); one point that seems very clear is that readers cannot acquire what does not exist. At a different level of access, the threat to public libraries in the United Kingdom, for example, where many libraries are shutting to save taxpayer's money, or being turned over to volunteers for the same reason, has raised widespread alarm that is not just confined to that country. For a quick overview of the situation, a newspaper article by the chair of The Library Campaign sums up some of the chaos that currently swamps library planning in the U.K. (Swaffield, 2017). School libraries are also part of an ongoing political argument. Again in the U.K., a new three-year campaign hopes to make the provision of a school library a statutory requirement (Allen-Kinross, 2018); but this dispute is not just a British one. The issue of bookstores in many different countries is also a complicated one, featuring an uneven playing field on which independent bookstores, big box corporate chains, and the online behemoth of Amazon, all compete for the attention of book buyers; Nobel (2017) offers a brief history of some of this battle in the United States.

- Smartphones and tablet computers represent a disruptive force.

The textual world of the digital, with all its interactive and multimodal potential, is now as mobile and portable as a book. In July 2016, Apple announced the sale of its billionth iPhone, since the initial launch of 2007 (www.statista.com/chart/5390/cumulative-iphone-sales/). The iPad was also astonishingly successful, selling 308 million between its launch in April 2010 and March 2016 (http://ipod.about.com/od/ipadmodelsandterms/f/ipad-sales-to-date.htm). The sales numbers for Apple's competitors must also be factored in, and the overall totals mark a key change in reading access.

Mobile phones are increasingly ubiquitous, and not just in the developed West. Two-thirds of the 7.6 billion people in the world now have a mobile phone, and more than half of the handsets in use today are smartphones (Kemp, 2018, n.p.). Young people are particularly apt to use them on an ongoing basis, as eMarketer reported in late 2017:

According to the survey, which polled 2,000 US internet users ages 18 to 75, most people check their device approximately 47 times per day. And younger users? Well, they tend to check it with a significantly higher frequency – roughly 86 times a day. That's an increase from the 82 times per day reported in 2016.

(https://www.emarketer.com/Article/Obsessed-Much-Mobile-Addiction-Real/101November 16, 6759, 2017)

The rise of smartphones enables a variety of textual activities. Ypulse surveyed 1000 13–33-year-old Americans, 80% of whom owned a smartphone, and reported in 2016 that their daily activities include messaging first and foremost, followed by social networking (www.ypulse.com/post/view/what-millennials-teens-are-doing-on-their-smartphones-every-single-day1).

These young people are reading across a variety of modalities as part of their regular daily activities, and frequently encountering what this report calls "snackable content" (n.p.).

But even as access to the Internet expands exponentially, not all reading comes in "snack" size. Book reading continues to be important, though to different degrees in different countries, and mobile phones are the portal to long-form reading in many places. A UNESCO report comments on this trend:

> Why mobile phones? Because people have them. … Collectively, mobile devices are the most ubiquitous information and communication technology (ICT) in history. More to the point, they are plentiful in places where books are scarce.
>
> *(UNESCO, 2014, 16)*

The UNESCO report, of course, is considering the advantages of mobile reading in situations where access to paper reading is very limited. Merga and Roni (2017) point out that we need to know much more about the advantages and drawbacks of e-reading in comparison to paper reading, and suggest that the virtues of the electronic space are not quite so clear-cut in circumstances where more choice is possible. Their survey of nearly a thousand young Australians (in Year 4 and Year 6) indicates that "access to eReading devices does not appear to increase reading frequency and in the case of mobile phone access, may in fact be associated with infrequency" (195). They suggest that schools and libraries should establish a clearer understanding of child preferences before making substantial conversions away from paper and towards digital books.

- The World Wide Web turned 25 in the summer of 2016.

A report in early 2018 reveals that more than 4 billion people around the world are using the Internet:

> Well over half of the world's population is now online, with the latest data showing that nearly *a quarter of a billion* new users came online for the first time in 2017. Africa has seen the fastest growth rates, with the number of internet users across the continent increasing by more than 20% year-on-year.
>
> *(Kemp, 2018, n.p.)*

These rapid increases in access are not neutral, however; in mid-2018, Sambuli reported that the African digital divide is gender-based: "Just 22% of Africa's citizens are online and the continent has the widest gender gap in connectivity" (n.p.).

How people make use of their online access is perhaps a more complex question. In September 2016, Google introduced Penguin 4.0, a new version of its algorithm for filtering search results (https://webmasters.googleblog.com/2016/09/penguin-is-now-part-of-our-core.html). That year, a British survey by Ofcom (2016), of adults' media use and attitudes, established that 62% of users thought that a Google search would return some reliable websites and some that were not trustworthy. 18% (nearly one in five) thought that if the search engine returned a result, the listed websites would offer accurate and unbiased information. Respondents were shown a screenshot of results of a Google search for "walking boots." The first three results were "distinguished by an orange box with the word 'Ad' written on it" (150). They were prompted to comment on whether these first three results were advertisements/sponsored links, or were the best/most relevant results, or were the most popular results. 60% correctly identified the entries as advertisements; 23% thought they represented the best or most relevant results, and 20% considered them to be the most popular. Clearly there is room for improved information literacy in such a scenario.

But children do not turn first to Google, according to David Kleeman, who is quoted in Howard's (2016) analysis of children's media preferences:

> today's children use YouTube as Google because when they're curious about something, they don't want text: they want images, sound, and/or video … YouTube is one of the most influential factors on children, second only to their friends.
>
> *(2016, n.p.)*

Readily available access to information that does not require reading marks a significant point of change in children's textual experience.

- The exploitation of algorithms on social media was already a concern in 2016.

Herrman (2016) and Tynan (2016) separately describe organizations explicitly designing political content in order to exploit Facebook's algorithms for news story promotion. Herrman describes the impact of this material as "gigantic," with cumulative audiences of tens of millions of people. He calls these specialist sites "perhaps, the purest expression of Facebook's design and of the incentives coded into its algorithm – a system that has already reshaped the web and has now inherited, for better or for worse, a great deal of America's political discourse" (n.p.).

These 2016 commentaries were prescient of scandal to come. The 2018 public perspective on Facebook's algorithms is more broadly distrustful, and it remains to be seen if the company can recover from revelations that the data of 87 million Facebook users were improperly "harvested" and exploited by the British consulting company Cambridge Analytica, with effects on assorted elections that are yet to be fully determined.

Part II: Why It Matters: The Role of Reading Choice

What people choose to read is a vitally important element of the reading experience. Choice of reading materials links to reading pleasure, and studies from many countries attest that reading pleasure correlates with reading achievement (Cullinan, 2000; Education Standards Research Team, 2012; Meiers, 2004; Sullivan & Brown, 2015).

Perhaps the most substantial international figures on both young people's achievements and their attitudes to reading come from PISA, the Programme for International Student Assessment, organized by the Organization for Economic Co-operation and Development (OECD). PISA conducts large-scale international assessments of 15-year-olds around the globe and issues many influential comparative tables. The most recent 2015 results (OECD, 2016) show the largest number of countries holding steady, rather than marking improvement:

> Of the 64 countries and economies with comparable data in reading performance, 20 show a positive trend in mean reading performance across the most recent PISA assessments, 31 show a stable trend, and the remaining 13 countries and economies show a deteriorating trend in average student performance.
>
> (OECD, 2016, 152)

Much national commentary focuses obsessively and unhelpfully on the "league table" elements of the PISA results, but by themselves they represent only a single snapshot. PISA investigates achievement in mathematics and science as well, and rotates a deeper look between these three subject areas. Reading was last explored in depth in 2009 (it is due for another special investigation in 2018); and these broader findings offer subtler insight into the state of reading than the comparative and competitive statistics. About two-thirds of the students reporting in 2009 say that they read for pleasure on a daily basis, but that number is unevenly distributed. "On average across OECD countries, 72% of socio-economically advantaged students… reported that they read daily for enjoyment while only 56% of disadvantaged students reported doing the same" (OECD, 2011, 2). PISA also reports that reading daily for enjoyment, had a stronger correlation with reading achievement than the amount of time students spend reading. The trend between 2000 and 2009, however, was downwards, especially among boys; PISA reported that the percentage of students reading daily for enjoyment dropped, on average, from 69% to 64%. Twenty-two countries saw the number drop, but ten reported an increase (OECD, 2011, 2–3).

Domestic access to books also connects to academic achievement; M. D. R. Evans and collaborators investigated the connection between book ownership at home and education, first in 27 countries (2010), and later in 42 countries (2014). Ownership of even a modest number of books at home correlates with more years of schooling, even after taking account of other contributing factors.

But an understanding of what people are reading is no longer simply a case of tallying decisions about book selection and ownership. The issue of who is reading what, has probably never included more diverse materials. Much academic research to date has considered the impact of books on reading success. We know less about the implications of access to other forms of text, though a suggestive study in India discovered that "time spent on the computer and internet was consistently and positively associated with academic achievement, while television viewing, regardless of content viewed, was negatively associated" (Malhi, Bharti, & Sidhu, 2016, 73). An OECD report on the PISA findings of 2015 said, "Between 2012 and 2015, the time that 15-year-olds reported spending on the Internet increased from 21 to 29 hours per week, on average across OECD countries" (2018, 2). But too much time on the Internet correlates with poorer achievement in science. Moderate Internet usage correlates with higher achievement (2018, 4–5). We simply do not yet know if and/or how the advantage of access to books translates to access to interactive screens.

UNESCO is confident that mobile screen reading represents a breakthrough in the pursuit of global literacy:

> Among other conclusions, UNESCO has learned that people read more when they read on mobile devices, that they enjoy reading more, and that people commonly read books and stories to children from mobile devices. The study shows that mobile reading represents a promising, if still underutilized, pathway to text. It is not hyperbole to suggest that if every person on the planet understood that his or her mobile phone could be transformed – easily and cheaply – into a library brimming with books, access to text would cease to be such a daunting hurdle to literacy.
>
> (UNESCO, 2014, 17)

Reading on a mobile phone may link more easily to other media forms such as sound and moving images. Of course, reading has never been purely verbal. Design and layout have always contributed to meaning, and context has always framed interpretation. Today, however, words on a page or screen may be part of a much more multimodal array:

> The increasingly multimodal ecosystem through which we filter news, social networks, and both visual and textual entertainment makes *reading* a much slipperier term than ever before. … What is a text, and how do you read it? are two questions that are increasingly in flux today.
>
> *(Garcia, 2016, 95)*

Some people's reading is closely implicated with other activities. Much videogame-playing, for example, calls for a great deal of conventional reading and writing (Steinkuehler, 2007). Gamers also produce reading material for each other; for example, the knowledge production by players for players in relation to a massive online game such as *World of Warcraft* is remarkable. In early 2018, the WOWWiki boasted 298,252 pages of content much of it created by players (http://wowwiki.wikia.com/wiki/Portal:Main); and a breakaway site, WOWpedia, is also enormous, though no figures were readily available (https://wow.gamepedia.com/Portal:Main). For younger readers, *Minecraft* offers a similar gateway to numerous reading activities (Italie, 2014; Maughan, 2015; Revoir, 2016). Game-related reading (and writing) may occur within the diegetic story world or in a larger zone of strategic decision-making. In related ways, fan collectives turn an original reading experience into a panoply of further reading, writing, and responding.

With such a range of options, young people are almost certainly learning to take multimodality very much for granted as part of their reading lives. There is much we need to learn about how families select the materials they load onto their screens. A child who regularly visits a library full of paper books will choose from a huge array of possibilities; in contrast, even to find out that a particular electronic text exists may involve complex browsing and searching skills (Vaala, Ly, & Levine, 2015). The alternative may be simply to download an uncritical sample of whatever turns up at the top of the charts in the app store.

But choice remains important. Ming Ming Chiu and Catherine McBride-Chang (2006) demonstrate the powerful impact of that autonomous power to select. They conducted an analysis of students in 43 countries, basing their work on the 2002 instantiation of the PISA findings (338). Their massive data set came from a pool of 193,841 15-year-old students. Their main points are as follows:

> In every country, girls outscored boys in reading. The explanatory model further showed that gender, log GDP per capita [a statistical refinement of growth measurement], family SES [socio-economic status], schoolmates' SES, number of books at home, and reading enjoyment were all significantly associated with reading score. *Only reading enjoyment mediated the gender effect.*
>
> *(2006, 343, emphasis added)*

Reading enjoyment relates directly to *what* is being read, and is clearly a potent factor, across very large numbers of teens in a wide range of countries. Other age ranges also benefit from the ability to choose; adults often take it for granted, but the role of autonomous selection in reading pleasure is significant on many levels. To understand how contemporary reading is developing, therefore, it is important to establish ways of finding valid and timely information about what people are choosing to read.

Part III: How We Assess It: Defining Evidence in a Period of Change

This brief account has offered a glimpse of the complexity of our contemporary reading world. Within the parentheses of the citations listed above lies another complex world of researchers from a huge variety of institutional backgrounds, motivated by different goals, and drawing on an assortment of methodologies that may privilege currency in the cause of seizing a marketing opportunity, or focus on mining the big data of international assessment exercises, or draw on findings as a springboard for social action. A major challenge of working with such a multiplicity of sources is that just keeping up is a strenuous exercise. Finding ways to evaluate the trustworthiness of evidence from so many different informants is an equally enormous job.

There are, of course, many schools of thought on how to assess evidence, particularly in a field such as reading, where basing practice on evidence is held in great esteem. There is no room in this chapter to explore the many arguments in this arena. Instead, I turn to a small and simplified convenience sample, in order to address some of the issues in concrete, rather than abstract terms. My sample of two comprises, firstly, a long-term survey of reading behaviours, conducted by the National Endowment for the Arts in the United States, and, secondly, a very short-term and ephemeral global survey of app readership, conducted by a market research group called App Annie.

The International Literacy Association (now ILA; previously the International Reading Association – IRA) has produced a checklist listing five qualities that accrue to make evidence trustworthy; it must be objective, valid, reliable, systematic, and refereed. For the purposes of this chapter, I will focus on validity and reliability, because they raise the most interesting challenges for the kinds of research represented in this chapter. The IRA definition of "valid" is that the data "adequately represent the tasks that children need to accomplish to be successful readers" (International Reading Association, 2002, n.p.); the Association for Qualitative Research suggests that "validity … refers to how well a scientific test or piece of research actually measures what it sets out to, or how well it reflects the reality it claims to represent" (www.aqr.org.uk/glossary/validity). The IRA says that evidence is "reliable" if "data will remain essentially unchanged if collected on a different day or by a different person" (2002, n.p.); similarly, the Association for Qualitative Research defines reliability as the "repeatability of a particular set of research findings; that is, how accurately they would be replicated in a second identical piece of research" (www.aqr.org.uk/glossary/reliability). But such desirable elements may be challenging to establish as these two case studies demonstrate; and their value is waning in the face of contemporary complexity.

Case #1: The Missing Readers in the NEA Surveys

How researchers define appropriate parameters for their research questions serves to frame the answers in constitutive and sometimes reductive ways. A classic example of how research limitations may define issues of "who is reading what" lies in reports from the American organization, the National Endowment for the Arts – NEA (2004, 2007, 2009, 2013, 2016). Employing a survey of public participation in the arts, conducted by the United States Census Bureau at periodic intervals, the NEA reports on a sample size of many thousands of individuals aged 18 and over. Each time, the survey asks respondents if, during the previous 12 months, they have read any novels, short stories, plays, or poetry in their leisure time (not for work or school). This question throws into relief the vagueness of the Pew survey (http://newsbreaks.infotoday.com/Digest/Pew-Unveils-Latest-Survey-Results-on-Americans-Reading-Habits-123778.asp), which simply tallies "books." Such a very restrictive definition of literary reading, however, is highly fiction-oriented and excludes philosophy, history, biography, science writing, political analysis, essays, and other forms of nonfiction that may possess highly literary qualities, and that certainly represent categories of serious leisure reading; sports and hobbies are similarly barred from consideration, though they may elicit very dedicated reading activities. The NEA's characterization of "literary reading" allows for "any print format, including the Internet" (2004, n.p.), but it does not consider new forms of writing that might capitalize on the interactive affordances of online reading. The Internet counts only when it serves as a delivery mechanism for novels, short stories, plays, and poems.

The NEA report proves to be as slippery as most other research on what people read. The 2004 report warns that literary reading is declining drastically. The 2009 sequel describes "a decisive and unambiguous increase among virtually every group measured in this comprehensive national survey" (2009, n.p.). By 2013, the NEA is pessimistic again. Based on a survey of 35,735 American adults, they report only 47% reading at least one work of literature, as they define it. A short-form Basic Survey in 2016, reports a further drop to 43%, the lowest number in their entire reporting cycle (Ingraham, 2016).

The NEA findings and conclusions stirred substantial public and political debate in the United States, and it may be helpful to evaluate their work in terms of the evidence they offer. These reports would pass on four of the five criteria listed by the IRA, but it can be argued that the validity is limited because of the question mark over whether the data "adequately represent the tasks" of "successful readers."

What are possible consequences of the NEA's skew towards fictional categories? High on the list of potential implications are questions concerning gender. The 2013 report does not discuss whether that bias in favour of fictional materials might affect the numbers of male readers of "literature" (37%, compared to 56.1% of women), but it is a reasonable question to ask, given that the preference of boys and men for nonfiction is a well-known phenomenon, as I now clarify in a short but important digression. Available studies tend to draw on binary definitions of gender, but a more open set of categories would probably not substantially alter the significance of the pronounced differences that are manifest in many studies, though details might be more nuanced.

Research suggests that the male preference for reading nonfiction crosses all ages. For example, Sullivan (2009) says that:

> boys often see nonfiction not as a vehicle for finding specific information but as a way to better understand the world around them, a way of acquiring the understanding of the world around them that they so desire and believe will help them to succeed. In short, they read nonfiction the way we expect children to read fiction.
>
> *(9)*

Smith and Wilhelm (2002, 2006) confirm these proclivities among older adolescent boys, and Summers' small study found the number of men preferring nonfiction to be almost double the number of women (2013, 247). Given the PISA-based findings (Chiu & McBride-Chang, 2006) that reading enjoyment ameliorates gender effects, the NEA questionnaire's slant towards fiction takes on further significance.

And yet the NEA treats its fiction bias as something neutral. It is a salutary reminder that even when research methodology is exemplary, longitudinal information is scrupulously acquired, and samples are very large, the assumptions of the framing questions can limit the results. The facts presented by the NEA are "objective" within their limitations, but they are so selective that they mislead as much as they inform.

The decision to omit those who are reading for work or school also skews the results. Stebbins, in a study of the "committed reader" (2012), discusses the significance of reading for utility, for pleasure, and for fulfillment. This range of motivations may account for some of the gap – in surveys reported in the same month, September 2016 – between the NEA findings of 43% reading a work of literature and the Pew tally of 73% of Americans reading a book in the previous year. A committed reader need not be a literary reader. Stebbins draws on insights from two disciplinary fields: library and information studies and serious leisure studies. Perhaps this background accounts for his agnosticism about content, in contrast to the NEA's strong focus on literariness.

The power of saying what gets to "count" as valid reading is a significant but often invisible force in discussions about reading at all levels, and is a factor in the fields of literary studies and education in particular. The idea that truly literate and cultured people invariably read fiction is well entrenched, in classrooms as well as in national organizations – though this emphasis is now challenged by the Common Core Curriculum in the United States. A fiction bias excludes many potential readers. A classroom emphasis on fiction also fosters the possibility that students are taught significantly less about the deep and/or critical reading of nonfiction than they need to know in order to function as contemporary citizens (Topping, Samuels, & Paul, 2008; White, 2011).

Case #2: App Annie and the Strengths and Perils of Short-Termism

As the NEA categories remind us, there is a cultural tendency to regard literature as relatively timeless. With much contemporary reading material, however, the issue of replicability of research becomes significant because of temporal limitations. The IRA definition of reliability is that data will remain unchanged if collected on a different day. In our contemporary world of shifting platforms and formats, that concept of reliability is more and more unrealistic, as my next example shows.

Patterns of contemporary reading behaviour are the subject of many different research approaches, and the motivations for such research are as varied as the methodologies. To be current in this territory is to trade in the ephemeral, and many active researchers in this area have short-term commercial aims in mind. For example, a business organization called App Annie surveys apps downloaded in April 2016 by active iPhone users and produces a top-ten list that features three different #1 titles in three different countries: the United States (Facebook), Japan (LINE), and the United Kingdom (WhatsApp Messenger) (App Annie, 2016). The same survey measures the top ten apps by growth in usage penetration between April 2015 and April 2016; again the #1 title is different in each of these countries, and also different from the three titles featuring in the first table (in the U.S., Facebook Messenger; in Japan, Yahoo! Japan Weather; and in the U.K., TripAdvisor).

With the timelines for app readership so short, information about usage that is up-to-date is also temporary. Any study that presents such data via peer review is likely to be obsolete before it even gets to press. Yet, any account of what people read that deals only with "permanent" content that can be relied on to stay constant throughout the publication time lag of refereed research simply does not offer a true picture of our contemporary situation, just as overly conservative definitions of literary reading restrict the broad utility of the NEA surveys.

In the current policy climate, particularly in the U.S. and the U.K., the "replicability" of research findings is important for legislators ruling on curriculum decisions. The App Annie findings indicate that many "what" questions are unlikely to be replicated even month to month. It is frequently the case that the most detailed information about shifting public reading behaviors comes from commercially motivated researchers, whose work is never refereed past the point of assessing its utility to the sponsor. With so many forms and products of current reporting to assess, it is arguable that we need some temporary and provisional standards for assessing reliability in the short-term, while we attempt to discern the larger patterns at work. For example, in the early 2010s it did seem as if e-reading was making unstoppable inroads into paper reading, but that trend has stalled; it is useful to observe this pattern, but an unavoidable and very basic conclusion is that we do not know how it will all work out.

One solution to this ongoing problem of large amounts of short-term data of differing provenance would be for like-minded researchers to establish an online clearinghouse for information about what people are currently reading, in paper, online, and app form. Background information about the *bona fides* of the different commercial organizations supplying short-term data could also be incorporated. For reasons of space in this chapter, my IRA checklist of research evaluation tools is a simplistic one, but a more complex grid of quality checks would be relatively straightforward to establish. Such efforts would be more economical and more productive if conducted on a collaborative scale.

Such a clearinghouse could also provide context for the many surveys produced by research organizations such as Pew and the National Endowment for the Arts in the United States, Ofcom and the National Literacy Trust in the United Kingdom, MediaSmarts in Canada, and many other organizations, some of which are cited in this chapter. A trusted source for keeping up to date with contemporary reading shifts and mutations would be a huge help as researchers, educators, librarians, and others, struggle to attain some perspective on the fast-moving contemporary scene.

Part IV: How We Read What We Read in the 21st Century: Situated and Dedicated Contexts

A brief consideration of *how* we read today may aid our assessment of *what* we read. The concepts of "situated" reading and "dedicated" reading offer a useful distinction. These categories are not discrete and readers regularly move back and forth between them.

Situated reading is woven into daily life in fleeting and fragmented ways. In the middle of a conversation, someone will quickly google a relevant fact. As part of a social get-together, someone will message a photo to their friends. The live action of our daily affairs is frequently punctuated with brief mediated interludes. Digital technologies introduce portable interactivity in ways that inflect much daily living.

The impact of smartphones on what and how people read is difficult to overestimate. A 2015 Pew report says that 24% of American teens are online "almost constantly," and 92% go online daily. Nearly three-quarters of American teens "have or have access to a smartphone." Only 12% of teens aged 13 to 17 have no phone of any type. Pew reports that "African-American teens are the most likely of any group of teens to have a smartphone, with 85% having access to one, compared with 71% of both white and Hispanic teens" (Lenhart, 2015, n.p.). Young people who inherit parental phones are now more likely, by the year, to acquire a second-hand smartphone.

The World Bank (2016) provides international figures that indicate that cellphone use is not confined to the affluent West, but is globally distributed in surprising ways. Results are measured in terms of active mobile cellular subscriptions per 100 people. The highest number recorded (323 per 100 people) comes from Macao SAR, in China, and Hong Kong checks in at 234. A prosperous country like Canada (a latecomer to widespread cellphone use) records a score of only 81, while Vietnam, a country often perceived as developing, registers 147. The United States number is 110 and the United Kingdom is 124 (http://data.worldbank.org/indicator/IT.CEL.SETS.P2).

The extreme mobility and flexibility of smartphones feeds into a culture of situated reading. But such fragmentation of reading time is not neutral. No sliver of time is too small to be monetized. Google defines the "micro-moment" as "anytime you turn to an Internet-enabled device to find something, learn something, watch something or purchase something" (Selligent, n.d., n.p.). A real-life moment becomes open to commercial enhancement once it is mediated, for however brief a period.

> These spontaneous task-driven engagements ... represent critical opportunities for brands and marketers alike. It is in these small, fragmented, and reflexive moments that impressions are formed and choices made. Understanding how to measure, manoeuver, and master the micro-moment is mission critical for any brand or business looking to win customers in the digital age.
>
> *(Selligent, n.d., n.p.)*

Situated literacy, with its almost seamless movement in and out of textual engagement, may thus be framed by its marketing potential; consequently, it presents an associated need for more critical perspectives about these transitory encounters. The ability to move in and out of contact with other people also represents a shift in the social framing of much reading.

In contrast, *dedicated reading* is more familiar. It involves a deliberate choice to engage with text in a more extended way. The event can feature a novel, or it may involve a complex information text. Alternatively, dedicated encounters may be multimodal – instead or as well – entailing a decision to binge-watch an entire television series on Netflix, or to commit to a protracted computer game and all its associated texts. It may involve a transmedia experience, in which a complete text is distributed across a number of platforms (Jenkins, 2007), or call for extensive movement between fictional and informational sources. Sometimes what starts out as a small example of situated literacy morphs to the status of an event, as one link leads to another, or a Twitter exchange takes on a life of its own. Sometimes a dedicated encounter is punctuated by situated exchanges of comment and/or critique.

One example of a gap between in-school and out-of-school literacies is summed up by the fact that many educational discourses privilege dedicated literacy. The distinction between the two kinds of engagement is at the heart of the ongoing dispute between two perceptions voiced by the lay public: "Kids today aren't reading" versus "Kids today read and write more than they ever did." Young people's *situated reading* is obviously more extensive than it was even a decade ago. But most of the public discussion invoking a cultural crisis in reading is focused on a perceived decline in *dedicated* reading. I hope this chapter has shown that the overall situation is more complicated than either extreme of the popular argument.

Filling Gaps and Meeting Challenges

A radical instability in the cultural landscape of texts and formats has been normalized to the point of invisibility for many people. We download upgrades, we add a new platform or app, we pay less attention to an old one, we make incremental changes, and after a while, we forget that it wasn't always like this – whatever "this" looks like at that moment.

In short, there is little point here in discussing the daily details of participation in particular forms of social media. Keith Oatley suggests a broader perspective may be more useful: "rather than thinking about implementation in paper and print as compared with electronic words on a computer screen, we should think of psychological functions" (2013, 179). To some degree, the comparison between situated and dedicated reading is a question of psychological function. Three further sub-headings may help refine our attention to major gaps in and challenges to our current understanding of contemporary reading choices.

Social Reading

The portability of reading and writing facilities now permits both activities to be slid into daily life in very small doses as part of ongoing social exchange, the epitome of situated reading. Many of the exchanges that develop through texting or Twitter or Snapchat may be described as low-level in terms of actual content, though their social value is high.

It is easy to see such situated reading as social. But dedicated reading also rides on a social network of writers, publishers, booksellers, and other readers (Nelles, 2013, 42). Digitization explicitly opens the way for "readers to participate in the debate themselves" in rather more direct ways (Hammond, 2016, 13). Digital reading may be less private, as we may see from, for example, Goodreads discussion forums, the Kindle's group-underlining feature, Genius.com's interface for crowd-sourced annotations of any text, SocialBook's platform for threaded conversations in the "margins" of digital books (see Hammond, 2016, 80). Social reading skews in favor of the public, but the whole concept of readers' rights to privacy is suddenly the focus of urgent discussion after the March 2018 revelation of the Facebook and Cambridge Analytica misuse of reader data.

Reader exchanges on the platforms listed above may indeed deepen and enrich one's individual thoughtful reading – or they may perhaps substitute for it, with people reading social commentary with more attention than they devote to the initiating text. In this case, as in so many others represented in this chapter, knowing more about *what* people are reading does not necessarily illuminate *how* their reception processes work. A sophisticated understanding of the role of social exchanges in today's reading contexts would enormously improve our ability to draw on new social tools.

Deep Reading

A singular, extended intimacy with invented characters and settings, or with prolonged analysis of a serious nonfiction topic, represents the far end of a reading spectrum. The paper book, of course, survives. It is easy to associate dedicated reading with paper, but much sustained electronic reading is also a feature of our current culture, whether on single-use e-readers, or on phones, or tablets. We need to understand more about if and/or how the simple fact of digitization affects the solitary, private experience of what Wolf and Barzillai call deep reading – "the array of sophisticated processes that propel comprehension and that include inferential and deductive reasoning, analogical skills, critical analysis, reflection, and insight" (2009, 32). We are a long way from establishing a robust answer to that question. It is possible that the NEA's category of "literature" is intended to serve as a proxy for this kind of deep reading.

We may also question whether deep reading needs be confined to print alone. New publishing options expand what was once a print space to include adaptations and reworkings in assorted media, background materials, fan contributions, and much, much more. Audiobooks may offer another form of deep experience.

Wolf, a scholar of the neuroscience of reading, expresses concern that, in response to the prevalence of situated reading in contemporary society, the great plasticity of our minds may lead us away from the contemplative achievements of deep reading towards a more fragmentary cognitive arrangement (Rosenwald, 2014; Wolf & Barzillai, 2009; Wolf & Gottwald, 2016). Wolf and her various colleagues have not addressed the issue of listening to a book, nor commented on whether a reading that crosses many media boundaries should be classified as deep or shallow. There are also many questions about whether it is possible to conduct a deep reading experience across a range of related websites. To establish a satisfactory account of the parameters of successful deep reading in current times would be to plug a crucial gap in our understanding.

Critical Reading

The fate of critical reading in a world of situated textual encounters is also not clear. Alan Luke says, "Critical literacy has an explicit aim of the critique and transformation of dominant ideologies, cultures and economies, institutions, and political systems" (2014, 22).

It seems likely that our collective failure to take situated reading seriously leads to important gaps, both in our larger understanding and in our specific capacity to consider the need for critical literacy in this arena. Much situated information comes with the stamp of personal insider authority. Are people less likely to critique (say) a political observation masquerading as factual if it comes (say) from a Facebook friend? To what extent do contemporary readers overvalue the "eyewitness" vividness of personal insights, and underestimate the need to fact-check the data we glean from our friends and acquaintances on social media? Marketers have established that a personal recommendation is the surest way to make a sale to a potential customer, and have established market relations with private individuals posting online. The need for critical scrutiny of what our friends are telling us is counter-intuitive to many readers. We need a multifaceted awareness of the shape and potential of a contemporary critical literacy.

At its self-taught and instinctual extreme, some information-gathering behavior today may be described as "feral" rather than sceptical or critical (Mackey, 2008, 5). "Snackable content" is easily swallowed whole. It is important to develop a critical stance towards our information-seeking "micro-moments" and how they may be shaped by marketing imperatives, and to reflect on the warrant of the "facts" presented on social media. Sophisticated media literacy demands attention to small moments of textual exchange as well as to larger questions.

Conclusions

Answers to the question of what people are reading (on what format) and why (and how), can only be expressed provisionally as we move through an enormous change in technological and cultural affordances, frequently framed by commercial motivations. Readers, in both situated and dedicated contexts, are dealing with new challenges in the social and critical frameworks they move through; and the shape of deep reading needs to be clarified in productive ways to take account of new text forms and networks. Information about reading choices comes and goes at a dizzying rate; establishing a central clearinghouse where data can be readily found and intelligently evaluated would make a big difference to our ability to be as nimble as we need to be.

Markers to watch in the short-term future, as seen from mid-2018, include the large-scale findings about international reading attitudes that may be uncovered by PISA's 2018 special surveys, the ripples from the Facebook scandal, the impact of the Common Core on attitudes towards nonfiction, and the rise or subsidence of e-reading. No doubt many new issues will also arise. As we take account of them, we must continue to monitor how critical, social, and deep reading play out in both situated and dedicated reading conditions, in the ever-shifting textual universes of the 21st century.

References

Allen-Kinross, P. (2018, April 27). New campaign would make school libraries a statutory requirement. *Schools Week*. Retrieved from https://schoolsweek.co.uk/new-campaign-would-make-school-libraries-a-statu tory-requirement/
App Annie. (2016). Usage is the new currency: The most used iOS apps in April 2016. Retrieved from http:// files.appannie.com.s3.amazonaws.com/reports/Usage-Is-the-New-Currency-EN.pdf?mkt_tok=eyJpIjoiWVRZ MU5qaG1NMkkyWmpNMCIsInQiOiJZaGlyUUJzOTl2XC9tU1RBSGxtUDJwN243alZmbm42bEJTbkp0e GE4N3F5WXpLN2V4NjZQN0FTenlLYzlRTUZDT1VSc3NlWXRcL3RNb2FuYUdxNnVFQTd2XC9 FUlpCXC9kOExpSm0ra0d4bzdRQnM9In0%3D
Chiu, M. M., & McBride-Chang, C. (2006). Gender, context, and reading: A comparison of students in 43 countries. *Scientific Studies of Reading*, 10(4), 331–362.
Cullinan, B. E. (2000). Independent reading and school achievement. *Research Journal of the American Association of School Librarians*, 3, 1–23.
Education Standards Research Team. (2012). Research evidence on reading for pleasure. Department for Education. Retrieved from www.gov.uk/government/uploads/system/uploads/attachment_data/file/284286/ reading_for_pleasure.pdf
Evans, M. D. R., Kelley, J., & Sikora, J. (2014). Scholarly culture and academic performance in 42 nations. *Social Forces*, 92(4), 1573–1605.
Evans, M. D. R. J., Kelley, J., Sikora, J., & Treiman, D. J. (2010). Family scholarly culture and educational success: Books and schooling in 27 nations. *Research in Social Stratification and Mobility*, 28, 171–197.

Garcia, A. (2016, July/August). Why challenging texts? Why now? *Journal of Adolescent & Adult Literacy, 60*(1), 95–98.

Hammond, A. (2016). *Literature in the digital age: An introduction*. Cambridge: Cambridge University Press.

Herrman, J. (2016, August 24). Inside Facebook's (totally insane, unintentionally gigantic, hyperpartisan) political-media nachine. *New York Times Magazine*. Retrieved from www.nytimes.com/2016/08/28/magazine/inside-facebooks-totally-insane-unintentionally-gigantic-hyperpartisan-political-media-machine.html?hp&action=click&pgtype=Homepage&clickSource=story-heading&module=first-column-region&region=top-news&WT.nav=top-news&_r=1

Howard, S. (2016, October 31). What kids want: Nielsen's children's book summit 2016. *Publishing Trends*. Retrieved from www.publishingtrends.com/2016/10/what-kids-want-nielsens-childrens-book-summit-2016/

Ingraham, C. (2016, September 7). The long, steady decline of literary reading. *The Washington Post*. Retrieved from www.washingtonpost.com/news/wonk/wp/2016/09/07/the-long-steady-decline-of-literary-reading/

International Reading Association. (2002). *What is evidence-based reading instruction?* Newark, DE: Author. Position Statement www.literacyworldwide.org/docs/default-source/where-we-stand/evidence-based-position-statement.pdf?sfvrsn=cc4ea18e_6

Italie, H. (2014, September 3). From the screen to the page: Minecraft now a publishing sensation. The Canadian Press. Retrieved from http://eds.a.ebscohost.com.login.ezproxy.library.ualberta.ca/eds/detail/detail?vid=3&sid=d381ad91-edbb-4ec5-915a-49814084a469%40sessionmgr4007&hid=4111&bdata=JnNpdGU9ZWRzLWxpdmUmc2NvcGU9c2l0ZQ%3d%3d#AN=MYO125406178814&db=p3h

Jenkins, H. (2007, March 22). Transmedia storytelling 101. *Confessions of an Aca-Fan: The Official Weblog of Henry Jenkins*. Retrieved from http://henryjenkins.org/2007/03/transmedia_storytelling_101.html

Kemp, S. (2018, January 30). Digital in 2018: World's Internet users pass the 4 billion mark. *We Are Social*. Retrieved from https://wearesocial.com/blog/2018/01/global-digital-report-2018

Lenhart, A. (2015, April 9). Teens, social media & technology overview 2015. Pew Research Center. Retrieved from www.pewinternet.org/2015/04/09/teens-social-media-technology-2015/

Luke, A. (2014). Defining critical literacy. In J. Z. Pandya & J. Avila (Eds.), *Moving critical literacies forward: A new look at praxis across contexts* (pp. 19–31). New York: Routledge.

Mackey, M. (2008). Introduction to volume III. In M. Mackey (Ed.), *Media literacies: Major themes in education* (Vol. III, pp. 1–10). London: Routledge.

Malhi, P., Bharti, B., & Sidhu, M. (2016, January-March). Use of electronic media and its relationship with academic achievement among school going adolescents. *Psychological Studies, 61*(1), 67–75.

Maughan, S. (2015, January 27). Publishers still mining sales from Minecraft titles. *Publishers Weekly*. Retrieved from www.publishersweekly.com/pw/by-topic/childrens/childrens-book-news/article/65408-publishers-still-mining-sales-from-minecraft-titles.html

Meiers, M. (2004). Reading for pleasure and literacy achievement. *Research Developments, 12*(5). Retrieved from http://research.acer.edu.au/resdev/vol12/iss12/5

Merga, M., & Roni, S. M. (2017). The influence of access to eReaders, computers and mobile phones on children's book reading frequency. *Computers & Education, 109*, 107–196.

Minotti, M. (2017, June 30). Pokémon Go passes $1.2 billion in revenue and 752 million downloads. *VentureBeat*. Retrieved from https://venturebeat.com/2017/06/30/pokemon-go-passes-1-2-billion-in-revenue-and-752-million-downloads/

National Endowment for the Arts. (2004). *Reading at risk: A survey of literary reading in America*. Retrieved from www.arts.gov/sites/default/files/ReadingAtRisk.pdf

National Endowment for the Arts. (2007). *To read or not to read: A question of national consequence*. Research Report #47. Retrieved from www.arts.gov/sites/default/files/ToRead.pdf

National Endowment for the Arts. (2009). *Reading on the rise: A new chapter in American literacy*. Retrieved from www.arts.gov/sites/default/files/ReadingonRise.pdf

National Endowment for the Arts. (2013). *How a nation engages with art: Highlights from the 2012 survey of public participation in the arts*. Research Report #57. Retrieved from www.arts.gov/sites/default/files/highlights-from-2012-sppa-revised-oct-2015.pdf

National Endowment for the Arts. (2016). Arts data profile #10 (August 2016) – Results from the annual arts basic survey (AABS). Retrieved from www.arts.gov/artistic-fields/research-analysis/arts-data-profiles/arts-data-profile-10

Nelles, D. (2013). Solitary reading in an age of compulsory sharing. In P. Socken (Ed.), *The edge of the precipice: Why read literature in the digital age?* (pp. 42–52). Montreal: McGill-Queens University Press.

Nobel, C. (2017, November 26). How independent bookstores thrived in spite of Amazon. *Quartz Media*. Retrieved from https://qz.com/1135474/how-independent-bookstores-thrived-in-spite-of-amazon/

Oatley, K. (2013). Thinking deeply in reading and writing. In P. Socken (Ed.), *The edge of the precipice: Why read literature in the digital age?* (pp. 175–191). Montreal: McGill-Queens University Press.

OECD. (2011, September 8). Do students today read for pleasure? *PISA in Focus 8*, 1–4. Retrieved from www.oecd-ilibrary.org/docserver/5k9h3621hw32-en.pdf?expires=1525585803&id=id&accname=guest&checksum=DFA3C51CF1DBC7EFE60A4BF6B94C22AB

OECD. (2016). *PISA 2015 Results (Volume I): Excellence and equity in education*. Paris: Author. doi:10.1787/9789264266490-en

OECD. (2018, April). How has Internet use changed between 2012 and 2015? *PISA in Focus #83*. Paris: Author. Retrieved from www.oecd-ilibrary.org/docserver/1e912a10-en.pdf?expires=1526312426&id=id&accname=guest&checksum=692AC884A3C8000BE12424A2C45F6B38

Ofcom. (2016, April). *Adults' media use and attitudes: Report 2016*. Retrieved from www.ofcom.org.uk/__data/assets/pdf_file/0026/80828/2016-adults-media-use-and-attitudes.pdf

Perrin, A. (2016, September 1). Book reading 2016. Pew Research Center. Retrieved from www.pewinternet.org/2016/09/01/book-reading-2016/

Perrin, A. (2018, March 8). Nearly one-in-five Americans now listen to audiobooks. Pew Research Center. Retrieved from www.pewresearch.org/fact-tank/2018/03/08/nearly-one-in-five-americans-now-listen-to-audiobooks/

Revoir, P. (2016, February 19). More than 2.5m minecraft books sold by Egmont Publishing. *TheGuardian.com*. Retrieved from www.theguardian.com/media/2016/feb/19/more-than-25m-minecraft-books-sold-by-egmont-publishing

Rosenwald, M. S. (2014, April 6). Serious reading takes a hit from online scanning and skimming, researchers say. *Washington Post*. Retrieved from www.washingtonpost.com/local/serious-reading-takes-a-hit-from-online-scanning-and-skimming-researchers-say/2014/04/06/088028d2-b5d2-11e3-b899-20667de76985_story.html

Rowling, J. K., Tiffany, J., & Thorne, J. (2016). *Harry Potter and the cursed child, parts one and two*. New York: Arthur A. Levine Books.

Sambuli, N. (2018, May 7). Africa's offline gender gap is getting repeated online. *Science and Development Network*. Retrieved from www.scidev.net/global/icts/opinion/africa-s-offline-gender-gap-is-getting-repeated-online.html

Selligent. (n.d.). *The rise of the micro-moment: How brands can benefit from understanding the impact of micro-moments on customers*. Retrieved from www.selligent.com/sites/default/files/media/wp-the-rise-of-the-micro-moment.pdf

Smith, M. W., & Wilhelm, J. D. (2002). *Reading don't fix no Chevys: Literacy in the lives of young men*. Portsmouth, NH: Heinemann.

Smith, M. W., & Wilhelm, J. D. (2006). *Going with the flow: How to engage boys (and girls) in their literacy learning*. Portsmouth, NH: Heinemann.

Stebbins, R. A. (2012). *The committed reader: Reading for utility, pleasure, and fulfillment in the twenty-first century*. Lanham, MD: Scarecrow Press.

Steinkuehler, C. (2007, September). Massively multiplayer online gaming as a constellation of literacy practices. *E-Learning and Digital Media*, *4*(3), 297–318.

Sullivan, A., & Brown, M. (2015). Reading for pleasure and progress in vocabulary and mathematics. *British Educational Research Journal*, *41*(6), 971–991.

Sullivan, M. (2009). *Serving boys through readers' advisory*. Chicago, IL: American Library Association.

Summers, K. (2013). Adult reading habits and preferences in relation to gender differences. *Reference & User Services Quarterly*, *52*(3), 243–249.

Swaffield, L. (2017, October 19). The UK no longer has a national public library system. *The Guardian*. Retrieved from www.theguardian.com/voluntary-sector-network/2017/oct/19/uk-national-public-library-system-community

Topping, K. J., Samuels, J., & Paul, T. (2008). Independent reading: The relationship of challenge, non-fiction and gender to achievement. *British Educational Research Journal*, *34*(4), 505–524.

Tynan, D. (2016, August 24). How Facebook powers money machines for obscure political "news" sites. *The Guardian*. Retrieved from www.theguardian.com/technology/2016/aug/24/facebook-clickbait-political-news-sites-us-election-trump

UNESCO. (2014). *Reading in the mobile era: A study of mobile reading in developing countries*. Education Sector, United Nations Educational, Scientific, and Cultural Organization. Retrieved from http://unesdoc.unesco.org/images/0022/002274/227436e.pdf

Vaala, S., Ly, A., & Levine, M. H. (2015, Fall). Getting a read on the app stores: A market scan and analysis of children's literacy apps. The Joan Ganz Cooney Center at Sesame Workshop. Retrieved from www.joanganzcooneycenter.org/wp-content/uploads/2015/12/jgcc_gettingaread.pdf

White, L. (2011). The place of non-fiction texts in today's primary school. *Synergy*, *9*(1). Retrieved from www.slav.vic.edu.au/synergy/volume-9-number-1-2011/research/124-the-place-of-non-fiction-texts-in-todays-primary-school.html

Wolf, M., & Barzillai, M. (2009, March). The importance of deep reading. *Educational Leadership*, *66*(6), 32–37.

Wolf, M., & Gottwald, S. (2016). *Tales of literacy for the 21st century*. Oxford: Oxford University Press.

7

Digital Reading
A Research Assessment

Naomi S. Baron

I. Introduction

Victor Hugo's novel *The Hunchback of Notre Dame* has a famous scene in which the medieval church is pitted against the Gutenberg revolution. Historian Elizabeth Eisenstein describes the moment:

> the archdeacon first points to the great cathedral and then stretches out his right hand toward a fifteenth-century printed book and announces "*Ceci tuera cela;*" *This* (the printed book) will kill *that* (the cathedral which had served for centuries as an encyclopedia in stone).
>
> *(Eisenstein, 1997, 1055)*

Over the centuries, warnings of one communication medium killing off another have been common: Telephones would replace the written word, radio would replace newspapers, television would replace both radio and newsprint, and now the internet will replace the printed book.

History has, however, continued to prove that co-evolution (Roger Fidler's term – 1997), not replacement of media, generally occurs. This idea goes back at least a century, when Wolfgang Riepl, editor of Nuremberg's largest newspaper, argued in 1913 that instead of one medium replacing another, the older was likely to continue, though perhaps focused on niche uses (see De Waal & Schoenbach, 2010, 479). In assessing the relationship (and potential competition) between alternative media, we should keep in mind that when a new medium is introduced, its novelty may attract users who subsequently revert in whole or part to earlier media choices (De Waal & Schoenbach, 2010, 480).

The rise of digital media, including communication conveyed via the internet, introduced a new set of options for how people read. Many early adopters predicted the demise of print (be that printed newspapers or hardcopy books). However, reading opportunities – and preferences – have not borne out this forecast. Instead, the relationship between print and digital has become at once more complex and nuanced.

Central to the discussion is the difference between content and container: If the words are the same in both media, is it irrelevant whether the text appears in newsprint or on your mobile phone? The debate continues to generate arguments on both sides (see Baron, 2015, 15–18).

Although billions of people are now reading onscreen (if we include smartphones), researchers know relatively little about the pros and cons of reading in print versus digitally. In other words, does the container matter? This chapter tackles the question.

I begin with a brief overview of growth in the digital reading landscape, tracing the early days of electronic reading, following the rise and leveling off of eBook consumption, considering who is reading eBooks, and looking at the emergence of online social media. I then identify variables to consider in examining digital reading: medium, content, function, convenience, and cost. The next section reviews research as of mid-2017. The discussion is grouped with regard to four measures: demographic, cognitive, perceptual, and usage, with an additional section on digital reading and children. The chapter concludes by identifying meaningful research questions we need to address and suggesting issues relevant for translating research into practice.

II. Growth of the Digital Reading Landscape

The notion of "digital reading" is itself an evolving concept, reflecting changes in hardware and software technologies, commercialization of digital access, and emergence of new internet functions.

Evolution of Digital Reading

Technically, digital reading began with the first monitors connected to computers. However, reading what we commonly think of as "texts" dates to 1971, when Michael Hart launched a digital project called Project Gutenberg at the University of Illinois. Participants in the initiative typed in thousands of books that were out of copyright, making them freely available to anyone with access to ARPANET (progenitor of the internet).

With Tim Berners-Lee's invention of the World Wide Web in 1991, internet users had a convenient way of accessing information, including extended text. The internet became an increasingly public tool for reading and writing online. Libraries began digitizing their collections, and in 2002, Google undertook the project that came to be known as Google Books. Newspapers and periodicals started creating digital complements to – or substitutes for – print publications. Meanwhile, universities, colleges, and some in lower education introduced the use of computer-based "learning management systems" (such as Blackboard or Canvas) on which faculties posted online reading assignments.

Commercially, three major developments spurred digital reading among the general public. The first was Amazon's launch of the Kindle eReader in late 2007. The second was Apple's release of the iPad in 2010. And the third, which has been more of an evolution, was the development and proliferation of smartphones – that is, mobile phones that have internet access, among other features. Over time, as ownership levels and the technological sophistication of smartphones continued to grow, much digital reading that earlier took place on desktop or laptop computers, and then on eReaders or tablets, now occurs on smartphones.

Growth – and Decline – of eBook Sales

Amazon's Kindle was a game-changer in marketing books to the general public. Using aggressive pricing strategies, Amazon sold eBooks for significantly less than print counterparts, creating a strong eBook market. In the US, eBook sales grew over 4,000 percent between 2008 and 2012 (Milliot, 2013). At the same time, print sales were falling (Print units fell, 2013).

By the mid-2010s, the balance between digital and print book sales had shifted. After several years in which growth rates for both print and digital were roughly on par in the US (averaging

1 to 4 percent growth rates), print growth rate generally surpassed digital. The Association of American Publishers, which collects data on just over 1,200 publishers, reported that for calendar year 2016, overall revenue was flat. But differences surfaced in the book medium.

Compared with trade book sales in 2015, adult paperback revenue was up 5.3 percent, adult hardback was down 3.7 percent, and eBook revenue was down 13.9 percent. (Meanwhile, adult audio sales were up 24.9 percent.) For children's trade books, paperback revenue was up 0.9 percent, hardback up 10.7 percent, board book up 7.7 percent, and eBook down 32.6 percent (AAP StatShot, 2017). Sales in the UK, as reported by The Publishers Association, revealed similar trends. Again for 2016, UK consumer eBook sales were down 17 percent, whereas print books were up 8 percent. Audio downloads were up 28 percent year-on-year (Cocozza, 2017).

In interpreting these statistics, it is important to keep several considerations in mind. The first is that runaway best sellers predominantly purchased in print or in digital can significantly skew sales numbers from year to year. The second is that national publishers' associations don't report on all books that have been published, generally excluding self-published books – which are heavily digital-only (Data Guy, 2017). Third, there is a difference between revenues and units sold, which is important in that digital books are largely less expensive than print counterparts. And fourth, given fluctuations in pricing agreements between publishers and digital distributors such as Amazon, it has been argued that recent declines in eBook sales reflect rising eBook prices and discounting on print, not readers' preference for print (Alter, 2015).

Who Reads eBooks?

In thinking about digital reading, it is critical to recognize the variety among readers and their motivations for reading, as well as for reading in a particular medium. Age can make a difference, but so can gender, ethnicity, education level, cultural context, and whether one is reading because one has to (for school, for work) or is reading for entertainment or personal edification.

A simple illustration of the importance of such variables is eBook penetration in the United States versus Germany. For 2016, the US publishing industry's market share of eBooks was roughly 20 percent of revenues, again, using figures compiled by the Association of American Publishers (AAP StatShot Data, no date). For Germany – home of the more than 500-year-old Frankfurt Book Fair, not to mention of Johannes Gutenberg and Martin Luther – that proportion was only 4.6 percent (Anderson, 2017).

As we will see in the next section, other factors come into play as well, including cost and convenience. We also need to factor in aggressive marketing by publishers and encouragement by educators for eBook adoption.

When it comes to personal reading, data suggest that adult readers prefer some genres as eBooks over others. Fiction (especially romance, science fiction, and thrillers) sells well in digital (MobileRead, n.d.). Art, gardening, cooking, and travel books continue to attract print buyers.

The Case of Social Media

Discussions of digital reading tend to focus on long-form text, especially books. However, online social media platforms offer multiple additional opportunities for generating and reading digital text.

Narrowly defined, social media are interactive online platforms that paradigmatically use brief messaging. The list of platforms ranges from email, IM (instant messaging), and texting, to Facebook (and its myriad competitors) and Twitter. With the exception of texting, most of this communication (at least in the US) initially took place on computers, though it has significantly moved to mobile phones. Regardless of platform, though, the amount of text is generally sufficiently short that when we talk about "digital reading," we aren't referring to decoding these sorts of messages.

Broadly defined, online social media also include potentially longer texts. Today's social web encompasses blogs, commentary on online news stories, reviews on social reading sites such as Goodreads, and shared highlighting or annotations on eBooks. The social web is also a place for referring readers to other online textual sources, including news articles, reports, or even books.

But the social web is not just a place for reading. Given current technology, it also encompasses audio and video material, often interwoven with text. Therefore, when talking about "reading online," we need to be mindful whether we are only referring to words or to complementary media as well. What is more, there is a growing trend on social media to augment – or even replace – short textual messages such as status updates with visual elements (McHugh, 2017).

III. Defining the Variables

In thinking about what it means to read on a digital screen, it is important to keep in mind variables that may impact research findings. Studies to date tend to take into account only a handful of such variables, making it difficult to generalize about "digital reading."

Here are the major variables relevant to understanding how we read in an age of platform options.

Medium

The obvious initial distinction is between reading in print versus reading on a digital screen. While there are different types of print platforms (e.g., hardback versus paper, book versus newspaper versus magazine), there is also variation in digital screens.

The relevant difference here between types of digital screens is size: desktops versus laptops versus eReaders versus tablets versus mobile phones – all of which come in a variety of sizes. While some of the existing research distinguishes between digital platforms (and derivatively screen size), much does not. As digital reading increasingly moves to mobile phones, screen size – and the amount and manner in which we read on them – becomes especially relevant.

Content

The content of printed text influences how we approach the reading process (e.g., skimming, concentrated study, rereading). The same should be true of reading digitally. Among the dimensions to consider are:

- Genre: Relevant categories include:
    - Fiction (e.g., light versus serious, romance or science fiction versus historical fiction)
    - Non-fiction (e.g., history, news/analysis, philosophy, cooking, biography)
    - Poetry
    - Interpersonal correspondence
    - Reports or memoranda
    - Web pages
    - Consumer reviews

- Format: Is the work a book? An article? A newspaper? A magazine? A blog?
- Length: Is the work short, medium, or long – relative to genre?
- One-way or interactive: Is the text designed to be read linearly or interactively?
- Are there hyperlinks?
- Are responses to postings possible?

Function

Our reasons for reading can shape how we read and what we derive from the experience. To oversimplify, among the reasons for reading are:

- Learning/memory (that is, for education and/or personal enrichment)
- Work
- Entertainment
- Social connection (including networking, social reading)

The social connection motivation merits special comment. In the world of online social networking, social connection typically refers to sharing online something relating to reading (such as a news story, a book review, or a quotation). However, we should remember that in the physical world, people have long shared their reading experiences in personal conversations or organized book clubs. In addition, brick and mortar bookstores provide places for social connectivity among readers who may be strangers but share a common love of books (Sax, 2016, 128).

Convenience

Choice of reading platform is often shaped by convenience. While notions of what constitutes "convenience" show individual variation, there is no dispute that eBooks are simpler to transport and take up less space than print counterparts. Similarly, when asked what distinguishes online news from its print counterpart, users commonly mention accessibility and convenience (Chyi, 2013, 78).

Cost

As with convenience, cost is a major factor influencing readers' decisions whether to access (and acquire) digital versus print materials. I have already noted the possible negative effect of a rise in eBook prices on digital sales.

IV. Research to Date

Research comparing how people read on digital screens versus in print dates back several decades (see Dillon, 1992 for an early review). Among the findings Dillon summarized were reduced speed and accuracy when proofreading onscreen (Wright & Lickorish, 1983), as well as a slower rate of skimming stories when reading digitally (Muter & Maurutto, 1991). A subsequent review by Noyes and Garland (2008) noted a research shift to more cognitively sophisticated measures, including cognitive workload and memory. Noyes and Garland stressed the importance of determining platform equivalence if digital screens are to be used for educational testing purposes.

Much has changed over time, including both quality of digital screens and amount of user experience reading onscreen. Consequently, early findings are best seen as points of historical reference rather than indicators of contemporary reading patterns.

The present overview focuses on studies conducted from 2010 onward. The main review, summarizing research with adults, is organized with respect to four types of measures: demographic, cognitive, perceptual, and usage. I then turn to research with children.

Demographic Measures

Demographic parameters potentially include age, gender, education, ethnicity, and other cultural factors. However, age and gender have received the most research attention. Studies looking at age and/or gender largely focus on preference for reading medium.

First consider book reading. In their 2016 study of US adults, the Pew Research Center (Perrin, 2016) reported that adults of all ages and both genders were more likely to have read a print book than a digital one in the previous year. At the same time, age revealed differences in the likelihood of having engaged in book-reading the previous year. (Participants were asked how many books they had read "either all or part of the way through.") While 72 percent of 18–29 year-olds said they had read a print book and 35 percent a digital book, the numbers among readers 65 and older dropped to 61 percent for print and 19 percent for digital.

Gender differences were also noted in the Pew report. For print books, 61 percent of males indicated they had read a book over the previous year, compared with 70 percent of females. For digital books, the percentages were more similar: 27 percent of males and 29 percent of females. Combining print and digital reading, men reported reading an average (mean) of nine books a year, compared with 15 for women. (Median scores were three for men and five for women.)

Now consider patterns of reading news. Using data from 2010, Chyi and Lee (2012) found an age gradation in preference for reading newspapers in print rather than on the web, assuming the same content and price for both formats. While 54.5 percent of survey participants aged 18–34 favored print, preference rose to 72.1 percent for 35–54 year-olds and to 82.4 percent for 55+ years. A 2016 Pew Research Center study of news-reading habits (Mitchell et al., 2016, July 7) reported that among 18–29 year-olds, 50 percent said they often got news online, compared with only 5 percent reading print newspapers. By contrast, among participants 65 years and older, 20 percent often went online for news, while 48 percent often read print. When getting news online, younger users (18–29 year-olds) were nearly five times as likely to access online news from social networking sites than were those 65 years and older. Regarding gender, the same 2016 study reported that while 51 percent of males sought news online, only 37 percent of women did.

Cognitive Measures

Of central interest in comparing reading onscreen versus in print is cognitive consequences. Results from studies to date must be seen as preliminary, given a lack of consistency in testing parameters, including comprehension or memory metrics, sample selection, type of digital screen used, and differing levels of experience that study participants had with digital reading.

A personal anecdote illustrates the challenges of assessing how readers cognitively approach digital versus print reading under formal testing conditions. In a study designed to compare multitasking when reading onscreen versus in print, I asked university undergraduates to read two lengthy passages, one on a computer screen and the other in a printout. A computer with internet access was in the room for both tasks, and various distractors (e.g., magazines, toys, pictures on the walls) were placed within easy access, as were the participants' mobile phones. Cameras recorded the sessions, enabling us to compare levels of multitasking under the two conditions.

The results: No differences. In fact, there was essentially no multitasking. Instead, like good students, they followed instructions to do the reading. (There was no follow-on comprehension test.) Only once they had finished the assigned reading task did the students engage with the distractors.

Considering studies using comprehension tests, there are further challenges. We know there are many ways in which people read. We might approach a text casually (think of reading a thriller to pass the time on a long plane ride) or with focused concentration (so-called deep reading – Wolf & Barzillai, 2009). We might read a text once or go back and reread it. We might read without annotating or making notes as we go, or we might fill the margins. And we might do nothing else while reading or might multitask. Such multitasking could occur online when reading digitally or with our mobile phones at hand when reading in print.

The cognitive studies I am about to review largely followed the same design: Ask participants to read a passage, then test for comprehension directly afterwards or perhaps add a memory component after an interval of time. The basic design is akin to standardized testing students commonly undergo when applying for college. Results from this type of assessment tell us little about the larger consequences of reading that many parents and educators seek to foster, including ability to grapple with complexity, connection of the current reading with something you read or experienced previously, or the emotional impact a written work may have upon you, regardless of your ability to remember detail.

With these caveats, I turn to the current body of research.

The majority of studies have indicated no significant differences in the way participants comprehended or remembered digital versus print texts. Such research has been done in a variety of countries, including Israel (Ackerman & Goldsmith, 2011), Germany (Kretzschmar et al., 2013), Austria (Holzinger et al., 2011), France (Porion, Aparicio, Megalakaki, Robert, & Baccino, 2016), and the US (Daniel & Woody, 2013; Green, Perera, Dance, & Myers, 2010; Margolin, Driscoll, Toland, & Kegler, 2013; Rockinson-Szapkiw, Courduff, Carter, & Bennett, 2013; Schugar, Schugar, & Penny, 2011). In a related vein, Norman and Furnes (2016) reported no difference in metacognitive activity that occurs when readers use print versus digital texts. Regarding proofreading, Köpper, Mayr, and Buchner (2016) concluded that speed and accuracy were now on par in the two media, likely reflecting both improvement in digital screen technology and user familiarity with working onscreen.

Interestingly, if testing conditions were altered or additional questions were asked, differences sometimes arose. When Ackerman and Goldsmith (2011) allowed participants to choose how much time to spend on the digital versus print readings, participants devoted less time to reading onscreen, and their screen reading comprehension was lower. Similarly, Ackerman and Lauterman (2012) reported that when participants were put under time pressure during the two reading tasks, learning effectiveness declined in the onscreen condition. Furthermore, Daniel and Woody (2013) found that while comprehension levels were largely the same when reading an electronic textbook and a print counterpart, students took more time doing the digital reading, especially when they worked at home rather than in a laboratory. The authors surmised the extended time resulted from multitasking while working electronically, which has been widely documented to slow down task completion (e.g., Bowman, Levine, Waite, & Gendron, 2010; Subrahmanyam et al., 2013). Schugar et al. (2011) found that students reported diminished use of study strategies (such as highlighting, note-taking, or bookmarking) when reading texts digitally compared with reading in print. Moreover, the negative effects of multitasking on academic work are well-documented (e.g., Carrier, Rosen, Cheever, & Lim, 2015; Junco & Cotton, 2012).

Anne Mangen and her colleagues in Norway have argued that platform-based differences exist. In a study of high school students, Mangen, Walgermo, and Brønnick (2013) reported higher comprehension scores in the print condition. Exploring other cognitive parameters, Mangen and Kuiken (2014) compared participant responses when reading narrative nonfiction in a print booklet versus on an iPad. Readers noted higher levels of narrative coherence and feeling they could "lose" themselves in the story (so-called "transportation") in the print condition. A further pilot study (Mangen, Robinet, Olivier, & Velay, 2014; see Flood, 2014 for discussion) asked participants to read a mystery story in print or on a Kindle. Those reading in print were more successful in arranging story elements in chronological order.

Kaufman and Flanagan (2016) have also probed the cognitive question, this time by comparing how successfully participants respond to different sorts of questions when reading a short story in print versus on a digital platform. When reading print, participants did better on abstract questions, which required inferential reasoning. When reading digitally, they did better in answering concrete questions.

Other cognitively-oriented research has looked at memory for news stories. Santana, Livingstone, and Cho (2013) reported that study participants remembered more when they read news in print than online. An earlier study by D'Haenens, Jankowski, and Heuvelman (2004) had reported no difference. Going forward, it will be important to ascertain whether such discrepancies in reports for reading news reflect differences in the participant pool (here, US versus the Netherlands) or development in digital reading patterns over time (the D'Haenens et al. data were collected in 2000).

Perceptual Measures

Although researchers commonly chart tangible metrics such as reading comprehension, users themselves can provide a trove of information through self-reports on reading preferences and rationales behind them. I therefore present findings from two research initiatives focused on user perceptions, gathered through self-reporting.

The first initiative was a project known as COST Action FP1104: New Possibilities for Print Media and Packaging – Combining Print with Digital (COST Action FP1104, n.d.), sponsored by the European Union. Researchers from Europe and Asia used essays, surveys, and interviews to inquire of university students how their experiences in reading and writing differed when working digitally versus with paper. Here I consider only results relating to reading. Published studies deriving from this research initiative (Farinosi, Lim, & Roll, 2016; Fortunati & Vincent, 2014; Taipale, 2014, 2015; Vincent, 2016) report on participants in Italy, Germany, the UK, and Finland. Findings were generally consistent across countries.

In responses regarding the benefits of reading in print, participants noted it was simpler to underline and make marginal notes, it was less tiring on the eyes, it was preferable for longer and more complex texts, and it was an easier medium on which to concentrate. Drawbacks of print included lack of a search function and environmental concerns about using paper. Regarding the benefits of reading onscreen, students commented on ease of searching text, availability of hyperlinks, text resizability, and the convenience of storing many books in one place. As for drawbacks of reading on digital media, participants mentioned eyestrain, difficulty of keeping track of a location in a digital document, and challenges with distraction.

Summarizing observations of students in Germany, Italy, and the UK, Farinosi et al. (2016) wrote: "Students in all three samples feel that reading on screen creates a disconnection with the content and paper seems to allow readers to immerse themselves in the content better[,] which improves learning" (p. 418). This theme of immersion echoes observations by Mangen and Kuiken (2014), while also paralleling findings from my own research.

The second initiative was a cross-national study of print versus digital reading patterns and preferences that my colleagues and I undertook (Baron, Calixte, & Havewala, 2017). We surveyed 429 university students in the US, Japan, Germany, Slovakia, and India. Data were collected between Spring 2013 and Spring 2015. A major goal of the study was to identify and quantify student preferences for reading in one medium versus the other. Using both multiple choice and frequency questions, we queried participants about a number of variables potentially driving preference, including text length, whether the reading was for academic work or pleasure, and cost.

Additionally, we posed four open-ended questions regarding the one thing participants liked most and liked least about reading in print or onscreen. In the US and India, all data were collected in English. In Japan, Germany, and Slovakia, the survey was translated into Japanese, German, and Slovak, respectively, with fluent bilinguals then translating the open-ended responses into English.

For purposes of the present review, the most relevant multiple choice or frequency questions involved text length, rereading, multitasking, concentration, and cost:

- Regarding **text length**, participants were asked which reading platform they preferred (print or digital) when the text was short and when it was long. While results for reading short text were mixed, there was clear preference for reading long texts in print: 86.4 percent favored print for long-text schoolwork and 77.6 percent voiced the same preference when reading for pleasure.
- Regarding **rereading**, students were asked if they were more likely to reread a book if it were in print or on a digital device. Six out of ten indicated they were more likely to reread in print, both for schoolwork and for pleasure, with around one-quarter reporting they were equally likely to reread in either medium.
- Regarding **multitasking**, 66.5 percent reported multitasking "very often" or "sometimes" when reading digitally, compared with 41.2 percent when reading in hardcopy.
- Regarding **concentration**, participants were asked on which reading platform (print, computer, tablet, eReader, or mobile phone) they found it easiest to concentrate. The result: 91.8 percent said print.
- Regarding **cost**, subjects were asked if they would prefer to read in print or onscreen if the cost were the same. For academic reading, 86.9 percent chose print, while for pleasure reading, 80.9 percent indicated print.

For the study's four open-ended questions, a total of 1,503 responses were collected and coded, using a fine-grained scheme (with 53 different categories) developed by the authors. Specific categories were then grouped into layers of more general categories. The most general levels included emotional/aesthetic, physical, cognitive, access to material, convenience, and resources. Among the major findings:

- **Hardcopy – like most**: The largest number of "like most" comments about reading in print involved something physical (61.7 percent). Responses included reference to the ability to make annotations, to the book's physicality (such as being able to hold it or turn its pages), and to the fact reading print did not cause eyestrain. A smaller number of comments mentioned ease of concentration or feeling that print aided memory.
- **Hardcopy – like least**: The largest category of complaints about reading in print (43.5 percent) concerned lack of convenience, including issues of portability, storage, or organization. While responses regarding cognitive issues were sparse, those that did appear were telling, including "It becomes boring sometimes" or "it takes time to sit down and focus on the material."
- **Digital – like most**: The most common reason for liking digital reading (31.6 percent) related to the screen's physical characteristics. These attributes included lighting on the

screen, word search functions, and access to the internet. Not far behind were convenience (25.1 percent) and access to material (16.0 percent). About a dozen participants commented they liked the ability to multitask.
- **Digital – like least**: The bulk of complaints about reading digitally (64.6 percent) involved physical attributes of the medium. Among these, the primary concern was visual issues such as eyestrain. The next largest category of concerns (21.3 percent) was cognitive. Comments mentioned distraction or lack of concentration.

The study also invited additional comments, of which we received 125. While many mirrored responses already reported, a number shed more light on university students' perceptions of the two reading platforms. Several revealed conflicts when deciding whether to read in print or digitally. One participant noted, "I like that digital screens save paper but it is hard to concentrate when reading on them." Another remarked, "Reading in digital is faster, but bad for the eyes." In an earlier pilot study, yet another wrote, "While I prefer reading things in hardcopy, I can't bring myself to print out online material simply for the environmental considerations. However, I highly, highly prefer things in hardcopy – just to clarify."

Speed of reading digitally could negatively impact learning. (Recall Ackerman and Goldsmith's findings reported above.) One of our participants wrote that "It takes more time to read the same number of pages in print comparing to digital," while a student from an earlier pilot study complained that what she liked least about reading in print was that "It takes me longer because I read more carefully."

Findings from both COST Action FP1104 studies and Baron et al. (2017) address reader perceptions, not measurable outcomes. Neither body of research establishes whether, for example, participants actually learned more from reading in print, or whether in their own practices they chose digital over print for reasons of cost-savings or convenience. However, results from these projects mesh with those of other research initiatives.

On the issue of preference, multiple studies found that despite equivalent performance on cognitive, memory, or proofreading tasks, participants reported preferring print (Ackerman & Goldsmith, 2011; Green et al., 2010; Holzinger et al., 2011; Köpper et al., 2016; Kretzschmar et al., 2013). In other studies, participants indicated feeling that they focused more, learned more, or performed better with hardcopy (Ji, Michaels, & Waterman, 2014; Mizrachi, 2015). Mizrachi also reported that undergraduates (in the US) were far more likely to say they reviewed course readings that are in print. In a UK study, Ríos Amaya and Secker (2016) found that 70 percent of their university participants preferred to have all of their course materials in print, 80 percent indicated they focused better when reading print, and 71 percent felt they remembered more course information when they read in print.

While not directly related to comparisons of reading in print versus onscreen, other research on what people remember – or think they know – when reading online is relevant to the question of how we learn in a world of digital media. In 2011, Sparrow et al. reported on the effects on memory of doing online searches. Participants were more likely to remember their search path than the information itself. More recently, several scholars (including Sparrow) have asked whether doing online searching colors our perceptions of what we know. One concern is that we stop making an effort to remember things ourselves since the internet (or our digital devices, more broadly) "remembers" them for us (Sparrow & Chapman, 2013; Ward, 2013). Another is that using the internet leads us to have inflated beliefs about topics we have not even researched online (Fischer, Goddu, & Keil, 2015).

Regarding the issue of eyestrain when reading onscreen, several experimental studies have documented greater strain when reading onscreen. Among these are Chu, Rosenfield, Portello, Benzoni, and Collier (2011) and Köpper et al. (2016).

The role of cost as a basis for choosing between a print or digital text has been widely reported elsewhere. Student Monitor LLC (2014) found that among students in four-year American colleges, cost was the main reason for buying an eTextbook rather than a print copy. Similar results have been reported by Ji et al. (2014) and Rockinson-Szapkiw et al. (2013). When students were asked about preferences if cost were the same, Student Monitor LLC (2013) found the majority chose print. Similarly, for newspapers, Chyi and Lee (2012) reported on a 2010 national survey of internet users in the US in which 70 percent indicated preference for the print rather than online edition, if content and price were the same.

Beyond cognitive, visual, and fiscal issues, a host of other factors shape readers' perceptions regarding the superiority of print versus screens. Mangen (e.g., Mangen & Velay, 2010) has written extensively on the importance of physical touch (haptics) in the way readers interact with books, suggesting the benefits are cognitive as well as aesthetic. Linked to the issue of physical touch is the fact that print books retain an individuality of cover, size, design, and physical feel (e.g., because of paper selection), while electronic counterparts are still largely homogeneous. In my own research, a surprising number of students commented that what they liked most about reading print was the smell of books.

David Sax (2016) suggests that more generally, society is experiencing a "revenge of analog," whereby growing numbers of people are rejecting digital activity (such as iTunes, word processing, or online magazines) in favor of analog counterparts (here, vinyl records, bound notebooks, and print periodicals). In some instances, preference for physical tools reflects an "aspirational" desire to be perceived by others in particular ways. Regarding magazines, Sax cites Tom Standage, deputy editor of *The Economist*, who finds that younger readers are often choosing the print rather than digital edition:

> We assume younger people want *The Economist* as a social signifier. ... You cannot show others you're reading it with the digital edition. You can't leave your iPad lying around to show others how smart you are.
>
> *(Sax, 2016, 110)*

Another intangible but potentially relevant factor in choosing between digital and print reading is what Standage calls the "finishability" of hardcopy. With a print magazine, you can read through from cover to cover. By contrast, as Sax puts it, "A news website ... can never be finished" (Sax, 2016, 110). Sax notes a survey the *New York Times* conducted in 2014 of print subscribers, who commented favorably on the "contained reading experience" of the printed newspaper (Sax, 2016, 114).

Reader perceptions of advantages and disadvantages of print versus digital reading platforms naturally help shape their usage of these media. I therefore next turn to research on usage measures.

Usage Measures

How much reading are people actually doing in hardcopy and onscreen? Begin with books.

Both Gallop and the Pew Research Center survey people in the US on how many books they read. In January 2017, Gallop reported 48 percent of their sample indicated having read between one and ten books (either all or part of the way through) the previous year, and 35 percent had read 11 or more. These findings roughly match Gallop results from a similar survey in 2002. When the recent survey asked about reading platform, 73 percent of those who had read at least one book indicated they primarily read print, while 19 percent said digital. Another 6 percent said they most often listened to audio books (Swift & Ander, 2017).

The Pew Research Center frames its surveys somewhat differently, as well as conducting studies more frequently. (Like Gallop, Pew defines "reading a book" as meaning either all or part of the way through.) When US adults were asked in Spring 2016 if they had read a book in any format in the previous 12 months, 73 percent said yes. Of these, 65 percent specified they had read a print book, 28 percent reported having read an eBook, and 14 said they had listened to an audio book (Page & Rainie, 2016).

Regarding overall reading, the Pew survey reported an average (mean) of 12 books per year, with a median of four books. Compared with early surveys, digital reading had increased by 11 percent between 2011 and 2014 (moving from 17 percent to 28 percent), with no growth between 2014 and 2016. Pew also inquired about commitment to single or multiple reading platforms. While 38 percent reported they only read print and 6 percent responded they only read digitally, 28 percent said they read both formats. (Another 26 percent had read no books during the previous 12 months.) Interestingly, young adults were not more likely than older adults to only read digitally.

The major change in reading habits Pew reported was in the type of device used for digital reading. Between 2011 and 2016, those who read an eBook on a tablet rose from 4 percent to 15 percent, and those reading on a mobile phone grew from 5 percent to 13 percent. Reading on a desktop or laptop grew less dramatically (from 7 percent to 11 percent), and reading on a dedicated eReader remained largely stable (from 7 percent to 8 percent).

For book reading on a mobile phone, age was an important variable. The younger the readers, the more likely they were to have read a book on a mobile phone: 18–29 year-olds: 22 percent; 30–49 year-olds: 18 percent; 50–64 year-olds: 9 percent; 65+: 4 percent.

While studies such as these are valuable indicators of reading trends, they are limited in many ways. As the authors of the Gallop report note, "it is unclear if Americans are reading books only partially, reading shorter books or reading lower-quality books than they used to" (Swift & Ander, 2017). However, we can conclude that as of late 2016, the majority of Americans were undertaking to read at least one book a year, and most book reading was done in print.

Now consider newspapers. Digital use of newspapers is growing, but the story is nuanced, regarding time spent reading, digital hardware used, and age of reader. Citing data of the Newspaper Association of America from late 2012, Chyi (2013, p. 66) reported that in the US, online news site visits averaged 4.4 minutes each, totaling 39 minutes per month.

A more recent study by the Pew Research Center (Mitchell et al., 2016, July 7) of US adults 18 years and older offered both an update and more detail. Overall, only 20 percent of those surveyed often got their news from print, down from 27 percent in 2013. Age, however, made a difference. In this 2016 sample, only 5 percent of 18–29 year-olds indicated often getting news from print, compared with 48 percent of those age 65 and older. By contrast, 50 percent of 18–29 year-olds often turned to online news, compared with only 20 percent of those 65+.

The device favored for accessing digital news has shifted in recent years. According to Mitchell et al., in 2013, 54 percent reported ever getting news on a mobile device (generally a mobile phone or tablet); in 2016, that number rose to 72 percent. Moreover, for those accessing news digitally, age correlated with the digital device used. Among 18–29 year-olds, seven out of ten said they either preferred or solely used a mobile device for accessing digital news. The comparable number for those 65+ was 16 percent.

"Non-mobile" digital devices are desktops or laptops. A related Pew Research Center analysis (Lu & Holcomb, 2016) noted that although Americans are more often turning to mobile devices to access news, when they use desktop computers, they spend more time per digitally-native news site visit.

To summarize: Younger adults are the heaviest readers of mobile news, but overall, when reading on a stationary desktop, readers log more time. These findings raise the question of how much time people spend when reading on mobile devices.

Another Pew Research Center analysis (Mitchell et al., 2016, May 5) sheds light on this issue. The research examined how much time users devoted to reading short-form news pieces (defined as 101–999 words) versus long-form news (1,000 words or more) on mobile phones. Readers averaged 57 seconds on short-form and 123 seconds on long-form stories. Interestingly, readers spent more time reading long-form stories accessed from an internal link (average: 148 seconds) than reading stories reaching them through social media (111 seconds). Moreover, while Facebook was the biggest social media driver of news stories, readers accessing long-form pieces via Facebook only averaged 107 seconds with the content.

Research by Chyi and Tenenboim (2017), examined American news access through a different lens, namely the degree to which readers use both print and digital. Comparing US readership of 51 metropolitan daily newspapers, they concluded that in 2015, the print edition reached almost three times as many local adults as the online edition, and that between 2007 and 2015, online readership of local newspapers showed very little growth. However, online readers tended to be hybrid readers, more than twice as likely as the general public to be reading the print version.

Regarding age, Chyi and Tenenboim confirmed the familiar finding that older adults (here, 55+) were more likely to read the news in print than younger adults. However, those most likely to read digitally were 35–44 year-olds, not the youngest cohort. Among the youngest group (18–24 year-olds), 7.8 percent indicated reading local newspapers digitally, while 19.9 percent did so in print.

Comparative studies of print versus digital news reading have also been done in the UK, centering on UK national newspapers. Thurman (2014) reported that for 2011, domestic readers spent 96.7 percent of such reading time with print. More recently, Thurman (2017) found that the average percent time spent with print news (again, by individual readers within the UK) was now 88.5, with 7.5 percent on mobile devices and 4 percent on PCs. That translated into about 40 minutes of reading in print per day, compared with less than 30 seconds reading news online.

Why does print retain an appeal to news readers? Chyi (2013) suggests a variety of reasons, including print causing less eyestrain and being more relaxing to read, along with the perception that if online news is free, it must not be as good (pp. 78–79). Thurman (2017) mentions the superior resolution of paper, its contrast ratio in ambient light, its tangibility, and its recognizable "design grammar" (see Schafer, 2016).

Children

Much of the research comparing print versus digital reading has considered adult readers. However, a growing number of experimental and survey initiatives offer an expanding window onto reading issues for children, including those not yet old enough to read by themselves. (Besides the references below, see Kucirkova and Rvachew (2017) for their special issue on "Reading in the 21st Century," in the *International Journal of Child-Computer Interaction*.)

Results from research on children up to age 5 or 6 remind us how multifaceted and nuanced a meaningful comparison of print versus digital needs to be. A number of studies have reported diminished performance with electronic books. For example, Chiong, Ree, Takeuchi, and Erickson (2012) looked at pairs of parents and children aged 3–6 reading stories together via a print book, a "basic" eBook, and an eBook with "enhanced" multimedia features. Children remembered fewer details of stories they encountered on the enhanced eBooks than when co-reading in print or with a basic eBook, suggesting the enhancements detracted from the book's storyline content. In a similar study of parents co-reading with 3 and 5 year-olds, Parish-Morris, Mahajan, Hirsh-Pasek, Golinkoff, and Collins (2013) found use of eBooks correlated both with lower story comprehension and more parent-child behavioral dialogue (e.g., "Stop pressing the buttons"), rather than with conversation focused on story content. Also looking at preschoolers, Richter and Courage (2017) reported that children made more story-related comments when reading print, but more comments about the eBook (or the electronic device) itself when reading digitally.

At the same time, studies also point to benefits of digital books. Multiple researchers have noted that young children (ranging from infants to preschoolers) find eBooks more engaging than print, making the children more attentive (Richter & Courage, 2017; Strouse & Ganea, 2017). Schugar et al. (2013) comment on higher engagement with eBooks among children in grades K-6. As Strouse and Ganea note, it seems likely that attention and engagement in young children may well lead to developmental gains, including in language.

In their metastudy of the pros and cons of technology-enhanced storybooks, Takacs, Swart, and Bus (2015) remind us that not all technological features affect readers (and reading) the same way. For example, the research suggests that animations and sound effects may aid in both vocabulary development and story comprehension, while such features as built-in games or opportunities to click on a "hotspot" leading to another activity appear to detract from learning.

Regarding older children, Heather Schugar and Jordan Schugar concluded that the middle-school children they studied comprehended more when reading print than when using eBooks on an iPad (Paul, 2014). It appeared that interactive features of the digital platform proved to be distractions from the textual content.

Complementing experimental research with children are Scholastic's biannual surveys (Scholastic, n.d.) on reading attitudes and practices of both children and their parents. Initially, studies were restricted to the US, though now the UK, Australia, and India are included as well. I focus here on key findings directly relating to print versus digital reading. Although the question bases are very different, Scholastic's approach of querying (rather than testing) users parallels the approach I employed with university students in my own research (Baron et al., 2017).

The most striking finding in Scholastic's US data is that while exposure to digital books in homes and schools has increased, both children and parents continue to value print. In successive surveys, children were asked whether they agreed with this statement: "I'll always want to read books printed on paper even though there are eBooks available." Here are summed results (combining "agree a lot" and "agree a little") for 6 to 17 year-olds:

2010:	66% (note: only 9–17 year-olds were surveyed in 2010)
2012:	60%
2014:	65%
2016:	65%

A similar commitment was evidenced in the other countries Scholastic surveyed in 2016:

UK:	68%
Australia:	79%
India:	80%

For children who had read an eBook in the previous year, Scholastic asked about reading preferences. The US results were:

	Prefer print	Prefer digital	No preference
2012:	43%	19%	38%
2014:	55%	11%	34%
2016:	45%	16%	38%

Here are results from the other countries (2016):

UK:	49%	22%	28%
Australia:	55%	13%	32%
India:	44%	35%	20%

Interestingly, while children in India expressed the strongest preference for digital reading (35 percent), they were also the most likely (80 percent) to say they would always want to have print available.

V. Research Directions and Translating Research into Practice

Digital reading is still in its relative infancy. We can say little definitively about reading on digital versus print platforms, in part because our experience with digital reading continues to evolve, as do the hardware and software tools with which we read onscreen.

Clearer at this point is the fact we need to identify what constitute meaningful research questions about reading in the two media. Equally importantly, we should be responsible for devising strategies that translate what we discover into pedagogical practice. To begin with, though, we must first consider our pedagogical goals.

Pedagogical Goals

For purposes of discussion, I will assume that among our pedagogical goals for readers are these:

- Ability to focus on a text with concentration and without distraction
- Ability to comprehend a text at both concrete and abstract levels
- Ability to remember the content of one's reading beyond immediate recall
- Ability to integrate one's reading into one's broader cognitive and social experience

Identifying Meaningful Research Questions

Most of what we know to date about reading digitally versus in print reflects artificial measures of learning, namely comparing immediate comprehension of passages read on the two platforms. A smaller number of studies has been probing more cognitively interesting issues, such as the work of Mangen and her colleagues on mental "transportation" and on readers' ability to reconstruct a story line; similarly, the work of Kaufman and Flanagan on success in answering concrete versus abstract questions. However, there are many more issues to be addressed. Such issues include:

1. *Explanations for Readers' Perceptions*: Why do so many readers report that they prefer print, that they concentrate best with it, and that they retain more from reading hardcopy? Is the explanation simply one of having been socialized to read in print (but not digitally), or are other factors at play?
2. *Time Taken When Reading in Print versus Onscreen*: What can we learn from readers' comments about the amount of time they take (or perceive themselves to take) when reading in print versus digitally? Do they actually read print more slowly and/or more carefully? Why do readers spend less time when consuming digital newspapers than print counterparts, and what are the consequences?
3. *Genre and Goal*: What are the intellectual or emotional consequences, differentiating by genre and level of textual complexity, of reading on paper versus digital platforms? When the goal is deep reading, what are the pros and cons of using print versus digital text? To what degree is the reading platform itself a determining factor as opposed to the mindset readers are likely to bring when using each platform?
4. *Screen Size*: When reading digitally, how relevant is screen size? The question becomes especially relevant as mobile phones are becoming increasingly the digital reading platform of choice for pleasure reading, academics, and even professional work.
5. *Testing Equivalence*: Do readers perform equally well on screen-administered tests as on paper tests? Mangen and her colleagues (2013) argued not, and Noyes and Garland (2008) noted the importance of determining the answer.
6. *Research Testing Conditions*: Psychologists have long known that study participants commonly perform differently when tested in a laboratory versus under naturalistic conditions. While laboratory results comparing reading on print versus digital platforms may be suggestive (as are participant self-reports), we need to devise accurate measures of natural reading behavior.
7. *The Physicality Question*: In what ways does tangibility matter for pedagogy? Beyond reader self-reports of valuing the physicality of print, how can we meaningfully study the extent to which the physicality of print (versus the ephemeral nature of digital reading) might foster integration of what one has read into one's broader cognitive or social experience?
8. *"Finishability"*: If it is correct that print naturally entails a stronger potential for "finishability" of a text, of what value is such potential for either learning or personal enjoyment?
9. *Form Following Function*: Since digital media offer a wealth of content and structural options that print does not (including audio, video, and access to the internet, along with adaptive learning, augmented reality, and virtual reality), how can we creatively make use of these opportunities without compromising continuity, concentration, and comprehension when reading?

Translating Research into Practice

As use of digital reading materials continues to grow, particularly in education, researchers have begun asking how we can tackle some of the challenges that reading onscreen has engendered. Some translational issues we should address are these:

1. *Learning to Read Digitally*: Rather than assume readers will, untutored, know how to engage in meaningful and focused digital reading, we likely need to provide training. (By way of analogy, when word processing tools became readily available in the late 1980s and early 1990s, schools and colleges needed to train students how to use them effectively.) Work by

Schugar et al. (2013), Turner and Hicks (2015), and Guernsey and Levine (2015) represents a useful start.
2. *Priming strategies*: Can training enable readers to overcome possible cognitive disadvantages of screen reading? We need to build on work (e.g., Kaufman & Flanagan, 2016) that suggests priming for abstract understanding when reading digitally can improve subsequent performance.
3. *Mixed platforms*: For the foreseeable future, it seems likely that both print and digital platforms will co-evolve. Drawing upon research findings regarding the role that genre and reading goals play in predicting the efficacy of reading onscreen or in print, we need to shape appropriate pedagogical balances and publicize our research findings so the general public can make informed choices.
4. *Variation in Reading Preferences*: Research results offer statistical findings but sometimes do not account for variation in personal preferences and/or abilities. Such variance may be shaped by prior reading experience or personality, as well as by age, gender, ethnicity, education level, or culture. Recommendations, whether in academic or work settings, or for personal reading, should take individual variation into account.
5. *Avoiding Distraction*: The largest challenge when reading digitally remains our ability to concentrate and avoid distraction. Curiously, students seem more aware of the problem than do educators, who increasingly determine students' reading platforms. Informed collaboration between teachers and learners will be needed if we are to meet this challenge.
6. *The Cost Issue*: We must be realistic about the role of cost in driving choice of reading platform, particularly for students. While most digital books today are less expensive than their print counterparts, such eBooks are commonly mirrors of the print edition, being created as PDFs or EPUB3 files. To design digital works with enhanced functionality (such as adaptive learning or multimodal interaction) drives up production cost, and therefore pricing.

    The growth of Open Educational Resources (OERs) – available to all for free – is increasingly helping address the high cost of textbooks, but such materials are overwhelmingly digital. We therefore need to combine the pragmatic adoption of open materials with meaningful training in how to use them to foster effective learning. We also must be mindful that while many OERs are of high quality and have undergone review and editing before being posted online, others may be written by well-meaning authors but carry less educational value (Cavanagh, 2016). Given the relative newness of the OER movement, it may be many years before teachers' confidence in OERs matches their confidence in commercially-published materials.
7. *Engagement versus Addiction*: Digital reading, especially for children, is often described as more engaging than its print counterpart. Yet we also know that digital addiction is a growing challenge for device users of all ages. We need to construct strategies for building on the engagement potential of digital reading while recognizing that children – and adults – need breaks from continual screen use.

References

AAP StatShot. (2017, June 15). Book publisher trade sales flat for 2016. Association of American Publishers. Retrieved November 27, 2017, from http://newsroom.publishers.org/aap-statshot-book-publisher-trade-sales-flat-for-2016/

AAP StatShot Data. (no date). Association of American Publishers. Retrieved November 27, 2017, from http://newsroom.publishers.org/aap-statshot-data/

Ackerman, R., & Goldsmith, M. (2011). Metacognitive regulation of text learning: On screen versus on paper. *Journal of Experimental Psychology: Applied*, 17(1), 18–32.

Ackerman, R., & Lauterman, T. (2012). Taking reading comprehension exams on screen or on paper? A metacognitive analysis of learning texts under time pressure. *Computers in Human Behavior, 28*(5), 1816–1828.

Alter, A. (2015, September 22). The plot twist: E-book sales slip, and print is far from dead. *New York Times*. Retrieved May 16, 2017, from www.nytimes.com/2015/09/23/business/media/the-plot-twist-e-book-sales-slip-and-print-is-far-from-dead.html?_r=0

Anderson, P. (2017, June 15). Germany's 2016 book market report: 'Stable amid transformation.' *Publishing Perspectives*. Retrieved November 27, 2017, from https://publishingperspectives.com/2017/06/borsenverein-2016-market-report-germany/

Baron, N. S. (2015). *Words onscreen: The fate of reading in a digital world*. New York, NY: Oxford.

Baron, N. S., Calixte, R. M., & Havewala, M. (2017). The persistence of print among university students: An exploratory study. *Telematics & Informatics, 34*, 590–604.

Bowman, L. L., Levine, L. E., Waite, B. M., & Gendron, M. (2010). Can students really multitask? An experimental study of instant messaging while reading. *Computers & Education, 54*(4), 927–931.

Carrier, L. M., Rosen, L. D., Cheever, N. A., & Lim, A. F. (2015). Causes, effects, and practicalities of everyday multitasking. *Developmental Review, 35*, 64–78.

Cavanagh, S. (2016, May 16). Pearson CEO Fallon talks common core, rise of 'open' resources. *EdWeek Market Brief*. Retrieved November 27, 2017, from https://marketbrief.edweek.org/marketplace-k-12/pearson-ceo-fallon-talks-common-core-rise-open-resources

Chiong, C., Ree, J., Takeuchi, L., & Erickson, I. (2012, Spring). Comparing parent-child co-reading on print, basic, and enhanced e-Book platforms. Jane Ganz Cooney Center. Retrieved May 16, 2017, from www.joanganzcooneycenter.org/publication/quickreport-print-books-vs-e-books/

Chu, D., Rosenfield, M., Portello, J. K., Benzoni, J. A., & Collier, J. D. (2011). A comparison of symptoms after viewing text on a computer screen and hardcopy. *Ophthalmic and Physiological Optics, 31*(1), 29–32.

Chyi, H. I. (2013). *Trial and error: U.S. newspapers' digital struggles toward inferiority*. Pamplona, Spain: University of Navarra, Media Markets Monographs.

Chyi, H. I., & Lee, A. M. (2012). Will the Internet disrupt? A reality check on format preference for traditional and digital content across five media. *Presented at the 10th world media economics and management conference*, Thessaloniki, Greece.

Chyi, H. I., & Tenenboim, O. (2017). Reality check: Multiplatform newspaper readership in the United States, 2007–2015. *Journalism Practice*. Digital-first. Retrieved May 16, 2017, from www.tandfonline.com/doi/abs/10.1080/17512786.2016.1208056?needAccess=true&

Cocozza, P. (2017, April 27). How eBooks lost their shine: 'Kindles now look clunky and unhip.' *The Guardian*. Retrieved May 16, 2017, from www.theguardian.com/books/2017/apr/27/how-ebooks-lost-their-shine-kindles-look-clunky-unhip-

COST Action FP1104. (n.d.). New possibilities for print media and packaging – Combining print with digital. Retrieved May 16, 2017, from www.cost.eu/COST_Actions/fps/FP1104?management

D'Haenens, L., Jankowski, N., & Heuvelman, A. (2004). News in online and print newspapers: Differences in reader consumption and recall. *New Media & Society, 6*(3), 363–382.

Daniel, D. B., & Woody, W. D. (2013). E-textbooks at what cost? Performance and use of electronic v. print texts. *Computers & Education, 62*, 18–23.

Data Guy. (2017, January 17). How do book sales stack up genre by genre? Digital Book World.

De Waal, E., & Schoenbach, K. (2010). New sites' position in the mediascape: Uses, evaluations, and media displacement effects over time. *New Media & Society, 12*(3), 477–496.

Dillon, A. (1992). Reading from paper versus screens: A critical review of the empirical literature. *Ergonomics, 35*(10), 1297–1326.

Eisenstein, E. (1997). From the printed word to the moving image. *Social Research, 64*, 1049–1066.

Farinosi, M., Lim, C., & Roll, J. (2016). Book or screen, pen or keyboard? A cross-cultural sociological analysis of writing and reading habits basing on Germany, Italy and the UK. *Telematics and Informatics, 33*(2), 410–421.

Fidler, R. (1997). *Metamorphosis: Understanding new media*. Thousand Oaks, CA: Pine Forge Press.

Fischer, M., Goddu, M. K., & Keil, F. C. (2015). Searching for explanations: How the internet inflates estimates of internal knowledge. *Journal of Experimental Psychology: General, 144*(3), 674–687.

Flood, A. (2014, August 19). Readers absorb less on Kindles than on paper, study finds. *The Guardian*. Retrieved May 16, 2017, from www.theguardian.com/books/2014/aug/19/readers-absorb-less-kindles-paper-study-plot-ereader-digitisation/

Fortunati, L., & Vincent, J. (2014). Sociological insights on the comparison of writing/reading on paper with writing/reading digitally. *Telematics and Informatics, 31*(1), 39–51.

Green, T. D., Perera, R. A., Dance, L. A., & Myers, E. A. (2010). Impact of presentation mode on recall of written text and numerical information: Hard copy versus electronic. *North American Journal of Psychology, 12*(2), 233–242.

Guernsey, L., & Levine, M. H. (2015). *Tap, click, read: Growing readers in a world of screens*. San Francisco, CA: Jossey-Bass.

Holzinger, A., Baernthaler, M., Pammer, W., Katz, H., Bjelic-Radisic, V., & Ziefle, M. (2011). Investigating paper vs. screen in real-life hospital workflows: Performance contradicts perceived superiority of paper in the user experience. *International Journal of Human-Computer Studies, 69*(9), 563–570.

Ji, S. W., Michaels, S., & Waterman, D. (2014). Print vs. electronic readings in college courses: Cost-efficiency and perceived learning. *The Internet and Higher Education, 21,* 17–24.

Junco, R., & Cotton, S. R. (2012). No A 4 U: The relationship between multitasking and academic performance. *Computers & Education, 59*(2), 505–514.

Kaufman, G., & Flanagan, M. (2016). High-low split: Divergent cognitive construal levels triggered by digital and non-digital platforms. *CHI '16 Proceedings of the 2016 CHI conference on human factors in computing systems.* New York, NY: ACM, pp. 2773–2777.

Köpper, M., Mayr, S., & Buchner, A. (2016). Reading from computer screen versus reading from paper: Does it still make a difference? *Ergonomics, 59*(5), 615–632.

Kretzschmar, F., Pleimling, D., Hosemann, J., Füssel, S., Bornkessel-Schlesewsky, I., & Schlesewsky, M. (2013). Subjective impressions do not mirror online reading effort: Concurrent EEG-eyetracking evidence from the reading of books and digital media. *PLoS ONE, 8*(2), e56178.

Kucirkova, N., & Rvachew, S. (2017). Editorial (Introduction to special issue "Reading in the 21st century"). *International Journal of Child-Computer Interaction, 12,* 1–50.

Lu, K., & Holcomb, J. (2016, June 15). Digital news audience: Fact sheet. Pew Research Center. Retrieved May 16, 2017, from www.journalism.org/2016/06/15/digital-news-audience-fact-sheet/

Mangen, A., & Kuiken, D. (2014). Lost in an iPad: Narrative engagement on paper and tablet. *Scientific Study of Literature, 4*(2), 150–177.

Mangen, A., Robinet, P., Olivier, G., & Velay, J.-L. (2014). Mystery story reading in pocket print book and on Kindle: Possible impact on chronological events memory. *Conference presentation, international society for the empirical study of literature and media.* Turin, Italy, July 21–25.

Mangen, A., & Velay, J.-L. (2010). Digitizing literacy: Reflections on the haptics of writing. In M. H. Zadeh (Ed.), *Advances in haptics* (pp. 385–401). Rijeka, Croatia: InTech.

Mangen, A., Walgermo, B. R., & Brønnick, K. (2013). Reading linear texts on paper versus computer screen: Effects on reading comprehension. *International Journal of Educational Research, 58,* 61–68.

Margolin, S. J., Driscoll, C., Toland, M. J., & Kegler, J. L. (2013). E-readers, computer screens, or paper: Does reading comprehension change across media platforms? *Applied Cognitive Psychology, 27*(4), 512–519.

McHugh, M. (2017, April 21). Where Facebook's going, we don't need words. *The Ringer.* Retrieved May 16, 2017, from https://theringer.com/facebook-status-updates-visuals-over-text-ac4d6dd6dfc1

Milliot, J. (2013, May 29). BEA 2013: The E-book boom years. *Publishers Weekly.* Retrieved May 16, 2017, from www.publishersweekly.com/pw/by-topic/industry-news/bea/article/57390-bea-2013-the-e-book-boom-years.html

Mitchell, A., Gottfried, J., Barthel, M., & Shearer, E. (2016, July 7). The modern news consumer: News attitudes and practices in the digital age. Pew Research Center. Retrieved May 16, 2017, from www.journalism.org/2016/07/07/the-modern-news-consumer/

Mitchell, A., Stocking, G., & Matsa, K. E. (2016, May 5). Long-form reading shows signs of life in our mobile news world. Pew Research Center. Retrieved May 16, 2017, from www.journalism.org/2016/05/05/long-form-reading-shows-signs-of-life-in-our-mobile-news-world/

Mizrachi, D. (2015). Undergraduates' academic reading format preferences and behaviors. *Journal of Academic Librarianship, 41*(3), 301–311.

MobileRead. (n.d.). US ebook sales breakdown by genre. Retrieved May 16, 2017, from www.mobileread.com/forums/showthread.php?t=274899

Muter, P., & Maurutto, P. (1991). Reading and skimming from computer screens and books: The paperless office revisited? *Behaviour and Information Technology, 10*(4), 257–266.

Norman, E., & Furnes, B. (2016). The relationship between metacognitive experiences and learning: Is there a difference between digital and non-digital study media? *Computers in Human Behavior, 54,* 301–309.

Noyes, J. M., & Garland, K. J. (2008). Computer- vs. paper-based tasks: Are they equivalent? *Ergonomics, 51*(9), 1352–1375.

Page, D., & Rainie, L. (2016, September 1). Book reading 2016. Pew Research Center. Retrieved May 16, 2017, from www.pewinternet.org/2016/09/01/book-reading-2016/

Parish-Morris, J., Mahajan, N., Hirsh-Pasek, K., Golinkoff, R. M., & Collins, M. F. (2013). Once upon a time: Parent-child dialogue and storybook reading in the electronic era. *Mind, Brain, and Education, 7*(3), 200–211.

Paul, A. M. (2014, April 10). Students reading e-books are losing out, study suggests. *New York Times.* Retrieved May 16, 2017, from https://parenting.blogs.nytimes.com/2014/04/10/students-reading-e-books-are-losing-out-study-suggests/?_r=0

Perrin, A. (2016, September 1). Book reading 2016. Pew Research Center. Retrieved May 16, 2017, from www.pewinternet.org/2016/09/01/book-reading-2016/

Porion, A., Aparicio, X., Megalakaki, O., Robert, A., & Baccino, T. (2016). The impact of paper-based versus computerized presentation on text comprehension and memorization. *Computers in Human Behavior, 54,* 569–576.

Print units fell 9 percent in 2012. (2013, January 4). *Publishers Weekly.* Retrieved March 16, 2020, from https://www.publishersweekly.com/pw/by-topic/industry-news/financial-reporting/article/82630-print-units-fell-4-at-the-end-of-february.html

Richter, A., & Courage, M. L. (2017). Comparing electronic and paper storybooks for preschoolers: Attention, engagement, and recall. *Journal of Applied Developmental Psychology, 48,* 92–102.

Ríos Amaya, J., & Secker, J. (2016). Choosing between print and electronic or keeping both? Academic reading format international study (ARFIS) UK report. London, UK: Learning Technology and Innovation (LTI).

Rockinson-Szapkiw, A. J., Courduff, J., Carter, K., & Bennett, D. (2013). Electronic versus traditional print textbooks: A comparison study on the influence of university students' learning. *Computers & Education, 63,* 259–266.

Santana, A. D., Livingstone, R. M., & Cho, Y. Y. (2013). Print readers recall more than do online readers. *Newspaper Research Journal, 34*(2), 78–92.

Sax, D. (2016). *The revenge of analog: Real things and why they matter.* New York, NY: Public Affairs.

Schafer, J. (2016, September 10). Why print news still rules. Politico.com. Retrieved May 16, 2017, from www.politico.com/magazine/story/2016/09/newspapers-print-news-online-journalism-214238

Scholastic. (n.d.). Kids and family reading report, downloads. Retrieved May 16, 2017, from www.scholastic.com/readingreport/downloads.htm

Schugar, H. R., Smith, C. A., & Schugar, J. T. (2013). Teaching with interactive e-books in grades K-6. *The Reading Teacher, 66*(8), 615–624.

Schugar, J. T., Schugar, H., & Penny, C. (2011). A nook or a book? Comparing college students' reading comprehension levels, critical reading, and study skills. *International Journal of Technology in Teaching and Learning, 7*(2), 174–192.

Sparrow, B., & Chapman, L. (2013). Social cognition in the internet age: Same as it ever was? *Psychological Inquiry, 24,* 273–292.

Sparrow, B., Liu, J., & Wegner, D. M. (2011). Google effects on memory: Cognitive consequences of having information at our fingertips. *Science, 333*(6043), 776–778.

Strouse, G. A., & Ganea, P. A. (2017, May 16). Parent-toddler behavior and language differ when reading electronic and print picture books. *Frontiers in Psychology, 8.* Retrieved November 27, 2017, from www.ncbi.nlm.nih.gov/pmc/articles/PMC5432581/

Student Monitor LLC. (2013). *Lifestyle & media – Spring 2013.*

Student Monitor LLC. (2014). *Converting data to insight – Fall 2014.*

Subrahmanyam, K., Michikyan, M., Clemmons, C., Carrillo, R., Uhls, Y. T., & Greenfield, P. M. (2013). Learning from paper, learning from screens: Impact of screen reading and multitasking conditions on reading and writing among college students. *International Journal of Cyber Behavior, Psychology and Learning, 3*(4), 1–27.

Swift, A., & Ander, S. (2017, January 6). Rumors of the demise of books greatly exaggerated. Gallup. Retrieved May 16, 2017, from www.gallup.com/poll/201644/rumors-demise-books-greatly-exaggerated.aspx

Taipale, S. (2014). The affordances of reading/writing on paper and digitally in Finland. *Telematics and Informatics, 31*(4), 532–542.

Taipale, S. (2015). Bodily dimensions of reading and writing practices on paper and digitally. *Telematics and Informatics, 32*(4), 766–775.

Takacs, Z. K., Swart, E. K., & Bus, A. G. (2015). Benefits and pitfalls of multimedia and interactive features in technology-enhanced storybooks: A meta-analysis. *Review of Educational Research, 85*(4), 698–739.

Thurman, N. (2014). Newspaper consumption in the digital age: Measuring multi-channel audience attention and brand popularity. *Digital Journalism, 2*(2), 156–178.

Thurman, N. (2017). Newspaper consumption in the mobile age. *Journalism Studies*. Digital-first. Retrieved May 16, 2017, from www.tandfonline.com/doi/full/10.1080/1461670X.2017.1279028

Turner, K. H., & Hicks, T. (2015). *Connected reading: Teaching adolescent readers in a digital world*. Urbana, IL: National Council of Teachers of English.

Vincent, J. (2016). Students' use of paper and pen versus digital media in university environments for writing and reading – A cross-cultural explanation. *Journal of Print and Media Technology Research, 2*, 97–106.

Ward, A. F. (2013). Supernormal: How the internet is changing our memories and our minds. *Psychological Inquiry, 24*, 341–348.

Wolf, M., & Barzillai, M. (2009). The importance of deep reading. *Educational Leadership, 66*(6), 32–37.

Wright, P., & Lickorish, A. (1983). Proof-reading texts on screen and paper. *Behaviour and Information Technology, 2*(3), 227–235.

8

Multimodal Critical Inquiry
Nurturing Decolonial Imaginaries

Gerald Campano, T. Philip Nichols, and Grace D. Player

We approach the invitation of this handbook chapter – to discuss multimodality in reading research – with an acknowledgment that multimodal frameworks have a long history and numerous intellectual lineages that precede their influence in literacy studies. By "put[ting] images, gestures, music, movement, animation, and other representational modes on equal footing with language" (Siegel, 2006, p. 65), multimodal lenses offer an avenue for re-reading "literacy" beyond school-based notions of reading and writing, and underscore how individuals and collectivities mobilize literacy practices within and across specific contexts and in relation to power asymmetries. They also invite us to look forward, to consider how phenomena such as transnational migration, global neoliberal policies, and activist movements of resistance might be aligned with, and inform, the next phase of multimodal literacy research.

One of the well-established contributions of multimodality to reading research is a more expansive understanding of what constitutes a text (e.g. Gee, 2003; Harste, Woodward, & Burke, 1984; Kress, 2000; Rowe, 1988; Serafini, 2013; Siegel, 1995; Smagorinsky & Coppock, 1994). This idea has provided educators theoretical and empirical justifications to go beyond traditional books and support students in reading across semiotic modes (Alvermann, 2010; Hassett & Curwood, 2010; Mills, 2010). Multimodality has also placed a renewed emphasis on collaborative work and creation (e.g. Beach & O'Brien, 2015; Vasudevan, Schultz, & Bateman, 2010). What has perhaps been less explored are the ways in which multimodal inquiry, decoupled from critical and postcolonial perspectives, can reproduce the conventional hermeneutic it has claimed to upend: the individual, rational subject transacting with an autonomous text; the Eurocentric, liberal humanist subject. Indeed, multimodality can potentially re-inscribe schooling as usual – one need only witness the co-opting of digital and media literacies within new standards, "college readiness" discourses, and high-stakes accountability that serve to widen the achievement gap rather than expand who counts as literate in school (e.g. Buckingham, 2010).

This chapter argues for the need to more explicitly co-articulate multimodality with postcolonial theory. We first review the various scholarly lineages and debates that have shaped the literature on multimodality in literacy and reading education. The emerging literature on multimodality, in particular those that are informed by materialist philosophical traditions (e.g., Deleuze, 1994) and concerned with ontology (e.g. Leander & Boldt, 2013; Lenters, 2016; Stornaiuolo, Smith, & Phillips, 2017), provides an opportunity to (re)imagine and enact alternative pedagogical communities that value multiple and non-dominant ways on knowing. Much of the research on multimodality in education, however, has shied away from directly addressing issues of race and legacies of colonialism in the lives and learning of youth. One promising area of critical research is from scholars and educators who have been working at the intersection of critical literacy and participatory methods (e.g. Mirra, Garcia, & Morrell, 2015). This body of work, although not always explicitly in conversation with multimodal scholarship, provides rich examples of youth who are tapping into subaltern literate legacies, both to critique power and to create new educational communities. We believe one generative avenue for further research in multimodality is through an engagement with postcolonial theory. We offer examples from two research studies (Campano, 2007; Campano, Ghiso, & Welch, 2016) to bring together multimodal literacy frameworks with the postcolonial theories of Édouard Glissant. This pairing invites educators and literacy researchers to confront traumatic histories, tap into the agency of individual and collective literate identities, and imagine insurgent intellectual communities.

Multimodality and Reading Research

In one sense, approaches to multimodality that engage postcolonial perspectives are not far afield from previous research in reading and literacy studies that explicitly ties the concept both to the proliferation of new technologies and to the recent spread of globalization and neoliberal policies (e.g. Jewitt, 2008; New London Group, 1996; Siegel, 2012). This is not to say that multimodality is, itself, a new or recent phenomenon: researchers readily acknowledge that reading has always involved processes of decoding not only words, but also images, spatial layouts, and even tones as texts are read aloud (e.g. Johns, 1998; Palmeri, 2012). Indeed, as historians of literacy have argued, some of our earliest alphabetic characters emerged first as pictorial representations (Schmandt-Besserat & Erard, 2007), and it was not until the late Middle Ages that "silent reading" displaced the conventional practice of orally reciting written text (Clanchy, 1979). What scholars have signaled as unique, then, is not the existence of multimodality but rather the accelerated pace with which information technologies, transnational migration, and geo-political shifts have tested the limits of our previous frameworks for categorizing, analyzing, and understanding reading practices (Kress, 2010; Stornaiuolo et al., 2017).

Researchers have used different terms to characterize such cultural shifts. Kress (2003) deems it "the new media age," where the primary medium for reading has moved from printed text to the digital screen. This pivot, he argues, has put visual images at the center of human communication – which demands that we recalibrate our understanding of how modes combine in different contexts. Luke (2003), likewise, suggests that we are living in "new times," which call for "new literacy practices" for navigating a landscape for reading that does not fit nicely into formalized structures. Building on this idea, the New London Group (1996) articulates a notion of "multiliteracies" to suggest that these new practices must not only attend to emerging arrangements of modes, but also to the ways globalization has brought together a plurality of languages and cultures that challenge any singular approach to studying or teaching reading. While these approaches use different language to frame the central problems that multimodality addresses, their unifying thread is the recognition that the multiple modes and participatory nature of new technologies have made it difficult – if not impossible – to think of reading as a simple process of decoding symbols on a page. Much like earlier proponents of literacy study who had advocated for an expanded view of reading that took into account larger social contexts (e.g. Cole & Scribner, 1981; Heath, 1983), these technological and geopolitical developments elucidated the need for research frames to be expanded further still – to include those social dimensions that help to shape the interplay between multiple modes, media, and languages.

To do so, researchers of multimodal reading have drawn on different conceptual frameworks to guide their inquiries. Jewitt (2008) delineates three parallel traditions in educational literature that examine how modes interact: New Literacy Studies, Multiliteracies, and Multimodality. The first of these, New Literacy Studies (NLS), signals a body of scholarship that examines literacy not as a discrete bundle of skills, but as a complex, culturally-situated practice (Barton, Hamilton, & Ivanic, 2000; Gee, 1990; Street, 1995). "Multiliteracies" builds on the NLS tradition, arguing that the changing role of global capitalism has shifted what it means to be literate – and therefore demands new pedagogical approaches whereby literacy teaching and learning are understood as matters of "design" (New London Group, 1996). Multimodality, likewise, has been couched as a response to similar political phenomena. Siegel (2012), for example, views multimodality as a counterpoint to the "hard times" associated with globalization, neoliberalism, and the implementation of rigid academic standards in public education and an intervention that can open up curricular opportunities for meaning-making. As in the aforementioned traditions, scholars of multimodality have argued that meaning can be made and interpreted using a plurality of communicative resources and combinations thereof – including, but not limited to, language, image, gesture, body posture, sound, writing, music, and speech (Kress, 2010; Kress & van Leeuwen, 2001). Further, Hull and Nelson (2005) have stressed that the merging of different modes is not simply a discrete additive process, but one that results in new, generative combinations of meaning – or, put simply, that the whole of a multimodal artifact is more than the sum of its individual parts.

Given certain similarities across these terms, it is not surprising that they are, at times, used interchangeably; however, some have argued that there are subtle tensions that exist between them. Anderson (2013), for example, notes that the genealogies of New Literacy Studies and Multiliteracies stem from anthropological traditions that foreground the study of literacy events and practices as social exchanges. By contrast, Multimodality has roots in Systemic Functional Linguistics, which helps explain why some of its proponents have not simply used the term to denote descriptive studies of semiotic practice, but have developed elaborate frameworks or "grammars" for organizing and analyzing multimodal artifacts (e.g. Jewitt, 2014; Kress & van Leeuwen, 1996). According to Anderson, glossing over differences in such methodological approaches

> could lead to misinterpretations of the assumptions and priorities underlying a particular research study, which can become problematic when the findings are uncritically adapted from studies whose underlying premises are not commensurate with educators' own beliefs about learning and author.
>
> (p. 296)

Tensions within and between these traditions are not limited to their respective intellectual and academic lineages. Bazalgette and Buckingham (2013), for example, note that there is a tendency for multimodal research to reinscribe and reify the very divides between print and non-print texts that such perspectives are meant to dissolve. They argue that this is, in part, due to an elision of differences between multimodal analysis (which involves a process of trying to understand how distinct modes work together to achieve a particular social outcome) and multimodal texts (which, they suggest, is not a particularly useful category, since all texts are, in some sense, constituted by multiple modes). Street (2013), likewise, develops this claim further, positing that multimodal analysis must be careful not to grant too much autonomy to the individual modes themselves, as their meanings and functions cannot be disembedded from their situated social uses. For instance, talk of the "affordances" of a given mode that does not acknowledge the specific contexts in which the mode is put to use seems to assume certain limits and possibilities in the mode itself, not as something interdependent with the contingencies of social use. Recently, literacy researchers have tried to attend to these uncertainties by turning attention to those dimensions of use that have traditionally been harder to account for – materiality (Pahl & Rowsell, 2010), embodiment (Ghiso, 2015), and affect (Lenters, 2016), for instance. Leander and Boldt (2013) draw on "rhizomatic" assemblage theories of Gilles Deleuze (1994) to illustrate how multimodality is an emergent phenomenon – where meaning is not only something that unfolds through an interplay of aesthetic and linguistic modes, but also through the embodied experiences and practices of those who interact with such texts.

Multimodality and Critical Inquiry

The recent resonance of Deleuze's work in reading research on multimodality – with its emphasis on creativity and difference – could provide an opportunity for educators to embrace alternative forms of sociality and community in education. This is because, as May (2005) argues, Deleuze embraces ontology and larger questions about how one might conduct one's life beyond dominant scripts and ossified categories of identity, such as, in the field of education, "struggling readers". By contrast, much of reading research and pedagogy with a critical orientation draws on theorists who take a more detached and skeptical posture toward the world. For example, the traditions of critical literacy (e.g., Lewison, Flint, & Van Sluys, 2002) and critical discourse analysis in education (Janks, 2010), developed during an intellectual zeitgeist aptly characterized as a hermeneutics of suspicion (Ricoeur, 1970), are geared toward supporting students in questioning the idea of an essential nature to human life or existence. From this perspective, the great books of the Western Canon, for example, do not reveal timeless truths, but are themselves the products of particular historical and political forces. A high school English teacher may encourage the class to adopt a "postcolonial" lens in their reading of a "classic" such as *Heart of Darkness*, not only to expose its pretense to universality, but also to demonstrate how cultural "others" are dehumanized and regulated to the background in the dominant narratives of human history (Achebe, 1977). At an elementary level, a teacher may invite children to analyze Disney movies in order to question the ways in which gender normativity is reproduced in popular culture, or how representations of (dis)ability stand in for human vice or virtue. Thus, these critical "lenses", traditionally applied to canonical texts (Appleman, 2015), may also be employed to analyze multimodal texts as well (e.g., Baildon & Damico, 2009).

Challenging or Reproducing Reading-As-Usual?

These approaches have been invaluable in the field of literacy studies and reading, but they do not – in and of themselves – transcend a conventional hermeneutics and narrow notions of what it means to be educated. As the literary theorist Felski (2015) has argued recently, there are "limits" to dominant critical approaches aimed at "demystifying" and "deconstructing" texts; for example, they do not always point the way toward viable different futures. In primary and secondary schools, students may be invited to take a critical stance, but the literacy event itself may still involve an individual reader analyzing an autonomous text in a manner that can be assessed and evaluated quantitatively to justify sorting and ranking students according to normal-curve ideologies, too often along lines of race, class, and language (Simon & Campano, 2013). This is because, as the philosopher Linda Martin Alcoff (2006) reminds us, the notion of an individual rational self that can transcend social context – the Western liberal humanist subject – is pretty much hardwired into our educational institutions. A curriculum may use culturally relevant content, but students may nonetheless feel alienated because they are still experiencing schooling as usual. Even educational approaches informed by Deleuze, such as "assemblage theory", may just become another abstract analytical lens for students to "apply" to the interpretation of texts or for a researcher to analyze a classroom dynamic. Ironically, the renewed emphasis on embodiment, materiality, and affect in literacy studies, has not always translated into helping students and teachers address the realities of racism and colonialism in schooling (Nichols & Campano, 2017).

We believe a multimodal orientation can provide a pathway for reclaiming indigenous and subaltern literacies. Walter Mignolo's scholarship (1995) unpacks writing as a site of colonial struggle, whereby definitions of literacy cast solely in alphabetic terms served to inscribe a binary between those deemed "literate", and by implication "civilized", and those considered "illiterate" and thereby savages in need of "taming" and "salvation." A multimodal approach makes visible the multiple indigenous literate traditions of the Americas – from Mayan codices to Andean quipus, among others – and also brings into the relief the power relations inherent in what gets named as literacy (Saldívar, 2004). As an example, European colonizers often burned entire indigenous archives to instantiate a myth of "illiteracy" and fuel the colonial enterprise. As Rasmussen (2012) notes, "broadening the definition of writing in the Americas beyond a particular semiotic system – the alphabet – disrupts a whole complex of cultural meanings, as well as dynamics of dominance" (p. 4). It frames the colonial encounter as a "confrontation between different literate traditions" (Rasmussen, 2012, p. 3) or as colonial semiosis (Mignolo, 2000), a bi-directional exchange that puts alphabetic and non-alphabetic texts in dialogue and "mutual inter-animation" (Rasmussen, 2012, p. 10). These exchanges have relevance for understanding the literate practices of today's youth, whose multimodal textual productions potentially draw on visual literacies and indigenous legacies of resistance (e.g. Cowan, 2004; Jiménez & Smith, 2008), and whose school literacy trajectories may have too often been circumscribed by their acquiescence to, or deviation from, an idealized alphabetic literacy.

Subaltern Literacies and Insurgent Communities of Inquiry

Some of the most promising research in multimodal inquiry comes from scholars who are working at the intersection of critical literacy pedagogy and participatory/community-based research (e.g. Mirra et al., 2015). Because their methodologies involve collaborative inquiry alongside youth and families, they are concerned with nurturing more egalitarian communities, collectively embodying humanizing and decolonial forms of sociality, ones that value interdependence and are more conducive to students' holistic flourishing (e.g. Ghiso, 2016). The language of this scholarship, following Lorde (1984) and rich traditions of feminist critical thought that do not separate emotions from cognition, is one of connection, love, healing, joy – multiple ways of knowing and being – and asset orientations that honor youths' brilliance rather than its deficits (e.g., Alim & Haupt, 2017). Often theorizing from non-dominant activist, artistic, and intellectual legacies, what may be characterized as organic critical literacies (Campano, Ghiso, Sánchez, 2013), this emerging scholarship also goes beyond critique to prefigure other possible worlds of education. While it does not always invoke directly the academic conversations on multimodality per se – although some scholars certainly do – what does appear to be a salient pattern is that it documents how youth draw on and inter-animate a range of semiotic resources, including subaltern literacies, in culturally relevant (Ladson-Billings, 1995), sustaining (Paris & Alim, 2014), and procreative ways.

San Pedro (2017), for example, examines the context of a Native American literature class to inquire into the ways youth engaged in multimodal projects that sought to build on Native traditions and give students opportunities for expressing identities as "in-process." He documented how, through visual and verbal storytelling and humanizing dialogue, a new classroom culture emerged that prioritized trust and mutual relationships. Ghiso (2016) draws explicitly on theories of coloniality to analyze how young Latina/o children use photography as a form of multimodal inquiry to recenter their immigrant neighborhood as a place of innovative knowledge production, cross-cultural and multilingual exchange, and interdependence. Wong and Peña (2017)'s study of two classrooms utilizing performance arts, revealed that this medium fostered inquiry into aspects of students' cultures and enabled them to address contemporary topics that impacted them daily. In this reimagined and interdependent school space, students built cultures of sharing, storytelling, and listening, that served both to acknowledge shared traumas and to joyfully and collectively project images of the futures they desired and deserved. Enciso (2011) showcases how storytelling as a culturally-inflected literacy practice, can build connections and solidarity between immigrant and non-immigrant youth. In their ethnographic study of Hip Hop culture in South Africa, Alim and Haupt (2017) found that Black South Africans both reclaimed and retold their linguistic and cultural histories while validating and celebrating their Black/Indigenous discourses and forms of expression. In turn, they used these ways of expression to cast a vision of a pluralistic future that centered people of color. Korina Jocson (2005) framed a study of June Jordan's *Poetry for the People* around the perspectives of feminist poets such as Adrienne Rich, Gloria Anzaldúa, and Jordan herself. In this work, she explores the potential of the *Poetry for the People* curriculum to harness student and teachers' multiple literacies, voices, and cultural resources, and to help students see the connection between poetry, identity, and political action.

Maisha Winn (2011, Fisher, 2009) has investigated multimodal literacy pedagogy that builds on cultural practices of resistance, such as playwriting and spoken word poetry. Reading, writing, and performing poetry gave students an opportunity to reclaim often silenced histories of Black revolutionaries, share testimonials, participate in political action, and resist dominant narratives that deficitized their literacies and knowledges. In her work with incarcerated girls and their teaching artists, Winn (2011) observed the ways that the girls, who had been assigned deficit narratives based on their race, gender, and class – narratives further impacted by their incarcerated statuses – used playwriting and performance built on traditions of political theater to describe their worlds and engage in collective acts of resistance. Through these multimodal practices the young women brought their stories and perspectives to light, reimagined their futures, fostered a community and a sense of home with one another, and advocated for themselves. In both of these studies, Winn demonstrates how multimodal pedagogies that connect students to traditions of resistant arts can create opportunities for youth of color to enact change as they assert identities as literate and knowledgeable.

A number of literacy scholars have used Black feminist traditions as theoretical grounding for multimodal pedagogies that attend to students' evolving identities and seek to reimagine schooling as more communitarian and decolonial. For example, Price-Dennis (2016) highlights how Black girls use digital tools to explore their "multiple, political/critical, historical, intellectual, collaborative, and identity-laden literacies" (p. 337), and how these multimodal facilities might be leveraged in the curriculum to mediate teachers' relationships to students across boundaries of race, gender, class, and ability. Price-Dennis builds on the work of Elaine Richardson (2007), who studied the multimodal literacies of Black girls. Richardson argues for the importance of using a racial and gendered analytical lens, and highlights how their literacies not only draw from cultural histories, but are also a response to the ever-present racism and sexism of our contemporary society.

Carmen Kynard (2010) adds to this literature by attending to the ways the 13 Black women in her study appropriated modern tools to tap into historical legacies of resistance. Through a digital listserv, the young women created what Kynard refers to as a "hush harbor", a communicative dynamic that was not audible to the broader class, and through which they could use literacy to share counter stories and more freely engage in acts of individual and collective self-definition. These spaces strove to prefigure decolonial worlds within the hegemonic white space of the academy, allowing students to recreate and reimagine the academy from within. Similarly, Haddix, McArthur, Muhammad, Price-Dennis, and Sealey-Ruiz (2016) created a "virtual kitchen table talk" – a multimodal conversation in the form of recorded Zoom videos that transposed the gendered cultural epistemological practices of "kitchen table talk" to the context of higher education. In both these examples, multimodality became a vehicle through which to nurture what Harney and Moten (2013) characterize as an educational "undercommons," an alternative inquiry community informed by Black radical theory and liberation struggles operating within and against predominantly white institutions, autonomous notions of literacy, and conventional hermeneutics.

All these studies reflect how multimodal approaches, when fused with critical theories, might give rise to insurgent communities of inquiry (Cochran-Smith & Lytle, 2009) that mobilize reading and writing for social change. The aforementioned research examples attend to the histories of systemic racism and colonial oppression that continue to shape schooling and tap into the meaning-making traditions of non-dominant communities. As we look to the future of reading and literacy studies, we anticipate scholarship that will draw both from cutting edge research on multimodality and from a wider array of intellectual traditions that are concerned with issues of power.

Multimodality and Decolonial Imaginaries

The convergence of multimodality and critical literacy provides a foundation for understanding reading practices as a situated coming-together of identities, geographies, and semiotic resources. Such a framing echoes the work of postcolonial scholars who have examined the ways language and identity are bound up with "place" and "history." To understand how these intersections might expand our conceptions and uses of multimodal inquiry, one perspective we have found especially instructive is that of Édouard Glissant. Much like scholars of multimodality have looked at the ways texts are not monoliths, but rather, exist as a constellation of communicative modes, and critical literacy scholars have recognized the ways that readers' identities condition their engagement with texts, Glissant also attends to the ways observable practices are animated by rich and textured histories. In his theorizing of a "poetics of landscape," Glissant (1989) suggests that situated activities which appear to us as stable and knowable are, in fact, an assemblage of identities, materials, and labor that, together, produce a perceived sense of stasis. In this way, we see in Glissant a resource for examining multimodal reading, too, as a layered assemblage.

Glissant is perhaps best known for his conceptualization of creolization, borrowed from linguistics, to characterize broader social phenomena, including how cultures and identities come in contact with one another. Unlike créolité, which may refer to a new, reified identity made from two formally separate identities, creolization draws attention to a universal, though largely unpredictable, relational process, whereby identities do not become fixed and cultural transactions do not have an end point. In literacy research, Lemrow (2016) draws on Glissant to understand the critical literacy practices of youth in a "developmental" (i.e. remedial) reading class, many of whom identified as multiracial. She argues that:

> within the realm of education, and literacy education, in particular, créolization theory can be a useful tool to explore how our literacy practices are informed and created within classrooms, with a special focus on those who best articulate a créolised reality: students who draw their identities from the interstices of the more formerly rigid categories of race, ethnicity, language, and gender.
>
> *(p. 4)*

She documents, for example, students' engagement with literature from ethnic studies that "awake[ns] the opportunity to see across and within difference" (p. 7). Lemrow traces how one student, Jeremiah, drew on these openings to link his experiences of the Philippines with Junot Diaz's (2007) characterizations of the Dominican Republic in *The Brief Wonderous Life of Oscar Wao*, reminding us that geographically disparate spaces are linked by colonial histories and reframing his particular lived reality as part of a global phenomenon.

As "creolization" demonstrates, Glissant's work engages *both* poststructural and decolonial thought, theorizing from the particular location of Caribbean ideas that have increasing worldwide resonance during this current era of globalization, information technology, social networking, mass migration, war, xenophobia, cultural and linguistic interaction, and conflict. In reading research, a thinker such as Glissant can play an important role in helping to reconcile scholarship that has embraced post-humanism to think about multimodality, new literacies, and technologies, but has largely evaded issues of race and colonialism with the work of critical literacy scholars concerned with more humanizing and liberatory pedagogies.

Glissant himself was an anti-essentialist but also a critical realist, who situates identity within collective memory and trauma. He did not shy away from a direct confrontation with colonialism, including the genocide of the middle passage, such as, for example, his formulation of the rhizomatic identity. Glissant was in dialogue with Deleuze and Guattarri, and applies their metaphor of the rhizome – an image to characterize non-hierarchical thought that has multiple entry points for interpretation – to identity, a term seemingly at odds with their philosophical project. For Glissant, the rhizome becomes an apt way to critique the dominant views of identity as adherence to a "single root, of racial or linguistic purity" (Hiepko, 2011, p. 256), often tied to exclusionary origin myths of nationhood. Multifarious cultural influences, an entangled and ever-expanding root system, shape a person's identity through processes of creolization, as identities are not static but rather perpetually in the act of becoming, formed, and reformed through our contact and relations with others, "identity-as-relation" (Hiepko, 2011, p. 260). In the field of reading, an identity-as-relation framing underscores that there is no one-to-one correspondence between a student's identity and some easily identifiable "primary discourse" (Gee, 1989) – thus complicating, for example, assumptions about what books students may gravitate to or what background knowledge students have for accessing particular textual content. Rather, through Glissant's formulation, what becomes salient are students' multiple, ever-expanding literacies, which borrow and remix from a range of discursive contexts.

Conceiving identity as dynamic does not imply, however, a type of unfettered self-invention, unconstrained by history and the material word. Glissant's (2010) figure for subjectification in the opening pages of the *Poetics of Relation*, is the errant slave ship and the triple forms of abyss the captives' faced: that of the boat's hull, the ocean bottom underneath it, and the foreign "new" world to which the ship sailed, where survivors were sold into chattel slavery. This new world was not discovered, but conquered through the genocide of its inhabitants and repopulated, in part, by subsequent waves of settlers, many with their own colonial legacies. These historical images and referents set a different stage than that of ethereal Deleuzian nomadic lines of flight, at least as Deleuze has been taken up in literacy research. Glissant strikes a delicate balance of acknowledging the productive forms of agency that arise out of history's contact (and conflict) zones without romanticizing suffering. It was within the abyss that new identities and alternative modes of expression and resistance emerge. Glissant's unsentimental historicizing of identity is a reminder that language and literacy are never neutral, but always implicated in colonial legacies and relations of power.

Our histories are thus entangled and we are implicated in one another's fates, but differences matter and matter differently. In fact, according to Glissant (2010), a central compulsion of the colonial imaginary is to absorb differences by making them "transparent" or assimilable into dominant Western paradigms, an imperial scholarly project which is inherently reductive, employed to promote hierarchies and justify racism and colonial power. For example, the long history of high stakes testing in the US masks how concepts such "reading comprehension" and literacy assessments are tied to legacies of oppression (Willis, 2008), and sets Western notions of reading (e.g. the bedtime story routine, [Heath, 1982]) as the interrogated norm for interactions with texts. This is why Glissant privileges the "right to opacity" (2010, p. 190), a way of asserting one's irreducible singularity, that which is not fully transparent to others, even possibly to oneself. We can learn from others, become transfigured by others, work in solidarity with others, without having to finally "know" others, and speak essential truths about them which they do not wish to articulate for themselves.

Opacity is also necessary for "furtive" (Ramazani, 2001, p. 129) resistant communicative and literacy practices, especially under conditions of oppression and power asymmetry (e.g. San Pedro, 2015). Nurturing a decolonial imaginary would entail promoting genuine dialogue across differences in order to imagine a collective future not premised on the need to homogenize and control. It would also require a more poetic sensibility in our relations with others, one that is genuinely open to the unexpected, creative alchemy of thought and expression when the robust diversity of the world is embraced rather than standardized or excluded.

Youth Conveying Rhizomatic Identities through Multimodal Design

How might destabilizing linear associations between students' "visible identities" (Alcoff, 2006) and their presumed knowledge of and relationships with texts extend existing multimodal research in new directions? How might a decolonial approach, coupled with multimodality, offer a lens through which to understand how students read the word and the world (Freire, 1970)? In this section, we probe these questions and possibilities through examples from two studies (Campano, 2007; Campano et al., 2016).

Dancing across Borders

Twenty years ago, before the concept of multimodality had taken widespread hold in literacy research and policy, Gerald was a fifth grade teacher in California's Central Valley, conducting practitioner research into how the official reading curriculum might be more dialogically attuned to the diverse immigrant narratives of his students (Campano, 2007). During that time, under the guidance of Angelica, an undergraduate student teacher, Gerald's students formed a performance group they called "Dancing Across Borders" (DAB). The troupe organically embraced a multimodal approach to literacy, composing and performing spoken-word poetry, choreographing musical routines, sharing essays, and scripting and producing plays, including one about the braided history of Filipino and Mexican farmworkers in California's Central Valley. When Gerald was asked to facilitate a professional development at his school on "classroom management" – a topic which usually takes a behavioral orientation in identifying and disciplining individuals to fit a preconceived norm of academic participation – he enlisted the help of the Dancing Across Borders group. The youth wrote and staged a play titled "What the Teacher Didn't Know", which spotlighted a series of common "management" scenarios in the classroom between students and a fictionalized teacher, Mr. Sid (modeled after the Dickens character Mr. M'Choakumchild). After each conflict, all the actors would freeze, and then the character reprimanded by Mr. Sid recited a soliloquy – a device the class embraced from Shakespeare – about "What the Teacher Didn't Know." For example, when the teacher reprimands a student, Susana, for speaking in Spanish and proclaims that "This is the United States, so there will be no foreign languages!", she replies:

> What the teacher didn't know is that I just came from Mexico five months ago, so sometimes I don't know how to say things in English. He didn't know my language is an important part of me. Speaking Spanish is something I feel proud of, but he is cruel for not

encouraging me to maintain my traditions. Instead he put me down and made me feel like a stranger. And also, my teacher didn't know that people spoke Spanish here before English!

(Campano, 2007, p. 99)

The nationalistic English-only policy of the school does not take into account legacies of colonialism and students' embodied and affective relationships to language. The performance was both humorous and poignant, as each soliloquy raised critical consciousness inequities related to class, culture, gender, and language difference that often lurk beneath the surface of classroom dynamics. In an act of empathy and generosity, the Dancing Across Borders troupe reserved the final soliloquy for Mr. Sid himself who, a one-dimensional villain throughout most of the performance, became humanized as he recounted the challenges of being a teacher in a severely under-resourced school district.

The writing of the DAB troupe exemplified many characteristics of traditional academic reading and writing (e.g. use of evidence-based argumentation, academic language, point of view, summarizing, inferring) as the children met, and often surpassed, the demands of conventional English Language Arts standards. Their plays were also hybrid texts: shifting between English, Spanish, and Illocano languages; literary, comic, and conversational registers – all dramatically conveyed through gesture, movement, and voice. They reflected the literacy practices associated with the students' rhizomatic identities, which are often invisible in the official curriculum. It was only after some time spent with Angelica and the students that Gerald realized their creative labor was informed by El Teatro Campesino, an activist and artistic legacy that grew out of the local intellectual soil of nearby migrant labor camps. Similar to El Teatro, the plays of DAB were collectively produced living texts that were revised and improvised in the process of performance, sometimes in response to audience feedback (Broyles-González, 1994), a poetics of relation. Often there was no single author to their plays; all students would contribute to the collaborative process of authoring in unique and, ideally, complementary ways. These furtive literacies protected the students by making their individual critiques "opaque" to institutional power. DAB employed a collective creative process that transgressed the ideology of individual authorship that underpins so much schooling and the high-stakes testing paradigm in the United States. Many children who were positioned as struggling in the mandated, standardized literacy curriculum of the school blossomed in DAB, which cultivated an ethos of interdependence rather than competition and the individuation of learners as conforming to or deviating from a norm.

The DAB troupe was engaged in multimodal critical literacy inquiry. In a Freirean (1970) manner, they were reading their worlds, including their world of schooling. In "What the Teacher Didn't Know," the students critiqued the education system and employed political theater as a vehicle to educate educators. Their insights, in part, derived from inquiry into their own subaltern experiences and identities. The students wanted their audiences to take seriously their claims about schooling, particularly the ways in which it can dehumanize and perpetuate inequity. DAB became a "community of epistemic resistance" (McHugh, 2017, p. 272; Mohanty, 2003) to official institutional practices that too often deficitize and criminalize youth, and that do not take into account systemic causes of inequality, such as poverty, racism, xenophobia, and colonial legacies. In the process of critique, however, they were simultaneously prefiguring and enacting an alternative community, one that fosters cooperation and celebrates human variance, including the multifarious literate and intercultural resources which fertilized their creative and intellectual imaginations. Although the elementary students were courageously addressing serious topics, there was a good deal of joy and bonding in the troupe, both in their performance as well throughout the process of collaborative inquiry. As Audre Lorde (1984, p. 56) reminds us: "The sharing of joy, whether physical, emotional, psychic, or intellectual, forms a bridge between the sharers which can be the basis for understanding much of what is not shared between them, and lessens the threat of their difference." Through multimodal inquiry rooted in and repurposed from the decolonial artistic and activist traditions of migrant political theater, the children were able to merge physical, emotional, psychic, and intellectual ways of knowing to make the academic literacy curriculum their own.

The Collective Educational Futures Project

Our second example comes from a university-community research partnership, now entering its eighth year, between the University of Pennsylvania and St. Thomas Aquinas (STA), a multilingual, multi-ethnic Catholic Parish, school, and community center in South Philadelphia (Campano et al., 2016). South Philadelphia itself has become a sort of archipelago, not unlike Glissant's actual Antilles, where different cultural and linguistic communities live alongside one another and engage in everyday relations. There are longstanding African American and Italian communities, Vietnamese and Cambodian refugees that arrived in the 1980's and 1990's, an Indonesian population beginning in the late 1990's, newcomers from Latin America within the past ten years, and most recently, arrivals from Sudan and the Democratic Republic of Congo. STA itself has masses in five different languages – Indonesian, Vietnamese, English, Spanish, and Tagalog – and supports an active Concerned Black Catholic organization. While Christianity has historically been an instrument of imperialism, St. Thomas Aquinas is composed of (post-)colonial communities, with legacies of war and genocide, who now occupy formally exclusive church space – such as a convent converted to a community center – in order to organize for their survival and rights. They also use the space and its resources to sustain cultural traditions, celebrate community, and engage each other in often compassionate and joyful ways.

On an early summer afternoon, in the cool, fluorescent-lit basement of the church, the youth of the Collective Educational Futures Project are busily sorting, flipping through, and snipping apart the heaps of magazines, newspapers, old discount bin art books, print-outs of textiles, and photographs of South Philadelphia. They are creating collage self-portraits after having viewed and discussed the collage art of Kara Walker and Lorna Simpson, among others.

Mai sits quietly in a corner, deliberately cutting shapes from the mounds of colorful paper before her. With care, her fingers deftly shift her cuttings ever so slightly, millimeter by millimeter, until a face, with shoulder length ombre hair and wispy bangs emerges (Figure 8.1).

The hair is made of delicate slivers of traditional Indonesian Batik textiles and photographs of South Philadelphia, reflecting a creolized lived reality and the multiple roots of her ever-evolving identity that transverse political borders and cultural boundaries. Mai explains that her hair carries a lot of meaning for her and her family. When she cut it without telling her parents, her mother, who saw her hair as a symbol of her Indonesian tradition, was upset because she felt it indicated that Mai was cutting off her ties to her culture. Mai explains, though, as she runs her fingers over the tendrils of Indonesian Batik and shimmering South Philadelphia lights, that she still holds onto her Indonesian roots. She mentions, too, that she used a picture of the sky in collaging the shape of her ear, symbolizing her openness to new relationships, experiences, and the world. Her collage is one multimodal representation of her dynamic identity, her ongoing process of becoming. This visual rendition shows both her singularity and her relationship to an ever expanding root system of cultural influences in ways that complicate common dichotomies of "old" and "new" cultures used to describe the experiences of transnational youth. For someone who first encounters Mai's artwork, it may seem – following Glissant – opaque, because the complexity of Mai's experiences defy reductive institutional categories, such as "model minority" or "immigrant student". As we learn from listening to Mai, it is in fact replete with interpretive possibilities.

Figure 8.1 Mai's collage self-portrait

It was multimodal inquiry that enabled Mai and her peers to draw from the range of multifarious cultural influences that shape their identities, and inquire into where their experiences overlap and diverge, and what possible futures they may want to forge together (Gultom et al., 2019). Through the arts, youth are exploring and communicating their own processes of becoming, reading and interpreting their worlds, and negotiating their relationships to others. Through film and critical media making (Thomas, 2017), youth, families, and community leaders are collaborating to learn about the ways local knowledge has been used to challenge educational barriers and to collectively imagine the futures they desire and deserve.

Conclusion

Multimodality is ancient. As a key term in literacy education, it has gained prominence over the past several decades, but may even be waning in recent years. While a multimodal approach has the potential to expand reading and writing opportunities and who "counts" as literate, we have argued that there is nothing inherently liberatory about employing diverse semiotic modes in the literacy curriculum. Like any social practice, multimodality must be understood contextually. We have also suggested that its salient features – an expansive notion of the text, the ineluctable twinning of reading and creation, and collective meaning-making – are promising for inquiry into culturally sustaining as well as culturally procreative pedagogies, especially when informed by theorists of race and coloniality. Glissant reminds us that the multimodal worlds students inhabit – worlds characterized by a multiplicity of identities (even within the self), languages, literacies, and meaning-making practices, often in the same school or neighborhood block – is an outgrowth of violent colonial and imperial legacies. But despite the unpredictability and uncertainty of cultural interaction and conflict, there is also the potential, if educators put their fears aside, to help nurture decolonial imaginaries, collective forms of resistance, and communities that embrace, returning to Lorde, the "interdependence of (non-dominant) differences". This hope may seem utopian, especially as we are writing this handbook chapter in a political period marked by a vicious resurgence of nativism and (re)legitimization of racism in the United States and across the globe. The critical multimodal inquiries of The Dancing Across Borders troupe and the families and youth of Collective Educational Futures Project provide evidence, nonetheless, that there are alternative worlds being imagined and enacted in the shell of the old. Like multimodality, these struggles are both longstanding and new.

References

Achebe, C. (1977). An image of Africa: Racism in Conrad's *Heart of Darkness*. *The Massachusetts Review*, 18(4), 782–794.

Alcoff, L. M. (2006). *Visible identities: Race, gender, and the self*. Oxford, UK: Oxford University Press.

Alim, H. S., & Haupt, A. (2017). Reviving soul(s) with Afrikaaps: Hip Hop as culturally sustaining pedagogy in South Africa. In D. Paris & H. S. Alim (Eds.) *Culturally sustaining pedagogies: Teaching and learning for justice in a changing world* (pp. 157–174). New York, NY: Teachers College Press.

Alvermann, D. (2010). *Adolescents' online literacies: Connecting classrooms, digital media, and popular culture*. New York, NY: Peter Lang.

Anderson, K. (2013). Contrasting Systemic Functional Linguistics and situated literacies approaches to multimodality in literacy and writing studies. *Written Communication*, 30(3), 276–299.

Appleman, D. (2015). *Critical encounters in high school English: Teaching literary theory to adolescents* (3rd ed.). New York, NY: Teachers College Press.

Baildon, M., & Damico, J. S. (2009). "How do we know": Students examine issues of credibility with a complicated multimodal web-based text. *Curriculum Inquiry*, 39(2), 265–285.

Barton, D., Hamilton, M., & Ivanic, R. (2000). *Situated literacies: Reading and writing in context*. New York, NY: Routledge.

Bazalgette, C., & Buckingham, D. (2013). Literacy, media, and multimodality: A critical response. *Literacy*, 47(2), 95–102.

Beach, R., & O'Brien, D. (2015). Fostering students' science inquiry through app affordances of multimodality, collaboration, interactivity, and connectivity. *Reading & Writing Quarterly*, 31(2), 119–134.

Broyles-González, Y. (1994). *El teatro campesino: Theater in the Chicano movement*. Austin, TX: University of Texas Press.

Buckingham, D. (2010). The future of media literacy in the digital age: Some challenges for policy and practice. In P. Verniers (Ed.), *Media literacy in Europe: Controversies, challenges, perspectives* (pp. 13–24). Brussels: Euromeduc.

Campano, G. (2007). *Immigrant students and literacy: Reading, writing and remembering*. New York, NY: Teachers College Press.

Campano, G., Ghiso, M. P., & Sánchez, L. (2013). "No one knows the … amount of a person": Elementary students critiquing dehumanization through organic critical literacies. *Research in the Teaching of English*, 48(1), 98–125.

Campano, G., Ghiso, M. P., & Welch, B. (2016). *Partnering with immigrant communities: Action through literacy*. New York, NY: Teachers College Press.

Clanchy, M. T. (1979). *From memory to written record*. Cambridge, MA: Blackwell.

Cochran-Smith, M., & Lytle, S. L. (2009). *Inquiry as stance, practitioner research for the next generation*. New York, NY: Teachers College Press.

Cole, M., & Scribner, S. (1981). *The psychology of literacy*. Cambridge, MA: Harvard Education Press.

Cowan, P. (2004). Devils or angels: Literacy and discourse in lowrider culture. In J. Mahiri (Ed.), *What they don't learn in school: Literacy in the lives of urban youth* (pp. 47–74). New York, NY: Peter Lang.

Deleuze, G. (1994). *Difference and repetition*. New York, NY: Columbia University Press.
Díaz, J. (2007). *The brief wondrous life of Osca Wao*. New York, NY: Riverhead Books.
Enciso, P. (2011). Storytelling in critical literacy pedagogy: Removing the walls between immigrant and non-imigrant youth. *English Teaching: Practice and Critique, 10*(1), 21–40.
Felski, R. (2015). *The limits of critique*. Chicago, IL: University of Chicago Press.
Fisher, M. T. (2009). *Black literate lives: Historical and contemporary perspectives*. New York, NY: Routledge.
Freire, P. (1970). *Pedagogy of the oppressed*. New York, NY: Continuum.
Gee, J. P. (1989). What is literacy? *Journal of Education, 71*(1), 18–25.
Gee, J. P. (1990). *Social linguistics and literacies: Ideology in discourse*. Philadelphia, PA: Falmer Press.
Gee, J. P. (2003). *What video games have to teach us about learning and literacy*. New York, NY: St. Martin's Press.
Ghiso, M. P. (2015). Arguing from experience: Young children's embodied knowledge and writing as inquiry. *Journal of Literacy Research, 47*(2), 186–215.
Ghiso, M. P. (2016). The Laundromat as the transnational local: Young children's literacies of interdependence. *Teachers College Record, 118*(1), 1–46.
Glissant, E. (1989). *Caribbean discourse: Selected essays*. Translated by J. Michael Dash. Charlottesville, VA: University Press of Virginia.
Glissant, E. (2010). *Poetics of relation* (B. Wing, Trans.). Ann Arbor, MI: University of Michigan Press.
Gultom, F., Gultom, F., Kosasih, M., Li, M., Lie, J., Lorenzo, C., … Campano, G. (2019). What is home? A collaborative multimodal inquiry project by transnational youth in South Philadelphia. *In:cite journal, 1*(2), 4–24.
Haddix, M., McArthur, S., Muhammad, G., Price-Dennis, D., & Sealey-Ruiz, Y. (2016). At the kitchen table: Black women English educators speaking our truths. *English Education, 48*(4), 380–395.
Harney, S., & Moten, F. (2013). *The undercommons: Fugitive planning and Black studies*. New York, NY: Minor Compositions.
Harste, J., Woodward, V., & Burke, C. (1984). *Language stories and literacy lessons*. Portsmouth, NH: Heinemann.
Hassett, D. D., & Curwood, J. S. (2010). Theories and practices of multimodal education: The instructional dynamics of picture books and primary classrooms. *The Reading Teacher, 63*(4), 270–282.
Heath, S. B. (1982). What no bedtime story means: Narrative skills at home and at school. *Language in Society, 11*(1), 49–76.
Heath, S. B. (1983). *Ways with words*. New York, NY: Cambridge University Press.
Hiepko, A. S. (2011). Europe and the Antilles: An interview with Édouard Glissant (J. Everret, Trans.). In F. Lionnet & S. Shih (Eds.), *The creolization of theory* (pp. 255–261). Durham, NC: Duke University Press.
Hull, G., & Nelson, M. (2005). Locating the semiotic power of multimodality. *Written Communication, 22*(2), 224–261.
Janks, H. (2010). *Literacy and power*. New York, NY: Routledge.
Jewitt, C. (2008). Multimodality and literacy in school classrooms. *Review of Research in Education, 32*(1), 241–267.
Jewitt, C. (2014). *The handbook of multimodality analysis* (2nd ed.). New York, NY: Routledge.
Jiménez, R. T., & Smith, P. H. (2008). Mesoamerican literacies: Indigenous writing systems and contemporary possibilities. *Reading Research Quarterly, 43*(1), 28–46.
Jocson, K. M. (2005). "Taking it to the mic": Pedagogy of June Jordan's Poetry for the People and partnership with an urban high school. *English Education, 37*, 132–148.
Johns, A. (1998). *The nature of the book: Print and knowledge in the making*. Chicago, IL: University of Chicago Press.
Kress, G. (2000). Multimodality. In B. Cope & M. Kalantzis (Eds.), *Multiliteracies: Literacy learning and the design of social futures* (pp. 182–202). New York, NY: Routledge.
Kress, G. (2003). *Literacy in the new media age*. New York, NY: Routledge.
Kress, G. (2010). *Multimodality*. New York, NY: Routledge.
Kress, G., & van Leeuwen, T. (1996). *Reading images: The grammar of visual design*. New York, NY: Routledge.
Kress, G., & van Leeuwen, T. (2001). *Multimodal discourse: The modes and media of contemporary communication*. London: Arnold Publishers.
Kynard, C. (2010). From candy girls to cyber sista-cipher: Narrating Black females' color-consciousness and counterstories in and out of school. *Harvard Education Review, 80*(1), 30–53.
Ladson-Billings, G. (1995). Toward a theory of culturally relevant pedagogy. *American Educational Research Journal, 32*(3), 465–491.
Leander, K., & Boldt, G. (2013). Rereading "A pedagogy of multiliteracies": Bodies, texts, and emergence. *Journal of Literacy Research, 45*(1), 22–46.

Lemrow, E. M. (2016). Créolization and the new cosmopolitanism: Examining twenty-first-century student identities and literacy practices for transcultural understanding. *Journal of Multilingual and Multicultural Development*. doi:10.1080/01434632.2016.1186680

Lenters, K. (2016). Riding the lines and overwriting in the margins: Affect and multimodal literacy practices. *Journal of Literacy Research*, 48(3), 280–316.

Lewison, M., Flint, A. S., & Van Sluys, K. (2002). Taking on critical literacy: The journey of newcomers and novices. *Language Arts*, 79(5), 382–392.

Lorde, A. (1984). Uses of the erotic: The erotic as power. In A. Lorde, *Sister outsider: Essays and speeches* (pp. 53–59). Freedom, CA: The Crossing Press.

Luke, A. (2003). Literacy and the other: A sociological approach to literacy research and policy in multilingual societies. *Reading Research Quarterly*, 38(1), 132–141.

May, T. (2005). *Gilles Deleuze: An introduction*. Cambridge, UK: Cambridge University Press.

McHugh, N. A. (2017). Epistemic communities and institutions. In I. J. Kidd, J. Medina, & G. Pohlhaus, Jr. (Eds.), *The Routledge handbook of epistemic injustice* (pp. 270–278). New York, NY: Routledge.

Mignolo, W. (1995). *The darker side of the renaissance: Literacy, territoriality, and colonization*. Ann Arbor, MI: University of Michigan Press.

Mignolo, W. (2000). *Local histories/global designs: Coloniality, subaltern knowledge, and border thinking*. Princeton, NJ: Princeton University Press.

Mills, K. A. (2010). Shrek meets Vygotsky: Rethinking adolescents' multimodal literacy practices in schools. *Journal of Adolescent & Adult Literacy*, 54(1), 35–45.

Mirra, N., Garcia, A., & Morrell, E. (2015). *Doing youth participatory action research: Transforming inquiry with researchers, educators, and students*. New York, NY: Routledge.

Mohanty, C. (2003). *Feminism without borders* (2nd ed.). Durham, NC: Duke University Press.

New London Group. (1996). A pedagogy of multiliteracies: Designing social futures. *Harvard Educational Review*, 66(1), 60–92.

Nichols, T. P., & Campano, G. (2017). Posthumanism and literacy studies. *Language Arts*, 94(4), 245–251.

Pahl, K., & Rowsell, J. (2010). *Artifactual literacies: Every object tells a story*. New York, NY: Teachers College Press.

Palmeri, J. (2012). *Remixing composition: A history of multimodal writing pedagogy*. Carbondale, IL: Southern Illinois University Press.

Paris, D., & Alim, H. S. (2014). What are we seeking to sustain through culturally sustaining pedagogy? A loving critique forward. *Harvard Education Review*, 84(1), 85–100.

Price-Dennis, D. (2016). Developing curriculum to support Black girls' literacies in digital spaces. *English Education*, 48(4), 337–361.

Ramazani, J. (2001). *The hybrid muse: Postcolonial poetry in English*. Chicago, IL: University of Chicago Press.

Rasmussen, B. B. (2012). *Queequeg's coffin: Indigenous literacies and early American literature*. Durham, NC: Duke University Press.

Richardson, E. (2007). "She was workin like foreal": Critical literacy and discourse practices of African American females in the age of hip hop. *Discourse & Society*, 18(6), 789–809.

Ricoeur, P. (1970). *Freud and philosophy: An essay on interpretation*. New Haven, CT: Yale University Press.

Rowe, D. (1988). The literate potentials of book-related dramatic play. *Reading Research Quarterly* 33(1), 10–35.

Saldívar, J. D. (2004). Response to "devils or angels". In J. Mahiri (Ed.), *What they don't learn in school: Literacy in the lives of urban youth* (pp. 75–77). New York, NY: Peter Lang.

San Pedro, T. (2017). "This stuff interests me": Re-centering indigenous paradigms in colonizing school spaces. In D. Paris & H. S. Alim (Eds.) *Culturally sustaining pedagogies: Teaching and learning for justice in a changing world* (pp. 99–116). New York, NY: Teachers College Press.

San Pedro, T. J. (2015). Silence as shields: Agency and resistances among Native American students in the urban Southwest. *Research in the Teaching of English*, 50(2), 132.

Schmandt-Besserat, D., & Erard, M. (2007). Origins and forms of writing. In P. Smagorinsky (Ed.), *Handbook of research on writing* (pp. 81–96). New York, NY: Lawrence Erlbaum Associates.

Serafini, F. (2013). *Reading the visual: An introduction to teaching multimodal literacy*. New York, NY: Teachers College Press.

Siegel, M. (1995). More than words: The generative potential of transmediation for learning. *Canadian Journal of Education*, 20(4), 455–475.

Siegel, M. (2006). Rereading the signs: Multimodal transformations in the field of literacy education. *Language Arts*, 84(1), 65–71.

Siegel, M. (2012). New times for multimodality? Confronting the accountability culture. *Journal of Adolescent and Adult Literacy, 55*(8), 671–681.
Simon, R., & Campano, G. (2013). Activist literacies: Teacher research as resistance to the "normal curve." *Journal of Language and Literacy Education, 9*(1), 21–39.
Smagorinsky, P., & Coppock, J. (1994). Cultural tools and the classroom context: An exploration of an artistic response to literature. *Written Communication, 11*(3), 283–310.
Stornaiuolo, A., Smith, A., & Phillips, N. (2017). Developing a transliteracies framework for a connected world. *Journal of Literacy Research, 49*(1), 68–91.
Street, B. V. (1995). *Social literacies*. New York, NY: Routledge.
Street, B. V. (2013). Multimodality and New Literacy Studies: Exploring complementarity. In M. Bock & N. Pachler (Eds.), *Multimodality and social semiosis: Communication, meaning-making, and learning in the work of Gunther Kress* (pp. 99–106). New York, NY: Routledge.
Thomas, D. A. (2017). *Navigating transnational borderlands through critical media making* (Unpublished doctoral dissertation). Teachers College, Columbia University.
Vasudevan, L., Schultz, K., & Bateman, J. (2010). Rethinking composing in a digital age: Authoring literate identities through multimodal storytelling. *Written Communication, 27*(4), 442–468.
Willis, A. I. (2008). *Reading comprehension research and testing in the U.S.: Undercurrents of race, class, and power in the struggle for meaning*. New York, NY: Lawrence Erlbaum.
Winn, M. T. (2011). *Girl time: Literacy, justice, and the school-to-prison pipeline*. New York, NY: Teachers College Press.
Wong, C., & Peña, C. (2017). Policing and performing culture: Rethinking "culture" and the role of the arts in culturally sustaining pedagogies. In D. Paris & H. S. Alim (Eds.) *Culturally sustaining pedagogies: Teaching and learning for justice in a changing world* (pp. 117–138). New York, NY: Teachers College Press.

Part IV

How Do Expanding Conceptualizations of Readers Change the Game for Teachers, Leaders, and Reading Researchers?

9
The Language for School Literacy
Widening the Lens on Language and Reading Relations

Paola Uccelli, Emily Phillips Galloway, and Wenjuan Qin

Introduction

For this edition of the *Handbook of Reading Research*, we were asked to write a chapter on the topic of academic language and its relation to reading. This apparently simple request led us to a non-trivial question: *What are the limits of what we define as academic language proficiency?* The challenge we faced in delimiting the scope of this chapter emerged, to a large extent, from the vagueness that still surrounds the definition of academic language proficiency in research and practice. On the one hand, academic language proficiency is conceptualized as **a set of language skills** that support literacy and learning at school (e.g., understanding the meaning of the word *argument*, comprehending sentences with multiple clauses). These skills are typically examined in quantitative studies through a variety of language assessments informed by language development theories and psychological models of reading comprehension. The majority of studies in this line of research has assessed academic vocabulary as a sole index of academic language proficiency. However, recent efforts have proposed and empirically tested more comprehensive operational definitions that also include morpho-syntactic and discourse skills (Brisk & Zhang-Wu, 2017; Nagy & Townsend, 2012; Schleppegrell, 2002). On the other hand, academic language proficiency is understood as **socially-situated discourse practices** that respond to the cultural expectations of school learning and entail enacting a particular academic identity (e.g., participating in debates following academic norms). One line of empirical studies guided by this view investigates metalanguage, i.e., the language to talk about discourse practices, as a window into students' awareness and perceptions of academic discourse practices. Some recent studies qualitatively investigate how teaching academic metalanguage supports students' awareness of the situational expectations and functions of academic discourse practices as a way to facilitate text comprehension (e.g., Schleppegrell, 2013). Other studies investigate learners' metalanguage to reveal their agency and motivation for embracing, or resisting, discourse practices associated with identities embedded in the larger institutional and socio-political contexts of school (Heller & Morek, 2015; van Lier & Walqui, 2012). In reality, of course, becoming proficient in academic language entails both internalizing skills *and* enacting situated practices. It is, in fact, through participation in oral and written school-like discourse practices that learners expand their academic language skills.

The simultaneous consideration of these two broad conceptualizations suggests that learning challenges for students include not only mastering a repertoire of language skills, but also understanding when and, most importantly, why to embrace the often hidden norms of school discourse practices, which may be perceived by some as incompatible with their out-of-school practices and identities (e.g., requests to "explain X" may be satisfied by very different types of responses at home and at school) (O'Connor, Michaels, & Chapin, 2015). In this chapter, we introduce a new term, the **Language for School Literacy (LSL)**. **LSL proficiency (LSL-P)** refers to the repertoire of discourse practices and academic language skills that learners gradually internalize as they flexibly enact the socio-cultural norms of reading, writing, and learning at school. We argue in this chapter that researching opportunities to support LSL learning entails not only identifying which skills to teach, but also investigating the potential role of language awareness in supporting text comprehension, and understanding the conditions under which learners actively choose to enact school-relevant discourse practices.

We adopt this framework to address gaps in the field of academic language research. Research paradigms have focused on disciplinary language, as the context-specific language needed to operate in the content area classroom, *or* on cross-disciplinary language, often operationalized as general vocabulary knowledge. Our LSL proposal is both broader and more specific than prior conceptualizations: broader in the sense that LSL includes both disciplinary and cross-disciplinary language, and more specific in that we focus on the language forms that that are most relevant for academic discourse. Perhaps more importantly, our LSL proposal also aims to address the role of learner agency and identity in school-relevant language development, an important consideration in light of increasing cultural and linguistic diversity in school populations.

In this chapter, our review of quantitative and qualitative studies from the last 15 years is driven by two goals. First, we synthesize how adolescents' school-relevant language has been conceptualized and examined in relation to reading comprehension. Second, we introduce our proposed definition of the **Language for School Literacy (LSL)**, with the goal of highlighting the need for an integrated conceptualization as timely to advance research and practice. To delimit the boundaries of our review, we included only studies that examined either the contribution of adolescents' language skills to reading comprehension; or analyzed metalanguage to understand students' awareness or perceptions of academic discourse practices. The chapter is organized around four main questions: (1) *Which new directions are noticeable in the study of LSL in the last 15 years?*; (2) *How do we conceptualize LSL, as a more inclusive construct, in order to advance research and practice?*; (3) *Which academic language skills support reading comprehension?*; and (4) *What does metalanguage research reveal about adolescents' awareness and perceptions of academic discourse practices?* In response to the first question, we highlight four new directions that have moved the field toward broader conceptualizations and innovative approaches. To address our second question, we present our conceptualization of LSL within a brief discussion of our larger theoretical framework. In answering our third question, we focused on the variety of instruments used to measure language skills and synthesize the main quantitative findings on the contribution of language proficiencies to school reading comprehension. To answer our fourth question, we review evidence from qualitative studies focused on students' academic metalanguage (i.e., language to talk about school discourse practices) to reveal its potential to support reading comprehension, as well as insights from students' own reflective voices about their perceptions of LSL practices. Finally, we close the chapter with a *vision of a pedagogically relevant research approach*, and suggestions for future research areas.

1. Which New Directions Are Noticeable in the Study of the Language for School Literacy?

Our review of studies conducted in the last decade and a half reveals four major new directions in the study of LSL in relation to reading comprehension.

New Direction 1: From a Focus on Emerging Bilinguals to a Focus on Studying Both Bilingual and Monolingual Learners

More than three decades ago, Jim Cummins raised awareness of the importance of academic language for school achievement in emergent bilinguals, i.e., bilingual students with emerging proficiency in the language of school (these students are called *English language learners* in the U.S. educational system) (Cummins, 1979, 1980). Cummins drew a contrast between *Basic Interpersonal Communicative Skills* (BICS) and *Cognitive Academic Language Proficiency* (CALP).[1] In the last decade and a half, however, educational research has moved from conceptualizing academic language proficiency as pedagogically relevant only for emergent bilinguals, to realizing how pertinent this construct is for a much larger population that also includes monolingual learners. Accumulating evidence shows that the language of school texts poses a greater challenge than decoding or fluency for large proportions of bilingual and monolingual adolescents, in particular, but not exclusively, for students from economically underprivileged communities (August & Shanahan, 2008; Mancilla-Martinez & Lesaux, 2011; Uccelli, Phillips Galloway, Barr, Meneses, & Dobbs, 2015). These findings demonstrate that language development is far from complete by adolescence and that new learning at school entails expanding conceptual knowledge alongside language resources. In this area, research originally focused on emergent bilinguals has contributed to advance our current understanding of language and reading relations for all students, foregrounding that, in fact, all students are LSL learners. Now that the pedagogical implications of LSL research are understood as relevant for all students, new opportunities emerge for more far-reaching partnerships between researchers and practitioners in this field.

New Direction 2: From Measuring Language as Global Proficiency to Measuring School-Relevant Language as Context-Specific Proficiency

One salient shift in the empirical research from the last 15 years has been the move from using instruments that measure *global* language proficiencies to instruments intentionally designed to capture the specific language skills *relevant for the context of school literacy and learning*. This shift has been informed by a longstanding research tradition focused on measuring general language skills with the goal of testing psychological models of reading comprehension (Gough & Tunmer, 1986; Perfetti & Stafura, 2014). In these studies, target language skills are classified by formal linguistic levels (e.g., lexical, morpho-syntactic skills) (Geva & Farnia, 2012), but no special attention is given to selecting forms that are particularly useful for school literacy. Recent studies from this line of research reveal developmental relations between lexical, morphological and syntactic skills and reading comprehension in longitudinal samples followed from the early grades up to the middle school years (Farnia & Geva, 2013). Despite these important insights, it is arguably in the more specific emerging field of academic language proficiency, where the focus is squarely on identifying language resources useful for school learning, that promising pedagogically-relevant research has bloomed in these last years. For the first time, the field has produced operational definitions of academic language skill sets, as well as considerable accumulating empirical evidence that supports the hypothesis that the language of school texts poses unique challenges to comprehension (Uccelli et al., 2015). Especially substantial progress has been achieved as the result of sustained and ambitious efforts to more directly link emergent bilingual learners' language skills to school achievement. In contrast to generalized English proficiency tests that used to measure general grammatical rules or vocabulary, U.S. English proficiency assessments today measure, in more precise and informative ways, the academic language skills required by the different school content areas across grades (e.g., WIDA-ACCESS for ELLs, ELPA21) (Deville, Chalhoub-Deville, Fox, & Fairbairn, 2011; Linquanti & Cook, 2013). Guided by the most up-to-date school and career-readiness standards, initiatives such as WIDA, now offer sophisticated screening, monitoring, and summative assessments to measure and track bilingual English learners' progress in mastering the language needed in specific content areas. This move to measure subsets of language skills identified according to their relevance for discipline- and grade-specific reading and learning has begun to show the potential to revolutionize discipline-specific literacy instruction in important ways for emerging bilingual students.

New Direction 3: From the Study of Discipline-Specific Language to the Complementary Study of High-Utility Cross-Disciplinary Language Skill Sets

Another important new direction is the recent expansion from a focus on discipline-specific academic language (e.g., the language of science, the language of history) to also studying high-utility academic language across content areas. **Discipline-specific academic language** refers to the specialized language forms and functions used for discussing key concepts and engaging in the reasoning moves of specific disciplines. **Cross-disciplinary academic language**, in contrast, refers to the array of linguistic features prevalent in texts across content areas that enable precise, concise, and reflective communication (Bailey, 2007). One prolific research area has been the study of academic vocabulary knowledge (August & Hakuta, 1997; August & Shanahan, 2006; Lesaux, Crosson, Kieffer, & Pierce, 2010). Interestingly, these studies consistently show that beyond the discipline-specific words (e.g., *electrons, biosphere, hypotenuse*), to which teachers regularly pay attention, it is the general-purpose academic words (e.g., *structure, hypothesis, conclude*) that are often unknown to students. More recently, operational definitions of academic language proficiency have moved beyond vocabulary knowledge to include a broader array of high-utility cross-disciplinary language skills (Fang & Schleppegrell, 2010; Nagy & Townsend, 2012; Uccelli et al., 2015). Today, empirical studies investigate not only academic vocabulary, but also more inclusive arrays of school-relevant morphological, syntactic, and discourse skills that are being made increasingly visible for research and practice through innovative instruments within and across content areas.

New Direction 4: From an Exclusive Focus on Language Skills to a View of Language Learning as Situated Discourse Practices

Another contribution in this field is the widening of the analytic lens beyond skills and knowledge, to study school-relevant language learning as the learning of socio-culturally situated discourse practices. LSL learning is not seen as a purely cognitive-linguistic task, but as social action; more specifically, as an "expression of agency embodied and embedded" in an environment that is itself part of larger social, historical, political, and economic structures (van Lier & Walqui, 2012, p. 47). In classroom settings and beyond, learners not only develop language skills but also become increasingly aware of when, why, and with whom to use which language resources. Far from trivial, students' ability to reflect on the mapping of language forms to the communicative expectations of school is hypothesized to support students' text comprehension and production. Moreover, aligned with research on language and identity (Shin, 2012), recent work illustrates that as students expand the communicative contexts they navigate, different ways of using language afford them the opportunities to enact a wider array of identities that they might embrace or resist (Alim, Rickford, & Ball, 2016; Heller & Morek, 2015).

2. How Do We Conceptualize the Language for School Literacy?

The major shifts discussed above call for a more inclusive conceptualization of school-relevant language learning to guide pedagogically relevant research in this field. Our proposed definition of LSL is situated within a larger sociocultural pragmatics-based theoretical framework that we briefly discuss below.

We qualify our approach as pragmatics-based because we are informed by research that reveals that (1) individuals' language use varies across interactional contexts; (2) language learning is driven by learners' communicative needs and purposes for using language; and (3) language proficiencies are, to a large extent, the result of a learner's accumulated experiences with oral and written language practices (Bruner, 1983; Ninio & Snow, 1996). Aligned with this view, extensive research from functional linguistics shows that academic texts (written or oral) recurrently display an array of co-occurring language features (e.g., nominalizations, dense syntactic structures) that respond to situational expectations, i.e., the needs and norms of a communicative situation, in this case academic communication. These particular language features of texts predictably distinguish academic texts from colloquial ones (Berman, Ragnarsdóttir, & Strömqvist, 2002; Halliday, Matthiessen, & Matthiessen, 2014; Schleppegrell, 2004). Thus, to access the meaning of these texts, readers need to master academic language skills, i.e., language skills that correspond to the linguistic features of academic texts.

We further qualify our approach as socio-cultural to highlight that, beyond the immediate interactional contexts, language learners are immersed in larger ecosystems (both at school and outside of school), where they are socialized to participate in culturally shaped language practices. Whereas, arguably, school texts across many societies may follow similar institutionally shaped and functional ways of using language; communities and families vary widely in their uses of language (Heath, 1983; Schieffelin & Ochs, 1986). This sociocultural view shapes our understanding of LSL proficiency as only one aspect of an individual's much larger repertoire of language resources. Extensive evidence demonstrates that a speaker can be skilled in one context (e.g., conversational English), yet struggle to understand or produce the language characteristic of other contexts (e.g., English school texts) (Cazden, 2001; Heath, 2012). Emergent bilinguals, as well as large proportions of monolingual adolescents, indeed often struggle with the language of school texts, despite their fluent command of conversational English. It is important to add that this differential proficiency is associated with the specific opportunities to learn afforded to speakers/readers and thus, may occur in various directions. For instance, for some English-as-a-foreign-language learners, the English of academic texts is more accessible than more colloquial uses of English to which they have been minimally exposed in their formal classes (Chang, 2012; Qin & Uccelli, 2016). In sum, LSL proficiency, as language proficiency more generally, is the result of individuals' histories of language socialization and enculturation inside and outside of school.

Guided by this sociocultural pragmatics-based theoretical framework, we propose the following definition:

***Language for School Literacy* proficiency (LSL-P)** refers to the socio-cultural academic discourse practices and academic language skills that learners internalize gradually as they flexibly enact the situational expectations of reading, writing, and learning at school.

As illustrated in Figure 9.1, in our proposed definition, discourse practices, situational expectations and language skills are all interconnected and inseparable elements of becoming proficient in LSL:

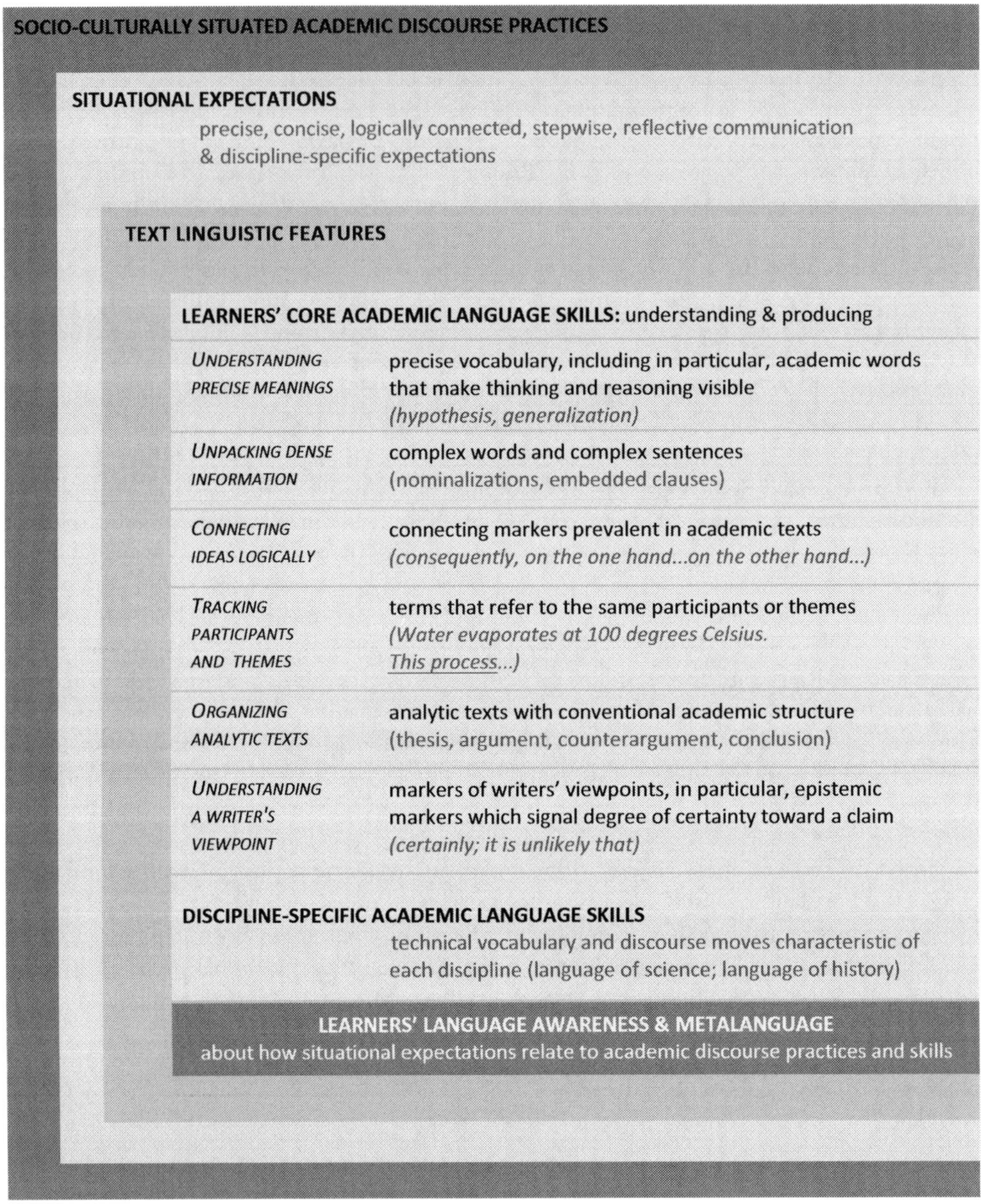

SOCIO-CULTURALLY SITUATED ACADEMIC DISCOURSE PRACTICES

SITUATIONAL EXPECTATIONS
precise, concise, logically connected, stepwise, reflective communication & discipline-specific expectations

TEXT LINGUISTIC FEATURES

LEARNERS' CORE ACADEMIC LANGUAGE SKILLS: understanding & producing

UNDERSTANDING PRECISE MEANINGS	precise vocabulary, including in particular, academic words that make thinking and reasoning visible *(hypothesis, generalization)*
UNPACKING DENSE INFORMATION	complex words and complex sentences *(nominalizations, embedded clauses)*
CONNECTING IDEAS LOGICALLY	connecting markers prevalent in academic texts *(consequently, on the one hand...on the other hand...)*
TRACKING PARTICIPANTS AND THEMES	terms that refer to the same participants or themes *(Water evaporates at 100 degrees Celsius. This process...)*
ORGANIZING ANALYTIC TEXTS	analytic texts with conventional academic structure *(thesis, argument, counterargument, conclusion)*
UNDERSTANDING A WRITER'S VIEWPOINT	markers of writers' viewpoints, in particular, epistemic markers which signal degree of certainty toward a claim *(certainly; it is unlikely that)*

DISCIPLINE-SPECIFIC ACADEMIC LANGUAGE SKILLS
technical vocabulary and discourse moves characteristic of each discipline (language of science; language of history)

LEARNERS' LANGUAGE AWARENESS & METALANGUAGE
about how situational expectations relate to academic discourse practices and skills

Figure 9.1 Interconnected discourse practices, situational expectations, text features and language skills involved in becoming proficient in the Language for School Literacy

Figure adapted from Uccelli (2019), Learning the Language for School Literacy Research Insights and a Vision for a Cross-Linguistic Research Program. In V. Grøver, P. Uccelli, M. Rowe, & E. Lieven (Eds.) *Learning through Language: Towards an Educationally Informed Theory of Language Learning* (pp. 95–109). Copyright 2019 by Cambridge University Press. Reprinted with permission.

- ***Participation in socio-cultural academic discourse practices*** refers to the uses of oral and written language for school learning that respond to the situational expectations of academic institutions, which entail enacting academic identities. In other words, academic discourse practices are cultural manifestations valued by academic institutions embedded in larger socio-political and historical structures; therefore, LSL involves learning cognitive-linguistic skills that are part of cultural discourse practices associated with particular identities, which learners may embrace or resist (Heller & Morek, 2015; van Lier & Walqui, 2012). For instance, participating in an academic debate requires students to adopt an academic identity in which they embrace not only how, but also why, using particular school-relevant discourse moves (e.g., evidence-based arguments) is relevant and functional.

- *Awareness of situational expectations* refers to the awareness of communicative norms that drive the use of oral and written language for school learning. Analogous to the pragmatic expectations of distant communication about complex ideas of the wider scientific community, school oral presentations and written texts are expected to be precise, concise, logically connected, and reflective, in addition to also conforming to discipline-specific expectations. As Mary Schleppegrell's work reveals, these situational expectations of school reading and writing often constitute a hidden curriculum that implicitly guides assessments and instruction, yet it is typically not made explicit for students, in large part, because teachers themselves may not be aware of them (Schleppegrell, 2002).
- *Academic language skills* refer to lexical, morpho-syntactic, and discourse-level skills that correspond to the linguistic features of academic texts and include both cross-disciplinary and discipline-specific language skills. Recent research has revealed considerable individual differences in students' mastery of these skills (August, Branum-Martin, Cardenas-Hagan, & Francis, 2009; Uccelli et al., 2015).

In addition, in order to internalize and embrace these academic discourse practices and academic language skills and to use them *flexibly*, learners need to gradually increase their **language awareness** about how and why the language choices speakers/writers make differ across different contexts. One of the most transparent ways in which this language awareness is made visible and can be scaffolded is through **metalanguage**.

Recent research to better understand how to scaffold adolescents' LSL can be grouped into studies that have broadly addressed two main questions: *Which academic language skills support reading comprehension? What does metalanguage research reveal about adolescents' awareness and perceptions of academic discourse practices?* In the next sections, we summarize the research findings so far generated to answer these questions.

3. Which Academic Language Skills Support Reading Comprehension?

In this section, we provide a review of quantitative studies that measure either general language skills (e.g., lexical and morpho-syntactic skills) or, more targeted, academic language skills in relation to reading comprehension. The brief review only includes research published through 2016 and is designed to provide an illustration of the range of assessments used across studies in this field, but it is not intended as an exhaustive literature review.[2] It is necessary to remind our readers that we only included studies that measured language skills in relation to reading comprehension, excluding those that measure language skills in relation to discipline-specific content knowledge. Table 9.1 offers an inventory of the instruments, and the studies that have used them, grouped into those that measure: first, general language skills (i.e., morpho-syntactic skills); then, academic vocabulary; and, finally, the most recent studies that measure academic language skill sets beyond vocabulary. As we will discuss below, the variety of instruments listed in Table 9.1 illustrates the considerable progress of the field, but it also signals an emerging need for consensus on constructs and instruments, so that the field moves towards producing more generalizable pedagogical implications.

Table 9.1 Instruments used to measure language skills in studies that tested the impact of a language-focused reading intervention or examined language and reading comprehension relations in upper elementary/middle school students

Instruments (instrument designers)	Skills measured (as described by researchers)	Target populations Grade	EL/EP	Empirical studies INTERVENTION tested: Name of Intervention
GENERAL MORPHOSYNTACTIC SKILLS				
Clinical Evaluation of Language Fundamentals (CELF) (Semel, Wiig, and Secord, 1995)	knowledge of word meanings and sentence processing	1–10	EL, EP	Cutting and Scarborough (2006) Foorman et al. (2015) Geva and Farnia (2012)
Compound Structure Test (Berninger and Nagy, 1999)	morphological knowledge/ awareness	2 & 4	EL, EP	Nagy et al. (2003)
Extract-the-Base task (Carlisle, 2000; adapted by Kieffer, 2009)	morphological knowledge/ awareness; morphological decomposition	4–6	EL, EP	Carlo et al. (2004) | INT: *Vocabulary Improvement Project (VIP)* Lesaux, Kieffer, Faller & Kelly (2010) | INT: *Academic Language Instruction for All Students (ALIAS)* Kieffer and Lesaux (2012) Kieffer et al. (2016) Goodwin et al. (2013) Lesaux et al. (2014) | INT: *ALIAS*
Finiteness Elicitation Task (Adlof & Catts, 2015)	morpho-syntax skills	4	EP	Adlof and Catts (2015)
Morphological Relatedness Test (Carlisle, 1995)	morphological knowledge/ awareness; understanding morphological relationship	2–6	EL, EP	Singson, Mahony & Mann (2000) Nagy et al. (2003) Goodwin (2016) | INT: *Word Detectives*
Suffix Choice Test (Tyler and Nagy, 1989)	morphological awareness; morphological derivation	4–9	EL, EP	Nagy et al. (2003) Nagy et al. (2006) Kieffer and Lesaux (2012) Kieffer (2014) Kieffer et al. (2016) Lesaux et al. (2014) | INT: *ALIAS* Goodwin (2016) | INT: *Word Detectives*
Test for Reception of Grammar (TROG) (Bishop, 2003)	comprehension of complex sentences	1–4	EP	Oakhill et al. (2003)
The Connectives Task		5	EL, EP	Crosson and Lesaux (2013)

(Continued)

Table 9.1 (Cont.)

Instruments (instrument designers)	Skills measured (as described by researchers)	Target populations Grade	EL/EP	Empirical studies INTERVENTION tested: Name of Intervention
(Droop and Verhoeven, 2003; adapted by Crosson, 2010)	understanding of connectives			
The Grammaticality Judgment Tasks (Johnson & Newport, 1989)	morpho-syntax skills; syntax skills	1–6	EL, EP	Geva and Farnia (2012) Farnia and Geva (2013) Adlof and Catts (2015)
The Oral Cloze Task (Siegel and Ryan, 1989)	syntactic awareness	6–7	EL	Lipka and Siegel (2012)
ACADEMIC VOCABULARY: DISCIPLINE-SPECIFIC				
Social Studies Vocabulary Test (Vaughn et al., 2009)	social studies vocabulary (intervention-specific)	7	EL, EP	Vaughn et al. (2009)	INT: *Social Studies Intervention*
Science Vocabulary Assessment (August et al., 2009)	science vocabulary (intervention-specific)	6	EL, EP	August et al. (2009)	INT: *Quality English and Science Teaching (QuEST)*
Science Vocabulary Measure (Cervetti et al., 2012)	science vocabulary (intervention-specific)	4	EL, EP	Cervetti et al. (2012)	INT: *Integrated Language & Science Instruction*
Vocabulary in the Content Area of Life Science (Taboada and Rutherford, 2011)	science vocabulary (intervention-specific)	4	EL	Taboada and Rutherford (2011)	INT: *Contextualized Vocabulary Instruction (CVI) vs. Intensified Vocabulary Instruction (IVI)*
ACADEMIC VOCABULARY: CROSS-DISCIPLINARY				
Academic Word Mastery (Lesaux et al., 2010)	academic vocabulary (intervention-specific)	6	EL, EP	Lesaux et al. (2010)	INT: *ALIAS* Lesaux, Kieffer, Faller, & Kelly (2010)	INT: *ALIAS* Lesaux et al. (2014)	INT: *ALIAS*
Academic Word Meaning-in-Context (Lesaux et al., 2010)	academic vocabulary in extended expository texts (intervention-specific)	6	EL, EP	Lesaux et al. (2010)	INT: *ALIAS* Lesaux, Kieffer, Faller, & Kelly (2010)	INT: *ALIAS* Lesaux et al. (2014)	INT: *ALIAS*
Vocabulary Breadth Test (VBT) & Vocabulary Depth Test (VDT) (Proctor et al., 2011)	breadth and depth of academic vocabulary (intervention-specific)	5	EL, EP	Proctor et al. (2011)	INT: *Improving Comprehension Online (ICON)*

(*Continued*)

Table 9.1 (Cont.)

Instruments (instrument designers)	Skills measured (as described by researchers)	Target populations Grade	EL/EP	Empirical studies INTERVENTION tested: Name of Intervention
Vocabulary Knowledge Scale – Measure of Academic Vocabulary (MAV) (Read, 2000)	academic vocabulary (intervention-specific)	6–8	EL, EP	Townsend & Collins (2009) | INT: Language Workshop Townsend, Filippini, Collins, & Biancarosa (2012)
Vocabulary Levels Test (VLT) (Schmitt, Schmitt, and Clapham, 2001)	general & academic vocabulary (intervention-specific)	6–8	EL, EP	Townsend & Collins (2009) | INT: Language Workshop Townsend, Filippini, Collins, & Biancarosa (2012)
Word Association Test (WAT) (Schoonen and Verhallen, 2008; adapted by Lesaux et al., 2010)	depth of academic vocabulary (intervention-specific)	5–6	EL, EP	Carlo et al. (2004) | INT: VIP Lesaux & Kieffer (2010) | INT: ALIAS Lesaux et al. (2014) | INT: ALIAS
Word Generation Academic Vocabulary Instrument (WG-AV) (Snow et al., 2009)	academic vocabulary (intervention-specific)	4–8	EL, EP	Snow et al. (2009) | INT: Word Generation (WG) Lawrence et al. (2015) | INT: WG
ACADEMIC SKILLSETS: DISCIPLINE SPECIFIC				
Academic English Language Proficiency Tasks (AELP) (Bailey et al., 2007)	knowledge of discipline-specific language features to be able to comprehend texts (not intervention-specific)	4–6	EL, EP	Bailey et al. (2007)
Assessing Comprehension and Communication in English State-to-State for English Language Learners (ACCESS for ELLs) (WIDA, 2004)	discipline-specific academic language and social language needed for college and career success	1–12	EL	WIDA (2004) – large-scale English proficiency assessment framework: website
English Language Proficiency Assessment for the 21st Century (ELPA21) (National Govenors Association, 2010)	discipline-specific academic language and social language practices that enable students to produce, interpret, and effectively collaborate on content-related grade-appropriate tasks	K-12	EL	ELPA (2016) - large-scale English proficiency assessment framework: website
ACADEMIC SKILLSETS: CROSS-DISCIPLINARY				
Core Academic Language Skills Instrument (CALS-I) (Uccelli et al., 2015)	high-utility academic language skills that support reading comprehension across content areas (not intervention-specific)	4–8	EL, EP	Uccelli et al. (2015) Uccelli, Phillips Galloway, et al.(2015) Phillips Galloway (2016) LaRusso et al. (2016) Jones et al. (under review) | INT: WG

General Linguistic Skills

A long research tradition has investigated general lexical and morpho-syntactic skills as predictors of reading comprehension. Most instruments used in these studies are repurposed from the field of clinical or general language development (e.g., *Clinical Evaluation of Language Fundamentals-* CELF). These instruments include skills that are representative of a specific, formal linguistic level (e.g., knowledge of word meanings, morphological skills, sentence comprehension), but without purposefully selecting forms for their relevance for school literacy.

At the **morphological level**, most instruments fall into versions of four types of tasks: a) *Morphological Decomposition Task* (e.g., *complexity* → complex) (Lesaux, Kieffer, Kelley, & Harris, 2014, p. 1172); b) *Morphological Derivation Task / Suffix Choice Test* (e.g., *complex* → complexity); (c) *Morphological Relatedness Test* (e.g., *deep* → depth, deeper, deepest); and d) *Compound Structure Test*, (e.g., "Which is a better name for a bee that lives in the grass? A grass bee? Or a bee grass?") (Nagy, Berninger, Abbott, Vaughan, & Vermeulen, 2003, p. 733). A number of empirical studies have found evidence for the unique and direct contribution of morphological skills to reading comprehension, controlling for vocabulary and reading fluency (Kieffer, 2014; Kieffer & Lesaux, 2012; Lesaux et al., 2014; Lipka & Siegel, 2012; Nagy, Berninger, & Abbott, 2006). However, other studies have either failed to find this relation across all participating groups (Nagy et al., 2003), or revealed only indirect contributions of morphological skills that were fully mediated by vocabulary. A recent morphological intervention showed a moderate positive effect on vocabulary knowledge and morphological skills, particularly for English learners; yet, researchers did not detect a meaningful effect of morphological instruction on reading comprehension (Goodwin, 2016; Goodwin, Huggins, Carlo, August, & Calderon, 2013; Kieffer, Petscher, Proctor, & Silverman, 2016; Neugebauer, Kieffer, & Howard, 2015).

At the **syntactic level**, across a variety of measures and studies, findings also show, overall, that students' syntactic skills are predictive of reading comprehension (Adlof & Catts, 2015; Cutting & Scarborough, 2006; Oakhill, Cain, & Bryant, 2003). Brimo, Apel, and Fountain (2017) find that syntax ability (i.e., the ability to understand or produce different grammatical structures within the context of a sentence), and metalinguistic knowledge of syntax (i.e., the ability to manipulate and reflect on the grammatical structures of language), both contribute to text comprehension. Syntactic skills also predict rate of growth in reading comprehension from the upper-elementary to the middle school years (Farnia & Geva, 2013). Nevertheless, similar to the findings with morphological skills, an association between syntactic skills and reading comprehension is not always detectable across groups that vary by English proficiency or grade level. Geva and Farnia (2012) found 5th-graders' syntactic skills (measured by the CELF *Formulated Sentences subtest*) were predictive of reading comprehension only for participants designated as English learners, but not for English proficient students. Moreover, this relation was significant in grade 5, but not in grade 2. It is also the case that the relation between syntax and other language skills has been found to vary across studies. Foorman and colleagues found that, in grade 5 to 10, syntactic skills (measured by the CELF *Recalling Sentence subtest* and *grammatical judgment* task) and vocabulary knowledge form a "general oral language factor" to predict reading comprehension; yet, only in grade 4, their syntax-specific factor was predictive of reading comprehension beyond general oral language and decoding (Foorman, Koon, Petscher, Mitchell, & Truckenmiller, 2015). Kieffer et al. (2016) found that syntactic, morphological, and vocabulary skills comprise a general language comprehension factor in grade 3–5 in their sample of monolingual and emergent bilingual students.

At the level of **inter-sentential relations**, knowledge of connectives that link ideas across sentences (e.g., *however, even though*) has also been shown to support text understanding. Crosson and Lesaux (2013) found that 5th-graders' knowledge of connectives explained unique variance in comprehension beyond that explained by breadth of vocabulary; yet, the relationship was stronger for monolingual learners than emergent bilinguals.

These studies reveal that general linguistic skills at the morphology, syntactic, and intra-sentential levels contribute to reading comprehension; yet, significant relations between these general linguistic skills and reading abilities are not always consistently found across grades or different socio-demographic groups. Given the various instruments used to measure morphosyntactic skills and the different populations tested, generalizing findings is problematic due to the scarcity of direct replication studies. Besides the need for replication, the discrepancies across studies also call for a line of research that examines not only general linguistic skills identified by formal linguistic levels, but also one that focuses, through purposeful and systematic design, on the particular skills relevant for the context of school literacy.

Beyond General Linguistic Skills: Academic Vocabulary Knowledge

A productive line of research has moved the field beyond the assessment of generalized linguistic skills to the purposeful identification of *academic vocabulary*, or the content words that are particularly relevant and useful in the context of school learning. The contribution of general vocabulary knowledge to reading comprehension has been extensively investigated. Numerous studies document considerable individual variability in readers' vocabulary repertoires and find vocabulary knowledge to be one of the most important predictors of reading comprehension (Biemiller & Slonim, 2001; Graves & Fink, 2007; Kieffer & Lesaux, 2007; Stahl & Nagy, 2007). Within the specific study of academic language, among the many potential lexical, syntactic, or discourse components of academic language proficiency, academic vocabulary has also been the most salient and, so far, the most widely studied (Nagy & Townsend, 2012). This body of research is meritorious for making the vague concept of academic language more concrete beyond general vocabulary knowledge. More specifically, this research has distinguished two basic categories of academic vocabulary: discipline-specific and cross-discipline academic vocabulary. **Discipline-specific academic vocabulary** refers primarily to content words (i.e., nouns, verbs, adjectives, adverbs) with specialized technical meanings (e.g., *antioxidant, rhombus, federalism*) that are distinctive of a discipline (e.g., science, math, social studies) (Nagy & Townsend, 2012). The discipline-specific vocabulary instruments listed in Table 9.1 were designed by researchers to assess gains in vocabulary words explicitly taught in interventions developed to improve reading comprehension and situated in a specific content area (August et al., 2009; Cervetti, Barber, Dorph, Pearson, & Goldschmidt, 2012; Vaughn et al., 2009). Discipline-specific vocabulary assessments evaluate students' knowledge of these words' meanings within the context of disciplinary knowledge.[3] **Cross-discipline academic vocabulary**, also called *all-purpose academic vocabulary*, refers to high-frequency academic words with a high dispersion index across content areas (Zeno, Ivens, Millard, & Duvvuri, 1995). These are high utility words found frequently in texts across content areas (Hiebert & Kamil, 2005; Snow, Lawrence, & White, 2009) (e.g., *process, convert, structure*). The majority of these instruments use the Academic Word List (Coxhead, 2000) to select academic vocabulary words with the goal of assessing the effectiveness of a vocabulary-focused reading intervention (e.g., *Academic Word Mastery, Word Generation Academic Vocabulary Instrument, Word Association Test*) (Lesaux et al., 2014; Snow et al., 2009). Not surprisingly, these studies consistently find a robust relation between academic vocabulary knowledge and reading comprehension. These studies have been particularly insightful in revealing that cross-discipline academic words are often unknown to adolescents and, thus, pose ubiquitous challenges to accessing the language of school texts.

Inspired by extensive developmental findings on the robust relation between vocabulary and reading comprehension, as well as by the lack of instruction focused on cross-disciplinary words, a prolific line of vocabulary-focused reading interventions has marked this last decade. Overall, these vocabulary interventions have been successful in leading to significant growth in taught academic vocabulary; yet, for the most part, they have detected only unsatisfactorily modest gains—if any—in reading comprehension (Deshler, Palincsar, Biancarosa, & Nair, 2007; Elleman, Lindo, Morphy, & Compton, 2009; Proctor et al., 2011).

By and large, interventions focused on a single facet of academic language—vocabulary or morphology—have failed to meaningfully increase reading comprehension. In response, researchers and educators called for more inclusive conceptualizations of academic language that would lead to pedagogies guided by the need to scaffold interrelated lexical, grammatical, and discourse skill sets, instead of isolated word meanings (National Research Council, 2010). After all, using a rich academic vocabulary repertoire entails interconnecting these words with other academic discourse resources in order to pack information concisely through subordination and nominalization, or to signal conceptual relations or stance through precise markers.

Beyond Academic Vocabulary: Academic Language Skill Sets

Two recent productive lines of research provide more inclusive conceptualizations and instruments to assess academic language: the first focuses on emerging bilinguals' discipline-specific skills; the second, on monolingual and bilingual learners' cross-disciplinary academic language skills.

Within the field of **emergent bilinguals**, researchers have made important strides in designing theoretically and psychometrically robust assessments that carefully attend to the **disciplinary language demands** of grade-specific content areas. One innovative effort was led by Bailey and colleagues, based on their analyses of classroom interactions, educational standards, and textbooks. Repurposing item formats typically used to test content, their *Academic English Language Proficiency (AELP)* instrument was designed to test knowledge of content-area specific language features (vocabulary, grammar, discourse functions characteristic of mathematics, science, or social studies texts) (Bailey, Huang, Shin, Farnsworth, & Butler, 2007). Large-scale English proficiency assessments administered to students identified as English learners (called emergent bilinguals in this chapter) also follow the same design rationale. As noted above, WIDA-ACCESS and ELPA21 are some of the most innovative tests available for emergent bilinguals. These assessments measure language proficiency in specific content areas (i.e., the language of language arts, mathematics, science and social studies) across grades and modalities (speaking, listening, reading and writing) (Deville et al., 2011; Linquanti & Cook, 2013). Adopted by a majority of U.S. states in order to comply with the federal requirement of monitoring U.S. emergent bilinguals' English proficiency,[4] these tests provide an unprecedented opportunity to move towards common definitions of "English proficiency", which will enable generalizations and comparisons across states, and promise to be transformational for pedagogy (Boals et al., 2015).

A more recent line of research focuses on understanding academic language proficiency for bilingual and monolingual students in Grades 4 to 8. Inspired by Bailey et al.'s (2007) assessment blueprint, this line of research has proposed an operational construct of **cross-disciplinary academic language skills**, the *Core Academic Language Skills* (CALS) and has designed a theoretically and psychometrically robust assessment, the *CALS Instrument* (CALS-I). CALS refer to a constellation of high-utility language skills called upon to understand the linguistic features prevalent in academic texts across content areas, but which are typically infrequent in colloquial conversations (Uccelli et al., 2015). As displayed in Figure 9.1, CALS consists of several domains of language skills that support reading, writing, and speaking at school (Uccelli & Phillips Galloway, 2017).

CALS-I assesses students' skills in each domain through different tasks, yet psychometric analyses have consistently revealed that a single factor model offers the best fit for CALS items, offering evidence of unidimensionality for the measured construct. Across studies, adolescents' performance on the CALS-I has been found to be a robust predictor of reading comprehension in grades 4 to 8, above and beyond the contribution of reading fluency, vocabulary knowledge, and students' socioeconomic status (Uccelli et al., 2015). Longitudinal studies have found strong, reciprocal links between CALS and reading comprehension, with growth from grades 6 to 8 in

CALS associated with growth in reading comprehension (Phillips Galloway, 2016). One finding in these studies demanding additional investigation is the relation between students' CALS and family socioeconomic status. Controlling for reading fluency, regression analyses have shown that the impact of SES on reading comprehension becomes non-significant once CALS and academic vocabulary knowledge are entered in the model. Finally, prior CALS studies reveal considerable individual variability within socio-economic groups, but overall significant associations with students' socio-economic status, such that students from low-income communities demonstrate lower performance in CALS-I than their more privileged peers attending the same urban public schools. Thus, instruments that tap a common, underlying school-relevant proficiency—like that captured by CALS tasks—are promising in delineating more precisely the knowledge about language to support all developing readers, and to design interventions for quality and equity in language and literacy instruction (Uccelli & Phillips Galloway, 2017).

The contribution of CALS to reading comprehension is aligned with other studies, including the work of Sánchez and colleagues (Sánchez, García, & Bustos, 2017), who found that for skilled readers between 11–13 years old, knowledge of anaphors and organizational signals uniquely contributed to reading comprehension while controlling for prior knowledge, working memory, and decoding skills. For struggling readers, though, only knowledge of organizational signals made a unique contribution (García, Bustos, & Sánchez, 2015; Sánchez et al., 2017).

The review from this section highlights the relevance and promise of having moved beyond general linguistic skills in order to identify not only discipline-specific but also cross-disciplinary skills, including vocabulary knowledge and other language skill sets. These studies suggest that knowledge of this broader constellation of academic language skills displays substantive individual differences, which are, in turn, associated with reading comprehension for both monolingual and bilingual populations. Yet, how to translate the current knowledge into practice is of the utmost importance, given the modest gains we have so far accomplished in moving the needle towards better comprehension for adolescent readers. As a complement to this quantitative review of academic language skills, in the next section we move to another, perhaps equally important, yet still understudied LSL component: metalanguage as a lever for, and a window into, students' awareness of language and context. We strongly believe that if we are to increase the impact of language research on pedagogical practices, we need to integrate quantitative and qualitative lenses and tools that address a highly complex developmental phenomenon and especially, we need to incorporate insights that come directly from students' own voices. The qualitative studies reviewed below offer an insightful starting point.

4. What Does Metalanguage Research Reveal about Adolescents' Awareness and Perceptions of Academic Discourse Practices?

Teaching language skills, such as those assessed by the CALS-I, is an important, though incomplete, approach to expand adolescents' LSL. Students also need to develop their language awareness in order to evaluate and interpret the language used by writers when reading, and to deploy LSL resources effectively and flexibly when writing or speaking. Indeed, deep text comprehension often hinges on a reader's ability to critically engage the writer's language (Graesser, 2007). In classrooms, this process of looking at language to dig deeper is made most visible when students and teachers use *metalanguage*, or language to talk about language (Schleppegrell, 2013). Students' metalanguage has been mostly examined via oral methods— discussions, interviews, and focus groups—or open-ended written tasks. As we discuss below, in analyzing metalanguage, the intertwinement of skills, practices, awareness, identity, and value judgments becomes salient and essential for supporting text comprehension, and for considering how to integrate students' perceptions into the design of culturally relevant and empowering LSL pedagogy.

The Language for School Literacy

What Role Does the Teaching of Metalanguage Play in Text Comprehension?

Several studies aim to cultivate *academic metalanguage*, or language to talk about school discourse practices, often in second language learners, to support students' understanding of how language is used in text to communicate meaning (Schleppegrell, 2013). Primarily drawing from Systemic Functional Linguistics (SFL) (Halliday et al., 2014), qualitative studies by and large examine if the explicit teaching of technical metalanguage (terms such as *nominalizations*) and the process of discussing text using the taught terminology heightens students' attention to, and awareness of, a text's language (Berry, 2004; Hammond, 2016). SFL-rooted instruction aims to help readers recognize that meaning is constructed by writers through lexical and grammatical choices that respond to the situational expectations—or communicative needs—of particular contexts (Hasan & Perrett, 1994; Schleppegrell, 2013). Following a long tradition of research on the use of metalanguage in the context of English-as-a-Foreign-Language classrooms, research conducted primarily in the U.S. and Australia demonstrates the utility of SFL metalanguage teaching in classrooms with first and second language learners (Brisk & Zisselsberger, 2010; de Oliveira, 2008; French, 2010; Gebhard, Harman, & Seger, 2007; Schleppegrell, 2013; Simard & Jean, 2011). For instance, in a qualitative study focused on emergent bilinguals and their English monolingual peers in grades 2–5, Moore and Schleppegrell (2014) illustrate how the teaching of SFL metalanguage terminology through frequent dialogic discussions that foregrounded meaning making from text aided students in seeing patterns in language that facilitated their learning from text. In addition, students were able to use these discoveries to inform their understanding of text's language later in the unit (Klingelhofer & Schleppegrell, 2016). Furthermore, Schleppegrell and colleagues have also demonstrated the value of these approaches to help students comprehend and critique the complex texts in math, science, social studies, and English language arts (Fang & Schleppegrell, 2010; Moore & Schleppegrell, 2014). This message is echoed in Gebhard, Chen, and Britton (2014), who find that the teaching of metalanguage to 3rd graders in history and science equips them with tools to write and understand disciplinary texts. Perhaps of greater relevance for this chapter is Gebhard's and colleagues' finding from case studies of focal students that the teaching of metalanguage also seems to support students' general language proficiency and reading comprehension. Gebhard and colleagues' work joins a host of others, including Gibbons (2006); Polias and Dare (2006); Quinn (2004), who find that the explicit teaching of SFL metalanguage terms aids transfer of knowledge about language gained through reading to writing, and back again, for emergent bilinguals and their classmates.

What Do Students' Own Metalanguage Reveal about Their Perceptions of LSL?

Our own work in this area suggests a complementary entry point to the direct teaching of linguistic terminology. By eliciting student-generated metalanguage, we have analyzed how students' every day, non-specialist language is re-purposed to describe the language features of school texts (e.g., students used "longer sentences" to describe a text's sentence with embedded clauses) (Berry, 2004; Niedzielski & Preston, 2000). Our work also departs from other studies in that we focus not only on those learning a second language, which is the dominant approach in the existing research (Berry, 2004; Couper, 2011; Fortune, 2005; Gánem-Gutiérrez & Roehr, 2011; Gebhard et al., 2014; Gutiérrez, 2016; Jessner, 2005), but also on monolingual English-speaking students, including speakers of non-mainstream as well as mainstream varieties of English. Our inquiry into middle graders' written and oral reflections on LSL find that, without explicit instruction in linguistic terminology, students already bring apt language to discuss the features and expectations of the language of academic texts (Galloway, Stude, & Uccelli, 2015). These elicited multi-party discussions provided a space for participants to use student-constructed metalanguage to build on the language of peers while negotiating the meaning of a text's language, and they emerged as potentially promising fertile contexts to foster language awareness. Moreover, in these conversations, out-of-school language resources are welcome in the conversation, and students are invited to reflect on and discuss who uses which language resources, and for what purposes, at school and in society at large (Clark & Ivanic, 1997; Fairclough, 1992, 2003). For instance, in one discussion focused on the register-switching practices of President Barack Obama, students drew from their knowledge of African American English and LSL to discuss the various reasons why speakers, and specifically our 44th president, would engage each set of language resources (Dobbs & Phillips Galloway, 2017).

Adolescents' metalanguage has also been studied using discourse analysis methods to identify learners' underlying beliefs about LSL and their motivations for using it (Heller & Morek, 2015; Phillips Galloway et al., 2015). This work has revealed that students often reflect on the language of school as "good," "proper" and "better" when contrasting the academic register mostly with colloquial language resources used in students' homes and communities (Bergin & Cooks, 2002; Flores-González, 2002; Galloway et al., 2015; Perry, 2003). Noticeably absent from students' comments was an acknowledgment of LSL as a functional set of language features. This suggests that students are not often exposed to a discussion of why academic language resources might be supportive—or not—for certain communicative tasks, an area that deserves pedagogical attention and intentional design to counter value judgments associated with various language resources.

Overall, metalanguage research illuminates promising ways in which LSL instruction in the service of text understanding can foster the understanding of academic language resources as functional choices for particular contexts. This instruction would promote a plural vision of language usage, where home and school language are viewed as equally useful depending on the message, context and audience.

5. A Vision to Advance Practice-Relevant Research

In this final section, we summarize the main lessons from this review, propose an emerging vision for an LSL pedagogical approach, and close our chapter by proposing areas for future research.

First, we highlight **four main insights** that emerge form our synthesis:

1. The substantial individual variability in adolescents' academic languages skills—both in emergent bilingual and monolingual populations—and their significant contribution to reading comprehension unequivocally shows that expanding adolescents' language skills to support text understanding needs to be a pedagogical priority. As reviewed in this chapter, academic language proficiency is predictive of reading comprehension above and beyond general vocabulary knowledge (in addition to word recognition skills). Extensive evidence demonstrates that beyond vocabulary, several other morphological, syntactic, and discourse skills contribute to reading comprehension. Perhaps more relevant for adolescent literacy pedagogy, the field has now identified high-utility skill sets within content areas (e.g., WIDA) and across content areas (e.g., CALS) that support text comprehension and can inform preservice and in-service teachers' professional training.
2. Relatedly, findings indicate that promoting vocabulary knowledge, morphological, or syntactic skills in isolation does not prepare readers to put these skills into use in the practice of understanding text. Language skills are actualized and learned in situated social practices where multiple interconnected skills are integrated in particular ways in order to accomplish specific purposes. Teaching skills in isolation without embedding them in authentic LSL

practices with plenty of opportunities to *"do things with LSL skills"* (Austin, 1962) counteracts what we know from extensive pragmatics-based research on language development.
3. Metalanguage emerges from these findings as a component of LSL-P that can be promoted to increase students' language awareness in the service of text comprehension. Teaching technical metalanguage for text analysis, as well as eliciting students' spontaneous metalanguage to elicit language-rich conversations about language and context, appear promising and deserve further research attention.
4. Minimal, but insightful, data from students' own voices suggest that adolescents are highly aware of the socio-political value judgments typically associated with LSL; yet, minimally, if at all, aware of the functionality of LSL or the potential to use it flexibly to sharpen their own meanings and dynamically construct their own identities.

Whereas theory and research need to isolate aspects of a phenomenon to study them in depth, educational research that seeks to improve pedagogy needs to go further to thoughtfully integrate different pieces of research. The integration of these findings, thus, call for future research focused on interventions that, while paying attention to academic language skills, understand that these skills are best fostered in the authentic context of situated language and literacy practices and pay close attention to adolescents' identities. Recent and promising initiatives (Palincsar & Schleppegrell, 2014; Snow et al., 2009; QTEL: Walqui & Van Lier, 2010) already implement more comprehensive approaches which promisingly locate the teaching of language in the authentic practices of text meaning-making. Furthermore, instructional approaches intently designed to invite students to sharpen their own meanings through reflective and functional language choices have the potential of achieving meaningful results (e.g., using academic language skills and practices, such as persuasive essays, to convince authorities of a problem they care about in their schools or communities).

An Emerging Vision for an LSL Pedagogical Approach

Informed by these findings, we propose an emerging *vision for a comprehensive pedagogical approach*. By focusing on language resources as functional and flexible choices that support effective communication, instruction inspired by the LSL framework departs from subtractive or prescriptive approaches (focused on "correct language"), and from appropriateness-based approaches (which see academic language as categorically distinct from colloquial language and, rigidly, as the appropriate language for academic contexts). Additive approaches have been criticized because they typically communicate to students that their home language is adequate for home and friends, but that there is no place for it at school. Critics rightly point out that these approaches run the risk of replacing the prescriptive lens of subtractive approaches with a sociolinguistically descriptive but rigid lens of appropriateness that continues to perpetuate the notion of linguistic hierarchies (Flores & Rosa, 2015). Our vision entails a "two-way street approach" in which students' academic discourse practices and skills are expanded, while also teachers' repertoire of practices is reframed and extended to understand how to explicitly value and leverage students' out-of-school language resources.

In our pedagogical vision, students' learning goal is not mastering academic language as a set of conventions to be followed, but achieving *critical rhetorical flexibility*. *Rhetorical flexibility* refers to the ability to use language flexibly and effectively to navigate an increasing variety of social contexts (Ferguson, 1994; Ravid & Tolchinsky, 2002). **Critical rhetorical flexibility** entails an increasing reflective attention to how language choices convey particular meanings in order to either embrace—or depart from—conventional academic language resources. Learners are, then, not passive absorbers or reproducers of academic practices, but agents who analyze and craft language reflectively to process and convey their own meanings. LSL is thus understood not as a fixed language variety or register,[5] but as a set of language resources that belong to the academic language register, but which language users choose to deploy flexibly to achieve specific communicative or learning purposes. Skilled multilingual or multidialectal speakers, as they "translanguage," draw resources from their multiple languages to communicate more effectively and to elicit or disrupt allegiances with specific communities (think about Gloria Anzaldúa's Borderlands/La frontera with its strategic mixing of English and Spanish or Barack Obama's multiple ways of speaking to address multiple audiences) (Alim et al., 2016). Inviting and empowering students to not only abide by the conventions of academic discourse, but also to encourage them to creatively depart from them through reflective choices and to use their multilingual language resources to make meaning from text, lies at the core of preparing them to be independent learners of content and language in an interconnected world, where not only information is constantly updated, but language also changes dynamically as the result of increased inter-language contact, new societal communicative needs, and innovative technologies. Figure 9.2 offers a visual display of learners' cumulative expansion of discourse practices and language skills across contexts, with ways of using language falling along a continuum where new academic language repertoires are incorporated and, of course, used in synchrony with familiar language structures. Slobin's classic developmental principle of "new forms first express old functions and new functions are first expressed by old forms" (Slobin, 1973, p. 184) is insightful here, as we reflect on the lack of rigid boundaries across contexts. Throughout development, often "old conversational forms" acquire "new academic functions," such as *first* used by young children in "I'll go first!" and used later in the upper grades as a discourse marker in a school essay.

Academic language skills have been described recently as "under the hood" skills, or enabling skills to access text (Compton & Pearson, 2016). However, the broader definition of LSL goes beyond skills to also encompass understanding how different language choices result in different

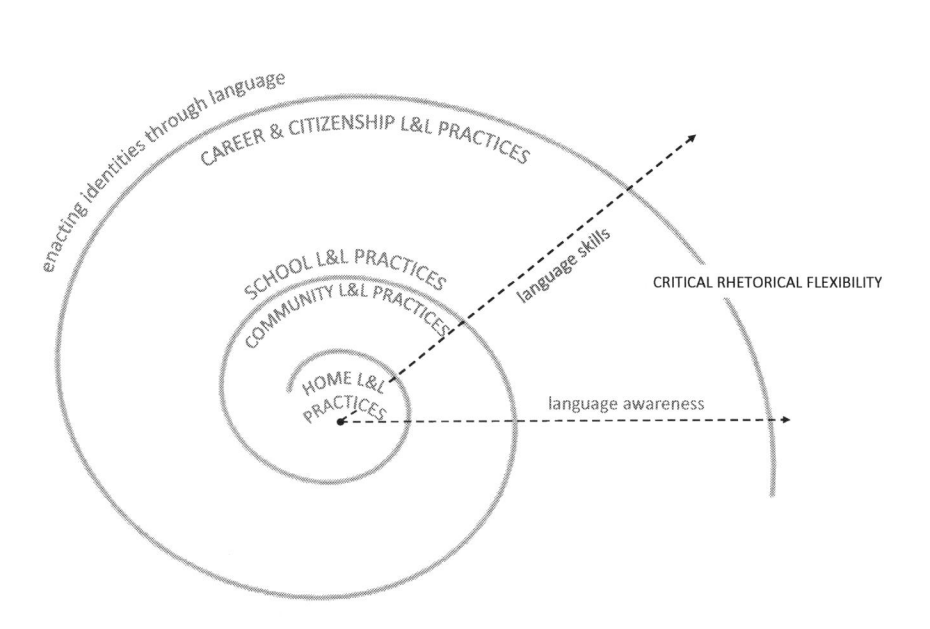

Figure 9.2 Learners' cumulative expansion of discourse practices and languages skills across contexts

meanings and identity choices (Heller & Morek, 2015; Schleppegrell, 2004). This entails a learning arc that goes beyond the "under the hood" characterization and constitutes an aspect of critical comprehension and self-expression (e.g., identifying detached stance as a way to hide responsibility or agency). We contend that grasping LSL learning in its full complexity and inviting students' full identities into the classroom is a fundamental ingredient to first convince them of the value of this learning enterprise.

Future directions: Widening the analytic lens to address current gaps

We end this chapter with a few suggestions to bridge research and practice in order to address current translation and implementation gaps.

- We advocate a ***four-legged educational research paradigm***: (1) genuine research-practitioner partnerships, (2) multidisciplinary teams, (3) multiple sources that represent multiple voices, and (4) methodologies that integrate qualitative and quantitative approaches.
- The field seems ready to work towards a ***consensus on operational definitions of LSL, its components, and a set of instruments*** that enables a systematic planning of replication studies that can gradually lead to cautious generalizations of findings to inform pedagogy.
- Moving from investigating and teaching reading and writing mostly independently to ***studying LSL as a multimodality construct***, examining how development and practice in one modality promotes or consolidates language skills in other modalities (for instance, while researchers and educators have internalized the idea that reading reflectively expands students' writing skills; the reversed direction of writing skills as promoting or consolidating language skills that can then be applied to reading is still much less investigated and infrequent in school practices).
- Designing and investigating the impact of ***a suite of tools that link students' assessment results to pedagogical dimensions*** is sorely needed. For example, a linked set of assessments, classroom observation protocols, and out-of-school surveys would be promising to monitor and learn about oral and written LSL learning opportunities that relate to students' advances in oral and written language proficiencies.
- ***Developmental and intervention studies that integrally analyze discourse practices, language skills, and language awareness*** are needed. The research undertaken thus far has focused on assessing the contribution of academic language skills to text understanding. This is a vital first step in designing research-informed instruction. However, we argue that the complexity of learners' LSL development calls for also investigating students' growth in their awareness of LSL as a set of socio-culturally situated, functional and flexible practices. Micro-linguistic analyses of interactions have the potential to greatly inform how, and why, intervention components work or fail under particular circumstances (O'Connor et al., 2015).
- In light of the most recent findings of LSL-P as a multifaceted developmental phenomenon, we contend the field will benefit from also analyzing **educators' understanding of LSL and how it translates into their situated classroom practices**. The available research provides findings that are precise enough to advance educators' awareness of the skills and practices that are teachable, malleable, and urgent to promote. A complementary, and perhaps more important aspect, is fostering educators' understanding of LSL from a socio-cultural perspective and an assets-based LSL pedagogy. This is essential to provide optimal conditions to motivate adolescents to embrace LSL in order to sharpen their own meanings, deepen their understanding of themselves in the world, and contest others' ideas by choosing reflectively from a wide repertoire of language choices.

To conclude, we remind our readers that in each situated social practice and context, speakers and writers draw from their multiple language repertoires with the triple purpose of establishing relations, transmitting information, and also constructing social identities in interaction with others. Understanding that welcoming students' out-of-school languages entails also welcoming who they are is an initial fundamental tenet for successfully inviting students to continue to expand their language resources. Scaffolding their understanding of LSL, not as prescriptive and rigid, but as functional and flexible—in other words, as expanding language choices to communicate more precisely, reflectively, and flexibly—seems to be an often overlooked, yet key, ingredient to encourage their LSL learning by empowering their own voices.

Notes

1 BICS refers to conversational fluency or proficiency in the language used for every day conversation; whereas CALP refers to and academic language proficiency or the language skills used, both in oral and written modes, for learning at school.
2 Articles published between 2000 and 2016 were searched in multiple databases (e.g., Academic Search Premier, Education Abstracts (H.W. Wilson), ERIC and Linguistics and Language Behavior Abstracts) first using the keywords '*academic language*' and '*reading comprehension*'. Then, we complemented the search by including keywords academic language sub-constructs including '*academic vocabulary*,' '*syntax*,' '*morphology*,' '*discourse*' in combination with '*reading comprehension*'. All studies focused on mid-adolescents (i.e., upper-elementary through middle/high school).
3 In our review, we identified fewer discipline-specific vocabulary measures as compared to cross-disciplinary measures, partially because discipline-specific vocabulary is often implicitly assessed within content knowledge assessments instead of as an isolated construct (Bailey, Huang, Shin, Farnsworth, & Butler, 2007). Thus, many more related initiatives are to be found in the field of disciplinary literacy, yet we only included studies that explicitly tested associations with a reading comprehension measure.
4 At the time of writing this chapter, 39 U.S. States belong to the WIDA consortium and ten belong to ELPA21 (South Carolina belongs to both).
5 Academic language is often described as a *register*, i.e., a language variety that is used regularly for specific purposes in the context of school learning (Biber & Conrad, 2009; Ferguson, 1994).

References

Adlof, S. M., & Catts, H. W. (2015). Morphosyntax in poor comprehenders. *Reading and Writing: An Interdisciplinary Journal, 28*(7), 1051–1070.

Alim, H. S., Rickford, J. R., & Ball, A. F. (2016). *Raciolinguistics: How language shapes our ideas about race*. New York, NY: Oxford University Press.

August, D., Branum-Martin, L., Cardenas-Hagan, E., & Francis, D. J. (2009). The impact of an instructional intervention on the science and language learning of middle grade English language learners. *Journal of Research on Educational Effectiveness, 2*(4), 345–376.

August, D., & Hakuta, K. (Eds.). (1997). *Improving schooling for language-minority children: A research Agenda*. Washington, DC: National Academy Press, 2101 Constitution Avenue, N.W..

August, D., & Shanahan, T. (2006). *Developing literacy in second-language learners*. Report of the National Literacy Panel on Language-Minority Children and Youth. Mahwah, NJ: Lawrence Erlbaum.

August, D., & Shanahan, T. (2008). *Developing reading and writing in second-language learners: Lessons from the report of the National Literacy Panel on Language-Minority Children and Youth*. New York, NY: Routledge.

Austin, J. L. (1962). *How to do things with words*. Oxford, UK: Clarendon Press.

Bailey, A. L. (2007). *The language demands of school: Putting academic English to the test*. New Haven, CT: Yale University Press.

Bailey, A. L., Huang, B. H., Shin, H. W., Farnsworth, T., & Butler, F. A. (2007). Developing academic English language proficiency prototypes for 5th grade reading: Psychometric and linguistic profiles of tasks. CSE technical report 727. *National Center for Research on Evaluation, Standards, and Student Testing (CRESST)*.

Bergin, D. A., & Cooks, H. C. (2002). High school students of color talk about accusations of "acting White". *The Urban Review, 34*(2), 113–134.

Berninger, V., & Nagy, W. (1999). Morphological awareness battery. Unpublished experimental test battery, University of Washington.

Berman, R., Ragnarsdóttir, H., & Strömqvist, S. (2002). Discourse stance: Written and spoken language. *Written Language & Literacy*, 5(2), 253–287.

Berry, R. (2004). Awareness of metalanguage. *Language Awareness*, 13(1), 1–16.

Biber, D., & Conrad, S. (2009). *Register, genre, and style*. Cambridge, UK: Cambridge University Press.

Biemiller, A., & Slonim, N. (2001). Estimating root word vocabulary growth in normative and advantaged populations: Evidence for a common sequence of vocabulary acquisition. *Journal of Educational Psychology*, 93(3), 498–520.

Bishop, D. (2003). Test for Reception of Grammar (TROG-2) Pearson Assessment.

Boals, T., Kenyon, D. M., Blair, A., Cranley, M. E., Wilmes, C., & Wright, L. J. (2015). Transformation in K-12 English language proficiency assessment: Changing contexts, changing constructs. *Review of Research in Education*, 39(1), 122–164.

Brimo, D., Apel, K., & Fountain, T. (2017). Examining the contributions of syntactic awareness and syntactic knowledge to reading comprehension. *Journal of Research in Reading*, 40(1), 57–74.

Brisk, M. E., & Zhang-Wu, Q. (2017). Academic language in K-12 contexts. In E. Hinkel (Ed.), *Handbook of research in second language teaching and learning* (3rd ed., pp. 82–100). New York, NY: Routledge.

Brisk, M. E., & Zisselsberger, M. (2010). We've let them in on the secret: Using SFL theory to improve the teaching of writing to bilingual learners. In T. Lucas (Ed.), *Teacher preparation for linguistically diverse classrooms: A resource for teacher educators* (pp. 111–126). New York, NY: Routledge.

Bruner, J. (1983). The acquisition of pragmatic commitments. In R. M. Golinkoff (Ed.), *The transition from prelinguistic to linguistic communication* (pp. 27–42). Hillsdale, NJ: Lawrence Erlbaum Associates Inc.

Carlisle, J. F. (1995). Morphological awareness and early reading achievement. In L. Feldman (Ed.), *Morphological aspects of language processing* (pp. 189–209). Mahwah, NJ: Erlbaum.

Carlisle, J. F. (2000). Awareness of the structure and meaning of morphologically complex words: Impact on reading. *Reading and Writing*, 12, 169–190.

Carlo, M. S., August, D., McLaughlin, B., Snow, C. E., Dressler, C., Lippman, D. N., … & White, C. E. (2004). Closing the gap: Addressing the vocabulary needs of English-language learners in bilingual and mainstream classrooms. *Reading Research Quarterly*, 39(2), 188–215.

Cazden, C. B. (2001). *The language of teaching and learning*. Portsmouth, NH: Heinemann.

Cervetti, G. N., Barber, J., Dorph, R., Pearson, P. D., & Goldschmidt, P. G. (2012). The impact of an integrated approach to science and literacy in elementary school classrooms. *Journal of Research in Science Teaching*, 49(5), 631–658.

Chang, C.-F. (2012). Fostering EFL college students' register awareness: Writing online forum posts and traditional essays. *Computer-Assisted Language Learning and Teaching*, 2(3), 17–34.

Clark, R., & Ivanic, R. (1997). Critical discourse analysis and educational change. In L. van Lier & D. Corson (Eds.), *Encyclopedia of language and education* (Vol. 6, pp. 217–227) The Netherlands: Kluwer Academic Publishers.

Compton, D. L., & Pearson, P. D. (2016). Identifying robust variations associated with reading comprehension skill: The search for pressure points. *Journal of Research on Educational Effectiveness*, 9(2), 223–231.

Couper, G. (2011). What makes pronunciation teaching work? Testing for the effect of two variables: Socially constructed metalanguage and critical listening. *Language Awareness*, 20(3), 159–182.

Coxhead, A. (2000). A new academic word list. *TESOL Quarterly*, 34, 213–238.

Crosson, A. C. (2010). *Pinpointing the challenging aspects of academic language for young adolescent English-language learners and English-only students*. Harvard University.

Crosson, A. C., & Lesaux, N. K. (2013). Does knowledge of connectives play a unique role in the reading comprehension of English learners and English-only students? *Journal of Research in Reading*, 36(3), 241–260.

Cummins, J. (1979). Linguistic interdependence and the educational development of bilingual children. *Review of Educational Research*, 49(2), 222–251.

Cummins, J. (1980). The cross-lingual dimensions of language proficiency: Implications for bilingual education and the optimal age issue. *TESOL Quarterly*, 14, 175–187.

Cutting, L. E., & Scarborough, H. S. (2006). Prediction of reading comprehension: Relative contributions of word recognition, language proficiency, and other cognitive skills can depend on how comprehension is measured. *Scientific Studies of Reading*, 10(3), 277–299.

de Oliveira, L. C. (2008). A linguistic approach in culturally and linguistically diverse classrooms: A focus on teacher education. *Linguistics & the Human Sciences*, 4, 2.

Deshler, D. D., Palincsar, A. S., Biancarosa, G., & Nair, M. (2007). Informed choices for struggling adolescent readers: A research-based guide to instructional programs and practices. *International Reading Association (NJ3)*.

Deville, C., Chalhoub-Deville, M., Fox, J., & Fairbairn, S. (2011). Test review: ACCESS for ELLs®. *Language Testing*, *28*(3), 425–431.

Dobbs, C., & Phillips Galloway, E. (2017). Explicit instruction in the language of school: An examination of students' metalanguage within academic language units. American Educational Research Association (AERA). San Antonio, TX.

Droop, M., & Verhoeven, L. (2003). Language proficiency and reading ability in first-and second-language learners. *Reading research quarterly*, *38*(1), 78–103.

Elleman, A. M., Lindo, E. J., Morphy, P., & Compton, D. L. (2009). The impact of vocabulary instruction on passage-level comprehension of school-age children: A meta-analysis. *Journal of Research on Educational Effectiveness*, *2*(1), 1–44.

Fairclough, N. (1992). *Discourse and social change (Vol. 10)*. Cambridge, MA: Polity Press.

Fairclough, N. (2003). *Analysing discourse: Textual analysis for social research*. New York, NY: Routledge.

Fang, Z., & Schleppegrell, M. J. (2010). Disciplinary literacies across content areas: Supporting secondary reading through functional language analysis. *Journal of Adolescent & Adult Literacy*, *53*(7), 587–597.

Farnia, F., & Geva, E. (2013). Growth and predictors of change in English language learners' reading comprehension. *Journal of Research in Reading*, *36*(4), 389–421.

Ferguson, C. A. (1994). Dialect, register, and genre: Working assumptions about conventionalization. In D. Biber, & E. Finegan (Eds.), *Sociolinguistic perspectives on register* (pp. 15–30). New York, NY: Oxford University Press.

Flores, N., & Rosa, J. (2015). Undoing appropriateness: Raciolinguistic ideologies and language diversity in education. *Harvard Educational Review*, *85*(2), 149–171.

Flores-González, N. (2002). *School kids/street kids: Identity development in Latino students*. New York, NY: Teachers College Press.

Foorman, B. R., Koon, S., Petscher, Y., Mitchell, A., & Truckenmiller, A. (2015). Examining general and specific factors in the dimensionality of oral language and reading in 4th–10th grades. *Journal of Educational Psychology*, *107*(3), 884.

Fortune, A. (2005). Learners' use of metalanguage in collaborative form-focused L2 output tasks. *Language Awareness*, *14*(1), 21–38.

French, R. (2010). Primary school children learning grammar: Rethinking the possibilities. In *Beyond the grammar wars: A resource for teachers and students on developing language knowledge in the English/literacy classroom* (pp. 206–229). New York, NY: Routledge.

Galloway, E. P., Stude, J., & Uccelli, P. (2015). Adolescents' metalinguistic reflections on the academic register in speech and writing. *Linguistics and Education*, *31*, 221–237.

Gánem-Gutiérrez, G. A., & Roehr, K. (2011). Use of L1, metalanguage, and discourse markers: L2 learners' regulation during individual task performance. *International Journal of Applied Linguistics*, *21*(3), 297–318.

García, J. R., Bustos, A., & Sánchez, E. (2015). The contribution of knowledge about anaphors, organisational signals and refutations to reading comprehension. *Journal of Research in Reading*, *38*(4), 405–427.

Gebhard, M., Chen, I.-A., & Britton, L. (2014). Miss, nominalization is a nominalization:" English language learners' use of SFL metalanguage and their literacy practices. *Linguistics and Education*, *26*, 106–125.

Gebhard, M., Harman, R., & Seger, W. (2007). Reclaiming recess: Learning the language of persuasion. *Language Arts*, *84*(5), 419.

Geva, E., & Farnia, F. (2012). Developmental changes in the nature of language proficiency and reading fluency paint a more complex view of reading comprehension in ELL and EL1. *Reading and Writing*, *25*(8), 1819–1845.

Gibbons, P. (2006). *Bridging discourses in the ESL classroom: Students, teachers and researchers*. New York, NY: Continuum.

Goodwin, A. (2016). Effectiveness of word solving: Integrating morphological problem-solving within comprehension instruction for middle school students. *Reading & Writing*, *29*(1), 91–116. doi:10.1007/s11145-015-9581-0

Goodwin, A. P., Huggins, A. C., Carlo, M. S., August, D., & Calderon, M. (2013). Minding morphology: How morphological awareness relates to reading for English language learners. *Reading and Writing: An Interdisciplinary Journal*, *26*(9), 1387–1415.

Gough, P. B., & Tunmer, W. E. (1986). Decoding, reading, and reading disability. *Remedial and Special Education*, *7*(1), 6–10.

Graesser, A. C. (2007). An introduction to strategic reading comprehension. *Reading Comprehension Strategies: Theories, Interventions, and Technologies*, *2579*, 3–26.

Graves, M. F., & Fink, L. S. (2007). Vocabulary instruction in the middle grades. *Voices from the Middle, 15*(1), 13.

Gutiérrez, X. (2016). Analyzed knowledge, metalanguage, and second language proficiency. *System, 60,* 42–54.

Halliday, M., Matthiessen, C. M., & Matthiessen, C. (2014). *An introduction to functional grammar.* New York, NY: Routledge.

Hammond, J. (2016). Dialogic space: Intersections between dialogic teaching and systemic functional linguistics. *Research Papers in Education, 31*(1), 5–22.

Hasan, R., & Perrett, G. (1994). Learning to function with the other tongue: A systemic functional perspective on second language teaching. *Perspectives on Pedagogical Grammar.* T. Odlin. Cambridge University Press, 179–226.

Heath, S. B. (1983). *Ways with words: Language, life and work in communities and classrooms.* Cambridge, UK: Cambridge University Press.

Heath, S. B. (2012). *Words at work and play: Three decades in family and community life.* New York, NY: Cambridge University Press.

Heller, V., & Morek, M. (2015). Academic discourse as situated practice: An introduction. Elsevier.

Hiebert, E. H., & Kamil, M. L. (2005). *Teaching and learning vocabulary: Bringing research to practice.* New York, NY: Routledge.

Jessner, U. (2005). Multilingual metalanguage, or the way multilinguals talk about their languages. *Language Awareness, 14*(1), 56–68.

Johnson, J. S., & Newport, E. L. (1989). Critical period effects in second language learning: The influence of maturational state on the acquisition of English as a second language. *Cognitive psychology, 21*(1), 60–99.

Kieffer, M. J. (2009). *The development of morphological awareness and vocabulary knowledge in adolescent language minority learners and their classmates.* Harvard University.

Kieffer, M. J. (2014). Morphological awareness and reading difficulties in adolescent Spanish-speaking language minority learners and their classmates. *Journal of Learning Disabilities, 47*(1), 44–53.

Kieffer, M. J., & Lesaux, N. K. (2007). Breaking down words to build meaning: Morphology, vocabulary, and reading comprehension in the urban classroom. *The Reading Teacher, 61*(2), 134–144.

Kieffer, M. J., & Lesaux, N. K. (2012). Direct and indirect roles of morphological awareness in the English reading comprehension of Native English, Spanish, Filipino, and Vietnamese speakers. *Language Learning, 62*(4), 1170–1204. doi:10.1111/j.1467-9922.2012.00722.x

Kieffer, M. J., Petscher, Y., Proctor, C. P., & Silverman, R. D. (2016). Is the whole greater than the sum of its parts? Modeling the contributions of language comprehension skills to reading comprehension in the upper elementary grades. *Scientific Studies of Reading, 20*(6), 436–454.

Klingelhofer, R. R., & Schleppegrell, M. (2016). Functional grammar analysis in support of dialogic instruction with text: Scaffolding purposeful, cumulative dialogue with English learners. *Research Papers in Education, 31*(1), 70–88.

LaRusso, M., Kim, H. Y., Selman, R., Uccelli, P., Dawson, T., Jones, S., … & Snow, C. (2016). Contributions of academic language, perspective taking, and complex reasoning to deep reading comprehension. *Journal of Research on Educational Effectiveness, 9*(2), 201–222.

Lawrence, J. F., Crosson, A. C., Paré-Blagoev, E. J., & Snow, C. E. (2015). Word Generation randomized trial: Discussion mediates the impact of program treatment on academic word learning. *American Educational Research Journal, 52*(4), 750–786.

Lesaux, N. K., Crosson, A. C., Kieffer, M. J., & Pierce, M. (2010). Uneven profiles: Language minority learners' word reading, vocabulary, and reading comprehension skills. *Journal of Applied Developmental Psychology, 31*(6), 475–483.

Lesaux, N. K., Kieffer, M. J., Faller, S. E., & Kelley, J. G. (2010). The effectiveness and ease of implementation of an academic vocabulary intervention for linguistically diverse students in urban middle schools. *Reading Research Quarterly, 45*(2), 196–228.

Lesaux, N. K., Kieffer, M. J., Kelley, J. G., & Harris, J. R. (2014). Effects of academic vocabulary instruction for linguistically diverse adolescents: Evidence from a randomized field trial. *American Educational Research Journal, 51*(6), 1159–1194.

Linquanti, R., & Cook, G. H. (2013). Toward a "Common Definition of English Learner": A brief defining policy and technical issues and opportunities for state assessment consortia.

Lipka, O., & Siegel, L. S. (2012). The development of reading comprehension skills in children learning English as a second language. *Reading and Writing: An Interdisciplinary Journal, 25*(8), 1873–1898.

Mancilla-Martinez, J., & Lesaux, N. K. (2011). The gap between Spanish speakers' word reading and word knowledge: A longitudinal study. *Child Development, 82*(5), 1544–1560.

Moore, J., & Schleppegrell, M. (2014). Using a functional linguistics metalanguage to support academic language development in the English Language Arts. *Linguistics and Education, 26,* 92–105.

Nagy, W., Berninger, V., Abbott, R., Vaughan, K., & Vermeulen, K. (2003). Relationship of morphology and other language skills to literacy skills in at-risk second-grade readers and at-risk fourth-grade writers. *Journal of Educational Psychology, 95*(4), 730.

Nagy, W., Berninger, V. W., & Abbott, R. D. (2006). Contributions of morphology beyond phonology to literacy outcomes of upper elementary and middle-school students. *Journal of Educational Psychology, 98*(1), 134.

Nagy, W., & Townsend, D. (2012). Words as tools: Learning academic vocabulary as language acquisition. *Reading Research Quarterly, 47*(1), 91–108.

National Governors Association. (2010). *Common core state standards*. Washington, DC.

National Research Council. (2010). *Language diversity, school learning, and closing achievement gaps: A workshop summary* (M. Welch-Ross, Rapp.). Washington, DC: National Academies Press.

Neugebauer, S. R., Kieffer, M. J., & Howard, E. R. (2015). Exploring multidimensionality and mediation in the roles of lexical knowledge in reading comprehension for spanish-speaking language minority learners. *Learning and Individual Differences, 39*, 24–38.

Niedzielski, N. A., & Preston, D. R. (2000). *Folk linguistics* (Vol. 122). Berlin: Walter de Gruyter.

Ninio, A., & Snow, C. E. (1996). *Pragmatic development*. Boulder, CO: Westview Press.

O'Connor, C., Michaels, S., & Chapin, S. (2015). "Scaling down" to explore the role of talk in learning: From district intervention to controlled classroom study. In L. Resnick, C. Asterhan, & S. Clarke (Eds.), *Socializing intelligence through academic talk and dialogue* (pp. 111–126). Washington, DC: American Educational Research Association.

Oakhill, J. V., Cain, K., & Bryant, P. E. (2003). The dissociation of word reading and text comprehension: Evidence from component skills. *Language and Cognitive Processes, 18*(4), 443–468.

Palincsar, A. S., & Schleppegrell, M. J. (2014). Focusing on language and meaning while learning with text. *TESOL Quarterly, 48*(3), 616–623.

Perfetti, C., & Stafura, J. (2014). Word knowledge in a theory of reading comprehension. *Scientific Studies of Reading, 18*(1), 22–37.

Perry, T. (2003). Up from the parched earth: Toward a theory of African-American achievement. In T. Perry, C. Steele, & A. G. Hilliard III (Eds.), *Young, gifted, and black: Promoting high achievement among African-American students* (pp. 1–108). Boston, MA: Beacon Press.

Phillips Galloway, E. (2016). *The Development of Core Academic Language and Reading Comprehension in Pre-Adolescent and Adolescent Learners* (Doctor of Education). Harvard University, Cambridge, MA.

Polias, J., & Dare, B. (2006). Towards a pedagogical grammar. In R. Whittaker, A. McCabe, & M. O'Donnell (Eds.), *Language and Literacy: Functional Approaches* (pp. 123–143). London: Bloomsbury Publishing.

Proctor, C. P., Dalton, B., Uccelli, P., Biancarosa, G., Mo, E., Snow, C., & Neugebauer, S. (2011). Improving comprehension online: Effects of deep vocabulary instruction with bilingual and monolingual fifth graders. *Reading and Writing, 24*(5), 517–544.

Qin, W., & Uccelli, P. (2016). Same language, different functions: A cross-genre analysis of Chinese EFL learners' writing performance. *Journal of Second Language Writing, 33*, 3–17.

Quinn, M. (2004). Talking with Jess: Looking at how metalanguage assisted explanation writing in the middle years. *The Australian Journal of Language and Literacy, 27*(3), 245.

Ravid, D., & Tolchinsky, L. (2002). Developing linguistic literacy: A comprehensive model. *Journal of Child Language, 29*, 417–447.

Read, J. (2000). *Assessing vocabulary*. New York, NY: Cambridge University Press.

Sánchez, E., García, J. R., & Bustos, A. (2017). Does rhetorical competence moderate the effect of rhetorical devices on the comprehension of expository texts beyond general comprehension skills? *Reading and Writing, 30*(3), 439–462.

Schieffelin, B. B., & Ochs, E. (1986). *Language socialization across cultures*. Cambridge, UK: Cambridge University Press.

Schleppegrell, M. J. (2002). Linguistic features of the language of schooling. *Linguistics and Education, 12*, 431–459.

Schleppegrell, M. J. (2004). *The language of schooling: A functional linguistics perspective*. New York, NY: Routledge.

Schleppegrell, M. J. (2013). The role of metalanguage in supporting academic language development. *Language Learning, 63*(s1), 153–170.

Schmitt, N., Schmitt, D., & Clapham, C. (2001). Developing and exploring the behaviour of two new versions of the Vocabulary Levels Test. *Language Testing, 18*(1), 55–88.

Schoonen, R., & Verhallen, M. (2008). The assessment of deep word knowledge in young first and second language learners. *Language Testing, 25*(2), 211–236.

Semel, E., Wiig, E. H., & Secord, W. (1995). *Clinical evaluation of language fundamentals: Examiner's manual*. San Antonio, TX: Psychological Corp.

Shin, S. J. (2012). *Bilingualism in schools and society: Language, identity, and policy*. New York, NY: Routledge.

Siegel, L. S., & Ryan, E. B. (1989). The development of working memory in normally achieving and subtypes of learning disabled children. *Child Development*, 973–980.

Simard, D., & Jean, G. (2011). An exploration of L2 teachers' use of pedagogical interventions devised to draw L2 learners' attention to form. *Language Learning*, 61(3), 759–785.

Singson, M., Mahony, D., & Mann, V. (2000). The relation between reading ability and morphological skills: Evidence from derivational suffixes. *Reading and Writing*, 12(3), 219–252.

Slobin, D. I. (1973). Cognitive prerequisites for the development of grammar. *Studies of Child Language Development*, 1, 75–208.

Snow, C. E., Lawrence, J. F., & White, C. (2009). Generating knowledge of academic language among urban middle school students. *Journal of Research on Educational Effectiveness*, 2(4), 325–344.

Stahl, S. A., & Nagy, W. E. (2007). *Teaching word meanings*. New York, NY: Routledge.

Taboada, A., & Rutherford, V. (2011). Developing reading comprehension and academic vocabulary for English language learners through science content: A formative experiment. *Reading Psychology*, 32(2), 113–157.

Townsend, D., & Collins, P. (2009). Academic vocabulary and middle school English learners: An intervention study. *Reading and Writing*, 22(9), 993–1019.

Townsend, D., Filippini, A., Collins, P., & Biancarosa, G. (2012). Evidence for the importance of academic word knowledge for the academic achievement of diverse middle school students. *The Elementary School Journal*, 112(3), 497–518.

Tyler, A., & Nagy, W. (1989). The acquisition of English derivational morphology. *Journal of Memory and Language*, 28(6), 649–667.

Uccelli, P., Barr, C. D., Dobbs, C. L., Galloway, E. P., Meneses, A., & Sanchez, E. (2015). Core academic language skills: An expanded operational construct and a novel instrument to chart school-relevant language proficiency in preadolescent and adolescent learners. *Applied Psycholinguistics*, 36(05), 1077–1109.

Uccelli, P., Galloway, E. P., Barr, C. D., Meneses, A., & Dobbs, C. L. (2015). Beyond vocabulary: Exploring cross-disciplinary academic language proficiency and its association with reading comprehension. *Reading Research Quarterly*, 50(3), 337–356.

Uccelli, P., & Phillips Galloway, E. (2017). Academic language across content areas: Lessons from an innovative assessment and from students' reflections about language. *Journal of Adolescent & Adult Literacy*, 60(4), 395–404.

van Lier, L., & Walqui, A. (2012). Language and the common core state standards. In K. Hakuta & M. Santos (Eds.), *Understanding language: Commissioned papers on language and literacy issues in the common core state standards and next generation science standards* (pp. 44–51). Palo Alto, CA: Stanford University.

Vaughn, S., Martinez, L. R., Linan-Thompson, S., Reutebuch, C. K., Carlson, C. D., & Francis, D. J. (2009). Enhancing social studies vocabulary and comprehension for seventh-grade English language learners: Findings from two experimental studies. *Journal of Research on Educational Effectiveness*, 2(4), 297–324.

Walqui, A., & Van Lier, L. (2010). *Scaffolding the academic success of adolescent English language learners: A pedagogy of promise*. San Francisco, CA: WestEd.

Wida Consortium. (2004). *WIDA English language proficiency standards*. Madison, WI: State of Wisconsin.

Zeno, S., Ivens, S., Millard, R., & Duvvuri, R. (1995). *The educator's word frequency guide. Inc. My Book*. New York, NY: Touchstone Applied Science Associates.

10
Readers' Individual Differences in Affect and Cognition

Emily Fox

Overview

As Ruth Strang made plain, it has long been accepted that the reader's feelings, beliefs, and emotions play a critical role in reading: "Obviously people read with their emotions, their prejudices, their suppressed desires, their loves, and their hates as well as with their intelligence and their background knowledge" (Strang, 1942, p. 102). In order to understand the particulars of why people read, what they read, how they read, and what they take away from their reading, it is necessary to take into account affect-related individual differences. Affective individual differences have a critical interactive role in reading experiences and outcomes. From think-aloud research in reading (e.g., Wyatt et al., 1993), there are strong indications that affect runs alongside of, informs, feeds into, gets feedback from, and sometimes fights with cognition during reading. Affect has a presence even in cognitively-oriented stories about reading processes, such as Kintsch's (1998) information-processing based construction-integration model of reading comprehension, which includes a role for emotional/affective response in relation to the construction of a situation model and also in relation to monitoring and evaluation of comprehension. Readers can differ not only in their personal affective or emotional responses, dispositions, tendencies, and preferences, but also in the role that these play, the importance that readers give them, and the control that readers have over this (e.g., See, Petty, & Fabrigar, 2008).

However, the research on individual differences in reading has been dominated by an emphasis on the cognitive; not nearly as much attention has been given to the affective side of the story, either in its own right, or in terms of interactions with cognitive processes and products (Afflerbach, 2016). On the curriculum and policy side, although the Common Core State Standards related to reading (Common Core State Standards Initiative, 2010) include wide reading, adoption of a critical stance, open-mindedness and empathetic perspective-taking, and becoming a self-directed learner among the desired outcomes of a K-12 education, the associated affective experiences and dispositions are not addressed in that document. Given the continued emphasis in the current educational climate on reading outcomes such as test scores or measurable learning of content, it appears that what is thought to matter with regard to reading is understanding the cognitive machinery at work; however, focusing exclusively or even primarily on that cognitive machinery seems short-sighted. Our understanding of individual differences in these cognitive outcomes and our ability to address them instructionally will have serious gaps if the role of affective individual differences is not taken into account.

As a step toward pointing out some of those possible gaps, and perhaps also toward directions for addressing them, the question this chapter will address is: What does the research show about the connection of affect-related individual differences in readers with readers' individual differences in cognitive processes and outcomes from reading? This question is an opportunity to highlight the critical role of affective individual differences on a number of levels, and to bring to the fore the urgency of addressing these instructionally and in educational policy, as well as in the research.

Setting Out the Territory

The types of individual differences in cognition that are involved here include differences related to the reader's intellectual functioning and capacities, as well as the outcomes of such functioning and capacities (for reading, this would include comprehension, evaluation, and learning from text). Individual readers can differ in cognitive capabilities and resources, in how these are deployed in a given reading situation and in their control over such deployment. They can also differ in how these capabilities and resources develop, in terms of rate of development, type of experience supporting development, or trajectory of development.

Affect-related individual differences, for the purposes of this chapter, will be broadly construed as differences related to the reader's feelings (considered as both state- and trait-like), which include emotions, beliefs, attitudes, and preferences. Individual readers can differ in the level or intensity of affect they tend to experience, and in the type or valence of the affect evoked by what is encountered in a given reading experience; they can also differ in their control over their own affective or emotional response. They can differ as well in the typical affect with which they approach both reading in general, and different types of reading experiences. They can differ in their preferences, attitudes, interests, and beliefs. A final important type of individual difference between readers that also needs to be considered here is that readers can differ in *how* affect and cognition are related for them, and in their ability to control or regulate that connection. For the purpose of generating an overview that addresses the question of this chapter, what counts as affect-related individual differences is framed broadly. In addition, setting out and maintaining strict categorical boundaries for the various constructs involved is beyond the scope of what is attempted here.

Chapter Organization

The review of literature is organized into three main parts, drawn from the RAND (RAND Reading Study Group, 2002) framework for reading comprehension that distinguishes the reader, the text, and the task as bound together in reading comprehension. The research on affective individual differences and their relation to cognitive individual differences in reading will be organized according to its focus on the reader's self, on the content of the text, and on the activity of reading. The research included in the review is drawn from publications in peer-reviewed journals since 2000, which is when the most recent chapter on motivation and engagement (Guthrie & Wigfield, 2000) appeared in the *Handbook of Reading Research*. For each part, what the recent research has had to say about how these affect-related individual differences in readers are associated with cognitive individual differences will be summarized, with regard to what types of things we know and how we know them. This will enable the identification of emergent or remaining questions that deserve attention, as well as barriers that might be standing in the way of meeting the needs for research in this area. Along with identifying gaps, the chapter will also address possible approaches to future research regarding affect-related individual differences in readers, and why this matters.

Review of Literature

Affect and the Reader's Self

Three general categories of affect-related individual differences centered on the reader's self were investigated regarding their connection with individual differences in cognitive reading processes or outcomes in the research. The first was self-beliefs, namely self-efficacy for reading and reading self-concept. The second was the reader's identified dispositional needs or preferences, primarily need for cognition. The third was the reader's emotionality, with regard to both sensitivity to specific emotions and more general sensitivity toward the experiences and feelings of others, or empathy.

Self-beliefs and Reading

Self-efficacy beliefs have a central position in expectancy-value theory, which posits that a person's achievement motivation related to a particular type of task will be driven by both the person's expectancy of success (typically measured as feelings of confidence about being able to complete the task) and the person's value for the task and its outcomes (Wigfield & Cambria, 2010). However, there are mixed results in the research regarding self-efficacy's hypothesized role as an affect-related predictor of reading achievement. The lack of coherence in the findings appears to be related to how self-efficacy is measured, in whom it is measured, what aspect of reading it is expected to predict, and what other contributing factors are taken into account. In general, though, it appears that self-efficacy beliefs may be linked to concurrent reading performance chiefly insofar as they reflect the reader's actual cognitive capabilities and prior reading achievement. In the studies reviewed, the anticipated independent role of self-efficacy beliefs as promoting engagement and persistence, and therefore achievement in reading, was not strongly established.

In a number of recent studies of school-age children investigating cognitive and motivational predictors of reading achievement, self-efficacy did not remain as an independent predictor of reading comprehension when relevant cognitive (such as reading ability, verbal skill, strategy use) and motivational (task value) factors were taken into account (Anmarkrud & Bråten, 2009; Cartwright, Marshall, & Wray, 2016; McGeown, Duncan, Griffiths, & Stothard, 2015). Similarly, in a study of undergraduates reading science texts, self-efficacy was not an independent predictor of generation of text-connecting inferences when controlling for reading comprehension skill (Clinton, 2015). Self-efficacy predicted other aspects of reading for younger readers, such as word/nonword reading (Cartwright et al., 2016) and reading speed (McGeown et al., 2015). However, in a study of 6- to 8-year-old poor readers, perceived reading competence was a negative predictor of scores for single word reading and spelling, which was hypothesized to reflect inflated self-beliefs that possibly served as a defense mechanism (Fives et al., 2014).

On the other hand, a number of studies found that self-efficacy predicted reading comprehension in certain circumstances. For example, in a study of different item formats (multiple choice and constructed response) on a reading comprehension measure, self-efficacy independently predicted fifth graders' performance on both types of items when also controlling for other cognitive factors (Solheim, 2011). This could be due to the inclusion of a specific self-efficacy item addressing expectancy for performance on reading comprehension tests, and to the lack of control for prior reading achievement. Self-efficacy for reading was an independent predictor of scores on a standardized reading test for middle school students when other predictors included the other aspects of motivation measured on the Motivation for Reading Questionnaire (MRQ) developed by Wigfield and Guthrie (1995); however, cognitive controls and prior achievement were not included (Mucherah & Yoder, 2008). A cross-sectional study with 8- and 12-year-olds found that participants' sense of self-efficacy in reading was moderately related to reading achievement for both age groups, but looked only at simple correlations (Smith, Smith, Gilmore, & Jameson, 2012). Finally, a large-scale longitudinal study found that perceived reading competence and intrinsic motivation for reading (at fifth grade) together predicted later achievement (at eighth grade), even when controlling for student background factors and prior reading achievement, although the effect was small (Froiland & Oros, 2014). The independent effect of self-efficacy was not determined, however.

The other self-belief addressed in this body of research was the very closely-related construct of reading self-concept, which also involves perceived reading competence, but the source of the perceptions can differ somewhat from those feeding into reading self-efficacy (Schiefele, Schaffner, Möller, & Wigfield, 2012). Self-concept has been considered to have a broader scope than self-efficacy, and to include perceived difficulty of reading and attitudes toward reading as well as perceived reading competence (Chapman, Tunmer, & Prochnow, 2000).

Studies investigating the role of reading self-concept tended to address questions about reading development and change over time. In studies with younger students, it appeared that reading self-concept can be somewhat unstable during the first year of school (e.g., Aunola, Leskinen, Onatsu-Arvilommi, & Nurmi, 2002); however, differences in reading self-concept that emerge, even in this early period, can persist where they are associated with poor reading-related skills such as knowledge of letter names and phonemic awareness (Chapman et al., 2000). It also appeared that changes in reading self-concept are driven by reading achievement (Aunola et al., 2002; Chapman et al., 2000). However, it appears that the converse relation, that reading self-concept predicts growth in reading performance, is not well supported by the evidence from longitudinal studies. No relation of reading self-concept to growth in comprehension was seen in a large-scale quantitative study with secondary students (Retelsdorf, Köller, & Möller, 2011), and a smaller qualitative study with middle school students (Hall, 2016). Reading self-concept was consistently associated with reading performance over time for first graders, in a study using a person-oriented approach to studying students' self-concept, intrinsic motivation, and achievement in reading and math, but its independent role as a predictor of reading performance was not addressed (Viljaranta, Aunola, & Hirvonen, 2016).

The concurrent relation between reading self-concept and reading performance for fifth graders was investigated by De Naeghel et al. (De Naeghel, Van Keer, Vansteenkiste, & Rosseel, 2012), who found that reading self-concept predicted reading comprehension both independently and as mediated by teacher-rated engagement, over and above the contribution of students' autonomous and controlled motivations for reading. The interactive role of intrinsic/extrinsic motivation for reading and self-concept was also investigated by Park (2011), using data for US fourth graders from the 2006 Progress in International Reading Literacy Study (PIRLS). Park distinguished self-referenced versus peer-referenced perceived competence in reading, based on the wording of the items, and found that both types of self-concept contributed to explaining reading performance, when controlling for motivation and reading habits. However, the positive relation between peer-referenced perceived competence and reading performance was stronger for students who also had a higher level of self-referenced perceived competence. In addition, independent reading of informational text outside of school was positively correlated with self-referenced perceived competence, but negatively correlated with peer-referenced perceived competence, suggesting that these two aspects of self-concept captured different perceptions about the self as reader.

Need for Cognition and Reading

Need for cognition (NFC) refers to an individual's dispositional preference for engaging in cognitive effort (Cacioppo, Petty, Feinstein, & Jarvis, 1996). An individual reader's propensity to exert cognitive effort while reading when it is required could reasonably be expected to make a difference in the reading processes and reading outcomes for that reader, and a number of studies, primarily with university students as participants, have investigated NFC as linked with individual differences in reading processes and outcomes. Overall, it appears that NFC is related to the reader's cognitive effort for certain types of processing during reading, and in that way can also emerge as a predictor of outcomes such as reading comprehension; its role in relation to persuasion is not yet clear, however, based on the findings from these studies.

NFC made an independent contribution to prediction of reading comprehension for undergraduates, over and above the variance accounted for by the reader's beliefs about reading, for both narrative and expository texts (Dai & Wang, 2007). A strong role for NFC in comprehension was similarly seen in a study with upper secondary students, which tested a model including both cognitive and affective individual difference variables (prior knowledge, individual interest, NFC, epistemic beliefs) and processing variables (deep strategy use, effort, situational interest). In this model, NFC predicted multiple text comprehension indirectly, through its contribution to deep strategy use (Bråten, Anmarkrud, Brandmo, & Strømsø, 2014).

The possible role for NFC in very specific types of effortful comprehension-related processing was investigated in eye-tracking studies (Kaakinen, Olkoniemi, Kinneri, & Hyönä, 2014; Olkoniemi, Ranta, & Kaakinen, 2016), in which it was found that NFC was not associated simply with expending cognitive effort; the type of effort seemed to matter. Interpretation of written irony involved extra reader effort, but working memory capacity (WMC), rather than NFC or self-perceived use of sarcasm, predicted whether readers returned to re-read the target ironic sentences (Kaakinen et al., 2014). NFC also did not predict rereading in texts including written sarcasm; on the other hand, NFC did predict rereading of metaphors in text (Olkoniemi et al., 2016), which the authors interpreted as due to the opportunity for reasoning offered by figuring out metaphors.

Several studies addressed the interaction of NFC and prior knowledge, with regard to readers' learning from text, evaluation of arguments, and response to persuasive texts (Diakidoy, Christodoulou, Floros, Iordanou, & Kargopoulos, 2015; Kendeou & van den Broek, 2007; Murphy, Holleran, Long, & Zeruth, 2005), with somewhat mixed findings. Diakidoy et al. (2015) found that half of their university student participants did not correctly identify the main claim in written arguments of better or worse quality; nonetheless, the students evaluated the texts positively and found them to be persuasive, regardless of the actual quality of the argument. In particular, students with higher NFC but lower topic knowledge were more likely to evaluate the text positively, regardless of the actual quality of the argument presented. In a study involving the reading of refutational or non-refutational science text by undergraduates, neither working memory capacity nor NFC made a difference in how readers read, or in their memory for the text (Kendeou & van den Broek, 2007). However, Murphy et al. (2005) found that NFC made an independent contribution to predicting students' change in beliefs after reading persuasive texts on social issues, over and above the contribution of the other motivational factors of topic interest, text interestingness, and topic beliefs.

A final line of research related to NFC looked at individual differences in readers' processing and persuasion depending on the readers' meta-bases, which refers to their interest in processing affective versus cognitive information. In one study, the role of meta-bases was compared to the role of structural bases, which refers to readers' efficiency at processing affective versus cognitive information (See et al., 2008). Meta-bases but not NFC, need for affect, or structural bases predicted reading time for affective versus cognitive information in persuasive texts; both meta-bases and structural bases predicted persuasion, with the text that matched the reader's meta-bases and structural bases being more persuasive for that reader. The authors suggested that future research is needed to determine the mechanisms behind these effects and the origins of people's meta-bases and structural bases.

Emotional Response and Reading

Two levels at which individual differences in the reader's emotional responses could be connected with differences in cognitive processing or outcomes were addressed in the research: sensitivity to particular emotions in the processing of emotional information, and the more general trait of empathy as a capacity to respond emotionally to others. Studies discussed here all used university students as participants.

Individual differences in sensitivity to particular types of emotion-related information influenced readers' processing of such information, in studies concerning anxiety (Calvo & Castillo, 2001) and disgust (Silva, Montant, Ponz, & Ziegler, 2012). In the study by Calvo and Castillo (2001), trait anxiety level biased the reader toward drawing predictive inferences that confirmed the expectations associated with that anxiety level, either the expectation of harm (high trait anxiety) or the expectation of a neutral outcome (low trait anxiety). The authors argued that this reflected the reader's prioritization of emotion-congruent information and sensitization to contexts evoking either vigilance (high anxiety) or threat avoidance (low anxiety). Similarly, responses to disgust-related words in a lexical decision task were predicted by sensitivity to disgust-related information, but not by features of the words themselves or the reader's level of empathy, interpreted as general emotion sensitivity (Silva et al., 2012). Reaction times and accuracy for lexical decisions on disgust-related words indicated response inhibition for high-disgust-sensitivity participants, but also facilitation for low-disgust sensitivity-participants. Looking at emotional processing more broadly, efficiency in processing of emotion-related information predicted readers' capabilities for processing written sarcasm, in an eye-tracking study (Olkoniemi et al., 2016).

The relation of empathy with other reading-related skills (phonemic awareness, decoding, and fluency) was addressed in a study of dyslexic and non-dyslexic readers (Gabay, Shamay-Tsoory, & Goldfarb, 2016). Empathy was measured as cognitive empathy (fantasy and perspective-taking) and emotional empathy (empathic concern and emotional distress). Total empathy and cognitive empathy were positively correlated with scores for phonemic awareness, decoding, and fluency, which the authors suggested could reflect an overlapping role for a particular brain region, the temporo-parietal junction, which has been implicated in both dyslexia and deficits in empathy. Alternatively, the types of school and social experiences associated with poor early reading skills could contribute to poor social and communicative development, making it harder to relate to the experiences of others.

Affect and the Reading Content

Readers' individual differences in affect related to the content of the text were addressed in research on the role of the reader's feelings about the content, principally interest in the topic or domain addressed by the text, and the reader's beliefs or opinions about the content addressed by the text. The role of domain and topic interest in reading is a well-established research area; the alignment (or not) of readers' topic beliefs or opinions with what is being said in the text is a relatively newer area of research, generally associated with investigations of conceptual change and multiple text comprehension.

Interest and Text Content

Individual differences in the reader's interest related to the content of the text can be at the broader level of a particular area of knowledge, such as an academic domain, or at the more focused level of a particular topic within a broader domain; in either case, this type of interest would be considered to reflect what is termed individual or personal interest in that domain, a stable trait-like individual characteristic (Alexander & Jetton, 1996). Topic interest can also be considered to be a type of situational interest that reflects a less stable affective response to the particulars of the reading situation (Ainley, Hidi, & Berndorff, 2002). In the recent research, studies of content-related interest as an affective individual difference factor connected with cognitive reading processes and outcomes have considered its direct or indirect role in reading comprehension, in learning new information from text, and in conceptual change, or change in topic beliefs. Studies discussed here used readers of varying ages, elementary or high school students as well as undergraduates. Overall, the evidence tends to support a connection of content-related interest and reading outcomes, but this often occurs indirectly through the motivational contribution of such interest to reading engagement in some form.

The contribution of interest in the content to reading comprehension has been investigated in a number of studies. For example, interest in the passages used in the assessment was positively related to performance on comprehension test items from the Iowa Test of Basic Skills (ITBS) across grade levels tested (fourth through eighth), when controlling for gender and verbal ability (Bray & Barron, 2003–2004). The authors suggested that using relatively low-interest passages might be the best way to assess comprehension without noise from interest effects, which were small but reliable in their large-scale study. The indirect contribution of topic interest to comprehension when taking into account participants' WMC, motivation, degree of mind wandering during reading, and prior experience related to the topic was investigated by Unsworth and McMillan (2013). Topic interest predicted motivation to do well on the task, which negatively predicted mind wandering. Mind wandering, in turn, negatively predicted comprehension for their undergraduate participants. In the two studies just discussed, however, interest was measured after the text had been read and the comprehension assessment completed, which makes it more difficult to interpret these results as indicating effects of interest on comprehension. For undergraduates reading a dual-positional text on a controversial issue (Kardash & Howell, 2000), participants' post-reading rating of their interest in the text was related to their use of comprehension-fostering reading strategies as evident in their think-alouds while reading, and also to their later level of recall of the text.

Moving beyond comprehension, several studies have addressed the role of content-related interest as supporting learning of new information from the text. When high school students were grouped by their level of prior topic knowledge and topic interest for science texts, higher interest only improved recall for readers with low topic knowledge, while it improved both recall and deeper-comprehension for readers with high topic knowledge (Boscolo & Mason, 2003). The role of content-related interest was unpacked further in studies that also considered the reader's affective and motivational response during the reading situation, where content-related interest was only an indirect contributor to learning from text. For example, content-related interest was related to students' affective response and persistence when reading, which was then related to learning from the text for high school students reading science or pop culture texts (Ainley et al., 2002). In studies considering the relative importance for learning from text of choice, topic interest (measured before reading, as expectation of interest in reading the text), and situational interest (measured after reading, as experienced interest in the text and its topic), the most important contributor to outcome performance was situational interest, or post-task interest in the text and its content (Flowerday, Schraw, & Stevens, 2004; Flowerday & Shell,

2015). This contribution was only indirect, through its association with attitude and engagement when reading (both also retrospectively reported).

A possible cognitive mechanism linking content-related interest with learning from text, amount of inference generation, was considered in a study by Clinton and van den Broek (2012), but this linkage was not conclusively supported by their findings. Topic interest did predict learning from text for their undergraduate participants, and was also related to learning from text through its association with inference generation (observed in think-alouds), when controlling for reading comprehension ability. However, this was only true for the more coherently-written of the two science texts used, and it was only true for higher-level comprehension questions, not recall.

Moving beyond the learning of new information from text, the role of content-related interest in readers' conceptual change, knowledge revision, or change in beliefs about a topic was investigated in several studies as well, with mixed findings. The degree to which high school students' beliefs about knowledge (epistemological understanding) and their topic interest contributed to their critical interpretation of a dual-position text on transgenic food, to their development of conceptual understanding and to change in their beliefs about the topic was investigated by Mason and Boscolo (2004). Topic interest made an independent contribution to students' development of conceptual understanding, but not to their critical interpretation or belief change after reading, which were both influenced by the students' level of epistemological understanding. Prior topic knowledge was included as a covariate in this study. Similarly, topic interest did not predict belief change for undergraduates reading persuasive texts, over and above the contribution of need for cognition and topic interestingness (Murphy et al., 2005). However, in a study with fifth graders reading traditional instructional texts or refutational texts intended to correct misconceptions about the scientific topic of light, topic interest did predict conceptual change, as did text type and level of epistemological understanding (Mason, Gava, & Boldrin, 2008). Reading comprehension ability was used as a covariate here. It appears, therefore, that the consistent, albeit indirect, association of topic interest with improvement in the reader's comprehension and learning from text, through increased engagement, positive affective response, and use of reading strategies, may not carry over to conceptual change. Readers may not necessarily adjust their misconceptions more readily for a more interesting topic.

Beliefs and Opinions about Text Content

A relatively new line of research has addressed how the reader's beliefs and opinions related to the content of texts might be implicated in how the reader (undergraduates, in all of the studies reviewed) understands, learns from, or is persuaded by the texts. Learners' beliefs about the topic addressed by the text were related to their comprehension processing when reading conflicting texts, as well as to their comprehension of what was read. For example, topic-specific beliefs were associated with more instances of monitoring for belief-consistent information and with more instances of evaluation for belief-inconsistent information, when reading a dual-positional text about HIV and AIDS (Kardash & Howell, 2000). A related difference in reading outcomes that suggests differential processing of information that conflicts with the learner's prior beliefs was observed in a study of undergraduates reading multiple conflicting science texts about global warming (Maier & Richter, 2013); readers did a better job on a post-reading verification task for inferred information (assessing the situation model level of comprehension) when it was belief-consistent, but did better on a verification task for explicitly stated information (assessing the text-base level of comprehension) when it was belief-inconsistent. However, differences in processing argumentative scientific texts were not based on the reader's prior beliefs about the topics discussed in the text (Wolfe, Tanner, & Taylor, 2013). Instead, what mattered was whether the reader reported holding the belief based on evidence or affect. Evidence-based belief was associated with more balanced processing (as far as attention to belief-inconsistent information), and with less biased summaries of a neutral text.

A related line of research has addressed reader preferences and biases in processing related to narrative texts; in particular, readers' preferences regarding particular characters influence their expectations regarding plot outcomes and drive some of their predictive inferences (Rapp & Gerrig, 2006). The reader's preferences are presumably driven, mostly normatively, by the author's intentions, although individual variability regarding which characters a reader will "root" for is also evident, and is not linked with trait empathy (Gerrig, Bagelmann, & Mumper, 2016).

Affect and the Reading Task

Several affective aspects of the reader's approach or response related to the reading task have been addressed in the research on affect-related differences in readers and their connection with cognitive outcomes. One is the reader's feelings about reading, primarily task value, attitude toward reading, and individual interest in reading. Another is the reader's specific motivations for reading, which can be categorized broadly as intrinsic and extrinsic, or autonomous and controlled. A third is the reader's affective response to the reading task, which includes situational interest and engagement. A final aspect is the reader's typical reading choices, which includes both frequency of reading and what is read.

Feelings about Reading

As discussed in the section above on self-efficacy beliefs, a number of studies have used an expectancy-value framework when considering the role of readers' affective individual differences as contributing to their reading performance. However, in contrast to the more variable findings regarding the expectancy component of self-efficacy or perceived competence, reading value has been more consistently found to contribute to the prediction of reading comprehension, even when controlling for other relevant cognitive and motivational factors (Anmarkrud & Bråten, 2009; Cartwright et al., 2016; Fives et al., 2014; Froiland & Oros, 2014; McGeown et al., 2015). This was seen for first graders on up to high school students, in both concurrent investigations in which predictors and outcomes were measured contemporaneously (Anmarkrud & Bråten, 2009; Cartwright et al., 2016; Fives et al., 2014; McGeown et al., 2015), and longitudinal investigations in which reading value measured at an earlier age was used to predict later reading comprehension performance (Froiland & Oros, 2014). There were divergent findings from several studies, though. Reading value did not make an independent contribution to predicting fifth graders' scores on a reading comprehension assessment (Solheim, 2011) or to 8- and 12-year-old students' performance on a performance-based reading assessment (Smith et al., 2012). In addition, first graders with profiles of low value but high perceived competence were nonetheless observed to show strong reading performance, which suggested to the authors that when beliefs and values are separate, beliefs matter more, at least in the early school years (Viljaranta et al., 2016).

In several longitudinal studies, it appeared that interest in reading or attitude toward reading has more of an influence on growth in reading ability in upper elementary school and beyond, and less of an impact in the earlier years of elementary school (Kirby, Ball, Geier, Parilla, & Wade-Woolley, 2011; Kush, Watkins, & Brookhart, 2005; Martínez, Aricak, & Jewell, 2008). Interest in reading measured in grade 1 was only weakly associated with students' reading ability when measured in grade 3 (Kirby et al., 2011). Further, Kush et al. (2005) found that attitude toward reading (ratings of liking of reading) measured in the fall of grade 3 did not predict spring grade 3 reading performance on the ITBS, but reading attitude in the third grade did predict seventh grade ITBS reading scores, even when controlling for prior reading achievement.

A developmental shift in the strength of the relation between reading attitude and growth in reading ability is also supported in the findings by Martínez et al. (2008), where reading achievement at the start of the fifth grade was predicted by reading attitude at the end of the fourth grade, even when controlling for prior reading ability.

These findings were seen to support a temporal-interactive model of reading development, in which early reading attitudes influence reading behaviors, which then influence later reading abilities. However, reading interest influenced growth in reading competence only for students in academic track schools, in a study with German fifth and sixth graders; this relation was not evident for students in the nonacademic track (Schaffner, Philipp, & Schiefele, 2016). Interest in reading did not predict undergraduates' immediate performance on a reading comprehension task (Patall, 2013), which is in line with the view that its influence, if any, is longer-term.

Motivations for Reading

Readers can differ not only in their attitudes and values related to reading, but also more broadly in their motivations for reading, which can include attitudes and values as well as other aspects such as those measured on the MRQ (Wigfield & Guthrie, 1995). These are typically grouped into intrinsic and extrinsic motivations, or sometimes autonomous and controlled motivations, within the context of self-determination theory (e.g., De Naeghel et al., 2012). In general, the findings from these studies indicate that the relation of individual differences in reading motivations to variability in reading performance and reading development is complex and conditional.

The concurrent relation of reading motivations to reading performance has been addressed in recent large-scale studies using fifth graders (De Naeghel et al., 2012) and fourth graders (Park, 2011). In the study by De Naeghel et al. (2012), reading motivation was assessed separately for recreational and academic reading contexts, and had somewhat different roles depending on the context. Reading motivation for the recreational reading context was related to reading comprehension, with a positive relation for autonomous motivation and a negative relation for controlled motivation. However, autonomous reading motivation for the academic reading context was not related to comprehension; there was also no significant indirect relation between any type of reading motivation and reading comprehension through reading frequency or teacher-rated engagement. The study by Park (2011) used US data from the 2006 PIRLS, and found an unequivocally positive role for intrinsic reading motivation; however, the contribution of extrinsic motivation to reading performance depended on the student's level of intrinsic motivation. Extrinsic motivation contributed positively to comprehension for students who also had at least a medium level of intrinsic motivation; for students with low intrinsic motivation, extrinsic motivation was negatively related to comprehension.

In a smaller-scale study relating scores on the MRQ to performance by middle school students on a standardized state reading assessment (Mucherah & Yoder, 2008), only certain aspects of intrinsic motivation predicted comprehension: reading for challenge and aesthetic enjoyment. Reading for social reasons (which includes sharing what is read, but also compliance as a driver of reading) was a negative predictor of comprehension scores. Finally, a study with undergraduates (Clinton, 2015) found that a certain type of cognitive processing during reading, generation of inferences related to connections within the text, was positively related to elements of both intrinsic motivation (reading as part of one's sense of self) and extrinsic motivation (reading to succeed at work or school), even when controlling for reading comprehension skill. Motivation was not independently related to generation of inferences involving the activation of background knowledge for the science texts read in this study, when reading ability was taken into account.

The role of reading motivation in the development of reading ability has also been investigated in longitudinal research. A short-term longitudinal study considered whether reading motivation mattered for third grade students' changes in level of reading competence over their summer vacation (Schaffner & Schiefele, 2016). Overall, there was not much change in students' scores for word and sentence comprehension from before to after the summer vacation. However, intrinsic motivation contributed to reading amount, which made an independent contribution to prediction of reading comprehension scores after the summer vacation, even when taking into account prior reading ability; extrinsic motivation was unrelated to end-of-summer reading scores, which the authors speculated could reflect the short timeframe involved. In more extended longitudinal research, intrinsic reading motivation predicted growth in reading comprehension over a school year when also taking verbal IQ and decoding skill into account, but only for lower-ability readers, in a study with 9–11-year olds (Logan, Medford, & Hughes, 2011). For somewhat older students (fifth to eighth graders), intrinsic reading motivation in the form of reading for enjoyment predicted initial reading performance but not growth over the school year, while the situation was reversed for intrinsic reading motivation in the form of reading for interest, which predicted growth but not initial performance (Retelsdorf et al., 2011). Additional controls included here were cognitive skills, family information, and demographic factors. Competition as a form of extrinsic motivation was negatively related to initial reading performance, but did not influence growth.

In a more extended view of growth in comprehension, vocabulary, and decoding skills from grades 3 to 6, reading performance in grade 3 predicted intrinsic reading motivation in grade 4, which predicted reading amount, which predicted reading skills in grade 6 (Becker, McElvany, & Kortenbruck, 2010). However, intrinsic motivation dropped out as a significant predictor of later skills when prior reading achievement was included in the model. Extrinsic reading motivation in grade 4 was negatively predicted by reading performance in grade 3, and remained a reliable negative predictor of later reading performance even when prior achievement was taken into account.

Feelings about the Reading Task

How the reader feels about the particular reading task at hand is thought to be another possible important affect-related contributor to differences in reading performance; these feelings can be measured as a form of individual or situational interest (e.g., Bråten et al., 2014), or as feelings of task engagement (e.g., Jones, Johnson, & Campbell, 2015). It appears to matter when these feelings about the reading task are assumed to exert their influence, and also when they are measured. In the study by Bråten et al. (2014), individual interest in learning from science texts predicted both reported interest in reading the specific science texts used in the reading task (situational interest), which was captured during reading, and reading time (effort). Effort and situational interest both predicted deep-level strategy use, which predicted multiple-text comprehension; effort also made an independent contribution to comprehension, as did prior knowledge. A variant of this pathway was seen in the study by Jones et al. (2015), who found that for their undergraduate participants reading a refutational text about the common cold, reading time (attention allocation) directly predicted self-reported level of engagement in the reading task (measured after task completion), which predicted conceptual change.

Reading Preferences and Habits

A final aspect of readers' feelings about reading is the role of the reader's preferences and habits related to reading; this can include the reader's choices about what to read and also about how often or how much to read. Research investigating the contribution of reading preferences and habits to other types of reading outcomes consistently shows that it matters what and how often people read. In particular, reading of fiction, reading of books, and reading of printed (rather than online) material have important benefits. One of the genre-specific benefits of reading fiction, particularly literary fiction, appears to be that it increases cognitive empathy (Djikic, Oatley, & Moldoveanu, 2013b) and the ability to understand the mental states of other, or theory of mind (Kidd & Castano, 2013); these studies were experimental, with adult participants, and compared literary fiction to other genres. A similar experimental study (Djikic, Oatley, & Moldoveanu, 2013a) found that reading fiction led to a decrease in need for closure, while reading nonfiction did not; this effect was stronger for participants who reported being regular readers of any type of text.

More traditional individual differences research has also found positive links of the reading of fiction with reading comprehension outcomes; for adolescents, reading of fictional books positively predicted performance on comprehension and summarization, even when taking word reading and text reading speed into account (McGeown et al., 2015). For sixth graders, weak comprehenders were more likely to be readers of nonfiction, while strong comprehenders were more likely to read fiction (Spear-Swerling, Brucker, & Alfano, 2010). Independent reading of extended print texts predicted inference-making and overall comprehension of fiction and nonfiction texts for 11- to 15-year-olds, although these students reported spending more time with digital than traditional texts (Duncan, McGeown, Griffiths, Stothard, & Dobai, 2016). Similarly, extracurricular reading of traditional printed texts was related to reading comprehension and vocabulary in a large-scale study of secondary students; in this study, time spent online was negatively related to reading achievement (Pfost, Dörfler, & Artelt, 2013). Finally, a large meta-analysis by Mol and Bus (2011) found that print exposure is related to improvements in reading skills and comprehension for students from pre-kindergarten through graduate school; they described the relation as a spiral in which initial levels of reading skill and success predict amount of reading, which then contributes to the development of greater reading skill and success. They found benefits of independent leisure reading for poor comprehenders as well; it is not only the rich who get richer, which is somewhat encouraging.

Identifying and Bridging the Gaps

Having overviewed the recent research on affect-related individual differences in readers with regard to the reader's self, the content, and the task, as far as the relation of such individual differences to variability in readers' cognitive processes and outcomes, what gaps, if any, appear? What are the practical/theoretical needs for research in this area, and are they being met? What potential new approaches could be taken to make the research or implementation of its findings fruitful, both in the current educational situation and the current conditions readers confront both in and out of the academic setting?

Many of the relations of cognitive and affective factors studied in this body of research appear to be interactive and bidirectional, which means that untangling paths of influence here is challenging. Intervention research was not included in this review, and the results of interventions could provide helpful evidence about what influences what. However, in terms of designing those interventions based upon what the research has shown, we do not, in many cases, have a clear story about which triggers should be the ones to try to manipulate in order to improve students' reading abilities and outcomes. One suggestion in this regard is to consider linking the cognitive and affective aspects even more closely in our theoretical models; affect and cognition appear to be commingled at the very heart of our thinking. We separate them in our stories and models, and think we are separating them in our measurements, but it is beginning to look as though they are interwoven all the way down; some of the newer lines of research related to reading are testing these borderlines, and this seems a very promising area for further investigations. Another suggestion for taking account of the interconnectivity among factors of interest is to support the large body of variable-centered research with more person-centered studies, in which multiple possibly meaningful patterns of relations among readers' characteristics can be explored and connected to how reading happens for those different types of readers.

With regard to the time course of what happens during reading, process-related approaches seem key, yet these are difficult to do and report. Think-alouds (e.g., Clinton & van den Broek, 2012; Kardash & Howell, 2000) and eye-tracking (e.g., Kaakinen et al., 2014; Olkoniemi et al., 2016; Scrimin & Mason, 2015), were used in a few studies in the reviewed research to capture differences in reading processes, along with online questionnaires and sampling of readers' in-the-moment feelings and responses. These are valuable techniques that add critical information about the possible mechanisms by which the relations seen between more static measures emerge. Without this type of information, our stories about what happens during reading remain speculative, to a greater degree than we should be comfortable with. In managing the interpretation of the multiplex phenomenon presented by a reader's response and performance, the use of a complex dynamic systems approach (e.g., Kaplan, Katz, & Flum, 2012) may be worth exploring. Another potential measurement issue is the general (but not total) lack of attention to negative affective responses; in recent work, Guthrie and colleagues have identified what they label as undermining forms of motivation and engagement (e.g., Guthrie, Klauda, & Ho, 2013). It seems very possible that readers' individual differences in negative affective responses and characteristics also matter, if we can figure out how to identify and measure these appropriately.

Considering the types of topics covered, focused attention on the role of the reader's capacity for emotional/motivational self-regulation was not directly evident in the research. It has been suggested that emotional control is important during the acquisition of a new skill, situations involving possible frustration, needing to cope with errors, or performance anxiety (such as testing), while motivational control is more important for persistence and improvement in skill development (Kanfer & Heggestad, 1999). Both of these seem like important areas for the reading research to address, in order to understand how individual affect-related differences can be implicated in reading outcomes; the evident strength of early reading experiences for what happens later in reading development suggests that understanding more about how readers work through the early stages of learning to read matters a great deal.

Understanding more about students' out-of-school reading habits and preferences seems ever more important, given their strong connection with reading abilities and other developmental outcomes, and the relentless pressure of new media for our children's attention. In connection with the explosion of unreliable yet widely available or even prominent sources of information on the internet, there is a lot of work being done on how affect is implicated in readers' evaluations of what they read (see, for example, the discussion of the role of motivation in biased information processing and rejection of information that conflicts with existing beliefs by Ecker, Swire, & Lewandowsky, 2014). It might be even more critical to uncover further how strongly readers' preferences for particular types of information or interactions with information influence what they end up believing to be true (see, for example, work by Hambrick, Meinz, Pink, Pettibone, & Oswald, 2010, about the influence of preferences for different types of information sources, such as television, newspapers, and radio, on people's acquisition of knowledge about politics). There are also many different purposes for reading in the real world; the contrast between academic tasks and leisure reading does not begin to capture what readers do. In those many other types of reading situations, there may well be different roles for affect and affective differences in readers; this is terra incognita at present.

Overall, it is evident that there is considerable thoughtful, careful, complex, research going on; perhaps not always with the strongest of tools for the job, in terms of measurement of affect and identification of what exactly the reader is doing. Reading this body of research creates a very powerful impression, with so many voices all arguing for the importance of consideration of affect-related factors in reading. Nonetheless, as far as the likelihood that the role of individual affect-related differences in reading will be acknowledged in curriculum or policy, it seems like a long road ahead. Teachers are enormously aware of the role of affect, but it tends to be viewed as either a serendipitous catalyst or enhancer, for those students who sit at the positive end of the spectrum, or as a roadblock to get around, for those who are at the other end. Teachers must also keep the bottom line of test scores in mind, and do not have much curricular flexibility or room for differentiation related to students' affective differences. Our educational system is not very good at change, and there seems no reason to think that this situation will improve any time soon.

However, one direction for possible change that would be a strong and integrative step toward bridging the gap between the manifold findings from what the research has shown about the importance of affective individual differences in reading and what should occur in classrooms and be prescribed in policy, was recommended by the late Jere Brophy (2008). Brophy recommended that motivational researchers turn their efforts toward how best to justify and promote students' appreciation and valuing of what they learn in school. He pointed out that, "Addressing value requires attention to the learners' beliefs and feelings about the content, as well as the processes involved in learning and applying it" (p. 132). Brophy suggested that one practical step toward accomplishing this integration of the affective and cognitive aspects of learning would be to return to including appreciation of what is learned as an intended outcome of instruction, as was the practice earlier in the 20th century (and even as late as the 1970's; see, e.g., Bloom, Hastings, & Madaus, 1971). If we consider what that might look like for reading, the possibilities that such a shift in instructional emphasis could open up with regard to how learners approach the reading that they do in and out of school are quite heartening. As Brophy explained it, for reading, appreciation can include the reader's sense that "reading and writing are not just basic skills needed for utilitarian applications but gateways to interest development, identity exploration, self-expression, and other enrichments to individuals' subjective lives" (2008, p. 138). That is something we would like all readers to be able to grasp.

References

Afflerbach, P. (2016). An overview of individual differences in reading: Research, policy, and practice. In P. Afflerbach (Ed.), *Handbook of individual differences in reading: Reader, text, and context* (pp. 1–12). New York: Routledge.

Ainley, M., Hidi, S., & Berndorff, D. (2002). Interest, learning, and the psychological processes that mediate their relationship. *Journal of Educational Psychology, 94*, 545–561.

Alexander, P. A., & Jetton, T. L. (1996). The role of importance and interest in the processing of text. *Educational Psychology Review, 8*, 89–121.

Anmarkrud, Ø., & Bråten, I. (2009). Motivation for reading comprehension. *Learning and Individual Differences, 19*, 252–256.

Aunola, K., Leskinen, E., Onatsu-Arvilommi, T., & Nurmi, J. (2002). Three methods for studying developmental change: A case of reading skills and self-concept. *British Journal of Educational Psychology, 72*, 343–364.

Becker, M., McElvany, N., & Kortenbruck, M. (2010). Intrinsic and extrinsic reading motivation as predictors of reading literacy: A longitudinal study. *Journal of Educational Psychology, 102*, 773–785.

Bloom, B. J., Hastings, J. R., & Madaus, G. F. (1971). *Handbook on formative and summative evaluation of learning*. New York: McGraw-Hill.

Boscolo, P., & Mason, L. (2003). Topic knowledge, text coherence, and interest: How they interact in learning from instructional texts. *The Journal of Experimental Education, 71*(2), 126–148.

Bråten, I., Anmarkrud, Ø., Brandmo, C., & Strømsø, H. I. (2014). Developing and testing a model of direct and indirect relationships between individual differences, processing, and multiple-text comprehension. *Learning and Instruction, 30,* 9–24.

Bray, G. B., & Barron, S. (2003–2004). Assessing reading comprehension: The effects of text-based interest, gender, and ability. *Educational Assessment, 9*(3&4), 107–128.

Brophy, J. (2008). Developing students' appreciation for what is taught in school. *Educational Psychologist, 43* (3), 132–141.

Cacioppo, J. T., Petty, R. E., Feinstein, J. A., & Jarvis, W. B. G. (1996). Dispositional differences in cognitive motivation: The life and times of individuals varying in need for cognition. *Psychological Bulletin, 119,* 197–253.

Calvo, M. G., & Castillo, M. D. (2001). Bias in predictive inferences during reading. *Discourse Processes, 32,* 43–71.

Cartwright, K. B., Marshall, T. R., & Wray, E. (2016). A longitudinal study of the role of reading motivation in primary students' reading comprehension: Implications for a less simple view of reading. *Reading Psychology, 37,* 55–91.

Chapman, J. W., Tunmer, W. E., & Prochnow, J. E. (2000). Early reading-related skills and performance, reading self-concept, and the development of academic self-concept: A longitudinal study. *Journal of Educational Psychology, 92,* 703–708.

Clinton, V. (2015). Examining associations between reading motivation and inference generation beyond reading comprehension skill. *Reading Psychology, 36,* 473–498.

Clinton, V., & van den Broek, P. (2012). Interest, inferences, and learning from texts. *Learning and Individual Differences, 22,* 650–663.

Common Core State Standards Initiative. (2010). *The Common Core State Standards for English language arts and literacy in history/social studies, science, and technical subjects.* Washington, DC: Council of Chief State School Officers and National Governors Association. Retrieved from www.corestandards.org/

Dai, D. Y., & Wang, X. (2007). The role of need for cognition and reader beliefs in text comprehension and interest development. *Contemporary Educational Psychology, 32,* 332–347.

De Naeghel, J., Van Keer, H., Vansteenkiste, M., & Rossel, Y. (2012). Relation between elementary students' recreational and academic reading motivation, reading frequency, engagement, and comprehension: A self-determination theory perspective. *Journal of Educational Psychology, 104,* 1006–1021.

Diakidoy, I. N., Christodoulou, S. A., Floros, G., Iordanou, K., & Kargopoulos, P. V. (2015). Forming a belief: The contribution of comprehension to the evaluation and persuasive impact of argumentative text. *British Journal of Educational Psychology, 85,* 300–315.

Djikic, M., Oatley, K., & Moldoveanu, M. C. (2013a). Opening the closed mind: The effects of exposure to literature on the need for closure. *Creativity Research Journal, 25*(2), 149–154.

Djikic, M., Oatley, K., & Moldoveanu, M. C. (2013b). Reading other minds: Effects of literature on empathy. *Scientific Study of Literature, 3*(1), 28–47.

Duncan, L. G., McGeown, S. P., Griffiths, Y. M., Stothard, S. E., & Dobai, A. (2016). Adolescent reading skills and engagement with digital and traditional literacies as predictors of reading comprehension. *British Journal of Psychology, 107,* 209–238.

Ecker, U. K. H., Swire, B., & Lewandowsky, S. (2014). Correcting misinformation: A challenge for education and science. In D. N. Rapp & J. L. G. Braasch (Eds.), *Processing inaccurate information* (pp. 13–37). Cambridge, MA: The MIT Press.

Fives, A., Russell, D., Kearns, N., Lyons, R., Eaton, P., Canavan, J., Devaney, C., & O'Brien, A. (2014). The association between academic self-beliefs and reading achievement among children at risk of reading failure. *Journal of Research in Reading, 37*(2), 215–232. doi:10.1111/1467-9817.12025

Flowerday, T., Schraw, G., & Stevens, J. (2004). The role of choice and interest in reader engagement. *The Journal of Experimental Education, 72,* 93–114.

Flowerday, T., & Shell, D. F. (2015). Disentangling the effects of interest and choice on learning, engagement, and attitude. *Learning and Individual Differences, 40,* 134–140.

Froiland, J. M., & Oros, E. (2014). Intrinsic motivation, perceived competence and classroom engagement as longitudinal predictors of adolescent reading achievement. *Educational Psychology, 34*(2), 119–132.

Gabay, Y., Shamay-Tsoory, S. G., & Goldfarb, L. (2016). Cognitive and emotional empathy in typical and impaired readers and its relationship to reading competence. *Journal of Clinical and Experimental Neuropsychology, 38,* 1131–1143.

Gerrig, R. J., Bagelmann, K. A., & Mumper, M. L. (2016). On the origins of readers' outcome preferences. *Discourse Processes, 53,* 603–631.

Guthrie, J. T., Klauda, S. L., & Ho, A. N. (2013). Modeling the relationships among reading instruction, motivation, engagement, and achievement for adolescents. *Reading Research Quarterly*, *48*, 9–26.

Guthrie, J. T., & Wigfield, A. (2000). Engagement and motivation in reading. In M. L. Kamil, P. B. Mosenthal, P. D. Pearson, & R. Barr (Eds.), *Handbook of reading research* (Vol. 3, pp. 403–422). Mahwah, NJ: Lawrence Erlbaum Associates.

Hall, L. A. (2016). The role of identity in reading comprehension development. *Reading & Writing Quarterly*, *32*, 56–80.

Hambrick, D. Z., Meinz, E. J., Pink, J. E., Pettibone, J. C., & Oswald, F. L. (2010). Learning outside the laboratory: Ability and non-ability influences on acquiring political knowledge. *Learning and Individual Differences*, *20*, 40–45.

Jones, S. H., Johnson, M. L., & Campbell, B. D. (2015). Hot factors for a cold topic: Exmaining the role of task-value, attention allocation, and engagement on conceptual change. *Contemporary Educational Psychology*, *42*, 62–70.

Kaakinen, J. K., Olkoniemi, H., Kinneri, T., & Hyönä, J. (2014). Processing of written irony: An eye movement study. *Discourse Processes*, *51*, 287–311.

Kanfer, R., & Heggestad, E. D. (1999). Individual differences in motivation: Traits and self-regulatory skills. In P. L. Ackerman, P. C. Kyllonen, & R. D. Roberts (Eds.), *Learning and individual differences: Process, trait, and content determinants* (pp. 293–309). Washington, DC: American Psychological Association.

Kaplan, A., Katz, I., & Flum, H. (2012). Motivation theory in educational practice: Knowledge claims, challenges, and future directions. In K. R. Harris, S. G. Graham, & T. Urdan (Eds.), *APA educational psychology handbook vol. 2: Individual differences, cultural considerations, and contextual factors in educational psychology* (pp. 165–194). Washington, DC: American Psychological Association.

Kardash, C. M., & Howell, K. L. (2000). The effects of epistemological and topic-specific beliefs on undergraduates' cognitive and strategic processing of dual-positional text. *Journal of Educational Psychology*, *92*, 524–535.

Kendeou, P., & van den Broek, P. (2007). The effects of prior knowledge and text structure on comprehension processes during reading of scientific texts. *Memory & Cognition*, *35*, 1567–1577.

Kidd, D. C., & Castano, E. (2013). Reading literary fiction improves theory of mind. *Science*, *382*, 377–380.

Kintsch, W. (1998). *Comprehension*. New York: Cambridge University Press.

Kirby, J. R., Ball, A., Geier, B. K., Parrila, R., & Wade-Woolley, L. (2011). The development of reading interest and its relation to reading ability. *Journal of Research in Reading*, *34*, 263–280.

Kush, J. C., Watkins, M. W., & Brookhart, S. M. (2005). The temporal-interactive influence of reading achievement and reading attitude. *Educational Research and Evaluation*, *11*(1), 29–44.

Logan, S., Medford, E., & Hughes, N. (2011). The importance of intrinsic motivation for high and low ability readers' reading performance. *Learning and Individual Differences*, *21*, 124–128.

Maier, J., & Richter, T. (2013). Text belief consistency effects in the comprehension of multiple texts with conflicting information. *Cognition and Instruction*, *31*, 151–175.

Martínez, R. S., Aricak, O. T., & Jewell, J. (2008). Influence of reading attitude on reading achievement: A test of the temporal-interaction model. *Psychology in the Schools*, *45*, 1010–1022.

Mason, L., & Boscolo, P. (2004). Role of epistemological understanding and interest in interpreting a controversy and in topic-specific belief change. *Contemporary Educational Psychology*, *29*, 103–128.

Mason, L., Gava, M., & Boldrin, A. (2008). On warm conceptual change: The interplay of text, epistemological beliefs, and topic interest. *Journal of Educational Psychology*, *100*, 291–309.

McGeown, S. P., Duncan, L. G., Griffiths, Y. M., & Stothard, S. E. (2015). Exploring the relationship between adolescents' reading skills, reading motivation and reading habits. *Reading & Writing*, *28*, 545–569.

Mol, S. E., & Bus, A. G. (2011). To read or not to read: A meta-analysis of print exposure from infancy to early adulthood. *Psychological Bulletin*, *137*(2), 267–296.

Mucherah, W., & Yoder, A. (2008). Motivation for reading and middle school students' performance on standardized testing in reading. *Reading Psychology*, *29*, 214–235.

Murphy, P. K., Holleran, T. A., Long, J. F., & Zeruth, J. A. (2005). Examining the complex roles of motivation and text medium in the persuasion process. *Contemporary Educational Psychology*, *30*, 418–438.

Olkoniemi, H., Ranta, H., & Kaakinen, J. K. (2016). Differences in the processing of written sarcasm and metaphor: Evidence from eye movements. *Journal of Experimental Psychology*, *42*, 433–450.

Park, Y. (2011). How motivational constructs interact to predict elementary students' reading performance: Examples from attitudes and self-concept in reading. *Learning and Individual Differences*, *21*, 347–358.

Patall, E. A. (2013). Constructing motivation through choice, interest, and interestingness. *Journal of Educational Psychology*, *105*, 522–534.

Pfost, M., Dörfler, T., & Artelt, C. (2013). Students' extracurricular reading behavior and the development of vocabulary and reading comprehension. *Learning and Individual Differences, 26*, 89–102.

RAND Reading Study Group. (2002). *Reading for understanding: Toward an R&D program in reading comprehension*. Santa Monica, CA: RAND.

Rapp, D. N., & Gerrig, R. J. (2006). Predilections for narrative outcomes: The impact of story contexts and reader preferences. *Journal of Memory and Language, 54*, 54–67.

Retelsdorf, J., Köller, O., & Möller, J. (2011). On the effects of motivation on reading performance growth in secondary school. *Learning and Instruction, 21*, 550–559.

Schaffner, E., Philipp, M., & Schiefele, U. (2016). Reciprocal effects between intrinsic reading motivation and reading competence? A cross-lagged panel model for academic track and nonacademic track students. *Journal of Research in Reading, 39*, 19–36.

Schaffner, E., & Schiefele, U. (2016). The contributions of intrinsic and extrinsic reading motivation to the development of reading competence over summer vacation. *Reading Psychology, 37*, 917–941.

Schiefele, U., Schaffner, E., Möller, J., & Wigfield, A. (2012). Dimensions of reading motivation and their relation to reading behavior and competence. *Reading Research Quarterly, 47*, 427–463.

Scrimin, S., & Mason, L. (2015). Does mood influence text processing and comprehension? Evidence from an eye-movement study. *British Journal of Educational Psychology, 85*, 387–406.

See, Y. H. M., Petty, R. E., & Fabrigar, L. R. (2008). Affective and cognitive meta-bases of attitudes: Unique effects on information interest and persuasion. *Journal of Personality and Social Psychology, 94*, 938–955.

Silva, C., Montant, M., Ponz, A., & Ziegler, J. C. (2012). Emotions in reading: Disgust, empathy and the contextual learning hypothesis. *Cognition, 125*, 333–338.

Smith, J. K., Smith, L. F., Gilmore, A., & Jameson, M. (2012). Students' self-perception of reading ability, enjoyment of reading, and reading achievement. *Learning and Individual Differences, 22*, 202–206.

Solheim, O. J. (2011). The impact of reading self-efficacy and task value on reading comprehension scores in different items formats. *Reading Psychology, 32*, 1–27.

Spear-Swerling, L., Brucker, P. O., & Alfano, M. P. (2010). Relationships between sixth graders' reading comprehension and two different measures of print exposure. *Reading & Writing, 23*, 73–96.

Strang, R. (1942). *Exploration in reading patterns*. Chicago, IL: University of Chicago Press.

Unsworth, N., & McMillan, B. D. (2013). Mind wandering and reading comprehension: Examining the roles of working memory capacity, interest, motivation, and topic experience. *Journal of Experimental Psychology, 39*, 832–842.

Viljaranta, J., Aunola, K., & Hirvonen, R. (2016). Motivation and academic performance among first-graders: A person-oriented approach. *Learning and Individual Differences, 49*, 366–372.

Wigfield, A., & Cambria, J. (2010). Students' achievement values, goal orientations, and interest: Definitions, development, and relations to achievement outcomes. *Developmental Review, 30*, 1–35.

Wigfield, A., & Guthrie, J. T. (1995). *Dimensions of children's motivations for reading: An initial study* (Research Rep. No. 34). Athens, GA: National Reading Research Center.

Wolfe, M. B., Tanner, S. M., & Taylor, A. R. (2013). Processing and representation of arguments in one-sided texts about disputed topics. *Discourse Processes, 50*, 457–497.

Wyatt, D., Pressley, M., El-Dinary, P. B., Stein, S., Evans, P., & Brown, R. (1993). Comprehension strategies, worth and credibility monitoring, and evaluations: Cold and hot cognition when experts read professional articles that are important to them. *Learning and Individual Differences, 5*, 49–72.

11

Continuities between Early Language Development and Reading Comprehension

Kiren S. Khan and Laura M. Justice

Language development and reading comprehension are two constructs of great interest to researchers, practitioners, and policy-makers, as both language and reading skill are critically associated with one's educational achievement and psychological well-being across the lifespan. Across these two dimensions of development, there are parallel interests in understanding individual differences in developmental trajectories, especially across languages and dialects; identifying risk factors that compromise development; and implementing interventions that mitigate difficulties when they arise within schooling and other institutions. However, theoretical and empirical discussions of language development and reading comprehension generally occur in isolation, with the former the focus of those who study early childhood education, linguistics, and developmental psychology, and the latter the focus of reading psychologists, and scholars in reading, elementary, and special education.

Yet, three conceptual shifts over the last decades have contributed to movement towards a more coherent and comprehensive recognition of the continuities between language acquisition and reading comprehension. First, theoretical perspectives on reading development have shifted from viewing reading skills as largely a result of visual-perceptual processes to recognizing that reading skill is largely a product of linguistic-cognitive processes. Viewing reading as linguistically based serves to highlight developmental continuities between young children's language acquisition and their future reading comprehension. Second, a considerable body of research involving prospective and retrospective longitudinal designs has carefully documented the strong, statistically reliable relations between young children's language skills during the preschool years and their reading comprehension in middle childhood, both within a given language and even across languages (e.g., Spanish to English; Proctor, August, Carlo, & Snow, 2006). From a prevention perspective, such work has also highlighted the prognostic importance of weak language skills early in life, to reading deficits in the primary grades, particularly with respect to reading comprehension (Justice, Mashburn, & Petscher, 2013). Finally, and possibly most importantly, those who study reading development from an intervention standpoint have begun to move away from a nearly exclusive focus on word recognition and its correlates, such as phonological awareness, towards investigating how to improve reading comprehension and its precursors, influenced in part by significant federal research investments (e.g., the Institute of Education Sciences' Reading for Understanding Consortium). Such work has served to highlight the developmental importance of children's language skills to their ability to read for meaning (e.g., Lesaux, Kieffer, Faller, & Kelley, 2010).

This chapter seeks to bridge the gap between these two bodies of work – language acquisition and reading comprehension – by describing what is known about these two constructs, identifying several big questions relevant to these constructs, and exploring challenges to developing a model of reading development and instruction that spans early childhood and elementary education. At the same time, this chapter seeks to consider what a long-range view of reading development might mean for how we conceptualize reading instruction across the preschool through early and middle childhood continuum. Ultimately, this chapter seeks to bridge language and reading research, as well as early and middle childhood practices that build skills in each of these domains.

Specifically, in the next few sections, we describe what is known about how language skills develop across the early childhood to middle childhood spectrum and speculate about the malleability of language skills across this developmental period. We then discuss relevant findings and existing gaps in our knowledge regarding the associations between lower- and higher-level language skills and reading comprehension and emphasize the importance of identifying aspects of language that are most influential for subsequent reading abilities. Within this discussion of lower- and higher-level language skills, we highlight the need for understanding the correlates of academic vocabulary, inference making, comprehension monitoring, and text-structure knowledge at even younger ages, so as to support these skills as early as possible, as well as the need for research on identifying aspects of language that show transfer across bilingual children's different languages.

The second half of this chapter deals with issues associated with the implementation gap, namely the inherent challenges associated with creating consistency in instructional and pedagogical practices across grade levels spanning early through middle childhood, in the service of supporting language and reading skills. We highlight the importance of continued investment in longitudinal work examining the effectiveness of research-based curricula that adopt a long-range view of development and target lower- and higher-level language skills as a route to improving reading comprehension, and we provide examples of some successful programs of research. We also discuss the importance of professional development that supports a longer range of view of language and reading development and provides opportunities for collaboration across the early to middle childhood education systems. Indeed, we suggest that the language-reading connection may provide a useful platform for bridging early childhood and elementary education, and share suggestions for synergistic efforts that may support this goal. Finally, we discuss some of the ways in which research and practice, particularly as they relate to supporting an extended and interconnected view of language and reading development, may be relevant to linguistically-diverse classrooms; the predominant context in which children are growing and learning today.

I. What's Known and How Do We Know It?

Language Development in Early Childhood

Language development is a multi-faceted phenomenon, encompassing the acquisition of a broad set of rules related to sounds and sound patterns, semantic units, sentence structures, as well as discourse-level processes and structures. These multiple dimensions of language have been extensively discussed and analyzed within the context of a number of disciplines, including developmental psychology, linguistics, speech and hearing sciences, among others; correspondingly, there is a considerable body of work delineating developmental progressions in each of these dimensions (Bavin, 2009; De Villiers & De Villiers, 1978; Khan et al., 2016; McKeown & Curtis,

2014; Stein & Glenn, 1979), such as a recent study by the authors describing age-related progressions in children's expression of story-grammar elements within narratives from 3- to 6-years of age (Khan et al., 2016).

A striking finding across much of this work is that the developmental sequence of acquisition of many linguistic rules and forms is fairly robust, even among children who are acquiring multiple languages at once (Hoff et al., 2012; Pearson & Fernandez, 1994) or acquiring language in another modality, such as sign language (Bohannon & Bonvillian, 1997). Perhaps the most well-known progression in language development is the achievement of key phonological, lexical, and syntactic milestones from infancy into toddlerhood, in which the emergence of babbling (gestural babbling in the case of deaf babies and verbal babbling in the case of hearing babies) is soon thereafter followed by a one-word stage in which children communicate by expressing single words (mama, up, kitty); a vocabulary spurt which emerges around 18 to 24 months of age, during which vocabulary size increases four-fold (Hoff, 2006); and production of multi-word utterances and use of grammatical inflections begins around age 3 (Behrens, 2009; De Villiers & De Villiers, 1978). Discourse-level skills, such as storytelling and narration of experienced events, similarly, adhere to a general developmental schedule, wherein children are able to construct more complete and coherent stories as age increases from 3 to 9 years (Berman, 2001; Castilla-Earls, Peterson, Spencer, & Hammer, 2015; Trabasso, Stein, Rodkin, Munger, & Baughn, 1992; Van Deusen-Phillips, Goldin-Meadow, & Miller, 2001).

Despite the evidence for, and extensive attention towards, describing universals in the developing child's route from vocabulary to grammar to narrative, there is also considerable evidence of individual differences in children's language skills and trajectories. Specifically, there are differences in starting points, such as the emergence of the first word and use of two-word utterances (McKean et al., 2015; Song et al., 2015), the nature of the first grammatical morphemes produced (Marchman, Martinez-Sussmann, & Dale, 2004), and velocity of shape of language growth over time (Rowe, Raudenbush, & Goldin-Meadow, 2012). Relevant to this chapter are longitudinal studies that have sought to understand these and other individual differences in early language development and to consider how these differences may relate to future achievements in areas closely related to language skill, particularly reading (ECCRN NICHD, 2005; Justice et al., 2013; McKean et al., 2015; Murphy, Language and Reading Research Consortium (LARRC), & Farquharson, 2016; Storch & Whitehurst, 2002).

One recent such study conducted by Song and colleagues (2015) investigated vocabulary development in Chinese children in relation to reading outcomes from age 4 to 11 years of age; an interest in this work was examining the interplay between vocabulary skill and growth trajectories and subsequent reading ability. The research methods identified three clearly distinguishable groups of children with respect to initial vocabulary skill and growth rate: a high-high group, a low-high group, and a low-low group. A finding relevant to the focus of this chapter is that children in the low-high group, who showed initially low vocabulary skills but a relatively steep trajectory, diverged from their low-low peers in terms of their vocabulary growth when they began formal schooling at age 7, which also coincided with the time at which they first demonstrated significantly higher phonological and morphological skills than their low-low counterparts. Longitudinal work such as this is necessary for understanding how child-level and environmental-level factors interact to influence children's language growth in the transitional period from pre-reader to reader, and to clarify how individual differences in language skill are associated with subsequent variability in reading skill.

To appreciate the continuities between early language and later reading skills, it is important to understand the trajectories of development for each of these skills. One approach to tackling this empirical question is to examine the extent to which the various dimensions of language skill, several of which were referenced earlier in this chapter, represent distinct components of language. Understanding the organization of the language system can provide information about the extent to which the various language dimensions represent distinct underlying systems, as suggested by modularist perspectives (e.g., Chomsky, 1965; Pinker, 1994), or whether language skills are built from the same mechanisms as suggested by emergentist perspectives on language acquisition (e.g., Marchman & Bates, 1994). Increased use of complex statistical modeling applied to large datasets representing children's language skills longitudinally has allowed researchers to ask fundamental questions regarding the dimensionality of language abilities across childhood, to include considering whether language comprises multiple dimensions (e.g., vocabulary, grammar, morphology) or whether it is a singular human capacity.

Such work is largely in its early stages, but generally finds that language ability comprises a unitary dimension when children are at younger ages (3 to 5 years; Tomblin & Zhang, 2006), but becomes increasingly *multidimensional* over time as children progress through the primary grades (Anthony, Davis, Williams, & Anthony, 2014; Bornstein, Hahn, Putnick, & Suwalsky, 2014; LARRC, 2015a) and into adolescence (Tomblin & Zhang, 2006). Such work suggests that during early childhood, language ability is best represented as a single, unitary construct, a phenomenon observed for preschool-aged children who are native English speakers (LARRC, 2015a) and who are native Spanish speakers (LARRC, 2015b). Importantly, however, with time grammar and vocabulary become independent systems, as will, eventually, discourse-level skills. Such work is important to the consideration of the relations between early language skill and future reading, as it suggests that children's language ability must be viewed as an *emergent system* that is affected by the increasing complexity of the forms and functions being acquired and increased variability in children's language-learning environments as they enter and progress through formal schooling and advanced curricula (Tomblin & Zhang, 2006).

The unidimensional nature of language ability at younger ages has potentially interesting implications for considering mechanisms that may influence language growth, as it suggests that affecting one aspect of language may, in turn, influence other dimensions of language due to shared underlying mechanisms. Indeed, emergentist perspectives on language development acknowledge the role of domain-general cognitive skills such as perception, memory, and attention in language acquisition (Bowerman & Levinson, 2001; MacWhinney, 1999). For instance, children's working memory capacities may impose limits on their ability to coordinate schemes into more complex and sophisticated patterns. Increases in working memory, in turn, allow for better integration of language structures (such as the use of coordinating conjunctions linking discrete sentences) which further support the use of higher-level reasoning strategies (such as chunking or inference-making). Similarly, advancements in one dimension of language (e.g., use of the present progressive inflection *-ing* to represent action) may simultaneously lead to concurrent developments in syntactic, lexical, and even discourse-level processes. Thus, simple linear progressions in one system make possible the learning of complex cognitive structures and accelerated learning in parallel systems. This notion of an iterative feedback loop leading to the acceleration of the overall pace of development has also been discussed in dynamic systems theory (Smith, 1999; Thelen & Smith, 1994). When examining associations and continuities between the development of early language and reading skills, an important question to consider, therefore, is to what extent shared mechanisms support interactions between these constructs.

As a counterpoint, the increasingly multidimensional nature of language ability at older ages and grades also has implications for considering mechanisms that may influence language growth as a potential route to improving reading skills. That is, with language ability increasingly multidimensional as children age, it is possible that skills become increasingly modularized, such that mechanisms that affect vocabulary skill may have little bearing on grammatical growth or discourse-level skills, and vice versa. As a result, recent efforts to affect children's language ability within the primary and later grades typically target numerous dimensions of language skill simultaneously (Clarke, Snowling, Truelove, & Hulme, 2010; Duff et al., 2014; LARRC, Jiang, & Logan, 2019), rather than focusing exclusively on a single dimension, especially vocabulary, as was a common focus in research over the last decade.

Reading Comprehension in the Primary Grades

In this chapter, we seek to bridge the gap between two bodies of work – language acquisition and reading comprehension – and both posit a developmental framework that extends from the early toddler/preschool years through the elementary grades, as well as describe how this may close the gap between early childhood education and reading instruction so as to promote continuity in reading instruction from early to middle childhood. Following our discussion of primary issues related to early childhood language acquisition, we now turn to discussing reading comprehension as an important developmental construct and instructional priority in the primary grades. Reading comprehension is the process by which an individual derives meaning from a written text, which occurs through developing (and continuing to update) a mental representation of text, or mental model (McNamara & Magliano, 2009). It is broadly recognized that reading comprehension draws upon, and is closely related to, one's language abilities, representing the skills and capabilities discussed in the prior section. It is also accepted that reading comprehension needs to be distinguished from another important reading process, namely word recognition. That is, comprehension of a text is distinct from, but dependent upon, the processes one employs to recognize or decode words in a text (word recognition). There is a developmental progression in the contribution of word recognition to reading comprehension, such that the contribution of word recognition to reading comprehension attenuates as children become more skilled as readers: when children are first beginning to read, during first grade, word recognition explains a considerable amount of the variance in concurrent reading comprehension (64%), whereas by third grade, word recognition explains quite modest amounts of variance (21%) (LARRC, 2015a). The attenuation in the contribution of word recognition to reading comprehension, reflects the gradually increasing importance of one's language skills to creating a mental representation of text and being able to read for meaning; by third grade, children's language skills explain a substantial portion of the variance in reading comprehension skill (61%).

To this end, both theory and research propose that for skilled readers, one's ability to read for meaning largely (but not entirely) approximates one's ability to comprehend spoken language (LARRC, 2015a; Perfetti, 2007). Of relevance to this chapter is considering those language skills that are among the most critical determinants of language comprehension. Addressing this question requires *bridging the gap* between scholarship focused on language acquisition during early childhood, when children are not able (yet) to read for meaning, and scholarship focused on reading comprehension in middle and later childhood, when language acquisition has generally slowed and many crucial linguistic milestones have been achieved, such as acquiring the native language's (L1) grammatical system and phonological inventory (Sakai, 2005).

Much of the literature on language acquisition has centered on the period of early childhood, during which linguistic competencies are rapidly developing during what is often referred to as a sensitive period (Huttenlocher, 2009). Researchers have attempted to not only document the precise linguistic competencies that children acquire, including those common across the world's languages (e.g., Caselli et al., 1995), but also the biological and environmental mechanisms that enable them to do so (Hoff, 2013; Kuhl & Rivera-Gaxiola, 2008). Largely, this body of work has focused on children's acquisition of "basic" or lower-level language skills across the linguistic domains of morphosyntax, semantics, and phonology, which were the focus of the initial content of this chapter. For instance, such work has helped to document the general order by which children acquire grammatical morphemes (De Villiers & De Villiers, 1973) and mechanisms through which young children acquire novel words (Akhtar, Jipson, & Callanan, 2001). This work has also been highly informative for describing distinctions and similarities in the acquisition of L1 and additional languages (Pierce, Genesee, & Paradis, 2013; Poulin-Dubois, Bialystok, Blaye, Polonia, & Yott, 2013).

Research concerned with understanding the role of language skills in reading comprehension often calls attention to the importance of distinguishing between *lower-level* and *higher-level* language skills. While the former skills are those most often studied by those interested in language acquisition, the latter are viewed as particularly important to reading for meaning and are referred to as higher-level comprehension processes (Perfetti & Adlof, 2012, p. 6). Lower-level language skills, as discussed in the reading-comprehension literature, are those basic, automatic processes that are acquired during early childhood, such as one's ability to efficiently process lexical information or comprehend syntactic forms. These skills are used to construct the literal meaning of a text, referred to by some as the *textbase* (Kintsch & Rawson, 2005). Whereas lower-level language skills, such as vocabulary, make unique, important contributions to reading comprehension, and are considered necessary for reading for meaning (Cain, Oakhill, Barnes, & Bryant, 2001; Verhoeven & Van Leeuwe, 2008), they are not assumed to be sufficient for arriving at a sophisticated, detailed model of the text.

Higher-level language skills, which are dependent upon the operation of lower-level skills, are those linguistic skills that the reader applies to arrive at a complex, coherent, and integrated mental model of the text (Cain, Oakhill, & Bryant, 2004). As a simple example, a student reading a novel involving the protagonist "Arnulfo" will apply the higher-level skill of inferencing to derive a coherent model of the actions and states of this character by integrating a number of pronominal references (e.g., he, him, his) that transcend multiple clauses, sentences, and paragraphs, to represent and update the actions and states of this protagonist (Cain et al., 2004). Creation of a mental model of a text – also called a *situation model* – draws upon a unique set of higher-level language skills that appear particularly crucial to higher-level comprehension because of the *integrative* role they play (Cain, Oakhill, & Bryant, 2004; Perfetti, 2007); these include *inferencing, comprehension monitoring*, and use of *text-structure knowledge* (Cain et al., 2004; Hogan, Bridges, Justice, & Cain, 2011).

Inferencing refers to the cognitive process of "filling in the gaps," which is essential for accurate comprehension of a text, given that much in a text is unstated and thus must be inferred in order to derive an integrated mental model of the text. Creation of a mental model of even a very simple proposition like "James was devastated when he saw the crumbled bike" requires a number of inferences, including that a crumbled bike can no longer be ridden and that James liked riding his bike a great deal. Types of inferences used to aid comprehension include cohesive references, knowledge-based references, and evaluative inferences (Bowyer-Crane & Snowling, 2005). Cohesive references are used to derive connections across a text, such as inferring that *he* is referring to Addie's cat in the sentences, *Addie threw the toy at the cat. He pounced on it quickly.* Knowledge-based inferences are used when one's background knowledge is drawn upon to fill in unstated information; using the sample example sentences above, a reader with knowledge about cats would likely infer that the toy thrown at the cat was a cat-toy rather than a child's toy, and that Addie is throwing the toy in a way to play with the cat. Finally, evaluative inferences are used by the reader to fill in missing information about a character's feelings, motives, and goals. Using our same example, it would be plausible for some readers to derive a mental model in which Addie is trying to hurt the cat by throwing things at it, based on the inference that when one throws objects at animals, the typical intent is to hurt them. However, such an inference in this case would not be correct and, ideally, would be corrected by the reader as he or she continues to read.

Comprehension monitoring references the higher-level language skill by which readers monitor their own comprehension of a text in an ongoing manner, and apply strategies to address any comprehension deficits. This is considered a higher-level metalinguistic skill as it involves one analyzing the act of comprehension as it occurs. Many good readers are aware of the comprehension-monitoring processes they apply when comprehension is compromised, such as re-reading a word or skimming back through the preceding paragraph; these are referred to as "fix-up strategies," and are a comprehension process consistently observed in good comprehenders, and less so in poor comprehenders (Oakhill, Hartt, & Samols, 2005).

Finally, text-structure knowledge is a higher-level language skill that references a reader's tacit understanding of how different texts are structured, to include recognition of relationships across sentences, paragraphs, and larger units of a text. Being able to navigate the organizational features of a given text is often central to one's comprehension of a text and the ability to derive the full meaning of a text. For instance, a cause-effect expository passage is organized in a way so that the reader is able to derive a mental model that situates a given cause with a given effect, with certain "clue" words used to highlight a cause and differentiate it from an effect, such as *because*, *then*, *thus*, and *therefore* (see Williams et al., 2007). For a fifth grader to read a passage describing the cause-effect relations between slavery and the civil war in the United States, and to comprehend the precise way in which the former led to the latter, he or she must draw on higher-level language skills that help to specify the sequences among events.

Measures of each of these three higher-level language skills explain significant amounts of unique variance in 8- to 11-year-old children's reading comprehension, even when controlling for lower-level language skills, working memory, and word-reading abilities (Cain et al., 2004). To this end, studies find that although, in the early years of reading development, an individual's ability to read for meaning is largely constrained by skills in word recognition, once these processes become automatized, reading comprehension is largely dependent upon one's skills in language comprehension (Catts, Hogan, Adlof, & Weismer, 2005), especially higher-level language skills. An important gap in the literature, and one that greatly compromises developing a model that captures continuity in language development and reading comprehension, is that these skills have seldom been examined in children who are not yet able to read. Thus, our understanding of inferencing, comprehension monitoring, and text-structure knowledge in children under the age of 6 or 7 years is extremely limited. At the same time, we have very little understanding of these higher-level language skills among dual language learners, to include whether these skills are likely to transfer across languages.

II. What are the Big Questions in This Area Relative to the Current Era?

Thorough understanding of continuities between early language acquisition and future reading comprehension is far from complete, and a number of big questions require serious scientific and theoretical attention to advance this understanding. We highlight three of these big questions here. First, it is unclear which precise language skills during the early childhood years are most influential to future reading comprehension. Put differently, does reading for meaning draw on certain linguistic abilities more so than others? The report of the National Early Literacy Panel aggregated longitudinal studies in an effort to identify prominent predictors of reading achievement from measures collected at or prior to kindergarten (Lonigan & Shanahan, 2009). The Panel identified 30 studies that examined predictive relations between language measures at or prior to kindergarten, and subsequent reading comprehension (average $r = .33$). However, this report was not able to precisely identify whether a specific aspect of language skill, such as vocabulary, is especially important to future reading comprehension, or whether all language skills are equally influential. Making progress on this question is essential, as it has direct bearing on how best to design early educational programs and practices directed towards improving children's early language skills. Should such programs focus exclusively on one aspect of language, such as vocabulary, or multiple skills? Increasing evidence of the unidimensionality of language skill prior to age 5 makes this question even more complicated; if young children's language skills are a unitary dimension of development, does it make sense to think about language dimensionally, as we so often do in our focus on distinct aspects of growth (e.g., grammar, vocabulary, phonology)?

Particularly important to such considerations is that relatively little work has examined the development of those "higher-level language skills" referenced earlier as especially important to reading comprehension. Higher-level language skills are those that a reader draws upon to arrive at a complex, coherent, and integrated mental model of the text, such as inferencing and comprehension monitoring. While it is evident that reading comprehension among skilled readers draws upon such higher-level language skills (Cain et al., 2004), we have limited understanding about the origins of these skills and their growth within pre-readers. For instance, comprehension monitoring – a metacognitive skill with high cross-linguistic transfer potential – has been examined almost exclusively in relation to the comprehension of written texts among school-aged children. No study to date has examined the role of comprehension monitoring of discourse during the preschool and kindergarten years, and its relation to later reading comprehension skills. However, there is some evidence from a recent study by Strasser and Del Río (2014) that comprehension monitoring, as assessed by the detection of inconsistencies in a story constructed to deliberately contain internally inconsistent actions and reactions, is related to narrative comprehension in kindergarteners. Based on this pattern of association, we may speculate that comprehension monitoring and inference-making strategies during the early preschool and kindergarten years would also be predictive of later reading comprehension skills. However, longitudinal research spanning early to middle childhood is needed to better understand the connections between oral language, comprehension monitoring (and other executive function skills), and reading comprehension.

Another important consideration is understanding the contribution and interplay of vocabulary knowledge in the processes supporting reading comprehension. Although referenced as a lower-level language skill in this chapter, vocabulary knowledge is paramount to listening and reading comprehension (Ouellette, 2006; Torppa et al., 2007), as it plays a key role in word-to-text (Perfetti & Stafura, 2014) or event-to-story integration. That is, individual concepts and words must be understood in order to derive appropriate inferences and ultimately build an accurate situation model of a text or story. Relating back to the example provided in the previous section, in order to draw accurate inferences regarding the meaning and significance of the statement "*James was devastated when he saw the crumbled bike*," the listener or reader must fully understand the definition and various connotations associated with the words "devastated" and "crumbled." A deep and broad vocabulary can therefore assist in developing higher-order associations within and across clauses of text. Thus, when examining the contribution of language skills to reading comprehension, an important question concerns the extent to which vocabulary knowledge supports and interacts with higher-level language skills to promote listening and reading comprehension.

A second big question that needs to be addressed concerns how best to represent continuities in language acquisition and reading comprehension for children who are acquiring multiple languages. Today, the majority of children in the world are multi-lingual, acquiring multiple languages simultaneously or sequentially. Although the United States has often been conceived as a monolingual society, with English as the sole official language, an estimated 65,000,000 Americans speak a language other than English in their homes today (Shin & Ortman, 2011). It is well understood that skills in one language often transfer to another; for example, sensitivity to the sound structure of language tends towards a high level of cross-linguistic transfer among bilingual individuals, especially for languages utilizing similar scripts, as with Spanish and English (Kuo, Uchikoshi, Kim, & Yang, 2016). Such work often focuses on how skills and understandings in a specific domain of language, such as Chinese vocabulary, transfer to another language, such as English vocabulary (Pasquarella, Chen, Lam, Luo, & Ramirez, 2011).

However, despite considerable extant work in the area of cross-linguistic transfer, a major question arises when considering continuity between language development and reading comprehension, namely, the extent to which there is cross-linguistic transfer in the component skills supporting development in these competencies. Some theoretical frameworks that delineate the nature of cross-linguistic transfer suggest that language and literacy skill development in one's second language (L2) is dependent on the child's proficiency in these skills in their L1 (Cummins, 1979, 1991), and that cross-linguistic transfer occurs more readily when concepts such as schemas are emphasized (see MacWhinney's unified competition model, 1987). In contrast, limited cross-linguistic transfer, or even negative transfer, may occur on language-specific concepts such as orthographic or syntactic patterns, which can vary considerably across languages. Consistent with this logic, skills that show transfer across a bilingual's two languages include metalinguistic skills such as phonological awareness (e.g., Atwill, Blanchard, Gorin, & Burstein, 2007; Cisero & Royer, 1995; Comeau, Cormier, Grandmaison, & Lacroix, 1999; Gottardo, Yan, Siegel, & Wade-Woolley, 2001), story grammar (e.g., Durgunoğlu, Mir, & Arino-Marti, 2002; Petersen et al., 2016; Squires et al., 2014), knowledge regarding the functions of print (e.g., Verhoeven & Aarts, 1998), and meaning-making strategies such as questioning, evaluating, and monitoring comprehension in both languages (e.g., Jimenez, et al., 1996).

If we draw our attention specifically to the oral language skills that demonstrate cross-linguistic transfer and have been shown to be related to reading comprehension, these include vocabulary breadth and depth (e.g., Davison, Hammer, & Lawrence, 2011; Mancilla-Martinez & Lesaux, 2010; Silverman et al., 2015), cognate awareness (Hipfner-Boucher, Pasquarella, Chen, & Deacon, 2016), and listening comprehension (Lesaux, Crosson, Kieffer, & Pierce, 2010). In fact, some researchers, such as Riches and Genesee (2006), argue that diversity of vocabulary and a deep understanding of text play a more influential role in explaining L2 literacy than general oral language abilities. However, it should be noted that the majority of this work has focused on school-aged children, and less attention has been paid to examining the associations between preschool language and later reading abilities. There is a strong need for developmental research examining the associations between aspects of early oral language skills in the preschool and early elementary years and later reading comprehension so as to better understand the continuities between early language abilities and reading. Indeed, understanding the relations between language skills and reading comprehension among individuals speaking and reading multiple languages requires a second-order of consideration, as we must consider the interplay among oral and written languages and script-universal and script-specific processes. Advances in this area will be instrumental for facilitating theoretical understandings of continuities in language acquisition and reading comprehension in bilinguals, as well as developing instructional paradigms that are relevant to this large population of students.

A third big question of interest concerns refining and improving our understanding of the construct of "academic language," an interest of emerging attention that strives to understand those language skills that are most important within the academic milieu. Promising areas of research include identifying early correlates of academic vocabulary (e.g., Lesaux et al., 2010) and the construct of academic language skills (Uccelli et al., 2015), given their theorized importance in school-relevant language and reading proficiency. For instance, one way to examine academic language skills, such as the ability to pack dense information through subordination, mark conceptual relations through connectives, and use referential strategies to link themes at younger ages, would be to assess the use of these devices in children's storytelling. Parallels can easily be found in the Core Academic Language Skills (CALS) proposed by Uccelli et al. (2015); for example, the six CALS areas, namely unpacking complex words, comprehending complex sentences, connecting ideas, tracking themes, organizing argumentative texts, and awareness of academic register correspond fairly well to the following children's narrative features: morphology, complex syntactic structure, use of connectives, pronominal references, story grammar, and awareness of narrative genre (personal, fictional, and expository). Furthermore, these early narrative skills, particularly the inclusion of story elements, story sequence, and perspective, may show cross-linguistic transfer (e.g. Uccelli & Paez, 2007) and help support the development of these competencies in the L2.

III. What are the Challenges to Bridging the Gaps in the Current Era?

In the current chapter, we highlight the importance of bridging the gap between two bodies of work – language acquisition and reading comprehension – by describing what is known about these two constructs. One possible outcome of this gap bridging would be to promote continuity in reading instruction from the toddler/preschool through the elementary grades. For instance, teachers from the preschool years forward could continuously ensure that the core literacy curriculum includes explicit attention to fostering children's inferencing skill, given its important role in skilled reading comprehension. Research finds that even very young children generate numerous inferences when listening to texts (Tompkins, Guo, & Justice, 2013), and that these early skills are predictive of future reading comprehension (Lepola, Lynch, Kiuru, Laakkonen, & Niemi, 2016). However, there is little evidence that preschool curricular programs and best practices include explicit attention to inferencing; for instance, inferential skills were not referenced in the report of the National Early Literacy Panel, which sought to identify those skills of young children that are most associated with future reading comprehension (Lonigan & Shanahan, 2009). To this end, it is important to acknowledge the need for better alignment between early childhood and elementary education in terms of pedagogical practices and perspectives related to language and reading comprehension, providing a more coherent learning pathway for children, which, theoretically, could exponentially catalyze learning. Having continuity in the expectations, contexts, and instructional approaches utilized, as well as in the set of skills being focused on during instruction, would help provide a consistent learning experience for children and support a long-term trajectory of deep and coherent learning. In important ways, the Common Core State Standards' English Language Arts standards for Kindergarten to Grade 12 served to align reading instructional practices for children across the primary grades, and served to highlight the relevance of oral language skills to reading for meaning; yet, these fall short in addressing the core need advanced in this chapter, namely the importance of bridging the gap between early childhood education, which is provided to children prior to kindergarten, and reading education in the primary grades.

An obvious challenge associated with achieving increased continuity between early childhood and elementary education, particularly in the area of reading, is that it necessitates achieving a common foundation of knowledge regarding the processes, sequences, variations, and long-term consequences of language development and its pathway to reading comprehension. In order to establish this common knowledge base, longitudinal research spanning early to middle childhood investigating the language skills most influential for reading development is needed, as we noted previously. Currently, longitudinal research has yet to precisely identify those language skills that are most influential to reading comprehension, and there is a lack of strong causal evidence relating language skills to reading comprehension. Thus, our models of reading development and instructional approaches that align to such models tend to begin in kindergarten, as do the Common Core State Standards. This results in significant discontinuities between early childhood education and elementary education with respect to pedagogy and practices specific to language and reading development. For instance, whereas language-focused pedagogies and practices in the elementary grades may provide extensive support towards helping children develop metalinguistic, higher-level understandings related to vocabulary (e.g., analysis of multiple-meaning words, exploration of shades of meaning), as these seem particularly important to reading comprehension, early childhood educators may focus very little time to expanding children's vocabulary breadth and depth (Pelatti, Piasta, Justice, & O'Connell, 2014).

Similarly, language-focused pedagogies in later grades focus on building academic language and explicitly teaching comprehension strategies such as summarizing, self-questioning, and comprehension monitoring (Dole, Duffy, Roehler, & Pearson, 1991; Solis et al., 2012). For instance, students are taught to ask and answer predetermined questions such as who or what the paragraph is about, what action is happening and why, and to create summary sentences or extract the gist of individual paragraphs (e.g., Bakken, Mastropieri, & Scruggs, 1997; Jitendra, Kay Hoppes, & Xin, 2000). Thus, by generating and answering questions related to the text, students are effectively engaged in self-monitoring their own comprehension. An important question that has received little empirical attention is to consider the developmentally-appropriate correlates of these comprehension strategies in the preschool and early elementary years.

Tasked with developing a research-based supplemental curriculum to intervene on language skills as a route to improving reading comprehension, the Language and Reading Research Consortium (LARRC) addressed this issue by including integration skills such as synthesizing information within texts, and monitoring comprehension and identifying when something does or does not make sense, into their scope of instruction for prekindergarten and kindergarten classrooms (LARRC, 2016). Specifically, teachers were instructed to scaffold children's abilities to identify the main idea, and two or more details, of an informational text for the synthesizing strategy. For comprehension monitoring, teachers were guided on how to encourage children to pause at various points during a story book reading and ask themselves if something does or does not make sense, and then to indicate their understanding using a clicking/clunking strategy (Klinger & Vaughn, 1998). An example of a teacher modeling this strategy might follow reading out loud the following sentence, "Bandit is a happy *canine*." At this point, the teacher reminds the children that if they are having trouble understanding the sentence, they should hold up their "does not make sense" sign and ask what the word *canine* means. The teacher can then help them "fix-up" what does not make sense by employing different "fix-up" strategies, such as looking at the pictures in the book, reading some more sentences, or asking questions to try to learn the word *canine*.

Thus, by explicit teaching of the strategy using clear explanations and steps, modeling examples for how to use the strategy, and providing practice, feedback, and support to individual children, higher-level language skills and metalinguistic skills may be taught effectively to children as young as 4 years of age. To support this point, results from the first cohort of a large, field-based randomized controlled trial ($N= 766$ students across grades) testing the impact of the Let's Know! curriculum supplement on children's comprehension skills, indicate large, consistent, and statistically significant effects on proximal measures of comprehension monitoring (Language and Reading Research Consortium, Jiang, & Logan, 2019). Developing and testing research-based curricula, as mentioned above, that cater to a long range view of development, and target both lower-level and higher-level language skills as a route to improving reading comprehension, is critical to changing how we conceptualize promoting children's language and reading skills, both in terms of theoretical models of development in these skill domains, as well as pedagogical practices adopted in daily teaching and learning from preschool through the primary grades.

A second and somewhat formidable challenge to bridging early childhood and elementary education with respect to language and reading continuities concerns the underlying capacity and educational preparation of the respective workforces. Many children participate in early childhood education programs that operate outside of the educational milieu, for instance in Head Start programs, private child-care programs, and home-based settings. Educators working in such settings may not have extensive, formal post-secondary training in early education pedagogies and disciplinary content, including language facilitation, and some evidence suggests that many educators working in these settings have somewhat under-developed understandings of core linguistic principles (for discussion of this issue, see Joshi, Cunningham, & Moats, 2009). It may take considerable efforts to ensure that early childhood educators have the skills they need to promote continuity in reading instruction from the toddler/preschool through the elementary grades. For instance, these continuities would entail ensuring that early childhood educators explicitly support those higher-level language skills important to future reading comprehension, yet there is evidence suggesting that language-focused instruction within early education settings is relatively scarce and of potentially low quality (Pelatti et al., 2014).

At the same time, it is not necessarily clear that primary-grade teachers of reading have a sophisticated understanding of language development themselves, to include those higher-level skills that appear especially crucial to reading comprehension. A focused course in language acquisition is not typically required within teacher-education programs, in the same way it is in other fields (psychology, speech and hearing sciences), and research finds that many elementary teachers do not have even basic understandings of language rules and forms (Moats & Foorman, 2003). Elevating all teachers' knowledge of language development and instruction appears necessary to improve continuities between early childhood language instruction and reading-comprehension instruction. Importantly, not only do teachers need to learn effective strategies for supporting the development of these skills, but they also need to support children's engagement and motivation towards reading by choosing appropriate learning materials and meaningful contexts for learning. For bilingual classrooms, this necessitates being mindful of cultural and linguistic diversity, and leveraging knowledge and skills acquired in the other language to support skill development across both languages.

Finally, we must also acknowledge that the task of establishing coherence between early childhood and elementary reading instruction presents logistical challenges as well. Traditionally, preschool education and elementary education have remained largely separate, in large part due to different funding sources and infrastructure and, to some extent, deeply entrenched differences in practices. In many states, early education programs are licensed through Jobs and Family Services rather than state education agencies, and federally, the nation's largest early childhood initiative – Head Start and Early Head Start – are operated by Health and Human Services. Although the language-reading connection could provide a solid platform and impetus for building a bridge, this work will necessitate close partnerships with educators, administrators in early education settings and elementary schools, and policy makers. As one example, synergistic efforts will be needed to support the necessary professional development (PD) and training opportunities for educators, so as to set coherent and developmentally appropriate instructional strategies based on empirical research. At the same time, state and federal learning standards could likely do a great deal to foster, if not require, attention to continuities in the language-reading continuum from early childhood through the primary grades by generating integrated standards rather than separate standards for early education (e.g., Ohio's Early Learning Standards) and education in the later grades (e.g., Common Core).

IV. New Approaches and Opportunities Relevant to the Current Era

We now highlight four new approaches and opportunities that hold promise for bridging the systems of early childhood education and elementary education with respect to reading instruction. First, there has been a substantial increase in the public interest and investment in improving reading comprehension, such as federal sponsorship of the Reading for Understanding initiative. This has resulted in collaboration among leading research teams at the forefront of studying reading development, as well as the development and testing of reading comprehension interventions that span preschool through the early primary grades. Importantly, these research teams have adopted a systematic approach to developing and testing curriculum supplements which, in the case of the Let's Know! curriculum, involved a thorough review of the extant research findings on various techniques of instruction, incorporated school administrator and teacher feedback in the development activities, and included pilot testing and formative evaluation work (see LARRC, 2016). Future curriculum-development work focused on incorporating instruction on both lower-level and higher-level language skills, as described earlier in this chapter, may benefit from adopting a similar framework. This line of research may also benefit from an even more extended view of development by considering language-reading connections and instructional strategies to support the development of these skills across the preschool through middle school continuum. Such work would help elucidate the learning pathways that lead to the strongest reading outcomes and provide opportunities to take advantage of the especially high plasticity of the language and cognitive systems at younger ages. Additionally, pending efficacy work demonstrating positive longitudinal impacts of this curricula on children's reading comprehension skills in later grades, as well as isolating the most effective practices for providing instruction on higher-level language skills in conjunction with lower-level language skills, the stage would be well set for translational research that focuses on bringing these evidence-based practices to scale. Thus, continuing to examine the effectiveness of language-focused interventions as a vehicle to improving reading outcomes, and extending the range of development to include prekindergarten through elementary and even middle school, would improve our understanding of the best instructional practices to support the development of these skills in a coherent and developmentally-appropriate manner across childhood.

Second, lessons may be learned from model schools, such as the Naval Avenue Early Learning Center in Bremerton, Washington, that provide comprehensive early childhood through third grade education to children and have been successful in increasing continuity and coherence across these grades. A particularly effective strategy that may be borrowed from this model is providing educators across the prekindergarten to grade 3 system with opportunities for joint professional development and learning opportunities, thus enabling dialogue and information sharing to facilitate grade-level transitions. Outside of such innovative models, there is little opportunity for early childhood educators and primary-grade teachers to have the opportunity to create professional learning communities. The federal government can help facilitate such synergistic efforts by offering grants to stimulate working partnerships that bridge the early education and elementary milieus. Policymakers can also play an important role by framing teacher certification policies that support ongoing teacher PD, specifically PD that has topical continuity and provides ongoing opportunities for collaboration with peers across the preschool–elementary school continuum.

Third, to ensure that children move from one grade to the next with the core set of knowledge and skills to be successful in the following year, efforts must be taken to align not just the curricula and pedagogical practices across the early childhood to elementary school continuum, but also to work on the alignment of educational standards and assessments. The development of literacy assessment systems across the prekindergarten through primary grade continuum to better inform instruction would be a particularly effective approach toward achieving such an alignment. For example, The McKnight Foundation's Education and Learning (E&L) Program has adopted use of a diagnostic literacy assessment system called STEP (Strategic Teaching and Evaluation of Progress), which was developed by the Urban Education Institute to meet a key objective of developing assessment systems across prekindergarten through third grade. A useful feature of an assessment system like the STEP is that it employs a set of leveled texts that increase in difficulty with each skill level or "step," which teachers use to help identify the skills that students need in order to become proficient, independent readers. Appropriate level texts can then be chosen to provide targeted instruction on skills that are shown to be weak (e.g., higher order thinking skills such as inferencing). Additional benefits reported by the program for using this assessment system include facilitating cross-grade conversations about teachers' expectations regarding children's literacy skills, providing teachers with a common language to communicate with each other and with parents about children's literacy skills, and aligning instructional approaches across different classrooms and grades (Golan et al., 2013).

Fourth, and particularly relevant to the current era in which dual language learners (DLLs) constitute a significant proportion of youth entering the education system, it is increasingly necessary to develop and implement effective cross-linguistic instructional strategies to support the development of higher-level language skills and reading comprehension among this population. Building higher-level language and listening comprehension skills in both the child's first and second languages in prekindergarten, prior to formal reading instruction in English, may be a particularly effective strategy for promoting positive transfer. At the same time, given the established developmental trends in DLLs showing language to be a continued source of reading difficulty in this population (Hammer, Lawrence, & Miccio, 2008; Mancilla-Martinez & Lesaux, 2011; Páez, Tabors, & López, 2007), it is increasingly important to create optimal learning conditions to build language and background knowledge in the L2 as early as possible to prevent future reading difficulties. One approach to facilitating language acquisition in DLLs is to create opportunities for these students to form connections between their knowledge and skills in their two languages. Other approaches that have been shown to be effective include direct vocabulary instruction focused on general-purpose academic words likely to be encountered across a variety of content areas (Beck, McKeown, & Omanson, 1987) and teaching strategies for inferring word meanings using contextual cues, cognate knowledge, morphological information, and using aids such as glossaries and dictionaries (e.g., Carlo et al., 2004; Jimenez et al., 1996).

Research in pedagogical practices for supporting literacy-skill development in DLLs suggests that a first step is for teachers to recognize that DLL's native language skills may interact with, and influence, their literacy development in English (e.g. Herrera, Perez, & Escamilla, 2010). This recognition of cross-linguistic effects on literacy development allows teachers to understand and remediate errors and misconceptions in English without attributing these to a lack of textual understanding or poor literacy skills. For example, at the word level, teachers can draw attention to and provide correct translations for false cognates like *rope/ropa*. Conversely, teachers could identify cognates (words with the same origin or root) across the child's two languages, thereby reinforcing knowledge of the word in their native language and building connections with the L2.

Another pedagogical practice recommended for use with DLLs is that teachers help contextualize new content to what is already familiar and known by the child (Ajayi, 2005; Calderón, 2007; Herrera et al., 2010). For instance, drawing connections between new vocabulary and prior experiences and background knowledge regarding the topic/word being taught helps children construct vocabulary meanings reflecting their life experiences and prior linguistic and educational backgrounds. When teaching academic vocabulary, in particular, the connections that teachers make with children's background knowledge and personal experiences can provide an important scaffold for the learning of more complex and abstract terms. Consistent with this suggestion, it is encouraged that teachers provide children with opportunities to practice using new words in multiple contexts. For instance, Hadaway, Vardell, and Young (2002) suggest integrating nonfiction literature such as poems, biographies, journals, and diaries into instruction, so as to provide DLLs opportunities to encounter academic vocabulary in more relevant and authentic contexts. Creating a collaborative classroom environment can also provide opportunities for children to practice their linguistic abilities, co-construct background and vocabulary knowledge, and make predictions during reading and writing activities. Other effective strategies that have been discussed as being especially beneficial for DLLs include implementing book clubs with culturally and linguistically diverse students in which they are allowed to choose age-appropriate, personally meaningful texts (e.g., Kong & Fitch, 2002), engaging in group dialogue around text, and modeling and scaffolding reading comprehension strategies such as questioning, inference-making, and monitoring text (Mokhtari & Reichard, 2002).

V. Concluding Comments

Over the course of this chapter, we have described the parallel interests, and recent shifts, in the conceptualization of continuities between language and reading. We argue that there is likely great benefit to continuing to improve our understanding of how early language skills support the development of reading skills across the primary grades so as to identify and develop instructional practices that would best support reading development across the preschool to elementary school (and potentially middle school) continuum. In particular, we highlight the importance of continued research examining the contribution of higher-level language skills relevant for forming a detailed and sophisticated mental model of text. We also emphasize the importance of continuity in pedagogical practices relevant to reading instruction across early childhood education and elementary education to ensure a coherent learning pathway for children, while also highlighting salient challenges and opportunities. Despite the breadth of topics covered in this chapter, it is important to highlight our central goal, which is to argue the necessity of recognizing the strong, central relations between language acquisition during early childhood and reading comprehension during the primary grades, which ought to lead to enhanced continuity in instructional targets and practices utilized in early childhood education and reading instruction in the primary grades.

References

Ajayi, L. J. (2005). A socioculture perspective: Language arts framework. vocabulary activities and english language learners in a second grade mixed classroom. *Journal of Instructional Psychology*, *32*(3), 180.

Akhtar, N., Jipson, J., & Callanan, M. A. (2001). Learning words through overhearing. *Child Development*, *72* (2), 416–430.

Anthony, J. L., Davis, C., Williams, J. M., & Anthony, T. I. (2014). Preschoolers' oral language abilities: A multilevel examination of dimensionality. *Learning and Individual Differences*, *35*, 56–61.

Atwill, K., Blanchard, J., Gorin, J. S., & Burstein, K. (2007). Receptive vocabulary and cross-language transfer of phonemic awareness in kindergarten children. *The Journal of Educational Research*, *100*(6), 336–346.

Bakken, J. P., Mastropieri, M. A., & Scruggs, T. E. (1997). Reading comprehension of expository science material and students with learning disabilities: A comparison of strategies. *The Journal of Special Education*, *31*(3), 300–324.

Bavin, E. L. (2009). *The Cambridge handbook of child language*. New York, NY: Cambridge University Press.

Beck, I., McKeown, M. G., & Omanson, R. C. (1987). The effects and uses of diverse vocabulary instructional techniques. In M. G. McKeown & M. E. Curtis (Eds.), *The nature of vocabulary acquisition* (pp. 147–163). Hillsdale, NJ: Erlbaum.

Behrens, H. (2009). Usage-based and emergentist approaches to language acquisition. *Linguistics*, *47*(2), 383–411.

Berman, R. A. (2001). Setting the narrative scene: How children begin to tell a story. In K. E. Nelson & A. Aksu-Koc (Eds.), *Children's language: Developing narrative and discourse competence* (Vol. 10, pp. 1–30). Mahwah, NJ: Lawrence Erlbaum.

Bohannon, J. N., III, & Bonvillian, J. D. (1997). Theoretical approaches to language acquisition. In J. B. Gleason (Ed.), *The development of language* (4th ed., pp. 259–316). Boston, MA: Allyn and Bacon.

Bornstein, M. H., Hahn, C. S., Putnick, D. L., & Suwalsky, J. T. (2014). Stability of core language skill from early childhood to adolescence: A latent variable approach. *Child Development*, *85*(4), 1346–1356.

Bowerman, M., & Levinson, S. (2001). *Language acquisition and conceptual development*. Cambridge, UK: Cambridge University Press.

Bowyer-Crane, C., & Snowling, M. J. (2005). Assessing children's inference generation: What do tests of reading comprehension measure? *British Journal of Educational Psychology*, 75(2), 189–201.

Cain, K., Oakhill, J., Barnes, M. A., & Bryant, P. E. (2001). Comprehension skill, inference-making ability, and their relation to knowledge. *Memory & Cognition*, 29(6), 850–859.

Cain, K., Oakhill, J., & Bryant, P. (2004). Children's reading comprehension ability: Concurrent prediction by working memory, verbal ability, and component skills. *Journal of Educational Psychology*, 96(1), 31.

Calderón, M. (2007). *Teaching reading to English language learners, grades 6-12: A framework for improving achievement in the content areas*. Thousand Oaks, CA: Corwin Press.

Carlo, M. S., August, D., McLaughlin, B., Snow, C. E., Dressler, C., Lippman, D. N., ... White, C. E. (2004). Closing the gap: Addressing the vocabulary needs of English-language learners in bilingual and mainstream classrooms. *Reading Research Quarterly*, 39(2), 188–215.

Caselli, M. C., Bates, E., Casadio, P., Fenson, J., Fenson, L., Sanderl, L., & Weir, J. (1995). A cross-linguistic study of early lexical development. *Cognitive Development*, 10(2), 159–199.

Castilla-Earls, A. P., Peterson, D., Spencer, T., & Hammer, K. (2015). Narratives and story grammar development in preschool Spanish-speaking children. *Early Education and Development*, 26(8), 1–21.

Catts, H., Adlof, S., Hogan, T., & Weismer, S. (2005). Are specific language impairment and dyslexia distinct disorders? *Journal of Speech, Language, and Hearing Research*, 48(6), 1378–1396.

Chomsky, N. (1965). *Aspects of the theory of syntax*. Cambridge, MA: MIT press.

Cisero, C. A., & Royer, J. M. (1995). The development and cross-language transfer of phonological awareness. *Contemporary Educational Psychology*, 20(3), 275–303.

Clarke, P. J., Snowling, M. J., Truelove, E., & Hulme, C. (2010). Ameliorating children's reading-comprehension difficulties a randomized controlled trial. *Psychological Science*, 21(8), 1106–1116.

Comeau, L., Cormier, P., Grandmaison, É., & Lacroix, D. (1999). A longitudinal study of phonological processing skills in children learning to read in a second language. *Journal of Educational Psychology*, 91(1), 29.

Cummins, J. (1979). Linguistic interdependence and the educational development of bilingual children. *Review of Educational Research*, 49(2), 222–251.

Cummins, J. (1991). Interdependence of first-and second-language proficiency in bilingual children. In E. Bialystok (Ed.), *Language Processing in Bilingual Children* (pp. 70–89). New York: Cambridge University Press.

Davison, M. D., Hammer, C., & Lawrence, F. R. (2011). Associations between preschool language and first grade reading outcomes in bilingual children. *Journal of Communication Disorders*, 44(4), 444–458.

De Villiers, J. G., & De Villiers, P. A. (1973). A cross-sectional study of the acquisition of grammatical morphemes in child speech. *Journal of Psycholinguistic Research*, 2(3), 267–278.

De Villiers, J. G., & De Villiers, P. A. (1978). *Language acquisition*. Cambridge, MA: Harvard University Press.

Dole, J. A., Duffy, G. G., Roehler, L. R., & Pearson, P. D. (1991). Moving from the old to the new: Research on reading comprehension instruction. *Review of Educational Research*, 61(2), 239–264.

Duff, F. J., Hulme, C., Grainger, K., Hardwick, S. J., Miles, J. N., & Snowling, M. J. (2014). Reading and language intervention for children at risk of dyslexia: A randomised controlled trial. *Journal of Child Psychology and Psychiatry*, 55(11), 1234–1243.

Durgunoğlu, A. Y., Mir, M., & Ariño-Marti, S. (2002). The relationships between Bilingual children's reading and writing in their two languages. In S. Ransdell & M. L. Barbier (Eds.), *New directions for research in L2 writing* (pp. 81–100). Dordrecht, Netherlands: Springer Netherlands.

ECCRN, NICHD (2005). A day in third grade: Classroom quality, teacher, and student behaviors. *Elementary School Journal*, 105(3), 305–323.

Golan, S., Wechsler, M., Cassidy, L., Chen, W. B., Wahlstrom, K., & Kundin, D. (2013). *The Mcknight Foundation Education and Learning Program PreK–third grade literacy and alignment formative evaluation findings*. Menlo Park, CA: SRI International.

Gottardo, A., Yan, B., Siegel, L. S., & Wade-Woolley, L. (2001). Factors related to English reading performance in children with Chinese as a first language: More evidence of cross-language transfer of phonological processing. *Journal of Educational Psychology*, 93(3), 530.

Hadaway, N. L., Vardell, S. M., & Young, T. A. (2002). Highlighting nonfiction literature: Literacy development and English language learners. *New England Reading Association Journal*, 38(2), 16.

Hammer, C., Lawrence, F. R., & Miccio, A. W. (2008). Exposure to English before and after entry into head start 1: Bilingual children's receptive language growth in Spanish and English. *International Journal of Bilingual Education and Bilingualism*, 11(1), 30–56.

Herrera, S. G., Perez, D. R., & Escamilla, K. (2010). *Teaching reading to English language learners: Differentiating literacies.* New York, NY: Allyn & Bacon.

Hipfner-Boucher, K., Pasquarella, A., Chen, X., & Deacon, S. H. (2016). Cognate awareness in French immersion students: Contributions to grade 2 reading comprehension. *Scientific Studies of Reading, 20*(5), 389–400.

Hoff, E. (2006). Language experience and language milestones during early childhood. In K. McCartney & D. Phillips (Eds.), *Blackwell Handbook of Early Childhood Development* (pp. 232–251). Hoboken, NJ: Wiley-Blackwell.

Hoff, E. (2013). Interpreting the early language trajectories of children from low-SES and language minority homes: Implications for closing achievement gaps. *Developmental Psychology, 49*(1), 4.

Hoff, E., Core, C., Place, S., Rumiche, R., Señor, M., & Parra, M. (2012). Dual language exposure and early bilingual development. *Journal of Child Language, 39*(01), 1–27.

Hogan, T. P., Bridges, M. S., Justice, L. M., & Cain, K. (2011). Increasing higher level language skills to improve reading comprehension. *Focus on Exceptional Children, 44*(3), 1.

Huttenlocher, P. R. (2009). *Neural plasticity.* Cambridge, MA: Harvard University Press.

Jimenez, R. T., García, G. E., & Pearson, P. D. (1996). The reading strategies of bilingual Latina/o students who are successful English readers: Opportunities and obstacles. *Reading Research Quarterly, 31,* 90–112.

Jitendra, A. K., Kay Hoppes, M., & Xin, Y. P. (2000). Enhancing main idea comprehension for students with learning problems: The role of a summarization strategy and self-monitoring instruction. *The Journal of Special Education, 34*(3), 127–139.

Joshi, R. M., Cunningham, A. E., & Moats, L. (2009). *Still wanted: Teachers with knowledge of language.* Los Angeles, CA: Sage Publications Sage CA.

Justice, L. M., Mashburn, A., & Petscher, Y. (2013). Very early language skills of fifth-grade poor comprehenders. *Journal of Research in Reading, 36*(2), 172–185.

Khan, K. S., Gugiu, M. R., Justice, L. M., Bowles, R. P., Skibbe, L. E., & Piasta, S. B. (2016). Age-related progressions in story structure in young children's narratives. *Journal of speech, language, and Hearing Research, 59*(6), 1395–1408.

Kintsch, W., & Rawson, K. A. (2005). Comprehension. In M. J. Snowling & C. Hulme (Eds.), *The science of reading: A handbook* (pp. 209–226). Oxford, UK: Blackwell. doi:10.1002/9780470757642.ch12

Klinger, J. K., & Vaughn, S. (1998). Using collaborative strategic reading. *Teaching Exceptional Children, 30*(6), 32–37.

Kong, A., & Fitch, E. (2002). Using book club to engage culturally and linguistically diverse learners in reading, writing, and talking about books. *The Reading Teacher, 56*(4), 352–362.

Kuhl, P., & Rivera-Gaxiola, M. (2008). Neural substrates of language acquisition. *Annual Review of Neuroscience, 31,* 511–534.

Kuo, L. J., Uchikoshi, Y., Kim, T.-J., & Yang, X. (2016). Bilingualism and phonological awareness: Re-examining theories of cross-language transfer and structural sensitivity. *Contemporary Educational Psychology, 46,* 1–9.

Language and Reading Research Consortium. (2015a). The dimensionality of language ability in young children. *Child Development, 86,* 1948–1965. doi:10.1111/cdev.12450

Language and Reading Research Consortium. (2015b). The dimensionality of Spanish in young Spanish-English dual-language learners. *Journal of speech, language, and Hearing Research, 58,* 754–766. doi:10.1044/2015_JSLHR-L-13-0266

Language and Reading Research Consortium. (2016). Use of the curriculum research framework (CRF) for developing a reading-comprehension curricular supplement for the primary grades. *Elementary School Journal, 116*(3), 459–486.

Language and Reading Research Consortium, Jiang, H., & Logan, J. (2019). Improving reading comprehension in the primary grades: Mediated effects of a language-focused classroom intervention. *Journal of Speech, Language, and Hearing Research, 62*(8), 2812–2828.

Lepola, J., Lynch, J., Kiuru, N., Laakkonen, E., & Niemi, P. (2016). Early oral language comprehension, task orientation, and foundational reading skills as predictors of grade 3 reading comprehension. *Reading Research Quarterly, 51*(4), 373–390.

Lesaux, N. K., Crosson, A. C., Kieffer, M. J., & Pierce, M. (2010). Uneven profiles: Language minority learners' word reading, vocabulary, and reading comprehension skills. *Journal of Applied Developmental Psychology, 31*(6), 475–483.

Lesaux, N. K., Kieffer, M. J., Faller, S. E., & Kelley, J. G. (2010). The effectiveness and ease of implementation of an academic vocabulary intervention for linguistically diverse students in urban middle schools. *Reading Research Quarterly, 45*(2), 196–228.

Lonigan, C. J., & Shanahan, T. (2009). Developing early literacy: Report of the national early literacy panel. Executive summary. A scientific synthesis of early literacy development and implications for intervention. *National Institute for Literacy*.

MacWhinney, B. (1987). The competition model. In B. MacWhinney (Ed.), *Mechanisms of language acquisition* (pp. 249–308). Hillsdale, NJ: Erlbaum Associates.

MacWhinney, B. (1999). The emergence of language from embodiment. In B. MacWhinney (Ed.), *The Emergence of Language* (pp. 213–256). Mahwah, NJ: Lawrence Erlbaum.

Mancilla-Martinez, J., & Lesaux, N. K. (2010). Predictors of reading comprehension for struggling readers: The case of Spanish-speaking language minority learners. *Journal of Educational Psychology, 102*(3), 701.

Mancilla-Martinez, J., & Lesaux, N. K. (2011). The gap between Spanish speakers' word reading and word knowledge: A longitudinal study. *Child Development, 82*(5), 1544–1560.

Marchman, V. A., & Bates, E. (1994). Continuity in lexical and morphological development: A test of the critical mass hypothesis. *Journal of Child Language, 21*, 339–366.

Marchman, V. A., Martinez-Sussmann, C., & Dale, P. S. (2004). The language-specific nature of grammatical development: Evidence from bilingual language learners. *Developmental Science, 7*(2), 212–224.

McKean, C., Mensah, F. K., Eadie, P., Bavin, E. L., Bretherton, L., Cini, E., & Reilly, S. (2015). Levers for language growth: Characteristics and predictors of language trajectories between 4 and 7 years. *PloS One, 10*(8), e0134251.

McKeown, M. G., & Curtis, M. E. (2014). *The nature of vocabulary acquisition*. New York, NY: Psychology Press.

McNamara, D. S., & Magliano, J. (2009). Toward a comprehensive model of comprehension. *Psychology of Learning and Motivation, 51*, 297–384.

Moats, L. C., & Foorman, B. R. (2003). Measuring teachers' content knowledge of language and reading. *Annals of Dyslexia, 53*(1), 23–45.

Mokhtari, K., & Reichard, C. A. (2002). Assessing students' metacognitive awareness of reading strategies. *Journal of Educational Psychology, 94*(2), 249.

Murphy, K., Language and Reading Research Consortium (LARRC), & Farquharson, K. (2016). Investigating profiles of lexical quality in preschool and their contribution to first grade reading. *Reading and Writing, 29*(9), 1745–1770. doi:10.1007/s11145-016-9651-y

Oakhill, J., Hartt, J., & Samols, D. (2005). Levels of comprehension monitoring and working memory in good and poor comprehenders. *Reading and Writing, 18*(7), 657–686.

Ouellette, G. P. (2006). What's meaning got to do with it: The role of vocabulary in word reading and reading comprehension. *Journal of Educational Psychology, 98*(3), 554.

Páez, M. M., Tabors, P. O., & López, L. M. (2007). Dual language and literacy development of Spanish-speaking preschool children. *Journal of Applied Developmental Psychology, 28*(2), 85–102.

Pasquarella, A., Chen, X., Lam, K., Luo, Y. C., & Ramirez, G. (2011). Cross-language transfer of morphological awareness in Chinese–English bilinguals. *Journal of Research in Reading, 34*(1), 23–42.

Pearson, B. Z., & Fernandez, S. C. (1994). Patterns of interaction in the lexical growth in two languages of bilingual infants and toddlers. *Language Learning, 44*(4), 617–653.

Pelatti, C. Y., Piasta, S. B., Justice, L. M., & O'Connell, A. (2014). Language-and literacy-learning opportunities in early childhood classrooms: Children's typical experiences and within-classroom variability. *Early Childhood Research Quarterly, 29*(4), 445–456.

Perfetti, C. (2007). Reading ability: Lexical quality to comprehension. *Scientific Studies of Reading, 11*(4), 357–383.

Perfetti, C., & Adlof, S. M. (2012). Reading comprehension: A conceptual framework from word meaning to text meaning. In J. P. Sabatini, E. Albro, & T. O'Reilly (Eds.), *Measuring up: Advances in how we assess reading ability* (pp. 3–20). Lanham, MD: Rowman & Littlefield Education.

Perfetti, C., & Stafura, J. (2014). Word knowledge in a theory of reading comprehension. *Scientific Studies of Reading, 18*(1), 22–37.

Petersen, D. B., Thompsen, B., Guiberson, M. M., & Spencer, T. D. (2016). Cross-linguistic interactions from second language to first language as the result of individualized narrative language intervention with children with and without language impairment. *Applied Psycholinguistics, 37*(03), 703–724.

Pierce, L. J., Genesee, F., & Paradis, J. (2013). Acquisition of English grammatical morphology by internationally adopted children from China. *Journal of Child Language, 40*(05), 1076–1090.

Pinker, S. (1994). *The language instinct: How the mind creates language*. New York: William Morrow.

Poulin-Dubois, D., Bialystok, E., Blaye, A., Polonia, A., & Yott, J. (2013). Lexical access and vocabulary development in very young bilinguals. *International Journal of Bilingualism, 17*(1), 57–70.

Proctor, C. P., August, D., Carlo, M. S., & Snow, C. (2006). The intriguing role of spanish language vocabulary knowledge in predicting English reading comprehension. *Journal of Educational Psychology, 98*(1), 159.

Riches, C., & Genesee, F. (2006). Crosslinguistic and crossmodal issues. In F. Genesee, K. Lindholm Leary, W. M. Saunders, & C. Donna (Eds.), *Educating English language learners: A synthesis of research evidence* (pp. 64–108). Cambridge, UK: Cambridge University Press.

Rowe, M. L., Raudenbush, S. W., & Goldin-Meadow, S. (2012). The pace of vocabulary growth helps predict later vocabulary skill. *Child Development*, *83*(2), 508–525.

Sakai, K. L. (2005). Language acquisition and brain development. *Science*, *310*(5749), 815–819.

Shin, H. B., & Ortman, J. M. (2011). April Language projections: 2010 to 2020. In *Federal forecasters conference* (pp. 1–12).

Silverman, R. D., Proctor, C. P., Harring, J. R., Hartranft, A. M., Doyle, B., & Zelinke, S. B. (2015). Language skills and reading comprehension in English monolingual and Spanish–English bilingual children in grades 2–5. *Reading and Writing*, *28*(9), 1381–1405.

Smith, L. B. (1999). Children's noun learning: How general learning processes make specialized learning mechanisms. In B. MacWhinney (Ed.), *The emergence of language* (pp. 277–304). Hillsdale, NJ: Erlbaum.

Solis, M., Ciullo, S., Vaughn, S., Pyle, N., Hassaram, B., & Leroux, A. (2012). Reading comprehension interventions for middle school students with learning disabilities: A synthesis of 30 years of research. *Journal of Learning Disabilities*, *45*(4), 327–340.

Song, S., Su, M., Kang, C., Liu, H., Zhang, Y., McBride-Chang, C., Tardif, T., Li, H., Liang, W., Zhang, Z., & Shu, H. (2015). Tracing children's vocabulary development from preschool through the school-age years: An 8-year longitudinal study. *Developmental Science*, *18*(1), 119–131.

Squires, K. E., Lugo-Neris, M. J., Peña, E. D., Bedore, L. M., Bohman, T. M., & Gillam, R. B. (2014). Story retelling by bilingual children with language impairments and typically developing controls. *International Journal of Language & Communication Disorders*, *49*(1), 60–74.

Stein, N. L., & Glenn, C. (1979). An analysis of story comprehension in elementary school children. In R. Freedle (Ed.), *New directions in discourse processing* (pp. 53–120). Hilldale, NJ: Ablex.

Storch, S. A., & Whitehurst, G. J. (2002). Oral language and code-related precursors to reading: Evidence from a longitudinal structural model. *Developmental Psychology*, *38*(6), 934.

Strasser, K., & Del Río, F. (2014). The role of comprehension monitoring, theory of mind, and vocabulary depth in predicting story comprehension and recall of kindergarten children. *Reading Research Quarterly*, *49*(2), 169–187.

Thelen, E., & Smith, L. B. (1994). *A dynamical systems approach to the development of perception and action*. Cambridge, MA: MIT Press.

Tomblin, J. B., & Zhang, X. (2006). The dimensionality of language ability in school-age children. *Journal of speech, language, and Hearing Research*, *49*(6), 1193–1208.

Tompkins, V., Guo, Y., & Justice, L. M. (2013). Inference generation, story comprehension, and language skills in the preschool years. *Reading and Writing*, *26*(3), 403–429.

Torppa, M., Tolvanen, A., Poikkeus, A. M., Eklund, K., Lerkkanen, M. K., Leskinen, E., & Lyytinen, H. (2007). Reading development subtypes and their early characteristics. *Annals of Dyslexia*, *57*(1), 3–32.

Trabasso, T., Stein, N. L., Rodkin, P. C., Munger, M. P., & Baughn, C. R. (1992). Knowledge of goals and plans in the on-line narration of events. *Cognitive Development*, *7*(2), 133–170.

Uccelli, P., Barr, C. D., Dobbs, C. L., Galloway, E. P., Meneses, A., & Sanchez, E. (2015). Core academic language skills: An expanded operational construct and a novel instrument to chart school-relevant language proficiency in preadolescent and adolescent learners. *Applied Psycholinguistics*, *36*(05), 1077–1109.

Uccelli, P., & Paez, M. M. (2007). Narrative and vocabulary development of bilingual children from kindergarten to first grade: Developmental changes and associations among English and Spanish skills. *language, speech, and Hearing Services in Schools*, *38*(3), 225–236.

Van Deusen-Phillips, S. B., Goldin-Meadow, S., & Miller, P. J. (2001). Enacting stories, seeing worlds: Similarities and differences in the cross-cultural narrative development of linguistically isolated deaf children. *Human Development*, *44*(6), 311–336.

Verhoeven, L., & Aarts, R. (1998). Attaining functional biliteracy in the Netherlands. In A. Y. Durgunoğlu & L. Verhoeven (Eds.), *Literacy development in a multilingual context: Cross-cultural perspectives* (pp. 111–133). Mahwah, NJ: Erlbaum and Associates.

Verhoeven, L., & Van Leeuwe, J. (2008). Prediction of the development of reading comprehension: A longitudinal study. *Applied Cognitive Psychology*, *22*(3), 407–423.

Williams, J. P., Nubla-Kung, A. M., Pollini, S., Stafford, K. B., Garcia, A., & Snyder, A. E. (2007). Teaching cause – Effect text structure through social studies content to at-risk second graders. *Journal of Learning Disabilities*, *40*(2), 111–120.

12

What Do We Know Today about the Complexity Of Vocabulary Gaps and What Do We Not Know?

Jeannette Mancilla-Martinez and Janna B. McClain

Organizer

I. Why Vocabulary Matters
II. Conceptualizing What We Mean by Vocabulary Knowledge
III. Language Environments, the Acquisition Process, and Disparities in Opportunity
IV. Promising Approaches to Building Vocabulary
V. Future Directions
VI. Conclusion

I. Why Vocabulary Matters

Before attending to gaps between what science reveals about vocabulary and its development and what effectively unfolds in practice, we begin with an overview of the importance of vocabulary for reading particularly and learning more generally. From models of reading to reading research, the importance of language comprehension is widely acknowledged—which encompasses vocabulary knowledge—for successful text comprehension (Baumann & Kame'enui, 2004; Gough & Tunmer, 1986; Just & Carpenter, 1987; Kintsch, 1998; National Reading Panel, 2000; Perfetti, 1999). More importantly, language comprehension helps explain more of the variance in reading comprehension outcomes once students exit the elementary school years (e.g., Catts, Hogan, & Adlof, 2005; Mancilla-Martinez & Lesaux, 2017; Vellutino, Tunmer, Jaccard, & Chen, 2007). Variation in reading achievement appears to undergo a developmental shift: while word-based skills influence reading outcomes early on, once word-based skills are automatic, language-based skills exert greater influence (Chall, 1983; Scarborough, 2001). This developmental shift has significant instructional implications regarding the emphasis of language-based skills over word-based skills. Because the demands of text increase over time, the early focus on language must be sustained throughout the school years (Stevens et al., 2015).

Unlike alphabetic word reading skills that can effectively reach a ceiling due to the finite number of letters in alphabets and the finite number of sounds those letters can make (Paris, 2005), language learning is essentially infinite, and the rate of language acquisition does vary across development. Language growth is generally faster during the (early) childhood years, with a slower rate of growth once students enter early adolescence and beyond (Mancilla-Martinez & Lesaux, 2011; Verhaegen & Poncelet, 2013). As an essential component of language comprehension, vocabulary has garnered increased attention over the years, but has proven to be challenging to define, to measure, and to support. With the acknowledgement that language comprehension is broader than knowing the meanings of words, this chapter focuses on what we currently know about vocabulary. Additionally, we raise questions concerning its development across the toddlerhood through adolescent years, given that other aspects of language comprehension hinge on vocabulary knowledge, at least to some extent.

Vocabulary as a Proxy for (Background) Knowledge

It would be a gross oversimplification to describe vocabulary as the mere acquisition of word meanings as isolated units. Instead, as individual word meanings are acquired, students begin to construct new conceptual understandings and build their background (or prior) knowledge (Glasersfeld, 1984; Harris, Golinkoff, & Hirsh-Pasek, 2011; Resnick, 1983). For instance, a student who is familiar with life on a farm has developed some conceptual understanding of what a farm is and, with that, has likely amassed a store of vocabulary specific to farm life (e.g., barn, windmill). For farm-related vocabulary that remains unknown (e.g., irrigation, trough), students with farm life background knowledge would likely have an easier time learning unknown farm life words as they can map on the new information to their existing background knowledge about farms. On the other hand, although students can and do learn unknown vocabulary without or with very limited background knowledge, the task of learning and retaining that new vocabulary would arguably be greater.

Because vocabulary learning is a process that involves the development of conceptual understandings that serve to build or extend background knowledge, vocabulary knowledge can be considered a general proxy for background or domain-specific knowledge. It is thus not surprising that students who have a large vocabulary knowledge on a given topic have an easier time, a) learning new words associated with that topic, b) comprehending the text they read about that topic, c) productively using those words, and d) developing and refining conceptual understandings (Langer, 1984; Lipson, 1982; Stanovich, 1986; Stevens, 1980). Indeed, the influence of background knowledge on reading comprehension outcomes is well-documented, for both native English speakers and ELLs (from hereof, used in reference to students whose native language is not English, independent of whether they are formally identified as limited English proficient or not for school purposes) (Anderson & Pearson, 1984; Hudson, 2007; Jiménez, García, & Pearson, 1996; Kintsch, 1988; Shapiro, 2004; Stanovich, 1986).

The importance of building background knowledge during the early childhood years has long been underscored (Neuman, 2003). The *lack of opportunity* for many children to develop this knowledge base contributes to later vocabulary and achievement gaps on account of limited concept and schema development, necessitating instruction on conceptual knowledge development alongside skill development. This point is especially pertinent to historically underserved populations, such as students from low-income homes and ELLs, given that they tend to be exposed to skills-based instruction (i.e., sounding out words) more so than to content (i.e., understanding concepts) (Lesaux, 2012). Of note, a heavy focus on skills-based competencies likely contributes to widening vocabulary gaps (Vellutino et al., 1996). Similarly, in understanding individual differences in reading comprehension, it is essential to differentiate constrained skills (i.e., alphabetic knowledge), which can effectively reach a ceiling of mastery, from unconstrained skills (i.e., vocabulary), which can never be fully mastered (Paris, 2005). On account of being easier to assess, Paris cautions against over-testing—and we would add over-instructing—the constrained skills, such as word reading, at the exclusion of the unconstrained skills such as vocabulary. Indeed, one of the difficulties of understanding vocabulary development is that there are numerous ways to conceptualize the construct, thereby complicating how we measure it and support its development. In the next section, we address how vocabulary is conceptualized in the literature.

II. Conceptualizing What We Mean by Vocabulary Knowledge

Defining Vocabulary

Vocabulary is defined and measured in myriad ways. In the simplest terms, vocabulary knowledge refers to knowledge of words. However, the conceptualization of vocabulary across academic disciplines and theoretical frameworks has proved more complex. The field of psycholinguistics, concerned primarily with the cognitive processing of language, defines vocabulary as mental representations of concepts (Menn, 2017). While psycholinguists have traditionally held vocabulary as synonymous with lexicon (words) and distinct from grammar (the syntactic system for organizing those words), cognitive psychological research holds a unified view of language that does not distinguish lexicon from grammar (Bates & Goodman, 1997). Cognitive theories of literacy have developed in a similar vein; Perfetti's (2007) Lexical Quality Hypothesis posits that high-quality mental representations of concepts attend to the grammatical form (syntactic and morphological), as well as to the semantic, phonological, and orthographic forms of the words.

In comparison with psycholinguistic definitions of vocabulary, sociolinguists attend to the intersection of societal norms and language use (Wardhaugh & Fuller, 2015). Thus, the field of sociolinguistics is more concerned about how word use is reflective of cultural norms, power structures, and identities. Sociocultural theories of literacy also emphasize the contextualization of vocabulary, arguing that "words are always integrally and inextricably integrated with ways of talking, thinking, believing, knowing, acting, interacting, valuing, and feeling associated with specific socially situated identities" (Gee, 2003, p. 31).

Adopting this perspective of language and literacy, some scholars critique research that quantifies the vocabulary of students from low-income backgrounds, arguing that ethnocentric bias inhibits researchers from considering language differences of marginalized communities "on its own terms" rather than "in reference to the language of dominant groups" (Dudley-Marling & Lucas, 2009, p. 336). This line of critique counters deficit orientations of the home language contexts among children living in poverty by drawing upon early sociolinguistic and ethnographic literacy research that describes rich story-telling practices of marginalized groups (Heath, 1983; Michaels, 1981; Miller, Cho, & Bracey, 2005). More recent research advocates for not only understanding, but also leveraging linguistic difference for school success (e.g. Dyson, 1993; Gonzalez, Moll, & Amanti, 2005; Michaels, 2005). However, while there is empirical evidence that "bridging home-school differences in interaction patterns or styles can enhance students' engagement, motivation, and participation in classroom instruction," the evidence that "bridging home-school differences improves literacy achievement or development" remains limited (August & Shanahan, 2006, p. 15).

Measuring Vocabulary

The wide spectrum of perspectives on defining vocabulary (Pearson, Hiebert, & Kamil, 2007) results in a similarly diverse set of measures for assessing this construct (Henriksen, 1999; Nation, 1990; Richards, 1976), from standardized to researcher-developed assessments. Even though the call for improved measures of vocabulary is hardly new, classroom-friendly measures that view vocabulary as a conceptually-rich construct remain scarce (Stahl & Bravo, 2010). Over seven decades ago, Cronbach (1943) pushed for the need to move beyond a dichotomous notion of vocabulary knowledge (i.e., the word is known vs. the word is unknown) to a more nuanced perspective, wherein conceptual development is at the core (i.e., to not only understand a word receptively, but also use it productively). This framing of vocabulary echoes a sociolinguistic perspective of vocabulary learning, underscoring the need to attend to the situated realities of vocabulary knowledge, explicitly noting that "correct" meanings require attention to both the context in which the words are used and the changing meanings of words (Beck, McKeown, & Omanson, 1987; Bravo & Cervetti, 2008; Dale, 1965).

Further elaborating on the challenges of assessing vocabulary knowledge, Schmitt's (2014) recent synthesis aligns with and builds on the work of Pearson and colleagues (2007). Measures of vocabulary breadth (or size) and depth (or quality) continually emerge as the most common targets. Although vocabulary breadth is arguably more straightforward to conceptualize and to measure compared to depth, it still presents challenges. For instance, is breadth of vocabulary in reference to the receptive or expressive domain? In either case, the bulk of breadth vocabulary assessments tap into form-meaning connections (also known as the process of *mapping*; see Carey, 1978; Clark, 1993). Yet, while the form-meaning connection is the first and central phase in vocabulary learning, vocabulary acquisition also relies on two slower, essential processes: packaging (discovery of things that can be packaged under the same label) and network building (discovery of links between words) (Henriksen, 1999). Hence, vocabulary depth measures, which have gained popularity over time, can be interpreted as an attempt to move towards a more nuanced understanding about word knowledge.

The more relevant characteristic to underscore in vocabulary measurement may be that measures of breadth include numerous items to reflect general vocabulary knowledge, while measures of depth focus on a limited number of items to allow for a more nuanced, in-depth examination. Furthermore, learner characteristics (e.g., lexicon size, dialectical differences) should be attended to in attempting to understand a student's vocabulary base, as even standardized vocabulary assessments with established psychometric properties are not sensitive to nuances in students' lexical knowledge, thereby undermining their instructional potential (Stahl & Bravo, 2010).

When it comes to vocabulary measurement among ELLs, the picture is considerably more complicated. Grosjean's (1982, 1989, 2013) seminal work has long cautioned researchers against the monolingual view on bilingualism (i.e., expecting that a bilingual is two monolinguals in one person, thus with roughly "equal" proficiency in both languages). Unlike their monolingual peers, ELLs' language environments are fundamentally different; they receive input in two languages, likely differing in quantity and quality. It is well-established that vocabulary knowledge among bilingual children is distributed across two languages, which severely limits the extent to which single-language vocabulary measures (typically English-only in the U.S. context) can accurately capture performance and development of *overall* vocabulary knowledge for this population of learners (e.g., Bedore, Peña, García, & Cortez, 2005; Mancilla-Martinez & Vagh, 2013; Pearson, Fernández, & Oller, 1995). In spite of this scientific understanding, bilinguals' performance is, thus, commonly measured on monolingual standards, likely due to the lack of measures that account for both languages in the field. Furthermore, common standardized English vocabulary assessments rarely attend to whether linguistically diverse speakers are included in the norming samples (Luk & Christodoulou, 2016). Given that studies have focused on quantifying vocabulary knowledge to predict and remedy trajectories that may lead to negative consequences for learners who fall outside the norm (Hoff, 2013), ensuring the validity of the measures for the population of students they are administered to is imperative.

In summary, while vocabulary measures have existed for a very long time with no shortage of assessments that tap into the receptive and productive domains, there continues to be a paucity of vocabulary assessments that can be utilized to effectively guide instruction and monitor growth, especially for ELLs. The next section summarizes extant research on vocabulary acquisition and the malleable factors that shape language learning.

III. Language Environments, the Acquisition Process, and Disparities in Opportunity

Genetic influences cannot be discounted in understanding vocabulary development and individual differences in that development (see De Zeeuw, de Geus, & Boomsma, 2015; Kovas et al., 2005; Olson et al., 2007). However, this chapter attends to *malleable environmental factors* that relate to differences in vocabulary knowledge and development, namely the language environment at home and school. Note that neither instructional nor intervention work is discussed in this section. The focus here is on describing what we know about children's home and school language environments, and the extent to which parent and teacher language practices relate to children's vocabulary achievement and growth. But first, a brief overview of language quantity and quality is provided, given that they emerge as central to discussions of vocabulary learning.

Language Quantity and Quality

To learn language, children need to be exposed to language. It is therefore of no surprise that the role of input, both the quantity and quality, has received considerable attention from the language and reading research community. Quantity of language input refers to the *amount* of words that children are exposed to, with higher quantities (or amounts of language input) generally associated with higher language attainment by children (Hurtado, Marchman, & Fernald, 2008; Huttenlocher, Haight, Bryk, Seltzer, & Lyons, 1991). On the other hand, quality of language input refers to the *types* of words children are exposed to, with more diverse and sophisticated types of words also generally associated with higher language attainment by children (Rowe, 2012). Thus, both the quantity and quality of language input help shape children's language learning (Hoff, 2006). Yet, children from diverse income backgrounds matched on quantity of language input demonstrate differential patterns of language use and growth based on the quality of the language they are exposed to (Cartmill et al., 2013; Rowe, 2012). This suggests that it is especially important to attend to the quality of language input rather than simply to the quantity. The sections that follow describe what we know about children's home and school language environments, with a focus on language quality.

Home Language Environment

The home is the first place in which children learn language. So what does quality language input look like in the home? While there is substantial evidence that children learn vocabulary from overheard speech between adults in their environment, "it remains that episodes of directed speech (or joint attention) make significant contributions to early word learning, even in communities in which overheard speech predominates" (Sperry, Sperry, & Miller, 2018, p. 3). In addition to the value of children's exposure to the diversity and quantity of words at home (e.g., Pan, Rowe, Singer, & Snow, 2005), developmental research consistently points to the value of engagement in interactive and responsive conversations between caretakers and children centered on topics of interest to the child (Cartmill et al., 2013; Dieterich, Assel, Swank, Smith, & Landry, 2006; Harris et al., 2011; Hirsh-Pasek et al., 2015; Pan et al., 2005; Weizman & Snow, 2001).

Studies that explore the relation between the home language environment and vocabulary development have commonly focused on the following areas: 1) types of parental input (e.g., Rowe, Leech, & Cabrera, 2016), 2) shared book reading (e.g., Hindman, Skibbe, & Foster, 2014), and 3) decontextualized talk, such as storytelling (e.g., Beals, 2001; Heath, 1983). In relation to parental input, parent use of *wh-* questions—often referred to as open-ended questions (versus closed-ended)—generally require more elaborate, linguistically complex responses from children, thus helping to build vocabulary (Rowe et al., 2016; Salo, Rowe, Leech, & Cabrera, 2016; Whitehurst et al., 1988). Additionally, increased rates of parents' other evocative techniques, such as asking questions about object functions or attributes and using elaborations or explanations, have been found to positively relate to children's vocabulary knowledge (Jordan, Snow, & Porche, 2000; Whitehurst et al., 1988). Regarding shared book reading (e.g., dialogic reading), the importance of children's *active* interaction (i.e., labeling and pointing during readings versus passively listening to book readings) with novel words during reading is underscored, as it helps enhance vocabulary development (Mol, Bus, de Jong, & Smeets, 2008; Sénéchal, Thomas, & Monker, 1995). Similarly, engaging in more *types* of meaning-related talk with children (e.g., labeling or describing pictures in the book, predicting the story) positively predicts vocabulary skills among children (Hindman et al., 2014).

Finally, while meaning-related talk about a book can be described as contextualized discourse (i.e., regarding objects and situations present in the immediate context; Curenton, Craig, & Flanigan, 2008), home language interactions involving decontextualized language—such as narrating or explaining something that is not immediately visible—have also been linked with improved vocabulary outcomes for young children (Rowe, 2012; Snow, Tabors, & Dickinson, 2001). In dialogic reading research, findings show that the more parents connected the story to children's own experiences and lives, the stronger children's vocabulary skills appeared (Hindman et al., 2014). Moreover, storytelling is a practice particularly worth noting, as rich storytelling practices not only rely on decontextualized language (Rowe, 2013) but also have been documented among socio-economically, culturally, and linguistically diverse populations (Heath, 1983; Miller et al., 2005). In fact, parents' storytelling to children was found to contain more decontextualized language than book reading (Curenton et al., 2008). Of note, maternal storytelling practices in predominantly Spanish-speaking homes have been shown to correlate positively with preschool dual language learners' conceptual vocabulary outcomes, signaling a potential cultural strength that could be leveraged for school success with this population of learners (Wishard Guerra, 2018).

Similar findings about the relationships between the quality and quantity of vocabulary emerge for children from linguistically diverse homes (Hurtado et al., 2008; Konishi, Kanero, Freeman, Golinkoff, & Hirsh-Pasek, 2014). However, it is important to note that the language input ELLs receive in *each* language, both in quantity and quality, varies widely (Bialystok, 2001; Grosjean, 1982, 1989, 2008; Romaine, 1999). Thus, vocabulary knowledge among ELLs is distributed across two (or more) languages, and is typically used in different social contexts. Thus, it is important to consider the context (e.g., home or school) in which children might encounter words, as it can play a role in priming bilinguals toward a more monolingual or bilingual language mode (Bialystok, Luk, Peets, & Yang, 2010; Grosjean, 1982, 1989, 2008). Further, Duursma and colleagues (2007) found that use of English at home was not required for English vocabulary development among elementary-age children from Spanish-speaking homes in the U.S. In contrast, both home language and instructional support was required for students to remain proficient in Spanish.

School Language Environment

Compared to research on the home language environment, work on the school language environment and its relationship to students' vocabulary development is not only less researched but also less conclusive. This is not surprising, given that teachers have fewer opportunities for one-on-one conversational engagement with individual students by the very nature of the schooling context (Bond & Wasik, 2009). Further, similar to the literature on home context, the bulk of the work to date is anchored on the early childhood years. These limitations notwithstanding, we do have some insight into the features of the school language environment that appear to be associated with student vocabulary achievement and/or growth.

In the preschool context, the quality of teacher-child interactions relates to children's language skills, specifically underscoring the importance of interactive stimulation (Mashburn et al., 2008). In a similar vein, Aukrust (2007) examined the relationship between teacher talk exposure in a Norwegian preschool and native Turkish speaking children's second language (Norwegian) vocabulary acquisition. Aukrust reports that the amount, diversity, and complexity of teacher talk in preschool predicted subsequent second language vocabulary skills in first grade. In another study that examined the growth of preschoolers' receptive lexical skills over a year in relation to teacher speech among ELLs and their monolingual English-speaking peers, different aspects of verbal input related to language growth of ELLs compared to monolingual English speakers (Bowers & Vasilyeva, 2011). For ELLs, vocabulary growth was positively related to the total number of words (i.e., quantity) produced by the teacher. For monolingual English speakers, vocabulary growth was positively related to the number of word types (i.e., quality) produced by the teacher. Also highlighting the role of quality of language in preschool settings, Gámez (2015) focused on teachers' and students' speech during English Language Development instruction, reporting that structural complexity and lexical diversity of teachers' speech positively related to Spanish-speaking ELLs' language gains, as did the lexical diversity of students' speech. Gámez underscores the importance of exposure to high-quality classroom-based English, together with opportunities for language interactions among teachers and students, for promoting ELLs' English development. Most recently, Justice, Jiang, and Strasser (2018) examined the contribution of linguistic environment features in Head Start classrooms, finding that only teachers' communication-facilitation behaviors (i.e., encouraging and facilitating children's conversational participation) predicted children's vocabulary growth from preschool to kindergarten. Finally, a longitudinal study followed 26 Turkish immigrant children in Norway from preschool to fifth grade (age 10) (Rydland, Grøver, & Lawrence, 2014). Findings showed that teacher-led and peer talk predicted children's Norwegian vocabulary skills at age five, with differences maintained up to age ten, underscoring the importance of preschool talk exposure for vocabulary development.

Turning to the formal school years, work focused on the school language environment and its relationship to students' vocabulary development is scant, in both U.S. and international contexts. In one of the few studies focused on elementary-age students, Cadima, Leal, and Burchinal (2010) examined associations between the quality of teacher-student interactions and first grade academic and adaptive behavior outcomes of Portuguese students. The findings showed that the quality of teacher-student interactions was positively associated with students' first grade vocabulary. In the U.S. context, only two studies could be identified that targeted teacher language use and student vocabulary outcomes. In the first study, Silverman et al. (2014) explored the relationship between teachers' instruction and students' vocabulary and comprehension in grades 3–5. They found that only teachers' instruction on definitions, word relations, and morphosyntax positively related to changes in students' vocabulary. In the second study, Gámez and Lesaux (2012) investigated the link between teachers' language use and early-adolescent students' vocabulary. Like the work in the home context, quality—more than quantity—of language appeared to be the stronger ingredient related to students' end-of-year vocabulary scores. In contrast, recent work evaluating the relationships between Chilean teachers' explicit vocabulary instruction and kindergarteners' vocabulary development did not find that the quantity or quality of teachers' language supported students' language growth (Bowne, Yoshikawa, & Snow, 2016). The authors point out that the nature of student-teacher interactions in the Chilean context may account for this divergent finding, given that teachers tended to have large groups of students in their classrooms.

In summary, most of the research on the relationship between the home or school language environment and students' vocabulary proficiency finds that both quantity and quality matter. Thus, for successful vocabulary acquisition and development, children must be provided with ample language learning opportunities; however, not all children have access to such opportunities. We also know that, in general, children with better reading skills early on tend to develop better reading skills over time (Stanovich, 1986), which likewise applies to vocabulary. In short, for students to develop their language skills, there must be ample and sustained language learning opportunities. In fact, it is estimated that students need between 12–15 exposures to new words to learn them (Templeton, Bear, Invernizzi, & Johnston, 2010); the importance of ensuring these learning opportunities cannot be overestimated. Nearly 30 years ago, Clay (1987) underscored the need to account for children's educational history when evaluating the etiology of reading disability, specifically asserting that quality of instruction must be at the forefront. The next section synthesizes research on instruction and intervention approaches to support and build students' vocabulary.

IV. Promising Approaches to Building Vocabulary

Mirroring our synthesis of research on malleable factors that shape vocabulary development from the previous section, we begin this section with home-focused interventions and then turn to school-focused interventions.

Home-Focused Approaches

A common element for promoting children's vocabulary development at home centers on interactions, particularly their quality (Dickinson & Tabors, 2002; Mol et al., 2008; O'Brien et al., 2014). Findings from two meta-analyses focused on family literacy interventions, one centered on a specific approach (i.e., dialogic reading) and the other much broader in scope (i.e., family literacy programs), hold promise for supporting children's vocabulary development.

Mol and colleagues (2008) conducted a meta-analysis of 16 experimental studies to examine whether variations in dialogic reading—in which the child becomes the storyteller (Whitehurst et al., 1988)—were specifically associated with vocabulary development. While the authors found dialogic reading promising, they noted that participant characteristics must be considered. The effects of dialogic reading appeared stronger for younger compared to older children and were more pronounced for children's expressive compared to receptive vocabulary. Neither of these findings is surprising, given that dialogic reading was designed for pre-literate children and effects have consistently been found on expressive vocabulary measures. Furthermore, the effects did not appear as promising for families from lower income homes nor for families of children with greater risk for compromised academic achievement. These findings are somewhat surprising, as others have found positive effects of dialogic reading for families from lower income homes (Lonigan & Whitehurst, 1998; Whitehurst et al., 1994) and, although much less researched, for children with disabilities (Towson, Gallagher, & Bingham, 2016). Mol and colleagues conclude that dialogic reading could promote young children's vocabulary development and assert that the quality of book reading matters.

Another meta-analysis examined the effects of 30 family literacy programs (FLPs) on children's literacy development, distinguishing their effects on code- and comprehension-related skills (including vocabulary) (Van Steensel, McElvany, Kurvers, & Herppich, S., 2011). Similar to Mol et al.'s meta-analysis (2008), it found a significant, though small, mean effect of the FLPs. However, effects on code- and comprehension-related measures were similar. The authors hypothesize that this may be attributed to the ways in which parents interact with their children. For instance, even if the program orients parents to focus on encouraging more child talk during reading, parents may default to simply reading the book to their child. Like Mol and colleagues, albeit with more reservation, the authors conclude that FLPs may have potential. But they underscore the need for further research into how programs are effectively carried out by parents and children, noting that implementation or treatment fidelity information is rarely provided.

Two quasi-experimental studies also identified the aspects of FLPs that may be most effective for closing vocabulary gaps. O'Brien and colleagues (2014) found that young ELLs from low-income, immigrant families who participated in an FLP had significantly higher vocabulary gains than their demographically-matched peers. Of note, children with the lowest vocabulary knowledge evidenced the greatest gains. The authors underscore that the FLP model utilized in the study emphasized authentic literacy practices and focused on ecologically-valid home literacy practices, such as direct parent-child interactions. The second study found that the participants in the Raising A Reader (RAR) program—an evidence-based, 12-week program that is designed to encourage parents to read to their children—experienced significant gains in students' receptive vocabulary (Chao, Mattocks, Birden, & Manarino-Leggett, 2015). RAR increased the number of questions parents asked about books, and the authors assert that their findings support the importance of quality of interaction.

Finally, Dickinson and Tabors (2002) provide a summary of findings from a longitudinal study that examined how parents (and teachers) support language development in children from low-income families, from preschool through high school (here, the focus is on the home context, although classroom data was also collected). The authors audiotaped home conversations, interviewed parents regarding their experiences with children, and administered several language and literacy measures from kindergarten through high school to identify the types of preschool interactions that related to later literacy development. They identified three dimensions of experiences that positively related to children's later literacy success: 1) exposure to varied vocabulary, 2) extended discourse, and 3) stimulating environments. Dickinson and Tabors stress the importance of ensuring that early oral language supports are provided for children given their long-term effects on literacy development.

School-Focused Approaches

This section focuses on efforts centered on improving the quality and quantity of language use in the classroom—from early childhood throughout the formal school years—to build students' vocabulary knowledge. Two promising approaches include improving classroom discussion and focusing vocabulary instruction on building conceptual understanding.

Targeting Talk

As with work in the home context, engaging children in meaningful conversations in classrooms is an effective way of supporting vocabulary learning (Jalongo & Sobolak, 2011; Sinatra, Zygouris-Coe, & Dasinger, 2012). Studies of preschool literacy time suggest that oral language and discussion take up a substantial portion of literacy instruction, second to book reading (Pelatti, Piasta, Justice, & O'Connell, 2014). Yet, research on oral language in early school settings generally focus less on classroom discussion per se and more on teacher-student talk in the context of shared book reading (e.g. Hindman, Wasik, & Erhart, 2012; Pollard-Durodola, Gonzalez, & Simmons, 2014; Wasik & Hindman, 2014) and dialogic book reading (Lonigan & Whitehurst, 1998; Whitehurst et al., 1994). We also know it is important for preschool teachers to follow students' conversational topics, such that students become conversational partners, not passive listeners (Schwanenflugel et al., 2005; Sinatra et al., 2012).

At the elementary, middle and high school level, researchers recognize that disrupting the pervasive teacher-driven discourse that positions students as passive recipients of knowledge requires considerable effort (Cazden, 2001; Reznitskaya & Wilkinson, 2015). Many researchers and practitioners have developed tools to help teachers improve the quality of classroom conversations, including explicit training on discursive talk moves (McElhone, 2015; Michaels & O'Connor, 2013), providing resources, such as lists of questions that can be used with any text (Beck, McKeown, Sandora, Kucan, & Worthy, 1996; McKeown & Beck, 2004), or utilizing curriculum that incorporates texts on topics that are conducive to academic conversations (Lawrence, Crosson, Paré-Blagoev, & Snow, 2015). Furthermore, organizational factors (e.g., positioning of desks, use of physical objects to moderate conversation) may also aid in scaffolding effective classroom conversation (Chiaravalloti, Frey, & Fink, 2010). Various pedagogical efforts to facilitate classroom discussions indeed contribute to student talk, as there appears to be a significant correlation between pre-service teachers' planned use of dialogic tools and increased student talk in high school English classrooms (Caughlan, Juzwik, Kelly, Fine, & Borsheim-Black, 2013). Additionally, teachers' commitment to consistently scaffolding classroom discussion over time has led to student uptake of discourse moves, thereby improving discussion quality (Jadallah et al., 2011).

Building Conceptual Understanding

As noted in the *Conceptualizing What We Mean by Vocabulary Knowledge* section, network building refers to the discovery of links between words (also referred to as semantic networks) (Henriksen, 1999). It seems useful to focus on the concept of network building when discussing how to support children's vocabulary development—particularly in the school context—because vocabulary learning involves more than a form-meaning connection. When children learn words, they begin to formulate an understanding of concepts associated with those words (Neuman & Dwyer, 2009; Stahl & Murray, 1994; Stahl & Nagy, 2006). Neuman and colleagues (2011) found that teaching academic vocabulary in the context of semantically related categories (e.g., healthy foods, wild animals) produced strong linguistic and conceptual learning. Similarly, although Bowne and colleagues (2016) did not find that the quantity nor quality of Chilean teachers' language supported language growth, it did find that only the *amount* of conceptual information about words made available during teacher discussions significantly predicted students' end-of-kindergarten vocabulary. This is an intriguing finding that supports the notion that a concerted focus on conceptual development has the potential to advance not only students' word knowledge, but also ultimately their world knowledge.

An example of an approach that targets language during content instruction and has the potential to advance students' vocabulary and conceptual knowledge is the Word Generation program (http://wordgen.serpmedia.org). While this vocabulary program was originally designed to support middle graders' (grades 6–8) vocabulary development, there is now also an upper-elementary curriculum targeting students in grades 4–5. The program is centered on embedding all-purpose academic words in the context of high-interest passages about a controversial topic. Aside from the importance of selecting cross-content words, a unique feature of this program is that implementation is a whole-school effort (Lawrence, White, & Snow, 2010), while vocabulary programs are typically implemented by individual classroom teachers. By virtue of having content-area teachers working with English language arts teachers, it is possible to build students' conceptual understanding of words, helping them identify relationships and nuanced meanings of words in authentic contexts applicable to their daily learning experiences. Indeed, the repeated exposures to target words—in varied contexts—and the opportunities to use the words orally and in writing represent the key features of the Word Generation program. In this way, Word Generation attends to students' conceptual development anchored on words, rather than on isolated word instruction.

The Academic Language Instruction for All Students (ALIAS) program represents another exemplary vocabulary intervention designed for middle school students from linguistically and socioeconomically diverse homes (Lesaux, Kieffer, Faller, & Kelley, 2010). Among other components, ALIAS utilizes collaborative learning activities to leverage the benefits of peer interaction on language development (see August & Hakuta, 1997; Ellis, 1994; McLaughlin, 1987). Weekly logs and interviews centered on teachers' perceptions of program implementation revealed that teachers found the use of appropriate and appealing texts very beneficial in promoting classroom talk and supporting students' vocabulary learning.

Taken together, quality interactions support children's vocabulary development, at home and in school. But there are gaps in the research on promising approaches that remain unaddressed. For instance, the precise nature of the interactions that unfold in homes remain an open question (Van Steensel et al., 2011), as does the role of discussion beyond book-reading in early childhood contexts. Further, the extent to which school-focused vocabulary approaches can influence other academic outcomes (e.g., reading comprehension)—beyond vocabulary development—remains inconclusive (Wright & Cervetti, 2017). The final section outlines additional areas that are ripe for further research to help move the vocabulary research field forward.

V. Future Directions

Building on what we currently know, several lines of vocabulary research could benefit from more in-depth studies, including how to improve instructional language environments, how technology can be leveraged to build vocabulary, how assessments can be revised to account for all of the linguistic resources multilingual children bring to school, and how teacher vocabulary knowledge shapes student vocabulary outcomes.

Improving Instructional Language Environments

We know that vocabulary is acquired via meaningful incidental encounters with words and explicit, purposeful, planned, and sustained support for monolingual English speakers and ELLs (Graves, 2006; Graves, August, & Mancilla-Martinez, 2013). However, research on *how* to effectively improve instructional practices for both incidental and direct vocabulary instruction remains limited.

Despite knowing that quality language interactions are important, classroom talk tends to be used to check student comprehension rather than help develop students' thinking (Fisher, Frey, & Rothenberg, 2008), and recitation remains the dominant form of teacher-led group talk (Cazden, 2001; Michaels & O'Connor, 2013). Furthermore, ELLs and students from low-income homes tend to be provided with few opportunities to engage in classroom talk (Ho, 2005; Lingard, Hayes, & Mills, 2003). The lack of quality classroom language interactions is not surprising, given that facilitating high-quality student discussion is a demanding pedagogical task. A major challenge to engaging students in conversations is that teachers are often not prepared to do so, especially in optimal ways (Ghousseini, 2015); in fact, doing so often relies on extensive planning (Caughlan et al., 2013; DeFrance & Fahrenbruck, 2015). In light of findings that show the positive influence of classroom talk on literacy outcomes and content-area learning from early childhood to high school years (for a review, see Lawrence & Snow, 2010), more research focusing on how teachers can support genuine language interactions during class discussions to help build students' conceptual understanding is essential.

In addition to the paucity of quality language interactions that support incidental vocabulary acquisition, a long line of research has documented the lack of high-quality explicit vocabulary instruction in classrooms that serve both monolingual English speakers and ELLs, from early childhood to high school (Beck & McKeown, 2007; Durkin, 1979; Dutro & Moran, 2003; Gersten & Baker, 2000; Scarcella, 1996; Scott & Nagy, 1997). Indeed, there appears to be a wide gap between what research recommends as best practice and what has been observed in actual classrooms, both in the quantity and quality of vocabulary instruction (Scott, Jamieson-Noel, & Asselin, 2003; Watts, 1995; Wright & Neuman, 2014). In addition, teachers have reported limited school- or district-level support for systematic vocabulary instruction (Berne & Blachowicz, 2008). Although there is generally acknowledgement of the importance of building vocabulary, more research is needed on developmentally-effective teaching strategies (Neuman & Dwyer, 2009).

The Role of Technology

Information and communication technologies (ICTs) are established as powerful instructional tools and can be expected to continue to play an increasingly central role in and out of school (Dalton & Grisham, 2011; National Institute for Literacy, 2008; Rideout, Lauricella, & Wartella, 2011). In fact, ICTs may provide particular benefits for students with special needs (Muligan, 2003; Sadao & Robinson, 2010) and ELLs (Lacina, 2004; Uchikoshi, 2006; Wong & Neuman, 2016). But more research on the relationship between the use of technology and student vocabulary development is necessary, including work that attends to issues of equity and access (NAEYC & Fred Rogers Center for Early Learning and Children's Media, 2012). Furthermore, research that elucidates *which* technological tools are most effective for vocabulary learning, and also *how* those tools can be implemented most effectively (Zhao, 2003) is needed. In other words, it is important to consider not only how much time (quantity) children spend with technology but also how (quality) they spend that time (Christakis & Garrison, 2009; Tandon, Zhou, Lozano, & Christakis, 2011) in order to gain more insight into the active ingredients that may promote vocabulary development. For example, research on using eBooks to promote early childhood vocabulary acquisition suggests that while multi-media features are beneficial, interactive elements may be distracting (Takacs, Swart, & Bus, 2015), and that language development is enhanced when adults mediate children's experiences during eBook reading (Reich, Yau, & Warschauer, 2016).

Assessment Considerations

Considering the large and growing population of students from linguistically diverse homes in U.S. classrooms, it is imperative that research carefully attends to the types of vocabulary assessments utilized to help us understand and best support students' vocabulary knowledge. As noted earlier (see *Conceptualizing What We Mean by Vocabulary Knowledge* section), common standardized English vocabulary assessments rarely attend to whether linguistically diverse speakers are included in the norming samples (Luk & Christodoulou, 2016). This point cannot be underestimated and has important implications. We cannot continue to assess students only in English and overlook the fact that they have knowledge, however limited or extensive, of their native language(s). Work focused on psycholinguistic aspects of bilingualism similarly points to the existence of a combined lexico-semantic storage that is similar to monolinguals' linguistic storage (Dijkstra & Van Heuven, 2002; Kroll & Sunderman, 2003). In spite of theoretical consensus about the importance of conceptual vocabulary, the dominance of English as the language of assessment remains pervasive; in practice, standardized conceptual vocabulary measures in which students can answer in either language are only now beginning to emerge and to be investigated for their utility (Mancilla-Martinez, Greenfader, & Ochoa, 2018).

Given the lack of appropriate measures for linguistically diverse learners, numerous studies and reports to date document Spanish-English bilingual children's low English *and* low Spanish vocabulary knowledge (e.g., Gross, Buac, & Kaushanskaya, 2014; Hammer, Lawrence, & Miccio, 2008; Mancilla-Martinez & Lesaux, 2011; Mancilla-Martinez & Vagh, 2013). For children from other language backgrounds, such as Kurdish or Arabic, we know even less about their vocabulary knowledge in their native language(s), leaving researchers and practitioners with only partial knowledge of what students know and thus limiting the instructional support they can provide. This is problematic for a variety of reasons, not the least of which is risking a deficit orientation in the instruction provided to linguistically diverse students. Teacher expectations matter; it may be that the quality of instruction may differ for students deemed to have sufficient English skills compared to those labeled as limited English proficient (Umansky, 2016). It is thus possible that measures that allow linguistically diverse students to demonstrate their conceptual knowledge base can potentially help inform instructional efforts and differentiate language difference from language disorder. There is much work left to do in this area, but given that standardized conceptual vocabulary assessments are now available, it seems like a worthy line of further investigation.

Teacher Vocabulary Knowledge

Finally, and much less explored, more work is need to understand the extent to which teacher knowledge of vocabulary is associated with students' vocabulary development. Minimal attention has been paid to the potential role that teachers' own understanding of vocabulary may have in being prepared to provide students with appropriate vocabulary support. With some exceptions (Carlisle, Correnti, Phelps, & Zeng, 2009), a growing body of research finds that teacher content knowledge influences teacher practice and positively contributes to student learning in that content-area (Hill, Rowan, & Ball, 2005; Lane et al., 2009; McCutchen et al., 2002; Sadler, Sonnert, Coyle, Cook-Smith, & Miller, 2013). Yet, no studies to date have directly examined whether teacher knowledge of vocabulary may relate to student vocabulary learning. Recent work by Duguay, Kenyon, Haynes, August, and Yanosky (2016) contributes to this issue via their design of a tool to measure teachers' knowledge of vocabulary development and instruction. The Teachers' Knowledge of Vocabulary Survey (TKVS) is designed for teachers of both monolingual English speakers and ELLs. While the TKVS's validity has yet to be established, pilot study results are encouraging, indicating that the measure appears to have content and construct validity. An important next step will be to examine the relationship between teacher knowledge of vocabulary development and instruction as assessed by the TKVS—and other measures that may emerge —and teacher practice, as well as student achievement.

VI. Conclusion

The increasing economic, racial, ethnic, cultural, and linguistic diversity in our U.S. child population highlights the importance of re-examining what we mean by vocabulary knowledge, and in turn, to revisit how best to measure it and help it unfold. Despite a lack of consensus in how vocabulary is precisely defined, we know that vocabulary learning is not about isolated acquisition of word definitions. Instead, when students amass a store of word knowledge, they are effectively building conceptual understandings and need interactions with others to build their vocabulary base. At the same time, we are still piecing together the elements of effective interactions, including the documentation of interactions in authentic contexts and how the nature of the interactions are, or can be, adapted across development for optimal learning. As evidenced by current vocabulary instructional efforts, we are moving in a direction of anchoring vocabulary learning on content instruction and, by extension, on opportunities for students to more explicitly make conceptual links. Furthermore, there is limited, but growing understanding of how technology could be used effectively to improve vocabulary learning. In addition, growing efforts to create more equitable and comprehensive assessments of students' vocabulary could shift researchers and practitioners away from deficit orientations of culturally and linguistically diverse learners and provide powerful guidance for instruction. These seem like promising directions to move toward for all our learners, and especially for historically underserved populations that have subsequently evidenced low vocabulary knowledge and low academic achievement across the school years and content areas.

References

Anderson, R. C., & Pearson, P. D. (1984). A schema-theoretic view of basic processes in reading comprehension. In P. D. Pearson (Ed.), *Handbook of reading research* (pp. 255–291). New York, NY: Longmann.

August, D., & Hakuta, K. (Eds.). (1997). *Improving schooling for language-minority children: A research Agenda.* Washington, DC: National Academy Press.

August, D., & Shanahan, T. (Eds.). (2006). *Developing literacy in second-language learners: Report of the national literacy panel on language minority children and youth.* Mahwah, NJ: Lawrence Erlbaum Associates.

Aukrust, V. G. (2007). Young children acquiring second language vocabulary in preschool group-time: Does amount, diversity, and discourse complexity of teacher talk matter?. *Journal of Research in Childhood Education, 22,* 17–38.

Bates, E., & Goodman, J. (1997). On the inseparability of grammar and the lexicon: Evidence from acquisition, aphasia, and real-time processing. *Language and Cognitive Processes, 12,* 507–586.

Baumann, J. F., & Kame'enui, E. J. (Eds.). (2004). *Vocabulary instruction: From research to practice.* New York, NY: Guilford Press.

Beals, D. (2001). Eating and reading: Links between family conversations with preschoolers and later language and literacy. In D. K. Dickinson & P. O. Tabors (Eds.), *Beginning literacy with language: Young children learning at home and school* (pp. 75–92). Baltimore, MD: Brookes.

Beck, I. L., & McKeown, M. G. (2007). Increasing young low-income children's oral vocabulary repertoires through rich and focused instruction. *The Elementary School Journal, 107*(3), 251–271.

Beck, I. L., McKeown, M. G., & Omanson, R. C. (1987). The effects and uses of diverse vocabulary instructional techniques. In M. G. McKeown & M. E. Curtis (Eds.), *The nature of vocabulary acquisition* (pp. 147–163). Hillsdale, NJ: Erlbaum.

Beck, I. L., McKeown, M. G., Sandora, C., Kucan, L., & Worthy, J. (1996). Questioning the author: A yearlong classroom implementation to engage students with text. *The Elementary School Journal, 96*(4), 385–414.

Bedore, L. M., Peña, E. D., Garcia, M., & Cortez, C. (2005). Conceptual versus monolingual scoring: When does it make a difference?. *language, speech, and Hearing Services in Schools, 36*(3), 188–200.

Berne, J. I., & Blachowicz, C. L. (2008). What reading teachers say about vocabulary instruction: Voices from the classroom. *The Reading Teacher, 62,* 314–323.

Bialystok, E. (2001). *Bilingualism in development: Language, literacy, and cognition.* New York, NY: Cambridge University Press.

Bialystok, E., Luk, G., Peets, K. F., & Yang, S. (2010). Receptive vocabulary differences in monolingual and bilingual children. *Bilingualism: Language and Cognition, 13,* 525–531.

Bond, M. A., & Wasik, B. A. (2009). Conversation stations: Promoting language development in young children. *Early Childhood Education Journal, 36,* 467–473.

Bowers, E. P., & Vasilyeva, M. (2011). The relation between teacher input and lexical growth of preschoolers. *Applied Psycholinguistics, 32*(1), 221–241.

Bowne, J. B., Yoshikawa, H., & Snow, C. E. (2016). Relationship of teachers' language and explicit vocabulary instruction to students' vocabulary growth in kindergarten. *Reading Research Quarterly, 52*(1), 1–23.

Bravo, M. A., & Cervetti, G. N. (2008). Teaching vocabulary through text and experience in content areas. In A. E. Farstrup & S. J. Samuels (Eds.), *What research has to say about vocabulary instruction* (pp. 130–149). Newark, DE: International Reading Association.

Cadima, J., Leal, T., & Burchinal, M. (2010). The quality of teacher–student interactions: Associations with first graders' academic and behavioral outcomes. *Journal of School Psychology, 48*(6), 457–482.

Carey, S. (1978). The child as word learner. In M. Halle, G. Miller, & J. Bresnan (Eds.), *Linguistic theory and psychological reality* (pp. 264–293). Cambridge, MA: MIT Press.

Carlisle, J. F., Correnti, R., Phelps, G., & Zeng, J. (2009). Exploration of the contribution of teachers' knowledge about reading to their students' improvement in reading. *Reading and Writing: An Interdisciplinary Journal, 22*, 457–486.

Cartmill, E. A., Armstrong, B. F., Gleitman, L. R., Goldin-Meadow, S., Medina, T. N., & Trueswell, J. C. (2013). Quality of early parent input predicts child vocabulary 3 years later. *Proceedings of the National Academy of Sciences, 110*(28), 11278–11283.

Catts, H. W., Hogan, T. P., & Adlof, S. M. (2005). Developmental changes in reading and reading disabilities. In H. W. Catts & A. G. Kamhi (Eds.), *The connections between language and reading disabilities* (pp. 25–40). Mahwah, NJ: Lawrence Erlbaum.

Caughlan, S., Juzwik, M. M., Borsheim-Black, C., Kelly, S., & Fine, J. G. (2013). English teacher candidates developing dialogically organized instructional practices. *Research in the Teaching of English, 47*(3), 212–246.

Cazden, C. B. (2001). *Classroom discourse: The language of teaching and learning* (2nd ed.). Portsmouth, NH: Heinemann.

Chall, J. S. (1983). *Learning to read: The great debate.* New York, NY: McGraw-Hill.

Chao, S. L., Mattocks, G., Birden, A., & Manarino-Leggett, P. (2015). The impact of the Raising A Reader Program on family literacy practices and receptive vocabulary of children in pre-kindergarten. *Early Childhood Education Journal, 43*, 427–434.

Chiaravalloti, L. A., Frey, N., & Fink, L. (2010). Wouldn't she notice he had mud on his shirt?": Scaffolding meaningful discussions. *Voices from the Middle, 18*(2), 16.

Christakis, D. A., & Garrison, M. M. (2009). Preschool-aged children's television viewing in child care settings. *Pediatrics, 124*, 1627–1632.

Clark, E. V. (1993). *The lexicon in acquisition.* New York, NY: Cambridge University Press.

Clay, M. M. (1987). Learning to be learning disabled. *New Zealand Journal of Educational Studies, 22*(2), 155–173.

Cronbach, L. J. (1943). Measuring knowledge of precise word meaning. *The Journal of Educational Research, 36*(7), 528–534.

Curenton, S. M., Craig, M. J., & Flanigan, N. (2008). Use of decontextualized talk across story contexts: How oral storytelling and emergent reading can scaffold children's development. *Early Education and Development, 19*(1), 161–187. doi:10.1080/10409280701839296

Dale, E. (1965). Vocabulary measurement: Techniques and major findings. *Elementary English, 42*(8), 895–901.

Dalton, B., & Grisham, D. L. (2011). eVoc strategies: 10 ways to use technology to build vocabulary. *The Reading Teacher, 64*(5), 306–317.

De Zeeuw, E. L., de Geus, E. J., & Boomsma, D. I. (2015). Meta-analysis of twin studies highlights the importance of genetic variation in primary school educational achievement. *Trends in Neuroscience and Education, 4*(3), 69–76.

DeFrance, N. L., & Fahrenbruck, M. L. (2015). Constructing a plan for text-based discussion. *Journal of Adolescent & Adult Literacy, 59*(5), 575–585.

Dickinson, D. K., & Tabors, P. O. (2002). Fostering language and literacy in classrooms and homes. *Young Children, 57*(2), 10–18.

Dieterich, S. E., Assel, M. A., Swank, P., Smith, K. E., & Landry, S. H. (2006). The impact of early maternal verbal scaffolding and child language abilities on later decoding and reading comprehension skills. *Journal of School Psychology, 43*(6), 481–494.

Dijkstra, T., & Van Heuven, W. J. (2002). The architecture of the bilingual word recognition system: From identification to decision. *Bilingualism: Language and Cognition, 5*(3), 175–197.

Dudley-Marling, C., & Lucas, K. (2009). Pathologizing the language and culture of poor children. *Language Arts, 86*, 362–370.

Duguay, A., Kenyon, D., Haynes, E., August, D., & Yanosky, T. (2016). Measuring teachers' knowledge of vocabulary development and instruction. *Reading and Writing, 29*(2), 321–347.

Durkin, D. (1979). What classroom observations reveal about reading comprehension instruction. *Reading Research Quarterly, 14*, 481–538.

Dutro, S., & Moran, C. (2003). Rethinking English language instruction: An architectural approach. In G. Garcia (Ed.), *English learners: Reaching the highest level of English literacy* (pp. 227–258). Newark, DE: International Reading Association.

Duursma, E., Romero-Contreras, S., Szuber, A., Proctor, P., Snow, C., August, D., & Calderon, M. (2007). The role of home literacy and language environment on bilinguals' English and Spanish vocabulary development. *Language Learning, 28*, 171–190.

Dyson, A. H. (1993). From invention to social action in early childhood literacy: A reconceptualization through dialogue about difference. *Early Childhood Research Quarterly, 8*(4), 409–425.

Ellis, R. (1994). *The study of second language acquisition*. New York, NY: Oxford University.

Fisher, D., Frey, N., & Rothenberg, C. (2008). *Content-area conversations: How to plan discussion-based lessons for diverse language learners*. Alexandria, VA: The Association for Supervision and Curriculum Development.

Gámez, P. B. (2015). Classroom-based English exposure and ELLs' expressive language skills. *Early Childhood Research Quarterly, 31*, 135–146.

Gámez, P. B., & Lesaux, N. K. (2012). The relation between exposure to sophisticated and complex language and early-adolescent English-only and language minority learners' vocabulary. *Child Development, 83*, 1316–1331.

Gee, J. P. (2003). A sociocultural perspective on early literacy development. In S. B. Neuman & D. K. Dickinson (Eds.), *Handbook of early literacy research* (pp. 30–42). New York, NY: The Guilford Press.

Gersten, R., & Baker, S. (2000). Effective instruction for English-language learners: What we know about effective instructional practices for English-language learners. *Exceptional Children, 66*, 454–470.

Ghousseini, H. (2015). Core practices and problems of practice in learning to lead class discussions. *Elementary School Journal, 115*(3), 334–357.

Glasersfeld, E. V. (1984). An introduction to radical constructivism. In P. Watlawick (Ed.), *The invented reality* (pp. 17–40). New York, NY: W.W. Norton.

Gonzalez, N., Moll, L. C., & Amanti, C. (2005). *Funds of knowledge: Theorizing practices in households, communities, and classrooms*. Mahwah, NJ: Laurence Erlbaum Associates.

Gough, P. B., & Tunmer, W. E. (1986). Decoding, reading, and reading disability. *Remedial and Special Education, 7*(1), 6–10.

Graves, M. F. (2006). *The vocabulary book: Learning & instruction*. New York, NY: Teachers College Press.

Graves, M. F., August, D., & Mancilla-Martinez, J. (2013). *Teaching vocabulary to English language learners*. New York, NY: Teachers College Press.

Grosjean, F. (1982). *Life with two languages: An introduction to Bilingualism*. Boston, MA: Harvard University Press.

Grosjean, F. (1989). Neurolinguists, beware! A bilingual is not two monolinguals in one person. *Brain and Language, 36*(1), 3–15.

Grosjean, F. (2008). *Studying Bilinguals*. New York, NY: Oxford University Press.

Grosjean, F. (2013). Bilingualism: A short introduction. In F. Grosjean & P. Li (Eds.), *The psycholinguistics of Bilingualism* (pp. 5–21). New York, NY: Wiley-Blackwell.

Gross, M., Buac, M., & Kaushanskaya, M. (2014). Conceptual scoring of receptive and expressive vocabulary measures in simultaneous and sequential bilingual children. *American Journal of Speech-Language Pathology, 23*(4), 574–586.

Hammer, C. S., Lawrence, F. R., & Miccio, A. W. (2008). Exposure to English before and after entry into Head Start 1: Bilingual children's receptive language growth in Spanish and English. *International Journal of Bilingual Education and Bilingualism, 11*(1), 30–56.

Harris, J., Golinkoff, R. M., & Hirsh-Pasek, K. (2011). Lessons from the crib for the classroom: How children really learn vocabulary. In S. B. Neuman & D. K. Dickinson (Eds.), *Handbook of early literacy research* (pp. 49–65). New York, NY: The Guilford Press.

Heath, S. B. (1983). *Ways with words: Language, life and work in communities and classrooms*. New York, NY: Cambridge University Press.

Henriksen, B. (1999). Three dimensions of vocabulary development. *Studies in Second Language Acquisition, 21*, 303–317.

Hill, H. C., Rowan, B., & Ball, D. L. (2005). Effects of teachers' mathematical knowledge for teaching on student achievement. *American Educational Research Journal, 42*, 371–406.

Hindman, A. H., Skibbe, L. E., & Foster, T. D. (2014). Exploring the variety of parental talk during shared book reading and its contributions to preschool language and literacy: Evidence from early childhood longitudinal study-birth cohort. *Reading and Writing, 27*, 287–313. doi:10.1007/s11145-013-9445-4

Hindman, A. H., Wasik, B. A., & Erhart, A. C. (2012). Shared book reading and Head Start preschoolers' vocabulary learning: The role of book-related discussion and curricular connections. *Early Education & Development, 23*, 451–474.

Hirsh-Pasek, K., Adamson, L. B., Bakeman, R., Owen, M. T., Golinkoff, R. M., Pace, A., ... Suma, K. (2015). The contributions of early communication quality to low-income children's language success. *Psychological Science, 26*(7), 1–13.

Ho, D. G. E. (2005). Why do teachers ask the questions they ask?. *RELC Journal: A Journal of Language Teaching and Research, 36*(3), 297–310.

Hoff, E. (2006). How social contexts support and shape language development. *Developmental Review, 26*(1), 55–88. doi:10.1016/j.dr.2005.11.002

Hoff, E. (2013). Interpreting the early language trajectories of children from low-SES and language minority homes: Implications for closing achievement gaps. *Developmental Psychology, 49*(1), 4.

Hudson, T. (2007). *Teaching second language reading.* Oxford: Oxford University Press.

Hurtado, N., Marchman, V. A., & Fernald, A. (2008). Does input influence uptake? Links between maternal talk, processing speed and vocabulary size in Spanish-learning children. *Developmental Science, 11*(6), F31–F39.

Huttenlocher, J., Haight, W., Bryk, A., Seltzer, M., & Lyons, T. (1991). Early vocabulary growth: Relation to language input and gender. *Developmental Psychology, 27*(2), 236–248.

Jadallah, M., Anderson, R. C., Nguyen-Jahiel, K., Miller, B. W., Kim, I. H., Kuo, L. J., ... Wu, X. (2011). Influence of a teacher's scaffolding moves during child-led small-group discussions. *American Educational Research Journal, 48*(1), 194–230.

Jalongo, M. R., & Sobolak, M. J. (2011). Supporting young children's vocabulary growth: The challenges, the benefits, and evidence-based strategies. *Early Childhood Education Journal, 38*(6), 421–429.

Jiménez, R. T., García, E. E., & Pearson, P. D. (1996). The reading strategies of bilingual Latina/o students who are successful English learners: Opportunities and obstacles. *Reading Research Quarterly, 31*(1), 90–112.

Jordan, G. E., Snow, C. E., & Porche, M. V. (2000). Project EASE: The effect of a family literacy project on kindergarten students' early literacy skills. *Reading Research Quarterly, 35*(4), 524–546.

Just, M. A., & Carpenter, P. A. (1987). *The psychology of reading and language comprehension.* Boston, MA: Allyn and Bacon.

Justice, L. M., Jiang, H., & Strasser, K. (2018). Linguistic environment of preschool classrooms: What dimensions support children's language growth?. *Early Childhood Research Quarterly, 42*, 79–92.

Kintsch, W. (1988). The role of knowledge in discourse comprehension: A construction-integration model. *Psychological Review, 95*(2), 163–182.

Kintsch, W. (1998). *Comprehension: A paradigm for cognition.* Cambridge: Cambridge University Press.

Konishi, H., Kanero, J., Freeman, M. R., Golinkoff, R. M., & Hirsh-Pasek, K. (2014). Six Principles of language development: Implications for second language Learners. *Developmental Neuropsychology, 39*(5), 404–420.

Kovas, Y., Hayiou-Thomas, M. E., Oliver, B., Dale, P. S., Bishop, D. V. M., & Plomin, R. (2005). Genetic influences in different aspects of language development: The etiology of language skills in 4.5-year-old twins. *Child Development, 76*, 632–651.

Kroll, J. F., & Sunderman, G. (2003). Cognitive processes in second language learners and bilinguals: The development of lexical and conceptual representations. In C. J. Doughty & M. H. Long (Eds.), *The Handbook of SLA* (pp. 104–129). Malden, MA: Blackwell Publishing.

Lacina, J. (2004). Promoting language acquisitions: Technology and English language learners. *Childhood Education, 81*(2), 113–115.

Lane, H. B., Hudson, R. F., Leite, W. L., Kosanovich, M. L., Strout, M. T., Fenty, N. S., & Wright, T. L. (2009). Teacher knowledge about reading fluency and indicators of students' fluency growth in reading first schools. *Reading & Writing Quarterly: Overcoming Learning Difficulties, 25*(1), 57–86.

Langer, J. A. (1984). Examining background knowledge and text comprehension. *Reading Research Quarterly, 19*, 468–481.

Lawrence, J. F., Crosson, A. C., Paré-Blagoev, E. J., & Snow, C. E. (2015). Word Generation randomized trial: Discussion mediates the impact of program treatment on academic word learning. *American Educational Research Journal, 52*(4), 750–786.

Lawrence, J. F., & Snow, C. E. (2010). Oral discourse and reading. In M. L. Kamil & P. D. Pearson (Eds.), *Handbook of reading research* (pp. 320–337). New York, NY: Routledge.

Lawrence, J. F., White, C., & Snow, C. E. (2010). The words students need. *Educational Leadership, 68*(2), 22–26.

Lesaux, N. K. (2012). Reading and reading instruction for children from low-income and non-English-speaking households. *The Future of Children, 22*(2), 73–88.

Lesaux, N. K., Kieffer, M. J., Faller, S. E., & Kelley, J. G. (2010). The effectiveness and ease of implementation of an academic vocabulary intervention for linguistically diverse students in urban middle schools. *Reading Research Quarterly, 45*(2), 196–228.

Lingard, B., Hayes, D., & Mills, M. (2003). Teachers and productive pedagogies: Contextualising, conceptualising, utilising. *pedagogy, Culture and Society, 11*(3), 397–422.

Lipson, M. Y. (1982). Learning new information from text: The role of prior knowledge and reading ability. *Journal of Reading Behavior, 14*, 243–261.

Lonigan, C. J., & Whitehurst, G. J. (1998). Relative efficacy of parent and teacher involvement in a shared-reading intervention for preschool children from low-income backgrounds. *Early Childhood Research Quarterly, 13*(2), 263–290.

Luk, G., & Christodoulou, J. A. (2016). Assessing and understanding the needs of dual-language learners. In N. Lesaux & S. M. Jones (Eds.), *The leading edge of early childhood education: Linking science to policy for a new generation* (pp. 67–90). Boston, MA: Harvard Education Press.

Mancilla-Martinez, J., Greenfader, C. M., & Ochoa, W. (2018). Spanish-speaking preschoolers' conceptual vocabulary knowledge: Towards more comprehensive assessment. *NHSA Dialog: A Research-to-Practice Journal for the Early Childhood Field, 21*(1).

Mancilla-Martinez, J., & Lesaux, N. K. (2011). The gap between Spanish-Speakers' word reading and word knowledge: A longitudinal study. *Child Development, 82*, 1544–1560.

Mancilla-Martinez, J., & Lesaux, N. K. (2017). Early indicators of later English reading comprehension outcomes among children from Spanish-speaking homes. *Scientific Studies of Reading, 21*(5).

Mancilla-Martinez, J., & Vagh, S. B. (2013). Growth in toddler's Spanish, English, and conceptual vocabulary knowledge. *Early Childhood Research Quarterly, 28*, 555–567.

Mashburn, A. J., Pianta, R. C., Hamre, B. K., Downer, J. T., Barbarin, O. A., Bryant, D., ... Howes, C. (2008). Measures of classroom quality in prekindergarten and children's development of academic, language, and social skills. *Child Development, 79*, 732–749.

McCutchen, D., Abbott, R., Green, L., Beretvas, S., Cox, S., Potter, N., ... Gray, A. (2002). Beginning literacy: Links among teacher knowledge, teacher practice, and student learning. *Journal of Learning Disabilities, 35*(1), 69–86.

McElhone, D. (2015). Using stems and supported inquiry to help an elementary teacher move toward dialogic reading instruction. *The Journal of Classroom Interaction, 50*(2), 156.

McKeown, M. G., & Beck, I. L. (2004). Transforming knowledge into professional development resources: Six teachers implement a model of teaching for understanding text. *The Elementary School Journal, 104*, 391–408.

McLaughlin, B. (1987). Reading in a second language: Studies with adult and child learners. In S. R. Goldman & H. T. Trueba (Eds.), *Becoming literate in English as a second language* (pp. 57–70). Norwood, NJ: Ablex.

Menn, L. (2017). *Psycholinguistics: Introduction and applications* (2nd ed.). San Diego, CA: Plural Publishing.

Michaels, S. (1981). Sharing time": Children's narrative styles and differential access to literacy. *Language in Society, 10*, 423–442.

Michaels, S. (2005). Can the intellectual affordances of working-class storytelling be leveraged in school? *Human Development, 48*(3), 136–145.

Michaels, S., & O'Connor, C. (2013). Conceptualizing talk moves as tools: Professional development approaches for academically productive discussions. In L. B. Resnick, C. Asterhan, & S. Clark (Eds.), *Socializing intelligence through academic talk and dialogue* (pp. 333–347). Washington, DC: American Educational Research Association.

Miller, P. J., Cho, G. E., & Bracey, J. R. (2005). Working-class children's experience through the prism of personal storytelling. *Human Development, 48*(3), 115–135.

Mol, S. E., Bus, A. G., de Jong, M. T., & Smeets, D. J. (2008). Added value of dialogic parent–child book readings: A meta-analysis. *Early Education and Development, 19*(1), 7–26.

Muligan, S. A. (2003). Assistive technology: Supporting the participation of children with disabilities. *Young Children, 58*(6), 50–51.

NAEYC & Fred Rogers Center for Early Learning and Children's Media. (2012). Technology and interactive mediate as tools in early childhood programs serving children from birth through age 8: A joint position statement of the National Association for the Education of Young Children and the Fred Rogers Center for Early Learning and Children's Media. Retrieved from www.naeyc.org/files/naeyc/file/positions/PS_technology_WEB2.pdf

Nation, I. S. P. (1990). *Teaching and learning vocabulary*. New York, NY: Newbury House.

National Institute for Literacy. (2008). *Developing early literacy: Report of the national early literacy panel. A scientific synthesis of early literacy development and implications for intervention*. T. Shanahan, Chair. Louisville, KY: National Center for Family Literacy.

National Reading Panel. (2000). *Teaching children to read: An evidence-based assessment of the scientific literature on reading and its implications for reading instruction*. Bethesda, MD: National Institute of Child Health and Human Development.

Neuman, S. B. (2003). The knowledge gap: Implications for early education. In D. K. Dickinson & S. B. Neuman (Eds.), *Handbook of early literacy research* (Vol. 2, pp. 29–40). New York, NY: The Guilford Press.

Neuman, S. B., & Dwyer, J. (2009). Missing in action: Vocabulary instruction in pre-k. *The Reading Teacher*, *62*(5), 384–392.

Neuman, S. B., Newman, E. H., & Dwyer, J. (2011). Educational effects of a vocabulary intervention on preschoolers' word knowledge and conceptual development: A cluster-randomized trial. *Reading Research Quarterly*, *46*(3), 249–272.

O'Brien, L. M., Paratore, J. R., Leighton, C. M., Cassano, C. M., Krol-Sinclair, B., & Green, J. G. (2014). Examining differential effects of a family literacy program on language and literacy growth of ELLs with varying vocabularies. *Journal of Literacy Research*, *46*(3), 383–415.

Olson, R. K., Keenan, J. M., Byrne, B., Samuelsson, S., Coventry, W. L., Corley, R., & Hulslander, J. (2007). Genetic and environmental influences on vocabulary and reading development. *Scientific Studies of Reading*, *20*, 51–76.

Pan, B. A., Rowe, M. L., Singer, J. D., & Snow, C. E. (2005). Maternal correlates of growth in toddler vocabulary production in low-income families. *Child Development*, *76*(4), 763–782.

Paris, S. G. (2005). Reinterpreting the development of reading skills. *Reading Research Quarterly*, *40*, 184–202.

Pearson, B. Z., Fernández, S. C., & Oller, D. K. (1995). Cross-language synonyms in the lexicons of bilingual infants: One language or two?. *Journal of Child Language*, *22*, 345.

Pearson, P. D., Hiebert, E. H., & Kamil, M. L. (2007). Vocabulary assessment: What we know and what we need to learn. *Reading Research Quarterly*, *42*, 282–296.

Pelatti, C. Y., Piasta, S. B., Justice, L. M., & O'Connell, A. (2014). Language-and literacy-learning opportunities in early childhood classrooms: Children's typical experiences and within-classroom variability. *Early Childhood Research Quarterly*, *29*, 445–456.

Perfetti, C. (2007). Reading ability: Lexical quality to comprehension. *Scientific Studies of Reading*, *11*, 357–383.

Perfetti, C. A. (1999). Comprehending written language: A blueprint of the reader. In C. M. Brown & P. Hagoort (Eds.), *The neurocognition of language processing* (pp. 167–208). London: Oxford University Press.

Pollard-Durodola, S. D., Gonzalez, J. E., & Simmons, D. C. (2014). Accelerating preschoolers' content vocabulary: Designing a shared book intervention in collaboration with teachers. *NHSA Dialog: A Research to Practice Journal for the Early Childhood Field*, *17*, 3.

Reich, S. M., Yau, J. C., & Warschauer, M. (2016). Tablet-based eBooks for young children: What does the research say?. *Journal of Developmental & Behavioral Pediatrics*, *37*(7), 585–591.

Resnick, L. B. (1983). Mathematics and science learning: A new conception. *Science*, *220*, 477–478.

Reznitskaya, A., & Wilkinson, I. (2015). Professional development in dialogic teaching: Helping teachers promote argument literacy in their classrooms. In D. Scott & E. Hargreaves (Eds.), *The SAGE handbook of learning* (pp. 219–232). Thousand Oaks, CA: SAGE.

Richards, J. C. (1976). The role of vocabulary teaching. *TESOL Quarterly*, *10*, 77–89.

Rideout, V. J., Lauricella, A., & Wartella, E. (2011). *Children, media, and race: Media use among White, Black, Hispanic, and Asian American Children*. Report of the Center on Media and Human Development School of Communication Northwestern University.

Romaine, S. R. (1999). Bilingual language development. In M. Barrett (Ed.), *The development of language* (pp. 251–276). New York, NY: Psychology Press.

Rowe, M. (2013). Decontextualized language input and preschoolers' vocabulary development. *Seminars in Speech and Language*, *34*(4), 260–266. doi:10.1055/s-0033-1353444

Rowe, M. L. (2012). A longitudinal investigation of the role of quantity and quality of child-directed speech in vocabulary development. *Child Development*, *83*, 1762–1774.

Rowe, M. L., Leech, K. A., & Cabrera, N. (2016). Going beyond input quantity: Wh-questions matter for toddlers' language and cognitive development. *Cognitive Science, 41*(S1), 162–179.

Rydland, V., Grøver, V., & Lawrence, J. (2014). The second-language vocabulary trajectories of Turkish immigrant children in Norway from ages five to ten: The role of preschool talk exposure, maternal education, and co-ethnic concentration in the neighborhood. *Journal of Child Language, 41*(02), 352–381.

Sadao, K. C., & Robinson, N. B. (2010). *Assistive technology for young children: Creating inclusive learning environments*. Baltimore, MD: Brookes.

Sadler, P. M., Sonnert, G., Coyle, H. P., Cook-Smith, N., & Miller, J. L. (2013). The influence of teachers' knowledge on student learning in middle school physical science classrooms. *American Educational Research Journal, 50*(5), 1020–1049.

Salo, V. C., Rowe, M. L., Leech, K. A., & Cabrera, N. J. (2016). Low-income fathers' speech to toddlers during book reading versus toy play. *Journal of Child Language, 43*(6), 1385–1399. doi:10.1017/s0305000915000550

Scarborough, H. (2001). Connecting early language and literacy to later reading (dis)abilities: Evidence, theory, and practice. In S. B. Neuman & D. K. Dickinson (Eds.), *Handbook of early literacy* (pp. 97–110). NY: Guilford Press.

Scarcella, R. C. (1996). Secondary education and second language research: ESL students in the 1990's. *The CATESOL Journal, 9*, 129–152.

Schmitt, N. (2014). Size and depth of vocabulary knowledge: What the research shows. *Language Learning, 64*(4), 913–951.

Schwanenflugel, P. J., Hamilton, C. E., Bradley, B. A., Ruston, H. P., Neuharth-Pritchett, S., & Restrepo, M. A. (2005). Classroom practices for vocabulary enhancement in prekindergarten: Lessons from PAVEd for success. In E. H. Hiebert & M. L. Kamil (Eds.), *Teaching and learning vocabulary: Bringing research to practice* (pp. 155–178). Mahwah, NJ: Lawrence Erlbaum.

Scott, J. A., Jamieson-Noel, D., & Asselin, M. (2003). Vocabulary instruction throughout the day in twenty-three Canadian upper-elementary classrooms. *The Elementary School Journal, 103*, 269–286.

Scott, J. A., & Nagy, W. E. (1997). Understanding the definitions of unfamiliar words. *Reading Research Quarterly, 32*, 184–200.

Sénéchal, M., Thomas, E., & Monker, J. A. (1995). Individual differences in 4-year-old children's acquisition of vocabulary during storybook reading. *Journal of Educational Psychology, 87*(2), 218–229. doi:10.1037/0022-0663.87.2.218

Shapiro, A. (2004). How including prior knowledge as a subject variable may change outcomes of learning research. *American Educational Research Journal, 41*, 159–189.

Silverman, R. D., Proctor, C. P., Harring, J. R., Doyle, B., Mitchell, M. A., & Meyer, A. G. (2014). Teachers' instruction and students' vocabulary and comprehension: An exploratory study with English monolingual and Spanish–English bilingual students in Grades 3–5. *Reading Research Quarterly, 49*, 31–60.

Sinatra, R., Zygouris-Coe, V., & Dasinger, S. B. (2012). Preventing a vocabulary lag: What lessons are learned from research. *Reading & Writing Quarterly, 28*(4), 333–357.

Snow, C. E., Tabors, P. O., & Dickinson, D. K. (2001). Language development in the preschool years. In D. K. Dickinson & P. O. Tabors (Eds.), *Beginning literacy with language: Young children learning at home and school* (pp. 1–25). Baltimore, MD: Brookes.

Sperry, D. E., Sperry, L. L., & Miller, P. J. (2018). Reexamining the verbal environments of children from different socioeconomic backgrounds. *Child Development*. Advance online publication. doi:10.1111/cdev.13072

Stahl, K. A. D., & Bravo, M. A. (2010). Contemporary classroom vocabulary assessment for content areas. *The Reading Teacher, 63*(7), 566–578.

Stahl, S. A., & Murray, B. (1994). Defining phonological awareness and its relationship to early reading. *Journal of Educational Psychology, 86*(2), 221–234.

Stahl, S. A., & Nagy, W. E. (2006). *Teaching word meanings*. Mahwah, NJ: Erlbaum.

Stanovich, K. E. (1986). Matthew effects in reading: Some consequences of individual differences in the acquisition of literacy. *Reading Research Quarterly, 22*, 360–407.

Stevens, K. C. (1980). The effect of background knowledge on the reading comprehension of ninth graders. *Journal of Reading Behavior, 12*(2), 151–154.

Stevens, R. J., Lu, X., Baker, D. P., Ray, M. N., Eckert, S. A., & Gamson, D. A. (2015). Assessing the cognitive demands of a century of reading curricula: An analysis of reading text and comprehension tasks from 1910 to 2000. *American Educational Research Journal, 52*, 582–617.

Takacs, Z. K., Swart, E. K., & Bus, A. G. (2015). Benefits and pitfalls of multimedia and interactive features in technology-enhanced storybooks a meta-analysis. *Review of Educational Research, 85*, 698–739.

Tandon, P. S., Zhou, C., Lozano, P., & Christakis, D. A. (2011). Preschoolers' total daily screen time at home and by type of child care. *Journal of Pediatrics, 158*, 297–300.

Templeton, S., Bear, D. R., Invernizzi, M., & Johnston, F. (2010). *Vocabulary their way: Word study with middle and secondary students* (1st ed.). New York, NY: Pearson.

Towson, J. A., Gallagher, P. A., & Bingham, G. E. (2016). Dialogic reading: Language and preliteracy outcomes for young children with disabilities. *Journal of Early Intervention, 38*(4), 230–246.

Uchikoshi, Y. (2006). Early reading in bilingual kindergartners: Can educational television help? *Scientific Studies of Reading, 10*, 89–120.

Umansky, I. M. (2016). To be or not to be EL: An examination of the impact of classifying students as English Learners. *Educational Evaluation and Policy Analysis, 38*, 714–737.

Van Steensel, R., McElvany, N., Kurvers, J., & Herppich, S. (2011). How effective are family literacy programs? Results of a meta-analysis. *Review of Educational Research, 81*, 69–96.

Vellutino, F. R., Scanlon, D. M., Sipay, E. R., Small, S. G., Pratt, A., Chen, R., & Denckla, M. B. (1996). Cognitive profiles of difficult-to-remediate and readily remediated poor readers: Early intervention as a vehicle for distinguishing between cognitive and experiential deficits as basic causes of specific reading disability. *Journal of Educational Psychology, 88*, 601.

Vellutino, F. R., Tunmer, W. E., Jaccard, J. J., & Chen, R. (2007). Components of reading ability: Multivariate evidence for a convergent skills model of reading. *Scientific Studies of Reading, 11*, 3–32.

Verhaegen, C., & Poncelet, M. (2013). Changes in naming and semantic abilities with aging from 50 to 90 years. *Journal of the International Neuropsychological Society, 19*(2), 119–126.

Wardhaugh, R., & Fuller, J. (2015). *An introduction to sociolinguistics* (7th ed.). New York, NY: Wiley-Blackwell.

Wasik, B. A., & Hindman, A. H. (2014). Understanding the active ingredients in an effective preschool vocabulary intervention: An exploratory study of teacher and child talk during book reading. *Early Education and Development, 25*, 1035–1056.

Watts, S. M. (1995). Vocabulary instruction during reading lessons in six classrooms. *Journal of Reading Behavior, 27*(3), 399–424.

Weizman, Z. O., & Snow, C. E. (2001). Lexical input as related to children's vocabulary acquisition: Effects of sophisticated exposure and support for meaning. *Developmental Psychology, 37*, 265–279.

Whitehurst, G. J., Arnold, D. S., Epstein, J. N., Angell, A. L., Smith, M., & Fischel, J. E. (1994). A picture book reading intervention in day care and home for children from low income families. *Developmental Psychology, 30*, 679–689.

Whitehurst, G. J., Falco, F. L., Lonigan, C. G., Fischel, J. E., DeBaryshe, B. D., Valdez-Menchaca, M. C., & Caulfield, M. (1988). Accelerating language development through picture book reading. *Developmental Psychology, 24*, 552–559.

Wishard Guerra, A. G. (2018, April). *Storytelling as an adaptive cultural practice that promotes vocabulary and self-regulation among dual language learning preschool children*. Symposium presentation at the meeting of the American Educational Research Association, New York, NY.

Wong, K. M., & Neuman, S. B. (2016). Educational media supports for preschool-aged English language learners. *Technology in Early Childhood Education, 19*(4), 28–31.

Wright, T. S., & Cervetti, G. N. (2017). A systematic review of the research on vocabulary instruction that impacts text comprehension. *Reading Research Quarterly, 52*(2), 203–226.

Wright, T. S., & Neuman, S. B. (2014). Paucity and disparity in kindergarten oral vocabulary instruction. *Journal of Literacy Research, 46*(3), 330–357.

Zhao, Y. (2003). Recent developments in technology and language learning: A literature review and meta-analysis. *CALICO Journal, 21*(1), 7–27.

13

The Role of Knowledge in Understanding and Learning from Text

Gina N. Cervetti and Tanya S. Wright

There is a wealth of theoretical and empirical evidence regarding the significant role of prior knowledge in reading comprehension. The purpose of this chapter is to examine the substantial body of research on knowledge in light of current models of comprehension. As such, we begin by describing theoretical accounts of the role of knowledge in reading comprehension. We then review the empirical evidence describing the role of knowledge in comprehension and the relationships among knowledge, reading skill, and language development in support of reading comprehension. In doing so, we both substantiate the critical role of knowledge in reading and also identify promising areas for future research and practice.

There is little question that the basic skills of decoding and interpreting words are essential for accessing and successfully comprehending text. This well-documented understanding has led to a strong emphasis on basic (word-level) skills in early reading instruction and to the design of skills-focused interventions for older students who struggle to make sense of grade-appropriate texts. This focus on basic skills has often overshadowed attention to other supports for comprehension and other possible explanations for comprehension difficulties—the skills and knowledge that are involved in comprehension itself, which assist students not just in reading and recalling text, but in *learning from text*. The focus on basic skills has sometimes caused educators and policymakers to overlook research demonstrating that basic skills, comprehension strategies, and knowledge develop simultaneously, rather than sequentially—and that instruction that supports the latter is essential even before students have mastered basic skills (e.g., Rapp, van den Broek, McMaster, Kendeou, & Espin, 2007). Moreover, the focus on word-level skills has diverted attention away from decades of research that have informed our understanding about how readers comprehend text and, in particular, the role of knowledge in comprehension.

Knowledge as a Predictor and Product of Reading

Theoretical Accounts of Knowledge and Reading Comprehension

Bartlett (1932) is often credited with laying the groundwork for later research on knowledge and comprehension in a series of studies examining the effect of knowledge on the processing of new information. Bartlett described "schemata" as organizations of past experiences that reside in memory and bias interpretation of new stimuli, such as stories. In the 1960's, Ausubel (1963, 1968) raised the status of prior knowledge as a factor in learning. In his widely-read 1968 educational psychology textbook, Ausubel represented learning as a cumulative process in which learners integrate new knowledge with existing knowledge, claiming that "the most important single factor influencing learning is what the learner already knows" (p. 18).

Ausubel's portrayal of the role of prior knowledge in learning powerfully influenced the cognitive models of reading comprehension that emerged in the subsequent decades. In particular, the leading model of the 1980's, schema theory, foregrounded prior knowledge as an explanation for comprehension. Schema theoretic models suggest that individuals have knowledge about things and events that provide a conceptual framework for understanding the world and a basis for comprehending text, filling in gaps in texts, and assimilating new information (Anderson & Pearson, 1984; Marr & Gormley, 1982). Several classic studies demonstrated that readers interpret new situations in text in light of their existing knowledge, experiences, and perspectives (e.g., Anderson, Spiro, & Anderson, 1978; Goetz, Schallert, Reynolds, & Radin, 1983). For example, Anderson, Reynolds, Schallert, and Goetz (1977) studied the effect of knowledge on interpretation of ambiguous passages. Participants enrolled in a weightlifting class or an educational psychology class for music education students read two ambiguous passages—each with two possible interpretations (prison/wrestling and cards/music). The participants retold the passages and completed multiple choice items for each passage, each of which had two possible correct answers, one for each of the interpretations. The weight-lifting students gave more correct wrestling-consistent answers than the music students on the prison/wrestling passage. The music education students gave more correct music-consistent answers than the weightlifting students on the cards/music passage. In addition, the inclusion of theme-revealing disambiguations in the retellings were significantly related to the subjects' background. That is, for example, more weightlifting students included statements that revealed a wrestling interpretation in the prison/wrestling passage. The authors interpret the findings as evidence that people's interpretation of messages is influenced by high-level schemata.

Contemporary cognitive models of reading describe the essential role of knowledge in text comprehension (Graesser, Singer, & Trabasso, 1994; Kintsch, 1998; van den Broek, Risden, Fletcher, & Thurlow, 1996). These models represent the relationship between knowledge and comprehension as one in which existing knowledge is continually activated and integrated with textual information in the interest of establishing a coherent mental representation of the text. The models also emphasize the malleability of knowledge, representing knowledge as a kind of network of associations that shifts continually during reading. Recent work describes in detail how memory of information encountered in a text (episodic memory) and existing knowledge (semantic memory) are activated and re-activated during reading, resulting in different kinds of inferences, as well as factors that influence these processes (e.g., Cook & Guéraud, 2005; Wolfe & Goldman, 2005). The most prominent contemporary model of comprehension, the Construction-Integration Model (Kintsch, 1988, 1998), portrays comprehension as having at least three levels. At the first level, readers identify the *surface structure* of the text, or the words and phrases that make up the text. The second level is the *textbase*, in which the reader uses information from the text and from their knowledge base to encode the semantic and rhetorical structures of the text, forming a set of basic propositions about the ideas and events in the text. The third level is the *situation model*, in which readers elaborate ideas and events described in a text by integrating them with prior knowledge, creating a fully fleshed out mental representation of the text (Kintsch, 1988, 1998). The Construction-Integration Model relies on the understanding that readers are in pursuit of a situation model, because it involves a rich and coherent understanding of the text.

Reading comprehension and knowledge have a reciprocal relationship in which knowledge supports comprehension and comprehension builds new knowledge through the development of situation models. The establishment of a situation model is important because it produces deeper understandings of a text, and because it is associated with *learning from* text, rather than simply *recalling* a text (Kintsch, 1986). That is, as readers integrate textual information with existing knowledge, their knowledge is being augmented and refined. These modifications of knowledge stored in long-term memory *are* learning and become the prior knowledge that the reader brings to subsequent reading (within the same texts and to new texts). While more basic encoding of propositions about the ideas and events in the text (i.e., a textbase) is often sufficient in order to produce retellings or summaries, it is a relatively shallow form of comprehension and is less likely to produce real learning than the development of a situation model.

The development of a situation model matters both because it supports students in building new knowledge, creating positive momentum toward comprehending future texts, and also because it enhances the experience of reading and interacting around texts. For example, readers who bring more knowledge to the text are better able to form connections among the ideas in the text, to make causal explanations (e.g., why things happen), and to infer global messages and deeper meanings (Graesser et al., 1994). In addition, in theory, establishing a situation model is associated with greater persistence; that is, readers may be less likely to abandon texts if they are able to establish a coherent understanding of the text (Graesser et al., 1994).

Empirical Accounts of Topic, Domain, and General World Knowledge on Comprehension

Over the last 40 years, a substantial body of empirical studies has examined the role of knowledge in comprehension. Consistent with theoretical accounts of comprehension, empirical studies provide strong evidence that having more knowledge related to a text better supports comprehension than having less knowledge. Across studies, researchers have operationalized knowledge in a number of different ways, varying in particular the proximity of readers' knowledge to the text being comprehended. These variations can be loosely clustered into studies of topic knowledge, domain knowledge, and general world knowledge (see Table 13.1 for a description of knowledge types).

Topic and Domain Knowledge

Dozens of studies have documented the impact of readers' topic knowledge and domain knowledge on reading comprehension across a wide range of age/grade-levels, e.g., second graders in Pearson et al., 1979; third graders in Taft & Leslie, 1985; middle school students in Reutzel & Morgan, 1990; Davis, Huang, & Yi, 2017; university students in Alexander, Kulikowich, and Schulze (1994), Chiesi, Spilich, and Voss (1979), and Gasparinatou and Grigoriadou (2013), and text genres (e.g., narrative in Pearson et al.; fictional narrative in Walker, 1987; more and less technical expository texts in Alexander et al.). Topic knowledge is often defined as knowledge that is closely related to the topic of the text (e.g., knowledge about spiders when reading a text about a spider), whereas domain knowledge is generally operationalized as knowledge that is related to the broader discipline or context in which the text's topic belongs (e.g., knowledge of biology when reading about spiders).

While topic knowledge often influences readers' ability to recall information from texts and to answer text explicit comprehension questions (e.g., Marr & Gormley, 1982; Pearson et al., 1979), the most consistent impact of topic knowledge is on readers' abilities to respond to questions that require bridging inferences (connecting information within texts, also called text implicit or gist questions) and connections to prior knowledge (often called script implicit or scriptally implicit questions). In one study demonstrating these effects, Taft and Leslie (1985) investigated the effects of third graders' prior knowledge of food chains on their

Table 13.1 Knowledge Types in Research on Knowledge and Reading Comprehension

Definition	Operationalization	Examples of Studies
Topic knowledge: Knowledge that is closely related to the topic of a text.	Topic knowledge has been assessed in a variety of ways across studies—e.g., using multiple choice items (e.g., Rydland, Aukrust, & Fulland, 2012), sorting tasks (e.g., McNamara, Kintsch, Songer, & Kintsch, 1996), fill-in-the-blank questions (McNamara et al.), open-ended questions (e.g., Ozuru et al., 2009), and free-association tasks (e.g., Reutzel & Morgan, 1990). In some studies, questions are drawn directly from the text used in the comprehension assessment (e.g., Levine & Hause, 1985; Marr & Gormley, 1982). In other studies, questions focus on knowledge that is judged by the researchers to be closely related to concepts or facts in the text (e.g., Pearson, Hansen, & Gordon, 1979). In a few cases, the knowledge assessed is close to the topic, but not the specific content, of the texts. For example, Hammadou (1991) used a multiple choice assessment that measured participants' knowledge of aspects of the topic that differed from those mentioned in the comprehension text. The questions demanded more in-depth knowledge of the topics than was addressed in the text. Sometimes topic knowledge is referred to as *specific knowledge* (e.g., Adams, Bell, & Perfetti, 1995).	Adams et al. (1995); Droop and Verhoeven (1998); Hammadou (1991); Kobayashi (2009); Levine and Hause (1985); Marr and Gormley (1982); McNamara, Kintsch, Songer, and Kintsch (1996; Experiment 1); Miller and Keenan (2009)[2]; Ozuru et al. (2009); Pearson et al. (1979); Recht and Leslie (1988); Reutzel and Morgan (1990); Rydland et al. (2012); Stevens (1980); Tarchi (2010); Usó-Juan (2006); Wolfe and Woodwyk (2010).
Domain knowledge: Knowledge that is related to a disciplinary area, such as history or biology, or broad topic, such as baseball, but not necessarily related to the content of a particular text being used to assess comprehension in the study.	Measures of domain knowledge include open-ended (e.g., Gasparinatou & Grigoriadou, 2013), multiple choice (e.g., Britton, Stimson, Stennett, & Gülgöz, 1998; Tarchi (2010), fill-in-the-blank (McNamara et al., 1996), free association (e.g., Stahl, Hare, Sinatra, & Gregory, 1992), and familiarity checklist (e.g., Stahl et al.) items. Across studies, the relationship of domain knowledge to the content of comprehension passages varies. For example, O'Reilly and McNamara	Britton, Stimson, Stennett, and Gülgöz (1998); Gasparinatou and Grigoriadou (2013); Haenggi and Perfetti (1992); McNamara et al. (1996; Experiment 2); O'Reilly and McNamara (2007); Stahl et al. (1992); Tarchi (2010).

(Continued)

Table 13.1 (Cont.)

Definition	Operationalization	Examples of Studies
	(2007) created a composite variable for domain knowledge using multiple choice questions about biology and open-ended questions about cells and used this variable to predict comprehension on a passage about cell mitosis. Stahl et al. (1992) used a free association task that was more topically related to the comprehension passage (a particular event in baseball history) and a vocabulary checklist of baseball terminology as measures of domain knowledge of baseball. Britton et al. (1998) administered prior knowledge items that were related to the same historical period as the comprehension text, but varied in their closeness to the event discussed in the text (a particular event in the Vietnam War).	
World knowledge: General academic knowledge in areas such as science and the humanities; not intended to relate to the comprehension passage.	In studies of knowledge and comprehension, world knowledge has been assessed using standardized knowledge assessments (e.g., the WJ III ACH Academic Knowledge test, Schrank et al., 2001, in Best, Floyd, & McNamara, 2008), or open-ended items based on lists of general knowledge and cultural literacy (Kozminsky & Kozminsky, 2001). World knowledge is sometimes referred to as *general knowledge* (e.g., Kozminsky & Kosminsky).	Best et al. (2008); Kozminsky and Kosminsky (2001); McNamara, Ozuru, and Floyd (2011).
Cultural knowledge: Knowledge that is based in the socio-cultural experiences of the reader. Readers' knowledge may or may not be congruent with the themes and imagery in the text being read.	Studies of cultural knowledge and comprehension have considered alignment between readers' African American and Latino socio-cultural knowledge (e.g., Bell & Clark, 1998; Kelley, Siwatu, Tost, & Martinez, 2015) or religious knowledge (e.g., Lipson, 1983; Markham & Latham, 1987), and themes in the text. Cultural knowledge is not measured in these studies, but is assumed based on student characteristics (i.e., student identifies as Latino; student identifies as Jewish) or community characteristics (student attends a conservative Christian school; e.g., Mosborg, 2002).	Bell and Clark (1998); Kintsch and Greene (1978); Kelley et al. (2015); Lipson (1983); Markham and Latham (1987); McCullough (2013); Mosborg (2002); Pritchard (1990); Pulido (2004).

comprehension of texts on that topic. The researchers did not find an effect of background knowledge on the number of propositions recalled in a retelling, but the high knowledge group had significantly higher scores on three types of comprehension questions—textually explicit, textually implicit, and scriptally implicit. The difference was greatest with scriptally implicit questions, which rely most on the knowledge readers bring to the text. Marr and Gormley (1982) examined fourth graders' comprehension of passages on more and less familiar topics. For some topics, the familiar passage produced higher scores for recall of textual information, but for some it was the unfamiliar passage. Students gave a greater number of scriptal responses (correct information not explicitly stated in the passage) for familiar passages. What is most interesting is that, when students read pairs of passages within a broad topic domain—one more familiar and one less familiar—prior knowledge about the more familiar topic prior to reading predicted post-reading scriptal comprehension of the less familiar passage. This suggests that readers can reason from familiar to unfamiliar texts by analogy when the familiar knowledge has been activated.

Studies of domain knowledge have also shown an effect of knowledge on comprehension, although the impacts are more variable (Britton, Stimson, Stennett, & Gülgöz, 1998; Haenggi & Perfetti, 1992). For example, Stahl et al. (1992) evaluated the relative contributions of vocabulary knowledge and baseball knowledge to high school students' recall of a text on the retirement of Mets pitcher Tom Seaver's jersey number. They found that, while students with low prior knowledge were able to recall as many facts as those with high prior knowledge, the high knowledge participants were more likely to include gist statements in their recalls. The gist statements involved the articulation of themes from the text. Vocabulary knowledge predicted total idea units recalled better than prior knowledge, but did not predict the inclusion of gist statements in the recall. Unlike Stahl et al., Haenggi and Perfetti (1992) found that prior domain knowledge about problem-solving and decision-making made a significant contribution to adult reader's ability to answer text explicit questions about texts on human decision-making, but it did not impact readers' responses to questions requiring bridging inferences (text implicit questions that rely on connecting information within a passage). Domain knowledge did positively impact the ability of readers to correctly answer script implicit questions (those that require background knowledge) after reading an expository text. Although the results are somewhat varied across these studies—perhaps due in part to the different ways of defining domain knowledge in relation to the texts—both show an advantage for entering the reading situation with relevant knowledge.

The role of topic and domain knowledge on more complex forms of comprehension, such as understanding intertextual relations is less studied, but preliminary evidence suggests similarly positive impacts. For instance, Kobayashi (2009) examined the impact of topic knowledge on college students' recall of intratextual arguments from two texts on a controversial issue and their comprehension of intertextual relationships among the arguments presented by the two authors. Topic knowledge influenced comprehension of intertextual relations—points of agreement or disagreement or a writer's opinion about an issue—with recall of intratextual arguments as a mediator.

General World Knowledge

General world knowledge, typically defined as breadth of knowledge of school type topics (arts, humanities, sciences, etc.), has also shown positive effects on comprehension, particularly comprehension of expository text. For instance, Best et al. (2008) examined third grade students' comprehension of narrative and expository texts, using general world knowledge as a predictor. Students completed free recall, cued recall, and multiple-choice comprehension measures after reading, all of which were focused on recall of textbase and bridging inferences. The textbase questions were based on explicit text content (e.g., What did Salvador use to make his fort?); while the bridging inference questions were operationalized in this study as questions that required readers to connect textual information with existing world knowledge (e.g., Why was Salvador's Mama worried about Salvador?). The general world knowledge score did not have an impact on any of the comprehension measures for the narrative text when decoding ability was also entered into the regression model. For the expository text, world knowledge was a stronger predictor than decoding, accounting for substantial variance in the comprehension scores across three measures. In a later study, world knowledge was found to impact fourth graders' comprehension of both narrative and science texts using both recall and multiple choice comprehension measures (McNamara et al., 2011).

Inconsistencies in Knowledge-Comprehension Relationships

Some of the inconsistencies in the relationships between particular types of knowledge and particular types of comprehension are certainly due to variation, both in defining the type of knowledge in relation to a text and in operationalizing particular types of comprehension, but they also expose the complex network of factors that influence any particular act of comprehension. For example, the inconsistent impact of knowledge on narrative text may simply be because comprehension of narratives often relies less on the kinds of specialized, academic knowledge that is typically assessed in these studies—knowledge is often measured as knowledge of academic topics and disciplines—and because most children have knowledge about the structure, characters, events, and settings of stories (McNamara et al., 2011). In addition, expository texts may induce readers to use their prior knowledge more than narrative (Wolfe & Woodwyk, 2010). Wolfe and Woodwyk (2010) examined the processing of narrative and expository text among high- and low- knowledge readers. College-age participants read a narrative or expository text related to the circulatory system, stopping after each sentence to think aloud. After reading, they were asked to retell the text. There were 43 sentences in each text, ten of which were common across the texts. For both the common sentences and the sentences that were unique to each passage, participants who read the expository text made significantly more prior knowledge elaborations in their think alouds than those who read the narrative text. In addition, participants who read the expository texts recalled more content from the common sentences and more often shifted the order of the text in retelling it. The researchers suggest that this is evidence that readers of the expository text were doing more to integrate the text with prior knowledge. The knowledge scores were correlated with participants' retelling scores for the expository but not the narrative text. In addition to genre, the particular domain may also influence the relationship between knowledge and comprehension. Tarchi (2010) examined the impact of different kinds of prior knowledge on seventh graders' comprehension of text in two domains: science and history. In science, prior knowledge of facts (knowledge of the topic of the text) did not impact comprehension of the text, but domain knowledge in science and prior knowledge of meanings (key vocabulary words) explained significant variance in comprehension of the science passage; prior knowledge of meanings explained the most variance. For the history passage, all three knowledge variables explained significant variance in comprehension, and prior knowledge of facts explained the most variance. Tarchi explains these differences in terms of differences in how the subjects are learned.

Inconsistencies in the impact of knowledge on retelling may be due to the limitations of recall as an assessment of comprehension; it reveals little about the degree of integration of textual information with existing knowledge. Topic and domain knowledge may improve memory for text (recalling text or answering text explicit questions) by making it possible for an individual to store new information with related information in memory (Kostons & van der Werf, 2015).

When new information is integrated with existing information, memory for ideas in the text is likely improved. However, recall is not always evidence of integration with existing knowledge. Relatively simple and cohesive texts can probably be recalled, particularly in the short-term, without substantial integration with existing knowledge. Integration may depend on the reading situation and may rely on other kinds of reading comprehension skills. Hence, some studies show an impact of topic and domain knowledge on memory for text and others do not.

From the perspective of contemporary theories of comprehension, making inferences within text (text implicit or bridging inferences that require connecting information within a text) places greater demands on prior knowledge compared with recall. Knowledge may allow readers to both selectively focus on the most important ideas in a text and form stronger connections among individual elements. This helps readers connect a series of discrete pieces of information into meaningful chunks and chains, such as sequences, cause-effect relationships, and plots. Bridging inferences, as well as the script implicit inferences that require integration of text with prior knowledge, are important because they are stronger evidence of developing a situation model and, thus, learning from text (Kintsch, 1986).

It is not entirely clear why general world knowledge, operationalized as knowledge of academic subjects, would impact comprehension of narrative and expository texts. It may simply be that possessing high levels of world knowledge increases the likelihood that a reader will have relevant topic or domain knowledge when encountering a new text. Kozminsky and Kozminsky (2001) suggest that a rich base of experiences and ideas gives readers easier access to a wide variety of reading materials, enhancing comprehension because they will more often bring relevant knowledge to texts they read. The impact of general knowledge on comprehension may also be evidence of analogous learning, or the idea that knowing information provides leverage for understanding related topics. Marr and Gormley's (1982) study (described above) found evidence of this: when students read topically related texts (sports) that were more and less familiar (e.g., about baseball and curling) in close time proximity, their understanding of the less familiar topic was enhanced.

Knowledge and Reading Ability

A number of studies have examined the relative contributions of knowledge and reading ability, seeking to determine which makes the strongest contribution to comprehension of a particular text and whether having knowledge may compensate for weaknesses in reading ability (comprehension or decoding) or vice versa. When general reading comprehension ability and topic knowledge are used to predict comprehension of a text, both typically make contributions to comprehension. However, knowledge has been shown to be a more powerful predictor among elementary school students (e.g., Taylor, 1979), middle school students (e.g., Recht & Leslie, 1988), high school students (e.g., Cromley & Azevedo, 2007; Stevens, 1980), and adults (e.g., Ozuru et al., 2009).[1,2] For example, Recht and Leslie (1988) studied the impact of baseball knowledge and comprehension ability on middle school students' comprehension of a baseball story. Students with high prior knowledge about baseball performed better than those with low baseball knowledge on a range of comprehension tasks, including retelling, summarizing, re-enacting a story using figures, and identifying sentences that represent the most important from a set. Notably, high knowledge participants' retellings, summarizations, and re-enactments were not only judged to be better quantitatively (i.e., number of correct propositions recalled or moved re-enacted), than lower knowledge readers, they were also judged qualitatively better in terms of the degree to which the propositions and moves recalled were important to the story. Moreover, reading ability did not compensate for low knowledge, but high knowledge did compensate for low reading ability. That is, students with high reading ability but low knowledge of baseball performed no better on the recall and summarization tasks than students with low reading ability and low knowledge of baseball. Moreover, there was no benefit for high reading ability over high knowledge. That is, students with high reading ability and high knowledge did not perform better than students with low reading ability and high knowledge. Thus, knowledge was a powerful determinant of comprehension, compensating even for low comprehension ability. O'Reilly and McNamara (2007) examined the relative impact of knowledge and comprehension skill on college students' comprehension of high and low coherence science texts. Among readers with low levels of science knowledge, those with stronger comprehension skill had better comprehension, suggesting that comprehension skill provided some compensation for low knowledge.

Other studies have also found that prior knowledge seems to provide some compensation for readers classified as less skilled. Adams et al. (1995) studied the contributions of domain knowledge and general reading skill, as measured by a standardized reading assessment to comprehension. Boys in grades 4, 6, and 7 identified as high or low in football knowledge and high or low in word reading skill read domain general (fire) and domain specific (quarterback) stories and completed a comprehension assessment that included retelling and questions that probed for theme, setting, and recollection of a specific episode. The researchers found that both domain knowledge and reading skill contribute to reading comprehension. Readers with high skill/low knowledge and low knowledge/high skill readers had similar comprehension of the football passage, suggesting the possibility of a "trading relationship" between knowledge and skills (p. 320). However, the best comprehension scores were obtained by the high knowledge/high skill readers, which provided evidence of a complementary relationship between knowledge and reading skill.

Miller and Keenan (2009) found that prior knowledge can help compensate for the "centrality deficit," the fact that poor decoders show a bigger deficit than good decoders in recalling central information than peripheral information. Fourth and fifth grade students were identified as having no prior knowledge or some prior knowledge about Amelia Earhart before reading a passage about Earhart and producing a free recall of the text. Miller and Keenan found that the difference in recall of central ideas between good and poor decoders (identified using a composite of two word reading assessments) was smaller when students possessed prior knowledge.

Although knowledge often has a stronger impact on comprehension of a topic or domain relevant text than general comprehension skill, as measured by a standardized assessment, it is likely that knowledge and skill make complementary contributions to comprehension. Evidence of this comes from Cromley and Azevedo (2007), who found that vocabulary knowledge and topic knowledge were the strongest predictors of high school students' reading comprehension among a set of five predictors (background knowledge, inference, strategies, vocabulary, and word reading). However, part of the contribution of background knowledge to comprehension was mediated by students' inferencing ability and use of reading strategies, such as summarizing and predicting. Tarchi (2010) similarly found that inferencing ability mediated some of the relationship between prior knowledge and comprehension. Ahmed et al. (2016) examined sources of variance in middle and high school students and, like Cromley and Azevedo, found that vocabulary knowledge and topic knowledge explained the most variance in comprehension of a set of reading-related variables. However, Ahmed et al. found that students who had more knowledge were better able to make the inferences that contribute to text comprehension.

Recent research is helping to explain the contributions of knowledge and reading skill to comprehension. For example, knowledge helps readers fill in gaps in a text (Ozuru et al., 2009), use the context of a text to form connections across ideas (Chiesi et al., 1979; Rapp et al., 2007), form the kinds of rich associations with textual information that make texts more memorable

(Long, Prat, Johns, Morris, & Jonathan, 2008), and more readily construct main ideas because they can anticipate the meaning of a text and generate accurate hypotheses about the content and structure of the text (Afflerbach, 1990). Although prior knowledge of the topic of a text, the domain within which that topic resides, and knowledge of the world have generally positive impacts on comprehension, activation of this knowledge from memory and integration of knowledge with information in a text are complex and unreliable processes. Reading skill likely supports readers' ability to use knowledge in the interest of comprehension.

As Cook and O'Brien (2014) explain, activation and integration are viewed in contemporary theories of comprehension as "continuous and overlapping" processes. Information in the text continually activates knowledge from memory, but this process is fairly indiscriminate; that is, information from the text activates existing knowledge based on general overlap, rather than relevance to the text being read. Kintsch (1986) describes the randomness of the activation process as having advantages for flexibility and context sensitivity in the comprehension process. However, readers do not always automatically activate relevant knowledge from long-term memory (Kendeou & O'Brien, 2015; Kostons & van der Werf, 2015), and they are not always skilled at integrating knowledge with text in ways that support comprehension and learning (Kozminsky & Kozminsky, 2001), even when they have the knowledge needed to make knowledge-based inferences (Barnes, Ahmed, Barth, & Francis, 2015).

Reading comprehension skill, in general, and inferencing skill, in particular, may support the reader's ability to form the kinds of meaningful connections that lead to coherence (Oakhill & Yuill, 1996; Rapp et al., 2007). Because younger readers and less skilled comprehenders are less able to generate relevant inferences, they are sometimes unable to draw on knowledge to fill in gaps and establish coherence. For example, Brandão and Oakhill (2005) studied how and to what extent children leverage prior knowledge and information from text when answering questions after reading narrative text. The researchers asked 7- and 8-year olds to read narrative stories, answer literal and inferential questions, and justify their answers. The results showed that students most often relied on the text in answering questions, even questions that were designed to require integration between prior knowledge and textual information (gap-filling or script implicit inferences).

Less skilled comprehenders generate fewer bridging inferences and fewer intertextual inferences than more skilled comprehenders, even when they are equally able to recall information from text (e.g., Cain, Oakhill, Barnes, & Bryant, 2001; Long, Oppy, & Seely, 1997). In a study of 7- and 8-year old children, Cain et al. found that even when less skilled comprehenders were taught the knowledge needed to generate inferences, they did not make the inferences as often as more skilled readers. In addition, the sources of difficulty in generating inferences in response to open-ended questions were different for less skilled and more skilled comprehenders. Less skilled comprehenders had difficulty in the initial stage of the inference generation process: recalling the information from the text that was necessary to generate the inference. When more skilled comprehenders had difficulty generating inferences, the breakdown tended to occur later in the process, at the stage of integrating the text information with background knowledge.

Overall, this research suggests that knowledge and reading ability make complementary contributions to reading comprehension. Knowledge can provide some compensation for low reading ability, and high levels of reading skill can support comprehension for readers with less knowledge of the topic of a text, but neither alone is ideal. That is, having knowledge does not ensure readers will use it unless they are skilled and active comprehenders, and having reading skill may not be sufficient to develop rich understandings of text when knowledge is less available. The strongest comprehenders are those who are equipped with knowledge and skilled enough to leverage it.

Knowledge and Text Cohesion and Quality

Several studies have expanded our understanding of the role of knowledge in comprehension through the inclusion of text factors, such as explicitness of causal relationships in text (e.g., Reutzel & Morgan, 1990) and text coherence/cohesion (e.g. Gasparinatou & Grigoriadou, 2013; McKeown, Beck, Sinatra, & Loxterman, 1992; O'Reilly & McNamara, 2007). These studies have generally found a positive impact of knowledge on comprehension across text types (Gasparinatou & Grigoriadou, 2013; Reutzel & Morgan, 1990). For example Reutzel and Morgan (1990) found that fifth and sixth graders with moderate to high levels of prior knowledge performed better than students with low prior knowledge on a range of explicit and inferential comprehension tasks after reading social studies passages adapted to have high or low levels of transparency in representing causal relationships (explicitly identifying causal relationships using the word "because" or not).

Other studies have found a benefit to high knowledge readers' comprehension from reading less cohesive texts. This has been called the "reverse cohesion effect." For example, McNamara et al. (1996) found that high knowledge junior high school readers had better comprehension of low cohesion texts compared with high cohesion texts. In particular, the high knowledge readers performed better on bridging inference and problem solving tasks. The opposite was true for low knowledge readers. The researchers suggest that lower cohesion texts encourage high knowledge readers to use their knowledge to do more inferential processing. Gasparinatou and Grigoriadou (2013) similarly found that high knowledge university-level readers performed better on bridging inference questions and elaborative inference questions (those requiring linking text information and information from background knowledge) when reading a low cohesion text compared with a high cohesion text. The opposite was true for low-knowledge readers. Less cohesive texts may increase high knowledge readers' need to spontaneously generate inferences, resulting in better comprehension (Best, Rowe, Ozuru, & McNamara, 2005). In contrast, O'Reilly and McNamara (2007) found that readers with high comprehension skill and high knowledge performed better on text-based questions when reading a high cohesion text compared with a low cohesion text. The authors suggest that high skill readers consistently use their knowledge in comprehending, but those with less skill are induced to use their knowledge by less cohesive texts. Relatedly, Ozuru et al. (2009) found that, when college-age readers have high knowledge, lower reading skill, and are reading a highly cohesive text, they tend to read shallowly, as evidenced by lower performance on text-based questions (compared with reading of low cohesion texts).

Knowledge and Comprehension among L2 Readers

Consistent with research involving mainly first language speakers of English (L1), studies of second language learners of English and other languages (L2) have largely shown a positive impact of topic and domain knowledge on comprehension across age levels and text types (e.g., Chen & Donin, 1997; Hammadou, 1991; Levine & Hause, 1985; Usó-Juan, 2006). Usó-Juan (2006) found that English language proficiency is a more powerful predictor of comprehension than knowledge among college students reading informational booklets about tourism/marketing, engineering, and psychology, and that higher L2 language proficiency provided some compensation for low knowledge. Burgoyne, Whiteley, and Hutchinson (2013) examined the impact of an instructed knowledge base (facts about the topic of the comprehension passage taught prior to reading) on the reading comprehension of third grade students learning English as an additional language (EAL), and monolingual students matched on word reading accuracy. The students were taught background knowledge that they would need to combine with textual information in order to answer inferential comprehension questions (about a fictional community, the Gan people). Although the monolingual students had higher scores on a standardized comprehension assessment and text explicit comprehension questions, the EAL students performed as well as their monolingual peers on the inferential questions. This suggests that EAL students benefited from having been taught general knowledge and were as likely as their monolingual peers to use this knowledge to facilitate comprehension.

The L2 knowledge research differs from L1 research in its focus on the relationship between language development (in L1 and L2) and knowledge in comprehension, asking whether language proficiency impacts the ability of L2 readers to leverage their knowledge during reading. For example, Droop and Verhoeven (1998) examined the role of background knowledge in first- and second-language reading comprehension of Dutch, Turkish, and Moroccan children in the Netherlands. Droop and Verhoeven found that culturally-relevant topic knowledge impacted third grade L2 learners' comprehension of linguistically simple texts, but not more linguistically complex texts. The researchers suggest that the children were unable to benefit from their background knowledge when the texts were too linguistically challenging. Similarly, Levine and Hause (1985) examined the impact of topic knowledge on text explicit and script implicit comprehension among high school students learning Spanish as an additional language. The researchers found that students at two levels of L2 language proficiency received similar benefits of background knowledge on text explicit questions. However, students with higher levels of language proficiency benefited more on the script implicit questions.

Recent studies have sought to directly investigate how the impact of background knowledge on comprehension is mediated by L2 language proficiency. Rydland et al. (2012) examined the contributions of word decoding, first-language (L1) and second-language (L2) vocabulary and prior topic knowledge to L2 reading comprehension. Norwegian fifth grade students who were first language speakers of Turkish and Urdu read multiple texts on global warming and answered text-based or inferential questions. Prior knowledge of global warming explained the most variance on the comprehension questions, explaining significant variance in comprehension. The researchers also found a significant interaction between L2 vocabulary depth and prior knowledge, suggesting that students with less depth of vocabulary knowledge may have been less able to leverage their prior knowledge for comprehension.

The idea that readers need to reach a certain level of proficiency—or threshold—in a second language in order to leverage their reading skills and knowledge effectively has been tested in several studies. In some studies, a second, upper threshold has also been hypothesized based on the idea that the most proficient L2 readers will need to rely less on background knowledge than those with more moderate proficiency (Carrell, 1983). Researchers have found inconsistent empirical evidence for the thresholds, though these studies have largely relied on familiarity ratings or experiential indicators of knowledge rather than direct assessments of knowledge (Clapham, 2000; Krekeler, 2006; Ridgway, 1997). Clapham found evidence for an upper and lower threshold. Ridgway found a lower threshold but not an upper one among Turkish college students who were learning English and reading academic texts in English. Krekeler found an association between language proficiency and the impact of knowledge on comprehension among adult learners of German as an additional language, but was unable to identify a threshold.

Activating Knowledge

As discussed above, readers with less developed comprehension skill may have difficulty integrating background knowledge with information in a text in order to make necessary inferences to support comprehension, even when they have relevant prior knowledge (e.g., Cain et al., 2001).

As such, researchers have posited that it may be necessary to support students in activating their prior knowledge. The idea has been that we should help students bring relevant prior knowledge into the foreground so it can be leveraged during reading. Activating relevant knowledge is a common component of instructional strategies or intervention studies that target comprehension (e.g., Brown, Pressley, Van Meter, & Schuder, 1996; Ogle, 1986; Paris, Cross, & Lipson, 1984). Activating prior knowledge can take various forms in different studies and interventions, which may include asking students what they know about the topic of the text (e.g., Alvermann, Smith, & Readence, 1985), discussing prior experiences related to the text (e.g., Hansen, 1981), giving students a problem to think through or perspective to take prior to reading (e.g., Alvermann & Hague, 1989; Schmidt, De Volder, De Grave, Moust, & Patel, 1989), concept mapping (e.g., Amadieu et al., 2015), or asking students to activate their prior knowledge in order to predict what might happen in a text prior to reading (e.g., Ogle, 1986; Peeck, Van den Bosch, & Kreupeling, 1982). While some studies have shown a benefit for knowledge activation, others call into question the idea that activating prior knowledge is always beneficial for readers.

Activating prior knowledge may be beneficial to comprehension when students have relevant and accurate knowledge (e.g., Bransford & Johnson, 1972; Hansen, 1981; Schmidt et al., 1989; Spires & Donley, 1998). For example, Hansen (1981) found that second grade students in two knowledge activation conditions out-performed a no treatment group on comprehension questions, but not on free recall, after reading a story. In one treatment condition, students were told that activating prior knowledge is important, asked to discuss a prior experience that related to the story, and then made predictions about the story before reading. In the second condition, students practiced answering questions during the story that required inferences that made use of prior knowledge. Spires and Donley (1998) found that when high school students were taught a knowledge activation strategy, they showed stronger performance on application comprehension questions (open-ended questions addressing issues not directly discussed in the text and requiring the application of background knowledge) than peers who learned a main idea strategy or were in a non-instruction treatment, although there were no differences on literal comprehension questions. This aligns with the idea that background knowledge may be particularly useful in supporting inferential comprehension.

Studies show inconsistent results on whether activating students' prior knowledge supports comprehension when students' knowledge is not aligned with the information in the text. For example, Peeck et al. (1982) found that when fifth graders activated knowledge prior to reading a passage, they were more successful than students who did not activate relevant knowledge at learning information from the text that was inconsistent with their prior knowledge. In contrast, other studies (e.g., Alvermann et al., 1985; Van Loon, de Bruin, van Gog, T, & van Merriënboer, 2013) suggest that activating inaccurate prior knowledge may negatively impact text comprehension. For example, Alvermann et al. (1985) found that when sixth grade students activated relevant background knowledge prior to reading text that contained ideas that were incompatible with their existing knowledge, their prior knowledge interfered with comprehension by overriding the information in the text. In a later study, Alvermann and Hague (1989) found that alerting students to the fact that a text may not align with their prior knowledge was more effective than simply activating prior knowledge for supporting developmental studies of college students' reading comprehension.

Recent studies have moved beyond simply activating prior knowledge before reading to support students in using their knowledge to make inferences (e.g., Barth & Elleman, 2017; Elbro & Buch-Iversen, 2013). For example, Elbro and Buch-Iversen (2013) studied sixth grade students who received an eight-lesson instructional program in which they were taught to consider what they might learn from the text and what they might learn from their prior knowledge in order to make gap-filling inferences. Students practiced using graphic organizers which included boxes for "information from the reader" and "information from the text," leading to a box containing the gap-filling inference. Therefore, rather than being told to activate knowledge or learning that they should activate knowledge, students in this study *learned how to activate* their prior knowledge in order to make inferences that support comprehension. Results indicated significant benefits to inferencing and reading comprehension compared to a business-as-usual control. The reading comprehension measure involved students in reading short fiction and nonfiction passages and responding to literal and inferential questions.

Overall, activating relevant prior knowledge can support students' text comprehension. Yet, instructional factors (method for activating knowledge), learner factors (e.g., high/low knowledge), and text factors (texts that affirm knowledge/contradict knowledge) may lead to differential effectiveness of knowledge activation attempts for promoting comprehension. Moreover, as teachers may not be able to analyze all of these factors for each text that is encountered, it may be more useful to focus on explicitly teaching students how to use their existing background knowledge to support comprehension (e.g., Elbro & Buch-Iversen, 203) or on building knowledge for all students, rather than only on activating knowledge which is differentially distributed based on students' past experiences.

Summary

A substantial body of research suggests that domain and topic knowledge support comprehension across age groups and across text types, and likely provide the most support for the bridging inferences and script implicit inferences that are most closely related to the development of a situation model and learning from text. World knowledge also provides a benefit to comprehension, though it is less clear *how* world knowledge supports comprehension.

Knowledge seems to have a greater impact on text comprehension than do general reading comprehension or decoding skill, and knowledge may help to compensate for lower levels of comprehension and decoding skill. High comprehension skill may also provide some compensation for lower knowledge; however, the degree to which readers utilize their knowledge to good effect in reading is variable. Given this variability in leveraging knowledge for comprehension, researchers have focused on supporting students to activate their knowledge before or during reading, yet the impact of knowledge activation on reading comprehension has been variable across studies. Reading skill seems to help readers leverage knowledge effectively. Based on this research, it is reasonable to suggest that intentionally building students' knowledge through and around reading and supporting their ability to use that knowledge might be particularly useful in setting the conditions for comprehension of particular texts and for fueling comprehension of future texts.

Future Directions: Building and Leveraging Knowledge for Literacy Development

In the following section, we address key questions relating to the role of knowledge in current literacy research. We address new approaches to considering knowledge that might be generative as well as challenges and gaps in the research in these areas. We focus on three key areas of research that might provide generative opportunities for innovative new research. These include opportunities to build knowledge in support of comprehension, to leverage cultural knowledge, and to support other aspect of literacy development.

Opportunities to Build Knowledge to Support Text Comprehension

Building Knowledge

In light of the large and longstanding body of research demonstrating a significant, positive impact of knowledge on reading comprehension, the most important question for the current era may be how to approach ELA instruction as an opportunity for knowledge building. There has been a strong emphasis in the research-and-practice literature in reading education on activating prior knowledge for reading, but less emphasis on finding ways to build knowledge in support of reading comprehension. With some notable exceptions (e.g., Guthrie et al., 2004; Romance & Vitale, 1992), little attention has been paid to building knowledge that students might later activate either before reading or through readers' interactions with text. As a number of prominent literacy researchers have pointed out (e.g., Neuman & Celano, 2006; Palincsar & Duke, 2004), we have often focused on using texts primarily as sites for strategy and skill development, even when reading content-rich texts (Norris et al., 2008).

One challenge for approaches that focus on building knowledge is the history of English language arts policy and practice, which has often involved an artificial divide between learning-to-read and reading-to-learn. The idea that there is a necessary developmental sequence in which readers must first gain mastery over word reading before reading for meaning stems in part from a misapplication of Chall's (1983) description of the developmental stages through which readers progress on the way to mature reading (Invernizzi & Hayes, 2012). The learning-to-read versus reading-to-learn paradigm has been fueled by policies, such as the No Child Left Behind Act (2001) and its associated Reading First policy, which emphasized the skills of early reading in grades K-3. Closing this divide and recognizing the reciprocal nature of learning-to-read and reading-to-learn is necessary if we are to capitalize on research demonstrating the significance of knowledge for reading.

Several approaches for concurrently building students' knowledge and literacy point to potentially generative future directions. What is common to all of these approaches is that they conceptualize the building of knowledge as the development of rich conceptual understandings, rather than the acquisition of litanies of facts. This approach is better supported by contemporary theories of comprehension, which suggest that better elaborated and more connected sets of ideas provide advantages to readers as they work to establish and maintain coherence (Kintsch, 1988). Possessing many interconnected ideas about a topic or domain allows greater flexibility in forming connections with textual information.

Integrated Literacy and Content Area Instruction

Programs that situate attention to literacy development in content-rich or disciplinary instruction have shown promise for advancing students' content knowledge, reading and writing (e.g., grades k-4 in Connor et al., 2017; grades 1–2 in Vitale & Romance, 2010; grade 4 in Cervetti, Barber, Dorph, Pearson, & Goldschmidt, 2012; grade 5 in Guthrie et al., 2009; grades 2–5 in Romance & Vitale, 2001; grades 6–8 in Fang & Wei, 2010; grades 8–10 in Greenleaf et al., 2011; for both English Learners and non-English Learners in; Vaughn et al., 2017; for students with reading difficulties in Swanson et al., 2017). In each of these studies, integrated approaches have had larger impacts on students' content area learning and at least some dimensions of students' literacy development compared with approaches that offered separate content and literacy instruction. In one of these studies, Guthrie et al. compared the impacts of a 12-week intervention using a Concept-Oriented Reading Instruction (CORI) approach to traditional instruction. In the CORI condition, fifth grade students participated in hands-on science activities and associated reading and writing activities about ecology and life science. CORI includes attention to comprehension strategy instruction and in-depth content-area study, a promising combination based on the research reviewed earlier in this chapter. The CORI program is also guided by a set of motivational practices, including choice and collaboration and, in this intervention, provided additional support for students who were designated as low-achieving based on a standardized reading comprehension assessment. Compared with students who received traditional, separate science and language arts instruction, both low- and high-achieving CORI students made greater growth in their reading comprehension, word recognition, and science knowledge.

Disciplinary Literacy

The disciplinary literacy movement has introduced new ways of conceptualizing the relationship between knowledge and literacy (Greenleaf, current volume). In particular, this work has advanced our understanding of how reading is necessarily shaped by the nature of text and the disciplinary practices in which reading is situated. In addition, this literature has explored how literacy in disciplines is shaped by disciplinary forms of reasoning, inquiry, and argumentation (e.g., Rainey, 2017; Shanahan, Shanahan, & Misischia, 2011). With its focus on high level reasoning with text and on using multiple texts and experiences to engage in disciplinary inquiry and produce disciplinary arguments, disciplinary literacy has the potential to produce new kinds of intervention that engage students with sophisticated reasoning within and across texts while building specialized content knowledge.

Refutation Texts

Researchers have examined whether texts can be structured in ways that support knowledge building and conceptual change, particularly in the area of science (see Kendeou & O'Brien, 2015; Sinatra et al., 2011). For example, refutation texts (i.e., texts that directly address and refute students' misconceptions) have been studied as a way to build knowledge that may contradict what students already know (e.g., Alvermann & Hague, 1989; Diakidoy, Kendeou, & Ioannides, 2003, 1989; Mason, Gava, & Boldrin, 2008; Maria & MacGinitie, 1987; Mikkilä-Erdmann, 2001). For example, Alvermann and Hague (1989) found higher comprehension when college students enrolled in developmental studies read refutation texts as compared to more traditional science texts. Similarly, Diakidoy et al. (2003) found that sixth grade students learned more science concepts when a refutation science text was included in their science instruction compared to a more typical expository text or no additional science texts. There have been studies that demonstrate that refutation texts are not always effective. For example, Kendeou and van den Broek (2007) found that college students with misconceptions remembered less information from a science text than readers without misconceptions, whether they read a refutation text or a more traditional science text. These inconsistent findings may be explained by additional recent research. For example, Diakidoy, Mouskounti, and Ioannides (2011) found that, when compared to expository texts, refutation texts support global bridging and elaborative inferences but not text recall. This mirrors the research on prior knowledge and reading comprehension in suggesting a stronger impact on the generation of inferences than recall. Mason et al. (2008) found that students' interest in the topic and beliefs about scientific knowledge may impact the ways in which students respond to refutation texts.

In their Knowledge Revision Components (KRec) framework, Kendeou and O'Brien (2015) present a theoretical description of the process by which existing knowledge is revised during reading. The framework suggests that revision can only take place if the incorrect existing knowledge is activated with the new knowledge being encountered in text and if the new knowledge is integrated with existing knowledge, such that the representation of information in long-term memory is revised to take into account the new information. With the addition of more new information, the correct information comes to dominate and increasingly draw activations to it, rather than the previously existing incorrect information. Over time, interference from the old, incorrect information decreases.

Opportunities to Leverage Cultural Knowledge to Support Text Comprehension

A critical question for current research is how we might think about leveraging students' cultural knowledge in the interest of their literacy development. Studies have demonstrated that cultural knowledge is one type of knowledge that supports students' text comprehension (e.g., Bell & Clark, 1998; Kelley et al., 2015; Kintsch & Greene, 1978; McCullough, 2013; Pritchard, 1990; Pulido, 2004). For example, Bell and Clark studied 109 first through fourth grade African American students who listened to texts with black characters and themes consistent with sociocultural experiences of African Americans, or texts with white characters and traditional Euro-American themes. Students showed better recall and comprehension of texts with black characters and African American themes. Kelley et al. (2015) studied seventh grade students who self-identified as Hispanic or multi-racial with Hispanic origins, as they read a culturally familiar text (a Latino themed short story by Sandra Cisneros) and a culturally unfamiliar passage (a Native American themed passage). Students performed better on recall and comprehension questions when reading the culturally familiar text. In addition, students had higher self-efficacy when reading the culturally familiar text compared to the unfamiliar text.

Similarly, studies have demonstrated that readers' religious knowledge impacts their comprehension of text (e.g., Lipson, 1983; Markham & Latham, 1987). For example, Lipson studied fourth through sixth grade Catholic and Jewish students who each read a culturally neutral text and then a text with specific knowledge related to one of the two religious groups (either a passage on Bar Mitzvahs or First Communion). Lipson found that participants recalled more explicit and implicit information and included fewer errors in their recalls when reading a culturally familiar passage. Moreover, students' own cultural knowledge seemed to limit their retelling of texts about the unfamiliar religion. Mosborg (2002) studied how high school students used their knowledge of history as they read newspaper articles on school prayer and Starbucks' treatment of Guatemalan coffee workers. Mosborg examined ten students' think alouds and interview responses. While students used the same textbook, they attended two different schools. One of the schools had an explicitly Christian mission and drew students from mainly socially conservative families, while the other school drew students from more socially liberal families and did not have a religious orientation. Mosborg found that while the two groups of students used some of the same approaches to leveraging history for the explication of ideas in the text, they ultimately interpreted the texts differently.

Therefore, there is promising research demonstrating that cultural knowledge impacts text comprehension, yet there is little evidence that this type of knowledge has been used purposefully in classroom instruction with the goal of supporting students' reading comprehension. While there is a growing body of literature focused on incorporating students' socio-cultural funds of knowledge (Moll, Amanti, Neff, & Gonzalez, 1992) to promote culturally sustaining (Paris, 2012) and culturally relevant (Ladson-Billings, 2014) literacy instruction, there remains substantial work to be done in bridging these lines of literature with the research on cultural knowledge and reading comprehension in order to build instructional programs that leverage these ideas.

Opportunities to Leverage Knowledge to Support Word Learning and Strategy Development

The research on knowledge and reading has focused primarily on the role of existing background knowledge in text comprehension, but recent research has started to explore the potential of knowledge to support other aspects of literacy development. This work is premised in part on the idea that possessing relevant knowledge contributes to the efficient allocation of attention, so attentional resources can be devoted to other aspects of literacy development. In addition, in helping students develop a coherent mental model of the text, knowledge provides a basis for engaging in sophisticated problem-solving with text, including inferring the meanings of unknown words and learning to apply cognitive strategies.

Several studies have demonstrated that strong background knowledge of a text supports higher rates of incidental vocabulary learning while reading (e.g., Pulido, 2003, 2004, 2007). For example, Pulido (2004) found that adult participants who read culturally familiar versions of everyday scenarios gained more knowledge of unknown (nonsense) words than did participants who read culturally unfamiliar narratives. Pulido (2007) examined the effect of topic familiarity and passage sight vocabulary on lexical inferencing and retention in a second language. Participants were adult second language learners of Spanish. Participants read narrative passages designed to be more and less familiar. Participants were asked to translate nonsense words embedded in the passages as they read and to indicate the level of difficulty in inferring the meaning of each word. Topic familiarity was a significant predictor of correct lexical inferencing, and higher scores on a retention task, though not on a production measure (translation). Cervetti, Wright, & Hwang (2016) found that when fourth grade students built knowledge by reading a set of conceptually related informational texts, they learned more vocabulary incidentally than peers who read an unrelated set of texts. Kaefer, Neuman, and Pinkham (2015) also found evidence with preschool children that knowledge facilitates vocabulary learning from text.

Diakidoy (1998) examined the relationship between comprehension of a particular text and word learning among sixth graders who read expository social studies passages. Diakidoy found that students who had higher comprehension of the text acquired more knowledge of low-frequency, target vocabulary word meanings from context than did students with poor comprehension of the text, independent of the students' breadth of prior word knowledge. However, Diakidoy did not control for other student factors, such as comprehension skill. Barnes, Ginther, and Cochran (1989) did account for comprehension skill in their examination of eighth graders' word learning from context when taught or not taught relevant information about the passage in advance. The researchers found that word learning from context did not differ between good and poor comprehenders when the readers' comprehension was fueled by teaching information relevant to the content of the passage in advance. Together, these studies suggest that knowledge and comprehension might be a particularly powerful combination in support of students' incidental vocabulary acquisition.

There is also preliminary evidence that knowledge provides a basis for students to become more skilled comprehenders. Gaultney (1995) asked whether prior knowledge can facilitate the acquisition of a reading comprehension strategy. Boys who were poor readers and who were baseball experts were trained in the comprehension strategy of asking why questions using either baseball stories or non-baseball stories. Compared with boys who were trained using non-baseball stories, boys who were trained on the strategy using baseball stories demonstrated better acquisition of the strategy, and they asked more why questions in both proximal and distal post-tests. Gaultney suggests that the use of materials for which participants had a great deal of expert knowledge facilitated comprehension, allowing more capacity to be devoted to strategy acquisition. Together, these findings suggest that there may be a "knowledge effect" (Cervetti, Wright,

& Hwang, 2016), whereby knowledge frees up attentional resources to enable students to focus on other aspects of reading (e.g., new words, new strategies). This is an important idea for further research to explore.

Conclusions

As we suggested at the outset of this review, theory and empirical research substantiate the significant role of knowledge in reading, casting doubt on approaches to literacy development that position skill-building as a prerequisite for engaging with texts as sources for acquiring knowledge about the world. Reading to learn is a support for learning to read and should be a focus of literacy instruction from the earliest years of schooling. This research also casts doubt on approaches to reading comprehension assessment that do not account for the knowledge students bring to the text.

The substantial research on knowledge and comprehension has largely impacted practice through instructional routines that activate students' knowledge prior to reading. Activating knowledge has shown promise for supporting comprehension, but knowledge activation advantages students who come to school with the type of knowledge that appears in school texts. Moving forward, we hope to see a shift toward knowledge building in literacy research and practice, as well as additional research exploring the potential of knowledge building to support other aspects of students' literacy development, such as the acquisition of word knowledge and strategic skill that has shown promise in existing research. As we further explore the potential of knowledge building, we should consider broader conceptions of knowledge, including the ways that conceptual knowledge, disciplinary knowledge, world knowledge, and cultural knowledge might be built and leveraged to support students' engagement with text.

While the research described in this chapter indicates that knowledge and inferencing skill are critical for reading comprehension (e.g., Cain et al., 2001), future research should also further examine the ways that they might interact to support text comprehension. In particular, research should continue to consider ways that students can be taught how to integrate their knowledge with the content of the text in order to make inferences that support comprehension (Elbro & Buch-Iversen, 2013). The interface of knowledge and skill development is a particularly generative area for future scholarship as we seek to support students in understanding and learning from text.

Notes

1 Ozuru et al. (2009), Recht and Leslie (1988), Taylor (1979), and Stevens (1980) used standardized comprehension measures as an indicator of reading ability. Cromley and Azevedo (2007) used a word reading composite score to study the relative contribution of reading ability and knowledge, as well as several other variables, to comprehension.
2 Use the term "topic domain knowledge" (p. 104) to refer to knowledge of the topic of the comprehension text.

References

Adams, B. C., Bell, L. S., & Perfetti, C. A. (1995). A trading relationship between reading skill and domain knowledge in children's text comprehension. *Discourse Processes*, *20*(3), 307–323.
Afflerbach, P. P. (1990). The influence of prior knowledge on expert readers' main idea construction strategies. *Reading Research Quarterly*, *25*, 31–46.
Ahmed, Y., Francis, D. J., York, M., Fletcher, J. M., Barnes, M. A., & Kulesz, P. (2016). Validation of the direct and mediation (DIME) model of reading comprehension in grades 7 through 12. *Contemporary Educational Psychology*, *44*, 68–82.

Alexander, P. A., Kulikowich, J. M., & Schulze, S. K. (1994). How subject-matter knowledge affects recall and interest. *American Educational Research Journal, 31*(2), 313–337.

Alvermann, D. E., & Hague, S. A. (1989). Comprehension of counterintuitive science text: Effects of prior knowledge and text structure. *The Journal of Educational Research, 82*(4), 197–202.

Alvermann, D. E., Smith, L. C., & Readence, J. E. (1985). Prior knowledge activation and the comprehension of compatible and incompatible text. *Reading Research Quarterly, 20*(4), 420–436.

Amadieu, F., Salmerón, L., Cegarra, J., Paubel, P. V., Lemarié, J., & Chevalier, A. (2015). Learning from concept mapping and hypertext: An eye tracking study. *Journal of Educational Technology & Society, 18*(4), 100–112.

Anderson, R. C., & Pearson, P. D. (1984). A schema-theoretic view of basic processes in reading comprehension. In P. D. Pearson, R. Barr, M. L. Kamil, & P. Mosenthal (Eds.), *Handbook of reading research* (pp. 255–292). New York, NY: Longman.

Anderson, R. C., Reynolds, R. E., Schallert, D. L., & Goetz, E. T. (1977). Frameworks for comprehending discourse. *American Educational Research Journal, 14*(4), 367–381.

Anderson, R. C., Spiro, R. J., & Anderson, M. C. (1978). Schemata as scaffolding for the representation of information in connected discourse. *American Educational Research Journal, 15*(3), 433–440.

Ausubel, D. P. (1963). *The psychology of meaningful verbal learning.* New York, NY: Grune & Stratton.

Ausubel, D. P. (1968). *Educational psychology: A cognitive view.* New York, NY: Holt, Rinehart, and Winston, Inc.

Barnes, J. A., Ginther, D. W., & Cochran, S. (1989). Schema and purpose in reading comprehension and learning vocabulary from context. *Reading Research and Instruction, 28*(2), 16–28.

Barnes, M. A., Ahmed, Y., Barth, A., & Francis, D. J. (2015). The relation of knowledge-text integration processes and reading comprehension in 7th- to 12th-grade students. *Scientific Studies of Reading, 19*(4), 253–272.

Barth, A. E., & Elleman, A. (2017). Evaluating the impact of a multistrategy inference intervention for middle-grade struggling readers. *language, speech, and Hearing Services in Schools, 48*(1), 31–41.

Bartlett, F. C. (1932). *Remembering: A study in experimental and social psychology.* Boston, MA: Cambridge University Press.

Bell, Y. R., & Clark, T. R. (1998). Culturally relevant reading material as related to comprehension and recall in African American children. *Journal of Black Psychology, 24*, 455–475.

Best, R. M., Floyd, R. G., & McNamara, D. S. (2008). Differential competencies contributing to children's comprehension of narrative and expository texts. *Reading Psychology, 29*(2), 137–164.

Best, R. M., Rowe, M., Ozuru, Y., & McNamara, D. S. (2005). Deep-level comprehension of science texts: The role of the reader and the text. *Topics in Language Disorders, 25*(1), 65–83.

Brandão, A. C. P., & Oakhill, J. (2005). "How do you know this answer?"—Children's use of text data and general knowledge in story comprehension. *Reading and Writing, 18*(7), 687–713.

Bransford, J. D., & Johnson, M. K. (1972). Contextual prerequisites for understanding: Some investigations of comprehension and recall. *Journal of Verbal Learning and Verbal Behavior, 11*(6), 717–726.

Britton, B. K., Stimson, M., Stennett, B., & Gülgöz, S. (1998). Learning from instructional text: Test of an individual-differences model. *Journal of Educational Psychology, 90*(3), 476–491.

Brown, R., Pressley, M., Van Meter, P., & Schuder, T. (1996). A quasi-experimental validation of transactional strategies instruction with low-achieving second-grade students. *Journal of Educational Psychology, 88*(1), 18–37.

Burgoyne, K., Whiteley, H. E., & Hutchinson, J. M. (2013). The role of background knowledge in text comprehension for children learning English as an additional language. *Journal of Research in Reading, 36*(2), 132–148.

Cain, K., Oakhill, J. V., Barnes, M. A., & Bryant, P. E. (2001). Comprehension skill, inference-making ability, and their relation to knowledge. *Memory & Cognition, 29*(6), 850–859.

Carrell, P. L. (1983). Three components of background knowledge in reading comprehension. *Language Learning, 33*(2), 183–203.

Cervetti, G. N., Barber, J., Dorph, R., Pearson, P. D., & Goldschmidt, P. (2012). The impact of an integrated approach to science and literacy in elementary school classrooms. *Journal of Research in Science Teaching, 49*(5), 631–658.

Cervetti, G. N., Wright, T. S., & Hwang, H. (2016). Conceptual coherence, comprehension, and vocabulary acquisition: A knowledge effect?. *Reading and Writing, 29*(4), 761–779.

Chall, J. S. (1983). *Stages of reading development* (1st ed.). Fort Worth, TX: Harcourt Brace College.

Chen, Q., & Donin, J. (1997). Discourse processing of first and second language biology texts: Effects of language proficiency and domain-specific knowledge. *The Modern Language Journal, 81*(2), 209–227.

Chiesi, H. I., Spilich, G. J., & Voss, J. F. (1979). Acquisition of domain related information in relation to high and low domain knowledge. *Journal of Verbal Learning and Verbal Behavior, 18*(3), 275–290.

Clapham, C. (2000). Assessment for academic purposes: Where next? *System, 28*(4), 511–521.

Connor, C. M., Dombek, J., Crowe, E. C., Spencer, M., Tighe, E. L., Coffinger, S., Zarger, E., Wood, T., & Petscher, Y. (2017). Acquiring science and social studies knowledge in kindergarten through fourth grade: Conceptualization, design, implementation, and efficacy testing of content-area literacy instruction (CALI). *Journal of Educational Psychology, 109*(3), 301–320.

Cook, A. E., & Guéraud, S. (2005). What have we been missing? The role of general world knowledge in discourse processing. *Discourse Processes, 39*(2&3), 265–278.

Cook, A. E., & O'Brien, E. J. (2014). Knowledge activation, integration, and validation during narrative text comprehension. *Discourse Processes, 51*(1-2), 26–49.

Cromley, J. G., & Azevedo, R. (2007). Testing and refining the direct and inferential mediation model of reading comprehension. *Journal of Educational Psychology, 99*(2), 311–325.

Davis, D. S., Huang, B., & Yi, T. (2017). Making sense of science texts: A mixed methods examination of predictors and processes of multiple-text comprehension. *Reading Research Quarterly, 52*(2), 227–252.

Diakidoy, I. A. N. (1998). The role of reading comprehension in word meaning acquisition during reading. *European Journal of Psychology of Education, 13*(2), 131–154.

Diakidoy, I. A. N., Kendeou, P., & Ioannides, C. (2003). Reading about energy: The effects of text structure in science learning and conceptual change. *Contemporary Educational Psychology, 28*(3), 335–356.

Diakidoy, I. A. N., Mouskounti, T., & Ioannides, C. (2011). Comprehension and learning from refutation and expository texts. *Reading Research Quarterly, 46*(1), 22–38.

Droop, M., & Verhoeven, L. (1998). Background knowledge, linguistic complexity, and second-language reading comprehension. *Journal of Literacy Research, 30*(2), 253–271.

Elbro, C., & Buch-Iversen, I. (2013). Activation of background knowledge for inference making: Effects on reading comprehension. *Scientific Studies of Reading, 17*(6), 435–452.

Fang, Z., & Wei, Y. (2010). Improving middle school students' science literacy through reading infusion. *The Journal of Educational Research, 103*(4), 262–273.

Gasparinatou, A., & Grigoriadou, M. (2013). Exploring the effect of background knowledge and text cohesion on learning from texts in computer science. *Educational Psychology, 33*(6), 645–670.

Gaultney, J. F. (1995). The effect of prior knowledge and metacognition on the acquisition of a reading comprehension strategy. *Journal of Experimental Child Psychology, 59*(1), 142–163.

Goetz, E. T., Schallert, D. L., Reynolds, R. E., & Radin, D. I. (1983). Reading in perspective: What real cops and pretend burglars look for in a story. *Journal of Educational Psychology, 75*(4), 500.

Graesser, A. C., Singer, M., & Trabasso, T. (1994). Constructing inferences during narrative text comprehension. *Psychological Review, 101*(3), 371–395.

Greenleaf, C. L., Litman, C., Hanson, T. L., Rosen, R., Boscardin, C. K., Herman, J., Schneider, S. A., & Jones, B. (2011). Integrating literacy and science in biology: Teaching and learning impacts of reading apprenticeship professional development. *American Educational Research Journal, 48*(3), 647–717.

Guthrie, J. T., McRae, A., Coddington, C. S., Klauda, S. L., Wigfield, A., & Barbosa, P. (2009). Impacts of comprehensive reading instruction on diverse outcomes of low- and high-achieving readers. *Journal of Learning Disabilities, 42*(3), 195–214.

Guthrie, J. T., Wigfield, A., Barbosa, P., Perencevich, K. C., Taboada, A., Davis, M. H., Scafiddi, N., & Tonks, S. (2004). Increasing reading comprehension and engagement through concept-oriented reading instruction. *Journal of Educational Psychology, 96*(3), 403.

Haenggi, D., & Perfetti, C. A. (1992). Individual differences in reprocessing of text. *Journal of Educational Psychology, 84*(2), 182–192.

Hammadou, J. (1991). Interrelationships among prior knowledge, inference, and language proficiency in foreign language reading. *Modern Language Journal, 75*(1), 27–38.

Hansen, J. (1981). The effects of inference training and practice on young children's reading comprehension. *Reading Research Quarterly, 16*(3), 391–417.

Invernizzi, M., & Hayes, L. (2012). Should the focus of literacy education be on "reading to learn" or "learning to read?" [The counterpoint position]. In A. J. Eackle (Ed.), *Curriculum and instruction: Debating issues in American education* (pp. 82–89). Thousand Oaks, CA: Sage.

Kaefer, T., Neuman, S. B., & Pinkham, A. M. (2015). Pre-existing background knowledge influences socio-economic differences in preschoolers' word learning and comprehension. *Reading Psychology, 36*(3), 203–231.doi:10.1080/02702711.2013.843064

Kelley, H. M., Siwatu, K. O., Tost, J. R., & Martinez, J. (2015). Culturally familiar tasks on reading performance and self-efficacy of culturally and linguistically diverse students. *Educational Psychology in Practice, 31*(3), 293–313.

Kendeou, P., & O' Brien, E. J. (2015). Prior knowledge: Acquisition andrRevision. In P. Afflerbach (Ed.), *Handbook of individual differences in reading: Text and context* (pp. 151–163). New York, NY: Routledge Publishing.

Kendeou, P., & van den Broek, P. (2007). The effects of prior knowledge and text structure on comprehension processes during reading of scientific texts. *Memory & Cognition, 35*(7), 1567–1577.

Kintsch, W. (1986). Learning from text. *Cognition and Instruction, 3*(2), 87–108.

Kintsch, W. (1988). The role of knowledge in discourse comprehension: A construction-integration model. *Psychological Review, 95*(2), 163–182.

Kintsch, W. (1998). *Comprehension: A paradigm for cognition*. London, UK: Cambridge University Press.

Kintsch, W., & Greene, E. (1978). The role of culture-specific schemata in the comprehension and recall of stories. *Discourse Processes, 1*, 1–13.

Kobayashi, K. (2009). The influence of topic knowledge, external strategy use, and college experience on students' comprehension of controversial texts. *Learning and Individual Differences, 19*(1), 130–134.

Kostons, D., & van der Werf, G. (2015). The effects of activating prior topic and metacognitive knowledge on text comprehension scores. *British Journal of Educational Psychology, 85*(3), 264–275.

Kozminsky, E., & Kozminsky, L. (2001). How do general knowledge and reading strategies ability relate to reading comprehension of high school students at different educational levels? *Journal of Research in Reading, 24*(2), 187–204.

Krekeler, C. (2006). Language for special academic purposes (LSAP) testing: The effect of background knowledge revisited. *Language Testing, 23*(1), 99–130.

Ladson-Billings, G. (2014). Culturally relevant pedagogy 2.0: Aka the remix. *Harvard Educational Review, 84*(1), 74–84.

Levine, M. G., & Hause, G. J. (1985). The effect of background knowledge on the reading comprehension of second language learners. *Foreign Language Annals, 18*(5), 391–397.

Lipson, M. Y. (1983). The influence of religious affiliation on children's memory for text information. *Reading Research Quarterly, 18*(4), 448–457.

Long, D. L., Oppy, B. J., & Seely, M. R. (1997). Individual differences in readers' sentence- and text-level representations. *Journal of Memory & Language, 36*(1), 129–145.

Long, D. L., Prat, C., Johns, C., Morris, P., & Jonathan, E. (2008). The importance of knowledge in vivid text memory: An individual-differences investigation of recollection and familiarity. *Psychonomic Bulletin & Review, 15*(3), 604–609.

Maria, K., & MacGinitie, W. (1987). Learning from texts that refute the reader's prior knowledge. *Literacy Research and Instruction, 26*(4), 222–238.

Markham, P., & Latham, M. (1987). The influence of religion-specific background knowledge on the listening comprehension of adult second-language students. *Language Learning, 37*(2), 157–170.

Marr, M. B., & Gormley, K. (1982). Children's recall of familiar and unfamiliar text. *Reading Research Quarterly, 18*(1), 89–104.

Mason, L., Gava, M., & Boldrin, A. (2008). On warm conceptual change: The interplay of text, epistemological beliefs, and topic interest. *Journal of Educational Psychology, 100*(2), 291.

McCullough, R. G. (2013). The relationship between reader response and prior knowledge on African American students' reading comprehension performance using multicultural literature. *Reading Psychology, 34*(5), 397–435.

McKeown, M. G., Beck, I. L., Sinatra, G. M., & Loxterman, J. A. (1992). The contribution of prior knowledge and coherent text to comprehension. *Reading Research Quarterly, 27*(1), 78–93.

McNamara, D. S., Kintsch, E., Songer, N. B., & Kintsch, W. (1996). Are good texts always better? Interactions of text coherence, background knowledge, and levels of understanding in learning from text. *Cognition and Instruction, 14*(1), 1–43.

McNamara, D. S., Ozuru, Y., & Floyd, R. G. (2011). Comprehension challenges in the fourth grade: The roles of text cohesion, text genre, and readers' prior knowledge. *International Electronic Journal of Elementary Education, 4*(1), 229–257.

Mikkilä-Erdmann, M. (2001). Improving conceptual change concerning photosynthesis through text design. *Learning and Instruction, 11*(3), 241–257.

Miller, A. C., & Keenan, J. M. (2009). How word decoding skill impacts text memory: The centrality deficit and how domain knowledge can compensate. *Annals of Dyslexia, 59*(2), 99–113.

Moll, L. C., Amanti, C., Neff, D., & Gonzalez, N. (1992). Funds of knowledge for teaching: Using a qualitative approach to connect homes and classrooms. *Theory into Practice*, *31*(2), 132–141.

Mosborg, S. (2002). Speaking of history: How adolescents use their knowledge of history in reading the daily news. *Cognition and Instruction*, *20*(3), 323–358.

Neuman, S. B., & Celano, D. (2006). The knowledge gap: Implications of leveling the playing field for low income and middle income children. *Reading Research Quarterly*, *41*(2), 176–201.

No Child Left Behind Act of 2001, ESEA, 2001, Title 1, Part B, Subpart 1.

Norris, S. P., Phillips, L. M., Smith, M. L., Guilbert, S. M., Stange, D. M., Baker, J. J., & Weber, A. C. (2008). Learning to read scientific text: Do elementary school commercial reading programs help. *Science Education*, *92*(5), 765–798.

O'Reilly, T., & McNamara, D. S. (2007). Reversing the reverse cohesion effect: Good texts can be better for strategic, high-knowledge readers. *Discourse Processes*, *43*(2), 121–152.

Oakhill, J., & Yuill, N. (1996). Higher order factors in comprehension disability: Processes and remediation. In C. Cornaldi & J. Oakhill (Eds.), *Reading comprehension difficulties: Processes and intervention* (pp. 69–92). Mahwah, NJ: Erlbaum.

Ogle, D. M. (1986). KWL: A teaching model that develops active reading of expository text. *The Reading Teacher*, *39*(6), 564–570.

Ozuru, Y., Dempsey, K., & McNamara, D. S. (2009). Prior knowledge, reading skill, and text cohesion in the comprehension of science texts. *Learning and Instruction*, *19*(3), 228–242.

Palincsar, A. S., & Duke, N. K. (2004). The role of text and text-reader interactions in young children's reading development and achievement. *The Elementary School Journal*, *105*(2), 183–197.

Paris, D. (2012). Culturally sustaining pedagogy: A needed change in stance, terminology, and practice. *Educational Researcher*, *41*(3), 93–97.

Paris, S. G., Cross, D. R., & Lipson, M. Y. (1984). Informed Strategies for Learning: A program to improve children's reading awareness and comprehension. *Journal of Educational Psychology*, *76*(6), 1239.

Pearson, P. D., Hansen, J., & Gordon, C. (1979). The effect of background knowledge on young children's comprehension of explicit and implicit information. *Journal of Reading Behavior*, *11*(3), 201–209.

Peeck, J., Van den Bosch, A. B., & Kreupeling, W. J. (1982). Effect of mobilizing prior knowledge on learning from text. *Journal of Educational Psychology*, *74*(5), 771–777.

Pritchard, R. (1990). The effects of cultural schemata on reading processing strategies. *Reading Research Quarterly*, *25*(4), 273–295.

Pulido, D. (2003). Modeling the role of second language proficiency and topic familiarity in second language incidental vocabulary acquisition through reading. *Language Learning*, *53*(2), 233–284.

Pulido, D. (2004). The relationship between text comprehension and second language incidental vocabulary acquisition: A matter of topic familiarity? *Language Learning*, *54*(3), 469–523.

Pulido, D. (2007). The effects of topic familiarity and passage sight vocabulary on L2 lexical inferencing and retention through reading. *Applied Linguistics*, *28*(1), 66–86.

Rainey, E. (2017). Disciplinary literacy in English Language Arts: Exploring the social and problem-based nature of literacy reading and reasoning. *Reading Research Quarterly*, *52*(1), 53–71.

Rapp, D. N., van den Broek, P., McMaster, K. L., Kendeou, P., & Espin, C. A. (2007). Higher-order comprehension processes in struggling readers: A perspective for research and intervention. *Scientific Studies of Reading*, *11*(4), 289–312.

Recht, D. R., & Leslie, L. (1988). Effect of prior knowledge on good and poor readers' memory of text. *Journal of Educational Psychology*, *80*(1), 16–20.

Reutzel, R. D., & Morgan, B. C. (1990). Effects of prior knowledge, explicitness, and clause order on children's comprehension of causal relationships. *Reading Psychology*, *11*(2), 93–114.

Ridgway, T. (1997). Thresholds of background knowledge effect in foreign language reading. *Reading in a Foreign Language*, *11*, 151–166.

Romance, N. R., & Vitale, M. R. (1992). A curriculum strategy that expands time for in-depth elementary science instruction by using science based reading strategies: Effects of a year long study in grade four. *Journal of Research in Science Teaching*, *29*(6), 545–554.

Romance, N. R., & Vitale, M. R. (2001). Implementing an in-depth expanded science model in elementary schools: Multi-year findings, research issues, and policy implications. *International Journal of Science Education*, *23*(4), 272–304.

Rydland, V., Aukrust, V. G., & Fulland, H. (2012). How word decoding, vocabulary and prior topic knowledge predict reading comprehension. A study of language-minority students in Norwegian fifth grade classrooms. *Reading and Writing: An Interdisciplinary Journal*, *25*(2), 465–482.

Schmidt, H. G., De Volder, M. L., De Grave, W. S., Moust, J. H., & Patel, V. L. (1989). Explanatory models in the processing of science text: The role of prior knowledge activation through small-group discussion. *Journal of Educational Psychology, 81*(4), 610.

Schrank, F., McGew, K., & Woodcock, R. (2001). *Woodcock Johnson achievement test III*. Itasca, IL: Riverside Publishing.

Shanahan, C., Shanahan, T., & Misischia, C. (2011). Analysis of expert readers in three disciplines: History, mathematics, and chemistry. *Journal of Literacy Research, 43*(4), 393–429.

Sinatra, G. M., & Broughton, S. H. (2011). Bridging reading comprehension and conceptual change in science education: The promise of refutation text. *Reading Research Quarterly, 46*(4), 374–393.

Spires, H. A., & Donley, J. (1998). Prior knowledge activation: Inducing engagement with informational texts. *Journal of Educational Psychology, 90*(2), 249–260.

Stahl, S. A., Hare, V. C., Sinatra, R., & Gregory, J. F. (1992). Defining the role of prior knowledge and vocabulary in reading comprehension: The retiring of number 41. *Journal of Reading Behavior, 23*(4), 487–508.

Stevens, K. C. (1980). The effect of background knowledge on the reading comprehension of ninth graders. *Journal of Reading Behavior, 12*(2), 151–154.

Swanson, E., Wanzek, J., Vaughn, S., Fall, A., Roberts, G., Hall, C., & Miller, V. L. (2017). Middle school reading comprehension and content learning intervention for below-average readers. *Reading & Writing Quarterly, 33*(1), 37–53.

Taft, M. L., & Leslie, L. (1985). The effects of prior knowledge and oral reading accuracy on miscues and comprehension. *Journal of Reading Behavior, 17*(2), 163–179.

Tarchi, C. (2010). Reading comprehension of informative texts in secondary school: A focus on direct and indirect effects of reader's prior knowledge, *Learning and Individual Differences, 20*, 415–420.

Taylor, B. M. (1979). Good and poor readers' recall of familiar and unfamiliar text. *Journal of Reading Behavior, 11*(4), 375–380.

Usó-Juan, E. (2006). The compensatory nature of discipline-knowledge and English- language proficiency in reading English for academic purposes. *Modern Language Journal, 90*, 210–227.

van den Broek, P., Risden, K., Fletcher, C. R., & Thurlow, R. (1996). A "landscape" view of reading. Fluctuating patterns of activation and the construction of a stable memory representation. In B. K. Britton & A. C. Greasser (Eds.), *Models of understanding text* (pp. 165–187). Hillsdale, NJ: Lawrence Erlbaum Associates.

van Loon, M. H., de Bruin, A. B., van Gog, T., & van Merriënboer, J. J. (2013). Activation of inaccurate prior knowledge affects primary-school students' metacognitive judgments and calibration. *Learning and Instruction, 24*, 15–25.

Vaughn, S., Martinez, L. R., Wanzek, J., Roberts, G., Swanson, E., & Fall, A. (2017). Improving content knowledge and comprehension for english language learners: Findings from a randomized control trial. *Journal of Educational Psychology, 109*(1), 22–34.

Vitale, M. R., & Romance, N. R. (2010). *Effects of an integrated instructional model for accelerating student achievement in science and reading comprehension in grades 1-2*. Paper presented at the Annual Meeting of the American Educational Research Association, Denver, CO.

Walker, C. H. (1987). Relative importance of domain knowledge and overall aptitude on acquisition of domain-related information. *Cognition and Instruction, 4*(1), 25–42.

Wolfe, M. B., & Woodwyk, J. M. (2010). Processing and memory of information presented in narrative or expository texts. *British Journal of Educational Psychology, 80*(3), 341–362.

Wolfe, M. B. W., & Goldman, S. R. (2005). Relations between adolescents' text processing and reasoning. *Cognition and Instruction, 23*(4), 467–502.

14

Defining Deep Reading Comprehension for Diverse Readers

Laura K. Allen and Danielle S. McNamara

Across both research and classroom contexts, the term *literacy* is often taken to hold vastly different meanings depending on the specific population being discussed (e.g., adolescent and adult readers, younger developing readers, second language (L2) learners, and adult literacy learners). For instance, *second language reading* is often treated as entirely separable from *first language reading*, drawing on different bodies of research and different foundational assumptions, which in turn lead to large differences in the types of interventions that are developed and implemented. However, reading comprehension processes share a number of similarities across these, and other, groups. In particular, prior knowledge, strategies, and language knowledge, all play important roles in the text comprehension process. Whereas the processes necessary to understand text and discourse are largely the same, what differs is what the reader brings to the table in terms of skills and knowledge.

The purpose of this chapter is to discuss the notion of deep text comprehension across a broad range of diverse readers. Most theories of comprehension assume that deeper comprehension is associated with a more coherent mental representation, which is comprised of multiple levels of understanding. One translation of the concept of levels of understanding into practice emphasizes a linear sequence of skill development, focusing on word decoding first, and then focusing on higher order strategies only after word and sentence decoding are fully developed. Another interpretation, focusing more on the reader's construction of a coherent mental representation, is that readers should be encouraged to use metacognitive reading strategies even at early stages of learning to read. In this chapter, we argue in favor of the latter interpretation.

Deep Comprehension

Reading is the process of interpreting and extracting meaningful information from written text. This complex process requires a number of cognitive abilities and language skills, including the ability to recognize and understand written words, as well as the ability to comprehend language at a deep level (McNamara & Magliano, 2009; Vellutino, 2003). A number of factors relate to an individual's ability to successfully comprehend a given text, such as morphological awareness (Carlisle & Stone, 2003), vocabulary knowledge (Allen, Snow, Crossley, Jackson, & McNamara, 2014), working memory (Berninger et al., 2006; Swanson & Ashbaker, 2000; Swanson & Siegel, 2001), and prior knowledge (Graesser, Gernsbacher, & Goldman, 2003; Kintsch, 1998). To understand the concepts within a given text, individuals must first be able to decode the written words. This requires individuals to use their knowledge of letter sounds to pronounce printed words. Beyond the processing of the words, the reader must understand the sentences in a text, as well as the relationships among the sentences.

A number of discourse models have been proposed to account for the cognitive processes that allow a reader to collect information from a text and develop a comprehensive understanding of that text at various levels (Gernsbacher, 1997; Graesser, Singer, & Trabasso, 1994; Kintsch, 1998; Myers & O'Brien, 1998; Zwaan, Langston, & Graesser, 1995). While these models diverge in more specific components, as well as their claims about the specific cognitive processes involved in reading, the majority of contemporary comprehension models highlight the constructive and active nature of the reading comprehension process and the importance of integrating information from a variety of sources (Graesser et al., 1994; Kintsch, 1998; McNamara & Magliano, 2009; Snow, 2002).

Indeed, a primary goal of reading is to understand the meaning of a text, such that this knowledge can be used later – requiring a reader to *deeply* comprehend a text.

But What Is Deep Comprehension?

This notion (at least partially) originates from theories on Levels of Processing proposed by Craik and Lockhart (1972), which was intended to describe memory recall based on the depth at which verbal stimuli were processed. Specifically, they proposed that people engage in three progressively deeper levels of processing: structural, phonemic, and semantic encoding. Structural encoding emphasizes the physical structure of the stimulus, and is thus considered to comprise relatively shallow processing. For example, if words are flashed on a screen, structural encoding might retain how they were printed (capital, lowercase, bold, italics) or the length of the words (e.g., the number of letters). By contrast phonemic encoding emphasizes what words sound like, such as the ee sound in beet and steal. Finally, semantic encoding emphasizes the meaning of the words, such as answering *yes* or *no* to the statement: *A beet is a red vegetable.*

Craik and Lockhart (1972) demonstrated that participants are more likely to remember words if they have been processed semantically. Their findings were replicated and the notion of levels of processing was refined in subsequent studies (e.g., Craik & Tulving, 1975; Morris, Bransford, & Franks, 1977; Nyberg, 2002; Tulving, 1979). The crux of the theory is that deeper levels of processing result in longer-lasting memory codes, particularly when the same processes are required when retrieving the information.

Within text comprehension literature, memory for information in a text (i.e., conceptual knowledge) is similarly assumed to be associated with the depth at which it is processed. The theoretical foundation for this assumption stems, in part, from the Construction-Integration model of comprehension (Kintsch, 1998) and its predecessor (Kintsch & van Dijk, 1978; van Dijk & Kintsch, 1983). According to the Construction-Integration model, readers construct multiple levels of understanding, including the surface structure, textbase, and situation model. The first level (the surface structure) contains the explicit words and sentence structures that are present in the text. If a mental representation is dominated by a surface structure, only a superficial understanding of the text can be represented. The words and syntax in this surface structure are integrated to build a mental model of the text propositions, comprising the second level of representation. This textbase represents the general ideas and concepts contained within the text itself. These generalizations of the textual concepts yield a series of propositions, which are only loosely, and perhaps inaccurately connected. This is because it is impossible to include all of the information and relations explicitly within a text. The activation and use of background knowledge is necessary to fill in the gaps and to add structure and stability to this network of concepts.

This third level of representation is referred to as the situation model, a higher-level representation of text that is related to its semantic meaning, rather than the specific words that were used. This model contains not only the information from the text itself, but also links between these concepts and a reader's prior knowledge. Thus, to establish a coherent representation of the text, individuals must integrate aspects of their knowledge, such as linguistic, world, and discourse knowledge, with information explicitly provided in the text.

Notably, the representation that is constructed after this construction-integration process is not necessarily composed of equal parts text-based and knowledge-derived information. Rather, it is entirely possible that the textbase or situation model dominate the ultimate mental representation. A primary assumption of the CI model is that deep comprehension requires readers to process texts at multiple levels. A reader's mental representation of a text is more coherent to the extent that inferences are generated to create links between concepts explicitly conveyed in the text (i.e., the textbase) and connections to prior knowledge (i.e., the situation model).

Just as it was established in the levels of processing literature for word recall, different levels of text processing have been shown to be associated with different levels and types of text memory and understanding of concepts. For example, van den Broek, Lorch, Linderholm, and Gustafson (2001) demonstrated that asking students to *read for entertainment* led them to generate more editorial comments and elaborative associations within their think alouds, whereas asking students to *read to study* led to an increase in bridging and predictive inference statements. In turn, better text recall was associated with a greater amount of inferencing. McNamara and colleagues (McNamara, 2004, 2006) have similarly found that students' generation of bridging inferences while explaining texts was associated with better performance on bridging inference comprehension questions.

In sum, reading comprehension involves processing the words and sentences in the text, activating related concepts, and generating a situation model, where background knowledge and experiences are integrated into the text for a specific purpose (Kintsch, 1998). Indeed, the objective of text comprehension is to make sense of it for a specific purpose. If the purpose of reading is to remember the sounds of the words, the words, or individual sentences, that objective may be met, but that is not deep comprehension. By contrast consider situations where a reader may be working toward the objective of learning from a text. To the extent that the reader attempts to make connections between ideas in the text, and to what the reader already knows, the reader is working toward a more coherent (deep) understanding of the text (McNamara, 1997). In essence the reader is working toward a coherent mental representation of the text. The reader is seeking to achieve deep comprehension.

What Factors Influence the Success of Deep Comprehension?

The potential success of a reader's drive to deeply understand a text depends on a number of factors. Deep text comprehension is achieved by calling upon prior knowledge and making strategic connections between ideas in the text and knowledge. If the reader lacks sufficient knowledge of the words, or sufficient prior knowledge to understand the relations between the concepts in the text, then it is unlikely that the reader will construct a deep understanding of the text. Hence, first and foremost, deep comprehension depends on what the reader brings to the table in terms of prior knowledge of the world and the domain (Afflerbach, 1986; Shapiro, 2004).

The features of the text can accentuate the effects of readers' knowledge and skills (Graesser, McNamara, & Kulikowich, 2011; McNamara, Graesser, McCarthy, & Cai, 2014). There are three main sources of text difficulty: word familiarity, syntax, and cohesion. Texts comprised primarily of words that are commonly used in day-to-day language are easier to understand compared to those that include more words that are uncommon or technical. Texts are also more challenging when they include more complex syntax, as opposed to short, simple sentences.

Cohesion is another important factor to consider (McNamara et al., 2014). Cohesion is the extent to which relationships between concepts and ideas are explicit in the text (Gernsbacher, 1990). Connectives (e.g., however, consequently, but, so, first, nonetheless) help to inform the reader on the nature of the relations between ideas. Overlap between words and concepts is another source of cohesion. When words, concepts, and ideas are repeated, and carried forward throughout a text, it is easier for the reader to make connections in the text. No text can spell out all of the information and connections, and thus knowledge is necessary for a reader to generate a coherent mental representation. Texts with many conceptual gaps are particularly challenging for low knowledge readers. Students with higher prior knowledge can readily compensate for gaps in text cohesion by generating inferences that help them comprehend the text (McNamara, 2004). Students with low domain knowledge, on the other hand, are often unable to make these inferences automatically.

Text Comprehension for Diverse Learners

Thus far, we have described the comprehension process and the processes involved in constructing a coherent mental representation (Gernsbacher, 1997; Graesser et al., 1994; Kintsch, 1998). This account, however, is primarily based on research conducted with college students who participate in laboratory experiments. Of course, some studies have extended to high school or middle school students, but these are rare in comparison to studies that have relied on convenience samples.

Various factors, including differences in the target populations as well as different fields of study (e.g., developmental psychology, cognitive science, education), have resulted in separate camps of literatures evolving over time. These camps are largely divided as a function of the target population, such as adolescent and adult readers, young developing readers, second language readers, and adult literacy learners. As a consequence, literacy is often viewed as a different cognitive process for members of these different groups. This is true on the part of researchers as well as educators. Researchers approach the investigation of reading comprehension differently as a function of the target population, and educators approach instruction and remediation differently as a function of the type of student. Indeed, learning to read can be quite different for individuals who comprise these four groups. Knowledge of language, vocabulary, domain knowledge, and metacognitive knowledge all play important roles and vary widely across these populations.

For each group of learners, this process of achieving deep comprehension can appear different because learners have different strengths and weaknesses in core aspects of comprehension. To illustrate this point, consider two learners, Sam and Leah, who are asked to read a text on "Cell Division" (see Figure 14.1). Sam is a high school student who possesses basic language knowledge (e.g., orthographic, syntactic knowledge); he speaks English and can decode words and most (but not all) syntactic constructions. His general vocabulary (i.e., world knowledge) is moderate, and he also has a low knowledge of Cell Division and academic topics in general; therefore, he has low domain knowledge. In addition, he is less knowledgeable of the metacognitive strategies needed to comprehend complex texts. When he has sufficient knowledge, he is able to make automatic inferences to connect ideas in the text. However, when he has less knowledge about the topic (like challenging science texts), he is unable to generate inferences because he does not know strategies to generate inferences that are not automatic. Further, he does not know about the other strategies that can help him understand these challenging texts, such as summarizing,

Knowledge Profiles for Sam and Leah

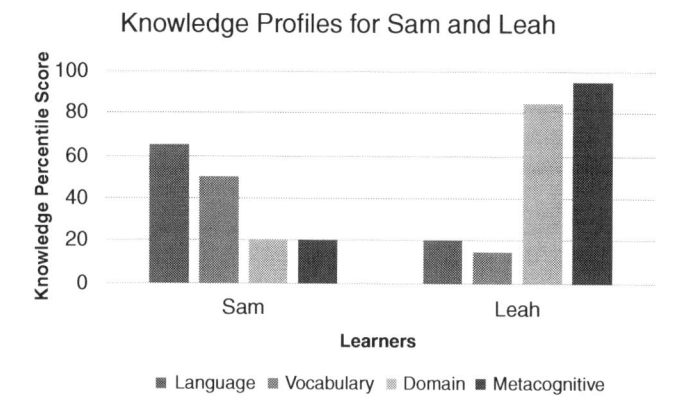

Figure 14.1 Cell Division text

asking and answering questions, and explaining text aloud while reading. We can compare Sam to Leah, an L2 reader who possesses strong comprehension skills in her native language (i.e., high metacognitive knowledge), and a high level of domain and academic knowledge. However, because she is a recent learner of English, Leah has poor language skills and a low level of English vocabulary knowledge.

In this example, both students receive similarly low scores on an assessment of their understanding of the Cell Division text; however, their different knowledge profiles suggest that they may have engaged in vastly different text comprehension processes. Accordingly, they may benefit from different feedback instruction from their teachers. Because Sam had moderate language knowledge, he did not struggle to decode the individual words or sentences in the text; however, his low prior knowledge of cell division, and science more broadly, led him to struggle to connect the text to prior knowledge. Additionally, his low metacognitive knowledge impaired his ability to generate these inferences when he encountered gaps in understanding. For example, when he did not understand the text, he continued reading, rather than working to understand the text by asking questions or generating an explanation using common sense or logic. Leah, on the other hand, struggled to understand the individual words and sentences in the text. However, she was able to achieve some comprehension success by generating connections between the words in the text (the ones she could understand) and her prior domain knowledge.

Importantly, despite the fact that Leah and Sam encountered different struggles while reading, they relied on a similar set of knowledge and skills during the text comprehension process. Specifically, both Sam and Leah activated their prior knowledge of the language and the domain integrated this knowledge with information from the text.

Sam and Leah provide two examples of individuals who come to reading tasks with widely varying sets of knowledge and skills. However, we can extend this example by considering the varying profiles that might be held by members of four primary groups of readers: adolescent and adult readers, younger developing readers, L2 learners, and adult literacy learners (see Figure 14.2).

Adolescent and Adult Readers

Adolescent and adult readers (ages 13 and above) are the target of the majority of prior research on deep text comprehension. This population can vary widely in terms of their

Knowledge Profiles for Four Example Learners

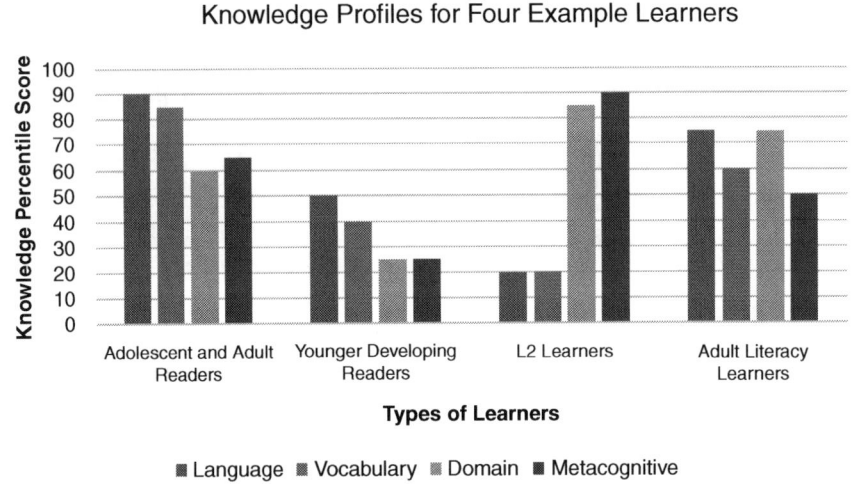

Figure 14.2 Four primary groups of readers

knowledge of language, vocabulary, domain knowledge, and metacognitive knowledge. Generally, however, they have been reading or learning to read for at least seven years, and can decode most words and process most sentence constructions. Hence, the variation in predicting comprehension for the general population lies less in lower-level factors, but in factors related to the readers' ability to generate inferences. While there is some evidence that working memory capacity is correlated with individuals' ability to understand text when the targets are standardized reading tests, there is little evidence that these working memory differences actually drive deep comprehension (McNamara, 2004; McNamara & O'Reilly, 2009). Instead, a substantial body of research on discourse comprehension points to the importance of higher-level cognitive processes, such as generating inferences, connecting information in the text (bridging), and using knowledge to make sense of the text (reasoning, elaboration). Further, this research also highlights the importance of knowledge across multiple dimensions, such as vocabulary (general world knowledge), domain knowledge, and knowledge of strategies to overcome knowledge deficits (metacognitive knowledge).

Younger Developing Readers

Young developing readers are learning how to decode words, process increasingly complex syntactic constructions, and generate inferences that make connections within the text and using prior knowledge. However, the bulk of the literature on developing readers has focused on decoding and vocabulary knowledge. There are only a few researchers who have investigated the importance of prior domain knowledge or metacognitive knowledge related to deliberate inference making. Importantly, however, reading research focused on this population has indicated that the importance of component skills for reading comprehension (e.g., decoding, listening comprehension) varies as a function of the type of assessment that is administered to students (Cutting & Scarborough, 2006; Keenan, Betjemann, & Olson, 2008). For instance, longer, passage-level assessments draw more on higher-level cognitive processes such as inferencing, whereas sentence-level assessments rely more heavily on lower-level, decoding skills (Keenan et al., 2008). In this sense, deliberate inferences are considered "higher level" cognitive processes.

Inferencing skills have been found to contribute to the reading comprehension skills of children across multiple grade levels, even after controlling for lower-level reading processes (Cain & Oakhill, 2007; Cain, Oakhill, & Bryant, 2004; Oakhill & Cain, 2012). For example, in a longitudinal investigation of 7- to 11-year-olds, Oakhill and Cain (2012) reported that inference and integration, comprehension monitoring, and knowledge of text structures contributed unique variance to later reading comprehension, independent of word reading, verbal IQ, and vocabulary knowledge. These findings suggest that higher-level, inference-based processes may influence later reading comprehension development as lower-level, word reading skills become more automatized.

Second Language Learners

A principal distinction between second (L2) and first language (L1) learners is the development stage at which reading comprehension (of the targeted language) is first required (Bernhardt, 1991). Native English speakers, for instance, begin instruction to read English texts after they have achieved some level of verbal fluency. According to Grabe and Stoller (2002), (L1) children are familiar with a large majority of grammatical sentence constructions and can recognize approximately 7,000 words before they begin to read. Thus, when these children first encounter written texts, they already have a great deal of English language knowledge readily available. On the other hand, L2 readers must develop L2 language skills, while simultaneously learning to read in that language. This can lead to a number of comprehension difficulties. For instance, because L2 readers do not have strong lexical knowledge, they may develop weaker associations among words and concepts and develop less coherent text representations.

As illustrated in Figure 14.2, an L2 learner may have a high knowledge of the text content, but may not know the meaning of all of the words or their syntactic derivations (e.g., past vs. conditional tense). Of course, the potential difficulties depend a great deal on the overlap between the languages (e.g., English vs. Spanish; English vs. Chinese). And of course, domain knowledge and metacognitive knowledge are likely to vary to the same degree as they do for L1 readers.

Researchers have identified several common difficulties encountered by L2 readers (Bernhardt, 1991, 2000; Grabe & Stoller, 2002; Oded & Walters, 2001; Walter, 2007). One problem is that these students typically rely much too heavily on bottom-up, rather than top-down processes when reading. Thus, they expend too much of their controlled effort on word decoding, sentence parsing, and the identification of other localized text features. Accordingly, these readers typically experience difficulties accessing the global strategies that they may use in their first language, such as making connections between distal ideas in the text and to prior knowledge (Walter, 2007). Rather, L2 readers spend a significant amount of their time decoding and translating the literal meaning of words and sentences, and also have problems ignoring irrelevant information from the text (Oded & Walters, 2001). The latter potentially stems from their inability to actively use their domain knowledge while reading, and thus generating a sparse mental representation of the text (McNamara, 2007; McNamara & McDaniel, 2004). In contrast, skilled L1 readers typically read for the purpose of constructing meaning; thus, they can extract the main purposes of the text more easily (Nassaji, 2002).

Adult Literacy Learners

There are approximately 30 million adults in the United States who cannot read. This means that they are unable to comprehend texts at an 8th grade reading level, and generally can read only simple text in terms of vocabulary and syntax. According to the National Assessment of Adult Literacy (NAAL; http://nces.ed.gov/naal), 14% of those surveyed scored below a basic level, demonstrating an inability to perform simple, everyday literacy activities. Moreover, estimates of illiteracy are far greater for students who do not graduate from high school (55%), English language learners (44%), Hispanic adults (39%), and black adults (20%). Many of the adults enrolled in adult education courses are adults who are learning English as a second language. Hence, adult literacy learners represent a broad spectrum of abilities in terms of the various types of knowledge displayed in Figure 14.2.

Of the four populations that we consider here, the least amount of research and the fewest empirically-based literacy interventions have been geared toward adult learners (Lesgold & Welch-Ross, 2012). The research studies, the few that have been conducted, have been correlational studies that have focused on the contributions of lower-level skills such as morphological awareness, phonological awareness, and word decoding to performance on reading comprehension tests. This is because the predominant assumption has been that adult literacy learners lack in lower-level skills. Indeed, this research has generally confirmed the importance of lower-level language skills (e.g., Tighe & Binder, 2015; Tighe & Schatschneider, 2016) as well as vocabulary knowledge (Mellard, Fall, & Woods, 2010); in terms of explaining variance in reading comprehension test performance.

There have not been any research studies (to our knowledge) that have examined adult literacy learners' inferencing skills or deep comprehension. Studies are needed that administer a broader array of measures to adult literacy learners, including domain knowledge and metacognitive knowledge. We would hypothesize in such a study that inferencing skills would contribute positively to performance on reading comprehension assessments, particularly on assessments that tap into deep comprehension as opposed to those that focus on shallow comprehension, such as those that solely require understanding single sentences.

Studies are also needed that examine the benefits of providing instruction in using higher-level strategies such as generating inferences. It has generally been assumed that adult literacy learners require instruction that focuses on lower-level skills, mirroring the correlational research that has been conducted thus far. A cascading relation among skills is traditionally assumed, wherein each higher-level skill depends on a lower-level skill. For example, making inferences depends on the ability to parse sentences, reading a sentence depends on the ability to read the words, and reading the words depends on the ability to read the letters (Snow, 2002). Accordingly, inference instruction would have little to no benefit because there would be a stop-gap at the lower levels of processing. This assumption has had a strong influence on adult literacy research. Whereas, theoretical accounts of adolescent and adult comprehension has long recognized top-down processes in text comprehension, the adult literacy literature has not. Hence, we recommend that further research is needed that explores the impact of higher-level processes, and the impact of providing instruction that enhances students' propensity to generate inferences, potentially compensating for struggles at the level of the words and syntax.

Implications for Education

The majority of contemporary theories of text comprehension assume that an individual's understanding of a text arises from cognitive and metacognitive processes at multiple levels, as well as interactions across these levels. Further, they rely on the assumption that deep comprehension depends on the construction of a coherent mental representation of the text. These assumptions have important implications for the ways in which reading is taught in the classroom – particularly with respect to diverse readers.

One consideration is a need for teacher education to place a greater priority and more time providing instruction on comprehension. Current and future instructors should be provided with a basic understanding of how comprehension processes emerge so that they can more easily adapt to their students' differential needs. Without this understanding, advancing the needs of diverse learners appears virtually impossible.

In turn, a greater focus of education needs to be on strategies to comprehend and learn rather than on feeding content to students. Students need to be provided with instruction and practice on strategies for achieving deep comprehension. In particular, students need to be taught *how* and *when* to use different strategies, depending on the context of various reading tasks (e.g., their native language, the text difficulty, etc.).

These educational implications point to two primary recommendations for educators tasked with training diverse groups of learners to read complex texts. The first is to teach students *strategies* that allow them to leverage the knowledge available to them across various reading contexts. By providing students with this training, they will be better equipped to successfully comprehend a variety of texts despite the variability in their knowledge across multiple dimensions. The second is to provide students with texts that have been adapted to them based on their particular strengths and weaknesses. This focus on text properties can help students to better understand the information they are reading, and can help to scaffold them toward more complex texts.

Reading Comprehension Strategies

Because reading comprehension is a cognitively demanding task that relies on multiple sources of knowledge, students must learn to compensate for their deficiencies across multiple reading contexts. One proposed method for alleviating these difficulties is through instruction and practice on reading strategies. Prior research has revealed that a primary difference between skilled and unskilled students is their efficient use of strategies during the comprehension process (Bransford, Vye, & Stein, 1984; Paris & Myers, 1981; Sheorey & Mokhtari, 2001). Skilled readers generate more inferences while reading and establish connections at a more global level (Millis, Magliano, & Todaro, 2006). Accordingly, a number of studies have investigated differences in strategy use based on native language (Block, 1986; Pritchard, 1990), as well as L2 language proficiency (Anderson, 1991; Carrell, 1989; Hosenfeld, 1977; for a review, see Brantmeier, 2002). Results of these studies reveal that students of low and high L2 proficiency levels utilize profoundly different strategies during the comprehension process.

A number of the reading strategies observed in these studies have been classified as either effective or ineffective for comprehension across multiple contexts. One primary distinction that has been made is in students' use of top-down (global) and bottom-up (local) strategies (Abbott, 2006; Barnett, 1988; Block, 1986, 1992; Carrell, 1989; Young & Oxford, 1997). Top-down reading strategies are those processes that lead readers to focus on the main idea of the text, often through an integration of background and discourse knowledge. The use of bottom-up strategies, on the other hand, leads readers to understand text at the local level, often through word decoding or sentence parsing. For example, Block (1992) investigated the comprehension-monitoring strategies of L1 and L2 readers of different L1 reading abilities. In the study, students were asked to think aloud while reading English texts; students' strategies were then coded according to strategy type. Results revealed that high proficiency L2 readers primarily utilized global reading strategies, such as accessing prior knowledge or using contextual cues to overcome vocabulary deficits. Low proficiency L2 readers, on the other hand, failed to utilize these top-down strategies and, accordingly, did not overcome their reading difficulties as successfully.

These studies, along with many others, have led researchers to develop a number of conclusions about the efficient use of reading strategies. First, high proficiency readers simply utilize more strategies overall than students at low proficiency levels (Anderson, 1991; Phakiti, 2003). Second, high and low proficiency readers utilize widely different forms of strategies. In particular, high proficiency readers utilize global strategies that focus on the overall purpose or meaning of the text, whereas low proficiency readers typically use local strategies when reading texts (Block, 1986; Carrell, 1989; Koda, 2005). In addition, these struggling L2 readers tend to use strategies incorrectly or inappropriately, and often indirectly weaken their text comprehension (Cohen, 1994).

Importantly, these comprehension differences can be manipulated through differences in the instructions provided to students before reading texts. For example, self-explanation is an instructional strategy that encourages the generation of inferences during reading, and has been shown to improve students' deep understanding of complex concepts (Pressley, McDaniel, Turnure, Wood, & Ahmad, 1987). When students produce high-quality self-explanations, they make inferences that link text content together and tie text ideas to their prior knowledge (McNamara, 2004). Thus, self-explanation instructions can prompt individuals to behave as skilled readers, whereas more general instructions do not necessarily promote the generation of these connections (Allen, Jacovina, & McNamara, 2016; Allen, McNamara, & McCrudden, 2015). Broadly, self-explanation has proven to be a beneficial strategy across a number of tasks, as it leads students to achieve greater success at problem solving (Bielaczyc, Pirolli, & Brown, 1995) and developing a stronger understanding of the concepts covered in texts (Chi, de Leeuw, Chiu, & LaVancher, 1994; Magliano et al., 2005; McNamara, 2004).

One problem is that many students do not effectively self-explain, and so they need instruction in how to produce effective self-explanations (McNamara, 2004). Self-explanation strategy training (SERT) combines self-explanation with comprehension strategies, including comprehension monitoring, paraphrasing, bridging, predicting, and elaborating. Instruction and practice in using the strategies, along with self-explanation, is synergistic because self-explanation externalizes the strategies and the strategies improve the quality of the students' explanations. SERT has proven to successfully improve comprehension at the middle school (O'Reilly, Best, & McNamara, 2004), high school (Jackson & McNamara, 2011; Jackson, Varner, Boonthum-Denecke, & McNamara, 2013; Jacovina, Jackson, Snow, & McNamara, 2016), and college (Magliano et al., 2005; McNamara, 2004) levels.

Because less-skilled readers tend to lack sufficient knowledge about strategy use, a number of researchers have recommended the addition of explicit strategy instruction to literacy curriculums. Research has demonstrated that such strategy instruction interventions can lead to significant improvements in students' comprehension. Taylor, Stevens, and Asher (2006) conducted a meta-analysis of 23 studies on L2 reading strategy interventions. They found that a number of strategies have led to successful L2 comprehension, such as semantic mapping, activating prior knowledge, and comprehension monitoring. The overall results of this review indicated that strategy instruction was, indeed, beneficial for L2 comprehension. They noted, however, that because these studies involve student groups with different ages, cultures, and native languages, it remains a question on how to identify the most appropriate strategies for specific students.

Text Readability

In addition to reading strategy instruction, the ability to comprehension texts deeply also relies on students' engagement in deliberate and persistent reading practice. Specifically, students need to be provided with opportunities to read numerous texts across a variety of different domains (Duke & Pearson, 2002). One method for maximizing the effectiveness of this practice is to assign students to read texts that specifically target their own sets of strengths and weaknesses. The difficulty of texts varies across a number of dimensions (Graesser et al., 2011; McNamara, Graesser, & Louwerse, 2012); therefore, students should read texts that have been appropriately matched to their specific knowledge and skills. Aligning text properties to students' abilities and needs allows them to capitalize on their strengths, while also fostering growth in specific comprehension skills. In this way, students will gradually come to recognize what makes texts rich and complex and how best to absorb what these texts provide. This outcome can only be achieved if teachers have the knowledge and tools available to appropriately adapt texts to their students' needs.

Consider the example students, Sam and Leah, from earlier in the chapter who received similarly low scores on their comprehension assessment. As a native English speaker, Sam has stronger language and vocabulary knowledge than Leah; however, he struggles to integrate information from across the text and has little knowledge of the text domain. Leah, on the other hand, has high metacognitive and domain knowledge and is therefore more skilled at generating inferences and integrating information from the text. Although Sam and Leah are classified as having similar reading levels, they are likely to be affected by different dimensions of text difficulty. For example, the sophistication of the words and the cohesion of the text will likely have differential effects on these students' comprehension of the text due to their varying knowledge profiles.

Given the importance of text properties on students' comprehension processes, it is important that educators have a means through which they can assign individual texts to students based on their strengths and weaknesses. Historically, these texts have been assigned based on grade level assessments, such as Flesch Kincaid. These assessments calculate basic indices related to the words and sentences in texts to estimate its appropriate grade level (Kincaid, Fisburne, Rogers, & Chissom, 1975). One weakness of these approaches, however, stems from their unidimensional nature. Text difficulty can be assessed at multiple levels, including challenges from the words and syntax, but also challenges that stem from the genre of the text and the cohesion of the text. For instance, increased cohesion tends to be positively associated with easier reading, and narrative texts tend to be easier to comprehend than expository texts. This assessment affords educators the ability to investigate these specific components that contribute to a text's difficulty. Importantly, the features that make texts more or less difficult vary from one text to the next. This can help to identify the more difficult elements of a particular text and determine whether specific texts are appropriate for different students. Once these components have been identified, educators can work with students to help them recognize and overcome the obstacles that the texts might present (Jackson, Allen, & McNamara, 2016).

For example, previous research has shown that readers with low prior knowledge on a topic benefit from a more coherent text (i.e., high percentile scores), while students with a high prior knowledge can benefit from texts with less cohesion, which require generating inferences while reading (McNamara, Kintsch, Songer, & Kintsch, 1996). Thus the information can be used to align appropriate texts with the skills and knowledge of particular students to improve their overall comprehension and retention. For instance, narrative text is easier to read, comprehend, and recall than informational text (Graesser & McNamara, 2011; Haberlandt & Graesser, 1985). If a passage is low in narrativity, students' prior domain knowledge should be considered. If the students have little domain knowledge, teachers may consider texts that help to compensate for these challenges, such as texts that are higher in narrativity, or have fewer sources of challenges on the other dimensions. Nonetheless, it is important that students are transitioned to more difficult (e.g., less narrative) texts over time (Best, Floyd, & McNamara, 2008; Sanacore & Palumbo, 2009). The reader must learn to understand increasingly complex and unfamiliar ideas. If the teacher wishes to move the students toward learning to use their prior knowledge and generating inferences to understand challenging text, the teacher may consider where the text falls on the spectrum of narrativity.

Similarly, more skilled readers are better able to process more complex sentences (e.g., Just & Carpenter, 1992), and, consequently, older readers are typically assigned texts with higher grade levels and more complex syntax. Highly narrative texts with challenging syntax may be optimal for tackling the pedagogical goal of learning to parse sentences. By contrast, if a syntactically challenging text is also low in narrativity, then the teacher may wish to consider whether the students' reading skill and prior knowledge are sufficient to tackle that text.

Conclusion

Despite suggested links between comprehension theories and educational practice, there are a number of translation gaps that inhibit their implementation. As a consequence, educational practice often emphasizes a linear sequence of skill development, focusing on word decoding first, and then focusing on higher order strategies, only after word and sentence decoding are fully developed (McNamara, Jacovina, & Allen, 2015). These stage-like models of reading pedagogy can be detrimental for students because they can result in a failure to provide instruction to students on the higher-level skills that they need in order to improve comprehension at deep levels and for complex text. The approaches that are motivated by stage-like models may be particularly ineffective for diverse groups of learners who have large variations in the profiles of knowledge and skills that interact in complex ways. It does not make sense, for example, to neglect to provide instruction to adolescent L2 students about inferencing strategies simply because they have a more limited vocabulary than their L1 peers. In fact, training and practice with these inferencing strategies may have a positive impact on L2 students' vocabulary growth and comprehension success more broadly.

Obviously, we must still account for the lower-level knowledge and skills that are sources of struggle for diverse sets of readers. We cannot ignore the fact that lower-level decoding processes may not be automatized for L2 readers (Yoshida, 2012), or that developing readers are less likely to have high domain knowledge. To more clearly understand the struggles of diverse readers, it is critical that researchers continue to examine the influences of these different sources of knowledge across readers.

It is a mistake, however, to develop or follow separate theories and different sets of assumptions for each population of readers. We believe that significant advances, both theoretically and practically, will follow from approaching reading and comprehension from a unified comprehension model. By accounting for diversity among readers under a similar set of theoretical assumptions, researchers will be poised to provide educational recommendations that lead to success for a broader range of readers. Further, teachers will have a more robust understanding of comprehension that allows them to flexibly adapt their instruction and feedback based on the needs of their students.

References

Abbott, M. L. (2006). ESL reading strategies: Differences in Arabic and Mandarin speaker test performance. *Language Learning, 56,* 633–670.

Afflerbach, P. (1986). The influence of prior knowledge on expert readers' importance assignment process. In J. A. Niles & R. V. Lalik (Eds.), *National reading conference yearbook: Vol. 35. Solving problems in literacy: Learners, teachers and researchers* (pp. 30–40). Rochester, New York, NY: National Reading Conference.

Allen, L. K., Jacovina, M. E., & McNamara, D. S. (2016). Cohesive features of deep text comprehension processes. In J. Trueswell, A. Papafragou, D. Grodner, & D. Mirman (Eds.), *Proceedings of the 38th Annual Meeting of the Cognitive Science Society in Philadelphia, PA* (pp. 2681–2686). Austin, TX: Cognitive Science Society.

Allen, L. K., McNamara, D. S., & McCrudden, M. T. (2015). Change your mind: Investigating the effects of self-explanation in the resolution of misconceptions. In D. C. Noelle, R. Dale, A. S. Warlaumont, J. Yoshimi, T. Matlock, C. D. Jennings, & P. Maglio (Eds.), *Proceedings of the 37th Annual Meeting of the Cognitive Science Society (Cog Sci 2015)* (pp. 78–83). Pasadena, CA: Cognitive Science Society.

Allen, L. K., Snow, E. L., Crossley, S. A., Jackson, G. T., & McNamara, D. S. (2014). Reading comprehension components and their relation to the writing process. *L'année psychologique/Topics in Cognitive Psychology, 114,* 663–691.

Anderson, N. J. (1991). Individual differences in strategy use in second language reading and testing. *Modern Language Journal, 75,* 460–472.

Barnett, M. A. (1988). Reading through context: How real and perceived strategy use affects L2 comprehension. *The Modern Language Journal, 73,* 150–162.

Bernhardt, E. B. (1991). *Reading development in a second language: Theoretical, research, and classroom perspectives.* Norwood, NJ: Ablex.

Bernhardt, E. B. (2000). Second language reading as a case study of reading scholarship in the twentieth century. In M. L. Kamil, P. B. Mosenthal, P. D. Pearson, & R. Barr (Eds.), *Handbook of reading research, Volume III* (pp. 791–811). Mahwah, NJ: Lawrence Erlbaum Associates.

Berninger, V., Abbott, R., Thomson, J., Wagner, R., Swanson, H. L., Wijsman, F., & Raskind, W. (2006). Modeling developmental phonological core deficits within a working-memory architecture in children and adults with developmental dyslexia. *Scientific Studies in Reading, 10,* 165–198.

Best, R. M., Floyd, R. G., & McNamara, D. S. (2008). Differential competencies contributing to children's comprehension of narrative and expository texts. *Reading Psychology, 29,* 137–164.

Bielaczyc, K., Pirolli, P. L., & Brown, A. L. (1995). Training in self-explanation and self-regulation strategies: Investigating the effects of knowledge acquisition activities on problem solving. *Cognition and Instruction, 13,* 221–252.

Block, E. (1986). The comprehension strategies of second language readers. *TESOL Quarterly, 20,* 463–494.

Block, E. (1992). See how they read: Comprehension monitoring of L1 and L2 readers. *TESOL Quarterly, 26,* 319–343.

Bransford, J. D., Vye, N. J., & Stein, B. S. (1984). A comparison of successful and less successful learners: Can we enhance comprehension and mastery skills? In J. Flood (Ed.), *Understanding reading comprehension* (pp. 216–231). Newark, DE: International Reading Association.

Brantmeier, C. (2002). Second language reading strategy research at the secondary and university levels: Variations, disparities, and generalizability. *The Reading Matrix, 2,* 1–14.

Cain, K., & Oakhill, J. (Eds.). (2007). *Children's comprehension problems in oral and written language: A cognitive perspective.* New York, NY: The Guilford Press.

Cain, K., Oakhill, J., & Bryant, P. (2004). Children's reading comprehension ability: Concurrent prediction by working memory, verbal ability, and component skills. *Journal of Educational Psychology, 96,* 31–42.

Carlisle, J. F., & Stone, C. A. (2003). The effects of morphological structure on children's reading of derived words in English. In E. Assink & D. Sandra (Eds.), *Reading complex words: Cross-language studies* (pp. 26–49). Kluwer: Dordrecht.

Carrell, P. L. (1989). Metacognitive awareness and second language reading. *Modern Language Journal, 73,* 121–134.

Chi, M. T. H., de Leeuw, N., Chiu, M. H., & LaVancher, C. (1994). Eliciting self-explanations improves understanding. *Cognitive Science, 18,* 439–477.

Cohen, A. D. (1994). *Assessing language ability in the classroom (2nd ed.).* Boston: Newbury House.

Craik, F. I. M., & Lockhart, R. S. (1972). Levels of processing: A framework for memory research. *Journal of Verbal Learning and Verbal Behavior, 11,* 671–684.

Craik, F. I. M., & Tulving, E. (1975). Depth of processing and the retention of words in episodic memory. *Journal of Experimental Psychology: General, 104,* 268–294.

Cutting, L. E., & Scarborough, H. S. (2006). Prediction of reading comprehension: Relative contributions of word recognition, language proficiency, and other cognitive skills can depend on how comprehension is measured. *Scientific Studies of Reading, 10,* 277–299.

Duke, N. K., & Pearson, P. (2002). Effective practices for developing reading comprehension. In A. E. Farstrup & S. Jay Samuels (Eds.), *What research has to say about reading instruction* (3rd ed., pp. 205–242). Newark, DE: International Reading Association, Inc.

Gernsbacher, M. A. (1990). *Language comprehension as structure building.* Hillsdale, NJ: Erlbaum.

Gernsbacher, M. A. (1997). Two decades of structure building. *Discourse Processes, 23,* 265–304.

Grabe, W., & Stoller, F. L. (2002). *Teaching and researching reading.* New York, NY: Longman.

Graesser, A. C., Gernsbacher, M. A., & Goldman, S. R. (2003). Introduction to the handbook of discourse processes. In A. C. Graesser, M. A. Gernsbacher, & S. R. Goldman (Eds.), *Handbook of discourse processes* (pp. 1–24). Mahwah, NJ: Erlbaum.

Graesser, A. C., & McNamara, D. S. (2011). Computational analyses of multilevel discourse comprehension. *Topics in Cognitive Science, 2,* 371–398.

Graesser, A. C., McNamara, D. S., & Kulikowich, J. M. (2011). Coh Metrix: Providing multilevel analyses of text characteristics. *Educational Researcher, 40,* 223–234.

Graesser, A. C., Singer, M., & Trabasso, T. (1994). Constructing inferences during narrative text comprehension. *Psychological Review, 101,* 371–395.

Haberlandt, K., & Graesser, A. C. (1985). Component processes in text comprehension and some of their interactions. *Journal of Experimental Psychology: General, 114,* 357–374.

Hosenfeld, C. (1977). A preliminary investigation of the reading strategies of successful and non-successful second language learners. *System, 5,* 110–123.

Jackson, G. T., Allen, L. K., & McNamara, D. S. (2016). Common core TERA: Text Ease and Readability Assessor. In D. S. McNamara & S. A. Crossley (Eds.), *Adaptive educational technologies for literacy instruction* (pp. 49–68). New York, NY: Taylor & Francis, Routledge.

Jackson, G. T., & McNamara, D. S. (2011). Motivational impacts of a game-based intelligent tutoring system. In R. C. Murray & P. M. McCarthy (Eds.), *Proceedings of the 24th International Florida Artificial Intelligence Research Society (FLAIRS) Conference* (pp. 519–524). Menlo Park, CA: AAAI Press.

Jackson, G. T., Varner, L. K., Boonthum-Denecke, C. & McNamara, D. S. (2013) The impact of individual differences on learning with an educational game and a traditional ITS, *International Journal of Learning Technology, 8*(4), 315–336.

Jacovina, M. E., Jackson, G. T., Snow, E. L., & McNamara, D. S. (2016). Timing game-based practice in a reading comprehension strategy tutor. In A. Micarelli, J. Stamper, & K. Panourgia (Eds.), *Proceedings of the 13th International Conference on Intelligent Tutoring Systems (ITS 2016)* (pp. 80–89). Zagreb, Croatia: Springer.

Just, M. A., & Carpenter, P. A. (1992). A capacity theory of comprehension: Individual differences in working memory. *Psychological Review, 99,* 122–149.

Keenan, J. M., Betjemann, R. S., & Olson, R. K. (2008). Reading comprehension tests vary in the skills they assess: Differential dependence on decoding and oral comprehension. *Scientific Studies of Reading, 12,* 281–300.

Kincaid, J., Fishburne, R., Rogers, R., & Chissom, B. (1975). *Derivation of new readability formulas for navy enlisted personnel.* Branch Report 8–75. Millington, TN: Chief of Naval Training.

Kintsch, W. (1998). *Comprehension: A paradigm for cognition.* Cambridge, MA: Cambridge University Press.

Kintsch, W., & van Dijk, T. A. (1978). Toward a model of text comprehension and production. *Psychological Review, 85,* 363–394.

Koda, K. (2005). *Insights into second language reading: A cross-linguistic approach.* New York, NY: Cambridge University Press.

Lesgold, A. M., & Welch-Ross, M. (Eds.). (2012). *Improving adult literacy instruction: Developing reading and writing.* Washington, DC: National Academies Press.

Magliano, J. P., Todaro, S., Millis, K., Wiemer-Hastings, K., Kim, H. J., & McNamara, D. S. (2005). Changes in reading strategies as a function of reading training: A comparison of live and computerized training. *Journal of Educational Computing Research, 32,* 185–208.

McNamara, D. S. (1997). Comprehension skill: A knowledge-based account. In M. G. Shafto & P. Langley (Eds.), *Proceedings of the Nineteenth Annual Conference of the Cognitive Science Society* (pp. 508–513). Hillsdale, NJ: Erlbaum.

McNamara, D. S. (2004). SERT: Self-explanation reading training. *Discourse Processes, 38,* 1–30.

McNamara, D. S. (Ed.). (2007). *Reading comprehension strategies: Theory, interventions, and technologies.* Mahwah, NJ: Erlbaum.

McNamara, D. S., Graesser, A. C., & Louwerse, M. M. (2012). Sources of text difficulty: Across genres and grades. In J. P. Sabatini, E. Albro, & T. O'Reilly (Eds.), *Measuring up: Advances in how we assess reading ability* (pp. 89–116). Lanham, MD: R&L Education.

McNamara, D. S., Graesser, A. C., McCarthy, P., & Cai, Z. (2014). *Automated evaluation of text and discourse with Coh-Metrix.* Cambridge: Cambridge University Press.

McNamara, D. S., Jacovina, M. E., & Allen, L. K. (2015). Higher order thinking in comprehension. In P. Afflerbach (Ed.), *Handbook of individual differences in reading: Text and context* (pp. 164–176). NY: Taylor & Francis, Routledge.

McNamara, D. S., Kintsch, E., Songer, N. B., & Kintsch, W. (1996). Are good texts always better? Interactions of text coherence, background knowledge, and levels of understanding in learning from text. *Cognition and Instruction, 14*, 1–43.

McNamara, D. S., & Magliano, J. P. (2009). Towards a comprehensive model of comprehension. In B. Ross (Ed.), *The psychology of learning and motivation* (pp. 297–384). New York, NY: Elsevier Science.

McNamara, D. S., & McDaniel, M. A. (2004). Suppressing irrelevant information: Knowledge activation or inhibition? *Journal of Experimental Psychology: Learning, Memory, & Cognition, 30*, 465–482.

McNamara, D. S., & O'Reilly, T. (2009). Theories of comprehension skill: Knowledge and strategies versus capacity and suppression. In A. M. Columbus (Ed.), *Advances in psychology research* (p. 62). Hauppauge, NY: Nova Science Publishers, Inc.

McNamara, D. S., O'Reilly, T., Best, R., & Ozuru, Y. (2006). Improving adolescent students' reading comprehension with iSTART. *Journal of Educational Computing Research, 34*, 147–171.

Mellard, D. F., Fall, E., & Woods, K. L. (2010). A path analysis of reading comprehension for adults with low literacy. *Journal of Learning Disabilities, 43*, 154–165.

Millis, K. K., Magliano, J. P., & Todaro, S. (2006). Measuring discourse-level processes with verbal protocols and latent semantic analysis. *Scientific Studies of Reading, 10*, 251–283.

Morris, C. D., Bransford, J. D., & Franks, J. J. (1977). Levels of processing versus transfer appropriate processing. *Journal of Verbal Learning and Verbal Behavior, 16*, 519–533.

Myers, J. L., & O'Brien, E. J. (1998). Accessing the discourse representation during reading. *Discourse Processes, 26*, 131–157.

Nassaji, H. (2002). Schema theory and knowledge-based processes in second language reading comprehension: A need for alternative perspectives. *Language Learning, 52*, 439–481.

Nyberg, L. (2002). Levels of processing: A view from functional brain imaging. *Memory, 10*, 345–348.

O'Reilly, T., Best, R., & McNamara, D. S. (2004). Self-explanation reading training: Effects for low-knowledge readers. In K. Forbus, D. Gentner, & T. Regier (Eds.), *Proceedings of the 26th Annual Cognitive Science Society* (pp. 1053–1058). Mahwah, NJ: Erlbaum.

Oakhill, J. V., & Cain, K. (2012). The precursors of reading ability in young readers: Evidence from a four-year longitudinal study. *Scientific Studies of Reading, 16*(2), 91–121.

Oded, B., & Walters, J. (2001). Deeper processing for better EFL reading comprehension. *System, 29*, 257–370.

Paris, S. G., & Myers, M. (1981). Comprehension monitoring, memory, and study strategies of good and poor readers. *Journal of Reading Behavior, 8*, 5–22.

Phakiti, A. (2003). A closer look at the relationship of cognitive and metacognitive strategy use to EFL reading achievement test performance. *Language Testing, 20*, 26–56.

Pressley, M., McDaniel, M. A., Turnure, J. E., Wood, E., & Ahmad, M. (1987). Generation and precision of elaboration: Effects on intentional and incidental learning. *Journal of Experimental Psychology: Learning, Memory, and Cognition, 13*, 291–300.

Pritchard, R. (1990). The effects of cultural schemata on reading processing strategies. *Reading Research Quarterly, 25*, 273–295.

Sanacore, J., & Palumbo, A. (2009). Understanding the fourth-grade slump: Our point of view. *The Educational Forum, 73*, 67–74.

Shapiro, A. M. (2004). How including prior knowledge as a subject variable may change outcomes of learning research. *American Educational Research Journal, 41*, 159–189.

Sheorey, R., & Mokhtari, K. (2001). Differences in the metacognitive awareness of reading strategies among native and non-native readers. *System, 29*, 431–449.

Snow, C. E. (2002). *Reading for understanding: Toward an R&D program in reading comprehension*. Arlington, VA: Rand Corporation.

Swanson, H. L., & Ashbaker, M. H. (2000). Working memory, short-term memory, speech rate, word recognition, and reading comprehension in learning disabled readers: Does the executive system have a role? *Intelligence, 28*, 1–30.

Swanson, H. L., & Siegel, L. (2001). Learning disabilities as a working memory deficit. *Issues in Education: Contributions from Educational Psychology, 7*, 1–48.

Taylor, A., Stevens, J. R., & Asher, J. W. (2006). The effects of explicit reading strategy training on L2 reading comprehension. In J. M. Norris & L. Ortega (Eds.), *Language learning and language teaching: Synthesizing research on language learning and teaching* (pp. 213–244). Amsterdam, The Netherlands: John Benjamin Publishing Company.

Tighe, E. L., & Binder, K. S. (2015). An investigation of morphological awareness and processing in adults with low literacy. *Applied Psycholinguistics, 36*(2), 245–273.

Tighe, E. L., & Schatschneider, C. (2016). A quantile regression approach to understanding the relations between morphological awareness, vocabulary, and reading comprehension in Adult Basic Education students. *Journal of Learning Disabilities, 49*, 424–436.

Tulving, E. (1979). Relation between encoding specificity and levels of processing. In L. S. Cermak & F. I. M. Craik (Eds.), *Levels of processing in human memory* (pp. 405–428). Hillsdale, NJ: Erlbaum.

van den Broek, P., Lorch, R. F., Linderholm, T., & Gustafson, M. (2001). The effects of readers' goals on inference generation and memory for texts. *Memory & Cognition, 29*, 1081–1087.

van Dijk, T. A., & Kintsch, W. (1983). *Strategies of discourse comprehension*. New York, NY: Academic Press.

Vellutino, F. R. (2003). Individual differences as sources of variability in reading comprehension in elementary school children. In A. P. Sweet & C. E. Snow (Eds.), *Rethinking reading comprehension* (pp. 51–81). New York, NY: Guilford Press.

Walter, C. (2007). First- to second-language reading comprehension: Not transfer, but access. *International Journal of Applied Linguistics, 17*, 19–35.

Yoshida, M. (2012). The interplay of processing task, text type, and proficiency in L2 reading. *Reading in a Foreign Language, 24*, 1–29.

Young, D. J., & Oxford, R. (1997). A gender-related analysis of strategies used to process written input in the native language and a foreign language. *Applied Language Learning, 8*, 43–73.

Zwaan, R. A., Langston, M. C., & Graesser, A. C. (1995). The construction of situation models in narrative comprehension: An event-indexing model. *Psychological Science, 6*, 292–297.

Part V

How Do Expanding Conceptions of Teacher, Reader, and Text Interaction Change the Game for Reading Researchers, Teachers, Leaders, and Policy Makers?

15

The Joint Development of Literacy and Self-Regulation in Early Childhood

Implications for Research and Practice

Emily C. Hanno, Stephanie M. Jones, and Dana C. McCoy

Successful reading relies on more than just literacy-specific skills. Skilled readers employ multiple competencies from outside of the domain, including elements of self-regulation, like maintaining attention and monitoring for errors. Much research has therefore sought to isolate the contribution of self-regulation to young children's reading development (Bohlmann & Downer, 2016; Eisenberg, Valiente, & Eggum, 2010; Kieffer, Vukovic, & Berry, 2013; McClelland et al., 2007) and to determine whether targeting self-regulation can, in turn, support reading (Rabiner, Murray, Skinner, & Malone, 2010; Raver et al., 2011). Whereas many studies assume a unidirectional relation from self-regulation to literacy, some recent work suggests that the relation between the two domains may be bidirectional, asserting that literacy is also foundational for self-regulation (Bohlmann, Maier, & Palacios, 2015; Cadima et al., 2018). The nature and direction of the association between literacy and self-regulation has implications for the types of practices and interventions that are likely to support competencies in both areas. This chapter summarizes current knowledge on the connection between literacy and self-regulation. We use that evidence to arrive at a conceptual model of the *bidirectional* relations between literacy and self-regulation occurring in, and influenced by, children's surrounding contexts.

Given its salience for the development of foundational literacy and self-regulation skills, we focus primarily on the early childhood period, from approximately ages three to eight years (Snow, 1983; Weintraub et al., 2013). As such, within the literacy domain, we concentrate on early literacy competencies that encompass both "conventional literacy skills," primarily the ability to read and write, and those considered precursors to conventional skills, such as language and phonological awareness (National Early Literacy Panel, 2008). These early competencies are thought to set the groundwork for both skill-based (e.g., decoding) and meaning-making (e.g., comprehension) aspects of conventional literacy (Lesaux, 2012; Snow, 1991).

We begin the chapter by defining self-regulation as encompassing a broad set of skills, including executive function and effortful control, that are often studied in relation to early literacy. We then present our conceptual model of the relations between self-regulation and early literacy. In particular, we argue that literacy and self-regulation development is interdependent and occurs within the same set of contexts. In this section, we present the theoretical and empirical evidence for the model's organizing principles. In the next section, we provide additional support for our conceptual model from experimental studies of interventions targeting the shared contexts of literacy and self-regulation development. We conclude the chapter by discussing the implications of current knowledge for classroom-based practices and outline directions for future research in the area. We suggest that integrated approaches, those targeting both literacy and self-regulation skills concurrently, are an effective method to promote their joint development.

What Is Self-regulation?

Numerous studies linking early reading skills to non-literacy competencies focus on self-regulation (e.g., Bohlmann & Downer, 2016; Connor et al., 2010; Eisenberg et al., 2010; Howse, Calkins, Anastopoulos, Keane, & Shelton, 2003; Konold & Pianta, 2005; Skibbe, Montroy, Bowles, & Morrison, 2018). These studies adopt varying definitions of self-regulation, using the term to connote a diverse set of skills. Some studies focus on cognitive aspects of self-regulation, such as executive functions. Executive functions are cognitive processes that support goal-directed behavior and include inhibitory control, working memory, and cognitive flexibility (Best & Miller, 2010; Diamond, 2013; Nigg, 2000). Other studies focus on the behavioral and emotional aspects of self-regulation, often characterized as effortful control. Effortful control is defined as behavioral regulation in the context of emotional arousal, marked by the ability to forgo a dominant thought, emotion, or response (i.e., an impulse) in favor of the subdominant (i.e., an intentional response; Lengua, 2009; Rothbart, Ellis, Rueda, & Posner, 2003). Although attentional and inhibitory processes are central to both executive function and effortful control, executive function is grounded primarily in the cognitive domain of social-emotional learning, whereas effortful control is grounded primarily in the emotional domain (Jones, Bailey, Barnes, & Partee, 2016).

Despite the relative precision of the terms executive function and effortful control, as compared to self-regulation, there exists little consensus about the specific constructs these terms represent or the appropriate measures to use in their operationalization. A comprehensive review of the self-regulation literature showed that researchers used over 50 distinct construct terms to represent and operationalize executive functions alone (Jones et al., 2016). It therefore comes as no surprise that the literature connecting executive function and effortful control to literacy also uses a variety of terms, defines these terms in varying ways, and uses different measures to represent the same stated construct. For instance, both Best and colleagues (2011) and Blair and Razza (2007) study the link between executive function and literacy development. Whereas the former adopts a definition of executive function that includes planning and goal-setting, the latter focuses on executive function's inhibitory control and cognitive flexibility components. A lack of consensus on self-regulatory concepts and measurement approaches poses a challenge for the creation of an integrated theory of literacy and self-regulation development, as findings based on a particular definition of self-regulation are not necessarily generalizable to a broader set of regulatory skills. Moreover, this confusion makes it difficult for policymakers and educators to identify and target specific regulatory skills that might be most important for reading development. To mitigate this terminological complexity, in the next section we review the current evidence on the relation between literacy and self-regulation, taking care to be explicit on the components of self-regulation (e.g., executive function or effortful control) used in any particular study.

What Do We Know about the Relation between Early Literacy and Self-regulation?

A vast body of research connecting literacy and self-regulation skills suggests the presence of cross-domain relations. Yet the conceptual complexity and related measurement challenges described above complicate our understanding of how and why literacy and self-regulation are linked. An understanding of the directionality and mechanisms of the relation between these domains is central to identifying adult practices that can promote children's development in both areas. Such an understanding also broadens the array of actionable explanations for observed variation in children's literacy competencies. That is, reading difficulties may not only be a function of deficits in literacy-specific skills, but also of non-literacy skills like self-regulation. To synthesize contemporary thought and evidence on the topic, we present organizing principles that underlie a conceptual model of the relation between early literacy and self-regulation.

Figure 15.1 depicts our conceptual model, and the three organizing principles, of the joint development of literacy and self-regulation in the early childhood period. First, the diagram shows that the development of literacy and self-regulation occur concurrently within individual children. Individual children, in turn, develop within multiple contexts, making the conditions for literacy development the same as those for self-regulation development. Second, the overlapping and interwoven developmental paths of literacy and self-regulation underscore the bidirectional dependencies between the two domains. Third, the shaded areas between the literacy and self-regulation pathways represent processes of reorganization and integration that are likely necessary as individuals develop increasingly complex literacy and self-regulation competencies over time. Children must learn to coordinate emerging skills in one area with prevailing skills in the other. Existing theoretical and empirical work offers support for each of these principles, which we summarize below.

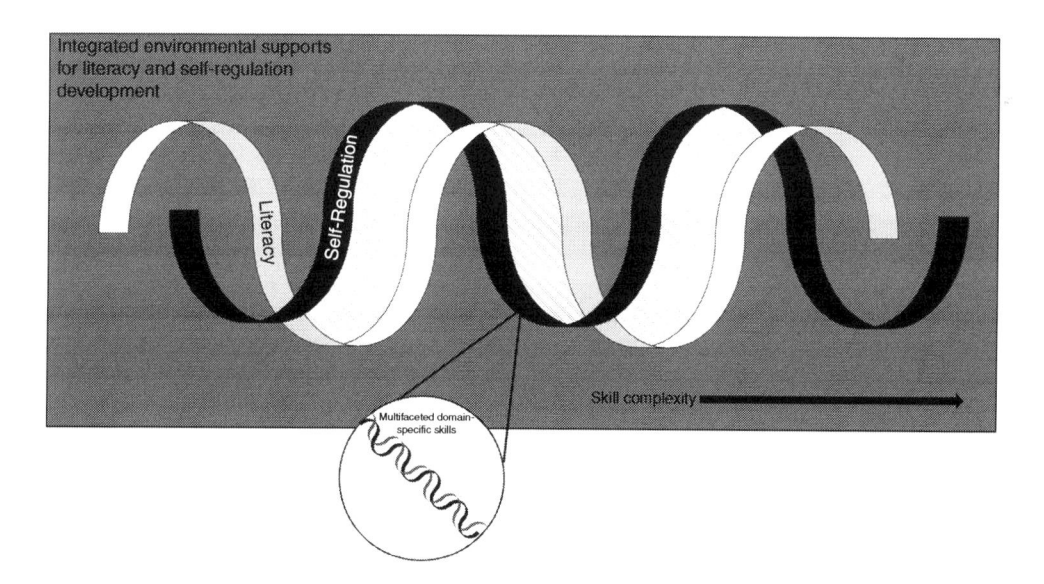

Figure 15.1 Conceptual model of the joint development of literacy and self-regulation

Note: This conceptual model represents our three organizing principles. First, the box around the skill pathways represents the shared environmental contexts of literacy and self-regulation development. Second, the intertwined pathways represent the hypothesized bidirectional relations between skills in the two domains. Third, the shaded areas between the pathways represent the hypothesized reorganizational processes that occur with the development of novel skills in either domain.

Principle 1. The Development of Literacy and Self-regulation Occur Concurrently within the Same Contexts

Children's self-regulation and early literacy skills both mature rapidly between the ages of three and five (National Early Literacy Panel, 2008; Weintraub et al., 2013). During this period, children acquire regulatory competencies that enable them to retain information, inhibit natural impulses, and flexibly follow rules (Best & Miller, 2010; Center on the Developing Child, 2011). At the same time, children's oral language and other pre-reading skills blossom (Dickinson & Tabors, 2001).

Because literacy and self-regulation skills develop simultaneously within individual children, the conditions of self-regulation development are naturally the conditions of literacy development. Work focused on self-regulation (e.g., Blair, 2010; Lengua, 2002) and literacy (e.g., Baker, Scher, & Mackler, 1997; Hart & Risley, 1992) independently identifies features of children's contexts as central to developmental progress in these domains. Dynamic and bioecological theories explain the role of context in propelling development (Bronfenbrenner & Morris, 2006; Fischer & Bidell, 2006; Sameroff, 2010). These theories are rooted in the notion that children live, and therefore develop, in a number of environments, including, most proximally, the home and school contexts. Children interact with these contexts and the individuals within them, which serves to encourage or inhibit development (Sameroff, 2010). These proximal relationships (e.g., with family, teachers, or peers) shape the quality of children's experiences, determine opportunities for learning, and expose children to new knowledge (Jones, Brown, & Aber, 2008).

A number of observational studies have found that features of children's background and socio-demographic context are related to developmental patterns in literacy and self-regulation. It is well documented that children arrive to kindergarten with varying levels of academic readiness, including in literacy, and that differences in readiness are associated with socioeconomic status and other family risk factors (Reardon & Portilla, 2016). A handful of studies has sought to determine whether differences in children's self-regulation skills explain socioeconomic-related gaps in early literacy competencies (Dilworth-Bart, 2012; Fitzpatrick, McKinnon, Blair, & Willoughby, 2014; Nesbitt, Baker-Ward, & Willoughby, 2013; Sektnan, McClelland, Acock, & Morrison, 2010). While unable to isolate causal relations between literacy and self-regulation, these studies suggest that differences in self-regulation account, at least in part, for socioeconomic variation in the acquisition of academic skills.

The studies noted above on socioeconomic status account for only one dimension of children's contexts and experiences. Of course, the conditions for development among children from low-income or at-risk families are heterogeneous. As such, another body of research focused mainly on school contexts has operationalized children's experiences in terms of the quality of their learning environments to understand how particular, and potentially malleable, features of these settings might influence development. The early childhood education field refers to the quality of children's learning environments, including their interpersonal relationships, as "process quality" (Phillipsen, Burchinal, Howes, & Cryer, 1997). However, most correlational studies linking commonly-used process quality measures to children's literacy and self-regulation have yielded either non-significant or small associations (e.g., Mashburn et al., 2008; Weiland, Ulvestad, Sachs, & Yoshikawa, 2013). These findings paired with the existence of socioeconomic-related differences in literacy and self-regulation skills underscore the importance of ongoing research into the mechanisms through which both home and school contexts influence children's development.

Principle 2. There Exist Bidirectional Dependencies between Literacy and Self-regulation

Literacy and self-regulation develop together within children, meaning growth in one domain cannot occur in isolation from growth in the other. This stands in contrast to the common approach of discussing literacy *or* self-regulation as independent, developing in parallel, or even in the absence of the other, as if each domain were capable of unfettered and insulated developmental spurts. As child advocate Marian Wright Edelman frequently notes, "Children do not come in pieces" (Children's Defense Fund, 2016). Growth and development of literacy and self-regulation are therefore not only concurrent but also likely intertwined. Below we summarize research documenting the links between literacy and self-regulation, paying particular attention to the regulatory constructs of executive function and effortful control.

Self-Regulation → Literacy

Executive Function → Literacy

The subcomponents of executive function (i.e., inhibitory control, working memory, and cognitive flexibility) are each thought to contribute to children's successful engagement in literacy-related tasks. Children who inhibit competing impulses while practicing foundational literacy skills may approach tasks with greater concentration for a longer period of time (McClelland & Cameron, 2012). Moreover, the ability to subvert dominant cognitive impulses, or appropriately deal with mental distractions, helps children filter, focus on, and retain relevant information from literacy tasks (Blair, Ursache, Greenberg, Vernon-Feagans, & Family Life Project Investigators, 2015; Morrison, Ponitz, & McClelland, 2010). Cognitive inhibitory control may, therefore, be most salient for the development of code-based literacy skills (e.g., phonological awareness and letter knowledge) that are often developed through tasks that require curtailing dominant responses in favor of a less natural but correct response (Blair & Razza, 2007; Foy & Mann, 2013; McClelland & Cameron, 2011). For example, an early literacy exercise might involve an adult stating a familiar word and then asking the child to replace the word's first sound with an alternative sound to generate a different or nonsensical word (e.g., replacing /c/ in "cat" with /l/). This task requires the child to inhibit the impulse to repeat back the same word or, in the nonsensical word case, the inclination to produce a meaningful word.

Working memory, another component of executive function, supports students in retaining the requisite knowledge for completing literacy tasks. Working memory involves the mental retention, employment, and manipulation of knowledge to inform thoughts and behaviors (Diamond, 2013; Jones et al., 2016). This executive functions sub-component is likely fundamental to the acquisition and retention of rote knowledge (e.g., letter sounds and print concepts) required of early literacy skills (Gathercole, Alloway, Willis, & Adams, 2006). It is also likely that working memory underlies complex literacy skills like comprehension by allowing students to make connections within texts (e.g., extract meaning from strings of words or build a mental representation of the story) and outside of texts (e.g., connect the text to other texts or lived realities; Goff, Pratt, & Ong, 2005; Just & Carpenter, 1980). In line with this hypothesis, several studies show that learning-disabled readers tend to have weaker working memories than their peers without learning delays (Swanson, 1999; Swanson, Zheng, & Jerman, 2009). Earlier theoretical work on working memory also underscores its relevance for simple (e.g., coding) and complex (e.g., comprehension) literacy skills through its facilitation of the storage, processing, and integration of verbal and visuo-spatial data (Baddeley, 1986; Baddeley & Hitch, 1974; Gathercole & Baddeley, 1993).

While less studied than either inhibitory control or working memory in relation to literacy, the third component of executive function – cognitive flexibility – additionally supports literacy development by allowing children to flexibly apply complex phonological rules, syntactic structures, and vocabulary (Cartwright, 2012; Colé, Duncan, & Blaye, 2014). For example, English-speaking children must be able to flexibly pronounce the same letter using a different sound (e.g., a hard and soft c), or a different letter using the same sound (e.g., s and c; Blair & Raver, 2015). Children must also distinguish between homonyms and homographs. A cognitively flexible child instantaneously applies the correct interpretation of a letter or word, or conversely understands that multiple words can be used to represent the same thing. Moreover, cognitive flexibility can facilitate the coordination of reading's multiple demands, such as engaging in decoding and meaning-making simultaneously (Cartwright, 2009, 2012).

Numerous cross-sectional and longitudinal studies have explored whether executive functions relate to contemporaneous and future literacy skills. Preschoolers' core executive functions have been linked to print, letter, and orthographic knowledge, as well as to phonological awareness and vocabulary (Blair & Razza, 2007; Fitzpatrick & Pagani, 2012; Fuhs, Farran, & Nesbitt, 2015; Fuhs, Nesbitt, Farran, & Dong, 2014; Kegel & Bus, 2014; Purpura, Schmitt, & Ganley, 2017; Shaul & Schwartz, 2014). Among elementary-aged children, executive functions have been linked to more complex literacy skills, including reading comprehension (Best et al., 2011; Gathercole, Pickering, Knight, & Stegmann, 2004; Goff et al., 2005; Kieffer et al., 2013; Sesma, Mahone, Levine, Eason, & Cutting, 2009; Swanson & Howell, 2001). A recent meta-analysis of nearly 30 studies linking executive function and reading comprehension found a moderate positive association between the two areas (Follmer, 2018).

Researchers have also examined the hypothesized mechanisms that account for the associations between executive function and early literacy. For example, some studies show that task engagement and attention partially explain the association between self-regulation and growth in early literacy outcomes (Bohlmann & Downer, 2016; Nesbitt, Farran, & Fuhs, 2015). Children with higher self-regulation tend to participate more in classroom activities – meaning they are more engaged, which in turn predicts literacy growth.

Effortful Control → Literacy

Executive functions are likely foundational to but insufficient for academic success given the emotional and social stimuli present in children's learning environments. As such, effortful control, which involves the regulation of thoughts, emotions, and behaviors, also supports children to manage the demands of learning environments (Kochanska, Murray, & Harlan, 2000; Lengua, 2009). Whereas cognitive inhibition (an executive function) supports children's concentration on pertinent aspects of a task, behavioral and emotional inhibition (an effortful control sub-component) likely enables children to eschew external distractions and behavioral impulses (Eisenberg et al., 2010; Rothbart & Jones, 1998). Moreover, behavioral and emotional inhibition may underlie students' persistence and motivation in the face of complex negative emotional arousal (e.g., frustration) that naturally occurs during challenging tasks, like learning to read (Blair, 2002; Pekrun, Elliot, & Maier, 2009; Ursache, Blair, & Raver,

2012). Such inhibitory skills can also facilitate students' sustained engagement in monotonous or routine tasks with delayed rewards (e.g., practicing sight words).

Relatedly, children with strong emotional and behavioral regulation are likely to build deeper relationships with peers and teachers, which affect their learning opportunities (Eisenberg et al., 2010; Hamre & Pianta, 2001; Pianta & Stuhlman, 2004). Children with high effortful control tend to operate in more socially desirable ways, leading to greater social acceptance and more positive relationships (Eisenberg, Fabes, Guthrie, & Reiser, 2000; Eisenberg et al., 2010). Positive relationships with other children encourage active engagement in peer-driven learning experiences (e.g., learning centers) and promote children's sense of belonging in school (Ladd, Herald, & Kochel, 2006). Positive relationships allow children to access content they would otherwise be unable to experience on their own (Pianta & Stuhlman, 2004; Torgesen, 2002; Vygotsky, 1978). Teacher-child relationships may also serve as a protective factor for children likely to have academic or behavioral difficulties (Sabol & Pianta, 2012). Furthermore, positive school-based relationships can promote literacy growth indirectly through their influence on students' perceptions of and connectedness to schooling (Hamre & Pianta, 2005; Ladd & Burgess, 2001).

Evidence from correlational studies shows that effortful control is related to a variety of literacy skills. Among preschoolers, effortful control has been linked to print knowledge, phonological awareness, and vocabulary (Allan & Lonigan, 2011). Among older children (i.e., elementary and middle school aged), effortful control is associated with decoding, fluency, and comprehension (Deater-Deckard, Mullineaux, Petrill, & Thompson, 2009; Mägi, Kikas, & Soodla, 2018). Some studies have explored potential mechanisms that account for the link between effortful control and literacy, like social functioning (Liew, McTigue, Barrois, & Hughes, 2008; Montroy, Bowles, Skibbe, & Foster, 2014; Trentacosta & Izard, 2007; Valiente et al., 2011). For example, the Montroy and Valiente studies showed that children's social skills, which likely underlie children's interpersonal and relational abilities, mediated the association between behavioral self-control and literacy growth.

Complex Executive Function and Effortful Control → Literacy

Complex executive function and effortful control skills (i.e., those requiring the integration and coordination of component skills) are likely more relevant to reading development than are the individual component skills reviewed above (Best et al., 2011; Blair & Dennis, 2010; Ursache et al., 2012). Complex executive function skills include planning, problem solving, and goal setting, whereas complex effortful control skills include delay of gratification, willpower, and resilience (Jones et al., 2016). Some complex skills integrate cognitive (executive function) and emotional (effortful control) skills concurrently (Blair & Dennis, 2010). For instance, error monitoring, which involves identifying and addressing errors, requires individuals to suppress dominant responses (i.e., inhibition), employ working knowledge to address mistakes, and sustain attention in the face of difficulties or frustrations (Zhou, Chen, & Main, 2012).

Complex executive function and effortful control likely underlie advanced reading skills, such as comprehension monitoring, which, unto itself, requires complex literacy skill integration (Miyake et al., 2000; Sesma et al., 2009). Comprehension monitoring involves the construction of complete mental representations of the text, which necessitates engaging working memory of prior parts of the text and of relevant outside content. It also requires inhibitory abilities so that readers are aware of gaps in their comprehension (Nagy, 2007).

Literacy → Self-Regulation

Although much research has focused on self-regulation as foundational to literacy, there is also reason to believe that certain literacy skills may promote children's self-regulation, particularly in early childhood. Specifically, language, which we consider a core element of early literacy (Snow, 1983, 1991), is thought to be a mental tool for self-regulation (Astington & Baird, 2005; Salmon, O'Kearney, Reese, & Fortune, 2016; Vygotsky, 1962; Zelazo et al., 2003). Language, primarily in the form of self-talk, allows children to reflect on, manage, and plan thoughts, emotions, and behaviors. Self-talk, or talking to oneself out loud or internally throughout daily activities, develops between the ages of three and five (Winsler, De León, Wallace, Carlton, & Willson-Quayle, 2003). Several empirical studies lend support for the notion that the emergence of linguistic strategies like self-talk facilitates growth in self-regulation (Fuhs & Day, 2011; Petersen, Bates, & Staples, 2015; Winsler, Diaz, Atencio, McCarthy, & Chabay, 2000). For example, Winsler and colleagues (2000) explored longitudinal patterns in self-talk and self-regulation among preschool-aged children, finding that improvements in self-talk were associated with task performance and executive functioning.

Even before preschool, early literacy skills likely support children's understanding of external regulatory-related interactions and imperatives from adults. Very young children rely on regulation by others, including soothing by adults in emotionally elevated moments and receiving guidance on socially acceptable behaviors. Through these regulation-related experiences with others, children learn appropriate emotional and behavioral responses (Sameroff, 2010; Sameroff & Fiese, 2000). Often, these regulation-related interactions are verbally intensive (e.g., involving explicit oral directives) and, in these instances, linguistic skills are necessary for children to understand what is expected of them. Linguistic deficits could therefore delay children's self-regulation development and undermine their capacity to respond to verbally intensive regulation tasks (Botting, Psarou, Caplin, & Nevin, 2013). Supporting this idea, Vallotton and Ayoub (2011) found that toddlers with higher vocabulary levels had stronger self-regulation growth.

Little research has considered the contributions of more advanced literacy skills, like decoding and reading comprehension, to self-regulation. However, it may be that learning to read also supports self-regulation. Connor and colleagues (2016) expanded on work showing that reading encourages ongoing language development between the ages of six and eight (Verhoeven, van Leeuwe, & Vermeer, 2011), hypothesizing that reading-induced changes in language, metacognition, and brain structure would, in turn, support self-regulation. Following children from first to second grade, the authors found a reciprocal relation between reading and self-regulation, suggesting that advanced literacy skills are not only supported by, but also support, self-regulation.

Toward a Bidirectional Theory

Evidence for the contribution of self-regulation to literacy and of literacy to self-regulation supports a bidirectional perspective. Importantly, the largely correlational studies on the two domains reviewed here do not provide definitive causal proof of the directionality of the relation between the two domains. Principally, it is impossible to determine whether omitted variables that affect both literacy and self-regulation explain the observed association between the two areas. For example, features of children's contexts may affect literacy and self-regulation independently and thus shared ecological features may explain the correlation between the domains. However, findings from the studies summarized here suggest the improbability of a purely context-driven or unidirectional relation from one area to the other.

Additionally, for students with low self-regulatory *and* literacy skills, there likely exists a mutually reinforcing downward cycle, or developmental cascade, between the two domains (Blair, 2002; Masten & Cicchetti, 2010). As students with low self-regulation struggle to read for the reasons outlined above, their lack of literacy competencies can exacerbate challenges with self-regulation (Blair & Diamond, 2008). These students receive explicit and implicit negative feedback via peers and teachers, which inculcates a negative perception of the self as learner and reader (Skinner, Zimmer-Gembeck, & Connell, 1998). Continued negative performance on literacy tasks could also inhibit children's belief in the rewards of cognitive and emotional investment in such tasks (Bandura, 1977).

Some longitudinal studies provide empirical support for bidirectionality between literacy and self-regulation (Bohlmann et al., 2015; Connor et al., 2016; Slot & von Suchodoletz, 2018). For example, Bohlmann and colleagues (2015) found that children's self-regulation and vocabulary skills were predictive of each other across three time points among preschoolers. Such studies validate the adoption of an integrated perspective in understanding individual differences in literacy and self-regulation development. That is, the potential existence of bidirectional dependencies between literacy and self-regulation development suggest that literacy-focused efforts alone may be insufficient to support all struggling readers, and vice versa. A child identified as a struggling reader may benefit from self-regulatory supports, whereas a child labeled as having behavioral issues could profit from literacy supports.

Principle 3. The Development of Novel Skills in either Area Results in a Process of Reorganization and Integration

Children's literacy and self-regulation skills progress from simple to complex over time. In the literacy domain, children learn to employ multiple foundational skills simultaneously, including code-based skills and meaning-based skills, to attack challenging texts. Similarly, in the self-regulation domain, children learn to integrate the component skills of executive function and effortful control to demonstrate more intricate regulatory skills like planning, goal-setting, and error monitoring (Jones et al., 2016). We contend that the development of more complex skills in either domain likely results in reorganizational processes during which individuals accommodate, combine, and ultimately apply complex domain-specific competencies in coordination with skills in the other domain. For example, when children develop the skill to engage in independent error monitoring, a complex self-regulatory process, the way they approach texts changes. Whereas previously, in the absence of these skills, children likely sped through challenging passages or ignored decoding and comprehension errors, children now can identify and address errors. Similarly, when children develop the literacy skill of incorporating background knowledge to make textual inferences, their working memory must adapt to accommodate inputs from both the text and their memory. Arguably, integration of newfound skills with existing skills will not be automatic, but rather will involve a gradual process of integration.

Dynamic skills theory provides theoretical backing for the existence of such reorganizational processes. It posits that over time, children develop increasingly complex skills in a range of domains, and that skills within and across domains influence each other, forming a complex web of interrelated competencies (Fischer & Bidell, 2006). As novel skills develop, individuals' dynamic cognitive organizational systems flexibly shift to incorporate new competencies (Bidell & Fischer, 2000). It is through a process of reorganization that individuals develop the ability to integrate new skills with existing skills. At present, little empirical evidence supports the existence of reorganizational processes, particularly among literacy and self-regulation skills, signifying an important area for future study.

What Do School-based Interventions Tell Us about the Relation between Literacy and Self-regulation?

Experimental studies of school-based interventions focused on literacy and self-regulation offer rigorous evidence in support of the first two organizing principles of our conceptual model. First, studies of interventions targeting the quality of children's environments show that the two domains develop within, and are influenced by, the same contextual features. Second, studies showing the efficacy of interventions that provide children opportunities to integrate literacy and self-regulation skills lend support for the interdependence of the domains. Intervention studies also suggest specific environmental conditions and school-based practices (via the components of the interventions) that are likely important to cross-domain development.

Despite the rapid increase in the number of experimental intervention studies in both the literacy and self-regulation fields, relatively few explore potential cross-domain impacts or integrate the two domains. We discuss six such intervention studies that simultaneously captured self-regulation, literacy, and their contexts. Table 15.1 summarizes these studies, including their design, sample, and measures.

The Chicago School Readiness Project (CSRP) had positive effects on children's literacy and self-regulation by supporting Head Start teachers to establish regulated and well-managed classroom environments (Raver et al., 2008, 2011). Teachers in the treatment group also received ongoing consultation from a mental health consultant to support their own well-being (e.g., managing stress). Such teacher-focused interventions were hypothesized to improve classroom environments to ultimately promote children's self-regulation. Indeed, students of treatment teachers had higher self-regulation *and* literacy skills as compared to those in other Head Start classrooms. Improvements in self-regulation only partially accounted for the treatment's impact on literacy skills, suggesting that improvements in environmental quality also led to direct or unmeasured, indirect impacts on literacy. CSRP's findings underscore that classroom conditions (e.g., approaches to classroom management) that positively affect self-regulation might also be those that support literacy.

Two additional classroom-based interventions targeting adult competencies lend support for the importance of children's environments in concurrently shaping children's literacy and self-regulation. The first, Head Start REDI, was designed to enrich instruction in preschool classrooms to promote early literacy and social-emotional skills, including self-regulation (Bierman et al., 2008a, 2008b). The intervention encouraged pedagogical approaches such as positive behavioral supports, explicit emotion coaching, and interactive readings on social-emotional themes. Teachers received curricular supports (e.g., the Preschool PATHS curriculum), plans for implementing student-driven learning centers, and on-going training in executing and integrating the program components. The program had positive effects on children's vocabulary and emergent literacy skills, as well as on task engagement. These effects were larger for children who began the intervention with low self-regulation skills (Bierman, Nix, Greenberg, Blair, & Domitrovich, 2008). Providing such children with explicit regulation-focused lessons and scaffolds may have had a compounding impact through directly improving children's self-regulation while increasing their engagement in literacy activities.

Similar to Head Start REDI, 4Rs (Reading, Writing, Respect and Resolution) integrated social-emotional and literacy learning in classroom settings (Jones et al., 2011, 2010). Participating K-5 teachers received on-going supports to implement a sequence of literacy-based lessons focused on social-emotional skills and conflict resolution. After a second year of implementation, the evaluation of 4Rs program indicated positive impacts on a host of child social-emotional

Table 15.1 Overview of experimental studies on literacy and self-regulation development

Intervention name	Summary of intervention	Number of experimental groups	Assignment level	Sample size	Age during intervention	Location	Sample description	Self-Regulation Measures	Early Literacy Measures
Chicago School Readiness Project (Raver et al., 2008, 2011)	Randomized control trial of intervention with Head Start teachers aimed to support management and teacher wellbeing	1	School	602[1]	Preschoolers	Chicago	-Children in 35 classrooms in 18 Head Start centers -Racially and ethnically diverse (67% African American; 26% Hispanic) -Low SES (Head Start eligible)	-Preschool Self-Regulation Assessment (PSRA; Smith-Donald et al., 2007) -Balance Beam (Murray & Kochanska et al., 2000) -Pencil Tap (Diamond & Taylor, 1996) -Toy Wrap, Toy Wait, Snack Delay, and Tongue Task (Murray & Kochanska et al., 2000) -Disruptive Behavior -Diagnostic Observation Schedule (Wakschlag et al., 2005)	-Peabody Picture Vocabulary Test (Dunn & Dunn, 1997) -Letter naming task

(Continued)

Table 15.1 (Cont.)

Intervention name	Summary of intervention	Number of experimental groups	Assignment level	Sample size	Age during intervention	Location	Sample description	Self-Regulation Measures	Early Literacy Measures
Computerized Attention Training (Rabiner et al., 2010)	Randomized controlled trial of 1) Computerized Attention Training (CAT) and 2) Computer Assisted Instruction (CAI)	2	Child	77	First graders	Southeastern United States	-Children in five public schools -Children reported as have attentional difficulties -Racially and ethnically diverse (58% African American; 24% Hispanic; 11% White) -67% Free or Reduced Price Lunch (FRPL) eligible	-Conners' Teacher Rating Scale-Revised (CTRS-R:L) DSM-IV Inattentive, Hyperactive-Impulsive, Oppositional, Social Problems, and Anxious/Shy subscales (Conners et al., 1997)	-Woodcock Johnson III – Letter Word Identification, Word Attack, Reading Fluency, and Passage Comprehension (Woodcock, McGrew, & Mather, 2001) -Dynamic Indicators of Basic Early Literacy Skills (DIBELS 2019; Good & Kaminski, 2002) -Teacher-rated Academic Performance Rating Scale (ARPS; DuPaul, Rapport, & Perriello, 1991)
Computer-Based Early Literacy Training (van de Sande, Segers, & Verhoeven, 2016)	Randomized controlled trial of 1) software targeting early literacy with embedded EF supports and 2) an EL-focused software	2	Child	101	Kindergarteners	Netherlands	-Children in three schools -Middle to middle-high income SES	-Flanker Fish -Hearts and Flowers (Diamond, 2013)	-Rhyming task -Syllabic awareness task -Auditory blending -Phonemic segmentation task -Grapheme knowledge task (Verhoeven, 1995; Verhoeven & Van Kuyk, 1991)

Head Start REDI (Bierman et al., 2008a; Bierman et al., 2008b)	Randomized control trial of Head Start REDI intervention in Head Start classrooms aimed at enriching social-emotional and literacy skills	1	Classrooms	356	Preschoolers	Pennsylvania	-Children in 44 Head Start classrooms -Racially and ethnically diverse (25% African American; 17% Hispanic; 42% White) - Low SES (Head Start eligible)	-Backward Word Span (Davis & Pratt, 1995) -Peg Tapping Task (Diamond & Taylor, 1996) -DCCS (Frye, Zelazo, & Palfai, 1995) -Walk-a-line Slowly Task (Kochanska, Murray, Jacques, Koenig, & Vandegeest, 1996) -Task Orientation (Smith-Donald, Raver, Hayes, & Richardson, 2007) -Social Competence Scale (Conduct Problems Prevention Research Group, 1995) -Teacher Observation of Child Adaptation – Revised (Werthamer-Larsson, Kellam, & Wheeler, 1991)	-Expressive One-Word Picture Vocabulary Test (Brownell, 2000) -Test of Language Development - Grammatical Understanding and Sentence Imitation subtest (Newcomer & Hammill, 1997) -Test of Preschool Literacy (TOPEL)- Blending, Elision, and Print Knowledge subtests (Lonigan, Wagner, Torgesen, & Rashotte, 2007)

(Continued)

Table 15.1 (Cont.)

Intervention name	Summary of intervention	Number of experimental groups	Assignment level	Sample size	Age during intervention	Location	Sample description	Self-Regulation Measures	Early Literacy Measures
Individualized Literacy Instruction (Connor et al., 2010)	Randomized control trial of individualized literacy instruction software (A2i) to support teachers in implementing individualized instructional approaches	1	School	445	First graders	Mid-sized city in Florida	-Children in 46 classrooms in ten schools -Racially and ethnically diverse (47% African American; 35% White) -Over half of students in study schools eligible for FRPL	-Head-Toes-Knees-Shoulders Task (Ponitz et al., 2009) -Social Skills Rating System (SSRS; Gresham & Elliott, 1990)	-Woodcock Johnson III -Letter Word Identification, Passage Comprehension, and Picture Vocabulary (Woodcock et al., 2001)
4Rs (Jones, Brown, & Aber, 2011; Jones, Brown, Hoglund, & Aber, 2010)	Randomized control trial of 4Rs intervention with elementary schools aimed at integrating social-emotional learning and literacy instruction	1	School	1,184[2]	Elementary school aged	New York City	-Children working with 146 teachers across 18 public schools -Racially and ethnically diverse (41.3% African American; 45.8% Hispanic; 4.3% White)	-Home Interview Questionnaire – Hostile attribution bias and Aggressive interpersonal negotiation strategies (Dahlberg, Toal, & Behrens, 1998)	-Early Childhood Longitudinal Study-Kindergarten Cohort, 3rd Grade Assessment -New York State standardized reading assessment

- Predominantly low SES

- Normative Beliefs About Aggression scale (Huesmann & Guerra, 1997)
- What I Think Instrument – Aggressive Fantasies and Prosocial Sub-scale (Rosenfeld, Huesmann, Eron, & Torney-Purta, 1982)
- ADHD Symptomatology Scale (Milich, Loney, & Landau, 1982)
- Diagnostic Interview Schedule for Children (Lucas et al., 2001)
- Behavioral Assessment System for Children (Reynolds & Kamphaus, 1998)
- Social Competence Scale (CPPRG, 1999)

---

1 Information on sample size and composition for Chicago School Readiness Project comes from Raver et al. (2008).
2 Information on sample size and composition of 4Rs study come from the second-year impact analyses presented in Jones et al. (2011).

competencies, including attention and social competence (Jones et al., 2010). Moreover, the program had positive effects on reading for those students identified by teachers as having the most challenging behaviors at baseline. Like Head Start REDI, the effects of 4Rs suggests that integrated approaches may have compounding effects by having direct *and* indirect impacts on skills in the two domains. Additional research on 4Rs suggests the intervention also had effects on classroom process quality, which might partially explain positive impacts on child outcomes (Brown, Jones, LaRusso, & Aber, 2010).

4Rs, Head Start REDI, and CSRP each suggest that helping educators create nurturing classroom environments, marked by positive teacher-child relationships and rigorous content instruction, supports children's literacy and self-regulation (Jones et al., 2008). Head Start REDI and 4Rs also highlight the potential value of integrating literacy and self-regulation instruction to promote growth in both domains. However, these studies do not provide evidence on the domains' bidirectionality, as it is unclear whether these forms of integrated instruction improved skill development above and beyond domain-specific approaches or whether development in one domain *led* to development in the other.

It is thought that evidence on the latter may come from intervention studies focused primarily on one domain. Interventions targeting primarily either literacy or self-regulation skills illustrate whether intervention-related gains in the targeted domain also cause growth in the non-targeted domain (Jacob & Parkinson, 2015). Nonetheless, these studies are limited in two principal ways. First, even interventions that target only one domain are likely to influence the other. For example, self-regulation-focused interventions are likely to expose children to verbal and written language, which could result in improvements in their literacy skills. At the same time, literacy-focused interventions provide children with opportunities to practice self-regulation through structured tasks. Second, interventions targeting one domain could indirectly influence the non-targeted domain by altering features of the learning environment.

A recent study of an individualized literacy instruction intervention illustrates the second case. The literacy-focused intervention positively affected children's self-regulation, particularly among those with low baseline regulatory levels (Connor et al., 2010). In this study, treatment teachers received the Assessment to Instruction (A2i) software to help tailor instruction to students' literacy skills. Individualized instruction allows students to access the types and intensity of instruction most likely to promote their development (Connor, Morrison, Fishman, Schatschneider, & Underwood, 2007; Connor, Morrison, & Slominski, 2006). Consistent with this hypothesis, several prior studies found individualized instruction to positively affect literacy development (Connor et al., 2009; Connor, Morrison, & Katch, 2004; Connor, Morrison, & Petrella, 2004). The designers of this intervention also hypothesized that individualized instruction might also improve children's self-regulation by improving classroom structures and increasing students' task engagement. It is therefore impossible to disentangle whether the observed effects on self-regulation were the result of improvements in literacy and/or due to changes in the classroom environment. Regardless, these results suggest that practices that support literacy also support self-regulation.

Experimental studies that directly compare the effects of domain-focused and domain-integrated interventions provide the most compelling evidence on the domains' interdependence. For example, a study with two interventions targeting literacy, one of which is primarily literacy-focused and the other of which also integrates self-regulation supports and learning, can help us understand whether literacy benefits from the integration of self-regulation. One such study of a computer-based literacy program tested the added contribution of embedding executive function-related activities in the program (van de Sande et al.,

2016). The study included two intervention groups: one that used software to practice early literacy skills (EL) and another that used a similar software program to practice early literacy skills with executive function-related tasks (EL+EF). Students in the EL+EF group were asked to stop, think, and verbally explain their thoughts on literacy tasks before selecting a response, activating inhibitory control. Whereas children in both groups experienced larger early literacy gains than those in the control group, the literacy gains of the EL+EF group were greater than those of the EL group. Children in the EL+EF group completed more computer activities, were less reliant on the software's "help" function, and performed less irrelevant mouse clicks. These findings suggest the integration of regulatory-related activities into literacy-based activities can improve literacy development by increasing children's attention and focus on literacy-related tasks.

Another multi-armed study of computer-based attention training similarly suggests that integrated approaches may be superior to domain-specific strategies. The Project CLASS (Children Learning Academic Success Skills) intervention isolated the relative impact of Computerized Attention Training (CAT) and Computerized Assisted Instruction (CAI) on first graders' attention and literacy skills (Rabiner et al., 2010). CAT involved the completion of computerized training exercises aimed at auditory and visual attention. Like CAT, CAI tasks were designed to improve children's attention, but did so in the context of literacy and mathematics tasks. Children identified by their teachers as having attentional challenges were randomized to receive one of the two attention-focused interventions or to be added to a waitlist. Both interventions led to a decline in teacher-reported attention issues. However, only the CAI – the integrated intervention – resulted in academic improvements. This study highlights the potential for academic-based attention interventions (e.g., CAI) to affect both attention and academics and shows the limitations of attention-only interventions for academic outcomes.

In sum, these classroom-based experimental studies emphasize the importance of children's contexts in simultaneously shaping literacy and self-regulation. They also provide support for the notion that literacy and self-regulation are interdependent, and relatedly underscore the promise of integrated approaches for improving skills in both domains. Nevertheless, additional research is needed to untangle these processes using robust experimental methods.

Implications for Classroom-based Practice

The research summarized above offers several potential directions for improving children's literacy and self-regulation, particularly within early childhood classroom settings. First, supporting teachers' well-being may be a mechanism for promoting children's literacy and self-regulation. Positive classroom environments marked by supportive relationships can help to build children's emotional health and afford children greater opportunities to learn academic skills like reading (Bohlmann & Downer, 2016; Valiente et al., 2011). In particular, adult-child interactions that ensue from strong relationships are thought to spur children's literacy development through language exposure and to promote self-regulation by improving task engagement and knowledge of acceptable emotional and behavioral responses (Bronfenbrenner & Morris, 2006; Downer, Sabol, & Hamre, 2010; Hamre, 2014; Sabol & Pianta, 2012). However, poor psychological functioning can prohibit adult caregivers from developing positive relationships with children (Friedman-Krauss, Raver, Neuspiel, & Kinsel, 2014; Hamre & Pianta, 2004; Li Grining et al., 2010; Sandilos, Goble, Rimm-Kaufman, & Pianta, 2018). A failure to adequately cope with stress can ignite a "burnout cascade" in which ineffective interactions with students result in more student misbehaviors (i.e., a less regulated classroom), which in turn increase teacher stress

(Jennings & Greenberg, 2009). Investing in adult well-being, such as in the CSRP intervention, can ensure children have strong relationships with teachers, which in turn support children's literacy and self-regulation development (Jones, Bouffard, & Weissbourd, 2013; Raver et al., 2008, 2011).

Second, in addition to well-being, focusing on building adults' knowledge of and ability to implement effective integrated instructional practices can also support the joint development of literacy and self-regulation. Teaching is a complex task that involves multiple, and at times competing, demands (Phillips, 2016). Providing educators with explicit guidance, via ongoing professional supports like coaching and trainings, can help educators negotiate competing demands to implement high impact pedagogical practices like those of the Head Start REDI and 4Rs interventions (Egert, Fukkink, & Eckhardt, 2018; Fukkink & Lont, 2007; Hamre, Downer, Jamil, & Pianta, 2012; Kraft, Blazar, & Hogan, 2016). Professional supports are thought to be most effective when they target specific pedagogical practices, such as integrated literacy and self-regulation approaches, over a sustained period of time using strategies that encourage adult behavioral change (Hamre, Partee, & Mulcahy, 2017; Weiland, McCormick, Mattera, Maier, & Morris, 2018). Both Head Start REDI (Bierman et al., 2008, 2008) and 4Rs (Jones et al., 2011, 2010) centered on providing adults with knowledge of instructional practices that concurrently support literacy and self-regulation along with ongoing professional supports to improve children's classroom-based learning opportunities.

Third, this body of research begins to shed light on the pedagogical practices that are most impactful for literacy and self-regulation. In addition to teacher-child interactions, integrated instructional practices that simultaneously target literacy and self-regulation development may have amplifying effects for development in both domains (Jones et al., 2011). Examples of integrated practices include the inclusion of rich texts in direct instruction on self-regulatory skills (as in Head Start REDI; Bierman et al., 2008, 2008) or regulatory-related scaffolds in literacy exercises (as in the computer-based early literacy training; van de Sande et al., 2016). If literacy and self-regulation are reciprocally and directly related as we assert, then targeting both domains simultaneously may capitalize on correlated strengths or interrupt correlated deficits. Indeed, some research suggests that such integrated practices may work best for children with low baseline skills in literacy and/or self-regulation (e.g., Bierman et al., 2008; Connor et al., 2010). In these cases, integrated practices may disrupt negative, mutually reinforcing cycles experienced by children with low literacy and/or self-regulation skills.

Directions for Future Research

Despite the current body of research linking self-regulation to literacy, there is a great deal that we do not yet know. For example, more research is needed to understand the mechanisms underlying the association between literacy and self-regulation. Whereas some work has explored the mediating role of other *skills* like task engagement and social competence (e.g., Bohlmann & Downer, 2016; Valiente et al., 2011), less work has considered the *developmental processes* through which these domains interact. In particular, there is little empirical evidence about how the development of novel skills in one domain may affect existing skills in another domain or, as suggested here and by dynamic skills theory (Fischer & Bidell, 2006), may drive processes of cognitive reorganization. Understanding these processes could highlight future targets for intervention in and out of the classroom.

Additional research is also needed to build our knowledge of why integrated instructional approaches may be more effective than domain-specific methods. Multi-armed experimental studies, like the two-computer based interventions discussed (Rabiner et al., 2010; van de

Sande et al., 2016), provide the opportunity to examine the relative contributions of integrated cross-domain practices versus domain-specific approaches. Within such studies, researchers should examine intervention effects on children's outcomes *and* on contextual quality to understand the ecological conditions that promote literacy and self-regulation development. For example, the 4Rs intervention had a positive impact on the instructional aspects of classroom quality, which may have accounted for its impact on child outcomes across domains (Brown et al., 2010).

Methodological Considerations for Future Research

In addition to addressing long-standing conceptual questions, future research on literacy and self-regulation can address a set of important methodological gaps. First, as suggested above, existing research on literacy and self-regulation has largely relied on observational studies, which substantially limits causal inference. More experimental studies are needed to clarify whether domain-specific interventions contribute to skills in the non-targeted domain (Jacob & Parkinson, 2015). For example, a literacy-focused intervention that also improves self-regulation might suggest that literacy development contributes to self-regulation. Nevertheless, as noted above, there are limits to this approach as any intervention intended to focus on literacy or self-regulation will incorporate elements that could directly influence the non-targeted domain. In the literacy-focused example, we would expect the intervention to include opportunities for students to explicitly practice self-regulation (e.g., practicing inhibition while participating in group activities). Thus, experimental research is unlikely to isolate an unbiased causal estimate of the direct relations between literacy and self-regulation but may suggest directionality and illuminate practices that effectively promote the domains' joint development.

A second challenge relates to the measurement of literacy and self-regulation. The research reviewed here employs numerous measures of literacy and self-regulation, each of which captures distinct sub-skills. The use of multiple measures within and across studies complicates our understanding of the specific dimensions of literacy and self-regulation development that are related. It also limits our ability to understand the domains' relations across developmental periods (e.g., Are differences across age groups due to age-related differences or the use of distinct measures for different ages?; Ahmed, Tang, Waters, & Davis-Kean, 2018). Moreover, studies that employ multiple measures of both domains tend to focus on statistically significant results, which may constitute only a fraction of the pairs of literacy and self-regulation skills tested.

These measurement-related challenges emphasize the importance of intentionality in choosing and analyzing measures. In selecting measures for a particular study, researchers should adopt an interdisciplinary perspective to more fully capture development in both domains, rather than disproportionally assessing outcomes in one domain or the other. For example, many studies conducted from a self-regulation perspective often focus only on vocabulary outcomes in the literacy domain. Measure selection should also be informed by the study or intervention's theory of change (i.e., choosing measures that capture only relevant constructs). Relatedly, in analysis, researchers should only test associations outlined in the theory of change and should adjust for multiple hypothesis testing to account for the increased probability of false-positive findings in the presence of multiple tests. To reduce the number of associations tested, researchers may also adopt data reduction approaches that combine measures, including latent variable methods.

A third challenge relates to the external validity, or generalizability, of work linking literacy and self-regulation. The majority of studies in this area are conducted with small samples in select populations (as illustrated in Table 1). It is therefore unknown whether such interventions may have different effects for particular subpopulations of children and within different contexts (Hanno & Surrain, 2019). In addition to limiting our understanding of how the two domains relate to each other in understudied populations, the use of small, non-representative samples minimizes our understanding of the feasibility of conducting such integrated interventions at a larger scale (e.g., at the district-level). In light of these challenges, there is the need for more systematic reviews that not only provide meta-analytic effect sizes of the relation between literacy and self-regulation, but also summarize measures and populations to illuminate understudied populations and constructs within the two domains.

Summary and Conclusions

In this chapter, we reviewed the literature on the link between literacy and self-regulation with a particular focus on how this body of research might inform school-based practices that support the two domains' joint development in early childhood. Specifically, research suggests that literacy and self-regulation development are intertwined and bidirectionally interdependent. Whereas self-regulation underlies children's ability to engage in literacy-related learning opportunities, early literacy (particularly language) also underlies children's ability to engage in self-regulatory processes. The existence of mutual dependencies – as well as research emphasizing the importance of context in shaping both domains – in turn suggests that integrated classroom-based practices that provide learning opportunities for both literacy and self-regulation growth are likely to drive the greatest impacts for skills in both domains, particularly for students struggling in either domain. High-quality randomized experiments of integrated instructional approaches, such as 4Rs and Head Start REDI, provide initial support for this hypothesis. Despite the wealth of research in this area, more work should investigate how integrated practices influence the full range of literacy and self-regulation skills and whether or not such pedagogical approaches are scalable.

References

Ahmed, S. F., Tang, S., Waters, N., & Davis-Kean, P. (2018). Executive function and academic achievement: Longitudinal relations from early childhood to adolescence. doi:10.31234/osf.io/xd5jy

Allan, N. P., & Lonigan, C. J. (2011). Examining the dimensionality of effortful control in preschool children and its relation to academic and socioemotional indicators. *Developmental Psychology, 47*(4), 905–915. doi:10.1037/a0023748

Astington, J. W., & Baird, J. A. (2005). *Why language matters for theory of mind.* New York, NY: Oxford University Press.

Baddeley, A. (1986). Oxford psychology series, No. 11. Working memory.

Baddeley, A., & Hitch, G. (1974). Working memory. In G. A. Bower (Ed.), *Psychology of learning and motivation* (Vol. 8, pp. 47–89). New York, NY: Elsevier.

Baker, L., Scher, D., & Mackler, K. (1997). Home and family influences on motivations for reading. *Educational Psychologist, 32*(2), 69–82. doi:10.1207/s15326985ep3202_2

Bandura, A. (1977). Self-efficacy: Toward a unifying theory of behavioral change. *Psychological Review, 84*(2), 191.

Best, J. R., & Miller, P. H. (2010). A developmental perspective on executive function. *Child Development, 81*(6), 1641–1660.

Best, J. R., Miller, P. H., & Naglieri, J. A. (2011). Relations between executive function and academic achievement from ages 5 to 17 in a large, representative national sample. *Learning and Individual Differences, 21*(4), 327–336.

Bidell, T. R., & Fischer, K. W. (2000). The role of cognitive structure in the development of behavioral control: A dynamic skills approach. *Control of Human Behavior, Mental Processes, and Consciousness: Essays in Honor of the 60th Birthday of August Flammer,* 183–201.

Bierman, K. L., Domitrovich, C. E., Nix, R. L., Gest, S. D., Welsh, J. A., Greenberg, M. T., Blair, C., Nelson, K. E., & Gill, S. (2008a). Promoting academic and social-emotional school readiness: The Head Start REDI program. *Child Development, 79*(6), 1802–1817.

Bierman, K. L., Nix, R. L., Greenberg, M. T., Blair, C., & Domitrovich, C. E. (2008b). Executive functions and school readiness intervention: Impact, moderation, and mediation in the Head Start REDI program. *Development and Psychopathology, 20*(03). doi:10.1017/S0954579408000394

Blair, C. (2002). School readiness: Integrating cognition and emotion in a neurobiological conceptualization of children's functioning at school entry. *American Psychologist, 57*(2), 111.

Blair, C. (2010). Stress and the development of self-regulation in context. *Child Development Perspectives, 4*(3), 181–188.

Blair, C., & Dennis, T. (2010). An optimal balance: The integration of emotion and cognition in context. *Child Development at the Intersection of Emotion and Cognition*, 17–35.

Blair, C., & Diamond, A. (2008). Biological processes in prevention and intervention: The promotion of self-regulation as a means of preventing school failure. *Development and Psychopathology, 20*(03). doi:10.1017/S0954579408000436

Blair, C., & Raver, C. C. (2015). School readiness and self-regulation: A developmental psychobiological approach. *Annual Review of Psychology, 66*(1), 711–731. doi:10.1146/annurev-psych-010814-015221

Blair, C., & Razza, R. P. (2007). Relating effortful control, executive function, and false belief understanding to emerging math and literacy ability in kindergarten. *Child Development, 78*(2), 647–663.

Blair, C., Ursache, A., Greenberg, M., & Vernon-Feagans, L.; Family Life Project Investigators. (2015). Multiple aspects of self-regulation uniquely predict mathematics but not letter–word knowledge in the early elementary grades. *Developmental Psychology, 51*(4), 459–472.

Bohlmann, N. L., & Downer, J. T. (2016). Self-regulation and task engagement as predictors of emergent language and literacy skills. *Early Education and Development, 27*(1), 18–37. doi:10.1080/10409289.2015.1046784

Bohlmann, N. L., Maier, M. F., & Palacios, N. (2015). Bidirectionality in self-regulation and expressive vocabulary: Comparisons between monolingual and dual language learners in preschool. *Child Development, 86*(4), 1094–1111.

Botting, N., Psarou, P., Caplin, T., & Nevin, L. (2013). Short-term memory skills in children with specific language impairment: The effect of verbal and nonverbal task content. *Topics in Language Disorders, 33*(4), 313. doi:10.1097/01.TLD.0000437940.01237.51

Bronfenbrenner, U., & Morris, P. A. (2006). The bioecological model of human development. In *Handbook of Child Psychology*. John Wiley & Sons, Inc.. doi:10.1002/9780470147658.chpsy0114

Brown, J. L., Jones, S. M., LaRusso, M. D., & Aber, J. L. (2010). Improving classroom quality: Teacher influences and experimental impacts of the 4Rs program. *Journal of Educational Psychology, 102*(1), 153–167. doi:10.1037/a0018160

Brownell, R. (2000). *Expressive one-word picture vocabulary test: Manual*. Academic Therapy Publications Novato, CA.

Cadima, J., Barros, S., Ferreira, T., Serra-Lemos, M., Leal, T., & Verschueren, K. (2018). Bidirectional associations between vocabulary and self-regulation in preschool and their interplay with teacher–child closeness and autonomy support. *Early Childhood Research Quarterly*. doi:10.1016/j.ecresq.2018.04.004

Cartwright, K. (2009). The role of cognitive flexibility in reading comprehension: Past, present, and future. In S. E. Israel & G. G. Duffy (Eds.), *Handbook of Research on Reading Comprehension* (pp. 115–139).

Cartwright, K. (2012). Insights from cognitive neuroscience: The importance of executive function for early reading development and education. *Early Education & Development, 23*(1), 24–36.

Center on the Developing Child. (2011). *Building the brain's "air traffic control" system: How early experiences shape the development of executive function* (Working Paper #11). Cambridge, MA.

Children's Defense Fund. (2016, February 9). Marian Wright Edelman says: President's budget would change the odds for children in America. Retrieved July 17, 2018, from https://www.childrensdefense.org/2016/marian-wright-edelman-says-presidents-budget-would-change-the-odds-for-children-in-america/

Colé, P., Duncan, L. G., & Blaye, A. (2014). Cognitive flexibility predicts early reading skills. *Frontiers in Psychology, 5*, 565.

Conduct Problems Prevention Research Group. (1995). Psychometric properties of the social competence scale-teacher and parent ratings. *Fast Track Project Technical Report*. University Park, PA: Pennsylvania State University.

Conduct Problems Prevention Research Group. (1999). Initial impact of the fast track prevention trial for conduct problems: I. the high-risk sample. *Journal of Consulting and Clinical Psychology, 67*, 631–647.

Conners, C. K., Wells, K. C., Parker, J. D., Sitarenios, G., Diamond, J. M., & Powell, J. W. (1997). A new self-report scale for assessment of adolescent psychopathology: Factor structure, reliability, validity, and diagnostic sensitivity. *Journal of Abnormal Child Psychology, 25*(6), 487–497.

Connor, C. M., Day, S. L., Phillips, B., Sparapani, N., Ingebrand, S. W., McLean, L., ... Kaschak, M. P. (2016). Reciprocal effects of self-regulation, semantic knowledge, and reading comprehension in early elementary school. *Child Development, 87*(6), 1813–1824. doi:10.1111/cdev.12570

Connor, C. M., Morrison, F. J., Fishman, B. J., Ponitz, C. C., Glasney, S., Underwood, P. S., ... Schatschneider, C. (2009). The ISI classroom observation system: Examining the literacy instruction provided to individual students. *Educational Researcher, 38*(2), 85–99. doi:10.3102/0013189X09332373

Connor, C. M., Morrison, F. J., Fishman, B. J., Schatschneider, C., & Underwood, P. (2007). Algorithm-guided individualized reading instruction. *Science-new York Then Washington, 315*(5811), 464.

Connor, C. M., Morrison, F. J., & Katch, L. E. (2004). Beyond the reading wars: Exploring the effect of child-instruction interactions on growth in early reading. *Scientific Studies of Reading, 8*(4), 305–336. doi:10.1207/s1532799xssr0804_1

Connor, C. M., Morrison, F. J., & Petrella, J. N. (2004). Effective reading comprehension instruction: Examining child x instruction interactions. *Journal of Educational Psychology, 96*(4), 682.

Connor, C. M., Morrison, F. J., & Slominski, L. (2006). Preschool instruction and children's emergent literacy growth. *Journal of Educational Psychology, 98*(4), 665.

Connor, C. M., Ponitz, C. C., Phillips, B. M., Travis, Q. M., Glasney, S., & Morrison, F. J. (2010). First graders' literacy and self-regulation gains: The effect of individualizing student instruction. *Journal of School Psychology, 48*(5), 433–455. doi:10.1016/j.jsp.2010.06.003

Dahlberg, L. L., Toal, S. B., & Behrens, C. B. (1998). *Measuring violence-related attitudes, beliefs, and behaviors among youths: A compendium of assessment tools*. Division of Violence Prevention, National Center for Injury Prevention and Control, Centers for Disease Control and Prevention Atlanta, GA.

Davis, H. L., & Pratt, C. (1995). The development of children's theory of mind: The working memory explanation. *Australian Journal of Psychology, 47*(1), 25–31.

Deater-Deckard, K., Mullineaux, P. Y., Petrill, S. A., & Thompson, L. A. (2009). Effortful control, surgency, and reading skills in middle childhood. *Reading and Writing, 22*(1), 107–116.

Diamond, A. (2013). Executive functions. *Annual Review of Psychology, 64*(1), 135–168. doi:10.1146/annurev-psych-113011-143750

Diamond, A., & Taylor, C. (1996). Development of an aspect of executive control: Development of the abilities to remember what I said and to "do as I say, not as I do." *Developmental Psychobiology, 29*(4), 315–334.

Dickinson, D. K., & Tabors, P. O. (2001). *Beginning literacy with language: Young children learning at home and school*. Baltimore, MD: Paul H Brookes Publishing.

Dilworth-Bart, J. E. (2012). Does executive function mediate SES and home quality associations with academic readiness?. *Early Childhood Research Quarterly, 27*(3), 416–425. doi:10.1016/j.ecresq.2012.02.002

Downer, J., Sabol, T. J., & Hamre, B. (2010). Teacher–Child interactions in the classroom: Toward a theory of within- and cross-domain links to children's developmental outcomes. *Early Education & Development, 21*(5), 699–723. doi:10.1080/10409289.2010.497453

Dunn, L. M., & Dunn, L. M. (1997). *PPVT-III: Peabody picture vocabulary test*. Circle Pines, MN: American Guidance Service.

DuPaul, G. J., Rapport, M. D., & Perriello, L. M. (1991). Teacher ratings of academic skills: The development of the academic performance rating scale. *School Psychology Review, 20*(2), 284–300.

Dynamic Indicator of Basic Early Literacy Skills (DIBELS). (2019). University of Oregon Center for Teaching and Learning. Eugene, Oregon. Retrieved from https //dibels.uoregon.edu

Egert, F., Fukkink, R. G., & Eckhardt, A. G. (2018). Impact of in-service professional development programs for early childhood teachers on quality ratings and child outcomes: A meta-analysis. *Review of Educational Research, 88*(3). doi:0034654317751918

Eisenberg, N., Fabes, R. A., Guthrie, I. K., & Reiser, M. (2000). Dispositional emotionality and regulation: Their role in predicting quality of social functioning. *Journal of Personality and Social Psychology, 78*(1), 136.

Eisenberg, N., Valiente, C., & Eggum, N. D. (2010). Self-regulation and school readiness. *Early Education & Development, 21*(5), 681–698. doi:10.1080/10409289.2010.497451

Fischer, K. W., & Bidell, T. (2006). Dynamic development of action and thought. *Handbook of Child Psychology: Theoretical Models of Human Development, 1*, 467–561.

Fitzpatrick, C., McKinnon, R. D., Blair, C. B., & Willoughby, M. T. (2014). Do preschool executive function skills explain the school readiness gap between advantaged and disadvantaged children? *Learning and Instruction, 30*, 25–31. doi:10.1016/j.learninstruc.2013.11.003

Fitzpatrick, C., & Pagani, L. S. (2012). Toddler working memory skills predict kindergarten school readiness. *Intelligence, 40*(2), 205–212. doi:10.1016/j.intell.2011.11.007

Follmer, D. J. (2018). Executive function and reading comprehension: A meta-analytic review. *Educational Psychologist, 53*(1), 42–60. doi:10.1080/00461520.2017.1309295

Foy, J. G., & Mann, V. A. (2013). Executive function and early reading skills. *Reading and Writing, 26*(3), 453–472. doi:10.1007/s11145-012-9376-5

Friedman-Krauss, A. H., Raver, C. C., Neuspiel, J. M., & Kinsel, J. (2014). Child behavior problems, teacher executive functions, and teacher stress in Head Start classrooms. *Early Education and Development, 25*(5), 681–702. doi:10.1080/10409289.2013.825190

Frye, D., Zelazo, P. D., & Palfai, T. (1995). Theory of mind and rule-based reasoning. *Cognitive Development, 10*(4), 483–527.

Fuhs, M. W., & Day, J. D. (2011). Verbal ability and executive functioning development in preschoolers at Head Start. *Developmental Psychology, 47*(2), 404–416. doi:10.1037/a0021065

Fuhs, M. W., Farran, D. C., & Nesbitt, K. T. (2015). Prekindergarten children's executive functioning skills and achievement gains: The utility of direct assessments and teacher ratings. *Journal of Educational Psychology, 107*(1), 207–221. doi:10.1037/a0037366

Fuhs, M. W., Nesbitt, K. T., Farran, D. C., & Dong, N. (2014). Longitudinal associations between executive functioning and academic skills across content areas. *Developmental Psychology, 50*(6), 1698–1709. doi:10.1037/a0036633

Fukkink, R. G., & Lont, A. (2007). Does training matter? A meta-analysis and review of caregiver training studies. *Early Childhood Research Quarterly, 22*(3), 294–311.

Gathercole, S., Alloway, T. P., Willis, C., & Adams, A.-M. (2006). Working memory in children with reading disabilities. *Journal of Experimental Child Psychology, 93*(3), 265–281. doi:10.1016/j.jecp.2005.08.003

Gathercole, S., & Baddeley, A. (1993). Phonological working memory: A critical building block for reading development and vocabulary acquisition? *European Journal of Psychology of Education, 8*(3), 259.

Gathercole, S., Pickering, S. J., Knight, C., & Stegmann, Z. (2004). Working memory skills and educational attainment: Evidence from national curriculum assessments at 7 and 14 years of age. *Applied Cognitive Psychology, 18*(1), 1–16. doi:10.1002/acp.934

Goff, D. A., Pratt, C., & Ong, B. (2005). The relations between children's reading comprehension, working memory, language skills and components of reading decoding in a normal sample. *Reading and Writing, 18*(7–9), 583–616.

Good, R. H., & Kaminski, R. A. (2002). *Dynamic indicators of basic early literacy skills: DIBELS*. Eugene, OR: Dynamic Measurement Group.

Gresham, F. M., & Elliott, S. N. (1990). *Social skills rating system: Manual*. Circle Pines, MN: American Guidance Service.

Hamre, B. (2014). Teachers' daily interactions with children: An essential ingredient in effective early childhood programs. *Child Development Perspectives, 8*(4), 223–230. doi:10.1111/cdep.12090

Hamre, B., Downer, J. T., Jamil, F. M., & Pianta, R. C. (2012). Enhancing teachers' intentional use of effective interactions with children: Designing and testing professional development interventions. In R. C. Pinata (Ed.), *Handbook of Early Childhood Education* (pp. 507–532). New York, NY: Guildford Press.

Hamre, B., Partee, A., & Mulcahy, C. (2017). Enhancing the impact of professional development in the context of preschool expansion. *AERA Open, 3*(4), 2332858417733686.

Hamre, B., & Pianta, R. (2004). Self-reported depression in nonfamilial caregivers: Prevalence and associations with caregiver behavior in child-care settings. *Early Childhood Research Quarterly, 19*(2), 297–318. doi:10.1016/j.ecresq.2004.04.006

Hamre, B., & Pianta, R. C. (2001). Early teacher–child relationships and the trajectory of children's school outcomes through eighth grade. *Child Development, 72*(2), 625–638.

Hamre, B. K., & Pianta, R. C. (2005). Can instructional and emotional support in the first-grade classroom make a difference for children at risk of school failure? *Child Development, 76*(5), 949–967.

Hanno, E., & Surrain, S. (2019). The direct and indirect relations between self-regulation and language development among monolinguals and dual language learners. *Clinical Child and Family Psychology Review, 22*(1), 75–89. doi:10.1007/s10567-019-00283-3

Hart, B., & Risley, T. R. (1992). American parenting of language-learning children: Persisting differences in family-child interactions observed in natural home environments. *Developmental Psychology, 28*(6), 1096.

Howse, R. B., Calkins, S. D., Anastopoulos, A. D., Keane, S. P., & Shelton, T. L. (2003). Regulatory contributors to children's kindergarten achievement. *Early Education & Development*, *14*(1), 101–120. doi:10.1207/s15566935eed1401_7

Huesmann, L. R., & Guerra, N. G. (1997). Children's normative beliefs about aggression and aggressive behavior. *Journal of Personality and Social Psychology*, *72*(2), 408.

Jacob, R., & Parkinson, J. (2015). The potential for school-based interventions that target executive function to improve academic achievement: A review. *Review of Educational Research*, *85*(4), 512–552.

Jennings, P. A., & Greenberg, M. T. (2009). The prosocial classroom: Teacher social and emotional competence in relation to student and classroom outcomes. *Review of Educational Research*, *79*(1), 491–525. doi:10.3102/0034654308325693

Jones, S., Bailey, R., Barnes, S., & Partee, A. (2016). *Executive function mapping project: Untangling the terms and skills related to executive function and self-regulation in early childhood (No. OPRE 2016-88)*. Washington, DC: Office of Planning, Research and Evaluation, Administration for Children and Families, U.S. Department of Health and Human Services.

Jones, S., Bouffard, S. M., & Weissbourd, R. (2013). Educators' social and emotional skills vital to learning. *Phi Delta Kappan*, *94*(8), 62–65.

Jones, S., Brown, J., & Aber, J. L. (2008). Classroom settings as targets of intervention and Research. In M. Shinn & H. Yoshikawa (Eds.), *Toward Positive Youth Development: Transforming Schools and Community Programs*. Retrieved from www.oxfordscholarship.com/view/10.1093/acprof:oso/9780195327892.001.0001/acprof-9780195327892-chapter-4

Jones, S., Brown, J. L., & Aber, J. L. (2011). Two-year impacts of a universal school-based social-emotional and literacy intervention: An experiment in translational developmental research. *Child Development*, *82*(2), 533–554. doi:10.1111/j.1467-8624.2010.01560.x

Jones, S., Brown, J. L., Hoglund, W. L. G., & Aber, J. L. (2010). A school-randomized clinical trial of an integrated social–emotional learning and literacy intervention: Impacts after 1 school year. *Journal of Consulting and Clinical Psychology*, *78*(6), 829–842. doi:10.1037/a0021383

Just, M. A., & Carpenter, P. A. (1980). A theory of reading: From eye fixations to comprehension. *Psychological Review*, *87*(4), 329.

Kegel, C. A. T., & Bus, A. G. (2014). Evidence for causal relations between executive functions and alphabetic skills based on longitudinal data: Executive functions and alphabetic skills. *Infant and Child Development*, *23*(1), 22–35. doi:10.1002/icd.1827

Kieffer, M. J., Vukovic, R. K., & Berry, D. (2013). Roles of attention shifting and inhibitory control in fourth-grade reading comprehension. *Reading Research Quarterly*, *48*(4), 333–348. doi:10.1002/rrq.54

Kochanska, G., Murray, K., Jacques, T. Y., Koenig, A. L., & Vandegeest, K. A. (1996). Inhibitory control in young children and its role in emerging internalization. *Child Development*, *67*(2), 490–507.

Kochanska, G., Murray, K. T., & Harlan, E. T. (2000). Effortful control in early childhood: Continuity and change, antecedents, and implications for social development. *Developmental Psychology*, *36*(2), 220.

Konold, T. R., & Pianta, R. C. (2005). Empirically-derived, person-oriented patterns of school readiness in typically-developing children: Description and prediction to first-grade achievement. *Applied Developmental Science*, *9*(4), 174–187. doi:10.1207/s1532480xads0904_1

Kraft, M. A., Blazar, D., & Hogan, D. (2018). The effect of teacher coaching on instruction and achievement: A meta-analysis of the causal evidence. *Review of Educational Research*, *88*(4), 547–588.

Ladd, G. W., & Burgess, K. B. (2001). Do relational risks and protective factors moderate the linkages between childhood aggression and early psychological and school adjustment? *Child Development*, *72*(5), 1579–1601.

Ladd, G. W., Herald, S. L., & Kochel, K. P. (2006). School readiness: Are there social prerequisites? *Early Education and Development*, *17*(1), 115–150.

Lengua, L. (2002). The Contribution of Emotionality and Self-Regulation to the Understanding of Children's Response to Multiple Risk. *Child Development*, *73*(1), 144–161. doi:10.1111/1467-8624.00397

Lengua, L. (2009). Effortful control in the context of socioeconomic and psychosocial risk. *Psychological Science Agenda*, *23*(1).

Lesaux, N. K. (2012). Reading and reading instruction for children from low-income and non-English-speaking households. *The Future of Children*, *22*(2), 73–88.

Li Grining, C., Raver, C. C., Champion, K., Sardin, L., Metzger, M., & Jones, S. M. (2010). Understanding and improving classroom emotional climate and behavior management in the "real world": The role of head start teachers' psychosocial stressors. *Early Education & Development*, *21*(1), 65–94. doi:10.1080/10409280902783509

Liew, J., McTigue, E. M., Barrois, L., & Hughes, J. N. (2008). Adaptive and effortful control and academic self-efficacy beliefs on achievement: A longitudinal study of 1st through 3rd graders. *Early Childhood Research Quarterly, 23*(4), 515–526. doi:10.1016/j.ecresq.2008.07.003

Lonigan, C. J., Wagner, R. K., Torgesen, J. K., & Rashotte, C. A. (2007). *TOPEL: Test of preschool early literacy*. Austin, TX: Pro-Ed.

Lucas, C. P., Zhang, H., Fisher, P. W., Shaffer, D., Regier, D. A., Narrow, W. E., Bourdon, K., Dulcan, M. K., Canino, G., & Rubio-Stipec, M. (2001). The DISC Predictive Scales (DPS): Efficiently screening for diagnoses. *Journal of the American Academy of Child & Adolescent Psychiatry, 40*(4), 443–449.

Mägi, K., Kikas, E., & Soodla, P. (2018). Effortful control, task persistence, and reading skills. *Journal of Applied Developmental Psychology, 54*, 42–52.

Mashburn, A. J., Pianta, R. C., Hamre, B. K., Downer, J. T., Barbarin, O. A., Bryant, D., … Howes, C. (2008). Measures of classroom quality in prekindergarten and children's development of academic, language, and social skills. *Child Development, 79*(3), 732–749.

Masten, A. S., & Cicchetti, D. (2010). Developmental cascades. *Development and Psychopathology, 22*(3), 491–495. doi:10.1017/S0954579410000222

McClelland, M. M., & Cameron, C. E. (2012). Self-regulation in early childhood: Improving conceptual clarity and developing ecologically valid measures. *Child Development Perspectives, 6*(2), 136–142.

McClelland, M. M., & Cameron, C. E. (2011). Self-regulation and academic achievement in elementary school children. *New Directions for Child and Adolescent Development, 2011*(133), 29–44. 10.1002/cd.302

McClelland, M. M., Cameron, C. E., Connor, C. M., Farris, C. L., Jewkes, A. M., & Morrison, F. J. (2007). Links between behavioral regulation and preschoolers' literacy, vocabulary, and math skills. *Developmental Psychology, 43*(4), 947–959. doi:10.1037/0012-1649.43.4.947

Milich, R., Loney, J., & Landau, S. (1982). Independent dimensions of hyperactivity and aggression: A validation with playroom observation data. *Journal of Abnormal Psychology, 91*(3), 183.

Miyake, A., Friedman, N. P., Emerson, M. J., Witzki, A. H., Howerter, A., & Wager, T. D. (2000). The unity and diversity of executive functions and their contributions to complex "Frontal Lobe" Tasks: A latent variable analysis. *Cognitive Psychology, 41*(1), 49–100. doi:10.1006/cogp.1999.0734

Montroy, J. J., Bowles, R. P., Skibbe, L. E., & Foster, T. D. (2014). Social skills and problem behaviors as mediators of the relationship between behavioral self-regulation and academic achievement. *Early Childhood Research Quarterly, 29*(3), 298–309. doi:10.1016/j.ecresq.2014.03.002

Morrison, F. M., Ponitz, C. C., & McClelland, M. M. (2010). Self-regulation and academic achievement in the transition to school. In M. A. Bell & S. D. Calkins (Eds.), *Child development at the intersection of emotion and cognition* (pp. 203–224). Washington, DC: American Psychological Association.

Nagy, W. (2007). Metalinguistic awareness and the vocabulary-comprehension connection. In R. Wagner, A. Muse & K. Tannenbaum (Eds.), *Vocabulary acquisition: Implications for reading comprehension* (pp. 52–77). New York: Guildford Press.

National Early Literacy Panel. (2008). *Developing early literacy: Report of the National Early Literacy Panel* (p. 260). National Institute for Literacy and National Center for Family Literacy. Retrieved from https://lincs.ed.gov/publications/pdf/NELPReport09.pdf

Nesbitt, K. T., Baker-Ward, L., & Willoughby, M. T. (2013). Executive function mediates socio-economic and racial differences in early academic achievement. *Early Childhood Research Quarterly, 28*(4), 774–783. doi:10.1016/j.ecresq.2013.07.005

Nesbitt, K. T., Farran, D. C., & Fuhs, M. W. (2015). Executive function skills and academic achievement gains in prekindergarten: Contributions of learning-related behaviors. *Developmental Psychology, 51*(7), 865–878. doi:10.1037/dev0000021

Newcomer, P., & Hammill, D. (1997). *Test of language development-primary*. Austin, TX: PRO-ED.

Nigg, J. T. (2000). On inhibition/disinhibition in developmental psychopathology: Views from cognitive and personality psychology and a working inhibition taxonomy. *Psychological Bulletin, 126*(2), 220.

Pekrun, R., Elliot, A. J., & Maier, M. A. (2009). Achievement goals and achievement emotions: Testing a model of their joint relations with academic performance. *Journal of Educational Psychology, 101*(1), 115.

Petersen, I. T., Bates, J. E., & Staples, A. D. (2015). The role of language ability and self-regulation in the development of inattentive-hyperactive behavior problems. *Development and Psychopathology, 27*(1), 221–237. doi:10.1017/S0954579414000698

Phillips, D. (2016). Stability, security, and social dynamics in early childhood environments. In N. Lesaux & S. M. Jones (Eds.), *The leading edge of early childhood education: Linking science to policy for a new generation* (pp. 7–28). Cambridge, MA: Harvard Education Press.

Phillipsen, L. C., Burchinal, M. R., Howes, C., & Cryer, D. (1997). The prediction of process quality from structural features of child care. *Early Childhood Research Quarterly, 12*(3), 281–303.

Pianta, R. C., & Stuhlman, M. W. (2004). Teacher-child relationships and children's success in the first years of school. *School Psychology Review*, *33*(3), 444.

Ponitz, C., McClelland, M., Matthews, J., & Morrison, F. (2009). A structured observation of behavioral self-regulation and its contribution to kindergarten outcomes. *Developmental Psychology*, *45*(3), 605–619.

Purpura, D. J., Schmitt, S. A., & Ganley, C. M. (2017). Foundations of mathematics and literacy: The role of executive functioning components. *Journal of Experimental Child Psychology*, *153*, 15–34. doi:10.1016/j.jecp.2016.08.010

Rabiner, D. L., Murray, D. W., Skinner, A. T., & Malone, P. S. (2010). A randomized trial of two promising computer-based interventions for students with attention difficulties. *Journal of Abnormal Child Psychology*, *38*(1), 131–142. doi:10.1007/s10802-009-9353-x

Raver, C. C., Jones, S. M., Li-Grining, C., Zhai, F., Bub, K., & Pressler, E. (2011). CSRP's impact on low-income preschoolers' preacademic skills: Self-regulation as a mediating mechanism: CSRP's impact on low-income preschoolers' preacademic skills. *Child Development*, *82*(1), 362–378. doi:10.1111/j.1467-8624.2010.01561.x

Raver, C. C., Jones, S. M., Li-Grining, C. P., Metzger, M., Champion, K. M., & Sardin, L. (2008). Improving preschool classroom processes: Preliminary findings from a randomized trial implemented in Head Start settings. *Early Childhood Research Quarterly*, *23*(1), 10–26. doi:10.1016/j.ecresq.2007.09.001

Reardon, S. F., & Portilla, X. A. (2016). Recent trends in income, racial, and ethnic school readiness gaps at kindergarten entry. *AERA Open*, *2*(3), 2332858416657343.

Reynolds, C. R., & Kamphaus, R. W. (1998). *Behavioral assessment system for children – Manual*. Circle Pines, MN: American Guidance Service.

Rosenfeld, E., Huesmann, L. R., Eron, L. D., & Torney-Purta, J. V. (1982). Measuring patterns of fantasy behavior in children. *Journal of Personality and Social Psychology*, *42*(2), 347.

Rothbart, M. K., Ellis, L. K., Rueda, M. R., & Posner, M. I. (2003). Developing mechanisms of temperamental effortful control. *Journal of Personality*, *71*(6), 1113–1144. doi:10.1111/1467-6494.7106009

Rothbart, M. K., & Jones, L. (1998). Temperament, self-regulation, and education. *School Psychology Review*, *27*(4), 479–491.

Sabol, T. J., & Pianta, R. C. (2012). Recent trends in research on teacher–child relationships. *Attachment & Human Development*, *14*(3), 213–231.

Salmon, K., O'Kearney, R., Reese, E., & Fortune, C.-A. (2016). The role of language skill in child psychopathology: Implications for intervention in the early years. *Clinical Child and Family Psychology Review*, *19*(4), 352–367. doi:10.1007/s10567-016-0214-1

Sameroff, A. (2010). A unified theory of development: A dialectic integration of nature and nurture. *Child Development*, *81*(1), 6–22.

Sameroff, A., & Fiese, B. H. (2000). Transactional regulation: The developmental ecology of early intervention. *Handbook of Early Childhood Intervention*, *2*, 135–159.

Sandilos, L. E., Goble, P., Rimm-Kaufman, S. E., & Pianta, R. C. (2018). Does professional development reduce the influence of teacher stress on teacher–child interactions in pre-kindergarten classrooms? *Early Childhood Research Quarterly*, *42*, 280–290. doi:10.1016/j.ecresq.2017.10.009

Sektnan, M., McClelland, M. M., Acock, A., & Morrison, F. J. (2010). Relations between early family risk, children's behavioral regulation, and academic achievement. *Early Childhood Research Quarterly*, *25*(4), 464–479. doi:10.1016/j.ecresq.2010.02.005

Sesma, H. W., Mahone, E. M., Levine, T., Eason, S. H., & Cutting, L. E. (2009). The contribution of executive skills to reading comprehension. *Child Neuropsychology*, *15*(3), 232–246. doi:10.1080/09297040802220029

Shaul, S., & Schwartz, M. (2014). The role of the executive functions in school readiness among preschool-age children. *Reading and Writing*, *27*(4), 749–768. doi:10.1007/s11145-013-9470-3

Skibbe, L. E., Montroy, J. J., Bowles, R. P., & Morrison, F. J. (2018). Self-regulation and the development of literacy and language achievement from preschool through second grade. *Early Childhood Research Quarterly*, *46*, 240–251.

Skinner, E. A., Zimmer-Gembeck, M. J., & Connell, J. P. (1998). Individual differences and the development of perceived control. *Monographs of the Society for Research in Child Development*, i–231.

Slot, P. L., & von Suchodoletz, A. (2018). Bidirectionality in preschool children's executive functions and language skills: Is one developing skill the better predictor of the other? *Early Childhood Research Quarterly*, *42*, 205–214. doi:10.1016/j.ecresq.2017.10.005

Smith-Donald, R., Raver, C. C., Hayes, T., & Richardson, B. (2007). Preliminary construct and concurrent validity of the Preschool Self-regulation Assessment (PSRA) for field-based research. *Early Childhood Research Quarterly*, *22*(2), 173–187. doi:10.1016/j.ecresq.2007.01.002

Snow, C. (1983). Literacy and Language: Relationships during the Preschool Years. *Harvard Educational Review, 53*(2), 165–189. doi:10.17763/haer.53.2.t6177w39817w2861

Snow, C. (1991). The theoretical basis for relationships between language and literacy in development. *Journal of Research in Childhood Education, 6*(1), 5–10. doi:10.1080/02568549109594817

Swanson, H. L. (1999). Reading comprehension and working memory in learning-disabled readers: Is the phonological loop more important than the executive system? *Journal of Experimental Child Psychology, 72*(1), 1–31. doi:10.1006/jecp.1998.2477

Swanson, H. L., & Howell, M. (2001). Working memory, short-term memory, and speech rate as predictors of children's reading performance at different ages. *Journal of Educational Psychology, 93*(4), 720.

Swanson, H. L., Zheng, X., & Jerman, O. (2009). Working memory, short-term memory, and reading disabilities: A selective meta-analysis of the literature. *Journal of Learning Disabilities, 42*(3), 260–287. doi:10.1177/0022219409331958

Torgesen, J. K. (2002). The prevention of reading difficulties. *Journal of School Psychology, 40*(1), 7–26.

Trentacosta, C. J., & Izard, C. E. (2007). Kindergarten children's emotion competence as a predictor of their academic competence in first grade. *Emotion, 7*(1), 77–88. doi:10.1037/1528-3542.7.1.77

Ursache, A., Blair, C., & Raver, C. C. (2012). The promotion of self-regulation as a means of enhancing school readiness and early achievement in children at risk for school failure: Promotion of self-regulation in school. *Child Development Perspectives, 6*(2), 122–128. doi:10.1111/j.1750-8606.2011.00209.x

Valiente, C., Eisenberg, N., Haugen, R., Spinrad, T. L., Hofer, C., Liew, J., & Kupfer, A. (2011). Children's effortful control and academic achievement: Mediation through social functioning. *Early Education & Development, 22*(3), 411–433. doi:10.1080/10409289.2010.505259

Vallotton, C., & Ayoub, C. (2011). Use your words: The role of language in the development of toddlers' self-regulation. *Early Childhood Research Quarterly, 26*(2), 169–181. doi:10.1016/j.ecresq.2010.09.002

van de Sande, E., Segers, E., & Verhoeven, L. (2016). Supporting executive functions during children's preliteracy learning with the computer: EFs in computerized literacy learning. *Journal of Computer Assisted Learning, 32*(5), 468–480. doi:10.1111/jcal.12147

Verhoeven, L. (1995). Drie Minuten Toets en Toets Voor auditieve synthese en grafementoets [three minutes test and test for blending and grapheme knowledge test]. *CITO, Arnhem*.

Verhoeven, L., & Van Kuyk, J. (1991). Peiling van conceptuele en metalinguïstische kennis bij de aanvang van het basisonderwijs [Assessment of conceptual and metalinguistic knowledge at the entrance of kindergarten]. *Pedagogische Studiën, 68*(9), 415–425.

Verhoeven, L., van Leeuwe, J., & Vermeer, A. (2011). Vocabulary growth and reading development across the elementary school years. *Scientific Studies of Reading, 15*(1), 8–25. doi:10.1080/10888438.2011.536125

Vygotsky, L. (1962). *Language and thought*. Ontario, Canada: Massachusetts Institute of Technology Press.

Vygotsky, L. (1978). Interaction between learning and development. *Readings on the Development of Children, 23*(3), 34–41.

Wakschlag, L. S., Leventhal, B. L., Briggs-Gowan, M. J., Danis, B., Keenan, K., Hill, C., Egger, H., Cicchetti, D., & Carter, A. S. (2005). Defining the "disruptive" in preschool behavior: What diagnostic observation can teach us. *Clinical Child and Family Psychology Review, 8*(3), 183–201.

Weiland, C., McCormick, M., Mattera, S., Maier, M., & Morris, P. (2018). Preschool curricula and professional development features for getting to high-quality implementation at scale: A comparative review across five trials. *AERA Open, 4*(1), 233285841875773. doi:10.1177/2332858418757735

Weiland, C., Ulvestad, K., Sachs, J., & Yoshikawa, H. (2013). Associations between classroom quality and children's vocabulary and executive function skills in an urban public prekindergarten program. *Early Childhood Research Quarterly, 28*(2), 199–209. doi:10.1016/j.ecresq.2012.12.002

Weintraub, S., Dikmen, S. S., Heaton, R. K., Tulsky, D. S., Zelazo, P. D., Bauer, P. J., … Gershon, R. C. (2013). Cognition assessment using the NIH Toolbox. *Neurology, 80*(11 Suppl 3), S54–64. doi:10.1212/wnl.0b013e3182872ded

Werthamer-Larsson, L., Kellam, S., & Wheeler, L. (1991). Effect of first-grade classroom environment on shy behavior, aggressive behavior, and concentration problems. *American Journal of Community Psychology, 19*(4), 585–602.

Winsler, A., De León, J. R., Wallace, B. A., Carlton, M. P., & Willson-Quayle, A. (2003). Private speech in preschool children: Developmental stability and change, across-task consistency, and relations with classroom behaviour. *Journal of Child Language, 30*(3), 583–608. doi:10.1017/S0305000903005671

Winsler, A., Diaz, R. M., Atencio, D. J., McCarthy, E. M., & Chabay, L. A. (2000). Verbal self-regulation over time in preschool children at risk for attention and behavior problems. *Journal of Child Psychology and Psychiatry, 41*(7), 875–886. doi:10.1111/1469-7610.00675

Woodcock, R. W., McGrew, K. S., & Mather, N. (2001). *Woodcock-Johnson III Test*. Itasca, IL: Riverside Publishing Company.

Zelazo, P. D., Müller, U., Frye, D., Marcovitch, S., Argitis, G., Boseovski, J., Chiang, J. K., Hongwanishkul, D., Schuster, B. V., Sutherland, A., & Carlson, S. M. (2003). *The development of executive function in early childhood. Monographs of the Society for Research in Child Development*, i–151.

Zhou, Q., Chen, S. H., & Main, A. (2012). Commonalities and differences in the research on children's effortful control and executive function: A call for an integrated model of self-regulation. *Child Development Perspectives*, *6*(2), 112–121.

16

Literacy Instruction and Individual Differences in Students' Cognitive Development

Jin Kyoung Hwang and Carol McDonald Connor

In this chapter, we will discuss individual differences in children's cognitive development, the multiple sources of influence that help create and sustain these differences, and how literacy instruction can be individualized to meet each student's developmental needs, and take into account their unique constellations of skills and aptitudes. For the purpose of this chapter, we conceptualize cognitive development as encompassing a wide array of proficiencies that children develop and learn throughout childhood and beyond. These include language, text-specific processes, self-regulation and executive functioning, and metacognition. We discuss each below and how they work synergistically to support the development of proficient literacy skills.

Language

Language development is a foundational aspect of cognitive development. As social beings, we pay special attention to the language we hear around us and continue to learn from birth to adulthood. Learning a language does not happen all at once. There are dimensions of language development that researchers have identified, including phonological awareness, vocabulary, semantics, morphosyntactic, and pragmatics. More recent research suggests that, at least for typically developing children, these dimensions can be represented by two constructs; a lexical/vocabulary construct (i.e., vocabulary, semantics) and a grammatical or higher order construct (i.e., morphosyntactic, pragmatics) (Language and Reading Research Consortium, 2015; Lonigan & Milburn, 2017).

Phonological development, the ability to distinguish, recognize, and manipulate the sounds of specific languages, is one of the beginning stages of language development that is highly relevant to literacy development. Babies, as early as a few weeks old, start to recognize familiar and unfamiliar sounds in their surroundings. For instance, they tend to pay greater attention to familiar sounds such as their mother's voice than unfamiliar sounds, such as a stranger's voice. Phonological skills continue to develop through early elementary years. By then, most children have sophisticated skills to distinguish slight differences in speech sounds. Children who are not able to distinguish between these sounds are at serious risk for both language and literacy disabilities as children begin to learn sound-symbol correspondence (Connor & McCardle, 2015).

Semantic development refers to children's ability to relate vocabulary words to referred subjects and their meaning. Children at around 12 months start saying high-frequency words that they hear often from their caregivers such as *mommy* and *hi*. Children typically acquire nouns with concrete meanings before they understand verbs and nouns with abstract meanings. There is almost no limit on the number of vocabulary words we can learn in our lifespan. Children vary greatly in the size of their vocabulary, and this happens early in life, before they receive any formal schooling. In their second year, when children generally know about 50–60 vocabulary words, they start combining words together. Children learn that they can convey meanings in these multi-word combinations and start being aware of the morphological and syntactic rules (i.e., morphosyntax), or grammatical rules about how words and sentences should be formed, of a language. Certain rules are acquired before others (Brown, 1973). For instance, children learn to use regular plurals before they know how to use possessives and auxiliary verbs in their utterances. Children who have delayed vocabulary development or smaller vocabularies have serious difficulty comprehending what they read (Duff et al., 2008). Vocabulary also influences the amounts and types of literacy instruction that are effective for individual children (Connor, Morrison, Fishman, Schatschneider, & Underwood, 2007). Language development does not end here. Children's knowledge of using language appropriately in different contexts – communicative competence or pragmatics – is also a part of a developmental process. Once children have some mastery of language skills, they learn to distinguish the difference between speaking to a peer and speaking to a stranger and understand when to use a polite language.

Text-Specific Processes

Text-specific processes are skills children only need to learn in societies where reading and writing are required. Reading and writing are not skills that we are naturally born to learn (i.e., our brain is not naturally primed to read and write text). Literacy development is *experience dependent* – it only develops when children are explicitly taught text specific processes (Adams, 1990). Reading and writing are human inventions. Thus, the relation between letter and sound (grapheme-sound correspondence) is arbitrary in any given language, and children need explicit instruction in order to learn to read and write fluently. In contrast, language is *experience expectant* (i.e., our brain is primed to develop these skills if we experience appropriate linguistic input and interaction during the critical period) and develops even in the face of serious barriers, such as deafness.

There are salient developmental phases in learning to read and write (Chall, 1996; Fitzgerald & Shanahan, 2000), although children vary in how they proceed through the phases, and the phases may be overlapping and simultaneous. In the emergent literacy phase, while children are still rapidly developing early language, they also learn about letters and how these letters correspond to sounds in spoken language. In reading, preschoolers pretend to read or read environmental print (Lonigan, Farver, Phillips, & Clancy-Menchetti, 2011; Teale & Sulzby, 1986). They scribble, draw letter-like symbols to represent syllables, or write invented spelling in their writing. Children then begin to develop their decoding and encoding skills. They learn that there is a specific relation between letters and sounds. Understanding this arbitrary set of rules in letter-sound correspondence is critical in learning how to read and write and is supported by children's growing phonological awareness skills. Most children master decoding texts, and their process of decoding becomes fluent and automatic – hopefully by the time they are about eight years old. Those children who are not reading fluently by the end of second grade are much less likely to attain proficient literacy skills (Connor et al., 2013; Spira, Bracken, & Fischel, 2005). Comprehension and focus on making-meaning through texts was thought to develop during middle childhood; at about nine years of age (Fitzgerald & Shanahan, 2000). However, new research shows that focus on attaching meaning to the text children can decode can be taught much earlier (Connor et al., 2014a); and that language and literacy development are intertwined (Scarborough, 2001). Throughout early literacy development, as early as kindergarten, ideally, reading and writing increasingly become a medium for learning new concepts in content areas (Connor et al., 2017). As children's metacognitive skills develop, they learn to understand multiple viewpoints in texts and synthesize different arguments coherently. Again, research shows that these skills can be taught during early and middle childhood and into adolescence. By the time students reach high school and university, it is too late to begin instruction on these crucial skills because students need to have a good command of these skills already in order to succeed academically at this age. Thus, the stage theory of literacy development is a useful template for thinking about crucial aspects of proficient literacy development. However, the stages overlap much more than was previously conceived and new models, such as the Lattice Model (Connor et al., 2016), suggest that the stages are likely developing, reciprocally and simultaneously. We discuss the Lattice Model in more detail later in this chapter. Language and literacy development discussed thus far are considered to be typical, normative development. However, there could be variations in children's development in these domains based on amount and type of input and instruction they receive at home, in-, and out-of-school environments. We explain potential factors that may cause individual differences in children's development later in this chapter.

Self-Regulation and Executive Functioning

Self-regulation is the ability to monitor, control, and evaluate one's behavior, goals, emotions, attention, and thoughts (McClelland & Cameron, 2012). Children develop self-regulatory skills as they get older, and these skills continue to develop through adulthood. Some researchers, in specific disciplines, refer to self-regulatory skills as "non-cognitive skills." However, self-regulation is indeed a part of cognitive development as it requires the coordination of inhibitory skills, working memory, and cognitive flexibility, which are critical components of executive functioning (Connor et al., 2016). Self-regulation is a broad construct that overlaps with other psychological constructs and has been studied under several different names such as social-cognitive skills, grit, mindset, consciousness, will power, motivation, and engagement – although there are nuances for each term (Lin, Coburn, & Eisenberg, 2016). Self-regulation has been found to be highly predictive of children's literacy skill development, school readiness, and academic achievement (Allan, Hume, Allan, Farrington, & Lonigan, 2014) – likely because it sets the stage for more sophisticated approaches to learning from instruction and practice. For instance, children who have strong self-regulation skills are able to control their behavior (e.g., sit still) and attention (e.g., listen to the teacher) to benefit more from formal literacy instruction than those who cannot and get distracted easily (Connor et al., 2010). Additionally, there may be a reciprocal association between self-regulation and learning to read such that learning to read supports the development of executive functioning and self-regulation (Connor et al., 2016).

Metacognition

Metacognition, or the ability to think about one's thinking, may provide an important foundation for learning to connect language to literacy (Efklides & Misailidi, 2010). Metacognition skills specific to language – or metalinguistic skills – play an important role as children learn to speak a new language. Metalinguistic skills can be simply defined as knowledge about the language system. Children with strong metalinguistic skills have a good understanding that language is an arbitrary system that can be broken into small parts (phonemes, syllables, morphemes, and so forth) and can be manipulated in many ways. Metalinguistic skills play an important role as children learn oral and written language. For instance, children who have good phonological awareness skills understand that our language system is comprised of small units of sounds that can be blended, broken apart, and manipulated in different ways, which is a critical skill they need to encode and decode text. Metacognitive skills also contribute to stronger reading comprehension. For example, monitoring and repairing understanding (i.e., comprehension monitoring) and the ability to understand what is known and unknown (i.e., meta-knowledge), are aspects of cognition that facilitate reading for understanding (Connor, 2016; Efklides & Misailidi, 2010).

Multiple Sources of Influence on Cognitive Development

Researchers have identified multiple sources of influence on children's cognitive development during early and middle childhood. Increasing evidence shows that differences in children's cognitive development, especially in language development, emerge early on (Fernald, Marchman, & Weisleder, 2013; Hart & Risley, 1995; Hoff, 2013). During early childhood, one of the most prominent factors that influences children's cognitive development is the socioeconomic status (SES) of the family the child is raised in – such that differences in SES are strongly correlated with differences in children's cognitive development (Buckingham, Beaman, & Wheldall, 2014; Fernald et al., 2013; Hoff, 2013; Strang & Piasta, 2016). Compared to children from middle- and high-SES homes, children from low-SES homes tend to have weaker language skills such as small vocabulary size (Fernald et al., 2013; Nelson, Welsh, Trup, & Greenberg, 2011) and use of less complex syntactic structures (Huttenlocher, Waterfall, Vasilyeva, Vevea, & Hedges, 2010; Nelson et al., 2011). Specifically, Fernald and colleagues (2013) found a significant gap in vocabulary knowledge and language processing skills as early as 18 months between infants raised in low- and high-SES homes.

One of the well-documented factors that mediate the effect of SES on children's cognitive development is their home learning environment (Hamilton, Hayiou-Thomas, Hulme, & Snowling, 2016; Mistry, Benner, Biesanz, Clark, & Howes, 2010; Rodriguez & Tamis-LeMonda, 2011; Son & Morrison, 2010; Ziol-Guest & McKenna, 2014). Home learning environment includes different variables such as parental behaviors toward children, amount of learning activities at home, and learning materials accessible at home. Home learning environment is dynamic and may change over time to meet children's cognitive needs (Son & Morrison, 2010). Research studies show that family's SES is associated with its home learning environment (Chazan-Cohen et al., 2009) – families with lower income would find it more difficult to purchase materials that stimulate learning at home than families with higher income, and parents who need to work extra hours to keep their household would not be able to invest as much time interacting with their children. Children raised in families with lower levels of home learning environment have been found to show delays in their language development and self-regulation skills (Chazan-Cohen et al., 2009; Mistry et al., 2010). Another crucial part of the home learning environment is language exposure and language use in the home. Specifically, parental speech and verbal communication between parents and children have a strong impact on children's language development (Newman, Rowe, & Bernstein Ratner, 2016; Rowe, 2012). It has been well documented that quantity and quality of verbal communication in the home varies by the family's SES (Hoff, 2003; Huttenlocher et al., 2010; Weisleder & Fernald, 2013). Research studies underscore that the quality of verbal interaction is more critical and has more predictive power than quantity of word use (Hirsh-Pasek et al., 2015; Rowe, Leech, & Cabrera, 2016). For instance, asking children wh-questions that elicit children's responses and engaging children in high-quality communicative interactions are more likely to build children's vocabulary and language skills, than repeating simple words or sentences multiple times.

Schooling is a principal source of influence on early child cognitive development, second only to the home environment (Morrison, Griffith, & Alberts, 1997; Skibbe, Connor, Morrison, & Jewkes, 2011). Accumulating research on early child care and schooling show that the amount and quality of time spent in preschools is associated with children's cognitive development (Auger, Farkas, Burchinal, Duncan, & Vandell, 2014; Burchinal, Vandergrift, Pianta, & Mashburn, 2010; Dickinson & Porche, 2011; Keys et al., 2013; Li, Farkas, Duncan, Burchinal, & Vandell, 2013; Skibbe et al., 2011; Skibbe, Grimm, Bowles, & Morrison, 2012). Children who experience high-quality early schooling are more likely to show stronger cognitive skills that lead to school readiness than those who receive low-quality early childhood care. Researchers found that there are variations in literacy instruction that happen in school during children's early childhood (Pelatti, Piasta, Justice, & O'Connell, 2014; Wright & Neuman, 2014), and the amount and quality of such instruction is often associated with the schools and centers' socioeconomic background (Wright & Neuman, 2014).

Similar to the home learning environment where parental behaviors and parent-child interactions play an important role in children's cognitive development, how much positive (or negative) influence schooling has on children's development depends on what happens in the actual classrooms and how teachers support the learning environment. Specifically, teachers' language practices and instruction and quality of teacher-child interactions are found to be important predictors for children's language and cognitive development (Bowers & Vasilyeva, 2011; Bowne, Yoshikawa, & Snow, 2016; Burchinal et al., 2008; Dickinson, 2011). For instance, Burchinal et al. (2008) found that responsive, supportive, and stimulating teacher-child interaction and quality of instruction at pre-kindergarten predicted children's language skills at the end of their kindergarten year. Such foundational aspects of the classroom learning environment are necessary but not sufficient – what, as well as how children are taught is important to consider (Connor et al., 2014), as we discuss in the next section.

These factors – SES, home learning environment, language use at home, and the amount and quality of schooling – continue to exert influence on children's cognitive development through middle childhood and beyond. Not only do they have short-term effects (Gámez & Lesaux, 2015) – e.g., teachers' language use in middle schools affects middle school students' reading and vocabulary outcomes – they also have long-term effects on children's cognitive development in adolescence (Dickinson & Porche, 2011; Sammons et al., 2015; Sorhagen, 2013; Vandell, Belsky, Burchinal, Steinberg, & Vandergrift, 2010) – e.g., the quantity and quality of early child care has effects on adolescent students' reading skills. Thus, children who are provided with learning environments both at home and schools/child care centers that are specifically designed to meet their learning needs are more likely to be successful academically and in life.

Literacy Instruction

Literacy instruction has received much attention in the research literature as a critical factor that may positively influence children's cognitive development at any given time point. Research on literacy instruction is often investigated in several ways – observational studies, correlational/longitudinal studies, and randomized controlled trials of literacy-related interventions. Observation is one way to examine how learning takes place in an educational setting and which teacher practices are effective for children's cognitive development (Cohen, Manion, & Morrison, 2011). The topics that are covered in literacy-related observation studies are diverse. There have been studies on examining teachers' instructional practices in the classroom (Barnes, Dickinson, & Grifenhagen, 2016; Connor et al., 2009; Jacoby & Lesaux, 2014; Lawrence, Crosson, Paré-Blagoev, & Snow, 2015; Pelatti et al., 2014; Wright & Neuman, 2014), teachers' use of vocabulary and academic language and its impact on students' language skills (Dickinson & Porche, 2011; Gámez & Lesaux, 2012, 2015; Gonzalez et al., 2014), child-teacher interaction in a literacy-related activities (Justice, McGinty, Zucker, Cabell, & Piasta, 2013; Tompkins, Zucker, Justice, & Binici, 2013), and so forth. Some studies are more qualitative (e.g., observing classroom instruction, coding teachers' and students' language use) whereas others are quantitative that use measurable outcomes such as children's vocabulary and/or reading comprehension test scores. Longitudinal studies follow children over time and help us understand typical and atypical development.

Randomized controlled trials (RCT) are the most rigorous and effective way to test theories by examining whether specific and multi-component instructional practices effectively enhance student-level literacy outcomes (Murnane & Willett, 2011). RCT is a golden rule in educational research if the objective is to evaluate the program/intervention effectiveness, and the underlying theories, with minimal selection bias. A successful RCT is one in which participants are randomly assigned to either a treatment or control condition. In other words, no third variable is associated with the treatment condition and the assignment is only due to chance. There would be no statistically significant difference between two groups (e.g., participants' ability levels, demographics, SES) when a random assignment is done successfully. However, in educational research, true random assignment is difficult to carry out in school settings. Hence, random assignment is conducted at the classroom or school level, and this may result in unequal treatment and control condition. There have been many RCT studies that aim to demonstrate improved children's literacy-related skills, including phonological awareness and decoding (Connor et al., 2013; Lonigan et al., 2011), vocabulary knowledge (Kim, Capotosto, Hartry, & Fitzgerald, 2011; Neuman, Newman, & Dwyer, 2011), and reading comprehension (Connor et al., 2013; Kim et al., 2011). The findings from these RCT studies show that when instruction is well designed using research-based principles, and well implemented with fidelity, taking into account individual child differences, children do benefit from these educational resources and show gains in their literacy-related outcomes.

Children bring to the learning opportunities different constellations of skills and abilities, which moderate the effects of instruction they receive in any educational setting (Connor & Morrison, 2016; Duncan & Vandell, 2012). Such child X instruction interactions, originally known as aptitude X treatment interaction (Cronbach, 1957), and also known as skill X instruction interactions (Burns, Codding, Boice, & Lukito, 2010), have been found in multiple literacy research studies (Connor et al., 2013, 2011; Lawrence, Capotosto, Branum-Martin, White, & Snow, 2012; Lesaux, Kieffer, Kelley, & Harris, 2014; Miller, Farkas, Vandell, & Duncan, 2014). For instance, in a meta-analysis of vocabulary intervention on young children (preschool-kindergarten), Marulis and Neuman (2010) found that children at-risk for language and literacy disorders from middle- and upper-income homes were more likely to demonstrate stronger gains from vocabulary intervention than those from low-income homes.

In a specific test of whether individualizing literacy instruction based on children's skills is more effective than business-as-usual, non-personalized instruction, individualizing instruction was more effective with effect sizes ranging from .2 to .4 in seven RCT studies (Al Otaiba et al., 2011; Connor et al., 2013, 2011, 2007, 2011). Moreover, the effects of individualizing student instruction based on assessment accumulated from first through third grade. The overall effect size accumulated over the three years to an effect size of .7 (Connor et al., 2013). In these studies, teachers used Assessment-to-instruction (A2i) technology, which provided algorithm-computed recommended amounts of code and meaning focused instruction (min/day) for each child based on the constellation of skills (Connor et al., 2013). Thus, literacy instruction that is personalized, differentiated, or individualized to take into account children's individual differences in cognitive strategies (i.e., a plan to achieve one's goal in a certain task) and skills (e.g., ability, proficiency) (Afflerbach, Pearson, & Paris, 2008), is generally more effective than the one-size-fits-all instruction observed in many classrooms today.

Big Questions: Bridging Gaps

How Do We Make Instruction Adaptive and Responsive to Students' Individual Cognitive Differences?

If assessment-informed personalized instruction is more effective than one-size-fits-all instruction, why is personalized instruction not ubiquitous throughout schools? Here we suggest three key reasons: first, because learning to read and reading for understanding is complex, calling on multiple cognitive, social, and linguistic processes, it is not always clear what children's learning needs actually are, why they are or are not struggling, and how to adapt instruction to meet those needs (Connor et al., 2014a). Thus, we present a new model of literacy that may be useful in informing more effective instruction. Second, personalizing instruction is more difficult than following the scope and sequence of a core literacy curriculum. Teachers report that using assessment to guide practice is difficult (Roehrig, Duggar, Moats, Glover, & Mincey, 2008) and they frequently receive inadequate training in how to administer and interpret assessments results in a meaningful way. Plus, using best practice teaching methods for accomplishing individualized instruction are described as extremely difficult (Farkas & Duffett, 2008) and rarely maintained (Pianta, Belsky, Houts, & Morrison, 2007) in general classroom settings. Thus, in this section we present a number of new technologies designed to facilitate personalized instruction. Finally, there are barriers to bringing evidence-based practices into the classroom that are created by researchers, vendors, and educators. Promising solutions include researcher-school partnerships (Coburn, Penuel, & Geil, 2013) and implementation science (Fixsen, Blase, Metz, & Dyke, 2013), although more research toward understanding and alleviating the implementation gap is needed.

Developing More Useful Models of Literacy to Inform Instruction

As we have discussed, there are multiple sources of influence on how children will respond to various types of literacy instruction. These include home learning environment, which directly influences children's linguistic and literacy development; and family SES and access to community resources, including good preschool and schools (NICHD-ECCRN, 2004), which directly influences self-regulation, general world knowledge, language, and literacy development. Most of the differentiated instruction we observe today (e.g., multi-tiered systems of support) rely solely on reading assessments (Kratochwill, Volpiansky, Clements, & Ball, 2007; Petscher, Kim, & Foorman, 2011). The Individualizing Student Instruction (ISI) instructional regime, which uses the A2i technology, relies on measures of semantic knowledge (i.e., vocabulary), of letter-sound knowledge, word reading, encoding, sentence construction, and of reading comprehension

(Connor et al., 2013). We argue here that metacognition and self-regulation are important child characteristics that might be considered in addition to language and literacy skills.

There are a number of useful models of literacy that are helpful in understanding how to personalize the instruction we provide to children as they learn to read and write. But there is a paradox – language, cognition, and reading comprehension are highly related; children with weaker skills in one area tend to have weaker skills in the others; yet instruction that targets specific language or cognitive skills does not necessarily lead to stronger performance on other language and cognitive components, nor on reading comprehension (Connor et al., 2011, 2014b; Connor, Phillips, Kim, Al Otaiba, & Lonigan, 2015). Metacognitive interventions, such as comprehension monitoring, have met with more success (Kim & Phillips, 2014) and have a stronger effect on the target – for example, detecting implausibilities in text – than on reading comprehension itself (Connor et al., 2015).

These conflicting results appear to call for a new way of thinking about the links between language, cognition, and literacy. In addition to the Stage Theory of Reading (Chall, 1996; Fitzgerald & Shanahan, 2000), one of the most influential theories of reading is the Simple View of Reading and other component models of reading, which holds that proficient reading comprehension is the product of fluent decoding and strong language comprehension (Hoover & Gough, 1990). To this simple model has been added cognitive skills, such as working memory, attention, executive functioning, and metacognition; cognitive-motor skills such as rapid automatic naming; social-cognitive skills including motivation, self-regulation, and engagement; and other influences, including family and parenting; genetics; and instruction (Connor et al., 2014; Gough & Tunmer, 1986; Kintsch, 1998; Perfetti & Stafura, 2014; Rapp & van den Broek, 2005; Taylor, Roehrig, Hensler, Connor, & Schatschneider, 2010). The suggested causal direction in every case is that the more basic processes, such as language (e.g., phonological, morphological, and semantic knowledge), and cognitive (e.g., attention and working memory) processes, along with other environmental, genetic, and social-emotional sources of influence work together to support the development of proficient literacy skills.

This one-way directional view of proficient literacy is pervasive throughout the literature and informs the thinking behind virtually every literacy intervention (NICHD National Reading Panel, 2000). But might learning to read with understanding also influence the more basic underlying skills? Previously, Connor and colleagues have suggested that a more complex view might be useful in resolving the language-cognition-literacy paradox and informing more effective instructional programs (Connor et al., 2014b). They have conceptualized reading comprehension as a "complex activity that requires the reader ... to call on the coordination of cognitive, regulatory, linguistic, and text-specific processes, including decoding of text, which are developing over time and that have reciprocal and interacting bootstrapping effects on one another" (p. 2). This conceptual framework was referred to as the Lattice Model, because these interacting effects resemble a lattice when they are drawn (see Figure 16.1). What they were trying to depict in this figure is the dynamic and complex nature of the associations among linguistic, cognitive, text-specific process (e.g., decoding, text structure, writing), instruction, and reading comprehension. Note that home, school, and community sources of influence are held to be ongoing, as is the child's maturation or development. Thus, any part of the system can, potentially, influence any other part of the system.

To be supported, the Lattice Model would require evidence of reciprocal effects – for example, not only would language and cognitive skills have to predict reading comprehension; in turn, reading comprehension would have to predict language and cognitive skills. This requires, at a minimum, longitudinal studies. To make causal directional claims,

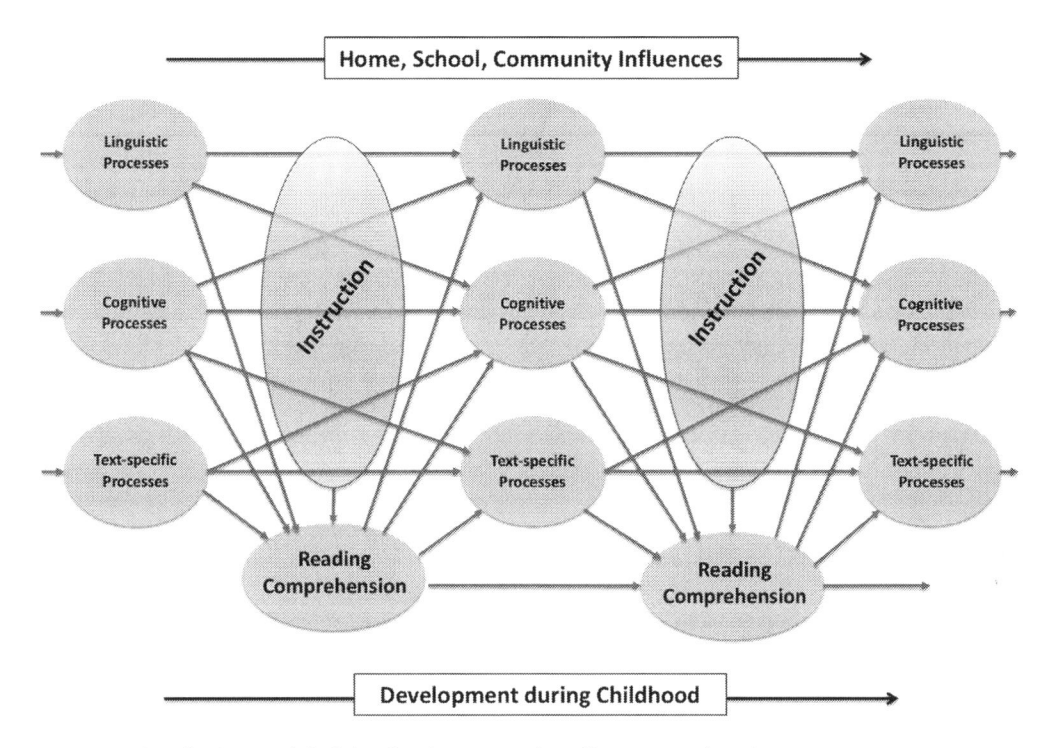

Figure 16.1 A lattice model of the development of reading comprehension

instructional experiments would be needed (Shadish, Cook, & Campbell, 2002). There is consistent and accumulating correlational and longitudinal evidence that children's language ability contributes to proficient reading comprehension (Anderson & Freebody, 1981; Cain, Oakhill, & Bryant, 2004; Hoover & Gough, 1990; Kintsch, 1988; Moreno et al., 2011). There is also longitudinal evidence of reciprocal effects, with reading predicting language. In many studies, reciprocal effects appear to emerge around second or third grade, which is between the ages of seven and eight years (Storch & Whitehurst, 2002; Verhoeven, van Leeuwe, & Vermeer, 2011), just as metacognitive skills are coming online. In the Lattice Model, reciprocal effects might emerge earlier in the context of instruction and there have been arguments for this.

There are, however, very few studies that examine whether reading comprehension predicts developing cognitive skills such as self-regulation and metacognition (Swanson & O'Connor, 2009). One of the first studies to demonstrate that reading comprehension and executive functioning are reciprocally related was a longitudinal study (Connor et al., 2016). In this study, surprisingly, semantic knowledge and executive functioning were not associated. Importantly, there were reciprocal effects for literacy and semantic knowledge, as well as reciprocal effects for literacy and self-regulation, specifically attention, working memory, and task inhibition.

In general, US schools have been successful in teaching children how to decode text fluently but have been less successful in teaching comprehension and academic language skills (Gamse, Jacob, Horst, Boulay, & Unlu, 2008). At least part of the reason is that substantially less time is spent in more meaning-focused and content area instruction. And it is these types of instruction that tend to support developing academic language and comprehension skills (Connor & Morrison, 2012; Connor et al., 2011, 2009). Early support for language and academic knowledge, along with executive functioning and self-regulation development is warranted – but in the context of, and integrated with, efforts to improve reading comprehension.

Following the Lattice Model further, improving reading comprehension instruction might promote the development of metalinguistic and metacognitive skills. In turn, improving these metaskills should support reading comprehension. But how do we teach, for example, metacognitive skills in a way that is integrated with reading comprehension instruction in order to take advantage of reciprocal and bootstrapping effects? Discussion about text that includes challenging children to think and reason, is one possible way (Carlisle, Dwyer, & Learned, 2014; Connor, Ingebrand, & Sparapani, 2015; Graham & Herbert, 2011). Connor and colleagues have found that teachers' discourse moves predict students' participation in learning opportunities and it is student participation that predicts reading comprehension gains in second through third grade (Connor et al., in press). Think aloud strategies may facilitate metacognition, specifically comprehension monitoring and meta-knowledge, and comprehension development (Baumann, Seifert-Kessell, & Jones, 1992).

What does this mean for personalizing instruction? This new research suggests that considering children's self-regulation and metacognitive skills may help to elucidate more optimal learning opportunities. For example, children with weaker metacognitive skills may make greater gains toward proficient literacy if they receive literacy instruction that is designed to foster comprehension monitoring. Such explicit instruction might not be necessary for children with stronger metacognitive skills. There is preliminary evidence that such explicit focus on comprehension monitoring might support stronger reading comprehension (Connor et al., 2014a, 2015; Kim & Phillips, 2014).

Use of Technology in Personalizing Student Instruction

How do we support teachers' effort to using assessment to personalize student instruction? With the current advances and innovations in technology, we are now able to use diverse approaches in assessing students' skills and performance, supporting teachers to better prepare their lessons according to their students' ability levels and needs, and developing curriculum programs and systems to supplement teacher instruction.

An example of how technology can facilitate useful and more meaningful assessment is Global Integrated Scenario-Based Assessment (GISA). GISA is a scenario-based reading assessment intended for elementary and middle school students that has been developed by the Reading for Understanding Network (O'Reilly & Sabatini, 2013). Whereas most of the traditional pencil-and-paper reading assessments aim to measure students' ability to comprehend text in a decontextualized and unidirectional way (i.e., students read a short passage and choose the best answer among multiple choices), GISA intends to assess students' reading abilities in a more dynamic way using an online, scenario-based test format (for a sample GISA item, visit www.ets.org/research/topics/reading_for_understanding/assessments/gisa_samples/).

Below is a brief description of a sample GISA item. Each GISA begins by providing a short introduction of the purpose and the context of the task. Then, students are asked to read a longer text with a general overview on the given topic and write a short summary. In asking students to provide a short summary, GISA provides guidelines of what should be included in the summary so that students do not find this task too difficult, yet learn to extract main ideas from the text they have just read. A model summary is also provided to them. To help students comprehend long and complicated texts, GISA asks students to fill out graphic organizers with some cells already being filled out to provide scaffolding. To mock-up real life situations where students interact with one another and have an opportunity to gather and synthesize information, GISA provides multiple mediums, such as message boards and online forums, to simulate peer interaction. In this assessment, we are not only able to see what students are able and not able to do when appropriate resources (e.g., background information, cognitive strategies) are provided to them, but also what students are able to learn about 21st century literacy skills as they complete each task. GISA is distinct from other traditional types of reading comprehension assessments in that it attempts to incorporate the dynamic and complex relationships that are associated in reading comprehension (c.f., Lattice Model). Hence, GISA may seem to assess constructs in addition to students' reading skills to some people. However, such perspectives would depend on one's view on theoretical foundations of reading.

Technology can also support teachers so they can better tailor their instruction to meet their students' needs. One example is Assessment-to-instruction (A2i) technology. A2i is a technology that is specifically designed and developed to support teachers' efforts in individualizing instruction based on students' needs. A2i uses dynamic forecasting intervention (DFI) algorithms. DFI algorithms use individual students' test scores on word reading, vocabulary, and reading comprehension, and calculate the amount and type of literacy instruction (i.e., teacher-centered, student-centered, code-focused, meaning-focused) students need in order to achieve the target outcome by the end of the school year. The assessments that are used are adaptive and embedded in the A2i program. Based on the recommendation, teachers can track their students' performance, form small homogeneous skill groups, and plan their lessons to optimize student learning in school more easily. A2i also provides lesson plans and activities that are aligned with the Common Core State Standards (Common Core State Standards Initiative, 2010) and can be shared publicly to make it easier for teachers to implement individualized instruction on a daily basis. The use of A2i has been found to be effective in enhancing students' reading outcomes in K-3 classrooms (Al Otaiba et al., 2011; Connor et al., 2013, 2011, 2007, 2011). In addition, the effect was greater when teachers adhered closely to the recommendations that were estimated by the DFI algorithm (Connor et al., 2009).

There are intelligent tutoring systems and instructional programs that have technological components and are found to be effective in enhancing students' literacy outcomes. Here, we overview four programs – Read 180, Intelligent Tutoring Structure Strategy (ITSS), Interactive Strategy Trainer for Active Reading and Thinking (iSTART), and Word Knowledge e-Book (WKe-Book). Different features and formats have been incorporated in these programs, however, the end goal of them is the same – to improve students' ability to read for understanding.

Read 180 is a curricular program that is designed for struggling readers in grade 4 and up. Students can use the application along with the booklet component of the program. The application includes videos that promote interests and engagement about the topic across content areas and build background knowledge, texts for close reading, activities to foster academic vocabulary knowledge, and writing instruction. There are also teacher booklets that teachers can use and teachers can incorporate whole-group, small-group, and independent reading time during their instruction based on their students' level of understanding. Recent efficacy studies of Read 180 suggest that this technology-assisted intervention may have positive effects on students' reading outcomes (Kim et al., 2011; Kim, Samson, Fitzgerald, & Hartry, 2010).

ITSS is a web-based program that was designed to enhance upper elementary and middle-school students' text comprehension by explicitly teaching them how to identify the text structure in expository texts (Meyer et al., 2010). In ITSS, students learn about how to attend to cues that inform us about the organization of the text. Students are also asked to write a summary of, or recall, what they read according to the structure they have learned. Automated feedback is generated when students' responses are entered to the program. The findings from recent studies of ITSS indicate that this intervention can help students better understand the structure of the text, which would lead to better text comprehension (Meyer, Wijekumar, & Lin, 2011; Meyer et al., 2010; Wijekumar, Meyer, & Lei, 2012). In their large-scale randomized controlled trial with fourth grade students from rural and suburban schools, Wijekumar et al. (2012) found that students in the treatment condition scored higher on the standardized reading comprehension test and also on researcher-developed reading comprehension measures at post-test (effect sizes ranged from .11 to .28). Previous studies also showed positive effects of the ITSS with older students (Meyer et al., 2011, 2010), and effect sizes were larger (effect sizes around .5). The authors noted that fourth grade students lacked the typing skills that were required to fully participate in this intervention, and had to modify the ITSS program. This finding suggests that young students may improve their reading comprehension by using the ITSS program, but sufficient typing skills are crucial in order to fully benefit from this technology-assisted intervention.

iSTART is an interactive tutoring system that focuses on strategy instruction so that adolescent and college-level students learn how to make appropriate inferences when they read (McNamara, O'Reilly, Rowe, Boonthum, & Levinstein, 2007). Using different characters (i.e., instructor, students) in a simulated setting, iSTART teaches students self-explanation and five main reading strategies – comprehension monitoring, paraphrasing, prediction, elaboration, and bridging – and helps students to practice using those strategies while reading texts. iSTART provides adaptive feedback based on students' responses. Previous RCT on iSTART has shown that students in the iSTART condition comprehended texts more than those in the control condition (McNamara, O'Reilly, Best, & Ozuru, 2006). More recently, iSTART-ME was developed in order to maintain students' interest and engagement over time by incorporate game-based principles (Jackson, Dempsey, & McNamara, 2010; Jackson & McNamara, 2013). Students can earn points, obtain rewards, and play mini-games to practice the learned strategies in iSTART-ME. In their study of comparing the impact of iSTART and iSTART-ME on high school students, Jackson and McNamara (2013) found that the effects of these programs on the reading comprehension were equivalent, however, the students in the iSTART-ME condition showed higher levels of motivation than those in the iSTART condition.

Connor and colleagues have developed an interactive e-book for third to fifth graders, designed to build word knowledge and comprehension monitoring (Connor et al., 2015, 2019). The Word Knowledge e-Book (WKe-book), which is read on an iPad, uses unfamiliar vocabulary, embedded comprehension questions, and a choose-your-own-adventure format. In this choose-your-own-adventure e-book, the child needs to pay attention to the path they are choosing or there are consequences – choosing a particular vocabulary word (e.g., surreptitious vs. boisterous) changes the plot of the story and they are required to re-read the pages when they answer comprehension questions incorrectly. Results reveal that students' word knowledge, comprehension monitoring, and reading comprehension improve after reading the WKe-Book (Connor et al., 2015). The user logs allow teachers to monitor children's reading, their progression through the book, how long they spend on a page, and whether they answer the comprehension questions correctly. In this way, the WKe-Book also operates as a stealth assessment (Schute, 2011), providing teachers insights into children's thinking processes.

The Implementation Gap: How do We Overcome Barriers To Bringing Evidence-Based Practices into the Classroom That Are Created By Researchers, Vendors, and Educators?

Although only a brief discussion, this chapter demonstrates the complexity of considering individual child differences as they impact the effect of particular types of literacy instruction on children's outcomes. Of course, if the problems were not complex, we would have solved the challenge of student underachievement long ago. Silver bullets are appealing but rarely provide lasting solutions. Perhaps the only way to ensure that all children are provided optimal learning opportunities is to continue to conduct meaningful research that has both research and practical implications (i.e., address the relevance gap), and then find ways to bring these practices to classrooms. Here we discuss two promising initiatives that may help to overcome barriers to bringing effective instructional practices into the classroom. These are research-practice partnerships (Coburn et al., 2013; Fishman, Penuel, Allen, Cheng, & Sabelli, 2013) and implementation science (Coburn et al., 2013; Fixsen, Blase, Metz, & Van Dyke, 2011).

Research-Practice Partnerships

Research-practice partnerships are long-term collaborations among researchers, frequently at universities, and school districts. These partnerships are designed to last a long time – not just the length of a study initiated by a research – to focus on problems that are relevant to the school and designed to improve student outcomes. They take an approach with which all partners benefit, and contribute not only to, for example, improving instructional practices and student outcomes, but also to developing new theories and ideas.

Coburn and colleagues (2013) describe three kinds of partnerships: research alliances, design research, and networked improvement communities. They define a research alliance as a "long-term partnership between a district and an independent research organization focused on investigating questions of policy and practice that are central to the district" (p. 4). Design research is described as a "form of educational research that is similar to engineering research … the aim is to build and study solutions at the same time in real world contexts" (p. 8). Building on design-based research (e.g., Cobb, Confrey, diSessa, Lehrer, & Schauble, 2003), design-based implementation research (DBIR) was developed in an effort to better understand the problem of why so many educational interventions are relatively fragile (Fishman, Marx, Blumenfeld, Krajcik, & Soloway, 2004). There are four key principles behind DBIR. First, there must be a common commitment to solving problems of practice that are important to educators and educational leaders; that is, development from the perspective of those who will ultimately be responsible for implementing interventions. Second, DBIR engages in iterative, collaborative design of solutions, targeting multiple levels of the system: design that is informed by ongoing and systematic inquiry into implementation and outcomes. Third, there is a common commitment to building theory and knowledge within the research community. And fourth, there is a focus on developing sustainable change within systems. In conducting DBIR, the procedures involve iterating between design and testing in order to continually refine the instructional practices. Networked improvement communities (NICs) are a third type of research-practice partnership where districts band together to solve problems. As Coburn and colleagues (2013) note, "A core feature of NICs is that they are formed as networks that are not tied to a single district or community … a NIC forms to address a problem that is common to many different communities." (p. 10).

Implementation Science

Implementation Science is an approach designed to bring sustained implementation of evidence-based practices into schools and districts. Fixsen and colleagues (2013) define implementation practices as "purposeful and … described in sufficient detail" (p. 5), with two sets of outcomes: one to assess the effectiveness of the intervention when implemented; and another to assess the process of implementation (Fixsen, Naoom, Blase, Friedman, & Wallace, 2005). Implementation science experts (Fixsen et al., 2013; National Implementation Research Network (NIRN), 2013) define four stages of implementation: *Exploration*, where the evidence-based practices are identified; *Installation*, acquiring or repurposing the resources needed to do the work ahead (nirn.fpg.unc.edu); *Initial Implementation*, schools make school-wide systematic changes and begin to implement the evidence-based practices; and *Full Implementation*, when at least 50% of the teachers and educational leaders are implementing the evidence-based practices with fidelity. Implementation science relies on teams that include practitioners, educational leaders, and researchers that work together across the system, understanding that unless the system is changed, effective practice cannot be sustained. Implementation Science relies on strong research–practice partnerships.

Summary and Implications

In this chapter, we discussed children's cognitive development and potential factors that may cause individual differences in children's cognitive growth. We also reviewed how literacy instruction has been studied and how children's individual differences can be taken into account when we plan and implement literacy instruction. In so doing, we discussed how we can bridge gaps between the research and practice. We implicitly and explicitly referred to different gaps: the implementation gap, translational research gap, relevance gap, and bridging gap.

Implementation gap refers to the gap between what the research community knows about literacy instruction and how such knowledge is used in school settings to inform practice in a meaningful way; and *translational research gap* refers to the gap between the research conducted in controlled settings and using findings from such research to inform practice in actual, uncontrolled settings. *Relevance gap* is the gap between the questions that drive research conducted in controlled settings and everyday conditions in school settings that may serve students from diverse backgrounds. One way that we recommended to close these different gaps in literacy research is through strong research–practice partnerships. By including school and district personnel in designing and implementing research-based interventions, not only can researchers effectively communicate their knowledge to practitioners on reading research, they can also think about the adjustments that are needed for evidence-based practices to work in real-life settings. Another way to close these gaps would be to incorporate implementation science. Implementing research-based programs gradually in stages would give sufficient time for practitioners to understand and adjust to the evidence-based practices that are to be implemented and to bring about systemic change. *Bridging gap* refers to the lack of communication across disciplines relevant for literacy research. We discussed how different disciplines (e.g., education, cognitive science, developmental psychology, computer science, etc.) can collaborate to achieve one goal: understand children's constellation of skills and deliberately consider these individual differences when designing effective literacy instruction.

Thanks to accumulating research, we are better understanding children's literacy development and what we can do to support their learning. Continuing to conduct high-quality research and expanding our knowledge in cognitive development, language, and literacy is important. By closing gaps, we apply our knowledge and expertise in real-life settings across different contexts to appropriately serve all children, particularly those who are most vulnerable.

References

Adams, M. J. (1990). *Beginning to read: Thinking and learning about print*. Cambridge, MA: The MIT Press.
Afflerbach, P., Pearson, P. D., & Paris, S. G. (2008). Clarifying differences between reading skills and reading strategies. *The Reading Teacher*, *61*(5), 364–373. doi:10.1598/RT.61.5.1
Al Otaiba, S., Connor, C. M., Folsom, J. S., Greulich, L., Meadows, J., & Li, Z. (2011). Assessment data-informed guidance to individualize kindergarten reading instruction: Findings from a cluster-randomized control field trial. *Elementary School Journal*, *111*(4), 535–560. doi:10.1086/659031
Allan, N. P., Hume, L. E., Allan, D. M., Farrington, A. L., & Lonigan, C. J. (2014). Relations between inhibitory control and the development of academic skills in preschool and kindergarten: A meta-analysis. *Developmental Psychology*, *50*(10), 2368–2379. doi:10.1037/a0037493
Anderson, R. C., & Freebody, P. (1981). Vocabulary knowledge. In J. T. Guthrie (Ed.), *Comprehension and teaching: Research reviews* (pp. 77–111). Newark: International Reading Association.
Auger, A., Farkas, G., Burchinal, M. R., Duncan, G. J., & Vandell, D. L. (2014). Preschool center care quality effects on academic achievement: An instrumental variables analysis. *Developmental Psychology*, *50*(12), 2559–2571. doi:10.1037/a0037995
Barnes, E. M., Dickinson, D. K., & Grifenhagen, J. F. (2016). The role of teachers' comments during book reading in children's vocabulary growth. *The Journal of Educational Research*, 1–13. doi:10.1080/00220671.2015.1134422
Baumann, J. F., Seifert-Kessell, N., & Jones, L. A. (1992). Effect of think-aloud instruction on elementary students' comprehension monitoring abilities. *Journal of Literacy Research*, *24*(2), 143–172. doi:10.1080/10862969209547770
Bowers, E. P., & Vasilyeva, M. (2011). The relation between teacher input and lexical growth of preschoolers. *Applied Psycholinguistics*, *32*(1), 221–241. doi:10.1017/S0142716410000354
Bowne, J. B., Yoshikawa, H., & Snow, C. E. (2016). Relationships of teachers' language and explicit vocabulary instruction to students' vocabulary growth in kindergarten. *Reading Research Quarterly*, n/a-n/a. doi:10.1002/rrq.151
Brown, R. (1973). *A first language: The early stages*. London: George Allen & Unwin.
Buckingham, J., Beaman, R., & Wheldall, K. (2014). Why poor children are more likely to become poor readers: The early years. *Educational Review*, *66*(4), 428–446. doi:10.1080/00131911.2013.795129
Burchinal, M., Howes, C., Pianta, R., Bryant, D., Early, D., Clifford, R., & Barbarin, O. (2008). Predicting child outcomes at the end of kindergarten from the quality of pre-kindergarten teacher–child interactions and instruction. *Applied Developmental Science*, *12*(3), 140–153. doi:10.1080/10888690802199418
Burchinal, M., Vandergrift, N., Pianta, R., & Mashburn, A. (2010). Threshold analysis of association between child care quality and child outcomes for low-income children in pre-kindergarten programs. *Early Childhood Research Quarterly*, *25*(2), 166–176. doi:10.1016/j.ecresq.2009.10.004
Burns, M. K., Codding, R. S., Boice, C. H., & Lukito, G. (2010). Meta-analysis of acquisition and fluency math interventions with instructional and frustration level skills: Evidence for a skill-by-treatment interaction. *School Psychology Review*, *39*(1), 69–83.
Cain, K., Oakhill, J., & Bryant, P. (2004). Children's reading comprehension ability: Concurrent prediction by working memory, verbal ability, and component skills. *Journal of Educational Psychology*, *96*(1), 31–42.
Carlisle, J. F., Dwyer, J., & Learned, J. (2014). Discussion as a means of learning to reason, read, and write analytically. In B. Miller, P. McCardle, & R. Long (Eds.), *Teaching reading and writing: Improving instruction and student achievement* (pp. 83–92). Baltimore, MD: Paul H. Brookes.
Chall, J. S. (1996). *Stages of reading development* (2nd ed.). Orlando, FL: Harcourt Brace.
Chazan-Cohen, R., Raikes, H., Brooks-Gunn, J., Ayoub, C., Pan, B. A., Kisker, E. E., Roggman, L., & Fuligni, A. S. (2009). Low-income children's school readiness: Parent contributions over the first five years. *Early Education and Development*, *20*(6), 958–977. doi:10.1080/10409280903362402
Cobb, P., Confrey, J., diSessa, A., Lehrer, R., & Schauble, L. (2003). Design experiments in educational research. *Educational Researcher*, *32*(1), 9–13. doi:10.3102/0013189X032001009

Coburn, C. E., Penuel, W. R., & Geil, K. E. (2013). Research-practice partnerships: A strategy for leveraging research for educational improvement in school districts. Retrieved from http://forumfyi.org/files/R-P%20Partnerships%20White%20Paper%20%20Jan%202013%20-%20Coburn%20Penuel%20&%20Geil.pdf

Cohen, L., Manion, L., & Morrison, K. (2011). *Research methods in education* (7th ed.). New York, NY: Routledge.

Common Core State Standards Initiative. (2010). *Common core state standards for English language arts & literacy in history/social studies, science, and technical subjects.* Washington, DC: Authors.

Connor, C. M. (2016). A lattice model of the development of reading comprehension. *Child Development Perspectives, 10*(4), 269–274. doi:10.1111/cdep.12200

Connor, C. M., Day, S. L., Phillips, B., Sparapani, N., Ingebrand, S. W., McLean, L., Barrus, A., & Kaschak, M. P. (2016). Reciprocal effects of self-regulation, semantic knowledge, and reading comprehension in early elementary school. *Child Development, 87*(6), 1813–1824. doi:10.1111/cdev.12570

Connor, C. M., Day, S. L., Zargar, E., Wood, T. S., Taylor, K. S., Jones, M. R., & Hwang, J. K. (2019). Building word knowledge, learning strategies, and metacognition with the Word-Knowledge e-Book. *Computers & Education, 128,* 284– 311. https://doi.org/10.1016/j.compedu.2018.09.016

Connor, C. M., Dombek, J., Crowe, E. C., Spencer, M., Tighe, E. L., Coffinger, S., ... Petscher, Y. (2017). Acquiring science and social studies knowledge in Kindergarten through fourth grade: Conceptualization, design, implementation, and efficacy testing of Content-Area Literacy Instruction (CALI). *Journal of Educational Psychology, 109*(3), 301–320. doi:10.1037/edu0000128

Connor, C. M., Fishman, B. J., Crowe, E., Underwood, P., Schatschneider, C., & Morrison, F. J. (2013). Teachers' use of Assessment to Instruction (A2i) software and third graders' reading comprehension gains. In A. Shamir & O. Korat (Eds.), *Technology as a support for literacy achievements for children at risk* (Vol. 7, pp. 123–139). Netherlands: Springer.

Connor, C. M., Ingebrand, S. W., & Sparapani, N. (2015). What does effective teaching really look like? In R. Gabriel & R. Allington (Eds.), *Evaluating literacy instruction* (pp. 151–175). New York, NY: Routledge.

Connor, C. M., Kelcey, B., Sparapni, N., Petscher, Y., Siegal, S. W., Adams, A., Hwang, J. K., & Carlisle, J. F. (in press). Predicting second and third graders' reading comprehension gains: Observing students' and classmates talk during literacy instruction using COLT. *Scientific Studies of Reading.* https://doi.org/10.1080/10888438.2019.1698583

Connor, C. M., & McCardle, P. (Eds.). (2015). *Reading intervention: Research to practice to research.* New York, NY: Brookes Publishing.

Connor, C. M., & Morrison, F. J. (2012). Knowledge acquisition in the classroom: Literacy and content area knowledge. In A. M. Pinkham, T. Kaefer, & S. B. Neuman (Eds.), *Knowledge development in early childhood: Sources of learning and classroom implications* (pp. 220–241). New York, NY: Guilford Press.

Connor, C. M., & Morrison, F. J. (2016). Individualizing student instruction in reading implications for policy and practice. *Policy Insights from the Behavioral and Brain Sciences, 3*(1), 54–61. doi:10.1177/2372732215624931

Connor, C. M., Morrison, F. J., Fishman, B., Giuliani, S., Luck, M., Underwood, P. S., Bayraktar, A., Crowe, E., & Schatschneider, C. (2011). Testing the impact of child characteristics × instruction interactions on third graders' reading comprehension by differentiating literacy instruction. *Reading Research Quarterly, 46*(3), 189–221. doi:10.1598/RRQ.46.3.1/epdf

Connor, C. M., Morrison, F. J., Fishman, B. J., Crowe, E. C., Al Otaiba, S., & Schatschneider, C. (2013). A longitudinal cluster-randomized controlled study on the accumulating effects of individualized literacy instruction on students' reading from first through third grade. *Psychological Science, 24*(8), 1408–1419. doi:10.1177/0956797612472204

Connor, C. M., Morrison, F. J., Fishman, B. J., Schatschneider, C., & Underwood, P. (2007). The early years: Algorithm-guided individualized reading instruction. *Science, 315*(5811), 464–465. doi:10.1126/science.1134513

Connor, C. M., Morrison, F. J., Schatschneider, C., Toste, J., Lundblom, E. G., Crowe, E., & Fishman, B. (2011). Effective classroom instruction: Implications of child characteristic by instruction interactions on first graders' word reading achievement. *Journal of Research on Educational Effectiveness, 4*(3), 173–207. doi:10.1080/19345747.2010.510179

Connor, C. M., Phillips, B., Kaschak, M., Apel, K., Kim, Y.-S., Al Otaiba, S., Crowe, E., Thomas-Tate, S., Cooper Johnson, L., & Lonigan, C. (2014a). Comprehension tools for teachers: Reading for understanding from prekindergarten through fourth grade. *Educational Psychology Review, 26*(3), 379–401. doi:10.1007/s10648-014-9267-1

Connor, C. M., Phillips, B., Kaschak, M., Apel, K., Kim, Y.-S., Otaiba, S., Crowe, E., Thomas-Tate, S., Cooper Johnson, L., & Lonigan, C. (2014b). Comprehension tools for teachers: Reading for understanding from prekindergarten through fourth grade. *Educational Psychology Review*, 1–23. doi:10.1007/s10648-014-9267-1

Connor, C. M., Phillips, B., Kim, Y.-S., Al Otaiba, S., & Lonigan, C. J. (2015). *Comparative efficacy study-1: Examining impacts of component interventions on comprehension-related skilsl for students at risk for comprehension difficulties*. San Diego: Paper presented at the Pacific Coast Research Conference.

Connor, C. M., Piasta, S. B., Fishman, B., Glasney, S., Schatschneider, C., Crowe, E., Underwood, P., & Morrison, F. J. (2009). Individualizing student instruction precisely: Effects of child× instruction interactions on first Graders' literacy development. *Child Development*, *80*(1), 77–100. doi:10.1111/j.1467-8624.2008.01247.x

Connor, C. M., Ponitz, C. E. C., Phillips, B., Travis, Q. M., Day, S. G., & Morrison, F. J. (2010). First graders' literacy and self-regulation gains: The effect of individualizing instruction. *Journal of School Psychology*, *48*, 433–455. doi:10.1016/j.jsp.2010.06.003

Connor, C. M., Romain, L., Ingebrand, S., McLean, L. E., Barrus, A., & Day, S. (2015). *Patterns of learning and the word knowledge e-book: Leveraging student usage data to inform desing and enhance achievement*. Philadelphia: Paper presented at the Biennial Meeting of the Society for Research in Child Development.

Connor, C. M., Spencer, M., Day, S. L., Giuliani, S., Ingebrand, S. W., McLean, L., & Morrison, F. J. (2014). Capturing the complexity: Content, type, and amount of instruction and quality of the classroom learning environment synergistically predict third graders' vocabulary and reading comprehension outcomes. *Journal of Educational Psychology*, *106*(3), 762–778. doi:10.1037/a0035921

Cronbach, L. J. (1957). The two disciplines of scientific psychology. *American Psychologist*, *12*(11), 671–684. doi:10.1037/h0043943

Dickinson, D. K. (2011). Teachers' language practices and academic outcomes of preschool children. *Science*, *333*(6045), 964–967. doi:10.1126/science.1204526

Dickinson, D. K., & Porche, M. V. (2011). Relation between language experiences in preschool classrooms and children's kindergarten and fourth-grade language and reading abilities. *Child Development*, *82*(3), 870–886. doi:10.1111/j.1467-8624.2011.01576.x

Duff, F. J., Fieldsend, E., Bowyer-Crane, C., Hulme, C., Smith, G., Gibbs, S., & Snowling, M. J. (2008). Reading with vocabulary intervention: Evaluation of an instruction for children with poor response to reading intervention. *Journal of Research in Reading*, *31*(3), 319–336.

Duncan, G. J., & Vandell, D. L. (2012). Understanding variation in the impacts of human capital interventions on children and youth. *Irvine Network on Interventions in Development Working Paper*.

Efklides, A., & Misailidi, P. (Eds.). (2010). *Trends and prospects in metacognitive research*. New York, NY: Springer.

Farkas, S., & Duffett, A. (2008). *High-achieving students in the era of NCLB: Part 2 results from a national teacher survey*. Washington, DC. Retrieved from http://edex.s3-us-west-2.amazonaws.com/publication/pdfs/20080618_high_achievers_7.pdf

Fernald, A., Marchman, V. A., & Weisleder, A. (2013). SES differences in language processing skill and vocabulary are evident at 18 months. *Developmental Science*, *16*(2), 234–248. doi:10.1111/desc.12019

Fishman, B. J., Marx, R., Blumenfeld, P., Krajcik, J. S., & Soloway, E. (2004). Creating a framework for research on systemic technology innovations. *The Journal of the Learning Sciences*, *13*(1), 43–76. doi:10.1207/s15327809jls1301_3

Fishman, B. J., Penuel, W. R., Allen, A.-R., Cheng, B. H., & Sabelli, N. (2013). Design-based implementation research: An emerging model for transforming the relationship of research and practice. *Yearbook of the national society for the study of education*, *112*(2), 136–156.

Fitzgerald, J., & Shanahan, T. (2000). Reading and writing relations and their development. *Educational Psychologist*, *35*(1), 39–50. doi:10.1207/S15326985EP3501_5

Fixsen, D. L., Blase, K., Metz, A., & Dyke, M. V. (2013). Statewide implementation of evidence-based programs. *Exceptional Children*, *79*(2), 213–230.

Fixsen, D. L., Blase, K., Metz, A., & Van Dyke, M. (2011). Mobilizing communities for implementing evidence-based youth violence prevention programming: A commentary. *American Journal of Community Psychology*, *48*(1-2), 133–137. doi:10.1007/s10464-010-9410-1

Fixsen, D. L., Naoom, S. F., Blase, M. A., Friedman, F. M., & Wallace, F. (2005). *Implementation research: A synthesis of the literature (FMHI Publication No. 231)*. Tampa, FL: University of South Florida, Louis de la Parte Florida Mental Health Institute, National Implementation Research Network.

Gámez, P. B., & Lesaux, N. K. (2012). The relation between exposure to sophisticated and complex language and early-adolescent English-only and language minority learners' vocabulary. *Child Development*, *83*(4), 1316–1331.

Gámez, P. B., & Lesaux, N. K. (2015). Early-adolescents' reading comprehension and the stability of the middle school classroom-language environment. *Developmental Psychology*, *51*(4), 447.

Gamse, B. C., Jacob, R. T., Horst, M., Boulay, B., & Unlu, F. (2008). *Reading First impact study final report (NCEE 2009-4038)*. Washington, DC: National Center for Education Evaluation and Regional Assistance, Institute of Education Sciences, U.S. Department of Education.

Gonzalez, J. E., Pollard-Durodola, S., Simmons, D. C., Taylor, A. B., Davis, M. J., Fogarty, M., & Simmons, L. (2014). Enhancing preschool children's vocabulary: Effects of teacher talk before, during and after shared reading. *Early Childhood Research Quarterly*, *29*(2), 214–226. doi:10.1016/j.ecresq.2013.11.001

Gough, & Tunmer. (1986). Decoding, reading, and reading disability. *Remedial and Special Education*, 7, 6–10.

Graham, S., & Herbert, M. (2011). Writing to read: A meta-analysis of the impact of writing and writing instruction on reading. *Harvard Educational Review*, *81*(4), 710–744.

Hamilton, L. G., Hayiou-Thomas, M. E., Hulme, C., & Snowling, M. J. (2016). The home literacy environment as a predictor of the early literacy development of children at family-risk of dyslexia. *Scientific Studies of Reading*, *20*(5), 401–419. doi:10.1080/10888438.2016.1213266

Hart, B., & Risley, T. R. (1995). *Meaningful differences in the everyday experience of young American children*. Baltimore, MD: Paul H. Brookes Publishing.

Hirsh-Pasek, K., Adamson, L. B., Bakeman, R., Owen, M. T., Golinkoff, R. M., Pace, A., ... Suma, K. (2015). The contribution of early communication quality to low-income children's language success. *Psychological Science*, *26*(7), 1071–1083. doi:10.1177/0956797615581493

Hoff, E. (2003). The specificity of environmental influence: Socioeconomic status affects early vocabulary development via maternal speech. *Child Development*, 74, 1368–1378.

Hoff, E. (2013). Interpreting the early language trajectories of children from low-SES and language minority homes: Implications for closing achievement gaps. *Developmental Psychology*, *49*(1), 4. doi:10.1037/a0027238

Hoover, W. A., & Gough, P. B. (1990). The simple view of reading. *Reading and Writing*, *2*(2), 127–160.

Huttenlocher, J., Waterfall, H., Vasilyeva, M., Vevea, J., & Hedges, L. V. (2010). Sources of variability in children's language growth. *Cognitive Psychology*, *61*(4), 343–365. doi:10.1016/j.cogpsych.2010.08.002

Jackson, G. T., Dempsey, K. B., & McNamara, D. S. (2010). The evolution of an automated reading strategy tutor: From classroom to a game-enhanced automated system. In M. S. Khine & I. M. Saleh (Eds.), *New science of learning: Cognition, computers and collaboration in education* (pp. 283–306). New York, NY: Springer.

Jackson, G. T., & McNamara, D. S. (2013). Motivation and performance in game-based intelligent tutoring system. *Journal of Educational Psychology*, *105*(4), 1036–1049. doi:10.1037/a0032580

Jacoby, J. W., & Lesaux, N. K. (2014). Support for extended discourse in teacher talk with linguistically diverse preschoolers. *Early Education and Development*, *25*(8), 1162–1179. doi:10.1080/10409289.2014.907695

Justice, L. M., McGinty, A. S., Zucker, T., Cabell, S. Q., & Piasta, S. B. (2013). Bi-directional dynamics underlie the complexity of talk in teacher–child play-based conversations in classrooms serving at-risk pupils. *Early Childhood Research Quarterly*, *28*(3), 496–508. doi:10.1016/j.ecresq.2013.02.005

Keys, T. D., Farkas, G., Burchinal, M. R., Duncan, G. J., Vandell, D. L., Li, W., Ruzek, E., & Howes, C. (2013). Preschool center quality and school readiness: Quality effects and variation by demographic and child characteristics. *Child Development*, *84*(4), 1171–1190. doi:10.1111/cdev.12048

Kim, J. S., Capotosto, L., Hartry, A., & Fitzgerald, R. (2011). Can a mixed-method literacy intervention improve the reading achievement of low-performing elementary school students in an after-school program?: Results from a randomized controlled rrial of READ 180 Enterprise. *Educational Evaluation and Policy Analysis*, *33*(2), 183–201. doi:10.3102/0162373711399148

Kim, J. S., Samson, J. F., Fitzgerald, R., & Hartry, A. (2010). A randomized experiment of a mixed-methods literacy intervention for struggling readers in grades 4–6: Effects on word reading efficiency, reading comprehension and vocabulary, and oral reading fluency. *Reading and Writing*, *23*(9), 1109–1129. doi:10.1007/s11145-009-9198-2

Kim, Y.-S., & Phillips, B. (2014). Cognitive correlates of listening comprehension. *Reading Research Quarterly*, 49, 269–281. doi:10.1080/10888438.2015.1007375

Kintsch, W. (1988). The role of knowledge in discourse comprehension: A construction-integration model. *Psychological Review*, *95*(2), 163–182. doi:http://dx.doi.org/10.1037/0033-295X.95.2.163

Kintsch, W. (1998). *Comprehension: A paradigm for cognition*. New York, NY: Cambridge Unviersity Press.

Kratochwill, T. R., Volpiansky, P., Clements, M., & Ball, C. (2007). Professional development in implementing and sustaining multitier prevention models: Implications for response to intervention. *School Psychology Review*, *36*(4), 618–631.

Language and Reading Research Consortium. (2015). The dimensionality of language ability in young children. *Child Development*, *86*(6), 1948–1965. doi:10.1111/cdev.12450

Lawrence, J. F., Capotosto, L., Branum-Martin, L., White, C., & Snow, C. E. (2012). Language proficiency, home-language status, and English vocabulary development: A longitudinal follow-up of the Word Generation program. *Bilingualism: Language and Cognition*, *15*(3), 437–451. doi:10.1017/S1366728911000393

Lawrence, J. F., Crosson, A., Paré-Blagoev, E. J., & Snow, C. E. (2015). Word Generation randomized trial: Discussion mediates the impact of program treatment on academic word learning. *American Educational Research Journal*, *52*(4), 750–786. doi:10.3102/0002831215579485

Lesaux, N. K., Kieffer, M. J., Kelley, J. G., & Harris, J. R. (2014). Effects of academic vocabulary Instruction for linguistically diverse adolescents evidence from a randomized field trial. *American Educational Research Journal*, *51*(6), 1159–1194. doi:10.3102/0002831214532165

Li, W., Farkas, G., Duncan, G. J., Burchinal, M. R., & Vandell, D. L. (2013). Timing of high-quality child care and cognitive, language, and preacademic development. *Developmental Psychology*, *49*(8), 1440–1451. doi:10.1037/a0030613

Lin, B., Coburn, S. S., & Eisenberg, N. (2016). Self-regulation and reading achievement. In C. M. Connor (Ed.), *The cognitive development of reading and reading comprehension* (pp. 67–86). New York, NY: Routledge.

Lonigan, C. J., Farver, J. M., Phillips, B. M., & Clancy-Menchetti, J. (2011). Promoting the development of preschool children's emergent literacy skills: A randomized evaluation of a literacy-focused curriculum and two professional development models. *Reading and Writing*, *24*(3), 305–337. doi:10.1007/s11145-009-9214-6

Lonigan, C. J., & Milburn, T. F. (2017). Identifying the dimensionality of oral language skills of chilren with typical development in preschool through fifth grade. *Journal of Speech, Language and Hearing*. doi:10.1044/2017_JSLHR-L-15-0402

Marulis, L. M., & Neuman, S. B. (2010). The effects of vocabulary intervention on young children's word learning: A meta-analysis. *Review of Educational Research*, *80*(3), 300–335. doi:10.3102/0034654310377087

McClelland, M. M., & Cameron, C. E. (2012). Self-regulation in early childhood: Improving conceptual clarity and developing ecologically-valid measures. *Child Development Perspectives*, *6*(2), 136–142.

McNamara, D. S., O'Reilly, T., Rowe, M., Boonthum, C., & Levinstein, I. (2007). iSTART: A web-based tutor that teaches self-explanation and metacognitive reading strategies. In D. S. McNamara (Ed.), *Reading comprehension strategies: Theories, interventions, and technologies* (pp. 397–421). Mahwah, NJ: Lawrence Erlbaum Associates.

McNamara, D. S., O'Reilly, T. P., Best, R. M., & Ozuru, Y. (2006). Improving adolescent students' reading comprehension with iSTART. *Journal of Educational Computing Research*, *34*(2), 147–171. doi:10.2190/1RU5-HDTJ-A5C8-JVWE

Meyer, B. J. F., Wijekumar, K., Middlemiss, W., Higley, K., Lei, P.-W., Meier, C., & Spielvogel, J. (2010). Web-based tutoring of the structure strategy with or without elaborated feedback or choice for fifth- and seventh-grade readers. *Reading Research Quarterly*, *45*(1), 62–92. doi:10.1598/RRQ.45.1.4

Meyer, B. J. F., Wijekumar, K. K., & Lin, Y. (2011). Individualizing a web-based structure strategy intervention for fifth graders' comprehension of nonfiction. *Journal of Educational Psychology*, *103*(1), 140–168. doi:10.1037/a0021606

Miller, E. B., Farkas, G., Vandell, D. L., & Duncan, G. J. (2014). Do the effects of Head Start vary by parental preacademic stimulation? *Child Development*, *85*(4), 1385–1400. doi:10.1111/cdev.12233

Mistry, R. S., Benner, A. D., Biesanz, J. C., Clark, S. L., & Howes, C. (2010). Family and social risk, and parental investments during the early childhood years as predictors of low-income children's school readiness outcomes. *Early Childhood Research Quarterly*, *25*(4), 432–449. doi:10.1016/j.ecresq.2010.01.002

Moreno, S., Bialystok, E., Barac, R., Schellenberg, E. G., Cepeda, N. J., & Chau, T. (2011). Short-term music training enhances verbal intellignece and exceecutive function. *Psychological Science*, *22*, 1425–1433.

Morrison, F. J., Griffith, E. M., & Alberts, D. M. (1997). Nature-nurture in the classroom: Entrance age, school readiness, and learning in children. *Developmental Psychology*, *33*(2), 254–262.

Murnane, R., & Willett, J. (2011). *Methods matter: Improving causal inference in educational and social science research*. New York, NY: Oxford Uniersity Press.

National Implementation Research Network (NIRN). (2013). Retrieved from www.nirn.fpg.unc.edu

Nelson, K. E., Welsh, J. A., Trup, E. M. V., & Greenberg, M. T. (2011). Language delays of impoverished preschool children in relation to early academic and emotion recognition skills. *First Language, 31*(2), 164–194. doi:10.1177/0142723710391887

Neuman, S. B., Newman, E. H., & Dwyer, J. (2011). Educational effects of a vocabulary intervention on preschoolers' word knowledge and conceptual development: A cluster-randomized trial. *Reading Research Quarterly, 46*(3), 249–272. doi:10.1598/RRQ.46.3.3

Newman, R. S., Rowe, M. L., & Bernstein Ratner, N. A. N. (2016). Input and uptake at 7 months predicts toddler vocabulary: The role of child-directed speech and infant processing skills in language development. *Journal of Child Language, 43*(5), 1158–1173. doi:10.1017/S0305000915000446

NICHD National Reading Panel. (2000). *Teaching children to read: An evidence-based assessment of the scientific research literature on reading and its implications for reading instruction.* Washington DC: U.S. DHHS, PHS, NICHD.

NICHD-ECCRN. (2004). Multiple pathways to early academic achievement. *Harvard Educational Review, 74* (1), 1–29. doi:10.17763/haer.74.1.k845735459043543

O'Reilly, T., & Sabatini, J. (2013). Reading for understanding: How performance moderators and scenarios impact assessment design. *ETS Research Report RR-13-31.* Retrieved from http://www.ets.org/Media/Research/pdf/RR-13-31.pdf

Pelatti, C. Y., Piasta, S. B., Justice, L. M., & O'Connell, A. (2014). Language- and literacy-learning opportunities in early childhood classrooms: Children's typical experiences and within-classroom variability. *Early Childhood Research Quarterly, 29*(4), 445–456. doi:10.1016/j.ecresq.2014.05.004

Perfetti, C., & Stafura, J. (2014). Word knowledge in a theory of reading comprehension. *Scientific Studies of Reading, 18*(1), 22–37. doi:10.1080/10888438.2013.827687

Petscher, Y., Kim, Y.-S., & Foorman, B. R. (2011). The importance of predictive power in early screening assessments: Implications for placement in the response to intervention framework. *Assessment for Effective Intervention, 36*(3), 158–166.

Pianta, R. C., Belsky, J., Houts, R., & Morrison, F. J. (2007). TEACHING: Opportunities to learn in America's elementary classrooms. *Science, 315,* 1795–1796.

Rapp, D. N., & van den Broek, P. (2005). Dynamic text comprehension: An integrative view of reading. *Current Directions in Psychological Science, 14*(5), 276–279.

Rodriguez, E. T., & Tamis-LeMonda, C. S. (2011). Trajectories of the home learning environment across the first 5 years: Associations with children's vocabulary and literacy skills at prekindergarten. *Child Development, 82*(4), 1058–1075. doi:10.1111/j.1467-8624.2011.01614.x

Roehrig, A. D., Duggar, S. W., Moats, L. C., Glover, M., & Mincey, B. (2008). When teachers work to use progress monitoring data to inform literacy instruction: Identifying potential supports and challenges. *Remedial and Special Education, 29,* 364–382. doi:10.1177/0741932507314021

Rowe, M. L. (2012). A longitudinal investigation of the role of quantity and quality of child-directed speech in vocabulary development. *Child Development, 83*(5), 1762–1774.

Rowe, M. L., Leech, K. A., & Cabrera, N. (2016). Going beyond input quantity: Wh-questions matter for toddlers' language and cognitive development. *Cognitive Science.* doi:10.1111/cogs.12349

Sammons, P., Toth, K., Sylva, K., Melhuish, E., Siraj, I., & Taggart, B. (2015). The long-term role of the home learning environment in shaping students' academic attainment in secondary school. *Journal of Children's Services, 10*(3), 189–201. doi:10.1108/jcs-02-2015-0007

Scarborough, H. S. (2001). Connecting early language and literacy to later reading (dis)abilities: Evidence, theory, and practice. In S. B. Neuman & D. K. Dickinson (Eds.), *Handbook of early literacy research* (pp. 97–110). New York, NY: Guilford Press.

Schute, V. J. (2011). Stealth assessment in computer-based gams to support learning. In S. Tobias & J. D. Fletcher (Eds.), *Computer games and instruction* (pp. 503–523). Charlotte, NC: Information Age Publishing.

Shadish, W. R., Cook, T. D., & Campbell, J. R. (2002). *Experimental and quasi-experimental designs for generalized causal inference.* New York, NY: Houghton Mifflin Company.

Skibbe, L. E., Connor, C. M., Morrison, F. J., & Jewkes, A. M. (2011). Schooling effects on preschoolers' self-regulation, early literacy, and language growth. *Early Childhood Research Quarterly, 26*(1), 42–49. doi:10.1016/j.ecresq.2010.05.001

Skibbe, L. E., Grimm, K. J., Bowles, R. P., & Morrison, F. J. (2012). Literacy growth in the academic year versus summer from preschool through second grade: Differential effects of schooling across four skills. *Scientific Studies of Reading, 16*(2), 141–165. doi:10.1080/10888438.2010.543446

Son, S.-H., & Morrison, F. J. (2010). The nature and impact of changes in home learning environment on development of language and academic skills in preschool children. *Developmental Psychology, 46*(5), 1103–1118. doi:10.1037/a0020065

Sorhagen, N. S. (2013). Early teacher expectations disproportionately affect poor children's high school performance. *Journal of Educational Psychology, 105*(2), 465–477. doi:10.1037/a0031754

Spira, E. G., Bracken, S. S., & Fischel, J. E. (2005). Predicting improvement after first-grade reading difficulties: The effects of oral language, emergent literacy, and behavior skills. *Developmental Psychology, 41*(1), 225–234. doi:10.1037/0012-1649.41.1.225

Storch, S. A., & Whitehurst, G. J. (2002). Oral language and code-related precursors to reading: Evidence from a longitudinal structural model. *Developmental Psychology, 38*(6), 934–947.

Strang, T. M., & Piasta, S. B. (2016). Socioeconomic differences in code-focused emergent literacy skills. *Reading and Writing, 29*(7), 1337–1362. doi:10.1007/s11145-016-9639-7

Swanson, H. L., & O'Connor, R. (2009). The role of working memory and fluency practice on the reading comprehension of students who are dysfluent readers. *Journal of Learning Disabilities, 42*(6), 548–575.

Taylor, J. E., Roehrig, A. D., Hensler, B. S., Connor, C. M., & Schatschneider, C. (2010). Teacher quality moderates the genetic effects on early reading. *Science, 328*, 512–514.

Teale, W. H., & Sulzby, E. (Eds.). (1986). *Emergent literacy: Writing and reading*. Norwood, NJ: Ablex.

Tompkins, V., Zucker, T. A., Justice, L. M., & Binici, S. (2013). Inferential talk during teacher–child interactions in small-group play. *Early Childhood Research Quarterly, 28*(2), 424–436. doi:10.1016/j.ecresq.2012.11.001

Vandell, D. L., Belsky, J., Burchinal, M., Steinberg, L., & Vandergrift, N. (2010). Do effects of early child care extend to age 15 years? Results from the NICHD study of early child care and youth development. *Child Development, 81*(3), 737–756.

Verhoeven, L., van Leeuwe, J., & Vermeer, A. (2011). Vocabulary growth and reading development across the elementary school years. *Scientific Studies of Reading, 15*(1), 8–25. doi:10.1080/10888438.2011.536125

Weisleder, A., & Fernald, A. (2013). Talking to children matters: Early language experience strengthens processing and builds vocabulary. *Psychological Science, 24*(11), 2143–2152. doi:10.1177/0956797613488145

Wijekumar, K. K., Meyer, B. J. F., & Lei, P. (2012). Large-scale randomized controlled trial with 4th graders using intelligent tutoring of the structure strategy to improve nonfiction reading comprehension. *Educational Technology Research and Development, 60*(6), 987–1013. doi:10.1007/s11423-012-9263-4

Wright, T. S., & Neuman, S. B. (2014). Paucity and disparity in kindergarten oral vocabulary instruction. *Journal of Literacy Research, 46*(3), 330–357. doi:10.1177/1086296x14551474

Ziol-Guest, K. M., & McKenna, C. C. (2014). Early childhood housing instability and school readiness. *Child Development, 85*(1), 103–113. doi:10.1111/cdev.12105

17

Social and Cultural Differences in Reading Development

Instructional Processes, Learning Gains, and Challenges

Allison Skerrett

Schools have long restricted learning opportunities for minoritized student groups in varied pernicious ways. One practice is framing students' racial, cultural, linguistic, immigrant, and transnational identities and competencies as deficits and barriers to learning (Lee, 2006; Moll & Gonzalez, 1994; Orellana & Gutiérrez, 2006; Skerrett, 2015; Valencia, 1997). Another is the refusal to prioritize curricula that reflect students' diverse sociocultural community experiences and capacity for knowledge production (Ladson-Billings, 1998/2009; Lee, 1997, 2007; Moll & Gonzalez, 1994). Furthermore, classroom-level instructional practices and district policies often adopt only superficial acknowledgement of the diverse ways students', families', and communities' histories and linguistic and cultural practices inform learning, such that Eurocentric middle class discourse patterns are privileged in daily interactions (Heath, 1983; Lee, 2006, 2007; Reese, Arauz, & Bazan, 2012).

Since the mid-1980s, scholars have amassed ground-breaking theoretical frameworks and empirical evidence to support social and cultural factors as significant contributors to reading development (Cole, 1996; Gonzalez, Moll, & Amanti, 2005; Heath, 1983; Lee, 1997, 2007; Moll & Gonzalez, 1994; Moll, 2014; New London Group [NLG], 1996; Scribner & Cole, 1978; Street, 1984). Recent research has applied and extended these assets-oriented sociocultural theories to investigate instructional approaches to reading, and documented the learning gains associated with them (e.g., Ivey & Johnston, 2013; Lee, 1997, 2007; Martínez-Roldán, 2003; Moll, 2014; Skerrett, 2012; Tatum, 2014). Yet literacy instruction policy mandates linked to Eurocentric values continuously constrain large-scale recognition and implementation of sociocultural approaches to reading instruction. Perhaps the most compelling example of the exclusion of youths' sociocultural ways of learning is that schools continue to perseverate on high-stakes standardized tests that are biased toward Eurocentric, middle class, English language skills and cultural knowledge (Au, 2009; Darling-Hammond, 2007). Schools' responses to students vulnerable to failing these tests—overwhelmingly represented by minoritized groups—have been to structure test-driven instructional spaces, content, and approaches for these students that further limit students' access to their sociocultural resources and thus their opportunities to learn (Gutiérrez, 2009; Nichols, Berliner, & Noddings, 2007).

Far from accepting things as "just the way schools are" (Tyack & Tobin, 1994, p. 454), this chapter offers some proposals that hold potential to advance knowledge and practice related to reading instruction that accounts for social and cultural differences within the current educational milieu. The chapter explores the following questions:

- How does an understanding of social and cultural differences provide opportunities and challenges for supporting students' reading development?
- What is the research on reading instruction that is responsive to social and cultural differences?

The chapter reviews selected foundational and contemporary scholarship that adopts a sociocultural perspective on literacy learning and learners (e.g., Cole, 1996; Gonzalez et al., 2005; Heath, 1983; Lee, 1997, 2007; Moll & Gonzalez, 1994; Moll, 2014; NLG, 1996; Scribner & Cole, 1978; Street, 1984; Tatum, 1999) and describes how this theoretical perspective has foregrounded the significance of the social and cultural dimensions of reading development. The chapter then reviews selected instructive research emerging from the early 2000's to the present that describes research on varied socioculturally-informed instructional approaches literacy researchers and teachers have employed to promote students' reading development, and the learning gains and challenges associated with each of these approaches. Given that a large number of these studies are conducted in literacy classrooms by researchers, often in collaboration with literacy teachers, much of this research is published in literacy teacher research journals and more general education journals. This pattern reflects the historical and ongoing dominance of individualistic cognitive-based perspectives on literacy learning (Street, 1984) and attendant privileging of quasi-experimental studies in reading research and publications. This phenomenon was recently discussed by P. David Pearson and his colleagues (Frankel, Becker, Rowe, &, Pearson, 2016), who documented the slow, and still growing, accommodation of the field of reading research of socioculturally-based theories of reading development.

After reviewing the research that draws upon sociocultural theories of reading development, the chapter identifies the major questions that persist in this area. It explores these questions through the framework of the four gaps—implementation, translational, relevance, and bridging—that organize the chapters in this volume and illuminates some pathways as well as challenges for bridging these gaps.

Sociocultural Perspectives on Literacy Learning and Reading Development

Literacy scholars, often working with marginalized communities, have led the ground-breaking sociocultural turn in literacy (Cole, 1996; Heath, 1983; Moll & Gonzalez, 1994; Scribner & Cole, 1978; Street, 1984). These foundational investigations have contributed understandings about the varied ways in which literacy takes form and is learned, used, and adapted within and among families, communities, and broader sociocultural contexts, such as educational institutions. This theoretical turn toward literacy as practice has critiqued the idea of a singular autonomous perspective on literacy (Street, 1984) that is print- and text-centric and that conceptualizes literacy as an individually acquired discrete set of cognitive skills that can be universally taught and applied across all learners and contexts. Literacy scholars have complicated this autonomous conceptualization of literacy learning by adding an ideological perspective. The ideological perspective privileges the social, linguistic, and cultural identities and features of particular learners and communities; their literacy goals, values, resources, and practices; and the technologies for making meaning available to them (Cole, 1996; Heath, 1983; Lee, 2006; Moll & Gonzalez, 1994; Scribner & Cole, 1978; Street, 1984; Tatum, 1999).

Foundational scholars have further investigated the design, processes, and outcomes of reading instruction that attends to the sociocultural dimensions of literacy learners and learning. For example, Cole (1996) reported on a study in which he and his colleagues, Courtney Cazden and Hugh Mehan, conducted an experiment based on Vygotsky's (1978) concept of the zone of proximal development (ZPD) with young children and adults. In this experiment, the task of reading was spread across participants, for instance, with distinct, shared, and/or partial cognitive and social roles for children and adults, depending upon cognitive and sociocultural factors such as participants' reading skill or confidence levels to take on specific roles at particular times. Cole (1996) and his colleagues found that the children were able to participate in the full act of reading and understanding texts in this shared mediated learning space.

Moll and his colleagues (Gonzalez et al., 2005; Moll & Gonzalez, 1994) introduced the concept of funds of knowledge, which framed Latina/o students' homes and communities as contexts rich with varied forms of knowledge, practices, and competencies that could support students' learning in school. Moll and his colleagues positioned teachers as researchers of their students' homes and communities who would learn about these resources, theorize how these could be used to facilitate teaching and learning the academic curriculum, and design and enact literacy learning experiences that reflected this funds of knowledge approach. More recently, Moll (2014) returned to the influential work of Lev Vygotsky (1978), on which much of sociocultural theories of literacy learning rely, to emphasize understandings of Vygotsky's (1978) concepts of cultural mediation of thinking and development in relation to bilingual and bicultural youths' reading development.

Moll (2014) re-analyzed a formative experiment he and his colleagues designed in which students labeled as ELLs were provided instruction in separate English and Spanish classes. The original study's focus was on how teachers' constructions of students' English language identities as either high, middle, or low, led to teachers' provision of instruction and learning tasks that yielded varied opportunities and constraints on students' ZPDs for generating high levels of cognitive thinking, including in reading and writing. Drawing upon Vygotsky's (1978) theory, Moll (2014) hypothesized that:

> [T]he students' Spanish reading level would be a useful indicator of the top of their zone of proximal reading development [suggesting] that the way English reading was taught should reflect what the children could do in Spanish…with students' English reading represent[ing] their actual developmental level.
>
> *(p. 64)*

Working alongside the English and Spanish teachers in these classrooms, Moll and his colleagues facilitated a redesign of curriculum and instruction that created greater opportunities for students to mediate their thinking and learning through the bilingual resources they possessed for becoming competent readers in English.

Likewise, Carol Lee (1997), (2006), (2007) developed a cultural modeling framework through working as both a scholar and teacher of African American students. Lee and her students first engaged the everyday cultural texts of students' lives to facilitate students' notice of their already existing skills of reading and interpreting texts. Students, equipped with this knowledge, and supported by their use of African American language in discussing texts, became increasingly sophisticated at conducting high quality analyses with challenging literary texts, including those texts that schools have historically valued. Other scholars, concerned with the language and literacy development of culturally and linguistically diverse youths, expound that language practices are continuously changing, for example, in response to shifting cultural demographics in local communities and digital interactions in multilingual global contexts (NLG, 1996; Paris, 2009). In a related vein, another group of scholars have pointed out the new social, functional, and political demands that individuals and families encounter as a result of immigrant and transnational lifestyles that help generate a wealth of linguistic, intercultural, and sociopolitical world knowledge (Enciso, Volz, Price-Dennis, & Durriyah, 2010; Guan, Nash, & Orellana, 2016; Sanchez & Orellana, 2006; Skerrett, 2015). Taken together, these scholars propose that these multilingual, multicultural, and transnational resources can be useful for reading instruction and development.

Theoretical conversations pertaining to how instructional approaches based in sociocultural theories may become more prominent in literacy education are actively ongoing. Central to these discussions are the possibilities for acknowledging and bridging the strengths that the ideological and autonomous perspectives offer for students' literacy development. Street (2012) proposed a concept of society reschooling in which schools accept their responsibility to enhance learners' literate capacities to participate effectively in the various social contexts of their lives, and that also acknowledges that students have much to learn from formal educational institutions. In this sense, although Street (2012) does not explicitly name this lineage, his ideas are quintessentially sociocultural/Vygotskian. Street's (2012) framework also aligns with Freire's (1990) concepts of reading word and world relationships. For Street (2012) is hopeful that if literacy education could "embrace both the everyday aspect of learning and that to be found in more formal educational institutions… the two fields… instead of being polar opposites, might embrace and build on the strengths of each other" (pp. 225–226).

Research on Socioculturally-Informed Instructional Approaches to Reading, Learning Gains, and Challenges

This body of research presents a variety of approaches to reading instruction that attend to social and cultural differences among students, and documents the learning gains and challenges associated with varied approaches. In this chapter, these approaches to reading instruction, although not always mutually exclusive, have been organized into the following categories:

- A focus on students' reading identities
- Choice/Independence in student reading
- Shared texts that invite students' sociocultural identities and experiences
- Reading instruction across home, school, and community contexts
- Blending sociocultural and cognitive factors in reading instruction.

The categories are consequently organized to illustrate the emphasis on the individual learner in sociocultural theories of reading instruction and development, and then portray the importance of situating the reader and his/her reading instruction and development within and across multiple social contexts with others including reading classrooms, the home, and community spaces. The category of blending sociocultural and cognitive dimensions in reading instruction is treated last for two reasons. First, this approach is currently the least employed in socioculturally-informed research on reading instruction. Second, though least utilized, the approach of attending to both the sociocultural and cognitive dimensions of reading in instruction raises important questions about the future (opportunities and challenges) of sociocultural approaches to reading instruction. As such, this category provides a fitting transition into the chapter's concluding discussion that is structured around the four gaps that serve as the organizing frame for this volume.

Students' Reading Identities

One line of research that takes a sociocultural approach to reading instruction, focuses on the relationship between students' reading identities and their reading development. Studies in this area demonstrate why students' social, cultural, and linguistic backgrounds, and their communities' sociopolitical histories and contemporary experiences, should be accounted for in the reading instruction they receive, and how doing so can promote students' investments and gains in reading. For example, Tatum (1999, 2014) has long studied African American males' identities in relation to reading. Tatum's (1999, 2014) work emphasizes the sociohistorically significant role of reading in African American communities, homes, and peer groups for religious, sociopolitical, social, and culturally meaningful purposes. Tatum (1999, 2014) critiques reading instruction practices that deny African American males' access to identities as readers—such as deficit thinking about their interests in, and capabilities to have high quality experiences with print texts and refusal to provide African American males with socially and culturally meaningful texts.

Studies on reading identity conducted with students who come from minoritized groups also reveal the multiplicity of reading identities that students can hold, including those they claim for themselves and those that are ascribed to them, for example "struggling readers," by teachers and schools (Enriquez, 2014; Kim & Viesca, 2016; Skerrett, 2012). Such studies illustrate the detrimental effects on students' reading development by labeling students as struggling readers. For example, Kim and Viesca (2016) illustrated how three reading intervention teachers' different positioning of their emergent bilingual learners (for example as individuals, a monolithic group, or as learners), resulted in differentiated reading instruction practices of motivating and engaging their students that ranged from more dynamic to tightly controlled. At the same time, research on students' reading identities often demonstrate the agency of students (and teachers) in contesting labels of struggling readers and crafting, through their engagements with reading across school and other social contexts, stronger reading identities and skills. Enriquez (2014) described how two middle school students, an African American girl and a boy of Middle Eastern descent, who were labeled as struggling readers, experienced this identity through feelings of loss and exclusion during reading in the classroom. Yet these students also worked toward creating more positive reading identities for themselves through performances of reading with print texts.

Thus, researchers advocate for an approach to reading instruction that involves teachers and students inquiring into the construct of reading identity and how it impacts reading instruction and reading achievement (Kim & Viesca, 2016; Skerrett, 2012; Tatum, 2014). This approach has the benefit of promoting students' and teachers' metacognitive awareness of how social, cultural, linguistic, and sociopolitical factors shape the reading identities and attendant learning opportunities that students are given, or withheld, by social actors such as schools and teachers. Researching with students into their reading identities promotes student agency in recognizing and rejecting deficit perspectives about themselves and claiming more productive reading identities. However, the effectiveness of this instructional approach is also dependent upon whether and how other positioning agents such as schools, teachers, and peers take on more generative perspectives on students as readers and the provision of high quality reading instruction.

As one example, I presented a case of a Latina student's reading history and identity across her early years of schooling into the ninth grade, as well as in her life outside school

(Skerrett, 2012). Angelica described how the standardized-test driven reading instruction she experienced beginning in grade three, resulted in her disenchantment with reading and her school's positioning of her as a struggling reader. Angelica herself took on this identity of a struggling reader despite the rich family literacies (such as writing and performing plays and reading with siblings) that she participated in at home. Studying Angelica in her ninth grade reading classroom with a teacher who took a sociocultural perspective on reading, I observed the gradual transformation of Angelica's taking on, for herself, the identity of reader. Part of the reading teacher's pedagogy involved critical exploration with students into the construct of reading identity and facilitation of how their identities as readers were not simply static or school-assigned labels. "Students considered how their emotional states, social and instructional interactions with their peers and teacher, the features of their texts, and their applications of cognitive and metacognitive skills positioned them, from moment to moment… as a particular kind of reader" (Skerrett, 2012, p. 71).

The final project for this reading class, was for students to reflect on how their identities as readers had changed over the course of the year. Angelica, working with a peer, developed a power point, with the last two slides demonstrating how she and other students had (re)claimed identities as readers in school and also outside school.

> On one power point slide, the two girls inserted an image of a chicken breaking out of its shell to depict the birth of their academic identities as readers and writers in Molly's class. Under the image they inserted the caption, "This Reminds Us About When We First Got Here And We Hatched In This Class." On the subsequent slide they wrote in large font, "We Don't Think Reading And Writing Is BORING 263A!!!!"
>
> *(Skerrett, 2012, p. 72)*

Choice and Independent Reading

As the section above suggested, different texts provide a range of opportunities and constraints for students developing their reading identities and skills. Another popular sociocultural approach to reading instruction is teachers making available to students, or inviting them to bring to school, a range of texts that reflect their social and cultural identities and interests. This instructional approach, often called independent or choice reading (Bomer, 2011), is especially beneficial for students who have historically disengaged from reading because it lacks relevance to their social and cultural identities and lived experiences. Reading instruction that centers students' reading independence and textual choice is credited with increasing student motivation and reading engagement (Bomer, 2011; Ivey & Johnston, 2013), building positive school and classroom reading cultures (Francois, 2013), growing students' reading competencies (Bomer, 2011), and strengthening students' identities as readers (Bomer, 2011; Francois, 2013). Francois (2013) conducted an ethnographic study of an urban school under pressure to raise the standardized test reading scores of its primarily Latina/o and Black student population. Her research discovered that daily independent reading promoted students' reading skills and generated a community where reading became a shared and valued literacy activity among administration, teachers, and students.

Ivey and Johnston's (2013) study is particularly instructive about the outcomes of choice in independent reading. Ivey and Johnston's (2013) study on adolescents' engaged reading occurred across four middle school language arts classrooms with 71 adolescents. Student ethnicities comprised 72% Caucasian, 16% African American, and 11% Hispanic, with 47% of the student body qualifying for free or reduced priced lunch. In the researchers' words, four English teachers "abandoned whole-class assigned classic texts in favor of student-selected, self-paced reading within a collection of materials dealing with issues and concepts of high interest to students" (p. 258). Rather than the comprehension quizzes and other assignments and projects typically attached to adolescents' reading in school, the simple homework assignment each night was encouragement to students to read their books at home. Teachers' instructional interactions focused on engagement by pursuing lines of inquiry important to students that were related to their texts. Ivey and Johnston (2013) found strong relationships among student choice in reading an array of young adult fiction; social structures for peer reading and discussing texts together; and development of students' academic and social identities, agency, and intellectual growth.

A choice reading instructional approach requires teachers to equip and support students with the tools they need to be agentive in their reading lives and reading development. For example teachers do not merely teach reading strategies; they also facilitate learners' increasing capabilities to recognize when and how to apply appropriate strategies to make sense of their independent reading (Bomer, 2011; Skerrett, 2012). A student choice approach further requires teachers with strong knowledge of children's and young adult literature. Lewis (1999) raised important cautions about choice in independent reading. In the middle school classrooms she observed, students brought in texts and other materials that adults considered inappropriate for engaging in school. Therefore, Lewis (1999) critiqued the assumption in choice reading that students are truly free to pursue the identities and interests that matter to them in school. Lewis (1999) added another important instructional role for the teacher who employs choice reading—that of a mediator who helps students understand and navigate the tensions between the invitation to choose and constraints on that freedom within the larger sociopolitical context of schooling.

Shared Texts that Invite Students' Sociocultural Identities and Experiences

In this instructional approach, teachers select texts for whole-class or small group reading that will encourage students to draw upon their racial, cultural, linguistic, social class, and other identities and experiences, to promote engagement and reading comprehension. In relation to race, Blue (2012) studied reading comprehension through oral reading and literary interpretation activities in a diverse classroom. Based in her findings, Blue (2012) proposed that literature that provided cultural cues for African American students and that valued their personal literary interpretations, allowed students to display their metacognitive competencies, reading achievement, and development.

Rogers and Mosley (2006) conducted research in a racially diverse second grade classroom where teachers used whole-class texts that evoked issues of race and racism to guide their young students, including White children, to deploy and further develop their racial literacies (understandings of how race shapes individual and group experiences and societal power relations) to make deeper meanings of texts. Thomas (2013, 2015) researching in racially mixed classrooms, and Borsheim-Black in a primarily White context (2015), also found that shared reading of texts with racial themes challenged students and teachers to apply a racial literacy lens to their reading and push their interpretative capacities as readers.

Linguistic resources as tools for building reading comprehension have also been studied in the shared texts reading instruction practice (Martínez-Roldán, 2003; Martínez-Roldán & Sayer, 2006). Martínez-Roldán (2003) studied the reading development of a Mexican-born girl across her year in a second grade bilingual classroom. She found that the learning context, which employed bilingual literature, as well as encouraged students' uses of bilingual oral narratives to discuss these texts in small groups, were key to the student's reading development. Martínez-Roldán and Sayer (2006) later explored how bilingual third grade students used language during story retellings. The researchers concluded that students demonstrated greater comprehension of the stories when they used Spanglish (Spanish-English code-switching) to mediate their retellings than they did when retelling stories using only English. Finally, in relation to social class, Thein, Guise, and Sloan (2012) observed the salience of social class identity on the literary interpretations of four white, socioeconomically diverse secondary school students who read Allison's *Bastard Out of Carolina* in a six-week literature circle. Findings from this set of studies provide evidence that using shared texts that facilitate students' access to their sociocultural identities, knowledge, and experiences for reading instruction promotes students' reading competencies.

Reading research, in line with using shared texts, also demonstrates the learning outcome of critical literacy, which includes students' abilities to read the word and the world, develop critical sociopolitical knowledge, and take action to redress injustices in their worlds (Freire, 1990). Such an outcome is highly significant for historically and contemporarily minoritized student populations. In the context of growing numbers of refugees into Australia, Boas (2012) organized literature circles in which she and her eighth grade students engaged with a variety of texts—newspaper articles, web resources, and an anchor novel—to explore the issue of human rights for this population. Although Boas (2012) did not indicate her students' racial or cultural backgrounds, transcripts of students' initial talk at the beginning of the unit suggest they were Australian-born, likely primarily White, and viewed refugees as othered. Boas (2012) found that this study enabled her to teach reading, writing, and thinking skills, including critical literacy. For example, as she and her students read and discussed letters to the editors of newspapers and articles that contained opposing perspectives on the topic of refugees, some of Boas' (2012) students moved toward advocacy and social-justice oriented positions for this marginalized group.

Enciso's (2011) participants included racially and culturally diverse sixth grade students representing a range of immigrant backgrounds (e.g., Somalia and the Dominican Republic), as well as African American and White Appalachian students. In this project, Enciso (2011) worked in collaboration with literacy teachers across two classrooms, as these students read various texts that invoked issues of immigration with the goal of spurring students' critical thinking and storytelling about their own experiences of and perspectives on immigration. One significant textual production from this work was the co-authorship of a text by immigrant and US-born students addressing the injustices inherent in xenophobia. Also taking on dual roles, Souto-Manning (2010) worked as a first grade teacher and researcher in her own literacy classroom, responding to her students' observations of different "pull out" learning opportunities offered to students at her elementary school that fell along the lines of social class, race, and language backgrounds. Souto-Manning (2010) created a curriculum where students read and discussed multiple texts that encouraged their critical thinking and discussion of these issues. Furthermore, she and her students took on roles of change agents at their schools, successfully advocating for all students to receive high quality instruction within their home classroom community.

A challenge to reading texts that invites students' sociocultural identities and experiences as meaning-making tools, is teachers' abilities to effectively engage students with varied forms of marginalization and privilege in students' and teachers' own lives and in society. Skerrett (2011), in a study of English teachers' practices of teaching racial literacy, found that teachers' own identities and lived experiences with diversity and inequality, professional preparation for teaching literacy in culturally responsive and antiracist ways, and opportunities for ongoing professional learning, impacted their preparedness and willingness to select such texts and effectively navigate the issues they raised with students. As one example of preparing literacy teachers to undertake such instruction, Martínez-Roldán and Heineke (2011) engaged a diverse group of educators in a graduate teacher education course, who were either "insiders" or "outsiders" to Latina/o or other communities that had experienced oppression and disenfranchisement in a literature discussion about Alvarez' "Before We Were free." Martínez-Roldán and Heineke (2011) concluded that using such literature in teacher education provides opportunities for mediating teacher learning about how to use such literature with their own K-12 students in productive ways. K-12 teachers report the continuing difficulties of undertaking literature study that invoke issues of racism and other forms of oppression in multicultural classrooms as well as in primarily White settings, where ideologies of Whiteness and White privilege are typically left undisturbed (Borsheim-Black, 2015; Thomas, 2013, 2015).

Reading Instruction across Home, School, and Community Contexts

Moving beyond classroom communities, researchers are studying how students' reading development can be accelerated by creating bridges among their schools, homes, and communities, and the resources for learning available within and across these contexts (Lima, Da Silva, & Freire De Carvalho, 2014; Reese et al., 2012; Singh, Sylvia, & Ridzi, 2015). This instructional approach builds upon the tradition of studying literacy development as it occurs across multiple social contexts, including attending to the resources available for literacy development across those settings (Gonzalez et al., 2005; Heath, 1983; Moll & Gonzalez, 1994). Lima et al. (2014) studied the unfolding of an experience called "Reading in areas out of school: A proposal for the expansion of reading practices in public squares," in Teresina, the densely populated capital of the Brazilian state of Piauí. The goal of this project was to expand the contexts for reading beyond school for children aged seven and ten, to encourage their curiosity, motivation, and enjoyment pertaining to reading. Lima et al. (2014) found grave differences between students' displayed reading practices in schools and those in community social contexts, leading them to argue for the importance of creating multiple spaces for children to read as a means to promote reading development.

Singh et al. (2015) presented a case of their active intervention into supporting the literacy lives of Burmese refugee families through a book distribution program coupled with a ten-month intergenerational family literacy program. Singh et al. (2015) employed the well-known Storycircles approach in which parents and caregivers were invited to participate weekly in a community-based literacy program with their children. The primary goals of this work were to influence children's literate lives at home in order to prepare them to participate successfully in schooling practices in their new homeland, and equip parents with the cultural knowledge and tools to engage with teachers and the larger institution of schooling. Singh et al. (2015) observed that the Burmese families' home literacy practices privileged oral traditions, and critiqued schools, from a funds of knowledge perspective (Gonzalez et al., 2005), for not capitalizing on these home literacies to teach students the academic practices schools value.

Singh et al. (2015) used an approach that valued the families' existing literacies and helped them make connections between these and the literacies of school. For example, adults were instructed through a reading method of story circles and encouraged to check out picture books from the library and engage in talk about texts with their children using all of their language repertoires. Singh et al. (2015) found that families' home language and literacy practices expanded to include use of print-based texts and parents' intentional practices of creating shared reading experiences with their children at home. Singh et al. (2015) pointed to the constraints and challenges of doing this work, citing the need for teachers' willingness to become knowledgeable about the cultural, linguistic, sociocultural, and other identities and circumstances of their diverse students and their families. They also pointed out the importance of teachers' capacities to appreciate and link, rather than devalue and disconnect, these families' socioculturally-informed ways with literacies from academic learning. Singh et al.'s (2015) work also indicates that the current sociopolitical contexts of schools contribute little support to such efforts curtailing the broad implementation of such a generative approach to reading instruction and development. At the same time, Singh et al.'s (2015) study illustrates the possibilities for researchers' strategic involvement with existing community organizations and engaged educational stakeholders for creating opportunities to expand contexts for reading instruction and development.

Studies in this category emphasize the need for all literacy partners to hold appreciative (Bomer, 2011), rather than deficit (Valencia, 1997), perspectives on minoritized groups to reap learning gains from this approach to reading across contexts. Reese et al. (2012), in two different urban contexts in Mexico (one working class, the other middle class), examined the relationships among the literacy practices of first-grade children and parents at home and the ways in which these practices were influenced and perceived by teachers and administrators. Reese et al. (2012) discovered disturbing connections related to teachers' deficit perspectives on the literacy practices of working class families and their provision of rote literacy instruction for these students. In contrast, the teachers offered more substantial literacy instruction to students who came from middle class backgrounds and whose families' literacy practices reflected the traditional literacy practices of schools.

Blending Sociocultural and Cognitive Factors in Reading Instruction

Socioculturally-based approaches to reading instruction acknowledge the cognitive processes involved in meaning-making (which, as noted above, schools traditionally and contemporarily emphasize), while stressing that the teaching and learning of reading is greatly strengthened by attending to its social and cultural dimensions (e.g., Cole, 1996; Moll, 2014). A few studies provide methodological models of research as well as examples of instructional practices that illuminate how the sociocultural and cognitive aspects of reading jointly influence students' reading development (Hall, 2016; Lesaux, Harris, & Sloane, 2012; Levine, 2014).

Given her earlier findings on the importance of students' reading identity to their efforts with reading and reading development Hall (2012, 2016) designed a one-year formative experiment study using mixed methods, in which she worked with a teacher in one eighth grade language arts classroom. The purpose of this work was to provide a form of reading instruction that was responsive to students' reading identities (oriented toward helping them become the readers they wanted to be), while providing them with the skills they needed to become successful readers. The focal class was selected because, of all the teacher's classes, it served the highest percentage of students deemed as underperforming in reading. The class population consisted of five African Americans, one Hispanic, and 15 White students. One student identified English as his/her second language, but was considered proficient and not in need of English language learning supports. The teacher took the lead instructional role with Hall serving as a participant observer. The instructional design included: 1) making identity explicit, 2), developing and refining reading identities, and 3), connecting reading instruction and assignments to students' goals as readers (Hall, 2016, p. 60). Data sources included classroom observations, teacher interviews, standardized reading assessments, and student questionnaires and written reflections across the year.

Just as with her 2012 findings, Hall's 2016 analysis found that most students identified as particular kinds of readers (very good, average, or poor) regardless of their reading assessment scores. Yet Hall (2016) also noticed the stronghold that the concept of reading level had on some students' definitions of their reader identities and their enacted reading practices (e.g. choosing leveled books). Students also had particular goals for themselves as readers, for example becoming faster readers, gaining more complex vocabulary, and for one student, increasing comprehension.

Hall (2016) detailed how the teacher navigated students' (often narrow) goals for reading development with reading instruction that assisted students' acquisition of more robust reading competencies. With students regularly reflecting on their reading identities and learning processes across the year, students began claiming more positive reading identities, articulating more substantive goals as readers, and grew in their reading skills and practices. Most students, reported Hall (2016), came to recognize and exercise their own agency and role in accomplishing their reading goals and contested the idea that their reading level on standardized tests was the definitive marker of their reading identity or ability.

Levine's (2014) work is also grounded in the assumption that students possess varying levels of knowledge and expertise in literary analysis that differentially impact the quality of their literary interpretations and overall textual experiences. Levine (2014) thus hypothesized that more novice readers can benefit from explicit strategy instruction in conducting literary analysis. In line with the work of Carol Lee (2007), Levine (2014) described an affect-based interpretive heuristic through which students draw upon their everyday social interpretive practices to identify and justify their selections of textual portions of literature that are especially rich for literary analyses. This four-week long quasi-experimental study involved using this intervention in one twelfth grade urban high school class and comparing student outcomes to a comparative class that also engaged with a unit of literary analysis, but did not use that heuristic. Levine (2014) found that the experimental group was able to apply their everyday affect-laden experiences and interpretations in their reading to go beyond basic summaries of texts and posit a range of figurative interpretations and thematic inferences. Pre- and post-study interpretive writing tasks and think-aloud protocols from both groups revealed that the students who were taught the heuristic, increased their skills in interpretive analysis in contrast to the comparison group.

Lesaux et al.'s (2012) two-year study, situated within 21 linguistically diverse, urban middle school classrooms, provided strong evidence for the importance of attending to students' academic, social, and cultural identities and competencies, in using targeted cognitive interventions to support students' reading development. Lesaux et al's (2012) approach focused on building language and reading skills through an academic vocabulary intervention called Academic Language Instruction for All Students (ALIAS) that lasted approximately 18 weeks. A sociocultural perspective was reflected in this research, in that the authors intentionally sought out the perspectives of students on how the intervention had influenced their academic motivation. Furthermore, the researchers' design included an instructional environment that facilitated learning through structured social and collaborative interactions, such as role play and dialogue; and the use of texts that reflected students' social and cultural interests and lived experiences.

In relation to the academic intervention, Lesaux et al. (2012) found positive effects of the treatment, for example, growth in students' "academic vocabulary knowledge, morphological skills, and reading comprehension of expository texts, including academic words" (p. 235), with students who began at the lowest levels of vocabulary experiencing the most growth in their vocabulary knowledge and writing. However, the intervention's impact on students' text comprehension based in "researcher-developed measures of academic vocabulary knowledge, morphological skills, and reading comprehension of expository texts, including academic word reading tasks… were largest and significant for students who began the intervention with slightly below average and average vocabulary levels" (Lesaux et al., 2012, p. 235). Importantly, across 20 focus groups, many students made positive associations between the development of their academic skills and their academic motivation, confidence, and senses of both personal and academic identity. For instance, one student reported "The words, they're becoming more natural to us, and you learn how to put them in sentences more. So you feel smart and stuff, … like, you know a lot of stuff'" (Lesaux et al., 2012, p. 236). Lesaux et al. (2012) proposed to teachers that adolescents' desire for academically rigorous work should be paired with appropriate instructional supports. These instructional supports should attend to sociocultural dimensions, such as collaborative learning, as well as opportunities for students to inquire into and recognize growth in their academic skills and identities both within, and outside, classrooms.

A challenge in studies that address both sociocultural and cognitive dimensions of reading is that one aspect may likely be foregrounded or back-staged, depending on the research questions and study design including the processes, amount, and kinds of data collected; and analysis procedures. Furthermore, tensions can arise if the ultimate goal or priority of the teachers/researchers is the effectiveness of the strategy intervention. This leaning can diminish attention to social and cultural differences, contributing to their treatment as secondary factors in research designs and student outcomes. Handsfield and Jimenez (2009), based in their ethnographic study of a multiracial, multilingual third grade literacy classroom, raised important cautions about the use of cognitive strategy instruction (CSI) with culturally and linguistically diverse learners. The authors conceptualized CSI as a site of "struggle for the monopoly of legitimate discourse" (Bourdieu, 1983, p. 317, in Handsfield & Jimenez, 2009, p. 160). This assertion was based in the researchers' findings that CSI was often implemented in ways that narrowed conceptions of literacy to an autonomous perspective that did not adequately account for how thinking and understanding might be shaped by students' sociocultural ways of making-meaning in their homes and communities.

Handsfield and Jimenez (2009) further raised concerns about the role of CSI in standardizing students' language and cognition processes to align with Euro-Western patterns that, historically and contemporarily, are most valued by schools. Data from this study also raised questions related to the extent to which students' uses of cognitive strategies may have been as much about performances of literacy required by their teacher rather than actual understanding and integration of these ways of thinking while reading. Handsfield and Jimenez (2009) admit the important benefits of CSI for students who struggle with reading. However, they call for an expanded conception of CSI in which strategies are modeled and practiced within socially meaningful conversations and context. They further propose that teachers invite students to consider how they make meaning of texts in their literacy engagements outside school which can facilitate students' awareness and uses of a wider array of socially and culturally informed ways of making-meaning that can build student agency and reading competencies while enriching the stock of learning resources available within the classroom.

Gaps, Challenges, and Opportunities to Bridging the Gaps in Research on Reading Instruction that Accounts for Social and Cultural Difference

The studies reviewed demonstrate a strong knowledge base related to teaching and learning reading from a sociocultural perspective. However, the gaps that are used to frame this volume—implementation, relevance, bridging, and translational—also manifest in this reading research domain.

The Implementation and Translational Gaps

A number of the studies reviewed involved in-depth research with small numbers of participants in time periods ranging from a few weeks to one year. Additionally, researchers played varied roles such as observer, participant-observer, and teacher/co-teacher (Hall, 2016; Skerrett, 2012; Souto-Manning, 2010; Thein et al., 2012). Thus a major challenge pertains to how *teachers* implement and sustain socioculturally-based reading instruction beyond the life of a study and how these practices can spread beyond individual classrooms and schools to promote the reading development of greater numbers of students. One way forward in broadening implementation of socioculturally-informed approaches to reading instruction is through more robust research designs that span several years and that are implemented within and across multiple classrooms and schools (e.g. Lesaux et al., 2012). It would also be important that such research designs create opportunities for teacher participation as co-researchers and co-learners that will improve the possibility of sustained implementation by teachers after a study concludes. Researchers could include in their research designs collaborative professional learning/inquiry spaces for teachers and researchers around the instructional approach being implemented and these learning communities could extend beyond a study's endpoint with teachers' leading their own learning and growth.

Support from school administration in redressing the implementation gap, especially in spaces under severe accountability pressures, cannot be overstated (Au, 2009; Nichols et al., 2007). The already plentiful body of research providing evidence of students' reading development emerging from instruction that attends to social and cultural differences can be used to educate and entice school and district literacy leaders to legitimize these instructional practices in their literacy policies and instructional guidelines. Beyond researchers and teachers, powerful levers for broad implementation of socioculturally-informed approaches to reading instruction include stakeholders invested in students' reading development who hold social and political capital. These groups include students themselves, families, religious and community leaders, and other social justice oriented partners—e.g., local non-profit educational organizations.

Yet it is important to recognize the deep socialization of literacy policy makers and leaders into privileging and implementing cognitive-based approaches to reading instruction (that often derive from post-positivist research methodologies) with minoritized students who are challenged by high-stakes standardized reading assessments. In relation to the translational gap, then, consider that few classroom-based studies pertaining to sociocultural approaches to reading instruction employed quasi-experimental, quantitative, or mixed methodologies (Hall, 2016; Lesaux et al., 2012; Levine, 2014). Studies that include these methodologies and prioritize sociocultural perspectives on reading development are important to the field in that they challenge researchers to operationalize the constructs of social and cultural differences among students. Such studies require innovating research designs that allow for understanding how social and cultural differences are addressed by varied socioculturally-informed approaches to reading instruction and the affects on students' reading development. This kind of research, and its instructional recommendations, can provide a viable alternative to literacy policy makers who hold a traditional understanding of empirical research.

To grow this body of work in reading research, it seems important to bring together teams of scholars with expertise in diverse methodologies; who can recognize and work within the strengths as well as limitations of different theoretical perspectives and research methodologies; and who understand and value multiple approaches to reading instruction and development. Within the larger sociopolitical context of education, particular definitions of empirical research, including in reading research, drives the distribution of federal funding (National Institute of Health and Human Services, 2013; US Department of Education, 2015), although some funding language can be interpreted as more open to reading research that includes attention to social and cultural differences (Institute of Education Sciences, 2016). As such, researchers who take a sociocultural perspective on reading instruction and development stand to benefit from improved flexibility and abilities to speak to multiple discourse communities about the significance of this approach and its already robust evidence base.

The Relevance and Bridging Gaps

There is wide recognition of sociocultural theory as a relevance-based framework for teaching and learning. This assertion holds for socioculturally-based approaches to reading education for all students, and especially those from culturally and linguistically minoritized groups. Culturally and linguistically diverse students will continue having difficulties developing and demonstrating their reading competencies, including on standardized curricula and assessments that fail to account for sociocultural differences (Au, 2009; Darling-Hammond, 2007). The primary challenge to the relevance gap remains the legitimation of the framework and attendant practices in literacy policy that directs mainstream reading education practices.

Moving beyond any given local or national literacy policy context is one way of understanding and responding to the bridging gap. There is a global movement toward revisioning national curriculum policies to improve students' reading and writing skills according to the traditional autonomous perspective, but also in acknowledgment of sociocultural theories and broader literacy competencies. Educational goals for teachers and students include learning how to learn collaboratively as well as independently; valuing and drawing upon the cultures, languages, and community resources of diverse learners to support instruction and learning; equipping students to engage with work and social life outside school, including its technological demands; and engaged citizenship, including a sense of global responsibility (Education Scotland, 2016; Finnish National Board of Education, 2016; Government of Sint Maarten, D.E.R.P.I., 2008). Yet the challenge to the success of such progressive curricula is professional guidance and support for teachers in how to design and implement a curriculum that addresses these varied competencies and how to assess student learning in domains that are unfamiliar in the schooling arena (Lam, 2011; OECD, 2015; Seunarinesingh, 2015; Skerrett, 2016).

In redressing the bridging gap, literacy researchers can consider making inroads into national educational contexts where policy conditions are supportive of advancing research and practice relative to sociocultural approaches to literacy education. Sub-fields within educational research that can inform literacy scholars moving into newer territory include the fields of educational policy and educational leadership/school change. These fields address systems level change, including in the areas of curriculum, instruction, and building learning cultures among teachers and schools (e.g., Hargreaves & Shirley, 2014). The knowledge base within these fields would be vital for literacy researchers' abilities to integrate pragmatic epistemologies and related research designs into their work. Literacy researchers would be further equipped to more fully engage with the sociopolitical factors and agents that shape the nature of reading instruction determined for schools. This challenge can be understood as a shift away from a narrow perspective of field (reading education) into a perspective of reading education as one of many components of the broader arena of educational research, policy, and practice.

References

Au, W. W. (2009). High-stakes testing and discursive control: The triple bind for non-standard student identities. *Multicultural Perspectives*, *11*(2), 65–71.

Blue, E. V. (2012). Reading and interpretive response to literary text: Drawing upon sociocultural perspectives. *Reading & Writing Quarterly*, *28*(2), 164–178.

Boas, E. (2012). Using literature circles to inquire into the big themes: Exploring the refugee experience. *English in Australia*, *47*(3), 25–28.

Bomer, R. (2011). *Building adolescent literacy in today's English classrooms*. Portsmouth, NH: Heinemann.

Borsheim-Black, C. (2015). "It's pretty much white": Challenges and opportunities of an antiracist approach to literature instruction in a multilayered white context. *Research in the Teaching of English*, *49*(4), 407–429.

Cole, M. (1996). *Cultural psychology: A once and future discipline*. Cambridge, MA: Harvard University Press.

Darling-Hammond, L. (2007). Race, inequality, and educational accountability: The irony of "no child left behind". *Race, Ethnicity, and Education, 10*(3), 245–260.

Enciso, P. (2011). Storytelling in critical literacy pedagogy: Removing the walls between immigrant and non-immigrant youth. In H. Janks & V. Vasquez (Eds.), *Special issue: Critical literacy revisited: Writing as critique for English teaching: Practice and critique, 10*(1), 21–40.

Enciso, P., Volz, A., Price-Dennis, D., & Durriyah, T. (2010). Story club and configurations of literary insights among immigrant and non-immigrant youth. In R. Jiménez, D. Rowe, V. Risko, & M. Hundley (Eds.), *59th Yearbook of the National Reading Conference* (pp. 354–366). Oak Creek, WI: National Reading Conference.

Enriquez, G. (2014). Embodiments of "struggle": The melancholy, loss, and interactions with print of two "struggling readers". *Anthropology & Education Quarterly, 45*(1), 105–122.

Finnish National Board of Education. (2016). Curriculum reform 2016. Retrieved October 12, 2016, from www.oph.fi/english/education_development/current_reforms/curriculum_reform_2016.

Francois, C. (2013). Reading is about relating: Urban youths giving voice to the possibilities for school literacy. *Journal of Adolescent and Adult Literacy, 57*(2), 141–149.

Frankel, K. K., Becker, B. C., Rowe, M. W., & Pearson, P. D. (2016). From "What is reading?" To what is literacy? *Journal Of Education, 196*(3), 7–17.

Freire, P. (1990). *Pedagogy of the oppressed*. New York, NY: Continuum.

Gonzalez, N., Moll, L. C., & Amanti, C. (Eds.). (2005). *Funds of knowledge: Theorizing practices in households, communities, and classrooms*. Mahwah, NJ: Lawrence Erlbaum.

Government of Sint Maarten Department for Educational Research, Policy, and Innovations (D.E.R.P.I). (2008). A practical handbook on exploring foundation based education: Putting children at the center of learning. D.E.R.P.I. Philipsburg, Sint Maarten.

Guan, S. A., Nash, A., & Orellana, M. F. (2016). Cultural and social processes of language brokering among Arab, Asian, and Latin immigrants. *Journal of Multilingual and Multicultural Development, 37*(2), 150–166.

Gutiérrez, K. (2009). A comprehensive federal literacy agenda: Moving beyond inoculation approaches to literacy policy. *Journal of Literacy Research, 41*(4), 476–483.

Hall, L. A. (2012). The role of reading identities and reading abilities in students' discussions about texts and comprehension strategies. *Journal of Literacy Research, 44*(3), 239–272.

Hall, L. A. (2016). The role of identity in reading comprehension development. *Reading & Writing Quarterly, 32*(1), 56–80.

Handsfield, L. J., & Jimenez, R. T. (2009). Cognition and misrecognition: A Bourdieuian analysis of cognitive strategy instruction in a linguistically and culturally diverse classroom. *Journal of Literacy Research, 41*(2), 151–195.

Hargreaves, A., & Shirley, D. (2014). *The global fourth way: The quest for educational excellence*. Thousand Oaks, CA: Corwin Press.

Heath, S. B. (1983). *Ways with words: Language, life and work in communities and classrooms*. Cambridge, UK: Cambridge University Press.

Institute of Education Sciences. (2016). Reading and writing. Retrieved June 25, 2017, from: https://ies.ed.gov/ncer/projects/program.asp?ProgID=18

Ivey, G., & Johnston, P. (2013). Engagement with young adult literature: Outcomes and processes. *Reading Research Quarterly, 48*(3), 255–275.

Kim, J., & Viesca, K. M. (2016). Three reading-intervention teachers' identity positioning and practices to motivate and engage emergent bilinguals in an urban middle school. *Teaching & Teacher Education, 55*, 122–132.

Ladson-Billings, G. (1998/2009). *The dreamkeepers: Successful teachers of African American children*. San Francisco, CA: Jossey-Bass.

Lam, E. (2011). Sharing best practices in Barbados and Trinidad and Tobago: Patterns of policy implementation and resistance. *Compare: A Journal of Comparative and International Education, 41*(1), 25–41.

Lee, C. D. (1997). Bridging home and school literacies: A model of culturally responsive teaching. In J. Flood, S. B. Heath, & D. Lapp (Eds.), *A handbook for literacy educators: Research on teaching the communicative and visual arts* (pp. 330–341). New York, NY: McMillan.

Lee, C. D. (2006). Every good-bye ain't gone: Analyzing the cultural underpinnings of classroom talk. *International Journal of Qualitative Studies in Education, 19*(3), 305–327.

Lee, C. D. (2007). *Culture, literacy, and learning: Blooming in the midst of the whirlwind*. New York, NY: Teachers College Press.

Lesaux, N. K., Harris, J. R., & Sloane, P. (2012). Adolescents' motivation in the context of an academic vocabulary intervention in urban middle school classrooms. *Journal of Adolescent & Adult Literacy, 56*, 231–240.

Levine, S. (2014). Making interpretation visible with an affect-based strategy. *Reading Research Quarterly, 49*(3), 283–303.

Lewis, C. (1999). The social and ideological construction of "free-choice reading". Retrieved ERIC/EBSCO host, September 28, 2016.

Lima, F. R., Da Silva, J., & Freire De Carvalho, M. A. (2014). Leitura em praças públicas: Uma proposta para a expansão de eventos de oralidade e letramento em espaços extraescolares. *Revista FSA, 11*(3), 287–306. doi:10.12819/2014.11.3.12

Martínez-Roldán, C., & Sayer, P. (2006). Reading through linguistic borderlands: Latino students' transactions with narrative texts. *Journal of Early Childhood Literacy, 6*(3), 294–322.

Martínez-Roldán, C. M. (2003). Building worlds and identities: A case study of the role of narratives in bilingual literature discussions. *Research in the Teaching of English, 37*(4), 491–526.

Martínez-Roldán, C.M., & Heineke, A.J. (2011). Latino literature mediating teacher learning. *Journal of Latinos and Education, 10,* 245–260.

Moll, L. C. (2014). *L. S. Vygotsky and education.* New York, NY: Routledge.

Moll, L. C., & Gonzalez, N. (1994). Lessons from research with language-minority children. *Journal Of Reading Behavior, 26*(4), 439–456.

National Institute of Health and Human Services. (2013). NIH fact sheet: Reading difficulty and disability. Retrieved November 23, 2016, from https://report.nih.gov/NIHfactsheets/ViewFactSheet.aspx?csid=114.

New London Group. (1996). A pedagogy of multiliteracies: Designing social futures. *Harvard Educational Review, 66,* 60–92.

Nichols, S. L., Berliner, D. C., & Noddings, N. (2007). *Collateral damage: How high-stakes testing corrupts America's schools.* Cambridge, MA: Harvard Education Press.

Orellana, M. F., & Gutiérrez, K. D. (2006). What's the problem? Constructing "different" genres for the study of English learners. *Research in the Teaching of English, 41*(1), 118–123.

Organization of Economic Cooperation and Development (OECD). (2015). Improving schools in Scotland: An OECD perspective. Retrieved October 12, 2016, from www.oecd.org/edu/school/improving-schools-in-scotland.htm

Paris, D. (2009). "They're in my culture, they speak the same way": African American Language in multiethnic high schools. *Harvard Educational Review, 79*(3), 428–448.

Reese, L., Arauz, R. M., & Bazan, A. R. (2012). Mexican parents' and teachers' literacy perspectives and practices: Construction of cultural capital. *International Journal Of Qualitative Studies In Education (QSE), 25*(8), 983–1003.

Rogers, R., & Mosley, M. (2006). Racial literacy in a second-grade classroom: Critical race theory, whiteness studies, and literacy research. *Reading Research Quarterly, 41*(4), 462–495.

Scribner, S., & Cole, M. (1978). Literacy without schooling: Testing for intellectual effects. *Harvard Educational Review, 48*(4), 448–461.

Sanchez, I. G., & Orellana, M. F. (2006). The construction of moral and social identity in immigrant children's narratives-in-translation. *Linguistics And Education: An International Research Journal, 17*(3), 209–239.

Scotland, E. (2016). Curriculum for excellence. Retrieved October 12, 2016, from www.educationscotland.gov.uk/learningandteaching/thecurriculum/whatiscurriculumforexcellence/index.asp

Seunarinesingh, K. (2015). Managing a paradigm shift in language arts pedagogy: A case study of effective literacy practice. *Caribbean Curriculum, 9,* 47–64.

Singh, S., Sylvia, M., & Ridzi, F. (2015). Exploring the literacy practices of refugee families enrolled in a book distribution program and an intergenerational family literacy program. *Early Childhood Education Journal, 43* (1), 37–45.

Skerrett, A. (2011). English teachers' racial literacy knowledge and practice. *Race, Ethnicity, and Education, 14* (3), 313–330.

Skerrett, A. (2012). "We hatched in this class": Repositioning of identity in and beyond a reading classroom. *The High School Journal, 95*(3), 62–75.

Skerrett, A. (2015). *Teaching transnational youth: Literacy and education in a changing world.* New York, NY: Teachers College Press.

Skerrett, A. (2016). Refiguring a Caribbean school within and across local and global communities. *Journal of Professional and Community Capital, 1*(4), 254–269.

Souto-Manning, M. (2010). *Freire, teaching, and learning: Culture circles across contexts.* New York, NY: Peter Lang.

Street, B. V. (1984). *Literacy in theory and practice.* NY: Cambridge University Press.

Street, B. V. (2012). Society reschooling. *Reading Research Quarterly, 47*(2), 216–227.

Tatum, A. W. (1999). Reading and the African American male: Identity, equity, and power. *Journal of Adolescent & Adult Literacy, 43*(1), 62–64.

Tatum, A. W. (2014). Orienting African American male adolescents toward meaningful literacy exchanges with texts. *Journal of Education, 194*(1), 35–47.

Thein, A. H., Guise, M., & Sloan, D. L. (2012). Exploring the significance of social class identity performance in the English classroom: A case study analysis of a literature circle discussion. *English Education, 44*, 215–253.

Thomas, E. E. (2013). Dilemmatic conversations: Some challenges of culturally responsive discourse in a high school English classroom. *Linguistics and Education, 24*(3), 328–347.

Thomas, E. E. (2015). "We always talk about race": Navigating race talk dilemmas in the teaching of literature. *Research in the Teaching of English, 50*(2), 154–175.

Tyack, D., & Tobin, W. (1994). The "grammar" of schooling. *Why Has It Been so Hard to Change? American Educational Research Journal, 31*(3), 453–479.

US Department of Education. (2015). Every Student Succeeds Act (ESSA). Retrieved November 23, 2016, from www.ed.gov/ESSA.

Valencia, R. (1997). Conceptualizing the notion of deficit thinking. In R. Valencia (Ed.), *The evolution of deficit thinking* (pp. 1–12). London: Falmer Press.

Vygotsky, L. S. (1978). *Mind in society: The development of higher psychological processes*. Cambridge, MA: Harvard University Press.

18

Learning Academic Language, Comprehending Text

Dianna Townsend, Ana Taboada Barber, and Hannah Carter

Introduction

When did educators start attending to academic language, and why? Depending on the definition or set of attributes assigned to *academic language* as a construct, it can be argued that academic language has been a prominent focus of instruction since the beginning of compulsory, state-funded education in the U.S. in the 19th century. Alternatively, academic language instruction can be framed as a more recent practice to support the diverse student population in America's schools. While previous versions of the *Handbook of Reading Research* have explored issues related to academic language, the current volume is the first with chapters dedicated to academic language, both as a research construct and as an instructional target. Additionally, like many foundational constructs in the field of literacy, academic language has been studied from a number of perspectives, each of which pushes the construct in different, and sometimes opposing, directions.

To the extent that academic language is, simply, the language of school environments, K-12 schools in the U.S. have always attended to the academic language development of students. While academic language may be part of a hidden curriculum that some students have more access to than others, K-12 schools have always required students to use the language of school environments to access information and display their knowledge. Students have consistently encountered academic texts, including literary and informational texts—both of which use and require understanding of academic language. However, as efforts to support *all* learners have gained momentum in recent decades, academic language instruction has been pulled into many research, practice, and policy arenas. In some ways, academic language instruction has been treated as an ideological football, serving multiple and sometimes disparate purposes. For example, academic language instruction is often viewed as a tool to address academic inequities and school language disparities across students' language backgrounds (Zwiers, 2014). At the same time, academic language instruction is also viewed as a symptom of an oppressive schooling system that rewards the powerful, those students who begin school with a clear advantage because their home and community language environments are aligned with the language expectations of K-12 schooling (Flores & Rosa, 2015).

Further problematizing the scholarship around academic language instruction are the many terms that are used with, and as proxies for, academic language. Academic language instruction research has been conducted with all of the following phrases as labels for an overlapping set of language and literacy components: academic language, academic vocabulary, academic English, academic literacy, content area language/literacy, and disciplinary language/literacy. Baumann and Graves (2010) have parsed many of these terms, exploring their related and unique components based on traditions of use in different fields and frameworks. Given the variations in how academic language is conceptualized, academic language *instruction* research ranges from a focus on individual academic vocabulary words to the discourse patterns and academic habits that support students' participation and success in school. This broader set of language and literacy skills is most often recognized as academic literacy. Within extant research, instructional targets generally fall into these two expansive, overlapping categories: *academic vocabulary* and *academic literacy*. In other words, the instructional research leans heavily towards either developing students' academic vocabulary knowledge with a focus on building rich knowledge of academic words, or developing a broader set of literacy skills for academic settings with several foci, including higher order comprehension skills within and across texts in the disciplines. Figure 18.1 illustrates these categories, using a nested model to demonstrate that, while the research does fall into these categories with some consistency, they are not mutually exclusive.

The rationale for focusing on academic language instruction spans a broad set of issues including preparing new teachers, addressing standards, meeting the needs of diverse students, and pushing research forward. EdTPA, a measurement of teacher candidates' readiness to teach that is growing in popularity across the U.S., prioritizes demonstrating skill helping students "develop and use academic language" (Lim, Stallings, & Kim, 2015, p. 3). Similarly, the Common Core State Standards (CCSS; National Governors Association Center for Best Practices & Council of Chief State School Officers, 2010) emphasize both informational texts and attention to academic language proficiency. Along with the CCSS, the linguistic, cultural, and socioeconomic diversity in schools calls for attention to academic language instruction, as academic language can be used as "a vehicle for communicating and learning within sociocultural contexts" (WIDA, 2014, p. 4).

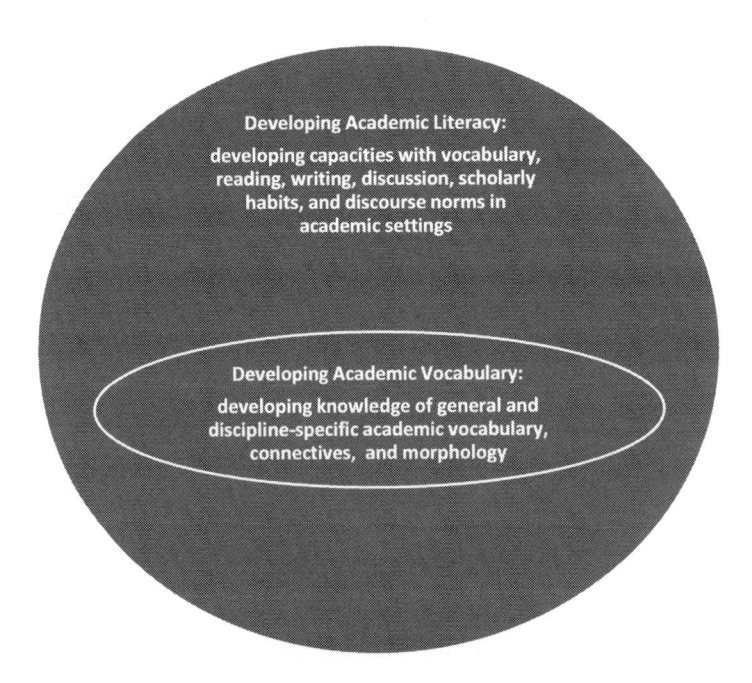

Figure 18.1 Instructional targets for academic language instruction in the extant research

Finally, research on academic language instruction is approaching a critical mass of findings and related theories, particularly in the last decade; it is time to take stock of what we know in order to support teachers and move the research forward.

Organization of Chapter

Our chapter begins by defining the two constructs of interest, academic language and reading comprehension. Next, we provide an explanation of the two instructional targets for academic language instruction, academic vocabulary and academic literacy, and we review the research on both targets within elementary and secondary settings. Gaps in and critiques of the literature are also addressed. Finally, we share implications of the research on instruction and recommendations for a path forward to maximize all students' language experiences in K-12 schools.

Defining Academic Language from a Systemic Functional Linguistics (SFL) Perspective

Academic language, as explained with a Systemic Functional Linguistics (SFL) framework, is a register of language comprised of a set of linguistic features that are used to communicate ideas in academic settings. According to SFL, varieties or registers of language and the contexts in which they are used, realize (i.e. *make real*) each other (Eggins, 2004). In other words, language is not used in a vacuum. Rather, specific contexts (e.g. cultural, social, academic) influence, reify, and reinforce the use of particular language structures. At the same time, those particular language structures create meaning within, and reinforce, the context. Academic language researchers (Achugar & Schleppegrell, 2005; Eggins, 2004; Fang, Schleppegrell, & Cox, 2006; Schleppegrell, 2004b; Snow & Uccelli, 2009) often apply these tenets of SFL to the language of schooling. They explore how academic contexts inform academic language, and vice versa, and they unpack the language of schooling to identify specific linguistic features that are used to create meaning in academic settings. In short, SFL allows for an articulation of what makes academic language *academic*. There are cross-cutting features that are used across academic disciplines, and features that are unique to, or used in unique ways in, each academic discipline (Fang, 2012; Schleppegrell, 2004b; Snow & Uccelli, 2009; Uccelli, Phillips Galloway, Barr, Meneses, & Dobbs, 2015).

Reading Comprehension, Academic Vocabulary, and Academic Literacy

A major outcome of interest for academic language instruction is reading comprehension, which the RAND Reading Study Group (Snow, 2002) defines as "the process of simultaneously extracting and constructing meaning through interaction and involvement with written language" (p. xiii). Comprehension is conceptualized as an active process, unique to each reader, text, activity, and sociocultural context. Academic vocabulary, one of the instructional targets in academic language research, is a direct correlate of students' reading comprehension (August, Artzi, & Barr, 2016; Ford-Connors & Paratore, 2015; Lesaux, Kieffer, Faller, & Kelley, 2010; Stahl & Fairbanks, 1986; Townsend, Filippini, Collins, & Biancarosa, 2012). Academic literacy, the other instructional target in academic language instruction research, also informs text comprehension. The linguistic features of academic texts (Bailey, 2007; Barnes, 2015; Fang, 2012; LaRusso et al., 2016; Schleppegrell, 2004b; Uccelli et al., 2015), the discourse norms and sociocultural contexts of the disciplines (Fang, 2006, 2012; Fang & Schleppegrell, 2008b; Goldman et al., 2016; Lee & Spratley, 2010; Moje, 2015; Neal, 2015; Schleppegrell, 2004a, 2007; Schleppegrell & de Oliveira, 2006; Shanahan & Shanahan, 2012), and students' linguistic resources each relate to comprehension.

Academic Vocabulary as an Instructional Target

Academic vocabulary includes words used primarily in academic settings that are often characterized by abstraction, technicality, and/or morphological complexity. The most common types of academic vocabulary are general academic words and discipline-specific academic words (Baumann & Graves, 2010; Gardner & Davies, 2014; Hiebert & Lubliner, 2008). General academic words are primarily used in academic settings and across all disciplines (e.g., *function, procedure, system*). Discipline-specific academic words are used primarily in academic settings, but are typically unique to one discipline only (e.g., *rhombus, isotope, habeas corpus*). However, this dichotomy is imperfect, with many words blurring boundaries. For example, a polysemous word (a word that has multiple meanings) like *function* is used in general ways across disciplines but also in mathematics with a technical, discipline-specific meaning. To address some of the gray area in function and usage, Baumann and Graves (2010) broadened the dichotomy to include five categories of academic words: "(1) domain-specific academic vocabulary, (2) general academic vocabulary, (3) literary vocabulary, (4) metalanguage, and (5) symbols" (p. 9).

Knowledge of academic words includes both semantic knowledge as well as knowledge of how words operate in relation to other, semantically-related words in connected text (Gardner & Davies, 2014; Nagy & Townsend, 2012). Also included in academic vocabulary knowledge is knowledge of morphology (Kieffer & Box, 2013) and connectives (Crosson & Lesaux, 2013), given the prominence of both morphologically complex words and cohesive devices in academic language (Snow & Uccelli, 2009). Finally, two other dimensions of word knowledge that impact academic vocabulary knowledge are polysemy (Logan & Kieffer, 2017) and cognates (Carlo et al., 2004).

Early investigations into academic vocabulary included a focus on identifying high utility academic vocabulary words that emerged in the literature (Coxhead, 2000; Xue & Nation, 1984). Most recently, Gardner and Davies (2014) offered a new Academic Vocabulary List. Much of the related earlier research included efforts to support ESL students in university settings, but these resources were quickly adopted as potential supports for K-12 students. Following is a review of the instructional research that, generally, targets academic vocabulary knowledge in elementary and secondary settings.

Developing Academic Vocabulary Knowledge in Elementary Settings

Studies focusing on the academic word level in elementary settings (K-5th grades) have emphasized morphological awareness, explicit teaching of word meanings, and, to a lesser extent, implicit word learning, or learning words in the context of reading or discussion activities. Morphological awareness refers to the ability to consider and manipulate the smallest units of meaning in language including word roots and affixes (e.g., Apel & Lawrence, 2011; Carlisle, 2000; Wolter et al., 2009). Morphology instruction research does not always state an aim of improving academic language. The high frequency of morphologically complex words in academic language, however, closely relates this line of research to the literature on academic language. Empirical studies and systematic reviews (Bowers et al., 2010; Goodwin & Ahn, 2013) provide evidence that morphological awareness interventions lead to moderate improvements in morphological awareness skills, including morphological problem-solving and awareness via generation of morphologically-related words, across a range of students' ages and abilities in the elementary grades (Apel et al., 2013, 2014; Carlisle & Stone, 2005; Goodwin, 2016). However, effects of morphological awareness instruction on reading comprehension in the elementary grades are somewhat small, but promising (e.g., Goodwin et al., 2013).

Explicit teaching of word meanings for discipline-specific (mostly science) and general academic words in the elementary grades, has taken place as part of interventions that, in their majority, included emergent bilinguals[1] and monolingual English speakers. August and colleagues (2016) compared two approaches to vocabulary instruction with 3rd and 4th grade Spanish-speaking emergent bilinguals. The first approach, embedded vocabulary instruction, consisted of providing clear definitions for target words as part of interactive shared reading of science text passages. In the second approach, extended vocabulary instruction, teachers provided explicit, rich, and multimodal instruction. Findings indicated that although extended instruction was more effective in terms of gains in target vocabulary, embedded instruction also helped emergent bilinguals acquire general and science-specific academic vocabulary. The two interventions in the August et al. (2016) study are similar to the two intervention groups designed by Taboada and Rutherford (2011) a few years earlier. With a smaller sample size of 4th grade ELs, this earlier study emphasized comparing explicit and implicit general and science-specific vocabulary. Findings indicated that explicit vocabulary instruction increased students' academic vocabulary even three weeks after the intervention was over; whereas the implicit condition, with emphasis on other components of reading comprehension, increased students' reading comprehension more than the explicit vocabulary instruction alone.

In addition to these two studies on older elementary students, three studies targeted science vocabulary in early elementary settings. Spycher (2009) explored the impact of intentional science vocabulary instruction with implicit science vocabulary instruction for kindergarteners. Students in the intentional/explicit instruction condition learned more science words and were better at expressing their conceptual knowledge in science.

With students in kindergarten through grade two, Silverman and Hines (2009) provided the same science texts and vocabulary instruction to their treatment and control groups over 12 weeks, but the treatment groups also received multimedia support for the vocabulary. While all students made gains, emergent bilinguals in the treatment group effectively closed the science vocabulary gap between their monolingual English speaking peers, providing evidence for the importance of multimedia support for elementary emergent bilinguals' academic language development. In another science-focused intervention, Parsons and Bryant (2016) developed an eight-week intervention for kindergartners that targeted science-specific vocabulary in the context of read alouds, peer conversations during authentic activities, and hands-on science activities. Using a formative experiment, the researchers found that students increased their use of the target words after each cycle of instruction (two weeks) and also showed improved depth of knowledge after the eight-week intervention.

Interventions focused on general academic vocabulary, often referred to as Tier 2 words (Beck, McKeown, & Kucan, 2002), have also shown vocabulary gains in elementary schools. In a study with kindergarteners and 1st graders, Beck and McKeown (2007) showed the importance of more exposures and opportunities to practice with academic words. All students received similar instruction, but some words were targeted for twice as many instructional exposures. When students had more opportunities to practice with words, they made greater gains with that word knowledge. Finally, Carlo et al. (2004) found that both emergent bilinguals and monolingual English speaking 5th graders made gains on multiple measures of word knowledge, and comprehension of text with target words embedded, when they were the beneficiaries of rich vocabulary instruction.

Developing Academic Vocabulary Knowledge in Secondary Settings

Studies focusing on academic vocabulary in secondary settings (6th–12th grades) include two recent large-scale interventions, as well as individual smaller-scope studies. ALIAS (Lesaux et al.,

2010; Lesaux, Kieffer, Kelley, & Harris, 2014) and Word Generation (Lawrence, Crosson, Pare-Blagoev, & Snow, 2015; Lawrence, Rolland, Branum-Martin, & Snow, 2014; Mokhtari & Velten, 2015; Snow, Lawrence, & White, 2009) have been studied in the initial implementation stage and in the scale-up stage. In the first iteration of ALIAS ($N = 476$), an 18-week intervention was facilitated by classroom teachers in 13 classrooms across seven middle schools; eight matched classrooms served as controls. The intervention was rooted in high-interest informational texts, and students participated in reading, writing, discussion, morphology study, direct instruction of vocabulary, and independent word learning strategies (i.e. using context clues). The intervention resulted in significant impacts on the researcher-designed measures of target word knowledge, morphology, and target-words-in-context (a contextualized vocabulary assessment with a comprehension component). There were marginally significant gains on depth of word knowledge and on a standardized measure of reading comprehension. Monolingual English speaking students and emergent bilinguals made similar gains. Noting that a writing outcome would be valuable, researchers added this to the next iteration of ALIAS (Lesaux et al., 2014), which was a scaled-up ($N = 2,082$), randomized field trial of the intervention. For this iteration, the same instructional components were used. Significant differences between the treatment and control groups were found on vocabulary, morphology, writing, and reading comprehension, for the passages that included the taught words, but not on the standardized comprehension measure.

Word Generation is an intervention organized around "engaging and discussable dilemmas" that are implemented across content area classes (Lawrence et al., 2015, p. 750). Instruction in each content area includes the target words, the controversial topic, and content-specific tasks and problems. An average week in Word Generation includes a high interest text on a controversial topic with explicit practice, in each academic content area, with academic target words from the text (Lawrence, Capotosto, Branum-Martin, White, & Snow, 2012). Reading, writing, and discussion are utilized throughout the week with scaffolds and guidance from all content area teachers. An initial examination of the effectiveness of Word Generation (Snow et al., 2009) revealed a treatment effect on the target vocabulary measures, and gains made in vocabulary predicted performance on state-level achievement tests. Additionally, emergent bilinguals benefitted more than monolingual English speaking students from the intervention.

Lawrence et al. (2012) also found that emergent bilinguals who were more proficient in English made gains in target academic words and maintained them a year later. However, those emergent bilinguals who were less proficient in English did neither. In the most recent, and largest, research iteration of Word Generation (Lawrence et al., 2015), the intervention was facilitated in 28 schools across two districts, with a total of 932 treatment students (control $n = 622$). Dramatic treatment effects on the quality of classroom discussions, small effects on target vocabulary, and no effects on general breadth of vocabulary knowledge were found. Finally, in a smaller and independent application of Word Generation, Mokhtari and Velten (2015) modified the approach for an after-school tutoring session to support students reading two or more years below grade level. Students ($n = 36$) made gains in target word vocabulary and a standardized reading comprehension measure, and appeared to close the gap with the control group ($n = 36$; peers were matched demographically but were not struggling readers).

Beyond ALIAS and Word Generation, a number of studies on smaller interventions have been published on academic vocabulary instruction. In their intervention Robust Academic Vocabulary Encounters (RAVE; Crosson & McKeown, 2016), McKeown and her colleagues created 11 seven-day cycles of direct instruction of academic words. Authentic texts from a variety of domains were used, and students were provided with multiple exposures of words in multiple contexts. Treatment students ($n = 64$ seventh graders) outperformed control students ($n = 44$) on experimenter-designed measures of word knowledge, lexical decision speed, and comprehension of passages including target words. For students who experienced two years of the intervention,

RAVE also showed promising impacts on a standardized measure of comprehension. One component of the RAVE was a voluntary activity called "In the Media" (McKeown, Crosson, Artz, Sandora, & Beck, 2013), in which students were encouraged to find the target words outside of school and share where, and how, they saw those words being used. Many students participated in the activity, and those who found ten or more RAVE words outside of school had higher overall gain scores in the experimenter-designed measures. In another intervention guided by the same principles of rich vocabulary instruction, Language Workshop, Townsend and Collins (2009) developed and facilitated a five-week afterschool program for middle school emergent bilinguals. As with other academic vocabulary interventions, the target words were general academic words, and instructional activities were designed to initiate from high-interest texts and to include reading, writing, speaking, and listening. Participants ($N = 37$) made significant gains on the measure aligned with the target words.

In a year-long professional learning (PL) project, Townsend (2014) facilitated a study with middle school teachers ($n = 8$) from all academic content areas. The initiative, Developing Content Area Academic Language (DCAAL), focused on supporting students' academic vocabulary development and used multiple data sources to measure the impact of PL on middle school students' ($n = 304$) academic vocabulary gains. Analyses indicated that teachers shifted their practice to include more scaffolds for academic vocabulary in their respective content areas. Additionally, all students made statistically significant gains on measures of academic vocabulary, and there were "dosage" effects. In other words, those students who had classes with more than one participating teacher from DCAAL made greater gains than those students who only had one class with a participating DCAAL teacher. There were no significant differences between monolingual English speakers and emergent bilinguals.

In a correlational study by Gamez and Lesaux (2015) designed to record the use of sophisticated vocabulary in classrooms, speech transcripts from 24 middle school classrooms were analyzed. Findings of note include that an average of 8% of class time was spent on direct vocabulary instruction, and about 80% of the words targeted during that time were taught by requiring students to define words or make sentences. However, despite this traditional vocabulary instruction, a teacher's use of sophisticated vocabulary still explained significant variance in students' reading comprehension; this finding held even when controlling for the percentage of time dedicated to vocabulary instruction.

Academic Literacy as an Instructional Target

The term academic literacy is often used as an omnibus label for the many language and literacy skills and habits students need to successfully participate in academic settings (Baker et al., 2014; Short & Fitzsimmins, 2007). Instructional approaches and interventions targeting academic literacy typically include academic vocabulary, as well as reading, writing, discussion, and other literacy dimensions within the academic content areas. These comprehensive approaches to academic literacy are often undergirded by Cummins' work on Basic Interpersonal Communication Skills (BICS) and Cognitive Academic Language Proficiency (CALP; Cummins, 1979). This groundbreaking work, while not free from critique (e.g. Aukerman, 2007), established academic literacy as a target for explicit instruction for bilingual students. Early efforts in this explicit instruction went well beyond word meanings and linguistic features of the register of academic language, encompassing a broad range of written and oral language skills and habits. For example, Chamot and O'Malley (1994) developed an instructional model, the Cognitive Academic Language Learning Approach (CALLA), which supported bilingual students with the academic literacy demands of schools. Around the same time frame, beginning in 1996, the Sheltered Instruction Observation Protocol (SIOP; Short, Fidelman, & Louguit, 2012) was developed and is still widely used to support teachers in scaffolding bilingual students with the academic literacy demands of school. Instructional approaches for developing academic literacy, including disciplinary literacy (Goldman et al., 2016), often incorporate elements of vocabulary. However, these instructional approaches also include both general (e.g., identifying main ideas) and discipline-specific (e.g., thinking like a historian) academic skills and habits (Baker et al., 2014; Chamot & O'Malley, 1994; Greenleaf, Brown, Goldmand, & Ko, 2013; Short, Echevarria, & Richards-Tutor, 2011).

Developing Academic Literacy in Elementary Settings

Empirical studies that target the broader category of academic literacy are less common in elementary settings than in secondary settings. However, due to the focus of the CCSS on informational texts starting in the early grades, there is an emerging literature that fits this category. Butler and Hakuta (2009) explored the nature of the relationship between oral English language proficiency and reading performance with two categories of linguistic features: meaning-related (content and key concepts) and formal (grammatical) aspects of 4th graders' academic language in science. After participation in two science lessons, the researchers found that monolingual English speaking students had better command of formal syntax, but monolingual English speaking students and emergent bilinguals had a similar command of new information learned from science texts. With respect to struggling versus typical readers, typical readers were more adept at expressing new information and academic vocabulary learned from text. The combination of both factors (limited oral English and struggles with reading) lead to a complex scenario that a great deal of intervention research is designed to address.

In a different approach to science instruction, Brown and colleagues (2010) examined what they called *disaggregate instruction*, which consists of separating science instruction into conceptual and discursive components. The researchers developed an intervention aimed at improving writing and oral explanations using scientific language in 5th graders of varied language backgrounds. The intervention explicitly provided experience with scientific phenomena using everyday language, and then supported students' development of science language after their initial experience with the phenomena. Students in the comparison group participated in instruction including the same concepts in both everyday and scientific language simultaneously. Findings indicated that both groups of students scored highest on questions designed to measure their conceptual understanding of photosynthesis in everyday language. However, the intervention group showed greater learning gains across all measures, including the science language measure, compared to the control group.

Developing Academic Literacy in Secondary Settings

Empirical research on the broader target of academic literacy in the secondary setting includes descriptive studies, intervention studies, and discipline-specific intervention studies. Peercy (2011) conducted a descriptive study on the practices of two junior high English as a Second Language (ESL) teachers, exploring their practices around essential approaches for helping emergent bilinguals develop academic literacy. Peercy found that the two teachers did attend to many recommended approaches for supporting the academic literacy development of emergent bilinguals, including attending to mainstream content in their classrooms, teaching students academic language, providing support in students' first language, teaching students explicit reading strategies, and using culturally responsive teaching methods. In another descriptive study, Zwiers (2007) found that middle school teachers supported students with "questioning, gestures, connecting to background knowledge with examples and analogies, and personifying" (p. 93). Both Peercy and

Zwiers concluded with a strong call for richer teacher education in these practices and a sociocultural and integrated approach to supporting emergent bilinguals' academic literacy.

Short et al. (2011) reported on three studies with the Sheltered Instruction Observation Protocol (SIOP), a professional learning and instructional approach designed to help emergent bilinguals build academic language and literacy skills in content area classrooms. The three studies reported in 2011 all looked at impacts on academic literacy, which were measured by standardized achievement tests in writing, oral language, reading, and the content areas. The first two studies ($N = 318$ and $N = 580$, respectively) demonstrated student gains on measures of academic achievement, and sustained PL resulted in higher fidelity of implementation on the part of teachers. The third study ($N = 1021$), involved a nine-week intervention; no significant differences between treatment and control students were found.

With respect to discipline-specific interventions, Vaughn et al. (2009) developed a set of instructional routines for middle school emergent bilinguals in social studies that included explicit vocabulary and concept instruction, strategic use of videos and purposeful discussion to build concept knowledge, and use of writing with graphic organizers. Participants made significant gains in experimenter-designed vocabulary and comprehension measures that aligned with the social studies content. Zwiers (2007) also explored the integration of academic language and social studies with an action research study exploring students' responses to instruction in six dimensions of historical thinking. With intentional scaffolding and modeling, students made progress in academic language and historical thinking.

In QuEST, another middle school intervention related to science, August, Branum-Martin, Cardenas-Hagan, and Francis (2009) developed four- and five-week units on Living Systems and the Environment. A number of scaffolds were integrated to support emergent bilinguals ($n = 562$; monolingual English speakers, $n = 328$), including visuals, graphic organizers, experiments and demonstrations, modeling, ongoing discussion, textbook support, explicit vocabulary instruction (both general and discipline-specific), glossaries with Spanish translations, and guided reading. All treatment students made gains on curriculum-based measures of vocabulary and science knowledge, but not on the standardized measures of vocabulary or comprehension. One possible explanation was the small sample of teachers ($n = 10$) and inconsistent fidelity with the intervention. In a second iteration of QuEST, August and her colleagues (2014) facilitated a larger PL component and modified their measures to include an academic language measure specific to science. Emergent bilinguals in the intervention made gains in academic language, but monolingual English speakers, on average, made greater gains.

In another science intervention, Reading Apprenticeship (Greenleaf et al., 2011), ten days of content-focused PL on a range of reading and inquiry activities, including textual features that shape literacy practices in the academic disciplines was completed. A group-randomized experimental study included a multitude of teacher- and student-level data sources, and results revealed that treatment teachers (N = 56), when compared to control teachers (N = 49), were more knowledgeable about how to integrate science reading and science content, create classrooms with collaborative inquiry and meaning-making through disciplinary texts, engage students in text inquiry, and promote comprehension strategies. Students who received instruction from the treatment teachers saw growth in ELA, reading comprehension, and biology state tests.

Finally, Levine and Horton (2015) conducted a month-long intervention in a 12th grade English class with primarily struggling readers. The purpose of the study was to determine if opportunities to learn from experts' models of reading would enhance students' reading. Using literary short stories, students were exposed to think-alouds from five expert English teachers. The expert think-alouds were guided by the experts' "identification of patterns, tensions, generally striking language, and lines in privileged positions" (p. 146). Students, on average, made gains in all of these areas. These last two secondary studies with academic literacy targets (Greenleaf et al.,

2011; Levine & Horton, 2015), are part of the growing body of literature in disciplinary literacy. Goldman et al. (2016) list "discourse and language structures" as one of five core constructs of disciplinary literacy. A full review of disciplinary literacy research is beyond the scope of this chapter, but we acknowledge the potential for garnering new insights on academic language instruction via explorations into disciplinary literacy.

What Have We Learned from Academic Language Instruction Research in K-12 Settings?

When organized by the two instructional targets, academic vocabulary and academic literacy, the research on academic language instruction suggests trends about instruction, students, and teachers. One clear trend is the effectiveness of rich and robust vocabulary instruction (Beck, McKeown, & Kucan, 2013; Graves et al., 2014), which includes multiple opportunities to practice and personalize word meanings in multiple contexts, along with independent word-learning strategies. With respect to academic vocabulary instruction in elementary settings, this rich and explicit instruction in academic vocabulary does lead to significant gains in students' academic word knowledge (August et al., 2016; Spycher, 2009; Taboada & Rutherford, 2011). While explicit instruction has a clear impact on academic word knowledge, the research suggests that more implicit instruction, or vocabulary instruction that is embedded within the study of text, serves a slightly different purpose. Embedded or implicit instruction has a less pronounced (but still significant) impact on word knowledge but may target comprehension performance more effectively (August et al., 2016; Taboada & Rutherford, 2011). Two additional trends are the value of multimodal and multimedia resources to enhance academic word learning (August et al., 2016; Silverman & Hines, 2009) and the importance of more increased frequency of exposure to word meanings across contexts (Beck & McKeown, 2007).

In secondary settings, there is evidence that rich academic vocabulary instruction does yield significant gains in word knowledge (Lawrence et al., 2012; Lesaux et al., 2014; McKeown et al., 2013; Townsend, 2014; Townsend & Collins, 2009) and, potentially, comprehension (Lesaux et al., 2010; Mokhtari & Velten, 2015). Furthermore, engaging secondary teachers across content areas in working toward common academic vocabulary targets appears to impact student word knowledge and academic discussions (Lawrence et al., 2014; Townsend, 2014).

The trends in the instructional research that targets academic literacy are less conclusive. Overall, the academic literacy research is aligned with Baker et al.'s (2014) four recommendations for supporting academic content and literacy development. There is clear evidence for using rich vocabulary instruction, multiple discussion and writing opportunities, explicit instruction with academic writing, and small group interventions for struggling readers (Baker et al., 2014). However, these recommendations are in the service of academic literacy more broadly. Specific impacts on global, standardized reading comprehension are much less robust.

Only two interventions, ALIAS (Lesaux et al., 2010) and Reading Apprenticeship (Greenleaf et al., 2011), showed gains in standardized measures of reading comprehension. Several other studies showed relationships, and possible causality, with standardized achievement measures that suggest comprehension gains (Short et al., 2011; Snow et al., 2009). Taboada and Rutherford (2011), Beck and McKeown (2007), and Vaughn et al. (2009) each showed gains on experimenter-designed passage comprehension measures that included the intervention target words. Other intervention studies did not measure comprehension, or showed no relationships with comprehension, but did yield gains in academic vocabulary (Townsend & Collins, 2009), academic discussions (Lawrence et al., 2015), and analysis skills (for reading specific disciplines; Levine & Horton, 2015).

Several past and recent multi-component reading comprehension interventions for elementary EL struggling readers (e.g., Proctor, Dalton & Grisham, 2007) point to the conclusion that improvements in reading comprehension are difficult to produce unless many components of comprehension are targeted as part of the intervention (e.g., Proctor et al., 2007; Vaughn et al., 2009; Taboada & Rutherford, 2011). When comprehension gains are achieved, gains are typically on passages including the target words, and very rarely on global comprehension measures. There are two potential explanations for the weak link, and both may be in play to varying degrees depending on the study. First, as suggested by Lesaux et al. (2014), it is entirely possible that standardized reading comprehension measures are too distal to pick up on gains made via robust vocabulary instruction. Reading comprehension measures may require such a large overall lexicon that they are not sensitive to even significant gains in academic vocabulary knowledge. Another possible explanation is that improved word knowledge, while a necessary ingredient, is not sufficient for improved global comprehension performance. Intervention research that aims to improve comprehension may need to expand to capture sentence and paragraph level structures, and other comprehension processes (e.g., local and global inferences), in order for students to apply their newfound word knowledge to larger sections of texts.

The instructional research that targeted academic literacy typically emphasized authentic texts, opportunities to read and write, use of graphic organizers, multimedia, and well-structured discussions. But, outcomes on comprehension differed; it is unclear which combination of strategies, or which intervention design, may have led to gains or lack thereof. Furthermore, interventions designed to support students' overall academic and disciplinary literacy often have broad goals that represent multiple constructs. There are simply not enough studies on any specific literacy objectives to draw confident conclusions across studies. For example, QuEST was designed to support students' science word knowledge and science comprehension, whereas Greenleaf et al. (2011) were specifically working toward scientific reasoning and discourse norms. Both studies yielded positive results, but their learning goals, while both related to science literacy, were somewhat disparate from each other. These trends suggest a need for clarity in future intervention research with respect to the purpose of each new or replicated intervention, with careful links to the research with common purposes that came earlier.

In addition to conducting more research that explores common purposes and compares different approaches in academic language instruction to meet those purposes, there are two gaps in the literature that require attention. The first is an implementation gap between what research suggests and what pre- and in-service teachers have opportunities to learn. The second gap is a bridging gap between the body of work on academic language instruction and the critiques of academic language from a raciolinguistics perspective.

Bridging the Implementation Gap: From Research to Practice

A troubling implementation gap in academic language research exists between what the field of literacy knows about academic language development and instruction, and what we see enacted in classrooms. Halliday (1999) provides strong guidance for teachers regarding the role language plays in learning by describing the three forms of language in schooling: (1) in learning language (first and/or second language development); (2) in learning *through* language (subject matter); (3) and in learning *about* language (metalanguage). Considering language in this threefold way has important implications for pre- and in-service teachers; teachers must have opportunities to develop their own knowledge about language, both language acquisition and language specific to the disciplines. There are multiple professional learning (PL) models that have affected change in teachers' practice, as well as several models that have impacted student learning. At the pre-service level, one emerging component of teacher certification is edTPA, which spotlights teacher candidates' understanding and implementation of four components of academic language including: vocabulary, language function, discourse, and syntax (Lim et al., 2015). Additionally, a number of practitioner publications draw on concepts and principles related to SFL to provide practical resources for educators (Buehl, 2011; Fang & Schleppegrell, 2008a; Zwiers, 2014). Established models that have broadened and improved teachers' practices with language development in general are also in place (Baker, Lewis, Uysal, Purzer, Lang, & Baker, 2011; Bowers, Fitz, Quirk, & Jung, 2010; Correnti, 2007; Gebhard, Willett, Jimenez, & Piedra, 2010; Gersten et al., 2010; Heinrichs & Leseman, 2014; Kindle, 2013; Masters et al., 2010). Additionally, several PL initiatives have shown impacts on both teachers' practice and students' learning, specifically related to academic language (Achugar, Schleppegrell, & Oteiza, 2007; Greenleaf et al., 2011; Short et al., 2011; Short, Cloud, Morris, & Motta, 2012, p. 407; Townsend, 2014). Specifically, de Oliveira (2012) suggests that teachers have knowledge in identifying discipline-specific academic language and designing scaffolding activities to help students build competencies with that language.

One additional approach to bridge this research to practice gap is to investigate the impact of PL that addresses academic sentences and paragraphs. As evidenced by the research reviewed in this chapter, studies that have investigated the impact of academic language instruction have generally focused narrowly on academic vocabulary or broadly on academic literacy. Few studies have included specific instruction on the kinds of linguistic features that characterize academic sentences and paragraphs (see Uccelli et al., 2015, and Uccelli, Phillips Galloway, & Qin in this volume, for an overview of selected features). There are likely reasons for this. First, the relationship between vocabulary and comprehension is well-established, making vocabulary an important instructional target for any learning objective. Second, identifying and teaching the grammatical structures that communicate meaning in academic language poses a unique challenge; to unpack sentences and paragraphs requires some degree of comfort with syntax and pragmatics. However, just as vocabulary researchers have identified effective ways of building abstract and technical vocabulary knowledge through work with authentic reading, writing, speaking, and listening, the same approach could potentially be used with features like connectives, anaphoric references, embedded clauses, nominalizations and noun phrases, and tracking ideas through text. These linguistic features are hallmarks of academic language (Uccelli et al., 2015), and they directly relate to comprehension (LaRusso et al., 2016). There is a need for interventions that support students with academic sentences and academic paragraphs, in addition to the current targets in the instructional research literature, academic vocabulary and academic literacy. Interventions that support dissection and comprehension of sentences and paragraphs, from authentic texts that are worth reading in their own right, are a logical next line of inquiry and may have potential to capture those elusive comprehension gains. Though the field is not without models for this work (Achugar, Schleppegrell, & Oteiza, 2007; Schleppegrell & de Oliveira, 2006), there is little related to reading comprehension. However, many researchers in the area of writing have explored how explicit instruction in the *functions* of language can support students' production of academic language (Coxhead & Byrd, 2007; Gebhard, Harman, & Seger, 2007; Schleppegrell & Go, 2007; Spycher, 2007). Certainly, PL of this kind would require a commitment, especially when considering the history of vocabulary instruction. Despite the evidence for robust, interactive, and authentic vocabulary instruction since the early 1980s (Beck, Perfetti, & McKeown, 1982), passive and outdated approaches to vocabulary hold sway (Gamez & Lesaux, 2015; Scott, Jamieson-Noel, & Asselin, 2003). Supporting teachers through pre- and in-service PL on bringing both embedded and explicit sentence/paragraph comprehension supports into their classrooms will require a commitment of time and resources.

Bridging the Gap between Academic Language and Raciolinguistics

The second gap that needs attention is the scarce communication between, and among, complementary fields relevant for academic language research. With respect to critiques of academic language as an instructional goal for students, we include a consideration of *raciolinguistics* (Avineri et al., 2015; Flores & Rosa, 2015). Flores and Rosa (2015) argue that K-12 schooling in the U.S. operates within a raciolinguistic ideology. To elaborate, by identifying academic language as the "appropriate" register for school, all students who have not been socialized into academic language contexts fall into a "deficient" category. Raciolinguistics, as applied to public schools, positions some students as "haves" and some as "have nots"; identifying academic language as necessary for success reifies these structures. Even as emergent bilingual learners build academic language proficiency, they are still judged within systems of power that privilege white, middle class students. Flores and Rosa refer to the phenomenon of "white gaze" (Morrison, 1998, cited in Paris & Alim, 2014, p. 86), a perspective that "privileges dominant white perspectives on the linguistic and cultural practices of racialized communities" (Flores & Rosa, p. 151). The problem, as viewed with a raciolinguist lens, is that the system of schooling in the U.S. is pervasively tainted with racist ideologies that are intrinsically intertwined with language practices. Even in the midst of much research demonstrating the cognitive advantages of bilingualism (Brito & Barr, 2012; Pelham & Abrams, 2014), raciolingusitic scholars aptly highlight the many studies that cite the academic needs and deficits of non-native English speakers (Flores & Rosa, 2015). There are similar discourse patterns for low-SES students (Avineri et al., 2015). The central tension, and question, is that linguistic readiness for academic work is often and inextricably tied to some groups of students and families and not others, creating inequity from the start.

Those scholars working within the tradition of SFL and academic vocabulary research could be perceived as "at odds" with those working from a critical stance and exploring the raciolinguistic framework that serves to reify inequities. And this conflict exists despite the purported neutrality of scholarship in the SFL tradition. An important theme in SFL scholarship is that different registers of language are not positioned as superior or inferior to each other. In the SFL tradition, registers are not privileged or ranked as more or less complex or decontextualized. All language is complex and all language is contextualized. Scholars operating within an SFL framework strive to maintain a neutrality to these discussions of academic language (Bailey, 2007). Based on the research reviewed for this chapter, academic vocabulary and language researchers are working from this perspective. In no research reviewed for this chapter did any researcher advocate for a replacement approach in which home, community, and social registers of language were not recognized as important and vitally related to students' identities.

Academic language, then, can be positioned as either a component of systemic inequity (via raciolinguistics) or as a more neutral set of linguistic resources (via SFL). We seek to mediate these seemingly irreconcilable differences. Our first recommendation is that academic language researchers working from an SLF perspective, or within the tradition of vocabulary research, consider working within two frames. First, academic language instruction research should operate from an open platform, an open instructional space, that encourages multiple ways of using, and analyzing, language and linguistic choices. In this open platform, academic language instruction can then provide *all* students opportunities to enhance their existing linguistic repertoires to support communication in academic settings.

Simultaneously, however, academic language research can, and arguably should, make space for students and teachers to identify, challenge, and dismantle the systemic inequities identified by raciolinguistics scholars. Scholars within this framework typically ask what might be accomplished if "the goal of teaching and learning with youth of color was not ultimately to see how closely students could perform on White middle-class norms but to explore, honor, extend, and problematize their heritage and community practices" (Paris & Alim, 2014, p. 86). By way of moving forward, academic language instruction researchers may want to address the notion of "lack" or "absence" that so often characterizes work in academic language with multilingual students. Research on emergent bilinguals often casts a broad net and identifies emergent bilinguals as any student who speaks another language, or a combination of English and another language, outside of school. While this broad net has been a good faith effort to support *all* multilingual students and not just newcomers to the U.S., it may also have led to lower expectations of a large group of students that is very diverse with respect to their academic language strengths. Indeed, there are important and divergent patterns related to emergent bilingual students in the academic language instruction research. Several studies yielded larger gains for emergent bilinguals who were more proficient in English than for their peers who were less proficient in English (August et al., 2014; Lawrence et al., 2012; Townsend & Collins, 2009). These studies, among others (Butler & Hakuta, 2015), dismantle the misconception that emergent bilinguals are a monolithic group. Reflection on the ways that academic language research has inadvertently promoted, or unintentionally fueled, a deficit model could enhance conversations among researchers and establish more open and equitable norms for moving forward. In the spirit of leaning in to reflective and critical work, we see two opportunities for bridging this gap. First, we recommend opening pathways of communication with raciolinguistics scholars, and scholars working from other Critical Theory frameworks. Reading, writing, and designing interventions together can allow for language instruction and analysis in inclusive spaces. Second, as recommended by Flores (2016), teachers need support in hosting classrooms that engage in language exploration; such classrooms would support students in analyzing language choices made by authors and themselves, and the relationships between those choices and the contexts and audiences for which they are used.

A Final, Integrated Model for Moving Forward

To bridge these gaps in the research related to teacher knowledge about language and the systemic inequities that are entangled with academic language, we recommend an approach forward. This approach is illustrated by a new figure (see Figure 18.2), which adds two new instructional targets, *Academic Sentences/Paragraphs* and *Critical Spaces*, to our original figure.

Again, these instructional targets for academic language research are not mutually exclusive, but the lack of intervention studies on academic sentences and paragraphs suggests a renewed focus on the specific linguistic features that make academic language *academic*. Research on morphology (Goodwin, Lipsky, & Ahn, 2012; Kieffer & Box, 2013; Kieffer & Lesaux, 2010), connectives (Crosson & Lesaux, 2013), and sentence, paragraph, and register levels of academic language (LaRusso et al., 2016; Uccelli et al., 2015) can be used to build language goals. Additionally, the new waves of research on disciplinary literacy can be used to help situate academic sentence/paragraph interventions within authentic disciplinary contexts.

With these recommendations for future directions, we offer two notes of caution. First, there is the possibility that attention to specific linguistic features will lead interventions away from disciplinary content in favor of specific language outcomes. Just as vocabulary instruction should be in the service of comprehension and production (rather than vocabulary for the sake of vocabulary), any focus on specific linguistic features should be situated in meaningful contexts. Second, efforts to invest in the kinds of interventions that can affect change in reading comprehension and achievement require policy and administrator support. Studies on ALIAS, Word Generation, SIOP, and QuEST all described the systemic challenges with garnering enough time for students' instruction and teachers' PL. The large-scale PL initiatives that have been successful have required serious commitments of time and resources.

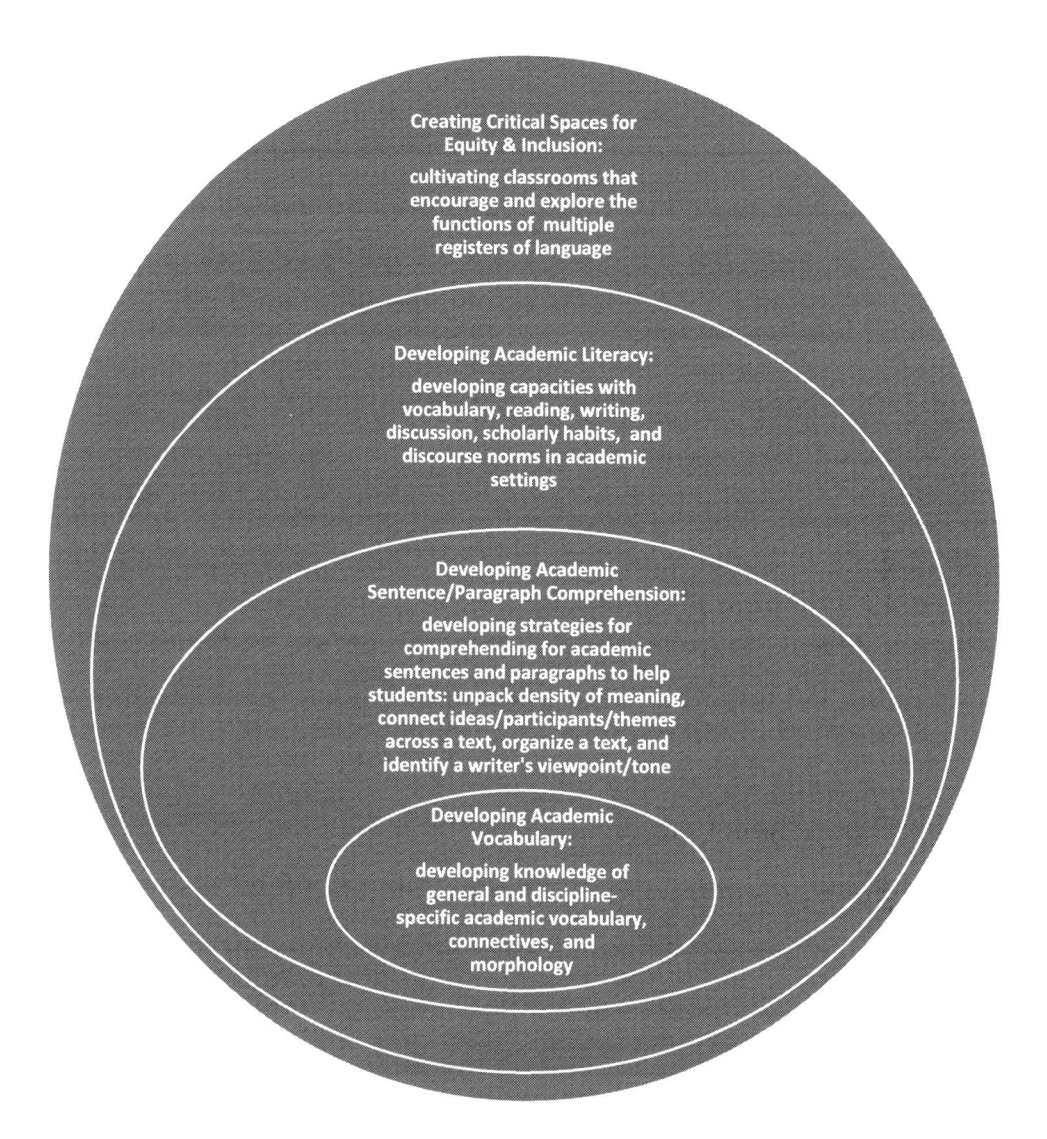

Learning Academic Language, Comprehending Text

Creating Critical Spaces for Equity & Inclusion:
cultivating classrooms that encourage and explore the functions of multiple registers of language

Developing Academic Literacy:
developing capacities with vocabulary, reading, writing, discussion, scholarly habits, and discourse norms in academic settings

Developing Academic Sentence/Paragraph Comprehension:
developing strategies for comprehending for academic sentences and paragraphs to help students: unpack density of meaning, connect ideas/participants/themes across a text, organize a text, and identify a writer's viewpoint/tone

Developing Academic Vocabulary:
developing knowledge of general and discipline-specific academic vocabulary, connectives, and morphology

Figure 18.2 Recommended instructional targets for academic language instruction in future research

To conclude, we draw attention to the top level of the new figure, that of *Critical Spaces*. By nesting all three instructional targets for academic language research within this level, we are calling for more attention to the sociolinguistic contexts of academic language (see Uccelli, Phillips Galloway, & Qin, this volume, for a similar argument for developing critical rhetorical flexibility). The scholarship operating within a raciolinguistics frame, as well as research that has explored the intersection of reading comprehension and race (see, for example, Lee, 2015), provide for a much richer conversation of language and literacy goals than is typically included in academic language pedagogy. We do see ways forward with research that involves all stakeholders and seeks to understand the academic language and learning experiences of students, families, and teachers. We think there are important opportunities, and a compelling rationale, to collaborate across different frameworks from SFL, raciolinguistics, literacy, and other fields and theories. We live in a world in which academic language is necessary for academic and career success, and, simultaneously, in a world that includes systemic inequities. This tension can be generative; we believe that by listening and making space for multiple ways of knowing and using language, we can effect change both *inside* and *to* the educational system.

Note

1 Many labels have been ascribed to students who speak more than one language at varying levels of proficiency. For ease of reading this chapter, we consistently use the term "emergent bilingual" to refer to students that are learning English and who also speak one or more other languages they speak. Some emergent bilinguals may have spoken English for years, but not as their dominant language. Others may be newcomers to the U.S. and in the early stages of learning English. In the current review of the literature, emergent bilingual learners are typically classified in their school districts as English Language Learners.

References

Achugar, M., & Schleppegrell, M. J. (2005). Beyond connectors: The construction of cause in history textbooks. *Linguistics and Education, 16*, 298–318.

Achugar, M., Schleppegrell, M. J., & Oteiza, T. (2007). Engaging teachers in language analysis: A functional linguistics approacj to reflective literacy. *English Teaching: Practice and Critique, 6*, 8–24.

Apel, K. (2014). A comprehension definition of morphological awareness: Implications for assessment. *Topics in Language Disorders, 34*(3), 197–209.

Apel, K., Brimo, D., Diehm, E., & Apel, L. (2013). Morphological awareness intervention with kindergarteners and first- and second-grade students from low socioeconomic status homes: A feasibility study. *Language Speech and Hearing Services in Schools, 44*(2), 161–173.

Apel, K., & Diehm, E. (2014). Morphological awareness intervention with kindergarteners and first and second grade students from low SES homes: A small efficacy study. *Journal of Learning Disabilities, 47*(1), 65–75.

Apel, K., & Lawrence, J. (2011). Contributions of morphological awareness skilsl to word-level reading and spelling in first-grade children with and without speech sound disorder. *Journal of Speech, Language and Hearing Research, 54*(5), 1312–1327.

August, D., Artzi, L., & Barr, C. (2016). Helping ELLs meet standards in English language arts and science: An intervention focused on academic vocabulary. *Reading & Writing Quarterly: Overcoming Learning DIfficulties, 32*(4), 373–396.

August, D., Branum-Martin, L., Cadenas-Hagan, E., Francis, D. J., Powell, J., Moore, S., & Haynes, E. (2014). Helping ELLs meet the common core state standards for literacy in science: The impact of an instructional intervention focused on academic language. *Journal of Research on Educational Effectiveness, 7*(1), 54–82.

August, D., Branum-Martin, L., Cardenas-Hagan, E., & Francis, D. (2009). The impact of an instructional intervention on the science and language learning of middle grade English language learners. *Journal of Research on Educational Effectiveness, 2*(4), 345–376.

Aukerman, M. (2007). A culpable CALP. *The Reading Teacher, 60*, 626–635.

Avineri, N., Johnson, E., Brice-Heath, S., McCarty, T., Ochs, E., Kremer-Sadlik, T., … Paris, D. (2015). Invited forum: Bridging the laguage gap. *Journal of Linguistic Anthropology, 25*(1), 66–86.

Bailey, A. L. (2007). *The language demands of school: Putting academic English to the test*. New Haven, CT: Yale University Press.

Baker, D. R., Lewis, E. B., Uysal, S., Purzer, S., Lang, M., & Baker, P. (2011). Using the communication in science inquiry project professional development model to facilitate learning middle school genertics concepts. *Professional Development in Education, 37*(3), 453–468.

Baker, S., Lesaux, N., Jayanthi, M., Dimino, J., Proctor, C. P., Morris, J., … Newman-Gonchar, R. (2014). *Teaching academic content and literacy to English learners in elementary and middle school (NCEE 2014-4012)*. Washington, DC: National Center for Education Evaluation and Regional Assistance (NCEE), Institute of Education Sciences, U.S. Department of Education.

Barnes, M. A. (2015). What do models of reading comprehension and its development have to contribute to a science of comprehension instruction and assessment for adolescents? In K. L. Santi & D. K. Reed (Eds.), *Improving reading comprehension of middle and high school students* (pp. 1–18). New York: Springer.

Baumann, J. F., & Graves, M. F. (2010). What is academic vocabulary? *Journal of Adolescent & Adult Literacy, 54*(1), 4–12.

Beck, I. L., & McKeown, M. G. (2007). Increasing young low-income children's oral vocabulary repertoires through rich and focused instruction. *The Elementary School Journal, 107*, 251–271.

Beck, I. L., McKeown, M. G., & Kucan, L. (2002). *Bringing words to life*. New York: The Guilford Press.

Beck, I. L., McKeown, M. G., & Kucan, L. (2013). *Bringing words to life: Robust vocabulary instruction, 2e*. New York: Guilford.

Beck, I. L., Perfetti, C. A., & McKeown, M. G. (1982). Effects of long-term vocabulary instruction on lexical access and reading comprehension. *Journal of Educational Psychology, 74*, 506–521.

Bowers, E., Fitts, S., Quirk, M., & Jung, W. (2010). Effective strategies for developing academic English: Professional development and teacher practices. *Bilingual Research Journal, 23*(1), 95–110.

Bowers, P. N., Kirby, J. R., & Deacon, H. (2010). The effects of morphological instruction on literacy skills: A systematic review of the literature. *Review of Educational Research, 80*(2), 144–179.

Brito, N., & Barr, R. (2012). Influence of bilingualism on memory generalization durig infancy. *Developmental Science, 15*(6), 812–816.

Brown, B. A., Ryoo, K., & Rodriguez, J. (2010). Pathway towards fluency: Using 'disaggregate instruction' to promote science literacy. *International Journal of Science Education, 32*, 1465–1493.

Buehl, D. (2011). *Developing readers in the academic disciplines*. Newark, DE: International Reading Association.

Butler, Y., & Hakuta, K. (2009). The relationship between academic oral proficiency and reading performance: A comparative study between English learners and English-only students. *Reading Psychology, 30*, 412–444.

Carlisle, J. F. (2000). Awareness of the structure and meaning of morphologically complex words: Impact on reading. *Reading and Writing: An Interdisciplinary Journal, 12*, 169–190.

Carlisle, J. F., & Stone, C. A. (2005). Exploring the role of morphemes in word reading. *Reading Research Quarterly, 40*(4), 428–449.

Carlo, M. S., August, D., McLaughlin, B., Snow, C., Dressler, C., Lippman, D., … White, C. (2004). Closing the gap: Addressing the vocabulary needs of English language learners in bilingual and mainstream classrooms. *Reading Research Quarterly, 39*, 188–215.

Chamot, A. U., & O'Malley, J. M. (1994). *CALLA handbook: Implementing the cognitive academic language learning approach*. Reading, MA: Addison-Wesley Publishing Company.

Correnti, R. (2007). An empirical investigation of professional development effects on literacy instruction using daily logs. *Educational Evaluation and Policy Analysis, 29*(4), 262–295.

Coxhead, A. (2000). A new academic word list. *TESOL Quarterly, 34*, 213–238.

Coxhead, A., & Byrd, P. (2007). Preparing writing teachers to teach the vocabulary and grammar of academic prose. *Journal of Second Language Writing, 16*, 129–147.

Crosson, A. C., & Lesaux, N. (2013). Does knowledge of connectives play a unique role in the reading comprehension of English learners and English-only students? *Journal of Research in Reading, 36*(3), 241–260.

Crosson, A. C., & McKeown, M. G. (2016). Middle school learners' use of Latin roots to infer the meaning of unfamiliar words. *Cognition and Instruction, 34*(2), 148–171.

Cummins, J. (1979). Linguistic interdependence and the educational development of bilingual children. *Review of Educational Research, 49*, 222–251.

de Oliveira, L. (2012). What history teachers need to know about academic language to teach English language learners. *Social Studies Review, 51*, 70–76.

Eggins, S. (2004). *An introduction to systemic functional linguistics, 2nd edition*. New York: Continuum.

Fang, Z. (2006). The language demands of science reading in middle school. *International Journal of Science Education, 28*(5), 491–520.

Fang, Z. (2012). Language correlates of disciplinary literacy. *Topics in Language Disorders, 32*(1), 19–34.

Fang, Z., & Schleppegrell, M. J. (2008a). *Reading in secondary content areas*. Ann Arbor, MI: The University of Michigan Press.

Fang, Z., & Schleppegrell, M. J. (2008b). *Reading in secondary content areas: A language-based pedagogy*. Ann Arbor, MI: University of Michigan Press.

Fang, Z., Schleppegrell, M. J., & Cox, B. E. (2006). Understanding the language demands of schooling: Nouns in academic registers. *Journal of Literacy Research, 38*(3), 247–273.

Flores, N. (2016). Combatting marginalized spaces in education through language architecture. *Perspectives on Urban Education, 13*(1), 1–3.

Flores, N., & Rosa, J. (2015). Undoing appropriateness: Raciolinguistics ideologies and language diversity in education. *Harvard Educational Review, 85*(2), 149–171.

Ford-Connors, E., & Paratore, J. R. (2015). Vocabulary instruction in fifth grade and beyond: Sources of word learning and productive contexts for development. *Review of Educational Research, 85*(1), 50–91.

Gamez, P. B., & Lesaux, N. K. (2015). Early-adolescesnts' reading comprehension and the stability of the middle school classroom-language environment. *Developmental Psychology, 51*(4), 447–458.

Gardner, D., & Davies, M. (2014). A new academic vocabulary list. *Applied Linguistics, 35*(3), 305–327.

Gebhard, M., Harman, R., & Seger, W. (2007). Reclaiming recess: Learning the language of persuasion. *Language Arts, 84*, 419–430.

Gebhard, M., Willett, J., Jimenez, J., & Piedra, A. (2010). Systemic functional linguistics, teachers' professional development, and ELLs' academic literacy practices. In T. Lucas (Ed.), *Teacher preparation for linguistically diverse classrooms: A resource for teacher educators* (pp. 91–110). Mahwah, NJ: Erlbaum/Taylor & Francis.

Gersten, R., Dimino, J., Jayanthi, M., Kim, J. S., & Santoro, L. E. (2010). Teacher study group: Impact of the professional development model on reading instruction and student outcomes in first grade classrooms. *American Educational Research Journal, 47*(3), 694–739.

Goldman, S. R., Britt, M. A., Brown, W., Cribb, G., George, M., Greenleaf, C., … Project READI (2016). Disciplinary literacies and learning to read for understanding: A conceptual framework for disciplinary literacy. *Educational Psychologist, 51*(2), 219–246.

Goodwin, A. (2016). Effectiveness of word solving: Integrating morphological problem-solving within comprehension instruction for middle school students. *Reading and Writing: An Interdisciplinary Journal, 29*, 91–116.

Goodwin, A., & Ahn, S. (2013). A meta-analysis of morphological interventions in English: Effects on literacy outcomes for school-age children. *Scientific Studies of Reading, 17*(4), 257–285.

Goodwin, A., Lipsky, M., & Ahn, S. (2012). Word detectives: Using units of meaning to support literacy. *The Reading Teacher, 65*(7), 461–470.

Graves, M. F., Baumann, J. F., Blachowicz, C. L. Z., Manyak, P., Bates, A., Cieply, C., … Von Gunten, H. (2014). Words, words everywhere, but which ones do we teach? *The Reading Teacher, 67*(5), 333–346.

Greenleaf, C., Brown, W., Goldmand, S. R., & Ko, M. K. (2013). *READI for science: Promoting scientific literacy practices through text-based investigations for middle and high school science teachers and students.* Washington, DC: National Research Council.

Greenleaf, C. L., Litman, C., Hanson, T. L., Rosen, R., Boscardin, C. K., Herman, J., … Jones, B. (2011). Integrating literacy and science in biology: Teaching and learning impacts of reading apprenticesheup professional development. *American Educational Research Journal, 48*(3), 647–717.

Halliday, M. A. K. (1999). The notion of "context" in language education. In M. Ghadessy (Ed.), *Text and context in functional linguistics*. Amsterdam: John Benjamins.

Heinrichs, L. F., & Leseman, P. P. M. (2014). Early science instruction and academic language development can go hand in hand: The promising effects of a low-intensity teacher-focused intervention. *International Journal of Science Education, 36*(17), 2978–2995.

Hiebert, E. H., & Lubliner, S. (2008). The nature, learning, and instruction of general academic vocabulary. In A. E. Farstrup & S. J. Samuels (Eds.), *What research has to say about vocabulary* (pp. 106–129). Newark, DE: International Reading Association.

Kieffer, M. J., & Box, C. D. (2013). Derivational morphological awareness, academic vocabulary, and reading comprehension in linguistically diverse sixth graders. *Learning and Individual Differences, 24*, 168–175.

Kieffer, M. J., & Lesaux, N. K. (2010). Morphing into adolescents: Active word learning for English-language learners and their classmates in middle school. *Journal of Adolescent and Adult Literacy, 54*(1), 47–56.

Kindle, K. (2013). Interactive reading in preschool: Improving practice through professional development. *Reading Improvement, 50*(4), 175–188.

LaRusso, M., Kim, H. W., Robert, S., Uccelli, P., Dawson, T., Jones, S., … Snow, C. E. (2016). Contributions of academic language, perspective taking, and complex reasoning to deep reading comprehension. *Journal of Research on Educational Effectiveness, 9*(2), 201–222.

Lawrence, J. F., Capotosto, L., Branum-Martin, L., White, C., & Snow, C. E. (2012). Language proficiency, home-language status, and English vocabulary development: A longitudinal follow-up of the word generation program. *Bilingualism: Language and Cognition, 15*(3), 437–451.

Lawrence, J. F., Crosson, A. C., Pare-Blagoev, J., & Snow, C. E. (2015). Word generation randomized trial: Discussion mediates the impact of program treatment on academic word learning. *American Educational Research Journal, 52*(4), 750–786.

Lawrence, J. F., Rolland, R. G., Branum-Martin, L., & Snow, C. E. (2014). Generating vocabulary knowledge for at-risk middle school readers: Contrasting program effects and growth trajectories. *Journal of Education for Students Placed at Risk, 19*(2), 76–97.

Lee, C. D. (2015). Influences of the experience of race as a lens for understanding variation in displays of competence in reading comprehension. In P. Afflerbach (Ed.), *Handbook of individual differences in reading: Reader, text, and context* (pp. 286–304). New York, NY: Taylor & Francis.

Lee, C. D., & Spratley, A. (2010). *Reading in the disciplines: The challenges of adolescent literacy*. New York, NY: Carnegie Corporation of New York.

Lesaux, N. K., Kieffer, M. J., Faller, S. E., & Kelley, J. G. (2010). The effectiveness and ease of implementation of an academic vocabulary intervention for linguistically diverse students in urban middle schools. *Reading Research Quarterly, 45*, 196–228.

Lesaux, N. K., Kieffer, M. J., Kelley, J. G., & Harris, J. R. (2014). Effects of academic vocabulary instruction for linguistically diverse adolescents: Evidence from a randomized field trial. *American Educational Research Journal, 51*(6), 1159–1194.

Levine, S., & Horton, W. (2015). Helping high school students read like experts: Affective evaluation, salience, and literary interpretation. *Cognition & Instruction, 33*(2), 125–153.

Lim, W., Stallings, L., & Kim, D. J. (2015). A proposed pedagogical approach for preparing teacher candidates to incorporate academic language in mathematics classrooms. *International Education Studies, 8*(7), 1–10..

Logan, K., & Kieffer, M. J. (2017). Evaluating the role of polysemous word knowledge in reading comprehension among bilingual adolescents. *Reading and Writing: An Interdisciplinary Journal. 30*, 1687–1704.

McKeown, M. G., Crosson, A. C., Artz, N. J., Sandora, C., & Beck, I. L. (2013). In the media: Expanding students' experience with academic vocabulary. *The Reading Teacher, 67*(1), 45–53.

McKeown, M. G., Crosson, A. C., Beck, I. L., Sandora, C., Artz, N. J., & Moore, D. (2013). *Word knowledge and comprehension outcomes for the second year of implementation of an academic word vocabulary intervention*. Paper presented at the American Educational Research Association, Vancouver, BC, Canada.

Masters, J., De Kramer, R. M., O'Dwyer, L. M., Dash, S., & Russell, M. (2010). The effects of online professional development on fourth grade English language arts teachers' knowledge and instructional practices. *Journal of Educational Computing Research, 43*(3), 355–375.

Moje, E. B. (2015). Doing and teaching disciplinary literacy with adolescent learners: A social and cultural enterprise. *Harvard Educational Review, 85*, 254–278.

Mokhtari, K., & Velten, J. (2015). Strengtheneing academic vocabulary with Word Generation helps sixth-grade students improve reading comprehension. *Middle Grades Research Journal, 10*(3), 23–42.

Nagy, W., & Townsend, D. (2012). Words as tools: Learning academic vocabulary as language acquisition. *Reading Research Quarterly, 47*(1), 91–108.

National Governors Association Center for Best Practices, Council of Chief State School Officers (2010). *Common Core State Standards*. Washington DC: Author.

Neal, H. N. (2015). Theory to practice: Cultivating academic language proficiency in developmental reading classrooms. *Journal of Developmental Education, 39*(1), 12–34.

Paris, D., & Alim, S. (2014). What are we seeking to sustain through culturally sustaining pedagogy? A loving critique forward. *Harvard Educational Review, 81*(1), 85–100.

Parsons, A. W., & Bryant, C. L. (2016). Deepening kindergarteners' science vocabulary: A design study. *The Journal of Educational Research, 109*(4), 375–390.

Peercy, M. M. (2011). Preparing English Language Learners for the mainstream: Academic language and literacy practices in two junior high school ESL classrooms. *Reading & Writing Quarterly: Overcoming Learning DIfficulties, 27*(4), 324–362.

Pelham, S. D., & Abrams, L. (2014). Cognitive advantages and disadvantages in early and late bilinguals. *Journal of Experimental Psychology: Learning, Memory, and Cognition, 40*(2), 313–325.

Practices, N. G. A. C. F. B., & Officers, C. O. C. S. S. (2010). Common core state standards.

Proctor, C. P., Dalton, B., & Grisham, D. L. (2007). Scaffolding English language learners and struggling readers in a universal literacy environment with embedded strategy instruction and vocabulary support. *Journal of Literacy Research, 39*(1), 79–93.

Schleppegrell, M. J. (2004a). Challenges of the science register for ESL students: Errors and meaning-making. In M. J. Schleppegrell & M. C. Colombi (Eds.), *Developing advanced literacy in first and second languages* (pp. 119–142). Mahwah, NJ: Lawrence Erlbaum Associates, Inc.

Schleppegrell, M. J. (2004b). *The language of schooling: A functional linguistics perspective*. Mahwah: NJ Lawrence Erlbaum Associates.

Schleppegrell, M. J. (2007). The linguistic challenges of mathematics teaching and learning: A research review. *Reading and Writing Quarterly, 23*, 139–159.

Schleppegrell, M. J., & de Oliveira, L. C. (2006). An integrated language and content approach for history teachers. *Journal of English for Academic Purposes, 5*, 254–268.

Schleppegrell, M. J., & Go, A. L. (2007). Analyzing the writing of English learners: A functional approach. *Language Arts, 84*, 529–538.

Scott, J. A., Jamieson-Noel, D., & Asselin, M. (2003). Vocabulary instruction throughout the day in twenty-three Canadian upper-elementary classrooms. *The Elementary School Journal, 103*, 269–312.

Shanahan, T., & Shanahan, C. (2012). What is disciplinary literacy and why does it matter? *Topics in Language Disorders, 32*(1), 7–18.

Short, D., Cloud, N., Morris, P., & Motta, J. (2012). Cross-district collaboration: Curriculum and professional development. *TESOL Journal, 3*(3), 402–424.

Short, D. J., Echevarria, J., & Richards-Tutor, C. (2011). Research on academic literacy development in sheltered instruction classrooms. *Language Teaching Research, 15*(3), 363–380.

Short, D. J., Fidelman, C. G., & Louguit, M. (2012). Developing academic language in English language learners through sheltered instruction. *TESOL Quarterly, 46*(2), 334–361.

Short, D. J., & Fitzsimmins, S. (2007). *Double the work: Challenges and solutions to acquiring language and academic literacy for adolescent English language learners.* Washington, DC: Alliance for Excellent Education.

Silverman, R., & Hines, S. (2009). The effects of multimedia-enhanced instruction on the vocabulary of English-language learners and non-English-language learners in pre-kindergarten through second grade. *Journal of Educational Psychology, 101*(2), 305–314.

Snow, C. (2002). *Reading for understanding: Toward an R&D program in reading comprehension.* Santa Monica, CA: RAND.

Snow, C., Lawrence, J. F., & White, C. (2009). Generating knowledge of academic language among urban middle school students. *Journal of Research on Educational Effectiveness, 2*, 325–344.

Snow, C., & Uccelli, P. (2009). The challenge of academic language. In D. R. Olson & N. Torrance (Eds.), *Cambridge handbook of literacy* (pp. 112–133). New York: Cambridge University Press.

Spycher, P. (2007). Academic writing of adolescent English learners: Learning to use "although". *Journal of Second Language Writing, 16*, 238–254.

Spycher, P. (2009). Learning academic language through science in two linguistically diverse kindergarten classes. *The Elementary School Journal, 109*(4), 359–379.

Stahl, S., & Fairbanks, M. M. (1986). The effects of vocabulary instruction: A model-based meta-analysis. *Review of Educational Research, 56*(1), 72–110.

Taboada, A., & Rutherford, V. (2011). Developing reading comprehension and academic vocabulary for English language learners through science content: A formative experiment. *Reading Psychology, 32*, 113–157.

Townsend, D. (2014). Who's using the language? Supporting middle school students with content area academic language. *Journal of Adolescent and Adult Literacy, 58*(5), 372–383.

Townsend, D., & Collins, P. (2009). Academic vocabulary and middle school English learners: An intervention study. *Reading and Writing: an Interdisciplinary Journal, 22*, 993–1019.

Townsend, D., Filippini, A., Collins, P., & Biancarosa, G. (2012). Evidence for the importance of academic word knowledge for the academic achievement of diverse middle school students. *The Elementary School Journal, 112*(2), 497–519.

Uccelli, P., Phillips Galloway, E., Barr, C. D., Meneses, A., & Dobbs, C. L. (2015). Beyond vocabulary: Exploring cross-disciplinary academic-language proficiency and its association with reading comprehension. *Reading Research Quarterly, 50*(3), 337–356. doi: 10.1002/rrq.104.

Vaughn, S., Martinez, L. R., Linan-Thompson, S., Reutenuch, C. K., Carlson, C. D., & Francis, D. J. (2009). Enhancing social studies vocabulary and comprehension for seventh-grade English language learners: Findings from two experimental studies. *Journal of Research on Educational Effectiveness, 2*, 297–324.

WIDA. (2014). *The WIDA standards framework and its theoretical foundations.* Madison, WI: Board of Regents of the University of Wisconsin.

Wolter, J. A., Wood, A., & D'zatko, K. (2009). The influence of morphological awareness on the literacy development of first-grade children. *Language Speech and Hearing Services in Schools, 40*(3), 286–298.

Xue, G., & Nation, I. S. P. (1984). A university word list. *Language Learning and Communication, 3*, 215–229.

Zwiers, J. (2007). Teacher practices and perspectives for developing academic language. *International Journal of Applied Linguistics, 17*, 93–116.

Zwiers, J. (2014). *Building academic language, 2e: Meeting common core standards across disciplines.* San Francisco, CA: Jossey-Bass.

19

High Quality Language Environments Promote Reading Development in Young Children and Older Learners

Perla B. Gámez

Given the global demographic shifts and accelerating advancements in technology, the occupations held by the current workforce will inevitably undergo fundamental transformations, which will lead to changes in the demands of work-related skills (World Economic Forum [WEF], 2014). Of the skills that will be in high demand across a variety of fields, critical thinking has been highlighted as a top skill that will determine academic and life success. Yet, today's youth are not being adequately equipped with the critical thinking skills requisite for success in the workforce, as is evident by the low reading rates worldwide (Gurria, 2016). In the U.S., about 37% of 12th graders score at or above proficient levels in reading comprehension, in line with the numbers in 8th and 4th grade (National Center for Education Statistics, 2015). These statistics imply that a majority of students in U.S. classrooms cannot engage in high-level comprehension, that is, "critical, reflective thinking about text" (Murphy, Wilkinson, Soter, & Hennessey, & Alexandar, 2009).

We now know that engaging students in deep and meaningful language interactions, particularly around text, promotes critical thinking and reading comprehension (Murphy, Firetto, Wei, Li, & Croninger, 2016; Murphy et al., 2009). In fact, the widely adopted standards-based practices aimed at increasing reading rates call for immersing students in language-rich classroom environments, ones that provide frequent opportunities for exposure to and use of high quality language (National Governors Association Center for Best Practices [NGA Center] & Council of Chief State School Officers [CCSSO], 2010). These recommendations are partly based on the well-documented link between language and reading skills (NICHD Early Child Care Research Network, 2005; Storch & Whitehurst, 2002). Despite the critical importance of language to reading, not *all* students have access to language-rich classroom environments. Thus, without a transformation of the classroom language environments in which students are learning to read, there will be a large skills mismatch between the demands of future jobs and what the entering workforce will be able to supply (National Research Council, 2013; WEF, 2014).

Indeed, the findings from existing research on the classroom language environment suggest that this foundational process of the classroom setting serves as a promising lever for improving language and reading outcomes. The goals of this chapter are twofold: to provide an overview of the research findings from separate, but related, sets of literature that reveal the features of the high-quality classroom language environment that promote children's language and reading development as well as discuss the implications of these findings on educational practice and research. Specifically, this chapter includes an overview of the empirical literature on language input (i.e. children's exposure to language), which makes the case that teacher and peer language input influence children's language and reading skills. This chapter also includes an overview of the empirical literature on the language-facilitating techniques that teachers can use to promote students' high-quality language use. The first section of this chapter theoretically motivates the connection between children's exposure to high quality language and their language and reading development. The chapter concludes by identifying critical gaps in our knowledge about the impact of the classroom language environment and suggests future directions for comprehensively exploring how the classroom language environment functions to promote language and reading development.

Connection between High Quality Language and Reading Development

Theoretical Underpinnings

There are numerous theories of reading comprehension that describe the key skills and multi-faceted processes involved in comprehending text (McNamara & Magliano, 2009; RAND Reading Study, 2002). Central variables include the text, which contains high quality language (e.g. sophisticated vocabulary, complex syntactic structures) and the reader, who comes equipped with a host of cognitive and linguistic skills (e.g. knowledge of sophisticated and complex language structures) (Snow, Corno, & Jackson, 1996). A long line of research has established that, of the many reader variables involved, young children's decoding (i.e. word recognition and fluency) and oral language skills (i.e. vocabulary) are crucial to reading comprehension (Gough & Tunmer, 1986; Hoover & Gough, 1990; Joshi & Aaron, 2000; Kirby & Savage, 2008; Language and Reading Research Consortium, 2015; Tunmer & Hoover, 1992; Vellutino, Tumner, Jaccard & Chen, 2007). With age, word recognition skills become more automatic as the vocabulary and syntax demands of the required reading materials increase. Longitudinal studies of reading development underscore the importance of linguistics skills in predicting later reading comprehension (Catts, Herrera, Nielson, & Bridges, 2015; Kendeou, Van den Broek, White, & Lynch, 2009; Ouellette & Beers, 2010; Storch & Whitehurst, 2002). In other words, reading for understanding requires students' knowledge of the language of text (Freebody & Anderson, 1983; Nagy, Anderson, & Herman, 1987), in particular, sophisticated vocabulary and complex syntax (Schleppegrell, 2004; Snow & Uccelli, 2009).

The critical role of high-quality linguistic representations in supporting successful reading comprehension has theoretical support. As explained by the *Lexical Quality Hypothesis* (Perfetti, 2007; Perfetti & Hart, 2002), good reading comprehension depends on the quality of the reader's lexical representations. Quality refers to the extent to which lexical representations include not only orthographical and phonological, but also morphological, syntactic and semantic components of a word. Quality also refers to how integrated these word components are with one another. If lexical representations are high quality, that is, well-specified and redundant (i.e. include all components), then the activation of one component (e.g. syntactic) leads to the activation of the other components (e.g. semantic). The (in)efficiency in retrieving words will lead to (un)successful comprehension of texts.

The more comprehensive *Reading Systems Framework* (RSF; Perfetti & Stafura, 2014) emphasizes a broader set of knowledge sources during reading, with a particular focus on word knowledge, and the cognitive and reading processes that act on these knowledge sources. Within the RSF, the reader's linguistic, orthographic, and general knowledge sources (i.e. about the world, text forms, etc.) are used by a multitude of reading processes (i.e. decoding, word identification, meaning retrieval, sentence parsing, inferencing, and comprehension monitoring) within a cognitive system with limited processing resources. Critically, the mental lexicon, where lexical representations (including semantic and syntactic) are stored, is a central connection point between the word identification system and the comprehension system in the RSF. That is, the interaction between the word identification system and the comprehension system is mediated by lexical knowledge.

An implication of these claims is that a critical foundation to successful reading comprehension is access to high-quality language experiences. In other words, successful reading comprehension depends on children's access to language environments that create high-quality language experiences, ones in which words and their multiple components (e.g. semantics, syntax) are encountered frequently. In the classroom setting, opportunities for children to encounter words arise through their exposure to and use of written (i.e. texts) and oral language (i.e. oral discussions).

The Features of High Quality Language

In particular, academic language permeates the entire school curriculum and therefore, opportunities that ensure children's exposure to and use of academic language is central to their academic success. Academic language is typically referred to as the language of schooling; a set of registers (oral, written) used at school to engage with disciplinary content (Bailey, Butler, Stevens, & Lord, 2007; Barnes, Grifenhagen, & Dickinson, 2016; Cummins, 1979; Nagy & Townsend, 2012; Schleppegrell, 2009; Snow & Uccelli, 2009; Valdes, 2004). Unlike more informal language, which is typically conveyed through contextual cues and face-to-face conversation, academic language is often decontextualized (i.e. removed from the here and now) and thus, relies more heavily on the use of linguistic over contextual cues in the environment (Snow, 1983). Of the many linguistic expectations of academic language, its use requires knowledge of specific vocabulary and syntactic structures (Snow & Uccelli, 2009). More expansive definitions of academic language are offered elsewhere, for example, that cover what students understand about the morphology and discourse function of academic language (Uccelli, Galloway, Barr, Meneses, & Dobbs, 2015).

Descriptions of High Quality Language Features

Two widely cited features of academic language include sophisticated vocabulary and complex syntax. Sophisticated vocabulary refers to low-frequency words that fall outside of the most commonly heard words in everyday interactions (Weizman & Snow, 2001), but which are characteristic of text (Dickinson, Hofer, Barnes, & Grifenhagen, 2014). Syntax refers to the set of rules for combining words into sentences in any given language. A principal feature of academic language is its syntactic complexity, which is typically characterized as the use of various syntactic structures and different patterns of embedded structures (Barnes et al., 2016; Huttenlocher, Vasilyeva, Cymerman, & Levine, 2002; Scarcella, 2003; Schleppegrell, 2001; Snow & Uccelli, 2009). For example, in academic language, sentences contain multiple clauses (i.e. a verb phrase and other accompanying elements) that are either embedded in or conjoined with one another. Snow and Uccelli (2009), like Halliday (1994), argue that a distinctive feature of academic language is embeddedness, where one element of a sentence is a structural part of another element, as opposed to being dependent on (but not part of) another clause. Structures like embedded clauses allow for the expression of a density of information, and thus, complex sentences are typically (but not necessarily) longer than simple sentences.

In fact, syntactic complexity is thought of as linguistic tool that allows for the expression of complex ideas within one sentence (Huttenlocher et al., 2002). Halliday (1994) explains that children are simultaneously engaged in learning language and learning through language (i.e. form and meaning). The progression from mastering simple to complex syntax is viewed as a process of "learning how to mean." In other words, with new forms of language come new forms of knowledge because in learning to use varied grammatical forms, children can construct meanings for a range of purposes. Learning the complex syntactic forms that are typical of the academic register thus allows children to express and think about more complex ideas than they would with simple sentences.

High Quality Language Measures

Various measures are available for estimating children's use of and exposure to sophisticated vocabulary and complex syntax across different ages. Existing word lists are useful in identifying sophisticated or rare words from high-frequency words (e.g. words commonly known to 4th graders: Chall & Dale, 1995; Academic Word List (AWL): Coxhead, 2000; General Service List: West, 1953). These lists can be used to filter out high-frequency words in order to calculate the diversity of sophisticated words, commonly referred to as the number of different sophisticated words (i.e. types), in a sample of speech or text; this is versus the total number of words or words (i.e. tokens). A smaller set of different sophisticated word types reflects low diversity; a higher set of different sophisticated word types reflects greater diversity.

Common methods for estimating the syntactic complexity of speech and text include calculating the mean length of utterance (MLU) and proportion of complex utterances. An utterance refers to an uninterrupted stream of speech that is typically bounded by pauses, intonation, and conversational turns (MacWhinney, 2007). MLU quantifies utterance length in either words (MLUw) or morphemes (MLUm), which are the smallest units of meaning in an utterance (e.g. "books" consists of one word, but two morphemes: the word form book and the plural marker "s"). These two measures of utterance length are highly correlated with each other (Parker & Brorson, 2005), at least at early stages of language development. According to the rules set forth by Brown (1973), the total number of morphemes (or words) is divided by the total number of utterances in a sample of at least 100 intelligible utterances (Miller & Chapman, 1981). These calculations can be done by hand or with free and publicly-available computer software (e.g. Computerized Language ANalysis; CLAN; MacWhinney, 2007). MLU is considered a broad indicator of syntactic complexity as larger values indicate longer utterances and thus, greater syntactic complexity.

Some scholars suggest that MLU provides a less accurate assessment of syntactic complexity at later stages of language development, in comparison to earlier stages (Scarborough, 1990; Scarborough, Rescorla, Tager-Flusberg, Fowler, & Sudhalter, 1991; Vasilyeva, Waterfall, & Huttenlocher, 2008). Huttenlocher and colleagues (Huttenlocher et al., 2002; Vasilyeva et al., 2008) thus offer an alternative measure of syntactic complexity that can be used across ages, specifically, the proportion of complex utterances in speech or text. This figure is calculated over the total number of utterances in the speech or text sample. In order to derive this measure of syntactic complexity, each utterance is classified as either multi-clause (i.e. containing more than one clause) or not (i.e. zero-clauses or one-clause). Multi-clause utterances are generally considered complex. The type of complex utterance can be further categorized based on the structural relations between the clauses, for example, embeddedness. In the following section we review the bodies of literature on language input that use these principle measures of high quality language, specifically sophisticated vocabulary and complex syntax, and provide evidence for the connection between language interactions and language development.

Connection between Language Development and Language Exposure

The social-cultural framework emphasizes the importance of both the learner and the environment in shaping language development (Bruner, 1983; Vygotsky, 1978). Language is considered a by-product of social interaction as well as the primary social tool for communication. In strong opposition to the proposal that language acquisition is innate (Chomsky, 1981), interactionists (Snow, 1994; Tomasello, 2000) emphasize the joint contribution of children's innate language learning capacities and their exposure to and use of language in the language learning process. According to the interactionist approach, the optimal language learning environment is one in which children are provided with scaffolded language interactions, in which more knowledgeable people (e.g. caregivers, teachers, and more advanced peers) expose children to language that is slightly above the child's current level of linguistic skill. Specifically, language-rich environments lead to exposure to the increasingly sophisticated and complex language that children are expected to master with age.

The *Emergentist Coalition Model* (Hirsh-Pasek, Golinkoff, & Hollich, 2000) of language learning further explains the connection between language input and language development. The ECM posits that the language learner relies on a "coalition" of information sources, which shift in importance across development. At the earliest stages of language development, children rely heavily on the perceptual features of words that "stand out" and grab their attention (e.g. Smith, 2000). Over time, children shift their reliance onto social (e.g. eye gaze, gestures; Tomasello, 2000) and linguistic cues, such as the vocabulary and syntax of language input. As they mature, the linguistic cues provided by input become the prominent sources of information that inform learning (Hoff & Naigles, 2002). For example, word learners use their knowledge of syntactic structures and/or known words in the input to figure out the meaning of unknown words (Gleitman, 1990; Landau & Gleitman, 1985).

The Home Language Environment: Caregiver Language Input

A long line of descriptive and longitudinal research on young children's language development shows evidence of a relation between children's language skills and the language input provided by caregivers at home (Hart & Risley, 1995; Hoff, 2003; Huttenlocher, Haight, Bryk, Seltzer, & Lyons, 1991; Pan, Rowe, Snow & Singer, 2005; Weizman & Snow, 2001). While the amount of caregiver language input is thought to be important at the earliest stages of language learning (Huttenlocher et al., 1991), indicators of the quality of input appear to be more potent predictors of language skills as children age (Hirsh-Pasek et al., 2015; Pan et al., 2005). In particular, caregivers' sophisticated word types is predictive of their children's vocabulary skills, above and beyond their amount of input (Weizman & Snow, 2001). The idea is that exposure to a diverse set of sophisticated words provides children with multiple exemplars of words and how they are used to convey different meanings across contexts.

Another indicator of the quality of language input is the syntactic complexity of caregivers' speech. Caregivers' longer MLUs—in words and morphemes—are typically associated with children's syntactic as well as vocabulary development (Bornstein, Haynes, & Painter, 1998; Hoff, E., 2003; Hoff & Naigles, 2002; Hoff-Ginsberg, 1998). The proportion of caregivers' complex utterances also predicts young children's syntactic development (Bornstein et al., 1998; Hoff &

Naigles, 2002; Hoff-Ginsberg, 1998). Of note, a longitudinal study of caregiver–child interactions showed a relation between caregivers' use of syntactic structures when the children were 14 months, and the corresponding syntactic structures in the children's speech at 46 months (Huttenlocher, Waterfall, Vasilyeva, Vevea, & Hedges, 2010). In that study, the child's earlier syntax did not significantly predict later caregiver syntax. Of note, this unidirectional association points to a causal role of caregivers' use of a particular syntactic structure on children's subsequent learning of those syntactic structures.

These findings of a positive relation between young children's language skills and their caregivers' language use lend credence to the argument that children's foundational reading skills, including vocabulary and syntax, are shaped by their early language experiences. In particular, young children with access to high quality language environments, in which they hear more diverse and complex language, will develop more advanced vocabulary and syntactic skills. Thus, a promising way to improve children's language skills and reading development is to improve their early access to high-quality language experiences.

The Classroom Language Environment: Teacher Language Input

The language-rich classroom environment is an additional source of exposure to the sophisticated vocabulary and complex syntax that school-age children are expected to comprehend, particularly in text (Snow & Uccelli, 2009). Exposure to high-quality, language-rich classrooms may be particularly important for children with limited opportunities for English language exposure at home, for example, if the primary home language does not match the language of instruction (e.g. dual language learners [DLLs], English language learners, second language learners). In fact, DLLs[1] with limited English proficiency are generally characterized, as a group, as "at risk" for English-related reading difficulties (National Center for Education Statistics [NCES], 2015), in part due to their insufficient command of English. Indeed, research highlights the importance of well-developed language skills in preventing reading difficulties in young DLLs akin to the relation observed for English-only (EO) children (August & Shanahan, 2006; Hammer et al., 2014; Lonigan, Farver, Nakamoto, & Eppe, 2013).

Decades of research show that teachers consume the majority of the total classroom talk time (Cazden, 2001; Chaudron, 1988; Mehan, 1979; Mercer, 1995), thus implicating teachers' language use as a significant input source across the school years. At the same time, classroom observation studies reveal wide variation in terms of the quality of teacher language input (e.g., Dickinson et al., 2014; Gámez & Lesaux, 2015), which appears to be stable over the school year (Gámez & Lesaux, 2015). This variability across classrooms in terms of teacher language input indicates substantial disparities in children's access to high-quality classroom language environments. These classroom-based language disparities are significant in light of research findings that suggest a long-lasting influence of early high-quality classroom language experiences on children's development (Burchinal et al., 2008; Dickinson & Porche, 2011; NICHD Early Child Care Research Network, 2000; Mashburn et al., 2008; Peisner-Feinberg et al., 2001; Pianta, La Paro, Payne, Cox, & Bradley, 2002).

Teacher Input and Young Children's Language Development

In particular, exposure to teachers' syntactic complexity is associated with young EO and DLL children's vocabulary and syntactic skills (Bowers & Vasilyeva, 2011; Gámez & Levine, 2013; Huttenlocher et al., 2002). In a seminal study of teacher input in preschool classrooms, Huttenlocher and colleagues (Huttenlocher et al., 2002) found a positive relation between teachers' syntactic complexity and their EO students' growth on a syntactic comprehension task, from fall to spring of the preschool year. In that study, children's syntactic comprehension was measured using a researcher-developed assessment with items that increased in length and complexity. During the middle of the school year, teachers' language was audio-recorded in order to calculate their number of multi-clause utterances and derive the proportion of complex utterances. The results revealed more syntactic growth in the preschoolers who were exposed to teachers with a higher proportion of complex utterances, in comparison to preschoolers with teachers with a lower proportion of complex utterances. Gámez and Levine (2013) also relied on naturalistic observation techniques to measure teachers' language use, including syntactic complexity, in kindergarten classrooms designed expressly for DLLs; the language of instruction was the DLLs' native language (Transitional Bilingual Education program; TBE). The DLLs' native Spanish skills were assessed in the fall and spring, using standardized vocabulary and sentence-level assessments. The study results revealed that the TBE teachers' proportion of complex utterances was positively associated with their DLL students' Spanish language skill gains, including in the domains of vocabulary and syntax.

In another study of teacher language input in English-speaking preschools, Bowers and Vasilyeva (2011) audio-recorded teachers' language use with their EO and limited-English proficient DLL students. The study findings showed that teachers' syntactic complexity, as measured by MLUw, was negatively related to their DLL students' gains on a standardized measure of vocabulary, from the fall to the spring of the academic year. There was no significant relation between teachers' MLUw and EO children's skill gains. The negative association with MLUw in that study contends with the results from the only other study—to date—that assesses the relation between teachers' MLUw in English and young DLLs' English skills (Gámez, 2015). Specifically, Gámez (2015) found a positive association between limited-English proficient DLLs' gains in English vocabulary and sentence-level skills and their teachers' vocabulary diversity. Teachers' vocabulary diversity in English was measured during the English Language Development (ELD) blocks, which are portions of the school day that are designated for English language instruction in an otherwise Spanish-speaking classroom.

It is worth noting that, on average, the TBE teachers in Gámez's (2015) study used lower MLUw's (~4 words) than did the teachers in Bowers and Vasilyeva's (2011) study (~5 words). This pattern of results suggests that teachers tailored their speech to match their students' language skills, a hypothesis that is supported by developmental theories that outline the adults' role in scaffolding children's learning experiences (Bruner, 1983; Vygotsky, 1978). It is also worth noting that in line with the methodology used in this line of research, the measures of teacher input in these two studies were gleaned from portions of the school day when whole-group instruction was taking place. Thus, the differences in teachers' syntactic complexity between these studies reflect the differences in the skill level of the respective classrooms, as a whole, and not individual students' language skills. In this case, the non-TBE teachers may have tailored their speech toward their EO students, who are English proficient, whereas the TBE teachers tailored their speech toward their limited-English proficient students.

The results from a recent study of teachers' MLUw in Head Start classrooms, where teachers used, on average, almost nine words per utterance (Barnes, Dickinson, & Grifenhagen, 2017), provide further support for the idea that the optimal language environment is one in which language input is slightly beyond, but not too far from, a child's current level of independent performance (i.e. Zone of Proximal Development; Vygotsky, 1978). That study involved children who performed below the national mean on a standardized receptive vocabulary measure. The results showed that children in classrooms where teachers used, on average, longer utterances evidenced lower vocabulary outcomes than did children with teachers who used shorter utterances. The authors explained this negative relation of teachers' increased MLUw to their students' decreased vocabulary gains as an artifact of the processing demands that are required by longer sentences. That is, overly long utterances may be too challenging for children with still-developing language skills.

The hypothesis that teachers' high quality language serves to extend children's language skills is also supported by research findings of a relation between preschool teachers' sophisticated vocabulary and their EO and DLL students' vocabulary development (Barnes et al., 2017; Bowers & Vasilyeva, 2011; Dickinson & Porche, 2011; Dickinson & Smith, 1994). Specifically, Bowers and Vasilyeva's (2011) study findings revealed a positive association between preschool teachers' vocabulary diversity and their EO students' vocabulary skill gains from fall to spring. Whereas there were null effects of the diversity of their teachers' vocabulary diversity for DLLs, their English vocabulary skill gains were positively related to teachers' amount of input (i.e. word tokens). In contrast, Gámez and Levine (2013) found that DLLs' Spanish skill gains were positively associated with their teachers' vocabulary diversity. The differential influence of vocabulary diversity on DLLs' native and second (English) language skills suggests that input might function differently for children at different stages of development, akin to the findings from home-based language input studies. That is, the quantity of teachers' language may matter more at the early stages of language development, whereas later stages of language development are better supported by exposure to high quality language, which includes sophisticated and complex language features.

Teacher Input and Older Learners' Language Development

Indeed, a smaller, but growing research-base shows a link between the high-quality language input provided by teachers and older learners' language and reading skills. In a series of studies conducted in middle schools serving high numbers of DLLs (up to 93% DLL), Gámez and Lesaux (2012; 2015) found a positive relation between ELA teachers' language use and their 6th grade EO and DLL students' vocabulary and reading outcomes. These studies were conducted in classrooms where instruction was provided exclusively in English and teachers' use of high quality language, for example, vocabulary diversity, was gleaned from video-recorded observations of English Language Arts (ELA) classes. The findings revealed a link between teachers' sophisticated vocabulary and students'—DLLs and EOs alike—English outcomes on standardized measures of reading and researcher-developed measures of vocabulary. Yet, there was no significant relation between these outcome measures and the total amount of teacher language input.

Another noteworthy finding from these classroom-based input studies is that the influence of teachers' complex syntax differed for DLLs as a function of their English language proficiency (Gámez & Lesaux, 2012). Specifically, while teachers' vocabulary diversity was positively associated with DLLs' English vocabulary skills, regardless of students' language proficiency, teachers' syntactic complexity (as measured by the proportion of complex utterances) was positively associated with English vocabulary outcomes for DLLs, specifically those who had attained "advanced" levels of English proficiency (as measured on a state-level test of language proficiency). Important to note is that there were null effects of teachers' syntactic complexity for DLLs with less-than-advanced levels of language proficiency; it was not the case that the relation was negative. These results suggest that teachers may extend older learners' language skills by exposure to sophisticated vocabulary and complex syntax, and that learners may filter out—without negative consequences—input that is not finely-tuned to the learners' language skill (i.e. may be too complex); a similar process that has been proposed for young children (Hoff, 2006).

Summary of Research on Teacher Input

The findings from studies on teacher input indicate that teachers can promote the development of sophisticated vocabulary and complex syntax by providing ample opportunities for exposure to high quality language that includes sophisticated and complex language features. In particular, this line of research suggests that in order to effectively support and extend children's language skills, teachers should aim to fine tune their speech to meet the language needs of their students, not only in early childhood, but also in early adolescence. Given the connection between reading and language, gaining exposure to high quality language environments is a critical step toward improving school-age children's language and reading difficulties.

The Classroom Language Environment: Peers' Language Use

Within the context of language interactions, the expert-learner imbalance of knowledge that is thought to propel learning forward can also take the form of a relationship between the student, as the learner, and more advanced peers, as the experts. Classroom observation studies that document teacher–student interactions demonstrate that children are most likely to be involved in whole-group configuration led by teachers, in comparison to any other configurations (Pianta et al., 2005). When not involved in whole-group classroom configurations, children are in small groups of peers where an adult is rarely present (Powell, Burchinal, File, & Kontos, 2008). Thus, like teacher-student interactions, student-peer interactions can serve as sites for linguistic exploration. Peer interactions can provide opportunities for language modeling, where learners are exposed to a variety of linguistic forms, including diverse vocabulary and complex syntax. Peer interactions can also provide opportunities for children to practice stretching their current linguistic repertoire.

While less research has examined the influence of peer talk, over teacher talk, a few studies—albeit mostly in preschool classrooms—point to the positive influence of peer language input on children's language skills (Grøver, Lawrence, & Rydland, 2016; Rydland, Grøver, & Lawrence, 2014). For example, in a study of DLL-peer interactions in preschool classrooms, Palermo and Mikulski (2014) found that peers' amount of English use in the fall was related to DLLs' performance on a standardized measure of English vocabulary in the spring. Specifically, using a time-sampling method, the researchers measured target children's English exposure as the number of times their peers used English during play sessions in preschool classrooms. Also, in the aforementioned study of the classroom language environment in TBE kindergarten classrooms, Gámez (2015) found a positive association between DLLs' gains in English (i.e. vocabulary and sentence-level skills) and the vocabulary diversity of classroom peers. Thus, the quantity and quality of peers' language use may be important for promoting young DLLs' language development.

It is worth noting that the findings from these studies that include a fine-grained linguistic analysis of children's classroom-based language interactions are in line with large-scale studies that document the relation of children's language skills to their preschool language environments, for example, as measured by the level of their peers' language ability (Justice, Petscher, Schatschneider, & Mashburn, 2011; Mashburn, Justice, Downer, & Pianta, 2009). In one study, Mashburn and colleagues (2009) assessed EO preschoolers' expressive and receptive language (i.e. vocabulary and sentence-level skills) from fall to spring in preschool and found that the average level of peers' language skill in the class predicted the spring scores of the children in that classroom. Justice and colleagues (2011) further showed that while there was not a significant peer effect for students with already-high levels of language skills, it was particularly strong for children with low language skills at the start of the school year.

These findings of a positive influence of peer input in preschool classrooms indicate that peers serve as potentially critical sources of information for learning language, including development of precursor literacy skills such as vocabulary. Notably, these findings indicate that increasing the frequency of children's interactions with their peers (input quantity), who provide high quality input (input quality), is particularly influential for children with low language skills. Thus, a promising avenue for improving children's language and reading skills is a targeted effort to create classroom activities that allow for peer interactions, particularly ones in which children can hear and practice using high quality language.

Practice Recommendations: Implementing Language-Facilitating Techniques

One widely recommended activity for promoting language development is shared book reading, in part because it affords children opportunities to not only hear vocabulary embedded in various grammatical structures, but also practice producing language. In shared book reading contexts, adults read books aloud to children and actively engage them with text (National Research Council, 1998; What Works Clearinghouse, 2013). Several meta-analyses of shared book reading in early childhood classrooms show a robust relation between children's participation in shared book reading and their vocabulary development (e.g. Mol, Bus, De Jong, & Smeets, 2008). Accumulating research also reports significant, but smaller, effects than for vocabulary, including narrative production, which encompasses skill in a variety of other language domains, including syntax (Gamez, Gonzalez, & Urbin, 2017; Sénéchal, Pagan, Lever, & Ouellette, 2008; Zevenbergen, Whitehurst, & Zevenbergen, 2003).

Particularly for struggling readers, teacher read alouds that consist of sophisticated vocabulary and complex language can serve as a scaffold that bridges the gap between children's current linguistic abilities and what reading tasks require. During reading, teachers' behaviors that facilitate language use, for example, highlighting or discussing the language of the text as well as expanding on students' own language use, have been shown to support language learning (review in Pentimonti et al., 2012). In particular, expanding on or recasting children's short or incomplete utterances into complete and/or more complex and grammatically correct sentences may help young children practice and then acquire more complex syntactic structures (Barnes et al., 2017).

In general, shared reading experiences play an important role in promoting children's oral language when children are actively involved in discussions (e.g., Wasik & Bond, 2001; Wasik, Bond, & Hindman, 2006; Whitehurst et al., 1994). In fact, interactive styles of shared book reading produce larger effects on oral language skills than do non-interactive styles (Gerde & Powell, 2009; Zucker, Cabell, Justice, Pentimonti, & Kaderavek, 2013). For example, young children in preschool and kindergarten classrooms with teachers who engage in more extra-textual talk (i.e., talk around text) make greater gains in vocabulary, in comparison with children in classrooms with teachers who rely less on extra-textual talk, and this is the case not only for EOs, but DLLs as well (Gamez et al., 2017).

For the older learner, the opportunity to engage in text-based classroom discussions, particularly if they are small-group, has also been shown to be a critical factor in text comprehension (Murphy et al., 2009; Wolf, Crosson, & Resnick, 2006). Middle and high-school students' reading skills are positively related to the amount of time spent in classroom discussion (Applebee, Langer, Nystrand, & Gamoran, 2003; Gamoran & Nystrand, 1991). However, recent meta-analyses reveal that not all discussion approaches generate the type of talk that is associated with high-level comprehension and critical thinking (Murphy et al., 2009).

Instead, this line of research identifies several language-facilitating techniques that teachers of older learners can use to promote classroom discussion, and thus, text comprehension (Nystrand, Wu, Gamoran, Zeiser, & Long, 2003; Soter et al., 2008). For example, when teachers ask open-ended questions, they allow for extended responses from the student. Students' extended responses allows them to practice producing different language forms, including sophisticated vocabulary and complex syntax. A distinction is made between "authentic" and unauthentic questions, the latter which typically are represented by "test" questions, which require only brief responses with pre-specified answers from the student. Authentic questions do not seek pre-specified answers and instead, require extended responses from students. Another category of questions is labeled "uptake" questions because they incorporate a previous response into a question (Boyd & Rubin, 2006).

In their analysis of discussion approaches that lead to high-level text comprehension, across a range of grade and age levels, Soter et al. (2008) found that authentic questions tended to lead to more opportunities for students' to engage in elaborated explanations and thus, "high-level thinking" (Nystrand, Gamoran, Kachur, & Prendergast, 1997). The authors took Webb's (Webb, Farivar, & Mastergeorge, 2002) stance that elaborated explanations fosters students' "cognitive restructuring" because it encourages them to reorganize the material presented to the class in order to ensure that it will be comprehensible (Soter et al., 2008). In addition, elaborated explanations force students to recognize the gaps in their understanding.

Taken together, the findings from the literature base on language-facilitating techniques—that can be used with young children as well as older learners—suggest that teachers must share the floor with their students by gradually releasing their control and allowing students to take on more responsibility for the discussion. That is, a high-quality language environment is one in which the teacher exposes students to sufficiently sophisticated and complex language, while also incorporating language-facilitating techniques that invite students to produce such speech and engage in high-level thinking. Thus, increasing students' opportunities to engage in classroom discussions is one way to augment and elevate the classroom language environment, which can function as a support for language and reading development.

Future Directions that Address the Gaps in Our Knowledge-Base

The research findings on the importance of high-quality classroom language environments for promoting language and reading skills—in young children and older learners—reinforce the need to study the foundational processes of the classroom setting, in addition to specific instructional practices. The research studies reviewed here suggest that a critical lever for improving children's language and literacy skills is access to high-quality language environments, ones that allows for exposure to and use of the sophisticated and complex language features that children are expected to comprehend in text, in particular, through fine-tuned teacher and peer language input as well as teachers' language-facilitating techniques. Questions remain, however, regarding when, for whom, and how the classroom language environment functions to promote language and reading development. Identifying these critical gaps in our knowledge base will help improve learning for *all* students and will provide the basis for future research directions.

For example, much of the existing classroom language research employs correlational designs, where language input and children's language use have not been systematically manipulated (i.e. in which classroom language interactions unfold naturally), and thus, these findings cannot be interpreted as causal. While the associations between the classroom language environment and children's language and reading outcomes are consistent findings in the literature, it is possible that unmeasured variables account for some results. Research studies employing experimental designs are thus needed in order to rule out competing explanations.

One candidate experimental technique for examining the relation of input to children's language skills comes from the psycholinguistics literature. Specifically, the structural priming technique—in which children are asked to describe pictures after exposure to one of two alternating syntactic forms (e.g., actives, passives)—allows researchers to systematically manipulate children's language input in a controlled environment (Bock, 1986; review in Pickering & Ferreira, 2008). Making the case for providing finely-tuned complex syntactic input, the results of these studies show that the modeling of developmentally-advanced syntactic forms, including passives, in comparison to actives, leads to an increase in the comprehension and production of passives, not only for preschool- and kindergarten-age monolingual speakers (Huttenlocher, Vasilyeva, & Shimpi, 2004), but DLLs as well (Gámez & Shimpi, 2016; Gámez & Vasilyeva, 2015). Other manipulations to consider in experimental research are to systematically vary children's language exposure in terms of the number and diversity of vocabulary and syntactic forms that are presented to children of different ages.

On this note, much of the existing classroom language literature has focused on the domain of vocabulary, at the expense of other language domains, both in terms of language input and children's language skills. In fact, while there has been an increase in the number of curriculum intervention studies that are focused on vocabulary learning in the early grades (Beck & McKeown, 2007; Biemiller & Boote, 2006), there has been less of an emphasis on syntax interventions in classrooms. Yet, there is evidence to suggest that syntax can be improved through classroom interventions (Vasilyeva, Huttenlocher, & Waterfall, 2006). For example, in one syntax intervention study, preschool children heard stories that contained a high proportion of passive sentences; a control group heard the same stories with a high proportion of active sentences. At post-test, the children who heard more passive sentences outperformed the children who heard more active sentences on the production and comprehension of passives. Given the low frequency of passives in children's speech, children's improved passive production and comprehension, after exposure to passives, shows that children's syntax is sensitive to changes in the language environment. Future research should explore the effectiveness of classroom interventions that vary the structural complexity and sophistication of language interactions, paying attention to vocabulary and syntax that is common in academic texts and discourse.

Also, the classroom-based language input studies that include fine-grained linguistic analyses—in order to identify specific features of the classroom language environment that promote development—typically include observations of language interactions at one time-point. Otherwise, large-scale studies that include more than one time-point typically rely on broader indicators of language input (e.g., the existence and frequency of teacher–student interactions), which are gleaned from coding schemes that are applied to in-class or videotaped language interactions (e.g. Castro, 2005; Pianta, Karen, Paro, & Hamre, 2008; Sprachman, Caspe, & Atkins-Burnett, 2009; Smith, Dickinson, Sangeorge, & Anastasopoulos, 2002). Of note, limiting the number of participant observations in classroom-based language research limits the laborious transcription and coding efforts required of fine-grained analyses. Yet, in order to begin to answer questions related to the consistencies and changes in teachers' and students' language use over time, studies that include multiple classroom observations are needed. Recent advances in technology (such as audio and video) have already made the collection of data more cost-effective and feasible than in years past. Further advances in computing technology (such as artificial intelligence) may facilitate fine-grained analysis given its potential to dramatically increase transcribing and coding productivity. Thus, a worthwhile direction for future research is to examine whether and how language use changes over time by increasing the number of observation time-points and sample sizes that are typically used in these lines of research.

The existing classroom language literature base also does not fully elucidate why high-quality classroom language promotes children's language and reading development, in part because the two sets of literature on language input and language-facilitating techniques tackle different variables of interest. For example, it is possible that teacher's use of language-facilitating techniques, including asking authentic questions, is also more syntactically complex and includes more sophisticated vocabulary than other linguistic forms. In order to tackle the question of whether particular utterance types (e.g. open-ended questions) evoke complex and sophisticated language use, a logical next step is to comprehensively explore the multiple features of the classroom language environment and co-vary the different candidate linguistic forms. To do so will not only require large study sample sizes, but also that researchers harness the diversity in theoretical assumptions, methodology, and discipline-specific conventions that are represented by their respective fields.

Moreover, the theoretical models reviewed here make it clear that the characteristics of the learner and the group interact with text to impact development. Yet, many of the studies of the classroom language environment have emphasized the importance of language interactions, particularly within whole-group settings, with a primary focus on the teachers' language use. While the sophistication and complexity of vocabulary and syntax may differ by instructional contexts (e.g., book reading vs. centers) or topics (e.g., science vs. ELA), only recently have researchers attempted to explore the different settings that evoke different types of talk (Dickinson et al., 2014). Emerging work has also begun to explore the interdependencies of teachers' and students' use of complex language (Justice, McGinty, Zucker, Cabell, & Piasta, 2013) and reveals a complex, bi-directional relation between teachers' and students' language use. Additional research is needed to explore the different instructional contexts, topics, and classroom configurations (e.g. small-group vs. whole-group; teacher-led vs. student/peer-led) that promote high-quality language use.

Given the linguistic and cultural diversity in today's classrooms (Krogstad & Lopez, 2014; Suitts, 2015), another timely direction for future research is to extend these lines of research and comprehensively explore the classroom language environments of different learners. In particular, more research is needed to better understand how classroom language functions to promote reading development for children with different language profiles, including English-only and DLLs, and in classrooms with students of different cultural and ethnic backgrounds. The available research suggests that the average quality of DLLs' language learning environments is less than good (Jacoby & Lesaux, 2014), especially in programs serving the lowest-income families (NICHD, 2000; Peisner-Feinberg et al., 2001; Scarr, Eisenberg, & Deater-Deckard, 1994). Given their fast growth rate, further investigations into how the classroom language environment promotes language and reading development, particularly in classrooms that serve high numbers of DLLs, represents an investment in the U.S.' future.

Conclusions

In the meantime, the bodies of literature reviewed in this chapter suggest that efforts to improve language and reading skills should include augmenting and elevating the language of the classroom. In order to become skillful in the language of text, children must experience language-rich environments that include the diverse set of words and variety of syntactic structures that are common in text. The responsibility to create high-quality, language-rich classrooms will fall mostly on teachers, who will need to to lead deep and meaningful classroom conversations with their students. Therefore, teachers will require professional development opportunities to learn about what makes for, and how to create, high-quality language environments with different learner profiles. Of note, previous efforts to change teachers' language practices have proven to be challenging (Dickinson, 2011; Wasik et al., 2006). Changing, and later supporting, the changes in teachers' language practices likely involves changes in educational policy and teacher preparation, not only practice, which will require extensive resources, including investments in time and funding. Of note, many of the studies reviewed here rely on naturalistic observation techniques, which means that many teachers are already well-versed in the language practices that make for a high-quality classroom language environment. Thus, transforming classrooms into high-quality language environments, ones that provide frequent opportunities for exposure to and use of the high quality language that promotes reading, is a feasible way to prepare our nation's students for successful academic and life outcomes.

Note

1 Given the lack of consensus in the field about terminology, the term Dual Language Learner (DLL) is used here to refer to children negotiating two language systems; who learn two languages, including English from birth or sequentially, or who are in the process of learning English as second language.

References

Applebee, A. N., Langer, J. A., Nystrand, M., & Gamoran, A. (2003). Discussion-based approaches to developing understanding: Classroom instruction and student performance in middle and high school English. *American Educational Research Journal, 40*(3), 685–730.

August, D., & Shanahan, T. (Eds.). (2006). *Developing literacy in second language learners: Report of the national literacy panel on language minority children and youth.* Mahwah, NJ: Erlbaum.

Bailey, A. L., Butler, F. A., Stevens, R., & Lord, C. (2007). Further specifying the language demands of school. In A. L. Bailey (Ed.), *Language demands of school: Putting academic language to the test* (pp. 103–156). New Haven, CT: Yale University Press.

Barnes, E. M., Dickinson, D. K., & Grifenhagen, J. F. (2017). The role of teachers' comments during book reading in children's vocabulary growth. *The Journal of Educational Research, 110*(5), 515–527.

Barnes, E. M., Grifenhagen, J. F., & Dickinson, D. K. (2016). Academic language in early childhood classrooms. *The Reading Teacher, 70*(1), 39–48.

Beck, I. L., & McKeown, M. G. (2007). Increasing young low-income children's oral vocabulary repertoires through rich and focused instruction. *The Elementary School Journal, 107*(3), 251–271.

Biemiller, A., & Boote, C. (2006). An effective method for building meaning vocabulary in primary grades. *Journal of Educational Psychology, 98*(1), 44.

Bock, K. (1986). Syntactic persistence in language production. *Cognitive Psychology, 18*, 355–387.

Bornstein, M. H., Haynes, M. O., & Painter, K. M. (1998). Sources of child vocabulary competence: A multivariate model. *Journal of Child Language, 25*(2), 367–393.

Bowers, E., & Vasilyeva, M. (2011). The relation between teacher input and lexical growth of preschoolers. *Applied Psycholinguistics, 32*, 221–241.

Boyd, M., & Rubin, D. (2006). How contingent questioning promotes extended student talk: A function of display questions. *Journal of Literacy Research, 38*(2), 141–169.

Brown, R. W. (1973). *A first language: The early stages.* Cambridge, MA: Harvard University Press.

Bruner, J. (1983). *Child's talk.* New York: Norton.

Burchinal, M., Howes, C., Pianta, R., Bryant, D., Early, D., Clifford, R., & Barbarin, O. (2008). Predicting child outcomes at the end of kindergarten from the quality of pre-kindergarten teacher-child interactions and instruction. *Applied Developmental Science, 12*(3), 140–153.

Castro, D. C. (2005). *Early language and literacy classroom observation: Addendum for English language learners.* Chapel Hill, NC: The University of North Carolina, FPG Child Development Institute.

Catts, H. W., Herrera, S., Nielsen, D. C., & Bridges, M. S. (2015). Early prediction of reading comprehension within the simple view framework. *Reading and Writing, 28*(9), 1407–1425.

Cazden, C. B. (2001). *Classroom discourse: The language of teaching and learning* (2nd ed.). Portsmouth, NH: Heinemann.

Chall, J., & Dale, E. (1995). *Readability revisited: The new Dale-Chall readability formula.* Cambridge, MA: Brookline.

Chaudron, C. (1988). *Second language classrooms: Research on teaching and learning.* New York, NY: Cambridge University Press.

Chomsky, N. (1981). *Lectures on government and binding.* Dordrecht, The Netherlands: Foris.

Clearinghouse, W. W. (2013). *WWC review of the report "The impact of collaborative strategic reading on the reading comprehension of grade 5 students in linguistically diverse schools."* Washington, DC: Institute of Education Sciences, U.S. Department of Education. Retrieved from http://ies.ed.gov/ncee/wwc/Docs/SingleStudyReviews/wwc_csr_071613.pdf

Coxhead, A. (2000). A new Academic Word List. *TESOL Quarterly, 34*, 213–238.

Cummins, J. (1979). Linguistic interdependence and the educational development of bilingual children. *Review of educational research, 49*(2), 222–251.

Dickinson, D. K. (2011). Teachers' language practices and academic outcomes of preschool children. *Science, 333*(6045), 964–967.

Dickinson, D. K., Hofer, K. G., Barnes, E. M., & Grifenhagen, J. F. (2014). Examining teachers' language in Head Start classrooms from a Systemic Linguistics Approach. *Early Childhood Research Quarterly, 29*(3), 231–244.

Dickinson, D. K., & Porche, M. V. (2011). Relationship between language experiences in preschool classrooms and children's kindergarten and fourth grade language and reading abilities. *Child Development, 82*, 870–886.

Dickinson, D. K., & Smith, M. W. (1994). Long-term effects of preschool teachers' book readings on low-income children's vocabulary and story comprehension. *Reading Research Quarterly, 29*, 105–122.

Freebody, P., & Anderson, R. (1983). Effects of vocabulary difficulty, text cohesion, and schema availability on reading comprehension. *Reading Research Quarterly, 18*(3), 277–294.

Gámez, P. B. (2015). Classroom-based English exposure and English Language Learners' expressive language skills. *Early Childhood Research Quarterly, 31*(2), 135–146.

Gamez, P. B., Gonzalez, D., & Urbin, L. M. (2017). Shared book reading and English Language Learners' narrative production and comprehension. *Reading Research Quarterly, 52*(3), 275–290.

Gámez, P. B., & Lesaux, N. K. (2012). The relation between exposure to sophisticated and complex language on early-adolescent English-only and language minority learners' vocabulary knowledge. *Child Development, 83*(4), 1316–1331.

Gámez, P. B., & Lesaux, N. K. (2015). Early-adolescents' reading comprehension and the stability of the middle school classroom-language environment. *Developmental Psychology, 51*(4), 447–458.

Gámez, P. B., & Levine, S. C. (2013). Oral language skills of Spanish-speaking English Language Learners: The impact of high-quality native language exposure. *Applied Psycholinguistics, 34*(4), 673–696.

Gámez, P. B., & Shimpi, P. M. (2016). Structural priming in Spanish as evidence of implicit learning. *Journal of Child Language, 43*(1), 207–233.

Gámez, P. B., & Vasilyeva, M. (2015). Increasing second language learners' production and comprehension of developmentally-advanced syntactic forms. *Language Learning & Development, 11*(2), 128–151.

Gamoran, A., & Nystrand, M. (1991). Background and instructional effects on achievement in eighth-grade English and social studies. *Journal of Research on Adolescence, 1*(3), 277–300.

Gerde, H. K., & Powell, D. R. (2009). Teacher education, book-reading practices, and children's language growth across one year of head start. *Early Education and Development, 20*(2), 211–237.

Gleitman, L. (1990). The structural sources of verb meanings. *Language Acquisition, 1*, 3–55.

Gough, P. B., & Tunmer, W. E. (1986). Decoding, reading and reading disability. *Remedial and Special Education, 7*, 6–10.

Grøver, V., Lawrence, J., & Rydland, V. (2016). Bilingual preschool children's second-language vocabulary development: The role of first-language vocabulary skills and second-language talk input. *International Journal of Bilingualism, 22*(2), 234–250.

Gurria, A. (2016). PISA 2015 results in focus. *PISA in Focus, 67*, 1.

Halliday, M. A. K. (1994). *An introduction to functional grammar.* London: Edward Arnold.

Hammer, C. S., Hoff, E., Uchikoshi, Y., Gillanders, C., Castro, D. C., & Sandilos, L. E. (2014). The language and literacy development of young dual language learners: A critical review. *Early Childhood Research Quarterly, 29*(4), 715–733.

Hart, B., & Risley, T. R. (1995). *Meaningful differences in the everyday experience of young American children.* Baltimore, MD: Paul H. Brookes.

Hirsh-Pasek, K., Adamson, L. B., Bakeman, R., Owen, M. T., Golinkoff, R. M., Pace, A., ... Suma, K. (2015). The contribution of early communication quality to low-income children's language success. *Psychological Science, 26*(7), 1071–1083.

Hirsh-Pasek, K., Golinkoff, R. M., & Hollich, G. (2000). An emergentist coalition model for word learning: Mapping words to objects is a product of the interaction of multiple cues. In R. M. Golinkoff, K. Hirsh-Pasek, L. Bloom, L. Smith, A. Woodward, N. Akhtar, & G. Hollich (Eds.), *Becoming a word learner: A debate on lexical acquisition* (pp. 136–164). New York: Oxford University Press.

Hoff, E. (2003). The specificity of environmental influence: Socioeconomic status affects early vocabulary development via maternal speech. *Child Development, 74*(5), 1368–1378.

Hoff, E. (2006). How social contexts support and shape language development. *Developmental Review, 26*, 55–88.

Hoff, E., & Naigles, L. (2002). How children use input to acquire a lexicon. *Child Development, 73*(2), 418–433.

Hoff-Ginsberg, E. (1998). The relation of birth order and socioeconomic status to children's language experience and language development. *Applied Psycholinguistics, 19*(4), 603–629.

Hoover, W. A., & Gough, P. B. (1990). The simple view of reading. *Reading and Writing, 2*, 127–160.

Huttenlocher, J., Haight, W., Bryk, A., Seltzer, M., & Lyons, T. (1991). Early vocabulary growth: Relation to language input and gender. *Developmental Psychology, 27*(2), 236–248.

Huttenlocher, J., Vasilyeva, M., Cymerman, E., & Levine, S. (2002). Language input and child syntax. *Cognitive Psychology, 45*, 337–374.

Huttenlocher, J., Vasilyeva, M., & Shimpi, P. (2004). Syntactic priming in young children. *Journal of Memory and Language, 50*(2), 182–195.

Huttenlocher, J., Waterfall, H., Vasilyeva, M., Vevea, J., & Hedges, L. (2010). Sources of variability in children's language growth. *Cognitive Psychology, 61*(4), 343–365.

Jacoby, J. W., & Lesaux, N. K. (2014). Support for extended discourse in teacher talk with linguistically diverse preschoolers. *Early Education and Development, 25*(8), 1162–1179.

Joshi, R. M., & Aaron, P. G. (2000). The component model of reading: Simple view of reading made a little more complex. *Reading Psychology, 21*(2), 85–97.

Justice, L. M., McGinty, A. S., Zucker, T., Cabell, S. Q., & Piasta, S. B. (2013). Bi-directional dynamics underlie the complexity of talk in teacher–child play-based conversations in classrooms serving at-risk pupils. *Early Childhood Research Quarterly, 28*(3), 496–508.

Justice, L. M., Petscher, Y., Schatschneider, C., & Mashburn, A. (2011). Peer effects in preschool classrooms: Is children's language growth associated with their classmates' skills? *Child Development, 82*(6), 1768–1777.

Kendeou, P., Van den Broek, P., White, M. J., & Lynch, J. S. (2009). Predicting reading comprehension in early elementary school: The independent contributions of oral language and decoding skills. *Journal of Educational Psychology, 101*(4), 765.

Kirby, J. R., & Savage, R. S. (2008). Can the simple view deal with the complexities of reading?. *Literacy, 42*(2), 75–82.

Krogstad, J. M., & Lopez, M. H. (2014). *Hispanic nativity shift: US births drive population growth as immigration stalls*. Washington, DC: Pew Research Center's Hispanic Trends Project.

Landau, B., & Gleitman, L. (1985). *Language and experience*. Cambridge, MA: Harvard University Press.

Language and Reading Research Consortium. (2015). Learning to read: Should we keep things simple? *Reading Research Quarterly, 50*(2), 151–169.

Lonigan, C. J., Farver, J. M., Nakamoto, J., & Eppe, S. (2013). Developmental trajectories of preschool early literacy skills: A comparison of language-minority and monolingual-English children. *Developmental Psychology, 49*(10), 1943.

MacWhinney, B. (2007). *The CHILDES project: Tools for analyzing talk*. Mahwah, NJ: Erlbaum.

Mashburn, A. J., Justice, L. M., Downer, J. T., & Pianta, R. C. (2009). Peer effects on children's language achievement during pre-kindergarten. *Child Development, 80*(3), 686–702.

Mashburn, A. J., Pianta, R. C., Hamre, B. K., Downer, J. T., Barbarin, O. A., Bryant, D., … Howes, C. (2008). Measures of classroom quality in prekindergarten and children's development of academic, language, and social skills. *Child Development, 79*(3), 732–749.

McNamara, D. S., & Magliano, J. (2009). Toward a comprehensive model of comprehension. *Psychology of Learning and Motivation, 51*, 297–384.

Mehan, H. (1979). *Learning lessons*. Cambridge, MA: Harvard University Press.

Mercer, N. (1995). *The guided construction of knowledge: Talk amongst teachers and learners*. Multilingual matters.

Miller, J. F., & Chapman, R. S. (1981). The relation between age and mean length of utterance in morphemes. *Journal of speech, language, and Hearing Research, 24*(2), 154–161.

Mol, S. E., Bus, A. G., De Jong, M. T., & Smeets, D. J. (2008). Added value of dialogic parent–child book readings: A meta-analysis. *Early Education and Development, 19*(1), 7–26.

Murphy, P. K., Firetto, C. M., Wei, L., Li, M., & Croninger, R. M. (2016). What really works: Optimizing classroom discussions to promote comprehension and critical-analytic thinking. *Policy Insights from the Behavioral and Brain Sciences, 3*(1), 27–35.

Murphy, P. K., Wilkinson, I. A., Soter, A. O., Hennessey, M. N., & Alexander, J. F. (2009). Examining the effects of classroom discussion on students' comprehension of text: A meta-analysis. *Journal of Educational Psychology, 101*(3), 740–764.

Nagy, W., & Townsend, D. (2012). Words as tools: Learning academic vocabulary as language acquisition. *Reading Research Quarterly, 47*(1), 91–108.

Nagy, W. E., Anderson, R. C., & Herman, P. A. (1987). Learning word meanings from context during normal reading. *American Educational Research Journal, 24*(2), 237–270.

National Center for Education Statistics. (2015). *The Nation's Report Card: 2015 mathematics and reading assessments (NCES 2015-136)*. Washington, DC: Author.

National Governors Association Center for Best Practices, & Council of Chief State School Officers. (2010). *Common core state standards for English language arts and literacy in history/social studies, science, and technical subjects.* Washington, DC: Authors.

National Institute of Child Health and Human Development Early Child Care Research Network. (2000). *Report of the national reading panel. Teaching children to read: An evidence-based assessment of the scientific research literature on reading and its implications for reading instruction (NIH Publication No. 00-4769).* Washington, DC: U.S. Government Printing Office.

National Institute of Child Health and Human Development Early Child Care Research Network. (2005). Pathways to reading: The role of oral language in the transition to reading. *Developmental Psychology, 41*(2), 428–442.

National Research Council. (1998). *Preventing reading difficulties in young children.* Washington, DC: National Academy Press.

National Research Council (2013). *Education for life and work: Developing transferable knowledge and skills in the 21st century.* Washington, DC: National Academies Press.

NICHD Early Child Care Research Network. (2000). The relation of child care to cognitive and language development. *Child Development, 71,* 960–980.

Nystrand, M., Gamoran, A., Kachur, R., & Prendergast, C. (1997). *Opening dialogue: Understanding the dynamics of language and learning in the English classroom.* New York: Teachers College Press.

Nystrand, M., Wu, L., Gamoran, A., Zeiser, S., & Long, D. (2003). Questions in time: Investigating the structure and dynamics of unfolding classroom discourse. *Discourse Processes, 35*(2), 135–198.

Ouellette, G., & Beers, A. (2010). A not-so-simple view of reading: How oral vocabulary and visual-word recognition complicate the story. *Reading and Writing, 23*(2), 189–208.

Palermo, F., & Mikulski, A. M. (2014). The role of positive peer interactions and English exposure in Spanish-speaking preschoolers' English vocabulary and letter-word skills. *Early Childhood Research Quarterly, 29*(4), 625–635.

Pan, B. A., Rowe, M. L., Singer, J. D., & Snow, C. E. (2005). Maternal correlates of growth in toddler vocabulary production in low-income families. *Child Development, 76*(4), 763–782.

Parker, M. D., & Brorson, K. (2005). A comparative study between mean length of utterance in morphemes (MLUm) and mean length of utterance in words (MLUw). *First Language, 25*(3), 365–376.

Peisner-Feinberg, E. S., Burchinal, M. R., Clifford, R. M., Culkin, M. L., Howes, C., Kagan, S. L., & Yazejian, N. (2001). The relation of preschool child-care quality to children's cognitive and social developmental trajectories through second grade. *Child Development, 72*(5), 1534–1553.

Pentimonti, J. M., Zucker, T. A., Justice, L. M., Petscher, Y., Piasta, S. B., & Kaderavek, J. N. (2012). A standardized tool for assessing the quality of classroom-based shared reading: Systematic Assessment of Book Reading (SABR). *Early Childhood Research Quarterly, 27*(3), 512–528.

Perfetti, C. (2007). Reading ability: Lexical quality to comprehension. *Scientific Studies of Reading, 11*(4), 357–383.

Perfetti, C., & Stafura, J. (2014). Word knowledge in a theory of reading comprehension. *Scientific Studies of Reading, 18*(1), 22–37.

Perfetti, C. A., & Hart, L. (2002). The lexical quality hypothesis. *Precursors of Functional Literacy, 11,* 67–86.

Pianta, R., Howes, C., Burchinal, M., Bryant, D., Clifford, R., Early, D., & Barbarin, O. (2005). Features of pre-kindergarten programs, classrooms, and teachers: Do they predict observed classroom quality and child-teacher interactions? *Applied Developmental Science, 9*(3), 144–159.

Pianta, R. C., Karen, M., Paro, L., & Hamre, B. K. (2008). *Classroom assessment scoring system (CLASS) manual, pre-K.* Baltimore, MD: Paul H. Brookes Publishing Company.

Pianta, R. C., La Paro, K. M., Payne, C., Cox, M. J., & Bradley, R. (2002). The relation of kindergarten classroom environment to teacher, family, and school characteristics and child outcomes. *The Elementary School Journal, 102*(3), 225–238.

Pickering, M. J., & Ferreira, V. S. (2008). Structural priming: A critical review. *Psychological Bulletin, 134*(3), 427–459.

Powell, D. R., Burchinal, M. R., File, N., & Kontos, S. (2008). An eco-behavioral analysis of children's engagement in urban public school preschool classrooms. *Early Childhood Research Quarterly, 23*(1), 108–123.

RAND Reading Study Group. (2002). *Reading for understanding: Toward an R&D program in reading comprehension.* Santa Monica, CA: RAND Corporation.

Rydland, V., Grøver, V., & Lawrence, J. (2014). The second-language vocabulary trajectories of Turkish immigrant children in Norway from ages five to ten: The role of preschool talk exposure, maternal education, and co-ethnic concentration in the neighborhood. *Journal of Child Language, 41*(2), 352–381.

Scarborough, H. S. (1990). Index of productive syntax. *Applied Psycholinguistics, 11*(1), 1–22.
Scarborough, H. S., Rescorla, L., Tager-Flusberg, H., Fowler, A. E., & Sudhalter, V. (1991). The relation of utterance length to grammatical complexity in normal and language-disordered groups. *Applied Psycholinguistics, 12*(1), 23–46.
Scarcella, R. (2003). *Academic English: A conceptual framework*. Los Angeles, CA: Language Minority Research Institute.
Scarr, S., Eisenberg, M., & Deater-Deckard, K. (1994). Measurement of quality in child care centers. *Early Childhood Research Quarterly, 9*(2), 131–151.
Schleppegrell, M. J. (2001). Linguistic features of the language of schooling. *Linguistics and Education, 12*(4), 431–459.
Schleppegrell, M. J. (2004). *The language of schooling: A functional linguistics perspective*. Mahwah, NJ: Lawrence Erlbaum.
Schleppegrell, M. J. (2009). *Language in academic subject areas and classroom instruction: What is academic language and how can we teach it?* Paper prepared for the workshop on the role of language in school learning: implications for closing the achievement gap. Hewlett Foundation, Menlo Park, CA.
Sénéchal, M., Pagan, S., Lever, R., & Ouellette, G. P. (2008). Relations among the frequency of shared reading and 4-year-old children's vocabulary, morphological and syntax comprehension, and narrative skills. *Early Education and Development, 19*(1), 27–44.
Smith, L. B. (2000). Learning how to learn words: An associative crane. In R. M. Golinkoff, K. Hirsh-Pasek, L. Bloom, L. Smith, A. Woodward, N. Akhtar, & G. Hollich (Eds.), *Becoming a word learner: A debate on lexical acquisition* (pp. 51–80). New York, NY: Oxford University Press.
Smith, M., Dickinson, D., Sangeorge, A., & Anastasopoulos, L. (2002). *Early literacy and language classroom observation scale (ELLCO)*. Baltimore, MD: Paul Brookes.
Snow, C. E. (1983). Literacy and language: Relationships during the preschool years. *Harvard Educational Review, 53*(2), 165–189.
Snow, C. E. (1994). Beginning from baby talk: Twenty years of research oninput and interaction. In C. Gallaway & B. Richards (Eds.), *Input and interac-tion in language acquisition* (pp. 3–12). Cambridge, UK: Cambridge University Press.
Snow, C. E., & Uccelli, P. (2009). The challenge of academic language. In D. R. Olson & N. Torrance (Eds.), *The Cambridge handbook of literacy* (pp. 112–133). New York: Cambridge University Press.
Snow, R. E., Corno, L., & Jackson, D. (1996). Conative and affective functions in educational psychology (243-310). In D. C. Berliner, & R. C. Calfee (Eds.) *Handbook of Educational Psychology* (pp. 243–310). New York: Macmillan.
Soter, A. O., Wilkinson, I. A., Murphy, P. K., Rudge, L., Reninger, K., & Edwards, M. (2008). What the discourse tells us: Talk and indicators of high-level comprehension. *International Journal of Educational Research, 47*(6), 372–391.
Sprachman, S., Caspe, M., & Atkins-Burnett, S. (2009). *Language interaction snapshot (LISn) field procedures and coding guide*. Princeton, NJ: Mathematica Policy Research.
Storch, S. A., & Whitehurst, G. J. (2002). Oral language and code-related precursors to reading: Evidence from a longitudinal structural model. *Developmental Psychology, 38*(6), 934.
Suitts, S. (2015). *A new majority research bulletin: Low income students now a majority in the nation's public schools*. Atlanta, GA: Southern Education Foundation.
Tomasello, M. (2000). Do young children have adult syntactic competence? *Cognition, 74*(3), 209–253.
Tunmer, W. E., & Hoover, W. (1992). Cognitive and linguistic factors in learning to read. In P. B. Gough, L. C. Ehri, & R. Treiman (Eds.), *Reading acquisition* (pp. 175–224). Hillsdale, NJ: Erlbaum.
Uccelli, P., Galloway, E. P., Barr, C. D., Meneses, A., & Dobbs, C. L. (2015). Beyond vocabulary: Exploring cross-disciplinary academic-language proficiency and its association with reading comprehension. *Reading Research Quarterly, 50*(3), 337–356.
Valdes, G. (2004). Between support and marginalisation: The development of academic language in linguistic minority children. *International Journal of Bilingual Education and Bilingualism, 7*(2-3), 102–132.
Vasilyeva, M., Huttenlocher, J., & Waterfall, H. (2006). Effects of language intervention on syntactic skill levels in preschoolers. *Developmental Psychology, 42*(1), 164.
Vasilyeva, M., Waterfall, H., & Huttenlocher, J. (2008). Emergence of syntax: Commonalities and differences across children. *Developmental Science, 11*(1), 84–97.
Vellutino, F. R., Tunmer, W. E., Jaccard, J. J., & Chen, R. (2007). Components of reading ability: Multivariate evidence for a convergent skills model of reading development. *Scientific Studies of Reading, 11*(1), 3–32.

Vygotsky, L. S. (1978). *Mind in society: The development of higher mental psychological processes.* Cambridge, MA: Harvard University Press.

Wasik, B. A., & Bond, M. A. (2001). Beyond the pages of a book: Interactive book reading and language development in preschool classrooms. *Journal of Educational Psychology, 93*(2), 243.

Wasik, B. A., Bond, M. A., & Hindman, A. (2006). The effects of a language and literacy intervention on head start children and teachers. *Journal of Educational Psychology, 98*(1), 63–74.

Webb, N. M., Farivar, S. H., & Mastergeorge, A. M. (2002). Productive helping in cooperative groups. *Theory into Practice, 41*(1), 13–20.

Weizman, Z. O., & Snow, C. E. (2001). Lexical output as related to children's vocabulary acquisition: Effects of sophisticated exposure and support for meaning. *Developmental Psychology, 37*(2), 265.

West, M. (1953). *A general service list of English words.* London: Longman.

Whitehurst, G. J., Arnold, D. S., Epstein, J. N., Angell, A. L., Smith, M., & Fischel, J. E. (1994). A picture book reading intervention in day care and home for children from low-income families. *Developmental Psychology, 30*(5), 679–689.

Wolf, M. K., Crosson, A. C., & Resnick, L. B. (2006). Accountable talk in reading comprehension instruction. CSE Technical Report 670. *National Center for Research on Evaluation, Standards, and Student Testing (CRESST).*

World Economic Forum. (2014). *The global competitiveness report 2014–2015.* Geneva, Switzerland: World Economic Forum.

Zevenbergen, A. A., Whitehurst, G. J., & Zevenbergen, J. A. (2003). Effects of a shared-reading intervention on the inclusion of evaluative devices in narratives of children from low-income families. *Journal of Applied Developmental Psychology, 24*(1), 1–15.

Zucker, T. A., Cabell, S. Q., Justice, L. M., Pentimonti, J. M., & Kaderavek, J. N. (2013). The role of frequent, interactive pre-kindergarten shared reading in the longitudinal development of language and literacy skills. *Developmental Psychology, 49*(8), 1425–1439.

20
Expanding Teaching and Learning with Disciplinary Texts
The Case of Reading and Science

Cynthia Greenleaf and Kathleen Hinchman

Since the publication of the last *Handbook of Reading Research*, there have been many new studies of teaching and learning with disciplinary texts. At the same time, controversies about the roles of subject-area teachers in fostering specialized literacies with increasingly diverse student populations have also been renewed, with lecturing, memorizing, and recitation persisting as primary instructional approaches. This chapter reviews this research, taking a social practices view of how texts are used in secondary school classrooms; their characteristics; potential benefits for students' engagement, reading repertoire, and disciplinary learning; and how teachers can help students to reap these benefits. It focuses on science text use because this has not been addressed in earlier *Handbooks*. The review addresses three questions: What is the research base with disciplinary texts in general and in science-focused subject-area classrooms? What are the gaps in this research? What research is needed to address these gaps and expand teaching and learning with disciplinary texts?

Methods of Review

We began our review by rereading related chapters in previous editions of this handbook to identify potential search terms. These included Alvermann and Moore's (1991) chapter in Volume II on "Secondary School Reading," Wade and Moje's (2000) "The Role of Text on Classroom Learning," Alexander and Jetton's (2000) "Learning from Text: A Multidimensional and Developmental Perspective" from *Volume III*, and Moje, Stockdill, Kim, and Kim's (2011), "The Role of Text in Disciplinary Learning" in Volume IV. We searched ProQuest, EBSCO, Google Scholar, Academia.edu, and Researchgate.net with an extensive set of search terms that included literacy in the disciplines, disciplinary texts, reading in disciplines, academic literacies, content-area reading and literacy, classroom use of text, and domain-specific text use. Additional search terms included reading, literacy, and text use in science and subspecialties such as biology, chemistry, and physics; reading in science; and literacy and science. Though we limited our examples here to science, we also searched on literacy and history, literary studies, engineering, mathematics, and mathematics communication for added insight into current practice and emerging possibilities toward disciplinary text classroom use. We also looked at germane work in elementary and post-secondary settings, even though this review is confined to secondary school settings.

A Social Practices View of Teaching and Learning with Disciplinary Texts

When K-12 textbooks were developed to address standardized literary, language, mathematics, and science content more than a century ago (Elliott & Woodward, 1990), decades of practical scholarship followed to help students read and study them successfully (Moore, Readence, & Rickelman, 1983). This was followed by a theoretical shift that refocused research on how to develop students' independent metacognitive reading comprehension strategies (Paris, Lipson, & Wixson, 1983) and construction of mental models of texts (Van Dijk & Kintsch, 1983). Little of this work was widely replicated, a circumstance that Alvermann and Moore (1991) blamed on lack of attention to social contexts and constraints, a lack of attention that has been addressed by more recent studies of how language and literacy is situated in social contexts.

Early work exploring language's social nature included Bernstein's (1971) and Labov's (1972) analyses of how individuals used language differently, depending on context. This was followed by Cazden's (1979) and Mehan's (1979) descriptions of teacher-student classroom interactions. Subsequent researchers, like Scribner and Cole (1981), Heath (1983), Street (1984), and Barton, Hamilton, and Ivanič (2000), described how people situated language, literacies, and texts in social practices. Later studies described how youth engaged in literacy practices using varied personal resources, funds of knowledge, and strategies (Alvermann, 2001; Hull & Schultz, 2002; Moje, Ciechanowski, Kramer, Ellis, Carrillo, & Collazo, 2004), including knowledge of classroom procedural display (Bloome, Puro, & Theodorou, 1989). Grossman and Stodolsky (1995) explored how teachers' knowledge of their subjects and pedagogy was situated in schools, and O'Brien, Stewart, and Moje (1995) described institutional and social constraints on curriculum, pedagogy, and secondary school culture, yielding calls for explorations of how to give students access to disciplinary cultures, especially in post-secondary (Bartholomae, 1986; Bazerman, 1985; Lea, 1999) and secondary (Geisler, 1994; Guzzetti, Snyder, Glass, & Gamas, 1993; Moje, 2007) education settings.

Recently, O'Brien and Ortmann (2017) reviewed the history of work that ensued as investigators from varied philosophical traditions and from inside and outside the disciplines they studied attempted to describe discipline-embedded forms of literacy for academic literacy teaching. For example, from linguistic traditions, researchers such as Fang and Schleppegrell (2010) described language elements characteristic of specific disciplinary texts. Literacy researchers such as Shanahan, Shanahan, and Misiscia (2011), studied disciplinary experts' mathematics, chemistry, and history reading to identify expert strategies to teach in subject area classrooms. Studies by disciplinary insiders noted how disciplinary experts read literature (Lee, 1993; Rabinowitz, 1998; Rosenblatt, 1978), history (Lee, 2005; Monte-Sano, 2011; Wineburg, 1991; Young & Leinhardt, 1998), mathematics (Schoenfeld, 1992; Shepherd & van de Sande, 2014; Weber & Mejia-Ramos, 2011), and science (Osborne, 2002; Lemke, 1990), using particular habits of mind that allowed disciplinary knowledge to be constructed (Chick, Haynie, & Gurung, 2012; Coll, Taylor, & Lay, 2009; Wineburg, 1999).

Observations of how people used media also provided new insight into what could be counted as texts (Cope & Kalantzis, 2000; New London Group, 1996). Texts are now understood to draw on multiple semiotic modalities, including oral, print, graphic, and video forms, as well as observed discussions and other enactments (Kress & van Leeuwen, 2001). Youth have been observed communicating via tagging, 'zine writing, and purposefully selecting apparel to communicate ideas (e.g., Finders, 1997; Moje, 2000; Schultz, 2002). The digital age augmented further what counted as disciplinary texts to include models, illustrations, diagrams, simulations, and explanations in a variety of media and multimodal forms (Beach & Castek, 2015; Giroux & Moje, 2017; Kress, 2013; Manderino, 2012), along with evolving conventions of argumentation using these sources (Goldman et al., 2016; Newell, Beach, Smith, Van Der Heide, Kuhn, & Andriessen, 2011).

How Teaching and Learning from Disciplinary Texts are Situated in Classroom Practice

Despite these recent understandings of literacy and of texts, literacy tasks and texts remain in limited use in secondary schools. The most frequently used texts in subject areas are textbooks, which continue to occupy center stage as they did a century ago. They "are simultaneously surrogate curricula, cultural artifacts, and commercial products" that delimit learning (Venezky, 2001, p. 256). Textbook assignments remain pervasive in English language arts, math, history, and science (ACT Inc., 2013a; Applebee, Langer, Nystrand, & Gamoran, 2003; Bain, 2006; Banilower et al., 2013; Polikoff et al., in press; Reisman, 2012).

Instructional practices continue to constrain students' opportunities for reading – whether textbooks or other sources. A recent observational study found that tenth grade students spent a majority of class time listening to lectures or watching films (Fisher, 2009). An average of 3.4 minutes per class were spent reading textbooks or class-assigned novels in English language arts, with most students reporting that they read only for homework. Discussions were led by teachers and focused on content knowledge, with few student contributions. Valencia (2014) more recently found Advanced Placement teachers using lectures, videos, Internet sources, and short handouts to avoid relying on students' extended reading of textbooks or other sources, which was cast as homework and was not central to learning. Recent surveys by ACT confirmed that secondary teachers prioritize content mastery over development of disciplinary literacy and reasoning (2013a; ACT Inc., 2009, 2013b), using lecture as the predominant mode of instruction and socializing students to skim for information rather than reading texts more thoroughly (ACT Inc., 2006; Ness, 2008).

Recent literacy standards pressed for developing students' ability to read complex texts across content areas to prepare them for college and careers. However, a RAND study of Common Core Aligned Standards (CCAS) implementation (Opfer, Kaufman, & Thompson, 2016) found that secondary ELA teachers were less likely than elementary teachers to use district instructional materials, including textbooks, and more likely to select other instructional materials. The study also indicated that teachers navigated demands of new standards with little support or time. Teachers in high poverty or linguistically diverse schools (98% and 82%, respectively) often assigned reading from relatively easy texts simplified for readability according to what they understood of students' reading abilities. These teachers used easy-to-read sources from LearnZillion, Newsela, EngageNY, RAZ-Kids, Reading A-Z, Read 180, or Accelerated Reader, as well as data aggregation tools, like Google, Teacherspayteachers, and Pinterest, suggesting they had limited other resources. Hiebert (2017) is among those who have critiqued such practices as constraining students' opportunities to learn to engage with deep learning from complex disciplinary texts.

Two recent observational studies also suggested that secondary students had little opportunity in school to puzzle through ideas or discuss reading–practices that contribute to literacy learning and independence. Vaughn and colleagues (2013) observed social studies and English language arts teachers who had participated in reading–related professional development and found they invited students to read 10.4% of the time, with sources limited mostly to textbooks and anthologized excerpts. Teacher-led comprehension strategy instruction was observed 20%–25% of the time, however, text-based discussion took less than 20% of the time. Litman and colleagues (2017) observed lessons in which subject-area teachers allocated three times as much class time to working with texts as to lectures, with tasks that had a disciplinary, knowledge-building focus about half the time, and argumentation and cross-textual analysis more than half the time. Despite more frequent use of texts, contribution of this use to learning was limited, with teachers using leading questions and a selective uptake of students' contributions to subtly draw students to required information or their own interpretations. Limited text use may be especially problematic given the way science teaching and learning is now being conceptualized in the science education literature.

A Social Practices View of Science, Literacy, and Texts

Across its multiple domains and sub-disciplines, science is fundamentally focused on explaining the natural and designed worlds (Rutherford & Ahlgren, 1990). Science knowledge develops as scientists accrue evidence for potential explanations of phenomena, usually communicating these in communities of similarly engaged scientists (Berland & Reiser, 2009; Cavagnetto, 2010; Latour & Woolgar, 1986; Ryu & Sandoval, 2012), using knowledge claims to argue that their explanatory models account for data (Bricker & Bell, 2008; Osborne, 2010; van den Broek, 2010; Windschitl, Thompson, & Braaten, 2008). However, science is also a theory building endeavor. Scientific explanation connects data to interpretations by drawing on existing science principles and theories (Braaten & Windschitl, 2011; Chin & Osborne, 2010). Scientific knowledge accumulates through generating and revising models and explanations from evidence. This means science knowledge is tentative, based on the best accounts from investigation and theorizing to date. Scientific habits of mind assume these epistemological stances with orientations toward skepticism and critical evaluation (Osborne, 2010).

Reading in multiple modalities is also central to science. Scientists engaged in inquiry processes use multiple semiotic forms (e.g., graphs, data charts, and exposition) to represent ideas and build models and explanations of phenomena (Cromley, Snyder-Hogan, & Luciw-Dubas, 2010; Lemke, 1990, 1998; Waldrip, Prain, & Carolan, 2010). Primary data recorded from scientists' investigations, secondary data derived from others' work, and texts that include explanations, graphs, data tables, and scientific models, are all valued epistemic tools for generating scientific knowledge. As data recording becomes increasingly technologically sophisticated, the artifacts of scientific work to be read and interpreted become, likewise, more complex. Skillful science reading thus includes the ability to make sense of scientific terminology; interpret arrays of data; comprehend scientific texts that convey information through verbal exposition, graphs, tables, visual models, and diagrams; interpret models and illustrations; and evaluate scientific explanations (Lemke, 1990; Osborne, 2002). Given these knowledge-building practices, and especially the role that reading multimodal texts plays, we reviewed learning opportunities students are currently offered so as to engage in these practices.

Science education researchers have long called for science teaching that engages students in science inquiry to learn about the nature of science, including thinking and discourse practices central to the discipline (Bybee, 2013; Duschl, Schweingruber, & Shouse, 2007; Ford & Wargo, 2012; Rutherford & Ahlgren, 1990; Von Aufschnaiter, Erduran, Osborne, & Simon, 2008). The Next Generation Science Standards (NGSS) were derived from a conception of science as both a body of knowledge and a model and theory building enterprise that continually extends, refines, and revises knowledge through evidence-based argumentation (NGSS Lead States, 2013). These standards specify that students learn science by engaging in the practices of science: asking questions; developing and using models; planning and carrying out investigations; analyzing and interpreting data; using mathematics and computational thinking; constructing explanations;

engaging in argument from evidence; and obtaining, evaluating, and communicating information. A National Research Council panel convened a conference on connections between the Common Core State Standards for literacy in science and the NGSS in 2013 (Council, 2014). While the consensus report acknowledged the relevance of literacy to obtaining, evaluating, and communicating information alone, language and literacy practices are arguably central to all NGSS practice standards, which can be viewed as constituting a set of design principles to inform disciplinary literacy instruction. The report advocates that teachers help students unpack the specialized forms of science texts they need to be able to read and produce but offers little detail about how teachers might support students in learning how to read these texts, nor the nature of the texts students should read. Similarly, promoting inquiry experiences for science teachers was seen as a route to building necessary knowledge and pedagogical repertoire to support NGSS and CCSS, but again, little detail about how to do so was offered.

How Teaching and Learning from Science Texts are Situated in Classroom Practice

Science educators charged that traditional textbooks presented science as a body of knowledge without attention to the ways such knowledge developed and changed over time (Chiappetta & Fillman, 2007). Moreover, little attention was paid in science textbooks to the practices of systematic investigation and explanation, or to the role of argumentation in advancing explanations of the natural and designed worlds (Myers, 1992). While encyclopedic in nature, textbooks omitted well-established science theories when they ran counter to beliefs embraced by state legislatures. As in other subject areas, textbooks often served as *de facto* curriculum, determining topics science teachers taught, in what order, and with what materials. Given the investment necessary to their development, science textbooks were slow to change in the face of advancing science, sometimes including erroneous information (Penney, Norris, Phillips, & Clark, 2003). These critiques resulted in science educators' wholesale rejection of reading in science under a banner of doing rather than reading about science.

Literacy researchers have also critiqued science textbooks for being too complex, advocating that they be redesigned with properties more considerate to readers. For example, van den Broek (2010) argued that science texts be designed to optimize their purported purpose, the learning of science content, recommending minimizing challenges students encounter when reading by placing visual illustrations and other examples close to relevant verbal explanations to foster coherence-building, for instance. Similarly, Moje and colleagues (Moje et al., 2004) developed science readings to accompany investigations, designing considerate texts for ease of comprehension in a project linking literacy and science explanation. Others argued that such alterations could make learning information from science texts easier but also fail to prepare students for actual science communication practices (Kerlin, McDonald, & Kelly, 2010). Authentic science texts are multimodal and conceptually dense, laden with science-specific meanings for common vocabulary, technical language, and syntactic complexity. Education researchers operating from a linguistic perspective advocate preparing students for making-meaning with such features, eventually independently; however, examples of such practices are just now beginning to emerge (Fang & Schleppegrell, 2010; O'Hallaron, Palincsar, & Schleppegrell, 2015; Snow, 2010).

How Reading Can Support Science Learning

Refutational Texts and Reform-oriented Curriculum

Textbook and curriculum redesign advocated by science researchers has foregrounded different concerns. Osborne (2010) advocated that texts present what is wrong and why it is wrong, as well as what is right, in order to foster robust conceptual change. Such refutational texts embody aspects of science explanation and argumentation by bringing common misconceptions into view while showing why they are incorrect (Broughton, Sinatra, & Reynolds, 2010; Sinatra & Broughton, 2011). Two decades of research indicate that reading refutational text is more likely to result in readers' conceptual change (Tippett, 2010). Reform curriculum developers have also sought to make visible the nature of science investigation and knowledge building, designing textual components with these elements in mind. For example, Krajcik and Sutherland (2009) designed curriculum texts around science practices, foregrounding the role of questions in driving investigations and making explicit connections across multiple sources of information, including students' investigation data and everyday experiences.

Targeted Instructional Approaches to Integrating Literacy and Science

Integrating literacy and science has shown benefits for elementary, middle, and high school students and for English language learners. The In-Depth Expanded Applications of Science (IDEAS) project replaced time devoted to ELA, with two hours of science exploration, reading, and writing, finding treatment effects in both reading and science across multiple studies in grades 2 through 5 (Romance & Vitale, 1992, 2001; Vitale & Romance, 2011). Similarly, a large-scale study of a science writing program for low SES elementary students, many of whom were English learners, showed impacts at grades 4 and 6 (Amaral, Garrison, & Klentschy, 2002). Multiple evaluation studies of the Seeds of Science/Roots of Reading curriculum for elementary students have demonstrated gains in reading comprehension, writing, and science knowledge for diverse learners, including English learners (Bravo & Cervetti, 2014; Cervetti, Barber, Dorph, Pearson, & Goldschmidt, 2012; Girod & Twyman, 2009; Wang & Herman, 2005). The Science Writing Heuristic approach to writing to make sense of inquiry-based science has shown consistently positive benefits from primary school to university (Gunel, Hand, & Prain, 2007; Hand, Yore, Jagger, & Prain, 2010).

Integrating science inquiry practices with English reading, writing, and argumentation in South Africa, where science teaching and learning take place in a second language for both teachers and students, has shown robust benefits for elementary and middle school students' achievement in both English literacy skills and science (Villanueva & Webb, 2008; Webb, 2009; Webb & Treagust, 2006; Webb, Williams, & Meiring, 2008). In post-secondary science education, attention to literacy aspects of science have similarly paid off (Fredlund, Airey, & Linder, 2015; Hill, Sharma, & Johnston, 2015). These many endeavors illustrate that students of all ages, English language proficiencies, SES levels, and prior literacy accomplishment can learn to read and write science texts as they learn science content, engage in science investigations, and learn how science is done. These studies demonstrate that rather than building a set of skills and proficiencies before engaging in disciplinary literacy practices (Fang, 2014; Shanahan & Shanahan, 2008), students benefit from opportunities to carry out approximations of real science knowledge-building practices throughout their tenure in school, simultaneously building the specialized literacy capacities these practices entail.

Widening recognition of reading, writing, discourse, and reasoning practices in the practice of science and the work of scientists has been influential in reshaping the role of literacy in science education reform (Cervetti et al., 2012; Duschl & Osborne, 2002; McNeill, 2009; McNeill & Krajcik, 2011; Norris & Phillips, 2003; Yore, 2004). Not coincidentally, science education researchers have identified problems in the implementation and learning outcomes resulting from hands-on science inquiry alone (Chinn & Malhotra, 2002; Jimenez-Aleixandre, Rodriguez, & Duschl, 2000). Science education research and curricular design have increasingly focused on integrating science inquiry and literacy to engage students in disciplinary practices of investigation and explanation (Braaten & Windschitl, 2011; Webb, 2010; Yore, Bisanz, & Hand, 2003). Investigation and explanation shape purposes for literacy in these efforts. The use of multiple representations has been especially central to this embrace of literacy in science (Gunel, Hand, & Gunduz, 2006; Hand & Choi, 2010; Putra & Tang, 2016; Tang & Moje, 2010). Research has focused on engaging students in developing multimodal texts and in transforming texts from one modality to another as they attempt to understand and explain their hands-on investigations, and the concept of representing to learn has become prominent in science curricula (Prain & Hand, 2016; Tytler, Prain, Hubber, & Waldrip, 2013). Yet we know comparatively little about the forms of texts or reading instruction offered to students to support their understandings of the phenomena they investigate.

Targeted Instructional Approaches with a Focus on Reading and Science

Two models for designing science reading experiences to embody the practices of science have been developed, with studies attesting to their promise. The first is the approach known as Adapted Primary Literature (APL), which draws on scientist's writing for professional journals (Norris, Stelnicki, & de Vries, 2012; Phillips & Norris, 2009; Yarden et al., 2009). This approach exploits the canonical structure of science journal reports, which typically include an abstract briefly describing the research questions, methodology, findings, and interpretations. This is followed by a description of the study methodology and its findings, including data that are often represented in multimodal textual forms. Finally, the discussion section makes an evidence-based argument that interprets the findings in the light of existing science principles and theory and refutes alternative explanations for these data. In the APL approach, students spend multiple class periods reading and discussing the abstract, findings, and discussion sections of such articles, and in the process grapple with multiple modes of communication and textual structures. They construct their own interpretations and evidence-based arguments based on the findings and compare these arguments to those of published authors.

One study of this approach described the discourse moves of an all-female chemistry class over the course of the eight-day lesson, showing how their work reflected disciplinary practices of multimodal representation, coordination across multiple sources, evidence-based argumentation, and reference to scientific principles and theory (Falk & Yarden, 2009). APL researchers also described work to build teachers' understanding and independent use of APL and resulting teacher-made adaptations of science literature (Koomen, Weaver, Blair, & Oberhauser, 2016). Of note, the principles used to modify scientific journal articles were not completely transparent from the studies reported. The authors described reducing barriers to comprehension for secondary students, but not precisely how, and importantly, warned against reducing complexity overmuch. Indeed, Yarden et al. (2009) suggested that the more complex elements of the text provoked more scientific reasoning and discourse among the chemistry students. This resonated with Kerlin et al. (2010), who found that use of more authentic, complex forms of texts promoted deeper science learning.

A second approach was based on Palincsar and Magnussen's (2001) work, in which they designed texts for elementary students to accompany hands-on investigation experiences with science phenomena. Whereas Palincsar and Magnussen authored "scientists'" notebooks to demonstrate the inquiry and multimodal practices of science and to support students' conceptual understanding of science phenomena, "text-based investigations" engaged students in reading authentic science texts of varied genres and modalities – data tables, maps, diagrams, informational texts (exposition), case studies, and science research reports, often in excerpted form – to explain phenomena (Greenleaf, Brown, Goldman, & Ko, 2013; Greenleaf, Hale, Charney-Sirott, & Schoenbach, 2007). For example, in the Reading Apprenticeship Academic

Literacy (RAAL) course, students investigated factors contributing to the epidemic of obesity and diabetes among youth. Instruction focused on how to make sense of demographic data tables, BMI charts, science reports, monographs from the CDC, textbook descriptions of digestive processes, models of insulin regulation, and arguments about dietary recommendations. Students synthesized these sources to write an evidence-based explanation of factors contributing to epidemic levels of obesity and diabetes among youth and to make a recommendation for reducing the risk of diabetes or obesity to an audience of their choosing. In a study of the RAAL course, 9th grade students reading two to five years below grade level made statistically significant progress in reading comprehension and science (Corrin, Somers, Kemple, Nelson, & Sepanik, 2008; Somers et al., 2010).

Building on the text-based investigation strategy from RAAL, the Project READI science design team added a focus on reading to model a phenomenon of study (Greenleaf et al., 2013). Organized around developing evidence-based arguments from multiple sources, these investigations provided students with intentionally varied forms of texts and multiple opportunities to develop and critique their own and their peers' causal explanations for phenomena such as the emergence of antibiotic resistant strains of bacteria or the contamination of water sources in agricultural and industrial areas impacting city water supplies. Culminating tasks focused on constructing and critiquing visual and verbal explanatory models for the phenomena. Underlying this work was a conceptual model of the epistemological stances and forms of knowledge scientists bring to their reading of texts and learning goals focused on simultaneously developing students' science knowledge, science literacy proficiencies, and science investigation practices (Goldman et al., 2016).

Importantly, science teachers in Project READI were engaged in ongoing professional learning inquiries that involved articulating their own sense making as they enacted text-based investigations and experienced metacognitive discourse routines they could implement in their own classrooms. Case studies of their implementation showed a dramatic shift in teachers' practices supporting students to build knowledge from the multiple text sources and work to develop explanations, as well as in students' science reading and modeling practices (Greenleaf, Brown & Sexton, 2013). An efficacy study tested the inquiry-based professional learning model and investigation materials in a semester-long sequence that progressively built students' science reading dispositions and processes, understanding of the role of models in science, and engagement in text-based investigations. The 9th grade biology students in the text-based investigation condition outperformed controls in classrooms covering the same topics on two measures of multi-source science comprehension that required reading, synthesizing, explanatory model building, and argumentation (Goldman, Greenleaf, et al., 2019).

Implications

Gaps in What We Know about Teaching and Learning with Disciplinary Texts

Developmental Concerns

Based on expert/novice studies, Shanahan and Shanahan (2008) proposed a progression of disciplinary literacy skills that posits that specialized literacy practices rely on a foundation of basic literacy skills. Accordingly, Shanahan and Shanahan (2012) described skills and strategies, such as academic vocabulary skills, that might be taught in early grade levels to pave the way for later disciplinary literacy. However, Fagella-Lucy, Graner, Deshler, and Drew (2012) point out that generalized literacy skills continue to develop as texts and tasks grow in complexity. Fagella-Lucy and colleagues argue that a focus on disciplinary literacy without attention to supporting more general literacy development could leave many students without either set of skills, making disciplinary literacy available only to the highest achieving students who extrapolate the more complex generalized literacy skills on their own.

From a social practices view of literacy, texts and literacy practices do not become specialized in middle and high school. Instead, every text is a form of communication with attendant genre and discourse properties for specialized social purposes, requiring specialized strategies and attention to language (Scribner & Cole, 1981; Street, 1984). From a very young age, in virtually all communities and cultures, children are invited to participate in reading, writing, and discourse for a variety of purposes, such as invitations to birthday parties, lists that serve as reminders for grocery shopping, and stories and study in religious traditions (Dyson, 1997; Heath, 1983). They use literacy in increasingly specialized ways to support their own social interests, as anyone who knows a Minecraft or Anime devotee will attest. These language and literacy experiences constitute resources to recruit for further development and learning (Gonzalez, Moll, & Amanti, 2005; Lee, 1995).

Athanases and de Oliveira (2014) explained that underprepared secondary school students are especially vulnerable to hierarchical skill approaches to disciplinary literacy development. They argue that Latino/a students need instructional scaffolding that taps cultural and linguistic resources, supports co-construction of knowledge, is contingent upon learners' contributions, and transfers responsibility for learning to students. Moll and Gonzalez (1997), Abedi and Gándara (2006), and de Schonewise and Klingner (2012) similarly advocate drawing on students' existing proficiencies in comprehensible ways and using scaffolds that connect to students' prior knowledge, life experiences, and interests so that disciplinary literacy and learning can occur. Similarly, Brozo and colleagues (2013) argue that learning to adapt reading strategies in multiple subject areas is likely needed for the development of discipline-specific literacies.

Developing knowledge and independent learning dispositions is similarly uncharted terrain. O'Brien and Ortmann (2017) and Greenleaf and colleagues (Greenleaf, Schoenbach, Cziko, & Mueller, 2001; Schoenbach & Greenleaf, 2009), called for the development of generalizable strategies and dispositions – academic literacies – that can be deployed across disciplines but that may be best learned in domain-specific settings. Alexander's (2003) Model of Domain Learning posited that learners attain knowledge and expertise through fragmented, limited, decontextualized bits of insight in the initial stages of learning, and then use strategies across domains to find personal connections and motivation to work toward domain-specific competence and, eventually, proficiency. Moje (2007) argued for socially-just disciplinary literacy teaching to help youth bridge everyday knowledge and practice to subject-area learning, navigate discourse communities, and help to reshape curriculum. These perspectives advocated, not for reducing expectations for struggling learners, but rather for increasing the challenge and support through instruction that is motivating and responsive to student needs and interests, favoring inquiry-oriented approaches (Araújo & Maeso, 2012; Bazzul & Sykes, 2011; Brozo, 2017; Leubner, Alber, & Schupfer, 1988; Mills & Bradley, 1993). To deny access to some students of the chance to contemplate complex ideas if they do not yet know how to read particular sentence structures or words may mean denying them access to authentic reasons to read and thereby improve reading.

Implementation Issues

Cervetti (2014) suggested that creating impactful learning experiences for students requires tasks that are authentic approximations of disciplines and that give students access to learning in the disciplines, as well as to concepts and dispositions of work in the disciplines. These approximations should draw on texts that reflect the unique purposes of the discipline. Engaging in such approximations of text-based learning will require both teachers and students to take on unfamiliar roles (Hall & Comperatore, 2014; Litman & Greenleaf, 2008; Porter, McMaken, Hwang, &

Yang, 2011). For teachers to engage students in disciplinary literacy instruction that supports these approximations, they must themselves have experienced discipline-shaped inquiry practices using text. Such instructional practice will require knowledge of the epistemologies and practices of disciplines, including the contribution literacy makes.

Unfortunately, professional development for teachers is often characterized by transmission pedagogy, with a focus on presenting bodies of knowledge, techniques, and prescriptions for teaching rather than on building teachers' understandings (Anderson & Herr, 2011; Lefstein, 2008). Such a focus may produce short-term change; however, impact on instruction is rare (McLaughlin & Marsh, 1978). One meta-analysis found that, in contrast to traditional professional development that offered prescriptions or bodies of knowledge, models that engaged teachers in inquiry improved instruction and increased student achievement (Kennedy, 2016). Another study demonstrated that capacity for teaching complex subject-area literacies endured long past initial inquiry-based professional learning (Greenleaf, Litman, & Marple, 2018). These studies demonstrate that lasting instructional change requires not only re-understanding but re-enacting core teaching practices.

Even when teachers have the knowledge of epistemologies and practices of their disciplines needed to support students' learning with texts, finding texts can also be challenging. Textbooks can be useful for building students' background knowledge, especially when they include embedded primary sources and visual and graphic models. Trade books, websites, and other news and research sources can also be useful for students building knowledge and reading capacity; however, locating texts to support students' disciplinary learning and advance needed literacies, including print literacies, is challenging (Heller & Greenleaf, 2007). As the RAND study (Opfer et al., 2016) showed, teachers spend a lot of time on this even though we have little idea of the efficacy of their practices. The question remains, what knowledge do teachers need to make their selections, and how can this be facilitated? Observations of text dis-use in subject-area classrooms raise questions about the proportion of time teachers should allocate to reading instruction within disciplines. Existing research is silent on such matters.

Much as O'Brien et al. (1995) found over 20 years ago, teachers may also be confronted with required pacing guides, end-of-course content examinations, and course evaluations that hold them accountable for limited kinds of student performance. Being underprepared to facilitate the reading of students who do not appear to possess needed skills and strategies, or to defend their innovative text-based practices in light of students, parents, and administrators who expect different kinds of instruction may also cause teachers to abandon practices learned in teacher education or professional development. They need, instead, professional development and sustained support for intentional and authentic use of disciplinary texts to support students' learning.

One promising strategy for building this needed capacity has involved collaborations of teachers, literacy and disciplinary education researchers, and disciplinary practitioners in designing pedagogical practices to approximate disciplinary knowledge-building practices. In this approach, teachers are invited to build their capacities via collaboration (Wells, 1999) and to study their own literacies and disciplinary knowledge building (Graves, 1990; Greenleaf & Schoenbach, 2004; Litman & Greenleaf, 2018; Schoenbach, Greenleaf, & Murphy, 2016). For example, Chandler-Olcott and colleagues (Chandler-Olcott, Doerr, Hinchman, & Masingila, 2015; Doerr & Temple, 2016) worked with secondary school mathematics teachers to identify ways teachers could support students' abilities to address literacy demands of mathematics curriculum materials. Wilson-Lopez worked with engineers and teachers to address literacy and engineering practices for elementary and middle school students (Wilson-Lopez, Gregory, & Larsen, 2016; Wilson-Lopez & Minichiello, 2017). Dobbs, Ippolito, and Charner-Laird (2016) described how literacy scholars worked with high school social studies teachers to delineate intermediate and disciplinary literacy work to engage students in history reading. Bain and Moje (Bain, 2012; Bain & Moje,

2012) developed an approach to preservice teacher education that used clinical rounds with a focus on discipline-specific literacy, a collaboration among disciplinary, literacy education experts and school-based partners. Draper and several disciplinary colleagues (Draper, 2012; Draper & Wimmer, 2015; Siebert & Draper, 2008; Siebert et al., 2016), collaborated to design preservice and inservice disciplinary literacy teacher education. Providing students with learning experiences that make the social practices and knowledge-building processes of disciplinary literacy work transparent are promising, but also require collaborations to draw on ways disciplines enact their own enterprises (Lehrer, 2009). O'Brien and Ortmann (2017) point out that such collaborations entail power differentials that need to be carefully mitigated.

Needed Studies of Teaching and Learning with Disciplinary Texts

Longstanding secondary school instructional practices virtually guarantee that students have little opportunity to grapple with complex texts when collaboration with peers and support from teachers might build the dispositions and skills of sustained sense-making. Most teachers and students appear to be profoundly inexperienced at doing the kind of teaching and learning with texts, respectively, that disciplinary knowledge building literacies entail. We need research that takes seriously the degree and level of challenge it will take to move the promise of disciplinary literacy instruction into practice.

Urgently needed is research on literacy instruction in subject areas that simultaneously develops requisite skills, strategies, and dispositions for discipline-specific reading and reasoning; builds knowledge about subjects of study; and meaningfully engages with the lives and languages students bring to the classroom. Discipline-specific literacy instruction promises to appeal to teachers' disciplinary commitments and value for text use to support student learning, while also drawing on and building students' purposeful engagement with texts, literacy proficiencies, and subject-area knowledge. The RAND study of CCAS implementation (Opfer et al., 2016) indicated differential use of curriculum, practices, and texts for low income students and English learners, suggesting that American schools may be continuing their long history of curricular segregation with too limited expectations for such students. Also vital is research on developing generalizable academic literacies, with a focus on shifting students' epistemic stances and dispositions toward using texts for learning across disciplines (e.g. Greenleaf & Valencia, 2017; Kiili, Mäkinen & Coiro, 2013; O'Brien & Ortmann, 2017; Schoenbach & Greenleaf, 2009), calls for which have resonated for decades (O'Brien & Stewart, 1992).

Simultaneously teaching and supporting students' learning of disciplinary concepts and practices, as well as disciplinary literacies alongside generalizable academic literacies, will require significant curricular and instructional change. As Cervetti and Pearson (2012) and Moje (2015) argue, such instruction must aim for fidelity to the ways that language and literacy are commingled with knowledge development in the disciplines. The texts students use in subject areas must include a range of authentic disciplinary texts across modalities. This means not only helping students to decipher and make meaning with the multiple modalities of textual forms specific to disciplines, but also fostering reasoning practices, shaped by disciplinary forms of inquiry and knowledge production. The tasks students engage in must move toward developmentally appropriate approximations of knowledge-building practices within disciplines. Thus, research is needed on text selection and use, curricular design, developmentally appropriate learning progressions, and most importantly, the teacher preparation and ongoing development necessary to bring the preceding to life.

Needed Studies of Teaching and Learning with Science Texts

Many exemplary science education curriculum interventions offer promising methods of teaching and learning with science texts, including APL and the text-based investigation approaches described above. The digital age has brought with it many quality science texts that are available on university- and government-sponsored public websites, where scientists publish their work, in science journals written for scientists and students, and through high quality newspaper outlets. Advancements in communication technologies are rapidly adding 3D models, new forms of imagery, and complex visuals to the mix. Yet, few of these texts or interventions are reaching classrooms within which often dated textbooks still serve as *de facto* curricula and the only source of reading, reinforcing the idea that teaching science is a knowledge delivery enterprise. Litman and colleagues (2017) found no close reading or argumentation in their science class observations, and a recent study of over 500 K-8 teacher leaders implementing the NGSS found that only 28% selected "reading informative/explanatory texts", when asked how they were integrating Common Core State Standards and science (Tyler, Britton, Iveland, Ngyuen, Hipps & Schenider, 2017). We need research on the spread of innovative science literacy integrations and the forms of texts in use in education settings.

Science text sets on offer, on many state and district websites, often collected by well-meaning literacy specialists, present sides of issues that involve science phenomena, such as whether to ban soda sales or mandate vaccinations (e.g. Sadler & Donnelly, 2006; Reading and Writing Project, undated). Weighing in on policies offers students opportunities to apply science learning and see how it is relevant. To argue well about such matters, however, students need to know the underlying science, and science teachers may be understandably reluctant to spend time engaging students in arguing policy rather than investigating and explaining phenomena to build understanding. Aligning the reading of science texts with disciplinary practices and purposes would require using texts in the service of scientific knowledge-building practices – such as argumentation to justify and support an explanation of a phenomenon, to raise alternative interpretations of data, or to question the validity of a set of methods or measures – rather than to take a side on a controversial issue. Science education research has long faced the need to develop content knowledge in the discipline, as literature about threshold concepts and common misconceptions attests (e.g. Land, Cousin, Meyer, & Davies, 2005; Meyer & Land, 2003; Sadler, Sonnert, Coyle, Cook-Smith, & Miller, 2013). Attempts to build understandings about how core concepts of science might develop over time are relatively new and evolving (e.g. Berland & McNeill, 2012; Gotwals, Songer, & Bullard, 2012). Studies contrasting purposes for spending time using texts in these pursuits would help to delineate central organizing principles of a disciplinary literacy approach that is well integrated into science teaching more generally.

As Cervetti (this handbook) argues, knowledge matters. To develop knowledge and construct arguments from textual evidence, students need to read science texts of various kinds attentively and deeply. This reading requires puzzling through the semiotic display to make sense of what it conveys about phenomena. To this end, textbooks can serve purposeful learning if they are current and used well. Students can use these traditional forms of exposition to gain breadth of knowledge in the discipline so they can, in turn, ask informed questions and link their own investigations to the work of other scientists. Students, therefore, need a repertoire of strategies, including informed scanning for relevance, evaluation of source reliability, and purposeful text use to build knowledge, as well as stamina, persistence, and will to deeply engage in problem solving to make meaning across complex and extended texts. Studies attending to roles and contributions to student learning for different forms of science texts are needed. Especially promising is research into instructional approaches that draw on teaching and learning from texts to make clear to students "how school science relates to relevant contexts and social practices beyond the classroom" (Sørvik & Mork, 2015, p. 274).

Such work entails expanding science teachers' knowledge and regard for disciplinary literacy, expanding their pedagogical repertoire, and expanding forms of instructional support available to varied learners to acquire needed knowledge, dispositions, and skills. These seismic changes in science curriculum and instruction will require concomitant investments in teacher capacity development through initial teacher preparation and ongoing professional development. Emerging examples of research that engages teachers in disciplinary inquiry so that they learn to address students' needs in instruction includes work by Reiser et al. (2017), who have developed a web-enabled professional learning environment for science teachers to carry out investigations of phenomena, post results for other teacher learning groups, and share student work on pertinent investigations. Windschitl and colleagues engage prospective science teachers in science investigations that include textual research to build their understandings of science practices (Windschitl et al., 2008; Windschitl, Thompson, & Braaten, 2011). Greenleaf and science colleagues have designed professional development to engage secondary science teachers in metacognitive inquiry into their own reading and reasoning processes with disciplinary texts, with a demonstrated impact on teachers' text use and support for students' text use (Fancsali et al., 2015; Greenleaf et al., 2011). Studies of the disjuncture between preservice teachers' understandings of their disciplines and needed education practices (Bain & Moje, 2012; Conley & Kang, 2015; Windschitl et al., 2011) make it especially important to identify effective ways to support inservice teacher learning.

Collaborative design research may also have the potential to advance the field on multiple fronts. Teachers in such collaborations work together with researchers to co-design, implement, and study effects of educational innovations and how to make them work within authentic, richly complex contexts of practice (Goldman et al., 2016; Klingner, Boardman, & McMaster, 2013; Ormel, Roblin, McKenney, Voogt, & Pieters, 2012). The opportunity to take an active part in co-designing or adapting curriculum and instruction can also deepen teachers' understanding of underlying principles (Burch & Spillane, 2005; Debarger et al., 2017; Voogt et al., 2015), support instructional decision-making (Fullan & Langworthy, 2014), promote teachers' sense of ownership and agency (Cviko, McKenney, & Voogt, 2014; Henson, 2001; Voogt et al., 2015), and foster knowledge utilization (Easton, 2014; Weiss, 1993). These factors may contribute to a more effective implementation of innovations and student learning, as well as greater sustainability (Penuel, Fishman, Cheng, & Sabelli, 2011; Penuel, Gallagher, & Moorthy, 2011; Roderick, Easton, & Sebring, 2009). Design research can thus produce new knowledge and create professional learning experiences that support teachers in ongoing design and implementation of curricular reforms (Cviko et al., 2014; Ormel et al., 2012; Penuel et al., 2011, 2011).

Conclusions

Research that expands teaching and learning with disciplinary texts holds the promise of improving youth's literacy, academic, and disciplinary competence. Classroom use of disciplinary texts must aim to expand the repertoire and agency of young people as they encounter specialized academic practices within and across disciplines. Such texts – a wide array of them – must also be made readily available to teachers and students. Expanding teaching and learning with disciplinary texts will depend on the mentorship of those who know best how to support them – teachers who have studied in these disciplines. This work, thus, also requires building the knowledge, capacity, and regard of subject-area teachers for generalized academic and discipline-specific literacies to support student learning. It also requires carefully qualified expectations for subject-area teachers' attention to these literacies by literacy advocates.

In short, future research to expand teaching and learning from disciplinary texts needs to aim toward expanding the literate repertoires of disciplinary teachers and their students. This means research needs to continue to look beyond the literacy research community to attend to ways that disciplines invoke literacy practices to build knowledge, to what it takes for students to gain expertise with this in developmentally appropriate ways, and to professional development that invites teachers to experience disciplinary knowledge building so they can orchestrate such practices for their students. Disrupting the long history of lecturing, memorizing, and recitation in secondary subject areas also requires situating research in partnerships of literacy researchers, disciplinary researchers, and classroom teachers. Such collaborations can design and test literacy pedagogies that build from the social practices of youth's lives and the work of schools, as well as ensure that youth engage in the kinds of disciplinary knowledge-building approximations that invite them to become the next generation of disciplinary experts.

References

Abedi, J., & Gándara, P. (2006). Performance of English language learners as a subgroup in large-scale assessment: Interaction of research and policy. *Educational Measurement: Issues and Practice, 25*(4), 36–46.

ACT Inc. (2006). *Reading between the lines: What the ACT reveals about college readiness in reading.* Iowa City, IA: ACT, Inc.

ACT Inc. (2009). *ACT national curriculum survey 2009.* Iowa City, IA: ACT, Inc.

ACT Inc. (2013a). *ACT national curriculum survey 2012: English language arts.* Iowa City, IA: ACT, Inc.

ACT Inc. (2013b). *ACT national curriculum survey 2012: Science.* Iowa City, IA: ACT, Inc.

Alexander, P. A. (2003). The development of expertise: The journey from acclimation to proficiency. *Educational Researcher, 32*(8), 10–14.

Alexander, P. A., & Jetton, T. L. (2000). Learning from text: A multidimensional and developmental perspective. In M. L. Kamil, P. B. Mosenthal, P. D. Pearson, & R. Barr (Eds.), *Handbook of reading research* (Vol. III, pp. 285–310). Mahwah, NJ: Erlbaum.

Alvermann, D. E. (2001). Reading adolescents' reading identities: Looking back to see ahead. *Journal of Adolescent & Adult Literacy, 44*(8), 676–690.

Alvermann, D. E., & Moore, D. W. (1991). Secondary school reading. In R. Barr, M. Kamil, P. Mosenthal, & P. D. Pearson (Eds.), *Handbook of reading research* (Vol. II, pp. 951–983). New York, NY: Longman.

Amaral, O. M., Garrison, L., & Klentschy, M. (2002). Helping English learners increase achievement through inquiry-based science instruction. *Bilingual Research Journal, 26*(2), 213–239.

Anderson, G. L., & Herr, K. (2011). Scaling up "evidence-based" practices for teachers is a profitable but discredited paradigm. *Educational Researcher, 40*(6), 287–289.

Applebee, A. N., Langer, J. A., Nystrand, M., & Gamoran, A. (2003). Discussion-based approaches to developing understanding: Classroom instruction and student performance in middle and high school English. *American Educational Research Journal, 40*(3), 685–730.

Araújo, M., & Maeso, S. R. (2012). History textbooks, racism, and the critique of Eurocentrism: Beyond rectification or compensation. *Ethnic and Racial Studies, 35*(7), 1266–1286.

Athanases, S. Z., & de Oliveira, L. C. (2014). Scaffolding versus routine support for latina/o youth in an urban school: Tensions in building toward disciplinary literacy. *Journal of Literacy Research, 46*(2), 263–299. doi:10.1177/1086296X14535328

Bain, R. B. (2006). Rounding up unusual suspects: Facing the authority hidden in the history classroom. *Teachers College Record, 108*, 2080–2114.

Bain, R. B. (2012). Using disciplinary literacy to develop coherence in history teacher education: The clinical rounds project. *The History Teacher, 45*(4), 513–532.

Bain, R. B., & Moje, E. B. (2012). Mapping the teacher education terrain for novices. *Phi Delta Kappan, 93*(5), 62–65. doi:10.1177/003172171209300514

Banilower, E. R., Smith, P. S., Weiss, I. R., Malzahn, K. A., Campbell, K. M., & Weis, A. M. (2013). *Report of the 2012 national survey of science and mathematics education.* Chapel Hill, NC: Horizon Research, Inc.

Bartholomae, D. (1986). Inventing the university. *Journal of Basic Writing, 5*(1), 4–23.

Barton, D., Hamilton, M., & Ivanič, R. (Eds.). (2000). *Situated literacies: Reading and writing in context.* UK: Psychology Press.

Bazerman, C. (1985). Physicists reading physics: Schema-laden purposes and purpose-laden schema. *Written Communication, 2*(1), 3–23.

Bazzul, J., & Sykes, H. (2011). The secret identity of a biology textbook: Straight and naturally sexed. *Cultural Studies of Science Education, 6*(2), 265–286.

Beach, R., & Castek, J. (2015). Use of apps and devices for fostering mobile learning of literacy practices. In B. Guzzetti & M. Lesley (Eds.), *Handbook of research on the societal impact of digital media* (pp. 343–370). Hershey, PA: IGI Global.

Berland, L. K., & McNeill, K. L. (2012). For whom is argument and explanation a necessary distinction? A response to Osborne and Patterson. *Science Education, 96*(5), 808–813.

Berland, L. K., & Reiser, B. J. (2009). Making sense of argumentation and explanation. *Science Education, 93*(1), 26–55.

Bernstein, B. (1971). *Class, codes, and control, Vol. 1. Theoretical studies towards a sociology of language*. London, UK & Boston: MA: Routledge and Kegan Paul.

Bloome, B., Puro, P., & Theodorou, E. (1989). Procedural display and classroom lessons. *Curriculum Inquiry, 19*(3), 265–291.

Braaten, M., & Windschitl, M. (2011). Working toward a stronger conceptualization of scientific explanation for science education. *Science Education, 95*(4), 639–669.

Bravo, M., & Cervetti, G. (2014). Attending to the language and literacy needs of English Learners in science. *Equity and Excellence in Education, 47*(2), 230–245. doi:10.1080/10665684.2014.900418

Bricker, L. A., & Bell, P. (2008). Conceptualizations of argumentation from science studies and the learning sciences and their implications for the practices of science education. *Science Education, 92*(3), 473–498.

Broughton, S. H., Sinatra, G. M., & Reynolds, R. E. (2010). The nature of the refutation text effect: An investigation of attention allocation. *The Journal of Educational Research, 103*(6), 407–423.

Brozo, W. G. (2017). *Disciplinary and content literacy for today's adolescents: Honoring diversity and building competence* (6th. ed.). New York, NY: Guilford Press.

Brozo, W. G., Moorman, G., Meyer, C., & Stewart, T. (2013). Content area reading and disciplinary literacy: A case for the radical center. *Journal of Adolescent & Adult Literacy, 56*(5), 353–357.

Burch, P., & Spillane, J. P. (2005). How subjects matter in district office practice: Instructionally relevant policy in urban school district redesign. *Journal of Educational Change, 6*, 51–76.

Bybee, R. W. (2013). *The case for stem education: challenges and opportunities*. Arlington, VA: NSTA Press.

Cavagnetto, A. R. (2010). Argument to foster scientific literacy: A review of argument interventions in K-12 science contexts. *Review of Educational Research, 80*(3), 336–371.

Cazden, C. (1979). Language in education: Variation in the teacher-talk register. In J. E. Alatis & G. R. Tucker (Eds.), *Language in public life* (pp. 144–162). Washington D.C.: Georgetown University Press.

Cervetti, G. (2014, December). *Content area literacy and disciplinary literacy in elementary school science: Reconciling the divide*. Paper presented at the conference of the Literacy Research Association, Marco Island, FL.

Cervetti, G. N., Barber, J., Dorph, R., Pearson, P. D., & Goldschmidt, P. G. (2012). The impact of an integrated approach to science and literacy in elementary school classrooms. *Journal of Research in Science Teaching, 49*(5), 631–658.

Cervetti, G., & Pearson, P. (2012). Reading, writing, and thinking like a scientist. *Journal of Adolescent & Adult Literacy, 55*(7), 580–586.

Chandler-Olcott, K., Doerr, H. M., Hinchman, K. A., & Masingila, J. O. (2015). Bypass, augment, or integrate: How secondary mathematics teachers address the literacy demands of standards-based curriculum materials. *Journal of Literacy Research, 47*(4), 439–472.

Chiappetta, E. L., & Fillman, D. A. (2007). Analysis of five high school biology textbooks used in the United States for inclusion of the nature of science. *International Journal of Science Education, 29*(15), 1847–1868.

Chick, N. L., Haynie, A., & Gurung, R. A. (2012). *Exploring more signature pedagogies: Approaches to teaching disciplinary habits of the mind*. Sterling, VA: Stylus.

Chin, C., & Osborne, J. (2010). Supporting argumentation through students' questions: Case studies in science classrooms. *Journal of the Learning Sciences, 19*(2), 230–284.

Chinn, C. A., & Malhotra, B. A. (2002). Epistemologically authentic inquiry in schools: A theoretical framework for evaluating inquiry tasks. *Science Education, 86*(2), 175–218.

Coll, R. K., Taylor, N., & Lay, M. C. (2009). Scientists' habits of mind as evidenced by the interaction between their science training and religious beliefs. *International Journal of Science Education, 31*(6), 725–755.

Conley, M. W., & Kang, H. (2015). What beginning teachers' narratives about video-based instruction tell us about learning to teach science and literacy. In E. Ortlieb, L. Shanahan, & M. McVee (Eds.), *Video research in disciplinary literacies* (pp. 21–40). Cambridge, MA: Emerald Group Publishing.

Cope, B., & Kalantzis, M. (Eds.). (2000). *Multiliteracies: Literacy learning and the design of social futures* (pp. 201–234). New York, NY: Routledge.

Corrin, W., Somers, M. A., Kemple, J., Nelson, E., & Sepanik, S. (2008). *The enhanced reading opportunities study: Findings from the second year of implementation*. Washington DC: National Center for Education Evaluation And Regional Assistance, Institute of Education Sciences, U.S. Department of Education. Retrieved from http://ies.ed.gov/ncee/pubs/20094036/

Council, N. R. (2014). *Literacy for science: Exploring the intersection of the next generation science standards*. Washington, DC: National Academies Press.

Cromley, J. G., Snyder-Hogan, L. E., & Luciw-Dubas, U. A. (2010). Reading comprehension of scientific text: A domain-specific test of the direct and inferential mediation model of reading comprehension. *Journal of Educational Psychology, 102*(3), 687–700. doi:10.1037/a0019452

Cviko, A., McKenney, S., & Voogt, J. (2014). Teacher roles in designing technology-rich learning activities for early literacy: A cross-case analysis. *Computers & Education, 72*, 68–79.

de Schonewise, E. A., & Klingner, J. K. (2012). Linguistic and cultural issues in developing disciplinary literacy for adolescent English language learners. *Topics in Language Disorders, 32*(1), 51–68.

Debarger, A. H., Penuel, W. R., Moorthy, S., Beauvineau, Y., Kennedy, C. A., & And Boscardin, C. K. (2017). Investigating purposeful science curriculum adaptation as a strategy to improve teaching and learning. *Science Education, 101*, 66–98. doi:10.1002/sce.21249

Dobbs, C. L., Ippolito, J., & Charner-Laird, M. (2016). Layering intermediate and disciplinary literacy work: Lessons learned from a secondary social studies teacher team. *Journal of Adolescent & Adult Literacy*. doi:10.1002/jaal.547

Doerr, H. M., & Temple, C. (2016). "Its a different kind of reading": Two middle-grade teachers evolving perspectives on reading in mathematics. *Journal of Literacy Research*. doi:10.1177/1086296X16637180

Draper, R. J. (2012). Professional resources. *Journal of Adolescent & Adult Literacy, 56*(4), 337–339. doi:10.1002/jaal.00148

Draper, R. J., & Wimmer, J. J. (2015). Acknowledging, noticing, and reimagining disciplinary instruction: The promise of new literacies for guiding research and practice in teacher education. *Action in Teacher Education, 37*(3), 251–264.

Duschl, R. A., & Osborne, J. (2002). Supporting and promoting argumentation discourse in Science education. *Studies in Science Education, 38*(1), 39–72.

Duschl, R. A., Schweingruber, H., & Shouse, A. (2007). *Taking science to school: Learning and teaching science in grades K-8*. Washington, DC: The National Academies Press.

Dyson, A. H. (1997). *Writing superheroes: Contemporary childhood, popular culture, and classroom literacy*. New York, NY: Teachers College Press.

Easton, J. (2014, April). *IES: Promises and challenges*. Presented at the Annual meeting of the American Educational Research Association, Philadelphia, PA. Retrieved from http://ies.ed.gov/director/pdf/Easton040514.pdf

Elliott, D. L., & Woodward, A. (Eds.). (1990). *Textbooks and schooling in the United States* (Vol. 89). Chicago, IL: The National Society for the Study of Education.

Faggella-Luby, M. N., Graner, P. S., Deshler, D. D., & Drew, S. V. (2012). Building a house on sand: Why disciplinary literacy is not sufficient to replace general strategies for adolescent learners who struggle. *Topics in Language Disorders, 32*(1), 69–84.

Falk, H., & Yarden, A. (2009). "Here the scientists explain what I said." Coordination practices elicited during the enactment of the results and discussion sections of adapted primary literature. *Research in Science Education, 39*(3), 349–383.

Fancsali, C., Abe, Y., Piatigorsky, M., Ortiz, L., Chan, V., Saltares, E., … Jaciw, A. (2015). *The impact of the Reading Apprenticeship Improving Secondary Education (RAISE) project on academic literacy in high school a report of a randomized experiment in pennsylvania and california schools (evaluation)*. Impaq International and Empirical Education, Inc.

Fang, Z. (2014). Preparing content area reachers for disciplinary literacy instruction: The role of literacy teacher educators. *Journal of Adolescent & Adult Literacy, 57*(6), 444–448.

Fang, Z., & Schleppegrell, M. J. (2010). Disciplinary literacies across content areas: Supporting secondary reading through functional language analysis. *Journal of Adolescent & Adult Literacy, 53*, 587–597.

Finders, M. J. (1997). *Just girls: Hidden literacies and life in junior high*. New York, NY: Teachers College Press.

Fisher, D. (2009). The use of instructional time in the typical high school classroom. *The Educational Forum, 73*(2), 168–176. doi:10.1080/00131720902739650

Ford, M. J., & Wargo, B. M. (2012). Dialogic framing of scientific content for conceptual and epistemic understanding. *Science Education, 96*(3), 369–391.

Fredlund, T., Airey, J., & Linder, C. (2015). Enhancing the possibilities for learning: Variation of disciplinary-relevant aspects in physics representations. *European Journal of Physics, 36*(5), 055001.

Fullan, M., & Langworthy, M. (2014). *A rich seam: How new pedagogies find deep learning*. London: Pearson.

Geisler, C. (1994). Literacy and expertise in the academy. *Language and Learning across the Disciplines, 1*(1), 35–57.

Girod, M., & Twyman, T. (2009). Comparing the added value of blended science/literacy curricula to inquiry based science curricula in two 2nd grade classrooms. *Journal of Elementary Science Education, 21*(3), Summer, 13–32.

Giroux, C. S., & Moje, E. B. (2017). Learning from the professions: Examining how, why, and when engineers read and write. *Theory into Practice, 56*(4), 300–307.

Goldman, S. R., Britt, M. A., Brown, W., Cribb, G., George, M., & Greenleaf, C. (2016). Disciplinary literacies and learning to read for understanding: A conceptual framework for disciplinary literacy. *Educational Psychologist*, *51*(2), Project READI, 219–246.

Goldman, S. R., Greenleaf, C., Yukhymenko-Lescroat, M., Brown, W., Ko, Mon-Lin M., Emig, J. M., George, M., Blaum, P. W. D., & Britt, M. A. (2019). Explanatory modeling in science through text-based investigation: Testing the efficacy of the Project READI Intervention Approach. *American Educational Research Journal*, *56*(4), 1148–1216.

González, N., Moll, L. C., & Amanti, C. (Eds.). (2005). *Funds of Knowledge: Theorizing practices in households, communities, and classrooms*. Mahwah, NJ: Erlbaum.

Gotwals, A. W., Songer, N. B., & Bullard, L. (2012). Assessing students' progressing abilities to construct scientific explanations. In A. C. Alonzo & A. W. Gotwals (Eds.), *Learning progressions in Science* (pp. 183–210). Rotterdam: SensePublishers. Retrieved from www.springerlink.com/index/10.1007/978-94-6091-824-7_9

Graves, D. (1990). *Discover your own literacy*. Portsmouth, NH: Heinemann.

Greenleaf, C., Brown, W., Goldman, S. R., & Ko, M.-L. (2013). READI for science: Promoting scientific literacy practices through text-based investigations for middle and high school science teachers and students. Presented at the NRC Workshop on Literacy for Science, Washington DC.

Greenleaf, C., Brown, W., & Sexton, U. (2013). *Studying the implementation of text-based investigations on MRSA in high school science classrooms: Lessons from collaborative design based research*. Project READI Technical Report #20. Oakland, CA: Strategic Literacy Initiative, WestEd. Retrieved from projectreadi.org

Greenleaf, C., Hale, G., Charney-Sirott, I., & Schoenbach, R. (2007). *Reading apprenticeship academic literacy curriculum*. San Francisco, CA: WestEd.

Greenleaf, C., Hanson, T., Herman, J., Litman, C., Rosen, R., Schneider, S., & Silver, D. (2011). *A study of the efficacy of reading apprenticeship professional development for high school history and science teaching and learning*. Final report to Institute for Education Sciences.

Greenleaf, C., Litman, C., & Marple, S. (2018). The impact of inquiry-based professional development on teachers' capacity to integrate literacy instruction in secondary subject areas. *Teaching and Teacher Education*, *71*, 226–240.

Greenleaf, C., & Schoenbach, R. (2004). Building capacity for the responsive teaching of reading in the academic disciplines: Strategic inquiry designs for middle and high school teachers' professional development. In D. Strickland & M. L. Kamil (Eds.), *Improving reading achievement through professional development* (pp. 200–226). Norwood, MA: Christopher-Gordon Publishers.

Greenleaf, C., Schoenbach, R., Cziko, C., & Mueller, F. (2001). Apprenticing adolescent readers to academic literacy. *Harvard Educational Review*, *71*(1), 79–130.

Greenleaf, C., & Valencia, S. (2017). Missing in action: Learning from texts in subject-matter classrooms. In K. A. Hinchman, & D. A. Appleman (Eds.), *Adolescent literacy: A handbook of practice-based research* (pp. 135–155). NY: Guilford Press.

Grossman, P. L., & Stodolsky, S. S. (1995). Content as context: The role of school subjects in secondary school teaching. *Educational Researcher*, *24*(8), 5–23.

Gunel, M., Hand, B., & Gunduz, S. (2006). Comparing student understanding of quantum physics when embedding multimodal representations into two different writing formats: Presentation format versus summary report format. *Science Education*, *90*(6), 1092–1112.

Gunel, M., Hand, B., & Prain, V. (2007). Writing for learning in science: A secondary analysis of six studies. *International Journal of Science and Mathematics Education*, *5*(4), 615–637.

Guzzetti, B. J., Snyder, T. E., Glass, G. V., & Gamas, W. S. (1993). Promoting conceptual change in science: A comparative meta-analysis of instructional interventions from reading education and science education. *Reading Research Quarterly*, *26*(2), 117–159.

Hall, L. A., & Comperatore, A. (2014). Teaching literacy to youth who struggle with academic literacies. In K. Hinchman & H. Sheridan-Thomas (Eds.), *Best practices in adolescent literacy instruction* (2nd., pp. 80–96). New York, NY: Guilford Press.

Hand, B., & Choi, A. (2010). Examining the impact of student use of multiple modal representations in constructing arguments in Organic Chemistry laboratory classes. *Research in Science Education*, *40*(1), 29–44.

Hand, B., Yore, L. D., Jagger, S., & Prain, V. (2010). Connecting research in science literacy and classroom practice: A review of science teaching journals in Australia, the UK and the United States, 1998–2008. *Studies in Science Education*, *46*(1), 45–68.

Heath, S. B. (1983). *Ways with words: Language, life and work in communities and classrooms*. UK: Cambridge University Press.

Heller, R., & Greenleaf, C. (2007). *Literacy instruction in the content areas: Getting to the core of middle and high school improvement*. Washington, DC: Alliance for Excellent Education.

Henson, R. K. (2001). The effects of participation in teacher research on teacher efficacy. *Teaching and Teacher Education, 17*(7), 819–836.

Hiebert, E. H. (2017). The texts of literacy Instruction: Obstacles to or opportunities for educational equity? *Literacy Research: Theory, Method, and Practice, 66*(1), 117–134. doi:10.1177/2381336917718521

Hill, M., Sharma, M. D., & Johnston, H. (2015). How online learning modules can improve the representational fluency and conceptual understanding of university physics students. *European Journal of Physics, 36*(4), 045019.

Hull, G. A., & Schultz, K. (Eds.). (2002). *School's out: Bridging out-of-school literacies with classroom practice*. New York, NY: Teachers College Press.

Jimenez-Aleixandre, M. P., Rodriguez, A. B., & Duschl, R. A. (2000). "Doing the lesson" or "doing science": Argumentation in high school genetics. *Science Education, 84*(6), 689–799.

Kennedy, M. M. (2016). How does professional development improve teaching? *Review of Educational Research, 86*(4), 945–980. https://doi-org/10.3102/0034654315626800

Kerlin, S. C., McDonald, S. P., & Kelly, G. J. (2010). Complexity of secondary scientific data sources and students' argumentative discourse. *International Journal of Science Education, 32*(9), 1207–1225.

Kiili, C., Mäkinen, M., & Coiro, J. (2013). Rethinking academic literacies. *Journal of Adolescent & Adult Literacy, 57*(3), 223–232.

Klingner, J. K., Boardman, A. G., & McMaster, K. L. (2013). What does it take to scale up and sustain evidence-based practices? *Exceptional Children, 79*(2), 195–211.

Koomen, M. H., Weaver, S., Blair, R. B., & Oberhauser, K. S. (2016). Disciplinary literacy in the science classroom: Using adaptive primary literature: Disciplinary literacy in the science classroom. *Journal of Research in Science Teaching, 53*(6), 847–894. doi:10.1002/tea.21317

Krajcik, J. S., & Sutherland, L. (2009). IQWST materials: Meeting the challenges of the 21st century. In Workshop on Exploring the Intersection of Science Education and the Development of 21st Century Skills, National Research Council. Retrieved May 2009, from: www7.nationalacademies.org/bose/Krajcik_Sutherland_Comm%20Paper.pdf

Kress, G. (2013). Recognizing learning. In I. deSaint-Georges & J. J. Weber (Eds.), *Multilingualism and multimodality* (pp. 119–140). Rotterdam, ND: Sense Publishers.

Kress, G., & van Leeuwen, T. (2001). *Multimodal discourse: The modes and media of contemporary communication*. London, UK: Arnold.

Labov, W. (1972). *Language in the inner city: Studies in the Black English vernacular* (Vol. 3). Philadelphia, PA: University of Pennsylvania Press.

Land, R., Cousin, G., Meyer, J. H., & Davies, P. (2005). Threshold concepts and troublesome knowledge (3): Implications for course design and evaluation. In C. Rust (Ed.), *Improving student learning: Diversity and inclusivity* (pp. 53–64). Oxford, UK: Oxford Centre for Staff & Learning Development.

Latour, B., & Woolgar, S. (1986). *Laboratory life: The construction of scientific facts*. Princeton, NJ: Princeton University Press.

Lea, M. R. (1999). Academic literacies and learning in higher education: Constructing knowledge through texts and experience. In C. Jones, J. Turner, & B. V. Street (Eds.), *Students writing in the university: Cultural and epistemological issues* (pp. 103–124). Amsterdam: John Benjamins Publishing.

Lee, C. D. (1993). *Signifying as a scaffold for literary interpretation: The pedagogical implications of an African American discourse genre*. Urbana, IL: National Council of Teachers of English.

Lee, C. D. (1995). A culturally based cognitive apprenticeship: Teaching African American high school students skills in literary interpretation. *Reading Research Quarterly, 30*(4), 608–630.

Lee, P. (2005). Putting principles into practice: Understanding history. In M. S. Donovan, & J. D. Bransford (Eds.), *How students learn: History in the classroom* (pp. 31–77). Washington, DC. The National Academies Press.

Lefstein, A. (2008). Changing classroom practice through the English national literacy strategy: A micro-interactional perspective. *American Educational Research Journal, 45*(3), 701–737.

Lehrer, R. (2009). Designing to develop disciplinary dispositions: Modeling natural systems. *American Psychologist, 64*(8), 759–771.

Lemke, J. (1998). Multiplying meaning. In J. R. Martin & R. Veel (Eds.), *Reading science: Critical and functional perspectives on discourses of science* (pp. 87–113). London, UK: Routledge.

Lemke, J. L. (1990). *Talking science: Language, learning, and values*. Norwood, NJ: Ablex Publishing Corporation.

Leubner, C., Alber, M., & Schupfer, N. (1988). Critique and correction of the textbook comparison between classical and quantum harmonic oscillator probability densities. *American Journal of Physics, 56*, 1123–1129.

Litman, C., & Greenleaf, C. (2008). Traveling together over difficult ground. In K. Hinchman & H. Sheridan-Thomas (Eds.), *Best practices in adolescent literacy instruction* (pp. 275–296). New York, NY: Guilford Press.

Litman, C., & Greenleaf, C. (2018). Argumentation tasks in secondary English language arts, history, and science: Variations in instructional focus and inquiry space. *Reading Research Quarterly, 53*(1), 107–126.

Litman, C., Marple, S., Greenleaf, C., Charney-Sirott, I., Bolz, M. J., Richardson, L. K., … Goldman, S. R. (2017). Text-based argumentation with multiple sources: A descriptive study of opportunity to learn in secondary English language arts, history, and science. *Journal of the Learning Sciences, 26*(1), 79–130.

Manderino, M. (2012). Disciplinary literacy in new literacies environments: Expanding the intersections of literate practice for adolescents. In P. Dunston, L. Gambrell, K. Headley, S. Fullerton, & P. Stecker (Eds.), *Sixty-first yearbook of the literacy research association* (pp. 69–83). Oak Creek, WI: Literacy Research Association.

McLaughlin, M. W., & Marsh, D. D. (1978). Staff development and school change. *Teachers College Record, 80*(1), 69–94.

McNeill, K. L. (2009). Teachers' use of curriculum to support students in writing scientific arguments to explain phenomena. *Science Education, 93*(2), 233–268.

McNeill, K. L., & Krajcik, J. S. (2011). *Supporting grade 5-8 students in constructing explanations in science: The claim, evidence, and reasoning framework for talk and writing.* Boston, MA: Pearson.

Mehan, H. (1979). *Learning lessons: Social organization in the classroom.* Cambridge, MA: Harvard University Press.

Meyer, J., & Land, R. (2003). *Threshold concepts and troublesome knowledge: Linkages to ways of thinking and practising within the disciplines.* University of Edinburgh Edinburgh. Retrieved from www.utwente.nl/ces/vop/archief_nieuwsbrief/afleveringen%20vanaf%20okt%202005/nieuwsbrief_17/land_paper.pdf

Mills, G. C., & Bradley, W. L. (1993). Origin of life & evolution in biology textbooks: A critique. *The American Biology Teacher, 55*(2), 78–83.

Moje, E. B. (2000). "To be part of the story": The literacy practices of gangsta adolescents. *Teachers College Record, 102*(3), 651–690.

Moje, E. B. (2007). Developing socially just subject-matter instruction: A review of the literature on disciplinary literacy teaching. *Review of Research in Education, 31*(1), 1–44.

Moje, E. B. (2015). Doing and teaching disciplinary literacy with adolescent learners: A social and cultural enterprise. *Harvard Educational Review, 85*(2), 254–278. doi:10.17763/0017-8055.85.2.254

Moje, E. B., Ciechanowski, K. M., Kramer, K., Ellis, L., Carrillo, R., & Collazo, T. (2004a). Working toward third space in content area literacy: An examination of everyday funds of knowledge and discourse. *Reading Research Quarterly, 39*(1), 38–70.

Moje, E. B., Peek-Brown, D., Sutherland, L. M., Marx, R. W., Blumenfeld, P., & Krajcik, J. (2004b). Explaining explanations. In D. Strickland & D. Alvermann (Eds.), *Bridging the literacy achievement gap, grades 4–12* (p. 227). Norwood, MA: Christopher-Gordon Publishers.

Moje, E. B., Stockdill, D., Kim, K., & Kim, H. J. (2011). The role of text in disciplinary learning. In *Handbook of reading research* (Vol. IV, pp. 479–512). New York, NY: Routledge.

Moll, L. C., & Gonzalez, N. (1997). Teachers as social scientists: Learning about culture from household research. *Race, Ethnicity, and Multiculturalism: Policy and Practice, 1,* 89–114.

Monte-Sano, C. (2011). Beyond reading comprehension and summary: Learning to read and write by focusing on evidence, perspective, and interpretation. *Curriculum Inquiry, 41*(2), 212–249.

Moore, D., Readence, J., & Rickelman, R. (1983). An historical exploration of content area reading instruction. *Reading Research Quarterly, 18*(4), 419–438. doi:10.2307/747377

Myers, G. A. (1992). Textbooks and the sociology of scientific knowledge. *English for Specific Purposes, 11*(1), 3–17.

New London Group. (1996). A pedagogy of multiliteracies: Designing social futures. *Harvard Educational Review, 66*(1), 60–93.

Ness, M. K. (2008). Supporting secondary readers: When teachers provide the "what," not the "how." *American Secondary Education, 37*(1), 80–95.

NGSS Lead States. (2013). *Next generation science standards: For states, by states.* Washington, DC: National Academies Press.

Newell, G. E., Beach, R., Smith, J., VanDerHeide, J., Kuhn, D., & Andriessen, J. (2011). Teaching and learning argumentative reading and writing: A review of research. *Reading Research Quarterly, 46*(3), 273–304.

Norris, S. P., & Phillips, L. M. (2003). How literacy in its fundamental sense is central to scientific literacy. *Science Education, 87*(2), 224–240.

Norris, S. P., Stelnicki, N., & de Vries, G. (2012). Teaching mathematical biology in high school using adapted primary literature. *Research in Science Education, 42*(4), 633–649.

O'Brien, D. G., & Ortmann, L. (2017). Disciplinary literacy: A multidisciplinary synthesis. In K. A. Hinchman & D. Appleman (Eds.), *Adolescent literacy: A handbook of practice-based research* (pp. 182–198). New York, NY: Guilford Press.

O'Brien, D. G., & Stewart, R. A. (1992). Resistance to content area reading instruction: Dimensions and solutions. *Reading in the Content Areas, 3,* 30–40.

O'Brien, D. G., Stewart, R. A., & Moje, E. B. (1995). Why content literacy is difficult to infuse into the secondary school: Complexities of curriculum, pedagogy, and school culture. *Reading Research Quarterly, 30*(3), 442–463.

O'Hallaron, C. L., Palincsar, A. S., & Schleppegrell, M. J. (2015). Reading science: Using systemic functional linguistics to support critical language awareness. *Special Issue on Critical Language Awareness Approaches in the Americas: Theoretical Principles, Pedagogical Practices and Distribution of Intellectual Labor, 32,* 55–67. doi:10.1016/j.linged.2015.02.002

Opfer, V. D., Kaufman, J. H., & Thompson, L. E. (2016). *Implementation of K-12 standards for Mathematics and English language arts and literacy.* Santa Monica, CA: RAND Corporation.

Ormel, B. J., Roblin, N. N. P., McKenney, S. E., Voogt, J. M., & Pieters, J. M. (2012). Research–practice interactions as reported in recent design studies: Still promising, still hazy. *Educational Technology Research and Development, 60*(6), 967–986.

Osborne, J. F. (2002). Science without literacy: A ship without a sail? *Cambridge Journal of Education, 32,* 203–215.

Osborne, J. F. (2010). Arguing to learn in science: The role of collaborative, critical discourse. *Science, 328*(5977), 463–466.

Palincsar, A. S., & Magnusson, S. J. (2001). The interplay of first-hand and text-based investigations to model and support the development of scientific knowledge and reasoning. In S. M. Carver & D. Klahr (Eds.), *Cognition and instruction: Twenty-five years of progress* (pp. 151–194). Mahwah, NJ: Lawrence Erlbaum Associates.

Paris, S. G., Lipson, M. Y., & Wixson, K. K. (1983). Becoming a strategic reader. *Contemporary Educational Psychology, 8*(3), 293–316.

Penney, K., Norris, S. P., Phillips, L. M., & Clark, G. (2003). The anatomy of junior high school science textbooks: An analysis of textual characteristics and a comparison to media reports of science. *Canadian Journal of Math, Science & Technology Education, 3*(4), 415–436.

Penuel, W. R., Fishman, B. J., Cheng, B. H., & Sabelli, N. (2011). Organizing research and development at the intersection of learning, implementation, and design. *Educational Researcher, 40*(7), 331–337.

Penuel, W. R., Gallagher, L. P., & Moorthy, S. (2011). Preparing teachers to design sequences of instruction in earth systems science a comparison of three professional development programs. *American Educational Research Journal, 48*(4), 996–1025.

Phillips, L. M., & Norris, S. P. (2009). Bridging the gap between the language of science and the language of school science through the use of adapted primary literature. *Research in Science Education, 39*(3), 313–319.

Porter, A. C., McMaken, J., Hwang, J., & Yang, R. (2011). Common core standards: The new U.S. intended curriculum. *Educational Researcher, 40*(3), 103–116.

Prain, V., & Hand, B. (2016). Learning science through learning to use its languages. In V. Prain, M. McDermott, & B. Hand (Eds.), *Using multimodal representations to support learning in the science classroom* (pp. 1–10). Cham, CH: Springer International Publishing.

Putra, G. B. S., & Tang, K.-S. (2016). Disciplinary literacy instructions on writing scientific explanations: A case study from a chemistry classroom in an all-girls school. *Chemistry Education Research and Practice, 17*(3), 569–579. doi:10.1039/C6RP00022C

Rabinowitz, P. J. (1998). *Before reading: Narrative conventions and the politics of interpretation.* Columbus, OH: The Ohio State University Press.

Reiser, B. J., Michaels, S., Moon, J., Bell, T., Dyer, E., Edwards, K. D., … Park, A. (2017). Scaling up three-dimensional science learning through teacher-led study groups across a state. *Journal of Teacher Education, 68*(3), 280–298. doi:10.1177/0022487117699598

Roderick, M., Easton, J., & Sebring, P. (2009). *The consortium on Chicago school research: A new model for the role of research in urban school reform.* Chicago, IL: CCSR.

Romance, N. R., & Vitale, M. R. (1992). A curriculum strategy that expands time for in-depth elementary science instruction by using science-based reading strategies: Effects of a year-long study in grade four. *Journal of Research in Science Teaching, 29*(6), 545–554.

Romance, N. R., & Vitale, M. R. (2001). Implementing an in-depth expanded science model in elementary schools: Multi-year findings, research issues, and policy implications. *International Journal of Science Education, 23*(4), 373–404.

Rosenblatt, L. (1978). *The reader. the text, the poem: A transactional theory of the literary work.* Carbondale, IL: Southern Illinois University Press.

Rutherford, F. J., & Ahlgren, A. (1990). *Science for all Americans.* Washington, DC: American Association for the Advancement of Science.

Ryu, S., & Sandoval, W. A. (2012). Improvements to elementary children's epistemic understanding from sustained argumentation. *Science Education, 96*(3), 488–526.

Sadler, P. M., Sonnert, G., Coyle, H. P., Cook-Smith, N., & Miller, J. L. (2013). The influence of teachers' knowledge on student learning in middle school physical science classrooms. *American Educational Research Journal*, *50*(5), 1020–1049. doi:10.3102/0002831213477680

Sadler, T. D., & Donnelly, L. A. (2006). Socioscientific argumentation: The effects of content knowledge and morality. *International Journal of Science Education*, *28*(12), 1463–1488.

Schoenbach, R., & Greenleaf, C. (2009). Fostering adolescents' engaged academic literacy. In L. Christenburg, R. Bomer, & P. Smagorinsky (Eds.), *Handbook of adolescent literacy research* (pp. 98–112). New York, NY: The Guilford Press.

Schoenbach, R., Greenleaf, C., & Murphy, L. (2016). *Leading for literacy: A reading apprenticeship approach*. Jossey-Bass. Retrieved from www.wiley.com/WileyCDA/WileyTitle/productCd-1118437268.html

Schoenfeld, A. H. (1992). Learning to think mathematically: Problem solving, metacognition, and sense making in mathematics. In D. A. Grouws (Ed.), *Handbook of research on mathematics teaching and learning* (pp. 334–370). New York, NY: MacMillan.

Schultz, K. (2002). Looking across space and time: Reconceptualizing literacy learning in and out of school. *Research in the Teaching of English*, *36*(3), 356–390.

Scribner, S., & Cole, M. (1981). *The psychology of literacy*. Cambridge, MA: Harvard University Press.

Shanahan, C., Shanahan, T., & Misischia, C. (2011). Analysis of expert readers in three disciplines: History, mathematics, and chemistry. *Journal of Literacy Research*, *43*(4), 393–429.

Shanahan, T., & Shanahan, C. (2008). Teaching disciplinary literacy to adolescents: Rethinking content-area literacy. *Harvard Educational Review*, *78*(1), 40–59.

Shanahan, T., & Shanahan, C. (2012). What is disciplinary literacy and why does it matter? *Topics in Language Disorders*, *32*(1), 7–18.

Shepherd, M. D., & van de Sande, C. C. (2014). Reading mathematics for understanding—from novice to expert. *The Journal of Mathematical Behavior*, *35*, 74–86.

Siebert, D., & Draper, R. (2008). Why content-area literacy messages do not speak to mathematics teachers: A critical content analysis. *Literacy Research and Instruction*, *47*(4), 229–245.

Siebert, D. K., Draper, R. J., Barney, D., Broomhead, P., Grierson, S., Jensen, A. P., ... Wimmer, J. (2016). Characteristics of literacy instruction that support reform in content area classrooms. *Journal of Adolescent & Adult Literacy*, *60*(1), 25–33.

Sinatra, G. M., & Broughton, S. H. (2011). Bridging reading comprehension and conceptual change in science education: The promise of refutation text. *Reading Research Quarterly*, *46*(4), 374–393.

Snow, C. E. (2010). Academic language and the challenge of reading for learning. *Science*, *328*(5977), 450–452.

Somers, M. A., Corrin, W., Sepanik, S., Salinger, T., Levin, J., Zmach, C., & Wong, E. (2010). *The enhanced reading opportunities study final report: The impact of supplemental literacy courses for struggling ninth-grade readers*. Washington, DC: National Center for Education Evaluation And Regional Assistance, Institute of Education Sciences, U.S. Department of Education.

Sørvik, G. O., & Mork, S. M. (2015). Scientific literacy as social practice: Implications for reading and writing in science classrooms. *Nordic Studies in Science Education*, *11*(3), 268–281.

Street, B. V. (1984). *Literacy in theory and practice* (Vol. 9). Cambridge, UK: Cambridge University Press.

Tang, K.-S., & Moje, E. B. (2010). Relating multimodal representations to the literacies of science. *Research in Science Education*, *40*(1), 81–85. doi:10.1007/s11165-009-9158-5

Tippett, C. D. (2010). Refutation text in science education: A review of two decades of research. *International Journal of Science and Mathematics Education*, *8*(6), 951–970. doi:10.1007/s10763-010-9203-x

Tyler, B., Britton, T., Iveland, A., Nguyen, K., Hipps, J., & Schneider, S. (2017). *The synergy of science and English language arts: means and mutual benefits of integration*. San Francisco, CA: WestEd.

Tytler, R., Prain, V., Hubber, P., & Waldrip, B., (Eds.). (2013). *Constructing representations to learn in Science*. Rotterdam: SensePublishers. Retrieved from http://link.springer.com/10.1007/978-94-6209-203-7

Valencia, S. (2014, April). *Disciplinary literacy and learning from text: Now you see it, now you don't*. Presented at the American Educational Research Association annual meeting, Philadelphia, PA.

van den Broek, P. (2010). Using texts in science education: Cognitive processes and knowledge representation. *Science*, *328*(5977), 453–456.

Van Dijk, T. A., & Kintsch, W. (1983). *Strategies of discourse comprehension*. New York, NY: Academic Press.

Vaughn, S., Swanson, E. A., Roberts, G., Wanzek, J., Stillman-Spisak, S. J., Solis, M., & Simmons, D. (2013). Improving reading comprehension and social studies knowledge in middle school. *Reading Research Quarterly*, *48*(1), 77–93.

Venezky, R. L. (2001). Procedures for evaluating the impact of complex educational interventions. *Journal of Science Education and Technology*, *10*(1), 17–30.

Villanueva, M. G., & Webb, P. (2008). Scientific investigations: The effect of the "Science Notebooks" approach in grade 6 classrooms in Port Elizabeth, South Africa. *African Journal of Research in Mathematics, Science and Technology Education, 12*(2), 3–16.

Vitale, M. R., & Romance, N. R. (2011). Adaptation of a knowledge-based instructional intervention to accelerate student learning in science and early literacy in grades 1 and 2. *Journal of Curriculum and Instruction, 5*(2), 79–93.

Von Aufschnaiter, C., Erduran, S., Osborne, J., & Simon, S. (2008). Arguing to learn and learning to argue: Case studies of how students' argumentation relates to their scientific knowledge. *Journal of Research in Science Teaching, 45*(1), 101–131.

Voogt, J., Laferrière, T., Breuleux, A., Itow, R. C., Hickey, D. T., & McKenney, S. (2015). Collaborative design as a form of professional development. *Instructional Science, 43*(2), 259–282.

Wade, S. E., & Moje, E. B. (2000). The role of text in classroom learning. In M. L. Kamil, P. B. Mosenthal, P. D. Pearson, & R. Barr (Eds.), *Handbook of reading research* (Vol. III, pp. 609–627). Mahwah, NJ: Erlbaum.

Waldrip, B., Prain, V., & Carolan, J. (2010). Using multi-modal representations to improve learning in junior secondary science. *Research in Science Education, 40*(1), 65–80.

Wang, J., & Herman, J. (2005). *Evaluation of seeds of science/roots of reading project: Shoreline science and terrarium investigations* (CRESST Report 676). Los Angeles, CA: University of California, National Center for Research on Evaluation, Standards, and Student Testing (CRESST).

Webb, P. (2009). Towards an integrated learning strategies Approach to promoting scientific literacy in the South African context. *International Journal of Environmental and Science Education, 4*(3), 313–334.

Webb, P. (2010). Science education and literacy: Imperatives for the developed and developing world. *Science, 328*(5977), 448–450.

Webb, P., & Treagust, D. F. (2006). Using exploratory talk to enhance problem-solving and reasoning skills in grade-7 science classrooms. *Research in Science Education, 36*(4), 381–401.

Webb, P., Williams, Y., & Meiring, L. (2008). Concept cartoons and writing frames: Developing argumentation in South African science classrooms? *African Journal of Research in Mathematics, Science and Technology Education, 12*(1), 5–17.

Weber, K., & Mejia-Ramos, J. P. (2011). Why and how mathematicians read proofs: An exploratory study. *Educational Studies in Mathematics, 76*(3), 329–344.

Weiss, C. H. (1993). Politics and evaluation: A reprise with mellower overtones. *American Journal of Evaluation, 14*(1), 107–109. doi:10.1177/109821409301400120

Wells, G. (1999). *Dialogic inquiry: Towards a socio-cultural practice and theory of education*. Cambridge, UK: Cambridge University Press.

Wilson-Lopez, A., Gregory, S., & Larsen, V. (2016). Reading and engineering: Elementary students' co-application of comprehension strategies and engineering design processes. *Journal of Pre-College Engineering Education Research (J-PEER), 6*(2), 3.

Wilson-Lopez, A., & Minichiello, A. (2017). Disciplinary literacy in engineering. *Journal of Adolescent & Adult Literacy, 61*(1), 7–14.

Windschitl, M., Thompson, J., & Braaten, M. (2008). Beyond the scientific method: Model-based inquiry as a new paradigm of preference for school science investigations. *Science Education, 92*(5), 941–967.

Windschitl, M., Thompson, J., & Braaten, M. (2011). Ambitious pedagogy by novice teachers: Who benefits from tool-supported collaborative inquiry into practice and why. *Teachers College Record, 113*(7), 1311–1360.

Wineburg, S. S. (1999). Historical thinking and other unnatural acts. *The Phi Delta Kappan, 80*(7), 488–499.

Wineburg, S. S. (1991). Historical problem solving: A study of the cognitive processes used in the evaluation of documentary and pictorial evidence. *Journal of Educational Psychology, 83*(1), 73–87.

Yarden, A., Falk, H., Federico-Agraso, M., Jiménez-Aleixandre, M. P., Norris, S. P., & Phillips, L. M. (2009). Supporting teaching and learning using authentic scientific texts: A rejoinder to Danielle J. Ford. *Research in Science Education, 39*(3), 391–395.

Yore, L., Bisanz, G. L., & Hand, B. M. (2003). Examining the literacy component of science literacy: 25 years of language arts and science research. *International Journal of Science Education, 25*(6), 689–725.

Yore, L. D. (2004). Why do future scientists need to study the language arts? In E. W. Saul (Ed.), *Crossing borders in literacy and science instruction: Perspectives on theory and practice* (pp. 71–94). Newark, DE: International Reading Association.

Young, K. M., & Leinhardt, G. (1998). Writing from primary documents: A way of knowing in history. *Written Communication, 15*(1), 25–68.

21

Literacy Instruction and Digital Innovation

Trends and Affordances for Digital Equity in Classrooms

Silvia Noguerón-Liu and Jayne C. Lammers

This chapter examines the adoption of digital tools in literacy instruction in K-8 classrooms. In this review of research, we answer the question: *How is the work of classroom literacy teaching mediated by new forms of and practices for reading texts?* by summarizing studies about the features and affordances of digital tools, and their implications for classroom-based practices within U.S. schools. As literacy researchers and teacher educators, our particular interest in this question stems from our commitment to digital equity, as well as our goal to empower teachers to consider their role in inclusive digital literacy instruction.

We situate this review in the context of academic standards that increasingly call on teachers to incorporate digital literacies in the English Language Arts—e.g., Common Core State Standards (CCSS), International Society for Technology in Education (ISTE) standards. With the adoption of the CCSS in many U.S. states, comprehension in reading instruction shifted, in part, to emphasize higher level thinking (such as evaluation, synthesis, interpretation, and application skills), as well as online reading comprehension (e.g., skills to research online to solve problems, locate information, and answer questions); furthermore, reading instruction now connects to the use of digital tools for collaboration, production, and dissemination of texts to authentic audiences (Leu et al., 2014). The reading anchor standards (NGACBP & CCSSO, 2010) expect students to evaluate information in "diverse media and formats" (p. 10), while for writing, they are expected to "use technology, including the Internet" to collaborate, produce, and publish their writing (p. 18). Similarly, the latest ISTE standards position students as "knowledge constructors" and "creative communicators," who curate resources using digital tools, and express themselves using various platforms and formats (ISTE, 2016). These standards signal the increasing role of technology in mediating access to information and new ways to design and communicate meaning. In this research review, informed by sociocultural and new literacies frameworks, we examine work that investigates the mediational role of digital tools, and make recommendations towards an equity-oriented approach to technology integration.

Within classrooms, new tools reconfigure learning practices and shape other elements in the classroom system, such as the rules governing classroom activity, or the expectations for division of labor (Engeström, 1987; Jewitt, 2006; Wertsch, 1991). Literacy practices within classrooms, then, can be understood as activities mediated by a wide range of meaning-making tools—including multiple languages, media, texts in various platforms (e.g., print books, CD-ROMs, websites), and devices to access content (Razfar & Yang, 2010). By framing new technologies as mediational tools, researchers can better understand the history embedded in digital platforms and software, and the ways they are adopted, changed, and constructed by subjects (Kaptelinin & Nardi, 2006).

In our review, we pay close attention to the affordances of digital tools (Kress, 2010) and the literacy practices central in the studies, including the integration of tablet devices, smartphones, and web-dependent laptops (Chromebooks) in classrooms, which at the time of this publication, are popular adoptions in school districts (Cavanagh, May 8, 2017; Singer, May 13, 2017). However, while the gap of Internet adoption has narrowed across racial groups, disparities remain across income, education level, and rural/suburban/urban areas (Pew Research Center, 2018). Furthermore, Hispanic and Black adults are more likely to be smartphone-dependent than white adults—respectively, 34%, 24%, and 14%, do not use broadband at home, but rely on smartphones for online access (Pew Research Center, 2018). These disparities matter, as digital solutions in schools may steer users to one-device, one-student initiatives, such as smartphones that have different affordances from computers with keyboards (e.g., it may be easier to type an essay in the latter). Hence, the research featured in this review includes some classroom-based studies conducted with nondominant student populations, informed by sociocultural perspectives that capitalize on their knowledge.

In this chapter, by "devices" we refer to the hardware used to interface with digital content (e.g., laptop, tablet). By "platforms," we refer to any website or other online repository that hosts educational content (e.g., digital portfolios and social media). By "texts," we focus on both print-based and digital documents (e.g., interactive e-books). The term "tool" reflects our theoretical approach to mediation through sociocultural theory, and it may encompass digital devices, platforms, and texts that potentially mediate literacy instruction. We share key findings from literature reviews and empirical studies, and conclude by emphasizing the need to conduct research alongside teachers and nondominant students and families.

Methods to Conduct This Review

To begin, we provide a summary of the theoretical frameworks that inform empirical work exploring the relationship between literacy and technology, in- and out- of school settings. We then connect these frameworks to previous literature reviews in past editions of this handbook and elsewhere, in order to provide a broader look at the themes identified in those reviews, including those related to sociocultural and new literacies' approaches. Next, we describe, in more depth, 11 empirical studies we found that specifically address the practices of reading and making sense of digital tools within classroom literacy instruction. We focus solely on articles, listed in Appendix A, drawing on sociocultural or new literacies theories, given our goal of representing work that illustrates the experiences of culturally and linguistically diverse learners.

We used academic search engines (ProQuest, EBSCO, and university-based library engines) to retrieve peer-reviewed articles that either reported empirical work conducted in kindergarten through middle school or made research-informed recommendations about the mediational roles of digital devices for literacy instruction. We then narrowed the scope to articles published in the last 12 years (2006–2018), to explore tools that remain most relevant in classrooms today, as older technologies may no longer be useful, or available, in classrooms (e.g., CD-ROMs). We mostly focused on research in the United States, in order to analyze how classroom practices are enacted within standards and assessment shaping schools in this country. However, in our outline of themes in literature reviews, we consider some international studies.

Silvia Noguerón-Liu and Jayne C. Lammers

Theoretical Frameworks and Research on Reading and Technology

Before we discuss the review findings, we briefly define three instrumental perspectives for theorizing practices related to learning mediated by technology. These approaches draw from qualitative and ethnographic research paradigms. We review these three perspectives, due to this chapter's emphasis on mediation, using key tenets in these theories as a lens to select and summarize the featured studies.

Sociocultural Theory and Mediation

According to Vygotsky's sociocultural approach to learning, both technical, tangible (e.g., a computer keyboard), and psychological tools (e.g., language) mediate human action and mental functions, and these tools are shaped by cultural, historical, and institutional forces (Wertsch, 1991). For instance, Wertsch (1991) explains that the QWERTY keyboard design ensured inefficiency, slowing down typists who jammed keys constantly; hence, common letters are widely distributed. The historical context and dominance of the QWERTY structure remains, even on computer keyboards that do not jam keys. While mediated action refers to the individuals acting with tools, both tools and action should be examined in relation to their history and to practices and values in social contexts. Sociocultural theory has shaped theories of literacy development by illuminating cultural contexts where children grow and learn how to read, as well as their relationships with peers, teachers, and literacy tools (Pérez, 2004). This perspective highlights how readers act and interact with their contexts and peers using tools (Razfar & Yang, 2010), including digital technologies, texts (both print-based and digital), and multiple languages.

While this review focuses on formal classroom practice, relevant work using mediation to organize literacy learning environments has been conducted in after-school contexts. One seminal ongoing project is the Fifth-Dimension model of after-school programs (Cole, 2006), made possible by university-community collaborations, where undergraduate students engage in face-to-face interactions with children using computer-based games. In this model, mediation is facilitated by computers, tasks, and a learning environment featuring games and culturally relevant content. In *La Clase Mágica*, the Fifth-Dimension redesign for bilingual communities (Flores, Vasquez, & Clark, 2014; Vásquez, 2003), mediational tools also include the linguistic and cultural knowledge children bring to interactions with digital content. *La Clase Mágica* connects community resources, families, and university personnel, by offering after-school activities where adults and children collaborate in digitally-mediated learning tasks, featuring culturally-relevant content. As we analyze how digital tools mediate learning tasks within classroom settings, we draw on this work as a reference to frame how activities could potentially be organized within larger social contexts and institutions.

New Literacies

The new literacies approach has become an influential orientation in the field, and shapes many of the studies highlighted in the articles in this review. Its roots rely on sociocultural perspectives on learning, and thus, new literacies scholars view literacies as multiple, situated, social practices informed by the historical, cultural, and political contexts in which they are enacted (e.g., Gee, 1996; New London Group, 1996; Street, 1984). As technology and the Internet began to play increasingly important roles in everyday lives, the focus of many with this orientation turned toward making sense of the changing nature of literacies in digital contexts. Theorization resulting from this "digital turn" (Mills, 2010) has offered the field some guiding principles for thinking of literacies as "new."

One influential set of such principles comes from Coiro, Knobel, Lankshear, and Leu (2008), who argue the following:

- new technology requires new practices to access the literacy potential of these devices and platforms,
- new literacies are crucial to civic, economic, and personal participation in a global world,
- literacies have always changed in response to the introduction of new technologies, but the pace of change has accelerated with the Internet's capability to disseminate new technology, and
- new literacies are multiple, multimodal, and multifaceted, therefore, they must be studied and enacted in ways that honor multiple perspectives. (p. 14)

Relatedly, Lankshear and Knobel (2011) differentiate between the "new technology stuff" (i.e., the devices and platforms) and the "new ethos stuff", which points to the practices and ways of thinking shaped by new literacies. Some key ethos include the ways in which literacies have evolved to be more participatory and collaborative, rather than individual and expert-centric.

Connected Learning

Mimi Ito's Connected Learning model (Ito et al., 2013) stems from a series of large-scale, ethnographic studies of youth practices in digital media production (Ito et al., 2010), and rests on a foundation of sociocultural learning theory that recognizes learning as "embedded within social relationships and cultural contexts" (Ito et al., 2013, p. 43). As such, Connected Learning highlights the connected nature of learning across young people's three key "spheres of learning"—interests, peer culture, and academics—with an eye toward equity and the relevance of learning to youth lives.

Though not technology-dependent, Connected Learning accounts for the myriad learning opportunities in an information age by recognizing that technology connects young people to networked spaces where they can engage in meaningful, interest-driven, production-centered learning. Connected Learning sets forth an agenda for equitable, social, and participatory learning (Ito et al., 2013). While our review centers on practices within classroom spaces, we pay attention to the potential for texts, practices, and dispositions in the articles we review that lend support to Connected Learning. Furthermore, we also notice how recent updates of technology and learning standards and models (e.g., ISTE, 2016 Standards for Students) move towards the conceptualization of tools as resources to facilitate students' engagement with networked communities and interest-driven inquiry.

Overall, these three approaches to learning emphasize the relevance of social contexts, by recognizing how digital tools expand social practices, including literacy practices, beyond classroom boundaries. They account for the multiple communities in which youth participate and use various tools to compose, access texts, and engage with multiple information sources. Empirical studies with youth informed by these approaches have reported their practices in after-school and outside-of-school programs designed with these learning principles in mind. In the following section, we examine how past literature reviews represent these theories and learning principles, before delving into specific studies illustrating how these theories inform classroom instruction and the design of digital tools.

Historical Overview of the Field through Literature Reviews

Here, we highlight the main themes identified in previous literature reviews, primarily published in handbooks such as the present volume (including its previous editions), and in peer-reviewed journals (see Table 21.1). These reviews explored the intersection between technology and literacy instruction in K-12 settings, and some offered international perspectives (e.g., Burnett, 2010; Takacs, Swart, & Bus, 2015). We categorized their main themes, identifying those emphasizing classroom literacy practices mediated by technology, the features of digital tools, as well as other themes—e.g., social, motivational, or critical aspects of technology adoption in literacy instruction. We focused on practices and tools as key categories to guide our analysis of the research paradigm, theoretical frames, and types of technologies central to previous research, even when such studies were not informed by sociocultural, new literacies, or Connected Learning approaches.

Research on the relationships between technology and literacy in the 1990s primarily drew from cognitive and psychological perspectives for studying how computers were used in reading and writing instruction (Reinking & Bridwell-Bowles, 1991) and the effect of other digital tools on instruction, with particular attention to at-risk populations (Kamil, Intrator, & Kim, 2000). In the early 2000s, researchers began to consider the historical, social, and policy contexts for technology and literacy instruction, calling for theoretical perspectives that acknowledge the transformative and transactional aspects of digital tools, as well as literacy's deictic nature (Labbo & Reinking, 2003; Leu, 2000). Leu (2000) defined deictic as "continuously changing as new technologies appear and as new envisionments for their use are crafted" (p. 746). While Leu included several studies reporting the effectiveness of specific applications on reading skills, he noted that studies tended to focus on the tools themselves, rather than on their use in classroom settings. Furthermore, the outcomes measured were mostly print-based instead of capturing new outcomes related to a "global information environment" (p. 758).

The shift toward sociocultural and new literacies approaches became more pronounced in literature reviews from the past decade. Warschauer and Ware (2008) pointed to research informed by a "change" framework, bringing to light the deictic and transformative nature of technology outlined by Leu in 2000. Studies reviewed described literacy and contexts more broadly from a sociocultural lens including out-of-school settings, and online communication and videogame playing (Burnett, 2010; Razfar & Yang, 2010). Overall, in these reviews, the scope of methods and theories expanded to include social contexts where digital tools were used, and the ways they facilitated and transformed literacy practices.

Lastly, the particular features of digital texts and tools—such as multimodal, interactive, and hypertextual components—are central in reviews about the effect of digital texts on literacy development and instruction. Reviews that make comparisons between traditional print texts and technology-mediated reading, not only argued that the portability, touchscreen functions, and availability of apps on tablets positively impacts readers' comprehension and engagement (Miller & Warschauer, 2014), but also uncovered concerns that some interactive features may be distracting, especially to children labeled as "at-risk" (Takacs et al., 2015). Relatedly, Colwell and Hutchison (2015) focused on specific digital tools (including tablet devices), but instead of comparing them with print-based equivalents, they examined the affordances (Kress, 2010) of nine tools for literacy instruction, guiding teachers about how to adopt these tools in their practice.

Overall, this summary shows the effects of changing research paradigms and conceptions of literacy from cognitive/psychological perspectives (e.g., Kamil et al., 2000; Takacs et al., 2015), sociocultural perspectives (e.g., Razfar & Yang, 2010), and new literacies (e.g., Colwell & Hutchison, 2015), and, more recently, to critical approaches (e.g., Warschauer & Ware, 2008). The predominant paradigm in the studies reviewed includes measures of effectiveness of particular applications—tools that have evolved over time, from CD-ROMs to tablet apps—on reading skills such as comprehension, vocabulary knowledge, fluency, or early decoding skills. However,

Table 21.1 Themes in past literature reviews on technology and literacy (1991–2015).

Authors	Themes related to reading and writing instructional practices/skills	Themes related to features of digital tools	Other themes
Reinking and Bridwell-Bowles (1991)	General studies of computer effectiveness in instruction; computer-based reading curricula; effectiveness of specific instructional applications.	Comparison of electronic and conventional texts from convergent and divergent perspectives.	
Kamil et al. (2000)	Word processing, collaborative writing, intervention benefits for special populations, and multimedia effects on literacy instruction	Hypermedia, hypertexts, and literacy.	Motivational effects of technology environments; motivating special populations at risk.
Leu (2000)	Literacy and learning tasks: closed and open tasks, search and browsing tasks; specific applications and their effect on comprehension, decoding.		Interest and motivational factors, teacher and student engagement; cognitive learning styles; teachers' beliefs and technology integration.
Labbo and Reinking (2003)	Computers supporting: writing development, phonological abilities, independent reading.		Computers supporting social interaction and collaboration; transforming and introducing new skills.
Warschauer and Ware (2008)	Learning framework: focus on raising learning outcomes.	Change framework: focus on new nature of literacy, including nature of texts and tools.	Change framework: focus on out-of-school literacies. Power framework: focus on issues of access and social inequality in relation to digital tools.
Razfar and Yang (2010)		Digital mediation through CD-ROMs, hypertexts, comparison with print formats.	Mediation through hybrid languages and literacies as mediational tools.
Burnett (2010)	Technology as a deliverer of literacy (content).	Technology as a medium for meaning-making.	Technology as a site of interaction around texts.
Miller and Warschauer (2013)	Pre-tablet era technology studies and e-book studies. Tablet era: technology studies and e-book/app studies at home and schools.		
Colwell and Hutchison (2015)	Guidelines for technology integration in reading comprehension, promoting discussion, and encouraging collaborative learning.	Review of uses and affordances of nine digital tools.	
Takacs et al. (2015)		Effects of technology-enhanced stories on literacy development, when compared with print-like stories.	Effects of technological additions for disadvantaged groups of students.

sociocultural perspectives reposition digital tools as mediums for students to participate in different kinds of practices, to reach new audiences, and to collaborate in the classroom in different ways. In the following sections, we feature studies that describe how digital tools mediate and transform classroom instruction.

Key Questions and Findings in Empirical Work

In this section, we closely examine the 11 empirical studies that represent detailed descriptions of classroom practice and innovation, informed by concepts related to sociocultural theory, new literacies, or Connected Learning. We focus on the articles that draw on sociocultural or new literacies, and which (re)define features, functions, and affordances of digital tools, including texts presented in tablet devices. Due to our focus on technology adoption by teachers in collaboration with researchers, several of these studies come from practitioner-oriented journals with high visibility and rigorous expectations for publication (e.g., the International Literacy Association's *The Reading Teacher*). Furthermore, some of the studies also address the experiences of nondominant students engaging with digital tools in the classroom, as teachers and researchers consider the ways digital tools and practices can capitalize on their knowledge. When reading and reviewing the articles, we used the following guiding question(s):

- What are the **features** of focal digital tools in these studies? How can these features mediate classroom instruction?
- How is the work of classroom instruction **mediated** by digital tools and practices?

In the first section, articles center on the **affordances of digital tools**, allowing both researchers and practitioners to identify new digital features to support students during literacy instruction, within the rapidly changing market of apps for mobile devices. In the second, we describe studies about **classroom-based practices**, where research questions explore specific instructional goals, and then examine how digital tools played a role in achieving such goals, particularly for youth whose access and use of technology has been underreported.

Tool-Centered Questions and Findings

The selected articles included questions focused on the features of digital tools (texts, platforms, and apps), particularly considering: (a) the nature of the affordances of these tools, and how such affordances mediate literacy instruction for readers at various developmental stages; and (b) how such affordances mediate the development of new and digital literacies with a goal of equity in mind.

As mentioned above, from sociocultural and new literacies' perspectives, mediated action is shaped by the affordances of the tools (Kress, 2010) and historical/cultural forces shape the use of the tools (Wertsch, 1991). The articles we analyzed describe specific features of digital tools, as well as some description of the classroom settings where such tools can be used, for instance, in whole-group, small group, and independent work settings.

In this section we present research that describes a range of frameworks or criterion for selecting and evaluating digital tools. The ten-year range that these studies represent allows us to see the increasing development of applications for mobile devices, as they were more frequently adopted in classrooms. Some studies based their criteria on particular theories of learning and literacy (e.g., Baker, 2007; Israelson, 2015; Rowsell & Wohlwend, 2016), while others took a more grounded approach and generated categories based, for example, on the coding of features in existing apps (e.g., Javorsky & Trainin, 2014). The digital tools described include classroom websites (Baker, 2007), scaffolded text environments (Dalton, Proctor, Uccelli, Mo, & Snow, 2011), technology-enhanced storybooks (Takacs et al., 2015), iPad apps (Israelson, 2015; Rowsell & Wohlwend, 2016), and digital story applications (Javorsky & Trainin, 2014).

The earliest study we reviewed explored how website features align with various literacy instructional approaches and classroom social practices. Informed by sociocultural, transformative, and new literacies' approaches, Baker (2007) examined 40 elementary (K-6) classroom websites, defined as sites maintained and published by a teacher, and titled accordingly (e.g., Ms. Elementary Classroom), or linked to the school/district site. Baker framed websites as tools facilitating online support and instructional opportunities *within* and *beyond* classrooms. Baker identified literacy instruction components or related activities and instructional approaches represented in the sites. Her analysis accounted for various modalities or textualities (e.g., including drawings and/or multimedia). She found every site had at least one feature supporting skills-oriented approaches to literacy instruction, such as studying spelling words or memorizing sight words, with links to specific literacy standards, and links to websites for practicing skills, including many commercial sites. Almost half of the sites (43%) were used to publish students' writing in alignment with process-based approaches—for instance, photos with captions, or students' emulation of a pattern in a children's book. About 35% of the sites included links to authors' websites, a feature aligned with student enjoyment and understanding of contemporary children's literature. Lastly, 70% of the websites had some type of information for parents, extending literacy support beyond the classroom. Baker noted that website content did not reflect the changing nature of interactive literacy platforms because links and newsletters are primarily non-communicative technologies. While the websites mediated access to literacy resources beyond school boundaries (for families with technology access), the study did not explore how these websites were used in the social contexts of home or school.

In Dalton et al. (2011), the authors examined the effects of scaffolded digital text on monolingual and bilingual students' reading achievement. The study richly described the features of the Improving Comprehension Online (ICON) reading environment used in six fifth grade classrooms in the north-eastern U.S. The ICON prototype—developed with universal design features for scaffolded digital reading, including multiple means of representation, expression, and engagement—provided essential components of accessible design for learning. The digital environment included eight multimedia texts with text-to-speech read-aloud functions in both English and Spanish. Bilingual readers were supported by bilingual and English-speaking virtual "coaches" who served as models, and could listen to Spanish narrations of the texts, as well as translations of key vocabulary. Dalton et al. compared reading performance in three conditions: using the program with scaffolds for reading comprehension only, vocabulary only, or a combination of comprehension strategies and vocabulary. They found that bilingual students' reading performance benefitted from the vocabulary and combined strategies' conditions. The study highlighted how the ICON reading environment provided several mediational means for the reader to engage with content, such as support through bilingual virtual coaching, vocabulary hyperlinks and translations, and multimodal means to represent ideas (images, audio, highlighting).

These two studies examined digital content designed by teachers or researchers, with features directly supporting literacy instruction (phonics, vocabulary, comprehension), and particular approaches to learning and teaching (e.g., universal design for learning, process-writing approaches). From a sociocultural approach to mediated action, these studies acknowledged the social and historical practices associated with digital tools and highlighted some innovations unique to multimodal, digital content. However, only the second study (Dalton et al., 2011) involved designing tools with expansive visions of culturally and linguistically diverse readers, providing specific ideas for future software design that can allow students to capitalize on their multiple linguistic resources.

Another trend in digital research concerning the analysis of digital tools comes from journals aimed for literacy practitioners, where articles provided teachers with guidelines to evaluate resources to integrate technology into literacy instruction. With the increased presence of tablets in early literacy classrooms, and a growing market of apps developed for educational purposes (Miller & Warschauer, 2013), some of these studies proposed heuristics to identify scaffolds and features that support instruction.

Javorsky and Trainin (2014) explored 20 story applications for mobile devices created for young children. Their study, informed by cognitive flexibility theory, frames how readers transfer skills from a familiar reading environment to a changing environment—navigating texts in a screen—and analyzed text features and book handling skills necessary to browse a digital book. Their findings showed that unlike with print-based texts, where concepts of print behaviors can be applied consistently across books with the same physical features, navigating digital texts presented young readers with more challenges. Digital applications have no consistency in their icons (e.g., each app used different icons to navigate a story or open a menu), nor in their interactivity (some animations happened automatically, some were user-activated). Thus, Javorski and Trainin explained that readers need to be flexible and persist when exploring story apps. Considering digital stories as mediators for literacy, this variability has implications for instruction: teachers cannot rely on students' familiarity with navigation icons, when such icons vary from app to app.

Israelson (2015) and Rowsell and Wohlwend (2016) designed rubrics for teachers to evaluate tablet apps. Israelson (2015) referred to the "value-added and affordances" (p. 341) of multimodal texts and developed an evaluation framework informed by these concepts. The rubric provided continua for multimodal features (distracting to engaging), intuitiveness of app navigation (confusing/unclear to clear displays, examples, and steps), user interactivity (minimal to high interactivity), and accuracy of literacy content (e.g., spelling of words). In addition, Israelson described various steps a teacher could take before examining value added and affordances: (a) consider instructional objectives and grouping structure (e.g., small group, whole group), and whether teachers seek to enhance or transform (e.g., modify, redesign) with technology; (b) situate the app in a category (e.g., e-book, mind-mapping), and consider how it may target early literacy skills (e.g., word recognition, vocabulary); and then (c) examine for value added and specific affordances. This framework illuminated the potential of digital text affordances within instructional contexts, where teachers consider their goals, interactions with students, and content demands. Hence, the framework considered more than text features mediating access to content in app selection; it also accounted for the social context of literacy instruction within the classroom.

Rowsell and Wohlwend (2016) built on Israelson's (2015) model by examining apps from an ideological perspective of literacy (Street, 1984), describing apps' "impact on children's opportunities to develop skills and dispositions as producers rather than consumers" (p. 197). They examined apps that mediate "participatory literacies," in which children can share, interpret, and use digital media to connect with various learning and digital cultures. They proposed six dimensions of app evaluation: whether an app allows multiple people to interact (multiplayer), supports content creation (productive), allows immersion through exposure to image, sound, motion, or animation features (multimodal), allows freedom to navigate alternative paths (open-ended), encourages affective and embodied interactions (pleasurable), and allows sharing on social networks (connectivity). Like Israelson (2015), they explored these dimensions in relation to classroom literacy practices (e.g., e-book reading), but they also included composition practices with multiple modes (e.g., video animation). They called for an expansive view of literacy that situates app use within contexts with shared cultural frameworks and models, drawing on anthropological and sociolinguistic literacy approaches (e.g., Street, 1984), and they explained how readers can benefit from various apps to engage with multimodal content, and to communicate and discuss what they have learned. Students' ability to participate in online communities is central in this evaluation framework.

Overall, these articles showcase how new forms and practices for reading texts can be shaped by the features of available digital tools. Most address the importance of new features that support readers' experience with digital tools (e.g., multimodal sound effects), as well as how specific skills and content are integrated into the digital tools. They showcase how app and digital tool integration are shaped by multiple goals, as teachers select apps based on their needs to meet curriculum standards, as well as their efforts to introduce new literacy dispositions and knowledge. For most researchers, the classroom setting is the social context for app integration, with the teacher as a designer and gatekeeper of app and digital text content. Baker (2007) expanded the audience of classroom websites to the household, where families can be potential consumers and users of literacy sites, and Dalton et al. (2011) described the design of online environments for bilingual students. Rowsell and Wohlwend (2016) stressed the importance of apps that connect students to wider communities online, beyond classroom boundaries. However, a limitation of studies centered on digital tools, is that design features and content that are culturally relevant for diverse, nondominant communities are under explored; for instance, other than Dalton et al. (2011), none of the other studies or apps consider specifically translation or multilingual features.

Classroom-Centered Practices: Questions and Findings

Within the collection of articles that focus on classroom practice more broadly, many centered on questions about how teachers integrated technology into their literacy instruction. Often deriving from case study approaches, this research highlights teachers' perspectives and experiences in planning and implementing technology-mediated literacy instruction. The devices explored in these studies included tablets and desktop computers, and their corresponding literacy-related applications (e.g., Hutchison, Beschorner, & Schmidt-Crawford, 2012; Price-Dennis, 2016; Rowsell, Saudelli, Scott, & Bishop, 2013) and flip cameras (Hagood, 2012). These readings also shed light on a variety of platforms that facilitated students' multimodal content production (e.g., Hagood, 2012; Handsfield, Dean, & Cielocha, 2009).

Through examples of classroom implementation, this research illuminates the affordances of technology in literacy instruction. For example, Hutchison and her colleagues (2012), describe the case of Mrs. Dill, a fourth grade teacher, whose practices show how iPads gave students access to digital libraries for independent reading and, using selected apps, facilitated development of reading comprehension skills—e.g., retelling, sequencing, and identifying main ideas and details. From the onset of her planning with the researchers, Mrs. Dill expressed a desire to enhance students' opportunities to engage with literacy content, by including new literacy skills. She discussed the affordances of an app to draw illustrations of students' visualizations, noting how they would have more options than crayons or paper, and she would be able to enlarge and share images with ease. With a mind-mapping app, students could manipulate the placement of boxes on a screen and in diagrams. With a virtual bookshelf app, students could communicate their text choices with others using virtual sticky notes. The researchers also discussed the apps' features with students in focus groups, gaining insights about their thoughts on the apps' potential. In this collaboration, the teacher and researchers planned their print-based literacy and new literacies' goals prior to selecting an app, and analyzed, and reflected on, how the selected apps mediated access to texts and offered students new ways to interact with, analyze, and produce texts.

Another teacher-researcher collaboration was conducted by Rowsell et al. (2013), who represents an international team of Australian, Canadian, and U.S.-based researchers, and thus highlights the potential of transnational collaborations. The article featured an action research project with two Canadian teachers in elementary and middle school, who analyzed professional readings and reflections in blog posts with the research team, focused on their students' development of print and digital literacies using iPads and apps. While the intent of the teachers' inquiry addressed how iPads were used in word study instruction (e.g., vocabulary, spelling), the teachers' reflections described how students engaged in critical conversations about app selection for particular purposes. They also noticed students' collaboration in face-to-face interaction using word-building and vocabulary apps. Rowsell et. al.'s research, in particular, highlights the potential for students to engage in local, social practices with each other, beyond the literacy-focused purposes of the apps.

Hagood (2012) also worked with teachers, drawing on a year-long professional learning group she facilitated with middle school content area teachers who learned about new literacies. Her research spotlights stories from nine teachers and offers direction to teachers interested in integrating digital tools and practices into their instruction. Like Rowsell et al. (2013), teachers' exploration of digital literacies began with reading common texts about new and media literacies. Teachers' exploration of various tools and platforms followed, culminating with their design and implementation of new literacies in their content-area instruction, which included reading intervention, English Language Arts, and ELA Honors. Hagood (2012) shared stories of middle school students using a range of devices and platforms to produce multimodal content, through digital storytelling research projects, visual representations of vocabulary, and video-recorded reading fluency exercises. This research illustrates how literacy instruction might successfully incorporate both consumption and production of digital tools as students produce, respond to, and interpret multiple texts.

While these studies describe the process of teachers adopting and examining digital tools, others address how teachers included the voices or perspectives of nondominant students. Price-Dennis (2016) grounded her two year qualitative study in theoretical frameworks that conceptualize Black girls' literacies as multimodal, critical, social practices. Instead of foregrounding the tools and their affordances, Price-Dennis' work began with a framework outlining how literacies are tied to Black girls' identities, how they are enacted collaboratively, and how they are shaped by power and politics (Muhammad & Haddix, 2016). Drawing on this framework, Price-Dennis collaborated with a fifth grade teacher to design English language arts instructional units, looking for ways to use digital tools to explore issues of equity, race, and power. Their curriculum integrated print-based and digital texts, such as children's literature, TEDx talks, poetry, and music videos. In analyzing these instructional units, Price-Dennis showcased how digital tools, apps, and platforms such as YouTube, Newsela, Flipboard, or Google forms, mediated Black girls' exploration and reflection on social issues. For instance, by accessing news, digital images, and media, students juxtaposed and curated multiple texts related to #BlackLivesMatter, and engaged in dialogue, responding to embedded questions in a digital lesson platform. In this research, nondominant students' lived experiences guided inquiry, and digital tools (together with print-based resources) helped mediate access, curation, and dialogue about culturally relevant resources. Students were not necessarily mirroring print-based literacies. They engaged in critical literacy practices drawing on their knowledge and critical and social justice concerns, while curating and responding to multiple platforms and types of texts. Their end-of-unit assessments reflected transformative shifts, as students' final products were digital and multimodal, including podcasts, stop-motion animation, and memes. These products showed the sense Black girls made of what they read, and the new and digital repertoire of practices they were building. This research reveals the importance of centering students' identities at the onset of planning a digital literacy project, instead of starting with standards or tools.

Handsfield et al. (2009) offered the example of fourth graders in a self-contained bilingual (Spanish-English) class that included a few students also receiving special education services. The researchers found that by using two platforms—Comic Creator and Blogger—the teacher worked to position these students as critical consumers and producers of texts. While the overall study centered on the exploration of multilingualism, multiliteracies, and teacher development, this article described how the focal teacher customized the use of two web platforms to engage her students in purposeful writers, and how they navigated together the affordances and limitations of the tools. For instance, students relied on print-versions of comic strips, as the comic-strip platform did not allow them to save their work. Valuable affordances included students' opportunities to engage in social interaction at their own pace (via written blog posts), to look up unfamiliar words, and to craft responses in their first or second language. Implications for emergent bilingual students include the multiple opportunities for them to use language in authentic ways: for social interaction, storytelling, and description of their reading practices and preferences.

Lastly, Martin-Beltrán, Tigert, Peercy and Silverman (2017) explored the digital literacy practices of seven students (in kindergarten and fourth grade) labeled as English learners, most of whom reported Spanish as their first language. In their design-based research study, the researchers and teachers developed a cross-age peer learning program (reading buddies), where students used print-based books, tablet texts, and videos to read together in pairs and/or triads. The digital texts allowed reading buddies to listen to a voice narration, and to tap on highlighted vocabulary for definitions, and access animations in some pages. Informed by sociocultural theory, they framed buddies' text-based interactions as "mediational episodes" (p. 137), where students co-constructed meaning together, using digital and print-based text to mediate their language and literacy learning. Their mixed methods analysis showed that buddies engaged in more turns of talk and engaged more deeply with the text when the text was print-based; with digital texts, buddies did quick vocabulary checks, tapping on word definitions embedded in the text. Buddies were more likely to re-read print-based books, arguing that re-reading took too long on a tablet, as they sometimes went back to the beginning of the book. Younger buddies (kindergarteners) were more likely to notice sight words or familiar text in the print-based books, than in the digital books. The authors stressed the need for instruction where students are shown how to develop strategies to engage with digital text. As mentioned above, the variability of navigation tools in digital books or apps, makes it hard for readers to maximize their engagement with digital features (Javorsky & Trainin, 2014). Hence, teacher's modeling is necessary to build dispositions for flexibility and persistence in these new reading environments.

Overall, this collection of classroom-centered research showcases the potential of teacher-researcher collaborations, as teachers' knowledge and experience with their students served as resources in designing instructional interventions. While not the focus of all of these studies, we see an emphasis on equity-oriented instructional practice in many of these articles, because they illustrate visions of digital literacy instruction that goes beyond remedial digital solutions, and place students' strengths at the center of planning (Handsfield et al., 2009; Martin-Beltrán, et al., 2017; Price-Dennis, 2016). Such work encourages the exploration of how digital tools can mediate literacy instruction for empowering purposes for nondominant students.

New Approaches and Opportunities

In starting this chapter, we outlined and described theoretical perspectives that center mediation and social contexts of learning. Like Rowsell and Wohlwend (2016), and previous reviews in this handbook (Reinking & Bridwell-Bowles, 1991; Leu, 2000; Kamil et al., 2000), we see value in studies that account for the transformative and deictic (Leu, 2000) nature of digital texts and practices. While most studies cited focused on the potential of features and scaffolds in digital devices and platforms to support reading skills, we found that teachers and students go beyond emphasis on foundational reading skills, to explore what is "transformative" and novel about digital tools.

Selection of Digital Tools: Expanding Visions of Design, Evaluation, and Decision-Making

Promising approaches to research and practice were found in resources aimed at helping teachers evaluate apps and digital books. These powerful checklists, rubrics, and frameworks aid teachers in making informed decisions about products and platforms they can adopt in whole-group, small-group, or independent work/centers for students. These rubrics index the various factors and considerations deemed relevant by multiple stakeholders, while demonstrating underlying theoretical understandings of literacy, technology, and learning. In the work we reviewed, descriptions of scaffolds and features heavily include multimodality, interactivity, and alignment with focal literacy skills or strategies (e.g., concepts of print, visualizing). Yet few studies consider features related to first-language support (e.g., Dalton et al., 2011), and aesthetic, pleasurable, and participatory affordances of apps (Rowsell & Wohlwend, 2016).

In our review of tool-centered studies, some of the digital tools had been designed by teachers (classroom websites) or a team of researchers (online environment in Dalton et al., 2011); however, in the app market, the apps reviewed were retrieved and evaluated from an app marketplace, where less information is available about the designers. McKenna (2006) pointed out the tension between established instructional practices, mirrored in the design and content of some school-based applications (e.g., a sight-word game), and a marketplace of more interactive, exploration-oriented apps (e.g., a blog). This tension is also present in the decisions school districts have to make about technology adoption, based on goals, cost, technical support, and infrastructure requirements (Demski, 2012; Owens, 2015). Furthermore, as standardized state reading assessments now offer adaptive computer-based testing (e.g., PARCC, Smarter Balanced), new demands pose challenges for schools to have an adequate technological infrastructure and readiness to conduct large-scale assessments (Davis, 2012). Hence, digital tools are not only mediating access to particular subject-area content (like reading and writing), but they are also, increasingly, part of larger school- and district-based instructional and assessment initiatives.

When large technology companies (e.g., Amazon, Google, Apple, Microsoft) are competitive in grand-scale adoption of devices and platforms in schools (Cavanagh, May 8, 2017, Singer, May 13, 2017), we need local, culturally situated studies that examine teachers' potential to customize tools and to design culturally and linguistically sustaining literacy experiences for all students. An analysis of vendors and large technology contracts should consider whether students, parents, and teachers are able to access and adopt digital education platforms, and it should examine closely the evidence of outcomes for nondominant students (Burch & Good, 2014). Further studies exploring the ways teachers can design, curate, and implement customized online content can provide much more insight on culturally responsive ways to integrate technology content for all students.

Classroom-Based Digital Literacy Instruction: Centering on Students' Experiences and Teacher-Researcher Collaboration

The reviewed studies point to the promise of collaboration and co-design of technology integration efforts in ELA with classroom teachers (see Hagood, 2012; Handsfield et al., 2009). Some of the classroom-based studies described the ways researchers balanced their entry and decision-making process with teachers and administrators, including their review of curriculum standards, as they also offered more expansive views of technology in their projects. For instance, Hutchison et al. (2012), and Price-Dennis (2016) report that their planning conversations with experienced teachers began with a focus on the relationships between literacy and social justice goals; once instructional units or lessons including content and strategies were designed, the teams explored digital tools and media (iPad and web apps, search engines) that could support these goals. All authors made some reference to inclusion of standards or curriculum guides in their planning. Their projects illustrate the benefits of translating research to practice in collaboration with teachers as co-researchers, including the alignment of digital projects with academic standards. Throughout this chapter, we argue that technology integration should go beyond efforts to enhance print-based literacy outcomes. However, alignment with literacy standards is a key component of the choices teachers make everyday; hence, we emphasize fruitful teacher-researcher collaborations through innovative practices that are not solely standards-driven, but also grounded on students' knowledge, interests, and potential.

Another area of new research could foster teacher-researcher collaboration in the development of checklists and rubrics to evaluate digital content, and to investigate the trajectories of app/digital text selection based on co-designed parameters. As the nature of apps and texts is constantly evolving in a competitive and fast-paced app market, these resources need to be made available in multiple venues for the greatest impact on practice. Instead of remaining locked behind the paywalls of peer-reviewed journals, practitioners and researchers should be allowed to share and enhance these helpful resources through online communities, professional conferences, social networks, and online professional development.

We do see great opportunity in the joint inquiry by researchers and teachers; however, digital equity can only be addressed when the voices, concerns, and experiences of nondominant students and families are invited into the conversation. In all the studies we reviewed, only Price-Dennis's (2016) work explicitly addressed the inclusion of critical and racially conscious approaches to digital literacy in their theoretical framing and focal units. Furthermore, decision-making processes at district- or school-levels may not always include the concerns of those on the receiving end of digital access initiatives—families perceived as having limited or no technology and internet connectivity. When studies showcase ways to leverage the knowledge of diverse students in the design of online environments (e.g., Dalton et al., 2011) or curriculum (Price-Dennis, 2016), implications of such work showcase how digital tools are not always a one-size-fits-all resource for literacy instruction. Nondominant children and their families navigate multiple social contexts, languages, and literacies, engaging in syncretic, hybrid, multimodal nepantla (or, in between, thriving at the boundary) literacies (Lizárraga & Gutiérrez, 2017, p. 39), drawing on their full linguistic and cultural repertoires, and repositioning themselves and their communities in powerful, expert ways.

Such situated practices have been central in research on mediation in after-school programs such as the Fifth Dimension and *La Clase Mágica*. For instance, Schwartz and Gutiérrez (2015) draw on Connected Learning and situated approaches to literacy to document how Latinx children and their mothers use cell phones to access the Internet and social media, elaborating on how new media practices are shaped by the rules of the household, gender roles, and beliefs about children's media use. They connect these insights from households to the ways children engage with media at an after-school program. Similarly, Nogueron-Liu (2017) explored the various sociopolitical and cultural factors shaping Latinx families' access to devices and connectivity, and their responses to a 1:1 (one-laptop, one-child) district initiative, also noticing how parents' beliefs about their roles and everyday practices did not always align with expectations of academic digital reading at home. Theoretical approaches that put cultural practices in the forefront, together with critical literacy perspectives illuminating issues of power, are both crucial to interrogate common assumptions about technology as a potential tool to support nondominant children's literacy learning.

Finally, this review revealed the untapped potential of out-of-school research studies and their implications for classroom instruction. For instance, out-of-school studies with adolescents show digital literacy and media production to be highly motivating for youth (see Curwood, Magnifico, & Lammers, 2013; Lammers, Magnifico, & Curwood, 2018; Lammers & Marsh, 2015); it also points to the potential of digital practices to give emergent bilinguals access to literate identities (Black, 2008; Lam, 2004). Despite the literature demonstrating how teachers can incorporate digital spaces and practices into literacy instruction, research about middle-school writing instruction still shows technology use to be very teacher-centered, focused on editing and revision, and sharing only with local, not global or connected, audiences (Graham, Capizzi, Harris, Hebert, & Morphy, 2014). Further connections between the out-of-school/after-school research literature and the classroom-based work is necessary to inform future studies going beyond the expectations of assessment in most literacy classrooms.

Conclusion and Connection to Entries in This Volume

Literacy instruction needs to prepare readers to widen their choices, opportunities, and access to various types of texts—as emphasized in the CCSS anchor standards, for students to "integrate and evaluate content presented in diverse media and formats" (CCSS.ELA-LITERACY.CCRA.R.7). Furthermore digital reading is shifting with the availability of digital content in libraries (Baron, Chapter 7 this volume; Mackey, Chapter 6, this volume). Research on mediation of digital texts should also account for factors and practices shaping the availability of digital texts beyond the classroom, considering access in public spaces like libraries, after school programs, as well as the growing marketplace of content tied to specific devices (e.g., Kindle, nook, Google, and Apple smartphones). As Mackey (this volume) explains, reading choices are now shaped by "an enormous change in technological and cultural affordances, frequently framed by commercial motivations" (p. 122). Mediation of digital literacies in the classroom should extend beyond learning scaffolds, and be inclusive of the critical exploration of titles, platforms, and media in an increasingly complex landscape of texts and ideas.

References

Baker, E. A. (2007). Elementary classroom web sites: Support for literacy within and beyond the classroom. *Journal of Literacy Research, 39*, 1–36.
Black, R. W. (2008). *Adolescents and online fan fiction.* New York, NY: Peter Lang.
Burch, P., & Good, A. (2014). *Equal scrutiny: Privatization and accountability in digital education.* Cambridge, MA: Education Press. Introduction.
Burnett, C. (2010). Technology and literacy in early childhood educational settings A review of the research. *Journal of Early Childhood Literacy, 10*(3), 247–270.
Cavanagh, S. (May 8, 2017). Amazon, Apple, Google and Microsoft battle for K-12 markets and loyalties of educators. *EdWeek Market Brief.* Retrieved from: https://marketbrief.edweek.org/special-report/amazon-apple-google-and-microsoft-battle-for-k-12-market-and-loyalties-of-educators/
Coiro, J., Knobel, M., Lankshear, C., & Leu, D. J. (2008). Central issues in new literacies and new literacies research. In J. Coiro, M. Knobel, C. Lankshear, & D. J. Leu (Eds.), *Handbook of research on new literacies* (pp. 1–21). New York, NY: Routledge.
The Distributed Literacy Consortium; Cole, M. (2006). *The fifth dimension: An after-school program built on diversity.* New York, NY: Russell Sage.
Colwell, J., & Hutchison, A. C. (2015). Supporting teachers in integrating digital technology into language arts instruction to promote literacy. *Journal of Digital Learning in Teacher Education, 31*(2), 56–63. doi:http://doi.org/10.1080/21532974.2014.991813

Curwood, J. S., Magnifico, A. M., & Lammers, J. C. (2013). Writing in the wild: Writers' motivation in fan-based affinity spaces. *Journal of Adolescent & Adult Literacy, 56*, 677–685.

Dalton, B., Proctor, C. P., Uccelli, P., Mo, E., & Snow, C. E. (2011). Designing for diversity: The role of reading strategies and interactive vocabulary in a digital reading environment for fifth-grade monolingual English and bilingual students. *Journal of Literacy Research, 43*, 68–100.

Davis, M. R. (2012, Spring). Ready or not. *Education Week's Digital Directions, 5*(4-4), 43, 45.

Demski, J. (2012). The Hard(ware) Choice. *T.H.E. Journal, 39*(9), 28–35.

Engeström, Y. (1987). *Learning by expanding: An activity-theoretical approach to developmental research*. Helsinki: Orienta-Konsultit.

Flores, B., Vasquez, O., & Clark, E. (Eds). (2014). *Generating transworld pedagogy: Reimagining la Clase Mágica*. Lanham, MD: Lexington Press.

Gee, J. P. (1996). *Social linguistics and literacies: Ideology in discourses* (2nd ed.). London: Taylor & Francis.

Graham, S., Capizzi, A., Harris, K. R., Hebert, M., & Morphy, P. (2014). Teaching writing to middle school students: A national survey. *Reading and Writing, 27*, 1015–1042.

Hagood, M. C. (2012). Risks, rewards, and responsibilities of using new literacies in middle grades. *Voices from the Middle, 19*(4), 10–17.

Handsfield, L. J., Dean, T. R., & Cielocha, K. M. (2009). Becoming critical consumers and producers of text: Teaching literacy with Web 1.0 and Web 2.0. *The Reading Teacher, 63*, 40–50.

Hutchison, A., Beschorner, B., & Schmidt-Crawford, D. (2012). Exploring the use of the iPad for literacy learning. *The Reading Teacher, 66*, 15–23.

International Society for Technology in Education. (2016). ISTE Standards for Students. Retrieved from: www.iste.org/standards/standards/for-students-2016

Israelson, M. H. (2015). The app map: A tool for systematic evaluation of apps for early literacy learning. *The Reading Teacher, 69*, 339–349.

Ito, M., Baumer, S., Bittanti, M., Boyd, D., Cody, R., Herr-Stephenson, B., ... & Tripp, L. (2010). *Hanging out, messing around, and geeking out: Kids living and learning with new media*. Cambridge, MA: The MIT Press.

Ito, M., Gutiérrez, K., Livingstone, S., Penuel, B., Rhodes, J., Salen, K., ... Watkins, S. C. (2013). *Connected learning: An agenda for research and design*. Irvine, CA: Digital Media and Learning Research Hub.

Javorsky, K., & Trainin, G. (2014). Teaching young readers to navigate a digital story when rules keep changing. *The Reading Teacher, 67*, 606–618.

Jewitt, C. (2006). *Technology, literacy and learning: A multimodal approach*. New York, NY: Routledge.

Kamil, M., Intrator, S., & Kim, H. (2000). The effects of other technologies on literacy and literacy learning. In M. Kamil, P. Mosenthal, D. Pearson, & R. Barr (Eds.), *Handbook of reading research* (Vol. III, pp. 771–790). New York, NY: Routledge.

Kaptelinin, V., & Nardi, B. (2006). *Acting with technology: Activity theory and interaction design*. Cambridge: MIT Press.

Kress, G. (2010). *Multimodality: A social semiotic approach to contemporary communication*. New York, NY: Routledge.

Labbo, L., & Reinking, D. (2003). Computers and early literacy education. In N. Hall, J. Larson, & J. Marsh (Eds.), *Handbook of early childhood literacy* (pp. 338–354). Thousand Oaks, CA: Sage.

Lam, W. S. E. (2004). Second language socialization in a bilingual chat room: Global and local considerations. *Language Learning & Technology, 8*(3), 44–65.

Lammers, J. C., Magnifico, A. M., & Curwood, J. S. (2018). Literate identities in fan-based online affinity spaces. In K. Mills, A. Stornaiuolo, A. Smith, & J. Z. Pandya (Eds.), *Handbook of writing, literacies, and education in digital cultures* (pp. 174–184). New York, NY: Routledge.

Lammers, J. C., & Marsh, V. L. (2015). Going public: An adolescent's networked writing on Fanfiction.net. *Journal of Adolescent & Adult Literacy, 59*, 277–285.

Lankshear, C., & Knobel, M. (2011). *New literacies: Everyday practices and social learning* (3rd ed.). New York, NY: Open University Press.

Leu, D. (2000). Literacy and technology: Deictic consequences for literacy education in the information age. In M. Kamil, P. Mosenthal, D. Pearson, & R. Barr (Eds.), *Handbook of reading research* (Vol. III, pp. 743–770). New York, NY: Routledge.

Leu, D., Forzani, E., Burlingame, C., Kulikowich, J., Sedransk, N., Coiro, J., & Kennedy, C. (2014). The new literacies of online research and comprehension: Assessing and preparing students for the 21st Century with Common Core State Standards. In S. Neuman & L. Gambrell (Eds.), *Quality reading instruction in the age of common standards* (pp. 219–236). Newark, DE: International Reading Association.

Lizárraga, J. R., & Gutiérrez, K. D. (2017). Centering Nepantla literacies from the borderlands: Leveraging "in-betweenness" toward learning in the everyday. *Theory Into Practice, 57*(1). doi:http://doi.org/10.1080/00405841.2017.1392164

Martin-Beltrán, M., Tigert, J. M., Peercy, M. M., & Silverman, R. D. (2017). Using digital texts vs. paper texts to read together: Insights into engagement and mediation of literacy practices among linguistically diverse students. *International Journal of Educational Research, 82*, 135–146. doi: http://doi.org/10.1016/j.ijer.2017.01.009

McKenna, M. (2006). Introduction: Trends and trajectories of literacy and technology in the new millenium. In M. McKenna, L. Labbo, R. Kieffer, & D. Reinking (Eds.), *International handbook of literacy and technology* (Vol. 2, pp. xi–xviii). Mahwah, NJ: Lawrence Erlbaum.

Miller, E., & Warschauer, M. (2014) Young children and e-reading: Research to date and questions for the future. *Learning, Media and Technology, 39*(3), 283–305. doi:10.1080/17439884.2013.867868

Mills, K. A. (2010). A review of the "digital turn" in the new literacy studies. *Review of Educational Research, 80*, 246–271.

Muhammad, G. E., & Haddix, M. (2016). Centering Black girls' literacies : A review of literature on the multiple ways of knowing of Black girls. *English Education, 48*(4), 299–336.

National Governors Association Center for Best Practices, & Council of Chief State School Officers. (2010). *Common core state standards- English language arts*. Washington, DC: National Governors Association Center for Best Practices, Council of Chief State School Officers.

New London Group. (1996). A pedagogy of multiliteracies: Designing social futures. *Harvard Educational Review, 66*(1), 60–92.

Noguerón-Liu, S. (2017). Expanding notions of digital access: Parents' negotiation of school-based technology initiatives in new immigrant communities. *Equity & Excellence in Education, 50*(4), 387–399.

Owens, D. (2015). It's not the device, it's what it can do. *THE Journal* (October), 27–28. Retrieved from https://thejournal.com/articles/2015/10/27/its-not-the-device-its-what-the-device-can-do.aspx

Pérez, B. (2004). *Sociocultural contexts of language and literacy*. Mahwah, NJ: Lawrence Erlbaum Associates.

Pew Research Center. (2018, February 5). Internet/Broadband fact sheet. Retrieved from www.pewinternet.org/fact-sheet/internet-broadband/

Price-Dennis, D. (2016). Developing curriculum to support Black girls' literacies in digital spaces. *English Education, 48*, 337–361.

Razfar, A., & Yang, E. (2010). Digital, hybrid, and multilingual literacies in early childhood. *Language Arts, 88*(2), 114–124.

Reinking, D., & Bridwell-Bowles, L. (1991). Computers in reading and writing. In R. Barr, M. Kamil, P. Mosenthal, & D. Pearson (Eds.), *Handbook of reading research* (Vol. II, pp. 310–340). New York, NY: Routledge.

Rowsell, J., Saudelli, M. G., Scott, R. M., & Bishop, A. (2013). iPads as placed resources: Forging community in online and offline spaces. *Language Arts, 90*, 351–360.

Rowsell, J., & Wohlwend, K. (2016). Free play or tight spaces? Mapping participatory literacies in apps. *The Reading Teacher, 70*, 197–205.

Schwartz, L., & Gutiérrez, K. (2015). Literacy studies and situated methods: Exploring the social organization of household activity and social media use. In J. Roswell & K. Pahl (Eds.), *The Routledge handbook of literacy studies* (pp. 575–592). New York, NY: Routledge.

Singer, N. (May 13, 2017). How Google took over the classroom. *The New York Times*. Retrieved from www.nytimes.com/2017/05/13/technology/google-education-chromebooks-schools.html

Street, B. V. (1984). *Literacy in theory and practice*. Cambridge, UK: Cambridge University Press.

Takacs, Z. K., Swart, E. K., & Bus, A. G. (2015). Benefits and pitfalls of multimedia and interactive features in technology-enhanced storybooks: A meta-analysis. *Review of Educational Research, 85*, 698–739.

Vásquez, O. A. (2003). *La clase mágica: Imagining optimal possibilities in a bilingual community of learners*. Mahwah, NJ: Erlbaum.

Warschauer, M., & Ware, P. (2008). Learning, change, and power: Competing discourses of technology and literacy. In J. Coiro, M. Knobel, C. Lankshear, & D. J. Leu (Eds.), *Handbook of research on new literacies* (pp. 215–240). New York, NY: Lawrence Erlbaum Associates.

Wertsch, J. (1991). *Voices of the mind: A sociocultural approach to mediated action*. Cambridge, MA: Harvard University Press.

Appendix A: Studies Reviewed

Authors and year	Method of inquiry	Grade level	Mediational tool (device or platform used)	Guiding theoretical frameworks
Tool-centered studies				
Baker (2007)	Analysis of classroom website features.	Elementary students (k-6)	Websites	Sociocultural perspectives, transformative and new literacies' stances
Dalton et al. (2011)	Mixed methods	Fifth-grade monolingual and bilingual children	Scaffolded text environment	Universal design for learning, simple view and compensatory models of reading, sociocultural context factors
Israelson (2015)	Development of framework for app selection	Elementary education	Apps	Affordances and value added; substitution, augmentation, modification and redefinition (SAMR) model.
Javorsky and Trainin (2014)	Exploratory study of digital story applications	Young, early readers	Digital texts, digital stories	Cognitive flexibility theory; references to multiple modalities
Rowsell and Wohlwend (2016)	Comparison of four app-mediated literacy practices and introduction of rubric	Elementary students	Apps	Participatory literacies, ideological model of literacy
Classroom-based studies				
Hutchison et al. (2012)	Exploratory case study	Fourth grade	Wikis, video production, blogs, apps, games, e-readers, podcasts, cartoon creators, e-mail	TPACK framework, new literacies and affordances
Price-Dennis (2016)	Qualitative case study	Fifth grade	Web 2.0 platforms and apps, digital and print-based media, tablets and desktops	Black girls' literacies framework
Handsfield et al. (2009)	Qualitative two-year research project.	Fourth grade	Comic creator and Blogspot	Sociocultural theory, affordances of digital text
Hagood (2012)	Qualitative study of teachers' experiences and risks	Grades 6-8	Photostory, Glogster, flip cameras, e-readers	new literacies
Martin-Beltrán et al. (2017)	Design-based research study of reading buddies program, mixed-methods analysis	Cross-age peers: kindergarten and 4th grade	Digital text in tablet	Sociocultural theory
Rowsell et al. (2013)	Longitudinal action research of teacher learning group	3rd & 6th grades	iPads and apps	New Literacy Studies; anthropological perspectives

22
Restorying Critical Literacies

*Ebony Elizabeth Thomas,
Jane Bean-Folkes, and James Joshua Coleman*

Despite increasing restrictions on curriculum, testing imperatives, and other aspects of neoliberal policies, today's students are recasting stories in their own images, experiences, perspectives, and mindsets (Thomas & Stornaiuolo, 2016). By the end of the 2010s, Black girls like Marley Dias were engaging in hashtag activism like #1000BlackGirlBooks, to push for more diversity in children's and young adult literature (Stornaiuolo & Thomas, 2017). Eleven year old Dias created the online campaign #1000BlackGirlBooks because she did not see herself in the books she was reading (Flood, 2016). While also inspiring other young people, Dias drew attention to the broader issue of representation in children's literature. According to the Cooperative Book Center's statistics for 2018, only 180 titles featured African or African American characters out of 3,500 books published (Campbell, 2017; CCBC, 2018). In her public declaration that these statistics must change, she displayed critical awareness of persistent disparities in the kinds of texts that are validated by schooling.

Dias is by no means alone. When today's young people are misrepresented or erased from mainstream media, they are now creating and finding new venues to represent themselves and others to create counter narratives of resistance as a matter of course (Duncan-Andrade, 2007). Whether "bending" the race, gender, or sexual identity of characters they find (Thomas & Stornaiuolo, 2016), engaging in "lifestreaming" to gain voice and visibility online (Wargo, 2015), or taking "selfies" to circulate self-representations (Brager, 2015), young people are now writing themselves into the media that have excluded them. Queer youth and young adults are remixing popular stories and cultures to better reflect the ways that all people live – and love – today (Wargo, 2015). Native youth are centering silence, testimony, and nonviolent action as a way to resist narratives that erase their cultures and presence (San Pedro, 2015). Most recently, at the time of this writing, students from all backgrounds at Marjory Stoneman Douglas High School in Florida emerged as leaders in the fight against gun violence after one of the nation's worst mass school shootings, using the hashtags #NeverAgain and #MarchForOurLives (Arndt & Tesar, 2018). Truly, this is an age of restorying and reclamation of narrative. However, this reclamation of narrative has been largely read as youth activism, without explicitly connecting this action to educational practice.

It must be noted that many of us – peoples of color, Indigenous peoples, LGBTQ folk, women and nonbinary folk, children of undocumented workers, descendants of the enslaved – have *always* had to read ourselves into canons that excluded us historically, and all too often, continue to exclude our perspectives. Many canonical texts historically assumed a White male readership as their primary audience, and, in turn, people from other groups had to read (through) those narratives to attain print literacies and acquire the codes of power (Delpit, 1995). Not only was it necessary for people from the margins to identify and comprehend the societal metanarratives and metadiscourses contained within the canon in order to gain access to the professions, but often familiarity with canonical White male subjectivity was also vital for their very survival. Whether by reading literary prose, borrowing and transforming religious metaphors, or secretly violating edicts and laws, would-be readers and writers from nondominant groups had to accommodate textual self-erasure while reading written prose, viewing artwork, and the like. Thus, there arose an imperative to read and write marginalized selfhoods into textual existence. Literacy for nondominant people began then, with intergenerational narratives of sustenance and resilience, and continued with counter-storytelling that recognized mainstream narratives as inadequate and often damaging.

In this chapter, we situate our review of the literature on critical literacies within Black and Indigenous traditions of struggle over literacy (Fisher, 2009; Reese, 2013; Rooks, 1989; Thomas & Stornaiuolo, 2016). In doing so, we place the Black literate tradition in conversation with Freirean critical pedagogy, invite critical Indigenous literacies to interrogate New Literacy Studies, and nod toward the existence of other traditions of criticality that can also be brought to bear on considerations of literacy and power. From there, we turn toward examining how today's children, youth, and young adults are reading the word and the world critically (Freire & Macedo, 1987), both in their embodied lifeworlds and in digital spaces (Kinloch, 2010; Lipman, 2004, 2013; Stornaiuolo & Thomas, 2017; Winn, 2010). We connect youth and teachers' visible action to critical reader response theory (Beach, Appleman, Fecho, & Simon, 2016; Botelho & Rudman, 2009; Dávila, 2012; Leland, Lewison, & Harste, 2013; Lewis, 2000; Lewis, Enciso, & Moje, 2007) and critical sociolinguistics (Gee, 1990; Hall, 2001; Luke, 2012; Luke & Freebody, 1997). Next, we locate critical literacies within the contemporary research landscape, suggesting bridges between the gaps of educational theory and practice. Our final section ends on a somber note as we ponder the task of narrating critical literacies itself from a critical perspective – now and in the future.

Restorying the History of Critical Literacy: Centering the Margins

Critical literacy has been defined as "the social practice of reading, interpreting, and analyzing texts, discourses, and society to understand how, where, and why power operates, circulates, and reproduces itself" (Coffey, n.d.). This definition focuses on power, because the idea of reading from a critical lens was first ignited by people from the margins – including children and youth – not represented within the official discourses and curricula of schooling itself (Thomas & Stornaiuolo, 2016). Thus, we recontextualize critical literacy within landscapes of educational struggle within and beyond the United States that have not always been highlighted in educational research (Anderson, 1988; Fisher, 2009). One such example comes from the Black literacy tradition. Slave narratives provide glimpses into the existence of critically literate traditions that predated the Civil War (Gates, 1987). For example, Noliwe Rooks observes the agency of Black women writers who

> have begun the task of reshaping and redefining the patriarchy's notions regarding slave women by offering an alternative view of history – a vision which has Black women at its center. While they have not as yet answered all of the stereotypes of Black women that we

> have come to accept, they have made a definite start... *Black women have begun to write themselves into existence.*
>
> (Rooks, 1989, p. 62)

These acts of interpretative freedom – inscribing the self into existence when the very selfhood of Black women and girls was recognized neither legally nor socially – predate most histories of critical literacies by over a century.

After the US Civil War, in the segregated South, the teachers of the freedmen, their children, and their children's children, pulled back the curtain of the United States literary canon and held it up to scrutiny. bell hooks attested to this agency within the segregated classrooms of her childhood:

> To be changed by ideas was pure pleasure. But to learn ideas that ran counter to values and beliefs learned at home was to place oneself at risk, to enter the danger zone... School was the place where I could forget that self and, through ideas, reinvent myself.

She describes her teachers as linguistically and culturally similar "women on a mission" (hooks, 1994). This mission of providing critical education for students – humanizing them, their culture, and the world around them, in the face of state-sanctioned dehumanization – is something that Jacqueline Jordan Irvine (1999) further historicizes:

> In 1903, Du Bois wrote: "In the Black world, the preacher and teacher embodied once the ideals of this people – the strife for another and a more just world, the vague dream of righteousness, the mystery of knowing" (Du Bois, 1903/1973, p. 57). As Du Bois's statement indicates, teachers in the African American community were held in high esteem and saw teaching as a moral act reminiscent of the "lifting as we climb" philosophy of late 19th- and early 20th-century Black women educators like Lucy Laney, Charlotte Hawkins Brown, Fanny Jackson Coppin, and Anna J. Cooper (Irvine & Hill, 1990). The African American teachers in my research have a strong and apparent sense of spirituality and use phrases and words like "special Godly anointing" and "sacred calling" to describe their work. The interviews with these teachers are replete with references to words like "blessings" and "mission."

Scholarship on the history of Black education, including the burgeoning literature on critical race theory in education and asset-based pedagogies, is sometimes considered separately from critical literacies. Yet this rich historical account is evidence of the emancipatory dimension of critical literacy, which Freire saw "as one of the major vehicles by which 'oppressed' people are able to participate in the sociohistorical transformation of their society" (Walmsley, 1981, p. 84, as quoted in Freire & Macedo, 1987). Published in 1970, Freire's *Pedagogy of the Oppressed*, shifted the landscape of teaching and learning as it called for critical praxis rooted in humanization and social transformation. Challenging a "banking model of education" (2016, p. 73), Freire's work focused on student agency by addressing power as it relates to epistemology – what counts as knowledge – and to the development of critical consciousness. No longer "vessel[s] to be filled" (p. 79), students within Freire's framework are repositioned as active constructors of knowledge, critical agents consciously reshaping both the world and the word.

Freire and Macedo's notion of "reading the world and reading the word," bridged critical pedagogy with studies of literacy as it linked the social world with the study of text (Freire, 2016; Freire & Macedo, 1987). In a sense, this work textualized the social world, making legible the operations of power such that readers – in Freire's case students – might challenge, harness, or even "rewrite" power in more equitable ways. Drawing upon this radical repositioning of the learner, scholars have extended Freire and Macedo's work on critical pedagogy and critical literacy to address the cultural politics of democratic citizenship (Giroux, 1992, 2016), the dialogical methods of literacy education for liberation (Shor & Freire, 1987), and even the implications of literacy as a critical endeavor for equity (Shor, 1999). Re-articulated in a myriad number of directions and forms, Freire's address of critical pedagogy serves as a foundation for critical readers as it positions students as active interpreters of power, power made legible by reading both the world and word. And yet, Freire himself hailed from the poorest and Blackest region of Brazil – the Northeast – and his landmark work was inspired and informed by his interactions with sugarcane workers, many of whom were the Afro-Brazilian descendants of slaves. It is therefore impossible to narrate emancipatory critical traditions in education without hailing the Middle Passage, the Atlantic slave trade, and the ways that literacy was – quite literally – emancipatory for millions of people.

Moving to another literate tradition that has been neglected within academic considerations of reading, literacy, and English education, the conceptualization of literacy among Native/Indigenous peoples has long been critical. Debbie Reese, founder of the influential American Indians in Children's Literature website, notes the need for the indigenization of critical literacies (Reese, 2013). Critical Indigenous Literacies is neither concerned with acquiring power within the dominant culture, nor being interpellated as minoritized "people of color." Instead, the focus of Critical Indigenous Literacies is the preservation of tribal sovereignty, as well as focusing on Indigenous issues, concerns, and communities (Reese, 2013, p. 251). As with parallel traditions, this work has gone on for centuries.

> Calls for change go back to the 1800s. In 1829, William Apes, a Pequot man raised by whites, wrote that he was afraid of his own people because of "the many stories I had heard of their cruelty toward the whites" and that if the whites "had told me how cruel they had been to the 'poor Indian,' I should have apprehended as much harm from them" (Apes & O'Connell, 1829, p. 11). Less than a hundred years later, Native parents in Chicago wrote to the mayor, objecting to what their children were being taught in Chicago schools. In part, they wrote "We do not know if school histories are pro-British, but we do know that they are unjust to the life of our people – the American Indian. They call all white victories, battles, and all Indian victories, massacres," and the parents asked that history be taught in a balanced way (Costo & Henry, 1927). Apes and the Chicago parents were engaged in what we know today as critical literacy.
>
> *(Reese, 2013, p. 253)*

Reese, as well as other scholars of Critical Indigenous Literacies and Critical Indigenous education, trace Native, Indigenous, and First Nations ways of knowing and being that are inherently social in nature (Brayboy, 2005; Reese, 2013). The writings of Apes in the 19th century, and the advocacy of Native parents in early 20th century Chicago, predate, and anticipate, Brian Street's ideological model of literacy, which reshaped the field of reading research by forging a novel, agentive framework for the study of students' literate practices (1984). Re-conceptualized as a social practice "embedded in social conceptions of knowledge, identity, [and] being" (2006, p. 2), Street demonstrated that literacy cannot be excised from social context and thus could not be characterized as universal: the singular conception of literacy must be transformed into a theory of multiple literacies. Challenging an "autonomous model of literacy" predicated on cognitivist principles of discrete skills, Street's anthropological approach made visible the monolithic Western ideologies undergirding literacy study – that literacy and literacy research should be concerned with the neutral acquisition of universalized reading skills. Within Street's model, literacy operates as a series of "literacy events" and "literacy practices" interwoven within social contexts. Street's foundational work recasts the epistemological foundations of prior literacy research, thus providing a novel framework for considerations of power and reading (Gee, 1990; Street, 2003). The work of Street and followers, known as the New Literacy Studies (NLS), informed subsequent research in critical literacy for three decades.

New Literacy Studies has since been applied to broader social theory (Bartlett & Holland, 2002), discussions of discourses and intertextuality (Maybin, 2000), and to theories of multimodality (Kress & Street, 2005). NLS repositioned considerations of power as intimately tied to the social practice of literacy, and thus propelled reading research focused on student and community literacies operating inside and outside of classroom spaces. New Literacy Studies is defined by its turn to ideological and social aspects of literacy. Shaping nearly all critical literacy projects that emerged in its wake, NLS has brought new attention to student agency by recognizing social practices both in and outside of school spaces, in the material or digital world. And yet the work of Reese, Brayboy and others reminds us that the centrality of the social has been inherent to the ways that Native and Indigenous cultures read the world around them for millennia. Long before European colonization and academic interpretation, Native peoples were living literacy as a social practice.

These are but two examples demonstrating that literacy as a means to advocate for social justice, political power, sovereignty, and humanization, is not solely a 20th and 21st century academic phenomenon. The idea that literacy can be both emancipatory and social is central to Black/African and Native/Indigenous experiences in settler-colonial North America, as well as in other Indigenous and minoritized experiences from around the world. We believe that research on similar resistant readings of oppressive dominant cultures, as well as concomitant critical pedagogies, is necessary. For the idea of reading from a critical lens was first ignited by people from the margins – especially children, youth, and teachers – not within the official discourses and curricula of schooling itself. Considering the agency of the *people* – human actors – within schooling and society, and how human agency informs academic conceptualizations of criticality, is vital for understanding critical literacies today.

Restorying the Word and the World: How are Today's Students Transforming Critical Literacies?

What does critical literacy look like in an era of profound social and technological change? Chinua Achebe suggests that one form of resistance has always been for those who have been dispossessed or silenced to "restory" themselves in order to establish "a balance of stories where every people will be able to contribute to a definition of themselves, where we are not victims of other people's accounts" (Bacon, 2000, para. 17). Restorying has been conceptualized in the narrative analysis tradition in qualitative research as a method for researchers to break down the stories that participants tell them into their constituent parts – plot, characters, and themes – and then synthesize them in new ways to make meaning of myriad experiences of the same phenomenon (cf. Connelly & Clandinin, 2006; Daiute & Lightfoot, 2004; Ollerenshaw & Creswell, 2002). However, restorying can also characterize the complex ways that contemporary young people are critically narrating "the word and the world" (Enciso, 2011; Freire & Macedo, 1987), analyzing their lived experiences, then synthesizing and recontextualizing a multiplicity of stories in order to form new narratives. In other words, as young readers imagine themselves into stories they *reimagine the very stories themselves*, reimagining time, place, identity, perspective, mode, and metanarratives through retold stories.

This process of restorying, or reshaping narratives to better reflect a diversity of perspectives and experiences, is an act of asserting the importance of one's existence in a world where subaltern voices are often silenced by those in power (Thomas & Stornaiuolo, 2016). Today's social issues are viewed with concern by young people, and they are increasingly engaged online and in the real world (Kinloch, 2010; Lipman, 2004, 2013; Stornaiuolo & Thomas, 2017; Winn, 2010), using media sites like Twitter, Instagram, and Tumblr to voice their concerns, provide a critical perspective on political and social issues, and organize to take action. Outside of schools, students' agentive restorying practices are transforming what it means to read the word and the world through a critical lens – lenses that they then bring into classroom spaces.

These and other digital age acts of interpretative freedom are connected to the long tradition of transactional theory in reading (Rosenblatt, 1995), as well as to critical reader response. Critical reader response considers the selection of and pedagogy involved in the teaching of diverse literature and media for young people, as well as reading context and readers' identities (Beach et al., 2016; Botelho & Rudman, 2009; Enciso, 1997, 1998; Garcia, 2013; Leland et al., 2013; Lewis, 2000; Moje & Luke, 2009; Naidoo & Dahlen, 2013; Willis, 1998). Typified in the work of Richard Beach (cf. 1993; 2000), critical reader response scholars infuse educational research with literary theory, creating space for critical meaning-making. Critical reader response challenges the separation of text and reader, instead emphasizing the connections among personal experience, reading practices, and the social world. Through his address of cultural models (1995), Beach echoes Street's ideological model of literacy, asserting that sociocultural experiences shape student interpretations of literature within classroom spaces. Placing pressure on New Criticism, the predominating mode of literary interpretation taught in K-12 classrooms, Beach challenged the separation of text and reader, instead emphasizing the connections among personal experience, reading practices, and the social world.

Important contributions to the literature on critical reader response have come from Cynthia Lewis, Carol D. Lee, Patricia Enciso, Deborah Appleman, Maria Franquiz, Wanda Brooks, Miriam Martinez, Jonda McNair, Marjorie Orellana, Carmen Medina, Denise Dávila, and Angie Zapata in recent years, to name a few – women scholars, many of color, who are honoring the ways that children from diverse families and backgrounds respond to texts through highlighting the counterstories these students tell. These scholars place emphasis on critical reader response as praxis, arguing for expanded curricula that increase diverse representation and thus the range of possible interpretative responses (cf. Bean-Folkes & Lewis-Ellison, 2018; DeNicolo & Franquiz, 2006; Dutro, 2008, 2011; Leland, Harste, Ociepka, Lewison, & Vasquez, 1999; Medina, 2010; Zapata, Sánchez & Robinson, 2016).

Another burgeoning area of critical reader response scholarship has embraced student responses to digital texts. We take the position that many of today's students are arriving in our classrooms with *some* critical lenses already, due to the ubiquity of personal devices like smartphones and tablets (Mascheroni & Ólafsson, 2016). Recognizing the agency afforded by out of school digital spaces, researchers are now considering how reader response interfaces with the digital to shape the development of critical reader lenses (Beach & Bruce, 2002; Myers & Beach, 2001). Examining what students are already doing, and how they respond to texts critically in out-of-school spaces, especially online, will become increasingly important for scholars interested in critical literacies. Recent work by Donna Alvermann, Ernest Morrell, Antero Garcia, Nicole Mirra, Tisha Lewis Ellison, Danielle Filipiak, and Jon Michel Wargo in critical media studies is welcome (Alvermann, 2008; Garcia, 2013; Lewis Ellison, 2017; Mirra, Morrell, & Filipiak, 2018; Wargo, 2017), but much more research is needed in this area.

Outside of the United States, scholarship on critical literacies emerged from the critical sociolinguistics tradition, which was influenced by the work of French philosopher Michel Foucault and British sociologist Stuart Hall (Hall, 2001), and typified in the work of Australian language and literacies scholars Allan Luke (2012), Peter Freebody (2017), and Barbara Comber (2015). This work focused on the connections between discourse and power, and developing student agency within the reading and writing classroom, which was positioned as a site of sociopolitical contestation. From a critical sociolinguistic perspective, students' best demonstrated their role as active shapers of discursive power as they became critical readers and producers of texts.

In the United States, James Paul Gee (1989, 1990) built on the work of Pierre Bourdieu to connect critical considerations of social linguistics, literacies, and orality to issues of domination made possible by the slippage between "learning" and "acquisition" of primary and secondary discourses, then moved toward researching the literate practices of online affinity groups, such as gaming communities (Gee, 2003). In South Africa, Hilary Janks drew upon the linguistic tradition of Norman Fairclough's (1989, 1995, 2003) model of critical discourse analysis to suggest critical reading and writing as a means to challenge domination, gain access, embrace diversity, and engage in the agentive act of (re)design (Janks, 2009). Finally, in recent years, linguists such as H. Samy Alim, Suresh Canagarajah, Nelson Flores, and Jonathan Rosa have influenced critical literacies, moving the needle forward toward considerations of language diversity, second language learners, and the needs of immigrant and refugee students.

Restorying the Gaps in Critical Literacies: What We Have vs. What We Need

Much has changed in the decade that has passed since the fourth edition of this handbook, where Peter Freebody and Jill Freiberg usefully characterized critical literacy as powerful educator action, defining it as "a range of attempts on the part of educators to prepare young people for societies that conduct much of their daily business via texts" (2011, p. 432). Situating schools as epicenters for the dissemination of power, Freebody and Freiberg delineated how knowledge – both of and about texts – leads to the circulation of power. While we concur that schools and other sites of learning are indeed critical for the teaching of critical literacies (pun intended), the seismic shifts in the culture during the 2010s have called into question the educator's role.

Definition Gap

While scholars in recent decades have extended Freire and Macedo's work on critical pedagogy and critical literacy to address the cultural politics of democratic citizenship (Giroux, 2016), the dialogical methods of literacy education for liberatory education (Shor & Freire, 1987), and even the implications of literacy as a critical endeavor for equity (Shor, 1999), more is needed as we move into the 2020s. Indeed, given current clarion calls within schooling and society for diversity, equity, and social justice, we question whether definitions of critical reading, critical literacy, and critical English language arts education *should* continue to be rooted primarily within the work of educators and educational researchers recognized within the academy of the final half of the 20th century, with subsequent work merely viewed as add-ons specific to the cultures and communities where research and teaching is taking place.

At this juncture, we advocate for situating academic research and scholarship on critical literacies within a much broader context – as part of centuries-long conversations about what it means to be *literate*, what it means to be *critical*, what it means to be *human*, and even what it means to *mean*. Although social and technological change is certainly not, in itself, indicative of increased criticality, this new landscape contests the idea that even the most critical educators could ever be primary arbiters of meaning for today's children and teens. Imperatives of testing and static measures of reading achievement imperil our collective understanding of what children, teens, and adults need to know. In an age where meaning itself is increasingly being determined by the whims of algorithms, and interpretation being influenced by the whims of crowdsourcing, this is unfortunate. By foregrounding voices from the margins – Black, Indigenous, and youth online – and their critical address of literacy through counterstories, we are seeking to bridge this particular gap.

Implementation and Translation Gaps

Although the value of critical literacy education is supported by the research literature, how it has been taken up in practice is less well known. Our review of the literature on critical literacies revealed a significant gap between qualitative and quantitative studies. We do not mean to suggest that laboratories or controlled settings are necessarily imperative for the development of actionable critical literacy praxis, and yet, there are ways that small-scale ethnographies and case study research documenting effective practice can be considered across contexts to inform ways to scale up critical literacy curricula. Critical literacy inherently challenges generalizability, since what is critical is dependent upon context.

Relevance and Bridging Gap

Reading curriculum is facing a crisis of relevance. Rather than allowing those shaped by the past to dominate narratives on the issues facing adolescents today, young users of participatory media sites like Twitter, Instagram, and Tumblr, are using these platforms to engage in advocacy and social activism. They are increasingly choosing their own reading that reflects their interests, while questioning canonical reads. Teaching critical lenses for analyzing the word and the world is one way to bridge this gap (Botelho & Rudman; Leland et al.). Also, there are many complementary fields beyond education that can inform research on critical literacies. Established fields, such as linguistics, English literary studies, media and communications, and ethnic and area studies, as well as emerging fields, such as fan studies, social movement studies, and the digital humanities can provide much insight as we look toward the future.

Conclusion

Critical literacies, like our world, is at a crossroads. Rather than allowing those shaped by the past to dominate narratives on the issues facing adolescents today – including gentrification, mass incarceration, neoliberal educational reform, and socioeconomic precarity in an age of global capitalism (Kinloch, 2010; Lipman, 2004, 2013; Winn, 2010) – young users of participatory media sites are using these platforms to engage in advocacy and social activism. Within their communities, they are taking action by becoming politically involved. They are increasingly choosing their own reading that reflects their interests, while questioning canonical reads. More importantly, they are demanding that the texts that they read and write about have relevance to the everyday concerns of their lives. While such demands are nothing new, the acute economic, social, and political pressures of the contemporary moment, as well as the ways that children and teens are engaged in the textual landscapes of the digital age brings such concerns into sharp relief.

It is difficult to predict what will happen on the next page in the long story of critical literacies. While we have attempted to show the myriad ways that critical ways of reading, writing, knowing, and being have influenced the past and present, all too often, critical literacies have taken a backseat during our current era of neoliberal educational reform. Traditional measures of literate success are aligned with a world that no longer exists. All of these factors of change are intimately tied to power.

As Chimamanda Ngozi Adichie noted in her influential TED talk, "The Danger of a Single Story":

> Power is the ability not just to tell the story of another person, but to make it the definitive story of that person. The Palestinian poet Mourid Barghouti writes that if you want to dispossess a people, the simplest way to do it is to tell their story and to start with, "secondly."

> Start the story with the arrows of the Native Americans, and not with the arrival of the British, and you have an entirely different story. Start the story with the failure of the African state, and not with the colonial creation of the African state, and you have an entirely different story.
>
> (Adichie, 2009)

In this chapter, we have attempted to tell the story of critical literacies differently, for the place where a story *begins* influences the meaning that can derive from that story. Restorying critical literacies means starting with critical traditions that predate the mid-20th century. It means documenting what children and teens in today's digitally networked world are bringing with them before they arrive in the classroom. And it means embracing teaching practices that disrupt the status quo, question established viewpoints, focus on sociopolitical issues, and promote social justice.

Maisha Winn reminds us of the words of Mary Rose O'Reilly, that one potential outcome of transformative literary pedagogy is to "teach literature so that people stop killing each other" (quoted in Winn, 2013, p. 128). If this is the case, we are encouraged by the growing number of critical literacy educators who embrace culturally relevant (Ladson-Billings, 1995), responsive (Gay, 2000), and sustaining (Paris, 2012) pedagogies that frame teaching and learning as centrally concerned with nurturing the language, literacy, and cultural practices students bring with them, positioning them as the center of their own literate worlds. For literacy itself must be reconsidered at a time when young people are entering schools with the power to restory the world.

References

Adichie, C. (2009). *The danger of a single story*. New York, NY: TED Global. Retrieved from www.ted.com/talks/chimamanda_adichie_the_danger_ofN_a_sing_story.htmlx

Alvermann, D. E. (2008). Why bother theorizing adolescents' online literacies for classroom practice and research? *Journal of Adolescent & Adult Literacy, 52*(1), 8–19.

Anderson, J. D. (1988). *The education of Blacks in the South, 1860–1935*. Durham: University of North Carolina Press.

Arndt, S., & Tesar, M. (2018). True fake news: Reshaping educational policies with the #MarchofOurLives. *Policy Futures in Education, 16*(3), 233–236.

Bacon, K. (2000, August 2). An African voice. *The Atlantic*. Retrieved from www.theatlantic.com/magazine/archive/2000/08/an-african-voice/306020/

Bartlett, L., & Holland, D. (2002). Theorizing the space of literacy practices. *Ways of Knowing, 2*(1), 10–22.

Beach, R. (1993). *Reader-response theories: A teacher's introduction to reader-response theories*. Urbana, IL: National Council of Teachers of English.

Beach, R. (1995). Constructing cultural models through response to literature. *English Journal, 84*(6), 87–94.

Beach, R. (2000). Critical issues: Reading and responding to literature at the level of activity. *Journal of Literacy Research, 32*(2), 237–251.

Beach, R., Appleman, D., Fecho, B., & Simon, R. (2016). *Teaching literature to adolescents*. New York, NY: Routledge.

Beach, R., & Bruce, B. C. (2002). Using digital tools to foster critical inquiry. In D. E. Alvermann (Ed.), *Adolescents and literacies in a digital world* (pp. 147–163). New York, NY: Peter Lang.

Bean-Folkes, J., & Lewis-Ellison, T. (2018). Teaching in a culture of love: An open dialogue about African American student learning. *School Community Journal, 8*(2), 213–228.

Botelho, M. J., & Rudman, M. K. (2009). *Critical multicultural analysis of children's literature: Mirrors, windows, and doors*. New York, NY: Routledge.

Brager, J. (2015). The selfie and the other: Consuming viral tragedy and social media (after) lives. *International Journal of Communication, 9*, 1660–1671.

Brayboy, B. M. J. (2005). Toward a tribal critical race theory in education. *The Urban Review, 37*(5), 425–446.

Campbell, E. (2017, March 11). #kidlitwomen: Black girls economics in young adult fiction. [web log comment]. Retrieved from https://campbele.wordpress.com/2018/03/11/black-girls-economics-in-young-adult-fiction/.

CCBC. (2018). Publishing statistics on children's books about people of color and first/native nations and by people of color and first/native nations authors and illustrators. *Cooperative Children's Book Center*. Retrieved from https://ccbc.education.wisc.edu/books/pcstats.asp.

Coffey, H. (n.d.) Critical literacy. *Learn NC: K-12 Teaching and Learning from the UNC School of Education*. Retrieved from http://econowha.ie/wp-content/uploads/2014/04/Critical-literacy-Heather-Coffey.pdf.

Comber, B. (2015). Critical literacy and social justice. *Journal of Adolescent & Adult Literacy*, 58(5), 362–367.

Connelly, F. M., & Clandinin, D. J. (2006). Narrative inquiry. In J. L. Green, G. Camilli, P. B. Elmore, & E. Grace (Eds.), *Handbook of complementary methods in education research* (pp. 477–487). Mahwah, NJ: Lawrence Erlbaum.

Daiute, C., & Lightfoot, C. (Eds.). (2004). *Narrative analysis: Studying the development of individuals in society*. London, UK: Sage.

Dávila, D. (2012). In search of the ideal reader for children's non-fiction books about el Día de Los Muertos. *Journal of Children's Literature*, 38(1), 16–26.

DeNicolo, C. P., & Franquiz, M. E. (2006). "Do I have to say it?": Critical encounters with multicultural children's literature. *Language Arts*, 82(2), 157–170.

Delpit, L. (1995). *Other people's children: Cultural conflict in the classroom*. New York, NY: W. W. Norton.

Du Bois, W. E. B. (1903/1973). *The souls of black folk*. New York, NY: Penguin.

Duncan-Andrade, J. M. R. (2007). Urban youth and the counter-narration of inequality. *Transforming Anthropology*, 15(1), 26–37. doi:10.1525/tran.2007.15.1.26

Dutro, E. (2008). "That's why I was crying on this book": Trauma as testimony in responses to literature. *Changing English*, 15(4), 423–434.

Dutro, E. (2011). Writing wounded: Trauma, testimony, and critical witness in literacy classrooms. *English Education*, 43(2), 193–211.

Enciso, P. (2011). Storytelling in critical literacy pedagogy: Removing the walls between immigrant and non-immigrant youth. *English Teaching: Practice and Critique*, 10(1), 21–40.

Enciso, P. E. (1997). Negotiating the meaning of difference: Talking back to multicultural literature. In R. Rogers & A. O. Soter (Eds.), *Reading across cultures: Teaching literature in a diverse society* (pp. 13–41). New York, NY: Teacher College Press.

Enciso, P. E. (1998). Good/Bad girls read together: Pre-adolescent girls' co-authorship of feminine subject positions during a shared reading event. *English Education*, 30(1), 44–66.

Fairclough, N. (1989). *Language and power*. London, UK: Longman.

Fairclough, N. (1995). *Media discourse*. London: Edward Arnold.

Fairclough, N. (2003). *Analysing discourse: Textual analysis for social research*. London: Routledge.

Fisher, M. T. (2009). *Black literate lives: Historical and contemporary perspectives*. New York, NY: Routledge.

Flood, A. (2016, February 16). Girl's drive to find 1000 "black girl books" hits target with outpouring of donations. *The Guardian*. Retrieved from www.theguardian.com/books/2016/feb/09/marley-dias-1000-black-girl-books-hits-target-with-outpouring-ofdonations.

Freebody, P. (2017). Critical-literacy education: "The supremely educational event". In B. Street & S. May (Eds.), *Literacies and language education. Encyclopedia of language and education* (pp. 95–107). New York, NY: Springer, Cham.

Freebody, P., & Freiberg, J. M. (2011). The teaching and learning of critical literacy: Beyond the "show of wisdom". In M. L. Kamil, P. D. Pearson, E. B. Moje, & P. P. Afflerbach (Eds.), *Handbook of reading research* (Vol. IV) (pp. 432–452). New York, NY: Routledge.

Freire, P. (2016). *Pedagogy of the oppressed*. New York, NY: Bloomsbury.

Freire, P., & Macedo, D. (1987). *Literacy: Reading the word and the world*. New York, NY: Routledge.

Garcia, A. (2013). *Critical foundations in young adult literature*. Boston, MA: Sense.

Gates, H. L. (Ed.) (1987). *The classic slave narratives*. New York, NY: Penguin.

Gay, G. (2000). *Culturally responsive teaching theory, research, and practice*. New York, NY: Teachers College Record.

Gee, J. P. (1989). What is literacy? *Journal of Education*, 171(1), 18–25.

Gee, J. P. (1990). *Social linguistics and literacies*. London, UK: Falmer Press.

Gee, J. P. (2003). *What video games have to teach us about learning and literacy*. New York, NY: Palgrave/Macmillan.

Giroux, H. A. (1992). Literacy, pedagogy, and the politics of difference. *College Literature*, 19(1), 1–11.

Giroux, H. A. (2016). When schools become dead zones of the imagination: A critical pedagogy manifesto. *High School Journal*, 99, 351–359.

Hall, S. (2001). Encoding/decoding. In M. G. Durham & D. M. Keller (Eds.), *Media and cultural studies: Keyworks* (pp. 163–173). Malden, MA: Blackwell Publishing.

hooks, b. (1994). *Teaching to transgress: Education as the practice of freedom*. New York, NY: Routledge.
Irvine, J. (1999). The education of children whose nightmares come both day and night. *Journal of Negro Education, 68*(3), 244–253. doi:10.2307/2668099
Irvine, J. J., & Hill, L. B. (1990). From plantation to schoolhouse: The rise and decline of Black woman teachers. *Humanity and Society, 14*(3), 244–256.
Janks, H. (2009). *Literacy and power*. London, UK: Routledge.
Kinloch, V. (2010). *Harlem on our minds: Place, race, and the literacies of urban youth*. New York, NY: Teachers College Press.
Kress, G., & Street, B. (2005). Multi-modality and literacy practices. In K. Pahl & J. Rowsell (Eds.), *Travel notes from the new literacy studies: Instances of practice* (pp. vi–x). Bristol, UK: Multilingual Matters.
Ladson-Billings, G. (1995). Toward a theory of culturally relevant pedagogy. *American Educational Research Journal, 32*(3), 465–491.
Leland, C., Harste, J., Ociepka, A., Lewison, M., & Vasquez, V. (1999). Talking about books: Exploring critical literacy: You can hear a pin drop. *Language Arts, 77*(1), 70–77.
Leland, C., Lewison, M., & Harste, J. (2013). *Teaching children's literature: It's critical!* New York, NY: Routledge.
Lewis, C. (2000). Critical issues: Limits of identification: The personal, pleasurable, and critical in reader response. *Journal of Literacy Research, 32*(2), 253–266.
Lewis, C., Enciso, P. E., & Moje, E. B. (2007). *Reframing sociocultural research on literacy: Identity, agency, power*. New York, NY: Routledge.
Lewis Ellison, T. (2017). Digital participation, agency, and choice: An African American youth's digital storytelling about minecraft. *Journal of Adolescent & Adult Literacy, 61*(1), 25–35. doi:10.1002/jaal.645
Lipman, P. (2004). *High stakes education: Inequality, globalization, and urban school reform*. London, UK: Psychology Press.
Lipman, P. (2013). *The new political economy of urban education: Neoliberalism, race, and the right to the city*. New York, NY: Taylor & Francis.
Luke, A., & Freebody, P. (1997). Shaping the social practices of reading. In S. Muspratt, A. Luke, & P. Freebody (Eds.), *Constructing critical literacies: Teaching and learning textual practice* (pp. 185–225). Cresskill, NJ: Hampton.
Luke, A. (2012). Critical literacy: Foundational notes. *Theory Into Practice, 51*(1), 4–11. doi:10.1080/00405841.2012.636324
Mascheroni, G., & Ólafsson, K. (2016). The mobile internet: Access, use, opportunities and divides among European children. *New Media & Society, 18*(8), 1657–1679.
Maybin, J. (2000). The new literacy studies, context, intertexuality and discourse. In D. Barton, M. Hamilton, & R. Ivanič (Eds.), *Situated literacies: Reading and writing in context* (pp. 199–209). London, UK: Routledge.
Medina, C. (2010). "Reading across communities" in biliteracy practices: Examining translocal discourses and cultural flows in literature discussions. *Reading Research Quarterly, 45*, 40–60. doi:10.1598/RRQ.45.1.3
Mirra, N., Morrell, E., & Filipiak, D. (2018). From digital consumption to digital invention: Toward a new critical theory and practice of multiliteracies. *Theory Into Practice, 57*(1), 12–19. doi:10.1080/00405841.2017.1390336
Moje, E. B., & Luke, A. (2009). Literacy and identity: Examining the metaphors in history and contemporary research. *Reading Research Quarterly, 44*(4), 425–437.
Myers, J., & Beach, R. (2001). Hypermedia authoring as critical literacy. *Journal of Adolescent & Adult Literacy, 44*(6), 538–546.
Naidoo, J. C., & Dahlen, S. P. (2013). *Diversity in youth literature: Opening doors through reading*. Chicago, IL: American Library Association Editions.
Ollerenshaw, J. A., & Creswell, J. W. (2002). Narrative research: A comparison of two restorying data analysis approaches. *Qualitative Inquiry, 8*(3), 329–347. doi:10.1177/10778004008003008
Paris, D. (2012). Culturally sustaining pedagogy: A needed change in stance, terminology, and practice. *Educational Researcher, 41*, 93–97.
Reese, D. (2013). Critical indigenous literacies. In J. Larson & J. Marsh (Eds.), *The SAGE handbook of early childhood literacy* (pp. 251–262). London, UK: SAGE Publications.
Rooks, N. (1989). Writing themselves into existence: The intersection of history and literature in writings on black women. *Iowa Journal of Literary Studies, 10*, 51–63. doi:10.17077/0743-2747.1298
Rosenblatt, L. M. (1995) (Original work published 1938). *Literature as exploration* (5th ed). New York, NY: Modern Language association.
San Pedro, T. J. (2015). Silence as shields: Agency and resistances among native American students in the urban Southwest. *Research in the Teaching of English, 50*(2), 132–153.

Shor, I. (1999). What is critical literacy? *Journal for Pedagogy, Pluralism & Practice, 4*(1), 1–26.
Shor, I., & Freire, P. (1987). What is the "dialogical method" of teaching? *Journal of Education, 169*(3), 11–31.
Stornaiuolo, A., & Thomas, E. E. (2017). Disrupting educational inequalities Through youth digital activism. *Review of Research in Education, 41*(1), 337–357. doi:10.3102/0091732X16687973
Street, B. (1984). *Literacy in theory and practice*. Cambridge, UK: Cambridge University Press.
Street, B. (2003). What's "new" in new literacy studies? Critical approaches to literacy in theory and practice. *Current Issues in Comparative Education, 5*(2), 77–91.
Street, B. (2006). Autonomous and ideological models of literacy: Approaches from new literacy studies. *Media Anthropology Network*. Retrieved from https://pdfs.semanticscholar.org/1957/884a4cad853a1c6eff5bf148671e45f6af4f.pdf
Thomas, E. E., & Stornaiuolo, A. (2016). Restorying the self: Bending toward textual justice. *Harvard Educational Review, 86*(3), 313–338. doi:10.17763/1943-5045-86.3.313
Walmsley, S. (1981). On the purpose and content of secondary reading programs: Educational and ideological perspectives. *Curriculum Inquiry, 11*(1), 73–93.
Wargo, J. M. (2015). "Every selfie tells a story": LGBTQ youth lifestreams and new media narratives as connective identity texts. *New Media & Society*, 1–19. doi:10.1177/1461444815612447
Wargo, J. M. (2017). Designing more just social futures or remixing the radical present? Reading LGBTQ youths' multimodal (counter)storytelling as activist practice. *English Teaching: Practice & Critique, 16*(2), 145–160.
Willis, A. (Ed.) (1998). *Teaching multicultural literature in grades 9–12: Moving beyond the canon*. Norwood, MA: Christopher-Gordon Publ.
Winn, M. (2013). Toward a restorative English education. *Research in the Teaching of English, 48*(1), 126–135. Retrieved from: www.jstor.org/stable/24398649
Winn, M. T. (2010). 'Our side of the story': Moving incarcerated youth voices from margins to center. *Race Ethnicity and Education, 13*(3), 313–325.
Zapata, A., Sánchez, L., & Robinson, A. (2016). Examining young children's envisionment building responses to postmodern picturebooks. *Journal of Early Childhood Literacy*, 1–26. doi:https://doi.org/10.1177/1468798416674253

23

More Connected and More Divided than Ever

Toward a Cosmopolitan Ethics of Digital Literacies

David B. Sabey and Kevin M. Leander

In this chapter, we consider the relations of ethics, digital literacies, and education. On a personal level, the occasion for these considerations was the contentious 2016 presidential election in the United States. Though we have somewhat different political orientations, we were both disturbed by the election—and as scholars of digital literacies, we realized that our subject matter was profoundly implicated in the discourse and outcome of the election. At the same time, we recognize that the 2016 election is not an entirely unique or isolated phenomenon, but is symptomatic of ongoing global dynamics with extensive histories, economies, and politics. These broader global dynamics have come to be, for us, the broader situation of this chapter—its occasion. After sketching this context, we approach questions of digital literacies, ethics, and education in two key ways. First, after a brief foray into ethical considerations in literacy studies, we review relatively recent work that draws on theories of cosmopolitanism (an ethical framework which will be introduced subsequently), most of which was published since the previous edition of this volume. In this review, we outline an emerging theory regarding ethical (digital) literacy practices. Second, we apply this framework to a projective description of topics in digital literacies that we believe to be important, and we raise questions for literacy research and practice.

Globalization and Digital Literacy

In sketching a backdrop for this chapter, we turn to the work of Arjun Appadurai, a leading theorist of globalization. In his seminal work, Appadurai (1996) asserted that, in processes of globalization, there is a central tension between cultural homogenization and heterogenization which responds to five different "flows": ethnoscapes (migration of people), mediascapes (use of media that shapes our imagined world), technoscapes (cultural interactions due to the promotion of technology), financescapes (flux of capital), and ideoscapes (global flow of ideologies). As he later suggests, one response to the massive change and intensified anxiety accompanying these flows is a sometimes violent swing to the extreme political right (Appadurai, 2006). Amid the radical circulations of globalization, the tension between homogenization and heterogenization easily shifts toward homogenizing paradigms like nationalism and xenophobia. One of the strange ironies of globalization is that, as the world becomes increasingly connected via these global flows, it is simultaneously becoming increasingly divided.

Digital literacies are present everywhere we look in the course of these tensions and flows, and in the politics that accompany and drive them. How might we understand these relations, especially in so far as they might inform education? Broadly speaking, we posit two different approaches to considering how the homogenizing and heterogenizing responses to globalization are tied up with digital literacies. First, everyday uses of literacy—as social practices (Gee, 1989; Barton & Hamilton, 2000; Street, 1984)—produce localizing and globalizing movements (Brandt & Clinton, 2002). New technologies have connected us as never before across social, cultural, and national boundaries. Many of us have experienced how social practices with everyday technologies—Instagram, commercial websites, games, e-mail, and Zoom—have become related to other movements as well, including opportunities to make and spend money ("financescapes"), or opportunities to move about the world more frequently, contributing to the creation of new "ethnoscapes". At the same time, social practices that include digital literacies have also been routinely marshalled to create and harden boundaries. Online literacy practices on Facebook and Twitter, for instance, have been used as effective means for consolidating and organizing groups around different ideological positions—the use of literacy toward new and often competing "ideoscapes". As social practices, digital literacies may open up and expand our ideologies just as they may reassert traditional orthodoxies or give birth to radicalized movements; they connect us globally and also create particular cultural networks and boundaries of social formation (e.g., de Haan, Leander, and Ünlüsoy, 2014).

In addition to focusing on the work of digital literacies as social practices, a second approach to the co-production of digital literacies and globalizing flows is to consider how digital literacies have been used to create stories with homogenizing or heterogenizing tendencies, or new forms of the "global imaginary". We use this term to refer to a socially and culturally produced realm of interpretation—the values, symbols, and narratives through which people understand themselves and their society. This expanded conception of literacy practice as having meaning and value in relation to a shared imaginary was argued by Bartlett and Holland (2002). For instance, "functional illiterates," "good readers," and other categories of "readers" are invoked and deployed in schools as participants in the narratives of school literacy. These partially imagined worlds—realms of interpretation—also connect digital literacy practices within political, social, and cultural realms of interpretation. The "figured worlds" (Holland, Lachicotte, Skinner, & Cain, 1998) reified by a single President's tweet, an individuals' Facebook feed, or an entire online media outlet (e.g., Breitbart, Huffington Post), shape both simplified models of the world and also more expansive cultural imaginaries, operating at individual and collective scales.

Appadurai (1996), who was influenced by Anderson's (1983) notion of the "imagined community," writes that the "imagination has become an organized field of social practices" which acts as a powerful homogenizing and/or heterogenizing force (p. 31). Implicitly responding to some of the extreme homogenizing movements that have emerged recently (e.g., the "alt-right"), Appadurai (2006) underscores this idea saying, "It requires some serious effort and attention on how to shape the imagination and this imaginary in a constructive manner, so as to not make it a terrain only of fear, anxiety, hate, anger" (np). In this chapter, we hope to offer this kind of "serious effort and attention" regarding digital literacy studies. In particular, we consider how digital literacy education might be shaped through a broad ethical vision that is responsive to present social, cultural, and political dynamics. We begin addressing these questions by considering the relationship between ethics and literacy.

Ethics and Literacy

The field's "social turn" has taught us that literacy is always situated within particular social contexts and tied up in relationships between people (e.g., Gee, 1990). But what is true of literacy in general is becoming increasingly evident in an age of social media: We read, write, remix, and share texts in relation to other people, and we read, write, and imagine people into being through social practices. This understanding of the social nature of literacy leads rather straightforwardly to ethical considerations. Once we acknowledge that literacy mediates/constitutes self-Other relationships, we must consider the qualities of those relationships. Indeed, ethics and literacy can be viewed as largely co-constitutive. While there may be some ethical obligations that transcend language, by and large we relate and respond to the Other semiotically and discursively.

The profound relationship between literacy and ethics has always been a part of the field—we need look no further than the classic notion of "ethos" as a rhetorical appeal. More recently, critical theorists have pointed out how literacy is always entangled in questions of politics and power. Consider how Freire and Macedo (1987) implicitly connect literacy and ethics when they say, "Reading the world always precedes reading the word, and reading the word implies continually reading the world" (p. 35). From this perspective, to read is to trace, respond to, and transform asymmetrical social relations. Street (1984) similarly argues that literacy is not "autonomous," but "ideological"—models he uses to distinguish between a view of literacy abstracted from sociocultural practice, and one that situates literacy in the dynamic and often troubled social world. Social practice theory and its ideological critique of literacy (e.g., Collins & Blot, 2003; Larson, 2001) is but one branch of literacy studies that has considered relations of identity, power, access, and equity in literacy studies—all questions of profound ethical meaning. Thus, we see a more direct engagement with ethics in literacy research as the development of a line of inquiry with a rich history, but which, in a field dominated by psychological and sociological perspectives, foregrounds philosophical resources and conversations.

But what kind of ethics might guide our digital literacies practices? To be clear, critical theory, critical race theory, cultural studies, and poststructuralisms have by now substantial histories of raising questions of ethics and value with respect to texts, the socio-cultural imaginary, identities, and relationships. But with our Janus-like assignment in this tense socio-political moment, we sense the field of digital literacies as needing a more explicitly worked out prospective ethical stance—a robust vision that includes, but also moves beyond, ideological critique. We want to consider how literacy education and scholarship can engage more directly with the development of ethical social practices, including how to create just and humane publics in which a pluralistic "we" can come together. One promising line of theory development and early research that offers such a prospective vision, and that has recently emerged in the field, draws on and expands a renewed vision of cosmopolitanism.

Cosmopolitanism and Literacy

The term "cosmopolitanism," though contested, generally refers to one's ethical responsibility toward distant and different others. Because of the relative novelty of the theory in educational research, many of the authors who draw on cosmopolitanism provide a brief history of the concept, tracing it back to the iconoclastic Cynic, Diogenes, who declared himself a "citizen of the world" (cosmopolitan) and not a single city-state. Although Diogenes' provocative questions about one's obligations toward distant others and toward humanity in general, in addition to/transcendence of more local loyalties, were by no means unique, his term stuck. The typical genealogy of the idea skims over Diogenes' immediate successors, the Stoics, and highlights

Enlightenment philosophers such as Immanuel Kant (1903) and more recent thinkers who grappled with these ethical questions (e.g., Derrida, 2001), as well as others in business and politics who have invoked "cosmopolitanism" as an ideal. With such a long and predominantly Western and masculine history, it is no wonder that some articulations of cosmopolitanism are problematic. As educational theorists and researchers have sifted through this history, they have tended to situate their versions of cosmopolitanism in contrast to Enlightenment era and contemporary neoliberal versions of cosmopolitanism, which they cast as elitist, essentializing, universalizing, and/or ahistorical for the way they invoke privileged and uncritical visions of humanity and a unified world (see Stornaiuolo and Nichols (2018) for a critical review and reframing of cosmopolitanism in education research).

Empirical work related to cosmopolitanism in language and literacy studies has thus far been entirely descriptive and ethnographic; it has focused on articulating an appropriate version of cosmopolitanism for educational research and on identifying, describing, and characterizing its various manifestations "on the ground" as young people interact with others and communicate across difference of various scales and kinds (e.g., transnational, linguistic, cultural). As one might expect with a relatively early body of research, much of this work has focused on developing analytical frameworks that help to operationalize cosmopolitanism and illuminate its constituent parts and multiple permutations. Although the scholars cited below develop a variety of such frameworks, they are united in proposing cosmopolitanism as an ethical touchstone for communicating across differences in an increasingly globalized world, and they aspire to understand and encourage dynamic relations in which self and Other, the known and the new, the local and the distant are imagined, represented, and responded to with an ethic of hospitality and dialogue.

Although these are undoubtedly high standards, a common conclusion underscored across this literature is that young people are already "cosmopolitan" in many ways—and that they can enact and further develop their cosmopolitan dispositions and literacies when they are positioned as competent (e.g., Campano & Ghiso, 2011; Juzwik & McKenzie, 2015; Vasudevan, 2014), empowered to draw on the multimodal semiotic resources available to them (e.g., Canagarajah, 2012; De Costa, 2014; Hull, Stornaiuolo, & Sterponi, 2013; Stornaiuolo, 2016), and provided with appropriate scaffolding and forms of reflection as they attempt to communicate with those who seem different or distant in some respect (e.g., Hansen, 2014; Hawkins, 2014; Hull & Stornaiuolo, 2014; Hull, Stornaiuolo, & Sahni, 2010). This work asks researchers and practitioners to begin with the assumption that young people, even (and perhaps especially) those that are traditionally marginalized, already possess the seeds of "cosmopolitan genius" (Campano & Ghiso, 2011).

This asset-based orientation does not, however, preclude the possibility that young people may require pedagogical support for their cosmopolitan genius to flourish. Indeed, as described below, the desire to pedagogically cultivate cosmopolitanism is continually present in this research, if not always explicitly so. While we agree with Hull and Stornaiuolo (2014) that "We are still a distance away from knowing how to foster a cosmopolitan citizenry" (p. 40), looking across this literature, we see a field-wide emergent theory about the contexts and conditions in which cosmopolitanism emerges and is manifest. In our synthesis of this literature, we suggest that much of the field's discussion of the emergence of cosmopolitanism resonates with three broad practices, which we label as "unsettling encounters," "critical reflections," and "hospitable dialogues." These practices will be discussed more fully below, but as an initial articulation of this nascent theory, we might say that cosmopolitan interactions and dispositions emerge and develop in and through these "cosmopolitanizing practices," especially as they are brought together in concert.

Cultivating Cosmopolitanism

What follows is a synthetic review of the educational research literature that draws on cosmopolitanism, with sections corresponding to each cosmopolitanizing practice. While we will discuss these practices in separate sections, they should not be considered as entirely distinct or related in stepwise fashion; rather, as will become evident, they are overlapping, interrelated, recursive, and rhizomatic. In offering this synthesis, we will refer to digital literacy, but not exclusively. The principal focus here is on outlining an ethically-inflected framework and illustrating its constituent parts in hopes that this will catalyze and channel efforts to further understand and cultivate the kinds of (digital) literacy practices that are increasingly urgent in this moment of simultaneous connection and division. Following our review, we will use this framework to explore more directly possible directions for reimagining digital literacy studies and pedagogies.

Unsettling Encounters

Authors drawing on cosmopolitanism repeatedly identify that an important aspect of cosmopolitan interactions is a certain unsettledness, often described in terms of openness and willingness to engage with, learn from, and relate differently to the new, distant, and Other. We use this word with negative connotations intentionally because encounters with otherness can indeed be unsettling in this sense, but we also intend it more positively here as a contrast to sedimentation, ossification, and entrenchment. To be unsettled may be disconcerting, but it can also be enlivening. References from across the field which we would characterize as "unsettling encounters" include decentering the self (Ong, 2009; Rizvi, 2009); destabilizing common sense ways of thinking (Campano & Ghiso, 2011); disrupting stereotypical, pre-determined, or otherwise simplistic perspectives (Choo, 2014, 2016); and reframing/denaturing the world (Cheah, 2008). Within digital literacies, for example, Wohlwend and Medina (2017) analyze how problematic cultural imaginaries are often thickened and reproduced in transmedia children's play, but also how they can be disrupted, making normative ideals visible and available for reworking.

By unsettling understandings of self, other, and world, individuals and collectives make room for the reconfiguration of these relationships (Hansen, 2014) and the imagination of how things could be otherwise (Stornaiuolo, 2015; Yaman Ntelioglou, 2017). While there is broad agreement that some unsettledness is a necessary feature of cosmopolitan dispositions and interactions, these authors do not advocate for entirely open and unrooted ways of being. In one of the most influential articulations of cosmopolitanism for literacy studies, Hansen (2010) glosses "cosmopolitan artfulness" as a reflective loyalty to the known and openness to the new, and clarifies, "It is out of the question to try to be open at all times to everything new, or loyal at all times to everything known. The former posture dissolves life, the latter petrifies it" (p. 5). Unsettling encounters facilitate the productive expression of openness and loyalty, preventing petrification while avoiding dissolution.

While many authors discuss unsettling encounters between people separated by vast geographical distance, Vasudevan (2014) considers the way a theater program for court-involved youth provided scaffolded opportunities to "unsettle" and remediate participants' narratives related to common scenarios in the local community. One of the ways program facilitators did this was to engage participants in improvisation activities built around their lived experiences (e.g., an altercation between two young men) and then to introduce "unsettling" conditions that required participants to question, reinterpret, and reimagine the typical trajectory of these experiences. Vasudevan characterizes this improvisation activity as an example of cosmopolitan pedagogy that, within an environment of belonging, put different perspectives in direct dialogue with each other, disrupted default ways of being and thinking, and helped participants productively navigate the space between the new and the known.

Saito (2010) discusses a curriculum that, however different from the one discussed above, likewise demonstrates aspects of unsettling encounters. He suggests identifying student interests and then "unsettling" them by tracing the threads that connect them transnationally (à la actor-network theory). For example, he helped grade 2 students in Japan begin exploring their embeddedness in global networks by looking at where their clothes were manufactured. The students were surprised to find out that the clothes they were wearing did not originate in Japan. Saito explained to them that the objects around them, like their clothes, were a "tug of a net … a starting point of connections to the world outside Japan. You pull that tug, you pull it and pull it, and then, you will catch a glance of what's happening outside Japan" (p. 342). This kind of unsettling encounter opened opportunities for (re)considering Japan's relationship to other countries and, more generally, the nature of the world.

Critical Reflections

As illustrated in the above examples, when individuals and collectives unsettle understandings of self, Other, and the world, they become available for critical engagement. Note that, in this literature, the word "critical" is employed in both the generic sense (which we will refer to with a lower-case "critical") to indicate thoughtful reflection upon, for example, similarities and differences between what seems normal to one and what is apparently normal to others; and in the theoretical sense (which we will refer to with an upper-case "Critical"), pointing toward explicitly liberationist and materialist perspectives derived from the Frankfurt School. In the first sense, for example, David Hansen has written eloquently about how a critical reflective distance allows for reconsideration and renegotiation of the new and the known (e.g., Hansen, 2010, 2014). In digital literacy research, a critical stance that stays close to a focal text and to reading process analysis, is well-represented by work on online reading comprehension (Leu et al., 2004; Coiro & Dobler, 2007), examining tasks that include children locating information online, critically evaluating that information, and synthesizing it. In the second sense of the Critical within digital literacy research, scholars are just beginning to consider, for instance, how software operates primarily out of sight, and that new "sub-screnic" literacies are needed to interpret the work of software and the associated interests of software companies that shape literacy practices (Lynch, 2015). Related Critical work on the role of algorithms and big data as relevant to digital literacy practice is also just emerging (Carrington, 2018).

Critical perspectives on digital literacies informed by cosmopolitan theory are just emerging, although a number of literacy researchers traverse cosmopolitan thinking and notions of Freirean praxis to theorize a Critical cosmopolitanism (Campano & Ghiso, 2011; Choo, 2014; Darvin & Norton, 2017; Hull & Stornaiuolo, 2010; Hull et al., 2010; Lemrow, 2016; Rizvi, 2009; Stornaiuolo, Hull, & Hall, 2017). This Critical perspective is at least in part a corrective response to Enlightenment era and contemporary neoliberal cosmopolitanism, training an analytical eye not on differences per se, but on the histories and material conditions that circumscribe those differences—including the ways one may be implicated in global inequities and other problematic power dynamics. Drawing on feminist and poststructuralist thinking to theorize Critical cosmopolitanism, a notable example of Critical reflections that implicates digital literacies is Whitty's (2017) grappling with dominant and subjugated histories of the University of New Brunswick. Whitty narrates her confrontation with the colonial narrative her university presents on its website, which she recognized as whitewashed, and her subsequent exploration of decolonizing/indigenizing histories and pedagogies. Her underlying approach to cosmopolitanism suggests that it may be necessary to locate what from the past has been "lost, hidden, removed, and written out"

(p. 18) before one can truly change future understandings and relationships. This Critical (un) learning takes place for Whitty as she encounters and enters into dialogue with alternative perspectives that unsettle and problematize dominant ways of thinking and being.

Aspects of C/critical reflections (along with unsettling encounters and hospitable dialogue) are likewise evident in Yaman Ntelioglou's (2017) description of a drama unit in an ELL class. The teacher of the class had students in small groups collectively write and perform mini-plays about Canadian holidays and other holidays students celebrated (e.g., religious holidays not officially recognized by Canada). In one of these mini-plays, students portrayed a family's preparation for the Eid, a Muslim holiday, and represented female characters doing housework while the male characters relaxed. In this performance, a female character confronts her brother about the household division of labor and requests that he helps. The content of this play derived from the social realities of students' lives, and the imaginative scripting and performing allowed them to reciprocally share, explore, and critique aspects of their own cultures. These dramatic productions became opportunities not only to put aspects of students' diverse cultures in conversation with each other, but also to critically consider how they might be otherwise.

Hospitable Dialogues

In characterizing cosmopolitan interactions, authors rely on the sometimes metaphorical, sometimes literal image of an ongoing dialogue in which all participants can express themselves and respond hospitably to each other, and they are optimistic about such dialogues, especially when they are combined with C/critical reflections (Darvin & Norton, 2017; Hansen, Burdick-shepherd, Cammarano, & Obelleiro, 2009; Hull & Stornaiuolo, 2010) and scaffolded to help interlocutors repair inevitable communicative missteps (Hull & Stornaiuolo, 2014; Hull et al., 2010). The first example we offer regards a dialogue as conventionally imagined—a face-to-face discussion—while the second considers hospitality in the context of the private social network Space2Cre8, which has been a digital proving ground for many of the ethical principles and practices we consider in this chapter.

Crampton, Lewis, and Tierney's (2017) analysis of a classroom discussion highlights characteristics of hospitable dialogue. The discussion concerned a photograph of a white couple posing with a Black lawn jockey. The couple, who had adopted a Black son, purportedly bought the problematic item in hopes of demonstrating solidarity with their son and Black culture. As the class explored a variety of justifications and criticisms regarding the parents' behavior, including charges of racism, the authors report that students achieved a "proper distance" in relation to the subjects of the picture: "the students were not so close that they couldn't see and critique the others in the photo for their display of an offensive statue, but they were close enough to extend hospitality to them, conceding their humanity" (p. 185). In this account, students' willingness to share honest opinions and their hospitality toward each other allowed them to collectively demonstrate a critically-informed hospitality toward the subjects of the photograph.

While dialogue remains the image par excellence of cosmopolitan exchange, it implies a certain oppositional relationship between interlocutors—not necessarily a contentious one, but one in which participants diametrically face each other. Although this kind of exchange may often be beneficial, it is also limited insofar as it maintains a relationship of distance and opposition. Reimagining the "shape" of this exchange, some authors encourage a move away from dialogue per se toward dialogic collaboration (Rizvi, 2009; Saito, 2010; Yaman Ntelioglou, 2017), a move that reconfigures the interlocutors' relationship, and figuratively places them on common ground in joint service of a shared cause. We note here that this reimagining of dialogue is especially fitting for digital contexts, where conventions (e.g., turn-taking), scale, and mode of communication transcend the two-way verbal exchange of face-to-face dialogue.

Stornaiuolo (2016) illustrates many of these ideas in her description of the hospitable dialogues among the international group of teachers involved in Space2Cre8 and the learning opportunities (for both teachers and students) that emerged from these conversations. She describes how these teachers discussed the complications of allowing students to write about sensitive topics (e.g., sexuality) and their desire to "deepen" engagement between students. In these discussions, teachers had to be willing to make explicit their differences of opinion, collaboratively develop shared goals, and sustain these challenging conversations over time. As they did this, they ultimately decided to allow students to write about sensitive topics, but also to provide some training about cultural differences among participants in Space2Cre8, including different understandings of what topics are appropriate to share publicly. They also decided to engage students in collaborative video exchanges in addition to single-author text messages as a means of "deepening" their interactions. The resulting video exchanges involved collaborative work at various scales as Space2Cre8 participants began to remix and respond to each other's videos. While Stornaiuolo is careful not to suggest that teacher collaboration or video exchanges alone will always yield hospitable dialogues, she asserts that they can be (and were, in the cases she highlights) conducive to cosmopolitan interactions.

Reflections on Digital Literacy Studies and Education

Taken together and sustained over time and space, unsettling encounters, C/critical reflections, and hospitable dialogues engender (and are largely constitutive of) cosmopolitan interactions and dispositions. This broad tripartite framework represents our field's current theory about the nature and emergence of cosmopolitanism and, as such, provides a useful onramp for elaborating the implications of cosmopolitan theory for digital literacy education. We attempt, in what follows, to consider some of the implications for digital literacies through the ethical lens that cosmopolitanism provides. As we do so, we attend to dimensions of digital literacies that are emergent and that we feel will play an increasingly significant role, and that, hence, should be the focus of further research and practice. For each part of the cosmopolitan framework, and in light of our own perceptions of how digital technologies and practices are changing, we have offered a new direction or re-orientation for the field, along with some discussion of related practices and tools.

Unsettling Encounters by Reading Networks

The page has long held a central place in our imagination within literacy studies and pedagogical practice. Even digital literacy technologies have often been informed by the idea of a (web)page as being designed and organized as a certain amount of content to read in one instance. For literacy, the page is perhaps the most comfortable place to settle in our imagination of what a "text" is. On the one hand, literacy scholars for some time have been attempting to disrupt text- or page-centered approaches to literacy, in particular through work on intertextuality and multivocality (see Baron, this volume). Yet, digital literacy texts and practices offer still further opportunity to unsettle the page and the common sense ways of reading and thinking it implies.

In digital media, every text is always already a "site" that is brought into relation with other sites. Internet firewalls cut some things out and bracket some things in, money and advertising boost sites in search rankings, and algorithms do their work behind the scenes. While the authors we have reviewed, in line with much of the broader field, recommend practices such as pairing thematically-related canonical and marginalized texts as a promising means of cultivating cosmopolitanism (e.g., Choo, 2016), online digital texts demand that we attend not only to the way different authors/texts treat a common theme, but also to the ways in which money, power, discourses, and material goods move across networks (see Mackey, this volume). This suggests a movement from reading "pages" to reading networks.

A networked image of the practice of reading might attend to the position of the text in relation to other connected texts, reading these connections in terms of how, together, they create cultural, historical, ideological, racial, or other differences. Yet, differences are read (or written) not merely as "positions" coming into contact; rather, networked lines may be imagined as creating movements or lines of flight that are neither one text nor the other. Reading networks, in this sense, means finding ways to read the (actual and imagined) lines between texts—to see reading as not merely a resting place for the collection of meanings in situ, but as travel between them. In this sense, network readers are "wayfarers," understanding that (digital) lives are led "not inside places but through, around, to and from them, from and to places elsewhere" (Ingold, 2000, p. 229). Practically speaking, this "unsettled" networked view of reading, as a cosmopolitan practice and image, calls out literacy educators and researchers for bounding online spaces too tightly and too quickly. Students cannot understand networks, their positions in them, and the ways that these networks connect them to others, by becoming skilled at the work of individual page-reading and writing.

As the individual page needs to be unsettled and networked, so must the individual actor. The shift we are proposing to the assemblage, at the nexus of digital literacy research and cosmopolitanism, involves assuming that the social "group," digitally connected at various scales, should be a principal "unit of analysis" for research and pedagogy. Due to the structuring of school around individual work and assessment, and for other reasons, the notion of inherently collective digital activity, or the learning digital assemblage, is a poor fit in the traditional school context. Still, moves in this direction are not impossible nor merely theoretical. As we write, digital tools are being developed that can be used to conceive of how individuals and groups come together in large, discursive Conversations (Gee, 2014). One example is a new add-on to widely-shared news articles published online by BuzzFeed, a news and entertainment company. BuzzFeed developed this add-on feature, called Outside Your Bubble (www.buzzfeed.com/outsideyourbubble), in February 2017, in response to trends of civic and political polarization. The tool appears as a module at the bottom of select news articles, where it collects and categorizes the multiple ways people are responding to the article across social media sites. For instance, a story recent to the writing of this chapter ("Trump Says Transgender People Cannot 'Serve In Any Capacity' In The Military," July 26, 2017) is followed by links to eight divergent responses. The first four of these are captioned as follows:

1. Many people disagree with Trump's decision and feel it poorly represents American values.
2. Several have pointed out that there are already transgender people in the military and say they feel Trump is disrespecting their service.
3. Many feel Trump is affronting the entire LGBT community, and one person pointed to an example of the community's impact in the military.
4. One person says he is in the Army and that he feels it's not a "good environment" for trans people.

As we consider cosmopolitan digital literacies, what is most interesting about this and similar tools is that a multiplicity of perspectives is curated and offered, avoiding rants or binary arguments. Moreover, these perspectives are not artificially shaped argument types for learning, but are connected to real people and lived experiences—they serve to exemplify how people, texts, and material practices are organized and assembled. Other media network analysis tools could also be used pedagogically, to make evident the routine structures or "conversational archetypes" of social media topic networks (e.g., "polarized crowd," "tight crowd," "community cluster," and "broadcast network," Smith et al., 2014). While there are problems with these early tools, they also offer digital literacy educators a developing means through which to show their students that conversations and positions online are worked out in complex, rhizomatic movements with others, rather than clear argumentative outlines contained on the page.

Finally, the critical reading of social-digital networks themselves is one way in which typified encounters, sedimented online or offline, can be unsettled and re-interpreted for who they include and exclude, and what their social and cultural practices are. In one project, Leander, together with colleagues, engaged migrant and non-migrant youth in analyzing their social networks, online and offline (de Haan, Leander, & Ünlüsoy, 2014). Such work made evident many of the differences in social networks between youth with different cultural practices and backgrounds. For instance, Turkish-Dutch youth were more inclined to practice family-oriented networks than were either Dutch or Moroccan-Dutch youth, and both groups of migrant youth had fewer networked connections nationally than did the non-migrant youth. Such differences, of course, are not static, and they are also not wholly invisible to youth. Yet, there are surprises that come to light when we make social-digital networks explicit, and thereby make them available to unsettling. Every day, most literacy students are not merely reading and writing "within" networks—they are in fact reading and writing the networks themselves. These are critically significant movements of their lives that can be marshaled as readable/writable networks in cosmopolitan digital literacies.

Critical Reflections: From Multiple Resources to Multi-Agency

As mentioned previously, authors drawing on cosmopolitanism often pair this theory with more explicitly Critical theories. Along with these Critical perspectives, other C/critical reflections in the field have made more explicit and developed pedagogies around the diverse multiple resources through which language and literacy are produced. In the literature cited above, authors contribute to these reflections, emphasizing different kinds of productive multiplicity (e.g., multimodality, multivocality, multilingualism) in cosmopolitan interactions. These forms of multiplicity afford what Hull et al. (2013) call "generative polysemy and indeterminacy" (p. 1234). Texts with these kinds of multiplicity are "generative" because they allow various points of entry, possible interpretations, and potential responses, and therefore are conducive to hospitable dialogues, C/critical reflections, and unsettling encounters.

In order to deeply engage with C/critical reflection in digital literacies, in addition to these more familiar types of productive multiplicity, presently there is a pressing need for more direct C/critical engagement with computer-based agents that act along with humans and guide much of human action. Such a shift requires attending not simply to the individual *qua* producer/consumer of texts, but to assemblages that bring together humans and non-humans alike (See Knox, 2016; Spector, 2015). A significant non-human participant in digital interactions, worthy of critical and ethical consideration, is the algorithm. Algorithms are ubiquitous in digital interactions, although they are often overlooked. To return to "Outside Your Bubble," for instance, the divergent comments on a given BuzzFeed article are gathered through the working of algorithms on BuzzFeed's official accounts on platforms such as Reddit, Twitter, and Facebook, and later summarized at the bottom of the original, selected article. Once clicked on, these topical links show the text of the actual comment and links to it. Considering "Outside Your Bubble" in this way highlights how different media platforms are involved in "reading" this kind of news, all of which are powered by algorithms that assesses popularity (likes, up votes, etc.) and determine visibility.

When discussing their work behind the scenes, early research suggests that students often have problematic understandings of algorithims (Jones, 2019). More explicitly, Jones catalogues how undergraduates in the UK and Hong Kong attribute different roles to algorithms: as agent, authority, adversary, audience, and even as oracle (2019, p. 11). Our own work on social media, and especially Facebook (e.g., Burriss & Leander, 2017), suggests youth with several years of practice on Facebook have a variety of divergent understandings of how, when, and why its algorithms function.

Researchers in education and media studies have taken different approaches to the study of algorithms and the questions they pose for learning and interaction, including Critical approaches to their presence and functioning (Finn, 2017; Noble, 2018), affect theoretical approaches (Bucher, 2017), and pragmatic approaches concerning how algorithms are used and engaged by humans (Jones, 2019). Across these approaches, however, is general agreement on the massive expansion of algorithms and other types of computational agents within everyday interaction. The anthropocentric history of digital literacy studies allows too little consideration of non-human actants. Outside of education, post-human theorist and artist Trevor Paglen (2018) calls to our attention that "the overwhelming majority of images are now made by machines for other machines, with humans rarely in the loop" (p. 89). How such computer interpretation is unlike human seeing, and how human/nonhuman interpretation function in relation to one another, is of significant importance to the practice of literacy education, as well as to the ongoing evolution of literacies. In Paglen's terms, "If we want to understand the invisible world of machine-machine visual culture, we need to unlearn how to see like humans" (Paglen, 2018, p. 17).

One of many possible practical arenas for a C/critical cosmopolitan practice in digital literacy education is the area of advertising. In addition to moving from a text-to-network perspective, argued above, and also from a linguistic to a multimodal perspective, which has become commonplace in advertising and propaganda analysis, a C/critical analysis of practice and ethics involved in everyday advertising and marketing might take up the following topics:

- How is offline data on users collected (e.g., through credit card purchases)?
- What kinds of online data are collected through cookies when using websites?
- How has timing, perhaps more than content, become important in online advertising, so as to reach users when they are further down what marketers call the "purchasing funnel"?
- What kind of identity "bucket" is being made about a user through targeted ads and an ongoing online marketing profile developed through cookies?

Studying new forms of digital marketing is an important form of digital literacy pedagogy not merely because such marketing is ubiquitous, but because these new practices unsettle our presumptions of either the mass consumer or individual reading the ad. Instead, in current practices there are massively individualized consumers, for whom data is being mined, analyzed, and put to use in real time, in ongoing cycles involving humans, non-humans, digital action, literacy, material action, and ethical consequences.

Hospitable Dialogues: Listening across Online and Offline Practices

As a third dimension for the ethical transformation of pedagogy at the nexus of cosmopolitan theory and digital literacies, we draw attention to the value of listening as an integral part of hospitable dialogue. Though attentive listening is mentioned repeatedly in the literature that draws on cosmopolitanism (e.g., Stornaiuolo, 2016; Vasudevan, 2014; Yaman Ntelioglou, 2017), the predominant focus thus far has been on the *productive side* of dialogue. This is reflective of the broader field, with its abundance of literacy research and practice in terms of text/utterance production and relatively little research or pedagogical work on listening. As we explore the nature of listening in cosmopolitan exchanges, we counter-pose the idea of close reading—and the closures of meaning that it may support—with the notion of "open listening." By this, we intend listening that is ethically and dialogically committed to the possibility of being changed by an interaction. Open listening conceives of both self and Other as unfixed, and yet related in their becoming through interaction. Ethically speaking, open listening runs much deeper than listening comprehension, as it does not fix a particular notion of content in advance of a listening occasion. Rather, open listening is envisioned as emergent and relational. It is worth noting that structures of dialogue can get in the way of open listening, including those designed to break I-R-E patterns for teacher-student exchange. For instance, student-student-student exchanges, bypassing teacher participation, can easily become topical commentary given to a common theme—with students waiting their respective turn—rather than practices of open, dialogic listening.

What might the shape of (online) interactions be that support open listening, and how might such interactions be scaffolded? One route into this difficult problem is through studying social practices, on- or offline, that appear to be especially given to knowing through intentional, open listening. While we retain the value of argumentation, persuasion, and debate for academic and scientific purposes, shifting our genres of literacy practice to those more supportive of open listening may be generative. For example, Enciso (2017) examines how significant the imagination is, to "borrow from and invent linguistic, artistic, and narrative forms," in story-telling among immigrant and non-immigrant youth (p. 34). Enciso's use of co-narration (Ochs & Capps, 2001) among culturally marginalized youth disrupts the notion of a separate listening moment from that of speaking; rather, listening, problem-solving, questioning, evaluating, and enacting are intertwined in the ensemble of relating. Also deeply connected to the imagination, in recent research, we have begun to study improvisational theater as a site for ethical engagement (Tanner, Leander & Carter-Stone, in press). Skilled improvisational artists must listen intently to know what to do next—their next move must build on the last, given by another in their group. Thus, in the flow of real time, skilled improvisational artists must both form responses and continually be open to omitting their responses as the situation ceaselessly evolves. Other literacy research in drama has a more developed history for showing the ways in which pedagogical mimetic practices involve engagement with real and imagined others that can deepen ethical sensibilities, including open listening (e.g., Edmiston, 2013). A grounded ethics of (new) everyday relationality could be supported by further research in such contexts, as well as by school-situated experimentation with open forms of dialogue, located at the nexus of online and offline interaction.

We have deliberately begun the discussion of pedagogical possibilities in this section in offline practices, because while we wish to maintain a focus on digital literacies, we believe in the case of dialogue in particular that the "online" problem of polarization must be addressed pedagogically within both online and offline spaces. As an experiment in this direction (Sabey and Leander, in preparation), in a recent course for university freshmen, we actively recruited students from across the political spectrum and engaged them in discussions of polarized topics (e.g., gun control). In cycles of participation and analysis, students were given the task of analyzing pieces of their own political dialogues and online interactions, in light of a developing set of reflective conversations and readings concerning cosmopolitan ethics. One realization from this work was simply that open listening is a challenging practice in both online and offline contexts. As students, teachers, social-media users, etc., we are not accustomed to being present with others and responding to their dialogic contributions openly; we tend to be much more comfortable in more predictable and controlled interactions. If, as we believe, open listening is an important aspect of cosmopolitan literacy practices, there is much to learn about how it can be developed and supported, perhaps especially online.

Yet another approach for the cultivation of hospitable dialogues online is to inquire about the development of new digital tools that might support open listening. The potential danger of filter-bubbles and echo-chambers in social media has received notable media and scholarly attention of late, with pundits and academics considering the role the Internet and social media may play in socio-political polarization (e.g., Boxell, Gentzkow, & Shapiro, 2017; Lee, Choi, Kim, & Kim, 2014). In response to this concern, a number of app developers have begun to create tools that attempt to disrupt filter-bubbles and allow users to "hear" other conversations. For instance, FlipFeed, developed by researchers in the MIT Media Lab, is a Google Chrome Extension that allows users to replace their own Twitter feed with that of another actual Twitter user. Feeds are selected based on users' inferred political ideology so that "a right-leaning user ... may load and navigate a left-leaning user's feed, observing the news stories, commentary, and other content they consume" (http://flipfeed.media.mit.edu). As a pedagogical opportunity, the idea of the feed seems both to shift attention from text to network—to provide a critical and ethical understanding of how individual texts participate in relations to myriad other texts (postings, advertisements, corporate media channels, etc.) in real time—and, perhaps, to encourage open listening. We are not, of course, suggesting that FlipFeed (or any other tool) stands on its own as a pedagogy. However, given an immersive pedagogy in forms of practice leading toward open listening and dialogue, tools like these may have untapped potential.

Concluding Thoughts

Digital literacy practices are profoundly implicated in the tense moment in which we find ourselves increasingly connected and divided. Recognizing this, we have explored how researchers and educators might contribute to the cultivation of more cosmopolitan ways of being with and relating to the Other. To this end, we reviewed the scholarly literature in literacy and language studies that draws on cosmopolitanism to outline a field-wide emergent theory regarding practices that cultivate and constitute these ways of being and relating. We have then employed this theory to frame our forward-looking commentary on the field of digital literacies, suggesting ways the research and education communities might refocus their attention to more fully understand the ever-evolving worlds of digital literacy and to contribute to the development of ethical relations within and across these worlds.

A number of pedagogical implications follow from this discussion: First, if we expect a given curriculum to cultivate cosmopolitan ways of being and relating, that curriculum will likely need to both typify and afford these cosmopolitanizing practices. While we find these practices compelling and believe they are full of pedagogical potential, we also recognize that they entail some risk. Some unsettling encounters may, for example, be traumatic for certain learners—an especially important consideration with regard to already vulnerable populations. With this in mind, we invite educators and researchers to explore and document forms of instructional scaffolding that appropriately support particular students' and teachers' participation in cosmopolitanizing practices.

As we have sought to apply this framework to ongoing and potential studies of digital literacy practices, we have had cause to re-examine the notion of dialogue which underlies much of the work on cosmopolitanism and on literacy more generally. The quintessential image of dialogue, as mentioned above, involves a verbal exchange between diametrically opposed individuals. In broad strokes, what we have suggested here offers a radical revision of this image, one that involves assemblages of human and non-human actors interacting in and across networks, modes and media. What it means to read, write, listen, dialogue, etc. in this context—let alone to do so ethically—are by no means settled. We hope that shifting our focus from the page to the network, from the (human) individual to the (human and non-human) assemblage, and from close(d) reading to open listening will prove not only to be useful redirections for further research, but will ultimately promote more cosmopolitan ways of being.

While we remain hopeful that such ethical relations are possible, and that ongoing teaching and research along the lines we have proposed may facilitate their realization, we are also deeply, painfully aware of how far we have to go. Although we believe there are gaps in the field's theoretical and empirical understanding, and gaping holes in our collective public discourse and modes of relating across difference, this awareness most poignantly relates to our own personal failings to live the cosmopolitan ethic we have articulated here. And so we temper our hope with humility, acknowledging that we settle too often into unreflective and inhospitable patterns of thought and behavior, rather than truly engaging with the reality of others. But we must do better—to understand more fully, to listen more openly, and to respond more lovingly to fellow citizens of the world.

References

Anderson, B. (1983). *Imagined communities: reflections on the origin and spread of nationalism*. London: Verso.

Appadurai, A. (1996). *Modernity at large: Cultural dimensions of globalization*. Minneapolis: University of Minnesota Press.

Appadurai, A. (2006). *Fear of small numbers: An essay on the geography of anger*. Durham: Duke University Press.

Bartlett, L., & Holland, D. (2002). Theorizing the space of literacy practices. *Ways of Knowing, 2*(1), 10–22.

Barton, D., & Hamilton, M. (2000). Literacy practices. In D. Barton, M. Hamilton, & R. Ivanič (Eds.), *Situated literacies: Reading and writing in context* (pp. 7–15). London: Routledge.

Boxell, L., Gentzkow, M., & Shapiro, J. (2017). *Is the internet causing political polarization? Evidence from demographics* (Political Economy No. 23258). doi:10.3386/w23258

Brandt, D., & Clinton, K. (2002). Limits of the local: Expanding perspectives on literacy as a social practice. *Journal of Literacy Research, 34*(3), 337–356.

Bucher, T. (2017). The algorithmic imaginary: Exploring the ordinary affects of Facebook algorithms. *Information, Communication & Society, 20*(1), 30–44.

Burriss, S. K., & Leander, K. M. (2017, March). "On This Day": Personal memory and social media. Paper presented at the National Council of Teachers of English Assembly for Research (NCTEAR) Annual Conference, Towson, MD.

Campano, G., & Ghiso, M. P. (2011). Immigrant students as cosmopolitan intellectuals. In S. A. Wolf, K. Coats, P. Enciso, & C. A. Jenkins (Eds.), *Handbook of research on children's and young adult literature* (pp. 164–176). New York: Routledge.

Canagarajah, S. (2012). *Translingual practice: Global Englishes and cosmopolitan relations*. New York: Routledge.

Carrington, V. (2018). The changing landscape of literacies: Big data and algorithms. *Digital Culture and Education, 10*(1), 67–76.

Cheah, P. (2008). What is a world? On world literature as world-making activity. *Daedalus, 137*(3), 26–38.

Choo, S. S. (2014). Cultivating a hospitable imagination: Re-envisioning the world literature curriculum through a cosmopolitan lens. *Curriculum Inquiry, 44*(1), 68–89. doi:10.1111/curi.12037

Choo, S. S. (2016). Fostering the hospitable imagination through cosmopolitan pedagogies: Reenvisioning literature education in Singapore. *Research in the Teaching of English, 50*(4), 400–421.

Coiro, J., & Dobler, E. (2007). Exploring the online reading comprehension strategies used by sixth-grade skilled readers to search for and locate information on the Internet. *Reading Research Quarterly, 42*(2), 214–257.

Collins, J., & Blot, R. (2003). *Literacy and literacies: Texts, power, and identity* (Vol. 22). Cambridge: Cambridge University Press.

Crampton, A., Lewis, C., & Tierney, J. D. (2017). Proper distance and the hope of cosmopolitanism in a classroom discussion about race. In R. Zaidi & J. Rowsell (Eds.), *Literacy lives in transcultural times* (pp. 175–190). New York: Routledge.

Darvin, R., & Norton, B. (2017). Investing in new literacies for a cosmopolitan future. In R. Zaidi & J. Rowsell (Eds.), *Literacy lives in transcultural times* (pp. 89–101). New York: Routledge.

De Costa, P. I. (2014). Reconceptualizing cosmopolitanism in language and literacy education: Insights from a Singapore school. *Research in the Teaching of English, 49*(1), 9–30.

de Haan, M., Leander, K., Ünlüsoy, A., & Prinsen, F. (2014). Challenging ideals of connected learning: The networked configurations for learning of migrant youth in the Netherlands. *Learning, Media and Technology, 39*(4), 507–535.

Derrida, J. (2001). *On cosmopolitanism and forgiveness*. London: Routledge.

Edmiston, B. (2013). *Transforming teaching and learning with active and dramatic approaches: Engaging students across the curriculum*. New York: Routledge.

Enciso, P. E. (2017). Stories lost and found: Mobilizing imagination in literacy research and practice. *Literacy Research: Theory, Method, and Practice, 66*(1), 29–52.
Finn, E. (2018). *What algorithms want: Information in the age of computing*. Cambridge, MA: The MIT Press.
Freire, P., & Macedo, D. P. (1987). *Literacy: Reading the word and the world*. South Hadley, MA: Bergin & Garvey Publishers.
Gee, J. P. (1989). Literacy, discourse, and linguistics: Introduction. *Journal of Education, 171*(1), 5–17.
Gee, J. P. (1990). *Social linguistics and literacies*. London: Falmer Press.
Gee, J. P. (2014). *An introduction to discourse analysis: Theory and method* (4th ed.). London: Routledge.
Hansen, D. T. (2010). Cosmopolitanism and education : A view from the ground. *Teachers College Record, 112*(1), 1–30.
Hansen, D. T. (2014). Cosmopolitanism as cultural creativity: New modes of educational practice in globalizing times. *Curriculum Inquiry, 44*(1), 1–14. doi:10.1111/curi.12039
Hansen, D. T., Burdick-shepherd, S., Cammarano, C., & Obelleiro, G. A. (2009). Education, values, and valuing in cosmopolitan perspective. *Curriculum Inquiry, 39*(5), 587–612. doi:10.1111/j.1467-873X.2009.00461.x
Hawkins, M. R. (2014). Ontologies of place, creative meaning making and critical cosmopolitan education. *Curriculum Inquiry, 44*(1), 90–112. doi:10.1111/curi.12036
Holland, D., Lachicotte, W., Jr, Skinner, D., & Cain, C. (1998). *Identity and agency in cultural worlds*. Cambridge, MA: Harvard University Press.
Hull, G. A., & Stornaiuolo, A. (2010). Literate arts in a global world: Reframing social networking as cosmopolitan practice. *Journal of Adolescent & Adult Literacy, 54*(2), 85–97. doi:10.1598/JAAL.54.2.1
Hull, G. A., & Stornaiuolo, A. (2014). Cosmopolitan literacies, social networks, and "proper distance": Striving to understand in a global world. *Curriculum Inquiry, 44*(1), 15–44. doi:10.1111/curi.12035
Hull, G. A., Stornaiuolo, A., & Sahni, U. (2010). Cultural citizenship and cosmopolitan practice: Global youth communicate online. *English Education, 42*(4), 331–367. doi:10.2307/23018017
Hull, G. A., Stornaiuolo, A., & Sterponi, L. (2013). Imagined readers and hospitable texts; Global youths connect online. In D. E. Alvermann, N. J. Unrau, & R. B. Ruddell (Eds.), *Theoretical models and processes of reading* (pp. 1208–1240). Newwark, DE: International Reading Association.
Ingold, T. (2000). *The perception of the environment: Essays on livelihood, dwelling and skill*. London: Routledge.
Jones, R. (2019). The text is reading you: Teaching language in the age of the algorithm. *Linguistics and Education*, (xxxx), 100750. doi:10.1016/j.linged.2019.100750
Juzwik, M. M., & McKenzie, C. (2015). Writing, religious faith, and rooted cosmopolitan dialogue: Portraitsof two American evangelical men in a public school english classroom. *Written Communication, 32*(2), 121–149.
Kant, I. (1903). *Perpetual peace: A philosophical essay* (M. Cambell Smith Trans.). London: George Allen & Unwin LTD.
Knox, J. (2016). *Posthumanism and the massive open online course: Contaminating the subject of global education*. New York: Routledge.
Larson, J. (Ed.). (2001). *Literacy as snake oil: Beyond the quick fix*. New York: Peter Lang Publishing Inc.
Lee, J. K., Choi, J., Kim, C., & Kim, Y. (2014). Social media, network heterogeneity, and opinion polarization. *Journal of Communication, 64*(4), 702–722. doi:10.1111/jcom.12077
Lemrow, E. M. (2016). Créolization and the new cosmopolitanism: Examining twenty-first-century student identities and literacy practices for transcultural understanding. *Journal of Multilingual and Multicultural Development, 4632*(June), 1–15. doi:10.1080/01434632.2016.1186680
Leu, D. J., Jr. Kinzer, C. K., Coiro, J. L., & Cammack, D. W. (2004). Toward a theory of new literacies emerging from the internet and other information and communication technologies. In R. B. Ruddell & N. J. Unrau (Eds.), *Theoretical models and processes of reading* (5th ed., pp. 1570–1613). International Reading Association.
Lynch, T. L. (2015). *The hidden role of software in educational research: Policy to practice*. New York: Routledge.
Noble, S. U. (2018). *Algorithms of oppression: How search engines reinforce racism*. New York, NY: New York University Press.
Ochs, E., & Capps, L. (2001). *Living narrative: Creating lives in everyday storytelling*. Cambridge, MA: Harvard University Press.
Ong, J. C. (2009). The cosmopolitan continuum: Locating cosmopolitanism in media and cultural studies. *Media, Culture, & Society, 31*(3), 449–466. doi:10.1177/0163443709102716
Paglen, T. (2018). *Machine visions*. Naucalpan, Mexico: Servicios Tepemex.
Rizvi, F. (2009). Towards cosmopolitan learning. *Discourse: Studies in the cultural politics of education, 30*(3), 253–268. doi:10.1080/01596300903036863

Saito, H. (2010). Actor-network theory of cosmopolitan education. *Journal of Curriculum Studies, 42*(3), 333–351. doi:10.1080/00220270903494261

Smith, M. A., Rainie, L., Himelboim, I., & Shneiderman, B. (2014). Mapping Twitter topic networks: From polarized crowds to community clusters. In *PEW Internet Research Project*. Retrieved from http://www.pewinternet.org/2014/02/20/mapping-twitter-topic-networks-from-polarized-crowds-to-community-clusters

Spector, H. (2015). The who and the what of educational cosmopolitanism. *Studies in Philosophy and Education* (September 2014), 423–440.

Stornaiuolo, A. (2015). Literacy as worldmaking: Multimodality, creativity and cosmopolitanism. In K. Pahl & J. Roswell (Eds.), *The Routledge handbook of literacy studies* (pp. 561–571). New York: Routledge.

Stornaiuolo, A. (2016). Teaching in global collaborations: Navigating challenging conversations through cosmopolitan activity. *Teaching and Teacher Education, 59*, 503–513. doi:10.1016/j.tate.2016.07.001

Stornaiuolo, A., Hull, G., & Hall, M. (2017). Cosmopolitan practices, networks, and flows of literacies. In K. Mills, A. Stornaiuolo, A. Smith, & J. Pandya-Zacher (Eds.), *Handbook of writing, literacies and education in digital culture* (pp. 1–16). New York: Routledge.

Stornaiuolo, A., & Nichols, T. P. (2018). Cosmopolitanism and education. In G. Noblit (Ed.), *Oxford research encyclopedia of education* (pp. 1–32). New York: Oxford University Press.

Street, B. V. (1984). *Literacy in theory and practice*. Cambridge: Cambridge University Press.

Tanner, S., Leander, K. M., & Carter-Stone, L. (in press). Ways with worlds: Bringing improvisational theater into play with reading. *Reading Research Quarterly*.

Vasudevan, L. M. (2014). Multimodal cosmopolitanism: Cultivating belonging in everyday moments with youth. *Curriculum Inquiry, 44*(1), 45–67. doi:10.1111/curi.12040

Whitty, P. (2017). Complicating literacies: Settler ways of being with story(ies) on Wabanaki lands. In R. Zaidi & J. Rowsell (Eds.), *Literacy lives in transcultural times* (pp. 17–31). New York: Routledge.

Wohlwend, K. E., & Medina, C. L. (2017). Monster high: Converging imaginaries of girlhood in tweens' digital doll play. In R. Zaidi & J. Rowsell (Eds.), *Literacy lives in transcultural times* (pp. 75–88). New York: Routledge.

Yaman Ntelioglou, B. (2017). Examining the relational space of the self and other in the language-drama classroom: Transcultural multiliteracies, situated practice and the cosmopolitan imagination. In R. Zaidi & J. Rowsell (Eds.), *Literacy lives in transcultural times* (pp. 58–72). New York: Routledge.

Part VI
How Do Research Methods Change the Game for Reading Researchers and Policy Makers

24
The Use of Video Data in Reading Research

Brian Rowan, Bridget Maher, and Mark White

This paper discusses the use of video data in research on reading, as well as future directions for research in the area. In the paper, we view video as a medium for collecting, transmitting, and storing research data, just like photography, audio recording, live observation with field notes, artifact collection, in-person interviewing, questionnaires, and administrative records, are media through which data are collected, transmitted, and stored. The purpose of this paper is to point the reader to some existing resources on the collection of video data and to discuss some trends in the use of video data in research on teaching and learning in the area of reading. Our central argument is that video recording technologies are evolving rapidly, providing particular affordances—and challenges—for the use of video data in qualitative and quantitative research on reading. We argue that some of these affordances might also help address the "gaps" in reading research identified in this handbook, gaps that now exist with respect to what has been studied in reading research, gaps in the translation of research findings from the reading research to reading practice communities, and gaps in how results from reading research are implemented in schools and classrooms. As we discuss below, new affordances in video data collection, management, and data analysis have the potential to address these gaps by allowing for research on new topics in the field, by allowing for different ways to communicate research results to different communities of practice, and by providing different ways to guide practitioners as they implement findings from reading research in classrooms.

Resources Describing Video Data Collection and Use in Research

Several publications have described the growing (and varied) uses of video data in research on teaching and learning broadly. A review by Erickson (2011) discussed the emergence and early use of video data in qualitative and ethnographic research. Stigler and colleagues discussed the use of "video surveys" in comparative cross-national research on teaching (Jacobs, Kawanaka, & Stigler, 1999; Stigler, Gallimore, & Hiebert, 2000). An edited volume by Kane, Kerr, and Pianta (2014) included several chapters on methodological issues arising in video-based studies of teaching effectiveness and their bearing on the practical evaluation of teachers. Goldman and colleagues' (2014) book-length monograph described the uses of video data in learning sciences research, and an edited volume by Janík and Seidel (2009) described the use of video data in European research on classroom teaching and learning.

Overall, this published work points to some special affordances of video in comparison to other modes of data collection for research on teaching and learning generally and, by inference, for reading research. Like direct observation, video data can be used to record the rich detail of real-time events. Of course, the features of events actually captured by video data depends on how, and how often, video tools are deployed, but holding those important features of research constant, video records preserve the exact timing and sequencing of observed events with less editing and more contextual detail than photographs, audio recordings, field notes, transcriptions, interviews, or questionnaires. Moreover, unlike most other data collection tools, video data are used in both qualitative and quantitative research. In qualitative research, video preserves the immediate visual and auditory phenomena inherent in events, allowing researchers to revisit basic data as they develop and refine coding schemes and check on the internal validity of developing hypotheses about a case. In quantitative research, especially large-sample studies of teaching practice, the preservation and re-use of video data allows analysts to more easily (and less obtrusively) deploy multiple raters to code the same events, allowing for estimation and correction for rater error in data analyses. Video also facilitates simultaneous use of multiple, structured coding schemes to characterize the same teaching and learning events, helping validate score interpretations arising from observation instruments. Further, in both quantitative and qualitative research, setting participants (or others) can view video recordings of events, and participant insights can be used (alongside observer accounts of the data) to better understand event participants' motives, cognition, decision-making, or knowledge use during the events under analysis. Finally, video data can be clipped and processed in a variety of ways that allow researchers to communicate their results visually—both to researchers and to practitioners.

Evolution of Video Technologies

Although many studies in education have used video data, we expect the number of such studies to increase rapidly in the next decade, both as a result of the rapid advances in video recording technology evident in the research reviews just cited and because developments in video technology allow researchers to address research questions they could not study previously. Much of this is due to a continuing miniaturization of video and audio recording devices, as well as continuing decreases in the costs of purchasing good video resolution, and the improved compatibility of video devices with other digital devices. Because of these trends, camera equipment has become easier to transport and set up. In many research settings, a trained camera operator is no longer required because respondents (or analysts) can easily position, turn on, and use video equipment according to research protocols. Multiple cameras can easily be deployed in classroom research and video subjects can wear pedants that allow cameras to follow them as they move around (Derry, 2007). Some camera systems even remove the need to make decisions about zooming and panning the camera during recording as they allow 360 degrees of panning and zooming upon video playback (see DIVER project; Pea, et al., 2004). Cameras can even be mounted on respondents' heads to capture what they see (Blikstad-Balas & Sørvik, 2015; Blikstad-Balas, 2017; see also Burris, 2017 for a broader discussion of "Point-of-View" camera usage). Connections to other equipment (like tablets or laptops), along with growth in internet access and bandwidth, make moving video records from field site to laboratory easier. Moreover, video data files are now more easily processed and analyzed using commercially developed and widely available tools for clipping, annotating, coding, and organizing video data (Derry, 2007). Finally, the costs of storing large quantities of video data have decreased and should continue to do so in the future.

Such advances in video technology may allow for reading researchers to deploy cameras across multiple contexts more efficiently and to conduct multi-site research more affordably. This, in turn, could provide insights into how different classrooms, teachers, and schools implement reading curricula, research-based teaching strategies, or other approaches to supporting readers. Researchers would also have the ability to use video as a part of understanding individual readers within a single classroom through use of evolving video technologies. Indeed, it is only recently possible to position multiple cameras (or even individual student cameras) so as to simultaneously capture and then sync video records of classroom dynamics, reading approaches, and interactions. The affordances are thus many and varied for reading researchers, as the opportunities to develop a complex record of classroom and readers' processes is only a recent possibility.

Video Data in Qualitative Reading Research

Previous volumes of the *Handbook of Reading Research* have mentioned the use of video as an approach to data collection and analysis but have not had a chapter focused on these video research methods. However, our review of qualitative (and mixed methods) studies in the field of reading research over the last ten years found that video data have been used to investigate a range of substantive topics in the field. We found studies using video data that: documented reading and writing processes among young people using multiple and varied texts (e.g., Cho, Woodward, & Li, 2018; Goldman, et al., 2012; Ivey & Johnston, 2013); examined instructional and pedagogical practices in the service of reading and literacy (e.g., Aukerman & Schuldt, 2016; Magnusson, Roe, & Blikstad-Balas, 2018); analyzed language exchanges, discourse, and other detailed and complex interactions in classrooms (e.g., Moore & Schleppegrell, 2014); and investigated the implementation of literacy interventions (e.g., Amendum, Bratsch-Hines, & Vernon-Feagans, 2018; Levine, 2014). As in prior research, video data in the studies we reviewed were used to document phenomena in rich detail and to attend to patterns and meaning within and across video records. Video data were also used alongside other data sources to triangulate findings.

Reading researchers have also used an extensive body of data analysis practices with video data, but several fundamental issues remain unresolved. One of the most vexing issues arises from qualitative researchers' interest in coupling video with other data sources to arrive at a "thick description" of events and cultures (Geertz, 1973). As video data becomes more available to qualitative reading researchers, questions about the validity and reliability of thick descriptions drawn from video data remain. Just how much video data is needed to arrive at "thick" description? Can someone not present in the community at the time of events, or not fully a member of the community, truly understand, analyze, and interpret the sociocultural (or even temporal) context of phenomena under study using video? What specific aspects of sociocultural and temporal context, community context, or social interactions can video capture well and which does it ignore? How might video records be treated similarly or differently from the interpretation and analysis of field notes, photographs, and other media? How might classroom video document (some) aspects of reading, literacy, and interaction, while at the same time failing to document other aspects, and what choices would a researcher make in light of such limitations? Answers to any of the questions raised here depend, of course, on a reading researcher's specific theoretical perspective, research topic, and methods of video data analysis. In our view, what is needed moving forward is more explicit discussion of these issues within specific reading research communities. It would also constitute growing evidence of maturity in the use of video data in the field.

Video Data in Quantitative Research on Reading

Over the past decade, video data have also come into wide use in quantitative research on teaching, especially research using structured observation instruments to examine classroom instruction.

The miniaturization of video equipment, and the easy setup and operation of such equipment by teachers, have made live observation of teaching less necessary and led to innovative uses of camera (and audio) equipment. The positioning of equipment is quite variable in this research, sometimes involving use of panoramic cameras, sometimes synchronization of cameras at the front and back of a classroom, sometimes the distribution of cameras to capture group work, and sometimes the mounting of cameras on students to capture the texts they are interacting with as they read or work on computers. The videos from all cameras can be synchronized, and as a result, many concerns about what can (or cannot) be captured in video studies of classrooms has been addressed (Derry, 2007). Still, the positioning of cameras depends in large part on the research questions being addressed, and we expect camera-positioning strategies to change in the coming years. What we hope evolves is some consensus about best practices in deployment of camera and video recording equipment in research on the teaching and learning of reading. However, best practices for video capture should be based on rigorous comparisons of alternatives. Unfortunately, comparative studies of video technologies and their effects on basic research processes such as measurement and statistical analysis is largely missing in current research. Thus, herein lies an additional opportunity for reading researchers to make progress in the field.

Beyond data collection, a major benefit of video data collection in quantitative research on classroom instruction is the increased ability to store video data for use in training and on-going certification. In research, viewing videos is now a central part of classroom observer training and calibration, with groups of observers frequently scoring common videos previously coded to a "gold standard" by experts. In heavily managed research projects, the scoring of videos is also sometimes monitored in real time, and coders who make large errors are pulled from scoring until they are re-certified (Park, Chen, and Holtzman, 2014). Video data collection further allows for easier (and less obtrusive) estimation of rater error in classroom observation studies than live observation, because two or more raters can now score videos without those raters being present in the same classroom on the same day.

Collection of video data can also address another methodological problem in classroom research—the fact that both the quality of instruction and the ways observers score instructional quality often change systematically over time (e.g., Casabianca et al., 2013). With live observation and live scoring, there is no way to unconfound these potentially correlated trends, and this makes it impossible to study changes over time in teaching practice using live observation (without large assumptions about time trends in rater error). With video scoring, however, videos for particular days can be distributed randomly to raters, making time of video recording and time of scoring uncorrelated.

Despite these affordances, some fundamental questions remain about the structured scoring of videos in reading research. For example, research suggests that video and live observations of the same classroom teaching sessions are scored differently (Casabianca et al., 2013; Curby, Johnson, Mashburn, & Carlis, 2016), although the correlations between live and video scores for teachers are often quite high after adjusting for measurement error. Interestingly, items measuring features of instruction that involve social interaction tend to show the largest differences between live and video scoring, but this does not appear to be affected by issues related to audio or video quality (White, 2017). Beyond these few studies, however, little research has explored why scores might vary across live and video observations or whether such variation differs across particular observation systems. Holding constant the sampling features of live and video research design, it is possible that differences between live and video scoring are due to scoring protocols (e.g., raters can pause and revisit videos but not live events). Alternatively, differences could vary across specific camera systems used in a study or be sensitive to the observation instruments in use.

These last points are especially important because, with the rapid change in video technology, each new project seems to use a new camera setup, and yet, we are unaware of any studies comparing the impact on scoring of different camera systems. It would not be surprising to find that different camera systems have large impacts on observation scores or to find that differences vary across observation instruments. These differences are due to the varied opportunities to see the board, teacher, student-student interactions, and what students are actually reading and doing during lessons afforded by the different tools. Thus, in reading research, where cumulative evidence from many studies is often used to evaluate the effectiveness of particular reading interventions and practices, it would be useful to give careful attention in reporting of study results to the equipment, observation instruments, and scoring procedures used in particular video studies. Such attention could help the field better understand any potential relationships between research results and video data collection/analysis procedures and might ultimately result in more agreement about best practices for video research within the field.

Other Developments in the Use of Video in Research

Other developments in the use of video in research are worth mentioning briefly, and we offer these as a way for imagining how to address various "gaps" in the field mentioned earlier. To begin, advances in software and technology for processing and streaming videos has made it easier to embed short clips of classroom practice within questionnaires. This has led to the embedding of video scenarios into surveys intended to measure teachers' knowledge, allowing teachers to respond to video representations of practice rather than text-based representations (Jamil, Sabol, Hamre, & Pianta, 2015; Kersting, 2008). Video data are also being combined with other kinds of data as well. Mobile eye-tracking technology, which overlays a teacher's gaze onto video data, is the most prominent example (see Beach & McConnel, 2018 for a review of this research), but we expect other combinations to become common, such as the synchronization of video data with screen capture technology that can provide new viewpoints on how students work with technology-based reading interventions.

Technology is sure to develop in other interesting ways as well. One interesting path is the automatic processing and coding of video data. Commercially available software already exists to automatically code facial expressions and (animal) behavior from videos (e.g., www.noldus.com). While these applications currently require the object under study to be center-frame and facing the camera, technology is sure to develop to reduce this limitation. Further, there are attempts in sports broadcasting to develop technology that tracks objects (i.e. a soccer ball) and players in real-time from video data. Technology for automatic transcription of audio is also progressing quickly and may soon develop to the point that conversational turn-taking, wait time, and the timing of discourse events can be coded automatically. Last, the technology to create three-dimensional representations of what is captured on video has been available since at least the release of the X-Box 360 in 2005, which could expand the ways that video is used in research. Application of these new technologies to reading research remains to be explored.

Archiving and Sharing Video Data

A final set of issues in the use of video data in research are related to the increased demand by research sponsors, scholarly journals, and researchers to archive video data for re-use. The rationale and practices for archiving quantitative data from video studies are well established (Johnston, 2017). Issues associated with archiving and re-using qualitative data from video studies, however, are somewhat more controversial, even though practices for archiving qualitative data have been in place in fields outside of education for decades (see Irwin, 2013 for discussion). The archiving and re-use of raw video records, however, raise special concerns. At present, it is difficult to identify any venue other than local repositories to house video data from reading research, and the costs of storing large amounts of video data could slow the development of centralized institutional arrangements for video storage and re-use. A notable exception to this trend is the establishment of a video data enclave at the Inter-University Consortium for Political and Social Research, a virtual data enclave that houses video records from the Gates Foundation's *Measures of Effective Teaching* (MET) project (www.icpsr.umich.edu/icpsrweb/METLDB/). This enclave has been the site of many re-uses of MET video data.

In addition to the complex problem of finding institutional support for video data archiving, there is currently no agreed upon template for the meta-data to be associated with video records (although standard templates make for a good start). Meta-data is the term for the data and information about videos that are archived so that searching, locating, and retrieving from a large source is efficient and possible. Meta-data may include information such as content, date, research participant ID, school location, classroom numbers, and other aspects that describe the videos. Both the storage and meta-data problems make discovery and re-use of relevant video data in the field of reading research difficult.

Equally important are concerns about the privacy and confidentiality of the human subjects of video research, concerns that are making some school districts and many potential subjects of video research reluctant to participate in video studies. Much video research does not depend crucially on knowing the exact identities of participants, but shielding subjects from re-identification is obviously difficult in video work, raising questions about how much context data to associate with video data, how to share video data with other users, and how to use video exemplars of findings in published research (Derry, 2007). Technological solutions to some of these problems (e.g., altering video and audio in ways that obscure subjects' identities) are available, but the effects of such practices on data analysis and inferences from data are unknown. Compounding these problems is the wide cross-national variation in human subjects' protections, which makes comparative cross-national video research more difficult. In light of these problems, researchers planning to engage in video data collection need to think very carefully (and in advance of data collection) about these ethical and practical concerns. Particularly important is the crafting—well in advance—of consent forms for video research that clarify exactly how data will be used, by whom, and for how long.

The use of archived videos and video repositories could also serve as one approach to closing the translational gap in reading research. This gap exists when research findings in controlled, laboratory settings are not ultimately integrated into other research settings or into practice. As one example, *My Teaching Partner*, a coaching tool for classroom teachers, uses video illustrations of particular teaching domains from the observation tool CLASS-S (Gregory et al., 2017). These videos are shared with novice teachers as they gain skills for beneficial teacher-student interactions; novices also share their own videos of attempts at these interactions as well as clips requesting feedback and support of a challenging issue in the classroom. Although *My Teaching Partner* did not particularly focus on reading research, it could model a possible direction of this research and use of video resources in the future.

Video libraries of reading instruction—videos within controlled research settings or videos of the translation of reading instruction to classroom environments—could serve as helpful training and illustration tools for practice and future teaching. Labeling and tagging video collections (or segments of videos) can provide helpful ways for teachers and instructors to search within archives for particular practices related to reading and teaching (see MET-X video repository within the *Teaching and Learning Exploratory* at the University of Michigan as one example). Video is often used in teacher education programs as assessment or reflection tools, but is typically not used beyond a single course or beyond a single teacher's training or portfolio. Establishing a video repository of exemplary practice or illustrations of specific practices may prove useful in demonstrating reading and literacy instruction, especially in ways that could establish common language and understandings around teaching and learning in reading. Teacher education programs could create examples of the development of teachers-in-training to show what is possible, even if not yet at exemplary practice, particularly around the area of reading instruction. Researchers and teachers alike could use such video resources to begin sharing practice and establishing shared language and vision about reading instruction and those beneficial practices to best serve students.

An Example of Video Data in Research

As a way of offering one example of the use of video data collection and analysis advancements, we describe a research project being conducted presently by the authors which uses video data collection, storage, and analysis tools, as well as research practices described in this chapter. The study, which we call *Teaching over Time* (TOT),[1] is a longitudinal, mixed-method study investigating the changes in teaching practice over the course of a ten-year period among a group of approximately 100 teachers of English Language Arts in grades 4 through 8, who earlier submitted video teaching records during the 2009–2011 school years as part of the well-known *Measures of Effective Teaching* (MET) study (MET Project, 2009). We followed up with a subset of 100 of these teachers during the 2017–2019 school years by collecting additional video records of teaching using a sampling plan similar to the one used in the MET study. We then coded all MET and TOT videos using the Protocol for Language Arts Teaching Observation (PLATO)[2] instrument for rating the quality of English Language Arts instruction (Grossman, Loeb, Cohen, & Wyckoff, 2013), as well as a team-developed scoring protocol that measured the extent to which teachers' lessons covered specific learning targets in the Common Core State Standards in reading and writing. As in many other studies, we also collected additional information about text use, approaches to reading, professional development experiences of teachers, the standards and objectives addressed in these teaching videos, and other details using both surveys and (in a subsample of teachers) interviews. Ultimately, we asked the question: How has teaching changed over the time interval of this study and to what should we attribute these changes?

Our research effort offers one example of how a previous repository of videos has been resurrected for additional research efforts and research questions; such an opportunity would not be possible without the use of a storage repository with clear and useful metadata to find appropriate files. It also provides an example of the way classroom video might be deployed and collected across multiple sites, thus raising statistical power to make claims about what is happening in classrooms across multiple contexts. The study also shows how video camera equipment has evolved over the past ten years. In the MET study, a camera operator was present and a somewhat cumbersome panoramic camera was used for video recording. In TOT, by contrast, camera equipment was sent directly to teachers for setup and use, with technological support offered through remote communication. The TOT camera system also had multiple audio tracks to better record both student and teacher voices, and also allowed for the camera to automatically follow the teacher via infrared technology. Researchers on this study also conducted follow-up interviews with individual teachers as a part of the qualitative research component, allowing us to consider the influences, approaches, constraints, and affordances of different professional development opportunities, school contexts, curricular and instructional materials, among other influences. The video data provided the research team several records of teaching practice from two time periods so as to provide a longitudinal record of approaches in classroom. In combination, we hope to use the video data, interviews, documents, and questionnaires to gain insight into the influences on English Language Arts teaching among TOT teachers. Ten years ago, such research would have been far more costly and difficult to conduct. It is only through increased miniaturization of camera and audio technologies, a decline in costs of these new technologies, and better ability to obtain low cost video storage and playback capacity, that a study like *Teaching over Time* became feasible. We therefore anticipate additional developments in video research by other reading researchers and a growing use of video technologies and data in order to address existing gaps and remaining questions in the field.

Notes

1 *Teaching over Time* is a part of a larger research effort entitled *Under Construction: The Rise, Spread, and Consequences of the Common Core State Standards Initiative in the U.S. Education Sector*. It is a Spencer Foundation and WT Grant Foundation endeavor across multiple universities and principal investigators.
2 PLATO stands for the Protcol for Language Arts Teaching Observations, which is a classroom observation protocol for English Language Arts teaching and instruction.

References

Amendum, S., Bratsch-Hines, M., & Vernon-Feagans, L. (2018). Investigating the efficacy of a web-based early reading and professional development intervention for young English learners. *Reading Research Quarterly*, *53*(2), 155–174. doi:https://doi.10.1002.rrq.188

Aukerman, M., & Schuldt, L. C. (2016). "The pictures can say more things": Change across time in young children's references to images and words during text discussion. *Reading Research Quarterly*, *51*(3), 267–287. doi:https://doi.10.1002.rrq.138

Beach, P., & McConnel, J. (2018). Eye tracking methodology for studying teacher learning: A review of the research. *International Journal of Research & Method in Education*, *0*(0), 1–17. doi:10.1080/1743727X.2018.1496415

Blikstad-Balas, M. (2017). Key challenges of using video when investigating social practices in education: Contextualization, magnification, and representation. *International Journal of Research & Method in Education*, *40*(5), 511–523. doi:10.1080/1743727X.2016.1181162

Blikstad-Balas, M., & Sørvik, G. O. (2015). Researching literacy in context: Using video analysis to explore school literacies. *Literacy*, *49*(3), 140–148. doi:10.1111/lit.12037

Burris, A. (2017). A child's-eye view: An examination of point-of-view camera use in four informal education settings. *Visitor Studies*, *20*(2), 218–237. doi:10.1080/10645578.2017.1404352

Casabianca, J. M., McCaffrey, D. F., Gitomer, D. H., Bell, C. A., Hamre, B. K., & Pianta, R. C. (2013). Effect of observation mode on measures of secondary mathematics teaching. *Educational and Psychological Measurement*, *73*(5), 757–783. doi:10.1177/0013164413486987

Cho, B.-Y., Woodward, L., & Li, D. (2018). Epistemic processing when adolescents read online: A verbal protocol analysis of more and less successful online readers. *Reading Research Quarterly*, *53*(2), 197–221. https://doi/10/1002/rrq.190

Curby, T. W., Johnson, P., Mashburn, A. J., & Carlis, L. (2016). Live versus video observations: Comparing the reliability and validity of two methods of assessing classroom quality. *Journal of Psychoeducational Assessment*, *34*(8), 765–781. doi:10.1177/0734282915627115

Derry, S. J. (Ed.). (2007). Guidelines for conducting video research in education: Recommendations from an expert panel. Chicago: Data Research and Development Center. Retrieved May 2, 2009, from http://drdc.uchicago.edu/what/video-research.html

Erickson, F. (2011). Uses of video in social research: A brief history. *International Journal of Social Research Methodology*, *14*(3), 179–189.

Geertz, C. (1973). Thick description: Toward an interpretive theory of culture. In *The interpretation of cultures* (pp. 310–323). New York, NY: Basic Books.

Goldman, R., Pea, R., Barron, B., & Derry, S. J. (Eds.). (2014). *Video research in the learning sciences*. Routledge.

Goldman, S. R., Braasch, J. L., Wiley, J., Graesser, A. C., & Brodowinska, K. (2012). Comprehending and learning from Internet sources: Processing patterns of better and poorer learners. *Reading Research Quarterly*, *47*(4), 356–381.

Gregory, A., Ruzek, E., Hafen, C. A., Mikami, A. Y., Allen, J. P., & Pianta, R. C. (2017). My teaching partner-secondary: A video-based coaching model. *Theory Into Practice*, *56*(1), 38–45. doi:10.1080/00405841.2016.1260402

Grossman, P., Loeb, S., Cohen, J., & Wyckoff, J. (2013). Measure for measure: The relationship between measures of instructional practice in middle school English language arts and teachers' value-added scores. *American Journal of Education, 119*(3), 445–470.

Irwin, S. (2013). Qualitative secondary data analysis: Ethics, epistemology and context. *Progress in Development Studies, 13*(4), 295–306.

Ivey, G., & Johnston, P. H. (2013). Engagement with young adult literature: Outcomes and processes. *Reading Research Quarterly, 48*(3), 255–275. doi:https://doi.10.1002/rrq.46

Jacobs, J. K., Kawanaka, T., & Stigler, J. W. (1999). Integrating qualitative and quantitative approaches to the analysis of video data on classroom teaching. *International Journal of Educational Research, 31*(8), 717–724.

Jamil, F. M., Sabol, T. J., Hamre, B. K., & Pianta, R. C. (2015). Assessing teachers' skills in detecting and identifying effective interactions in the classroom: Theory and measurement. *The Elementary School Journal, 115*(3), 407–432. doi:10.1086/680353

Janík, T., & Seidel, T. (Eds.). (2009). *The power of video studies for investigating teaching and learning in the classroom*. Münster: Waxmann Publishing.

Johnston, L. R. (Ed) (2017). *Curating research data volume one: Practical strategies for your digital repository*. Chicago, IL: Association of College and Research Libraries.

Kane, T., Kerr, K., & Pianta, R. (2014). *Designing teacher evaluation systems: New guidance from the measures of effective teaching project*. Hoboken, NJ: John Wiley & Sons.

Kersting, N. (2008). Using video clips of mathematics classroom instruction as item prompts to measure teachers' knowledge of teaching mathematics. *Educational and Psychological Measurement, 68*(5), 845–861. doi:10.1177/0013164407313369

Levine, S. (2014). Making interpretation visible with an affect-based strategy. *Reading Research Quarterly, 49*(3), 283–303. doi:https://doi.10.10021.rrq.71

Magnusson, C. G., Roe, A., & Blikstad-Balas, M. (2018). To what extent and how are reading comprehension strategies part of language arts instruction? A study of lower secondary classrooms. *Reading Research Quarterly, 0*(0), 1–26. doi:10.1002/rrq.231

MET Project. (2009). *Learning about teaching: Initial findings from the measure of effective teaching project*. Seattle, WA: Bill & Melinda Gates Foundation.

Moore, J., & Schleppegrell, M. (2014). Using a functional linguistic metalanguage to support academic language development in the English language arts. *Linguistics and Education., 26*(1), 92–105. doi:10.1016/j.linged.2014.01.002

Park, Y. S., Chen, J., & Holtzman, S. (2014). Evaluating efforts to minimize rater bias in scoring classroom observations. In K. Kerr, R. Pianta, & T. Kane (Eds.), *Designing teacher revaluation systems: New guidance from the Measures of Effective Teaching Project* (pp. 383–414). San Francisco, CA: Jossey-Bass.

Pea, R. D., Mills, M., Rosen, J., Dauber, K., Effelsberg, W., & Hoffert, E. (2004). The diver project: Interactive digital video repurposing. *IEEE MultiMedia, 11*(1), 54–61. doi:10.1109/MMUL.2004.1261108

Stigler, J. W., Gallimore, R., & Hiebert, J. (2000). Using video surveys to compare classrooms and teaching across cultures: Examples and lessons from the TIMSS video studies. *Educational Psychologist, 35*(2), 87–100.

White, M. (2017). *Generalizability of scores from classroom observation instruments*. Ann Arbor, MI: University of Michigan. http://hdl.handle.net/2027.42/138742

25
Examining the Process of Reading in Media Text Environments
A Methodological Perspective

Byeong-Young Cho

This chapter focuses on methods of inquiry into processes of reading across media. The discussion conceives of media as both forms or channels of communication, and the system and structure of communication through which texts of varying quality, mostly online, are presented as potential sources of information to readers. The chapter concerns reading in a broad sense, drawing on the research literature that seeks to understand and describe reading by examining how readers access, learn from, and reason about diverse texts in media. My goal is to review process-oriented research methods of examining media reading and thereby offer a précis of ideas that may be useful for specifying and integrating various inquiry methods with differing merits and limits.

Kinds of Reading that We Study in Media Text Environments

What kinds of reading do we wish to better understand? This question deserves attention from those engaged in reading inquiry because our response to it drives our decisions about methods, tools, techniques, and procedures. Comprehending reading in digital media often means moving beyond single reader-text-task parameters (Britt, Goldman, & Rouet, 2013; Buckingham, 2006; Lankshear & Knobel, 2003; Leu, Kinzer, Coiro, Castek, & Henry, 2013; New London Group, 1996). For example, the digital media environment forces readers to make choices of texts as untested sources of information that await, attract, or hide from our attention (Kwon, Cha, & Jung, 2017; Miller & Record, 2013; Simon, 2010). In addition, reading news reports, journal articles, and open sources is oftentimes situated in goal-driven inquiry cycles of locating, evaluating, and using relevant information to investigate problems and questions (Metzger & Flanagin, 2013; Renear & Palmer, 2009). Further, active readers keenly interact with other readers, responding to media texts critically, which reminds us how easily individuals may become biased as they choose what to read in media and how to use reading to make important decisions (Bakshy, Messing, & Adamic, 2015; Mocanu, Rossi, Zhang, Karsai, & Quattrociocchi, 2015).

The kinds of reading described above are distinct from reading in which an individual applies processing skills to a given text in a strictly defined task environment. This means that our assumptions about reading need to be revisited if we want to adequately explain the multifaceted opportunities for learning from media texts that people commonly experience today (Greenhow, Robelia, & Hughs, 2009; Leu et al., 2013). What is central to reading in media text environments is how readers identify, understand, and use the range of media texts available as sources of knowledge and learning that may be useful for attaining their goals. A burgeoning field of research seeks to describe the wide variety of reading and literacy tasks that include both daily use of media texts, such as newspapers, documentary films, scientific animations, and websites (Boucheix, Lowe, Putri, & Groff, 2013; Glaser, Garsoffky, & Schwan, 2012; Johnson, Azevedo, & D'Mello, 2011; Kesler, Tinio, & Nolan, 2016; Mosborg, 2002), and learning with digital media to make textual inquiries, secure reliable sources, and construct new questions worth investigating (Cho, Woodward, Li, & Barlow, 2017; Mercier & Frederiksen, 2018; Wopereis & van Merriënboer, 2011).

It is noteworthy that the foci of reading inquiry as described here, are not necessarily confined to *cognitive processes*, but can subsume readers' *thinking about*, *feeling about*, *reacting to*, and *interacting with* the demands of reading in a media space. In particular, media text environments often engage readers' epistemologies, as readers scrutinize many unsubstantiated knowledge claims through interactions with multiple texts (Bråten, Britt, Strømsø, & Rouet, 2011; Hofer, 2004; Ikuenobe, 2003; Lankshear, Peters, & Knobel, 2000). In this context of epistemological uncertainty, media readers are often required to grasp arguments from different texts and reason about evidence to analyze and evaluate the knowledge claims that the authors build in the texts. Therefore, when carrying out reading inquiry, we deal with epistemic thinking engagement (e.g., how readers come to know and justify their understandings through evaluating varied texts as potential sources of evidence) in addition to cognitive processes and metacognitive experiences. Examinations of these aspects of reading depend on context: who reads what texts for what goals and interests.

In brief, our examinations of reading in media text environments require special attention to how these environments evoke, engage, and constrain readers' thinking processes in and across the cognitive, metacognitive, and epistemological dimensions of reading. The following section recounts some methodological approaches and their affordances and advantages that can potentially aid in advancing our knowledge with regard to how readers engage in thought processes while responding to, and interacting with, media text environments.

Useful Methods for Examining Reading in Media Text Environments

Reading inquiry over the past century has offered compelling theories and models to advance our knowledge of how people read (for a comprehensive review, see McNamara & Magliano, 2009). Every such advance is entwined with the development and refinement of our methodologies. For example, we are now confident that tracking a reader's eye gaze indicates how the reader's attention shifts as she processes information (Just & Carpenter, 1980; Rayner, 2009). We have also benefited from evidentiary inferences about text-processing strategies from the analysis of readers' think-aloud protocols (Afflerbach & Johnston, 1984; Pressley & Afflerbach, 1995). That said, our ability to determine the optimal research methods to investigate media reading with multiple sources and tasks will be limited if we settle for established ideas of reading that are solely based on single-text processing (Bråten et al., 2011; Cho, Afflerbach, & Han, 2018; Goldman, 2010; Rouet, 2006).

This section addresses methodological needs that arise when we examine and evaluate how people read media texts (see Table 25.1). The approaches reviewed here were identified in a range of empirical work on diverse reading situations across media. While previous work demonstrates the scientific merits of these different approaches (Afflerbach, 2000; Hofer, 2004; Smagorinsky, 1998; Van Gog, Paas, van Merriënboer, & Witte, 2005; Veenman, 2005), this review details their potential uses and benefits for examinations of reader cognition and thinking engagement, and situates them in relation to prominent (con)textual features of media.

Table 25.1 Methods of Inquiry into Reading Across Media

Methods	What procedures and techniques can be used?	What kinds of data can be collected?	What aspects of reading can this approach address?	What needs to be considered for data analysis?
Verbal reporting and verbal protocol analysis	Concurrent verbal reporting during reading	Spontaneous think-aloud (e.g., "What are you thinking, feeling, and doing as you navigate on the Internet?")	Relatively automatized processing of information when skimming paragraphs, browsing a series of images, or scanning a list of hyperlinks.	Processing complexity (e.g., basic and higher-order), thinking level (e.g., surface and deep), and strategic effectiveness (e.g., success and failure) may be judged and coded for each processing type.
			Instantiations of prior knowledge use (e.g., what the reader knew and didn't know about particular links, sites, web tools, or media functions while making literal-level inferences about what they are about and for).	Knowledge types (e.g., topic knowledge, domain knowledge, media knowledge such as information publishing and sharing, information system knowledge), knowledge sources (e.g., prior learning, previous reading, personal experience, other human resources such as teachers), and effectiveness in knowledge use (e.g., (in)accurate association of (in)correct knowledge with the information being processed) may be inferred and coded.
			Pre-planned reading paths taken by readers to gather information and solve problems (e.g., starting Internet research by locating and processing easier links and texts first, following a tentative plan for online searching and information reading, rejecting difficult texts regardless of their importance and value for reading goals).	Readers' comments on chosen pages and links can be integrated into a map of reading paths, and this map can be judged in terms of its (non)linearity and (in)flexibility. The map patterns may be identified and compared among the individuals.

(Continued)

Table 25.1 (Cont.)

Methods	What procedures and techniques can be used?	What kinds of data can be collected?	What aspects of reading can this approach address?	What needs to be considered for data analysis?
			Initial noticing of, and attention to, new and eye-catching information (e.g., images and graphics, audiovisual resources, technical terms and jargon) and text features (e.g., hyperlinks and menus, headings and subheadings, previews and overviews).	Patterns of noticing may indicate readers' preferred modes of information gathering (e.g., visual or written representation), habits of reading (e.g., selective reading, skimming, close reading), or reasons for being distracted or diverted (e.g., information overload, disorientation during navigation, ill-defined focus of information-knowledge seeking).
			Reactive (rather than critical) judgments of the content relevance of media information and decisions about its source utility (e.g., keyword-text matching, text-content comparison) in the course of online searching and information location.	Opportunities that readers might have missed in the course of accessing novel, unexplored information spaces may be considered in the data analysis when reactive judgments are observed repeatedly.
			Motivations for navigational jumping and switching between pages in a routine cycle (e.g., browsing, clicking, site opening, bookmarking, checking-leaving).	Motivational shift can be considered in data analysis in that media environments may facilitate readers' development of situational interest (e.g., interest changing through the task) beyond personal interest (intrinsic interest independent of the task).

(Continued)

Table 25.1 (Cont.)

Methods	What procedures and techniques can be used?	What kinds of data can be collected?	What aspects of reading can this approach address?	What needs to be considered for data analysis?
		Elicited self-explanation (e.g., "Why are you thinking, feeling, and doing that in that way at this moment of your website reading?")	Degree of intentional and goal-directed thinking, which is likely to be involved in evidence-based reasoning about texts and sources (e.g., understanding webpage content, developing new thoughts, citing and referencing to support claims, imposing and revising a point of view as part of text interpretation, challenging and updating a mental model of previous and current web sources).	Data analysis should consider readers' verbal proficiency and willingness to talk in front of others because elicited verbal reporting largely involves self-explanation, and articulation, of one's thoughts and behaviors. Interpretation of these verbal data needs to be complemented by prior measures of individual differences with regard to readers' cognitive, motivational, and verbal abilities and tendencies.
			Emerging self-reflection that readers may bring in to judge their own reading processes and behaviors related to their information searching, online navigation, and media interaction (e.g., refocusing, progress judgment, judgment of success and failure, reader engagement).	Accuracy of self-reflection should be judged and coded because not all readers' self-reflection is well-calibrated with their actual reading performance, especially for readers who are metacognitively inexperienced in relation to media tasks and environments.
			Metacognitive monitoring processes and self-regulatory planning in which readers engage while navigating the media space and negotiating multiple media sources (e.g., evaluating aspects of reading against task goals and situations of reading, detecting information needs and implementing follow-up actions to meet the needs, evaluating the challenges and difficulties presented by specific media contexts).	Monitoring may be interpreted in two ways: (a) monitoring as an independent category of strategic processing (e.g., problem detection, fix–it strategy use, goal specification), or (b) monitoring as assumed to be a latent competence that allows coordination of cognitive strategies.

(Continued)

Table 25.1 (Cont.)

Methods	What procedures and techniques can be used?	What kinds of data can be collected?	What aspects of reading can this approach address?	What needs to be considered for data analysis?
			Intentional management of multiple media texts in which readers shift their reading focus and attention between sources and develop meaning toward evidentiary understanding of the topics, issues, or problems investigated through media inquiry.	Because verbal reports often include unclear pronouns (e.g., it, this, they, that), data analysis should clarify as much as possible what sources of information a specific verbal utterance refers to in order to delineate and trace how each source is read and used.
	Retrospective verbal reporting after the focal task of reading is done	Spontaneous think-aloud (e.g., "How would you describe the process of your reading as you navigate the Internet?") and/or elicited self-explanation (e.g., "How did you strive to make sense of conflicting news reports?")	Reasons for particular actions taken in the course of reading, especially at important and culminating moments of reading retained in the reader's mind (e.g., rejecting a certain website, spending a relatively long time to read a particular article, changing search terms several times, seeking specific media publishing types and authorities such as news media, personal blogs, tweets and postings by lay people, expert columns, government sites).	Post-reading recall of actions may rely heavily on readers' interpretation and judgment of their reading and of themselves, and be contextualized within their entire process of reading. Therefore, retrospective protocols may best be used as complementary data that describe, support, and verify the inferences made from other, unobtrusive real-time process data such as eye movements and logging history.
			Important information learned from media reading and integrated into readers' schemas and experience.	Readers' memories do not necessarily represent what happened during reading accurately and in detail, and oftentimes, they are constructed (and thus biased) through the verbal reporting process. Therefore, the

(Continued)

Table 25.1 (Cont.)

Methods	What procedures and techniques can be used?	What kinds of data can be collected?	What aspects of reading can this approach address?	What needs to be considered for data analysis?
				verbal data should be triangulated with reader attention data, including reading times and logging history. Also, the importance and relevance of the retained information may be judged based on post-hoc analysis of the media texts accessed by readers. Such judgments may be informative about reading effectiveness and reader understanding as the result of their media text investigation.
	Cued retrospective verbal reporting or stimulated recall	Think-aloud and self-explanation in response to external visual cues (e.g., videorecorded performance) with examiner prompts	Self-reflection in relation to focal moments (e.g., searching), actions (e.g., clicking), choices (e.g., choosing a media text), and decisions (e.g., shifting a reading focus from searching to comprehension) triggered by external cues.	Richer verbal reporting may be stimulated by the cues, and the resulting verbal data may allow for more in-depth analysis of focal acts of reading and the underlying motivation. Close observations of during-reading processes are required because the important stimuli and cues need to be chosen immediately after the reading task is done. Cued retrospective verbal reporting is particularly useful in media reading situations that involve multilayered information spaces in which readers perform fast and dynamic moves along a series of nodes and links.

(Continued)

Table 25.1 (Cont.)

Methods	What procedures and techniques can be used?	What kinds of data can be collected?	What aspects of reading can this approach address?	What needs to be considered for data analysis?
			Self-assessment based on the recognition, analysis, and evaluation of perceived missteps, errors, and failures, using cues as supporting evidence.	Unconstrained talking aloud may facilitate readers' continual revision of self-reflection (considering the factors of the task, goal, and context), which may lead them to inaccurate judgments or self-justifying biases (e.g., under- or overestimation of skills, knowledge, and success as opposed to actual performance).
	Spontaneous verbalizations during real-life tasks	Think-aloud situated in an authentic context of task performance (e.g., by approaching a learner reading digital media during class and eliciting personal talk from the learner on his/her performance)	Microgenetic analysis of moment-to-moment processes of reading situated in authentic, everyday problem-solving tasks (e.g., in-school literacy tasks, home literacy practices).	Reader factors that affect moment-to-moment reading processes must be considered in the data analysis (e.g., how individuals' history of media learning may come into play in reading with a variety of media sources—ontogenetic influence on microgenetic moves).
			Thinking or wandering, engagement or indifference, and agreement or refusal in the course of media text reading as contextualized with the authentic task, goal, setting, and ways of interacting with authentic problems.	Data analysis may consider how readers' awareness and identification of authentic problems are situated within real-world constraints and affordances (e.g., micro-, meso-, and macro-contextual influences).

(Continued)

Table 25.1 (Cont.)

Methods	What procedures and techniques can be used?	What kinds of data can be collected?	What aspects of reading can this approach address?	What needs to be considered for data analysis?
			Ways readers approach media texts as potentially useful sources of information as they select, prioritize, or reject certain texts and materials (e.g., given texts, self-chosen texts, world knowledge, topic knowledge in use).	The scope and boundaries of the chosen media texts may be analyzed in terms of their usefulness, relevance, and significance for readers' progress toward achieving their goals.
Task-based discourse analysis	Recorded peer discussion and discourse	Verbal comments on texts and media	Mental models built as reading makes progress toward an understanding, and the use of meaning-making strategies of varying complexities and roles (e.g., commenting, noticing, summarizing, elaborating, analyzing and synthesizing, contextualizing word meanings, questioning and challenging text ideas).	Discourse analysis allows researchers to identify readers' use of key information, and to analyze their sensemaking processes. This is because the mental models built within individuals' minds are evidenced through intellectual exchanges and verbal interactions between the individuals.
			Processes of identifying and determining relationships among mental models built at difference stages of reading (e.g., mutually (dis)agreeing, complementary or conflicting perspectives) and the involved cognitive dissonances (e.g., confusion, tension, tentativeness, resolution of disparate ideas and perspectives represented in mental models).	Data analysis may consider the course of engagement in which readers become more and more involved in intertextual meaning-making processes. Discourse analysis allows tracing the origins and relationships of ideas (e.g., keeping records of sources of information used to build within- and cross-textual models).

(Continued)

Table 25.1 (Cont.)

Methods	What procedures and techniques can be used?	What kinds of data can be collected?	What aspects of reading can this approach address?	What needs to be considered for data analysis?
		Verbal comments referring to sourcing and referencing	Contribution of media sources to the overall learning process, and the accompanying epistemic processes (e.g., (in)consistent judgments in claim-making, evidence use through reasoning about the sources of information).	Comments including certain vocabulary that indicates epistemic processing and justification (e.g., reliable, truth, believe, depend, reason, evidence, data, claim, fake, false, wrong, know, think) may be analyzed. Such words and comments often accompany judgments of media's utility and credibility.
		Lexical transitions in speech (e.g., pronoun shifts)	Transactional commitment to text understanding at a critical level. For example, pronoun shifts may indicate shifts in readers' stances toward history, from considering it as lists of fossilized facts and events (e.g., their, it) to considering it as personalized and culturally reinterpreted narratives (e.g., our, I) as a result of working with diverse written and visual accounts of current and historical issues found in media.	Data analysis may be informed by a preliminary analysis of the chosen media texts in terms of how they are relevant to readers' experience and knowledge and hidden assumptions, motives, or biases in the texts.
		Verbal comments on partners (and the self), and processes and sequences of verbal exchanges	Shared metacognition that facilitates monitoring, control, regulation, and negotiation of textual decision-making processes in relation to what sources to choose and how to make use of those sources (e.g., shared goals, division of labor, unique and joint contributions to the progress of knowing).	Data analysis may focus on readers' responsive reactions to each other's language and their underlying thoughts and perspectives about pursuing knowledge together (e.g., if/how they invite thoughts and opinions, if/how they accept presented claims, if/how they offer evidence to support objections).

(Continued)

Table 25.1 (Cont.)

Methods	What procedures and techniques can be used?	What kinds of data can be collected?	What aspects of reading can this approach address?	What needs to be considered for data analysis?
Ethnographic methods	Interviews	Pre-reading interviews (e.g., "How do you plan to read as you work with media sources to do this upcoming task?")	Individual differences and tendencies that readers bring to the task of reading and the goals that they set up prior to performance.	Data analysis may include the assessment of reader factors such as knowledge (e.g., prior knowledge and funds of knowledge regarding topics, content, text features, task environments), motivation (e.g., topic interest, reading attitudes, task engagement), self-efficacy (e.g., skills, knowledge, performance), and task impressions (e.g., available materials and resources, spatio-temporal and physical constraints, expected outcomes).
		Post-reading interviews (e.g., "What new information did you find during your online reading?")	What readers learned from reading: major take-away in terms of content learning of new information, novel insights, puzzling ideas, unresolved issues, and remaining questions.	Data analysis may include distinguishing new and old information. The acquisition of new information may be traced by analyzing the process of choosing, reading, and evaluating media sources, while old information may be identified in pre-reading interviews or during-reading verbal protocols.
			Self-reflection on task performance, including readers' feeling of success or failure, self-reported learning experience and engagement, and judgment of task-text complexity and difficulty.	Reader judgment may be assessed both explicitly and implicitly. Explicit questions may elicit direct responses from readers, but the responses might be biased. Specified follow-up questions may be necessary.

(Continued)

Table 25.1 (Cont.)

Methods	What procedures and techniques can be used?	What kinds of data can be collected?	What aspects of reading can this approach address?	What needs to be considered for data analysis?
		Focus group interviews (e.g., "What would you like to share about your media reading experience?")	Typical, shared reactions among the participants in response to the reading task performed.	Focus groups can be done with participants who worked together on collaborative tasks, or participants who performed the same task individually.
			Conflicting experiences and reflections of participants, and the sources of the conflicts.	Data analysis may include interpretation of focus group data along with pre-reading interviews and during-reading observations.
	Observations	Fieldnotes on during-reading behaviors	Noticeable reader utterances that help to identify critical moments and episodes of reading in the media space.	Close observation is required: watching what readers are doing and noting the texts they are reading. Photographing computer screens and making quick notes on reader behaviors and researcher insights can be helpful to preserve moments of reading to be analyzed later.
			Readers' feelings and engagement at specific moments of reading.	Data analysis may include inferences from embodied non-verbal language such as facial expressions, physical actions, and gestures that may not be captured by screen-recording or verbal reporting (e.g., how readers arrange their surroundings when reading; how readers position their bodies; how readers handle objects such as a book, printed paper, computer, or mouse; what readers look for first and last; what makes readers stop or continue browsing).

(Continued)

Table 25.1 (Cont.)

Methods	What procedures and techniques can be used?	What kinds of data can be collected?	What aspects of reading can this approach address?	What needs to be considered for data analysis?
		Post-hoc analysis of videorecorded reader performance	Dynamic use of explicit strategic behaviors that accompany a series of cognitive strategies and processes (e.g., search term use, site visits, web-browser use, page transitions, mouse use, scrolling).	Data analysis may assess the quality and complexity of the web sources that readers visited, read, and used (post-hoc qualitative analysis of source relevance, credibility, and usefulness) and the order in which these web sources were visited and used.
Automatized, unobtrusive collection of nonverbal data	Eye-tracking within and across areas of interest (AOIs)	Fixation (and duration) and saccade	Extensiveness and intensiveness of reader attention to reading within an AOI, which can be predetermined either spatially (e.g., frames, sections) or functionally (e.g., figures and tables, titles, topic sentences, keywords, paragraphs).	Within-AOI reader attention may be analyzed by calculating the amount of reading time and the density of eye-mind attention (e.g., percentage of total viewing time, mean duration of all fixations).
		Eye-movement sequence	How distinctively the reader processes different AOIs according to their relevance and importance: The mean difference in total fixation and duration times between different AOIs can be examined.	The linear and nonlinear order of reading and relevant metacognitive and self-regulatory processes (e.g., monitoring, fix-up strategy use) may be analyzed by charting the reader's revisiting-reviewing-rereading patterns across the AOIs (e.g., number of times a reader returns to each AOI, comparison of time spent at the first-place fixation and subsequent fixations).
	Log-file analysis	Log files	Readers' management of reading time and adjustment of reading attention when processing multiple texts and sources.	Data analysis includes the assessment of dwell time (when one's eye lands on a specific site and page and how long one's attention to the text continues) as well as total numbers of websites loaded, unique URLs loaded, and clicks on links.

(Continued)

Table 25.1 (Cont.)

Methods	What procedures and techniques can be used?	What kinds of data can be collected?	What aspects of reading can this approach address?	What needs to be considered for data analysis?
			Whether readers visit websites that meet certain quality criteria, according to post-hoc analysis (e.g., (ir)relevant or (un)reliable website visits).	Pre-task textual analysis is required if readers work within a closed-ended system (e.g., hypertext), whereas post-hoc analysis must be undertaken if readers work in an unconstrained, authentic media text environment (e.g., the Internet).
			Readers' choices and solution paths or diversions.	Logging history may be delineated into a series of separate page visits and then integrated into a map that represents the sequence of reading choices. Coherence of the choices may be judged in relation to their relevance and importance.
		Search term use (keystroke data)	How extensively readers engage in online searching (e.g., the total number of keystroke activities and search terms entered).	Quantitative analysis may be performed on the number of search term modifications, the number of site visits, and the amount of reading time within each search term use.
			How readers use prior knowledge (e.g., topic knowledge, domain knowledge, text knowledge, Internet knowledge) to generate relevant search terms (mostly in the beginning phase of reading).	Data may be analyzed to identify the categories of the typed search terms (e.g., by topic, publishing type, expertise or authority) as well as their qualities (e.g., relevance, significance).

(Continued)

Table 25.1 (Cont.)

Methods	What procedures and techniques can be used?	What kinds of data can be collected?	What aspects of reading can this approach address?	What needs to be considered for data analysis?
			How readers modify search terms at the metacognitive level by responding to changing situations of reading and evolving goals for reading.	Qualitative analysis is required to judge the flow of thinking demonstrated by readers (e.g., a flow of changes in search term use as compared to verbalized thoughts).
	Post-click interaction analysis	Cursor (mouse pointer) movement and scrolling	How readers spend their time on the landing page and subsequently viewed documents (e.g., close reading versus scanning according to document relevance).	Data analysis may ask whether consistent patterns in scroll bar and mouse use (e.g., frequent shifts in direction and duration, moving down-pausing-moving up, scrolling down from top to bottom of the page) are observed across texts and among readers, which may show reader tendencies.

Note. Empirical studies contributing to this review include: Baron (2016); Barzilai and Zohar (2012); Biedert, Dengel, Buscher, and Vartan (2012); Boucheix et al. (2013); Brand-Gruwel, Kammerer, van Meeuwen, and van Gog (2017); Bulger, Mayer, and Metzger (2014); Cho (2014); Cho, Kucan, Rainey, and Han (2018); Cho, Woodward, and Li (2018); Cho et al. (2017); Cutrell and Guan (2007); Ferguson, Bråten, and Strømsø (2012); Fitzgerald and Palincsar (2017); Gerjets, Kammerer, and Werner (2011); Glaser et al. (2012); Goldman, Braasch, Wiley, Graesser, and Brodowinska (2012); Greene, Yu, and Copeland (2014); Guo and Agichtein (2012); Hillesund (2010); Hollis and Was (2016); Jian (2015); Johnson et al. (2011); Kesler et al. (2016); Kiili, Laurinen, Marttunen, and Leu (2012); Kiili, Leu, Marttunen, Hautala, and Leppänen (2018); Kruger and Steyn (2013); Lawless, Schrader, and Mayall (2007); Lewis and Fabos (2005); Lipponen, Rahikainen, Lallimo, and Hakkarainen (2003); Marsh (2011); Mason, Ariasi, and Boldrin (2011); Mason, Tornatora, and Pluchino (2015); McEneaney, Li, Allen, and Guzniczak (2009); Mercier and Frederiksen (2018); Minguela, Solé, and Pieschl (2015); Mosborg (2002); Pan et al. (2004); Paul and Morris (2011); Salmerón and García (2011); Salmerón, Naumann, García, and Fajardo (2017); Song and Cho (2019); Sung, Wu, Chen, and Chang (2015); Trevors, Feyzi-Behnagh, Azevedo, and Bouchet (2016); and Zhang and Duke (2008).

The review suggests verbal data analysis as a culminating approach to media-based reading inquiry. This approach uses language data generated by readers in more or less authentic, spontaneous, and interactive conditions. Its specific methods include:

- *concurrent thinking aloud*—readers verbalize their thoughts and actions spontaneously while engaged in a reading process, for example, using the Internet to conduct research on a controversial topic (e.g., Cho, 2014);
- *cued retrospective verbal reporting*—after reading, readers explain their processing of digital texts by responding to external cues they themselves generated while reading, such as

videorecorded screen moves or visual displays of eye movements on a screen (e.g., Salmerón et al., 2017);
- *ethnographic interviews and think-aloud*—readers talk to researchers about their interactions with digital technologies as an authentic experience of sensemaking through reading, writing, and communicating (e.g., Lewis & Fabos, 2005); and
- *task-oriented group discourse*—readers' recorded (non)verbal exchanges during joint meaning construction while reading in an online media context (e.g., Kiili et al., 2012).

Such verbal data analysis research notably manifests trends in data triangulation, one way or another. For example, two or more sources of verbal data are regularly used together (e.g., metacognitive web sourcing strategies inferred from think-aloud reports and epistemic interviews in Barzilai & Zohar, 2012). In addition, verbal data can be coordinated with behavioral data (e.g., think-aloud reports with eye movements and Internet log files in Gerjets, Kammerer, & Werner's 2011 study to measure sourcing strategies in web searches).

Further, unconventional and creative adaptations of these verbal data approaches have contributed to theoretical discussions about the construct of reading in media text environments. Specifically, a growing body of work looks into readers' epistemic engagement in working with multiple sources of information in media. Scholars have demonstrated the utility of interpreting readers' elicited verbal reports, retrospective interviews, or task-oriented discourses to describe readers' epistemic (meta)cognition in action while reading digitally (Barzilai & Zohar, 2012; Cho et al., 2018; Ferguson et al., 2012; Greene et al., 2014; Mason et al., 2011).

Verbal data are uniquely valuable for observing the operation of epistemic processes when readers' latent theories of knowledge and knowing may surface and work toward source judgments, conflict resolution, justification for knowing, or additional evidence-seeking during media reading. Such uses of readers' verbal data to describe epistemic cognition as a situated construct help address the lack of authenticity inherent in the self-report surveys typically used in learner epistemology studies (Greene, Muis, & Pieschl, 2010; Hofer, 2004). At best, readers' survey responses describe perceived epistemic beliefs—but verbal data approaches can reflect how such beliefs are enacted along with (meta)cognitive processes in an intertextual media space.

Research on media reading is increasingly informed by current technologies, including eye-tracking (Gerjets et al., 2011; Salmerón et al., 2017; Sung et al., 2015) and automatized collection of navigational indicators such as dwell time, logging history, cursor movements, and keystrokes (Bulger et al., 2014; Lawless, Brown, Mills, & Mayall, 2003; McEneaney et al., 2009; Paul & Morris, 2011). Technological advancement has also extended the affordances of our methods with increasingly sophisticated and reliable tools. For instance, recent studies explore ubiquitous practices of media reading on mobile devices such as smartphones (e.g., see Biedert et al., 2012; Guo & Agichtein, 2012, for methods combining data from log files, touch screen use, cursor movements, and gaze estimation to examine reading process patterns in smartphone reading).

Adaptive eye-tracking is among the most promising methods to detect when, where, and to what the reader becomes attentive to while processing digital sources. Readers' gazes can be tracked according to predetermined areas of interest (AOIs), which are chosen to address specific research questions and goals (Goldberg & Helfman, 2010; Holmqvist et al., 2011; Jian, 2015; Sung et al., 2015). By selecting the sizes, shapes, and locations of text components on a page of electronic text, AOIs can be constructed to investigate how readers attend to spatial information (e.g., frames, sections, divisions), semantic and functional information (e.g., titles, topic sentences, keywords, hyperlinks, menus, and tabs), or the forms of information representation (e.g., tables, diagrams, charts, images, sounds, videos, and animations). For example, author information on a blog post could be designated a focal AOI to observe whether, and how closely, readers examine source reliability. The reader's control of attention transitions can also be analyzed by calculating the amount of time spent gazing at AOIs and the density of eye fixations in and across them. Along with additional unobtrusive methods such as web tracking, AOI-based eye-tracking could improve interpretation of reader-text interactions in digital media. In addition, eye-tracking can be paired with retrospective verbal protocols, which can offer clues for inferences about why readers fix their attention on, and move across the, AOIs. Most desirably, advancing technology may soon make possible methods of representing a reader's sequential (often nonlinear) attention shifts across AOIs, sites of interest, and even media of interest.

The brief review thus far is meant to clarify our understanding of current methods useful for future inquiries drawing on theories and conceptions of reading across different media contexts. Game-changing methodologies are realized when researchers commit to creativity and criticality in designing, testing, and validating novel adaptations of these existing methodological approaches, as detailed in Table 25.1. Such trials and errors require scientific rigor if we desire to understand the complexities and nuances of media text reading.

Toward a Methodological Advancement in the Study of Reading across Media

An important task in our methodological innovation is to close the gaps we perceive between what we wish to know, what data we actually have at hand, and how we interpret the data (Messick, 1989; Pellegrino, Chudowsky, & Glaser, 2001). As implied in this review of methods of inquiry into media reading, such inferential gaps could be filled in, at least partly, by considering the principles that shape our methodological tasks, especially the tasks of prediction, contextualization, and triangulation.

Prediction

Media environments present novel complexities and uncertainties, so researchers should be able to anticipate how details of task implementation, tool administration, participant observation, and the collection, organization, and analysis of data will interact with such environmental features (Leander, 2008; Murthy, 2008; Williams, Rice, & Rogers, 1988). Because no methodology is perfect, research processes can depart drastically from the original research designs and intentions, and from the "pure" form and content we might assume when we study methodology apart from actual use. Methodological prediction cannot correct missteps that emerge and interact in the actual research process. However, cogent predictions of research processes, informed by relevant theories and methodologies, can help researchers think proactively to anticipate what they might need to do when issues and questions arise. Therefore, making predictions about what might happen when employing specific methods, and about how each method and procedure might influence data collection and interpretation, is a necessary step for researchers.

Particularly important to reading inquiry is theoretical task analysis before the research begins (Veenman, Van Hout-Wolters, & Afflerbach, 2006). Task analysis helps examiners anticipate how reading will begin, go, and end given the task, goal, and setting within a media environment. Through task analysis, researchers can (a) define what counts as focal data, (b) discern how to fit separate data analyses into a cohesive theory, (c) decide how to value contextual information as a source of alternative explanations against known conclusions, and finally, (d) determine an optimal methodological approach. Therefore, a thorough task analysis not only helps researchers make informed predictions for research processes but also prepares them to respond if their data challenges their prior knowledge, beliefs, and assumptions about reading, readers, texts, and environments.

Contextualization

Detailed methodological contextualization can help researchers improve the design of their inquiries into reading in media text environments. Contextualization can be performed in two ways: (a) bringing methods to natural contexts of reading, and (b) accounting for the context in which methods are used in data interpretation. First, because reading is a context-bound practice with particular reader goals (Brown, Collins, & Duguid, 1989), researchers need to contextualize their methodologies when readers work with authentic texts, tasks, and situations. Taking a sociocultural perspective (Cross, 2010; Smagorinsky, 1998), for example, verbal reporting approaches could be reframed in order to gain access to the moment-to-moment processes readers engage in while they conduct authentic, everyday problem-solving tasks (e.g., in-school science projects using the Internet, digital news reading at home, reference searching at a community library). When researchers thus look into readers' thinking or wandering, engagement or indifference, and agreement to or refusal of what texts mean to be, they need to contextualize what they observe in terms of the authentic reading tasks and goals.

Second, data analysis is better situated when researchers report when, where, and how specific methods and procedures were used during the study (Afflerbach, 2000). For example, common criticisms of verbal reporting methodologies concern their validity (e.g., how precisely do verbal reports capture readers' thinking processes?), reliability (e.g., how consistently does what readers say match what they do?), generalizability (e.g., how completely do verbal reports demonstrate consistencies across readers, texts read, and reading tasks?), and authenticity (e.g., how spontaneously do readers report their thinking and actions?). These are valid criticisms that point out threats to research quality that can compromise and otherwise influence the inferences we make from data. Researchers can address them through situated data analysis and reporting of the results—for example, fully disclosing the contexts of verbal reporting (e.g., participants' individual differences, whether goals are given or self-initiated, the scope and boundary of textual choices, task prompting and instruction, researcher-participant relationships, who else other than the focal participants is involved in interactive media environments) and the details of the protocol analysis (e.g., data reduction and segmentation, units of coding and their hierarchies, multilevel coding and qualities of thinking, sequential relations of codes and the flow of thinking, non-codable utterances and the possibility of unnoticed meanings).

Triangulation

Triangulation (Denzin, 1970; Flick, 2004) is a valuable feature of the current body of reading research, as noted in the review of inquiry methods. It usually refers to *data triangulation*, through which data of multiple types are integrated into a coherent body of evidence. Each dataset may yield disparate kinds of information, and they may conflict with each other, depending on whether they are experimental or natural, and qualitative or quantitative. For example, a study could be designed to integrate meanings and insights at the intersection of theoretical task analysis (anticipatory), verbal protocol analysis (exploratory), and measures of reading behaviors and outcomes (confirmatory) (Magliano & Graesser, 1991). The task analysis would offer a framework for predicting reading complexities in a media text environment, the validity of which would later be demonstrated with the verbal report data. Detailed descriptions of the effectiveness of acts of reading and thinking engagement would be produced through the analyses of reading behaviors such as fixation, duration, and sequence of readers' eye gazes, or on-screen navigational moves in a media space (e.g., Sung et al.'s 2015 study on fifth-graders' web-based reading processes integrated analyses of eye movements, screen recordings, and retrospective verbal protocols).

Theoretical triangulation exploiting the intersection of different perspectives and approaches also has potential. For example, different approaches to discourse analysis can be intermingled across the phases of separate data interpretations, as demonstrated in a study of students' peer interactions about multiple digital sources (Cho et al., 2018). An analysis of discourse data from a cognitive approach (Tenbrink, 2015) discusses how readers build mental representations at different phases of understanding (e.g., within-text situation models, intertext models of source relations), their sensemaking processes (e.g., commenting, noticing, elaborating, critiquing, questioning), and any cognitive dissonance they might experience at transitions (e.g., confusion, tension, tentativeness). Another analysis of the same discourse from a social linguistic approach (Bloome & Carter, 2014) offers a nuanced interpretation of how these readers push and pull their ideas and perspectives while collaborating to reason about multiple and contentious digital sources (e.g., through epistemic practices such as building claims, examining relevant evidence, and making appropriate objections). Such dual-layered discourse analysis can demonstrate how the same case may reflect distinctive reader interactions, and how this distinctiveness may enrich a theory-building process (Yin, 2009).

Concluding Remarks

This chapter has provided a review of diverse methods for investigating the reading processes involved in media text environments. It has also offered some notes suggesting approaches to methodological prediction, contextualization, and triangulation that may be useful in future inquiries. Throughout, the chapter has sought to remind us that theory and methodology are symbiotic. We must continue to update our ideas of reading to augment the singular reader-text-task paradigm, and, further, move forward to foreground the multidimensional, complex, and even complicated nature of reading taking place across different media text environments. A paradox we face is that as we build more sophisticated understandings of such reading, we reveal ever more intricate reader-text-task relationships, which the methods we design and choose for our reading inquiry must be able to address. At the same time, thus refining our theories and frameworks allows us to carry out more theory-sensitive, methodologically authentic research. Taking the opportunities that thus arise, we will be better positioned to move the field forward by continuing to test, alternate, and refine our conceptions of reading when it is situated in constantly changing media contexts.

References

Afflerbach, P. (2000). Verbal reports and protocol analysis. In M. L. Kamil, P. B. Mosenthal, P. D. Pearson, & R. Barr (Eds.), *Handbook of reading research* (Vol. 3, pp. 163–179). New York, NY: Routledge.

Afflerbach, P., & Johnston, P. (1984). On the use of verbal reports in reading research. *Journal of Reading Behavior, 16*, 307–322.

Bakshy, E., Messing, S., & Adamic, L. A. (2015). Exposure to ideologically diverse news and opinion on Facebook. *Science, 348*(6239), 1130–1132.

Baron, C. (2016). Using embedded visual coding to support contextualization of historical texts. *American Educational Research Journal, 53*(3), 516–540.

Barzilai, S., & Zohar, A. (2012). Epistemic thinking in action: Evaluating and integrating online sources. *Cognition and Instruction, 30*(1), 39–85.

Biedert, R., Dengel, A., Buscher, G., & Vartan, A. (2012). Reading and estimating gaze on smart phones. In *Proceedings of the 2012 Symposium on Eye Tracking Research and Applications* (pp. 385–388). New York, NY: ACM.

Bloome, D., & Carter, S. P. (2014). Microethnographic discourse analysis. In P. Albers, T. Holbrook, & A. S. Flint (Eds.), *New methods of literacy research* (pp. 3–18). New York, NY: Routledge.

Boucheix, J.-M., Lowe, R. K., Putri, D. K., & Groff, J. (2013). Cueing animations: Dynamic signaling aids information extraction and comprehension. *Learning and Instruction, 25*, 71–84.

Brand-Gruwel, S., Kammerer, Y., van Meeuwen, L., & van Gog, T. (2017). Source evaluation of domain experts and novices during web search. *Journal of Computer Assisted Learning, 33*(3), 234–251.

Bråten, I., Britt, M. A., Strømsø, H. I., & Rouet, J. F. (2011). The role of epistemic beliefs in the comprehension of multiple expository texts: Toward an integrated model. *Educational Psychologist, 46*(1), 48–70.

Britt, M. A., Goldman, S. R., & Rouet, J.-F. (2013). *Reading: From words to multiple texts*. New York, NY: Routledge.

Brown, J. S., Collins, A., & Duguid, P. (1989). Situated cognition and the culture of learning. *Educational Researcher, 18*(1), 32–42.

Buckingham, D. (2006). Defining digital literacy: What do young people need to know about digital media? *Digital Kompetanse, 1*(4), 263–276.

Bulger, M. E., Mayer, R. E., & Metzger, M. J. (2014). Knowledge and processes that predict proficiency in digital literacy. *Reading and Writing, 27*, 1567–1583.

Cho, B.-Y. (2014). Competent adolescent readers' use of Internet reading strategies: A think-aloud study. *Cognition and Instruction, 32*(3), 253–289.

Cho, B.-Y., Afflerbach, P., & Han, H. (2018). Strategic processing in accessing, comprehending, and using multiple sources. In J. Braasch, I. Bråten, & M. McCrudden (Eds.), *Handbook of multiple source use* (pp. 133–150). London, UK: Routledge.

Cho, B.-Y., Kucan, L., Rainey, E., & Han, H. (June, 2018). *Historical learning through multisource text inquiry: A study of middle school learners using an online repository of historical sources*. Paper presented at the 6th International Workshop on Advanced Learning Sciences, Pittsburgh, PA.

Cho, B.-Y., Woodward, L., & Li, D. (2018). Epistemic processing when adolescents read online: A verbal protocol analysis of more and less successful online readers. *Reading Research Quarterly, 53*(2), 197–221.

Cho, B.-Y., Woodward, L., Li, D., & Barlow, W. (2017). Examining adolescents' strategic processing during online reading with a question-generating task. *American Educational Research Journal, 54*(4), 691–724.

Cross, R. (2010). Language teaching as sociocultural activity: Rethinking language teacher practice. *Modern Language Journal, 94*(3), 434–452.

Cutrell, E., & Guan, Z. (2007). What are you looking for? An eye-tracking study of information usage in web search. In *Proceedings of the SIGCHI Conference on Human Factors in Computing Systems* (pp. 407–416). New York, NY: ACM.

Denzin, N. K. (1970). *The research act: A theoretical introduction to sociological methods*. Chicago, IL: Aldine.

Ferguson, L. E., Bråten, I., & Strømsø, H. I. (2012). Epistemic cognition when students read multiple documents containing conflicting scientific evidence: A think-aloud study. *Learning and Instruction, 22*, 103–120.

Fitzgerald, M. S., & Palincsar, A. S. (2017). Peer-mediated reading and writing in a digital multimodal environment. *Reading & Writing Quarterly, 33*(3), 309–326.

Flick, U. (2004). Triangulation in qualitative research. In U. Flick, E. von Kardorff, & I. Steinke (Eds.), *A companion to qualitative research* (pp. 178–183). London, UK: SAGE.

Gerjets, P., Kammerer, Y., & Werner, B. (2011). Measuring spontaneous and instructed evaluation processes during web search: Integrating concurrent thinking-aloud protocols and eye-tracking data. *Learning and Instruction, 21*, 220–231.

Glaser, M., Garsoffky, B., & Schwan, S. (2012). What do we learn from docutainment? Processing hybrid television documentaries. *Learning and Instruction, 22*, 37–46.

Goldberg, J. H., & Helfman, J. I. (2010). Comparing information graphics: A critical look at eye tracking. In *Proceedings of the 3rd BELIV '10 Workshop: Beyond time and errors: Novel evaluation methods for information visualization* (pp. 71–78). New York, NY: ACM. doi:10.1145/2110192.2110203

Goldman, S. R. (2010). Literacy in the digital world: Comprehending and learning from multiple sources. In M. G. McKeown & L. Kucan with Lawless, K. A., Gomez, K. W., Braasch, J., MacLeod, S., & Manning, F. Eds., *Bringing reading research to life* (pp. 257–284). New York, NY: Guilford Press.

Goldman, S. R., Braasch, J., Wiley, J., Graesser, A. C., & Brodowinska, K. (2012). Comprehending and learning from internet sources: Processing patterns of better and poorer learners. *Reading Research Quarterly, 47*(4), 356–381.

Greene, J. A., Muis, K. R., & Pieschl, S. (2010). The role of epistemic beliefs in students' self-regulated learning with computer-based learning environments: Conceptual and methodological issues. *Educational Psychologist, 45*(4), 245–257.

Greene, J. A., Yu, S. B., & Copeland, D. Z. (2014). Measuring critical components of digital literacy and their relationships with learning. *Computers & Education, 76*, 55–69.

Greenhow, C., Robelia, B., & Hughs, J. E. (2009). Web 2.0 and classroom research: What path should we take now? *Educational Researcher, 38*(4), 246–259.

Group, N. L. (1996). A pedagogy of multiliteracies: Designing social futures. *Harvard Educational Review, 66*(1), 60–93.

Guo, Q., & Agichtein, E. (2012). Beyond dwell time: Estimating document relevance from cursor movements and other post-click searcher behavior. In *Proceedings of the 21st International Conference on World Wide Web* (pp. 569–578). New York, NY: ACM.

Hillesund, T. (2010). Digital reading spaces: How expert readers handle books, the Web, and electronic paper. *First Monday, 15*(4–5), 1–16.

Hofer, B. K. (2004). Epistemological understanding as a metacognitive process: Thinking aloud during online searching. *Educational Psychologist, 39*(1), 43–55.

Hollis, R. B., & Was, C. A. (2016). Mind wandering, control failures, and social media distractions in online learning. *Learning and Instruction, 42*, 104–112.

Holmqvist, K., Nyström, M., Andersson, R., Dewhurst, R., Jarodzka, H., & van deWeijer, J. (2011). *Eye tracking: A comprehensive guide to methods and measures.* Oxford, UK: Oxford University Press.

Ikuenobe, P. (2003). Optimizing reasonableness, critical thinking, and cyberspace. *Educational Philosophy and Theory, 35*(4), 407–424.

Jian, Y.-C. (2015). Fourth graders' cognitive processes and learning strategies for reading illustrated biology texts: Eye movement measurements. *Reading Research Quarterly, 51*(1), 93–109.

Johnson, A. M., Azevedo, R., & D'Mello, S. K. (2011). The temporal and dynamic nature of self-regulatory processes during independent and externally assisted hypermedia learning. *Cognition and Instruction, 29*(2), 471–504.

Just, M. A., & Carpenter, P. A. (1980). A theory of reading: From eye fixations to comprehension. *Psychological Review, 87*(4), 329–354.

Kesler, T., Tinio, P., & Nolan, B. T. (2016). What's our position? A critical media literacy study of popular culture websites with eighth-grade special education students. *Reading & Writing Quarterly, 32*(1), 1–26.

Kiili, C., Laurinen, L., Marttunen, M., & Leu, D. J. (2012). Working on understanding during collaborative online reading. *Journal of Literacy Research, 44*(4), 448–483.

Kiili, C., Leu, D. J., Marttunen, M., Hautala, J., & Leppänen, P. (2018). Exploring early adolescents' evaluation of academic and commercial online resources related to health. *Reading and Writing, 31*, 533–557.

Kruger, J.-L., & Steyn, F. (2013). Subtitles and eye tracking: Reading and performance. *Reading Research Quarterly, 49*(1), 105–120.

Kwon, S., Cha, M., & Jung, K. (2017). Rumor detection over varying time windows. *PLoS One, 12*(1), 1–19.

Lankshear, C., & Knobel, M. (2003). *New literacies: Changing knowledge and classroom learning.* Buckingham, England: Open University Press.

Lankshear, C., Peters, M., & Knobel, M. (2000). Information, knowledge and learning: Some issues facing epistemology and education in a digital age. *Journal of Philosophy of Education, 34*(1), 17–39.

Lawless, K. A., Brown, S. W., Mills, R., & Mayall, H. J. (2003). Knowledge, interest, recall and navigation: A look at hypertext processing. *Journal of Literacy Research, 35*(3), 911–934.

Lawless, K. A., Schrader, P. G., & Mayall, H. J. (2007). Acquisition of information online: Knowledge, navigation and learning outcomes. *Journal of Literacy Research, 39*(3), 289–306.

Leander, K. M. (2008). Toward a connective ethnography of online/offline literacy networks. In J. Coiro, M. Knobel, C. Lankshear, & D. Leu (Eds.), *Handbook of research on new literacies* (pp. 33–65). New York, NY: Routledge.

Leu, D. J., Kinzer, C. K., Coiro, J., Castek, J., & Henry, L. A. (2013). New literacies: A dual-level theory of the changing nature of literacy, instruction, and assessment. In D. E. Alvermann, N. J. Unrau, & R. B. Ruddell (Eds.), *Theoretical models and processes of reading* (6th ed., pp. 1150–1181). Newark, DE: International Reading Association.

Lewis, C., & Fabos, B. (2005). Instant Messaging, literacies, and social identities. *Reading Research Quarterly, 40*(4), 470–501.

Lipponen, L., Rahikainen, M., Lallimo, J., & Hakkarainen, K. (2003). Patterns of participation and discourse in elementary students' computer-supported collaborative learning. *Learning and Instruction, 13*, 487–509.

Magliano, J. P., & Graesser, A. C. (1991). A three-pronged method for studying inference generation in literary text. *Poetics, 20*(3), 193–232.

Marsh, J. (2011). Young children's literacy practices in a virtual world: Establishing an online interaction order. *Reading Research Quarterly, 46*(2), 101–108.

Mason, L., Ariasi, N., & Boldrin, A. (2011). Epistemic beliefs in action: Spontaneous reflections about knowledge and knowing during online information searching and their influence on learning. *Learning and Instruction, 21*, 137–151.

Mason, L., Tornatora, M. C., & Pluchino, P. (2015). Integrative processing of verbal and graphical information during re-reading predicts learning from illustrated text: An eye-movement study. *Reading and Writing, 28*, 851–872.

McEneaney, J. E., Li, L., Allen, K., & Guzniczak, L. (2009). Stance, navigation, and reader response in expository hypertext. *Journal of Literacy Research, 41*, 1–45.

McNamara, D. S., & Magliano, J. (2009). Toward a comprehensive model of comprehension. *The Psychology of Learning and Motivation, 51*, 297–384.

Mercier, J., & Frederiksen, C. H. (2018). Individual differences in graduate students' help-seeking process in using a computer coach in problem-based learning. *Learning and Instruction, 17*, 184–203.

Messick, S. (1989). Validity. In R. L. Linn (Ed.), *Educational measurement* (3rd ed., pp. 13–103). London, UK: Collier Macmillan.

Metzger, M. J., & Flanagin, A. J. (2013). Credibility and trust of information in online environments: The use of cognitive heuristics. *Journal of Pragmatics, 59*, 210–220.

Miller, B., & Record, I. (2013). Justified belief in a digital age: On the epistemic implications of secret Internet technologies. *Episteme, 10*(2), 117–134.

Minguela, M., Solé, I., & Pieschl, S. (2015). Flexible self-regulated reading as a cue for deep comprehension: Evidence from online and offline measures. *Reading and Writing, 28*, 721–744.

Mocanu, D., Rossi, L., Zhang, Q., Karsai, M., & Quattrociocchi, W. (2015). Collective attention in the age of (mis)information. *Computers in Human Behavior, 51*, 1198–1204.

Mosborg, S. (2002). Speaking of history: How adolescents use their knowledge of history in reading the daily news. *Cognition and Instruction, 20*(3), 323–358.

Murthy, D. (2008). Digital ethnography: An examination of the use of new technologies for social research. *Sociology, 42*(5), 837–855.

Pan, B., Hembrooke, H. A., Gay, G. K., Granka, L. A., Feusner, M. K., & Newman, J. K. (2004). The determinants of web page viewing behavior: An eye-tracking study. In *Proceedings of the 2004 Symposium on Eye Tracking Research & Applications* (pp. 147–154). New York, NY: ACM.

Paul, S. A., & Morris, M. R. (2011). Sensemaking in collaborative web search. *Human-Computer Interaction, 26* (1–2), 72–122.

Pellegrino, J., Chudowsky, N., & Glaser, R. (2001). *Knowing what students know: The science and design of educational assessment*. Committee on the Foundations of Assessment, Center for Education, Division on Behavioral and Social Sciences and Education, National Research Council. Washington, DC: National Academy Press.

Pressley, M., & Afflerbach, P. (1995). *Verbal protocols of reading: The nature of constructively responsive reading*. Hillsdale, NJ: Lawrence Erlbaum.

Rayner, K. (2009). Eye movements and attention in reading, scene perception, and visual search. *The Quarterly Journal of Experimental Psychology, 62*(8), 1457–1506.

Renear, A. H., & Palmer, C. L. (2009). Strategic reading, ontologies, and the future of scientific publishing. *Science, 325*(5942), 828–832.

Rouet, J.-F. (2006). *The skills of document use: From text comprehension to web-based learning*. Mahwah, NJ: Lawrence Erlbaum.

Salmerón, L., & García, V. (2011). Reading skills and children's navigation strategies in hypertext. *Computers in Human Behavior, 27*, 1143–1151. doi:10.1016/j.chb.2010.12.008

Salmerón, L., Naumann, J., García, V., & Fajardo, I. (2017). Scanning and deep processing of information in hypertext: An eye tracking and cued retrospective think-aloud study. *Journal of Computer Assisted Learning, 33*(3), 222–233.

Simon, J. (2010). The entanglement of trust and knowledge on the Web. *Ethics and Information Technology, 12* (4), 343–355.

Smagorinsky, P. (1998). Thinking and speech and protocol analysis. *Mind, Culture, and Activity, 5*(3), 157–177.

Song, K., & Cho, B.-Y. (2019). Exploring bilingual adolescents' translanguaging strategies during online reading. *International Journal of Bilingual Education and Bilingualism*. doi:10.1080/13670050.2018.1497008

Sung, Y.-T., Wu, M.-D., Chen, C.-K., & Chang, K.-E. (2015). Examining the online reading behavior and performance of fifth-graders: Evidence from eye-movement data. *Frontiers in Psychology*. doi:10.3389/fpsyg.2015.00665

Tenbrink, T. (2015). Cognitive discourse analysis: Accessing cognitive representations and processes through language data. *Language and Cognition, 7*, 98–137.

Trevors, G., Feyzi-Behnagh, R., Azevedo, R., & Bouchet, F. (2016). Self-regulated learning processes vary as a function of epistemic beliefs and contexts: Mixed method evidence from eye tracking and concurrent and retrospective reports. *Learning and Instruction, 42*, 31–46.

Van Gog, T., Paas, F., van Merriënboer, J., & Witte, P. (2005). Uncovering the problem-solving process: Cued retrospective reporting versus concurrent and retrospective reporting. *Journal of Experimental Psychology: Applied, 11*(4), 237–244.

Veenman, M. V. J. (2005). The assessment of metacognitive skills: What can be learned from multi-method designs? In C. Artelt & B. Moschner (Eds.), *Lernstrategien und metakognition: Implikationen fur forschung und praxis* (pp. 77–99). Munster, Germany: Waxman.

Veenman, M. V. J., Van Hout-Wolters, B. H. A. M., & Afflerbach, P. (2006). Metacognition and learning: Conceptual and methodological considerations. *Metacognition & Learning, 1*, 3–14.

Williams, F., Rice, R. E., & Rogers, E. M. (1988). *Research methods and the new media*. New York, NY: The Free Press.

Wopereis, I., & van Merriënboer, J. (2011). Evaluating text-based information on the World Wide Web. *Learning and Instruction, 21*, 232–237.

Yin, R. K. (2009). *Case study research: Design and methods* (4th ed.). Thousand Oaks, CA: SAGE.

Zhang, S., & Duke, N. K. (2008). Strategies for Internet reading with different reading purposes: A descriptive study of twelve good Internet readers. *Journal of Literacy Research, 40*, 128–162.

26

How Can Neuroscience Bridge Gaps in Reading Research?

Kimberly G. Noble and Katrina R. Simon

As neuroscientists, we are often asked to explain what our methods offer, above and beyond existing tools. Brain imaging is far costlier than teacher surveys, paper-and-pencil measures, or computerized assessments. Is this cost justified? And, beyond the cost, what are we really learning by employing neuroscience techniques? Is there scientific or other value to understanding the neural underpinnings of typical reading development, reading impairment, and achievement gaps more broadly?

In the context of these questions, there are many reasons to continue to pursue research using neuroscience methods. Early work investigating the neural underpinnings of reading provided critical insights into the structural and functional circuitry involved in reading development, and how this circuitry goes awry in cases of reading impairment. However, today's neuroscientific insights go far beyond simply elaborating the "neural correlates" of reading development and impairment. Here, we argue that neuroscience provides a means for researchers to get "under the hood" to study reading development in a way that would be impossible through behavioral measures alone. Three key aspects of the neuroscience of reading highlight the novel and generative understanding that this methodology can provide:

(1) Neuroscience may shed light on mechanistic differences that would be undetectable through behavioral investigations alone.
(2) Neuroscience may allow for early prediction of impairments in skills, such as reading, that cannot be measured until children are older.
(3) Neuroscience may provide compelling evidence for policymakers, educators, and other stakeholders, providing an impetus for effecting change.

Below, we discuss each of these in turn.

Neuroscience May Elucidate Mechanistic Differences that Behavioral Techniques Cannot

In some cases, similar behavioral phenotypes may be the product of different underlying neural structural or functional characteristics. For example, several lines of research have suggested that neuroscience methods may be more sensitive to socioeconomic differences than behavioral methods. This is important, to the extent that these neural differences provide information that is meaningful in interpreting behavioral skill.

For instance, in one study, we recruited a group of children who were at-risk for reading impairment, and invited them to complete a reading task while we imaged their brains (Noble, Wolmetz, Ochs, Farah, & McCandliss, 2006). We found that children who were struggling with reading in the context of family socioeconomic disadvantage showed *typical* brain-behavior relationships. In contrast, children who were struggling despite the access to resources of more socioeconomically advantaged environments showed *atypical* brain-behavior relationships. This suggested that the latter group's difficulties were perhaps more likely to be rooted in atypical neurobiological development, whereas the former group's difficulties may have been rooted in low levels of home-based reading exposure and/or high-quality school-based reading instruction. In other work investigating the neural basis of selective attention, researchers instructed children to pay attention to one aurally-presented story, while simultaneously ignoring another (Stevens, Lauinger, & Neville, 2009). The authors found that, while all children performed equivalently well on comprehension questions about the target story's content, children's neural responses varied as a function of family socioeconomic background. Specifically, children from more socioeconomically disadvantaged backgrounds showed less evidence of neural suppression of the irrelevant story – suggesting that, in the context of disadvantage, it may be more challenging to focus and ignore distractions. In both of these studies, neuroscience provided more information about the ways children process information than would have been available through behavioral assessments alone. Put another way, neuroscience provides insights into *mechanisms*, and, as discussed below, these mechanisms may ultimately be quite powerful in predicting trajectories of achievement, particularly when they are triangulated with information gleaned from other sources or methodologies.

Neuroscience May Allow for Early Prediction of Reading Impairments

The second line of evidence supporting the use of neuroscience derives from the fact that neuroscience approaches to examining reading development may yield "biomarkers" – that is, biological indices that predict subsequent cognitive or behavioral development (Pavlakis, Noble, Pavlakis, Ali, & Frank, 2014). Such biomarkers could be put into place for early screening of reading impairments or other potential cognitive difficulties, long before it would be possible to assess children behaviorally on these skills.

For instance, Molfese (2000) showed nearly two decades ago that brain activity recorded at birth predicted, with over 80% accuracy, which infants would be characterized as dyslexic, poor readers, or typically-developing readers eight years later. More recently, researchers have used neuroscience methods (in this case, structural magnetic resonance imaging (MRI) and diffusion tensor imaging (DTI)) to examine variations in brain development between kindergarten and grade 3 (Myers et al., 2014). Increases in volume of two white matter clusters uniquely predicted reading outcomes over and above family history, socioeconomic background, and baseline cognitive and pre-literacy measures. In another prospective, longitudinal study – in this case focusing specifically on children identified with dyslexia – children's brain activation pattern during phonological processing predicted, with over 90% accuracy, which children would show improved reading skills 2.5 years later (Hoeft et al., 2011). In contrast, behavioral measures, including widely used and standardized assessments of reading and language, were at chance at predicting children's improvement. Other work has also shown that brain function in pre-instruction children with a familial risk of reading impairment (i.e., at least one first-degree relative self-identified as dyslexic) predicted reading ability five years later, whereas early behavioral measures did not (Maurer, Bucher, Brem, Benz, & Brandeis, 2009). Finally, recent work has shown that, among a large sample of children referred to a clinic for learning difficulties, whole-brain structural imaging was able to classify children into one of four distinct cognitive profiles, whereas children's cognitive profiles were not predicted by diagnosis or referral reason (Astle, Bathelt, CALM Team, & Holmes, 2019).

Of course, historically, reading impairment has been diagnosed *after* a child undergoes reading instruction. Yet, taken together, the above studies suggest that neural structure and function may serve as sensitive early biomarkers that have the power to predict subsequent reading trajectories, before formal instruction begins. Indeed, brain-based classification may be more useful than standardized reading and language measures or clinical diagnostic criteria, both in predicting outcomes and, perhaps, in guiding interventional strategies. For example, reading remediation has been shown to ameliorate dysfunctional neural mechanisms in children with dyslexia, and these neural changes have been correlated with changes in behavior (Keller & Just, 2009; Romeo et al., 2018; Temple et al., 2003). In another study of a math tutoring intervention, baseline neuroimaging measures predicted improvement in response to the tutoring program, whereas baseline math scores, IQ, and working memory did not (Supekar et al., 2013).

As with any diagnostic measure used to predict outcomes or inform intervention, it is important to consider how the results of brain-based classification align with those gathered using other methods or criteria. In sum, if neuroscience tools can be useful for predicting future reading impairment, it may be possible to screen and implement targeted early intervention that could alleviate the risk of reading impairment. Furthermore, paired with more traditional or standardized measures of children's reading abilities and skills, neuroscience techniques may allow for early tracking of the efficacy of interventional approaches.

Neuroscience May Provide Compelling Evidence for Stakeholders

Finally, empirical evidence suggests that laypeople find neuroscience data highly compelling. While environmental influences on cognitive development or school achievement, such as socioeconomic status, may seem obvious, the fact that such influences are reflected in our *brains* – our physical selves – is, for many, more captivating. Why is that? On the one hand, any rational person would expect that school achievement would reflect function of the brain and not, say, function of the kidney. On the other hand, knowing how experience helps to shape the very structure and function of our brains provides a window into our personal and societal development that is rarely accessible through other kinds of metrics. Such glimpses into ourselves are appealing to the public, and indeed, neuroscience findings relevant for education and social policy have been covered extensively by the popular media (Hayasaki, 2016; The Economist, 2018).

One frequently cited study investigated participants' responses when they were given two otherwise identical explanations of psychological phenomena – one of which included neuroscience information, while the other did not (Weisberg, Keil, Goodstein, Rawson, & Gray, 2008). Non-experts judged that explanations with neuroscience information – even when that information was logically irrelevant – were more satisfying than explanations without such information. Some scholars have derided this phenomenon as "the seductive allure of neuroscience." Indeed, scientific, journalistic, and policy communities have a responsibility to mitigate or prevent misunderstandings or misuse of neuroscience data by ensuring the integrity and accuracy of the information and related messaging they share. That is, in light of the numerous competing demands for the attention of policymakers, practitioners, and educators, we argue that, when neuroscience helps to underscore scientific findings that are relevant for education practices, public policy, or other endeavors that are beneficial to society, then their use is justified. For example, a great deal of research centers on best practices for screening and intervention among children with reading impairment. If research employing the tools of neuroscience naturally garners increased attention to these issues, then advocates would be well served to capitalize on this attention to help spark conversations about educational intervention and policy. Further, neuroscience studies may be more likely to capture the attention and interest of teachers, parents, and school administrators, making evidence-based interventions more likely to be accessible to a greater number of students.

Conclusions

In conclusion, we posit that neuroscience research has the power to bridge important gaps between research and practice in the field of reading development. Specifically, neuroscience sheds light on mechanistic differences that are frequently undetectable through behavioral investigations alone, and these neuroscientific insights are often predictive of subsequent growth (or failure) in reading skill. Finally, by capturing the attention of policymakers, educators, parents, and teachers, neuroscience has the power to cast a spotlight on critical issues inherent in reading education and remediation.

References

Astle, D. E., Bathelt, J., CALM Team, & Holmes, J. (2019). Remapping the cognitive and neural profiles of children who struggle at school. *Developmental Science*, 22(1), e12747. doi:10.1111/desc.12747

The Economist. (2018, May). Does growing up poor harm brain development? *The Economist*. Retrieved from www.economist.com/united-states/2018/05/03/does-growing-up-poor-harm-brain-development

Hayasaki, E. (2016, August). How poverty affects the brain. *Newsweek*. Retrieved from www.newsweek.com/2016/09/02/how-poverty-affects-brains-493239.html

Hoeft, F., McCandliss, B. D., Black, J. M., Gantman, A., Zakerani, N., Hulme, C., Lyytinen, H., Whitfield-Gabrielie, S., Glover, G., Reiss, A. L., & Gabrieli, J. D. (2011). Neural systems predicting long-term outcome in dyslexia. *Proceedings of the National Academy of Sciences of the United States of America*, 108(1), 361–366. doi:10.1073/pnas.1008950108

Keller, T. A., & Just, M. A. (2009). Altering cortical connectivity: Remediation-induced changes in the white matter of poor readers. *Neuron*, 64(5), 624–631. doi:10.1016/j.neuron.2009.10.018

Maurer, U., Bucher, K., Brem, S., Benz, R., & Brandeis, D. (2009). Neurophysiology in preschool improves behavioral prediction of reading ability throughout primary school. *Biological Psychiatry*, 66(4), 341–348. doi:10.1016/j.biopsych.2009.02.031

Molfese, D. L. (2000). Predicting Dyslexia at 8 years of age using neonatal brain responses. *Brain and Language*, 72(3), 238–245. doi:https://doi.org/10.1006/brln.2000.2287

Myers, C. A., Vandermosten, M., Farris, E. A., Hancock, R., Gimenez, P., Black, J. M., Castro, B., Drahos, M., Tumber, M., Hendren, R. L., Hulme, C., & Hoeft, F. (2014). White matter morphometric changes uniquely predict children's reading acquisition. *Psychological Science*, 25(10), 1870–1883. doi: https://doi.org/10.1177/0956797614544511

Noble, K. G., Wolmetz, M. E., Ochs, L. G., Farah, M. J., & McCandliss, B. D. (2006). Brain-behavior relationships in reading acquisition are modulated by socioeconomic factors. *Developmental Science*, 9(6), 642–654. doi:https://doi.org/10.1111/j.1467-7687.2006.00542.x

Pavlakis, A. E., Noble, K., Pavlakis, S. G., Ali, N., & Frank, Y. (2014). Brain imaging and electrophysiology biomarkers: Is there a role in poverty and education outcome research? *Pediatric Neurology*, 52(4), 383–388. doi:10.1016/j.pediatrneurol.2014.11.005

Romeo, R. R., Christodoulou, J. A., Halverson, K. K., Murtagh, J., Cyr, A. B., Schimmel, C., Chang, P., Hook, P., & Gabrieli, J. (2018). Socioeconomic status and reading disability: Neuroanatomy and plasticity in response to intervention. *Cerebral Cortex*, 28(7), 2297–2312. doi:10.1093/cercor/bhx131

Stevens, C., Lauinger, B., & Neville, H. (2009). Differences in the neural mechanisms of selective attention in children from different socioeconomic backgrounds: An event-related brain potential study. *Developmental Science*, 12(4), 634–646. doi:10.1111/j.1467-7687.2009.00807

Supekar, K., Swigart, A. G., Tenison, C., Jolles, D. D., Rosenberg-Lee, M., Fuchs, L., & Menon, V. (2013). Neural predictors of individual differences in response to math tutoring in primary-grade school children.

Proceedings of the National Academy of Sciences of the United States of America, 110(20), 8230–8235. doi:10.1073/pnas.1222154110

Temple, E., Deutsch, G. K., Poldrack, R. A., Miller, S. L., Tallal, P., Merzenich, M. M., & Gabrieli, J. D. (2003). Neural deficits in children with dyslexia ameliorated by behavioral remediation: Evidence from functional MRI. *Proceedings of the National Academy of Sciences of the United States of America, 100*(5), 2860–2865. doi:10.1073/pnas.0030098100

Weisberg, D. S., Keil, F. C., Goodstein, J., Rawson, E., & Gray, J. R. (2008). The seductive allure of neuroscience explanations. *Journal of Cognitive Neuroscience, 20*(3), 470–477. doi:10.1162/jocn.2008.20040

27
Qualitative Case Study Methodology Driven by Sociocultural Perspectives

Carmen M. Martínez-Roldán

My inquiry into bilingual children's use of language(s) to make meaning of texts involves the combination of already familiar methods, in a research design driven by sociocultural theoretical tenets. In this chapter, I describe the methods I have found most useful in examining bilingual learning and literacy among culturally diverse students, with a focus on reading as a mediated cultural activity. While my approach could be described as a traditional qualitative case study design that employs ethnographic methods, Critical Discourse Analysis (CDA), and narrative analysis, it also draws on a sociocultural approach influenced by Vygotsky's concept of mediation and by Cultural-Historical Activity Theory (CHAT). My incorporation of this theoretical framework is characterized by movement back and forth, from analysis that foregrounds the role of cultural tools in individual learning, to analysis of learning as an activity system. In some respects, this movement resembles Rogoff's (2003) description of the three levels of analysis involved in sociocultural research that focuses on learning, as changes of participation in sociocultural practices—the individual, the interpersonal, and the cultural-institutional level—in which the researcher may foreground any of these while keeping the other two levels in the background. More recently, my efforts to widen the lenses of analysis has expanded my research scope to include more than one activity system, following Engeström and Sannino's (2011) theorization of expansive learning, while still anchoring the findings in cases of bilingual learning and literacy of immigrant and bilingual Latino students.

I preface this description by bringing to the forefront a key axiological assumption that has informed my work and that is embedded in a qualitative research paradigm that embraces critical perspectives, namely, that research has the potential to generate social change and combat inequalitites. Qualitative and interpretive methods emerged out of researchers' concerns for the lives and perspectives of people in society whose voices were absent in the research being conducted (Erickson, 1986). From a critical sociocultural stance (Lewis, Enciso, & Moje, 2007), I embrace this concern in my research through a commitment to uncover and transform contexts for learning that stifle bilingual students' potential, and document those literacy engagements that support students' learning and identities. The research methods described here have enabled me to address three main concerns: first, the use of prescriptive curricula that prioritize bilingual students' oral English language proficiency while relegating reading comprehension and more engaging literacy learning to the upper grades; second, the tendency to overlook or dismiss the role of students' home-based language(s) in their academic learning; and third, the low expectations and deficit perspectives still seen in schools, in scholarly discussions, and in society's discourses regarding immigrants, Latino students, and children from working class communities.

Overview of the Methodology, Key Assumptions, and Goals

This methodology is theoretically grounded; therefore, this discussion is organized around some principles from sociocultural theories that have driven my methods and analysis over the past 20 years. In particular, I highlight some of the elements addressed when we shift the unit of analysis from the individual to the activity system in which the individual engages in learning. Using CHAT constructs, the description of methods refers to the *subject* (the actors as agents), the *tools*, the *community*, the *roles*, and the *rules* that have organized the reading activities studied: elements that come together around a partially shared motive or *object* that drives participants' actions (Engeström, 1987, 2001; Leontyev, 1979/1981). Changes in any of these elements play a role in students' learning. The theoretical principles outlined, below, also point to changes in my research foci: as my theoretical frameworks have expanded, so too, have my research questions and, in turn, the scope of my reseach or unit of analysis.

From the Individual Interacting with Tools to the Activity System

A key principle guiding my methodology is the role of mediation in learning, which addresses the interplay between individual agency and society (Moll, 2014; Vygotsky, 1978, 1987; Wertsch, 1985). My methods have focused on analyzing and documenting children's learning as mediated by material and psychological *tools*: language (Spanish/English), texts, interactions (with peers and adults), and ideologies (ideological beliefs about languages and about gender issues) (e.g., Martínez-Roldán, 2003, 2005a, 2005b). In my study findings, I view children's agentic roles in appropriating or rejecting the cultural tools available to them, as equally salient.

In attempting to understand young bilingual children's ways of approaching and interpreting texts, I have designed longitudinal classroom-based studies in which the learners interact with a variety of texts, either as part of regular instruction or in spaces created by the researcher, such as after-school programs. I have focused on children's literature (fiction and expository texts) and the role of bilingual students' home language as they interpret and discuss texts—specifically, the ways in which emergent bilingual students' linguistic repertoire serves as a resource for meaning-making and for supporting their academic identities (Martínez-Roldán, 2003). This interest in addressing readers' interpretations of texts from a transactional perspective (Goodman, 1994; Rosenblatt, 1995), that highlights meaning-making led me to the following question at the outset of my research journey: What is the nature of the talk in which second grade bilingual Spanish/English students engage as they discuss children's literature in small groups? In a study examining this "nature of the talk," I focused on the following subquestions: What types of responses do students have to literature in small group discussions? What content and issues(s) are discussed by the children? In keeping with an emic perspective, the small groups in this study were called *pláticas literarias*, a name generated by the teacher and the children together, to refer to literature circles or small group discussions. In a second study, I organized the reading events differently, in a one-on-one reading setting, to conduct miscue analysis and research (Goodman, Watson, & Burke, 2005). I sought to answer the following question: How is second-language learners' comprehension of expository texts in their second language (English) enhanced or impeded by discussing their meanings of texts in their first language (Spanish)? While the two settings had different purposes, reading in small groups offered many more opportunities for horizontal learning, with peer mediation playing a critical role in supporting students' meaning-making. The one-on-one work, however, provided important insights into, and opportunities for, targeted instruction. Over time, I have moved back and forth between the two settings, leaning more toward research in small-group reading events.

In this iteration of qualitative case methodology (Dyson & Genishi, 2005), driven by sociocultural historical tenets, I have always used purposive samples. I have chosen classrooms where I could learn about, or explore, bilingual children's potential for meaning-making of texts–classrooms, where they could use their linguistic repertoires as part of the activity of learning. The *object* or motive of my research activity has been bilingual children's learning or, at times, bilingual teachers' and teacher candidates' learning. I have always selected children from working class communities or families, given my interest in challenging low expectations for immigrants, Latinos, and working class children. The young, participants in my studies, have always been considered as bringing a variety of intellectual and cultural resources to the reading process, in particular linguistic resources. At times, the students have become the *subjects* of the activity system, not in the experimental sense of the word, but in the CHAT sense of becoming agentive actors who lead the activity. The research design has not only documented these shifts in students' position within the studies but also supported them.

Given my concern regarding reading curricula that narrows the kinds of texts and kinds of discussions around texts that young bilingual children are often expected to engage with in schools, the books I select move away from the leveled (basic skills–oriented) texts that tend to be at the center of primary classrooms' reading instruction. My selection of books considers whole texts as opposed to fragments of texts, or texts in which the language has been simplified. I select children's literature, available in English and Spanish, with the potential to support students as critical readers on a variety of topics; sometimes I have also used digital texts. Whenever possible, the students' interests are explored before the selection of texts. In one study this process led to a selection of books that addressed issues related to family, language, race, and gender, in which the children had shown interest (Martínez-Roldán, 2005b). In another study, the selected books focused on animals the children wanted to learn about to explore the concept of habitats. With regard to the dimension of *roles* in the classroom activity system, I strive whenever possible to include the participants in the selection of text topics, bridging pedagogical practice and research. The goal is to expand opportunities for the children to talk about books as well as increase opportunities for data collection and triangulation.

These aims led me, in one classroom, to organize with the teacher, 75 small-group literature discussions of 20–40 minutes each, all audio and video recorded; years later, in another classroom, I organized 70 small groups that read and talked about a variety of texts focusing on habitats. The groups were organized by students' interests rather than by reading proficiency. With regard to *rules* for language use and participation, the groups in the first study were initially organized according to language dominance; eventually, however, the groups were linguistically heterogeneous, and students could use whatever language they felt more comfortable with. In other studies, the use of the minoritized language was purposefully privileged, but learners were able to engage in translanguaging using the linguistic resources that were at their disposal to make meaning of texts and participate in literacy and science learning events (Martínez-Roldán, 2015).

As I believe that we are not independent from our inquiries, I embrace being involved as a participant in many of my studies, which has supported bridging teaching and research. The *roles* of researcher and teacher are often blurred. Whenever possible, the blurring of roles also applies to the classroom teacher, who may choose the level of participation in the study that feels most comfortable to them. The roles of teacher and learner are also often blurred for the researcher, as children have much to teach researchers. These role distributions do not preclude the researcher from organizing sufficient opportunities for observation. Epistemologically, I feel the urgency to document the knowledge and ways of knowing of Latino children, and this entails opportunities for observing, listening to, and learning from them.

Focusing on the individual learner has enabled me to document the ways in which Spanish, English, and code switching, have become semiotic resources that enable emergent bilinguals to participate in reading events to the same degree as their English-speaking peers; however, shifting the focus to context and the classroom *community* has permitted me to see the role of peer interaction in meaning-making among small groups, in which emergent bilinguals use one language or the other in their interpretations. In one study, the aspects of context I considered included the linguistic composition of the groups, and the types of texts used in the discussions (Martínez-Roldán, 2005a). Therefore, one of the research questions I pursued was: In what ways did the linguistic composition of the small groups (whether Spanish dominant or English dominant) shape the children's responses? The linguistic composition of the groups indeed played an important role in the types of responses generated by some bilingual children. Bilingual students self-regulated their talk and discourse according to the group's linguistic composition. Such successful self-regulation suggests a notion of achievement that departs from that of policymakers who choose to interpret achievement only in terms of standardized test scores. Participation in these reading events supported children's development of situated identities in two arenas: academic identities as skillful students who participated effectively in literature discussions and cultural identities rooted in their countries of origin and the Spanish language.

In the process of opening up the unit of analysis, I found it extremely useful to incorporate critical discourse analysis (Gee, 1990, 2011) and narrative analyses (Riessman, 2008) into my research design, to complement the traditional thematic analysis. These analytical tools enabled me to conduct a close language analysis while addressing the role of larger contexts in children's interpretations of texts. In my studies, CDA and narrative analyses contributed new knowledge of the ways in which children negotiate with other children and also with adults when they encounter different and sometimes contradictory discourses on language, gender, and identities (Martínez-Roldán & Malavé, 2004, 2011).

Expansive Learning: Studying Mobilization of Knowledge across Activity Systems

My most recent project involves methods that document generation of knowledge across activity systems involved in student learning (e.g., teacher education classrooms, classroom settings, and students' homes). This type of investigation requires collaboration among researchers given the many layers and systems involved in the analysis. In spite of its methodological complexity, this methodology provides opportunities for the development of case studies to examing learning in general and literacy in particular. For instance, we are currently developing case studies of teacher candidates interacting with bilingual learners in which three activity systems are relevant to the child's learning (the teacher-education program, the classroom, and the funds of knowledge of the student's family). This type of research project can contribute to the ongoing search for apprenticeship models that more effectively prepare our bilingual teaching candidates to analyze and address, creatively, the needs of an increasingly diverse student population with differing language and literacy strengths and needs.

What Counts as Innovation?

While my research approach may not be particularly novel, it has been generative. The flexible ways in which this methodology enables the researcher to move from focusing on cultural tools or individuals to focusing on learning within activity systems and social discourses, have allowed me to learn about the complexities of bilingual children's reading learning, while foregrounding the roles of language, texts, and ideologies. Qualitative inquiry into the role of language and texts as cultural tools in Latino children's learning has been a strong thread in my scholarly work, with children's perspectives and linguistic resources brought to the forefront, bringing new insights into bilingual students' reading. In this methodology, there are no linear steps to be followed that I can list. While the research questions always drive the methods, in a design driven by sociocultural theories, the theory signals the scope of settings, participants, and the unit of analysis.

Bridging Gaps

This methodology has helped me explore possibilities for bridging gaps among reading research methodologies (qualitative research designs, narrative analysis, and critical discourse analysis); epistemologies (Vygotskian theories and Latina epistemologies that view learners as producers of knowledge); instructional practices, texts, and contexts (when the research is part of pedagogical practices in educational settings); and readers' identities and experiences. The methodology especially addresses translational and implementation gaps.

The scant preparation for teaching students of nondominant backgrounds that many teachers in the United States receive, makes this type of research relevant. This research design and methodology, which involves not only the researcher but also teachers and teacher candidates participating in studies and working with children, has yielded examples of the sophisticated interpretations of texts that bilingual children can produce when they are provided with texts addressing their interests and with instructional organization offering opportunities for meaning-making and horizontal learning. In an effort to bridge research and pedagogies, I have taken my research results, and the body of scholarship sharing similar approaches, into my teacher education courses, inviting teacher candidates and teachers to look for the particular reading strengths, and not just the needs, of the emergent bilingual students they teach.

In sum, the discussion presented here shows my still-evolving understanding of theories and methods as useful for understanding Latino children's interpretation of texts, and bilinguals' use of their linguistic repertoires to make meaning of texts. The term evolving, as I use it here, echoes the ever-changing theoretical landscape in literacy research today. A major force leading this change, in my own scholarship, comes from the very sociocultural contexts in which the studies take place, contexts that have increasingly required me to highlight even more critical and anti-colonial approaches within sociocultural driven studies.

References

Dyson, A., & Genishi, C. (2005). *On the case: Approaches to language and literacy research.* New York, NY: Teachers College Press & NCRLL.
Engeström, Y. (1987). *Learning by expanding: An activity-theoretical approach to developmental research.* Helsinki, Finland: Orienta-Konsultit. Retrieved from http://lchc.ucsd.edu/MCA/Paper/Engestrom/expanding/toc.htm
Engeström, Y. (2001). Expansive learning at work: Toward an activity theoretical reconceptualization. *Journal of Education and Work, 14*(1), 133–156.
Engeström, Y., & Sannino, A. (2011). Discursive manifestations of contradictions in organizational change efforts. *Journal of Organizational Change, 24*(3), 368–387.
Erickson, F. (1986). Qualitative methods in research on teaching. In M. C. Wittrock (Ed.), *Handbook of research on teaching* (pp. 119–161). London: MacMillan.
Gee, J. P. (1990). *Social linguistics and literacies: Ideology and discourses.* New York, NY: Routledge.
Gee, J. P. (2011). *An introduction to discourse analysis: Theory and method* (3rd ed.). New York, NY: Routledge.
Goodman, K. S. (1994). Reading, writing, and written texts: A transactional sociopsycholinguistic view. In R. Rudell, M. R. Rudell, & H. Singer (Eds.), *Theoretical models and processes of reading* (pp. 1093–1130). Newark, DE: International Reading Association.
Goodman, Y., Watson, D., & Burke, C. (2005). *Reading miscue inventory.* Katonah, NY: Richard C. Owen Publishers.

Leontyev, A. N. (1979/1981). The problem of activity in psychology. In J. V. Wertsch (Ed.), *The concept of activity in Soviet psychology* (pp. 37–71). Armonk, NY: Sharpe.

Lewis, C., Enciso, P., & Moje, E. (2007). *Reframing sociocultural research on literacy: Identity, agency, and power.* Mahwah, NJ: Lawrence Erlbaum.

Martínez-Roldán, C. M. (2003). Building worlds and identities: A case study of the role of narratives in bilingual literature discussions. *Research in the Teaching of English, 37*(4), 491–526.

Martínez-Roldán, C. M. (2005a). The interplay between context and students' self-regulation in bilingual literature discussions: A case study. In J. Cohen, K. T. McAlister, K. Rolstad, & J. MacSwan (Eds.), *ISB4: Proceedings of the 4th International Symposium on Bilingualism* (pp. 1501–1521). Somerville, MA: Cascadilla Press.

Martínez-Roldán, C. M. (2005b). Examining bilingual children's gender ideologies through critical discourse analysis. *Critical Inquiry in Language Studies: an International Journal, 2*(3), 157–178.

Martínez-Roldán, C. M. (2015). Translanguaging practices as mobilization of linguistic resources in a Spanish/English bilingual after-school program: An analysis of contradictions. *International Multilingual Research Journal, 9*, 43–58. doi:10.1080/19313152.2014.982442

Martínez-Roldán, C. M., & Malavé, G. (2004). Language ideologies' mediating literacy and identity in bilingual contexts. *Journal of Early Childhood Literacy, 4*(2), 155–180.

Martínez-Roldán, C. M., & Malavé, G. (2011). Identity construction in the borderlands: The Acosta family. In V. Kinloch (Ed.), *Urban literacies: Critical perspectives on language, learning, and community* (pp. 53–71). New York, NY: Teachers College Press.

Moll, L. C. (2014). *L. S. Vygotsky and education.* New York, NY: Routledge.

Riessman, C. K. (2008). *Narrative methods for the human sciences.* Thousand Oaks, CA: Sage.

Rogoff. (2003). *The cultural nature of human development.* New York, NY: Oxford University Press.

Rosenblatt, L. M. (1995). *Literature as exploration* (5th ed.). New York, NY: The Modern Language Association of America.

Vygotsky, L. S. (1978). *Mind in society. The development of higher psychological processes.* (M. Cole, V. John-Steiner, S. Scribner, & E. Souberman, Eds.). Cambridge, MA: Harvard University Press.

Vygotsky, L. S. (1987). *Thinking and speech.* In L. S. Vygotsky, Collected works (vol. 1, pp. 39-285) (R. Rieber & A. Carton, Eds; N. Minick, Trans.). New York, NY: Plenum.

Wertsch, J. V. (1985). *Vygotsky and the social formation of mind.* Cambridge, MA: Harvard University Press.

Part VII
Minding the Gaps
Translating Reading Research as the Game is Changing

28
Concluding Thoughts from the Editors

Much has changed since the initial meetings in which we conceptualized the framework and chapter foci of the *Handbook of Reading Research, Volume V*, and much has remained the same. On the change front, even since our first meetings, research is increasingly informed by the diverse disciplines affiliated with and focused on reading—their paradigms and theories, and their methodological approaches. In turn, the knowledge emanating from these disciplines changes our understanding of what reading "is." Moreover, reading is increasingly acknowledged as more than an array of cognitive strategies and skills used to comprehend text, with attention given to the role of reader purpose, readers' affective and cognitive characteristics, sociocultural and political contexts, traditional and digital media, and texts themselves in the reading process. The dynamics associated with this evolution can be observed in competing models of reading, the waxing and waning of large-scale standards-based initiatives, the related changes in reading instruction as teachers pivot in relation to standards, and claims about what teachers need to learn and do to teach reading well.

As the conditions for reading research and education continue to shift, traditions of reading research that contribute to our understanding of how reading is situated and how readers development continues to progress. This research refines our understanding of many of the aspects of reading development and achievement previously discussed. What also hasn't changed are the filters and outlets through which much reading research is processed for consumption by teachers and school communities, parents and families, policymakers, as well as engaged and concerned citizens. Finally, there remains the need for research that informs our understanding of reading and acts of literacy, that situates reading in relation to diverse students and their characteristics, and that describes effective means for teaching reading for all students. The dynamics of stasis and change in reading research take place in the context of stagnant test scores; questioning of teachers' professionalism, a diminished and underprepared teaching force; the politicization of reading research, policy and practice; and declining or inequitably distributed funding for research and schools. It is in this environment of stasis and change, coupled with the tremendous contributions featured in this handbook for the 21st century, that we offer this Conclusions chapter.

Addressing the Gaps

To close, we remind the reader that a central purpose of *Handbook of Reading Research, Volume V*, is to address critical *gaps* that reflect the lack of consistent and positive student reading performance, in spite of burgeoning reading-focused research. These gaps include the *translational research gap*, or the space between the research conducted in laboratories or other controlled settings and approaches, and how other researchers, professional developers, and teachers and leaders make sense of—or translate—the findings for real-world conditions. Underlying our identification of this gap are the questions, "To what end is reading research conducted?" and "How applicable is the knowledge gained from research conducted in controlled settings for actual classrooms and other learning spaces?"

A further gap is the *implementation gap*, or what research describes as effective practice and what actually transpires in classrooms as findings are implemented. In other words, how does one actually *do* the things that we know from research that could make a difference in an individual's reading development and ultimately, their life, especially when trying to make individual change for 35 people at a time? What changes occur to the principles and practices of a research-based program in the process of implementation? Can strong fidelity to the original goals and principles of reading research findings be maintained over time as a program is implemented?

A third gap is the *relevance gap*, which describes disparities among reading research conducted under the agenda of a funding agency, the researchers' own interests or the research questions that follow from the last study conducted, or research that speaks directly to address classroom teachers' and administrators' needs. Related, how relevant are studies conducted in near-optimal conditions (e.g., research including significant teacher professional development, well-resourced curriculum development, or both) to the often less-than-optimal conditions in today's schools and classrooms? The answers to these questions might have strong implications for the translational and implementation gaps.

A final gap is the *bridging gap*, which focuses the degree of communication between and among complementary research fields, each of which could contribute to closing other gaps. How might diverse research traditions, with their attendant paradigms, methodologies, epistemologies, and research foci coalesce to best advance knowledge and ensure greater impact?

Advancing Our Understanding of Reading: The Lens of Key Gaps

With a frame of the gaps previously described, the contents of the *Handbook of Reading Research V* reflect an expansion of how we come to know reading. This research informs a changing perspective on what reading "is," marking an evolution from information processing to cognition to situated cognition, and from cognition to diverse and related aspects of historical and sociocultural dimensions of human development. Contributing to this evolution has been the building in of research from affiliated fields that expands our understanding of how reading develops and how to best teach reading. This dynamic is evident in the chapters of this handbook. In each iteration and across the prior volumes of the *Handbook of Reading Research*, we find cycles of investigation. A cycle may begin with the determination that research of a particular aspect of reading has reached critical mass—that mass indicated by a research and theory literature of sufficient breadth and depth. The critical mass of research may be homegrown, such as that focused on reading comprehension strategies or phonemic awareness. Alternatively, the research may be imported initially from affiliated fields, such as motivation and learning, and sociocultural influences on cognition, and then serve as foundation for ensuing inquiry focused on reading.

The knowledge produced by these traditional and innovative approaches to reading research is apparent in the chapters of this *Handbook of Reading Research*. The first set of chapters provide varied perspectives on the nature of diverse student populations and the implications for reading instruction and policy. The next set of chapters focuses on changes in text, from traditional to digital to multimedia, as well as everyday communications and the challenges and affordances that diverse texts and communications represent. Following, chapters focus on research that describes the continually evolving understanding of readers' strategies, skills, linguistic repertoires, knowledge, and stances—and then readers are described in relation to cognitive, affective, and cognitive development. The next set of chapters describes teacher, reader, text, and task interactions that mark successful instruction and resultant student reading, especially among multilingual and racially and ethnically diverse readers. Finally, reading research methodologies, bearing strong potential for breakthrough research and evolving in parallel with the foci of research, are described.

As demonstrated by a large body of knowledge, including this collection of chapters, we know much about the process of reading. We know much about the purposes and values of reading, and we know much about effective reading instruction, even in the face of game changing conditions of the contexts of teaching and learning. And yet the gaps we have outlined remain. Are the gaps only a product of a failure to communicate across different communities of practice (i.e., research to practice, discipline to discipline, etc.)? Or do other influences mediate the closing of these gaps by presenting obstacles to a fair and full representation of reading research? One such influence worth pointing out is the media, which has a role in shaping how certain issues related to reading are framed and disseminated, or in how specific designs and results gain favor (and assume legitimacy) as they are certified by one authority or another. Just as acts of reading are situated in relation to reader ability, purposes, texts, tasks, and contexts, reading research is situated in relation to the media, testing, economics, politics, and their complex interrelationships.

Consider a recent Public Broadcasting Service (PBS) presentation, "What parents of dyslexic children are teaching schools about literacy," which appeared on the nationally syndicated PBS News Hour (Public Broadcasting Service, 2019). In this presentation, parents and relatives of children in Arkansas describe the struggles encountered as their children try to read. The PBS report defines dyslexia as "a learning disability that makes it difficult to spell and read. It affects 1 in 5 individuals," with the implication that 20% of American school children experience reading disabilities. The piece makes the case that the problem stems from the lack of teaching guided by the *science of reading*. In this case, the PBS presenters defined the "science of reading" as intensive and systematic phonics instruction in the early years.

A lack of intensive and systematics phonics teaching may well have been a contributing factor to the outcomes of the children featured in the piece; there is a robust line of research that links under-developed phonological awareness to word reading difficulties. That, however, is just one piece of the puzzle in what is a complex scenario with respect to sources of reading problems—rarely one-dimensional and uniform in profile—and the appropriate solutions, which are also anchored in a science of reading, as evidenced by the chapters in this handbook. It is also just one piece of the puzzle of reading outcomes in the state of Arkansas. The state ranks 40th in the United States in regard to quality of the state's education system (Ziegler, 2019); 36th in per pupil spending (Governing, 2018); 46th for average starting teacher salary (National Education Association, 2019); and 47th in poverty rate (World Population Review, 2019). Such numbers point to concerns regarding teachers' working conditions, professional learning opportunities to develop teacher knowledge of reading and its instruction, student poverty and what that means for classroom instruction and the design of the educational system, and education funding, overall. Acknowledgment of these factors harks back to our Introduction chapter, in which we argued for examination of broad educational and societal contexts and their influence both reading research and practice.

Indeed, the students featured in the piece have many peers, potentially many more peers, with similar profiles—students who themselves are struggling in reading, though may not have been identified as dyslexic. All of those students need and depend on a science of reading instruction—a science that simultaneously focuses on developing a multitude of strategies, skills, and competencies (e.g., vocabulary and language development, phonological and word reading skills, knowledge of text and text-based strategies, etc.), using relevant, accurate, and engaging stories and texts;

characterized by strong cognitive press, knowledge-building opportunities, and attention to the ways different cultural practices and social contexts shape meaning-making from text. The big picture in which the PBS segment sits—arguably the umbrella issue—reflects a dire need to increase opportunities to learn in classrooms and the necessity of a multi-pronged approach to improve teaching and learning. The research reviews, research reports, and concluding implications produced by authors of this *Handbook of Reading Research* contribute to a well-developed science of reading research and help shape future directions.

Re-Centering Research

We know that the reading research conducted over the last 75 years has changed the way teachers teach, leaders lead, and how reading researchers do research. Consider, for example, the potential impact of this remarkable collection of chapters. From research on the demographics of classrooms around the world, on how reading develops both cognitively and culturally, on the texts through which information flows at top speed, to the current state of the art in reading instruction across the developmental spectrum, we know a great deal. As we consider this work, we can challenge ourselves to consider the mismatch among the students we teach, the teachers who teach them, the teacher educators who teach the teachers, and the researchers who study both teaching and learning to read. How might gaps be closed if we were to take seriously the need to recruit a diverse pool of teachers and to teach them how not only to recognize cultural differences, but also to celebrate and sustain them (cf. Paris, 2012)? How might reading research translate to reading practice if it actually helped teachers do this critical work?

How might reading research matter if it had a more robust and balanced presence in schools, and if the knowledge yielded by research informed classroom practice? What if this corpus of knowledge about how reading skill develops in individuals and how reading is also a product of social and cultural interactions (taken together, what we would call the "science of reading" as described above) were translated into practice? What would it look like if researchers developed interventions designed with attention to curriculum, instruction, and the contexts in which they operate? How might the implementation gap shrink if intervention took into account the range of experiences of children, the preparation (or lack thereof) of teachers? What if reading research more fully accounted for the conditions of classroom, school, and community life, where engaging text might be difficult to find, where children are hungry or experiencing trauma, and where teachers are pushed to prepare children for the next high-stakes assessment?

What could it look like if we built on what we know about how children learn language—not by being taught to memorize word meanings, but by engaging in rich, historically and culturally-informed, text-based conversations scaffolded by expert teachers? What if we helped teachers see what it looks like to engage students in disciplinary learning by focusing on learning the language practices of academic and disciplinary domains as youth engaged in inquiry? If we paid much more attention to such research, then our teacher education practice would change dramatically, as well as the resources we provide teachers. Finally, what might it mean to take research on texts seriously, from how text forms and media shape meaning-making, cognitive processes, and social practices, to what it looks like to support reading and synthesizing meaning across multiple forms? For each set of questions posed here, we remind readers to consider the gaps reading researchers need to help close if reading research is to truly address the game changers of the societal moment in which this handbook was produced.

As an editorial team, we are appreciative that the author teams agreed, *a priori*, to go beyond the more traditional research synthesis and critique to employ the gaps frame, and suggest school and classroom applications that hold promise for improving reading instruction and student achievement. By taking this approach to reviewing the research, the authors have taken important steps in addressing gaps and elaborating on the game changers of our time. We look forward to the next decade of further progress toward developing a body of useable knowledge that drives stronger learning and teaching and produces skills and competencies for an engaged and equipped next generation of readers.

References

Governing. (June, 2018). Education spending per student by state. Retrieved from: www.governing.com/gov-data/education-data/state-education-spending-per-pupil-data.html

National Education Association. (2019). 2017–2018 average teacher starting salaries by state. Retrieved from: www.nea.org/home/2017-2018-average-starting-teacher-salary.html

Paris, D. (2012). Culturally sustaining pedagogy: A needed change in stance, terminology, and practice. *Educational Researcher*, *41*(3), 93–97.

Public Broadcasting Service. (April, 2019). What parents of dyslexic children are teaching schools about literacy. Retrieved from: www.pbs.org/newshour/show/what-parents-of-dyslexic-children-are-teaching-schools-about-literacy

World Population Review. (2019). Poverty rate by state 2019. Retrieved from: http://worldpopulationreview.com/states/poverty-rate-by-state/

Ziegler, B. (2019). Education rankings: Measuring how well states are educating their students. Retrieved from: www.usnews.com/news/best-states/rankings/education

Contributor Biographies

Laura K. Allen is an Assistant Professor in the Department of Psychology at University of New Hampshire. The overarching aim of her research is to better understand the cognitive processes involved in language comprehension, writing, knowledge acquisition, and conceptual change, and to apply that understanding to educational practice by developing and testing educational technologies.

Ana Taboada Barber serves as Associate Professor in the Department of Counseling, Higher Education, and Special Education, at the University of Maryland. Her work centers on studying the influence of cognitive, linguistic, and motivation variables on the literacy and language development of students of diverse language backgrounds.

Naomi S. Baron is Professor of Linguistics Emerita at American University in Washington, DC. The latest of her eight books is *Words Onscreen: The Fate of Reading in a Digital World* (Oxford University Press).

Jane Bean-Folkes received her M.Ed. and Ed.D. from Teachers College, Columbia University in Curriculum and Teaching with a concentration in Reading and Language Arts. Her research interests involve multilingual classrooms, written academic language, African American Language, sociocultural and sociolinguistic perspectives of education for African American students and other non-dominant language speakers as they learn the academic language in urban settings.

Jason L. G. Braasch is an Associate Professor in the Department of Psychology at the University of Memphis. His research examines the cognitive processes that underlie learning from multiple, diverse sources we encounter every day.

Ivar Bråten is a Professor of Educational Psychology in the Department of Education at the University of Oslo, Norway. His research interests include academic motivation, self-regulated learning, epistemic cognition, and multiple document literacy.

Gerald Campano is Professor and Chair of the Literacy, Culture, and International Education Division at the Graduate School of Education, University of Pennsylvania. Gerald's scholarship focuses on community-based, practitioner and participatory research, critical literacy, and educational access and justice for immigrant families.

Hannah Carter, Ph.D., is an Assistant Professor at Boise State University. In addition to teaching courses in the Literacy, Language, and Culture Department, she is also a Co-Director of the Boise State Literacy Lab and works as a Clinical Supervisor for secondary teacher candidates. Her research interests include literacy in the disciplines, pre-service teacher learning, and teacher education supervision.

Gina N. Cervetti is an Associate Professor of Literacy, Language, and Culture at the University of Michigan. Her research focused on the roles of world knowledge, language, and disciplinary inquiry in reading comprehension.

Chris K. Chang-Bacon is an Assistant Professor at the University of Virginia Curry School of Education and Human Development. His research explores bilingualism, language policy, and critical literacies in teacher education.

Byeong-Young Cho is a Professor of Literacy in the College of Education at Hanyang University, Seoul, South Korea. His research focuses on understanding and supporting students' learning and development of sophisticated literacies in digital societies.

James Joshua Coleman is an Assistant Professor at San José State University where his research interests include critical literacy, English education, queer studies, and affect studies.

Carol McDonald Connor is a Chancellor's Professor at the University of California, Irvine and Director of the Center for Creating Opportunity through Education. Her research focuses on children's language and literacy development and understanding why some children have difficulty learning to read and write proficiently.

Tisha Lewis Ellison is an Associate Professor in the Department of Language and Literacy Education at the University of Georgia. Her research explores the intersections of family literacy, multimodality, and digital and STEM literacy practices among African American and Latinx families and adolescents.

Emily Fox is currently semi-retired; she does editing work for European researchers. Her research interest when she was at the University of Maryland was higher-level reading development, with regard to its affective, cognitive, epistemic, dispositional, and behavioral aspects.

Emily Phillips Galloway is an Assistant Professor at Vanderbilt University's Peabody School of Education. Phillips Galloway's research explores the relationships between school-relevant language development and language expression and comprehension during middle childhood with a particular focus on linguistically- and culturally-minoritized learners.

Perla B. Gámez is an Associate Professor in the Department of Psychology at Loyola University Chicago. Her current research examines the role of language exposure and use in the language and literacy development of dual language learners.

Cynthia Greenleaf is a Senior Research Scientist at WestEd, where she designs, studies, and disseminates models and approaches for the teaching and learning of literacies in the disciplines. Through collaborative design-based research with middle and high school as well as college teachers, she has developed and refined the Reading Apprenticeship Instructional Framework and professional learning model and tools to foster reading for inquiry purposes, build students' socio-emotional learning dispositions, and advance their literacy, agency, knowledge, and reasoning.

Contributor Biographies

Mary Guay, Ph.D., is a Clinical Associate Professor at the University of Georgia. She specializes in Early Literacy development and dyslexia.

Emily C. Hanno is a Doctoral Candidate at the Harvard Graduate School of Education. Her research focuses on understanding how early childhood educators can promote children's development in a number of domains.

Kathleen Hinchman is Professor in the Reading and Language Arts Department in the School of Education at Syracuse University. Her scholarship focuses on teachers' and youth's perspectives toward literacy instruction, including disciplinary literacy instruction.

Jin Kyoung Hwang is an Assistant Project Scientist in the School of Education at the University of California, Irvine. Her research centers on understanding language and literacy development of school-aged children, including dual language learners, and examining how research-based interventions can help improve their literacy outcomes.

Stephanie M. Jones is the Gerald S. Lesser Professor of Early Childhood Development at the Graduate School of Education at Harvard University. Her research, anchored in prevention science, focuses on the effects of poverty and exposure to violence on children and youth's social, emotional, and behavioral development. Over the last ten years her work has focused on evaluation research addressing the impact of preschool and elementary focused social-emotional learning interventions on behavioral and academic outcomes and classroom practices; as well as new curriculum development, implementation, and testing.

Laura M. Justice, Ph.D., is EHE Distinguished Professor of Educational Psychology at the Ohio State University. She is Executive Director of the Crane Center for Early Childhood Research and Policy, and is also the Editor-in-Chief of Early Childhood Research Quarterly. Justice is an active researcher of topics related to early childhood language and literacy development, preschool program quality, and developmental disabilities.

Kiren S. Khan is an Assistant Professor of Psychology at Rhodes College with research interests spanning narrative and language development, effective narrative instructional strategies, and school readiness interventions for children and families facing socio-economic disparities.

Michelle Kwok is a Clinical Assistant Professor at Texas A&M University and the Editorial Assistant for the *Handbook of Reading Research, Vol. V*. Her research draws on the intersections of literacy instruction, multicultural education, and teacher preparation.

Jayne C. Lammers (Ph.D. – Arizona State University) is an Associate Professor of Education and Director of secondary English teacher preparation at the University of Rochester's Warner School of Education and Human Development. She is a founding Associate Director of the Center for Learning in the Digital Age, and her research examines young people's interest-driven digital literacies to inform classroom instruction.

Kevin M. Leander is Professor of Language, Literacy, and Culture Education at Vanderbilt University in Nashville, Tennessee. His research focuses on affective, embodied engagements with literacy, dialogic and material approaches to digital media, and poststructural theory.

Contributor Biographies

Carol D. Lee is Professor Emeritus at Northwestern University in the School of Education and Social Policy, Learning Sciences. Her research addresses reading in the disciplines in K-12 settings informed by attention to ecological systems, human development, and cognitive processes with particular focus on issues of cultural diversity.

Margaret Mackey is Professor Emerita in the School of Library and Information Studies at the University of Alberta. Her most recent book is *One Child Reading: My Auto-Bibliography* (University of Alberta Press, 2016).

Bridget Maher holds a Ph.D. from the University of Michigan in Educational Studies specializing in Literacy, Language, and Culture, and she is currently a postdoctoral research fellow at the University of Michigan. Her research interests include studying teaching and learning in the disciplines from secondary into higher education, as well as studying the development and trajectory of teachers from novices through experienced practitioners, particularly as they implement literacy instruction within and across the disciplines.

Jeannette Mancilla-Martinez is an Associate Professor of Literacy, as well as Associate Dean of Graduate Education for Vanderbilt University's Peabody College. Her program of research is focused on advancing students' language and reading comprehension outcomes.

Carmen M. Martínez-Roldán is an Associate Professor and Director of the Bilingual Bicultural Education Program at Teachers College, Columbia University. Her research agenda addresses the literacy practices of Spanish/English speaking bilingual students, their use of Spanish as an intellectual resource for learning and identity development, and bilingual teacher education using qualitative methods, including case studies and narrative methodologies.

Janna B. McClain is a Doctoral Candidate in Teaching, Learning, and Diversity at Peabody College of Education and Human Development, Vanderbilt University. Her research explores the systems of belief and knowledge that teachers draw upon as they strive to enact equitable language instruction.

Dana C. McCoy is an Assistant Professor at the Harvard Graduate School of Education (HGSE). Her work focuses on understanding the ways that poverty-related risk factors in children's home, school, and neighborhood environments affect the development of their cognitive and socioemotional skills in early childhood.

Danielle S. McNamara, Ph.D., is a Professor of Psychology in the Psychology Department at Arizona State University. She is an international expert in the fields of cognitive and learning sciences, reading comprehension, writing, text and learning analytics, natural language processing, computational linguistics, and intelligent tutoring systems. She develops educational technologies and conducts research to better understand cognitive processes involved in comprehension, knowledge and skill acquisition, and writing.

T. Philip Nichols is an Assistant Professor in the department of Curriculum and Instruction at Baylor University. His research examines how science and technology condition the ways we practice, teach, and talk about literacy – and the implications for ethical and equitable education.

Kimberly G. Noble, M.D., Ph.D., is an Associate Professor of Neuroscience and Education at Teachers College, Columbia University. As a neuroscientist and board-certified pediatrician, she studies how socioeconomic inequality relates to children's cognitive and brain development.

Dr. Noble was elected a Fellow of the Association for Psychological Science and was awarded a 2017 Association for Psychological Science Janet Taylor Spence Award for Transformative Early Career Contributions.

Silvia Noguerón-Liu is an Assistant Professor at the University of Colorado, Boulder. Her research interests include family literacy and digital literacies in bilingual/immigrant communities.

Grace D. Player is an Assistant Professor in the Curriculum and Instruction Department at the University of Connecticut, Neag School of Education. Her work explores the ways that girls and women of color leverage literacies to enact resistance and solidarity in and beyond educational settings.

C. Patrick Proctor is Professor of Literacy and Bilingualism at the Boston College Lynch School of Education and Human Development. He works with bilingual children and youth, and their teachers, in varied linguistic contexts to promote equitable connections between research and practice.

Wenjuan Qin is an Assistant Professor at Fudan University, the College of Foreign Languages and Literature. She holds an Ed.D. and Ed.M. from Harvard Graduate School of Education. Her research focuses on investigating language skills relevant for successful reading and writing for academic purposes; and also, on understanding how English as foreign language (EFL) learners acquire a variety of linguistic and pragmatic resources to navigate across communicative contexts.

Brian Rowan is the Burke A. Hinsdale Collegiate Professor in Education at the University of Michigan and a Research Professor at the University of Michigan's Institute for Social Research. A sociologist by training (Ph.D. Stanford University), he studies the organization of schooling and its effects on teaching and learning.

David B. Sabey, a Doctoral Candidate at Vanderbilt University, brings an interest in ethics to his study of literacy, attending to the relational qualities and possibilities inherent in any literacy practice.

Ladislao Salmerón is currently Associate Professor at the Department of Developmental and Educational Psychology at the University of Valencia, Spain. His research focuses on the cognitive mechanisms of digital reading.

Katrina R. Simon is a Doctoral student in Developmental Psychology at Teacher's College, Columbia University. Broadly, her interests lie in how the environment influences the relationship between brain and cognitive development.

Allison Skerrett is a Professor in the Department of Curriculum and Instruction at the University of Texas, Austin. Her research interests include youth literacy practices across school and other social contexts, transnationalism and education, and secondary English teachers' preparation for and development in urban schools.

Peter Smagorinsky is Distinguished Research Professor at the University of Georgia, and Distinguished Visiting Scholar at the University of Guadalajara. He serves as the faculty advisor to the Journal of Language and Literacy Education, which is edited by graduate students in his department at UGA.

Ebony Elizabeth Thomas is Associate Professor in the Literacy, Culture, and International Educational Division at the University of Pennsylvania's Graduate School of Education. A former Detroit Public Schools teacher and National Academy of Education/Spencer Foundation Postdoctoral Fellow, she is an expert on diversity in children's literature, youth media, and fan studies.

Dianna Townsend is an Associate Professor of Literacy Studies at the University of Nevada, Reno. She conducts research in the areas of vocabulary, academic language, and adolescent literacy.

Paola Uccelli is a Professor at the Harvard Graduate School of Education. With a background in linguistics, she studies socio-cultural and individual differences in monolingual and multilingual learners' language and literacy development throughout the school years.

Mark White is a Post-Doc at the University of Oslo and is interested in how video data is used to study and understand instructional quality, especially biases generated from this approach.

Arlette Ingram Willis is a Professor and University Scholar at the University of Illinois, Urbana Champaign. Her scholarship draws on critical theories to examine African American literacies, reading policies, and reading research.

Tanya S. Wright is an Associate Professor of Language and Literacy in the Department of Teacher Education at Michigan State University.

Index

Page numbers in **bold** refer to content in **figures**; page numbers in *italics* refer to content in *tables*.

3S Model of Credibility 82, 84
4Rs (Reading, Writing, Respect and Resolution) 288–294, *292–293*

academic language instruction 345–347, **346**; academic literacy **346**, 351–354, 355; academic vocabulary 166–167, 210–211, **346**, 348–351, 354–355; integrated model for moving forward 358–360, **359**; and raciolinguistics 357–358; and reading comprehension definition 347; research-to-practice gap 355–356; trends in research 354–355
Academic Language Instruction for All Students (ALIAS) 226, 338, 349–350
academic language proficiency 155–156; conceptualization of 158–161, **160**; in early childhood 205–206; metalanguage research 168–170; new directions of study 156–158; skills for reading comprehension 161, *162–164*, 165–168; vision for practice-relevant research 170–174
academic literacy **346**, 351–354, 355
academic vocabulary 166–167, 210–211, **346**, 348–351, 354–355
Accavitti, M. 19
Achebe, Chinua 428
Ackerman, R. 89, 122
ACT Inc. 386
activating prior knowledge 248–250
Adams, B.C. 245
Adapted Primary Literature (APL) 390
Adichie, Chimamanda Ngozi 431–432
adult literacy learners **266**, 267–268
advertising, online 446
affective individual differences 180–181; bridging gaps in research 191–193; reader's self 182–185; reading content 185–188, 338; reading task 188–191
Afflerbach, Peter P. 3–12
African-American learners 46, 57–58; black literacy tradition 425–426; cultural knowledge 253; home reading 61–66; nature, nurture, and reading 66–68; and reading instruction 330, 332, 334; *see also* sociocultural diversity
age differences 121, 127–128
Ahmed, Y. 245
Alcoff, Linda Martin 140
Alexander, P.A. 89, 392
algorithms 103
Alim, H.S. 22, 48, 142
Allen, Laura K. 261–272
Alvarez, L. 22
Alvermann, D.E. 249, 252, 385
Amazon 117
Anderson, K. 139
Anderson, R. 44, 64, 238
App Annie 108
Appadurai, Arjun 436, 437
Apple 101, 117
apps, mobile 414–416, 418, 448
Arcia, E. 19
Asher, J.W. 270
assemblage theory 140
assessments: language proficiency 155, 157, 167; reading comprehension 268, 271; social and cultural gaps 37, 46; and sociocultural diversity 62, 65–66; standardized literacy 20, 23; of vocabulary knowledge 219–220, 227–228
Assessment-to-instruction (A2i) tool 317
Association for Qualitative Research (AQR) 106
Association of American Publishers (AAP) 118
attitudes, to reading 188–189
August, D. 29, 349, 353
Aukrust, V.G. 222
Ausubel, D.P. 238
authentic questions 374–375
Azevedo, R. 245

Babies (2010) 40, 48
Bailey, A.L. 167
Bain, R.B. 393–394
Baker, E.A. 413

Index

Baker, S. 354
Bang, M. 45
Baron, Naomi S. 116–132
Bartlett, F.C. 237–238
Bartlett, L. 437
Barzilai, S. 87
Basic Interpersonal Communication Skills (BICS) 351
Baumann, J.F. 346, 348
Bazalgette, C. 139
Beach, Richard 429
Bean-Folkes, Jane 424–432
Beck, I.L. 349
behavioral inhibition 284–285
beliefs: about text content 187–188; epistemological 81–82, 85, 86, 87, 479; self-efficacy beliefs 182–183
Bell, Y.R. 253
Berliner, D.C. 62
Best, J.R. 280
Best, R.M. 242–243
bilingual learners: academic language instruction 358; academic literacy 351–353; cross-linguistic transfer 204–205; digital literacy instruction 417; language for school literacy (LSL) 157, 167; qualitative case study 492–496; vocabulary knowledge 219, 228, 349; *see also* sociocultural diversity
black feminism 142
black radicalism 143
Blair, C. 280
Block, E. 269
blogs 90
Bloome, D. 67
Blue, E.V. 334
Boas, E. 335
Bohlmann, N.L. 287
book ownership 104
bottom-up (local) strategies 269–270
Bourdieu, P. 67
Bowers, E. 371, 372
Braasch, Jason L.G. 79–92
brain function *see* neuroscience
Brandão, A.C.P. 246
Bråten, Ivar 79–92, 87, 190
Brisk, M. 24
Brophy, Jere 193
Brown, B.A. 352
Brown, R.W. 368
Bryant, C.L. 349
Bu Bois, W.E.B. 426
Buch-Iversen, I. 249–250
Buckingham, D. 139
Bunch, G.C. 22
Burchinal, M. 311
burnout 9, 295
Butler, Y. 352
BuzzFeed 444, 445

Cain, K. 246
Callahan, R. 67
Calvo, M.G. 185
Campano, Gerald 137–149
Capitelli, S. 22
Carlo, M.S. 349
Carter, Hannah 345–360
Castillo, M.D. 185
cell phones *see* smartphones
Cervetti, Gina N. 237–255, 392
Chang-Bacon, Chris K. 5–6, 17–30
Chicago School Readiness Project (CSRP) 288, *289*, 294
child language development *see* early language development
child literacy 279–280; implications and future directions 295–298; relation with self-regulation 280–287, **281**; school interventions and self-regulation 288–295; text-specific processes 308–309; *see also* early language development; individualized literacy instruction
childhood self-regulation *see* self-regulation, in childhood
Chiu, Ming Ming 105
Cho, Byeong-Young 464–482
choices, reading 103–105, 333–334
Christian, B. 67
Chyi, H.I. 121, 126, 127
Civil Rights Act (1964) 66
Clark, T.R. 253
classroom conversation 224–225, 226–227, 374–375
Clay, M.M. 223
Coburn, C.E. 319–320
Cognitive Academic Language Learning Approach (CALLA) 351
Cognitive Academic Language Proficiency (CALP) 351
cognitive development, overview 307–311; *see also* cognitive individual differences; early language development; self-regulation, in childhood
cognitive flexibility 284
cognitive individual differences 180–181; affect and the reader's self 182–185; affect and the reading content 185–188; affect and the reading task 188–191; bridging gaps in affect-related research 191–193; and individualized literacy instruction 312–320; *see also* cognitive development, overview
cognitive strategy instruction (CSI) 339
Coiro, J. 409
Cole, M. 66, 330
Coleman, James J. 424–432
Collective Educational Futures Project 147–148, **148**
Collingridge, D.S. 28
Collins, P. 351
colonialism *see* decolonization
Common Core State Standards (CCSS) 8–9, 20; academic language proficiency 346; and affective individual differences 180; digital literacy 406; disciplinary texts 386; New Criticism 60; primary

513

Index

grades 206; reading comprehension 37, 42; science learning 388, 395; and sociocultural diversity 65
community reading 336–337
competition discourses 5
comprehension monitoring 203, 204, 314
comprehension standards 42–43
computer-based early literacy training *290*, 294–295
Computerized Attention Training (CAT) *290*, 295
Concept-Oriented Reading Instruction (CORI) 251–252
conditions, overview *see* game changers, overview
Connected Learning model 409
Connor, C.M. 286, 307–321
Construction-Integration (CI) Model 238, 262
content-related interest 186–187
contextualization, methodological 481
conversation 224–225, 226–227, 374–375
Cook, A.E. 246
Cooperative Children's Book Center (CCBC) 424
Core Academic Language Skills (CALS) 167–168, 206
corroboration, of texts 85
cosmopolitanism 438–443
COST Action FP1104 123, 125
Council of Chief State School Officers (CCSSO) 8
Craik, F.I.M. 262
Crampton, A. 442
creolization 143–144
critical literacy 47–48, 111–112, 424–425; and digital tools 416; restorying the gaps in 430–431; restorying the history of 425–428; restorying the words and the world 428–430; and shared texts 335
critical reader response 429
critical rhetorical flexibility 171–172
Cromley, J.G. 245
Cronbach, L.J. 219
cross-disciplinary language 158, *163–164*, 166, 167–168
cross-linguistic transfer 204–205
cultural diversity *see* sociocultural diversity
cultural knowledge 253
Cultural Modeling (CM) 44, 46, 330
Cultural-Historical Activity Theory (CHAT) 492, 493
Cummins, Jim 157
Cushman, E. 63
Cyphers for Justice 47

Dalton, B. 413
Dancing Across Borders (DAB) 145–147
Daniel, D.B. 122
Davies, M. 348
De Naeghel, J. 189
decoding 38, 266–267, 308
decolonization 137–138; critical inquiry and multimodality 141–143; decolonial imaginaries and multimodality 142–143; rhizomatic identities and multimodal design 145–148

deculturalization 60
dedicated reading 110–111
deep comprehension: and digitization 111; and diverse learners 264–268, **265**, **266**; implications for education 268–272; overview of 261–264
Del Río, F. 204
Deleuze, Gilles 140
Delpit, L.D. 62
demographics: age differences 121, 127–128; and digital reading 121; gender differences 107, 121, 142; and literacy 17–18; and literacy in teacher education 22–25; and literacy research 25–27, *26*; student and teacher paradox 18–21; *see also* sociocultural diversity
Department of Education (USA) 28
design-based implementation research (DBIR) 319
Developing Content Area Academic Language (DCAAL) 351
Dewey, J. 60
Diakidoy, I.N. 184, 252, 254
Dias, Marley 424
Dickinson, D.K. 224
digital literacy: and cosmopolitanism 438–443; critical reflections 445–446; and ethics 438; and globalization 436–437; listening across online and offline practices 446–448; reading networks 443–445; *see also* digital literacy instruction; digital reading
digital literacy instruction 406–407; historical overview of literature 409–412, *411*; key questions and findings 412–417; new approaches and opportunities 417–420; theory on reading and technology 408–409; *see also* digital literacy
digital reading 116–117; and critical literacy 429; future research 130–132; growth of 117–119; non-traditional text reading 79, 83, 87–91; and reading habits 100, 101–103; research to date 120–130; social media 110–111; variables of 119–120; *see also* media text environments, examinations of; printed vs. digital texts
digital tools 412–415; *see also* digital literacy instruction
Dillon, A. 120
Diogenes 438
disaggregate instruction 352
disaggregation, of test data 4–5
disciplinary literacy 252, 352, 354
Disciplinary Literacy Conceptual Framework 81–82, 84
disciplinary texts: future research directions 394–396; implications gaps 391–394; reading and science learning 388–391; social practices perspective 385–386, 387–388; use in classroom practice 386–387, 388
discipline-specific language 158, *163*, *164*, 166, 167–168, 348, 349, 353; *see also* disciplinary texts
discourse analysis *472–473*, 482, 495
discourse practices 168–170, 172, 173, 199, 200
discrimination 64

514

Documents Model Framework (DMF) 80–81, 83
domain knowledge 239–242, *240–241*, 245, 247–248
Donley, J. 249
Draper, R.J. 394
Driscoll, A. 23
dual language learners (DLLs) 210–211, 370, 371, 372, 373, 377
Duncan-Andrade, J.M. 47
Duursma, E. 221
dynamic forecasting intervention (DFI) algorithms 317
dynamic skills theory 287, 296
dynamic systems theory 200
dyslexia 67, 185, 488, 489, 503

early language development: approaches to building vocabulary 223–226; challenges to improving reading comprehension 206–208; knowledge and inferencing 266–267, **266**; and language environments 220–223, 370–372; major issues 198–201; new approaches and future directions 208–211, 226–228; primary grade reading comprehension 201–203; questions regarding reading comprehension 203–206; text-specific processes 308–309; *see also* child literacy; cognitive development, overview
early literacy *see* child literacy
eBooks *see* digital reading
ecological systems theory 41
Economic Policy Institute (EPI) 10
Economist, The 126
Edelman, Marian Wright 283
edTPA 346, 356
Educational Testing Service 37
effortful control 280, 284–285, 287
El Teatro Campesino 146
Elbro, C. 249–250
Ellison, Tisha Lewis 57–68
eMarketer 102
embedded structures 367–368
Emergentist Coalition Model (ECM) 369
emotional inhibition 284–285
emotional responses 185
Enciso, Patricia 3–12, 142, 335, 447
encoding 262
Engeström, Y. 492
English language learners (ELLs): classroom conversation 226–227; comprehension strategies 269, 270; and language for school literacy (LSL) 159; and literacy trends 26–27; metalanguage teaching 169; metalinguistic skills 44; and teacher education 23; topic and domain knowledge 247–248, **266**, 267; vocabulary knowledge 219, 221, 222, **266**, 349; and zone of proximal development (ZPD) 330
Enriquez, G. 332
environments *see* language environments

epistemology *see* knowledge
e-reading *see* digital reading
Erickson, F. 455
Eseth-Alkalai, Y. 87
Espinoza, Manuel 46
ethics 438
ethnic diversity 5–6, 18–20; *see also* African-American learners; decolonization; sociocultural diversity
Evans, M.D.R. 104
Every Student Succeeds Act (ESSA, 2015) 20
evidence, in research 105–109
executive function 280, 283–284, 285, 287, 309
expectancy-value theory 182
eye-tracking technology 479–480

Facebook 103, 128, 437
Fagella-Luby, M.N. 391–392
Fairclough, N. 22
family literacy programs (FLPs) 224
Farinosi, M. 123
Farkas, G. 67
Farnsworth, M. 29
Felski, R. 140
feminism 142
Ferguson, L.E. 87
fiction vs. nonfiction 191
Fifth-Dimension model 408, 419
Fillmore, L.W. 22
Fixsen, D.L. 320
Flanagan, M. 123, 131
Flesch-Kincaid assessments 271
FlipFeed 448
Flores, N. 21, 358
forums 90
Fox, Emily 180–193
franchises 99, 100–101
Francois, C. 333
Freebody, P. 430
Freiberg, J. 430
Freire, P. 331, 426–427, 438
Fry, R. 18

Galguera, T. 22
Galloway, Emily Phillips 155–174
Gallup 126, 127
Galton, F. 67
game changers, overview 3–5, **4**; decline in teacher workforce and preparation 10–11; effect on reading research 11–12; ethnic, racial, and socioeconomic changes 5–6; increasing demands for student learning 8–9; new forms of text and communication practices 6–7; student and teacher stress 9; testing 7–8; workforce and changes in economy 6
Gámez, P.B. 351, 365–377
Gándara, P. 23
Gantt, E.E. 28

515

Index

Garcia, A. 105
Gardner, D. 348
Garland, K.J. 120
Gates Foundation 460
Gaultney, J.F. 254
Gebhard, M. 169
Gee, James Paul 430
gender differences 107, 121, 142
general world knowledge *241*, 242–243, 354
Gilliam, W.S. 19
Ginsburg, A. 28
Glissant, Édouard 143–145
global economic changes 6
Global Integrated Scenario-Based Assessment (GISA) 37, 316–317
global strategies 269–270
globalization 436–437
Goals 200: Educate America Act (1994) 20
Goetz, E.T. 238
Goldman, S.R. 81–82, 354
Goldsmith, M. 122
Gonzalez, N. 392
Google 102–103, 109, 117
Gormley, K. 242, 244
Grabe, W. 267
Grapes of Wrath, The 45
Graves, M.F. 346, 348
Greenleaf, Cynthia 384–397
Griffin, P. 66
Grosjean, F. 219
Grossman, P. 38
group work 29, 373
Guay, Mary 57–68
Guise, M. 335
Guthrie, J.T. 182, 192, 251
Guttiérrez, Kris 46, 419

habits, reading 190–191, 192
Haddix, M.M. 23, 59
Haenggi, D. 242
Hagen, A.M. 87
Hagood, M.C. 416
Hague, S.A. 249, 252
Hakuta, K. 352
Hall, L.A. 337–338
Halliday, M.A.K. 355, 368
Handsfield, L.J. 339, 417
Hanno, Emily C. 279–298
Hansen, D. 440, 441
Hansen, J. 249
Harry Potter and the Cursed Child 99, 100–101
Head Start 208, 222, 371; REDI intervention 288, *291*, 294
Heath, S.B. 60–62, 65
Heineke, A.J. 335–336
Herrman, J. 103
heterogenization 436–437
Hiebert, E.H. 64, 386

high quality language 365–369; future research directions 375–377; and language environments 369–374; language-facilitating techniques in classrooms 374–375; *see also* academic language proficiency
higher-level language skills 202–203, 204, 208, 209, 210, 268; *see also* high quality language
Hinchman, Kathleen 384–397
Hines, S. 349
hip hop literacies 47–48, 142
Holland, D. 437
home language environments 220–221, 223–224, 310–311, 369–370
home reading 60–66, 221, 336–337
homogenization 436–437
Horton, W. 353–354
hospitable dialogue 442–443, 445, 446–448
Hull, G. 139, 439, 445
human development perspectives 39–42
Hunchback of Notre Dame, The 116
Hutchison, A. 415, 419
Huttenlocher, J. 370–371
Hwang, J.K. 307–321
hypertext 89

identities, reading 332–333, 337–338
immigration 18
impairments 488–489
implementation science 320
Improving Comprehension Online (ICON) 413
independent reading 333–334
In-Depth Expanded Applications of Science (IDEAS) 389
indigenous literacy 427, 428
individualized literacy instruction 311–313; initiatives for implementing classroom practices 319–320; models for aiding instruction 313–316, **315**; and self-regulation *292*, 294; use of technology 316–319
inferencing 244, 246; activating prior knowledge 249–250; adult literacy learners 268; early language development 202, 204, 266–267
information, availability of 4
inhibitory control 283
Institute of Education Sciences (IES) 25, 28, 29, 43
instructional approaches 331–339, 389–391; *see also* digital literacy instruction; individualized literacy instruction
Intelligent Tutoring Structure Strategy (ITSS) 318
interest: content-related 186–187; in reading 188–189; in reading tasks 190
International Literacy Association (ILA) 22, 106
International Society for Technology in Education (ISTE) 406
Internet reading 89–91, 102–103, 104; *see also* digital reading
Inter-University Consortium for Political and Social Research (ICPSR) 460

interventions 288–295, *289–293*, 338, 349, 350, 376
Iowa Test of Basic Skills (ITBS) 186
Irvine, Jacqueline Jordan 426
Israelson, M.H. 414
iSTART 318
Ito, Mimi 409
Ivey, G. 333–334

Jackson, G.T. 318
Janks, Hilary 430
Javorsky, K. 414
Jewitt, C. 138–139
Jiang, H. 222
Jimenez, R.T. 339
Johnson, Lyndon B. 66
Johnston, P. 333–334
Jones, R. 445–446
Jones, S.H. 190
Jones, Stephanie M. 279–298
Justice, Laura M. 197–211, 222, 373

Kaufman, G. 123, 131
Kaveh, Y. 24
Keenan, J.M. 245
Kelley, H.M. 253
Kemp, S. 102
Kendeou, P. 252
Kerlin, S.C. 390
Khan, Kiren S. 197–211
Kim, J. 332
kindergarten 206, 309
Kinloch, V. 48
Kintsch, W. 42, 180, 246
Kirkland, D.E. 62
Kleeman, David 103
Knobel, M. 409
knowledge: activation of 248–250; and beliefs 81–82, 85, 86, 87, 479; future research directions 250–255; general world knowledge *241*, 242–243; inconsistencies with reading comprehension 243–244; and L2 readers' comprehension 247–248, 267; prior knowledge 84–85, 86, 87, 186, *466*; and reading ability 244–246; and text cohesion/quality 247; theoretical accounts of 237–239; topic and domain knowledge 239–242, *240–241*, 245, 247–248, 254; *see also* deep comprehension
Knowledge Revision Components (KRec) framework 252–253
Kobayashi, K. 87, 242
Kochhar, R. 18–19
Kozminsky, E. 244
Kratochwill, T.R. 28
Kress, G. 138
Kush, J.C. 188
Kynard, Carmen 142

La Clase Mágica 408, 419
Lammers, Jayne 406–420
language acquisition *see* early language development
Language and Reading Research Consortium (LARRC) 207
language environments 220–227, 365–366; future research directions 375–377; high quality language and reading development 366–369; implementing language-facilitating techniques 374–375; language development and exposure 369–374
language for school literacy (LSL) 156, **160**; conceptualization of 158–161; in early childhood 205–206; metalanguage research 168–170; new directions of study 156–158; skills for reading comprehension 161, *162–164*, 165–168; vision for practice-relevant research 170–174
language proficiency *see* academic language proficiency
Language Workshop 351
Lankshear, C. 409
Latino learners 141–142, 330, 419; qualitative case study 492–496
Lattice Model 309, 314–315, **315**
Lauterman, T. 122
Lawrence, J.F. 350
Leander, Kevin M. 436–449
Lee, A.M. 121, 126
Lee, Carol D. 37–49, 330
Lemrow, E.M. 143–144
Lesaux, Nonie 3–12, 338–339, 351, 355
Leslie, L. 239–242, 244
Let's Know! 207, 209
Leu, D.J. 410
levels of processing theory 262
Levine, S. 338, 353–354, 371, 372
Lewis, C. 334, 442
Lexical Quality Hypothesis (LQH) 218, 366
Lima, F.R. 336
Lipson, M.Y. 253
listening, open 446–448
literacy 17–18; and content area instruction 251–252; demographic trends in reseach 25–27, *26*; demographics overview 18–21; disciplinary 252; methodological trends in research 27–29; models of 313–316, *315*; sociocultural perspectives 329–331; in teacher education 21–25; *see also* academic language proficiency; child literacy; critical literacy; individualized literacy instruction
literacy instruction *see* digital literacy instruction, individualized literacy instruction
Literary Research Association (LRA) 25
Litman, C. 387, 395
local strategies 269–270
Lockhart, R.S. 262
López, F. 20–21
Lorde, Audre 146–147
lower-level language skills 202, 209, 268

Index

Lucas, T. 22
Lucassen, T. 82
Luke, Alan 111, 138
Lyiscott, J. 47

Macedo, D. 426–427, 438
Mackey, Margaret 99–112
Magnussen, S.J. 390
Maher, Bridget 455–462
Majors, Y. 47
Mancilla-Martinez, Jeannette 216–229
Mangen, A. 122–123, 126, 130
market-based reforms 5, 7
marketing, online 446
Marr, M.B. 242, 244
Martín-Beltrán, M. 417
Martínez, R.S. 189
Martínez-Roldán, C.M. 334–336, 492–496
Marulis, L.M. 312
Mashburn, A.J. 373
Maupin, A.N. 19
Maxwell-Jolly, J. 23
May, T. 140
McBride-Chang, Catherine 105
McClain, Janna B. 216–229
McCoy, Dana C. 279–298
McKenna, M. 418
McKeown, M.G. 349, 350
McKnight Foundation 209
McNair, J. 65
McNamara, D.S. 247, 261–272, 263, 318
mean length of utterance (MLU) 368, 371
Measures of Effective Teaching (MET) project 460, 461
media text environments, examinations of 464–465; automatized non-verbal data collection *476–478*; ethnographic methods *474–476*; review of examination methods 478–480; task-based discourse analysis *472–473*; toward methodological advancements in research 480–482; verbal reporting and protocol analysis *466–472*
mental models 80, 201, 202, 262, 385, *472*
Merga, M. 102
metacognition 309–310, 314, 316, *468*, *473*
metalanguage 155, 161, 168–170
metalinguistic skills 44, 309–310
micro-blogging 90–91
micro-level comprehension processes 42–43, 48
Mignolo, Walter 141
Migrant Student Leadership Institute, UCLA 46
Mikulski, A.M. 373
Miller, A.C. 245
Mind in Society 58
mind wandering 186
Minecraft 105
mobile apps 414–416, 418, 448
mobile phones *see* smartphones

Model of Domain Learning (MDL) 392
Moje, Elizabeth Birr 3–12, 388, 392, 393–394
Mol, S.E. 223–224
Molfese, D.L. 488
Moll, L.C. 330, 392
monolingual learners 157, 167, 222, 349
Moore, D.W. 385
Moore, J. 169
Morell, E. 47
Morgan, P.L. 67
morphosyntactic skills *162–163*, 165–166
Mosborg, S. 253
motivation 189–190; and content interest 186; in media text environments 467; and multiple text reading 85, 86; and self-efficacy beliefs 182–183
Motivation for Reading Questionnaire (MRQ) 182, 189
Muller, C. 67
multilingualism 204–205, 331
multiliteracies 138, 139
multimodality 137–138; and critical inquiry 140–143; and decolonial imaginaries 143–145; digital tools 414–415, 416; and reading research 138–140; science texts 387, 390; youth conveying rhizomatic identities 145–148
multiple text reading 79–80; implications and future directions 91–92; individual and contextual factors 84–87; theoretical background 80–84; *see also* non-traditional text reading; printed vs. digital texts
Multiple-Document Task-based Relevance Assessment and Content Extraction Model (MD-TRACE) 81, 83
multi-tasking 121–122
Murphy, P.K. 184
My Teaching Partner (MTP) 460

narrative analysis 495
National Assessment of Adult Literacy (NAAL) 268
National Assessment of Educational Progress (NAEP) 7, 8, 64
National Center for Educational Reseach (NCER) 25–27
National Center for Educational Statistics (NCES) 64
National Council for Teacher Quality (NCTQ) 22
National Early Literacy Panel (NELP) 203, 206
National Endowment for the Arts (NEA) 106–108
National Governors Association (NGA) 8
National Reading Panel (NRP, 2000) 21, 24, 27
National Research Council (NRC) 388
National Teacher and Principal Survey (2015-2016) 10
Native American literacy 141, 427
nature vs. nurture 66–68
Naval Avenue Early Learning Center, Washington 209
need for cognition (NFC) 184–185
Nelson, M. 139
networked improvement communities (NICs) 319–320

networks, reading 443–445
Neuman, S.B. 225
neuroscience 487–490
New Criticism 59–60, 429
new literacies 82–83, 139, 408–409, 410, 416, 428
New London Group 138
New York Times 126
Newman, D. 66
Newman, S.B. 312
news reading 121, 126, 127–128
Next Generation Science Standards (NGSS) 20, 387–388, 395
Nichols, T. Philip 137–149
No Child Left Behind Act (2001) 8, 20, 66, 251
Noble, Kimberly G. 487–490
Noguera, P. 61, 63
Noguerón-Liu, Silvia 406–420, 419
nonfiction vs. fiction 191
non-traditional text reading 79–80; in digital contexts 89–91; implications and future directions 91–92; summer of 2016 reading habits 99–103; theoretical background 80–84; *see also* digital reading; printed vs. digital texts
Noyes, J.M. 120
Ntelioglou, Yaman 442

Oakhill, J. 246
Oatley, Keith 110
O'Brien, D.G. 385, 392, 393, 394
O'Brien, E.J. 246, 252
O'Brien, L.M. 224
Ofcom 103
online news comments 91
Open Educational Resources (OERs) 132
open listening 446–448
open-ended questions 374–375
O'Reilly, T. 247
Organization for Economic Co-operation and Development (OECD) 103–104
Ortmann, L. 385, 392, 394
Osborne, J. 388–389
Outside Your Bubble 444, 445

Paglen, Trevor 446
Palermo, F. 373
Palincsar, A.S. 390
PARCC testing 37
parents' role 64–65, 221, 310–311, 369–370
Paris, D. 48, 217–218
Park, Y. 183, 189
Parsons, A.W. 349
Pearson, P. David 329
Pedagogy of the Oppressed 426
Peeck, J. 249
Peercy, M.M. 352–353, 417
peers' language input 373–374
Perfetti, C. 218, 242
Pew Reseach Center 106, 109, 121, 126–128

phonology 307
physiological processes 40
Player, Grace D. 137–149
pleasure, reading for 104, 105
Poetry for the People 142
Pokémon GO 99, 100–101
policy landscapes 20–21, 66
Pomerantz, A. 21
positioning theory 65
postcolonialism *see* decolonization
poverty 19, 63, 66
predictions, in research 480
preferences, reading 190–191, 192
preschool curricula 206, 288
Pressley, M. 27
Preventing Reading Difficulties in Young Children 24
Price-Dennis, D. 142, 416, 419
printed vs. digital texts 88, 119–120; child readers 128–130; cognitive research 121–123; and demographics 121; future research 130–132; perceptual research 123–126; usage research 126–128
prior knowledge *see* knowledge
Proctor, C. Patrick 5–6, 17–30
professional development (PD) 23–25, 209
Programme for International Student Assessment (PISA) 103–104
Progress in International Reading Literacy Study (PIRLS, 2006) 183, 189
Project CLASS 295
Project Gutenberg 117
Protocol for Language Arts Teaching Observation (PLATO) 461
psycholinguistics 218, 228, 375–376
Public Broadcasting Service (PBS) 503
Pulido, D. 254
PVEST framework 41, 47

Qin, Wenjuan 155–174
qualitative case methodology 492–496
QuEST 353

Race to the Top 20, 66
racial diversity 5–6, 66–68, 334, 425; *see also* African-American learners; critical literacy; decolonization; sociocultural diversity
raciolinguistics 24, 357–358
racism 64, 357
Raising a Reader (RAR) 224
RAND Reading Study Group 181, 347, 386, 394
randomized-control trials (RCTs) 28, 29, 312
Rasmussen, B.B. 141
Razza, R.P. 280
Read 180 program 317
READI project 43, 46, 391
Reading Apprenticeship 353

Index

Reading Apprenticeship Academic Literacy (RAAL) 390–391
reading attitudes 188–189
reading comprehension 37–39; academic language instruction 347, 354–355; and high quality language 366–369; Lattice Model **315**; social and cultural diversity 39–49; strategies 269–270; *see also* deep comprehension
Reading First initiative 251
reading for pleasure 104, 105
Reading for Understanding initiative 209
Reading Research Quarterly 25–26, *26*
Reading Systems Framework (RSF) 366–367
Reading Wars 68
Recht, D.R. 244
Reese, Debbie 427
Reese, L. 337
refutation texts 252–253
Reiser, B.J. 396
religious knowledge 253
research-practice partnerships 319–320
resilience navigation 41–42
Reyes, C.R. 19
Reynolds, R.E. 238
rhetorical flexibility 171
rhizomatic learning 140, 144, 145–148, 445
Riehl, C. 28
Riepl, Wolfgang 116
risk navigation 41–42
Robust Academic Vocabulary Encounters (RAVE) 350–351
robust learning environments: design for supporting comprehension 42–43; features of 40–42; social contexts and diverse interaction 45–48
Rogers, R. 25
Rogoff, B. 492
Roni, S.M. 102
Rooks, Noliwe 425–426
Rosenblatt, L.M. 60
Rowan, Brian 455–462
Rowsell, J. 414–415, 416
Rutherford, V. 349
Rydland, V. 248
Rymes, B. 21

Sabey, David B. 436–449
Saito, H. 441
Salmerón, Ladislao 79–92, 90
San Pedro, T.J. 48, 141
Sannino, A. 492
Sax, D. 126
scaffolded text environments 413
Schallert, D.L. 238
schema theory 238
Schleppegrell, Mary 161, 169
Schmitt, N. 219
Scholastic 129–130

school language environments 222–223, 224–227
Schugar, H.R. 129
Schwartz, L. 419
science learning: academic language learning 349, 352, 353; in classroom practice 388; future research directions 394–396; reading to support science learning 388–391; refutation texts 252; social practices perspective 387–388
Science Writing Heuristic approach 389
Scientific Studies of Reading 25–26, *26*
Scott, J.A. 64
Sealy-Ruiz, Y. 59
Seeds of Science/Roots of Reading 389
segregation 64
self-beliefs 182–183
self-explanation strategy training (SERT) 270
self-regulation, in childhood 279–280, 309; implications and future directions 295–298; relation with literacy 281–287, *281*; school interventions and literacy 288–295, *289–293*
Selligent 109
semantics 225, 307, 348
Semantics, Surface, and Source (3S) Model of Credibility Evaluation 82, 84
Shanahan, T. 391
shared texts 334–335, 374
Sheltered Instruction Observation Protocol (SIOP) 351–352, 353
Shic, F. 19
Shifrer, D. 67
Short, D.J. 353
short-term research 108–109
Siegel, M. 139
Silverman, R. 349, 417
Simon, Katrina R. 487–490
Simple View of Reading (SVR) 314
Singer, L.M. 89
Singh, S. 336–337
situated reading 109–112
situation models 238–239, 263
Skerrett, Allison 328–341, 335
Sleeter, C. 21
Sloan, D.L. 335
Slobin, D.I. 172
Smagorinsky, Peter 57–68
Smarter Balanced 37
smartphones 100, 101–102, 104–105, 109, 117, 127, 414
Smith, M.S. 28
Snow, C.E. 22, 367
social interaction 90–91, 369
social media 118–119; algorithms 103, 445–446; and globalization 437; as situated reading 110–111
socially-situated discourse practices 155, 158, 160–161, **160**
sociocultural diversity 57–60, 328–329; affordances of human development perspectives 39–40;

conundrums of the paradigm shift 48–49; cultural knowledge *241*, 253; gaps in reading instruction research 339–341; instructional approaches to reading 331–339; language for school literacy (LSL) 159–161, **160**; literacy and reading development perspectives 329–331; and mediation 408; and multi-dimensional framing of reading comprehension 43–45; nature, nurture, and reading 66–68; policy context 66; qualitative case study 492–496; reading at home 60–66; robust learning environments 40–43; social contexts and robust learning environments 45–48, 336–337; *see also* African-American learners; critical literacy; decolonization
socioeconomic diversity 5–6, 66, 282, 310, 487–488
sociolinguistics 218, 219, 429–430
Song, S. 199
sophisticated vocabulary 367, 368, 372, 374
Soter, A.O. 375
sourcing, of texts 85, 86, 87
South Africa 142
Souto-Manning, M. 335
Space2Cre8 443
Sparrow, B. 125
special needs 19
Spencer, M.B. 41, 47
Sperling, R.A. 67
Spires, H.A. 249
Spycher, P. 349
Srasser, K. 204
St. Thomas Aquinas School (STA), Philadelphia 147
Stadler, M. 87
Stahl, S.A. 242
Standage, Tom 126
Stebbins, R.A. 107
STEP (Strategic Teaching and Evaluation of Progress) 209–210
Stevens, J.R. 270
Stoller, F.L. 267
Stornaiuolo, A. 439, 443
story apps 414
story circles 336
storytelling 205–206, 221
Stotsky, S. 59
Strang, Ruth 180
Strasser, K. 222
strategies, deep reading 269–270
Strategy Trainer for Active Reading and Thinking (iSTART) 318
Street, B.V. 139, 331, 427–428, 438
stress 9, 295
Strømsø, H.I. 85
Student Monitor LLC 126
student populations 18–19
Sullivan, M. 107
Summers, K. 107
symbolic reasoning 39, 43–44

syntax 367–368; and language environments 369–374, 376; and reading comprehension 165, 263–264
systemic functional linguistics (SFL) 139, 169, 347, 357

tablet computers 100, 101–102, 127, 414, 415–416
Taboada Barber, Ana 345–360
Tabors, P.O. 224
Taft, M.L. 239–242
Tarchi, C. 243, 245
task analysis 480
task instructions 87
tasks, reading 190
Tatum, A.W. 332
Taylor, A. 270
teacher-child relationships 285, 295–296, 311
teachers: demographics 19–20; digital literacy instruction 416, 419; and disciplinary texts 393, 395–396; and language for school literacy (LSL) 173; language input 370–373; literacy in teacher education 21–25; professional development (PD) 23–25, 209; sociocultural diversity of 335–336; stress and burnout 9; vocabulary knowledge of 228; workforce and preparation decline 10–11
Teachers' Knowledge of Vocabulary Survey (TKVS) 228
Teaching Over Time (TOT) 461–462
Technical Working Groups (TWGs) 27
technology 408–409; for classroom observations 376; and media reading 479–480; and personalizing student instruction 316–319; video data 455–462; and vocabulary 227; *see also* digital literacy instruction; digital reading
Tenenboim, O. 128
testing 7–8, 65–66; *see also* assessments
text considerations: cohesion 247, 264, 271; new forms 6–7; readability 270–272; structures 38, 43, 203; text-specific processes 308–309; *see also* multiple text reading; non-traditional text reading; printed vs. digital texts; text content
text content: beliefs and opinions about 187–188; interest in 186–187; refutation texts 252–253; *see also* disciplinary texts
Thein, A.H. 335
think-aloud *471*, 479
Thomas, Ebony E. 424–432
Thurman, N. 128
Tierney, J.D. 442
Tigert, J.M. 417
top-down (global) strategies 269–270
topic interest 186–187
topic knowledge 239–242, *240–241*, 244, 245, 247–248, 254
Townsend, Dianna 345–360
Trainin, G. 414
Transitional Bilingual Education (TBE) 371, 373
triangulation *470*, 479, 481–482
Tufis, P.A. 67

Index

Twitter 110, 437, 448
Tynan, D. 103

Uccelli, Paola 155–174, 206, 367
Understanding Language (Stanford) 21
UNESCO (United Nations Educational, Scientific and Cultural Organization) 102, 104
University of California (UCLA) 46
University of Pennsylvania 147
unsettledness 440–441, 443–445

Valdés, G. 22
Valenica, S. 386
values, reading-related 188
van den Broek, P. 252, 263, 388
Vasilyeva, M. 371, 372
Vasudevan, L.M. 440
Vaughn, S. 353, 386
verbal data analysis 478–479
video data 455–457; archiving and sharing 459–461; qualitative and quantitative research 457–459; research example 461–462
video games 105
Viesca, K.M. 332
Villegas, A.M. 22
vocabulary: academic vocabulary 166–167, 210–211, **346**, 348–351, 354–355; conceptualizing vocabulary knowledge 218–220; in early childhood 199, 204, 205, 210–211, 220–228; importance of 216–218; language environments and acquisition 220–223, 226–227, 369–374; sophisticated 367, 368, 372, 374; and textual knowledge 254
Vygotsky, L.S. 58, 59, 330, 408, 492

Ware, P. 410
Warschauer, M. 410

Ways with Words 60
We Need Diverse Books 101
Web 2.0 89–90
web forums 90
websites, classroom 413
Wertsch, J. 408
What the Teacher Didn't Know 145–146
What Works Clearinghouse (WWC) 27–28, 29
White, Mark 455–462
WIDA 157–158, 167
Wigfield, A. 182
Wijekumar, K.K. 318
Wilkinson, I.A.G. 64
Willis, Arlette I. 57–68
Windschitl, M. 396
Wineburg, S. 38, 84, 85–86
Winn, M.T. 47, 142, 432
Winsler, A. 286
Wohlwend, K. 414–415
Wolf, M. 111
Wolfe, M.B. 243
Woodwyk, J.M. 243
Woody, W.D. 122
Word Generation program 225–226, 350
Word Knowledge e-Book (WKe-Book) 318–319
working memory 283–284
World Bank 109
World of Warcraft 105
Wright, Tanya S. 237–255

Yarden, A. 390
Ypulse 102

zone of proximal development (ZPD) 330
Zwiers, J. 352–353